C.P.A. LAW REVIEW
Under the Uniform Commercial Code
as Amended

C.P.A. Law Review

under the Uniform Commercial Code as Amended

TEXT, UNIFORM COMMERCIAL CODE, OTHER STATUTES, PREVIOUS C.P.A.
LAW EXAMINATION QUESTIONS AND MODEL ANSWERS

JOSEPH L. FRASCONA, J.D.

*Member of the New York, Colorado, and
Federal Bars and Professor of Business Law,
University of Colorado*

FOURTH EDITION • 1972

RICHARD D. IRWIN, INC. *Homewood, Illinois 60430*

IRWIN-DORSEY LIMITED *Georgetown, Ontario L7G 4B3*

IRWIN-DORSEY INTERNATIONAL *London, England WC2H 9NJ*

Fourth Edition

First Printing, August 1972
Second Printing, June 1973

Library of Congress Catalog Card No. 72–185437
Printed in the United States of America

TO MY STUDENTS

PREFACE

THIS FOURTH edition has but one purpose—to continue to serve the great number of accountants and accounting students by revising and bringing previous editions of this book thoroughly up to date under the Uniform Commercial Code. As stated in previous editions, this book was motivated by students of accounting, in the practice and in school, and it is written for them. Whatever experience in teaching and writing the author has acquired in this area over the past twenty-five years is made available here for the help of those who plan to take the Business Law part of the Certified Public Accountant Examination and those accountants who need to keep up to date on Business Law.

Several factors make this fourth edition of still further outstanding importance to users. First, the material is current with authoritative up-to-date references. Second, Article 9 of the Uniform Commercial Code was extensively amended in 1971. That portion of the text on Consensual Property Security Transactions has been rewritten reflecting this change, and the amended Article 9 is included in this book. Third, excerpts from and references to the federal Consumer Credit Protection Act of 1968 and the Uniform Consumer Credit Code of 1969 occur throughout the text and footnotes where particularly applicable. Fourth, Part Thirteen on Accountant's Legal Responsibility has been largely rewritten, with more extensive coverage, including pertinent excerpts from various federal statutes reflecting civil and criminal liability to which accountants particularly are exposed. Fifth, the Frequency Chart, and previous C.P.A. Business Law examination questions and the author's model answers to them have been brought up to date as of the time when the manuscript for this edition was submitted to the publisher. The author hopes to keep adoptors of this book continually current with supplementary materials consisting of a cumulative Frequency Chart, and C.P.A. examination questions on Business Law and his model answers to them as each examination occurs. Sixth, every effort has been made to make the text more complete and understandable to readers. More illustrations have been included throughout. Also, there is greater cross-reference to the text via the footnotes. Seventh, all statutory material, e.g., the complete texts of the Uniform Commercial Code and the Uniform Partnership Act, are now at the back of the book for easy consolidated reference, and also to permit better sequential and connecting flow of textual subject matter throughout the book.

The author wishes to acknowledge again with deep appreciation the very extensive and helpful suggestions and advice offered by S. Darden Brown, formerly Professor and Acting Chairman of the Department of General Business, College of Business Administration, University of Washington. Acknowledgment again is also due to Professor Allen Sinsheimer, Jr., formerly of San Diego State College, San Diego, California, and to the many other professors, accountants, and students who have made constructive suggestions which have been so very helpful. The American Institute of Certified Public Accountants has been very helpful both through the personal assistance of its former director of examinations, Mr. William C. Bruschi, and also in kindly permitting the author to reproduce questions from the Business Law part of the Uniform Certified Public Accountant Examinations in this book and in supplementary materials thereto; the author expresses on behalf of his student candidates and for himself his acknowledgment and appreciation of this courtesy.

The author also gratefully acknowledges the permission of: The American Law Institute and the National Conference of Commissioners on Uniform State Laws to quote from the Comments of the 1962 Official Text of the Uniform Commercial Code as amended in 1971; and the National Conference of Commissioners on Uniform State Laws to reproduce the Uniform Partnership Act, and excerpts from the Uniform Limited Partnership Act, the Uniform Fraudulent Conveyance Act, and the 1969 Official Text of the Uniform Consumer Credit Code and to quote from the Code's Comments in this book.

Further, the author wishes to acknowledge again the helpful and friendly courtesy of the staff of, and the facilities made available by, the William M. White Business Library and the Law Library of the School of Law, University of Colorado; the help of Mrs. Helen Sayre for her typing of the manuscript draft; the constant, unstinted, and much needed encouragement and assistance of the author's wife, Jean Ezard Frascona, LL.B., without whose invaluable help this book could not have been written and rewritten in the various editions; and the patience and unselfish sacrifices of the younger members of the author's family in loss of recreation companionship.

May 1972   JOSEPH L. FRASCONA

FREQUENCY CHART
BRANCHES OF LAW COVERED IN RECENT PREVIOUS
C.P.A. EXAMINATION QUESTIONS

Examination Date	Contracts	PERSONAL PROPERTY				Commercial Paper	Agency	BUSINESS ORGANIZATIONS	
		Personal Property in General	Bailments	Sales	Bulk Transfers			Partnerships	Corporations
May 1971	6b			5,6a			8		1A–C,E–F
Nov. 1970	2			2B,3,7		8	4	6	
May 1970			8a(1)(2),b	4		6		1D(21)–(26)(28),3	2A–B,E,F
Nov. 1969	2C–F			2A,B,6b,c	6a	7	1,8c		1F(27),3D(76),4a,b(3)(6)
May 1969	4					3	1	5	7
Nov. 1968	2A,C–F			2B,3		4	7	6	1
May 1968	7a	8	5			2		1	
Nov. 1967	1,5c,d			2,6c		4	6a,b,d		3
May 1967	2A(63)(64),4			8		3		1	7
Nov. 1966	7d		4	3		5	1A–K,L(56)(59)(60)	1L(57)(58)	
May 1966	2,5					8		6	1
Nov. 1965	2A–G,4,7a–c	2H–K	8a(4)	8a(1)(3),b,c		6	5	3	
May 1965	4,8a(1)(2)		3I–L	4a(2),6			2G–L		3E–H,7

Examination Date	Security		Bankruptcy	Insurance	Real Property	Wills and Decedents' Estates	Trusts	Accountant's Legal Responsibility	Public Law
	Property Security Transactions	Suretyship							
May 1971	2,3A (61)– (66)	7			3A(67)–(70), B–E			4	1D
Nov. 1970	1C(15)			1A–B, C(11)–(14), D–F				5,7a(2), b(2)	
May 1970		5	7	1D(27), 8a(3)				1A–C, D(29)(30)	2C,D
Nov. 1969	3A–C, F(89)	3D(77)–(80), E,F(86)– (88)(90)		5				8a,b,d	4b(1) (2)(4) (5)
May 1969			2		6			8	
Nov. 1968	8	5	1D(17) (18)						
May 1968		6		3		4a(3), b	4a(1) (2)		7b
Nov. 1967	8b		8a,c	7				5a,b	3F
May 1967	2A(61) (62),F– L	2A(65),B– E			5,6				
Nov. 1966			2	6		8a	8b–d	7a–c	
May 1966	7	4			3J–L	3A–F	3G–I		
Nov. 1965		1J–L	8a(2)	1A–I	2L			7d	
May 1965		3A–D	1	5			2A–F	8a(3),b	

TABLE OF CONTENTS

B: Bailments

C: Sales

PART FOUR: COMMERCIAL PAPER

PART FIVE: AGENCY

PART EIGHT: BANKRUPTCY

PART NINE: INSURANCE

PART TEN: REAL PROPERTY

PART ELEVEN: WILLS AND DECEDENTS' ESTATES

PART TWELVE: TRUSTS

PART THIRTEEN: ACCOUNTANT'S LEGAL RESPONSIBILITY

PART FOURTEEN: PUBLIC LAW REFERENCES AND QUESTIONS

STATUTES

INDEX

INTRODUCTION

THE STATUS of being a certified public accountant is a certification of assurance by the State that the individual has the requisite competence and necessary professional responsibility to serve the public as a professional accountant. Those who have acquired this status have the obligation to be currently informed and continually updated on new developments affecting their profession. Such a status represents ability in terms of essential knowledge and of its application both on the Uniform Certified Public Accountant Examination and in practice. With respect to candidates for this status, the examination has solely one purpose—namely, to determine whether the candidate has the required knowledge and can properly apply it to factual situations. Accordingly, every candidate's preparation for the examination should be predicated, first, on the acquisition of this knowledge and, second, on its proper application.

The objective of this book is to assist the candidate both in the acquisition and in the application of knowledge of Business Law, regardless of the locality in which the candidate is taking the Business Law part of the examination. First, with regard to the acquisition of such knowledge, the author has attempted to bring together in one place all the pertinent legal material necessary for preparation, except for the field of Public Law where only some recent previous C.P.A. Law Examination questions have been reproduced with suggestions on how to acquire this information. This pertinent legal material consists of a comprehensive text, the entire 1962 Official Text of the Uniform Commercial Code as Amended, and other carefully selected statutory material. Extraneous legal material, not germane to the object of this book, has been omitted. Each field of law is treated separately and completely, consisting of a check list followed by the text for that particular field. The candidate's careful amplification of the check list as each part of the text is read will result in a complete outline of each particular field of law which, on final review, should serve to refresh the candidate's memory of the subject matter. The author is convinced by his experience in teaching candidates, by their results on the examinations, and by their reactions in his classes that the best method of remembering the large amount of legal material is first to go over the material carefully, preparing a detailed outline, then to examine the outline to check his knowledge, and finally to retain such knowledge of each particular field of law by remembering a simplified, brief check list therefor. For example, the Law of Contracts fundamentally consists of the four required elements of a contract, the principles applicable to third-party beneficiary contracts and assignments as two special types of contract, the enforceability of a contract affected by the statute of frauds, the condition on which performance of a promise depends, the nonperformance and breach of a contract, and the discharge of a contract. Accordingly, the check list would consist of these items with a knowledge of the material represented by them. Candidates have stated to the author repeatedly that, apart from the method of answering the questions, the check-list development has been the greatest asset in achieving success on the examination.

Second, with regard to the actual answering of questions, the author has reproduced and grouped by field of law recent previous C.P.A. Law Examination questions with the author's model answers to them as a guide. A definite method must be utilized in order to apply the check-list information to each particular question in a manner ensuring complete and accurate coverage to the satisfaction of the examiners. The method of answering a question may be divided into two parts: *what* information is required by the question, and *how* to supply such information. Questions vary in form and length. True-false and multiple-choice questions are answered easily; the essay-type question requires a methodical answer. Before any question is answered, two things should be done: first, the entire question should be read thoroughly and carefully in order to determine what field of law is applicable and the general nature of the question; and second, scratch paper should be utilized to block out the legal point or points involved. The scratch paper constitutes a work sheet on which should be listed the pertinent points as they appear and a word or two concerning the elements of each point. For example, a contract question may state that an oral contract for the sale of goods for $1,000 has been made and the first installment delivery occurred on January 2. A notation should be made on the scratch paper immediately as follows: "Sale goods, $1,000, oral, UCC Stat. of Frauds, needs writing for enforceability—A rec'd part of goods Jan. 2, Stat. of F. satisfied to that extent." After the question has been analyzed in this manner, a careful examination of the scratch paper should reveal the requisite material for inclusion in the answer. The question should be reread and the notes on the scratch paper reviewed in order to be certain that the question has been properly analyzed; then the answer should be written, predicated on such notes. It will be observed that approximately one half the time will have been used in analyzing the question; sufficient time remains for the careful writing of a good answer.

The author recommends an umbrella approach as the method to be used generally in answering a question. At the top of the umbrella is the protruding staff point; that point is the precise answer to the question. The question "Can A recover from B?" should be answered "Yes" or "No," followed by a period; the question should be answered exactly. In giving the reasons for the answer, first the broad, overall reason or principle of law should be given, and, in a sentence or two, it should be tied in to the particular question, resulting in a complete and accurate answer. *The examiners want to see whether or not the candidate can discern the important legal point or points involved in solving the question (not the legal points which are immaterial to such solution) and whether he can properly apply the pertinent principles of law to the solution of those points using good English in stating his answer.* First determine what is the predominant principle of law involved, state it, and then apply it to the question. For example, see the question and answer No. 8a(3) of May 1971, pages 593–95. First comes the point of the umbrella in "No." Then is stated the umbrella principle of law pertinent to the question; the principle is narrowed to its application to the question; it is then tied in to the question itself; and, finally, the concluding sentence at the bottom of the umbrella handle completes the answer.

The umbrella approach, with its graduated application of a principle of law to a legal question, is but the scientific approach of applying rules to facts. *Continuous classroom or home practice* in answering questions will result in facile ability to apply the rules. If a question is ambiguous, the candidate should take the approach which appears most reasonable to him and should explain it. Then, at the end of his answer, the candidate should indicate what the result would be if the other approach were taken. Similarly, if the answer to a question will depend upon whether the majority or minority view is adopted, the answer should be predicated on the majority view, although the minority view should be mentioned if it is a strong view and if the candidate can remember it. Careful exposition and application of the principles of law involved in the solution of the problem is the essential factor sought by the examiners. *Recently, the conceptual aspect of law has begun to be emphasized and some of the examination questions have asked that the issues be stated and then that they be discussed and applied to the facts in the questions.* This is but the umbrella approach in a slightly different format, first to see the pertinent legal points or issues involved, and then to apply the proper legal principles to the facts in order to resolve those legal points.

Previous recent examination questions have been answered by the author primarily to illustrate the method of answering such questions and, incidentally, to supply legal knowledge. The model answers all have the same basic format of the umbrella approach. A few questions have presented considerable difficulty because of the length of the question or of the answer required. The author has chosen to avoid a brief, sketchy, and inadequate answer to these few questions and, instead, has given a complete answer mainly for purposes of information rather than as a model of form; it is not expected that an accountant would answer such a question in that way and at such length. The author hopes that this type of question will not recur in the future.

Orderly assimilation of the required legal material, and the development of mental alertness to the legal significance of factual situations and of an ability to apply such knowledge in a careful, orderly, and relatively brief manner, should ensure successful completion of the Business Law part of the examination.

PART ONE

INTRODUCTION TO THE UNIFORM COMMERCIAL CODE

BACKGROUND, DEFINITIONS, AND PRINCIPLES OF INTERPRETATION

Background   THE Uniform Commercial Code, referred to as the "UCC," is the most recent product of society to further clarify and make uniform the law in *commercial transactions concerning personal property* throughout the United States. Prior to the Code, the desire of the various states for uniformity of various aspects of law prompted the formation of the National Conference of Commissioners on Uniform State Laws. Each state has representation on this body, which, after extensive study, formulated and recommended to each state for its adoption a proposed uniform law covering a particular area where uniformity was desired. To the extent of adoption by the various states, uniformity was achieved. In this way there was adopted the Uniform Negotiable Instruments Act, promulgated in 1896; Uniform Warehouse Receipts Act and Uniform Sales Act in 1906; Uniform Bills of Lading Act and Uniform Stock Transfer Act in 1909; Uniform Conditional Sales Act in 1918; Uniform Trust Receipts Act in 1933, and many other uniform laws.

While these uniform laws served very well, nevertheless with the passage of time it was realized that those uniform laws dealing with various aspects of *commercial transactions concerning personal property* needed updating in order to reflect the evolutionary progress of commercial transactions in society, and that a greater uniformity of law in this area was needed among the various states. The National Conference of Commissioners on Uniform State Laws combined with The American Law Institute, a body of outstanding judges and lawyers, to produce a Uniform Commercial Code "(a) to simplify, clarify and modernize the law governing commercial transactions; (b) to permit the continued expansion of commercial practices through custom, usage and agreement of the parties; (c) to make uniform the law among the various jurisdictions."[1] After great research and many drafts, the Code

---
[1] UCC 1–102(2).

3

appeared in its final form in 1958. It was changed subsequently, and today the 1962 Official Text with Comments is the standard reference work. The Code replaces the uniform laws mentioned in the above paragraph together with various miscellaneous state statutes on commercial transactions. A Permanent Editorial Board for the Uniform Commercial Code was established in 1961 to recommend future amendment of the Code as it deemed necessary and to preserve uniformity of the Code among the various states. The Code was amended in December, 1971; the amendments are in this book. Practicing accountants should carefully note changes in the Code which presently exist in each state.

It should be observed very carefully that the Code is concerned only with *commercial transactions concerning personal property.* Thus it does not disturb other branches of the law, except that to the extent they deal with any aspect of such commercial transactions they are modified by the Code. For example, the law of contracts deals with many kinds of contract, such as contracts to render services, contracts to sell an interest in land or goods, and contracts to sell commercial accounts receivable; the Code changes the law of contracts to sell goods and commercial accounts receivable. Also, it should be noted that Section 1–103 of the Code provides that, unless displaced by Code provision, the principles of law and equity, including the law merchant, shall apply and *supplement* the Code provisions. It should be noted carefully that the UCC in turn *supplements* the Uniform Consumer Credit Code (referred to in this book as U3C), which is dominant over the UCC.[2]

The Code consists of eleven Articles, each of which is subdivided into Parts, each Part having various Sections. References are by Section, each reference having 3 numbers—first the Article, then the Part, and lastly the Section. For example, the reference "Section 2–201" means that the material is in Article 2, Part 2 of that Article, Section 1 of that Part. "Section 3–112" means Article 3, Part 1, Section 12. Each Article deals with one facet of an over-all commercial transaction. The Articles are:

1. General Provisions.
2. Sales.
3. Commercial Paper.
4. Bank Deposits and Collections.
5. Letters of Credit.
6. Bulk Transfers.
7. Warehouse Receipts, Bills of Lading and Other Documents of Title.
8. Investment Securities.

---

[2] See U3C, sec. 1.103.

9. Secured Transactions; Sales of Accounts, and Chattel Paper.
10. Effective Date and Repealer.
11. Effective Date and Transition Provisions.

Parties to a transaction may, by their agreement, vary the legal effect of the Code except as the Code prohibits such variance.[3] For example, 1–102(3) of the Code provides that "the obligations of good faith, diligence, reasonableness and care prescribed by the Act may not be disclaimed by agreement but the parties may by agreement determine the standards by which the performance of such obligations is to be measured if such standards are not manifestly unreasonable." Also, the parties may agree that the law of any state or nation shall apply and govern their contract rights and duties as long as the transaction bears a *reasonable relation* to such state or nation; i.e., the state or nation ordinarily must be where a "significant enough portion of the making or performance of the contract is to occur or occurs."[4] However, 1–105(2) of the Code limits this right of the parties and specifies the applicable law in certain instances in connection with: rights of creditors against sold goods; bank deposits and collections; bulk transfers; investment securities; and secured transactions. Also, a party to a transaction may waive or renounce, in whole or in part, his claim or right against the other party arising out of an *alleged breach;* but to be effective as a release the waiver or renunciation if *oral* must be supported by *consideration,* or if *in writing* it must be signed and delivered by the aggrieved party without any requirement of consideration.

Definitions   Various words and terms are clearly defined in the Code. Those which are applicable generally throughout the Code are defined in 1–201, and those which are particularly applicable to a specific Article are defined in the introductory sections to such Article. In the event of conflict between the definitions of a term occurring in two or more Articles, which does occur because the same word has different meanings in different contexts, *it is very important to remember that the definition in a specific Article governs for that Article.* For example, the definitions of "goods" are different under the Sales portion of the Code (2–105(1)) and the Documents of Title portion of the Code (7–102(1)(f)). It is for this reason that the word "goods" is not included among the terms generally

---

[3] But cf. U3C, sec. 1.107, which generally prohibits a consumer from waiving or foregoing rights or benefits under that Act.

[4] UCC 1–105, *Comment 1.*

applicable throughout the Code (1–201). Again, it should be emphasized that *these definitions are applicable to the Code and not to other branches of the law not concerned with commercial transactions except as the Code refers to such other branches of the law.* For example, 1–201(11) of the Code defines "Contract" as meaning "the total legal obligation which results from the parties' agreement as affected by this Act and any other applicable rules of law." Some of these definitions are new, some modify, and some are basically the same as those previously used. *All definitions, whether of general or particular application to a specific Article, should be examined with great care because they control the meaning of the words used by parties in their dealings with each other.* Code definitions which are applicable generally are reproduced in Article 1, Part 2, of the Code.

Principles of Interpretation

In addition to various definitions to assist in clarifying the meaning of terms, the Code lays down certain fundamental rules of interpretation for general use. Thus, prima facie authenticity, genuineness, and truth of the facts stated is accorded to documents issued by third parties as authorized or required by the contract, e.g., a bill of lading issued by a carrier or a policy of insurance issued by an insurer as parties by their contract have agreed is to be issued by such third party carrier or insurer.[5] Also the Code provides for an obligation of good faith by the parties to a commercial transaction;[6] concepts of "reasonable time" and when action is taken "seasonably";[7] course of dealing and usage of trade;[8] performance or acceptance under reservation of rights;[9] and a very important option by a party to accelerate the other party's payment or performance at will when, in good faith, he believes that the other party will not perform.[10]

---

[5] UCC 1–202.
[6] UCC 1–203.
[7] UCC 1–204.
[8] UCC 1–205.
[9] UCC 1–207.
[10] UCC 1–208.

APPENDIX TO PART ONE

REFERENCES

1. Anderson, Ronald A. *Anderson's Uniform Commercial Code.* 2d ed. Rochester: Lawyers Cooperative Publishing Co., 1970.
2. Malcolm. "The Uniform Commercial Code," in *Uniform Commercial Code Handbook 1.* Chicago: American Bar Association, 1964.
3. *Uniform Laws Annotated,* Uniform Commercial Code, 1962.
4. Permanent Editorial Board for the Uniform Commercial Code, "Proposals for Changes in Article 9 of the Uniform Commercial Code and Related Changes in Other Articles." Philadelphia: The American Law Institute, December 20, 1971.

PART TWO

CONTRACTS

Chapter I

CONCEPT AND CLASSIFICATION

---

1. *CONCEPT OF CONTRACT*

THE law of contracts is concerned with promises and their legal effect. It would seem that any discussion of contracts should include: what a contract is; how contracts are formed; special kinds of contract in which third persons not parties thereto have an interest; proper proof of the existence of a contract; when a contract becomes performable by each of the parties; when nonperformance is wrongful and the legal remedies available to the injured party; and lastly, when a contract is terminated. Accordingly, this will be the order in which the subject will be discussed.

The subject of contracts is governed by the Common Law,[1] in the absence of statutory provision. The Uniform Commercial Code is a statute, operating in the area of its coverage. As stated previously,[2] the Code is concerned only with *commercial transactions involving personal property* and does not disturb other branches of the law except that, to the extent that they deal with any aspect of commercial transactions, they are modified by the Code. They supplement the Code. Thus, to make a sale of goods under the Sales portion of the Code it is necessary to make a contract. Accordingly, the Code is supplemented by the law of contracts.

Definition of Contract A *"contract" is a promise or set of promises creating a legal duty of performance*. It is a person's *promise* which induces action and reliance, and it is the *promise* to which the law attaches legal significance. Accordingly, by "contract" is meant a promise with a legal duty to perform its terms. Some promises create such a legal duty of performance, while others do not;

---

[1] The Common Law consists of those principles, rules, and usages which are sanctioned by the courts and found in their judicial decisions, and which are not dependent upon constitutional or legislative expression for their authority.

[2] See above, p. 4.

e.g., a promise to commit a crime. If more than one promise is made and they all relate to the same transaction, they all constitute the contract. Promises not relating to the same transaction are separate contracts. There must be at least two parties to a contract; but there may be only one promise, as where A promises B compensation for performance of a service which B then performs. Both A and B are parties to the contract—A because he made the promise and B because he relied on it—although there is only one promise. B is under no duty to perform because he did not make a promise, he rendered a service; but once he does perform, then A's promise becomes performable according to its terms. It is the promise which is the contract and which is sought to be enforced.

The Promise *A "promise" is an undertaking that something shall or shall not happen.* A promise is made by the promisor to the promisee. A *representation* is a statement of a past or present fact made to induce formation of a contract, while a promise is of future conduct. A's statement to B that X ship has arrived, which then induces the formation of a contract between A and B, is a representation. A *warranty* is essentially a promise or affirmation of a state of things, such as a statement that goods are or shall be of a certain quality.[3] A *condition* states a fact on the happening or nonhappening of which a promissory duty of immediate performance either arises or is extinguished. A's promise in a contract with B to reimburse B for any loss he sustains by fire imposes no duty on A to perform until damage occurs by fire. A's promise has a *condition precedent* to duty of performance—namely, fire loss to B. A's promise may have a *condition subsequent* the occurrence of which extinguishes the duty to perform the promise. Using the illustration immediately above, A's promise may also provide that, if A rejects B's claim for fire loss and B does not sue A within a specified period of time thereafter, A will have no duty to perform his promise. The necessity of B's suit within the specified period of time is a condition subsequent, and its nonoccurrence extinguishes A's duty to perform his promise. There is also a *condition concurrent*, e.g., unless otherwise agreed delivery and payment are concurrent conditions. The subject of conditions is considered in detail later.[4]

---

[3] For concept of warranties, see Samuel Williston, *A Treatise on the Law of Contracts* (3d ed., Williston and Jaeger; New York: Baker, Voorhis & Co., 1970), Vol. 5, sec. 673.

[4] See below, pp. 116–25.

An expression may take the form of a promise but not be a promise because it does not undertake that something shall or shall not happen. Such expressions are called *"illusory promises"* and have no legal effect as a promise. An employer's statement that he will pay the employee whatever salary the employer sees fit is not a promise to pay a salary.

A contract can be only executory because it is to be performed in the future. The phrase *"executory contract"* means that the promise or promises have not all been performed, while *"executed contract"* means that the promise or promises subsequently have been performed and no promissory duty remains.

The promise must be manifested by physical conduct. The conduct may be an *express promise,* as by an oral or written word, a gesture, a sign, or other manner. An *implied promise* is a promise implied from conduct, just as a promise to pay is implied from the act of a customer carrying away merchandise from the vendor's counter. *Silence* is not an expression; but under certain exceptional circumstances, discussed later,[5] silence may have legal effect as an expression of acceptance. *Express contracts* are promises expressly given, while *implied contracts* are promises implied from conduct. There is no difference in legal effect between such contracts. Implied contracts are sometimes called "contracts implied in fact," distinguishable from "contracts implied in law."

Quasi contract differs markedly from implied contracts and is the name of a legal duty or obligation imposed by law for reasons of justice and not because of any promise to perform. It is not a contract, because it lacks a promise and an agreement. Furthermore, damages are measured differently for breach of contract and for quasi contract, the damages for quasi contract being the reasonable value of what has been rendered. Illustrations of quasi contract are: obligations of parental or marital support; the obligation to surrender benefits received through unjust enrichment; and the obligation of an infant to pay the reasonable value of necessaries he has received.

A promise must create a legal duty to perform what has been promised. It must create a *legal obligation,* not just a moral obligation, in order to be a contract. Not all promises create legal obligations. Promises which are not contrary to law and which are supported by sufficient consideration are sanctioned by the law and become legal obligations. Promises are contrary to law when they are contrary to the law as provided by statute, or contrary to public policy as declared by the

---

[5] See below, pp. 36–38.

courts for reasons of social welfare and justice. Such promises are illegal and do not create legal obligations. They cannot be called contracts and are called merely *illegal promises.*

Agreement A promise by itself has no legal effect. It is the reliance on, and compliance with, the promise by someone else which causes the law to impose a duty of performance on the promisor. The promisor bargains his promise for something in return, and, when the promisee signifies his assent to the promise, there is an agreement. Accordingly, with but few exceptions, discussed later,[6] a contract must have an agreement manifested by the parties thereto. An *agreement* is a *manifestation of mutual assent* by two or more parties each to the other. This is often called a "meeting of the minds."

The courts are concerned only with the expressed intents of the parties, for that is the basis on which persons deal with each other and reach agreement. Their unexpressed mental intents are of no importance. There may be a manifestation of mutual assent when the parties are not mentally in accord. (A offers to sell B the house at 111 Walnut Street. There is only one 111 Walnut Street. B accepts, thinking of another house as 111 Walnut Street. The parties have manifested mutual assent to 111 Walnut Street and, accordingly, there is an agreement.)

While a contract requires an agreement, not every agreement is a contract. An agreement contemplating performance of illegal conduct or for an illegal purpose is void; and, as it does not create any legal obligation, it cannot be a contract. The term "agreement" should not be confused with the term "contract."

2. CLASSIFICATION OF CONTRACTS

Formal and Informal Contracts All contracts may be classified broadly as either *formal* or *informal* contracts. Formal contracts are called such because of their exceptional form, such form alone determining their validity as contracts. There are three kinds of formal contract: *contracts under seal, recognizances,* and *negotiable instruments. Contracts under seal* originated long before informal contracts and consist of the promisor's delivery of

---

[6] See below, pp. 80–89.

a contract in writing with a seal attached. They were called "deeds," "specialities," or "covenants." No consideration was necessary for a sealed instrument. Today the seal has greatly diminished in importance, and in most states the distinction between sealed and unsealed contracts is abolished. A *recognizance* is an undertaking made in court that payment will be made unless a certain condition occurs. One of the purposes of a recognizance is to assure attendance in court at a future day. *Negotiable instruments* are drafts, checks, negotiable promissory notes, and certificates of deposit under the Code. Warehouse receipts and bills of lading running to bearer or to the order of a specified person under the Code are *negotiable documents of title* and are considered formal contracts in the same category as negotiable instruments. These negotiable instruments and negotiable documents of title are promises expressed in a certain form. While corporate certificates of stock are of a negotiable character under the Code, they do not usually contain promises and, therefore, are not contracts.

Informal contracts are all contracts which are not formal contracts. They are sometimes called "simple contracts" and may be oral or written.

Unilateral and Bilateral Contracts

Contracts are classified more particularly as *unilateral, bilateral, voidable,* and *unenforceable.* All these contracts may be either under seal or be informal contracts. A *unilateral contract* is one in which only an act or a forbearance is rendered in return for a promise. A *bilateral contract* is one in which there are only mutual promises between the parties to the contract. By definition, a contract consists of a promise or set of promises creating a legal duty of performance. The promise or promises constitute the contract—not the manifestation of mutual assent or the sufficient consideration, which are necessary elements in the formation of the contract. A unilateral contract may have more than one promise on one side, and a bilateral contract may have more than one promise on each side. In unilateral contracts, only the promisor is bound by the contract; while in bilateral contracts, all promisors are bound to each other. If the promisor requests and receives a return promise from someone other than the promisee, or the promisor requests the promisee to make a return promise to someone other than the promisor which the promisee does, there cannot be a bilateral contract, inasmuch as each party must be a promisor and a promisee to the other. There can be a unilateral contract, however.

Voidable Contracts

At the time of its inception the contract may be *voidable,* but not "void." A contract means that a promise creates a legal duty. A void promise creates no legal duty and, therefore, cannot be a contract. The phrase "void contract" is a misnomer, a contradiction in terms, and should be avoided. A voidable contract has a promise which creates a duty to perform. *It is a contract in which one or more parties has the power to avoid the contract by manifesting his election to do so.* It is subject to the same obligations as a contract not voidable, and it differs only in the existence of a power to avoid the contract. Only the party who has this power of avoidance may exercise or waive it. By his exercise of this power, the contract is rescinded and made void. By his waiver of this power, the power thereby ceases to exist and the contract no longer is subject to it. By waiving this power, the party is said to "ratify" the transaction. Illustrative of grounds for avoidance are: infancy, duress generally, undue influence, fraud in inducing the formation of a contract, and a party's nondisclosure of facts when there is a legal duty to do so as in transactions between fiduciaries and beneficiaries.

Unenforceable Contracts

An unenforceable contract is a contract with no legal remedy for its enforcement. The contract exists, nevertheless, because the law recognizes its performance as a legal duty. Illustrations are: contracts in which the remedy of enforcement is gone, as where a statute of limitations bars the right of recovery; and contracts which do not comply with the statutory requisites of proof of the contract, as where a contract which is within the statute of frauds fails to comply with its requirements.

Divisible Contracts

A divisible contract is a contract which provides that performance of less than all the obligations on one side will become due by performance of less than all the obligations on the other side. An indivisible contract provides that performance of all obligations on one side will become due only by performance of all obligations on the other side. For example, a contract for the construction of a building for a fixed price to be paid to the builder in installments as he completes each story of the building is a *divisible* contract. If the contract provided that the total cost of constructing the building would be paid on the completion of the whole building, it would be an *indivisible* contract.

3. *REQUISITES OF CONTRACT*

A contract has four essential elements: (1) two or more parties with contractual capacity, (2) manifestation of mutual assent, (3) sufficient consideration, and (4) legally valid transaction. These four elements will be considered in turn, in the order indicated, in the chapter immediately following.

Chapter II

FORMATION OF CONTRACTS

---

1. PARTIES WITH CONTRACTUAL CAPACITY

Persons   ONE of the four essential elements in the formation of a contract is parties with contractual capacity. Parties to a contract may be either natural or juristic persons. Natural persons are human beings. Juristic persons are legal entities designated or personified as such by law. Corporations, political subdivisions such as state and county, partnerships, and other associations with a legal entity are persons, in the sense that they can be parties to a contract.

Persons with Limited Capacity to Contract   Juristic persons are limited to the powers granted to them and, accordingly, have capacity to contract as limited by such powers. Aliens may contract, but the contracts and contractual powers of enemy aliens are regulated by federal statute. Convicts serving long terms of imprisonment have their contractual powers limited by statute in many states. A married woman (feme covert) had no power to contract at common law, but today she is fully capable to contract. Infants, the insane, and drunkards in certain cases, have limited capacity to make contracts. Each of these last three will be considered.

Infants. An infant is a natural person, male or female, who has not yet attained his majority. In most states an infant is a person under twenty-one years of age. Exceptions are made by statutes which provide lower ages at which people may enter into a contract of marriage, enlist in military service, or execute wills; some state statutes provide that a woman becomes an adult at eighteen years of age. Except for a few instances the age of majority is twenty-one years.

Disaffirmance. An infant is legally capable of making a contract; but, because of his immaturity and inferiority in bargaining astuteness, as compared with adults, an infant's contracts are voidable at his election. Except for the power of avoidance, an infant's contract is like any other contract and is subject to the same rules of law. The infant's privilege of

18

avoidance, or of *"disaffirmance"* as it is often called in the case of infants' contracts, is absolute and personal only to the infant. Disaffirmance is an expression of intention to rescind or to avoid the contract and may be made expressly, or impliedly by conduct indicating avoidance. Once disaffirmance occurs, the contract is avoided and cannot be ratified subsequently. On disaffirmance, the adult party to the contract is entitled to whatever the infant received under the contract if the infant still has it, regardless of its changed form. If the infant no longer has what he received under the contract, he can disaffirm anyway. If the infant still has what he received under the contract or what he has received in exchange therefor, by the better view he must tender its return to the adult as a condition to disaffirmance, although many courts do not impose this as a condition.

An *executed* contract may be avoided during minority or within a reasonable period of time after majority, except a conveyance of real property which cannot be avoided during minority. State statutes usually specify what is a reasonable time; otherwise it is a question of fact for the jury. If the contract is *executory* on the infant's side, no expression of disaffirmance is necessary and the contract is unenforceable against him unless he ratifies the contract.

Generally, the effect of disaffirmance is to restore the parties to their position immediately prior to making the contract. However, if the property to which the infant is entitled is unavailable and has depreciated in value at the time of disaffirmance, there is a conflict among the courts as to whether the infant is entitled only to the value at the time of disaffirmance or he is to be made whole. A problem arises if, prior to disaffirmance, the adult party to the contract had transferred to a third person the property acquired from the infant. At Common Law the infant could disaffirm and regain the property, even if the transferee were a bona fide purchaser for value. This is still true today, except in the case of a good faith purchaser for value of *goods* from whom the infant cannot regain the property. The exception applies only to a good faith purchaser for value and only to goods, as provided in 2–403(1) of the Code: "A person with voidable title has power to transfer a good title to a good faith purchaser for value." (I, an infant, sold and delivered goods to A, an adult. A's sale and delivery of the goods to G, a good faith purchaser for value, cuts off I's power of avoidance as to G, who obtains good title to the goods.)

Ratification. The infant's waiver of his power of avoidance is called *"ratification"* or "affirmance," and is a manifestation of assent to the contract. Ratification may occur only after majority and may be express, or implied from the infant's affirmative or negative conduct. *Retention and use after majority* of what the infant has received under the contract implies ratification. Failure to exercise the power of avoidance within a statutory, or in the absence of statute a reasonable, period of time after majority impliedly waives the power. Ratification must be *in toto* and not partial; the infant cannot ratify part of the contract and also disaffirm part of it. Ratification cannot occur if, at the time, the infant is ignorant of some material fact.[1] The effect of ratification is merely to remove the power of avoidance; the contract is not disturbed by it.

Necessaries. Although an infant may avoid his contracts, he is liable in quasi contract for the reasonable value of *necessaries* he has *received.* On disaffirmance, an infant must retain the necessaries he has received and may recover from the adult what he has paid in excess of the market value. A "necessary" is that which is actually and reasonably needed for the personal general welfare of the infant, considering his status in life, at the time the contract was made by him. Food, clothing, lodging, medical care, and, to a certain extent, education are included among necessaries. An ordinary education is usually essential to an infant's welfare; but whether higher education is a necessary depends upon the circumstances in each particular case. A purchase of clothes might be a necessary in one case and not in another, depending on the status in life of the particular infant, the clothes he had previously, the price of the new clothes, and other factors.

Torts and Crimes. An infant, except one of tender years, is liable for his torts or wrongs just as is anyone else. Commission of a tort by an infant in connection with a contract does not preclude the infant from exercising his power to disaffirm the contract, although some courts hold to the contrary. The usual type of tort committed by an infant is deceit by misrepresentation of age. If the infant's tort is independent of the contract, such as deceit inducing the formation of a contract, the infant is liable for the damage caused by the tort. If the infant's tort is a part of the contract, as a warranty in a sales contract, the infant is not liable for the tort. A contract induced by fraud is voidable at the election of the party defrauded; and, if the infant has perpetrated such fraud, the adult may avoid the contract.

When Not Voidable. Public policy, as provided by statute or declared by the courts, has recognized the desirability that certain contracts of infants should not be voidable because of such infancy. Exam-

---

[1] For the effect of ignorance of a material fact on ratification in agency, see below, p. 537. See also, below, p. 88.

ples are: a contract of marriage; a contract of enlistment in military service; and a contract to do that which the infant was under a legal duty to do and which he could be legally compelled to do. Many states by statute recognize that self-supporting infants often engage in business and, accordingly, provide that such contracts are binding with no power of avoidance if the contract was reasonable and provident from the infant's point of view. Also by statute in many states, infants above a specified age are permitted to procure life insurance with certain specified persons as beneficiaries (e.g., mother, father, brother, sister), but they are deprived of any power to avoid such insurance contracts. While an infant partner may disaffirm a contract of partnership and a contract made by the partnership, nevertheless, he cannot thereby disturb the availability of his capital contribution to firm creditors and to his partners.

Emancipation of an infant means that the parents have given up their right to the custody and income of the infant and that the infant is self-supporting. Emancipation may be done expressly, or impliedly—as by marriage or enlistment in military service with parental consent. Emancipation does not affect the infant's limited capacity to make contracts nor, in the absence of statute to the contrary, his right to disaffirm contracts.

The Insane. For the purpose of contracts, insanity is such an absence of mental balance as prevents the particular person from comprehending the nature and effect of his act. It is not merely mental weakness. An insane person has limited contractual capacity and may make contracts which are voidable at his election during insanity or within a reasonable period of time after he becomes sane and after he learns of the contract. The law applicable to infants' contracts and liability for necessaries in general applies similarly to insane persons. However, a person who has been *adjudicated* insane and for whom a guardian or conservator is appointed has *no* legal capacity to contract; and, accordingly, he cannot make a contract. The power to contract for him is vested in the appointee.

Drunkards. Intoxication does not of itself make voidable a contract made by a drunkard. The degree of intoxication is important. If the intoxication is extreme, so that the drunkard does not appreciate the nature and consequences of his act, his contract is voidable and the law applicable to contracts by insane persons applies. If intoxication is not of such extreme degree, then the drunkard has no power of avoidance, unless the party dealing with the drunkard was aware of his condition and took advantage of it, in which case the contract is voidable by the drunkard as against the other contracting party only.

Joint, Several, and Joint and Several Parties   A contract requires two or more parties. If two or more parties to a contract are promisors or promisees of the *same* performance, such parties may be joint, several, or joint and several promisors or promisees.

The *intentions* of the parties determine whether their obligations or rights are joint, several, or joint and several.

Joint Liability.   Unless the parties expressly or impliedly indicate to the contrary, two or more parties who *together* promise the same performance to the same promisee or promisees are *jointly* bound. For example, partners in a partnership make their contracts with third persons and are bound jointly to them. The partners are an entity for the purpose of that contract. If the parties express no intention as to how they wish to be bound, then their contract will be interpreted in light of the terms thereof and the circumstances surrounding its formation in order to determine their intention. *If no intention is expressed or implied, they are joint parties.* The manner and extent to which the obligation is to be borne among the parties themselves does not preclude a joint obligation. In order to promote uniformity in the various branches of the law, *two exceptions are made to this principle of law if the parties do not indicate their intention. First,* if a written promise made together by more than one person uses solely *the first person singular,* the parties are *joint and several.* (A writing with the words "30 days after date *I* promise to pay to X $50" is signed by A, B, C, and D.)[2] *Second, joint payees* ("pay to the order of A and B") or *joint indorsees* of a *negotiable instrument,* who indorse such instrument, are deemed to indorse *jointly and severally.*[3] *Joint parties are a unit,* as one person. They sue and are sued as a group. The discharge of joint debtors is discussed later.[4]

Several Liability.   Unless the parties expressly or impliedly indicate to the contrary, two or more parties to a contract who promise the same performance by making *separate* promises, or who promise to make such performance *separately,* to the same promisee or promisees, are *severally* bound. "We each promise," "each of us promises," "we severally promise," are commonplace expressions indicating the intention to be bound severally.

Joint and Several Liability.   Unless the parties indicate to the contrary, two or more parties who promise, in the same contract, the

---

[2] See below, p. 395.
[3] *Ibid.*
[4] See below, pp. 146–47.

same performance to the same promisee or promisees, and who *also* make such promises separately or promise separate performance, are *jointly and severally bound.* "We and each of us promise" illustrates a joint and several liability. By statute in many states, obligations which are joint are interpreted to be joint and several,[5] unless the parties have expressed a contrary intention.

Joint, Several, and Joint and Several Rights.   Just as two or more parties may be jointly, severally, or jointly and severally liable as co-obligors, so two or more parties may have joint, several, or joint and several rights as co-obligees. Unless the promisor indicates to the contrary, his promise of performance to two or more parties creates several rights if the interests of the promisees are separate and distinct, or joint rights if the promisees have only a single interest in the performance. (A contracted with B, C, and D, a partnership, to erect a building on their land. A's promise created joint rights in B, C, and D.)

2. MANIFESTATION OF MUTUAL ASSENT

Parties must agree to a transaction, and such agreement must be manifested. In forming an informal contract, parties manifest to each other their mutual assent by offer and acceptance. An offer contains a promise which is bargained for something specific in return—an act, forbearance, or a return promise. An acceptance is the rendition of what was requested in the offer, manifesting assent through compliance with the offer and in reliance thereon. If the conduct requested and rendered by the offer is a return promise, the contract is bilateral; if the conduct is an act or forbearance, the contract is unilateral. In case of doubt whether the offer invites the formation of a bilateral or of a unilateral contract, the offer is interpreted by the courts as inviting a bilateral contract.

Offer

Expression of Intent to Contract.   An "offer" may be defined as a promise *proposed in exchange* for an act, forbearance, or return promise. An offer is the expression of a promise which would lead another reasonably to believe that it is a complete[6] proposal to him to buy or sell definite and certain conduct and that it invites definite and certain conduct (act, forbearance, or return promise) in return. An offer is made by an offeror to an offeree. The offer may be expressed wholly or partly by words, writings, acts, or other conduct and must be communicated to the offeree. The

---

[5] With respect to liability of partners, see below, p. 628.

[6] But see a different rule for Sales under the Code, below, pp. 247–48.

offeror's expressed intent to contract, as reasonably understood by the offeree, is important—not the offeror's unexpressed mental intent. The offeror's expression is tested objectively. Could a reasonable man in the position of the offeree reasonably understand the expression to invite certain conduct in exchange for the promise? If he can, the expression is an offer. If the addressee knows, or reasonably should know, from the expression or from the circumstances at the time of the expression that the utterer does not thereby intend to make an offer, there is no offer.

Inadequate Expressions. An expression made in anger, jest, or excitement, if so understood by the addressee, does not constitute an offer because the circumstances surrounding its utterance would not lead the addressee to understand the utterer to intend an offer—an intent to contract. Similarly, negotiations do not constitute offers. Negotiations are preliminary explorations indicating an inclination, not an intention, to buy or sell at the best price. They are inducements inviting offers. Advertisements, published price lists, and merchants' circulars, indicating that goods are for sale, are not offers; they invite offers. Quotations,[7] estimates, trade inquiries and answers thereto, *usually* are not offers. An invitation for bids on work to be done or property to be sold is not an offer. However, the bids usually are offers. Expressions or negotiations which are incomplete, vague, or indefinite, in that normally included terms are omitted, do not constitute offers. The phrase "$40 per week and a fair share of the profits of the business" is indefinite and not an offer. An offer must be a complete proposal contemplating definite and certain conduct, nothing remaining to be done but to accept the offer and thereby create a definite obligation. If the expression or manifestation is not complete, there can be no inference that it constitutes an offer to contract. However, the law invokes the standard of reasonableness whenever it can in order to make a promise sufficiently definite to be legally enforceable. Thus, omission of a provision for the time within which performance is to occur, or for the amount of the purchase price, does not necessarily render the promise indefinite and ineffective as an offer. The law interprets the intent to be for a reasonable time or a reasonable amount—namely, the fair value. If the terms of the promise exclude such an interpretation, the promise is indefinite and is not an offer. It should be noted that a promise is sufficiently definite if it refers to extrinsic facts for completeness.[8]

---

[7] But see "firm offers," below, p. 31, ftn. 12, and p. 248.

[8] However, under UCC 2–204(3): "Even though one or more terms are left open a contract for sale does not fail for indefiniteness if the parties have intended to make a contract and there is a reasonably certain basis for giving an appropriate remedy."

A problem sometimes arises when an indefinite or vague promise is made and, in reliance thereon, complete or partial performance is made by the addressee. There are two possible solutions. First, if the promisor benefits from the performance, he then has a quasi-contractual obligation to pay a fair value for the benefits he received. Second, it is possible that the performance made definite the otherwise indefinite promise. (X tells Y that he will pay Y $8.00 per day for work when X wants him. Y later works for X. There is a unilateral contract at $8.00 per day for each day Y worked. Although X's expression was too vague to be an offer because indefinite in time, yet Y's performance made X's offer definite as to when Y was to work.)

Auctions. Auctions are public sales of property by public outcry to the highest bidder. Advertisements of an auction are not offers but invitations to appear and bid. The auctioneer, by putting the goods up for sale, invites bids. The auctioneer may accept or reject any bid and may withdraw the property from the auction; this right is reserved to him, and such an auction is "with reserve." However, this right may be waived, and, when done, the auction is "without reserve." *An auction is with reserve unless indicated to be without reserve,* and a bid is an *offer.* An announcement of an auction *without reserve* is an *offer* that, if the property is put up for sale and a bid is made, the property will be sold to the highest bidder. The bid at an auction *without reserve* is an *acceptance* subject to the condition subsequent that no higher bids are made. After an announcement of an auction without reserve the auctioneer need not put up the goods for sale. In an auction without reserve, after the auctioneer calls for bids on an item the auctioneer cannot withdraw the item unless no bid is made within a reasonable time. Also, before a bid is made, he may announce that the auction is no longer without reserve. The auctioneer may do this just as any other offeror may withdraw or change his offer before acceptance. In an auction, whether with or without reserve, the bid may be withdrawn by the bidder before the auctioneer manifests his acceptance by the fall of the hammer or in other customary manner.[9] A bidder's retraction does not revive any previous bid.

---

[9] UCC 2–328: "(2) A sale by auction is complete when the auctioneer so announces by the fall of the hammer or in other customary manner. Where a bid is made while the hammer is falling in acceptance of a prior bid the auctioneer may in his discretion reopen the bidding or declare the goods sold under the bid on which the hammer was falling.

"(4) If the auctioneer knowingly receives a bid on the seller's behalf or the seller makes or procures such a bid, and notice has not been given that liberty for such bidding is reserved, the buyer may at his option avoid the sale or take the goods at the price of the last good faith bid prior to the completion of the sale. This subsection shall not apply to any bid at a forced sale."

Writings—Memorial or Contract. If the expression or manifestation under the circumstances reasonably leads the addressee to understand that the utterer does not intend it as a proposal binding upon him until the utterer manifests a further assent, it is not an offer. Difficulty is encountered, however, when the parties contemplate a subsequent writing. Do the parties intend the writing to be the contract, requiring their signed assent thereto; or do they intend it to be a memorial of the oral contract, or of the several writings constituting a written contract already made? If the writing is to be *the contract,* then the utterer's expression is not an offer. If the writing is to be *a memorial,* then the utterer's expression was an offer which has been accepted resulting in a contract. It is essentially a problem of interpretation of the intention of the parties as expressed by them. If the parties agree to a writing which shall contain solely the provisions already agreed upon, the contract has been made and the writing is merely a memorial thereof. If the agreement is incomplete, contemplating subsequent inclusion of necessary details at the time of the writing, the preliminary agreement constitutes merely negotiations and the writing is to be the contract. Circumstances which are considered in determining whether the parties intended the writing to be the contract or to be a memorial of a contract already made are:

. . . whether the contract is of that class which is usually found to be in writing, whether it is of such nature as to need a formal writing for its full expression, whether it has few or many details, whether the amount involved is large or small, whether it is a common or unusual contract, whether the negotiations themselves indicate that a written draft is contemplated as the final conclusion of the negotiations. If a written draft is proposed, suggested, or referred to during the negotiations, it is some evidence that the parties intended it to be the final closing of the contract. [*Mississippi & Dominion Steamship Co.* v. *Swift,* 86 Me. 248, 259, 29 A. 1063, 1067 (1894).]

Another problem of interpretation which has arisen is whether the offer contemplates one contract and, therefore, one acceptance, or a series of contracts requiring a series of acceptances. An offer can propose a series of contracts, but, because of its expression, there is sometimes difficulty in its interpretation.

Duration. An offer is legally operative—that is, capable of being accepted—until terminated. Termination may occur in four ways: *expiration* of the offer, *revocation* of the offer by the offeror, and either *rejection* or *acceptance* of the offer by the offeree. If the offer has expired or has been revoked, there no longer is any offer for the offeree to consider. *Until expiration or revocation, there is an offer outstanding* *which the offeree may either reject or accept.* Duration of the offer will be considered in the order of possible termination, as indicated.

Expiration of Offers. An offer may expire: pursuant to the terms of the offer; by delay in the communication of the offer; by supervening legal incapacity of the offeror or offeree to make a contract; by supervening destruction of a specific person or thing required for performance of the proposed contract; or by supervening illegality.

An offer may specify its duration. On the expiration of that time the offer is terminated. If the time is clearly expressed within which an acceptance must occur, expiration of that time terminates the offer and an acceptance cannot occur subsequently. An offer requiring immediate telegraphic acceptance, or acceptance by return mail, limits the duration of the offer to that time. There is a difference of opinion as to the duration of an offer which ambiguously expresses the time within which acceptance must occur. (A mailed written offer specifies that the offeree has eight days in which to accept or to reject the offer. Do the eight days begin to run from the date the offer was written or from the date of its delivery to the offeree?) An offer must be communicated to the offeree, and it is not legally effective as an offer until so communicated. However, whether or not the utterer's expression constitutes an offer and what constitutes the terms thereof are determined by *what the addressee reasonably can understand the expression to mean.* The objective test is applicable. Inasmuch as the offeree realizes and knows that an offeror may make the terms of his offer as he sees fit, the offeree should realize that the offeror *may* have intended the offer to begin from the date the offer was written or orally expressed. Accordingly, while some courts have held to the contrary, the better view is that such an offer begins to run from the date of its writing or oral expression and not from the date of its communication to the offeree.

If no time is expressed in the offer, then it is implied that the offeror intended its duration to be for a reasonable time. A reasonable time is determined by taking into consideration the nature of the offer and the circumstances under which it was made, of which the offeree either knows or reasonably should know. If the offer is for a unilateral contract, a reasonable time for acceptance is the time in which the act or forbearance can reasonably occur. If the offer is for a bilateral contract, what may be considered to be a reasonable time for acceptance varies. When the parties are not at a distance from each other, or are conversing over the telephone, a reasonable time for acceptance does not extend beyond the time of the occasion; acceptance must occur immediately or the offer thereupon expires. When the parties are at a distance from each other, a reasonable time for acceptance is determined by the haste by which the offer was sent, whether the subject matter is subject to rapid fluctuations in price, and the requirements of usage. Generally, in commercial transactions time is of the essence, and a reasonable period of time for acceptance of an offer sent by mail is return mail, the same day in which the offer was received.

Where communication of the offer has been delayed by fault of the offeror or of the communication channel utilized by the offeror, the offer expires if the time in which to accept has been expressed in the offer and has been exceeded or if a reasonable period of time to accept has elapsed and this is known or should be known by the offeree. If the offeree does not know, or has no means of knowing, of the delay, the period of time of acceptance is extended as though the delay had never occurred. If the offeree knows of the delay but the time expressed in the offer has not elapsed or if no time is expressed in the offer and a reasonable time has not gone by, the offeree may accept within the period of time remaining. The postmark on the letter, the date on the letter, and other circumstances surrounding the transmission of the offer are considered in determining whether the offeree had reason to know of the delay.

It is implied in an offer that, at the time of acceptance: the offeror is alive and legally capable of entering into a contract; where the proposed contract required the existence of a specific person or thing, that such person or thing was in existence; and the proposed contract would be a legally valid transaction. If between the time an offer is made and the time when a manifestation of assent is made by the offeree the offeror should die, the offer expires at that moment. An offeree takes the risk that the offeror is alive at the time of his acceptance. Inasmuch as an insane person is legally capable of making a voidable contract in most states, supervening insanity of the offeror, if not known to the offeree, does not affect the duration of the offer. If it is known to the offeree prior to his acceptance, the offer generally is considered void. As an offeree is required for an offer, the offeree's supervening death precludes acceptance and the offer thereby expires. Supervening insanity of the offeree, if known to the offeror, terminates the offer; if it is not known to the offeror, the offer continues in existence. If a specific thing required by the proposed contract for its performance is destroyed *prior to acceptance* of the offer, the offer expires. (A offers to supply B with all the goods produced by X factory. Prior to B's acceptance, X factory is destroyed. The offer has expired because the continued existence of X factory was required by the offer and by the proposed contract.) Generally, an agreement to perform an illegal transaction is legally void and therefore cannot create a contract. If the contemplated transaction becomes illegal subsequent to the making of the offer, the offer expires inasmuch as it cannot result in a contract.

Revocation of Offers. An offer for an informal contract, except for certain irrevocable offers, *may be revoked by the offeror at any time prior to acceptance.* Once acceptance has occurred an offer cannot be revoked, because the offer and acceptance have merged into an agreement creating a contract. Even though an offer expressly states a specific time in which to accept or states that the offer will not be withdrawn, it is still revocable at any time prior to acceptance.

No specific form of revocation by the offeror is required. It may be express, as by parol or writing, or may be implied from conduct. Any expression by the offeror which states or implies an intention not to be bound by the offer constitutes a revocation; the word "revoke" is not necessary.

A revocation is ineffective and does not terminate an offer until the revocation is communicated to the offeree. Such communication may be made by the offeror or by the offeree's acquisition of reliable information of the offeror's expression of revocation. Information is reliable when a reasonable man would believe it to be true or when it should reasonably cause him to make inquiry. (A offers to sell certain land to B. Subsequently, before any acceptance by B, A sells such land to C. B learned of the sale. B no longer can accept. The offer has been revoked by A's expression of intent to revoke—the sale from which such intent is implied—and by the communication of such intent through B's acquisition of knowledge of the sale.) *An offeror communicates his revocation to the offeree when the offeree receives*[10] *the revocation.* The offeree receives the revocation when it comes into his possession either personally, through his agent authorized to receive communications for him, or by deposit in a place authorized by him for deposit of this or similar communications. Deposit in the offeree's door mailbox or on his office desk, or delivery to his servant or office secretary is communication. There can be no *effective* revocation without communication of notice to the offeree either by the offeror or by the offeree's acquisition of such knowledge, with one exception. When an offer is made to people unidentified to the offeror, the better view is that the offer may be revoked even though the offerees do not receive actual

---

[10] See UCC 1–201 (26) (27).

notice of the revocation, as long as the offeror takes all reasonable means under the circumstances to give the offerees such notice. Use of the same channel for revocation as for making the offer, with a similar degree of publicity, usually is sufficient. A newspaper publication of an offer for reward may be revoked by the same degree of newspaper publicity of revocation. Use of a different channel, such as radio, for revocation of a newspaper published offer might not reach the offerees, who might not be expected to hear a radio revocation. If the offeror later learned the identity of the offerees, publication in any form would, in itself, be insufficient; direct, individual communication would have to be made by the offeror.

Sometimes there is difficulty in determining whether an offer is divisible, in that it invites a series of acceptances each acceptance to create a new contract, or contemplates a single acceptance covering a series of acts to be performed under the one contract. If the offer is divisible, it may be revoked except as to contracts formed by acceptances which have already occurred. This is often the case in suretyship.[11]

An offer is irrevocable by the offeror or by his death or insanity if it is an option, or if it has resulted in part performance or tender of part performance in reliance thereon. An irrevocable offer is exposed to the power of acceptance just as any revocable offer, the difference being that, in the case of an irrevocable offer, a legal duty not to revoke is present which will be enforced. This duty exists because an express or implied contract has been made in which the offeror promises to keep the offer open.

Option. The subject matter of a contract may be the continued existence of an offer for the period indicated in the contract. (A offers to sell certain land to B and states he will keep his offer open for 10 days if B will pay A $10 for this privilege. B pays A $10. There is a contract between A and B whereby A's offer to sell the land to B is to remain open for the 10-day period.) An offer is a promise which may contain two offers: one, a main offer—e.g., to sell land—and two, a subsidiary offer to keep the main offer open for a prescribed period of time if the offeree will pay for this privilege. The offeree's payment for the privilege is an acceptance of the subsidiary offer thereby making a contract, under the terms of which the main offer in the over-all promise is to remain open for the prescribed period. The main offer is irrevocable by the offeror during that period. Inasmuch as the over-all promise is the

---

[11] See below, p. 811.

offer containing the main irrevocable offer, the promise or offer is called an "option." Accordingly, *an option is an irrevocable offer as prescribed in the option contract.*

An option contract requires, among other things, sufficient consideration. Sufficient consideration is the price requested by, and for, the promise and is the name for the act, forbearance, or return promise requested. In the foregoing illustration it was the $10 requested by A. If the promise requests sufficient consideration which is rendered, then the promise is a contract. In some states a written promise under seal makes sufficient consideration unnecessary. A promise cannot become an option without sufficient consideration[12] or unless it is a written promise under seal in those few states where the sealed promise is binding without sufficient consideration, with the exception of promissory estoppel, which will be discussed later.[13] (A promised to sell certain land to B, such promise to remain open for the next 10 days if B paid A $10. B's payment of $10 makes the promise an option. Within the 10 days, B may accept A's promise or offer and thereby create a contract for the sale of the land. If A's promise were not under seal and did not request sufficient consideration—e.g., payment of $10—to keep the promise open, A's promise or offer is not an option and is revocable by A prior to its acceptance by B.) The essence of an option is that it is an irrevocable offer for the period prescribed therein; or, if no period is prescribed, then for a reasonable period of time.

If an offer for a *unilateral contract* is made and, in reliance thereon, part performance occurs or is tendered, can the offer be revoked by the offeror or by his death or insanity? An offeror may revoke his offer before acceptance occurs. Acceptance of an offer for a unilateral contract is full performance of the act or forbearance requested. Part performance is not acceptance of the offer. The offeror's promise is in exchange for performance of an act or a forbearance and, until performance occurs, there is no acceptance and no contract, and the promisor cannot be compelled to perform his promise. *When there is doubt concerning the meaning of the offer as to whether it requests a unilateral or a bilateral contract, the courts will interpret the transaction*

---

[12] UCC 2–205: "Firm Offers. An offer *by a merchant* to buy or sell goods in a *signed writing* which by its terms gives assurance that it will be held open is not revocable, for lack of consideration, during the time stated or if no time is stated for a reasonable time, but in no event may such period of irrevocability exceed *three months;* but any such term of assurance on a form supplied by the *offeree* must be *separately signed by the offeror*." (Author's italics)

[13] See below, pp. 87–88.

as a bilateral contract,[14] thereby protecting both parties. (A offers to pay B $100 for rendering certain services, to which B replies "I'll do it," or "All right," or words of similar import. The expressions of A and B create a *bilateral* contract.) However, when the offer clearly contemplates a unilateral contract and part performance occurs, can the offeror revoke the offer? Inasmuch as the offeror may limit his offer as he wishes, if the terms of the offer indicate that the offeror may revoke, clearly the offer is revocable at any time before full performance. *If the offer contains no such indication, once part performance occurs or is tendered in reliance on the offer the better view is that the offer is irrevocable by the offeror, by his death, or by his insanity.* The reasoning is that an offer for a unilateral contract implies a *subsidiary offer* to keep the main offer open if performance is begun. *Beginning of performance* is the act called for by the subsidiary offer and is consideration therefor, resulting in a contract to keep the main offer open. Any other approach would permit revocation after part performance and obviously would work injustice on the offeree. After performance has begun, the offer is irrevocable for the period stated in the offer within which full performance is to occur; or, if no period is stated, then for a reasonable period of time within which such performance can occur. When the offeree *tenders* part performance, may the offeror revoke his offer? The offeror may revoke at any time prior to tender; but once tender is made, the offeror cannot revoke. Again, the reasoning is that his offer implies a subsidiary offer to accept a tender of part performance. Once the tender of part performance is made, there is an acceptance of the subsidiary offer, and a contract is formed to keep the main offer open. Any other approach would be unjust to the offeree, who has gone to the trouble of making the tender in reliance on the offer, only to be subjected to the offeror's revocation. It should be noted carefully that preparation to tender and preparation to perform do not constitute tender or part performance.

Rejection of Offers. *Rejection of an offer by the offeree terminates the offer immediately.* If the offeror reasonably could infer from an offeree's expression, either by word or conduct, that the offeree does

---

[14] UCC 2–206: "(1) Unless otherwise unambiguously indicated by the language or circumstances
  (a) an offer to make a contract shall be construed as inviting acceptance in any manner and by any medium reasonable in the circumstances;
  (b) an order or other offer to buy goods for prompt or current shipment shall be construed *as inviting acceptance either by a prompt promise to ship or by the prompt or current shipment of conforming or non-conforming goods. . . .*" (Author's italics)

not intend to accept the offer, there is a rejection. The offeree's manifestation of rejection may expressly state a rejection, or it may be such conduct as to indicate to the offeror an intention to reject. A refusal to consider the offer any further is conduct implying no intent to accept. Similarly, a *counteroffer* implies a rejection. A "counteroffer" is an expression by the offeree of a new offer regarding the same subject matter as the original offer, but containing different terms.[15] To constitute an offer, the counteroffer must contain all the elements of an offer. A *conditional acceptance* is a counteroffer if it contains the elements of an offer. However, an *inquiry* by the offeree whether the offeror would consider other terms, or an offeree's request for further details, are not counteroffers, since they do not imply an intent to reject.

The rejection must be communicated by the offeree to the offeror in order to be legally effective, but there is a difference of opinion as to what constitutes communication. Does it mean actual receipt of the rejection by the offeror, similar to revocation which the offeree must receive to be legally effective; or merely deposit in the channel of communication authorized by the offeror, similar to the manner of effecting an acceptance? If an offer is sent by mail, the offeree mails a rejection, and then the offeree telegraphs an acceptance which the offeror receives before the rejection, does the mailing of the rejection terminate the offer? The better view is that the rejection is legally effective when mailed by the offeree, subject to the offeree's power to accept provided the offeror receives the acceptance before he receives the rejection. An acceptance sent subsequent to a previous rejection is solely a counteroffer, unless it arrives first, in which event it is an acceptance. If an acceptance is followed by a rejection, the rejection arriving first, later discussion[16] indicates that, although an acceptance is legally effective when mailed, nevertheless, if the offeror innocently *relies* on the earlier received rejection and changes his position before receipt of the acceptance, the offeree is estopped to allege the acceptance.

As previously stated, the law of contracts is concerned with the objective, rather than with the subjective, test of whether the parties have manifested mutual assent. It is what another reasonably can understand from an expression that is of the essence. Just as the objective test is used to determine the existence of an offer, so it is used to determine whether the offeror can understand the first communication he receives from the offeree to mean a rejection. If the offeror receives a communi-

---

[15] See below, p. 38, ftn. 18.
[16] See below, pp. 42–43.

cation of rejection, he need not do anything at all because the offer is thereby terminated. If by any chance an acceptance and a subsequent rejection have been sent, although the acceptance is effective when properly deposited in the channel authorized by the offeror, yet the objective test is the offeror's reasonable interpretation of the communication first received. If the acceptance arrives first, the offeror knows a contract was formed immediately on its dispatch, and any rejection which may have been made is ineffectual. If the rejection arrives first, the contractual status depends upon what the offeror reasonably does. The sending of the acceptance, unknown to the offeror, created a contract; but the offeree has misled the offeror by sending the rejection also and, if the offeror reasonably relies on the rejection not knowing of the acceptance, the offeree is estopped from alleging he sent the acceptance. In this way the offeror is protected for having acted reasonably. The objective test in contracts in effect estops the assertion of any mental intent or of other facts which contravene the manifested intent.

Acceptance   An "acceptance" is the offeree's manifestation of assent to an offer in reliance on, and in compliance with, the offer. The manifestation of mutual assent by the parties through offer and acceptance is essential to the formation of a contract. Once an acceptance occurs, there no longer is an offer; the acceptance merges with the offer, resulting in an agreement and in a contract if the other necessary elements are present. An acceptance is the consideration or price for the promise stated in the offer. Only the offeree to whom the offer is made may accept it.

Expression of Intent to Accept. The form of acceptance is that required by the offer and is either a promise or conduct other than a promise—namely, an act or forbearance.

Performance and Part Performance in Unilateral Contracts. The offer for a unilateral contract is a promise which requests an act or forbearance from the offeree. A unilateral contract is formed only by performance on the part of the offeree. Performance means complete performance, and nothing else constitutes an acceptance of a unilateral offer. However, as previously pointed out,[17] an offer for a unilateral contract is interpreted legally to imply a subsidiary offer promising to keep the main offer open for the time stated in the main offer, or for a reasonable time if no specific time is stated, and promising to accept a tender of part or full performance by the offeree. The beginning of

---

[17] See above, pp. 31 f.

performance, or a tender of part performance, by the offeree is an acceptance and performance of *the subsidiary offer* resulting in a contract to keep the main offer open and irrevocable for that time. On performance or tender of performance the main offer thereby is accepted, a contract is formed, and the promisor is obliged to perform his promise.

Performance and Tender of Performance in Bilateral Contracts. The offer for a bilateral contract is a promise which requests a return promise from the offeree. The offeree must give the return promise requested by the offer in order to form a contract; nothing else suffices except performance or tender of performance within the time in which the return promise of acceptance was to be made. The reasons for the exceptions are easily understandable. Performance is a sufficient acceptance complying with the offer because, inasmuch as the primary purpose of the offer was to obtain performance, the promise of performance being a temporary expedient to assure such performance, the offeror cannot complain if he obtains the performance primarily desired. Accordingly, such performance constitutes an acceptance resulting in a contract. Part performance is not an acceptance of an offer for a bilateral contract. However, a tender of performance is an offer to perform and thereby is a promise to perform, which is what the offer requests. A tender is an unconditional offer by one party to perform, with present ability to do so, what he is required to do under a bilateral contract or what is requested in an offer for a unilateral or a bilateral contract. When a tender is made in response to an offer for a unilateral or a bilateral contract, the tender is an acceptance and a contract is formed.

Objective Test of Acceptance. The acceptance, as a manisfestation of intent to accept, must be expressed clearly so that the offeror reasonably can understand it to constitute an acceptance of his offer. It is only when the parties—offeror and offeree—can understand the manifestation of each other to be in accord that there is an offer and an acceptance. If the offeree reasonably can understand the offeror's expression to be an offer, and the offeree's manifestation of assent thereto is reasonably clear to the offeror, there is a contract. It is immaterial that the offeree's mental and manifested assents are at variance; *the manifested assent controls.* The offeree may be ignorant of the nature, terms, and proper interpretation of the writing to which he assented; but if he reasonably could have ascertained the same, his negligence in not doing so and his resulting ignorance do not prevent the formation of a contract. However, if the offeree reasonably could not ascertain such facts, then his ignorance is not the result of his negligence and, even though he has manifested assent, he is not bound and there is no contract. The offeree may be blind and may sign the writing because of immediate urgency. If there were no urgency and the blind offeree signed the writing without having it read to him by an available impartial person, inasmuch as he reasonably could have been informed of the nature of the writing, his failure to do so is negligence and he is bound by the contract.

An offeree is held responsible for his examination of the terms of an offer made to him. His assent to such terms is an acceptance and such terms are a part of the contract, irrespective of whether or not he has examined and knows them. If he knows or reasonably should know that the contents of writings are a part of the offer, he should be aware that such writings contain contract terms; and his acceptance of such writings without objection is an implied acceptance of the contract terms contained therein. Some writings do, and some do not, purport to contain contract terms. Bills of lading, warehouse receipts, and telegraph message blanks are examples of writings which, throughout most of the United States, are held to purport to contain contract terms, and persons accepting them without objection are held to have impliedly assented to their terms. Whether or not a ticket of passage (e.g., railroad ticket) purports to contain contract terms depends upon the purpose and appearance of the ticket. If it is meant merely to show the beginning and ending points of passage, it does not purport to contain contract terms; while if it is covered with print and writing suggesting conditions concerning passage, it does purport to contain contract terms. With respect to baggage checks, the decisions are in conflict, but by the majority view the baggage check does not purport to contain contract terms. There is disagreement also on whether or not printed material on tags attached to goods, on catalogues, on letterheads, on invoices, and the like purport to contain contract terms. *The test on all this is whether or not the recipient of the writings reasonably can believe that the writings contain contract terms.* Of course, writings containing contract terms which are received by the offeree *after* the contract has been made are not binding upon him, unless he either expressly or impliedly agrees to reformation of the contract by his acceptance of such writings.

Silence. What an expression manifests is tested by what the addressee reasonably can understand it to mean. The same is true of silence. If an offeror reasonably can understand an offeree's silence to mean assent, then such silence is a manifestation of assent and an acceptance. *Silence, generally, is not a manifestation of assent.* An offeree is under no obligation to reply to offers or to do anything with services or property proffered or left with him, and his silence does not constitute assent.

There are exceptions, however, when an offeree's silence coupled with either activity or inactivity does constitute a manifestation of assent and, therefore, an acceptance.

1. Silence Coupled with Activity. *Silent use implies acceptance.* If the offeree receives property knowing, or having reasonable cause to know, that compensation is expected in return and, instead of rejecting such property, he exercises *dominion* over it, his silence is coupled with activity which manifests assent and is an acceptance. By "dominion" is meant the exercise of ownership by use, sale, destruction as opposed to discarding, or by other ways.

2. Silence Coupled with Inactivity. An offeree's silence and inactivity make more difficult a determination of the meaning of such silence. When the offeror indicates to the offeree that the latter's silence and inactivity will constitute acceptance and the offeree, understanding this, is silent thereby *intending* to accept, there is an acceptance and a contract. (A makes an offer to B for a unilateral contract requesting B's forbearance from instituting certain legal proceedings. In reliance thereon B forbears, silently and inactively. There is a contract because A reasonably can understand B's silent forbearance in reliance on his offer to be a manifestation of acceptance.) The parties may *agree* that silence shall be a manifestation of assent. An offeree, by *previous dealings* with the offeror or otherwise, may have led the offeror reasonably to believe that the offeree's silence and inactivity constitute a manifestation of assent; and if the offeror reasonably understands the offeree's present silence and inactivity to constitute assent, there is an acceptance. Thus, where an offeree *solicits* an offer, often in the form of an order, under circumstances which, because of the relations of the parties or otherwise, cause the offeror reasonably to believe that the offeree's silence is intended as a manifestation of assent, the offeree must indicate his rejection of the offer to the offeror within a reasonable time or his silence will constitute an acceptance. By court decision, and by statute in some states, insurance companies must notify applicants of rejection of their applications within a reasonable period of time; otherwise such delay constitutes acceptance. If an offeree receives property knowing, or having reasonable cause to know, that compensation is expected in return and, instead of rejecting it, he does nothing but takes the *benefit* of it, his silence and inactivity are held to manifest assent.

When the offeree's silence and either activity or inactivity constitute a manifestation of assent, the offeree is under a legal obligation to pay the compensation stated in the offer if he knows it; otherwise the reasonable value of what was offered. (A sends goods to B, stating that B's silence constitutes acceptance. If B silently does nothing, not intending to accept, there is no contract; if by his silence he intended to accept, there is a contract. If B silently takes and uses the goods, there is a contract.)

Adequacy of an Expression of Acceptance. A purported acceptance is legally inadequate and is not an acceptance if it does not comply exactly with the offer,[18] with the exceptions discussed previously in connection with part performance of an offer for a unilateral contract and the rendition of performance instead of a promise requested by an offer for a bilateral contract;[19] and with the additional exception, discussed later,[20] of an acceptance being effected by the offeror's receipt of the acceptance even though an improper channel of communication was used by the acceptor. An offer requesting an act is not accepted by a return promise. An expression of acceptance which is not clear or is equivocal, so that the offeror reasonably cannot understand it to constitute an acceptance, is not an acceptance. A *confirmation* that the offer has been received is not an acceptance.[21] If the offer requests the offeree to indicate a choice of amount or time of delivery, the acceptance must so indicate; "I accept" is not an acceptance in this instance. If an offer of reward is made for information leading to the apprehension of a criminal and for his conviction, both information and conviction are necessary for the acceptance of the unilateral offer. An expression of accept-

---

[18] UCC 2–207: "Additional Terms in Acceptance or Confirmation. (1) A definite and seasonable expression of acceptance or a written confirmation which is sent within a reasonable time operates as an acceptance even though it states terms additional to or different from those offered or agreed upon, unless acceptance is expressly made conditional on assent to the additional or different terms.
(2) The additional terms are to be construed as proposals for addition to the contract. *Between merchants* such terms become part of the contract unless:
    (a) the offer expressly limits acceptance to the terms of the offer;
    (b) they materially alter it; or
    (c) notification of objection to them has already been given or is given within
        a reasonable time after notice of them is received.
(3) Conduct by both parties which recognizes the existence of a contract is sufficient to establish a contract for sale although the writings of the parties do not otherwise establish a contract. In such case the terms of the particular contract consist of those terms on which the writings of the parties agree, together with any supplementary terms incorporated under any other provisions of this Act." (Author's italics) See below, p. 249.

[19] See above, pp. 34–35.

[20] See below, p. 41.

[21] See ftn. 18, above.

ance which also qualifies the acceptance or makes it *conditional* on something else happening is not an acceptance but is a counteroffer instead. However, a qualified or conditional expression of acceptance should be distinguished from an expression of acceptance which *requests* a change in the terms of the offer; the latter is an acceptance, the former is not. The two can be distinguished by asking the question: Does the expression of acceptance *require* a change in the offer's terms for the acceptance to take effect? If the answer is in the negative, it is an acceptance; if in the affirmative, it is not an acceptance. (A offers to sell goods to B for $1,000. B replies: "I accept, if the price is $900." There is no acceptance, but rather a counteroffer because the terms of the offer are qualified and the purported acceptance is qualified. Instead, B replies: "I accept, but you must give me good title." There is an acceptance, as a vendor impliedly warrants he has title and the offer makes such an implied warranty; the reply has not changed the offer. Instead, B replies: "I accept, but I hope you will send the goods in 10 days rather than in 20 days." There is an acceptance, since the reply does not require the goods to be delivered in 10 days.)

Knowledge of Offer for Acceptance. An acceptance is made by the offeree with knowledge of the offer and with an intent to accept that offer. Without such knowledge of a prior offer, an offeree cannot intend to accept that of which he does not know. An offeree may perform the act requested in an offer for a unilateral contract or give the promise requested in an offer for a bilateral contract; but, unless he knows of the offer, his conduct does not constitute an acceptance. (A makes a gift of goods to B, ignorant of B's offer to purchase such goods. There is no acceptance by A.) If performance is begun before an offeree learns of the offer, rendering the remainder is not acceptance because the complete performance as an acceptance was not made in reliance on the offer.

Communication of Acceptance. An acceptance, as a manifestation of assent, is in compliance with the offer. If the offer is for a bilateral contract, the offer requests a return promise which must be communicated to the offeror. If the offer is for a unilateral contract, the offer requests an act or a forbearance which need not be communicated to the offeror if not required by the offer. First, communication of acceptance in bilateral contracts, and then in unilateral contracts will be discussed.

In Bilateral Contracts. The parties contemplating a bilateral contract may or may not be at a distance from each other. Earlier discussion[22] indicated that when the parties are not at a distance from each other, or are conversing over the telephone, the occasion requires an immediate communication of a manifestation of assent, if the offer does not provide otherwise. In the case of a telephonic acceptance, the transaction is the same as though it were taking place between the parties in each other's presence, and the acceptance must be heard by the offeror to form a contract.

When the parties are at a distance from each other, the offer will indicate either expressly or impliedly the channel by which the acceptance is to be communicated to the offeror. If an offer authorizes the use of a specified channel by which to transmit an acceptance, the offer makes that channel the agent of the offeror for such purpose. By placing the acceptance in such channel, knowledge of such acceptance is given to the offeror through its agent. By complying with the offer, the offeree has given to the offeror such knowledge of the acceptance as the offeror required. Unless the offer states to the contrary, the law interprets an offer to imply authority to *use* a proper mode of communication; and the moment such channel is used, the offeror has knowledge of the acceptance and the offer has been complied with. Deposit of the acceptance in the proper channel forms the contract, unless the offer provides to the contrary. A contract is formed at that place where the last act necessary to form the contract occurs, and at that very time. If the offer authorizes telephonic acceptance, the transaction is the same as though it were taking place between the parties in each other's presence, and the acceptance must be heard by the offeror to form a contract. When the parties are at a distance from each other, the offer determines the method of transmitting such acceptance. If the offer expressly *prescribes* the method of transmittal, then no other method can be implied. If the offer expressly requires the offeror's *receipt* of the acceptance, then it cannot be inferred from the offer that mere use of the proper channel is sufficient; the acceptance must be *received* to be effective as such. When the offer does not *prescribe* expressly the channel of communication to be used for acceptance by the offeree, then the offer is interpreted to imply use of the same channel as for the offer, or whatever channel is customarily used for transactions of that nature at the place where the offer is received.[23]

It is incumbent on the offeree to observe every reasonable precaution

---

[22] See above, p. 27.

[23] See American Law Institute, *Restatement: Contracts,* 1932, sec. 66. Also see UCC 1–201(38) for "Send"; and above, p. 32, ftn. 14.

for the safe transmission of his acceptance. A letter of acceptance must be addressed properly and must be stamped. Insufficient postage does not prevent proper mailing, because it will be delivered and the deficient postage collected from the addressee; but a letter will not be transmitted without any postage. When the proper channel for acceptance is other than by mail—e.g., telegraph, railway express—and that channel does not require prepayment for transmittal, such fact does not affect the propriety of the dispatch even though a delay in delivery may be occasioned thereby. If the offeree knows or has reason to know of interruption in the authorized channel of communication, his use of that channel resulting in nondelivery of his acceptance is not compliance with the offeror's requirement that the offeree take reasonable precaution in his transmittal of the acceptance, and no contract is formed.

An acceptance dispatched for transmittal by a channel not expressly or impliedly authorized by the offer is ineffective, unless received by the offeror in the same time as by use of the authorized channel. Similarly, a misdirected acceptance is ineffective unless it is received by the addressee without undue delay in the same time as if properly directed. However, the offer expressly may so limit or prescribe the method of communicating an acceptance that, even if the offeror receives an expression of acceptance in an unauthorized manner, the expression does not constitute an acceptance. (A offers to sell goods to B if B personally will appear at A's office and accept before a stipulated time. There cannot be an acceptance unless B appears, personally, before that time, and accepts.) It is sometimes difficult to determine whether the offer *prescribes* or *suggests* a manner of acceptance. If it prescribes, the manner of acceptance must comply exactly with the offer; nothing else, not even the offeror's receipt of the acceptance, will suffice. If it suggests, then *use* of the suggested channel is sufficient of itself, while use of a channel other than the one suggested is ineffective unless the offeror received the acceptance within the same time as if the suggested channel had been used.

In Unilateral Contracts. An offer for a unilateral contract is accepted by performance. The offeree has no obligation to notify the offeror of performance, unless the offer requires notice. If the offeror does not require notice, then he has the burden of ascertaining whether performance has occurred. However, when the offeror cannot ascertain with reasonable promptness and certainty whether performance has occurred, and the offeree knows or has reason to know this, the offeree must exercise reasonable diligence in notifying the offeror,[24] or the offeror's duty to perform is discharged. For example, under the law of suretyship, if S offers to C that if C will advance credit to D to purchase lumber from C and D does not pay C then S will pay C, C has the duty to notify S of each purchase by D from C on credit within a reasonable time after each such purchase, and C's failure to do so will discharge S from liability as a surety on each such contract.[25] There is a contract by the offeree's performance, but giving such notice is a condition precedent to the offeror's duty *to perform* his promise and is a condition subsequent discharging his duty to perform his promise. Notification of performance is accomplished by utilizing any reasonable means of communication, regardless of whether the addressee ever receives the notice. If the offer is for a bilateral contract and the offeree performs or tenders performance instead of making a return promise, such performance or tender thereof must be made within the same time in which the offer could be accepted by a return promise in order to constitute an acceptance.

Estoppel. When one person represents or "holds out" to another person a material fact and the other person changes his position materially to his prejudice in reasonable reliance on the holding out, the first person is prohibited in law or "estopped" to deny what he had asserted previously. This principle of law is called "estoppel."[26] Its purpose is to prevent the obvious injustice which would otherwise result. (T stole O's horse and offered it for sale to B, who was ignorant of the theft and did not know that the horse belonged to O, who told B that it was not O's horse. In reliance on O's statement, B paid T and bought the horse from him. O is estopped to assert his title to the horse against B.)[27] It should be noted carefully that estoppel has two ingredients: a holding out by one person to another of a material fact; and the other person's material change of position in reasonable reliance on the holding out.

In the law of contracts, an offer ceases if acceptance does not occur within the expressed or implied time of its duration, and it cannot be accepted thereafter. Any subsequent manifestation of acceptance is a new offer. If the offeree dates his purported acceptance as of a time in which acceptance could occur, when in fact he is too late, there is no acceptance, because the offer has expired. Should the offeror reasonably

---

[24] Sending such notice by any reasonable means of communication, irrespective of whether or not it is received by the offeror, is sufficient notice.

[25] See below, pp. 811–12.

[26] See below, pp. 527–29. *Cf.* promissory estoppel, below, pp. 87–88.

[27] See UCC 2–403.

rely on the purported acceptance, the offeree will be *estopped* from asserting a defense of delay as negativing acceptance. In other words, the offeree previously having falsely asserted the date of his acceptance to be correct, and the offeror having relied on the offeree's assertion and believing that a contract has been formed, the offeree is prevented from varying from his original assertion. Any other approach would be manifestly unfair to the innocent offeror. To state it more broadly, if the offeree misrepresents any existing fact which is essential to the formation of a contract, and the offeror reasonably *relies* on it and changes his position, the offeree is estopped from asserting the reverse of what he misrepresented. (A mails an offer to B. B mails an acceptance and then telegraphs a rejection, the telegram arriving first. A, relying on the telegram, changes his position. A then receives B's acceptance. Although a contract was formed when the acceptance was mailed, A's ignorance of this and his reliance and change of position induced by the telegram estop B from alleging his acceptance.)

It is the manifestation of mutual assent, intentionally made, which is the key to offer and acceptance. If the parties reasonably can understand the manifestations to constitute mutual assent, and the other required elements of a contract are present, a contract has been formed. The reasonable understandings of the parties, predicated on their manifestations, are at the root of contract.

Fraud and Material Misrepresentation
Misrepresentation is a manifestation of what is not in accordance with fact. A contractual mistake may occur as a result of intentional or unintentional misrepresentation, usually made by one of the parties to the transaction; or it may occur without any such misrepresentation. Here we are concerned with such misrepresentation; later we will consider contractual mistake without such misrepresentation.[28] Sometimes this subject is treated under various headings, e.g., "reality of consent" and "genuineness of consent." While the parties have manifested mutual assent, nevertheless an element of reality or genuineness appears to be lacking.

The subject of misrepresentation at times is discussed by text writers separately from offer and acceptance. However, it seems more feasible to consider misrepresentation along with duress, undue influence, and mistake under the heading of "mutual assent" because these subjects essentially are concerned with offer and acceptance. Some of these

---

[28] See below, p. 51.

subjects preclude the formation of a contract, while others do not affect the formation of a contract but create a power to avoid a contract. These subjects will be discussed at this time, in the order indicated above.

When the term "fraud" is used, it may refer to a misrepresentation in connection with the law of torts or the law of contracts. In the law of torts, fraud is called "deceit," which is a tort,[29] and has a meaning slightly different from fraud as used in the law of contracts. The same transaction may involve the tort and contractual fraud.

In the law of contracts *fraud* signifies *intentional* misrepresentation to induce a contractual mistake. It may be defined as a misrepresentation of fact made by one person with the *intent* to induce another person to make a mistake in making, or in refraining from making, a contract. An intentional nondisclosure of facts when there is a duty to disclose, coupled with the intent to induce the mistake, is also fraud. Fraud may be stated more inclusively as the *intentional* misrepresentation of fact, or the *intentional* nondisclosure of fact in violation of a duty to disclose, with *intent* to induce a contractual mistake. If the misrepresentation, or the nondisclosure in violation of duty, is not intentional but innocent, then there is no fraud. However, there is a legal effect to such innocent misrepresentation or nondisclosure if the facts concerned are *material* facts. The term *"material misrepresentation"* means an *innocent* misrepresentation, or *innocent* nondisclosure in violation of a legal duty, of *material* facts. It should be noted that in fraud the fact need not be material; any fact is sufficient. Misrepresentation is a manifestation of what is not in accordance with fact. A material fact is a fact of such importance that, if known at the time of its representation, it would likely have influenced the conduct of a reasonable man.

Types of Fraud and Material Misrepresentation. Fraud and material misrepresentation are inoperative unless they produce a contractual mistake. They may either preclude the formation of a contract or render a contract voidable, depending on the type of fraud or material misrepresentation which occurs. There are two types: fraud or material misrepresentation *in the procurement*—which precludes the formation of a contract; and fraud or material misrepresentation *in the inducement*—which causes the contract to be voidable at the election of the party to whom the misrepresentation has been made.

---

[29] Deceit, sometimes described as "actionable fraud," may be defined as a misrepresentation of a material fact made by a person with knowledge of its falsity and with intent to mislead another person by inducing the latter to act in a particular business transaction in reliance thereon, which causes the other person so to act in justifiable reliance thereon and thereby to suffer pecuniary damage.

Effect of Fraud or Material Misrepresentation in the Procurement—No Contract. Fraud or material misrepresentation *in the procurement* (also called "fraud in the factum," "fraud in the execution," or "fraud in the inception") means that the fraud or material misrepresentation consisted of a misrepresentation of the *nature of the act* in which the injured party engaged. An example of fraud in the procurement is a misrepresentation that the paper to be signed has certain provisions or is of a certain character when, by subtle substitution, the paper signed contains different provisions or is of a different character. If the substitution of the paper were made innocently, it would be a material misrepresentation but not fraud; however, the result in both cases would be the same. The injured party is misled in his belief that his act was not a manifestation of assent to any transaction, or that his manifestation of assent was made to a particular transaction when, in fact, it was made to another transaction not intended by him. If the injured party is *not negligent* and reasonably relies on the fraud or material misrepresentation, there is *no contract.* If he is *negligent,* there is no fraud or material misrepresentation in the procurement; but there is a *contract* which, because of the fraud or misrepresentation in the inducement, is *voidable* at his election. (A cannot read the writing before him. B misrepresents the terms or the character of the writing to A. A has no opportunity to have someone other than B read it to him, or the person reading it is in collusion with B and misrepresents also. A signs. There is no contract.) In the foregoing illustration, if A had the opportunity to have the writing read to him by some impartial person and does not avail himself of this opportunity, he is negligent and there would be a voidable contract.

Effect of Fraud or Material Misrepresentation in the Inducement—Voidable Contract. Fraud or material misrepresentation *in the inducement* (also called "fraud in the treaty") means that the fraud or material misrepresentation consisted of something inducing the *formation of the contract.* (A's intentional misrepresentation of his available manufacturing equipment in a contract to manufacture, or of his financial position in obtaining an extension of credit, or of the book value of shares of stock in a contract for their sale, or his contractual promise made with no intention to perform it, which induces B to make a contract, is fraud in the inducement creating a contract *voidable* at B's election. If the misrepresentations were made innocently, there would be material misrepresentation with the same result.) There is a manifestation of mutual assent to do certain things, and a contract is created. The contract's *formation, not its subject matter,* was induced by the fraud or material misrepresentation. If the injured party as a reasonable man has relied on this inducement, the contract is voidable at his election. *When the word "fraud" is used without qualification it signifies fraud in the inducement.*

We have seen that when one of the parties to the transaction has perpetrated fraud or material misrepresentation upon the other, if it is *in the procurement,* there is no contract; while if it is *in the inducement,* the contract is voidable at the election of the party to whom the misrepresentation has been made. However, what is the effect if the fraud or material misrepresentation is perpetrated upon an innocent party to the transaction by a third person not a party to the transaction? (A fraudulently induced B to contract with C.) The effect of the fraud or material misrepresentation *in the procurement* has been indicated as not creating any contract, the result being the same whether the wrongful party is a party to the transaction or a third party. However, there is a difference if a third party commits the fraud or material misrepresentation in the *inducement.* If the third party induces the injured party to contract with another innocent party, it would be manifestly unjust to the other innocent party after he has *materially changed his position* in reliance on the contract to permit the injured party to avoid the contract. On the other hand, if the other innocent party had not yet materially changed his position, justice would be served best if the injured party were permitted to avoid the contract. Accordingly, the injured party may avoid the contract unless the other innocent party has already materially changed his position in reliance on the contract. If the injured party has no power of avoidance against the other party to the contract because of the latter's material change of position, there is no power of avoidance against the other party's assignee of the contract, unless the assignee has participated in inducing the fraud or material misrepresentation.

Summary. In summary, fraud or material misrepresentation *in the procurement* precludes the formation of a contract. However, fraud or material misrepresentation *in the inducement* causes the contract to be voidable at the election of the party to whom the misrepresentation has been made; but if a *third party* committed the wrong upon one of the innocent contracting parties, the injured party can avoid the contract provided the other innocent contracting party has not materially changed his position in reliance on the contract.

Exercise of the Power of Avoidance. The injured party may exercise his power of avoidance, or may affirm the contract and thereby extinguish such power. If he chooses to avoid, he must avoid the entire transaction. He cannot avoid part and affirm part unless it is a severable contract, one divisible part of which has been completely performed, when he can affirm the performed part and avoid the rest of the contract.

The injured party may avoid or affirm expressly or impliedly. The power of avoidance must be exercised promptly after the injured party learns of the fraud or material misrepresentation. It is a condition of disaffirmance, with certain exceptions not discussed here, that the injured party promptly offer to return the consideration he has received under the contract. Avoidance is implied from the wronged party's retention of property he was to deliver, or his reacquisition of property he already has delivered, under the contract after he has learned of the fraud or material misrepresentation. Affirmance may be made expressly or may be implied from his failure to notify the other party promptly, or from his exercise of dominion over the consideration he has received, after he has learned of the fraud or material misrepresentation. It should be noted that, if there is solely a material misrepresentation— i.e., the material misrepresentation was innocently made—and the misrepresented fact becomes a fact prior to the exercise of the power of avoidance, the power thereby ceases to exist.

Remedies. On avoidance the injured party has a right in quasi contract for the value of the performance he has rendered and, when a judgment for such value would be inadequate, a right to restitution or specific restoration of the land or things which he has delivered under the contract, at his election. Specific restoration will not be decreed against a subsequent bona fide purchaser for value of goods.[30] Until the power of avoidance is exercised, the other party to the contract has title to the property, although the title is subject to the power of avoidance. A sale of the title to a bona fide purchaser for value without notice of the power of avoidance cuts off this power. When there is fraud or material misrepresentation in the procurement and the injured party has been negligent, resulting in a voidable written contract, the injured party may rescind the contract by exercising his power of avoidance or he may obtain a decree reforming the writing to what it was represented to be.

Misrepresentation by Nondisclosure and by Opinion. Before leaving the subject of fraud and material misrepresentation a brief comment should be made about nondisclosure and about misrepresentation of opinion.

In the absence of a legal duty to speak, a party has no obligation to

---

[30] See UCC 2–403.

disclose that of which the other party is ignorant. Probably the most common instances in which a duty arises in connection with contracts are: when there is a fiduciary relationship between the parties wherein one party is acting on behalf of the other, such as between principal and agent, partners, trustee and beneficiary, executor and beneficiary, attorney and client, suretyship, director and the corporation; and when an innocent material misrepresentation is made, but before the contract is concluded the party misrepresenting learns of the misrepresentation, there is a duty to disclose the misrepresentation to the other party. Failure to disclose in violation of a duty is a material misrepresentation that there is nothing to disclose, thereby causing the contract to be voidable at the election of the party to whom disclosure should have been made. This type of misrepresentation is an illustration of what is called "constructive fraud," which is fraud as a matter of law and which occurs by failure of one party to exercise good faith in dealing with another. In contrast is what is called "actual fraud," which is intentional and direct fraud by one party upon another as a fact.

An "opinion" is a fact. The assertion that one has an opinion is an assertion of a fact—namely, that he has an opinion. An expression of opinion is subject to interpretation either as a statement of absolute truth—a fact—or as an expression of a belief in a fact. If the latter, then reliance upon such a statement is not justified because the representation of opinion is not a *material* fact and the addressee reasonably cannot rely upon it. (A, a layman, says that a certain provision is the law. As a layman, his expression of the law is understood only as his opinion, his belief that such is the law. The opinion cannot reasonably be relied on and is not the subject of fraud or material misrepresentation.) In the foregoing illustration, if A had been a lawyer, his expression is an assertion of a fact of which he should have knowledge. When an opinion is expressed by one who professes to be an expert on the subject matter, his opinion can reasonably be relied on, and such opinion may be the basis of fraud or material misrepresentation. (A, an expert on certain subject matter, misrepresents such subject matter with the intent to induce a contractual mistake. His misrepresentation is fraud.)

Compulsion to Disclose under U3C. In 1968, the federal Consumer Credit Protection Act (CCPA) became law. Title I is called the Truth-in-Lending Act, with the purpose of assuring "a meaningful disclosure of credit terms so that the consumer will be able to compare more readily the various credit terms available to him and avoid the uninformed use of credit" (sec. 102). Its purpose is consumer protection, and persons granting consumer credit must disclose certain required data concerning credit charges. The Board of Governors of the Federal Reserve System prescribes regulations to carry out the purposes of the Title. Chapter 2 is concerned with "Credit Transactions," and section 123 provides that the Board shall except from federal disclosure requirements under Chapter 2 "any class of credit transactions within any State if it determines that under the law of that State that class of transactions is subject to requirements substantially similar to those imposed under this chapter, and that there is adequate provision for enforcement." In 1969, the National Conference of Commissioners on Uniform State Laws and the American Bar Association approved of a revised final draft of the Uniform Consumer Credit Code, hereinafter referred to throughout this book as "U3C" so as not to confuse it with the UCC (Uniform Commercial Code), which covers only *commercial transactions concerning personal property.* The U3C is a comprehensive consumer protection law covering only *consumer and other credit transactions.* The U3C is much broader in its coverage than the CCPA. Pertinent references to the U3C appear in the footnotes throughout this book. It should be noted carefully that the UCC *supplements* the U3C, which is dominant over the UCC.

Duress
Duress is concerned with wrongful persuasion, either through the commission of a wrongful act or the threat of such an act, which deprives a person of free will. It may be defined as *a wrongful act, or the threat of a wrongful act, which induces a person to enter into a transaction without exercising his free will and judgment because of the act or the fear that the threat will be carried out.* If the duress is an act, the act must be wrongful, such as personal violence or imprisonment. If the duress is in a threat, the threat must be to commit a wrongful act either to the addressee or to his family. Fear is not measured by what would cause fear to a reasonable man but, rather, by what would cause fear to the particular addressee; it is a subjective test. A threat of civil suit, made in good faith with an honest belief in the claim, is not a threat of a wrongful act. There is a difference of view on whether or not a threat of criminal proceedings is a threat of a wrongful act. By the preferred view, such a threat is wrongful if its effect is to coerce (i.e., against free will) the other party's conduct, irrespective of whether or not he is guilty of the alleged crime.

Duress may either preclude the formation of a contract or render a contract voidable at the election of the wronged party. Duress *precludes* the formation of a contract if the wronged party reasonably cannot know the character of the transaction to which he is manifesting an assent. (A induces B by duress to sign a writing, the contents or character of which B does not know and reasonably cannot ascertain. The transaction is void.) Duress makes a contract *voidable* if the wronged party knows, or reasonably should know, the contents or character of the transaction and if the transaction did not involve a previous duty on his part. His manifestation here is voluntary, he knows what he is doing; but his free will and judgment have been affected by the duress. (A points a loaded gun at B and threatens to shoot him if B does not sign the proposed contract before him. B either knows the contract terms or has reasonable opportunity to ascertain them. B signs. The contract is voidable.) (A, by duress, induces B to pay his liquidated and undisputed debt to A. The transaction cannot be avoided.) Duress may be practiced by a party to the transaction or by a third party.

Undue Influence   "Undue influence" is another form of wrongful persuasion, rendering the transaction *voidable* at the election of the injured party. Undue influence is unfair persuasion by the exertion of influence obtained through the relationship between the parties and does not involve any fear. Undue influence may be defined as *unfair persuasion by the exertion of influence obtained either through domination over another, or by the reliance of one party on his relation with the wrongful party whereby the latter will not act contrary to the former's best interests and welfare.* It is the improper utilization of this influence which is unfair persuasion or undue influence. (A induces B, his son, to sign a contract with him, knowing that it is to B's great disadvantage to do so. A has utilized his parental relationship to his son's unreasonable disadvantage, which is undue influence. The contract is voidable by B.) Reliance on another's previous advice, the relationship of principal and agent or trustee and beneficiary, creates a duty in the person trusted not to exercise his influence unduly by unfair persuasion to the other party's disadvantage. If there is a fiduciary relationship between the parties—e.g., one party is either a trustee, executor, administrator, or guardian and the other is the beneficiary of this relationship—the transaction must be fair and reasonable and assented to by all the parties who must be legally capable of participating in the transaction; otherwise the transaction is voidable. Exercise of this power of avoidance and remedies thereunder are the same for duress and undue influence as in fraud and material misrepresentation.

Mistake

A contractual mistake may occur as a result of fraud, material misrepresentation,[31] or without fraud or material misrepresentation. We here are concerned with contractual mistake without fraud or material misrepresentation.

The effect of a *unilateral mistake* was discussed previously under "Objective Test of Acceptance."[32] A unilateral mistake does not affect the enforceability of a contract or the formation of a contract, unless assent is given in ignorance of the nature, terms, or proper interpretation of a writing and such assent is given without negligence, in which event there is no contract.

There are only two occasions when *mutual mistake* by the parties prevents the formation of a contract. First, when the parties mistakenly believe that certain material extrinsic facts exist and, *predicated on that assumption,* they manifest mutual assent, there is no contract. They obviously do not intend a contract to result unless such contemplated facts exist *at the time of their manifestation.* The facts may have been the existence of a thing, a person, or a set of circumstances. The person may be dead or the thing destroyed. The parties reasonably may have believed that performance was possible when in fact is was impossible. Such mistakes prevent the formation of a contract because, in spite of the apparent mutual assent, there is in fact no agreement. A mutual mistake of law does not affect the formation of a contract nor make a contract voidable.

Second, if either party's manifestation of intent is *ambiguous* or uncertain and this fact is *unknown* to the parties, or if the parties attach different meanings to the manifestation, there is no contract even though each party mistakenly believes from the manifestations that there is agreement. Both parties acted reasonably in making their differing interpretations of the innocently appearing, but in fact ambiguous or uncertain, manifestation. If both parties know, or reasonably should know, of the ambiguous or uncertain nature of the manifestation, they are on notice of a possibility of differing interpretations being mistakenly made by each other which would not result in a contract. If solely one party knows of the uncertainty or ambiguity, he is bound by the reasonable interpretation put upon it by the other party; but this is not a situation of mutual mistake because *both* parties have not made a mistake.

---

[31] See above, pp. 43–46.
[32] See above, pp. 35 ff.

Interpretation of Agreements

Once parties have manifested their intents, there is the problem of determining the meaning of their manifestations. After the meaning has been determined, legal effects flow from such determination. There are legal rules, called "standards of interpretation," which are applied in order to determine the meaning of what the parties have said or written, to determine their intents. Some of these rules follow:

1. In oral agreements, the meaning of the words or other manifestations used is that meaning which the utterer reasonably should know the addressee would understand from the employment of such manifestations. In written agreements, often called "integrations" to signify that the parties have reduced their agreement to a writing, the meaning which a reasonable person acquainted with the circumstances surrounding its formation would ascribe to the terms used is the meaning which would be applied to the writing.
2. If a word or other manifestation is ambiguous:
   a. If the ambiguity is unknown or known to both parties,
      (1) If each party gives a different meaning to the manifestation, there is no agreement for want of a manifestation of mutual assent.
      (2) If each party gives the same meaning to the manifestation, there is an agreement because of a manifestation of mutual assent and an accord in mental intent on the ambiguity.
   b. If the ambiguity is known, or should be known, to only one party, the meaning innocently attached to it by the other party is the meaning applied to the agreement and the first party is bound thereby.
3. The common, ordinary meaning of the language used everywhere applies.
4. Technical terms are given their technical meaning.
5. The manifested purpose of the parties is a very important factor in determining the parties' intentions.
6. A lawful, rather than an unlawful, interpretation will be given to the manifestations.
7. If the language used is susceptible of more than one meaning, and the above rules do not solve the difficulty, the language is interpreted most strongly against the party employing it. This is because the addressee of ambiguous words will interpret them as best suits himself.
8. Where there is inconsistency between printed or typewritten and handwritten provisions, the meaning of the latter prevails. If the inconsistency is between printed and typewritten provisions, the meaning of the latter prevails. If the inconsistency is between figures and written words, the meaning of the latter prevails.
9. If general terms are followed by specific terms, the specific provisions control and qualify the meaning of the general terms.
10. The circumstances surrounding the transaction are considered in interpreting the manifestations which occurred. Usage is a part of the circumstances.[33]

---

[33] See UCC 1–201(3) for "Agreement," and UCC 1–205 for course of dealing and usage of trade.

Law Applicable to Contracts. The place where a contract is made is the place where the last act necessary to make a contract has occurred by offer and acceptance. It is the law of that place which will determine its status as a contract. Generally, the validity of the following contracts is determined by the local state law as follows: contract to transfer an interest in land—the state where the land is situated; contract for the sale of an interest in a chattel—the state where by the contract terms the seller is to deliver the chattel; life insurance contract—the state where the insured was domiciled when he applied for the policy; contract of fire, surety, or casualty insurance—the state which the parties understood was to be the principal location of the insured risk during the term of the policy; contract for repayment of money—the state where the contract requires repayment to be made; contract for rendition of services—the state where the contract requires that the services, or a major portion of the services, be rendered.[34]

Under the Code. It should be noted carefully that, under the Code, with certain exceptions the parties may agree that the law of any state or nation shall apply and govern their rights and duties as long as the transaction bears a *reasonable relation* to such state or nation, i.e., the state or nation ordinarily must be where a "significant enough portion of the making or performance of the contract is to occur or occurs."[35] Also, under UCC 1–205(5), "An applicable usage of trade in the place where any part of performance is to occur shall be used in interpreting the agreement as to that part of the performance."

Parol Evidence Rule
The parol evidence rule is not a rule of interpretation nor of evidence. It is a rule with one simple purpose—to establish or determine what manifestations were made in written form. Once parties reduce their agreement to a writing intending that the writing is to constitute their contract, any oral (parol) or written agreement made prior to such written contract, and any oral agreement made contemporaneously with the written contract, which varies or adds to such written contract, are inadmissible in evidence and cannot be proved. In other words, a written contract is the final manifested intention of the parties, and it will not be varied or added to by prior agreements or by contemporaneous oral

---

[34] See American Law Institute, *Restatement: Conflict of Laws,* 2d 1969, secs. 186–97.
[35] UCC 1–105, *Comment 1.* But see U3C, sec. 1.201.

agreements. Two important factors should be noted carefully: first, that the parties intend the writing to be a contract; and, second, that the terms of the written contract cannot be varied or added to by any prior agreements or by contemporaneous oral agreements.

The writing must be a contract. If the writing is not a contract, then the parol evidence rule is inapplicable. Evidence is admissible to show that the parties do not intend the writing to be a contract, that the writing is not to be effective as a contract until a later time or on the occurrence of a contingency, or that the writing is void or voidable. Such evidence does not vary or add to any written contract; it proves that the writing is not a contract or that it is voidable.

The parol evidence rule prevents the admission into evidence of any prior agreements, or any contemporaneous oral agreements, which vary or add to the writing. Prior or contemporaneous agreements, and prior negotiations, which do not vary or add to the writing, are not covered by the parol evidence rule. Such agreements and negotiations may be admitted into evidence to explain the meaning of the written contract.

A written or oral contract may be modified or extinguished by a *subsequent* oral or written contract, and such subsequent contract is admissible in evidence to show the modification or nonexistence of the previous contract. It should be noted that writings which are executed as part of a single transaction are to be read and interpreted together as one agreement.[36]

Reformation. "If a written contract or conveyance does not reflect the intentions of the contracting parties because of a mistake of fact as to its contents or a mistake of law as to its legal effect, the writing may be reformed and extrinsic evidence not otherwise admissible to vary the writing is admissible solely for the purpose of reforming the contract so as to correct the mistake and reflect the intentions of the parties. But both parties must have been so mistaken, or one must know that the other was mistaken. However, a change of position by a person in reliance on the writing may preclude reformation, except reliance by persons who take the writing subject to equitable interests, such as assignees and transferees of instruments not of a negotiable character. The process by which a written contract is changed by court decree to reflect the previous intentions of all the contracting parties not properly expressed in the writing is called Reformation."[37]

---

[36] See UCC 3–119 concerning negotiable instruments.

[37] Joseph L. Frascona, *Agency* (Englewood Cliffs, N.J.: Prentice-Hall, Inc., 1964), p. 19.

3. SUFFICIENT CONSIDERATION

Common Law   The doctrine of consideration is a creature of English Common Law. Prior to 1285 an informal contract was not recognized by the English courts and the doctrine of consideration was unknown. Contracts under seal were recognized and enforced because of their formal nature and not because of the presence of consideration. After 1285 an informal contract was recognized and legally enforced, but consideration had to be present. The legal requirement of consideration limited the kind of promise which was legally enforceable. A promise without consideration was unenforceable, with certain exceptions.

    "Consideration" means price. If a promise is made
Price   which requests something in exchange, that some-
Exchanged   thing is the price for the promise. (A promises B
for a Promise $100 if B will do certain work. B's work is the consideration or price for A's promise.) The promise is being sold or exchanged for a price. If the price is rendered, then the promise should be performed because the promisee paid the requested price relying on the assurance that the promise would be performed. The price rendered which supports the promise is called "consideration." A promise may request as consideration an act, forbearance, or a return promise.

It was recognized early by the courts that, while the act, forbearance, or return promise requested and rendered constituted consideration, nevertheless, the consideration in and of itself in some instances was insufficient to justify the courts in enforcing the promise which requested it. (A promises $50 to B, a sheriff, if B will do a particular thing which the law already compels him to do by virtue of his office. B's performance is the act requested and, therefore, is consideration. However, B's act is only what B had to do. A in effect has obtained nothing in exchange for his promise. A's promise, while supported by consideration, is unenforceable.) If a promise is to be exchanged for consideration, the consideration must have some "value" as a price for the promise. If the consideration has value, it is deemed legally sufficient to make the promise enforceable. Accordingly, the legal principle emerged that for a promise to be enforceable it must be supported by *sufficient consideration;* consideration by itself is not enough. Courts often use the term "valuable consideration," which means sufficient consideration. *If the consideration has value, it is legally sufficient.*

Value—Detriment or Benefit. The courts have indicated clearly what is meant by "value"; it is a legal value, as distinguished from an actual value. By legal value is meant something which did not have to be given up or done previously but which was rendered (usually by the promisee) as consideration for a promise, or something to which the promisor was not entitled previously but which he received as consideration for his promise. (A promises B $10 to do a job. B does the job. B was under no legal obligation to do the job prior to the promise; and his act, therefore, is a legal detriment to him and is sufficient consideration for A's promise.) Consideration may have legal value and, therefore, be legally sufficient even though it has no actual value. (A, for sentimental reasons, offers to buy a certain map of his town from B for $10. The map may have no actual value at all; yet B's delivery of the map to A is an act which B was not obligated to do previously and, therefore, is valuable or sufficient consideration for A's promise to buy.) Courts do not inquire into the adequacy or actual value of the act, forbearance, or promises as fixed by the parties; that is for the parties to determine. Courts are concerned solely with legal value—namely, the legal detriment that has been experienced in compliance with the promise or the legal benefit received by the promisor. In a leading case the promisor requested the promisee to refrain from using tobacco and drinking liquor until the promisee became twenty-one years of age, in return for which the promisor would pay the promisee $5,000. The promisee abstained in compliance with the promise. The promisor contended that the promisee experienced no detriment, but rather a benefit in so abstaining, and that the promisor received no benefit from the promisee's forbearance. The court, holding that the promise was supported by sufficient consideration and enforceable, said:

. . . . the promisee used tobacco, occasionally drank liquor, and he had a legal right to do so. That right he abandoned for a period of years upon the strength of the promise of the testator that for such forbearance he would give him $5,000. We need not speculate on the effort which may have been required to give up the use of those stimulants. It is sufficient that he restricted his lawful freedom of action within certain prescribed limits upon the faith of his uncle's agreement, and now having fully performed the conditions imposed, it is of no moment whether such performance actually proved a benefit to the promisor, and the court will not inquire into it; but were it a proper subject of inquiry, we see nothing in this record that would permit a determination that the uncle was not benefited in a legal sense. [*Hamer* v. *Sidway,* 124 N.Y. 538, 546, 27 N.E. 256, 257 (1891).]

It is the detriment experienced by the promisee or the benefit received by the promisor, performed as requested by the promise, which causes the courts to enforce the promise as a contract. It is that *kind* of a price or consideration for which the courts look. The parties may agree upon any consideration they wish; but unless the consideration is legally sufficient in that it is a detriment to the promisee or a benefit to the promisor, the promise will not be enforced. *Informal promises must be supported by sufficient consideration in order to be enforceable.*

Mutuality of Obligation. Only promises require sufficient consideration. In unilateral contracts the promise requests an act or forbearance. The promisor does not think of the act or forbearance as having legal value; he wants that act or forbearance. Performance gives the promisor what he requested. It is *the law* which recognizes the act or forbearance as consideration and which determines whether it has legal value and thereby constitutes sufficient consideration to make the promise enforceable. The parties do not think in terms of legal value and sufficiency of consideration. The same reasoning applies to bilateral contracts. In bilateral contracts, one promise requests another promise. Each of the parties relies on the other's promise as assuring performance of what is stated in the promise. The parties do not think of "sufficient consideration," nor do they indicate that they rely on each other's promise as a "legal obligation." Each requests solely a promise assuring performance. It is the law which recognizes each expression as a promise and, therefore, as consideration; and it is the law which examines each promise to determine whether it is sufficient consideration for the other promise. *The law is that a promise is sufficient consideration for another promise if it is a legally binding obligation. It is legally binding if it promises an act or forbearance which would be sufficient consideration by itself for a unilateral contract and if it is legally valid.* A promise to pay a debt is consideration because it is a promise; but it does not promise sufficient consideration, because the duty to pay was already owing and, therefore, the promise is not binding. A promise to perform a criminal act is consideration for another promise to pay for such performance because it is a promise; but it is invalid and, therefore, is not binding. Similarly, a promise by one who has no legal capacity to contract is void—e.g., the promise of a person adjudicated to be insane is void, and in some states a married woman's promise to act as surety for her husband is void. It is a promise with no legal effect. When the promises are binding obligations, there is a contract. The courts speak of these binding promises as "mutual obligations" and of "mutuality of obligation" being present. What is meant is that each of the promises is sufficient consideration for the other because each is a legal obligation to perform sufficient consideration. If one of the promises is not a legal obligation, there is no mutuality of obligation, insufficient consideration for the other promise, and, therefore, no contract. An illusory promise precludes the existence of mutuality of obligation because it is not a promise and, therefore, is not consideration.

Consideration In determining whether a promise is supported by sufficient consideration it is important to determine *first whether there is any consideration.* Is the thing requested by the promise and provided in reliance thereon an act, forbearance, or a return promise? If it is, there is consideration. *Secondly, is the consideration sufficient?* If, pursuant to the promisor's request, someone experienced a detriment in that his act, forbearance, or return promise was not required of him previously, or the promisor received a benefit to which legally he was not entitled previously, there is sufficient consideration. The rest of this section on consideration is concerned, first, with a detailed discussion of *consideration* and, secondly, with a detailed discussion of *sufficient consideration.*

Defined. "Consideration" may be defined as *that act, forbearance, or return promise requested and rendered in exchange for a promise.* Whatever is requested by the promise must comply with the promise and be rendered in reliance on the promise, as in the case of acceptance of an offer, in order to constitute consideration. An acceptance is consideration for the promise in the offer. Rendering the thing requested without knowledge of the promise is a gift by the promisee. (A promises to pay B $100 for B's horse. B, ignorant of the promise, gives the horse to A. B's act is a gift, since B did not act in reliance on the promise and had no expectation of anything in return.) The thing rendered must be exchanged as the price for the promise and be induced by the promise.

Illusory Promises. The return promise must be a promise in fact and not merely a promise in form. A promise is an expression which undertakes that something shall or shall not happen. An expression in the form of a promise which does not give such undertaking is not a promise. It is called an "illusory promise" or "apparent promise." An illusory promise is not consideration. (A "promises" to buy and B promises to sell all the oil which A may "desire" to order from B during one year at a fixed price. A's "promise" is illusory because it does not undertake to do anything. It does not promise to order; and, even if A does order, he does not promise to order from B. Accordingly, A has not given a return promise as requested, and B's promise is unenforceable for lack of consideration.) Illusory promises are nugatory because it lies within the power of the promisor, at his election, to do nothing. If the expression undertakes that an act or forbearance will occur, it is a promise and, therefore, is consideration, regardless of any choice which the utterer may reserve to himself. (A promises to sell to B all the goods he manufactures, and B promises to buy from A whatever goods A produces. A's promise at first appears to be illusory in that A may or may not manufacture goods; A does not undertake to manufacture. But A's promise is not illusory because, even though he has such choice, nevertheless, he has undertaken that, in the event he manufactures goods, he will sell them only to B. A has promised to sell *exclusively* to B.) Promises to "buy from you all I may require" or "sell to you all I may produce" are not illusory, since they undertake to buy or sell *exclusively,* even though the other features of each promise are illusory in that nothing may be required if the buyer's business does not function, or nothing may be produced if the seller's business does not operate.

Gratuitous Promises. A promise which is gratuitous is unenforceable for lack of consideration; it requests nothing in return. It is sometimes difficult to determine whether a promise is gratuitous or whether the promise requests consideration in return. A promise may state a condition which may be either a price for the promise or merely an act to effectuate a gift. (A promises a tramp an overcoat if the tramp will walk to the store around the corner. If the tramp's walk is merely to obtain the gift, the promise is gratuitous and unenforceable as a conditional gift. If the walk is a price for the promise, the tramp's walking as requested is consideration for the promise which becomes enforceable.) If the promisee reasonably can believe that the condition expressed in the promise requests something as consideration, the courts so interpret the promise. (A's promise to pay B $100 if B's car has an accident, is a gratuitous conditional promise, since B reasonably could not understand it to be otherwise.) Promises to contribute to charity, usually in the form of subscription or pledge, are essentially gratuitous in that they ask for nothing in exchange and people understand the intention of such promises as gratuitous. Because such promises are not supported by consideration, they should be unenforceable. However, because the courts strongly favor enforcement of charitable subscriptions, an exception to the requirement of consideration is made, called *promissory estoppel.* Although the charitable promise requests no consideration, yet if such a promise reasonably can be expected to induce reliance thereon and such reliance in the form of an act or forbearance occurs, the promisor is estopped or barred from setting up insufficient consideration and the promise is enforceable. Contracts under seal constitute another exception to the requirement of consideration because of their formal nature, and they are enforceable in those few states where the seal still has its Common Law effectiveness.

Under the Code. It should be noted carefully that, under the Code, the Common Law effect of the seal is abolished. However, the seal still can be used to authenticate a signature, such as a corporate seal; and the seal may even be a signature when the party intends it as such. Also, a party to a transaction may waive or renounce, in whole or in part, his claim or right against the other party arising out of an *alleged* breach; but to be effective as a release the waiver or renunciation *if oral* must be supported by consideration, or if *in writing* it must be signed and delivered by the aggrieved party *without any requirement of consideration.*[38]

"Past" Consideration. There is no such thing as "past" consideration, although some of the courts use this phrase.[39] Consideration is the price requested by, and exchanged for, the promise. An act or forbearance rendered *prior* to the making of the promise is not consideration for the promise, although such act or forbearance sometimes is referred to as "past" consideration to indicate that it occurred in the past or prior to the making of the promise. (X renders certain services for Y. Subsequently, Z promises X to pay for such services. X's services are not consideration for Z's promise, which is, therefore, unenforceable.) However, a subsequent promise may be evidence of the value of the previous act or forbearance. (A requests B to do a certain act, which B does in reliance on A's request. Subsequently, A promises B $100 for B's act. A's request implies a promise to pay the reasonable value of B's act, and B's performance is consideration for A's implied promise to pay such reasonable value. B's act is not consideration for A's subsequent promise, and A's subsequent promise is unenforceable for lack of consideration. A's subsequent promise is evidence of what A estimates to be the reasonable value of B's act.) An antecedent debt does not constitute consideration for a debtor's promise to pay the debt. However, an antecedent or pre-existing debt constitutes value for a promise which is in the form of a negotiable instrument—e.g., check or negotiable promissory note—because under the Law Merchant,[40] which originally devel-

---

[38] See UCC 1–107.

[39] By state statute, "past" consideration may be recognized and, if it is the basis of a written promise, it causes the promise to be enforceable.

[40] The Law Merchant is that body of customs and usages of merchants sanctioned by the courts. Initially, this body of law was developed in English mercantile courts, and subsequently it became a part of the Common Law as recognized and declared by the Common Law Courts. Thus, the Law Merchant, along with the Common Law and Equity,

oped separately from the Common Law, the concept of consideration was unknown.

"Moral" or "Good" Consideration. What is often called "moral" consideration or "good" consideration is not consideration at all, and a promise based upon either of these is unenforceable for lack of consideration. (A, "in consideration of B's love and affection," promises to pay B $1,000. The promise is unenforceable for lack of consideration.) No price is being exchanged for the promise. The "moral" consideration is nothing more than an indication of the motive prompting the promise.

Motive. Motive for making the promise should not be confused with consideration. If the promisor is motivated by his friendship with the promisee in promising to sell an article at a price lower than its actual value, and the promisor receives the requested act, forbearance, or promise in return, his promise is enforceable. Motive cannot be substituted for consideration, although it may explain why the consideration is so small.

Failure, Compared with Want, of Consideration. Failure of consideration should be distinguished from lack or want of consideration. A contract cannot be formed unless the promise is supported by consideration; the promise is unenforceable for lack or want of consideration. If a bilateral contract has been formed by the exchange of promises and one of the promises is not performed, such nonperformance is a failure of consideration and the other promise thereby becomes unenforceable. Failure of consideration indicates that a contract has been formed, but one of the promises was not performed; while lack or want of consideration indicates that no contract has been formed because a promise was not supported by consideration.

By Whom and to Whom Consideration Is Rendered. Consideration may be given by the promisee or anyone else, and may be given to the promisor or to anyone he designates. If a promise requests consideration and the consideration is provided as requested, it is immaterial whether the consideration was to be provided by the promisee or by someone else. (A promises B $100 if C will do a certain act. C performs the act. C's act is consideration for A's promise. A just as well could have requested B to perform the act instead of C.) Similarly, the

---

became a part of the heritage of the American colonies and of each of the later independent American states. Since a merchant's promise to pay an antecedent debt was enforceable under the Law Merchant, today the Code provides that "value" for a promise causing it to be enforceable may be sufficient consideration or an antecedent or pre-existing debt. For example, see UCC 1–201(44)(b) and 3–303(b).

promise may request the consideration to be rendered to the promisor or to someone else. (A promises B that, if B will extend credit to C, A will pay B if C does not pay B. B extends the credit. B's act is consideration for A's promise, even though the consideration was rendered to C.) (A promises B that, if B will forbear instituting legal proceedings against C, A will pay B $100. B forbears. B's forbearance is consideration for A's promise.) Consideration is the price requested in exchange for the promise and, if rendered as requested, it is immaterial to whom or by whom it was given.

Third Party Beneficiary Contracts. A third party beneficiary contract is a contract made between two persons for the purpose of benefiting a third person who is not a party to the contract and who provides no consideration. The third person is called a "beneficiary." (A promises B that, if B will lend A $100, A will pay $100 to C in 10 days. B lends A $100. A's promise is supported by consideration—namely, B's delivery of $100 to A. C is a beneficiary of the contract in that A is to pay $100 to him.) Third party beneficiary contracts create no difficulty regarding consideration. They raise the sole problem of whether the beneficiary should be permitted to enforce the promise made in his favor. This problem is discussed later,[41] under the separate subject of third party beneficiary contracts.

Recital of Consideration. *Informal Contracts.* The law requires that an informal promise, to be enforceable, must be supported by sufficient consideration. If a written contract does not recite the consideration, it can be proved that the consideration was given. If a written agreement recites that the consideration has been given, the recital is prima facie evidence of that fact. However, a false recital that consideration has been given cannot evade the legal requirement of consideration, and the recital can be proved to be false. If the recital of consideration be false but a promise to pay the consideration can be implied, then the promise to pay the consideration is deemed sufficient consideration to support the other promise. (A, an insurance company, issues a policy to B insuring B's premises against fire, such policy stating it is effective only when B has paid the premium and falsely reciting that the premium has been paid. B accepts the policy. The falsity of the recital of payment can be shown; but inasmuch as B's promise to pay the premium can be inferred from B's acceptance of the policy, B's implied promise is the consideration supporting A's promise to insure.)

---

[41] See below, pp. 96 ff.

promisor, it is insufficient consideration for the promise to excuse a part of the debt. Therefore, *a promise to accept a lesser sum in satisfaction of a greater sum undisputedly owing to the promisor is not supported by sufficient consideration.* To state the principle more broadly and in another way, any promise to accept part of what is legally owing in satisfaction of it all, or to give something more than the contract requires in order to obtain performance of the other party's promise, is not supported by sufficient consideration and is unenforceable. (Under a contract between A and B, A is to design and superintend the construction of certain buildings for B for a commission of 5 per cent on the cost of the buildings. Subsequently, B desired the construction of an additional building and entered into a contract with C whereby C was to design and supervise the construction of the additional building for a commission of 5 per cent on its cost. A refused to perform his contract with B unless B promised to give A 5 per cent of the cost of the additional building in addition to C's 5 per cent. B so promised. A then performed his contract and demanded the additional 5 per cent. B's promise to pay A the additional 5 per cent is unenforceable because it is not supported by sufficient consideration. B's promise requested an act—namely, A's performance of his contract with B—which act was consideration for the promise. However, A's act was a legal duty previously owing to B; and as its performance did not constitute a detriment to A or a benefit to B, it is insufficient consideration for B's promise.)

Consideration Partly Sufficient. A promise may request consideration, part of which is sufficient consideration and part of which is not sufficient consideration. That part which is sufficient consideration will cause the promise to be enforceable; the fact that the other part is insufficient is immaterial. (A owes B money. B promises to discharge A if A will pay a certain portion of the indebtedness and deliver A's horse to B. A complies with the promise. B's promise requested two acts: part payment and delivery of a horse. These acts were rendered and, therefore, are consideration for the promise. Although the act of part payment is insufficient consideration because it is a legal duty already owing to B, nevertheless, A's delivery of the horse was not previously owing and is sufficient consideration to make B's promise enforceable.) As long as the consideration is sufficient in part, the promise is enforceable. Illustrations of this principle are numerous. Although a creditor's promise to discharge a debtor for part payment by the debtor is unenforceable for lack of sufficient consideration if such part payment is made, yet, if the creditor requests and receives something in addition to that legally owing, then his promise is enforceable because the addition is sufficient consideration. A debtor's part payment in a manner different from that required by the indebtedness obligation, as requested by the creditor, is sufficient consideration for the creditor's promise of discharge because the manner of paying is different from that required by the previous legal duty. A promise to pay a greater amount than that required by a contract, in exchange for a return promise by the other contracting party to perform his contract and to do additional work, is supported by sufficient consideration; the promise of additional work is sufficient consideration. A contract between creditor and debtor whereby an *interest-bearing* obligation is extended in time is supported by sufficient consideration. The consideration for the creditor's promise to postpone the date of payment consists of the debtor's promise to pay interest for a longer period of time and to pay the principal at a later date. That portion of the debtor's promise which assured payment of the principal promised performance of an act already due and, therefore, is insufficient consideration. That portion of the debtor's promise assuring the payment of interest for a longer period of time than was required previously is sufficient consideration, making the creditor's promise enforceable. It should be noted that, when an obligation—e.g., a promissory note—specifies that interest shall be paid, interest as it accrues becomes part of the principal; and payment only of the original principal, therefore, is merely part payment. Accordingly, a creditor's promise to discharge the debtor on the debtor's payment of only the original principal is not supported by sufficient consideration if such payment is made, because there is no sufficient consideration for the creditor's promise to forgive payment of the addition to the principal. However, if the obligation does not provide for interest, but in a legal action for the principal interest could be obtained as damages for nonpayment of the principal, such possible interest does not constitute part of the principal, and payment of the principal is payment in full.

Negotiable Instruments. Although it would seem that a creditor's promise to discharge a debt if the debtor will give to the creditor his negotiable instrument for the *full* amount would not be enforceable because it is not supported by sufficient consideration when such instrument is given—for the reason that the instrument is merely a new promise to pay what is already owing—such is not the case with respect to negotiable instruments. The law of negotiable instruments developed under the Law Merchant, separate from the Common Law. The Code reflects the Law Merchant by providing that a negotiable instrument is supported by value if the consideration is sufficient to support a simple contract or is an antecedent obligation. Accordingly, inasmuch as a debtor's negotiable instrument for the *full* amount is enforceable, the delivery of the instrument to the creditor in exchange for the latter's promise to accept it in full satisfaction of the debt is sufficient consideration for such promise, because the creditor was not previously entitled to the instrument. The debt is thereby discharged and the debtor has a new obligation—to pay the instrument. In the absence of any specific agreement a negotiable instrument for the full amount is not absolute payment but, rather, conditional payment—it is accepted on condition that it is paid. If the instrument is not paid, the original debt still exists; if it is paid, the original debt is discharged.

Although a debtor's instrument for a *smaller* amount is insufficient consideration for the creditor's promise of discharge of the total amount due, yet, if a third person's signature (either as co-maker, co-drawer, or indorser) appears thereon, the debtor is discharged from the debt. The creditor's promise to discharge is supported by consideration consisting of two promises—namely, the debtor's promise to make part payment, which is insufficient consideration because it is already legally owing; and the third person's promise to pay the face amount of the instrument, which is sufficient consideration for the creditor's promise because it was not previously owing. This type of instrument is called a "secured instrument" because the third person's obligation to pay is additional security to the creditor that the debt will be paid. It is clear that a creditor's promise to discharge a debtor if a third person pays the whole or a part of the debt, or if a third person delivers his negotiable instrument for such amount to the creditor, is supported by sufficient consideration if such act is performed.

Same Consideration for Several Promises. Several promises may request the same consideration. If the consideration is sufficient for at least one of the several promises, all of the promises are enforceable. The price for all of the promises was the consideration requested, and the rendition of such consideration should make all of such promises enforceable. This is true whether the consideration requested was an act, forbearance, or a return promise. (A promises B $5,000 if B will: promise to supply the goods he previously promised to supply under an existing contract with A; promise to supply the goods more quickly than the contract requires; and promise to supply special containers for the goods which the contract does not require. B so promises. B's promise to supply the goods as required under the existing contract is insufficient consideration for A's promise because B already was obligated to do this. However, B's other promises are sufficient consideration for A's promise. Inasmuch as A's promise did get something new—namely, B's promises to supply more quickly and to supply special containers—A's promise is enforceable. All B's promises are enforceable because they are supported by A's promise, which is sufficient consideration. It should be noted that, although there is mutuality of obligation by A's promise on one side, and all of B's promises collectively on the other, yet the promises first had to be examined for sufficiency of consideration.)

Compositions. A "composition" outside of bankruptcy[44] is an agreement whereby an insolvent or financially embarrassed debtor agrees with some or all of his creditors that, on his immediate payment to each of them of a part of his indebtedness to each, each will discharge the debtor. Composition agreements are socially useful and desirable and are enforced. Because of the obvious problem of sufficient consideration in compositions, various explanations have been advanced to justify the enforcement of such agreements. One explanation is that there is no sufficient consideration, because the debtor paid what was already owing, but that social policy makes an exception here to the requirement of sufficient consideration. Another explanation is that the mutual promises of the creditors, each to forego a part of his claim, are sufficient consideration for each other. Still another explanation is that the promise of the debtor not to pay each creditor more than his pro rata portion is sufficient consideration for each creditor's promise. Under the Bankruptcy Act, a composition is permitted between a debtor and his creditors with the approval of the court and the debtor is discharged from liability for such debts. The statute here represents public policy.

Prior Duty Owing to Public. A promise which requests as consideration that which is already owing to the public is not supported by sufficient consideration and is unenforceable. The person owing a legal duty is called the *obligor,* and the person to whom the obligation is owing is called the *obligee.* An obligor incurs no detriment to himself by rendering the promise to perform or by performing, inasmuch as he already was legally obliged to do so. Similarly, as the promisor is a member of the public, such legal duty was owed to him by the obligor and does not constitute a benefit to the promisor. People are under a legal duty not to commit torts, crimes, or other illegal acts; and forbearance from commission of such illegal acts, or performance of such illegal acts, or a promise to forbear from or to perform such acts, does not constitute sufficient consideration for a promise. A common carrier's promise to carry goods is insufficient consideration for a shipper's prom-

---

[44] For compositions under bankruptcy, see below, pp. 866–68.

ise to limit the carrier's liability for negligence, because common carriers are under a legal duty to carry goods for the public. Similarly, executors, trustees, and public officers are under a duty to perform; and a promise for such performance by an interested party is unenforceable for want of sufficient consideration. There seems to be an exception in the case of finders. Although a finder becomes an involuntary bailee under a legal duty to hold the property for the owner, nevertheless, the courts have held that an offer of reward for the return of the property is enforceable regardless of the doctrine of consideration. The law that a finder is entitled to the proffered reward is so old that it persists today. It should be noted careully that, if the promise requests and receives from the obligor something, however small, in excess of his legal duty, such thing is sufficient consideration and, accordingly, the promise is enforceable.

Prior Duty Owing to Third Persons. The great majority of American courts hold that performance of, or a promise to perform, an obligation already owing to third persons (obligees) is insufficient consideration for a promise of another person requesting such performance. A small minority of American courts; the *Restatement of Contracts;* Samuel Williston, the outstanding American authority on the law of contracts; and the English courts—all hold it is sufficient consideration. The conflict reduces itself to the simple question of whether a legal benefit to the promisor constitutes sufficient consideration. Usually benefit and detriment occur together; but in the case of a prior legal duty owing to third persons, there is no detriment. (A is under a contractual duty to B to build a building. A refuses to perform. C promises A $1,000 if A will perform his contract with B. A performs in reliance on the promise. Under the minority view, A's performance is sufficient consideration for C's promise; the majority of American courts hold it is insufficient consideration. A's performance was no detriment to A because he was under a legal duty to B to perform. However, under the minority view, A's performance is a benefit to C, for C obtained a performance to which he was not entitled previously.) The American courts consistently have stated that consideration which constitutes a detriment to the promisee or a benefit to the promisor is sufficient to render a promise enforceable. In view of such statements by the American courts and their application by the English courts, and because a person who has sold his promise and received consideration in exchange should pay for the benefit received, it is submitted that the minority American view is preferable. There is no question that, if a person *pays* consideration to the obligor for the latter's promise to perform his duty to the third party obligee, such payment is sufficient consideration for the obligor's promise, which is then enforceable by the person who has paid the obligor.

Exception 2—Invalid Claim or Defense Not Honestly and Reasonably Believed to Be Valid. *A forbearance to assert, or the surrender of, an invalid claim or defense made by a person who has no honest and reasonable belief in the possible validity of such claim or defense is insufficient consideration for the promise requesting it.* People have the legal right to institute legal proceedings for recovery on claims which they assert, be the claims valid or invalid. It is for the courts to determine the validity or invalidity of such claims. A promise to pay for forbearance to assert, or for forbearance from continuing to assert, such claim must be supported by sufficient consideration to be enforceable. If the claim is invalid, such forbearance or surrender gives nothing and is not suffiient consideration for the promise. Does it make any difference that the person so forbearing or surrendering honestly and reasonably believes that the claim is valid when in fact it is invalid? The law says it does make a difference. If a person honestly and reasonably believes that he has a valid claim, his giving up the right to institute legal proceedings thereon is a detriment to him and is sufficient consideration for a promise requesting such forbearance. Similarly, it constitutes a detriment to forbear continuing a legal proceeding already begun on the claim, or to surrender such a claim. If a person asserting an invalid claim has no honest and reasonable belief in its validity, he gives up nothing detrimental to himself. The same principle applies to legal defenses. If the defense is invalid, it is insufficient consideration; but if the person claiming the defense honestly and reasonably believes that the defense is valid, his waiver of, or promise to waive, such defense is sufficient consideration for the initial promise requesting it. Accordingly, *any forbearance to assert, or any surrender of, an invalid claim or defense is insufficient consideration, unless the person forbearing or surrendering honestly and reasonably believes the claim or defense to be valid, in which case the forbearance or surrender is sufficient consideration.*

Who May Assert Exception 2. The claim or defense may be asserted by the promisee against the promisor, by the promisee against a third person, or by a third person against a fourth person. (A promises B $10 if B will surrender his claim against A. Or A promises B $10 if B will not assert his claim against C. Or A promises B $10 if C will not assert his claim against D.) As long as a detriment has been experienced in reliance on the promise, regardless of who experienced the detriment, there is sufficient consideration for the promise.

Duration of Forbearance. There is no problem regarding the duration of forbearance if the period of time is stated in the contract. The specified period may be for a limited time or perpetually. However, some agreements do not specify the duration of the forbearance, and the courts must interpret the agreement in light of the circumstances surrounding its formation to determine the intent of the parties. If the agreement is unilateral in that the promise requests the forbearance, the courts interpret the forbearance to be for a reasonable period of time; otherwise the promisee would have to wait indefinitely before receiving payment for his forbearance. If the agreement is bilateral, the courts are inclined to interpret the agreement as requiring forbearance for a reasonable period of time, unless the amount of money involved indicated the contrary. A promise to pay $90 for a promise to forbear asserting a claim for $100 probably would be interpreted as requiring perpetual forbearance. Perpetual forbearance means discharge of the claim. If there is doubt whether the agreement contemplated a unilateral or a bilateral contract, the courts will interpret the intention as bilateral. A promise to forbear as long as the promisor wishes is an illusory promise, since he does not promise that he will forbear at all; it is not an undertaking to forbear and, therefore, is not a promise.

Disputed Claims. Claims may be disputed or undisputed. *A claim is disputed if it is honestly and reasonably believed not to be valid by the party against whom the claim is asserted.* When a claim is undisputed, a promise to discharge the claim for payment of a lesser amount than what is due is not supported by sufficient consideration, on the ground that a promise to accept a lesser sum in satisfaction of a greater sum is not supported by sufficient consideration. There was a previous legal obligation to pay the entire amount; and, accordingly, there is insufficient consideration for the promise to forgive a part of what is owing. However, when the claim is disputed, a promise to discharge the claim on payment of a compromised amount is supported by sufficient consideration if the payment is made. The reason is that the promisee thereby gives up an amount which he does not feel he is obligated to do. (A and B disagree on how much A owes B. A honestly and reasonably claims it is $10, while B claims it is $20. They compromise on $15, and A pays $15 in return for B's promise to discharge the debt. B's claim is disputed, and A paid more than he felt was due. A's payment is a detriment and is sufficient consideration for B's promise.) It is immaterial that the actual amount owing was smaller or larger than the compromise amount. It is what a party honestly and reasonably believed he was giving up or getting which is important and which constitutes the detriment or benefit. Courts do not inquire into the compromise amount except to see that is a bona fide compromise. Accordingly, *a compromise of a disputed claim is enforceable.*

Liquidated and Unliquidated Claims. A claim may be liquidated or unliquidated. *A claim is liquidated when the amount is either: fixed by the parties, certain, or ascertained by mathematical computation or by operation of law.* (A sold and delivered goods to B for $200. A claims B owes him $200. B honestly and reasonably asserts that he has, and A honestly and reasonably asserts that B has not, paid the $200. A's claim is *liquidated* inasmuch as its amount is fixed, but the claim is *disputed* by each party as to its payment.) If the claim is liquidated and undisputed, the full amount of the claim is owing and a promise to accept a lesser amount in satisfaction of the total amount due is unenforceable. If the claim is liquidated but disputed, a compromise agreement for a stipulated amount will be enforced. (A owed B $20 but asserted he had paid it. B disagreed. They compromised that, if A would pay B $5.00, B would discharge A. A paid B the $5.00. B's promise is enforceable. The amount owed was certain, $20. The dispute was concerned with its payment.) If the claim is unliquidated, whether disputed or not, a promise of discharge on payment of an amount agreed by the parties is enforceable on payment of such amount. (A's car injured B, and B claims $1,000 damages. B promised to discharge A on payment of $1,000. A paid B $1,000. B's promise is enforceable. The claim was unliquidated.) Therefore, *payment of an unliquidated claim or payment of a disputed claim in the amount stipulated by the promise of discharge is sufficient consideration for such promise.*

There is unnecessary conflict among the courts in connection with claims where part of a claim is undisputedly owing and part is either disputed or unliquidated. (A admits he owes B "at least" $50. B claims the debt is $75. B promises to discharge A if A will pay $50. A pays B $50. B now asserts a claim against A for $25. A states his payment of $50 was sufficient consideration for B's promise of discharge. The majority of the courts hold that A's payment is sufficient consideration; the strong minority holds it is insufficient consideration. The minority view is the preferable view.) Inasmuch as part is admittedly due, there is a legal obligation to pay that part; and any promise for payment of what is admittedly due is not supported by sufficient consideration if the payment is made. This is merely another illustration of the rule stated previously herein[45] that an act or forbearance which is undisputedly and legally owing to the promisor cannot be sufficient consideration for a promise, nor can a return promise to perform such act or forbearance be sufficient consideration for the initial promise. There is no dispute among the courts that, when there are two distinct claims—one of which is undisputed and the other either disputed or unliquidated—a promise of discharge for both claims on payment of the undisputed claim is not supported by sufficient consideration, inasmuch as the undisputed amount was a legal obligation previously owing. Insufficient consideration has been rendered for the promise to forgive either the disputed or unliquidated claim. Apparently the majority of the courts has failed to distinguish between (a) an unliquidated or disputed debt in which part is admittedly owing and (b) two claims, one of which is undisputedly owing and the other disputed or unliquidated. Essentially there is no difference between the two situations. Therefore, *when part of a claim is admittedly owing and the other part is disputed or unliquidated, or when one of two claims is admittedly owing and the other is disputed or unliquidated, a promise of discharge for all that is claimed on payment of what is admittedly due is not supported by sufficient consideration if such payment is made.*

Exception 3—Transfer of Like Goods or Money in Different Amounts. *The transfer of fungible goods or money in exchange for a promise to transfer a larger or smaller amount of the same thing at the same time and place is insufficient consideration.* It is obvious that parties who agree to a mutual transfer of things of the same nature, in the same condition, but in different amounts at the same time and place, cannot intend to enter into a bona fide bargain. The law inquires into such a transaction solely for the purpose of ascertaining whether the parties intended to bargain and whether fraud, duress, or undue influence is present. An agreement to exchange $10.00 for $1.00, or 100 bushels of grain of a certain quality for 150 bushels of similar grain and quality, at the same time and place, is not a bona fide bargain. The transaction is probably a disguise for a gift by one party for the difference in amount. However, if there is the smallest difference in the time or place of each party's delivery, or in the quality or nature of the goods, or in any other way, then the contract is enforceable if the parties intended a bona fide agreement of exchange. The word "fungible" is used to designate goods of a certain nature. The Code defines fungible goods as goods "of which any unit is, by nature or usage of trade, the equivalent of any other like

---

[45] See above, p. 64 f.

unit." In the absence of any difference other than amount in the things sought to be exchanged, the delivery of such things is insufficient consideration for a promise requesting it.

Adequacy of Consideration. The court's examination of an agreement contemplating the exchange of like things in different amounts appears to be an inquiry into the adequacy of the consideration involved in the agreement. The law does not inquire into the adequacy of the consideration agreed upon by the parties; it is concerned only with the sufficiency of the consideration and whether fraud, duress, or undue influence is present. The difference between adequacy and sufficiency of consideration is that adequacy is concerned with the actual value of the thing requested and rendered, while sufficiency is concerned with its legal value in terms of legal detriment and legal benefit. The parties may agree to buy and to sell goods at a price which is above or below the market value. They may fix as consideration any price they wish. The law does not make their contracts; they do. If one of the parties already owed an obligation to sell to the other or to buy from the other, then the law holds that there is insufficient consideration because nothing was being done, or promised to be done, which was not already owing; there is no detriment or benefit involved. Accordingly, the parties may provide for any consideration, whether adequate or inadequate, just so long as there is a bona fide intent to bargain and to exchange what amounts to a detriment or a benefit so that sufficient consideration is present to make the promises enforceable. *The parties determine the adequacy of the consideration; the law determines the sufficiency of the consideration.* There is no relation between adequacy and sufficiency of consideration, except at a point where the consideration is so entirely inadequate that the law finds insufficiency of consideration because the parties did not intend a bona fide agreement to make an exchange. (A promises B $1.00 for a horse worth $100.00. B delivers the horse to A. The court will not inquire into the adequacy of $1.00, but it will inquire to see whether the parties intended to bargain the horse for $1.00 *as consideration.* If there is a genuine intent to bargain for the $1.00 as consideration for the horse, then there is sufficient consideration and the promise is enforceable.)

The subject of adequacy of the consideration often arises in assignments or in the transfer of documents. A person may desire certain rights which he believes belong to another, and he promises a consideration to the other for assignment to him of *whatever rights* the promisee may have. After the assignment has taken place, the promisor may find that the promisee did not have the particular right desired. The promisor cannot raise the question of inadequate consideration when the promisee seeks to enforce the promise. The promisor must perform his promise even though he received an assignment of no value to him. The assignment is sufficient consideration, for it constituted a detriment to the promisee in that he gave up something he did not have to give up, and a benefit to the promisor in that he received something to which he was not previously entitled, regardless of the actual value to either party. If the promisor requested the assignment to him of *that particular right,* his promise is unenforceable for lack of consideration until that right is assigned. Similarly, a promise may request transfer of *a paper or document,* believing it to have a certain actual value. On transfer of the paper requested, the promisor finds it does not have the value he anticipated. His promise is enforceable because the transfer of the paper was sufficient consideration. If the promisor had requested the transfer of a paper containing *a certain right,* his promise is unenforceable for lack of consideration until that paper containing that right is transferred. Both parties may agree to effect a transfer of *a certain paper* containing *a certain right.* On transfer, it is found that the paper does not contain such right. There is no contract because of a mutual mistake of fact that the paper contained a particular right. Similarly, a promise of discharge may request the promisee's negotiable instrument—e.g., check, negotiable promissory note. If the promisor clearly indicates that the instrument alone is the consideration requested, then, regardless of whether the instrument is ever paid, the promise is enforceable. If the promisor does not clearly so indicate, then the law interprets the intent of the parties to be that the consideration requested is *the money* indicated in the instrument and the promise is unenforceable for lack of consideration until the instrument is paid. In the latter situation the instrument is called "conditional payment."

Exception 4—Promise to Render Consideration Insufficient for Unilateral Contract. *A promise to do an act or to forbear, which the promisor has reason to know would be insufficient consideration for a unilateral contract, is insufficient consideration for another promise.* Whether a promise contemplates a unilateral contract by requesting an act or forbearance, or contemplates a bilateral contract by requesting a return promise to perform an act or to forbear, the initial promise must be supported by sufficient consideration in order to be enforceable. A return promise is not in itself sufficient consideration; it must promise an act or forbearance which is sufficient consideration. If an act or forbearance is insufficient consideration, a promise requesting such act or forbearance, or requesting a return promise to perform such act or forbearance, is unenforceable because it is not supported by sufficient consideration. "If the performance is sufficient consideration for a contract, the promise of performance is likewise sufficient."[46] As an illustration, performance of an act previously owing to the promisor, or a return promise to perform such act, does not constitute sufficient consideration in support of the initial promise; while performance of an act not previously owing to the promisor, or a return promise to perform such act, does constitute sufficient consideration in support of the initial promise. Inasmuch as a return promise must be supported by sufficient consideration, the initial promise also must undertake to perform an act or forbearance which is sufficient consideration for a unilateral contract.

Reasonable and Honest Belief of Sufficiency. Difficulty arises when the promisor of consideration insufficient to support a unilateral contract honestly and reasonably believes that the consideration is sufficient to support a unilateral contract. (A asserts an invalid claim against B. B promises A $100 if A will forbear asserting his claim. A forbears. A's forbearance is insufficient consideration for B's promise, since it is no detriment to A and no benefit to B because the claim is invalid. If A honestly and reasonably believed that the claim was valid at the time he forbore, his forbearance constitutes sufficient consideration because he gave up a right to assert or litigate what he reasonably believed to be a claim, which is a detriment to him.) The law is concerned with what a party honestly and reasonably believes when he enters into an agreement. Performing an act which he honestly believed he did not have to do (A honestly believing he had paid B the $50 debt, when he really had not, but paying $25 in reliance on B's promise of discharge), or forbearing to do something he honestly and reasonably believed he did not have to do (forbearing to assert an invalid claim which he honestly believed to be valid, in reliance on a promise to pay), or promising to do such act or forbearance honestly and reasonably believing he was under no obligation so to promise—all constitute sufficient consideration regardless of the actual fact of insufficiency. Accordingly, to state the rule in a positive form, *a promise to render consideration which is insufficient for a unilateral contract is insufficient for a bilateral contract unless the promisor honestly and reasonably believes that such consideration is sufficient, in which case his promise is sufficient consideration for a bilateral contract.*

Exception 5—Promise with an Alternative of Insufficient Consideration. *A promise containing alternatives of performance at the*

---

[46] Samuel Williston, *A Treatise on the Law of Contracts* (rev. ed., Williston and Thompson; New York: Baker, Voorhis & Co., 1936), Vol. I, sec. 103D.

election of the promisor, at least one of such alternatives being insufficient consideration for a unilateral contract, is insufficient consideration for another promise. A promise must undertake to perform an act or forbearance which would be sufficient consideration for a unilateral contract in order for the promise to constitute sufficient consideration for another promise. A promise which reserves to the promisor a choice of several performances, each of which is sufficient consideration, constitutes sufficient consideration because there *shall* be performance and the performance *shall* be sufficient consideration. If one of the alternative performances reserved by the promisor is insufficient consideration, there is no certainty that the promisor will perform sufficient consideration, and that fact renders the promise itself insufficient consideration. *A promise must undertake to perform sufficient consideration as a certainty, not as a possibility, for it to be sufficient consideration.* A promise, to constitute sufficient consideration for another promise, must be a legal obligation to perform sufficient consideration.

A promise which undertakes alternative performances, one of which is sufficient consideration, at the election of the *promisee* is sufficient consideration. The promise is now a legal obligation to perform sufficient consideration if the promisee so chooses. The promise assures the promisee a certainty of performance of sufficient consideration if the promisee so desires.

Promises containing alternatives, one of which is insufficient consideration, at the election of the promisor are not by reason of that fact illusory. The word "promise" has been used in its proper legal sense, as undertaking that something shall or shall not happen. (A promises B to deliver a horse to B or to pay his debt to B, if B will promise to discharge the debt. B promises. A's promise contains two alternatives at A's election: to deliver a horse or to pay the debt. The first alternative is sufficient consideration, since delivery of the horse was not a previous legal obligation. The second alternative is insufficient consideration, since it was a legal obligation previously owing. As the election of the alternatives lies with A, A's promise is insufficient consideration for B's promise, and there is no contract. A's promise does undertake to perform one of two acts; and even though one is insufficient consideration, nevertheless, it does *promise* an act.) An illusory promise does not undertake to perform anything. (A promises to buy and B promises to sell all the coal which A may wish to order from B at $7.00 per ton during one year. B's promise is to supply coal to A at that price in amounts as A may order during that year, which act is sufficient consideration and makes the promise sufficient consideration. A's expression is not a promise; it is illusory, because it does not undertake to perform anything. A's expression is not even consideration, let alone insufficient consideration, for B's promise; and no contract results.)

In the last illustration, one promise was sufficient, and the other was insufficient, consideration. If the promise which is insufficient consideration were performed, there would be a unilateral contract because the act of ordering coal is sufficient consideration as an acceptance of the promise to sell, which is outstanding until revoked or rejected. Similarly, if one of the two parties to a promissory agreement has no legal capacity to contract but performs his promise, there is a unilateral contract, since such performance was sufficient consideration for the other party's promise. Only a promise requires sufficient consideration in order to be enforceable.

Exception 6—Promises Not Binding. *A promise which is not binding or capable of becoming binding, except when unenforceable or voidable solely by operation of law, is insufficient consideration for another promise.* Each promise in a bilateral contract is sufficient consideration for the other because it is a legal obligation; it is a binding promise. A bilateral promise is binding if it promises an act or forbearance which is a detriment or benefit and if it is legally valid. When a party reserves to himself the option of performing or not performing, the promise is illusory and obviously not binding because there is no promise to enforce. The law accords to infants and to parties who have been defrauded the power of avoidance at their election. The granting of such a privilege does not affect the existence of the contract, which continues until the privilege is exercised. Such contracts are called "voidable contracts." Inasmuch as a party has the option of performing or not performing his promise, the promise is illusory and not binding. Nevertheless, promises otherwise binding, but which are made voidable solely by operation of law, are treated as sufficient consideration because the purpose of the legal privilege is to give the power of avoidance to certain people in all fairness to them. If they wish to exercise the power, justice can be obtained. If they do not wish to exercise the power, then that is their right. Were the law to hold arbitrarily that promises made voidable solely by operation of law did not constitute sufficient consideration, the law would be superimposing its will upon the party sought to be protected and would be depriving him of the right to avoid exercising the protection. Accordingly, a promise which is voidable solely by operation of law is not, for that reason, insufficient consideration for another promise. For the same reason, promises otherwise binding but which are made unenforceable solely by operation of law are treated as sufficient consideration. Illustrations of such unenforceable promises are: promises which are within, but do not comply with, the statute of frauds requiring the promise to be proved in certain enumerated ways for it to be recognized and enforced by the courts; and promises which have not been enforced within the period allowed under a statute of limitations.

Summary of Sufficient Consideration

What Is Sufficient Consideration. A promise may request as consideration an act, forbearance, or a return promise. A promise is unenforceable unless the consideration requested and rendered is legally sufficient. Consideration is sufficient if it has a legal value, as distinguished from an actual value. Consideration has a legal value if it constitutes a legal detriment to the person rendering it, usually the promisee, or a legal benefit to the person to whom it is rendered, usually the promisor. A legal detriment is the performance of something which the promisee was under no previous legal obligation to do. A legal benefit is the performance of something to which the promisor was not legally entitled previously. While the courts speak of detriment and benefit as sufficient consideration, there is serious conflict when benefit alone is sought to be applied as sufficient consideration. Usually, what is a detriment to one is also a benefit to the other, and the conflict is avoided. All promises which are supported by a detriment or benefit are enforceable.

What Is Insufficient Consideration. All consideration is legally sufficient except for a few situations when it is insufficient. Accordingly, once it has been established that consideration in the form of an act, forbearance, or return promise is present, examination of the consideration should be made in order to determine if it is insufficient in terms of detriment and benefit. An act or forbearance which is a previous legal obligation owing to the promisor is insufficient consideration unless it is disputed by the promisee, in which event its performance is sufficient consideration. If an undisputed duty is owing by the promisee to a person other than the promisor, the majority, but not to be preferred, view is that its performance is insufficient consideration for the promise. A forbearance to assert an invalid claim or defense is insufficient consideration unless it is honestly and reasonably believed to be valid by the promisee, in which event it is sufficient consideration. A bargain must be bona fide, and a transfer of fungible goods or money in exchange for a promise to transfer a larger or smaller amount of the same thing at the same time and place is not pursuant to a bona fide bargain and, therefore, is insufficient consideration for the promise. Every promise given in exchange for another promise must constitute a legal obligation to be sufficient consideration for the other promise. The promises must be mutually obligatory to result in a contract. A promise is a legal obligation if it promises what would be sufficient consideration for a unilateral contract—namely, an act or forbearance which constitutes a detriment or benefit—and if it is legally binding on the promisor. A promise undertaking to perform an act or forbearance which is insufficient consideration for a unilateral contract is insufficient consideration for another promise. That consideration which is insufficient for a unilateral contract has just been discussed. A promise reserving election in the promisor of alternative performances is a promise in that it undertakes to perform one of the alternatives. If one of the alternatives is insufficient consideration for a unilateral contract, the promise is unenforceable; it does not undertake for a certainty that sufficient consideration will be performed, it does not promise value and, therefore, it is insufficient consideration. If at least one of the alternatives is sufficient consideration and the election is in the promisee, the promise is sufficient consideration because of the obligation to perform sufficient consideration if the promisee so chooses. A promise which is not binding because it is illegal or is made by one who has no legal capacity to bind himself by it is insufficient consideration. However, promises which are made voidable or unenforceable solely by operation of law are treated as sufficient consideration, even though they are illusory in that the privileged protection may be asserted in lieu of performance at the election of the promisor. A promise voidable or unenforceable solely by operation of law is an exception to the rule requiring a promise to be binding in order to be sufficient consideration. The act or forbearance must constitute a legal detriment or a legal benefit for it, or a binding promise, to constitute sufficient consideration.

4. WHEN CONSIDERATION AND MUTUAL ASSENT ARE UNNECESSARY

General There are certain promises which are enforceable although consideration[47] and mutual assent are not present. They are definite exceptions to the doctrine of sufficient con-

---

[47] UCC 2–205 provides that *merchants'* signed, written, firm offers to buy or sell goods for a period not exceeding three months are enforceable without consideration. See above, p. 31, ftn. 12.

sideration and to the requirement of mutual assent. The reason for such exceptions lies in the necessity for avoidance of obvious injustice and in the development of the law. A certain brief background is necessary to understand the reasons for these exceptions.

Past Consideration and Development of Promises Implied in Fact

The doctrine of consideration requires the exchange of sufficient consideration for a promise. If one person performed an act or forbore pursuant to a request made by a second person (e.g., at A's request, B rendered services to A), the early English courts developed the doctrine of "past consideration" whereby the promise was considered enforceable because of the consideration rendered in the past. The "past consideration" doctrine later became obsolete,[48] as it did in the United States except for a few jurisdictions, because the courts implied from such a request a promise to pay for the act or forbearance rendered in reliance on the request; and, the implied promise being supported by sufficient consideration, it was enforceable.

If a rule of law subsequently caused the promise to become unenforceable, the courts held that a subsequent express promise to perform the previous contractual obligation now barred by a rule of law would be enforceable without any consideration. Thus, if the statute of limitations barred enforcement of an implied promise, or if an implied promise to pay a debt was no longer enforceable because it had been discharged in bankruptcy, a subsequent express promise to perform the obligation would be enforceable. There are two theories for such enforcement. Under the waiver theory, which is used in the majority of states, the new express promise waives the statutory bar and revives the enforceability of the old obligation. Under the preferred view adopted by the *Restatement of Contracts*,[49] the new express promise itself is enforceable according to its terms, and the statutory bar is not waived. Inasmuch as the new promise can impose any limitations it wishes and also usually expressly promises to pay the debt and not to waive the statute, the new promise is the source of obligation and not the prior obligation barred by the statute.

---

[48] The doctrine of "moral consideration," under which a prior "moral" obligation was held to be consideration for a subsequent express promise, shared the same fate as the doctrine of "past consideration" and became obsolete and is not the law in the United States.

[49] Secs. 86, 87.

New Promise
Implied in Fact
Waives Statu-
tory Bar and
Is Enforceable
without Con-
sideration

Once the courts had decided to enforce a new express promise to perform an obligation barred by a rule of law, it was an easy step to imply such a promise from conduct. Today the new promise may be express or implied in fact. There is greater opportunity to imply such a promise when the statutory bar is the statute of limitations than there is when it is the Bankruptcy Act. It should be noted carefully that the new promise must refer to a prior obligation which had the elements of contract, not of tort. If an action on a tort is barred by the statute of limitations or discharged under the Bankruptcy Act, a new promise with respect to such tort must be supported by new sufficient consideration.

It was recognized that there were other situations or types of case in which promises should be held binding without consideration. The compelling motive was to avoid injustice. One of these situations involved new promises of ratification to perform existing voidable contractual obligations not barred by any rule of law—namely, voidable contracts. Illustrations of such contracts are contracts made by persons with limited capacity to contract, such as infants, to whom the law accords a power of avoidance because of their relatively inferior bargaining position; and contracts made under the influence of fraud, duress, or undue influence, a power of avoidance being accorded to those who have been wronged. A new promise by the person who previously had limited capacity to contract, or by the wronged person, to perform the existing contract ratified the contract and eliminated the power of avoidance. Another situation involved new promises ratifying previously unauthorized acts which did not necessarily create obligations binding on the promisor. An illustration is a contract purportedly made by one acting as an agent for a principal when in fact there was no agency relationship, yet the promisor subsequently ratified the purported contract by his promise to perform it. Still another situation involved new promises to perform obligations previously discharged because of a failure of a condition on which performance of the old promise was dependent, such condition mainly bearing on the time or manner of performance. Illustrations are: a surety's contract with a creditor in which the creditor is required to notify the surety of default by the principal debtor, the notice of default is not given and the surety is discharged, but the surety subsequently promises the creditor to perform the discharged contract; and a fire insurance policy requiring notice of fire loss within a specified period of time after such occurrence, the notice is not given and the insurer is discharged, but the insurer subsequently promises to perform the discharged obligation. A further situation involved gratuitous promises to perform something not previously obligatory and requesting nothing in return, the promisor reasonably expecting the reliance on his promise, which subsequently occurs. This is known as the "doctrine of promissory estoppel." An illustration is a gratuitous promise made to a charity contemplating the erection of a structure and, subsequently, work on the structure is begun.

All of these new promises, whether relating to contractual obligations barred by rules of law, ratifying voidable or unauthorized contracts, relating to previously discharged contractual obligations, or creating new obligations as in the case of promissory estoppel, will be considered in turn.

Promises Regarding Previous Contractual Obligations for the Payment of Money Barred by the Statute of Limitations
A voluntary promise to perform a contractual or quasi-contractual obligation for the payment of money, which obligation is either presently enforceable, or presently unenforceable solely because of the statute of limitations, is enforceable without consideration and without mutual assent. The promise must express an intent to make payment of all or part of such debt, whether it be liquidated or unliquidated, already barred by statute or not. The effect of such a promise is to extend the statutory period beginning from the date the new promise is performable according to its terms. The promise must be made by the debtor (obligor) or his authorized agent to the creditor (obligee), his surety or co-principal. A promise made by a joint debtor does not bind his co-debtors, but a promise made by a partner prior to dissolution binds the partnership. The promisor's ignorance of material facts at the time the promise is made renders the promise not binding, although ignorance of the legal effect of such facts in no way affects the enforceability of the promise. The promise must specify the indebtedness to which it relates in order for the statutory bar to be waived as to that particular indebtedness. If the promise specifies several debts to which it is to be applied, the statutory bar is waived as to all of such specified debts. If the promise specifies an account stated, the statute is waived as to that account stated, all the items therein being set forth in one balance or account. If the debtor does not specify to which of several debts the payment is to be made, the creditor may apply it to any or all of such debts,[50] but

---

[50] See below, pp. 139 ff.

the statute is not waived as to *any* debt because the payment did not specify to which debt it was to apply.

A promise may impose any conditions, and such conditions limit the performance of the promise. The waiver of the statute of limitations, or a promise so to waive, is a detriment and constitutes sufficient consideration for a promise in exchange. A debtor's promise to pay a lesser amount than that due and barred by the statute of limitations in exchange for the creditor's promise to accept such lesser amount is sufficient consideration for the creditor's promise because the debtor has experienced a detriment in waiving the statute of limitations. A promise to waive the statute and to pay a lesser amount than due *if the creditor will accept it* is not binding until the promisee complies with the promise's request by manifesting acceptance. A promise to pay a barred debt less an invalid claim asserted against the promisee is binding only to the extent of the difference between the barred debt and the invalid claim. If the promise requests the creditor's acceptance of such a proposition, then the promise is ineffective until the condition of acceptance has been made. A promise to pay a barred debt by installments is binding only on the occurrence of the due date of each installment.

The new promise to pay may be express or implied in fact; and it must be in writing in most states except in those few instances when it may be implied from the debtor's part payment, or from his issuance of a negotiable instrument or his giving of collateral security for any part or all of the indebtedness or for interest due thereon. The promise must be signed by the promisor or his authorized agent. If the new promise is supported by sufficient consideration, the promise is enforceable whether oral or written, just as in any unilateral or bilateral contract. Most states imply a promise to pay from either of the following, unless the circumstances preclude such implication:

1. An acknowledgment of the existence of a debt.
2. Payment of part of the debt, the issuance of a negotiable instrument—e.g., check, negotiable promissory note, draft—or the delivery of collateral security for part or all of the debt or for interest due thereon.

Any such acknowledgment or transfer as indicated above cannot imply a promise to pay if the debtor's manifested intent is to the contrary. An acknowledgment of the debt expressing an inability to pay it does not imply a promise to pay. However, an acknowledgment of the debt expressing a *present* inability to pay implies a promise to pay it in the future and is binding when the promisor becomes able or on the expiration of a reasonable time under the circumstances. An acknowledgment of the debt expressing inability to pay before the expiration of a year implies a promise to pay on the expiration of a year, and the statute is waived or extended to begin to run all over again on the expiration of the year. *The statute begins to run on a new promise from the time performance is due on the new promise.*

An express promise not to plead the statute of limitations as a defense to any action begun in the future for the recovery of a claim is valid and implies a promise to pay if the express promise is made after maturity of the claim. If such a promise is made before a claim's maturity, it is interpreted to mean a perpetual forbearance from pleading the statute, which is void. It is illegal to agree to limit, for an unreasonable period of time, a right to enforce a possible future claim. If the promise is made after maturity of the claim, then such a promise not to plead the statute is valid, for it is interpreted to mean a new promise to pay, which extends the statute. A promise to extend the statute beyond the next statutory period is valid.

It should be noted that the promise must be voluntarily made. It is not interpreted to be a voluntary promise if made under oath or in a pleading defending an action; nor is a judgment which is not by default or confession considered a voluntary promise.

Promises Regarding Previous Contractual Obligations for the Payment of Money Barred by a Discharge under the Bankruptcy Act
A promise to pay part or all of a debt discharged or dischargeable under the Bankruptcy Act, made subsequent to the commencement of bankruptcy proceedings, is enforceable without consideration and without mutual assent. The promise does not waive a discharge if made prior to the beginning of bankruptcy proceedings, which is the filing of a voluntary or involuntary petition in bankruptcy. The effect of the promise is to waive discharge of the specified debt if such discharge should occur. In most states the promise need not be in writing. In general, the promise is governed by the same principles applicable to a promise waiving the statute of limitations, except that the courts require more definite proof of such a promise. The promise to pay may be express or implied in fact, but no such implication may be made from an acknowledgment of the debt or part payment. It is often said that the promise, whether express or implied, must be clear and unequivocal. The debtor's preparation of a schedule of debts as required by the Bankruptcy Act does not imply a promise to pay. A promise to waive a discharge of a particular debt implies a promise to pay that debt; and, in the event of discharge in bankruptcy from such debt, the new promise is binding, effectively waiving the discharge.

Promises to Perform Voidable Obligations

A promise to perform a contractual obligation voidable by the promisor is enforceable without consideration and without mutual assent. Such a promise is binding and extinguishes the power of avoidance. In most states the promise need not be in writing. In general, the promise is governed by the same principles applicable to a promise waiving a bankruptcy discharge.

Voidable contracts contain a power of avoidance imposed by law and made available to infant or insane parties and to parties who have been subjected to fraud, duress, or undue influence in the inducement to make a contract. The waiver of such power of avoidance is called "ratification" or "affirmance" of the contract. The promise to perform the voidable obligation has a binding effect only if the power of avoidance has not been exercised previously by the promisor. The time within which an infant or insane person may exercise this power is indicated in a discussion of infants and insane persons as parties with limited capacity to contract.[51] The time for exercise of the power in the case of fraud, duress, and undue influence is indicated in a discussion of voidable contracts under manifestation of mutual assent.[52]

Ratification by a promise to assume an obligation not previously borne by the promisor also is enforceable without consideration or assent in many instances. A few examples are: a principal's ratification of an act performed on his behalf by one who was not his agent; a principal's ratification of an unauthorized act of his agent; and a promise to pay the original debt together with interest not exceeding the maximum legal rate, in substitution for an illegal usurious agreement. The promise of performance by the ratification is enforceable without consideration and mutual assent because justice is served best in that manner.

Promises of Performance of Discharged or Dischargeable Duties

A promise is binding without consideration and without mutual assent which undertakes to perform an obligation conditioned on something which has not happened if the condition was not an essential element in performance of the obligation and merely fixes the time or manner of performance. Again justice is served best if promises of this character, whether made before or after failure of the condition's occurrence, are enforced without consideration and without mutual assent. Illustrations of such promises are: a surety's expressed promise, or acknowledgment

---

[51] See above, pp. 18–20.

[52] See above, pp. 46 ff.

of a duty, to perform his suretyship obligation which has been discharged by conduct of the principal debtor or creditor; a promise to be liable by a party whose secondary liability on a negotiable instrument was discharged because he had not received due notice of dishonor or because improper presentment was made; and an insurer's promise that notification of loss in a manner other than as prescribed by an insurance contract will be proper.

Promissory Estoppel

The *Restatement of Contracts,* section 90, provides: *"A promise which the promisor should reasonably expect to induce action or forbearance of a definite and substantial character on the part of the promisee and which does induce such action or forbearance is binding if injustice can be avoided only by enforcement of the promise."* The doctrine of *promissory estoppel* is an exception to the rules requiring a manifestation of mutual assent and sufficient consideration in order to form a contract, and is designed as a device to achieve justice when the situation requires relief and no other legal remedy is available.

A gratuitous promise is not an offer, since it proposes nothing in exchange for the promise and, consequently, cannot be accepted. Without an acceptance there is no consideration, and the promise is unenforceable. Yet, often such promises are made which the promisor has reason to know may induce a substantial change of position by the promisee and which does induce such change of position in justifiable reliance thereon. In equity, such promises are enforced to achieve justice in certain cases involving land. A gratuitous promise to convey land which has induced the promisee to enter and make improvements upon the land and a gratuitous promise not to foreclose on a mortgage have been held binding in equity. At law the principle is well established that a gratuitous promise not to assert a defense, or a gratuitous promise to waive a contractual condition in favor of the promisee, which induces a change of position in reasonable reliance thereon, is binding. Accordingly, the presently enunciated principle of promissory estoppel includes these and all cases in which gratuitous promises of the nature described induce the change of position indicated in such principle.

The principle of promissory estoppel is a substitute for the requirement of sufficient consideration in the situations covered by it. It has pertinent application to charitable subscriptions. All courts wished to enforce such promises and, realizing the necessity of a manifestation of mutual assent and sufficient consideration to make the promise binding, used divers methods to comply with these requisites. Some courts held that the promise of one subscriber was in return for, and supported by, the promises of other subscribers even though the promise never expressed such an intention. Others held that acceptance of the subscription by the beneficiary imported a promise to apply the funds properly and that such promise supported the promises of other subscribers. The answer is the doctrine of promissory estoppel. At any time prior to reliance thereon, the gratuitous promise may be revoked or withdrawn. Once reliance occurs or partial reliance has begun, the promise is binding. (A subscribes $100 to a fund to build a church. Before the erection of the church is begun, the promise is revocable. Once the erection is begun, the promise is irrevocably binding.)

The principle has been extended to other than charitable subscriptions and applies not only to those legal and equitable examples given at the beginning of this discussion but also to gratuitous promises to anyone. (A promises $1,000 to B, knowing that B needs the money for a certain purpose. B relies on the promise and changes his position materially in reliance on the promise to accomplish that purpose. A's promise is binding.)

It should be noted carefully that *promissory* estoppel is a term used to estop a party from setting up lack of manifestation of mutual assent and lack of sufficient consideration as a defense to suit on his *promise*. It is not a true estoppel. "Estoppel" has been discussed previously[53] and means that a misrepresentation of a material fact has been made, reasonable reliance thereon has occurred, and the utterer of the misrepresentation is now estopped from denying the truth of what he previously had misrepresented. (A, in response to an inquiry by B, states that a certain horse is not A's, when in fact it is A's horse which has been stolen by C. In reliance on A's statement, B purchased the horse from C. A is estopped to assert that the horse is his.)

Here, as in all the other promises binding without manifestation of mutual assent and sufficient consideration, previously discussed, *ignorance of material facts renders the promise either unenforceable or merely voidable, there being a difference of view on this point.*

Contracts under Seal

In those few states where the seal still has its Common Law significance and the sealed promise is binding without consideration,[54] a contract under seal is enforceable without a manifestation of mutual as-

---

[53] See above, pp. 42–43.

[54] But see below, p. 141, ftn. 4, concerning the binding effect in some states of an unsealed signed writing, without consideration, purporting to modify or discharge an existing legal obligation.

sent. A contract under seal is a written promise under seal: indicating or describing the parties thereto each of whom has legal capacity to contract; undertaking to perform a legally valid transaction; delivered to the promisee or his agent or to someone in escrow; and presently performable according to its terms. If the promise requires an acceptance, then the promise is inoperative until such acceptance occurs. A seal is any substance, writing, sign, or impression affixed to a writing and intended as a seal by the promisor. The promisor may affix the seal or adopt one already there.

5. LEGALLY VALID TRANSACTION

A transaction is legally valid when the agreement is not legally void. An illegal agreement is void, generally, because usually it creates no legal duty or obligation to perform. An agreement is illegal when its formation or performance is contrary to law by being opposed to statute, or to public policy as declared by the courts.

Effect of Illegal Agreements Illegal agreements usually are void either because the statute so provides or because the courts will not enforce the agreement as against public policy. The reason why the courts usually refuse to enforce the agreement is because the plaintiff usually is a wrongdoer and courts deny relief to a wrongdoer. If the plaintiff is not a wrongdoer, then, in certain cases, the courts will grant relief, even by enforcing the agreement if justice so requires. The following are some of the principles in effect among courts regarding relief under illegal agreements:

1. If a statute bars recovery under an illegal agreement, then the courts can give no relief. If no statute bars recovery, then it is within the discretion of the courts to determine whether relief is justified and the kind of such relief.

2. Ordinarily, no recovery will be granted to either party under an illegal agreement. If the agreement is executed, it will not be opened; if it is executory, it will not be enforced.

3. Relief and recovery will be permitted to a party under an illegal agreement for whose protection and benefit the law exists. Recovery may be by rescission of the agreement and restitution of what has been parted with by the protected party, or by enforcement of the agreement and an award of damages for its breach. (A issues to B a policy of insurance containing terms which are contrary to law enacted for the benefit of people like B. On the occurrence of the event insured against, re-

lief should be given to B as the law was enacted for his benefit. Here the most appropriate relief would be enforcement of the policy.)

4. When one party justifiably is ignorant of the facts which make the agreement illegal and the other party is not ignorant, the ignorant party may refuse to perform after he has learned of the facts and may recover damages for breach of the executory portion of the agreement (the loss he sustained or the profit not made thereunder), or regain what he previously has performed or its value at the rate under the agreement. If both parties are ignorant, then relief is given only to the extent of performance already rendered, at the agreed rate.

5. When both parties are knowingly guilty of making the illegal agreement but are not of equal guilt—i.e., not *in pari delicto*—the less guilty party may repudiate the agreement and recover what he has performed or its value.

6. When a party is ignorant of the statutory provisions of a relatively minor nature and relies on the special knowledge that the other party should have of such provisions, the relief is the same as under paragraph 4, above. (A, an electrician, and B agree that A is to install electric connections in B's house according to B's specifications. Some of the specifications are not permitted by law. A later discovers this illegality and refuses to perform. B was ignorant of the illegality. B may enforce the agreement against A and obtain damages for A's breach, although the agreement is illegal.)

7. When an agreement is illegal because of the illegal use to which the performance thereunder will be put, the other party may repudiate the agreement and not be required to perform it; or he may perform it and recover under the agreement, provided he has not furthered the illegal use of the performance and provided the illegal use is not for a serious violation of the law.

8. When part of an agreement is valid and part illegal, if the main purpose of the agreement will not be affected, the valid portion of the agreement will be enforced by the courts. An agreement consisting of several valid distinct parts, all of which are supported by illegal consideration, is illegal and unenforceable as a whole. If one of such parts is supported by a valid sufficient consideration, that part is valid and enforceable.

9. If an agreement is legally valid but by a change of law it becomes illegal, all contract rights of performance and damages for breach which arose prior to the change of legal status continue in existence. Recovery is limited to the extent of the agreement prior to the change of legal status.

10. Once an agreement is illegal, it continues to be illegal unless a change in law specifically validates such agreement, or the fact causing the transaction to be illegal and of which both parties were ignorant at the time of the transaction is changed, no longer barring the agreement as illegal.

11. When consideration has been rendered under an illegal agreement but the illegal provisions are still executory, the party who has rendered the consideration may recover such consideration. (Under an illegal gambling agreement, A delivered his money bet to B, a stakeholder. A may recover the money from B at any time prior to B's delivery of it to the other party to the agreement.)

Kinds of Illegal Agreement There are various kinds of illegal agreement. A few of the more important ones will be considered here.

Commission of Crimes and Torts. Inasmuch as the law provides public punishment for the commission of a crime and civil relief for the commission of a civil wrong, called a "tort," agreements which contemplate performance of a crime or tort are illegal. Examples of such torts are: battery, assault, defamation (slander or libel), deceit, infringement of trade-mark or trade name.[55] Generally, a person may contract that another shall not owe a duty of care to the plantiff's interest and that the other will not be liable for harm to the plantiff's interest caused by conduct of the defendant which, but for the contract, would constitute negligence. The parties are free to contract as they wish, provided it is not illegal. An agreement is illegal if it provides against liability: for intentional infliction of harm; or for negligence with respect to performance of a public duty for compensation (e.g., railroad transporting goods or passengers for hire, public warehouseman for hire), or with respect to the employer's liability for harm negligently caused to an employee while acting within the scope of his employment.[56] The courts are divided concerning the legality of a

---

[55] It should be noted that while persons may deal or refuse to deal with other persons as they choose, in the absence of statute to the contrary (e.g., the federal Civil Rights Act of 1964), they may not, unless privileged, induce *other persons* to refuse to deal, to refuse to continue a business relationship, or to breach their contracts with third persons. Society recognizes the interest of persons to enter into business relations with each other, and it protects this interest by denouncing such interfering inducements as wrongful and tortious. Inducing breach of contract or refusal to deal are, therefore, torts and may be defined as intentionally and without privilege causing another person by inducement or otherwise to breach his contract, to refuse to continue a business relationship, or to refuse to deal, with a third person, which is a legal cause of special damage to the third person.

[56] American Law Institute, *Restatement: Contracts,* 1932, sec. 575.

contractual provision against liability for negligence in the case of bailees without a public duty.

Violation of Statute. Agreements which are prohibited by statute are illegal. Statutes may make such agreements illegal by prohibiting either the formation or the performance of such agreements. The prohibition of such formation or performance may be made expressly, or impliedly by providing penalties therefor, making it a crime, or requiring a license therefor. When a statute requires a license, an examination must be made of the legislative intent to determine whether the purpose of the statute was to protect the public or to obtain revenue. If the former, then an agreement violating the statute is illegal; if the latter, then usually the agreement is considered valid.

Usury. Usury is the taking of interest on a loan in excess of that maximum interest permitted by law. Three elements are necessary for usury: a loan of money, to be repaid, with interest in excess of that permitted by law. At Common Law there was no legal maximum of interest on a loan of money. Today, by statute,[57] most states provide for a maximum rate of interest on a loan and the taking of interest in excess of such rate is usury. Usurious agreements are illegal in most states. Such statutes usually specify two rates of interest: the legal rate and the maximum rate. When a contract provides for interest but does not specify the rate, the legal rate is applied.[58] The maximum rate is the highest rate permitted in that state. The rates of interest vary among the states.[59]

The effect of usury also varies among the states, as follows:

1. Forfeiture of principal and all interest.
2. Forfeiture of all interest.
3. Forfeiture of that portion of the interest in excess of what is permitted by law.
4. Forfeiture of interest, and a civil penalty is imposed on the lender to repay to the borrower double the interest charged.
5. Usurious interest once paid cannot be recovered.
6. Usury is a crime.

Because of public policy the various states except certain transactions from the usury rule. The following are usual exceptions:

1. Small personal loans for short duration may exact interest rates higher than those permitted by law for ordinary loans.

---

[57] See U3C, sec. 1.108, governing extension of consumer credit.

[58] UCC 3–118(d) prescribes, in the case of negotiable instruments, "the judgment rate at the place of payment. . . ."

[59] See U3C, Article 3, Part 2, for maximum charges on loans.

2. An innocent mistake in calculating interest resulting in interest in excess of the permitted rate. Only such excess is forfeited.
3. Addition of proper service charges to the interest due.
4. Deduction of interest at the permitted rate in advance of the loan.
5. Loans to corporations in excess of the permitted rate.
6. Imposition of collection charges in addition to permitted interest in the event of the borrower's default.
7. A higher price for bona fide credit sales than for cash sales.
8. Purchase of an annuity.
9. Discount of commercial paper by sale.
10. Calculation of interest on the basis of 360 days in the year.

Often a form different from a loan is utilized to color the nature of a transaction and thereby avoid the usury law. The courts examine a transaction and the circumstances surrounding its formation to determine the intent of the parties and to see if the transaction is meant to be usurious. When the transaction is in the form of a sale, the courts require an intent to loan on the part of the one advancing the credit before they will consider the transaction usurious. Some of the subterfuges to evade the usury laws are as follows:

1. Requiring the borrower to antedate his note to effect a usurious transaction.
2. The charging of fictitious fees in connection with the loan.
3. The sale on credit by the lender to the borrower of property far in excess of its fair value, the borrower to realize the cash by its sale.
4. Improper statement of the amount of the loan or of the rate of interest in the loan transaction.
5. Compelling the borrower to repay to the lender part of the loan immediately on making the loan.
6. The sale of property by the borrower to the lender at a low price on the condition that the borrower is to buy it back later at a higher price.

Sunday Statutes. In the absence of statutory provision to the contrary, contracts can be made and performed on Sunday. Many states have statutes which prohibit the formation or performance of agreements on Sunday. The extent of such statutes varies greatly. Such statutes usually except agreements to marry and agreements made of necessity or for charity. Matters of health, saving of property, religious ministry, and household work come within the exception. If a contract is made on other than a Sunday but performance is to occur on a Sunday, then, if performance on Sunday is not material to the contract, the contract is interpreted as requiring performance on the next day when performance is legally permissible. Such an agreement is legal. An offer made on Sunday and accepted on Monday creates a contract on Monday. An agreement made on Sunday but subsequently agreed to on Monday creates a contract on Monday, if all the elements of a contract are present, because the parties agreed anew and thereby created their contract.

Unreasonable Restraint of Trade. Agreements in unreasonable restraint of trade are illegal. The law permits contracts in restraint of trade, which is the restraint of competition in business or restraint in the exercise of one's occupation; yet such restraint must not be unreasonable. Restraint is unreasonable: if it is in excess of what is reasonably necessary in time, area, or subject matter to protect the promisee or imposes undue hardship on the promisor; if it tends to create a monopoly or to control prices; if it unreasonably restricts the alienation of property; or if it restrains competition and if such restraint is not made in connection with the sale of a business and its goodwill or similar transaction. While the courts are more ready to countenance restraints where they are part of a contract involving the sale of a business and goodwill than where they are part of an employment contract, nevertheless, the restraint must not be more than is reasonably necessary to protect the promisee.

Wagers. A wager is an agreement in which: the parties have no legal interest in the subject matter; one party is to win at the expense of the other; and performance of the agreement is subject to the condition of a fortuitous event. Gambling agreements and lotteries are wagers. Wagers are illegal in most states by statute. An insurance contract is not a wager because the insured has a legal interest to protect, either his property or his life and health, and by the insurance contract he is shifting to the insurer for sufficient consideration the insured's risk of harm to, or destruction of, such interest. If the insured has no legal interest, the agreement is illegal as a wager.[60] Speculative business agreements are valid, whether they be for the purchase of securities on margin or for "futures," provided the agreement does not preclude delivery of the subject matter and does not contemplate settlement dependent on the rise and fall of the market price. If the agreement precludes such delivery and contemplates such settlement, the agreement is a wager and illegal. However, the courts are in conflict concerning the validity of a hedging agreement for commodities, which is a common business transaction today precluding such delivery and contemplating such settlement. The purpose of the hedging agreement is to protect the value of commodities already acquired from being affected by a change in market prices. It would seem that such a transaction is of social value and should be protected; the federal courts, as well as some

---

[60] See below, p. 877.

state courts, have held the hedging contract as valid and not contrary to public policy. Inasmuch as the federal courts are concerned with this type of agreement in enforcing federal interstate commodity regulatory legislation, the federal view appears to be preferable.[61]

Interference with Governmental Process. Interference with governmental processes is improper, and agreements so to interfere are illegal. An agreement providing for unfair influence of a public official in carrying out a public duty is illegal. Fairly influencing such official is proper, and agreements so to influence are valid. (A employs B to urge favorable support by C, a congressman, of a legislative bill. Such an agreement is valid. However, if the agreement provided for the rendition of favors or of bribery, the agreement is illegal.) An agreement to pay a potential witness in a legal proceeding more than he is entitled to by law, unless he is an expert witness, is illegal. An agreement to conceal a crime, to testify falsely, to suppress evidence, or to induce assertion of a claim known to be false is illegal. An agreement to do business with an alien enemy residing in the enemy country or to aid an alien enemy country is illegal.

---

[61] See American Law Institute, *Restatement: Contracts,* 1932, 1948 Supplement, sec. 523 (3), *Comment c,* and Reason for Changes i and ii.

Chapter III

CONTRACTS AND THIRD PARTIES

1. *THIRD PARTY BENEFICIARY CONTRACTS*

CONTRACTS are binding upon the parties thereto and create rights and duties among those parties. Such parties are in "privity of contract" and may enforce the terms of their contract among themselves. A contract may provide that benefits are to be rendered to persons not parties thereto, called a "third party beneficiary contract."[1] Public policy favored the enforcement of such contracts by the third party beneficiary, but the accomplishment of this result was made difficult by the lack of any privity of contract between the third party beneficiary and the parties to the contract and by the absence of any Common Law precedent.

Requirements Just as the doctrine of promissory estoppel evolved as a new principle of law to meet a novel situation requiring legal relief,[2] so a new principle of law developed under which a third party acquired a direct right against the promisor of the benefit under the third party beneficiary contract, regardless of whether the contract was informal or under seal. There are two requirements. First, *the contract must be made specifically for the benefit of a third person not a party to the contract,* called the third party *"creditor beneficiary"* or the third party *"donee beneficiary."* It is not necessary that the creditor or donee beneficiary be identified at the time the contract is made in order to create rights in the beneficiary under the contract. Illustrations are: a building contract for the benefit of the laborers and materialmen to be hired by the building contractor; a contract for the benefit of employees; and a contract for the benefit of the promisee's children surviving him. Second, *the beneficiary must be either a creditor of the promisee who is to obtain the benefit under the contract or a donee of such promisee.*

---

[1] See UCC 2–318: "Third Party Beneficiaries of Warranties Express or Implied," in the sale of goods.

[2] See above, p. 87 f.

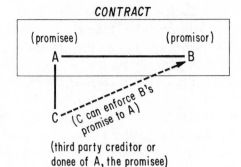

(third party creditor or
donee of A, the promisee)

**Types of
Third Party
Beneficiary**

Contracts may create three types of third party beneficiary: donee, creditor, and incidental. The type of
beneficiary in each contract is determined by the
intention of the parties as expressly or impliedly indicated in the contract and the circumstances surrounding its formation.

Donee Beneficiary. A third party beneficiary under a contract
which has the purpose of making a gift to the beneficiary of a right
against the promisor, not due or believed to be due by the promisee to
the beneficiary, is a *"donee beneficiary."* A donee beneficiary receives
as a gift from the promisee a right against the promisor under the contract. (A and B contract whereby A promises to supply B with goods
for $1,000, which B promises to pay to C. B is under an obligation to
C. C is a donee beneficiary of the contract.)

Creditor Beneficiary. A third party beneficiary under a contract
in which the purpose is to confer on the beneficiary a right against the
promisor, not as a gift but in order that the promisor's performance
will satisfy a duty actually, or believed to be, owing by the promisee to
the beneficiary, is called a *"creditor beneficiary."* A creditor beneficiary
is a creditor of the promisee and receives a right against the promisor
in order to satisfy the promisee's obligation due to the beneficiary. (A
owes C $100. A lends $100 to B on B's promise to pay $100 to C in
satisfaction of A's debt to C. The intent of the parties is to make B's
payment to C a satisfaction of A's obligation to C. C is a creditor beneficiary.) The right was not conferred on the creditor as a gift but in satisfaction of the claim; so the creditor is a creditor beneficiary. However, a right against the promisor may be conferred on the promisee's
creditor as a gift, making him a donee beneficiary. The express or implied intention of the contracting parties is the test. (A owes C $1,000
and D $5,000. A and B contract whereby B promises: to pay C $50 as

an expression of appreciation for waiting so long; to pay D $5,000 in satisfaction of A's indebtedness to D; and to pay $1,000 to E, who is A's brother. C, although a creditor of the promisee, is a donee beneficiary, for the intention is to pay the $50 as a gift rather than as payment on the indebtedness. D is a creditor beneficiary. E is a donee beneficiary.)

Incidental Beneficiary. A person who will benefit incidentally by the promisor's performance under a contract in which such person is neither a donee nor a creditor beneficiary is called an *"incidental beneficiary."* (A, a wholesaler, and B, a retailer, contract whereby A promises to sell and B promises to buy certain of X Company goods. X is an incidental beneficiary.) In many contracts the promisee is the United States government, a municipality, a state, or some other political subdivision. May the individuals who make up the population of the promisee be donee, creditor, or incidental beneficiaries? Again, the intention of the parties controls. Unless the parties clearly intend to confer rights on such individuals for injury sustained by them in the promisor's performance of such a contract, no such rights are created. The intent of the parties is determined by the terms of their contract in light of the circumstances surrounding its formation. If the promisor undertook to perform a duty owing by a municipality promisee to the public for failure of which the municipality would be liable to those persons injured thereby, the individual members of the public are creditor beneficiaries, since such was the implied intent of the contracting parties. If there is no such duty but the contract is solely for public advantage, the members of the public are incidental beneficiaries. (A, a municipality, contracts with B, a water company, which promises to keep a certain water pressure in fire hydrants. B fails to do so, and C's house is destroyed by fire because of B's failure. A had no duty to maintain such pressure. C is neither a donee nor a creditor beneficiary, but an incidental beneficiary.)

Rights of Donee and Creditor Beneficiaries

In the great majority of states, donee and creditor beneficiaries have a direct right against the promisor for the enforcement of his promise. Incidental beneficiaries have no rights under the contract. The donee and creditor beneficiaries have a right against the promisor subject to whatever defenses the promisor has against the promisee under the contract. The contract may be voidable at the election of the promisor, the promisor's duty of performance may have been discharged because of failure of consideration, or the contract may be unenforceable against the promisor. The promisor's defenses under the contract should be available to him regardless of whether or not there are any donee or creditor beneficiaries. The promisee may have defenses to the creditor beneficiary's claim against him. The promisee's ignorance of the invalidity or unenforceability of such a claim does not affect the creation of rights in the beneficiary as either a creditor or donee beneficiary. If the intent was that the promisor's performance was to satisfy a claim, then the beneficiary is a creditor beneficiary regardless of whether or not he had a claim. The promisee has determined that the debt exists, and the promisor cannot refute such a determination. The promisor cannot set up against the creditor beneficiary defenses available to the promisee as against the beneficiary, except in one type of case. If the contract between the parties provided that the promisor was to be liable for payment of the promisee's debts, then the promisor is to determine which debts may be properly asserted by the creditor beneficiary and the promisor may set up the promisee's defenses. (A assigns his business to B under a contract whereby B assumes all of A's debts. B can set up A's defenses to any debts asserted.)

Variation of Promisor's Obligation

The donee or creditor beneficiary may disclaim or assent to the benefit conferred. Assent is presumed unless the beneficiary disclaims within a reasonable period of time after learning of the benefit conferred. Once disclaimer occurs, the beneficiary's right is extinguished as of the time the contract was made. The promisor's duty is then performable to the promisee, unless such performance is rendered impossible by the disclaimer. Disclaimer can be set aside if it is a fraud on creditors of the beneficiary.

The promisor's obligation of performance can be varied by the promisor and promisee only to a limited extent. In the case of a donee beneficiary, the obligation cannot be varied unless the contract specifically provided for such power of variation. (A takes out a policy of insurance on his life, naming B as a donee beneficiary, reserving the power to change the beneficiary. B's rights as a donee beneficiary are defeasible by A, who subsequently may arrange with the insurance company for a change of beneficiary.)[3] In the case of a creditor beneficiary, such a variation is effective provided the beneficiary has not changed his position materially in reliance on the benefit conferred before he knows of the variation, and the variation is not a fraud on the creditor beneficiary and other creditors of the promisee.

---

[3] For assignment of interests under life insurance contracts, see below, p. 892.

2. *ASSIGNMENTS*

A contract creates rights and duties. The party having rights is called the *"obligee"* and the party owing duties is called the *"obligor."* Contract rights may be transferred, just as other property, and such a transfer is called an *"assignment."* The right assigned is called a *"chose in action"* (thing in action), because it is a right of action on the contract, a claim, e.g., an account receivable. Contract duties may be delegated but not assigned, because a party with contract duties cannot avoid his obligations merely by transferring them. An assignment is made by a person called an "assignor" to a person called an "assignee." In the assignment of contract rights, no particular form of assignment is necessary; it may be oral or in writing, as long as there is a manifestation of intent to transfer such rights. The assignment may be of the entire right or of only a portion, called a *"partial assignment."* (X owes Y $100. Y assigns $50 of the debt to Z.) An assignment is distinguished from a contract to assign in that the latter promises a future as-

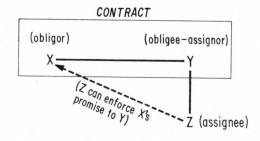

signment of a right and creates a present right to such assignment in the future. An assignment is effective when the assignee acquires the assignor's right to the obligor's performance. It is not necessary for the assignee to inform the obligor of such assignment in order to make it effective, nor need the person to whom duties are delegated notify the obligee of such delegation. Contract rights may be assigned and duties delegated unless:

1. Assignment or delegation is prohibited by law because it is contrary to statute, or to public policy as declared by the courts. It is for this reason that a public employee cannot assign future compensation or delegate performance of his public duties and that a person with a government pension cannot assign it.

2. The contract expressly or impliedly prohibits assignment or delegation.[4]

Assignment of Rights

Rights under a contract not personal in character are assignable. However, assignment is not possible unless there is a contract right capable of assignment.

Future rights expected to arise under an existing contract, such as compensation for employment,[5] are assignable; but expected future rights under a contract not in existence cannot be assigned, in the absence of statute to the contrary.

Personal Contracts are Nonassignable without the Obligor's Assent. A contract may or may not be personal in character. It is personal in character when its assignment is prohibited either by law or by the contract, expressly or impliedly. If prohibited by law, the contract cannot be assigned in any case. If prohibited by the contract, it cannot be assigned without the *obligor's* assent. *A contract which is personal in character other than by law is nonassignable by the obligee without the obligor's assent.*

Under the Code. It should be noted very carefully that the sale or assignment of *accounts* is governed by the Code. The Code favors assignment freely of accounts, and while a clause in a contract precluding assignment *of the contract* is valid, nevertheless "A term in any contract between an account debtor and an assignor is ineffective if it prohibits assignment *of an account* . . . ."[6] (Author's italics)

Impliedly Personal Contracts. Often there is difficulty in determining whether a contract impliedly prohibits assignment.[7] A contract is impliedly personal in character and the contract right is impliedly nonassignable without the obligor's assent if: *the personal taste, skill or fancy of the obligor is involved; or assignment would impose material additional risks or burdens on the obligor or change his duty.* (E employs S as his secretary, or A employs B as an artist to paint A's

---

[4] UCC 2–210(3): "Unless the circumstances indicate the contrary a prohibition of assignment of 'the contract' is to be construed as barring only the delegation to the assignee of the assignor's performance."

[5] But under U3C, sec. 2.410: "A seller or lessor may not take an assignment of earnings of the buyer or lessee for payment or as security for payment of a debt arising out of a consumer credit sale or a consumer lease. An assignment of earnings in violation of this section is unenforceable by the assignee of the earnings and revocable by the buyer or lessee. This section does not prohibit an employee from authorizing deductions from his earnings if the authorization is revocable."

[6] UCC 9–318(4).

[7] For assignment of a contract for the sale of goods under the Code, see UCC 2–210.

portrait, or X employs Y as his business representative. These contracts are of a personal character, and rights thereunder cannot be assigned by E, A, or X without the consent of S, B, or Y, respectively.) The right to fire protection in a contract of fire insurance is of a personal character because the insured's reliability as an insurance risk is an element considered by the insurer in issuing the policy, and the right to fire insurance is impliedly nonassignable. By the majority view, the purchaser under a contract *to purchase* on the *personal unsecured* credit of the purchaser cannot assign his contract right to make such purchase because credit was extended only to such purchasing party, and substitution of another party would subject the seller to a risk of loss through credit which he had not previously undertaken. In a contract for the sale of a business, the seller's promise not to compete with the buyer is interpreted to apply to the one owning the business, and the buyer may assign this right to such restraint to a subsequent purchaser of the business without thereby imposing any additional burdens on the seller. The usual type of assignment is of the right to be paid money, the right to have a contractor erect a building, and the right of restraint from competition, to mention only a few examples. These rights involve no personal taste or fancy and, therefore, are not personal in character; nor do they involve the imposition on the obligor of any materially increased burdens or risks.

Revocation of Assignment. An assignment may be made for value—i.e., for sufficient consideration—or it may be made gratuitously. By the former, the assignment is irrevocable and the right passes from the assignor to the assignee. The right acquired by a gratuitous assignment is revocable by the assignor and by his death unless: the assignee has already realized on the assignment by payment, judgment, or otherwise; or as a part of the assignment there was delivered to the assignee a document of title (e.g., negotiable bill of lading or negotiable warehouse receipt) or a token necessary to the obligor's performance (e.g., bank book, life insurance policy, certificate of corporate stock). An assignor of a revocable or voidable assignment may revoke or avoid such assignment by a subsequent assignment of the same right. An assignment cannot be foisted on an unwilling assignee who may refuse or disclaim the assignment within a reasonable period of time after he learns of it. An assignment is ineffective without the assignee's manifestation of assent, except when the assignment is for value or made with a token necessary to the obligor's performance.

Rights Acquired by Assignment. An assignee acquires the rights of his assignor; he stands in the shoes of his assignor; and the assignee may sue in his own name. If the assignor has a claim which has a priority in payment from the obligor's insolvent estate, assignment of the claim includes the priority feature. An assignee takes the assigned right subject to all defenses, setoffs, and counterclaims available to the obligor as against the assignor obligee.[8] (A contract between A and B is voidable by B. A assigns the contract right to C. B may avoid the contract.)[9]

Notice of Assignment to Obligor.   While an assignee is not required to give to the obligor notice of assignment, his failure to do so may affect his recovery on the right because third parties would be adversely affected. Ignorance of such assignment may cause the obligor to pay the obligee or the obligee's judgment creditor instead of the assignee, which discharges the obligor. Further, the obligee may assign the same right successively to different assignees. If the obligor innocently pays the first assignee who appears before him, not knowing of any previous assignment, the obligor is discharged. As between the two assignees, who has the assigned right? The first assignment in time transferred the right to that assignee. If the first assignment is revocable, then the subsequent assignment revoked the prior assignment. If the first assignment is irrevocable, a second assignee, who is either a gratuitous assignee or an assignee for value but with notice of the previous assignment, obviously should not be able to prevail over the assignee prior in time. However, if the second assignee is one for value and without notice of any prior assignment—i.e., a bona fide purchaser for value in good faith without notice of the prior assignment—whether or not he may prevail over the first assignee depends upon the jurisdiction. In some states the assignee who first gives notice of assignment to the obligor prevails. By the better view the assignee first in time prevails, unless a subsequent innocent assignee for value *obtains* payment or other performance from the obligor before the obligor has notice of the prior assignment. In short, as between an assignee and the obligor, the assignee acquires the right defeasible by the innocent obligor rendering performance to the obligee, to the obligee's judgment creditor, or to an assignee subsequent in time. As between an assignee and either a judgment creditor of his assignor or an assignee subsequent in time, the assignee prior in time has the right defeasible only by the obligor's innocent *performance* to such judgment creditor or subsequent assignee. *An assignee should give actual notice to the obligor and demand pay-*

---

[8] But see U3C, sec. 2.404, and pp. 740–42, 761–62.

[9] For a discussion of the assignment of accounts under the Secured Transactions Article of the Code, see below, pp. 761–63.

ment or performance from the obligor in order to protect his right, although such notice is not required in order to make an assignment effective as between the assignor and the assignee.[10]

Warranties. An assignment may include express warranties and, by operation of law, the following implied warranties as enumerated in section 175 of the *Restatement of Contracts:*

(1) An assignor of a right by assignment under seal or for value warrants to the assignee, in the absence of circumstances showing a contrary intention,

    (a) that he will do nothing to defeat or impair the value of the assignment;

    (b) that the right, as assigned, actually exists and is subject to no limitations or defenses other than those stated or apparent at the time of the assignment;

    (c) that any token, writing or evidence of the right delivered to the assignee as part of the transaction of assignment, or exhibited to him as an inducement to accept the assignment, is genuine and what it purports to be.

(2) An assignor does not by the mere fact of assigning warrant that the obligor is solvent or that he will perform his obligation.

(3) An assignor is bound by affirmations and promises to the assignee with reference to the right assigned, in the same way and to the same extent that one who transfers chattels is bound under like circumstances.

(4) An assignee's rights under his assignor's warranties are not assigned to a sub-assignee by the mere assignment of the right against the obligor, to which the warranties relate, but the rights under such warranties may be expressly assigned.

Delegation of Duties

Duties under a contract not personal in character are delegable.

Personal Contracts Are Nondelegable without the Obligee's Assent. A contract is personal in character when delegation of duties thereunder is prohibited either by law or by the contract, expressly or impliedly. If prohibited by law,

---

[10] See UCC 9–318(3). For a discussion of the effect of an assignment of an account on other creditors of the assignor, see Secured Transactions, below, pp. 761–63. UCC 9–205 should be noted at this point: "Use or Disposition of Collateral Without Accounting Permissible. A security interest is not invalid or fraudulent against creditors by reason of liberty in the debtor to use, commingle or dispose of all or part of the collateral (including returned or repossessed goods) or to collect or compromise accounts or chattel paper, or to accept the return of goods or make repossessions, or to use, commingle or dispose of proceeds, or by reason of the failure of the secured party to require the debtor to account for proceeds or replace collateral. This section does not relax the requirements of possession where perfection of a security interest depends upon possession of the collateral by the secured party or by a bailee."

contract duties cannot be delegated in any case. If prohibited by the contract, the duties cannot be delegated without the *obligee's* assent. *Duties under a contract which is personal in character other than by law are nondelegable by the obligor without the obligee's assent.*

Impliedly Personal Contracts. Often there is difficulty in determining whether a contract impliedly prohibits delegation of its duties. A contract is impliedly personal in character and contract duties impliedly nondelegable without the obligee's assent if: *the personal taste, skill or fancy of the obligor is involved; or delegation would vary materially the performance due to the obligee under the contract.* Under the heading *"Impliedly Personal Contracts"* on page 101 above, the first illustration refers to employment between E and S, A and B, X and Y. Neither S, B, nor Y could delegate his respective duties without the assent of E, A, or X, respectively. A building contractor can delegate his contract duty to erect a building for the other party because no special skill is involved, but a building contractor with certain special or unusual skills could not delegate his duty. A member of a professional athletic team could not delegate his duties, nor could an officer in a corporation. Because the duty cannot be delegated does not preclude the assignment of a right by the obligor. (In the illustration of E and S, A and B, X and Y, although neither S, B, nor Y could delegate his duties nor E, A, or X assign his rights to performance by the other parties, nevertheless, the employees could assign their rights to compensation.) However, if there is a personal relationship between the parties, the correlative right and duty cannot be assigned or delegated. (S, B, and Y cannot delegate; and E, A, and X cannot assign.)

Effect of Delegation. The obligor's delegation of a contract duty authorizes the delegated person to perform the duty. Such delegation does not extinguish the duty of the obligor to the obligee under their contract. The delegated person may have the option of performing the duty, or he may assume performance of the duty. He may also refuse to consent to such delegation. It is difficult sometimes to determine whether there is an assumption of the duties. By the better view and under the Code,[11] the assignment of an entire contract and its acceptance by the assignee is interpreted as an assumption of duties by the assignee and as creating a third party creditor beneficiary contract.[12] Some courts hold to the contrary, that an assumption of duties must be expressly manifested.

---

[11] UCC 2–210(4). Also see below, pp. 253–55.

[12] See above, p. 97 f.

Novation

The obligor, the obligee, and the delegated person may contract to extinguish the obligor's duty in exchange for the assumption of such duty by the delegated person. Repudiation by the obligor of his duty, coupled with the assumption of such duty by the delegated person and the obligee's silent acceptance of performance by such delegated person with knowledge of such repudiation, operate to extinguish the obligor's duty. The obligee could accept the substituted performance and inform the obligor or the delegated person that he did not thereby waive his right to continue to hold the obligor liable for performance of his duty; the obligor's duty would not be extinguished. The extinguishment of the obligor's duty and the substitution of another person in his place is accomplished by a *novation. A novation is a new contract in which one of the parties was not a party to the old contract and which immediately discharges the old contract.* Until novation occurs, the obligee can hold both the obligor and the delegated person who assumed the duty liable for the performance of such duty.[13]

---

[13] The obligee is a third party creditor beneficiary of the contract between the obligor and the delegated person who assumed the duty and, thus, he may enforce the contract. See above, p. 97 f.

Chapter IV

STATUTE OF FRAUDS

Background EACH state has a statute of frauds as a part of its law. It is not a principle of equity or of Common Law, but a statute following substantially some of the provisions in the old English Statute of Frauds of 1677. The statute of frauds is concerned not with frauds but rather with *certain methods of proof necessary to establish the existence of certain kinds of contract* in order to prevent the occurrence of fraud through perjured testimony to prove the existence of such alleged contracts. The statute provides that a contract of the kind indicated therein is *unenforceable* unless proved in a certain specified way. There are slight variations in the statutes of the various states, but for the most part they are alike. It is a "proof" statute.

Contents of the Statute The statute of frauds applies only to informal contracts. A contract within the provisions of the statute is *unenforceable* unless proved as prescribed.

Failure to comply with the requirements of proof affects enforceability, not validity, of the contract. The following five types of contract are *unenforceable unless the contract is in writing, or a note or memorandum thereof is in writing and signed by the party to be charged or by his lawfully authorized agent:*

1. A contract by an administrator or an executor to pay out of his own estate for a duty of the decedent's estate.
2. A contract to answer for the debt, default, or miscarriages of another person.
3. A contract made in consideration of marriage, not between the parties to be married (e.g., father's promise to pay groom to marry daughter).
4. A contract for the sale of land or of an interest in land.
5. A contract not performed by any party to it and which cannot be performed within one year from the date of its formation.

Under the Code. There are other types of transaction the enforceability of which is governed by the Code: a contract for the sale of goods for the price of $500 or more (UCC 2–201);[1] a contract for the sale of securities (UCC 8–319);[2] a security agreement for a non-possessory security interest (UCC 9–203);[3] a contract for general intangibles, e.g., goodwill, royalty rights, rights to performance (UCC 9–106),[4] and a contract for various types of security transaction (UCC 9–104),[5] for more than $5,000 are governed by UCC 1–206.[6] Reference should be made to those specific areas in the text to determine the proof necessary to make such contracts enforceable.

Contract to Answer for the Debt, Default, or Miscarriages of Another Person. There is no difficulty in understanding the first and third types of contract. The second type of contract is concerned with the relationship among three people: a creditor or obligee, a principal debtor or obligor, and a surety:

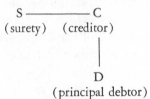

A "surety" is a person who makes his credit available to another, a debtor; and if he is compelled to pay because of the debtor's default, he has a right to be reimbursed by the debtor. (S contracts with C that, if C will sell goods to D on credit and D does not pay, then S will pay C. C sells the goods to D who does not pay C. When S has paid C, S has a right to be reimbursed by D.) When the surety contracts with the creditor whereby the surety will pay the creditor if the debtor fails to pay, the contract is within the statute.

The Contract Must Be for the Promisor (Surety) to Answer for the Debtor's Duty. If the contract does not appear to be for this purpose and the creditor has no reason for knowing otherwise, then the contract is not within the statute. (S and D agree that they will sign a contract with C for the purchase of certain goods to be deliverable to S. S and D have agreed that the goods will then be turned over to D, inasmuch as the only reason for S's participation in the contract is to induce

---

[1] See Sales, below, pp. 1005–6.

[2] See Investment Securities, below, p. 1117.

[3] See Secured Transactions, below, p. 1130.

[4] See *ibid.*, below, p. 1127.

[5] See *ibid.*, below, pp. 1124–25.

[6] See below, p. 1012.

C to sell the goods because of S's financial reliability. D will then reimburse S for the contract price. C is ignorant of this surety relationship between S and D. An oral contract is made by S and D with C. The contract is not within the statute, and S and D are both debtors to C under the contract.) If the promisor contracts to *assume* the debtor's duty, he thereby makes the duty his own and is not answering for the debtor's duty. He may do the latter by so contracting with the creditor, by a novation, or by doing so originally whereby he and the debtor become jointly liable to the creditor for an obligation. An oral contract between the promisor and the creditor whereby the promisor *undertakes to pay* the debtor's debt is not a contract to answer for the debtor's debt; the promisor has assumed and made the debt his own, and the contract is enforceable although oral. An unconditional promise to pay is different from a promise to pay *if* the debtor fails to pay. The first promise creates an absolute liability on the promisor for the debt; the second promise creates a contingent liability to answer for the debtor *if he* defaults. The first promise is not within the purview of the statute; the second is.

The Surety's Promise Must Be Made to the Creditor and Be Collateral to the Debtor's Duty. The surety's promise must be made to the creditor because the contract is to answer to the creditor for the debtor's duty. It is immaterial that the debtor's duty is voidable at his election, for, until avoidance, the duty is still owing. (D, an infant, makes a contract with C. S contracts with C to answer for D's default. S is bound.) A promise by one who holds the debtor's property to deliver it to the creditor is not a promise to answer for the debtor's duty as contemplated by the statute. The debtor's duty need not be in existence at the time the surety's promise is made to the creditor. (S orally contracts with C that, if C will sell goods to D on credit and D does not pay, then S will pay C. C sells the goods to D.) (D owes C money. S contracts with C that, if D does not pay his debt by a certain date, S will pay it.)

A contract made primarily for the benefit of the promisor and not for the benefit of the debtor is not within the statute. (D owes C money. C is about to proceed against D's property on the debt. X contracts with C that, if C will forbear from proceeding against D's property for a certain period and if D does not pay by that time, then X will pay. C forbears. Whether or not the contract is within the statute depends on X's relationship to D. If X is also a creditor of D and made the contract so that D's business would not be ruined and, if given time, D could pay X and C, then the contract is not within the statute. It was made for

X's benefit and not for D's benefit. If X is only a friend of D and made the contract to help D get on his feet, then the contract is within the statute.) However, if the promisor is a *paid surety,* e.g., an insurance company acting as a surety,[7] the contract is held to be within the statute, inasmuch as the purpose of the statute is to include this type of promise irrespective of premium benefit.

Contract for the Sale of Land or Interest Therein. A contract for the sale of land or of an interest therein is within the statute because of the great importance of land and the temptation to commit perjury to prove a contract for its sale. The statute covers not only land but interests therein. Easements, leases, mining rights, and the building of a railroad, in connection with land, are illustrations of interests in land. Licenses for the use of land are not interests in land. A theater ticket is merely a license to enter upon the land. A contract for board and lodging and a contract to erect a building or to make improvements on land are not contracts for an interest in land. They are merely contracts relating to the land. A "lease" is a contract for the sale of an interest in land, but most state statutes provide that a lease for a period less than a year is not within the statute and is enforceable if oral. Oil, gas, minerals, or a structure (e.g., building) affixed to land are land; but a contract for their sale, contemplating their severance from the land *by the seller* after the formation of the contract, causes them to be treated as goods *for the purpose of the contract.*[8] Such a contract is not considered as dealing with interests in land and, therefore, is not within the statute. Similarly, a contract for the sale of a house, but not of the land underneath it, contemplates severance from the realty and is not within the statute. A contract to give a mortgage is within the statute because a mortgage is an interest in land. A mortgage is different from the indebtedness it secures; it is a right to sell the land on the debtor's default and to apply the proceeds in satisfaction of the indebtedness. A contract to sell the debt is not within the statute even though the mortgage follows the indebtedness.

A contract to sell an equitable interest in land is within the statute (e.g., a contract to sell land creates an equitable interest in land in favor of the buyer because, in a court with equity powers, he can compel the seller to convey the land to him). While some courts consider an option

---

[7] The insurance company may be acting as a *surety* or as an *indemnitor.* If a surety, it is within the statute; if an indemnitor, it is not within the statute. For the distinction between surety and indemnitor, see below, pp. 806–7, 815, 877 ff., 883.

[8] See UCC 2–107(1), and below, pp. 243–44. *Comment 1: "If the buyer is to sever,* such transactions are considered contracts affecting land and all problems of the Statute of Frauds and of the recording of land rights apply to them." (Author's italics)

to buy land as not creating such an interest until the buyer accepts under the option, other courts hold that the option of itself creates such an interest.

Part Performance. Part performance of a contract for the sale of land or of an interest therein may take the contract *out of the statute* and permit its enforcement, depending upon the nature of the part performance, as in the following instances:

1. *Seller's conveyance to the buyer.* When that portion of an oral contract requiring performance by transfer of land or of an interest therein has been executed, the courts do not consider the contract as any longer within the statute, and they will enforce the remaining unexecuted portion of the contract. (A contracts orally with B for the purchase of B's land, A to pay the price 30 days after B has conveyed the land to A. B conveys the land to A, but A defaults in making payment. The contract is no longer within the statute of frauds and is enforceable by B.)

2. *Seller's delivery of possession to buyer and either buyer's payment or buyer's substantial improvements on the land with seller's consent.* By the better view, when under an oral contract a purchaser of land or of an interest in land acquires or retains *possession* of the land with the consent of the vendor *and pays* a portion or all of the purchase price, *or* a purchaser with the consent of the vendor makes *valuable improvements* thereon, the contract is specifically enforced[9] by the courts. Many courts consider permitted possession of the land sufficient to justify specific enforcement of the oral contract. The courts do this, regardless of the statute, in order to prevent the perpetration of injustice and fraud on the buyer. A buyer who pays a part or all of the purchase price but makes no valuable improvements and does not obtain possession may not enforce the oral contract and is entitled solely to the return of what he has rendered or its reasonable value as a quasi-contractual right. The purchase price need not be money; it may be services, chattels, or land.

Contract Not Performable within One Year. There have been divers conflicting interpretations of that portion of the statute which provides for contracts not performable *within* one year from the making thereof. The first difficulty is in the calculation of the one-year period. The law disregards fractions of a day. In calculating the one-year period some courts have disregarded the legal fiction of disregarding a fraction of a day and have computed exactly the period of one year. The

---

[9] See below, pp. 133 f.

better view is to disregard the fraction of a day so as to be most favorable to enforcement of the contract. Accordingly, the year begins to run from the end of the day when the contract was made and expires at midnight on the anniversary of the date of the contract's formation. All courts hold that a bilateral contract for a year, in which performance is to begin the day the contract is made, is not within the statute. By the better view, if performance is to begin the day after the contract was made, the contract is not within the statute. All courts agree that, if performance is to begin at any time later than the day following the contract's formation, the contract is within the statute. It should be noted that the date of the contract's formation is the date when the last act necessary to create the contract occurs. *The above discussion relates solely to executory bilateral contracts. A unilateral promise is not within the statute,* regardless of the period of time for the performance called for, because there is no contract until such performance occurs.

The second difficulty is in the determination of what contracts are not to be performed within the year's time. All courts agree that, if the contract literally *cannot* be completely performed within the year by the mode of performance agreed upon, then the contract is within the statute, regardless of the expectations and views of the parties concerning the probability of performance within the year. An illustration is an oral contract to sell a number of crops from the same land when it is physically impossible to grow that many crops from that land in one year. If performance within one year were conceivably possible by a method of performance different from the one contemplated by the parties in their contract, some courts hold the contract not to be within the statute, but most courts hold to the contrary. Contracts performable on a contingency which may or may not happen within a year are not within the statute, regardless of the duration of such contracts. Illustrations of such contracts are: insurance contracts on life or property, regardless of the term of years, because the contingency may occur within the year and the promise to pay become performable; and a contract to support another for life, because death may occur within a year and the contract thereby be performed. However, a contract to support another, or to forbear, for a term of years is within the statute. While it is true that a promise to support another for five years is discharged by the promisee's death, yet the promise has not been performed; its further performance is excused. In contrast, a contract to support for life is *performed* on the promisee's death. For the same reason, a contract not to compete for a period in excess of one year is, by the better view, within the statute.

Courts are in disagreement concerning the status of a contract performable on one side but not on the other within one year. (A and B orally contract whereby A is to render his performance now, e.g., pay money, and B is to render his performance over a period of 18 months.) Because the entire contract cannot be performed within one year, it is clearly within the statute. However, most courts hold that, if one side of the contract is performable within one year and such performance occurs within one year, the contract no longer is within the statute. Many courts hold that performance on one side within the year is not enough; if the remaining promise on the other side still is not performable within the year, the contract is still within the statute. The *Restatement of Contracts,* section 198, provides that performance on one side, made *at any time,* takes the contract out of the purview of the statute. In any case, if all or part performance is rendered on one side of an oral contract which is unenforceable, the party who has performed has a right of restitution of what he has rendered or the reasonable value thereof on the ground of quasi contract in order to prevent unjust enrichment.

The Memorandum
All five types of contract may be proved by the contract being in writing, or a note or memorandum thereof being in writing and signed by the party to be charged or by his lawfully authorized agent. The memorandum is sufficient if made at any time before a legal action is begun on the contract. (A and B make a signed written contract. On its expiration A and B orally contract to renew the contract previously made and now expired. The previous contract is a memorandum of the subsequent oral contract.) It may be a formal or informal writing and may be one writing or a series of related writings. If there is more than one writing, either all the writings must be attached to the signed writing or the signed writing must refer to all the other writings. (A writes to B complaining about B's failure to perform an oral contract within the statute of frauds and sets forth all the data regarding such contract. B's answering signed letter refers to A's letter and admits the formation of such a contract but refuses to perform it. B's signed letter refers to A's letter, and the two writings constitute the memorandum sufficient to satisfy the statute and to prove' the oral contract. The contract is enforceable by A against B. If B were seeking to enforce the oral contract against A, A's signed letter would be the memorandum.) The memorandum need not have been intended by the party as a memorandum of the contract.

The memorandum must be signed by the party to be charged or by his lawfully authorized agent.[10] Signature means any mark, sign, printing, or writing intended by the party making or adopting it to be his signature.[11] It may occur anywhere on the writing; and it is different from the word "subscribe," which means that the signature must occur at the bottom of the document. The memorandum may be asserted to prove the contract only against the party who has signed it. In the second illustration given in the paragraph above, if B had never answered A's letter, A could not assert the oral contract against B; but B could assert the contract against A and prove the contract by A's signed letter, which is a memorandum signed by the party to be charged—namely, A. One party cannot authorize the other party to sign the memorandum for him because of the temptation to assert authority fraudulently. However, a third person may be authorized to sign for both parties. In sales by auction, the auctioneer impliedly is authorized by both seller and buyer to prepare and sign on their behalf a memorandum of sale *immediately* after the sale.

The memorandum must state: the names of the parties or their agents, or provide a description sufficient for their identification, and their relationship (e.g., as buyer and seller); the subject matter of the contract (e.g., a horse, land, machinery, and the quantity and quality of such); and *all* the terms and conditions of each promise and to whom made.[12] (A is the agent of C, and B is the agent of D. C and D have made an oral contract within the statute of frauds. A and B are authorized to execute a memorandum of the contract, which they do, signing as "C" and "D." The memorandum is sufficient to prove the contract against C or D.) The contract price is a part of the terms and conditions. Omission of any of this required data causes the writing to be insufficient as a memorandum. A writing naming the parties but not indicating their relationship (e.g., who is the buyer and who the seller) is defective. A memorandum which has been destroyed or lost may be proved by other evidence.

---

[10] See below, p. 550, for the legal effect when an agent does not identify his principal in the memorandum signed by the agent.

[11] Under UCC 1–201(39) : " 'Signed' includes any symbol executed or adopted by a party with present intention to authenticate a writing."

[12] UCC 2–201(1) does not require the memorandum to indicate: which party is the buyer and which the seller; or the price, time and place of payment or delivery, or warranties, except that if the "price" consists of goods rather than money then the quantity of such goods must be stated. *Comment 1:* "Only three definite and invariable requirements as to the memorandum are made by this subsection. First, it must evidence a contract for the sale of goods; second, it must be 'signed,' a word which includes any authentication which identifies the party to be charged; and third, it must specify a quantity."

Summary

The statute of frauds is extremely important in the law of contracts. A contract within the purview of the statute is unenforceable unless proved as prescribed in the statute. The statute is concerned solely with methods of proving a contract. Failure of proof in compliance with the statute does not affect the validity of the contract. If the contract is executed completely, the effect is the same as though the statute had been satisfied. All five types of contract named at the beginning of this section may be proved by the contract being in writing or by a proper memorandum of the contract. Other types of contract governed by the Code may be proved only as prescribed by the Code.[13]

---

[13] For contracts for the sale of goods, see UCC 2–201, and below, pp. 255 ff.

Chapter V

CONDITIONS

Nature and Importance A "CONDITION" is a fact on the happening or nonhappening of which a promissory duty of immediate performance either arises or is extinguished. (A promises to pay B $100 for the construction of a shed. A has no duty of immediate performance of his promise until the condition for such performance has occurred—namely, B's construction of the shed.) (A insures B's house against fire, the policy providing that failure of the insured to bring an action against the insurer for fire loss within a prescribed period of time after the insurer has rejected the claim shall terminate the insurer's duty to pay. Fire occurs and B presents his claim, which A rejects. B does not bring an action against A within the prescribed time. A's promissory duty of immediate performance—i.e., to pay B for the fire loss—has been extinguished by B's failure to sue within the prescribed time, which is a condition extinguishing A's duty.) The subject of conditions is the key to the comprehension of performance and nonperformance, breach of contract, and discharge from the duty of performing one's promise. In brief, the occurrence or nonoccurrence of a condition determines whether or not a party has a legal duty of immediately performing his promise.

Absolute and Conditional Promises All promises are either absolute or conditional. They differ as to when a duty of immediate performance arises in each case. A promise performable only after the lapse of a certain period of time is an absolute promise. There are no conditions to its immediate performance; *the law does not consider a lapse of time as a condition.* A promise is conditional when something other than a lapse of time must occur. A promise which is not absolute is conditional. (A promises to pay B $1,000 on the expiration of 30 days, and B promises to deliver goods two months after such payment. A's promise is absolute, payable at the end of 30 days, and subject to no conditions. B's promise is conditional, no duty of immediate performance arising until two months after payment.) A conditional promise may have as a condition either the performance of another party's promise or the occurrence of an event or act. Conditional promises are often called "dependent promises" because there is no duty of their immediate performance until the occurrence of the condition on which such performance is dependent.

Conditions Precedent. Conditions may be preced-
Classification ent, subsequent, or concurrent; and they may be
of Conditions either expressly stated or implied in fact from the
contract, or implied in law. *A condition precedent
is a condition which must occur before there is a duty of immediate performance of the conditional promise.* (A promises to pay B $10,000 on
the arrival of a certain ship. Arrival of the ship is a condition precedent.) When the condition of a promise is the promisor's satisfaction of
the performance of the condition, it is a problem of interpretation as to
whether the satisfaction means personal satisfaction or the reasonable
satisfaction of a person in the promisor's position. Satisfaction is concerned solely with the performance of the condition, and nothing else.
(A contracts with B for the purchase of a suit to be made by B to A's
satisfaction for $75. B manufactures a suit for A. A, without examining
the suit, expresses his dissatisfaction. A's satisfaction is a condition precedent to A's immediate promissory duty to pay. A has not indicated any
satisfaction or dissatisfaction *of the performance,* and his repudiation of
the contract subjects him to damages for its breach.) Regardless of
whether the satisfaction is interpreted as personal or as reasonable, the
promisor must act in good faith and cannot be arbitrary or capricious.
In the event of doubt as to which satisfaction is meant, reasonable satisfaction is implied by law as the intent of the parties. If the purpose of
the contract is the personal taste, fancy, preference, or convenience of
the promisor, then the satisfaction is personal and, until he is personally
satisfied, there is no duty of immediate performance of his promise.
Whether or not another person would reasonably be satisfied is irrelevant. If the purpose of the contract is to accomplish a routine, ministerial, or mechanical result, then the satisfaction is that of a reasonable
man in the promisor's position. An architect's certificate is issuable on
the architect's reasonable satisfaction. (A contracts with B for B's construction of a building. On completion B is to obtain a certificate of satisfaction from C, an architect, and deliver it to A, who will then pay B
$10,000. C's satisfaction of performance is reasonable satisfaction.
If C's dissatisfaction is unreasonable, B need not produce the certificate

in order to obtain the $10,000.) A promise to do something on demand of the promisee is conditional on the making of such demand, except that, when the promise is to pay the promisor's money debt, the promise is not interpreted as conditional and the promisee need make no demand in order to hold the promisor liable. This is an odd exception which has come into the law. While the demand for payment of the debt need not be made, yet a demand for interest thereon is a condition precedent which must be made. It should be noted that a contract which does not expressly state when it is to be performed is impliedly performable within a reasonable time.

Conditions Subsequent. *A condition subsequent is a condition which, if occurring subsequent to the rise of a duty of immediate performance of a conditional promise, extinguishes such duty.* (A insures B's house against fire, the policy providing that B is to notify A of any loss by fire within a prescribed period of time thereafter or A's duty to pay will cease, and further providing that, if B's claim is rejected, B must sue A within a prescribed period of time thereafter or A's liability will cease. B's notice to A of fire loss is a condition precedent to the creation of any duty of immediate performance of A's conditional promise. On giving such notice A's duty arises; but it may be extinguished by B's failure to sue A within the prescribed period of time after his claim has been rejected, which is a condition subsequent.) A condition subsequent to the duty of immediate performance should be distinguished carefully from a condition subsequent to the creation of a contract but before the duty of immediate performance arises. (A insures B's house against fire, the policy providing that, if gasoline is kept on the premises, the policy is void. If gasoline is kept on the premises, the contract is ended. The gasoline provision is a condition subsequent to the creation of a contract.)

Conditions Concurrent. *Conditions concurrent are conditions which are to occur simultaneously, each a condition to performance of a promise.* (A contracts with B for the purchase of B's house for $10,000, the transfer of the deed and payment to occur at the same time. Transfer of the deed is the condition of the immediate promissory duty of performance by A, and payment is the condition of the immediate promissory duty of performance by B. Performance of each promise is a concurrent condition.)

Implied Conditions. Implied conditions may be implied in fact or implied in law. A condition implied in fact is implied from the contract of the parties. (A and B contract whereby A is to supply coal to B for one year; and B agrees to buy such coal exclusively from A as B requires it, for a certain price payable by B. It is implied in fact that a condition for the performance of A's promise is notice from B of his requirements.) A condition implied in law is a condition implied by the courts, when necessary, to assist in interpreting the contract. Conditions implied in law are concerned mostly with the order in which promises are to be performed.

Conditions Implied in Law—Order in Which Promises Are Performable.

1. The law implies that, in the absence of anything in the contract to the contrary, mutual promises are concurrently conditional *if they can be performed simultaneously* with the knowledge of both parties. (A and B contract whereby A is to deliver certain goods to B on a certain date. B is to pay A $100, but the contract does not state when such payment is to be made. The law implies that payment is to be made at the time of delivery. Performance of each promise is concurrently conditional.) If parts of such promises can be so performed, performance of each part is concurrently conditional. This applies to installment contracts.

2. However, *when a material part of the contract is to be performed on one side by installments and the last installment can be performed simultaneously with full performance by the other side,* such last installment and full performance are concurrent conditions. (A contracts with B for the sale of land whereby A is to pay for the purchase price by installments. The payment of the last installment by A and the transfer of the deed by B are concurrent conditions.)

3. *If performance of one promise will extend over a period of time, while the other promise, by its terms, is not to extend over any period of time,* performance of the promise taking time is implied as a condition precedent to performance of the other promise which will not take any time to perform. An illustration is an employment contract in which the employee is to receive a salary, the employee's services taking time to perform but not the employer's payment of salary. The employee's performance is a condition precedent to payment by the employer.

Failure of Condition

There is no immediate duty to perform a conditional promise until the condition occurs. The effect of failure of the condition to occur depends on whether or not the condition was promised. Damages are available to an injured party against a party who has wrongfully failed to perform his promise. If the condition was not promised, the failure is not a breach of any contractual duty and there can be no damages for breach of promise—i.e., of contract; the promise dependent on the condition's occurrence is extinguished. In the illustration of the fire insurance policy with the condition that, if gasoline were kept on the premises, the contract would be void, no promise was made that gasoline would not be kept on the premises; occurrence of the condition discharges the insurer from any duty to perform his promise, but he has no action for damages against the insured because the insured has neither made nor breached any promise regarding the presence of the gasoline. However, when a condition is *promised* and fails to occur, there is no duty to perform the conditional promise (the promisee has not performed the condition, nor is he ready, willing, and able to perform); except that the courts make a distinction between performance and substantial performance of the condition which directly affects the duty of performing the conditional promise.

Degrees of Nonperformance. "Performance" means complete performance. "Nonperformance" means a failure of performance, whether in small or great degree. When performance has not occurred, whether or not the injured party is discharged from his promissory duty to perform depends upon the express terms of the contract and the law regarding discharge of the duty of performance. If the parties have provided expressly in their contract that failure of performance in any detail whatsoever discharges the duty of the injured party, then any defect in performance discharges such duty. The parties have expressed themselves; it is their contract, and the law will not act contrary to their intentions. If there is no such express provision, the courts examine what has been done by the nonperforming party under the contract. In the event that nothing has been done in performing under the contract, then there is a *failure of consideration discharging* the injured promisor from any duty of performance. When something has been done under the contract but it is not performance, the courts are more inclined to see whether the conditional promisor got substantially what he was to receive under the contract. It would be less of a hardship on the conditional promisor to require him to keep the substantial performance which he has received and to give him a right to damages for breach of the contract, than to deprive the promisee of all compensation he was to receive after having performed his contractual duty to a very great extent. If substantial performance has occurred, the promisor's duty of performance is not discharged; if no substantial performance has occurred, there is a failure of consideration and his duty to perform is discharged. Restating this in another way, anything less than substantial performance creates a material failure of performance; substantial performance creates a nonmaterial failure of performance. A material failure of performance does not entitle the nonperforming promisee to any right of performance by the conditional promisor because there has been a *failure of consideration.* A nonmaterial failure of performance entitles the nonperforming promisee to performance of the conditional promise but subjects the promisee to damages for breach of contract if the nonperformance was wrongful.

Test of Materiality of Nonperformance. Often it is very difficult to determine whether or not the nonperformance is material. Determination of materiality is a question of fact for the jury. The thought is often expressed that, *if the main purpose of the contract has been performed, or not defeated,* then there is substantial performance and the failure to perform is nonmaterial; otherwise the failure to perform is material. That appears to sum up the attitude of the courts, which consider: (1) what the injured party actually received, his difficulty in rectifying the defective performance, and whether damages for such defects will be adequate considering his difficulty and inconvenience, as against the degree of the wrongful party's failure to perform; (2) the possibility of his completing performance; and (3) whether his nonperformance was willful. Willful failure to perform is a weighty factor inclining the courts to treat the failure to perform as material and discharging any immediate duty of performance of the injured promisor's conditional promise. Building a house with pine floors instead of oak floors, and installation in a building of a different brand of pipe equal in quality to that specified by the contract, have been held to be substantial performance. Delay in performance is material nonperformance only when time is of the essence. The parties may expressly provide in their contract that time is of the essence. In business contracts, time is of the essence. The circumstances surrounding the formation of the contract may indicate that time is of the essence. Installment contracts for the sale of goods are governed by the Code, and the effect of nonperformance in an installment is discussed later under Sales.[1]

Failure of Consideration. Less than substantial performance is a material failure of performance which constitutes a *failure of consideration* discharging the conditional promisor's duty of performance. The conditional promisor's right of action against the nonperforming promisee for damages for wrongful nonperformance is predicated on the assumption that the promisor can perform his promise. If, after the promisee's nonperformance, it appears that the promisor could not

---

[1] See below, pp. 315–16.

perform his promise, then the promisor's right of action is extinguished. (E and A made an employment contract on February 1, A's employment to begin March 1. On February 15, E repudiated the contract. On February 25, A died. While E had breached the contract thereby creating in A a right to damages from E, nevertheless, A's death prior to the date when A's performance was to begin extinguishes A's right, acquired by his estate, to bring such action.) Failure of consideration discharges the duty of the conditional promisor regardless of his ignorance of the existence of such failure of consideration. (A refuses to perform his contract with B, not knowing of B's material nonperformance. A has not acted improperly. B's material nonperformance was a failure of consideration discharging A's duty to perform.)

Prospective Failure of Consideration. When a strong likelihood of *material nonperformance* by the promisee arises subsequent to the formation of the contract, in some instances the promisor's duty of performance should be discharged and in other instances the promisor should have the opportunity to change his position materially in reliance thereon and thereby to be discharged of his duty of performance. This is called "prospective failure of consideration." However, if prospective failure of consideration is wrongfully caused by the conditional promisor, his duty to perform is not discharged. Prospective failure of consideration may occur in the following ways:

1. The promisee's manifestation of an intention not to render substantial performance (called "repudiation") or his manifestation of doubt concerning his ability to render substantial performance *and* the promisor's material change of position in reliance thereon. The promisee can retract his manifestation before the promisor's material change of position in reliance thereon and thereby cause the situation to be the same as it was prior to the manifestation.

2. The promisee is insolvent under the law of contracts when he is unable to pay his debts as they mature, and under the Uniform Commercial Code when he "either has ceased to pay his debts in the ordinary course of business or cannot pay his debts as they become due or is insolvent within the meaning of the federal bankruptcy law;"[2] or he has been adjudicated a bankrupt, or bankruptcy proceedings are pending against him; or his property is in receivership, or receivership proceedings are pending against him; *and* the promisor has materially changed his position in reliance thereon before performance by the promisee occurs, is tendered, or is secured.[3] However, if the contractual obligation of

---

[2] UCC 1–201(23).

[3] It should be noted that a promisee's insolvency or bankruptcy discharges the promisor of his obligation to continue to extend credit to the promisee, unless security is given to assure performance by the promisee. It should also be noted that, if the promisee has been adjudicated a bankrupt, the trustee in bankruptcy has 60 days after the bankrupt's adjudication within which to reject or assume any executory contract of the bankrupt and contracts not assumed within that time are deemed rejected. (See below, p. 860.)

the insolvent or bankrupt promisee is to render personal services and his insolvency or bankruptcy will not interfere with his rendition of such services, the promisor may not consider such insolvency or bankruptcy as a prospective failure of consideration and his duty to perform is not discharged.

3. In a contract to sell certain land or goods to the promisor purchaser, the promisee vendor contracts to sell the same to a third person, or so encumbers the same as to cause the promisor reasonably to believe that the promisee will not be able to remove the encumbrance by the time performance to the promisor becomes due. The promisor is not required to change his position materially to be discharged of his duty to perform; but by doing so the promisor precludes the promisee from canceling such discharge by his subsequent reacquisition of the land or goods, or removal of the encumbrance, before the time performance to the promisor becomes due.

4. The promisor purchaser neither knows nor has reason to know at the time a contract is made to sell him certain land or goods that the promisee vendor does not own the same *and,* on learning of this fact while it still continues, the promisor materially changes his position in reliance thereon.

5. Destruction or impairment of the requisite subject matter of the contract, or of the requisite means of performing the contract, making impossible rendition of substantial performance by the promisee. (A contracts with B to paint B's building, which subsequently is destroyed accidentally; A's duty to paint the building is discharged. Or X contracts with Y for the purchase of a product to be made by a certain factory or certain person, and subsequently the factory is destroyed or the person dies; X's duty to purchase is discharged.)

6. Death or physical incapacity of the promisee of a *personal service contract* rendering his performance impossible, or the promisor's material change of position in reliance on the physical condition of the promisee as making the latter's personal performance reasonably improbable. Whether or not a contract is for personal services is determined by whether or not the duty of performance is delegable.[4]

7. Supervening illegality of contractual performance by the promisee.

Excused Failure of Consideration. Previous discussion[5] has indicated that failure of consideration by material nonperformance of the promisee discharges the conditional promisor's duty of performance. However, if the promisee's failure to perform has been excused, then the promisor's duty of performance still exists and he is not dependent upon the promisee's performance as a condition. When the promisor has excused material nonperformance, he is deemed to have waived it. If the promisee substitutes a performance materially different from what the contract called for, the promisor's acceptance of the promisee's material nonperformance with knowledge of such, or his implied acceptance by his retention of such material nonperformance for an unreasonable period of time, excuses the failure of consideration and im-

---

[4] See above, p. 104 f.
[5] See above, pp. 121 f.

poses upon the conditional promisor the duty of performing his promise. (A contracts with B for the purchase of a certain machine for $100. The machine which is delivered to A is materially defective. A knows of the defect but retains the machine for an unreasonable period without objecting to B. A has excused the failure of consideration and is under a duty to pay the $100.) However, acceptance of material nonperformance is not, in itself, a manifestation of assent to further material nonperformance, unless the frequency of such acceptance reasonably induces the promisee to believe that such material nonperformance is satisfactory to the promisor and the promisee changes his position materially in reliance thereon. (A issued a noncancelable policy of insurance to B which provided that annual premiums must be paid in advance at the home office of A. For 10 years B had paid the premium each year by mailing a check to the home office, which accepted it. B mailed a check for the eleventh premium to A, which A never received. On the expiration of the due date, A informed B that the policy was canceled. B immediately tendered the eleventh premium and requested reinstatement of the policy. A must accept the check and reinstate the policy. A's promise to insure required payment at the home office. By accepting mailed checks for 10 years, which A did not have to do, A induced B to believe that such manner of performance was satisfactory to A. B's material change of position in reliance thereon by sending mailed checks to the home office is excusable nonperformance.) It should be noted that, if the promisor of a contract to be performed within a specified or a reasonable time waives the requirement or condition of such time or indicates he is willing to extend such time without specifying the length of the extension, he subsequently must inform the promisee of a reasonable time within which his performance is to occur if it is to have the same effect as though it were originally a term of the contract. In this way nonperformance which has been excused previously can be stopped from continuing indefinitely.

Other instances of excused material nonperformance are:

1. The promisor's manifestation of an intention not to render substantial performance (called "repudiation") or his manifestation of doubt concerning his ability to render substantial performance, which has induced nonperformance by the promisee or failure of the condition to occur. The promisor's retraction of his manifestation before the promisee's material change of position in reliance thereon extinguishes the effect of the manifestation as excusing material nonperformance by the promisee.

2. The promisor's hindrance or prevention of the promisee's performance or of occurrence of the condition which otherwise would have occurred, provided

such hindrance or prevention was not caused or justified by the promisee's financial condition or by his conduct.

3. Continued acceptance by the promisor of defective performance (e.g., delivery of defective installments) is such as causes the promisee reasonably to believe that such performance is satisfactory to the promisor and the promisee materially changes his position in reliance thereon.

4. Excusable impossibility of performance by the promisee which would discharge the promisee's duty of performance,[6] the promisor's duty to perform having arisen and the condition of its performance serving only to determine the time when such performance is to occur.[7]

5. The promisee's inability to produce a required architect's, or other expert's, certificate because of the architect's unreasonable refusal to deliver such a certificate to the promisee or because the architect is physically unable to do so.

Ordinarily, the promisor may reject material nonperformance without stating any reason therefor, and the giving of an insufficient reason is immaterial. However, if such rejection reasonably induces the promisee not to perform, which he could have done in proper time, then the promisor impliedly waives or excuses nonperformance. An illustration of this is the tender of payment by check[8] or in other form which is not legal tender when payment is to be made in legal tender. Rejection of nonlegal tender for this reason without explanation misleads the promisee, since he could have obtained such legal tender in proper time if he had been informed of the reason for the rejection. The promisor has excused the promisee's performance, and the promisor is under a duty to perform his promise.

Importance of Nonperformance to Conditions and Breach of Contract. Nonperformance is of importance to the subjects of conditions and breach of contract in different ways. In conditions, actual or prospective *material failure of performance affects the promisor's duty of performance;* it does not create a right of action for damages for such failure. In breach of contract, *any failure of performance which is wrongful creates a right of action for damages.* Accordingly, conditions are important in connection with the promisor's duty of performance and, if promised and wrongfully not performed, are important as constituting a breach of contract.

---

[6] See below, pp. 149 f.

[7] As an illustration of this kind of excusable material nonperformance, C, creditor, is to return to D, debtor, certain security of the debtor at which time D is to pay his debt to C. The security is destroyed through no fault of C. D's promise to pay C is performable without the condition of C's surrender of the security.

[8] For payment by check in contracts for sale of goods under the Code, see below, p. 309.

Chapter VI

BREACH OF CONTRACT

Wrongful Non-performance WRONGFUL nonperformance of a promissory duty under a contract is a breach of promise and, therefore, a breach of contract. The law is concerned only with the *wrongful* nonperformance of a contractual duty and does not impose liability for excused nonperformance. A breach occurs on the failure to perform an *immediate* duty under the contract. Prospective inability to perform is not a breach of contract because no breach of an immediate duty has occurred, although, if the conditional promisor wishes to change his position materially in reliance thereon, he can do so and thereby discharge his duty to perform his promise, as was discussed previously in "Conditions."[1] A contracting party's unjustified hindrance or prevention of another contracting party's performance or of the occurrence of a condition which otherwise would have occurred is a breach of contract. (A employs B under an employment contract for one year. A discharges B without cause before the expiration of the year. A's act not only excused B from further performing under the contract, but it also constituted a material breach of contract by A.)

Breach of contract is concerned with the *immediate* creation of a right of action for such breach available to the injured party against the wrongfully nonperforming party. The extent of this right of action depends upon the materiality[2] of the breach. A material breach is a breach of the entire contract, often called a "total breach," which creates a right to remedies (damages, specific performance, or restitution) which may be substituted for the rights under the contract; while a nonmaterial breach is a breach of only a part of the contract, often called a "partial breach," which thereby creates a right of action only for damages for the partial breach. A nonmaterial breach means that there has been substantial performance or nonmaterial failure of performance with no excuse for incomplete promised performance; it creates only the right of action for

[1] See above, pp. 122 ff.
[2] See above, p. 121.

damages, the contract remaining in existence and the injured party still having the duty of performing his promise. A breach of contract is material if either: substantial performance is not rendered when due; substantial performance which otherwise would have occurred is prevented or hindered by the other party; or the breach is accompanied or followed by a repudiation of the contract.

Repudiation. A party may repudiate his duty to perform under the contract. Repudiation is a manifestation of an intention not to render substantial performance of a contractual duty; it may be made expressly or impliedly by conduct. An express repudiation must be made to the other party or to any other beneficiary of the performance due under the contract, and it must clearly indicate such unwillingness to perform substantially. Repudiation is implied from voluntary conduct which causes substantial performance to be either actually or apparently impossible. *When unjustified repudiation accompanies or follows a breach of contract, it characterizes the breach as a material breach.* The injured party not only is discharged from the duty of performing his promise, but he also acquires a right of action for such breach. Until the injured party materially changes his position in reliance on the repudiation, the repudiating party may withdraw his repudiation. Withdrawal of the repudiation still leaves the nonperformance and a right of action therefor, the extent of which is determined by whether the nonperformance is a material, or a nonmaterial, breach. Reliance by material change of position may be made expressly or impliedly by conduct indicating an intent to do so. An illustration of implied reliance is: the injured party's bringing an action for the breach; or his purchase elsewhere of an article or services similar to that promised and not rendered; or his sale of the subject matter of the contract.

Anticipatory Breach. Unjustified repudiation may occur not only at the time when the duty is to be performed but also prior to such time; the latter is called an "anticipatory breach." Anticipatory breach is not really a breach because a breach occurs only on a failure to perform an immediate duty under the contract. However, a party's unjustified repudiation of his duty to perform under the contract exposes the injured party to a risk of nonperformance which he had not contemplated previously. He should not continue under a duty of performing his promise when the other party has indicated clearly wrongful refusal to perform his promise, if the injured party so wishes. The wrongful character of this repudiation stamps it as a "breach by anticipatory repudiation."[3] Accord-

---

[3] American Law Institute, *Restatement: Contracts*, 1932, sec. 318, *Comment d.*

ingly, an anticipatory breach gives to the other party the right to change his position materially in reliance thereon and thereby be discharged of his duty to perform his promise and preclude the repudiator's withdrawal of his repudiation. Until such reliance, the repudiation can be withdrawn. Timely withdrawal of the repudiation restores the parties to their status immediately prior to the anticipatory breach.[4] There remains no right of action to the other party because no duty of immediate performance has been breached. (On January 10, A contracted with B to buy a certain horse, the price to be paid and the horse to be delivered on January 30. On January 15, B sold the horse to C. On January 20, A, relying on B's sale to C, bought a horse from D. On January 25, B repurchased the horse he sold to C. On January 30, B tendered the horse to A. A refused to take it and refused to pay for it. B's sale to C was an implied repudiation constituting an anticipatory breach. A's purchase on January 20 was an implied material change of position in reliance on such breach thereby precluding B's withdrawal of his repudiation. B's tender of performance on January 30 was ineffectual. If A had not changed his position by January 25 and he knew of B's repurchase of the horse, B's repurchase would have been a withdrawal of the repudiation and A's duty to perform would have continued to exist with no right of action against B.) Tender of performance after material change of position in reliance on an anticipatory breach is ineffectual to restore the injured party's duty to perform his promise; the latter's duty is discharged. Withdrawal of the repudiation must be brought to the attention of the injured party before his reliance on the anticipatory breach in order to be effective. If the repudiation was made expressly, then the repudiator must inform the injured party; if made impliedly, then notice obtained by the injured party from any source is sufficient.

A party's insolvency and his manifestation of doubt concerning his ability to render substantial performance are not nonperformance; their occurrence gives to the other party an *opportunity* to discharge his contractual duty to perform by changing his position materially in reliance thereon, as discussed previously under "Conditions,"[5] but they do not constitute an anticipatory breach, for two reasons. First, anticipatory breach is concerned with a party's manifested *voluntary unwillingness* to perform, and is a breach of contract creating a right of action because of the *wrongful refusal* to perform. Second, breach of contract

---

[4] See UCC 2–611.
[5] See above, pp. 122 f.

is concerned with a right of action for wrongful *nonperformance,* and not with the *possibility of nonperformance.*

Anticipatory breach creates an immediate right of action for the breach of contract. The assertion of this right by bringing an action is a material change of position in reliance on the breach. Failure to exercise this right gives to the repudiator an opportunity to withdraw his repudiation; and, for this reason, the statute of limitations does not begin to run on the right of action until the time when there is a failure to perform an immediate duty under the contract.

When Nonperformance Is Wrongful. Nonperformance is wrongful when there is a contractual duty to render immediate performance, performance has not been rendered, and there is no legal justification or excuse for such nonperformance. "Justification may be due to the fact that the duty arising when the contract was formed has been discharged, or if that is not the case, to the fact that a duty of immediate performance has not arisen because some condition precedent has not occurred."[6] Accordingly, there cannot be a breach of contract if a contractual duty of immediate performance has not yet arisen, or the duty has been discharged. Discharge of a contractual duty may occur not only by failure of condition, discussed previously,[7] but in other ways, discussed later.[8]

Waiver   Waiver is the relinquishment of a known right. In the discussion of conditions,[9] it was indicated that the conditional promisor could excuse the condition on the occurrence of which performance of his promise was dependent. The excuse of such condition was, in effect, a waiver.[10] Similarly, after the occurrence of a breach of contract, the injured party may waive defective performance or nonperformance by manifesting, either expressly or impliedly, his intention not to insist on performance. The injured party can waive a nonmaterial breach or a material breach, or treat a material breach as a nonmaterial breach—e.g., accepting materially defective performance—except that, in the case of a material breach by repudiation, the injured party cannot waive the breach and continue to perform under the contract.[11] Delay in asserting a right of

---

[6] American Law Institute, *Restatement: Contracts,* 1932, sec. 132, *Comment a.*
[7] See above, pp. 119 ff.
[8] See below, pp. 139 ff.
[9] See above, pp. 123 ff.
[10] See UCC 2–208, 2–209.
[11] See below, p. 132.

action for a breach, and delay in changing one's position materially in reliance on a material breach, do not imply a waiver. Neither is the injured party's urging of performance after a breach a waiver of such breach.

Remedies   Breach of contract is wrongful nonperformance, creating an immediate *right of action for damages* for such breach. There are two other remedies which are available for proper cases: *specific performance* and *restitution*. These remedies are forms of relief to help the injured party. It is often said that damages are a form of relief at law and that specific performance and restitution are forms of relief in equity. These three forms of relief have different objectives. "Damages" is the money judicially awarded as compensation for injury or harm sustained. By "injury" is meant the invasion of another person's interest. Here the interest is in performance of the contract and the injury is the interference with the interest by nonperformance. Injury is distinguished from the words "damage" and "harm," which mean loss or tangible and material detriment. A decree of "specific performance" seeks to compel performance of the contract according to its terms as much as possible. "Restitution" means the return of what has been rendered, or its value, in order to place the parties in the positions they occupied prior to the contract's formation. These three remedies will be considered in turn.

Damages. Damages may be *nominal* or *trivial, exemplary* or *punitive,* or *compensatory.*

Nominal Damages. Immediately on breach of contract a right to an action for damages arises. The right exists although no damage may have been sustained, and statutory nominal damages will be awarded if an action is begun. Such damages are trivial and indicate that *injury without damage has occurred.* (A and B contract for the sale of a horse for $50. B refuses to take the horse, which is worth $75. A has suffered no damage.)

Punitive Damages. A judicial award for malicious, wanton, or intentionally wrongful conduct, which is in excess of compensation for injury or damage, is called "exemplary" or "punitive" damages. Punitive damages are not ordinarily available for breach of contract.

Compensatory Damages. Compensatory damages are to compensate the injured party for loss sustained or gains lost caused by the breach. The wrongful party should be liable only for the damage which he reasonably should or could foresee would naturally flow from the breach. If he knows or should know at the time the contract is made that breach may cause damage to the other party greater than the damage which would ordinarily occur, breach causing such damage makes him liable therefor. Such damage is called "special damage," which must be pleaded specially as well as proved. (A and B contract for the sale of certain gaskets. A, the seller, knows B has a contract to supply these gaskets to C. A breaches the contract. A is liable for the loss of profit which B would have made under his contract with C, as well as the loss which B may have experienced under his contract with A. If B were involved in litigation with C because of his failure to supply the gaskets, A would be liable for this damage also.)[12] In contracts for the sale of real or personal property, damages are measured by the difference between the contract price and the market price at the time when performance was due. In contracts for services, the measure of damages depends upon who is the injured party. If an employee has been improperly discharged under a contract, his damages are his salary due up to the time of his discharge plus his salary under the remainder of the contract, less what he has earned by other employment since the breach and what prospective earnings he can make in other employment for the remainder of the contract period. When a contract for services is for the life of the employee, the duration of the contract is measured by the employee's health and expected span of life, as determined by mortality tables at the time of the breach. If the employer is the injured party, his damages are the difference between the contract rate and what he must pay a substitute for the same services. Whatever expense is saved to one party by the other party's breach is deducted from the damages. (A contracts to manufacture an article for B for $1,000. After A has begun to manufacture, B repudiates the contract. A's damages are measured by $1,000 less the expense which A still would have to incur to finish the article. To state it in another way, A could recover the expense he has already incurred plus his loss of profit.)

Damages are fixed as of the time the breach occurred, except in the case of an anticipatory breach, when damages are fixed as of the time when performance was to have occurred. On the occurrence of a non-material breach the injured party immediately acquires a right of action for damages, but he must continue performance under the contract. If the breach is material, the injured party has a right of action for

---

[12] See UCC 2–715(2). It should be noted carefully that while general damage and special damage describe the loss or harm experienced, they are reflected in the judicial award of general damages or special damages. General damages are concerned with loss which usually accompanies the injury complained of; pleading the injury gives the defending party sufficient notice of the damage which need not be pleaded. Special damages are concerned with loss which does not usually accompany the injury complained of and which must be pleaded specially as well as proved.

damages for such breach. He may treat a material breach other than by repudiation as a nonmaterial breach and continue performance, his right of action for damages being reduced to the damages for a non-material breach. (A and B contract for the delivery of goods by install-ments. B's first deliveries are materially defective. The breach is mate-rial. A retains the goods delivered without objecting to B, or objects to B but retains the goods and awaits further deliveries. A has a right of action for damages for the defective deliveries he has already accepted.) When a material breach occurs by repudiation, the injured party cannot waive the breach and continue to perform under the contract. He must not perform any further.[13] He may change his position materially in reliance on the material breach by repudiation and thereby preclude the repudiator's withdrawal of his repudiation. Suit is such a change of position. His damages are for the entire contract. Alternatively, he may rescind the contract and demand restoration to his original position prior to the formation of the contract. The right of rescission is a quasi-contractual right of restitution. Immediately on breach of contract there arises the duty to mitigate damages. (A employs B for one year. After six months A discharges B without cause. B must seek employment elsewhere for the remaining six months; and his earnings therefrom, or what he could have earned in that period, are deducted from the amount of salary he would have received for the remainder of the contract's duration. B's damages are such loss in earnings for that period.) Breach of contract for the payment of money causes interest to accrue for the amount due from the time of such breach, unless the parties have provided to the contrary in their contract. Such interest is a part of the damages and is computed at the legal rate. If the parties provide in their contract for liquidated damages, interest accrues thereon.

Liquidated damages are the judicial award of that certain amount of money fixed by the parties as reasonable compensation for damage caused by wrongful conduct where it is difficult to determine the extent of such damage. The amount must not be a penalty to deter such conduct but, rather, it must be compensatory. A provision for a forfei-ture is void. (A and B contracted for the sale of oil to be delivered to B in 50-gallon drums. The contract provided that the drums were to be returned to A; and, if not returned, $5.00 was to be paid for every drum not so returned. The $5.00 provision was meant to be an indication of liquidated damages. If the drums reasonably were worth much less, the provision might be considered a forfeiture and therefore invalid.) Con-

---

[13] See UCC 2–704(2), and below, p. 333, when the aggrieved seller may complete the manufacture of unfinished goods on the buyer's default in order to avoid loss.

tracts for the sale of real estate usually provide that the amount of the buyer's deposit will be the liquidated damages in the event the buyer defaults and does not pay the balance of the purchase price.

In building construction contracts, if substantial performance has been rendered by the builder in good faith, damages will be either replacement cost or the difference between the value of what was to be performed and what was performed, whichever involves the lesser economic waste. (Under a contract between A and B, A installed pipe in a building which differed from the pipe specified under the contract only in the brand name. A may recover from B the contract price for his substantial performance less the damage sustained by B. B has not experienced any damage and the benefit to B by replacing the pipe would be far outweighed by the hardship occasioned thereby to A. The usual test of replacement cost would not be used here.)

Specific Performance. The object of a decree specifically enforcing performance of a contract is to achieve, as nearly as possible, the effect contemplated by the contract. A decree of specific performance is a form of equitable relief. It is an injunction granted against a party who has breached, or is threatening to breach, a contract when damages at law would be inadequate as relief to the injured party. The issuance of a decree lies solely within the discretion of the court handling each particular case. From the applied discretion of the courts certain guiding principles have emerged. Courts will not issue a decree of specific performance of a contract in favor of a party who has materially breached the contract. Both a decree for specific performance of a contract and an award of damages for the remainder of the contract may be made in the same case if such relief is deemed necessary. An agreement will not be specifically enforced if it is illegal or if enforcement would be contrary to public policy or welfare. An agreement to create an illegal monopoly will not be specifically enforced. A contract in which one party has the power of avoidance will not be ordered specifically enforceable against such party, inasmuch as that party has the legal power to nullify the effect of the decree. Courts will consider the difficulty of enforcing a decree before issuing one.

Land. Contracts are usually for the transfer of property or interests therein, or for the rendition of services. In contracts for the transfer of land or of interests therein a decree of specific enforcement is available only when the land has not yet been transferred. The vendor may compel the vendee to accept the transfer and to make payment therefor, and the vendee may compel the vendor to transfer the land. Inasmuch as the vendor can be compelled to transfer, the vendee should be compelled to accept transfer. If the land has been transferred but the vendee refuses to make payment, a decree of specific enforcement will not be issued, although a judgment for the money is obtainable by the vendor.

Chattels and Intangibles. Courts consider the following factors in determining the adequacy or inadequacy of damages for breach of contract for the transfer of chattels and intangibles or of interests therein: the sentiment associated with, and the unusual character of, the chattel or intangible; the availability of a substitute chattel or intangible;[14] the difficulty in estimating damages; and the probability of realizing on any award of damages. No decree of specific performance will be issued unless the chattel or intangible is unique, e.g., family heirlooms or works of art, or other proper circumstances exist where damages for non-delivery would be inadequate. Patents and copyrights are unique. Stock in a corporation is not unique; but if the same stock is not otherwise available for purchase and failure to acquire those particular shares will have a harmful effect that cannot be compensated by an award of damages, then such shares are unique and a decree will be issued. (A owns 48 percent, B owns 49 percent, and C owns 3 percent, of the shares in a corporation. A contracts with C for the purchase of his 3 percent of the shares. C refuses to transfer his shares to A. A can obtain a decree of specific performance because no other shares are available and C's shares are necessary to give A control of the corporation, which control is not contrary to public policy.)

Personal Services. Contracts for personal services are contracts of such a character that performance is nondelegable. Contracts made with artists, sculptors, musicians, doctors, lawyers, accountants, ball players, teachers, cooks, and valets are illustrations of contracts of a personal character. A decree of specific enforcement will never be issued for such contracts because of the difficulty of enforcement, the probability of creating an unworkable and undesirable relationship between the parties, and the U.S. Constitution's prohibition of involuntary servitude.

Injunctions are of two kinds: *mandatory* and *prohibitory.* A mandatory injunction compels the performance of an affirmative act and is called a "decree of specific performance" when used in the law of contracts. It will not be issued in contracts of personal service. A prohibitory injunction compels or enjoins the nonperformance of an act and, in the law of contracts, is a decree enforcing a negative promise. (A contracts to work for B and not for C. An injunction restraining A from working for C is a prohibitory injunction.) A promise not to

[14] For specific performance under the Sales provisions of UCC 2–716, see below, pp. 342–43.

render personal services for anyone else may be express or implied in a contract. If not implied, then a prohibitory injunction would not be issued. If implied, it is unusual for a prohibitory injunction to be issued in a personal service contract case unless irreparable harm will result. Courts generally will not issue such an injunction with the primary intention of enforcing the affirmative promise. Nor will a court usually issue a prohibitory injunction when its effect will be to deprive a person of the means of making a living. A court will consider the type of employment contract, the probability of a renewal of good employer-employee relations, the harm which will be caused in the event of issuance or nonissuance of an injunction, and the inadequacy of other legal remedies. Irreparable harm seems to be the over-all test of whether or not a prohibitory injunction will issue in personal service contract cases. (A, an auditor well known for his ability to detect defalcation in business firms, was employed by B, a firm of accountants, to work for them for a certain period. A refused to perform under the contract. B cannot obtain a mandatory injunction. B probably could not obtain a prohibitory injunction enjoining A from working elsewhere because no irreparable harm will result by A's employment elsewhere. A is not unique, and another accountant with his qualifications can be found. A's employment by some other firm of accountants will not affect B's business seriously.) (A, a well-known opera star, contracts with B to sing in B's theater for a specified period and not to sing in any competing theater. A refuses to perform and contracts to sing in a competing theater. B cannot obtain a mandatory injunction but can obtain a prohibitory injunction preventing A from singing in the competing theater because of the irreparable harm which otherwise would be caused to B. If A were to sing in a noncompeting theater, the prohibitory injunction would not be issued.) Violation of either a mandatory or a prohibitory injunction is a contempt of court; and the violator could be penalized by fine, imprisonment, or both, by the court which issued the injunction.

Restitution. Restitution is a noncontractual remedy made available in the law of contracts and is designed to restore an injured person to his original position prior to the particular transaction. It applies to other fields of law as well as to contracts. In the law of contracts, its purpose is to restore an injured party to his original position prior to the formation of the contract which is *materially breached* by the other party.

Restitution applies *when* (1) *the complaining party has rendered some performance which the other party has received under the con-*

tract, (2) *the other party has materially breached the contract,* (3) *the performance due from the other party is other than for the payment of a liquidated debt, and* (4) *the complaining party promptly tenders the return of whatever he has received and still has.* The complaining party can obtain the reasonable value of what he has rendered less the benefit that he has received from what was rendered to him by the defending party under the contract. The complaining party's expenses in preparing to perform the contract do not constitute anything that the defending party has received. If the complaining party is under a contractual duty to make a statue and prior to such performance the defending party repudiates the contract, the complaining party cannot obtain restitution for the reasonable value of the effort, labor, and materials already expended on the statue; the defending party has not yet received anything. If the statue had been completed and the title thereto or possession thereof had been transferred to the defending party, who then repudiated, restitution would be available as a remedy. A mistaken overpayment of money can be reacquired by restitution. In a case of promissory estoppel, where there is no contract, restitution is available if the defending party has received a benefit from the complaining party's performance.

A party in materially breaching his contract may leave unperformed either the payment of a liquidated debt—i.e., money—or something else. An action for damages for breach of contract will give adequate relief to the complaining party if the remaining performance due is the payment of a liquidated debt, but often it will not give adequate relief if the remaining performance is of a different nature. Restitution in money, either paid by the complaining party or as the reasonable value of what he has rendered and what is received by the defending party, is available as an alternative remedy to an action for damages only if the *remaining* performance or some part thereof due from the defending party is other than for the payment of a liquidated debt. (A employs B at $50 per week for ten weeks. B works one week, and then A repudiates the contract. B can bring an action for damages for breach of contract but cannot ask for restitution for the reasonable value of his week's work.) (A and B contract for the sale of land to A, who pays the purchase price of $10,000 at the time of the contract, a deed to be delivered by B to A in 30 days. B repudiates the contract. A can get restitution of the $10,000 he paid.) If only a part of the remaining performance due from the defending party is not for payment of a liquidated debt, restitution is available. (A and B contract whereby A is to render certain services to B for which B will pay $1,000 and convey certain land to A. A renders the services, and B then repudiates the contract. A may get restitution for the reasonable value of his services.) Specific restitution of land, or unique chattels or unique choses in action, may be allowed only if all other remedies are inadequate and justice so requires, if the property still exists, and if the property has not been sold by the defending party to a bona fide purchaser for value.

It is essential to restitution that, when the complaining party has performed, the defending party's nonperformance be a material breach of contract. However, if the complaining party has not performed and such nonperformance is a failure of consideration or a material breach of contract excusing the defending party's failure to perform, generally the complaining party may obtain restitution for the benefit received by the defending party from the part performance of the complaining party which is in excess of the damage sustained by the defending party caused by the complaining party's nonperformance.

The complaining party must act promptly after breach by the defending party and tender the return of whatever he has received and still has, unless he has previously disposed of the property without knowledge of the breach by the defending party, or unless the property is worthless. Unreasonable delay extinguishes the remedy of restitution. Acceptance of defective performance with knowledge of such defectiveness makes restitution unavailable. The performance must be accepted or rejected; acceptance precludes subsequent rejection. Disclaimer by a beneficiary in a third party beneficiary contract of the performance due him under the contract gives the promisee a right of restitution for what he has rendered to the promisor.

Election of Remedies. Restitution is available only when a material breach has occurred by the defending party. Where restitution is available, the complaining party has a choice of remedies between an action for damages for breach of contract or restitution. When specific performance also is available, the election of remedies must be made between restitution and damages and between restitution and specific performance.

In connection with election of remedies it should be noted that the occurrence of misrepresentation making a contract voidable also requires an election of remedies. The contract may be either avoided (rescinded) or affirmed. Exercise of the power of avoidance discharges the contract; and the remedy of restitution is available to recover what the complaining party has rendered, or its value, under the contract. Affirmance of the contract causes the complaining party to retain what he has received and accepted; and, if the misrepresentation amounts to fraud, the complaining party has an action for damages for the tort of deceit.[15] There is a difference of opinion as to the measure of such damages. In most states the "loss of bargain" rule applies whereby the measure of damages is the difference between the market value of what the defrauded party has received at the time of such receipt and the value that the property was represented to have. If the defrauded party still owes part of the purchase price, such amount owing will be deducted from the damages to be awarded. In the minority of states the "out-of-pocket" loss rule is applied under which the measure of damages is the difference between the purchase price and the market value of what was purchased as of the date of receipt of such property. Damages "for breach of warranty is the difference at the time and place of acceptance between the value of the goods accepted and the value they would have had if they had been as warranted, unless special circumstances show proximate damages of a different amount."[16]

---

[15] See above, p. 44, ftn. 29.
[16] See UCC 2–714(2), and below, p. 342.

Chapter VII

DISCHARGE OF CONTRACTS

THE termination of a contractual duty is called a "discharge." A "contract" is a promise or set of promises creating a legal duty of performance. Discharge of a contractual duty discharges the promise and, therefore, discharges the contract. Discharge may occur by act of the parties or by operation of law.

By Act of the Parties   Discharge of a contractual duty by act of the parties may occur in the following ways: *performance, failure of condition, material breach of contract, mutual agreement, assignment, exercise of a power of avoidance,* and *material alteration of the contract.*

Performance. Performance, meaning complete performance, of a contractual duty discharges that duty. When there is more than one matured debt and the debtor makes a payment, the creditor must apply the payment as directed by the debtor at or before the time of such payment. If no such indication is given by the debtor, then the creditor may apply the payment to any or all of the matured debts or distribute such payment among them,[1] provided he does so within a reasonable period of time and gives notice to the debtor of such application within a reasonable period of time. The creditor's subsequent suit on the debts, or his sending of a statement of the status of such debts, is notice to the debtor of his application of such payment. The creditor cannot apply such payment to an immature debt or to a disputed or illegal claim. He can apply the payment to a debt barred by the statute of limitations, but, if the payment is insufficient to satisfy the debt, the statute is not waived as to the remainder still due. If neither the debtor nor the creditor indicates to which of such matured debts the payment is to be applied, the law in most states is that the payment is to be applied as is most just. Usually, the payment is applied first to overdue interest, then to the earliest unsecured matured debt, and finally to the earliest secured debt,

---

[1] But see below, p., 807, for the effect in Suretyship if the surety advances the money to the principal debtor for payment to the creditor and the creditor knows this.

to which the creditor might have applied such payment. An appropriation once made cannot be changed except by the assent of both parties. Such assent may validate a previously improper application of payment. A debtor's silence for an unreasonable period of time after his receipt of notice of the application of a payment is interpreted as assent to such application, whether made properly or improperly.

Failure of Condition and Material Breach of Contract. As discussed previously under "Conditions,"[2] the duty of performance of a promise may depend upon the occurrence of a condition precedent, the nonoccurrence of a condition subsequent, or performance of a return promise. Unexcused failure of a condition precedent to occur prior to the time when performance of the promise is due discharges the promise. Occurrence of a condition subsequent discharges the promise. When the condition is the performance of a return promise, a promise is discharged by either: a material breach of contract; an unexcused failure of consideration—i.e., material nonperformance—or a prospective unexcused failure of consideration. It should be reiterated here, although previously discussed in "Conditions," that, once a material breach or an unexcused failure of consideration has occurred, the promissory duty is discharged without any change of position, while for *prospective* unexcused failure of consideration a material change of position in reliance thereon generally is necessary in order to discharge the promissory duty. Repudiation is a material breach of contract, and a material change of position is unnecessary except to preclude the repudiator from withdrawing his repudiation.

A promisor's improper refusal of a valid tender of performance by a promisee under a bilateral contract is a waiver of such performance, and the promisor has a duty to perform his promise without the occurrence of performance by the promisee. The tender has the effect of performance. The promisee's duty of performance is discharged, except when such performance is the payment of money. The effect of an improper refusal of a valid tender of performance by the payment of money is to halt the running of interest on the amount unpaid and to cause the creditor to pay for the court costs of any later suit he may bring to collect such payment from the debtor.[3] A tender is an unconditional offer by one party to perform, with present ability to do so, what he is required to do under a bilateral contract or what is requested in an offer

---

[2] See above, pp. 116 ff.

[3] For the effect of an improper refusal of a valid tender of performance by the payment of money in the law of: Commercial Paper, see below, pp. 468–69. Security, see below, pp. 790, 820.

for a unilateral or a bilateral contract. When a tender is made in response to an offer for a unilateral or a bilateral contract, the tender is an acceptance and a contract is formed.

Mutual Agreement. By agreement between the parties an existing contractual duty may be discharged. Such an agreement may apply to different types of situation, and, accordingly, it has a different name to identify each situation. The situations to be discussed here are: *release and contract not to sue, mutual rescission, accord and satisfaction, novation,* and *account stated.*

Release and Contract Not to Sue. A release is a voluntary relinquishment of a right by its owner to the person against whom it is exercisable. Relinquishment of a right discharges its correlative duty. A release is not a contract because it is not a promise of future performance; it operates immediately in accordance with its terms. If the terms specify a condition precedent before the release is to be operative, the release is ineffective as a relinquishment of a right until the occurrence of the condition. Although a release is not a contract, in the absence of statute to the contrary it must be supported by sufficient consideration, or be under seal in those few states preserving the Common Law effect of a seal.[4] In the absence of statute to the contrary, a release need not be in writing and may be oral, although in practice it usually is in writing so as to assure future proof of the release. If the release is in writing, it must be executed and delivered in order to be effective. A general release relinquishes all existing rights of the owner to the person against whom they are exercisable, and may include future and contingent claims. A mutual release is a discharge by each of two or more parties to the other or others, the consideration for each discharge being the discharge or discharges given by the others. The validity of a release may be attacked for fraud, duress, undue influence, mutual mistake, lack of capacity so to release, and lack of sufficient consideration. A receipt differs from a release in that a receipt is a written acknowledgment or admission that some thing has been received.

It should be noted carefully that, under the Code, the Common Law effect of the seal is abolished. Also, a party to a transaction may waive or renounce, in whole or in part, his claim or right against the other party arising out of an *alleged* breach; but to be effective as a release the

---

[4] However, because the Common Law effect of the seal as a method of causing a release or promise without consideration to be enforceable has largely disappeared and with it the opportunity of making a binding gratuitous discharge of an existing legal obligation, by statute or judicial decision in some states a signed written unsealed release or promise concerning an existing legal obligation, indicating an intention to be bound thereby, is enforceable without consideration.

waiver or renunciation *if oral* must be supported by consideration, or if *in writing* it must be signed and delivered by the aggrieved party *without any requirement of consideration.*[5]

The release may contain terms providing for the discharge of a future right. This portion of the release is a contract not to sue or not to enforce a right when it arises; it is a contract to forbear permanently. The terminology may be in the form of a release, a covenant not to sue, a promise, or a waiver. A contract not to sue permanently has the same net effect as a release. A contract not to sue may appear separate from inclusion in a release.

Mutual Rescission. A contract may be rescinded and all rights and duties thereunder discharged. When the parties to the contract agree to rescission, it is called "mutual rescission." The agreement to rescind is operative to discharge the duties immediately, and no promise is made of future action. Although the agreement of rescission is not a contract, there must be a manifestation of mutual assent and sufficient consideration. The parties may manifest mutual assent by a writing, by words, or by other conduct. Failure to object to another party's expressed intent to rescind may indicate assent. However, if repudiation is made by one party, the other party's silence or failure to object is not an expression of assent to rescission. Courts are careful to detect what apparently is rescission as a cover for repudiation by one party and silence by the other party. A contract containing a term or terms inconsistent with a term or terms in a previous contract is interpreted as an agreement of mutual rescission of such prior term or terms.

The sufficient consideration for mutual rescission is found in the mutual giving-up of rights to performance under the contract by each party, each relinquishment being sufficient consideration for the other. Each party must be entitled to some performance by the other, whether it be complete or part performance. If one party has completely performed, there cannot be mutual rescission without additional consideration because, while the party who has performed gives up his right to return performance, yet the other party has no right to give up in exchange. It is for this reason that unilateral contracts cannot be mutually rescinded without additional consideration.

Mutual rescission does not involve restitution unless the parties so agree. In the absence of any provision for restitution in their agreement of mutual rescission, the parties are left where they find themselves at the moment of rescission.

---

[5] UCC 1–107.

Accord and Satisfaction. An accord is a new *contract* whereby the parties to it agree to a specified performance in the future as satisfaction of an existing duty owing between them under a previous contract. (A owes B $100. A and B contract whereby A agrees to deliver and B agrees to take a horse in 30 days in satisfaction of the debt.) The previous contract is not discharged, but performance under it is suspended pending performance under the new contract. Performance of the new contract discharges the new and old contracts and is, therefore, a "satisfaction" of such contracts. Failure to perform the new contract has an effect dependent upon who breaks the new contract. If the debtor breaks the new contract, the creditor has the alternative remedies of suing on the new, or on the old, contract. If the creditor breaks the new contract, the debtor still has the duty of performing under the old contract; but the debtor may sue for damages for breach of the new contract or, in a proper case, obtain specific performance of the new contract. When the creditor has breached the new contract, specific performance of the accord usually is given as the best way to avoid circuity of action and to avoid the difficulty of ascertaining the debtor's damages at law.

Satisfaction is that performance which discharges a contractual obligation. Either the accord itself or performance of the accord may constitute the satisfaction of the previous contract, depending on the intention of the parties to the accord. An "accord and satisfaction" means that both an accord and a satisfaction of the previous contract have occurred and that the previous contract has been discharged. An accord which is also a satisfaction is called an "accord and satisfaction."

When the parties to an accord clearly manifest an intent that the accord is to be also a satisfaction, no problem is present, the accord constituting also a satisfaction of the previous contract which is now discharged by the accord and satisfaction. However, it is difficult sometimes to determine from the accord whether or not the parties intended it to be also a satisfaction. Unless the circumstances are to the contrary, it is but reasonable to infer that a creditor does not intend merely to exchange his present undisputed liquidated[6] claim or undisputed overdue unliquidated claim for a new claim against his debtor. However, the circumstances may be such as to lead to the inference that the creditor does wish an accord and satisfaction. Accordingly, the law provides that, in case of doubt of the creditor's intention, if the previous contractual

---

[6] A claim is liquidated when the amount is either fixed by the parties, certain, or ascertained by mathematical computation or by operation of law. A claim is disputed if it is honestly and reasonably believed not to be valid by the party against whom the claim is asserted. (See above, p. 71 ff.)

duty is *undisputedly* either to pay a *liquidated* debt or to perform an *unliquidated matured* obligation, the accord is solely an accord; otherwise the accord is also a satisfaction. (D owes C $1,000. D delivers his check for $1,000 to C. Because a check is deemed conditional payment in the absence of agreement to the contrary, the original contract debt is not discharged until the check is paid. The check is an accord but not a satisfaction until the check is paid.)

Debtors often offer to settle the claims of their creditors by sending their checks therefor. There cannot be any accord or accord and satisfaction without the creditor's acceptance of his debtor's offer. An offer to settle a disputed or unliquidated claim by sending a check therefor[7] is accepted by the creditor when he cashes it or otherwise manifests his assent to it; and an offer of something other than money to settle the disputed or unliquidated claim is accepted by the creditor when he expressly accepts it, or impliedly accepts it by exercising dominion over it. Such acceptance creates a contract of accord which is also a satisfaction. It must be manifested clearly to the creditor, however, that what has been sent is in satisfaction, otherwise there is no accord or agreement on the performance as satisfaction of the prior contractual obligation.

There is a conflict of authority regarding the effect of a creditor's *retention* of a debtor's check voluntarily sent by the debtor and indicated to be in full satisfaction of a *disputed* claim. Most courts hold that the mere silent retention is an implied acceptance creating an accord on that amount as due and payable. Other courts hold that there is no acceptance. All courts would agree that cashing the check was both an accord and a satisfaction. Unless the parties agree to the contrary, a contract *to take* a check or a negotiable promissory note for the *undisputed* full amount due, or a check or note for *less* than the amount claimed if the claim is *disputed* or *unliquidated,* is solely an accord, and satisfaction is to occur on payment of the check. A creditor cannot cash a check sent in settlement of a disputed or unliquidated claim and declare he is not accepting it as satisfaction. He must either accept or reject, and cashing the check or exercising dominion over whatever else he has received in settlement creates an accord and satisfaction.

Novation. A novation is a new *contract* in which one of the parties was not a party to the old contract and which immediately discharges the old contract.[8] It is an accord and satisfaction in which a new party

---

[7] For sufficient consideration, see above, pp. 71–73.

[8] The new party's *assumption* of the previous contractual obligation is not a promise to answer for the debt, default, or miscarriages of another under the statute of frauds. See above, pp. 108 ff.

participates. (A owes B money. C contracts with A and B that he will pay the debt in consideration of B's release of A. The new debtor, C, is being substituted for the old debtor, A.)

Account Stated. An account stated is an account which has been settled and the matured items and balance agreed to by the parties either expressly, or impliedly by failure to object thereto within a reasonable period of time after receipt of a statement of such account. The account stated discharges all matured debts up to the date of the account stated. An account stated is open to correction for innocent mistake, unless in the meanwhile the other party has changed his position in reliance on the account stated. (A receives his monthly bank statement with canceled checks and does not notice the forgery of his signature to one check payable to C. C has cashed the check and is solvent until A discovers the forgery, at which time C is insolvent. A requests B, the bank, to correct his bank balance and to add the amount of the forged check. A cannot regain such amount. There is an account stated between A and B; and though an innocent mistake has been made, B has relied on A's silence by refraining from doing anything and would be prejudiced in recovering from C, who is now insolvent.)[9]

An account stated must be distinguished from other types of account which have nothing to do with discharge of contracts. An *account* is a detailed statement of debits and credits between parties, usually arising out of contract or some fiduciary relationship. A *current running account* is an open or unsettled account; it has not been finally closed or stated. In the absence of agreement between the parties, statute, or trade custom or usage, interest cannot be charged on such an account because the amount due is uncertain; and it is not until the amount is certain that interest may be charged. In the case of an account stated, however, in the absence of any contrary agreement between the parties, interest may be charged, inasmuch as the amount due is certain. A *mutual account* is one which, pursuant to agreement between the parties, involves mutual credits. Each party's side of a mutual account may be set off against the other, and only the balance is recoverable. An *account rendered* is an account presented by the creditor to the debtor for his examination and acceptance.

Assignment. The subject of assignment has been discussed previously.[10] It was pointed out that assignment of a right and the assignee's demand for payment discharges the debtor's duty to the assignor and makes it performable to the assignee. The debtor's ignorance of such

---

[9] See below, pp. 471, 486–87.
[10] See above, pp. 101 ff., especially p. 103 f.

discharge because of his ignorance of the assignment may cause him innocently to render performance to the assignor, who tortiously and silently accepts it. The debtor's performance rendered to a known assignee, or to the assignor in ignorance of the assignment, discharges the debtor's contractual duty. A delegation of duty is not an assignment.

Exercise of a Power of Avoidance. Voidable contracts are subject to rescission by exercise of the power of avoidance on the part of the party who has such power. Previous discussion has indicated when voidable contracts are created.[11] Exercise of the power of avoidance discharges the contract and may give rise to a right of restitution.

Material Alteration of Contract. A fraudulent material alteration of a written contract, made by a party to the contract with *intent* to alter materially his rights or duties thereunder and made without the assent of the other contracting party, discharges the contractual duty owing to him and destroys his right. The wrongful party's alteration does not vary the innocent party's rights under the contract; but if a party to the contract, knowing of the alteration, asserts his rights under the contract, his duties and the wrongful party's rights and duties to him are revived as though no alteration had occurred. If a party manifests assent to the terms as changed by the other party, as to those parties the old contract is rescinded and the new changed contract takes its place. The authority to fill in a blank space in a contract may be express or implied, but the fraudulent insertion of material matter in such space which is contrary to such express or implied authority discharges the contractual duty of the other party to the contract.

Discharge of Joint Debtors. Joint promisors—i.e., joint obligors or debtors—as well as joint promisees—i.e., joint obligees or creditors —are a unit with the element of survivorship. All joint promisees must sue and all joint promisors must be sued, unless one or more is dead, beyond the jurisdiction of the court, or discharged in bankruptcy, in which event the remainder of such joint promisees or promisors available, respectively, sue or are sued. Joint promisors may object to the nonjoinder of all available joint promisors in a suit brought against them, but failure to object causes a judgment to be binding against the ones sued; the remaining available joint promisors are discharged because there no longer is any claim against them, the claim having been merged in the judgment obtained. In some states there are joint debtor statutes which provide that judgment against less than all the available joint debtors does not extinguish the claim against the others not sued.[12]

---

[11] See above, pp. 16, 18 ff., 43 ff.

[12] As applicable to partnerships, see below, pp. 629–30.

Death of a joint promisor causes the duty to survive in the remaining joint promisors; the estate of the deceased joint promisor no longer is bound by the joint promise, although in many states statutes are to the contrary. Death of the last surviving joint promisor causes the joint duty to survive to his estate. Death of a joint promisee causes the joint right to survive to the remaining joint promisees. A promisee's discharge of a joint promisor discharges all the joint promisors, unless the discharge reserves rights against the other joint promisors, in which case the reservation operates as a promise not to sue that joint promisor, and the others are still liable. Full or partial performance or satisfaction of a contractual duty by less than all the joint promisors operates for the benefit of all the joint promisors and discharges the joint duty of all of them to the extent of such performance or satisfaction. This last is equally true if the promisors are several, or joint and several, as well as joint.

By Operation of Law
A contractual duty is discharged by the rendition of a *judgment,* an *arbitration award,* a *bankruptcy discharge,* the *statute of limitations,* and *excusable impossibility.* Each of these methods of discharge will be considered briefly in turn.

Judgment. The rendition of a judgment discharges the contractual duty and substitutes for the claim to performance of such duty a final, judicial pronouncement of the validity of such claim and the liquidated nature of such duty. The contractual duty is merged in the judgment.

Arbitration Award. Arbitration is the determination of a controversy in a nonjudicial proceeding by persons selected to decide the matter, pursuant to the agreement of the parties whose controversy is to be determined. The decision of the arbitrators is called an "award" which is enforceable in the courts. If the purpose of the arbitration is to determine whether there is a duty alleged to exist, an arbitration award discharges the duty found to exist, and the award itself is enforceable in the courts as a new cause of action. If the purpose is not to determine the existence of a contractual duty but solely to determine the liquidated amount due under such duty, then the duty is not merged in the arbitration award and the effect of the award is to fix the limit of the duty. The duty was never in dispute and is not discharged; it exists, limited in liquidated amount by the award, and may be sued on in the courts. In some of the states permitting contracts to arbitrate, such contracts must be in writing. The arbitration clauses included in a contract must not be unfair or unconscionable. An arbitration award is to be made in good faith, and if the arbitrator has not acted in good faith a court may set aside the arbitration award.

Bankruptcy Discharge. The Bankruptcy Act provides that in a bankruptcy proceeding the debtor bankrupt may be discharged from all provable claims, with certain exceptions. A discharge in bankruptcy discharges the bankrupt from the contractual duties inherent in such discharged claims.

Statute of Limitations. The statute of limitations is a statute which provides certain specified periods of time within which matured claims may be asserted by legal action. The periods of time vary among the states. Failure to act within the prescribed time bars enforcement of such a claim in the courts.[13] The Bankruptcy Act and the statute of limitations often are described as discharging contractual duties and also as barring or suspending remedial rights for the nonperformance of such duties. In effect, and for all practical purposes, the duties are discharged.

The statute of limitations begins to run as soon as a cause of action for an amount accrues. In open book accounts, the statute begins to run from the date the last item was entered in the account, unless the parties agree to the contrary. In some states the statute begins to run on each item from the date of entry of such item. In contracts for the sale of goods, the amount payable is due at the time the goods are delivered, unless the parties agree to the contrary, and the statute begins to run at that time. In commercial paper, the statute begins to run from a date dependent upon whether it is a time or demand instrument. A cause of action against a maker or an acceptor accrues: in the case of a time instrument, on the day after maturity; in the case of a demand instrument, upon its date or, if no date is stated, on the date of issue.[14]

It should be noted that, by statute in many states, the running of the statute of limitations is halted or suspended: when a person with a cause of action is under legal disability to sue, e.g., an infant or insane person, at the time the cause of action accrues; during the imprisonment of a person with a cause of action; while the person against whom a cause of action has accrued is absent from the state or has absconded or concealed himself; until the person upon whom fraud has been perpetrated

---

[13] "Laches" is a non-statutory doctrine of equity that an equitable claim will not be enforced when the claimant has not been diligent in asserting it by an action. The purpose of the doctrine, like the legal equivalent the statute of limitations, is to bar the enforcement of stale claims.

[14] See UCC 3–122(1).

discovers the fraud or facts sufficient to put him on inquiry. Also, courts will suspend the running of the statute between citizens of states at war. The statute is "tolled" when the statutory bar to an action is removed or ended. This has been discussed previously.[15]

Excusable Impossibility. "Impossibility" means that performance is either a physical impossibility or impracticable because of the expense, difficulty, or loss which may be involved. A promise which is impossible of performance because of the *subjective* inability of the party with the duty to perform is no excuse for nonperformance, and his duty is not discharged. Impossibility may exist at the time the promise to perform is made, called "existing impossibility," or it may occur after the contract is made, called "supervening impossibility." If a promise is impossible of performance *when made,* not because of the subjective inability of the party with the duty to perform but, rather, because of facts of which he does not know or has no reason to know, the promise does not create a duty of performance and it is not a contract. (A promises to sell, and B promises to buy, a certain chattel which, unknown to them, has been destroyed previously. There is no contract because of a mutual mistake of fact concerning the nonexistence of the chattel. Neither promise created a duty of performance.)[16] Supervening impossibility other than by the subjective inability of the party with the duty to perform discharges his contractual duty to perform, and consequently that of the other contracting party, if the impossibility: is not wrongfully caused by him; could not reasonably be foreseen by him at the time the contract was made; occurred before performance was overdue; occurred before he has breached the contract other than by an anticipatory breach; and if the risk of the supervening impossibility has not been assumed by him. Illustrations of discharge by supervening impossibility[17] are:

1. Supervening illegality of contractual performance by legal prohibition, or by legal prevention, of performance by the party with the duty to perform. This may occur by governmental executive order, by legislation, or by judicial or administrative decision.

2. In *personal service* contracts, the supervening death of the party with the duty to perform, or his supervening illness which makes his performance impossible or seriously harmful to him, such death or illness not having been wrongfully caused by him. In personal service contracts, it is implied that personal performance will be rendered if the party is alive and well. A test of whether or not a contract is for personal services is whether or not the duty of performance is

[15] See above, pp. 83–85.
[16] See UCC 2–613(a).
[17] See American Law Institute, *Restatement: Contracts,* 1932, secs. 458–69.

delegable. In a contract of a personal character the duty is nondelegable without the obligee's assent.[18] (A, a building contractor, made a contract with B to build a house for B. No unusual or unique services were to be rendered by A. A died without rendering performance. A's duty to perform is not discharged because the contract was not of a personal character. A's personal services were not required; another capable building contractor could perform the contract.)

3. Supervening destruction or material impairment of the requisite subject matter of the contract or of the requisite means of performing the contract, making performance impossible by the party with the duty to perform, provided such destruction or impairment was not wrongfully caused by him. When the parties contemplate, or provide in their contract for, specific subject matter—e.g., *that* horse, *this* machine, or *that* building—or for a certain mode of performance—e.g., the arbitrator is to be A, or the product of *that* particular factory—the continued existence of such subject matter or mode of performance is requisite for performance. Destruction or material impairment thereof discharges the duty of the party to render performance.

4. Supervening nonexistence of certain facts other than requisite subject matter and requisite means of performance, making performance impossible by the party with the duty to perform, the parties having contemplated or provided in their contract for performance only on the continued existence of such facts, provided such nonexistence was not wrongfully caused by the party with the duty to perform. For example, a contract to ship goods from one country to a particular port in another country is made impossible of performance by an embargo or quarantine on the port of delivery, and the party with the duty to perform is discharged. The continued existence of the fact that the port of delivery would be available has ceased.

---

[18] See above, pp. 104–105.

APPENDIX TO PART TWO

REFERENCES

1. American Law Institute. *Restatement: Conflict of Laws* 2d, 1969.
2. American Law Institute. *Restatement: Contracts.* 1932.
3. Corbin, Arthur L. *Corbin on Contracts.* Rev. ed. St. Paul: West Publishing Co., 1964.
4. Williston, Samuel. *A Treatise on the Law of Contracts.* 3d ed., Williston and Jaeger. New York: Baker, Voorhis & Co., 1970.

PROBLEMS

1. You have been engaged by Stark Industries, Inc. to examine the financial statements of Murz Corporation for the six months ended June 30, 1965. The management of Stark Industries, Inc. is negotiating for the purchase of the outstanding capital stock of Murz Corporation. The purchase price will be determined, in part, by the book value of the stock. Your audit of Murz Corporation's records and books disclosed the following information:
   (a) The minutes of the December, 1964, meeting of the board of directors revealed approval of the employment, to begin January 1, 1965, of John Laurel as general manager. Upon further investigation, you determined that Laurel had orally accepted the Corporation's offer of this position which provided for compensation "at the rate of $1,000 per month plus a large percentage of the net income before income taxes." You also determined that no written contract of employment was executed.
   (b) Laurel had vehemently opposed the proposed merger with Stark Industries, Inc. and resigned on June 30, 1965. His letter of resignation demanded the payment of $15,000 as his percentage of the net income under his contract of employment. He computed the payment as 15 percent of $100,000. His estimate of the net income as $100,000 is close to the Corporation's actual net income for the period before any provision for profit-sharing and income taxes.
   (c) The management and board of directors of Murz Corporation refuse to recognize any liability to Laurel. They were dissatisfied with his services and would have discharged him if he had not resigned. Furthermore, they had intended that the profit-sharing computation would be very flexible and that the percentage would not exceed 5 percent.

a. (1) List four kinds of contracts to which the Statute of Frauds is applicable.
   (2) What is the basic requirement for contracts to which the Statute of Frauds is applicable?
   (3) What is the legal consequence if a contract to which the Statute of Frauds is applicable is not executed in compliance with it?
   (4) Is the Statute of Frauds applicable to the contract between Murz Corporation and Laurel? Explain.

b. Does Laurel have a cause of action in contract against Murz Corporation? Explain.

c. Does Laurel have a cause of action against Murz Corporation under any other theory of law? Discuss. (Former C.P.A. Examination question)

2. D borrowed $20,000 from C, secured by a real property mortgage, repayable monthly with interest over a period of 10 years. A higher rate of interest would apply to delinquent monthly payments. Five years later, C complained to D that there had been too many delinquent payments and that he was having a difficult time computing two sets of interest. C demanded immediate payment of all delinquent monthly payments together with regular and delinquent interest. At D's request, C computed the total interest and principal due to date, and D then mortgaged one of his other buildings in order to obtain the agreed amount. One month after the money was paid by D to C, C found that he had forgotten to include in the amount the delinquent interest, amounting to $700. C demanded the $700, but D refused to pay it.

   You are the accountant for C and you have kept his books on an accrual basis in the past. How will you carry this item on C's books, and why?

3. (a) Define contract.
   (b) Name the requisites of a contract.
   (c) How does a contract differ from quasi contract?
   (d) What is meant by the following:
       (1) Promise.
       (2) Agreement.
       (3) Formal and informal contracts.
       (4) Unilateral and bilateral contracts.
       (5) Voidable contract.
       (6) Unenforceable contract.

4. Define, or describe, any five of the following terms:
   (a) Novation.
   (b) Accord and satisfaction.
   (c) An account stated.
   (d) Laches.
   (e) Statute of limitations.
   (f) Usury. (Former C.P.A. Examination question)

5. L and E had an oral lease for a house and land for one year, rent to be paid by E to L monthly, with an option in E to purchase the premises at the end of the lease for a specified price, the rent already paid by E to be applied in reduction of the purchase price. E took possession of the premises, paid

his rent, and orally exercised his option to buy the premises. L refused to convey title to the premises to E, who was still in possession. Can E compel L to convey title to E? Explain.

6. (a) In January, 1971, A and B made a contract whereby A was to construct certain buildings for B by June 1, 1971, for which B would pay $100,000 by installments as the buildings were completed. In March, A unjustifiedly refused to construct the remainder of the buildings unless B promised to pay A an additional $10,000, which B promised to do if A would agree to complete the buildings by May 25; A so agreed. The buildings were completed by May 25, and B paid A the last installment of the agreed $100,000 but refused to pay the additional $10,000.
   (1) Is A entitled to the additional $10,000?
   (2) Why?
   (b) You are a certified public accountant and you find two papers in your client's files. The first paper is a written agreement between your client and X in which it was stated that, in connection with a $1,000 debt, although your client claimed that X still owed him $1,000 and X claimed that the debt was only for $500, they agreed to settle the matter for $750; the writing acknowledged your client's receipt of $750 and discharged X from the debt. The second paper is conclusive proof that X's debt was for $1,000 and not $500 as claimed by X.
   (1) Does X owe your client $250?
   (2) Why?

7. In January, 1971, Hitchcock, as manager of City Clinic having specific authority to conduct its affairs, engaged Jones, a C.P.A., to make an audit of the books of the clinic for the year ended December 31, 1970. At that time Jones stated he could begin the job soon after income tax time. On September 22, 1971, Hitchcock wrote Jones stating that he needed some figures and asking Jones to start the audit. Jones started the audit on October 7, 1971, and continued to work on it from time to time until March 31, 1972. During this period he conferred with Hitchcock several times and furnished him with some preliminary figures. The last of these conferences took place on February 17, 1972. At such conferences no indication was given to Jones that there was concern about the delay in the completion of the audit. On March 31, 1972, Hitchcock notified Jones by letter that his engagement was terminated because delay in completion of the audit rendered it worthless at that late date. At this time Jones could have completed the audit within four days. Hitchcock, for the clinic, refused to pay Jones any fee.
   Would Jones be entitled to any compensation? If so, on what grounds could he recover and how would the amount be determined? Explain fully.
   (Former C.P.A. Examination question)

8. D owes C five debts, two of which are barred by the statute of limitations. D pays C $100.
   (a) If D specified that the $100 was to be applied to a particular barred debt, is the remainder of that debt recoverable by C?

(b) If D did not specify to which debt the $100 was to be applied, what may C do and how would it affect the barred debts?

(c) If D had paid C $100 on C's promise to discharge the two barred debts totaling $500, is C's promise enforceable by D?

9. (a) What is the difference between a divisible and an indivisible contract?

(b) What is the effect of an improper refusal of a valid tender of performance?

(c) When does impossibility excuse performance of a contract?

(d) When may a contract be decreed to be specifically enforceable?

10. Green entered into an option agreement to purchase certain tracts of land. Before the expiration of the option period, Green exercised the right of election granted therein by giving the seller written notice that he would purchase the property. Subsequently, and before the expiration of the option period, Green entered into an oral agreement with R whereby Green agreed to sell and R agreed to purchase from Green all of Green's interest in and to said option agreement. R further orally agreed:

(a) to pay the consideration fixed by the option and to perform all of the terms and conditions of said option agreement; and

(b) to form a corporation which was to take title to said property; and

(c) to cause said corporation to issue 25 per cent of its capital stock to Green and further promised to pay to Green the par value of the stock at any time the market value of said stock should be less than 50 per cent of the par value of the stock; and

(d) to cause the corporation to employ Green for a period of five years at a salary of $20,000.

R was to retain a controlling interest in the capital stock of the corporation. Green performed his obligations under the agreement, but R refused to perform. Green brought suit and R set up the statute of frauds as a defense. Are the oral promises of R enforceable under the statute of frauds? Explain. (Former C.P.A. Examination question)

11. (a) A owed B $500. C promised A that, if A would lend $500 to C, C would discharge A's debt to B in 30 days by paying the $500 to B. A loaned $500 to C but C refused to pay B at the end of 30 days.

(1) Does B have any right against C?

(2) Why?

(b) X borrowed $100 from Y and agreed with Y to pay it to Z at the end of 30 days as a gift from Y to Z. X refused to pay Z at the end of 30 days.

(1) Does Z have any right against X?

(2) Why?

(c) R contracted with S to construct a building for S upon S's land adjoining T's land. Such a building would enhance materially the value of T's land; and T immediately made substantial improvements to his land, intending to sell it at a high price as soon as R had completed the building. R refuses to perform his contract.

(1) Does T have any right against R?

(2) Why?

12. (a) A, 20 years of age, wanted to drive to work on a motorcycle instead of using a streetcar. B and A contracted for the sale of B's motorcycle to A in exchange for A's watch and $300. B delivered the motorcycle to A and A paid the $300 and delivered the watch to B. B immediately sold and delivered the watch to C, a good faith purchaser for value. Two years later the motorcycle was destroyed in an accident while being driven by A, and A demanded the return of his watch and $300.
   (1) Can A enforce his demand?
   (2) Why?
   (b) Alex agreed with Bowers to relinquish a part of a debt due Alex from Bowers if Bowers would pay the balance. This was reduced to writing and signed by both. Is this a valid contract? Explain.

13. (a) C contracted to build an office building for O according to agreed specifications at a cost of $190,000. At a later date, C discovered that he had made a $15,000 error in his calculations. Before work starts, may he have his contract rescinded because of this mistake?
   (b) Assume in (a) above that no error had occurred, but that prior to the beginning of construction, material costs increased $20,000. If O promised in writing to pay that additional amount at the date of the completion of the building, is the promise enforceable?
   (c) If O leases to T a suite of rooms in a proposed new building at $130 a month, the lease to begin on October 1, but the building is not available for occupancy until December 1, is O liable in damages to T? (Former C.P.A. Examination question)

14. In August, 1971, X and Y duly made a legally valid written contract whereby X agreed to audit the books and accounts of Y for the calendar year 1972 for a fee fixed by this contract. At the time of the making of this contract and as a part of the negotiations leading up to it, X and Y orally agreed that said contract was to be effective only in the event that Y procured certain additional capital from Z prior to January 1, 1972. If Y is unable to procure such capital, is the written contract legally binding? (Former C.P.A. Examination question)

15. S and B executed a written contract which provided that S was to sell and convey, and B was to buy, certain land. Subsequently, S sold the land to C but later reacquired it in time to tender its conveyance to B in compliance with the terms of the contract. B knew of these transactions and refused the conveyance tendered by S.
   (a) May S enforce the contract against B?
   (b) Was B's silent inactivity a waiver?
   (c) Would it have made any difference if B had sued S for damages for breach of contract before S's reacquisition of the land?

16. A, an accountant, sent B a bill for $1,000 for personal services. There had been no agreement as to the price to be paid. B, on receiving the bill, sent a letter to A questioning the reasonableness of the amount charged but did not dispute the service, enclosing a check for $500 which he stated was in

full satisfaction of A's claim. A made no reply and deposited the check in the bank; it was paid. He subsequently sued B to recover the $500 as balance due. Is he entitled to recover? (Former C.P.A. Examination question)

17. A agreed in a written contract to erect for O an apartment building according to plans and specifications for a contract price of $100,000. For each of the following cases, state whether A's nonperformance would be excused. Give a brief reason for each answer.
    (a) A becomes paralyzed and bedridden as a result of an accident.
    (b) A refuses to complete the building because construction and labor costs have risen 25 per cent since the contract was made.
    (c) Because of possible war with a foreign power, Congress has passed a law forbidding the construction of such buildings.
    (d) O becomes bankrupt and will be unable to pay for the building when it is completed. (Former C.P.A. Examination question)

18. P's father entered into a written contract with S, a school district, whereby, for a period of five years, the father was to supply a bus and drivers to transport school children of the district to and from school each school day. On the father's death, the father's estate through P, the administrator, wished to continue performance of the contract for the remainder of the five-year period, which S refused to do. Does P, on behalf of the estate, have a right of action against S for damages for breach of contract?

19. An investment company sold certain bonds to Clark but refused to take Clark's check in payment, although Clark offered the check in time to enable the vendor to have it certified before delivery of the bonds. Clark refused to give a check already certified, but by agreement between the parties the vendor delivered the bonds to a bank in which the vendee had a balance sufficient to cover the purchase price and accepted that bank's cashier's check and the bank immediately delivered the bonds to the vendee. Thereafter, but before the cashier's check could be cashed, the bank failed. Can the vendor recover the purchase price from the vendee? (Former C.P.A. Examination question)

20. (a) On July 25, 1971, A, as president of Boston Company, and with the approval of his board of directors, engaged C, a certified public accountant, to examine the financial statements of Boston Company as at July 31, 1971, and to render his report in time for the annual stockholders' meeting to be held on September 5, 1971. C proceeded at reasonable speed but on August 10 objected to A that the company's staff was so inefficient and uncooperative that it might be impossible to meet the deadline. A said: "Don't worry! I'll fix that." C proceeded, but the Boston Company staff showed no improvement. Notwithstanding C's reasonable efforts, the report was not ready until September 7. A, acting on behalf of Boston Company, refused to accept or to pay for the report since it no longer served its intended purpose. A maintains that delivery of the report by September 5 was a condition of the contract. What are C's rights? Explain fully. (Former C.P.A. Examination question)
    (b) In June, A and B orally agreed that A should employ B beginning next August 1 for 10 months on a special research job which B agreed

to do. On July 1, A told B he had engaged someone else and would not need him.

On your paper list the numbers 1 through 12 and opposite each number write *"true"* if the statement is true and *"false"* if the statement is not true. Answer all parts. No penalty will be imposed for guessing.

(1) The contract is unenforceable for lack of a writing.

(2) B may sue A at once.

(3) If B sues A at once, he may then safely accept other employment without losing his right against A for breach of contract.

(4) Unless B does sue A at once, he must continue his preparations and be free and ready to perform his side until A's breach becomes actual by the arrival of August 1.

(5) Unless on August 1, B was ready to start work for A, he cannot sue A after August 1.

(6) If before B sues A or takes other employment A notified B on July 15 that he will employ him after all, A is bound.

(7) If B sues A at once but dies before August 1, a defense will arise in favor of A.

(8) If B dies September 1, not yet having sued A, B's administrator may nevertheless sue A.

(9) If B was under 21, there was no contract.

(10) B could get a decree specifically ordering A to perform.

(11) B could assign his prospective salary to C.

(12) C, by accepting an assignment of the salary from B, would be promising impliedly that he would do the work. (Former C.P.A. Examination question)

21. On March 1, 1972, A employed B to work as a stenographer for one year beginning March 25, 1972. On March 10, A informed B that he would not require B's services and that the contract was at an end. On March 12, A changed his mind and informed B to disregard his remarks made on March 10 and that the contract was still in effect. B subsequently refused to work for A; and, on March 15, B was employed as a stenographer by someone else at a salary lower than that provided in her contract with A. On March 20, A employed C as a stenographer on the same terms as his contract with B. B sued A for damages for breach of contract.

(a) Can B recover from A?

(b) Why?

SOME PREVIOUS C.P.A. LAW EXAMINATION QUESTIONS AND MODEL ANSWERS

MAY, 1971

No. 6 (b. Estimated time—12 to 15 minutes)

b. In examining the accounts receivable of the Mercury Publishing Company the following problem was discovered.

During the months of November and December, 1970, Famous Music Shops, Inc. ordered and was shipped sheet music and music books having a total invoice price of $565.29. The amount of Famous Music's indebtedness to Mercury has not been disputed.

Investigation revealed that on March 1, 1971, exasperated with the number and frequency of Mercury's written demands for settlement of the account, Famous Music sent Mercury a large number of the previously purchased books and a check for $255.04. The total price of the returned books on Famous Music's original invoice was $310.25, so that this amount plus the check equaled the amount owed. There was no dispute as to this point.

Famous Music's letter to Mercury included a list of the books being returned and stated that the credit for the return plus the enclosed check for the balance constituted payment of the account in full. The following was written on the face of the check: "Complete and final settlement of our account payable."

The letter and check reached Mercury in due course. Mercury cashed the check, but declined to accept the books for credit. On March 7, 1971 Mercury wrote Famous Music as follows: "We are not crediting your account with these books, but are holding them subject to your disposal."

On March 15, 1971, Famous replied reaffirming its position as indicated in its letter of March 1.

Famous claimed that there was a general custom throughout the United States permitting the return of such books. Mercury denied that such a custom existed. Mercury's counsel submitted a memorandum stating that there was authority supporting both sides of the proposition and that in fact there was a bona fide dispute as to whether such a custom existed. The attorney's memorandum concluded that "this issue can only be determined by litigation."

Famous Music has refused to accept the returned books or to pay any more on the account.

(1) What are the legal problems and implications of the above facts? Discuss.

(2) Is the Mercury account receivable valid and enforceable against Famous? State "yes" or "no" and explain.

Answer

b. (1) The legal question here is whether an accord and satisfaction has occurred.

An accord is a new contract, and if it discharges the previous contract it is an accord and satisfaction. A promise is unenforceable as a contract unless it is supported by sufficient consideration. While a creditor's promise to discharge an undisputed debt by the debtor's payment of less than what is due is unenforceable, nevertheless if the debt is disputed the creditor's promise is supported by sufficient consideration by the debtor's payment of the lesser amount. A claim is disputed if it is honestly and reasonably believed not to be valid by the party against whom the claim is asserted.

Here, there is a disputed claim with respect to the alleged custom. Mercury's cashing of the check, which stated it was in complete and final settlement, constituted an implied promise by Mercury so to discharge the entire disputed debt and, therefore, the promise is a contract and an accord and satisfaction. Mercury cannot avoid this legal effect by declining to accept the books for credit. Mercury should not have cashed the check.

(2) No. The accord and satisfaction terminated the account receivable. The cost of the returned books should be debited to Mercury's inventory.

NOVEMBER, 1970

No. 2 (Estimated time—20 to 25 minutes)

Each of the following numbered sentences states a legal conclusion relating to the lettered material. You are to determine whether the legal conclusion is true or false according to the *Uniform Commercial Code and the general principles of contract law.* Write on a separate sheet whether each conclusion is true or false. Your grade will be determined from your total of correct answers less a penalty for your incorrect answers; an omitted answer will not be considered an incorrect answer.

A. Davis, a CPA, has a one-year retainer agreement with Franklin Corporation. Davis is to examine the financial statements, prepare tax returns, and be available for consultation on financial matters. The retainer provides for an annual fee of $12,000. Davis has a claim for $3,000 for services rendered to the Corporation prior to the execution of the retainer agreement. Davis performs the required services for the first four months and is paid therefor. Davis then is required to retire completely from practice because of a severe heart attack and assigns to Leeds, another CPA, his $3,000 claim against the Franklin Corporation and his rights and duties under the retainer agreement.

31. Davis' assignment of his $3,000 claim against the Franklin Corporation is valid, even without Franklin's consent to such assignment.

32. Franklin Corporation is not legally obligated under the retainer agreement to accept Leeds as its CPA for the remaining period.

33. Franklin Corporation may recover a judgment against Davis for breach of contract.

34. If Leeds sues Franklin Corporation, the latter may assert against Leeds all defenses it had against Davis before Davis assigned the claim to Leeds.

35. The assignment to be valid must be in writing.

B. The following telegrams are exchanged among Gordon, a watch merchant, Andrews, another watch merchant, and Speculator.
  a. September 1, 1970. To Andrews: Offer you my collection of 25 original 1928 Mickey Mouse watches for $1,500. Offer will be held open until September 10.

                                                                    Gordon

    b. September 2, 1970. To Gordon: Mickey Mouse market is bearish now. I am still considering your offer, will advise shortly.

Andrews

    c. September 2, 1970. To Gordon: Understand you are offering for sale 25 original 1928 Mickey Mouse watches for $1,500. I accept your offer.

Speculator

    d. September 3, 1970. To Andrews: Your judgment of market condition is wrong. Offer withdrawn.

Gordon

    e. September 3, 1970. To Speculator: You know value when you hear about it. It's a deal.

Gordon

    f. September 7, 1970. To Gordon: You're a hard man to deal with. Accept your offer.

Andrews

36. Gordon's withdrawal of his offer to Andrews was effective when Andrews received Gordon's telegram dated September 3.

37. Andrews' telegram dated September 7 operated as an acceptance only when Gordon received that telegram.

38. Speculator's telegram dated September 2 created a contract between Gordon and Speculator when received by Gordon.

39. Gordon has entered into a contract with both Andrews and Speculator.

40. Assuming Gordon died on September 6, his offer to Andrews terminated on that date even if Andrews had no notice until September 15.

C. Ott owes Casey $6,000 which is past due. Casey offers to discharge this debt if Ott promises to pay $3,000 to Casey's wife, pay $2,000 to Milton, a creditor of Casey, and give Casey his stamp collection which has a market value of $500. Ott accepts the offer.

41. This contract is an example of a bilateral contract.

42. After Ott fully performs, Casey may recover a judgment against Ott for $500.

43. Assuming Ott defaults, Casey's wife and Milton may recover judgments against Ott for $3,000 and $2,000 respectively.

44. Casey's wife and Milton are both incidental beneficiaries.

45. If Ott fully performs, there is an accord and satisfaction.

D. In the presence of three witnesses, Boyd enters into an oral agreement with Stanley to purchase Stanley's house for $30,000 cash. Thereafter, Stanley refuses to sell the house to Boyd. Boyd sues Stanley for breach of contract and seeks a decree of specific performance from the court to compel Stanley to deliver a deed to the house. Stanley pleads the Statute of Frauds as a defense.

46. The oral agreement is void.

47. The oral agreement is valid and enforceable if the three witnesses testify in court that the oral agreement was entered into.

48. Assuming that the agreement has been signed only by Stanley, Boyd need not also sign it to satisfy the Statute of Frauds.

49. Assuming that the agreement is enforceable, Boyd is entitled only to an award of money damages.

50. Assuming that Boyd gave Stanley a cash deposit, the oral agreement is unenforceable.

E. Norton, a minor, purchased a car for his personal use for $1,000 cash from Adams, a car dealer. Norton also purchased an acre of unimproved land for $3,000 cash from Holmes. Adams and Holmes knew that Norton was a minor.

51. Norton may disaffirm both contracts at any time during his minority by tendering the car and the land to Adams and Holmes respectively.

52. A disaffirmation by Norton must be in writing and signed to be legally effective.

53. Norton's ratification of the two contracts during his minority would not legally bar him from disaffirming both contracts at any subsequent time.

54. Norton may ratify his contracts only by giving Adams and Holmes written notice to that effect when he reaches his majority or within a reasonable time thereafter.

55. Neither Adams nor Holmes may disaffirm his contract with Norton if Norton wants to affirm.

F. Peters, a car dealer, makes the following representations to Evans in selling a car to Evans for $900.
   a. The car has been driven 50,000 miles.
   b. The market value of the car is $1,000.
   c. The manufacturer's warranty on the car does not expire for one year.
The facts are:
   a. Peters turned back the odometer from 70,000 miles.
   b. The market value of the car is $800.
   c. Unknown to Peters the warranty has expired.

56. Peters' statement as to the value of the car constitutes fraud.

57. Peters' statement as to the warranty constitutes fraud.

58. Evans may rescind the contract at any time after he discovers that Peters turned back the odometer.

59. If Evans affirms the contract after discovering that Peters turned back the odometer, he is barred from recovering a judgment for damages against Peters.

60. There is a legal difference between innocent misrepresentation and fraud.

Answer

31. True	37. False	43. True	49. False	55. True
32. True	38. False	44. False	50. True	56. False
33. False	39. True	45. True	51. False	57. False
34. True	40. False	46. False	52. False	58. False
35. False	41. True	47. False	53. True	59. False
36. False	42. False	48. True	54. False	60. True

NOVEMBER, 1969

No. 2 (C–F. Estimated time—13 to 17 minutes)

Each of the following numbered sentences states a legal conclusion as it relates to the preceding related lettered fact situation. You are to determine whether each of the legal conclusions is true or false and write on a separate answer sheet whether each conclusion is true or false. Your grade will be determined from your total net score obtained by deducting your total of incorrect answers from your total of correct answers; an omitted answer will not be considered an incorrect answer. Write on a separate answer sheet whether the following numbered sentences are true or false according to the Uniform Commercial Code and general principles of contract law.

C. Strong made a contract with Johnston Drug Corporation for the sale of Strong's Drug Store. The terms of the sale called for a payment of $8,000 to Strong, a promise by Johnston Drug to pay all outstanding firm debts listed by Strong in the contract of sale and a $1,000 gift to Strong's faithful employee, Cramford.

41. Strong made a delegation of his duty to pay his former creditors.

42. Cramford is an incidental beneficiary and cannot recover on the contract.

43. Strong's creditors may sue Johnston Drug even though they have not given any consideration for Johnston's promise to pay them.

44. Strong's creditors are donee beneficiaries.

45. If the transaction were a novation, it would release Strong from his debts to the creditors.

D. Abrams sent Dawson a letter offering to sell twelve acres of land suitable for a construction site. Abrams stated that acceptance must be made within two weeks of receipt of the offer. Six days after receipt of the offer, Dawson posted a letter of acceptance. Shortly thereafter, and prior to Abrams' receipt of the letter of acceptance, Abrams telegraphed Dawson and advised that he was withdrawing the offer. The telegram arrived prior to the letter.

46. Abrams made a firm offer to Dawson and could not withdraw it for two weeks.
47. The Statute of Frauds applies to the above transaction regardless of the purchase price.
48. The telegram withdrawing the offer could not be effective until it was received.
49. The mail was the authorized means of acceptance.
50. Dawson can hold Abrams to the contract.
E. Evans gave Bishop the following letter of introduction to Frost, a wholesaler:
"This will introduce you to my good friend and former customer, Bishop, who desires to purchase about $5,000 worth of goods from you on open credit. If you will let him have the goods, I will make good any loss up to $5,000 if he is unable to pay.

(signed) *Evans*"

Bishop presented the letter to Frost on May 1 and Frost sold and delivered $4,500 worth of goods to Bishop.
51. Evans is a surety or guarantor.
52. It is essential that Frost have Evans' promise in a signed writing if Frost is to prevail.
53. The extension of credit by Frost constituted an acceptance of Evans' offer to enter into a unilateral contract.
54. Frost was obligated to communicate his acceptance of Evans' offer prior to the extension of credit.
55. Since Evans received no consideration for his promise, Frost will be unable to enforce it.
F. Barton, upon retiring from business, offered to sell his office equipment for $1,000. He told Francis, a prospective buyer, "The equipment is almost as good as new and a good buy at the asking price. I originally paid $3,000 for it." None of the statements were true and Barton knew he had originally paid only $1,200 for the equipment. The equipment was worth $750. Francis purchased Barton's office equipment relying on the above misrepresentations.
56. The statement that the equipment was "almost as good as new" was a material misrepresentation of fact.
57. Francis could sue Barton for damages based upon the tort of fraud (deceit) in that Barton knew he was lying.
58. Even if Barton honestly believed all the above statements, Francis could still rescind the contract.
59. In order to rescind, Francis would have to show he relied on Barton's statements.
60. Since the statements were oral, the Statute of Frauds will apply.

Answer

41. True	45. True	49. True	53. True	57. True
42. False	46. False	50. True	54. False	58. True
43. True	47. True	51. True	55. False	59. True
44. False	48. True	52. True	56. False	60. False

MAY, 1969

No. 4 (Estimated time—20 to 25 minutes)

You were engaged by Bridge Builders, Inc. to conduct a special study to project the net income or loss which the Corporation should expect from a contract to build a bridge and were shown the following documents:

1. A letter dated September 1, 1968, from Robert Jones, president of Bridge Builders, Inc., to Henry Adams, president of Allied Steel Company. The text of the letter read as follows:

   "We can use 10,000 #4 grade C 'Allied Brand' steel pipes for which we will pay the present market price.

   As in the past, unless we hear from you to the contrary by return mail, we will assume you have agreed to promise to deliver. The pipe must arrive before the end of September or we will lose a $100,000 bonus payment for early completion of work."

2. A letter dated September 25, 1968, from Henry Adams to Robert Jones. The text of the letter read as follows:

   "We were pleased to receive your order of September 1, for 10,000 #4 grade C 'Allied Brand' steel pipes. We have not contacted you before because until today we were sure we could deliver and intended to do so.

   Unfortunately, our last supply of pipe, which had been set aside for you, was shipped to another customer by mistake. Unless we go to great expense it will be impossible for us to produce new pipe for two months. But Master Steel Company, our competitor, has an equivalent pipe which meets all of your specifications except that it does not bear our brand name. Their price will be the same as ours and we have arranged to have them ship their pipe to you to meet our obligation."

3. A telegram dated October 5, 1968, from Robert Jones to Henry Adams. The text of the telegram read as follows:

   "Master never delivered. We lost our bonus. We intend to hold you responsible."

   a. Did Bridge Builders intend to create a bilateral or a unilateral contract? Explain.

   b. List the requirements for a valid contract and explain how each of these requirements was or was not met in the above.

   c. Assume a valid contract existed. Could Allied Steel Company successfully assert that (1) its mistake or (2) the doctrine of impossibility of performance excused its failure to perform?

   d. Assume a valid contract existed and that Master Steel made a timely delivery to Bridge Builders. Can Bridge Builders collect damages from Allied Steel Company for its failure to deliver "Allied Brand" steel pipe? Discuss the legal theory or theories which apply to your answer.

Answer

a. A bilateral contract. A bilateral contract consists of mutual promises between the parties, while a unilateral contract consists of a promise in exchange for an act of forbearance. Here, Bridge Builders is the offeror, whose promise indicated that Allied Steel's silence would, as in the past, be a promise to deliver.

b. (1) *Parties with contractual capacity.* Corporations are juristic persons with capacity to contract.

  (2) *Manifestation of mutual assent, consisting of an offer and acceptance.* Bridge Builders made an offer, namely a promise to purchase in exchange for Allied Steel's promise to sell and deliver. Allied Steel's silence was a manifestation of assent to the offer and an acceptance. Although silence, generally, is not a manifestation of assent, nevertheless, there are two exceptions when it is such. First, when previous dealings between the parties lead the offeror to believe that the offeree's silence is an acceptance. This has occurred here. Second, if the offeree intended his silence to be an acceptance. Here, Adam's letter of September 25th indicated that Allied Steel intended its silence to be an acceptance.

  (3) *Sufficient consideration.* The exchange of mutual promises to do that which the promisors were under no previous legal duty to perform causes the promises to be sufficient consideration for each other. This occurred here.

  (4) *Legally valid transaction.* There are no facts to indicate conduct contrary to public policy here, and therefore no illegality.

c. No. Unilateral mistake resulting in failure to perform a contractual duty does not excuse such nonperformance. Allied Steel's mistake is of this character. Also, subjective inability of a promisor to perform, especially if it occurs by his unilateral mistake, does not constitute excusable impossibility because of the additional expense Allied Steel would have to incur.

d. One issue is whether substantial performance has occurred. Another issue is the type of damages which can be recovered in a legal action. Although unexcused nonperformance is a breach of contract, nevertheless, if there is substantial performance by the nonperforming party, the innocent party must perform his promise less the damage he has sustained. If the main purpose of the contract has been performed or not defeated, there is substantial performance. Here, both brands of pipe were the equivalent of each other, and the main purpose of the contract has been performed. Nominal damages are awarded if no harm has been sustained by the innocent party. Here, there is substantial performance by Allied Steel, and Bridge Builders must pay the purchase price less the nominal damages that would be awarded if the case came to court.

PART THREE

PERSONAL PROPERTY

A. PERSONAL PROPERTY IN GENERAL

Chapter I

NATURE AND ACQUISITION OF PERSONAL PROPERTY

---

1. NATURE OF PERSONAL PROPERTY

PERSONAL property is concerned with things which are owned. First the nature of things and then the concept of ownership or property will be considered.

Things

Things may be owned. A "thing" may be an object which has corporeal or physical substance, as a horse, machinery, textiles, land. Such a thing is called a "tangible." Tangibles may be immovable, such as the surface and subsurface of the earth and that which is so annexed to it as to be a permanent part thereof (e.g., a building), usually described as "land." Tangibles also may be movable, as an automobile or furniture, usually described as "chattels" or "goods."[1] Goods and their transfer by sale are governed by the Sales portion of the Code. Goods are tangible, movable things, but do not include money, investment securities, and things in action. Goods does include the unborn young of animals and growing crops. Oil, minerals, or a structure (e.g., building) affixed to land are land; but a contract for their sale, contemplating their severance from the land *by the seller* after the formation of the contract, causes them to be treated as goods *for the purpose of the contract.* However, *if the buyer is to make severance,* the transaction is considered to be a contract affecting land.[2] All things which are not tangible are incorporeal and are known as "intangibles," such as goodwill, a contract right, a trade-mark, a patent, or a copyright.[3] A thing in action—i.e., a right of action—is called a "chose in action" (e.g., the right contained in a

---

[1] See UCC 2–105(1), and below, pp. 243–44.

[2] See UCC 2–107, and below, pp. 243–44.

[3] Under federal law, a patent is a grant by the federal government through its Patent Office to the inventor (and his heirs and assigns) of "any new and useful process, machine, manufacture, or composition of matter, or any new and useful improvement thereof," not previously patented or used, "of the right to exclude others from making, using, or selling the invention throughout the United States" for a nonrenewable period of seventeen years.

Under federal law, a copyright is a grant by the federal government through its

check, promissory note, bill of exchange, a simple contract, bond, account receivable). An intangible may be included in a chattel which evidences the intangible, as a certificate of stock evidences a share in the corporation and its ownership, and a check evidences the right to money in accordance with the terms of the check. Thus, all things are either land (a tangible immovable), chattels (tangible movables), or intangibles (rights).

Property
A person may have an interest in some thing. Such an interest is "property." Customarily, the object of the interest is called property, but technically only the interest therein constitutes property; the thing itself is the object of property. (A's interest in possession of a chattel or of land is property. The chattel or land is the object of property.) An owner is the person who has such an interest, and "ownership" describes the interest as belonging to a person. The purpose of business transactions is the transfer of property—i.e., interests in things.

It should be noted carefully, however, that because the word "property" usually is used to describe a thing rather than an interest in a thing, *throughout this book the word "property" refers to a thing rather than to an interest in a thing, except when otherwise indicated.*

Classification. Property may be classified in various ways. It may be classified on the basis of its physical substance either as tangible property (e.g., land, chattels) or as intangible property (e.g., a chose in action). Classification may be made on the basis of ownership, "public property" being property owned by a nation, state, or political sub-

---

Register of Copyrights to the author or proprietor of books, periodicals, compositions, maps, works of art and models or designs for works of art, drawings or plastic works of a scientific or technical character, photographs, prints and pictorial illustrations including prints or labels used for articles of merchandise, motion-picture displays, and motion pictures other than photoplays, of the exclusive right to print, publish, copy, sell, translate, dramatize, novelize, and otherwise reproduce or use the copyrighted work for a renewable period of twenty-eight years.

Goods often are identified by a trade-mark, which is a symbol, mark, device, or other designation which a person affixes to goods to identify them as being marketed by him. An interest in a trade-mark is acquired by the person who first uses it. Federal and state legislation provide for registration of trade-marks (federal—Patent Office), which assists the registrant to prove the time of his initial use. However, registration is not necessary to the acquisition of an interest in a trade-mark. The person with a trade-mark has the exclusive right to use it with respect to those goods which, by reason of the trade-mark, prospective customers would associate with the source identified by the trade-mark; and he has this exclusive right in those territorial areas in which he used it prior to anyone else. Registration is for renewable periods of twenty years.

The assignment of an interest in a patent, copyright, or trade-mark must be in writing, and the assignment of a trade-mark must also be acknowledged. Assignment is valid as between the assignor and the assignee, but it is void as against a subsequent bona fide purchaser for value unless it has been recorded. The assignment of a patent or trade-mark is recorded in the United States Patent Office, and the assignment of a copyright is recorded with the Register of Copyright, both in Washington, D.C.

division thereof, and "private property" being property owned by a private person. The broadest classification of property is "real property" and "personal property." In a strictly technical sense, the term "real property" describes a particular kind of interest in land, called a "freehold," which is an interest in land for a period of time the termination of which cannot be measured or computed exactly in terms of years, months, and days, and which is not terminable at the will of the transferor.[4] An interest in land which is not a freehold is a "chattel real." All chattels real and all interests in movables are "personal property." However, as indicated previously, the word "property" commonly is used to refer to a thing rather than to an interest in a thing, and so, unless otherwise indicated, *throughout this book "real property" refers to land while "personal property" refers to chattels and to intangible things.*

2. ACQUISITION OF PERSONAL PROPERTY

Ownership of personal property may be acquired in various ways, such as by: bailment,[5] sale,[6] will or intestacy,[7] bankruptcy,[8] trust,[9] a judgment *in rem*,[10] occupancy, finding, gift, accession, confusion, and satisfaction of a judgment for conversion. Only the last six will be considered at this time; the others are considered elsewhere in this book, at the places indicated.

By Occupancy Occupancy is a method of acquiring ownership of personal property which is unowned by acquiring possession of the property with the intention of owning it. Thus, wild animals (and fish) which are captured, dead or alive, belong to the captor. Should a captured animal escape and regain its wild state, it is again a wild animal owned by nobody. By the majority view and in the absence of statute to the contrary, a wild animal captured by a trespasser upon another person's land belongs to the landowner. The state has a public interest in wild animals within its boundaries and regulates their capture by game laws. Similarly, the federal government regulates interference with migratory birds.

Abandoned Personal Property. Personal property becomes unowned by abandonment. Personal property which has been voluntarily

---

[4] See below, p. 903.

[5] Below, pp. 183 ff.

[6] Below, pp. 244 ff.

[7] Below, pp. 929 ff.

[8] Below, pp. 845 ff.

[9] Below, pp. 947 ff.

[10] A judgment *in rem* affects the interests of all persons in some thing.

relinquished by an owner without any intent to reclaim it and which has not been acquired by another person is abandoned personal property. Abandoned personal property is subject to acquisition by the first occupant—i.e., the person who first accomplishes its occupancy.

By Finding

Lost personal property and mislaid or misplaced personal property are to be distinguished carefully from abandoned personal property and from each other. Abandoned personal property has been discarded intentionally and is unowned. Lost personal property describes personal property located at a place where it was not put by the owner and which is unknown to the owner. Mislaid or misplaced personal property describes personal property located at a place where it was put by the owner but now forgotten by him. (A placed her handbag upon a counter in a store as she examined some merchandise. She left the store forgetting to regain the handbag and she cannot remember where she left it. The property is mislaid or misplaced but still belongs to A. If another customer accidentally had pushed the handbag upon the floor, or if A carelessly had dropped the bag upon the floor and was unaware of it, the property is lost.)

The loss or mislaying of personal property has no effect upon the rightful owner's interests therein, but it does have an effect upon the finder's interests therein. If the property is lost, the finder thereby acquires ownership of the property good as against everyone except the rightful owner. The owner of the premises upon which the property was found has no right to its possession. If the property is mislaid, it is presumed that the rightful owner will return and reclaim the property, and the owner of the premises upon which the article was found has a right to its possession. The finder of lost property, and the owner of the premises upon which mislaid property has been found and who has possession of the property, have a legal obligation to hold the property for the rightful owner. They are in the position of an involuntary bailee[11] with a duty to exercise slight care for the preservation of the property. Often statutory provisions prescribe how the finder of lost property may perfect title to lost property in himself. If a finder knows the identity of the rightful owner, he has a duty to return the property; refusal to do so may constitute the tort of conversion and also a crime.

By Gift

Personal property may be acquired by gift. A gift is a voluntary transfer of ownership of personal property by one person to another without consideration. It is essential to a gift that possession of the property be transferred from one person to another with the intent to transfer ownership therein to the

[11] See below, p. 184.

donee, who accepts before revocation by the donor or by the donor's death. Possession need not be transferred to the donee but may be transferred to a third person for the donee; and if the donee already is in possession, a manifestation by the donor of intent thereby to make a gift to the donee is a gift. Also, if possession cannot be transferred because the property is not present or, if present, because of the article's size or weight, symbolical or constructive delivery may be made by delivery of the means of access to the property, as by the delivery of keys to the place where it is located.

A gift may be absolute or subject to a condition subsequent and may be either *inter vivos* or *causa mortis*. A gift *inter vivos* is a gift among living persons. A gift *causa mortis* is a gift among living persons in contemplation of impending death of the donor from a present illness or impending peril, subject to the condition subsequent that the donor's failure to die from *such* illness or peril shall revoke the gift.[12] Death of the donee prior to death of the donor revokes the gift. A gratuitous fraudulent transfer of personal property may be set aside by creditors of the donor,[13] or by the trustee in bankruptcy under certain circumstances.[14] A gift induced by fraud or undue influence is revocable by the donor.

By Accession   The increase in personal property by what it produces or by the addition to it of other personal property so as to become a permanent part thereof is called "accession." The term means augmentation, addition. The increase of animals by birth of their young and the increase in the value of chattels by labor or materials are illustrations of accession. There may be accession of real, as well as of personal, property, as by the erection of a building upon land, the building becoming a part of the land. Accession may change the identity of the original property.

Reference should be made to the matter of priorities among security interests in accessions under the Code, discussed later.[15]

By Confusion   When the chattels of more than one owner are intermingled so that the respective chattels of each are indistinguishable, there is "confusion of goods." The storage of grain of various owners in the same enclosure or bin in a

---

[12] It should be noted carefully that the unofficial objective type answers to the uniform C.P.A. examination questions on gift *causa mortis* have consistently considered an intent to pass present title to the property as *not* being a required element in order to make such gift. The author respectfully disagrees.

[13] See Uniform Fraudulent Conveyance Act, secs. 9, 10, below, pp. 1174 ff.

[14] See below, pp. 860–61.

[15] See Secured Transactions, below, pp. 755–61.

warehouse, and the mixture of oil of various owners in the same tank or other container, are examples of confusion. Fungible goods are the usual subject of confusion; they are goods of which any unit is, by nature or usage of trade, the equivalent of any other like unit,[16] such as oil or wine in a vat, grain in a bin, cotton or wool in a heap.

The legal effect of confusion depends upon whether confusion occurred by consent of the parties, by tortious conduct, by innocent mistake of fact, or by inevitable accident, and whether the proportionate share of each owner in the mass can be ascertained. Confusion by consent of the parties causes the owners to become owners or tenants in common of the mass and to have an undivided interest therein to the extent of the contribution of each; they share proportionately any damage or loss to the mass. A similar result occurs, by the majority view, when confusion is caused by an innocent mistake of fact. Confusion by tortious conduct may occur either intentionally or negligently. If intentionally, generally the property of the tortfeasor is forfeited and transferred to the innocent owner, unless the tortfeasor can prove that proportionate division of the mass can be made between them, in which case the owners are owners in common of the mass. In other words, as between the intentionally wrongful and the innocent owners the innocent owner shall not suffer, and the intentionally wrongful owner shall not profit, from the confusion. If confusion is caused by a party's negligence, while there is conflict, in general, the negligent party must sustain any loss caused by his negligent conduct. However, if the negligent party has a fiduciary obligation to other persons with respect to certain goods which he negligently confuses with his own, his negligence usually results in the forfeiture of his goods.

By Satisfaction of a Judgment for Conversion
Conversion is a tortious interference with another person's right to immediate possession of chattels and may be defined[17] as a person's unprivileged (unpermitted) act in interfering with possession of a chattel inconsistent with another person's right to its immediate possession and inconsistent with his right to control and dominion over the chattel. Conversion alone does not disturb a person's interests in a chattel. He has a right of action for repossession of the chattel, and he also has an alternative right of action against the tortfeasor for conversion of the chattel and may recover its value at the time of the latter's conversion. Rendition of a judgment for conversion

---

[16] See UCC 1–201(17).

[17] See below, p. 193, ftn. 18, for a fuller discussion of conversion.

and its satisfaction generally causes the plaintiff's title to the property to be transferred to the defendant. In a few states rendition of the judgment alone, irrespective of its satisfaction, causes such a transfer. Generally, transfer relates back to the time of conversion by the defendant.

APPENDIX TO PART THREE (A)

REFERENCES

1. American Law Institute. *Restatement: Conflict of Laws.* 2d., 1969.
2. Brown, Ray Andrews. *The Law of Personal Property.* 2d ed. Chicago: Callaghan & Co., 1955.

PROBLEMS

1. As to patents, trade-marks, and copyrights:
   - (a) (1) Can any interest in any of them be transferred?
     - (2) Which?
     - (3) How?
     - (4) Is any record required?
     - (5) Where? Explain.
   - (b) What is the life of a (1) patent? (2) trade-mark? (3) copyright; and are any of them renewable? If so, which, and how long?
   - (c) Of what value is this knowledge to the accountant? (Former C.P.A. Examination question)

2. B was on a business trip and, while packing his belongings in a hotel room where he was staying, he overlooked a brief case which he had left in the closet.
   - (a) Who owns the brief case?
   - (b) A maid found the brief case. As between the maid and the hotel, who is entitled to possession of the brief case?

3. (a) Is a promise to make a gift enforceable in law? (Give a legal reason to support your answer.) (Former C.P.A. Examination question)
   - (b) What elements or factors must be found to make a transaction a gift of personal property? (Former C.P.A. Examination question)
   - (c) H is ill in bed and knows he apparently is about to die from pneumonia. He handed to W, his wife, the keys to his safe deposit box in a bank located in a nearby city, telling her that the box contained H's valuables and that, inasmuch as he was about to die from pneumonia, W could have it all as hers.
     - (1) Who owns the contents of the safe deposit box?
     - (2) H recovered from pneumonia but died a few weeks later in an automobile accident. Who owns the contents of the safe deposit box?

SOME PREVIOUS C.P.A. LAW EXAMINATION
QUESTIONS AND MODEL ANSWERS

MAY, 1968

No. 8 (Estimated time—20 to 25 minutes)

a. You were requested by Charles to prepare a net worth statement for him as of December 31, 1967, which will be furnished to his bank. You must determine whether or not a truck having a fair market value of $20,000 should be included in Charles's net worth. Charles was in the trucking business as a sole proprietor during 1967. Filmore, Charles's uncle, looked upon Charles as his favorite nephew and wished to help Charles in business. Filmore decided to present Charles with a new truck which Charles needed but lacked the funds to purchase.

Filmore invited Charles to lunch and told him about the intent to make a gift of the truck to him. In fact, he told Charles he had hoped to give him the truck right after lunch, but delivery was not to be made to Filmore until the following week. To evidence his intent Filmore wrote the following on a piece of paper:

"I hereby acknowledge my intent to make a gift of a new truck to my favorite nephew, Charles. Therefore, for good and valuable consideration, consisting of my love and respect for him, I irrevocably promise to deliver said truck to Charles as soon as I receive it.

Daniel Filmore."

Filmore had two waiters sign the paper as witnesses and gave it to Charles.

Filmore later learned that sometime before the luncheon Charles had been complaining to other relatives that "Uncle Filmore is a tightwad and a cheapskate." Consequently, Filmore refused to turn the new truck over to Charles.

Charles asserts that a valid *inter vivos* gift was made at the luncheon or, in the alternative, that his uncle was equally bound by the promise he made.
(1) What are the requirements necessary to establish a valid *inter vivos* gift?
(2) Did Filmore make a gift to Charles at the luncheon? Explain.
(3) Did Filmore make a legally binding contract with Charles for delivery of the truck? Explain.
(4) Assuming that the truck had actually been delivered to Filmore prior to the luncheon, that he turned the keys over to Charles at the luncheon and that Charles drove the truck back to his own place of business after the luncheon, would Charles be entitled to the truck? Explain.

b. Pierre, owner of Ritz Restaurant, Inc., had in his possession several valuable items which wealthy patrons had lost or left in the restaurant. The total value of these items was in excess of $5,000.

Ritz Restaurant's financial position was poor. Consequently, Pierre decided to pledge the items in question as collateral for a loan. He took the items to Friendly Finance Company and obtained a loan of $3,500 on the property pledged.

(1) What is the legal relationship and duty of Pierre of Ritz Restaurant, Inc. to the original owners of the property in question? Explain.

(2) As between the original owners of the property and Friendly Finance Company, who is entitled to the property? Explain.

Answer

a. (1) (a) A donor who is legally competent to make a gift.

(b) The donor's intent to make a gift and transfer ownership to the donee.

(c) Actual or symbolic delivery of the chattel by the donor to the donee or to a third person for the donee.

(d) Acceptance of the gift by the donee.

(e) No consideration is furnished to the donor.

(f) The gift must be irrevocable, except in the case of a gift *causa mortis.*

(2) No. It is necessary to a gift that the chattel be delivered by the donor. Here, Filmore did not deliver the truck. The paper executed by him at the luncheon was not a symbolic delivery of the truck; it was solely a promise to make a gift.

(3) No. A promise is unenforceable unless it is supported by sufficient consideration. Love and respect are not consideration. Since Filmore's promise requested nothing in exchange, there is no consideration and his promise is not a contract.

(4) Yes. Symbolic delivery of a chattel occurs by delivery of the means of access to the chattel. Here, Filmore's delivery of the keys to the truck to Charles constituted a delivery of the truck to Charles. Since the other elements necessary to make a gift are present, a gift of the truck has been made to Charles and he has title and the right to its possession.

b. (1) Pierre is an involuntary bailee. As a finder and involuntary bailee, he has the duty, imposed upon him by law, to hold the items for the rightful owners, and to exercise slight care for their preservation. He has no right to pledge the items.

(2) The original owners. Loss or mislaying of chattels by the owners does not deprive them of their title and paramount right to possession. While the finder acquires various interests in such chattels, such interests are subordinate to that of the owners. The same is true of the finder's transferee.

NOVEMBER, 1965

No. 2

Each of the following numbered phrases or clauses states a legal conclusion as it completes the related lettered material. You are to determine whether each of the legal conclusions is true or false according to the general principles of personal property law. Blacken the appropriate space on the separate answer sheer to indicate whether each conclusion is true or false. Your grade will be determined by deducting your total of incorrect answers from your total of correct answers; if you omit an answer it will not affect either total.

H. Ownership of personal property may be acquired by
    96. Ownership of real property.
    97. Finding lost property.
    98. Being a bailee.
    99. Purchase or barter.
    100. Accession.

I. The following items constitute personal property:
    101. The right to income on land.
    102. A brick wall built around an undeveloped plot of land.
    103. A liquidated account.
    104. A quantity of nursery trees for planting but not as yet planted.
    105. Lumber salvaged from a wrecked building.

J. The validity of a gift *causa mortis*, i.e., made in contemplation of impending death, depends upon
    106. The intent to pass present title to the property.
    107. The death of the donor occurring before the death of the donee.
    108. The actual or constructive delivery of the property which is the subject matter of the gift.
    109. The death of the donor from the existing cause which induced him to contemplate the gift.
    110. The gift being made in contemplation of the approaching end of one's life in the normal course of things.

K. The owner of a brief case lost it.
    111. Losing property is the same as abandoning it.
    112. Title to the brief case remains with the owner.
    113. A finder of the brief case will acquire good title if the owner lost the case as a result of gross negligence.
    114. The person in charge of the property upon which the case was found has rights to the case superior to those of the finder.
    115. A finder of the case who takes it into his possession becomes a bailee by operation of law.

Answer

96. True	100. True	104. True	108. True	112. True
97. True	101. True	105. True	109. True	113. False
98. False	102. False	106. True	110. False	114. False
99. True	103. True	107. True	111. False	115. True

B. BAILMENTS

Chapter II

NATURE AND SCOPE OF BAILMENTS

---

1. BAILMENT DISTINGUISHED FROM OTHER LEGAL RELATIONSHIPS

A KNOWLEDGE of the law of bailments is necessary in the marketing and storage of goods. It indicates the rights and the duties involved in the handling of goods for other persons. The word "bailment" stems from the French word, *bailler,* which means to deliver. It should be noted very carefully that the subject of bailments is concerned with goods and that the bailee, that is the person to whom the goods have been delivered, may be a person engaged in the business of transporting or storing goods, e.g., a carrier or warehouseman, or a person not in such a business, e.g., a bank holding securities to assure payment on a loan or a person to whom a truck or machinery has been rented. Documents of title, to be discussed later under Chapter III, are issued by persons engaged in the business of transporting or storing goods, and such documents evidence that the holder is entitled to receive, hold, and dispose of such documents and the goods they cover. It is because of this difference in bailees that the subject of bailments is treated in two parts, Chapter II dealing with bailments without reference to documents of title, and Chapter III dealing with documents of title representing bailed goods for transportation or storage. Of great importance also is the fact that, while bailments without reference to documents of title do not come within the purview of the Code, documents of title do come within its purview and, therefore, two fields of law are involved. This must be kept in mind because of the difference in meaning of similar terminology used in each field of law. For example, the words "goods" and "bailee" have different meanings in each field of law. Under Chapter II, "goods" has a much broader meaning than under documents of title in Chapter III, which is concerned with a limited kind of goods as a subject of documents of title. Similarly, "bailee" has a much broader meaning in Chapter II than under documents of title in Chapter III,

183

which is concerned with a more limited class of persons who are engaged in the business of transporting and storing goods and who issue documents of title for such goods.

Definition   "Bailment" may be defined as a legal relationship whereby: one party, called a "bailor," delivers goods to another, called a "bailee," for an agreed purpose; the bailee accepts the goods; and, on the accomplishment of the purpose of the bailment, the goods are to be delivered by the bailee to the bailor or pursuant to his direction as provided in the agreement. Bailment is the result of an agreement between the parties; but bailment *duties* may be implied by law without agreement or delivery, creating an *involuntary bailment.* For example, the law imposes a duty on the finder of lost or misplaced goods to hold such goods as an involuntary bailee for the benefit of the owner. However, there is no bailment, because there is no agreement and no delivery.[1] If the finder has the intent to appropriate the goods to his own use, whether such intent occurs at the time the goods are found or subsequently, the finder may be held liable for the tort of conversion. For voluntary bailments the delivery may be actual or constructive, as when goods are not capable of manual delivery because of their physical size. Delivery means not only the voluntary transfer of possession but also the bailee's acceptance of such possession. Delivery of goods by a master to his servant for an agency purpose does not create a bailment, because the servant has "custody"[2] and not possession of the goods. The word "goods" has been interpreted generally as meaning tangible movable things, called "chattels."[3] In the law of bailments, goods include money only when treated as a commodity and not as a medium of exchange, and also documents and instruments[4] whether representing goods (e.g., bills of lading and warehouse receipts representing goods) or representing intangibles (e.g., certificates of stock representing shares in a corporation, and negotiable and nonnego-

---

[1] It should be noted carefully that the unofficial objective type answers to the uniform C.P.A. examination questions on bailments have consistently considered an involuntary bailment to be a bailment, meaning that it is a bailment by operation of law.

[2] "Custody is not the same as possession in connection with chattels. By custody is meant physical control over the chattel in order to care for it or to have charge of it for someone, without any claim to interests in the chattel adverse to another. An illustration is goods held by a servant for his master. By possession is meant physical control over the chattel together with a claimed interest in the chattel to retain physical control over it to the exclusion of others, in other words, a physical control with a property right to retain such physical control." Joseph L. Frascona, *Agency* (Englewood Cliffs, N.J.: Prentice-Hall, Inc., 1964), p. 104.

[3] See above, p. 169.

[4] See American Law Institute, *Restatement: Security,* 1941, sec. 2.

tiable instruments representing rights of action, such as checks, promissory notes, insurance policies, and savings bank books). The bailment agreement may be informal and need not be in writing. However, an agreement *to make* a bailment is unenforceable unless it has the requisites of a contract.

Bailment Distinguished

A bailment should be distinguished from certain other legal terms:

1. *A present sale and a contract to sell.* A present sale[5] effects the present transfer of title, and a contract to sell[6] contemplates the future transfer of title; transfer of possession is not essential to either. A bailment is not concerned with the transfer of title, but rather with the transfer of possession. (A and B contract for the sale of oil to B, the oil to be delivered in drums returnable to A. B is to pay A $5.00 for each drum not delivered. This is a contract to sell oil and for the bailment of the drums. The provision for $5.00 fixes liquidated damages for the nondelivery of each drum.) If goods are delivered under an agreement whereby they are *exchanged* for other goods, the transaction is one involving sale. If the goods delivered are to be *returned* in a different form, the transaction is one of bailment.

2. *A mortgage.* A mortgage[7] is a security device whereby one to whom an obligation is owing acquires the right of recourse to certain property on the other's failure to perform his obligation. A mortgage may be on real property, called a "real property mortgage," and on chattels, formerly called a "chattel mortgage" and now a "security interest." With reference to real property mortgages, most states are so-called "lien states"; the mortgage creates merely a lien on the real property, which is the right to have the property sold on the debtor's default in the performance of his obligation and the proceeds applied to such obligation. A minority of states are so-called "title states," and a mortgage transfers title to the real property to the mortgagee as security for performance of the obligation. In the real property mortgage a transfer of possession is neither usual nor necessary. A bailment requires a transfer of possession of goods regardless of the purpose therefor.

3. *A trust.* The creation of a trust[8] involves the transfer of title to property to be held and administered for the benefit of a person, called

---

[5] See below, p. 244.
[6] *Ibid.*
[7] See below, p. 779.
[8] See below, p. 950.

a beneficiary; transfer of possession is not necessary. In the creation of a bailment, transfer of possession is necessary.

4. *A gift.* A gift[9] is effected only by the transfer of title together with an actual or symbolical transfer of possession.

5. *A pledge, a factor, a warehouseman.* These all involve certain types of bailment and differ only in the purpose of their creation. A "pledge"[10] involves a transfer of possession as security for the performance of an obligation, usually the payment of a debt. A "factor"[11] is a person who is an agent usually with possession for the purpose of sale; the relationship is often called "factorage." A "warehouseman" is a person who, for compensation, has received possession for the purpose of storage.

2. CLASSIFICATION OF BAILMENTS

Bailments may be divided into two classes: *ordinary bailments,* often called "private bailments"; and bailments of a public character, often called *"special bailments." Special bailees hold themselves out to serve the public generally to the limit of their facilities in the type of bailment transactions in which they are engaged.* Private bailees do not make such a holding out; they agree to carry goods for customers as they choose in each particular transaction. These two classes of bailment are distinguished from each other also by their different rights and duties.

Ordinary Bailments   Ordinary bailments are of three kinds: for the *sole benefit of the bailor;* for the *sole benefit of the bailee;* and for the *mutual benefit* of the bailor and the bailee. The first two types of bailment are called *"gratuitous bailments";* the third is called a *"mutual-benefit bailment."* If the bailment agreement does not define the duties of the parties thereto, then the law implies a duty of care determined by the type of ordinary bailment. Whether the bailment is gratuitous or mutual-benefit is determined by the *intent of each of the parties regarding their primary expectation of benefit at the time of the formation of the bailment agreement.* If each *primarily* expects a benefit, it is a mutual-benefit bailment; otherwise it is a gratuitous bailment. The realization of benefit by either the bailor or the bailee, or both, is immaterial; the

---

[9] See above, pp. 172 ff.

[10] See below, pp. 775–76.

[11] See below, pp. 509–10.

test is their expectation of benefit. (A bails a picture to B for exhibition at a fair. A is not to receive any monetary compensation therefor, but B will profit by charging admission to view the picture. At the time of the bailment, A expected a benefit in the form of greater notoriety as an artist, and B expected a financial benefit. This is a mutual-benefit bailment.) Gratuitous transportation of certain articles as a part of an over-all agreement wherein the carrier expects a benefit does not create a gratuitous bailment of those articles; they are part of a mutual-benefit bailment. The fact that incidental benefit to one of the parties will occur does not make the bailment one of mutual benefit. It is the primary expectation of benefit which is important. (A bails goods to B subject to withdrawal by A as he desires from time to time. B accepts such goods as an accommodation to A and does not intend to receive a benefit thereby, although B derives an incidental benefit because B's position and reputation in the community will be enhanced by the bailment. It is a bailment for the sole benefit of the bailor.)

The bailee's duty of care in gratuitous bailments is *great* in the case of a bailment for the sole benefit of the bailee and *slight* in the case of a bailment for the sole benefit of the bailor. A mutual-benefit bailment imposes upon the bailee the care of *a reasonably careful man in the position of the bailee under the circumstances.* It is a question of fact for the jury whether the particular duty of care has been observed. Negligence is a failure to exercise that amount of care required under the circumstances, and what is negligence in one type of ordinary bailment would not be negligence in another type. A warehouseman is an ordinary bailee of a mutual-benefit bailment with a duty of ordinary, reasonable care even though warehousing is regulated by statute and often is considered to be a public duty. By the majority view, in the case of bailments without a public duty, a bailor and bailee generally may contract to relieve the bailee of a duty of care toward the bailed goods.[12] However, this does not permit the bailee so to act with respect to such goods as to abandon all care whatsoever and thereby negate the very purpose for which the bailment was made.

It is essential to a bailment that there be a transfer of possession of goods. A patron's deposit of clothing on a hanger provided by a restaurant or other establishment does not create a bailment, because the establishment never received possession of the clothing. The hanger is provided for the convenience of the patrons, and the clothing may be removed without the permission of the establishment. The patron's use

---

[12] Under the Code this does not apply to warehousemen. See UCC 7–204, and below, p. 203.

of checking facilities made available by an establishment whereby the patron surrenders possession of clothing to an authorized attendant creates a bailment because possession has been transferred. Similarly, the parking of an automobile in a parking lot is a bailment, if control of the automobile is surrendered to an authorized attendant; when no control is assumed by the attendants and merely a space is designated in which the driver is to park, there is no bailment but merely a license to use the designated space.

Special Bailments

Innkeepers. Today innkeepers are those who operate hotels, inns, and taverns. Innkeepers hold themselves out to accommodate all proper transient persons, called "guests," with lodging or with lodging and meals. Inns, or "hotels" as they are called today, are distinguished from lodging, or boarding, houses which do not hold themselves out to serve the public generally; they are ordinary bailees. There is a conflict of authority regarding the duty of care to be exercised by innkeepers over the baggage of their guests. By the better view, the liability is the same as that of the common carrier of goods who has the absolute liability of an insurer, with certain exceptions. Statutes in many states permit the innkeeper to limit his liability to that of an ordinary bailee by providing a place for the safe custody of guests' valuables and by giving reasonable publicity of the availability of such facilities. A guest who does not avail himself of such facilities can hold the innkeeper liable only for failure to exercise the care required in a mutual-benefit bailment. Guests are transients lodging at the inn or hotel. Guests do not include nonlodging guests of guests; people using the hotel's services, such as a person using solely a writing desk in the lobby, are not guests. The innkeeper is liable only for baggage of the guest, and not for goods for sale or exhibition.

Common Carriers. A common carrier is a special bailee which holds itself out for hire to transport goods or persons; it is called a "common carrier of goods" or a "common carrier of persons," respectively. The common carrier holds itself out to serve all who apply for the available services to the limit of its facilities. A common carrier of goods is distinguished from a private carrier of goods which does not hold itself out to serve the public generally and which is an ordinary bailee. Examples of common carriers of goods or of persons are: railroads, taxicabs, airplanes, boats, ferries, express companies, and bus companies. The person named in a bill of lading[13] as the person from

---

[13] For bill of lading, see UCC 1–201(6), and below, pp. 210 ff.

whom the goods have been received for shipment is called the "consignor," and the person named in a bill of lading to whom or to whose order the bill promises delivery is called a "consignee."[14]

While *a common carrier of goods is required by law to receive goods for transportation,*[15] nevertheless it is not required to receive for transportation goods which it is not equipped to carry, goods which are inherently dangerous, goods which have not been properly prepared for transportation, goods injurious to public health, or goods which cannot be transported legally. Similarly, while *a common carrier of persons is required by law to receive persons for transportation,* nevertheless it is not required to receive as passengers persons who require more than ordinary attention and care, such as drunkards, or insane, blind or otherwise physically incapacitated persons, without an attending assistant or guardian; also, persons with contagious diseases may be refused transportation.

Duties of Common Carriers of Persons. While a common carrier *of persons* is not a bailee of its passengers because only goods are the subject of bailment, nevertheless, it has certain duties in connection with the transportation of its passengers and of their baggage. A common carrier of persons has a great or extraordinary duty of care toward its passengers. It must make reasonable rules and regulations for the transportation of passengers, give reasonable notice of approach to stations, afford reasonable opportunity to alight and board, protect its passengers from harm, and avoid unreasonable delays. Passengers are those who have subjected themselves to the facilities of the common carrier with the carrier's permission. A person on a platform awaiting a railroad train is a passenger. Those persons on the carrier's premises without permission are trespassers and are not entitled to the same care as passengers.

The liability of a common carrier of persons for *checked baggage* being transported is the same as the absolute liability of a common carrier of goods in transporting goods, while its liability for *unchecked baggage* within the personal possession of the passenger is only for negligence because there is no bailment. A passenger must be permitted to bring a reasonable amount of baggage without charge. Baggage is that which is reasonably necessary for the convenience of the passenger for his personal use in making the journey, considering his station in life and the length, nature, and purpose of his journey. Thus, jewelry

---

[14] UCC 7–102 (b) (c).

[15] For the lien of such common carrier of goods, see below, pp. 215–18.

suitable to the condition in life of the passenger and intended for personal use on the journey is baggage; but it is not baggage when carried by a passenger for the use of another or for the purpose of business or sale. A lawyer's or accountant's brief case containing business papers in connection with the purpose of the journey is baggage; sample jewelry carried by a jewelry salesman is not baggage.

3. LIABILITY OF A COMMON CARRIER OF GOODS

Absolute Liability of an Insurer By state law for intrastate commerce in many states, and by federal law for interstate commerce, when goods have been delivered to a *common carrier* of goods for immediate shipment, a *shipper-carrier relationship* thereby is established, *imposing upon the carrier the absolute liability of an insurer, with certain exceptions.* The shipper has no way of proving negligence by the common carrier proximately causing damage to goods shipped. Public policy has determined that the common carrier is in a better position to take on this absolute liability and include a reasonable charge for indemnity in the shipping charges. The delivery of goods to the carrier not for immediate shipment does not create a shipper-carrier relationship; it creates an ordinary bailment. (A delivers goods to B, a common carrier, for shipment 10 days later. On the fifth day part of the goods are destroyed without B's negligence, and on the twelfth day the remainder of the goods is destroyed without B's negligence. During the 10 days the relationship is an ordinary mutual-benefit bailment, and, inasmuch as no negligence occurred, B is not liable for the loss. On the twelfth day the relationship was shipper-carrier because the goods were to be shipped on the tenth day and, B's liability being that of an insurer, B is liable for the loss occurring on the twelfth day.) If the common carrier transports goods outside its calling, or gratuitously, then it is a private carrier with the liability of an ordinary bailee. *The shipper-carrier relationship begins when a common carrier accepts goods for immediate shipment and ends when delivery is made as provided in the agreement between the shipper and the carrier.* If the agreement provides for delivery directly to the consignee, then only an actual delivery to the consignee within a reasonable period of time, at a reasonable hour, on a proper day, constitutes delivery. Delivery occurs either when the consignee or his agent for that purpose takes possession of the goods, or when the goods have been delivered at the depot or docks nearest to the destination point and a reasonable period of time has expired within which the consignee could have removed the goods after having received reasonable notice of their arrival. On the expiration of a reasonable period of time within which the consignee could have removed the goods, the shipper-carrier relationship ceases, the carrier becomes an ordinary bailee for the consignee, and the carrier may charge for storage thereafter. While the minority view does not require notice to be given to the consignee on the arrival of the goods, by the better view such notice must be given.

Often goods are transferred from one carrier to another in the process of carriage from the point of shipment to the point of delivery. The carrier who first receives the goods for shipment is called the *initial carrier;* the other carriers handling the goods are agents of the initial carrier and are called *connecting carriers.* The initial carrier is liable to the owner of the goods for loss of, or damage to, the shipped goods caused by a connecting carrier. When the initial carrier has paid the owner of the goods for such loss or damage, it is then subrogated—i.e., entitled—to the rights of the owner against the connecting carrier. In this way the owner of the goods is not subjected to the trouble of ascertaining which carrier was liable; it is easier for the initial carrier to determine this.

Exceptions to Absolute Liability of an Insurer. The law imposes the absolute liability of an insurer on a common carrier of goods because the carrier is in sole possession of the goods which it receives from the public generally and the shipper would experience great difficulty in proving fault on the part of the carrier through its agents. The following are five exceptions to the liability of a common carrier as an insurer:

1. Loss caused by an act of God.
2. Loss caused by an act of a public enemy.
3. Loss caused by an act of the shipper.
4. Loss caused by the inherent nature of the goods.
5. Loss of goods seized from the carrier pursuant to legal process.

Act of God. A common carrier is not liable for loss caused by an act of God. An act of God is an occurrence of nature, but in the law of bailments the phrase is used as an excuse from liability and means an occurrence of nature which reasonably could not have been foreseen by the carrier. Illustrations are tornadoes, hurricanes, lightning, earthquakes, unusual rains, and floods. If a human agency joins with an act of God in causing loss, the carrier is not excused. The act of God must be the sole cause of the loss in order to excuse the carrier's liability. When a carrier delays transportation of goods and loss occurs through an act of God, which loss would not have occurred but for the delay, most courts hold that the delay, although a human factor, did not create a risk of loss by an act of God and the carrier's liability for the delay does not extend to include such loss.[16] Loss caused by fire usually is not caused by an act of God because of the presence of a human agency; a fire caused by lightning or unforeseeable spontaneous combustion is caused by an act of God, and loss caused by such a fire is not borne by the carrier.

Act of Public Enemy. A common carrier is not liable for the loss caused by an act of a public enemy. By "public enemy" is meant an enemy of the United States, such as revolutionaries, or hostile military forces operating against the United States. Thieves, mobs, and rioters are not public enemies.

Act of Shipper. A common carrier is not liable for loss caused by an act of the shipper, irrespective of the shipper's negligence. (A ships horses accompained by B, a caretaker employed by A, by C, a common carrier. B's lantern causes fire, injuring the horses while in transit. A is liable for the loss regardless of whether or not A or B was negligent.) Damage caused by the improper preparation of goods for shipment must be borne by the shipper, unless the common carrier knew, or reasonably should have known, of such defective preparation and negligently failed to correct the defect or to refuse to ship the goods.

Inherent Nature of the Goods. A common carrier is not liable for loss caused by the inherent nature of the goods, unless the carrier is aware of the nature of the goods and fails to take adequate precautions to preserve them during their transportation. (A ships a barrel of molasses which fermented and exploded while being unloaded from the common carrier. A bears the loss.) The common carrier is under a duty to provide adequate facilities for the transportation of perishables of which the common carrier is aware.

Legal Process. A common carrier is not liable for the loss of goods seized from it pursuant to legal process—e.g., garnishment, execution, attachment. (A, a sheriff, seizes goods from B, a common carrier, in order to satisfy a judgment obtained by C against D, the owner of the goods. B is not liable for its inability to deliver the goods to D, or for any loss occurring after the goods have been taken from B by A.)

Reasonable Limitation of Liability. The right of a common carrier of goods reasonably to limit damages for the *amount* of liability in the case of loss of, or injury to, the transported goods with or without

---

[16] See William L. Prosser, *Handbook of the Law of Torts* (4th ed., St. Paul: West Publishing Co., 1971), pp. 285–86.

negligence on its part by contract with the shipper is discussed later under Documents of Title.[17]

The common carrier may issue reasonable rules and regulations for the operation of its business and may charge reasonable rates. Such rates usually are fixed by the federal government through the Interstate Commerce Commission for interstate transportation, and by state regulatory bodies for intrastate carriage. The common carrier cannot discriminate unfairly between shippers. A common carrier is permitted to fix its rates dependent upon the quantity, bulk, value, and special nature —e.g., explosives—of the goods transported. It may insist upon prepayment for the transportation of goods as well as for passengers. Reasonable rates include a reasonable charge for storage in connection with shipments and *demurrage* charges for unreasonable retention of cars by customers, as well as transportation rates.

4. *THE RIGHT TO POSSESSION AND USE OF BAILED GOODS*

The Right to Possession of Bailed Goods   The bailee's right to possession of bailed goods is determined by the bailment agreement. In the absence of agreement to the contrary, the bailee has the duty of delivering the goods to the bailor or pursuant to his direction. The bailee's misdelivery of the goods, whether innocent or intentional, subjects the bailee to liability to the bailor for damages for breach of the bailment contract or for damages for the tort of conversion,[18] unless the bailee made delivery pursuant to the au-

---

[17] See below, pp. 213 ff.

[18] "Conversion" is a tort (a civil, noncontractual wrong) and may be defined as a person's unprivileged (unpermitted) act in interfering with *possession* of a *chattel* inconsistent with another person's right to its *immediate possession* and inconsistent with his right to *control and dominion* over the chattel. The wrongdoer has converted the chattel to his own use. Interference is inconsistent with another person's control and dominion over a chattel when either:

1. A person intentionally and without privilege *disposseses* another person of a chattel. (A steals goods from B and bails them to C. A has committed conversion.)
2. A person in possession of a chattel *refuses to surrender possession* of the chattel to another person who is entitled to its immediate possession and who has *demanded* its possession. (A steals goods from B and bails them to C. B demands the goods from C who refuses to deliver them to B. C has committed conversion.)
3. A person in possession of a chattel *uses* the chattel either without authority, or with authority pursuant to a bailment agreement but so excessively as to constitute a material breach of the bailment agreement. (A bails goods to B for B's use in a way specified in the bailment agreement. B's use of the goods in an entirely different way is a conversion.) Although unprivileged commingling of chattels by one person with those of another is a conversion, nevertheless by contract, custom and usage, as provided in UCC 7–207, a warehouseman may

thority of a person with a right to their immediate possession superior to that of the bailor. (F, a factor of B, is directed by B to redeliver the goods to B by Railway Express. F innocently delivers the goods to C, an imposter representing that he is from the express company. C absconds with the goods. F is liable to B for damages for breach of contract or for conversion.) In the absence of agreement to the contrary, the bailor has a right to recover possession of the goods.[19] In the foregoing illustration, B had such a right against C.

The bailee also has a right to immediate possession of the bailed goods, and he may institute an action to recover their possession from one unlawfully possessing them. Even the bailor cannot recover possession of goods from the bailee unless the bailment is terminable at will and the bailor terminates it, or the bailee has materially breached the bailment contract, thereby entitling the bailor to repossession of the goods. However, the bailor does have a right of action against third persons for their tortious damage to his reversionary interest in the goods.[20] (A bails goods to B for a term during which they are stolen by C, who permanently damages the goods. B has rights of action

---

commingle fungible goods of the same kind and grade belonging to different persons.

4. A person *disposes* (delivers) of a chattel with the intent to transfer a *proprietary* interest in the chattel. "Proprietary interest" means an interest which entitles the owner to possession permanently or for a period of time. (A bails goods to B for safekeeping, and B leases or sells and delivers them to C. B has committed conversion.) However, as an exception, a bailee who misdelivers the bailed chattel to a person other than the one entitled to immediate possession, whether or not pursuant to the bailment agreement, is liable to the person entitled to immediate possession only if the latter had made a previous demand upon the bailee for surrender of possession and the bailee's delivery was unprivileged. (A stole goods from B and bailed them to C, who was unaware of the theft. C's redelivery of the goods to A prior to any demand by B is not a conversion by C, even if C had learned of the theft.)

5. A person *acquires* possession of a chattel with the intent to obtain a *proprietary* interest in the chattel either for himself or for a third person. (A bails goods to B for safekeeping, and B leases or sells and delivers them to C. C is liable to A for conversion for wrongful *receipt* of the goods, and B is liable to A for conversion for wrongful *disposal* of the goods.) However, as an exception, a bailee who receives a chattel on behalf of the bailor and who, at the time of his receipt, is innocent that another person is entitled to the immediate possession of the chattel, is not liable for conversion. This situation frequently arises in connection with the bailment of stolen goods.

Damages for the tort of conversion is for the full value of the chattel, in effect imposing a forced sale of the chattel upon the wrongdoer. Generally, the value is measured by its market value at the time and place of conversion with interest from that time.

[19] The legal form of action to recover possession of specific chattels was called "Replevin."

[20] It should be noted that a bailee's negligence is not imputed to his bailor, while a master is liable for damages caused by the negligence of his servants while acting within the scope of their employment. See below, pp. 574 f.

against C for repossession of the goods and for damage to his possessory interest in the goods caused by C's trespass. A has a right of action against C for the damage done to his reversionary interest in the goods. In the absence of agreement to the contrary, possession of the goods is to revert to A at the end of the bailment term, and A's interest in the return of the goods is called a "reversionary interest.") As between one unlawfully in possession and another who unlawfully obtains possession, the first person is entitled to immediate possession as against the second person and those who acquire possession through him. (A bails goods to B which C steals from B. D steals the goods from C. As between B and C or D, B is entitled to possession. As between C and D, C is entitled to possession.)

The bailee's failure to deliver the bailed goods to the bailor or pursuant to his direction subjects the bailee to liability except in the following instances:

1. In the case of carrier and warehouseman bailees, reference should be made to Documents of Title, discussed later.[21]

2. When the bailee has delivered the goods to a person whose right to their immediate possession is superior to that of the bailor. (A purchases goods from B under a contract voidable at the election of B. A bails the goods to C for a term. B avoids his contract with A and, at the end of the bailment term, *demands* possession of the goods from C. C must deliver the goods to B.)

3. When the goods have been damaged, destroyed, or lost by: an act of God; an act of a public enemy; an act of the shipper; the inherent nature of the goods; or seizure of the goods pursuant to legal process—e.g., garnishment, execution, or attachment—and the bailee gives the bailor prompt notice thereof.

A bailee acts at his peril when he delivers bailed goods to someone other than the bailor and not pursuant to the bailor's direction. If the recipient of the goods does not have a right to their immediate possession superior to the right of the bailor, the bailee is liable for such misdelivery. The bailee's primary duty is to deliver the goods to the bailor or pursuant to his direction. If the bailee is confronted by conflicting claims to possession asserted by the bailor and others, the bailee may avail himself of the remedy of *interpleader.* In a suit by the bailor against the bailee for refusual to redeliver possession of bailed goods at the end of the bailment term, the bailee may interplead, or bring in, any other party asserting the right to possession and make the goods available to the court for disposition on its determination of the one entitled to possession. The bailee itself may institute a proceeding joining the bailor and other parties who assert the right to possession of the goods.

---

[21] See below, pp. 220–21.

The Code provides for this right of interpleader on the part of a carrier or warehouseman.[22] A bailee is estopped to set up title in himself as adverse to the bailor because, by accepting the bailed goods, the bailee impliedly agrees that the bailor is entitled to the possession of the goods on the termination of the bailment term.

The Bailee's Right of Lien. A lien may be defined as a legal right in the property of another as security for the performance of an obligation. In the law of bailments this right of lien is a right to possession of the goods and a right to subject such goods to sale in payment for reasonable charges in connection with such goods; it is a security device. The lien may be provided for by contract or may be implied by law. In ordinary bailments for hire, the bailee acquires a right to retain possession of the goods and to sell such goods in order to obtain satisfaction for the charges owing. At Common Law a lien was accorded when services rendered in connection with bailed goods enhanced the value of such goods. Today it is not necessary that the value of such goods be enhanced; liens are prescribed by law when services, labor, skill, or material have been rendered in connection with bailed goods. A finder of goods who has incurred reasonable expense in connection with their preservation had a lien at Common Law only to the extent of the offer of reward if made, while by statute today a finder frequently has a lien for such expense.

Special bailees have liens on the goods in connection with which services have been rendered. An innkeeper has a lien on all the goods of its guests to the extent of reasonable charges for the accommodation furnished. Such a lien extends not only to baggage or luggage of the guest but to all goods that he may have. Similarly, a common carrier or a warehouseman has a lien as security for reasonable charges for goods transported, the storage of such goods, and for demurrage charges. These liens are *specific liens,* and not general liens,[23] in the sense that *these liens attach only to the specific goods to which services have been rendered.* For a common carrier, the lien extends to all parts of a shipment, and the surrender of one installment to the consignee permits the carrier to retain possession of the remaining installments as security for the amount owing for all the installments. Such a lien does not extend to goods which have been entrusted to the bailee without the consent of the real owner.[24] It is implied in a contract wherein credit is

---

[22] UCC 7–603.

[23] For an extended discussion of specific and general liens, see below, 789–90.

[24] But see variations in a warehouseman's lien, below, p. 206, and a carrier's lien below, pp. 216–17.

extended that there is no right of lien as security for the charges owing.

The right of lien is terminated in the following ways: by payment of the charges owing; by improper refusal of a valid tender of payment; or by a voluntary surrender of possession by the bailee to the bailor.

The Bailee's Right to Use the Bailed Goods

The extent to which the bailee may make use of bailed goods depends upon the bailment agreement. In ordinary bailments the degree of use of the bailed goods by the bailee depends in turn upon the kind of bailment. In a mutual-benefit bailment except for carriage or storage, and in a bailment for the sole benefit of the bailee, generally the bailee may make use of the goods for his primary benefit, limited by the terms of the bailment agreement. In a bailment for the sole benefit of the bailor, generally the bailee has the implied authority to use the bailed goods for their preservation even though by such use the bailee may derive an incidental benefit. The bailee, however, may not derive a primary benefit. (A bails his race horse to B for the sole benefit of A. B has the implied authority to exercise the race horse in order to keep it in good condition. He may not, however, use the race horse primarily for his own benefit. The fact that B derives an incidental benefit by the pleasure he obtains from the use of the race horse does not change the nature of the bailment; it still is a bailment for the sole benefit of the bailor.)

In ordinary mutual-benefit bailments except for carriage or storage, the bailor has the duty of providing goods which are reasonably suitable and fit for use in accordance with the purpose of the bailment. Damage caused by the bailor's failure to observe such duty subjects the bailor to liability therefor. (A rents a defective tool to B to be used for a known particular purpose. The defect causes the tool to break and damage other property of B. A is liable to B for such damage.) The bailee has the obligation of making ordinary and incidental repairs to the goods, while the bailor has the obligation of making unusual and extraordinary repairs to such goods if such repairs were not necessitated by any fault of the bailee. In the absence of any provision to the contrary in the bailment agreement or by custom and usage, the bailee is under no duty to insure the bailed property. The bailee may insure such property, however, because the bailee has an insurable interest in the property.[25] The bailee cannot recover from the bailor any insurance premiums which he has paid.

---

[25] For concept of insurable interest in property, see below, p. 879.

Deviation. The bailee may not deviate or depart from the terms of the bailment agreement. If the bailment was created by contract, the bailee's deviation subjects him to liability for damages for breach of contract. In tort, the bailee is liable in conversion for: his use of the goods when the bailment agreement does not permit his use; or, if his use is permitted, his excessive use amounting to a material breach of contract. If his use is permitted and his excessive use does not amount to a material breach of contract, he is absolutely liable for any damage to the goods during such deviation or caused by such deviation irrespective of his negligence. By custom and usage and usually by contract, a warehouseman may commingle fungible goods of the same kind and grade belonging to different persons, such owners thereby becoming owners or tenants in common of the mass, each with an undivided interest therein to the extent of his contribution. Such commingling is not a deviation from the terms of the bailment agreement.

5. TERMINATION

A bailment may be terminated in accordance with the terms of the bailment agreement or by the conduct of the parties. The bailment agreement may provide for the accomplishment of a certain purpose, and on the accomplishment of this purpose the bailment is at an end. The bailment agreement may provide for the duration of the bailment in terms of a period of time, and on the expiration of such period of time the bailment terminates. It is implied in a bailment agreement that the bailment relationship will continue as long as there are bailed goods. If there is a total destruction or loss of the subject matter of the bailment, or if such subject matter is partially destroyed or so changed as to be unfit and unsuitable for the purpose for which it was bailed, the bailment is terminated.

The parties themselves, acting together or individually, may terminate the bailment agreement. When a bailment agreement is for an indefinite period of time, the bailment is one that is terminable at will. Either the bailor or the bailee may terminate such a bailment at any time. In a bailment that is not terminable at will, the bailee may terminate the bailment by reason of his material failure to perform or because of his material deviation from the terms of the bailment agreement. If the bailment is a contract, then the act of the bailee in breaching such contract subjects him to liability for damages for such breach, just as in any other type of contract. Similarly, the bailor may terminate the bailment agreement; and if the bailment is a contract, he also is liable for damages for breach of the bailment contract. The bailor cannot wrongfully terminate a mutual-benefit bailment without the bailee's consent when the bailee has an interest in the subject matter. (A bails a machine to B for one year. B is to pay a rental for such machine during that period. On the expiration of six months A attempts to terminate the bailment agreement and repossess the machine. A cannot terminate the bailment agreement by himself because the bailee has an interest in the possession of the machine for one year.) The bailor and the bailee mutually may agree to rescind the bailment agreement, in which case the bailment thereby is terminated.

FORM 1585   12-47—100M Sets

(Uniform Domestic Order Bill of Lading, adopted by Carriers in Official, Southern, Western and Illinois Classification Territories, March 15, 1922, as amended August 1, 1930, and June 15, 1941.)

1st SHEET

UNION PACIFIC

UNIFORM ORDER BILL OF LADING
ORIGINAL

Shipper's No._____
Agent's No._____

UNION PACIFIC RAILROAD COMPANY

RECEIVED, subject to the classifications and tariffs in effect on the date of the issue of this Bill of Lading,

at_____194____

from_____

the property described below, in apparent good order, except as noted (contents and condition of contents of packages unknown), marked, consigned, and destined as indicated below, which said company (the word company being understood throughout this contract as meaning any person or corporation in possession of the property under the contract) agrees to carry to its usual place of delivery at said destination, if on its own road or its own water line, otherwise to deliver to another carrier on the route to said destination. It is mutually agreed, as to each carrier of all or any of said property over all or any portion of said route to destination, and as to each party at any time interested in all or any of said property, that every service to be performed hereunder shall be subject to all the conditions not prohibited by law, whether printed or written, herein contained, including the conditions on back hereof, which are hereby agreed to by the shipper and accepted for himself and his assigns.
   The surrender of this Original ORDER Bill of Lading properly indorsed shall be required before the delivery of the property. Inspection of property covered by this Bill of Lading will not be permitted unless provided by law or unless permission is indorsed on this Original Bill of Lading or given in writing by the shipper.

Consigned to ORDER OF_____

Destination_____ State of_____ County of_____

Notify_____

At_____ State of_____ County of_____

Route_____

Delivering Carrier_____ Car Initial_____ Car No._____

No. Packages	DESCRIPTION OF ARTICLES, SPECIAL MARKS AND EXCEPTIONS	*WEIGHT (Subject to Correction)	CLASS OR RATE	CHECK COLUMN	
					Subject to Section 7 of conditions, if this shipment is to be delivered to the consignee without recourse on the con-
					(The signature here acknowledges only the amount prepaid.)

*If the shipment moves between two ports by a carrier by water, the law requires that the bill of lading shall state whether it is "carrier's or shipper's weight."
NOTE—Where the rate is dependent on value, shippers are required to state specifically in writing the agreed or declared value of the property.
The agreed or declared value of the property is hereby specifically stated by the shipper to be not exceeding

_____ per _____

Charges Advanced:

$_____

_____Shipper. _____Agent

Per_____ Per_____

Permanent postoffice address of shipper_____

COURTESY, SAFETY AND RELIABLE SERVICE

ORDER BILL OF LADING (*front*)

Chapter III

DOCUMENTS OF TITLE

In General   THE subject of documents of title comes under Article 7 of the Uniform Commercial Code and is governed by its provisions.[1] On the receipt of bailed goods, common carriers and warehousemen issue a writing which constitutes both a receipt for such goods and also a contract containing the terms on which such goods were received. The writing issued by a common carrier is called a "bill of lading." A bill of lading is "a document evidencing the receipt of goods for shipment issued by a person engaged in the business of transporting or forwarding goods, and includes an airbill."[2] The writing issued by a warehouseman is called a "warehouse receipt." A warehouse receipt is "a receipt issued by a person engaged in the business of storing goods for hire."[3] Bills of lading and warehouse receipts are called "documents of title"[4] because they represent the goods and are symbols of title to such goods. Under the Code:[5] a bailee is "the person who by a warehouse receipt, bill of lading or other document of title acknowledges possession of goods and contracts to deliver them"; a consignor is "the person named in a bill as the person from whom the goods have been received for shipment"; a consignee is "the person named in a bill to whom or to whose order the bill promises delivery"; and goods "means all things which are treated as movable for the purposes of a contract of storage or transportation."

---

[1] UCC 7–103: "To the extent that any treaty or statute of the United States, regulatory statute of this State or tariff, classification or regulation filed or issued pursuant thereto is applicable, the provisions of this Article are subject thereto."

[2] " 'Airbill' means a document serving for air transportation as a bill of lading does for marine or rail transportation, and includes an air consignment note or air waybill." UCC 1–201(6).

[3] UCC 1–201(45).

[4] " 'Document of title' includes bill of lading, dock warrant, dock receipt, warehouse receipt or order for the delivery of goods, and also any other document which in the regular course of business or financing is treated as adequately evidencing that the person in possession of it is entitled to receive, hold and dispose of the document and the goods it covers. To be a document of title a document must purport to be issued by or addressed to a bailee and purport to cover goods in the bailee's possession which are either identified or are fungible portions of an identified mass." UCC 1–201(15).

[5] UCC 7–102(1) (a), (b), (c), (f).

Documents of title may be either negotiable or non-negotiable. A document of title is negotiable: if, by its terms, the goods are to be delivered either *to the order of* a named person, or *to bearer;* or, where recognized in overseas trade, if it runs to a named person or assigns. Any other document is non-negotiable. A bill of lading which states that the goods are *consigned to* a named person is not made negotiable by a provision that the goods are to be delivered only against a written order signed by the same, or another, named person. Also, "Deliverable on proper indorsement and surrender of this receipt" does not cause the document to be negotiable, although such a provision is often included by bailees in their documents in order to insure that they receive the non-negotiable document proving that delivery of the goods has been made. A document of title is either negotiable or non-negotiable at the time of its inception, and the indorsement of a non-negotiable document cannot thereby make it negotiable. A negotiable bill of lading often is called an "order bill." Inasmuch as a non-negotiable bill of lading states that the goods are to be delivered *to* the person specified in the bill, it is often called a "straight bill." It is very important to distinguish between negotiable and non-negotiable documents of title because different rights and duties are associated with each. These will be discussed later.[6] The law of documents of title is concerned mainly with warehouse receipts and bills of lading. Accordingly, first special rules applicable only to warehouse receipts, then special rules applicable only to bills of lading, and finally rules applicable to both warehouse receipts and bills of lading will be discussed, in that order.

Warehouse Receipts Only **Form.** A warehouse receipt is issued by a warehouseman,[7] and it need not be in any particular form. A warehouse receipt should contain the following information, and the warehouseman is liable for damages caused by any omission to a person injured thereby:

(a) the location of the warehouse where the goods are stored;
(b) the date of issue of the receipt;
(c) the consecutive number of the receipt;
(d) a statement whether the goods received will be delivered to the bearer, to a specified person, or to a specified person or his order;
(e) the rate of storage and handling charges, except that where goods are

---

[6] See below, pp. 223–29.

[7] However, a receipt issued by a non-warehouseman owner of goods (e.g., distilled spirits, agricultural commodities) under a statute requiring a bond against withdrawal or a license for the issuance of receipts in the nature of warehouse receipts has the same effect as a warehouse receipt.

stored under a field warehousing arrangement a statement of that fact is sufficient on a non-negotiable receipt;

(f) a description of the goods or of the packages containing them;

(g) the signature of the warehouseman, which may be made by his authorized agent;

(h) if the receipt is issued for goods of which the warehouseman is owner, either solely or jointly or in common with others, the fact of such ownership; and

(i) a statement of the amount of advances made and of liabilities incurred for which the warehouseman claims a lien or security interest. . . . If the precise amount of such advances made or of such liabilities incurred is, at the time of the issue of the receipt, unknown to the warehouseman or to his agent who issues it, a statement of the fact that advances have been made or liabilities incurred and the purpose thereof is sufficient.[8]

Additional terms may be inserted by the warehouseman in the receipt as long as they are not contrary to the provisions of the Code and they do not impair his obligation of delivery or his duty of care.

When a document of title other than a bill of lading is issued without the issuer[9] having received the goods or with a misdescription of the goods, the issuer is liable for damages caused by such non-receipt or misdescription to a party to the document or to a good faith purchaser for value of the document who relied upon the description of the goods in the document.[10] Of course, to the extent that the document conspicuously indicates that the issuer does not know whether any part or all of the goods in fact were received or conformed to the description,

---

[8] UCC 7–202(2).

[9] " 'Issuer' means a bailee who issues a document except that in relation to an unaccepted delivery order it means the person who orders the possessor of goods to deliver. Issuer includes any person for whom an agent or employee purports to act in issuing a document if the agent or employee has real or apparent authority to issue documents, notwithstanding that the issuer received no goods or that the goods were misdescribed or that in any other respect the agent or employee violated his instructions." " 'Delivery order' means a written order to deliver goods directed to a warehouseman, carrier or other person who in the ordinary course of business issues warehouse receipts or bills of lading." UCC 7–102 (g)(d).

[10] This is a reflection of the law of agency illustrating the application of inherent agency power subjecting a disclosed principal to liability for the unauthorized acts of his general agent. "Under the law of Agency, when a principal appoints another as a general agent in a position where, as a part of his regular employment, he is to issue commercial documents representing chattels or choses in action only when certain facts exist or on the occurrence of a certain event, such facts or event being within the peculiar knowledge of the general agent, if A [agent] issues such commercial documents unauthorizedly and they are purchased by innocent persons for value without notice of A's impropriety, P [principal] is bound by A's conduct as though A had acted authorizedly. Examples are: the agent of a common carrier or of a warehouseman with authority to issue bills of lading or warehouse receipts on receipt of goods for carriage or storage. . . ." (Author's brackets) Joseph L. Frascona, *Agency* (Englewood Cliffs, N.J.: Prentice-Hall, Inc., 1964), pp. 66–67.

if such indication be true, or the party or purchaser otherwise has notice, the issuer is not liable for such non-receipt or misdescription of the goods. For example, the description may be in terms of marks or labels or kind, quantity or condition, or the receipt or description is qualified by "contents, condition and quality unknown," "said to contain," or the like.[11]

Duty of Care. A warehouseman is an ordinary bailee of a mutual-benefit bailment, even though a warehouseman may be licensed by statute and is called a "public warehouseman." As such, he has a duty to exercise the care of a reasonably careful man in the position of the bailee under the circumstances, and he is liable for damages for loss of, or injury to, the goods caused by his negligence in failing to exercise such care. Unless the agreement of the parties or statute provides for a higher degree of care, the warehouseman is not liable for damages which could not have been avoided by the exercise of such reasonable care. *In the absence of state statute or judicial decision to the contrary, this duty of care of a warehouseman cannot be impaired by agreement.* However, damages for the *amount* of liability in the case of loss or damage by the warehouseman's failure to exercise such care may be limited by a term in the warehouse receipt or storage agreement, which must set forth a specific liability per article or item, or value per unit of weight, beyond which the warehouseman shall not be liable. However, on the bailor's written statement that the goods are of a greater value and his written request, made at the time of signing such storage agreement or within a reasonable time after receipt of the warehouse receipt, the warehouseman must increase his liability on part or all of the goods thereunder for which he may charge increased rates based on such increased valuation but not contrary to a lawful limitation of liability contained in the warehouseman's tariff, if any. The warehouse receipt or tariff may include reasonable provisions as to time and manner of presenting claims and instituting actions based on the bailment.

Any agreement to limit the warehouseman's liability for conversion[12] of bailed goods to his own use is contrary to public policy and, therefore, ineffective. However, it should be noted very carefully that, *if the warehouseman is also in the business of buying and selling fungible goods*[13] *and he unauthorizedly sells and delivers bailed fungible goods*

---

[11] UCC 7–203.

[12] For conversion, see above, p. 193, ftn. 18.

[13] Fungible goods are goods of which any unit is, by nature or usage of trade, the equivalent of any other like unit; for example, oil in a vat. However, goods which are not fungible shall be deemed fungible for the purposes of the Code to the extent that under a particular agreement or document unlike units are treated as equivalents. UCC 1–201 (17).

to a buyer in ordinary course of business,[14] *the buyer acquires title to such goods free from any claim under a warehouse receipt even if the receipt is negotiable.* This is consistent with that portion of the law of sales, discussed later,[15] concerned with entrusting possession of goods to a merchant who deals in goods of that kind. The warehouseman would be liable for the conversion by unauthorized sale of such fungible goods.

Except for fungible goods and as otherwise provided in the warehouse receipt, a warehouseman must not commingle the goods represented by the various warehouse receipts outstanding, but he must keep separate the goods covered by each receipt so as to permit their identification and delivery at all times. Unless otherwise agreed, fungible goods may be commingled; they are owned in common by the various persons entitled to them. The warehouseman is liable to each owner of commingled goods for that owner's share. Should the warehouseman overissue warehouse receipts for commingled fungible goods, so that the mass of fungible goods is insufficient to meet all the receipts which the warehouseman has issued against it, the persons entitled to the mass include all holders to whom overissued receipts have been duly negotiated. In such an event, each owner is an owner in common of such mass to the extent of his pro rata share based on the proportion that the amount stated on his receipt bears to the mass. The warehouseman is liable to each owner for his respective deficiency.

A warehouse receipt may not reflect the warehouseman's intent because of its unauthorized alteration, either by its issuance with blanks and subsequent unauthorized completion, or by other unauthorized alteration. The extent of the warehouseman's liability to the holder of the altered receipt depends upon the negotiable or non-negotiable character of the receipt and the type of alteration. The warehouseman must be careful in issuing warehouse receipts, particularly negotiable receipts, so as to insure that each warehouse receipt is complete and has no blanks. As between a warehouseman whose issued *negotiable* receipt has a *blank,* and a good faith purchaser for value without notice that the blank has been filled in without authority, the warehouseman will be held liable to such purchaser *who may treat the insertion as authorized.*[16] As between the warehouseman and such purchaser the risk falls on the warehouseman who, by leaving the blank and facilitating unauthorized completion, has misled the purchaser as to the correctness of

---

[14] As to who is a buyer in ordinary course of business, see below, 283–84.

[15] See below, pp. 283–84.

[16] But see below, p. 215, for a different effect if the document is a bill of lading.

the negotiable receipt and the warehouseman is estopped or precluded from asserting such unauthorized alteration by unauthorized completion of the blank.[17] Unauthorized completion of a *blank* on a *non-negotiable* warehouse receipt is disregarded as of no effect, and the receipt is enforceable against the issuer *according to its original tenor.* Any other unauthorized alteration on *any* warehouse receipt, whether negotiable or non-negotiable, is disregarded as of no effect, and the receipt is enforceable against the issuer *according to its original tenor.*

Warehouseman's Lien. *Nature of the Lien.* By Code provision *a warehouseman automatically acquires a statutory specific, possessory lien against the bailor on the goods covered by the warehouse receipt or on the proceeds thereof*[18] *in his possession,* "for charges for storage or transportation (including demurrage and terminal charges), insurance, labor, or charges present or future in relation to the goods, and for expenses necessary for preservation of the goods or reasonably incurred in their sale pursuant to law."[19] It is not necessary that the receipt refer to such lien; all persons have constructive notice of the law on this point and they take warehouse receipts subject to such lien. Should the warehouseman desire to increase the lien on such goods against the person on whose account the goods are held[20] to assure payment by such person of his liability for like charges and expenses for *other* goods, whether or not delivered to the warehouseman, then in order that holders of a *non-negotiable* warehouse receipt are put on notice of such a *general*[21] lien it is necessary that the warehouse receipt so state such lien for such additional charges and expenses. If the warehouse receipt is *negotiable,* as to persons to whom the receipt has been *negotiated*[22] the "warehouseman's lien is limited to charges in an amount or at a rate specified on the receipt or if no charges are so specified then to a reasonable charge for storage of the goods covered by the receipt subsequent to the date of the receipt."[23] Also, should the warehouseman desire to reserve a security interest against the bailor in the goods for a maximum amount for charges other than those just

---

[17] See below, p. 396–97, for similar reasoning when a material alteration of a negotiable instrument has been caused by the negligence of the drawer or maker.

[18] The proceeds may result from a proper sale of the goods by the warehouseman.

[19] UCC 7–209(1).

[20] The person on whose account the goods are held may be the bailor or a purchaser of the warehouse receipt from the bailor.

[21] It is a general lien because it is on goods on which services for the additional charges have not been rendered.

[22] For negotiation, see below, pp. 221–23.

[23] UCC 7–209(1).

mentioned, the receipt must so state such security interest and the maximum amount. Thus, the warehouseman may have advanced a loan of money to the bailor apart from the warehousing transaction.[24]

A warehouseman's lien is not so broad as a carrier's lien, discussed later,[25] the extent of the increased breadth of the carrier's lien depending on whether or not the carrier was required by law to receive the goods for transportation. The above warehouseman's lien is, to the extent indicated, effective against the bailor and subsequent third persons holding the warehouse receipt. However, the effect of the lien on parties with an interest in the goods *prior* to the lien varies. (O owns goods which are stolen by T and bailed to W, a warehouseman. Or O has entrusted his goods to M, a merchant dealing in such goods, with authority to sell the goods, and M unauthorizedly bailed them to W, a warehouseman.) The warehouseman's lien is not effective against a person who, *before* issuance of the receipt, had a legal interest or a perfected security interest[26] in the goods and who has not consented to nor authorized such bailment nor is precluded by his conduct from asserting his interest in the bailed goods.[27] Thus, in the first illustration given, T's theft of the goods from O and bailment to W created a lien effective as against T but ineffective as against O. O owns the goods and has not, by his conduct, jeopardized his interest in those goods and, therefore, W's lien is ineffective as to him.[28] However, his conduct may cause W's lien to be effective against him; the second illustration is an example. For conduct by a person prior to the bailment which causes the warehouseman's lien to be effective as against him, see later discussion.[29] Until the lien on the bailed goods is satisfied, the warehouseman is not obligated to deliver the goods. *His voluntary delivery of the goods or his unjustified refusal to deliver them terminates his lien on such goods.*

We have observed that the warehouseman's lien may be on the proceeds resulting from his proper sale of the bailed goods. Such sale terminates storage and may result from the exercise of the warehouse-

---

[24] Under UCC 7–209, *Comment 2:* "Such a security interest arises out of relations between the parties other than bailment for storage or transportation, as where the bailee assumes the role of financier or performs a manufacturing operation, extending credit in reliance upon the goods covered by the receipt. Such a security interest is not a statutory lien" (UCC 9–310), but is a regular security interest under Article 9 of the Code.

[25] See below, pp. 215–17.

[26] For perfected security interest, see below, p. 745.

[27] UCC 7–209(3), 7–503(1). But compare UCC 7–307(2).

[28] Compare the result if it were a carrier's lien instead of a warehouseman's lien. See below, pp. 215–17.

[29] See below, pp. 224 ff.

man's option to terminate storage under various circumstances, either for reasons other than non-payment of storage charges or because of non-payment of storage charges. First, termination of storage and sale other than for non-payment will be discussed and then sale in enforcement of the warehouseman's lien for non-payment.

Termination of Storage. First, the warehouseman may, on notifying the person on whose account the goods are held or any other person known to claim an interest in the goods, require that the goods be removed from the warehouse on the expiration of the period of storage fixed in the receipt, or, if there is no such fixed period, then within a period of time stated in the notification but which is not less than 30 days after the notification. If the goods are not removed before the expiration of such period, the warehouseman has the right to advertise and sell the goods in the same way as he would sell goods in the enforcement of his warehouseman's lien. The warehouseman's right to terminate storage includes a right to demand payment of storage charges, which demand may be included in the notification of termination of storage. But the warehouseman's right to terminate storage exists independently of any such right to payment. Most warehousing is for an indefinite term, terminable by delivery of the goods to the bailor on his reasonable demand. *Second,* the warehouseman may, in good faith, believe that the goods are about to *deteriorate or decline in value to less than the amount of his lien within the above-described period for notification, advertisment and sale.* If he so believes, he may specify in the notification any reasonable shorter time for removal of the goods. If the goods are not removed before the expiration of the specified shorter period of time, the warehouseman may sell them at public sale held not less than one week after a single advertisement or posting. *Third,* if the warehouseman had no notice at the time of deposit of the goods with him of a quality or condition of such goods which makes them a hazard to other stored property, to the warehouse, or to persons, he may, without advertisement and on reasonable notification to all persons known to claim an interest in the goods, sell the goods at public or private sale. If, after reasonable effort, he is unable to sell the hazardous goods, he may dispose of them in any lawful manner; he does not thereby incur any liability by reason of such disposition. The warehouseman's right of removal of stored goods is, however, subject to state regulatory statutes and their implementing regulations. For example, some state statutes forbid a warehouseman from ordering removal of goods for the purpose of discriminating among customers. Also, should any person who is entitled to the goods duly demand them at any time prior to sale or other disposition as described above, the warehouseman must deliver the goods to that person on payment of his lien for charges. If sale occurs, the warehouseman may utilize so much of the proceeds as is sufficient to satisfy his lien and, if there are any proceeds remaining, he must hold the balance for delivery on the demand of any person to whom he would have been bound to deliver the goods.

Enforcement of the Lien. In addition to all other rights allowed by law to a creditor against his debtor, a warehouseman has a right to enforce his lien by sale of the bailed goods after giving proper notification. It is important to determine at the outset whether the goods to be sold are commercially stored, i.e., stored by a merchant in the course of his business, or non-commercially stored, i.e., principally by private owners of household goods. The warehouseman's sale of commercially stored goods is faster, more flexible and less detailed in its requirements. While the warehouseman *may,* instead of selling under the rules for commercially stored goods, sell under the more detailed rules for non-commercial storage if he wishes, nevertheless if the goods are non-commercially stored he *must* follow the detailed rules for sale of the goods in non-commercial storage. The rules for sale of each type of goods differ only in the kind and content of notification of the sale and in the need for advertisement in a sale of non-commercially stored goods. First the rules governing solely sale of commercially stored goods will be discussed, then the rules governing solely sale of non-commercially stored goods, and finally the rules applicable to both commercially and non-commercially stored goods.

With respect to commercially stored goods, the warehouseman may enforce his lien by public or private sale of the goods after *notifying* all persons known to claim an interest in the goods. "A person 'notifies' or 'gives' a notice or notification to another by taking such steps as may be reasonably required to inform the other in ordinary course whether or not such other actually comes to know of it."[30] Thus, notification here means proper *sending* of the notice; it is not necessary that the addressees *receive* such notice. The notification must include a statement of the amount due, the nature of the proposed sale, and if it is to be a public sale the time and place of the public sale. *The sale of the goods must be commercially reasonable* and it may be in block or in parcels, at any time or place, and on any terms. He sells in a commercially reasonable manner: if he sells the goods in the usual manner in any recognized market therefor; or if he sells at the price current in such market

---

[30] UCC 1–201 (26).

at the time of his sale; or if he has otherwise sold in conformity with commercially reasonable practices among dealers in the type of goods sold. However, a sale of more goods than are apparently necessary to be offered for sale in order to insure satisfaction of the obligation is not commercially reasonable, except in cases covered by the preceding sentence. The fact that a better price could have been obtained by a sale at a different time or in a different method from that selected by the warehouseman is not of itself sufficient to establish that the sale was not made in a commercially reasonable manner.

With respect to non-commercially stored goods, the warehouseman's lien may be enforced only as follows:

(a) All persons known to claim an interest in the goods must be notified.

(b) The notification must be delivered in person or sent by registered or certified letter to the last known address of any person to be notified.

(c) The notification must include an itemized statement of the claim, a description of the goods subject to the lien, a demand for payment within a specified time not less than ten days after receipt of the notification, and a conspicuous statement that unless the claim is paid within that time the goods will be advertised for sale and sold by auction at a specified time and place.

(d) The sale must conform to the terms of the notification.

(e) The sale must be held at the nearest suitable place to that where the goods are held or stored.

(f) After the expiration of the time given in the notification, an advertisement of the sale must be published once a week for two weeks consecutively in a newspaper of general circulation where the sale is to be held. The advertisement must include a description of the goods, the name of the person on whose account they are being held, and the time and place of the sale. The sale must take place at least fifteen days after the first publication. If there is no newspaper of general circulation where the sale is to be held, the advertisement must be posted at least ten days before the sale in not less than six conspicuous places in the neighborhood of the proposed sale.[31]

The following discussion applies to all stored goods, whether commercially or non-commercially stored. It should be noted very carefully that, *despite non-compliance by the warehouseman with the rules for sale, a good faith purchaser for value takes the goods free of any rights of persons against whom the lien was valid.* (O stored his goods with W, a warehouseman. On W's enforcement of his lien and sale to B, a good faith purchaser for value, B acquires a title to the goods valid against O. However, if T stole O's goods and stored them with W, a warehouseman innocent of the theft, who then enforced his lien and

---

[31] UCC 7–210(2).

sold the goods to P, a good faith purchaser for value without notice of T's theft, P has a good title as against T but not as against O.[32]) However, the warehouseman is liable for damages caused by his failure to comply with requirements for sale and, in the case of willful violation, he is liable for conversion.[33] The warehouseman may utilize so much of the proceeds as is sufficient to satisfy his lien and, if there are any proceeds remaining, he must hold the balance for delivery on demand to any person to whom he would have been bound to deliver the goods. The warehouseman may buy at any *public* sale. If, before the sale, any person claiming a right in the goods wishes to pay the amount necessary to satisfy the lien and the reasonable expenses incurred by the warehouseman in the enforcement of his lien prior to sale, he may do so and the goods must not be sold; instead, they must be retained by the warehouseman subject to the terms of the warehouse receipt and subject to the Code rules on documents of title.

Bills of Lading Only

Form. The bill of lading issued by a carrier may take a variety of forms depending upon its purpose with consequent differing liability thereunder.

Through Bills of Lading. The bill may be a through bill of lading, which is a bill embodying an undertaking to be performed in part by persons other than the issuer. Such persons may be the issuer's agents or connecting carriers.[34] (D delivers goods to R railroad for delivery to a point not served by R but served by S railroad. R may issue a through bill of lading because R undertook the duty of transporting the goods which will occur over its own lines and over lines owned by S.)

The Code does not require that a through bill be issued in such a case, but its issuance affects the rights and liabilities of the issuer (initial carrier), its agents and connecting carriers. When the issuer's agent or a connecting carrier receives the goods covered by a through bill of lading, such person holds the goods under the terms of the through bill and he has the issuer's obligation to perform thereunder while the goods are in his possession. Such person discharges his obligation under the document by his delivery of the goods to another such agent or

---

[32] Compare the result if it were a carrier's lien instead of a warehouseman's lien; see below, p. 216. W is not liable to P for breach of warranty of title; see below, pp. 287–88.

[33] For discussion of conversion, see above, p. 193, ftn. 18.

[34] The carrier who first receives the goods for shipment is called the "initial carrier"; the other carriers handling the goods are called "connecting carriers."

connecting carrier pursuant to the document and he is not liable thereafter for subsequent breach under the document by such other person. Accordingly, the issuer is liable not only for *his* own breach of obligation under the document, but also for breach thereunder by his agent or *any* connecting carrier while the goods are in such person's possession if such person's breach would subject the latter to liability thereunder. In other words, the initial carrier has the liability of its agent or any connecting carrier for loss which occurred while the goods were in either's possession.[35] *This liability of the issuer of the through bill for its agent or any connecting carrier cannot be varied by agreement;* although to the extent that the bill covers an undertaking to be performed overseas or in territory not contiguous to the continental United States or an undertaking including matters other than transportation, this liability may be varied by agreement. If the issuer has been held liable under the through bill for loss occurring while the goods were in the possession of such agent or connecting carrier, the issuer has a right to recover from such agent or connecting carrier the amount which the issuer has paid or may be required to pay for such breach, together with any expense reasonably incurred by the issuer in defending any action brought by anyone entitled to recover on the document therefor. Proof of the issuer's liability for such loss may be established by any receipt, judgment, or transcript thereof.

Bills of Lading in a Set. The issuance of a bill of lading in a set of parts is prohibited, *except where customary in overseas transportation,* and the issuer is liable for damages caused by unlawful issuance. However, what is the form and legal effect of a *lawfully* issued bill in a set of parts? *Where customary in overseas transportation,* the bill may be lawfully issued in a set of parts if each part is numbered and expressed to be valid only if the goods have not been delivered against any other part. When so lawfully issued, the whole of the parts constitutes one bill. The bailee has the obligation of making delivery to the first holder who presents a part of the lawfully issued bill to the bailee, and such delivery discharges the bailee's obligation on the whole bill and on its parts still outstanding.

---

[35] "Where the obligations or standards applicable to different parties bound by a document of title are different, the initial carrier's responsibility for portions of the journey not on its own lines will be determined by the standards appropriate to the connecting carrier. Thus a land carrier issuing a through bill of lading involving water carriage at a later stage will have the benefit of the water carrier's immunity from liability for negligence of its servants in navigating the vessel, where the law provides such an immunity for water carriers and the loss occurred while the goods were in the water carrier's possession." UCC 7–302, *Comment 3.*

A single part of the lawfully issued bill may be negotiated or transferred, with a resulting legal effect on the person so negotiating or transferring a part and on the person acquiring the part. With respect to the person negotiating or transferring a part of the lawfully issued bill, the part is treated as if it were the whole set or a single bill of lading, and he is liable to a holder of that part as though it were a single bill. With respect to subsequent holders of different parts of a lawfully issued bill to whom the parts have been negotiated, the first person to whom a part has been negotiated prevails as to the entire document and the goods covered under it as against all later holders of other parts. Should a later holder of another part receive the covered goods from the carrier, even if received in good faith, he holds the goods subject to the prior holder's paramount right to them. The carrier's delivery to such later holder on surrender of his part discharges the carrier's obligation.[36]

Destination Bills of Lading. High-speed carriers may cause the transported goods to arrive at the destination point before the arrival there of documents for such goods issued by the carrier when such goods were initially delivered to the carrier for transportation. This requires storage of such goods by the carrier until the documents are received by the consignee at the destination point and presented for such goods, and also impedes the consignee buyer and the financing agency used by him from the use of such goods and in financing their purchase. Accordingly, instead of the consignor obtaining a bill of lading from the carrier on delivery of goods to it for shipment, he may request the carrier to issue a bill of lading at destination or any other place and to any person as indicated in the consignor's request.[37] Such a bill of lading is called a "destination bill." A destination bill may be issued by a carrier in exchange for the surrender of an ordinary bill of lading, previously issued by the carrier on its receipt of goods for shipment, upon the request of anyone entitled as against the carrier to

---

[36] "The statement of the legal effect of a lawfully issued set is in accord with existing commercial law relating to maritime and other overseas bills. This law has been codified in the Hague and Warsaw Conventions and in the Carriage of Goods by Sea Act, the provisions of which would ordinarily govern in situations where bills in a set are recognized by this Article." UCC 7–304, *Comment.*

[37] "Financing of shipments under this plan would be handled as follows: seller at San Francisco delivers the goods to an airline with instructions to issue a bill in New York to a named bank. Seller receives a receipt embodying this undertaking to issue a destination bill. Airline wires its New York freight agent to issue the bill as instructed by the seller. Seller wires the New York bank a draft on buyer. New York bank indorses the bill to buyer when he honors the draft. Normally seller would act through his own bank in San Francisco, which would extend him credit in reliance on the airline's contract to deliver a bill to the order of its New York correspondent." UCC 7–305, *Comment.*

control the goods while in transit. The Code permits the carrier to issue a destination bill; but the carrier has no legal obligation to do so.

Diversion of Transported Goods. The carrier's obligation is to deliver the transported goods to the person or destination as indicated in its issued bill of lading; it is liable for misdelivery. However, unless the bill of lading otherwise provides, the carrier may divert the goods and thereby effect a reconsignment by delivering them otherwise than as stated in the bill in accordance with instructions from any one of certain persons entitled to control the goods while in transit. Such persons are:

(a) the holder of a negotiable bill; or

(b) the consignor on a non-negotiable bill notwithstanding contrary instructions from the consignee; or

(c) the consignee on a non-negotiable bill in the absence of contrary instructions from the consignor, if the goods have arrived at the billed destination or if the consignee is in possession of the bill; or

(d) the consignee on a non-negotiable bill if he is entitled as against the consignor to dispose of them.[38]

The carrier is not obligated to divert the goods as requested. But, under the Code, the carrier is protected from a charge of misdelivery for not delivering the goods to the person or at the destination indicated in the bill if it diverts the goods in accordance with instructions by the proper person under the conditions indicated. However, if a *negotiable* bill of lading is outstanding, the carrier should make a notation on the bill itself of such instructions for diversion; the carrier's failure to do so exposes it to liability to a person innocent of the reconsignment to whom the bill has been subsequently negotiated and who is entitled to hold the carrier according to the original terms on the bill.

Duty of Care. *A carrier, whether a common carrier or a private carrier, has a duty to exercise the care of a reasonably careful man in the position of the bailee under the circumstances,* and the carrier is liable for damages for loss of or injury to the goods caused by its failure to exercise such care. If the carrier is also a common carrier in intrastate commerce, as previously discussed,[39] state law in many states imposes an absolute liability upon the carrier while there is a shipper-carrier relationship. *In the absence of state statute or judicial decision to the contrary, the carrier's duty of care cannot be impaired by agreement.* However, the damages for the *amount* of liability in the case of loss or damage by the carrier's failure to exercise such care may be limited by a

---

[38] UCC 7–303(1).

[39] See above, pp. 190–91.

provision in the bill of lading "that the carrier's liability shall not exceed a value stated in the document if the carrier's rates are dependent upon value and the consignor by the carrier's tariff is afforded an opportunity to declare a higher value or a value as lawfully provided in the tariff, or where no tariff is filed he is otherwise advised of such opportunity."[40] However, any agreement to limit the carrier's liability for conversion[41] of bailed goods to his own use is contrary to public policy and, therefore, ineffective. The bill of lading or tariff may include reasonable provisions as to time and manner of presenting claims and instituting actions based on the shipment.

Except as the issuer may avoid liability by proper notation on the bill of lading, the issuer is liable for damages caused by non-receipt or misdescription of the goods or misdating to a consignee of a non-negotiable bill who has given value in good faith or to a holder to whom a negotiable bill has been duly negotiated who has relied upon the description of the goods or the date as shown in the bill. The issuer may avoid liability *for non-receipt or misdescription* of the goods by *truthfully* making a notation on the bill that the issuer *does not know* whether any part or all of the goods were received or conformed to the description. The issuer's truthful notation on the bill so qualifying such liability of the issuer may be either: by the words used in the description of the goods, as in terms of marks or labels or kind, quantity, or condition; or by qualifying the description by the words "contents or condition of contents of packages unknown," "said to contain," "shipper's weight, load and count," or the like. If the issuer *truthfully* indicates in his notation on the bill *that the information contained in the bill is based on information supplied by the shipper,* to that extent the issuer is not liable for the inaccuracy in the information contained in the bill. If the issuer's qualifying notation is not true, then, to the extent of such falsity, his liability is not avoided. When goods are loaded by an issuer who is a *common* carrier, the issuer *must* count the packages of goods if it is package freight and ascertain the kind and quantity if it is bulk freight; if the issuer then makes a notation on the bill indicating that the description was made by the shipper, as by the words "shipper's weight, load and count" or other words of similar purport, such notation is not true and, therefore, it is ineffective to avoid the issuer's liability for misdescription, except as to freight concealed by packages. When bulk freight is loaded by a shipper who makes available to the

---

[40] UCC 7–309(2).
[41] For conversion, see above, p. 193, ftn. 18.

issuer adequate facilities for weighing such freight and, in writing, requests the issuer to use such facilities in order to ascertain the kind and quantity of the bulk freight, if the issuer is a *common* carrier it *must* comply with the request within a reasonable time after receiving such request. In such a case, the issuer's notation of "shipper's weight" or words of like purport indicating that the shipper had determined the weight is untrue and, therefore, it is ineffective to avoid the issuer's liability therefor. Similarly, although the issuer is liable for damages caused by *his* improper loading of the goods, nevertheless if the goods were loaded by the shipper and the issuer's notation on the bill so indicates, as by the words "shipper's weight, load and count" or other words of like purport, the issuer is not liable for such damages; although the omission of such a notation in this instance does not imply liability for such damages. To the extent that the shipper furnishes the issuer with a description, marks, labels, number, kind, quantity, condition, and freight, the shipper guarantees their accuracy at the time of shipment and has an obligation to indemnify the issuer against damage caused by inaccuracies in such particulars. It should be noted carefully that the issuer's right of indemnity against the shipper of itself in no way limits the issuer's responsibility and liability under the contract of carriage to any person other than the shipper.

A bill of lading may not reflect the issuer's intent because of its unauthorized alteration, either by its issuance with blanks and subsequent unauthorized completion, or by other unauthorized alteration. The issuer must be careful in issuing bills of lading so as to insure that each bill is complete and has no blanks. *An unauthorized alteration of any bill of lading, whether negotiable or non-negotiable and whether by unauthorized completion of a blank or otherwise, leaves the bill enforceable according to its original tenor.* It should be noted as discussed previously[42] that, in the case of unauthorized completion of a blank in a *negotiable warehouse receipt,* the warehouseman is liable at the election of a good faith purchaser for value without notice of the unauthorized completion as though such completion had been authorized.

Carrier's Lien. *Nature of the Lien. By Code provision a carrier automatically acquires a statutory specific, possessory lien on the goods covered by a bill of lading* "for charges subsequent to the date of its receipt of the goods for storage or transportation (including demurrage and terminal charges) and for expenses necessary for preservation

---

[42] See above, p. 204.

of the goods incident to their transportation or reasonably incurred in their sale pursuant to law."[43] It is not necessary that the bill of lading refer to such lien; all persons have constructive notice of the law on this point and they take bills of lading subject to such lien. If the bill of lading is *negotiable,* then as to a purchaser for value the carrier's lien is limited to charges stated in the bill or the applicable tariffs, or if no charges are stated then to a reasonable charge.

The above carrier's lien on transported goods is effective against the consignor and subsequent third persons holding the bill of lading. However, the effect of the lien on parties with an interest in the goods *prior* to the lien depends upon whether or not the carrier was required by law to receive such goods for transportation and whether or not the carrier had notice of any lack of authority in the consignor to deliver the goods to the carrier for transportation. *When the carrier is required by law to receive such goods for transportation (common carrier), the lien is effective against the consignor or any person entitled to the goods, unless the carrier had notice that the consignor lacked authority to subject the goods to such charges and expenses.* It should be noted very carefully that such a lien is effective against an owner who never consented to such transportation. (O owns goods which are stolen by T and delivered for transportation to C, a carrier who is required by law to receive such goods for transportation and who had no notice of the theft. C's lien is effective against both O and T.) Inasmuch as the carrier was legally required to receive and accept such goods for transportation, the consignor's mere possession is sufficient to justify the carrier's lien as effective not only against the consignor but also against persons with interests in the goods, provided the carrier had no notice of the consignor's lack of authority to subject the goods to such charges and expenses. *When the carrier is not required by law to receive such goods for transportation, the lien is effective against the consignor and any person who permitted the bailor to have control or possession of the goods, unless the carrier had notice that the consignor lacked authority to subject the goods to such charges and expenses.* (O owns goods which are stolen by T and delivered for transportation to C, a carrier without notice of the theft and not legally required to receive and accept such goods. Or O delivers his goods to A to hold for him and A unauthorizedly delivers the goods for transportation to C, a carrier not legally required to receive and accept such goods. In the first illustration, C's lien is effective against T but is not effective against O. In the second illustration, whether or

---

[43] UCC 7–307(1).

not C's lien is effective against O depends upon whether or not C had notice of A's lack of authority when the goods were delivered for transportation to C. If C did not have such notice, C's lien is effective against O; if C had such notice, C's lien is not effective against O.) *Until the lien on the bailed goods is satisfied, the carrier is not obligated to deliver the goods. The carrier's voluntary delivery of the goods or its unjustified refusal to deliver them terminates its lien on such goods.*

Enforcement of the Lien. In addition to all other rights allowed by law to a creditor against his debtor, a carrier has a right to enforce its lien by sale of the bailed goods after giving proper notification. The carrier may enforce its lien on the goods by public or private sale after *notifying* all persons known to claim an interest in the goods. Thus, notification here means proper *sending* of the notice; it is not necessary that the addressees *receive* such notice. The notification must include a statement of the amount due, the nature of the proposed sale, and, if it is to be a public sale, the time and place of the public sale. *The sale of the goods must be commercially reasonable,* and it may be in block or in parcels, at any time or place, and on any terms. The carrier sells in a commercially reasonable manner: if it sells the goods in the usual manner in any recognized market therefor; or if the carrier sells at the price current in such market at the time of its sale; or if it otherwise sells in conformity with commercially reasonable practices among dealers in the type of goods sold. However, a sale of more goods than are apparently necessary to be offered for sale in order to insure satisfaction of the obligation is not commercially reasonable, except in cases covered by the preceding sentence. The fact that a better price could have been obtained by a sale at a different time or in a different method from that selected by the carrier is not of itself sufficient to establish that the sale was not made in a commercially reasonable manner. It should be noted very carefully that, *despite non-compliance by the carrier with the rules for sale, a good faith purchaser for value takes the goods free of any rights of persons against whom the lien was valid.* (O delivered his goods for transportation to C, a carrier. On C's enforcement of its lien and sale to B, a good faith purchaser for value, B acquires a title to the goods valid against O. However, suppose T stole O's goods and delivered them for transportation to C, a carrier without notice of the theft. On C's enforcement of its lien and sale to B, a good faith purchaser for value without notice of the theft, B acquires a title to the goods valid against T; but whether or not B's title is valid against O depends upon whether or not C was legally required to receive and accept such goods for transportation. If C was so legally obligated, then B acquires title valid against O. If C was not so legally obligated, then B does not acquire a title valid against O.) Compare the result in these illustrations if a warehouseman's lien instead of a carrier's lien was involved, discussed previously.[44] However, the carrier is liable for damages caused by its failure to comply with requirements for sale and, in the case of willful violation, it is liable for conversion.[45] The carrier may utilize so much of the proceeds as is sufficient to satisfy its lien and, if there are any proceeds remaining, it must hold the balance for delivery on demand to any person to whom it would have been bound to deliver the goods. The carrier may buy at any *public* sale. If, before the sale, any person claiming a right in the goods wishes to pay the amount necessary to satisfy the lien and the reasonable expenses incurred by the carrier in beginning the enforcement of its lien prior to sale, he may do so and the goods must not be sold; instead, they must be retained by the carrier subject to the terms of the bill of lading and subject to the Code rules on documents of title. If the carrier wishes, it may enforce its lien under the same less flexible and more detailed rules for sale as are required for the exercise of a warehouseman's lien against non-commercially stored goods, discussed previously.[46]

Warehouse Receipts and Bills of Lading

Various Code rules are applicable equally to warehouse receipts and bills of lading. The issuance of such documents of title and their subsequent negotiation or transfer materially affect the rights and obligations of the issuer, bailee, and holders of the documents. First the general obligations of the issuer and bailee will be discussed, then the legal effects of the issuance, negotiation, and transfer of negotiable and non-negotiable documents of title, and finally missing documents of title.

General Obligations. *Irregularities in the Issue of Documents of Title or Issuer's Conduct. The issuer*[47] *of a document of title acquires the obligations imposed by the Code for such issuance and he cannot avoid them because of irregularities in the document, violation of the law by its issuance, or his own wrongful conduct.* The issuer cannot profit from his own wrong and use such wrong as a reason to escape obligation. The obligations of the issuer of a document of title are not affected by: non-compliance of the document with the require-

---

[44] See above, p. 206.

[45] For conversion, see above, p. 193, ftn. 18.

[46] See above, p. 209.

[47] For meaning of issuer, see above, p. 202, ftn. 9.

ments of the Code or any other statute or administrative regulation regarding its issue, form, or content; the issuer's violation of laws regulating the conduct of his business; ownership by the bailee of goods covered by the document at the time the document was issued; the issuer of a purported warehouse receipt not being a warehouseman at the time of its issuance.[48]

Duplicate Document of Title or Overissue. The issuance of a duplicate document of title or the overissue of documents of title does not confer any right in the covered goods, except in the case of a lawfully issued bill of lading in a set of parts,[49] overissue of documents for fungible goods,[50] and substitutes for lost, stolen or destroyed documents.[51] A duplicate document of title is an exact copy of another document of title outstanding. The issuance of a duplicate document of title should identify the document as a duplicate by conspicuous[52] notation of such fact on its face. Overissue occurs when a document of title is issued to cover goods already represented by an outstanding document of the *same* issuer. Two or more valid documents outstanding for the same goods at the same time but issued by *different* issuers do not constitute an overissue. "Thus freight forwarders commonly issue bills of lading to their customers for small shipments to be combined into carload shipments for which the railroad will issue a bill of lading to the forwarder. So also a warehouse receipt may be outstanding against goods, and the holder of the receipt may issue delivery orders against the same goods."[53] The issuer is liable for damages caused by his overissue or failure so to identify the document as a duplicate. It should be noted carefully that the issuer's liability for such damages is to *anyone,* which in the case of a non-negotiable document of title is an exception to the general rule that a transferee acquires only the rights of his transferor. (C issues a duplicate non-negotiable bill of lading without identification of its being a duplicate to A, who knows this. C is not liable to A. If A then transferred the duplicate to B, a good faith purchaser for value without notice of the document being a duplicate,

---

[48] "For example, a bailee will not be permitted to avoid his obligation to deliver the goods . . . or his obligation of due care with respect to them . . . by taking the position that no valid 'document' was issued because he failed to file a statutory bond or did not pay stamp taxes or did not disclose the place of storage in the document." UCC 7–401, *Comment.*

[49] Discussed previously, above, pp. 211–12.

[50] Discussed previously, above, p. 204.

[51] Discussed later, below, p. 230.

[52] See below, p. 391, ftn. 33.

[53] UCC 7–402, *Comment 3.*

while under the general rule B would get only what A had and, therefore, he could not hold C liable, nevertheless, by Code exception to the general rule here, B does not have to claim through A but may recover in his own right against C.)

Obligation to Deliver, Excuse. The bailee's obligation under the document is to deliver the goods covered by the document to a "person entitled under the document," provided such person complies with two conditions. If the document is *negotiable,* such person is the *holder*[54] of the document; if it is *non-negotiable,* such person is the one to whom delivery is to be made by the terms of, or pursuant to *written* instructions under, the document. *With respect to the first condition of such person,* if he has a right in the covered goods[55] and a *negotiable* document of title is outstanding, *he must surrender the document to the bailee* for cancellation or notation of partial deliveries. On his receipt of such negotiable document, the bailee must either cancel the document or conspicuously note the partial delivery thereon, and his failure to do so will make him liable to any innocent person to whom the document is duly negotiated.[56] *The bailee has no obligation to take up a non-negotiable document of title outstanding.* The obligation of the bailee of a non-negotiable document is to deliver the goods to the consignee, in the absence of knowledge of any previous transfer of the document. *With respect to the second condition of such person,* he must satisfy the bailee's lien where the bailee so requests or where the bailee is prohibited by law from delivering the goods until the charges are paid. It should be noted that the bailee, not the claimant of the goods, has the obligation to request payment of the amount of the lien, and only if the bailee's request is refused may the bailee lawfully refuse to deliver the goods to the claimant.[57]

The bailee is excused from delivering the covered goods to a person entitled to the goods under the document if the bailee establishes any of the following:

1. Delivery of the goods to a person whose receipt was rightful as against the claimant. (O owns goods which are stolen by T and delivered for

---

[54] See below, pp. 221–22.

[55] See below, pp. 224–25, when a document of title confers no right in the covered goods against a person who, before issuance of the document, had a legal interest or a perfected security interest in the goods.

[56] A bill of lading sometimes is called "spent" if the carrier had delivered the goods to a previous holder of the bill and the carrier had not taken up and canceled the bill.

[57] Apparently, under the Code, where the bailee is prohibited by law from delivering the goods until the charges are paid, the bailee's request for payment of his lien is not necessary.

transportation to C, a carrier without notice of the theft. D is the consignee named in the bill of lading issued by C. O paid C the amount of the lien and demanded the goods from C. C's delivery of the goods to O excuses C from delivering them to D.)

2. Damage to, or delay, loss, or destruction of, the goods for which the bailee is not liable.
3. Previous sale or other disposition of the goods in lawful enforcement of the bailee's lien.[58]
4. Previous sale or other disposition of the goods in lawful termination of storage.[59]
5. The seller's exercise of his right of stoppage of delivery.[60]
6. Diversion, reconsignment or other disposition as provided under the Code[61] or tariff regulating this right.
7. The bailee has a personal defense against the claimant of the goods, as by a release, satisfaction, or any other fact.
8. Any other lawful excuse. This "may well protect a bailee who delivers pursuant to oral instructions of the person entitled, despite the requirement of 'written instructions' in the definition of 'person entitled under the document' ".[62]

A bailee who in good faith has received goods and delivered or otherwise disposed of them according to the terms of the document of title or pursuant to the Documents of Title portion of the Code is not liable therefor. Good faith here includes observance of reasonable commercial standards, inasmuch as the bailee is a commercial warehouseman or carrier. It should be noted very carefully that such immunity from liability of the bailee applies "even though the person from whom he received the goods had no authority to procure the document or to dispose of the goods and even though the person to whom he delivered the goods had no authority to receive them"[63] but was a person entitled under the document. This is an exception to the Common Law liability for the tort of conversion[64] by an *innocent* bailee.

Negotiation and Transfer. *In General.* Before getting into negotiation and transfer of documents of title, let us thoroughly understand the meaning of a very important word, "holder." A person is a holder of a document of title if two things are present. First, he must possess the document; secondly, the document must flow to him either

---

[58] See above, for warehouseman, pp. 208–10, for carrier, pp. 217–18.

[59] See above, pp. 207–8.

[60] See below, pp. 333–35.

[61] See above, p. 213.

[62] Robert Braucher, "The Uniform Commercial Code—Documents of Title," *Uniform Commercial Code Handbook.* (Chicago: American Bar Association, 1964), p. 187.

[63] UCC 7–404.

[64] For conversion, see above, p. 193, ftn. 18.

by its issuance or by indorsement. An indorsement is a person's signature made alone or with other words on a document signed by the issuer. (S delivers goods to R railroad who signs and issues a document of title naming Frank Fay as the consignee. Frank Fay's signature in blank—without any additional words—on the document is an indorsement.) *The document flows to a person on its issuance:* to him ("to Frank Fay"); to his order ("to the order of Frank Fay"); to bearer ("to bearer") and he possesses the document; or in blank without designating any person or bearer and he possesses the document. *The document flows to him by indorsement:* to him ("to John Smith. [signed] Frank Fay"); to his order ("to the order of John Smith. [signed] Frank Fay"); to bearer ("to bearer. [signed] Frank Fay") and he possesses the document; or in blank, the indorsement not designating any person or bearer ("_____. [signed] Frank Fay") and he possesses the document. A person may be a holder of a document whether it be negotiable or nonnegotiable, and whether or not it is to order. This discussion of a holder should help in understanding its very compact definition under the Code:[65] " 'Holder' means a person who is in possession of a document of title or an instrument or an investment security drawn, issued or indorsed to him or to his order or to bearer or in blank." *A document is negotiated or transferred to a holder when it is delivered to a person in such form that the transferee becomes a holder.* He has possession and the document flows to him by name, as bearer, or by the blank indorsement of the specified person to whom the document previously flowed.

A document of title is *negotiable* if, by its terms, the goods are to be delivered either *to the order of* a named person, or *to bearer.*[66] A negotiable document of title may be either negotiated or transferred without negotiation, while a non-negotiable document of title can only be transferred. The rights acquired under a *negotiable* document of title depend upon whether the document has been negotiated or transferred without negotiation. A negotiable document of title may run to the order of a named person or, by its original terms, it may run to bearer. When the negotiable document runs to the order of a named person, it can be negotiated only by that person's indorsement and delivery of the document. His indorsement may be in blank or to bearer in which case any person can negotiate the document by delivery alone; and similarly, a negotiable document originally issued to bearer may be negotiated by delivery alone. On the other hand, his indorsement may be to a specified

---

[65] UCC 1–201(20).

[66] ". . . or where recognized in overseas trade, if it runs to a named person or assigns." UCC 7–104(1) (b). See above, p. 201.

person ("to John Smith. [signed] Frank Fay"), and the latter's indorsement and delivery of the document are necessary to further negotiation of the document. In the illustration given, John Smith will have to indorse the document before it can be further negotiated. When a negotiable document running to the order of a named person is delivered to him, the effect is the same as if the document had been negotiated. In brief, *a negotiable document of title is negotiated when it is transferred in such form that the transferee becomes a holder. A negotiable document of title is "duly negotiated" when it is negotiated to a holder who purchases it in good faith, without notice of any defense against, or claim to, it on the part of any person, and for value.*[67] A person to whom a negotiable document of title has been "duly negotiated" will thereby acquire rights in the document greater than if it had merely been negotiated to him. There is an exception to "duly negotiated"; if the negotiation is not in the regular course of business or financing, or involves receiving the document in settlement or payment of a money obligation, the document cannot be considered to have been "duly negotiated." For example, the transferor of the document may not be the kind of person with whom it is reasonable to deal in that type of transaction; he is not a person in the trade. Or the transaction may be one in which a person would not engage without inquiry, as a purchase for resale at an unusually low price or the document itself manifests irregularity. While a pre-existing claim is value and the pledge of a negotiable document of title to secure a past debt is normal, nevertheless the *payment* of a debt with the document as commodity paper is not commercially regular. It should be noted in passing that the indorsement of a non-negotiable document neither makes it negotiable nor adds to the transferee's rights. Also, the naming in a negotiable bill of a person to be notified of the arrival of the goods does not limit the negotiability of the bill nor constitute notice to a purchaser thereof of any interest of such person in the goods.

Rights Acquired by Due Negotiation. A negotiable document of title stands in the place of the goods, and the bailee cannot safely deliver the goods covered by the document to anyone as long as the negotiable document of title is outstanding. It is a symbol of title to the goods. Except for those instances where a document of title to goods may be defeated, to be discussed later,[68] and except for the power of a warehouseman of fungible goods to transfer title to such goods to a

---

[67] For the meaning of value, see UCC 1–201(44).

[68] See below, pp. 224–25.

buyer in ordinary course of business, discussed previously,[69] a holder of a negotiable document of title duly negotiated to him thereby acquires the following:

(a) title to the document;
(b) title to the goods;
(c) all rights accruing under the law of agency or estoppel, including rights to goods delivered to the bailee after the document was issued; and
(d) the direct obligation of the issuer to hold or deliver the goods according to the terms of the document free of any defense or claim by him except those arising under the terms of the document or under this Article. In the case of a [negotiable] delivery order the bailee's obligation accrues only upon acceptance and the obligation acquired by the holder is that the issuer and any indorser will procure the acceptance of the bailee. (Author's brackets and italics)[70]

The Code particularizes *the following defenses and claims which the issuer cannot assert against the holder of a negotiable document of title duly negotiated to him,* (subject to those instances where a document of title to goods may be defeated). They are: any stoppage of the goods represented by the document;[71] the bailee's unauthorized surrender of the goods to some other person; the negotiation or any prior negotiation of the document was in breach of a duty; a person was deprived of possession of the document by misrepresentation, fraud, accident, mistake, duress, loss, theft, or conversion; a previous sale or other transfer of the goods or the document has been made to a third person.

We have just discussed the general rule that the holder of a negotiable document of title duly negotiated to him acquires title to the document and to the covered goods. But the rule is general because it is subject to certain instances where title to the covered goods may be defeated because of the more righteous and, therefore, superior position of a claimant *prior to such holder.* The desirability of encouraging persons to accept negotiable documents of title with assurance that a holder to whom it was duly negotiated will thereby acquire title to the goods conflicts, however, with a legal fundamental that *the owner of an interest in goods continues as the owner until by his conduct he deprives himself of such ownership either by his disposition of his interest or by his conduct precluding himself from asserting his ownership against such a holder.* Where the conduct of a prior party "introduced the goods into the stream of commerce or carried them along that stream,"[72] as

---

[69] See above, pp. 203–4.

[70] UCC 7–502.

[71] For stoppage of delivery, see below, pp. 333–35.

[72] UCC 7–503, *Comment 1.*

between him and the holder of the negotiable document duly nego-tiated to such holder, the latter prevails because of the prior party's conduct to the prejudice of such subsequent holder. However, if the prior party is not guilty of such conduct, then his interest in the covered goods should prevail over the holder of the negotiable document duly negotiated to such holder. (T steals O's goods and delivers them for transportation to C, a carrier who issues a negotiable bill of lading to T as consignee. T duly negotiates the document to H, a holder. O and H now demand the goods from C. O has title to the covered goods and he will prevail over H and against C.) Accordingly, the Code states that *the holder of a negotiable document of title duly negotiated to him acquires title to the document and to the covered goods, but title to the goods is subject to a prior claimant with either a legal interest or a perfected security interest[73] in the goods, unless certain conduct of the prior claimant with respect to possession of the goods has occurred.* The nature of that conduct therefore becomes vitally important.

A person with a legal interest or a perfected security interest in goods *subsequently* covered by *any* document of title prevails over any rights acquired under such document, and the document confers no right in the goods *against such person unless the latter:* (a) *delivered or entrusted the goods or any document of title covering them to the bailor or his nominee* (1) *with actual or apparent authority to ship, store or sell them,[74]* or (2) *with power to obtain delivery under the Code provisions on Documents of Title,[75]* or (3) *with power of disposition under this Code generally,[76] or other statute or rule of law;[77]* or (b) *acquiesced in the procurement by the bailor or his nominee of any document of title.* This applies to non-negotiable, as well as to nego-tiable, documents of title.

Delivery orders and bills of lading issued by freight forwarders are documents of title, and title to the goods thereunder may be defeated. A delivery order is "a written order to deliver goods directed to a ware-houseman, carrier or other person who in the ordinary course of busi-ness issues warehouse receipts or bills of lading."[78] For example, the holder of a bill of lading may issue a delivery order to the carrier to

---

[73] For perfected security interest, see below, p. 745.

[74] For example, see Factors, below, p. 281.

[75] See Obligation to Deliver, Excuse, above, pp. 220–21.

[76] See Voidable Title, below, p. 281; Entrusting Goods to a Merchant, below, p, 283; Protection of Buyers of Goods, below, pp. 280–84.

[77] See Transfer of Title by Estoppel, below, p. 281.

[78] UCC 7–102(1) (d).

deliver the covered goods to another person named in the delivery order. On the bailee's acceptance of a delivery order, the delivery order has the same effect as a document of title issued by the bailee, the delivery order is for all practical purposes indistinguishable from a warehouse receipt, and *the bailee now holds the goods pursuant to the delivery order and not the document of title previously issued by the bailee.* A bailee who has issued a *negotiable* document of title outstanding should not accept a delivery order without the surrender of the negotiable document of title to him and either cancelling it or making a notation conspicuously thereon that partial delivery has been made; his failure to do so makes him liable to any person to whom the document is duly negotiated, as discussed previously.[79] The bailee's obligation accrues only on his acceptance of the delivery order, and the issuer and any previous indorsers of an unaccepted delivery order have an obligation to the holder of such order to procure the bailee's acceptance. Until the bailee accepts a delivery order, he is not bound thereon and has only the obligations of his contract with the depositor of the goods with him. *Title to goods based upon an unaccepted delivery order is subject to the rights of anyone to whom a negotiable warehouse receipt or bill of lading covering the goods has been duly negotiated. Also, the title to the goods covered by an unaccepted delivery order may be defeated as indicated in the next paragraph.* It should be noted carefully, with respect to bills of lading issued by freight forwarders, that *title to the goods covered by a bill of lading issued to a freight forwarder is subject to the rights of anyone to whom a negotiable bill issued by the freight forwarder is duly negotiated,* although delivery by the carrier pursuant to its own bill of lading in accordance with the Code[80] discharges the carrier's obligation to deliver. This seems but fair inasmuch as the bailee's bill of lading issued to the freight forwarder gives notice on its face that a freight forwarder is involved, which fact gives notice that the freight forwarder may issue or may have already issued his own bills of lading for the same goods.

The rights of a "transferee" of a negotiable document of title may also be defeated. A negotiable document of title may be either negotiated or transferred, but a non-negotiable document of title may only be transferred. A negotiable document of title is negotiated by its delivery to a holder,[81] who is the person in possession of the document and to whom the document runs either originally or by indorsement.

---

[79] See above, p. 220.

[80] See above, pp. 220–21.

[81] For holder, see above, pp. 221–22.

Lack of a required indorsement on a negotiable document precludes negotiation and the person to whom the document was delivered is solely a transferee. However, "the transferee of a negotiable document of title has a specifically enforceable right to have his transferor supply any necessary indorsement but the transfer becomes a negotiation only as of the time the indorsement is supplied."[82] A person is also a transferee of a negotiable document if, while it has been negotiated to him, it has not been "duly negotiated" to him.[83] *Thus, a transferee of a negotiable document of title is the person to whom the document has been delivered but not duly negotiated.* (T steals O's goods and delivers them for transportation to C, a carrier who issues a negotiable bill of lading to T as consignee. T delivers the bill for value to P, who is not aware of the theft. At this point P is a transferee. P then discovers the theft and obtains T's blank indorsement on the bill. P is a holder of the bill negotiated to him as of the time of T's indorsement and, since *at the time of negotiation* P knew of the theft, the bill has not been "duly negotiated" to him and he is still a transferee.) It is important to ascertain the status of the possessor of a document of title because, if he is only a *transferee,* his rights under the document are much narrower than those rights acquired by a holder of a negotiable document of title *duly negotiated* to such holder.

Rights Acquired in the Absence of Due Negotiation. A document of title can be only *transferred* if the document is non-negotiable or, if negotiable, it has not been properly indorsed. *A transferee of a document of title, whether negotiable or non-negotiable, acquires the title and rights which his transferor had or had actual authority to convey. With respect to non-negotiable documents of title, the transferee has the right to notify the bailee of the transfer of the document to him and thereby acquire whatever obligation the bailee owed to the transferor of the bill immediately before notification. Before such notification is given to the bailee* by the transferee or transferor, the transferee's rights under the non-negotiable document of title and his right to acquire the bailee's obligations to his transferor may be defeated by various persons. *First,* before notification to the bailee of the transfer to the transferee, the transferor's creditors may exercise their right to avoid the sale by the transferor, discussed later under Sales,[84] and thereby defeat the transferee's rights. *Second,* before notification to the bailee of

[82] UCC 7–506.

[83] UCC 7–504(1). For negotiation, see above, pp. 222–23; for due negotiation, see above, p. 223.

[84] See below, pp. 279–80.

the transfer to the transferee, the transferor may sell the goods to a buyer in ordinary course of business and the bailee either delivers the goods to such buyer or receives notification of such buyer's rights, thereby defeating the transferee's rights. *Third,* before notification to the bailee of the transfer to the transferee, the bailee may deal in good faith with the transferor, as by delivering the goods to him or otherwise, and thereby defeat the transferee's rights.

There are other instances in the case of non-negotiable documents of title where the consignee's rights under the document may be defeated either by the consignor or by the seller of shipped goods. The consignor of shipped goods under a non-negotiable bill of lading may divert the goods or otherwise change the shipping instructions, discussed previously,[85] which causes the bailee not to deliver the goods to the consignee, thereby defeating the consignee's rights against the bailee. Should the diverted or reshipped goods be delivered to a buyer in ordinary course of business, the consignee's title to the goods is thereby defeated, and the new buyer consignee acquires the title. The seller's exercise of his right to stoppage in transit or otherwise and the exercise of his legal remedies in the disposition of the goods thereby defeats the consignee's rights against the bailee and the consignee's rights against the goods. A bailee honoring the seller's instructions is entitled to be indemnified by the seller against any resulting loss or expense. However, it should be noted that the bailee cannot be compelled to deliver to creditors of the person who deposited with the bailee the goods covered by a *negotiable* document of title outstanding without the surrender, or the legal impounding, of such document. But there is an exception; a person with a legal interest or a perfected security interest in the goods who has not by his conduct caused the loss of his interest[86] has the right to such goods and, therefore, *his* creditors can reach such goods and obtain them from the carrier *without* having to surrender any document of title outstanding. Under the Code:

Except where the document was originally issued upon delivery of the goods by a person who had no power to dispose of them,[87] no lien attaches by virtue of any judicial process to goods in the possession of a bailee for which a *negotiable* document of title is outstanding unless the document be first surrendered to the bailee or its negotiation enjoined, and the bailee shall not be

---

[85] See above, p. 213.

[86] For when conduct causes loss of interest, see above, pp. 224–25.

[87] UCC 7–602, *Comment 1:* "However, if the document was issued upon deposit of the goods by a person who had no power to dispose of the goods so that the document is ineffective to pass title, judgment liens are valid to the extent of the debtor's interest in the goods."

compelled to deliver the goods pursuant to process until the document is surrendered to him or impounded by the court. One who purchases the document for value without notice of the process or injunction takes free of the lien imposed by judicial process. (Author's italics) [88]

Warranties. A person, other than a mere intermediary, who negotiates or transfers a document of title to a *purchaser for value* thereby makes various warranties with respect to the goods covered by the document and also with respect to the document itself, whether it be negotiable or non-negotiable. Unless otherwise agreed, his warranties are made *only* to his immediate purchaser. The transfer or negotiation of the document warrants the express and implied warranties made in selling goods under the Sales portion of the Code. [89] To the extent that the Sales portion of the Code permits disclaimer of any warranty, the parties may so provide in their agreement. In addition, unless otherwise agreed, the person negotiating or transferring the document makes *all* of the following warranties: that the document is genuine, i.e., "free of forgery or counterfeiting"; [90] that he has no knowledge of any fact which would impair its validity or worth; that his negotiation or transfer is rightful with respect to the title to the document and the goods it represents; that his negotiation or transfer is fully effective with respect to the title to the document and the goods it represents. When the person negotiating or transferring a document of title is an intermediary entrusted with the document, he thereby makes by such negotiation or transfer limited warranties and only with respect to the document. Under the Code: [91] "A collecting bank [92] or other intermediary [93] known to be entrusted with documents on behalf of another or with collection of a draft or other claim against delivery of documents warrants by such delivery of the document only its own good faith and authority. This rule applies even though the intermediary has purchased or made advances against the claim or draft to be collected."

With respect to indorsements on a document of title, whether negotiable or non-negotiable, the purpose of an indorsement is to perfect the rights of the transferee under the document rather than to impose any obligation upon the indorser. Accordingly, "The indorsement of a docu-

---

[88] UCC 7–602.

[89] See below, pp. 285–301.

[90] UCC 1–201(18).

[91] UCC 7–508.

[92] UCC 4–105(d): "'Collecting bank' means any bank handling the item for collection except the payor bank."

[93] UCC 4–105(c): "'Intermediary bank' means any bank to which an item is transferred in course of collection except the depositary or payor bank."

ment of title *issued by a bailee* does not make the indorser liable for any default by the bailee or by previous indorsers." (Author's italics)[94] However, there is "one case in which an indorsement given for value guarantees future action, namely, that in which the bailee has not yet become liable upon the document at the time of the indorsement. Under such circumstances the indorser, of course, engages that appropriate honor of the document by the bailee will occur."[95] We have already seen[96] that among the rights which a holder acquires under an *unaccepted negotiable delivery order*[97] duly negotiated to him is the obligation that the issuer and any indorser will procure the acceptance of the delivery order by the bailee. Once the bailee accepts the delivery order, the indorser has no further obligation under the delivery order.

Missing Documents of Title.   A document of title may be missing because it has been lost, stolen, or destroyed. If a document of title has been lost, stolen, or destroyed, action may be taken either by the bailee or by a court. The bailee may, without court order, deliver the goods to a person claiming under a missing document of title, but by doing so the bailee becomes liable to any person injured thereby. Also, if the bailee does not act in good faith in making such delivery without court order, he becomes liable for conversion. He makes delivery in good faith without court order and is not liable for conversion if either the delivery was made in accordance with a filed classification or tariff, or, where no classification or tariff is filed, the claimant posts security with the bailee in an amount at least double the value of the goods at the time of posting to indemnify any person injured by the delivery who files a notice of claim within one year after the delivery. Alternatively, at the request of either the bailee or a claimant and on the applicant's proof that the document of title has been lost, stolen, or destroyed, a court may order either delivery of the goods or the issuance of a substitute document of title to the claimant. The bailee must comply with the court order and, therefore, he is not liable to anyone by his compliance. If the document was negotiable, the claimant must post security approved by the court to indemnify any person who may suffer loss as a result of non-surrender of the document. If the document was not negotiable, such security is not required, although the court may, in its discretion, order payment of the bailee's reasonable costs and counsel fees. It should be noted that, unless otherwise indicated, the above

---

[94] UCC 7–505.

[95] UCC 7–505, *Comment.*

[96] See above, p. 226.

[97] For meaning of delivery order, see above p. 225.

discussion applies to all documents of title, whether negotiable or non-negotiable.

APPENDIX TO PART THREE (B)

REFERENCES

1. Anderson, Ronald A. *Anderson's Uniform Commercial Code.* 2d ed. Rochester: Lawyers Cooperative Publishing Co., 1970.
2. Braucher, Robert, revised by Davenport, "The Uniform Commercial Code— Documents of Title," in *Uniform Commercial Code Handbook 173.* Chicago: American Bar Association, 1964.
3. Goddard, Edwin C. *Outlines of the Law of Bailments and Carriers.* 2d ed., Charles E. Cullen. Chicago: Callaghan & Co., 1928.
4. *Uniform Laws Annotated,* Article 7, Uniform Commercial Code, 1962.

PROBLEMS

1. (a) What are the requisites of a bailment?
   (b) Distinguish a bailment from the following:
       (1) Present sale.
       (2) Mortgage.
       (3) Pledge.
   (c) May a bailment be created other than by agreement? Explain.
   (d) What is the difference between a public or special bailment and an ordinary or private bailment?
2. X requested Y for the use of Y's horse for a month as a favor to X. Y agreed to do the favor.
   (1) Is there a bailment? Why?
   (2) If Y later refused to deliver the horse to X, would X have any rights against Y? Why?
   (3) If Y delivered the horse to X, could Y require delivery of the horse to him after X had it one week only? Why?
   (4) If Y delivered the horse to X, what degree of care of the horse must X exercise?
   (5) While X has the horse, Y is called away for a week. Y is glad that X is taking care of the horse in Y's absence, inasmuch as Y would have had to pay someone to care for the horse. Does this change in circumstances alter X's duty of care? Why?
3. (a) A delivered goods to B for storage at an agreed charge. While in B's warehouse, the goods were destroyed without any fault of B.

(1) Is B liable to A for the loss of the goods?

(2) Why?

(b) X entered Y's restaurant, hung his hat and coat upon a coat hook on a nearby hanger, and ordered a meal. The coat was stolen while X was having his meal.

(1) Is Y liable to X for the loss of the coat? Why?

(2) If, instead of hanging his coat upon the hook, he had checked it with a checkroom attendant provided by the restaurant management and the coat were stolen, would the restaurant be liable for the loss? Why?

4. (a) A is a guest for the night at a hotel which is owned and operated by B.

(1) What is B's liability for the safety of A's property?

(2) How can B limit this liability?

(b) X delivers goods to Y, a common carrier of goods, for immediate shipment to Z.

(1) What is Y's liability for the safety of such goods?

(2) List any exceptions to this liability.

(3) How may Y limit such liability?

5. A delivers goods to B, a common carrier, in X city for shipment to C in Y city with instructions that such goods are to be held at X for five days and then sent on their way. During the five days, part of the goods is damaged without any negligence by B. After the expiration of five days and while the goods are being transported by B, further damage occurs without any negligence by B. While the goods are being transported by D, a connecting carrier, more damage occurs.

(1) Is B liable for such damage to the goods?

(2) Why?

6. A certified public accountant completed an out-of-town engagement and returned to his home-office city by railroad. He purchased a one-way ticket with Pullman accommodations and checked a large brief case and a suitcase as baggage. There was no excess-baggage charge. The brief case and the suitcase were carried on the same train with the accountant but for some unknown reason the brief case could not be found by the carrier at the end of the journey. No questions had been asked by the railroad agent concerning the contents of either case and the passenger had volunteered no information about them. The brief case contained working papers, the replacement of which would cost over $1,000. Is the carrier legally responsible for the loss of the brief case as baggage? (Former C.P.A. Examination question)

7. Allen rented an auto to Burt for a month. During that month the auto was destroyed in a collision with a truck owned by Carr, through the joint negligence of the servants of Burt and Carr. Allen sued Carr for damages. Could he recover? (Former C.P.A. Examination question)

8. (a) When is a bailee exempt from liability for his failure to deliver bailed goods pursuant to the bailment agreement?

(b) To what extent does a bailee have any right to use bailed goods?

(c) A delivered his automobile to B for repairs. The automobile was repaired; and B, not having his own automobile available, used A's automobile in going to a party. On the way, A's automobile was damaged in a motor vehicle accident without B's negligence.
(1) Does A have any right against B for such damage?
(2) Why?

9. (a) A delivered his truck to B under an agreement whereby B was to have the use of the truck for six months for a specified rental charge payable in advance. At the end of three months, A needed the truck and demanded its possession from B, tendering the return of one-half the rent received by him. B refused to deliver the truck to A, who forcibly repossessed the truck. What are the rights of the parties?

(b) X bailed goods to Y for one month for $100. Z stole the goods and damaged them. What are the rights of X and Y?

10. (a) What is a bill of lading?
(b) What is a straight bill of lading, and how is it distinguished from any other bill of lading?
(c) Name two documents of title other than a bill of lading.
(d) What are the rights of a holder of a bill of lading?

11. T stole goods from O and sold them to B, a good faith purchaser for value and without notice of the theft, and shipped them to B by C, a common carrier. T received from C a bill of lading drawn to the order of B and delivered it to B.
(1) If both O and B demand the goods from C, B tendering the bill to C, who is entitled to them? Why?
(2) May C assert a carrier's lien on the goods for the transportation charges? Why?
(3) If only O demands the goods, can he obtain them from C? Why?

12. A sold goods to B and shipped them to B by C, a common carrier—A receiving from C a straight bill of lading, drawn in favor of B, which he delivered to B. B sold the bill of lading to D, indorsed it in blank and delivered it to D. B then demanded the goods from C, representing that the bill had been destroyed. C delivered the goods to B without receiving the bill of lading and without knowledge of the transaction between B and D. D subsequently notified C of his possession of the bill of lading and demanded the goods.
(1) Does D have any right against C?
(2) Why?

13. O stored fungible goods in W's warehouse and obtained from W a negotiable warehouse receipt, to the order of O. W buys and sells the same kind of fungible goods.
(1) T stole the warehouse receipt from O, forged O's blank indorsement on the receipt and sold and delivered it for value to B, a purchaser innocent of the theft. B tendered the receipt to W and, at the same time as O, demanded the goods from W. Who will prevail, and why?
(2) O indorsed the receipt in blank, T stole it and sold and delivered it to B, a purchaser innocent of the theft, in satisfaction of T's debt to B.

B tendered the receipt to W and, at the same time as O, demanded the goods from W. Who will prevail and why?

(3) W misrepresented that he owned the goods and unauthorizedly sold and delivered the goods for value to X. The events in (2) above later having occurred, O and B now demand the goods from X. Who will prevail and why if:

(a) X is a good faith purchaser for value?

(b) X is a merchant who buys and sells this kind of fungible goods, and he bought the goods from W for value, innocent of the facts?

14. T stole O's goods. What is the extent of the lien of W and C if:

(1) T warehoused the goods as owner in W's warehouse, W being innocent of the facts? Explain.

(2) T shipped the goods as owner by C carrier, C being innocent of the facts? Explain.

(3) T were O's agent, instead of a thief, to whom O had delivered the goods with authority to retain them at T's establishment, and T had unauthorizedly asserted he owned the goods and warehoused or shipped the goods as indicated in (1) and (2) above? Explain.

SOME PREVIOUS C.P.A. LAW EXAMINATION QUESTIONS AND MODEL ANSWERS

MAY, 1970

No. 8 (Estimated time—20 to 25 minutes)

a. Korn, a fur coat manufacturer, wished to promote a new style of coat and approached Carter's Department Stores, Inc. with the following proposal: If Carter would allow Korn to sell the coats on a "special promotion" in Carter's store for two days, Korn would split all profits with Carter on a 50-50 basis and give Carter exclusive rights to sell the coats in the area thereafter if Carter so desired. The "special promotion" sale was to be conducted by Korn's personnel, Carter was to furnish Korn with counter space in the store and space in the fur storage vault of the store for keeping the coats during nonbusiness hours. Carter agreed to this proposition. After the close of business on the first day of the promotion, the fur storage vault having been secured in the usual manner, Carter's was burglarized and Korn's coats were stolen from the vault. Korn asserts that Carter must make good his loss.

(1) Describe the relationship between Carter and Korn.

(2) On the facts given, was Carter liable to Korn? Explain.

b. Devlin warehoused grain for Smith, Jones, and Roe, who were grain dealers. Devlin was also a grain dealer. In January, Devlin received 5,000 bushels of grain from Smith and issued a negotiable warehouse receipt to Smith for the grain. In February, Devlin received 10,000 bushels of grain from Jones and issued a negotiable warehouse receipt to Jones for the grain. In March, Devlin issued a negotiable warehouse receipt to Roe for 10,000 bushels of grain which Roe promised to deliver in April. Roe thereupon negotiated the receipt for value to Tucker. In April, there then being 15,000 bushels of grain in

Devlin's warehouse, Devlin sold and delivered 10,000 bushels to Mayberry, a local baker. Roe did not deliver the 10,000 bushels and has disappeared. Smith, Jones, and Tucker now present their receipts to Devlin and demand delivery of the grain evidenced thereby.

(1) Assuming none of the grain in the warehouse belonged to Devlin at any time, discuss the relationships, rights and liabilities between Devlin, Smith, Jones, and Tucker.

(2) Assume Devlin is insolvent. What are the rights of Smith, Jones, and Tucker in the 5,000 bushels remaining in Devlin's warehouse? May they, or any of them, recover the 10,000 bushels or their value from Mayberry? Explain.

Answer

a. (1) Korn is the owner and bailor of the coats; Carter is the bailee. There is an ordinary mutual benefit bailment between them inasmuch as both parties expect to get a benefit from the bailment. A bailment occurs when there is a delivery of goods pursuant to an agreement whereby the goods are to be returned to the bailor.

(2) No. An ordinary bailee is liable only for loss caused by his negligence, which is the failure to exercise the care of a reasonably careful man in the position of the bailee under the circumstances. The problem does not state any facts evidencing negligence by Carter.

b. (1) An ordinary mutual benefit bailment exists between Smith and Jones as bailors and Devlin as bailee. Devlin has the duty of returning 5,000 bushels of grain to Smith and 10,000 bushels to Jones on their demand and presentation of the two warehouse receipts. Devlin is liable to them for damages for breach of the bailment contract to the extent that he cannot perform his contract. Devlin wrongfully issued the negotiable warehouse receipt for 10,000 bushels to Roe for grain not received by Devlin. The problem states that this receipt was negotiated to Tucker; but it does not state whether it was "duly" negotiated to Tucker, which would occur if Tucker took it in good faith. Under the Uniform Commercial Code on Documents of Title, if the receipt was duly negotiated to Tucker, then he also has a valid claim against Devlin for breach of contract, like Smith and Jones. If not duly negotiated to Tucker, then Tucker has the rights only of Roe, his transferor, which amount to nothing because Roe never delivered the grain to Devlin.

(2) Smith and Jones are tenants in common of the 5,000 bushels. Owners of fungible goods commingled by the warehouseman bailee are tenants in common of the mass with an undivided interest therein to the extent of their individual contributions. Roe did not contribute anything, and so Tucker is not such a tenant.

Nobody may recover the 10,000 bushels or their value from Mayberry if he was a buyer in ordinary course of business. Under the Code, if fungible goods are entrusted to a merchant who deals in goods of that kind, his unauthorized sale and delivery of such goods to a buyer in ordinary course of business causes the buyer to acquire title to the goods free from any claim under a warehouse receipt.

MAY, 1960

No. 7

a. M operates a factory in which he manufactures sport shirts. His usual course of business is to have the customer furnish the cloth and patterns, while M furnishes the buttons, thread, linings, and other minor materials, in addition to performing all of the labor and machine work to make a completed garment.

    (1) Customer C delivered sufficient rare imported wool gabardine material to make up 1,000 dozen shirts for an exclusive trade. While the shirts were in process, a fire occurred in the building adjoining M's factory. The material was severely damaged by smoke and water, and there is no practical means of recovering damages from the persons at fault in causing the fire. Would M or C bear the burden of the damage done to the material? Apply the legal principles involved.

    (2) Customer D delivered sufficient standard broadcloth material for 10,000 dozen shirts. At the time of the fire M was using part of this material to complete a rush order for Customer E, knowing that there would be no difficulty in replacing the broadcloth in time to complete the order for D. Would M or D bear the burden of the damage done to the material? Apply the legal principles involved.

b. P owned a panel truck which he used to operate a parcel delivery service for several women's and children's low-priced specialty shops.

    (1) One day while he was making a delivery to an apartment house in the suburbs, a number of packages were stolen from the truck, which P had left unlocked. Would P bear the loss? Apply the legal principles involved.

    (2) Would your answer be any different if P had carefully placed a strong padlock on the truck door, which the thief had been obliged to break in order to steal the packages? Apply the legal principles involved.

    (3) Would your answer (to part 2) be different if P had been engaged by an exclusive jewelry store rather than a group of specialty shops? Apply the legal principles involved.

Answer

a. (1) C. This is a mutual-benefit bailment. There has been a delivery of goods pursuant to an agreement whereby the goods were to be returned to the bailor or pursuant to his direction in accordance with the bailment agreement. Each of the parties primarily expected a benefit at the time of the formation of the bailment agreement, C to have the shirts made and M to be paid for doing so. In a mutual-benefit bailment, the bailee has the duty to use the care of a reasonably careful man in the position of the bailee under the circumstances. Since M was not negligent, therefore C must bear the loss.

    (2) M. There is also a mutual-benefit bailment of D's goods. A bailee's deviation from the terms of the bailment in the use of the bailed goods subjects him to liability for damage to such goods, irrespective of no negligence on his part. Therefore, M is liable for the loss.

b. (1) Yes. This is also a mutual-benefit bailment of the packages. P's conduct in leaving the truck door unlocked was negligence in this type of bailment which caused the loss of the packages. Therefore, P is liable for the loss.

(2) Yes. Under these circumstances, P has exercised proper care and, not being negligent, he is not liable for the loss.

(3) Yes. The circumstances determine the care to be exercised by a mutual-benefit bailee. The very largely increased value of the goods here requires greater security than a strong padlock, such as a special set of locks or an alarm system.

C. SALES

Chapter IV

FORMATION OF THE CONTRACT

Subject Matter **Code Coverage.** THE law of sales of goods is governed by Article 2 of the Uniform Commercial Code entitled "Sales," which is concerned only with *transactions for the sale of goods.* That Article does not apply to transactions involving goods which are intended to operate only as security transactions; such transactions are considered under Article 9 on Secured Transactions. Goods may be a part of a stock in trade of a business and, when transferred in bulk by sale or otherwise, Article 6 of the Uniform Commercial Code entitled "Bulk Transfers" is applicable in order to prevent commercial fraud. First Sales under Article 2, and then Bulk Transfers under Article 6, will be discussed.

Goods. " 'Goods' means all things (including specially manufactured goods) which are movable at the time of identification to the contract for sale other than the money in which the price is to be paid, investment securities (Article 8) and things in action. 'Goods' also includes the unborn young of animals and growing crops and other identified things attached to realty as described in the section on goods to be severed from realty (Section 2–107)."[1] It should be noted carefully under UCC 2–107(1) that if the *seller* is to sever those enumerated items (oil, minerals, structure) related to the land, the contract is for the sale of goods and is under this Article of the Code; but if the

---

[1] UCC 2–105(1). UCC 2–107: "Goods to Be Severed From Realty: Recording. (1) A contract for the sale of minerals or the like (including oil and gas) or a structure or its materials to be removed from realty is a contract for the sale of goods within this Article if they are to be severed *by the seller* but until severance a purported present sale thereof which is not effective as a transfer of an interest in land is effective only as a contract to sell.

(2) A contract for the sale apart from the land of growing crops or other things attached to realty and capable of severance without material harm thereto but not described in subsection (1) or of timber to be cut is a contract for the sale of goods within this Article whether the subject matter is to be severed *by the buyer or by the seller* even though it forms part of the realty at the time of contracting, and the parties can by identification effect a present sale before severance.

(3) The provisions of this section are subject to any third party rights provided by the law relating to realty records, and the contract for sale may be executed and recorded as a document transferring an interest in land and shall then constitute notice to third parties of the buyer's rights under the contract for sale." (Author's italics)

243

buyer is to sever such items, the contract affects an interest in land, it is not a contract for the sale of goods under the Code, and it comes within that portion of the statute of frauds concerned with the transfer of an interest in land.[2] Subsection 2 of UCC 2–107 is concerned with different items related to the land (growing crops or other things attached to realty and capable of severance without material harm thereto and not included in subsection (1)) which may be severed by either the seller *or* the buyer, and a contract for their sale is for goods and is under the Code. Inasmuch as a third person may become a subsequent purchaser or creditor of the land innocent of the contract for sale of the goods related to the land and thereby adversely affect the original buyer's interest in the goods under his contract of purchase, the original buyer of goods to be severed from the realty may protect his interest in such goods from such subsequent impairment by recording his contract for sale against the land and thereby put all third persons on constructive notice of the contract. While money bargained for as a medium of exchange is not goods, it is goods if bargained for as a commodity.

The Code introduces the two new terms "lot" and "commercial unit." "Lot" means "a parcel or a single article which is the subject matter of a separate sale or delivery, whether or not it is sufficient to perform the contract."[3] For example, each chair in a contract for sale of 100 chairs is a lot; it is a single item. A "commercial unit" is "such a unit of goods as by commercial usage is a single whole for purposes of sale and division of which materially impairs its character or value on the market or use."[4] It may be a single unit, as a machine; a set of articles, as a suite of furniture or an assortment of sizes; a quantity, as a bale, gross, or carload; or any other unit treated in use or in the relevant market as a single whole.

Contracts for Sale

The transaction for the sale of goods is called a "contract for sale," which includes both a "present sale" of goods and a "contract to sell" goods at a future time. If the title to the goods passes from the seller to the buyer at the time the contract is made, the transaction is a present sale. In a contract to sell, the title does not pass at the time the contract is made but is to pass in the future. Inasmuch as the title to goods may be transferred as a gift, which does not come under the Code, the Code uses the term "sale" to mean the passing of title for a price.

---

[2] See above, pp. 110–11.

[3] UCC 2–105(5).

[4] UCC 2–105(6).

"Existing and Identified," and "Future" Goods.
Kinds of Goods The kind of goods in a contract for sale is determined as of the time the contract is made. If the goods exist *and* are identified to the contract at that time, they are called "existing and identified goods"; if not, they are called "future goods." It is irrelevant whether the seller has the potentiality of performing his contract. The kind of goods is important because *goods must be both existing and identified to the contract before any interest in them can pass.* An exception is a contract for sale of a part interest in existing and identified goods, discussed immediately below. Accordingly, a *contract to sell* goods may be concerned with existing and identified goods, the title to which is to be transferred at a future time, or it may involve future goods. When the future goods are subsequently identified to the contract, only then can title to such goods pass to the buyer. A *present sale* of goods involves only existing and identified goods or a part interest in existing and identified goods. Although the intention of the buyer and seller governs, nevertheless there cannot be a present sale of future goods. Should the parties' language attempt to do this, the purported present sale operates as a contract to sell.[5]

Sale of Part Interest in Goods. As an exception to the rule that goods must be existing and identified before any interest in them can pass, a present sale may occur of a part interest in existing and identified goods. (S owns an automobile and contracted for the sale to B of a one-half share in such automobile. The automobile is existing and identified and, although the undivided share exists but is not identified, nevertheless there is a present sale to B of a one-half share in the automobile.)

Fungible Goods. Existing and identified goods which are fungible in nature may also be the object of a present sale of an undivided share therein. " 'Fungible' with respect to goods or securities means goods or securities of which any unit is, by nature or usage of trade, the equivalent of any other like unit. Goods which are not fungible shall be deemed fungible for the purposes of this Act to the extent that under a particular agreement or document unlike units are treated as equivalents."[6] Oil or wine in a vat, grain in a bin, cotton or wool in a heap, are illustrative of fungible goods. However, while several bales of cotton, several barrels of butter, or several barrels of flour do not constitute fungible goods, nevertheless the parties may by their agreement specify

---

[5] UCC 2–105(2).
[6] UCC 1–201(17).

that such goods shall be considered as fungible goods, in which case they will be so considered. "An undivided share in an identified bulk of fungible goods is sufficiently identified to be sold although the quantity of the bulk is not determined. Any agreed proportion of such a bulk or any quantity thereof agreed upon by number, weight or other measure may to the extent of the seller's interest in the bulk be sold to the buyer who then becomes an owner in common."[7] (B examines S's 1,000 gallon vat of wine. If B contracts with S for the sale of 500 gallons from that vat, there is a present sale of 500 gallons to B. However, if B contracts with S for the purchase of 500 gallons of wine like that in the vat, there is a contract to sell future goods because there was no intent to sell an undivided share *of that* existing and identified wine but rather future wine *like that* in the vat.)

Contracts between Merchants

The Code recognizes the professional status of merchants and those who profess to be such or have the knowledge and skill of such. A merchant is "a person who deals in goods of the kind or otherwise by his occupation holds himself out as having knowledge or skill peculiar to the practices or goods involved in the transaction or to whom such knowledge or skill may be attributed by his employment of an agent or broker or other intermediary who by his occupation holds himself out as having such knowledge or skill. . . . 'Between merchants' means in any transaction with respect to which both parties are chargeable with the knowledge or skill of merchants."[8]

The Code "assumes that transactions between professionals in a given field require special and clear rules which may not apply to a casual or inexperienced seller or buyer. It thus adopts a policy of expressly stating rules applicable 'between merchants' and 'as against a merchant', wherever they are needed . . ."[9] There are several such rules and *they apply only to merchants*, not to non-merchants. These rules may be conveniently grouped into three categories. The rules in the first category are concerned with normal, non-specialized business practices of merchants acting in a mercantile capacity.[10] The rules for the second

---

[7] UCC 2–105(4). For the transfer of title to fungible goods by a warehouseman even though covered by a negotiable warehouse receipt, see below, p. 284.

[8] UCC 2–104(1)(3).

[9] UCC 2–104, *Comment 1*.

[10] UCC 2–201(2) is concerned with the Statute of Frauds; UCC 2–205 with firm offers; UCC 2–207(2) with the inclusion in a merchant's acceptance or written confirmation of terms additional to or different from those in the offer; UCC 2–209(2) with clauses excluding modification or rescission of a written agreement except by a signed writing.

category are concerned with the rights in goods which buyers may reasonably expect to acquire from merchant sellers and the rights of creditors in goods possessed by merchants.[11] The rules for the third category are concerned with a merchant's good faith, which means "honesty in fact and the observance of reasonable commercial standards of fair dealing in the trade."[12] They deal with responsibilities of merchant buyers to follow a seller's instructions, risk of loss, and adequate assurance of performance.[13]

Offer and Acceptance

Manifested Intention of the Parties. A contract for sale of goods will result if the manifestations of the parties show agreement to make a binding transaction. Their manifestations may be expressed in any form, whether oral, written, or otherwise, irrespective of whether or not they are enforceable under the statute of frauds. Their *conduct* may be sufficient not only to create a contract but also to recognize the *prior* existence of a contract. A contract may be made even though the time of its creation is undetermined. For example, while the conduct of the parties may show that a contract was made, nevertheless their writings may not clearly indicate the exact time when they finished bargaining. Even though the parties have left some terms open, this does not preclude the formation of a contract for indefiniteness, as long as: (1) *the parties have intended to make a contract, and* (2) *there is a reasonably certain basis for giving an appropriate remedy.* Commercial standards provide the basis for filling in the missing terms and giving an appropriate remedy, and the Code provides for such standards, e.g.,

---

[11] UCC 2–312(3) is concerned with the merchant-seller's express warranty against infringement; UCC 2–314(1) with the merchant-seller's implied warranty of merchantability; UCC 2–402(2) with the non-fraudulent legal effect of a merchant seller's retention in good faith of sold goods; UCC 2–403(2) with the legal power of a merchant seller unauthorizedly to transfer to a buyer in ordinary course of business the rights in the goods of the person entrusting their possession to the merchant seller; UCC 2–326(3) with the fixing of a transaction as a sale or return as to creditors of a merchant seller under certain conditions.

[12] UCC 2–103(b).

[13] UCC 2–327(1)(c) is concerned with the merchant buyer's obligation to follow reasonable instructions of the seller on the merchant buyer's election to return goods under a sale on approval; UCC 2–603 with a merchant buyer's duties as to rightfully rejected goods; UCC 2–605(1)(b) with waiver of a buyer's objections by failure to particularize defects in goods when the transaction is between merchants; UCC 2–509(3) with a merchant seller's risk of loss in the absence of breach for goods, physical delivery of which is to be made at the merchant seller's place; UCC 2–609(2) with the application of commercial standards in determining the reasonableness of grounds for insecurity and the adequacy of any assurance offered when the transaction is between merchants.

open price terms,[14] open delivery terms,[15] and open payment terms.[16] It should be noted, however, that the greater the number of terms left open the greater the likelihood that the parties did not intend to make a contract. Also, if the parties manifest an intent not to have a contract until the open terms become certain, then no contract is formed until this occurs. Auctions were considered under Contracts (p. 25).

The Offer. Under the law of contracts, in the absence of statute to the contrary, a promise is unenforceable unless supported by sufficient consideration, and an oral or written promise to keep an offer open is unenforceable without such consideration. If consideration for the promise is present, the promise is enforceable as a contract to keep the offer open, and the offer is an option.[17] This is also the law under the Code, with one exception.[18] When a *signed written* offer to buy or sell goods, made by a *merchant,* by its terms gives assurance that it will be held open, the offer is enforceable without consideration. The Code gives effect to the merchant's written intention to make his firm offer binding without consideration. A merchant's *oral* offer, and a non-merchant's oral or written offer, is governed by the law of contracts and requires consideration to be enforceable. Under the Code, the Common Law effect of the seal with respect to consideration is destroyed. However, a seal may still be used to authenticate a signature, or even to serve as a signature of a party who so intends it or if it is so provided by statute. The merchant's signed written firm offer without consideration is irrevocable for the time stated therein, or if no time is stated then for a reasonable time, but in no event is it irrevocable for more than three months. If such offer states that it is for a longer time, it is irrevocable without consideration only for three months. However, it can be renewed without consideration. Note that such offer is made *by* a merchant; it may be made *to* anyone. To protect a merchant from inadvertently signing an offer with an assurance that it will be held open *on a form supplied by the offeree,* the merchant offeror must *separately sign such assurance clause in the offer.* " 'Signed' includes any symbol executed or adopted by a party with present intention to authenticate a writing."[19]

---

[14] UCC 2–305.

[15] UCC 2–308.

[16] UCC 2–310.

[17] See above, pp. 30–31.

[18] UCC 2–205.

[19] UCC 1–201(39). "The circumstances surrounding the signing may justify something less than a formal signature or initialing but typically the kind of authentication involved here would consist of a minimum of initialing of the clause involved. A handwritten memorandum on the writer's letterhead purporting in its terms to 'confirm' a

It should be noted that an offer made by *anyone* which is supported by sufficient consideration becomes an option under the law of Contracts and is irrevocable for as long as the parties agree.

The Acceptance. When an offer clearly prescribes the manner or medium of acceptance, only the offeree's use of that manner or medium constitutes an acceptance. Under the Code, if the offer does not clearly indicate otherwise, an offer to make a contract shall be construed as inviting acceptance in any manner and by any medium reasonable in the circumstances.

The Code reflects commercial practice by providing that an order or other offer to buy goods for prompt or current shipment shall be construed as inviting acceptance either by a prompt promise to ship or by prompt or current shipment.[20] " 'Shipment' . . . does not include the beginning of delivery by the seller's own truck or by messenger."[21] The offeree seller may clearly manifest his intention to become bound by beginning to render the requested performance and, when this is a reasonable mode of acceptance, if he so notifies[22] the offeror buyer within a reasonable time, such beginning of performance is an acceptance. If the offeror buyer is not notified of acceptance within a reasonable time, he may treat the offer as having lapsed before acceptance.[23] It should be noted that, inasmuch as the offeree seller's shipment of goods manifests his intention to close the bargain and accept the offer, his shipment of conforming *or non-conforming* goods is an acceptance, although shipment of non-conforming goods is also a breach of contract. The offeree seller may protect himself from having his defective shipment constitute an acceptance and a breach by seasonably notifying the offeror buyer that the shipment is an offer for the accommodation of the offeror buyer. In effect, the seller is making a counteroffer.

When the buyer and seller have closed the deal there is a contract. A definite and seasonable expression of acceptance or a *written confirmation* which is sent within a reasonable time operates as an acceptance. However, a party's written confirmation or expression of acceptance

---

firm offer already made would be enough to satisfy this section, . . . Similarly an authorized telegram will suffice, and this is true even though the original draft contained only a typewritten signature." UCC 2–205, *Comment 2.*

[20] For a discussion of shipment, see below, pp. 304–5.

[21] UCC 2–206, *Comment 2.*

[22] UCC 1–201 (26): "A person 'notifies' or 'gives' a notice or notification to another by taking such steps as may be reasonably required to inform the other in ordinary course whether or not such other actually comes to know of it."

[23] Under the law of contracts, such beginning of performance may be an acceptance of a subsidiary offer of the main offer for a unilateral contract with its resulting legal effect. See above, pp. 34–35.

may state terms additional to, or different from, those offered or agreed upon; this does not stop the expression of acceptance or confirmation from being an acceptance, as long as it does not expressly make acceptance conditional on the other party's assent to the additional or different terms. For example, a party adds "Ship by Tuesday," "Rush," "Ship draft against bill of lading inspection allowed." The additional or different terms are construed as proposals or offers for addition to the contract and are available for acceptance or rejection by the offeree under the normal rules governing acceptance. However, *when the transaction is between merchants,* the additional terms become part of the contract, unless:

(a) the offer expressly limits acceptance to the terms of the offer;
(b) they materially alter it; or
(c) notification of objection to them has already been given or is given within a reasonable time after notice of them is received.[24]

The test of whether or not the additional terms *materially* alter the bargain between merchants is whether they would result in unreasonable surprise or hardship if so incorporated in the contract without express awareness by the other party.[25] Examples of additional terms materially altering the contract are: "a clause negating such standard warranties as that of merchantability or fitness for a particular purpose in circumstances in which either warranty normally attaches; . . . a clause reserving to the seller the power to cancel upon the buyer's failure to meet any invoice when due; a clause requiring that complaints be made in a time materially shorter than customary or reasonable."[26] Examples of additional terms not materially altering the contract are: "a clause fixing a reasonable time for complaints within customary limits, or in the case of a purchase for sub-sale, providing for inspection by the sub-purchaser; a clause providing for interest on overdue invoices or fixing the seller's standard credit terms where they are within the range of trade practice and do not limit any credit bargained for. . . ."[27] "Where clauses on confirming forms sent by both parties conflict each party must be assumed to object to a clause of the other conflicting with one on the confirmation sent by himself. As a result the requirement that there be notice of objection . . . is satisfied and the conflicting terms do not become a part of the contract. The contract

---

[24] UCC 2–207.
[25] See UCC 2–207, *Comments 3, 4.*
[26] UCC 2–207, *Comment 4.*
[27] UCC 2–207, *Comment 5.*

then consists of the terms originally expressly agreed to, terms on which the confirmations agree, and terms supplied by"[28] the Code.

There are occasions where the *conduct* of both parties recognizes the existence of a contract but their writings do not of themselves establish a contract. Inasmuch as the Code effects the manifested intent of the parties to have a contract, it provides that *a contract may be made by both parties' conduct recognizing the existence of such a contract.* When this occurs, the terms of the contract consist of those terms on which the writings of the parties agree, together with any supplementary terms incorporated under any other provisions of the Code.[29]

Interpretation. In order to interpret the meaning of an agreement which has resulted in a contract for sale of goods, various factors become important. The intent of the parties is best expressed by themselves: in the *express terms* of their agreement; by their conduct in the *course of performance* under the agreement; their *course of dealing;* and *usage of trade.* All of these are to be construed whenever reasonable as consistent with each other, but when such construction is unreasonable the express terms control course of performance, course of performance controls both a course of dealing and usage of trade, and course of dealing controls usage of trade.

During the course of performance under the agreement, the conduct of the parties will well reflect their understanding of whether or not such known "course of performance" is or is not in accord with their agreement, and if it is not in accord the performing party would reasonably expect the other party to object thereto. A course of performance involves repeated occasions of performance and not a single occasion. It is for this reason that the Code provides: "Where the contract for sale involves repeated occasions for performance by either party with knowledge of the nature of the performance and opportunity for objection to it by the other, any course of performance accepted or acquiesced in without objection shall be relevant to determine the meaning of the agreement."[30] It should be noted that a course of performance, and even conduct insufficient to constitute a course of performance, may not only assist in the interpretation of the meaning of an agreement, but it is also relevant to show a waiver or modification of a term in the agreement inconsistent with such course of performance or conduct. Where it is in doubt whether a course of performance is reflective of the meaning or is

---

[28] UCC 2–207, *Comment 6.*
[29] UCC 2–207(3).
[30] UCC 2–208(1).

a modification of the agreement on the one hand, or is a waiver on the other, because of the greater flexibility of a waiver (e.g., ease of retraction)[31] and to guard against surprise or other hardship, the course of performance is construed as a waiver.

While a course of performance consists of a sequence of conduct by the parties *subsequent* to the formation of their agreement, in contrast a "course of dealing" is a sequence of their conduct *prior* to the formation of their agreement. Their course of dealing is helpful in the interpretation of their expressions and other conduct resulting in their agreement.

Parties speak in a language and in an environment which are a part of the circumstances bearing upon the meaning of their agreement. Commercial usage, or "usage of trade" as it is usually called, is a part of such circumstances. The Code reflects this by providing: "A usage of trade is any practice or method of dealing having such *regularity of observance* in a place, vocation or trade as to justify an expectation that it will be observed with respect to the transaction in question. . . . An applicable usage of trade in the place where any part of performance is to occur shall be used in interpreting the agreement as to that part of the performance. . . . A course of dealing between parties and any usage of trade in the vocation or trade in which they are engaged or of which they are or should be aware give particular meaning to and supplement or qualify terms of an agreement." (Author's italics)[32]

Modification, Rescission, Waiver. The parties make their own agreement resulting in a contract for sale of goods and, except as precluded by law, they may agree to whatever terms they please. They may agree to various terms, subsequently *agree*[33] to modify them, waive any of them, or rescind the agreement. Consideration is not required to make binding an agreement modifying their contract, nor is consideration required if the modification is by their course of performance. However, any such modification whether with or without consideration *must be in "good faith,"* which means "honesty in fact in the conduct or transaction concerned,"[34] and in the case of a merchant it means "honesty in fact and the observance of reasonable, commercial standards of fair dealing in the trade."[35] For example, a market shift may have

---

[31] See below, p. 253.

[32] UCC 1–205(2)–(5). It should be noted that "regularity of performance" is the test of trade usage, and not the old English concept of custom as of ancient or immemorial origin.

[33] Note that modification cannot occur unilaterally; it can occur only mutually by agreement.

[34] UCC 1–201(19).

[35] UCC 2–103(1)(b).

occurred which would cause performance to result in a loss, or performance may have "become commercially impracticable because of unforeseen supervening circumstances not within the contemplation of the parties at the time of contracting."[36]

A contract for sale may be modified by agreement or by course of performance, irrespective of the form of the original agreement. The Code has special provisions to protect against misrepresentation that an oral agreement of modification has occurred. *First,* if the contract as modified comes within the statute of frauds as being a contract for the sale of goods for $500 or more, the agreement for modification itself comes within the statute and must be a proper, signed writing. If the modification agreement takes the contract *out* of the statute, it may be in any form. *Second,* a signed agreement which excludes its modification or rescission except by a signed writing cannot be otherwise modified or rescinded. However, when such exclusion is on a form *supplied by a merchant to a non-merchant,* the *clause* must be *separately signed* by the non-merchant; but as *between merchants,* such separate signing of the clause is not required.

It should be noted that if an attempt at modification or recission is ineffective because of the statute of frauds or because of the prohibiting clause in the contract, nevertheless the new agreement may operate as a waiver. However, reflecting the law of contracts, "a party who has made a waiver affecting an executory portion of the contract may retract the waiver by reasonable notification *received* by the other party that strict performance will be required of any term waived, unless the retraction would be unjust in view of a material change of position in reliance on the waiver." (Author's italics)[37] A person *receives* a notice or notification when "it comes to his attention; or . . . it is duly delivered at the place of business through which the contract was made or at any other place held out by him as the place for receipt of such communications."[38]

Delegation and Assignment. It is usual in commercial trade to have parties assign their rights under the contract and to delegate performance of their duties under the contract. Contract rights may be *assigned* but contract duties may only be *delegated;* responsibility for performance and for breach remains in the delegating party even though the person to whom the duty has been delegated may also be responsible for performance and breach under the contract. Inasmuch as the parties make their bargain and each relies on the other party's per-

[36] UCC 2–615, *Comment 1.*
[37] UCC 2–209(5).
[38] UCC 1–201(26).

formance, by their agreement they may prohibit assignment or delegation, except that a prohibition of assignment in the agreement is inoperative to prevent a party's assignment of his right to damages for breach of the whole contract or a right arising out of the assignor's due performance of his entire obligation (e.g., the commercial account receivable). Delegation by a party cannot occur if the agreement precludes delegation or if the other party has a "substantial interest" in having his original promisor perform or control the acts required by the contract. By "substantial interest" is meant that the non-delegating party had bargained for performance only by the original delegating promisor. To resolve possible ambiguity, the Code establishes a rule of construction that, *"unless the circumstances indicate the contrary a prohibition of assignment of 'the contract' is to be construed as barring only the delegation to the assignee of the assignor's performance."* (Author's italics)[39] Another Code rule of construction is that a *general assignment* operates as *both* an assignment of rights *and,* unless the language of the agreement or circumstances indicate the contrary, a delegation of the performance of duties. For example, an assignment of "the contract" or of "all my rights under the contract" or similar general terms is a general assignment. An assignment of rights that are no longer executory, such as a right to damages for breach of the entire contract or of an account receivable, or an assignment of rights for the purpose of security are circumstances which indicate that there is no delegation of duties. If the person to whom delegation has been made accepts such delegation, *his acceptance constitutes a promise to perform those duties* thereby creating a third party creditor beneficiary contract[40] and making him, as well as the delegating party, liable to the other party for performance of the contract duties and for breach of contract therefor.

The non-delegating party may treat delegation as creating reasonable grounds for insecurity and he may, without prejudice to his rights against the delegating party, demand adequate assurance of due performance from the party to whom delegation has been made. This reflects the well-established legal principle that each contracting party has an obligation not to impair the other's expectation of receiving due performance. "Between merchants the reasonableness of grounds for insecurity and the adequacy of any assurance offered shall be determined according to commercial standards."[41]

---

[39] UCC 2–210(3).
[40] See above, p. 105.
[41] UCC 2–609(2).

All rights of either the seller or the buyer can be assigned except where the assignment would *materially:*

1. Change the duty of the other party, or
2. Increase the burden or risk imposed on him by his contract, or
3. Impair his chance of obtaining return performance.

Form of the Transaction

Statute of Frauds. As discussed previously under the law of contracts,[42] the statute of frauds in each state has for its purpose the prevention of effective fraudulent allegation that a contract exists, and the statute accomplishes this by requiring that certain kinds of contract therein enumerated are *unenforceable* unless proved in a specified way. The statute of frauds is really a general description of those statutory provisions in various areas of the law prescribing proof of various kinds of contract in order for such contracts to be enforceable. Under the Code, the various types of transactions included are: a contract for the sale of goods for the price of $500 or more (UCC 2–201); a contract for the sale of securities (UCC 8–319)[43]; a security agreement for a non-possessory security interest, e.g., accounts receivable (UCC 9–203);[44] a contract for general intangibles, e.g., goodwill, royalty rights, rights to performance (UCC 9–106),[45] and a contract for various types of security transaction (UCC 9–104)[46] for more than $5,000 are governed by UCC 1–206.[47]

Under UCC 2–201(1), a contract for the sale of goods for the price of $500 or more is unenforceable unless: *there is a writing sufficient to indicate that a contract for sale has been made between the parties; and the writing is signed by the party against whom enforcement of the contract is sought or by his authorized agent or broker.* Also, if a contract as subsequently modified by the parties[48] is for the sale of goods for $500 or more, the contract as well as the agreement of modification comes within the statute. It should be noted that, inasmuch as "sale or return" contracts[49] are relatively so infrequent, in order to prove such a contract the "or return" term of a contract for sale

---

[42] See above, p. 107.
[43] See below, pp. 692–93.
[44] See below, p. 739.
[45] See below, p. 736.
[46] See below, pp. 729–30.
[47] See below, p. 1012.
[48] See above, p. 253.
[49] See below, p. 262.

irrespective of sales price is treated as a separate contract for sale under the statute of frauds and is unenforceable unless proved as required by the statute.

The Contract Price. Under the Sales Article of the Code, the statute of frauds provision is concerned only with goods with a sales price of $500 or more. It is the contract price of $500 or more that is important, and not the actual value of the goods. If a number of items are bought by the same buyer from the same seller at the same time, all the items are considered as forming part of one contract and a total price as being the contract price.

The Writing. The contract for sale itself may be in writing, or there may be an oral contract supported by a written memorandum indicating that the contract had been made and the memorandum has been signed by a party or his authorized agent or broker. Such writings are the best method of proving that the contract had been made by the party or parties who had signed them. The writing is proof only against a signatory. Accordingly, *the writing must be signed by the party against whom the contract is sought to be enforced.* If the seller is the signatory, the contract is enforceable against him by the buyer; if the buyer is the signatory, the contract is enforceable against him by the seller; if both buyer and seller are signatories, each may enforce the contract against the other. It should be noted carefully that the validity of the contract is not questioned; it is solely a matter of enforceability. (A and B make an oral contract for the sale of goods for $1,000. There is a contract; but unless the contract is proved by a proper writing, it is unenforceable.)

It is not necessary that the writing required by the statute state all the terms of the agreement. The writing is not insufficient because it omits or incorrectly states a term of the agreement. For example, the price, the time and place of delivery, and warranties may all be omitted. The Code fills in these items by reflecting commercial understanding in its implementing sections; course of performance, course of dealing, and usage of trade become important in this respect. The Code is interested in sufficient proof that a contract has been made, and the person who signs a writing so indicating should be responsible for the contract which he has indicated is in effect. Irrespective of whether or not the items in the writing are correct, a party signed it, and it is evidence against him. He is bound only to the extent of the quantity of goods shown in the writing as the object of the contract. *All that is required is that the writing contain three things: it must indicate that a contract for sale of goods has been made; it must be signed by the party against whom the contract is sought to be enforced; and it must specify a quantity of goods.*

Commercial understanding *between merchants* is reflected in the Code,[50] which provides that a merchant's written confirmation of the contract for sale of goods which is sufficient to make the contract enforceable against him will also be sufficient as a writing of confirmation against the merchant recipient *if he received the writing within a reasonable time after the transaction was made, he had reason to know its contents, and he did not give to the sender written notice*[51] *of his objection to the contents within ten days after he received the written confirmation.* In short, as between merchants, one merchant has a duty to manifest his objection to another merchant's timely erroneous confirmation and his failure to do so soon is an admission that the confirmation is correct and he thereby makes it a written manifestation of his own.

The writing may be made at or after the time that the contract has been made, and it may be in any tangible form, e.g., printing, typewriting, ink, pencil. It may be in the form of correspondence between the parties, e.g., letters and telegrams, or it may be by will or negotiable instrument. The writing may be formal or informal and may be one writing or a series of related writings. If there is more than one writing, either all the writings must be attached to the signed writing or the signed writing must refer to all the other writings. (A writes to B complaining about B's failure to perform an oral contract within the statute of frauds and sets forth all the data regarding such contract. B's answering signed letter refers to A's letter and admits the formation of such a contract but refuses to perform it. B's signed letter refers to A's letter, and the two letters constitute the writing sufficient to satisfy the statute and to prove the oral contract. The contract is enforceable by A against B. If B were seeking to enforce the oral contract against A, A's signed letter would be the writing.)

The writing must be signed by the party against whom the contract is sought to be enforced. " 'Signed' includes any symbol executed or adopted by a party with present intention to authenticate a writing."[52] For example, the signature may be any writing, seal, stamp, or mark which a party intends to adopt as his own, whether or not made by him, and irrespective of whether or not he intended such signature to be on a writing to satisfy the statute of frauds. The signature may occur any-

---

[50] UCC 2–201(2).

[51] For Notice, see UCC 1–201(25).

[52] UCC 1–201(39).

where on the writing; and it is different from the word "subscribe," which means that the signature must occur at the bottom of the document. A party's agent or broker may sign the writing for him only if such agent or broker is so authorized. Such authorization is a matter of the law of agency,[53] but briefly the authorization may be given by the party principal orally, in writing, by his other conduct (e.g., the agent's signing for the principal party in his presence and without his objection), by ratification, and by apparent authority. The agent may be a corporate employee[54] or a partner.[55] The agent need not disclose his principal's identity inasmuch as, under the law of agency,[56] the principal can be held liable as a party to the contract when his identity becomes known to the other contracting party. In sales by auction,[57] by law the auctioneer is the agent of both seller and buyer to prepare and sign on their behalf a memorandum of sale immediately after the sale, which is a writing sufficient to satisfy the requirements of the statute of frauds.

Transactions Excluded from the Statute of Frauds. The Code excepts four transactions concerning goods *from the statute of frauds provision under Sales,* but the other Sales sections of the Code apply to the transaction because goods are involved.

The first transaction excluded from the statute is concerned with non-resellable goods. The Code eliminates the difficulty of determining whether a contract which involves selling goods *and* performing services on such goods is essentially a contract for services and, therefore, is not within the statute of frauds; or whether it is esentially a contract for the sale of goods and is within the statute of frauds. (A contracts with B to paint B's portrait, or to make a suit for B, or to build a special vehicle for B.) A contract for services alone is not within this statute of frauds provision and is enforceable even though oral. A contract is not within the statute and is enforceable "if the goods are to be specially manufactured for the buyer and are not suitable for sale to others in the ordinary course of the seller's business and the seller, before notice of repudiation is received and under circumstances which reasonably indicate that the goods are for the buyer, has made either a substantial beginning of their manufacture or commitments for their procurement."[58] (A, a manufacturer of carriages, orally contracts with B to build B a carriage like the

---

[53] See below, pp. 511, 514–39.

[54] See below, pp. 523–24.

[55] See below, pp. 524, 623.

[56] See below, pp. 566–67.

[57] For Auction, see above, p. 25.

[58] UCC 2–201(3)(a).

carriages A usually builds. It is a contract to sell and is within the statute. If the carriage were to be made especially for B according to certain specifications different from the type of carriage A ordinarily makes and sells, and A so made the carriage, the contract is for services, is not within the statute, and is enforceable even though orally made. An oral contract to make a suit of clothes which the tailor then begins to make involves the same principle. Similarly, an oral contract between A, a dentist, and B whereby A was to make for B's use an artificial denture and which A subsequently so made is not within the statute and is enforceable.)

The second transaction excluded from the statute is concerned with a contract for the sale of goods and the buyer has received and accepted part or all of the goods. The buyer's receipt and acceptance of goods is good proof that a contract for their sale was made and, accordingly, *only to the extent of such goods the buyer's receipt and acceptance of them causes the contract for their sale to be enforceable without a writing.* A buyer has receipt when he has acquired possession, personally or through his agent, with the assent of the seller. Delivery of the goods to a warehouseman or to anyone else, as requested by the buyer, is a delivery to the buyer through his agent. In the absence of agreement to the contrary, delivery to a carrier for shipment to the buyer is delivery to the buyer, the carrier being the buyer's agent to transport the goods. In these instances the buyer has possession. Unless the circumstances indicate that the seller is a bailee for the buyer, the seller's possession of the goods awaiting the buyer's acquisition is not a receipt by the buyer; the seller is not his agent to receive the goods. *The buyer's possession* of a negotiable document of title (e.g., negotiable bill of lading or negotiable warehouse receipt) drawn or indorsed in his favor, or the buyer's possession of a non-negotiable document of title in which the buyer is the consignee, is a receipt of the goods. The document of title is a symbol of the goods to which it refers. A buyer has accepted the goods when he expressly or impliedly so indicates. Acceptance is implied from the buyer's exercise of dominion over the goods, or his retention of such goods for an unreasonable period of time without informing the seller that he has rejected them. Acceptance usually occurs after receipt, but it can precede receipt. (B, the buyer, selects 100 rolls of cloth and asks S, the seller, to send them to him. S sends the goods by railroad. There is a receipt by B through the railroad as his agent, and there is an acceptance which occurred when B selected and assented to those 100 rolls.)

The third transaction excepted from the statute is concerned with a contract where the buyer has made part or complete payment which has been accepted by the seller. The buyer's payment and the seller's acceptance is good proof that a contract for the sale of goods was made and, accordingly, *only to the extent of the apportioned value of the seller's goods, the buyer's part or full payment of the price causes the contract for the sale of such goods to be enforceable without a writing.* The price need not be in money but may be anything other than money.[59] If the price is in terms of money, delivery of a check or negotiable promissory note which the seller accepts is payment for the purpose of satisfying the statute, although it is only conditional payment as far as performance of a contract duty is concerned. Part payment is sufficient, but a tender of payment is not. Payment may be made at any time. If payment is to be made by cancellation of an existing claim by the buyer against the seller, the time when payment is made depends upon the intention of the parties. If cancellation is to occur when the goods are received, then no payment is made until the goods are received. If cancellation is to occur immediately on the making of the contract, then payment occurs at that time.

The fourth transaction excepted from the statute is concerned with a contract for sale which a party admits in court, e.g., by his pleading, testimony, or otherwise, *was made by him.* Such admission in court is good proof that a contract for the sale of goods was made and, accordingly, *only to the extent of the goods admitted, a party's admission in court of a contract for the sale of goods is enforceable against him without a writing.*

Parol Evidence Rule. The parol evidence rule has been discussed previously under the law of contracts.[60] The Code reflects this rule with modification. Terms which the parties have agreed upon in their confirmatory memoranda or final written agreement may not be *contradicted* by any prior oral or written agreement or by a contemporaneous oral agreement between such parties. However, such terms may be explained or supplemented by: course of performance, course of dealing, or usage of trade; and by consistent additional terms, unless the court finds the writing to have been intended as a complete and exclusive statement of the terms of the agreement. The writing may be reformed[61] by the court to reflect the previous intentions of the parties not properly expressed in the writing.

---

[59] See below, p. 264.

[60] See above, pp. 53–54.

[61] For Reformation, see above, p. 54.

Chapter V

CONSTRUCTION OF THE CONTRACT

---

1. *INTENTION OF THE PARTIES GOVERNS*

THE intention of the parties as expressed or implied in their sales agreement governs their transaction, except where it is contrary to law as prohibited by the Code. Many times the intention of the parties is not expressed on important factors involved in the particular transaction, or the legal import of the commercial terms used by them is not clearly understood. The Code prescribes certain rules for ascertaining the implied intention of the parties, and it clarifies the legal meaning and effect of commercial terms. All this is a matter of *construing* the agreement to reflect its meaning in light of the terminology used by the parties and the surrounding circumstances of course of performance, course of dealing, and usage of trade. First the general obligations of the contracting parties, open terms, shipment, and delivery will be considered, then title, creditors, and good faith purchasers.

2. *GENERAL OBLIGATIONS, OPEN TERMS, SHIPMENT, AND DELIVERY*

General Obligations   **Generally.** The Code seeks to observe carefully fair dealing in commercial transactions. It exacts good faith between parties dealing with each other which means honesty in fact and, in the case of a merchant, means also honesty in the observance of reasonable commercial standards of fair dealing in the trade. In dealing with each other, the seller has the obligation to transfer and deliver the goods and the buyer has the obligation to accept and pay for the goods in accordance with their contract, and they may provide for their risks and burdens as they wish unless prohibited by the Code as not reflective of fair dealing. *The Code's allocation of risks and burdens is so to provide only if the parties have not otherwise agreed.* When it is claimed by a party that the contract or a clause therein was unconscionable at the time the contract was made, as not reflecting fair dealing, the parties will be afforded reasonable opportunity to present evidence to assist the court to decide as a matter of law whether or not such contract or clause was unconscionable at the time it was made. The court, not the jury, may refuse to enforce the contract if it is permeated by unconscionability, it may delete the unconscionable clause and enforce the remainder of the contract, or it may so limit the application of an unconscionable clause as to avoid an unconscionable result.[1]

Sale on Approval and Sale or Return. Two types of transaction are different from other transactions involving sale of goods; they are "sale on approval" and "sale or return." In these two transactions, the parties are agreeing that the buyer has a power to turn back the goods to the seller, not because of non-conformity of the goods to the contract but, rather, because of the particular nature of the contract. *In a sale on approval,* the goods are delivered to the buyer but the seller retains the title and risk of loss for such goods until the buyer gives his approval of the goods and thereby accepts them. *In a sale or return,* the goods are delivered to the buyer, the title and risk of loss pass to the buyer, but the buyer may return the goods to the seller in lieu of paying the purchase price. Although the parties determine which transaction it is, often it is difficult to determine which transaction is meant by the parties. *Unless otherwise agreed,* the kind of transaction is determined primarily by the purpose for which the goods are delivered: *if primarily for use, it is a sale on approval; if primarily for resale, it is a sale or return.* The reason for this test is that, by commercial practice, when a returnable power is included in the sales agreement consumers take the goods subject to their approval and merchants take goods for resale and return if not resold. The sale "on approval," or "on trial," or "on satisfaction," or any other words of like import, is a contract with an option to purchase if the goods are satisfactory to the buyer; as distinguished from a sale or return, in which title passes on delivery with an option in the buyer to return the goods if they are not satisfactory to him, or for any other agreed reason. The sale on approval is a bailment of the goods with an option to buy. In a sale or return, there is no bailment but rather a sale with the option to revest title to the goods in the seller.

---

[1] UCC 2–302, *Comment 1:* "The basic test is whether, in the light of the general commercial background and the commercial needs of the particular trade or case, the clauses involved are so one-sided as to be unconscionable under the circumstances existing at the time of the making of the contract. . . . The principle is one of the prevention of oppression and unfair surprise . . . and *not of disturbance of allocation of risks because of superior bargaining power.* . . . A clause limiting time for complaints was held inapplicable to latent defects in a shipment of catsup which could be discovered only by microscopic analysis." (Author's italics)

In a sale on approval, if the buyer retains the goods without giving notice to the seller of his approval or acceptance, or of his rejection, within the agreed time in which the buyer is to return the goods, then such retention without any indication by the buyer beyond such period of time is the equivalent of approval or acceptance, and the title passes to the buyer. If no time has been specified within which the goods are to be returned to the seller, then on the expiration of a reasonable period of time the title passes to the buyer. Similarly, in a sale or return contract, the buyer may exercise his option of revesting title in the seller only by doing so within the agreed period of time, or within a reasonable period of time if no time has been fixed. On the expiration of such period of time, the option to revest the title in the seller can no longer be exercised. In a sale on approval, the buyer's use of the goods consistent with the purpose of trial is at the seller's risk and is not an acceptance; but the buyer's acceptance of any part of conforming goods is an acceptance of the whole. His return of the goods, *after due notification to the seller of his intention to do so,* is at the seller's risk and expense; but if he is a *merchant buyer,* he must follow any reasonable instructions of the seller. By contrast, in a sale or return the buyer has the option to return all *or* any commercial unit of the goods, and return is at the buyer's risk and expense. It should be noted that, inasmuch as it is most unusual for an ordinary contract for the sale of goods to include an "or return" clause, the Code stipulates: that *such clause* be treated as a separate contract for sale within the statute of frauds and unenforceable unless proved by a proper signed writing;[2] and that, when the sales agreement is in writing but the agreed "or return" provision is oral, such provision is contradictory of the written sales agreement and inadmissible in evidence under the parol evidence rule.[3]

Creditors' Rights. While the goods are in the buyer's possession, the buyer's creditors can resort only to the interest of the buyer in the goods, unless the buyer's business is such as to cause his creditors to be misled by the seller's delivery of the goods to the buyer. If it is a sale on approval, no title has passed to the buyer and, until he accepts the goods, the goods are not available to his creditors. If it is a sale or return, the buyer has the title to the goods and the goods are available to his creditors. *However, when the seller delivers goods for sale to a buyer-dealer who deals in goods of that kind and who maintains a place of business under a name other than that of the seller or person making*

---

[2] See above, pp. 255–56.
[3] See above, p. 260.

such delivery, then, as to the buyer's creditors, the transaction is treated as a sale or return irrespective of the intentions of the parties, and the goods are available to the buyer's creditors. In effect, if a seller delivers the goods for sale to such a buyer-dealer, he is estopped to assert *to the buyer's creditors* that it is anything other than a sale or return. This is true whether "on consignment," "on memorandum," or similar words of reservation of title in the seller are used. Of course, if the buyer's creditors are on notice of the interest of the seller in the goods, then, since they have not been misled by the seller's delivery of the goods to the buyer, the true nature of the transaction and the seller's interest in the goods prevail. Such notice to the buyer's creditors occurs when either: pursuant to local law, the seller posts a sign on the buyer's premises and thereby has his interests protected; the buyer or person conducting the business is generally known by his creditors to be substantially engaged in selling the goods of others, e.g., factor; or the seller gives notice of his security interest in the goods by proper filing.[4]

Open Terms
The Price. The parties determine by their agreement whether or not there is to be a contract for the sale of goods and also the price therefor. The price, that is the consideration, may be money or any other property or services. The price, in full or in part, may be bartered goods, services, or an interest in land. When all or part of the price is payable in an interest in land, the transfer of the goods and the seller's obligations with respect to them are subject to the Code's provisions on Sales, but not the transfer of the interest in land or the transferor's obligations in connection therewith. The agreement may specifically fix the price for the goods; however, *if the parties intend to conclude a contract for sale without determining the price, a contract is made even though there is indefiniteness concerning the price.* In such case, *the price is a reasonable price at the time and place where the goods were to be delivered to the buyer if:* nothing is said as to the price; or the price is left to be agreed by the parties and they fail to agree; or the price is to be fixed in terms of some agreed market or other standard as set or recorded by a third person or agency and it is not so set or recorded; or the price is to be determined by a particular person's judgment when there is no market standard for fixing the value or price for the goods and the third person does not so fix the price. An agreement to agree later on the price is perfectly reasonable, *as long as the parties intend to conclude a*

---

[4] See Property Security Transactions, below, p. 746, 763 ff.

contract for sale at the time of their initial agreement. If the parties agree that the price is to be fixed by the buyer or the seller, the price must be fixed by that party in good faith, which "includes observance of reasonable commercial standards of fair dealing in the trade if the party is a merchant. . . . But in the normal case a 'posted price' or a future seller's or buyer's 'given price,' 'price in effect,' 'market price,' or the like satisfies the good faith requirement."[5] When the price is to be fixed otherwise than by subsequent agreement of the parties but the buyer or the seller wrongfully prevents the fixing of such price, the other party may at his option treat the contract as cancelled or he himself may fix a reasonable price. Of course, *if the parties intend not to be bound unless the price be fixed or agreed* and the price is not fixed or agreed, there is no contract. The intention of the parties prevails. In such a case, the buyer must return any goods which he has already received or, if he is unable to do so, he must pay their reasonable value at the time of delivery to him, and the seller must return any portion of the price paid on account by the buyer. It should be noted that when the price is payable in whole or in part in goods, each party is a seller of the goods which he is to transfer.

Output, Requirements, and Exclusive Dealings. *Output, Requirements.* It is common for the parties to an agreement for the sale of goods not to provide for a specific quantity of goods to be supplied by the seller to the buyer but, rather, to provide that the quantity of goods is measured by the seller's output or the buyer's requirements. For example, the buyer agrees to buy 60 per cent of the seller's output. The indefiniteness of the quantity of goods does not preclude the agreement from resulting in a valid contract. In order to be on the safe side, the agreement may specify minimum or maximum amounts which may be tendered by the seller or demanded by the buyer. However, the parties may not feel that they can establish minimums or maximums and that the best that they can provide for is a stated estimate of the quantity to be furnished by the seller or demanded by the buyer, bearing in mind the seller's output and the buyer's requirements. If the agreement does not provide for a stated estimate, then the prior experience of the parties on output and requirements is to be examined in order to determine some reasonable limitiation on the quantity that may be tendered by the seller or demanded by the buyer. An output or requirements agreement contemplates good faith by the parties according to commercial standards of fair dealing and contem-

---

[5] UCC 2–305, *Comment 3.*

plates reasonable expansion or contraction of production or requirements. "A shut-down by a requirements buyer for lack of orders might be permissible when a shut-down merely to curtail losses would not. The essential test is whether the party is acting in good faith. Similarly, a sudden expansion of the plant by which requirements are to be measured would not be included within the scope of the contract as made but normal expansion undertaken in good faith would be within the scope of contemplation by the parties. One of the factors in an expansion situation would be whether the market price has risen greatly in a case in which the requirements contract contained a fixed price."[6] If the parties had made a stated estimate, reasonable variation in quantity is intended, as long as such variation is not unreasonably disproportionate to the stated estimate. Similarly, in the absence of a stated estimate, variation cannot be unreasonably disproportionate to the prior output or requirement experience of the parties. Improper demand by either party may be disregarded by the other party, who may insist that the contract be performed as agreed and also insist that, inasmuch as such improper demand constituted reasonable grounds for insecurity of performance by the demanding party, the latter furnish adequate assurance of due performance.[7]

Exclusive Dealings. In an exclusive dealing contract, the parties agree on a specified geographical territory in which the agent-buyer is to have the exclusive right to sell the principal-seller's goods. Whether or not the agreement results in a valid contract is determined by local law and, where applicable, by federal law. Unless the parties have agreed to the contrary, they have a duty to employ reasonable diligence and good faith in performing their contract, the principal-seller to use his best efforts to supply the goods and to refrain from supplying any other dealer or agent in the exclusive territory, and the agent-buyer to use his best efforts to promote the sale of his principal-seller's goods and to expand their market.

Payment. It is the duty of the seller to deliver the goods to the buyer, and it is the duty of the buyer to accept and pay for such goods as provided by their contract. Often the parties do not expressly provide in their agreement when and where payment is to be made by the buyer. *Unless otherwise agreed, payment is due at the time and place at which the buyer is to receive the goods,* even though the place of shipment is the place of delivery. When the seller has been authorized by the

---

[6] UCC 2–306, *Comment 2.*
[7] See below, pp. 322–24.

contract to send the goods to the buyer, the seller's delivery of the goods to the carrier or other suitable bailee constitutes a delivery to the buyer. However, inasmuch as this kind of a delivery is a special kind of delivery, the buyer is under no obligation to pay on the seller's delivery to the carrier; but after the goods have arrived and the buyer has had a reasonable opportunity to inspect the goods, then the buyer is under an obligation to make payment. *If, pursuant to the contract, the seller sends the goods to the buyer C.O.D. (collect on delivery) or the contract provides for payment against documents of title,*[8] *unless otherwise agreed the buyer is not entitled to inspect the goods before making payment.* When payment is to be made against documents of title, payment is due at the time and place at which the buyer is to receive the documents, regardless of where the goods are to be received. It should be noted that, *unless otherwise agreed, a seller who is authorized to send goods may ship them and reserve in himself a security interest in the goods by having the documents of title name the seller as the consignee.* Where the seller is required or authorized to ship the goods on credit, the credit period runs from the time of shipment. It is common commercial understanding that the dating of the invoice is recognized as a representation of the time of shipment, and postdating the invoice delays the starting of the credit period until the date on the invoice. If the seller delays sending the invoice to the buyer, inasmuch as the buyer will not have the opportunity of knowing when to pay, the credit period does not begin until the invoice has been sent to the buyer.

Shipment and Delivery

In General. We have already observed that an agreement for sale which is otherwise sufficiently definite to be a contract is not made invalid by the fact that it leaves particulars of performance to be specified by one of the parties. Any such specification, however, must be made in good faith and within limits set by commercial reasonableness. This applies also in connection with the shipment and delivery of goods. Unless otherwise agreed, specifications relating to assortment of goods are at the buyer's option and, except as otherwise provided by the Code,[9] specifications or arrangements relating to shipment are at the

---

[8] In the case of payment against documents (e.g., bill of lading), *payment is required before inspection,* "since shipping documents against which payment is to be made will commonly arrive and be tendered while the goods are still in transit." UCC 2–513, *Comment 5.*

[9] See F.O.B. and F.A.S. shipments, below, pp. 270–71.

seller's option. Where such specification would materially affect the other party's performance and the specification is not seasonably[10] made, or where one party's cooperation is necessary to the agreed performance of the other but such cooperation is not seasonably forthcoming, the other party in addition to all other remedies for breach of contract "is excused for any resulting delay in his own performance; and he may also either proceed to perform in any reasonable manner or, after the time for a material part of his own performance, treat the failure to specify or to cooperate as a breach by failure to deliver or accept the goods."[11]

Delivery by Installments. *Delivery means voluntary transfer of possession* from one person to another and may be made by one person through his authorized agent to another person through the latter's authorized agent. The agreement of the parties may provide expressly or impliedly whether or not delivery or payment is to be made by installments; but in the absence of any such provision, the buyer is under no obligation to accept delivery, and the seller is under no obligation to accept payment, by installments. All the goods called for by the contract for sale must be tendered in a single delivery, and payment is due only on such tender. An example of an agreement implying that delivery may be made by several lots[12] instead of a single lot of goods is an agreement in which the seller is to deliver the goods as required by the buyer. A buyer may accept delivery of several lots rather than a single lot and thereby waive his right to refuse such delivery by lots; similarly, the seller's acceptance of payment by installments may waive his right to refuse payment by installments. However, circumstances may indicate that it is not commercially feasible to deliver or to receive the goods in a single lot and, when this occurs, either party has the right to make or demand delivery in lots and the price, if it can be apportioned, may be demanded for each lot.[13] Where such circumstances exist, "a partial delivery is not subject to rejection for the defect

---

[10] UCC 1–204(3)(2): "An action is taken 'seasonably' when it is taken at or within the time agreed or if no time is agreed at or within a reasonable time. What is a reasonable time for taking any action depends on the nature, purpose and circumstances of such action."

[11] UCC 2–311(3)(a)(b).

[12] For Lot see above, p. 244.

[13] UCC 2–307, *Comment 3,* gives examples of such circumstances. ". . . where a contract calls for the shipment of ten carloads of coal and only three cars are available at a given time. Similarly, in a contract involving brick necessary to build a building the buyer's storage space may be limited so that it would be impossible to receive the entire amount of brick at once, or it may be necessary to assemble the goods as in the case of cattle on the range, or to mine" such goods.

in quantity alone, if the circumstances do not indicate a repudiation or default by the seller as to the expected balance or do not give the buyer ground for suspending his performance because of insecurity. . . . However, in such cases the undelivered balance of goods under the contract must be forthcoming within a reasonable time and in a reasonable manner. . . ."[14]

Place and Time of Delivery. *Place.* The agreement of the parties determines the place and time of delivery. Later discussion will consider delivery to be made by a carrier.[15] When goods are to be delivered other than by a carrier, "Unless otherwise agreed (a) the place for delivery of goods is the seller's place of business or if he has none his residence; but (b) in a contract for sale of identified goods which to the knowledge of the parties at the time of contracting are in some other place, that place is the place for their delivery; and (c) documents of title may be delivered through customary banking channels."[16] If the goods located in some other place are in the possession of a bailee, the seller has the additional obligation of obtaining the acknowledgment by the bailee of the buyer's right to possession in order to effect delivery to the buyer.

Time. The parties may agree on the time of delivery of goods either expressly, or impliedly by course of performance, course of dealing, usage of trade, or the circumstances under which the agreement was made. Should one party propose a time limit, the other party's failure to reply may constitute an assent to such time limit.[17] *If the time for shipment, delivery, or any other action under the contract is not agreed to by the parties then, unless otherwise provided by the Code, the time is a reasonable time.* Acceptable commercial conduct in light of the nature, purpose, and circumstances determines what is a reasonable time. Failure to deliver or tender delivery within a reasonable time is a breach of contract. An unreasonably early demand for, or offer of, delivery is not a breach of contract but constitutes a manifestation of intent requesting the other party's assent, whose subsequent silence may constitute assent. If such demanding or offering party *insists* on such unreasonably early delivery, such insistence may constitute conduct amounting to a breach of contract or justify a request for adequate assurance of

---

[14] *Ibid.*

[15] See below, pp. 304 ff.

[16] UCC 2–308. *Comment 3:* "Where 'customary banking channels' call only for due notification by the banker that the documents are on hand, leaving the buyer himself to see to the physical receipt of the goods, tender at the buyer's address is not required under paragraph (c)."

[17] See above, pp. 249 ff.

performance.[18] If both parties silently let a reasonable time go by, their conduct may enlarge such reasonable time.

When the contract is of a continuing nature, that is providing for successive performances but without agreement as to how long such performances are to continue, the contract continues for a reasonable time; however, unless otherwise agreed, either party may terminate the contract at any time. While the continuing contract may be justifiably terminated[19] by one party *for other than the occurrence of an agreed event,* the other party should have a reasonable opportunity for making substitute arrangements in his affairs because of such termination. Accordingly, the Code requires that the other party *receive* reasonable notification of such termination. While the agreement of the parties may dispense with such notification, such a provision for dispensing with notification will be invalid if its operation would be unconscionable. If the agreement of the parties had provided for termination on the happening of an agreed event, then no notification is required.

Shipping Terms. In commercial practice, various terms in connection with the shipment of goods have a well-defined meaning. While the parties to the transaction may vary this meaning and their intent governs, nevertheless, unless such variation is clearly indicated, the established meaning will prevail.

C.O.D. "C.O.D." means collect on delivery. In a C.O.D. shipment the carrier is the agent of the consignor seller for the purpose of collecting payment, and the carrier is also the agent of the consignee buyer for the purpose of transporting the goods. This contract term is interpreted to mean that payment to the carrier must precede transfer of *possession* from the carrier to the consignee buyer; it does not mean that such payment is to precede the transfer of title.

F.O.B. "F.O.B." means free on board. F.O.B. is at a named place, even though used only in connection with the stated price, and is a delivery term *indicating the extent of the consignor seller's obligation under the contract.* When the term is *F.O.B. the place of shipment,* the seller's obligation is to ship the goods at that place and bear the expense and risk of putting them into the possession of the carrier. When the

---

[18] See below, pp. 322–24.

[19] UCC 2–106: "(3) 'Termination' occurs when either party pursuant to a power created by agreement or law puts an end to the contract *otherwise than for its breach.* On 'termination' all obligations which are still executory on both sides are discharged but any right based on prior breach or performance survives. (4) 'Cancellation' occurs when either party puts an end to the contract *for breach* by the other and its effect is the same as that of 'termination' except that the cancelling party also retains any remedy for breach of the whole contract or any unperformed balance." (Author's italics)

term is *F.O.B. the place of destination,* the seller's obligation is to transport the goods to that designated place and there tender delivery of the goods, such transportation being at the seller's expense and risk. When the goods are to be shipped *F.O.B the place of shipment or F.O.B. the place of destination and, in addition, the term provides also for F.O.B. vessel, car or other vehicle,* the seller has the additional obligation of loading the goods on board at his own expense and risk. When the term is F.O.B. vessel: the seller has the obligation of obtaining a bill of lading in the proper form; and the buyer has the obligations of naming the vessel, seasonably giving any needed instructions for delivery including the loading berth of the vessel and in an appropriate case its name and sailing date, and unless otherwise agreed of making payment on the tender of the documents by the seller.

F.A.S. The term "F.A.S." means free alongside. *F.A.S. vessel* is at a named port and, even though used only in connection with the stated price, is a delivery term *indicating the extent of the consignor seller's obligation under the contract.* The seller's obligations are: to deliver the goods alongside the vessel in the manner usual in that port or on a dock designated and provided by the buyer; and to obtain a receipt for the goods which he is to exchange for a bill of lading to be issued by the carrier. The buyer's obligations are: seasonably to give any needed instructions for delivery, including the loading berth of the vessel and in an appropriate case its name and sailing date, and, unless otherwise agreed, to make payment on the tender of the documents by the seller.

It should be noted that in all of the F.O.B. and F.A.S. terms just discussed, except for F.O.B. place of destination, should the buyer fail to provide the needed instructions, the seller may treat such failure as a failure of cooperation[20] and, at his option, move the goods in any reasonable manner preparatory to delivery or shipment. Also, under F.O.B. vessel or F.A.S., unless otherwise agreed, the seller may not tender nor the buyer demand delivery of the goods in substitution for the documents.

C.I.F. and C. & F. Terms. The term "C.I.F." means cost, insurance, and freight, signifying that the seller is to ship the goods and to pay for insurance thereon and the freight charges to the point of destination. The lump sum sales price includes these charges. The intention of the parties to a C.I.F. contract is that the buyer desires insurance because he does not wish to bear the risk of loss, which has

---

[20] See above, p. 268.

shifted to the buyer under this type of contract, indicating that the intention is that title is to be transferred to the buyer on the seller's delivery of the goods to the carrier and on the seller's payment of the insurance and freight charges. Accordingly, the seller's compliance with the C.I.F. requirements in the contract causes the title to the goods to be transferred at the time of such compliance, even though the agreement has provided that the seller is to pay the freight to the point of destination. The term "C. & F." means cost and freight, signifying that the seller is to ship the goods and pay for the freight charges to the point of destination; insurance is not included in the lump sum sales price for these two charges.

Unless otherwise agreed, the term C.I.F. destination or its equivalent imposes upon the seller the following obligations at his own expense and risk:

(a) put the goods into the possession of a carrier at the port for shipment and obtain a negotiable bill or bills of lading covering the entire transaction to the named destination.

(b) load the goods and obtain a receipt from the carrier (which may be contained in the bill of lading) showing that the freight has been paid or provided for.

(c) obtain a policy or certificate of insurance, including any war risk insurance, of a kind and on terms then current at the port of shipment in the usual amount, in the currency of the contract, shown to cover the same goods covered by the bill of lading and providing for payment of loss to the order of the buyer or for the account of whom it may concern; but the seller may add to the price the amount of the premium for any such war risk insurance.

(d) prepare an invoice of the goods and procure any other documents required to effect shipment or to comply with the contract.

(e) forward and tender with commercial promptness all the documents in due form and with any indorsement necessary to perfect the buyer's rights.[21]

Unless otherwise agreed, the buyer's obligations are: to bear the risk of loss after the goods have been delivered to the carrier; and to make payment to the seller against tender of the required documents, without any right to inspect the goods prior to such payment. The seller may not tender, nor the buyer demand, delivery of the goods in substitution for the documents. Unless otherwise agreed, C. & F. has the same effect and imposes upon the seller the same obligations and risk as a C.I.F. term except the obligation as to insurance, and imposes upon the buyer the same obligations and risks as a C.I.F. term.[22]

---

[21] UCC 2–320(2).

[22] UCC 2–320, *Comment 8:* "The C.I.F. contract calls for insurance covering the value

The parties to a C.I.F. or C. & F. contract may wish to modify the effect of these terms only to such an extent as to shift to the seller the risk of loss for ordinary deterioration, shrinkage and the like which may occur during transportation. If this is done, the other ingredients of the C.I.F. and C. & F. contracts are not disturbed by such modification, e.g., the risk of loss other than by such modification is still with the buyer. "Where the price is based on or is to be adjusted according to 'net landed weights,' 'delivered weights,' 'out turn' quantity or quality or the like, unless otherwise agreed the seller must reasonably estimate the price. The payment due on tender of the documents called for by the contract is the amount so estimated, but after final adjustment of the price a settlement must be made with commercial promptness."[23] While payment is due on tender of the required documents without any right of prior inspection, nevertheless if the parties should otherwise agree that payment is to be made on or after arrival of the goods, the seller must before payment allow such preliminary inspection as is feasible; but if the goods are lost, delivery of the documents and payment are due when the goods *should* have arrived.

Delivery Ex-Ship. Delivery "ex-ship" means that the seller has the obligation of delivering the goods from a ship which has reached a place at the named port of destination where goods of the kind are usually discharged. Ex-ship is the reverse of F.A.S.[24] Unless otherwise agreed, the seller has the obligation of discharging all liens arising out of the carriage and of furnishing the buyer with a direction to the ship thereby putting the carrier under a duty to deliver the goods; the seller bears the risk of loss until the goods leave the ship's tackle or are otherwise properly unloaded, at which time the risk of loss passes to the buyer.

No Arrival, No Sale. The seller who has the risk of loss during shipment may wish to avoid liability to the buyer for their non-arrival. The contract term "no arrival, no sale" accomplishes this intention of

---

of the goods at the time and place of shipment and does not include any increase in market value during transit or any anticipated profit to the buyer on a sale by him.

"The contract contemplates that before the goods arrive at their destination they may be sold again and again on C.I.F. terms and that the original policy of insurance and bill of lading will run with the interest in the goods by being transferred to each successive buyer. A buyer who becomes the seller in such an intermediate contract for sale does not thereby, if his sub-buyer knows the circumstances, undertake to insure the goods again at an increased price fixed in the new contract or to cover the increase in price by additional insurance, and his buyer may not reject the documents on the ground that the original policy does not cover such higher price. If such a sub-buyer desires additional insurance he must procure it for himself."

[23] UCC 2–321(1).

[24] See above, p. 271.

the parties. The seller still must properly ship conforming goods and if they arrive he must tender them on arrival to the buyer, but the seller assumes no obligation that the goods will arrive. However, the seller must not be the cause of their non-arrival; he has a duty not to interfere with the arrival of the goods. If, during shipment and without the fault of the seller, the goods experience partial loss, or have so deteriorated as no longer to conform to the contract, or arrive after the contract time, the buyer may treat the loss, deterioration, or late arrival as if there had been a casualty to identified goods,[25] i.e., either treat the contract as avoided or accept the goods with due allowance from the contract price for the loss, deterioration, or late arrival. ". . . Where the seller is reselling goods bought by him as shipped by another and this fact is known to the buyer, so that the seller is not under any obligation to make the shipment himself, the seller is entitled under the 'no arrival, no sale' clause to exemption from payment of damages for non-delivery if the goods do not arrive or if the goods which actually arrive are non-conforming. This does not extend to sellers who arrange shipment by their own agents. . . . But sellers who make known that they are contracting only with respect to what will be delivered to them by parties over whom they assume no control are entitled to the full quantum of the exemption."[26]

"Letter of Credit" and "Confirmed Credit." Often the sales contract may provide that the buyer is to furnish a letter of credit. A "letter of credit" or "banker's credit" is an irrevocable credit issued by a financing agency[27] of good repute and, where the shipment is overseas,[28] of good international repute. The buyer's failure seasonably to furnish the agreed letter of credit is a breach of the contract. If the buyer seasonably delivers to the seller a proper letter of credit, the letter of credit is conditional payment[29] and the buyer's obligation to pay the purchase price is suspended pending presentation of the letter of credit for honor. If the letter of credit is dishonored, the seller must seasonably notify the buyer that payment is to be made directly by the buyer to the seller. The term "confirmed credit" means that the credit must also carry the direct obligation of such a financing agency which does business in the seller's financial market.

---

[25] See below, p. 325.

[26] UCC 2–324, *Comment 1.*

[27] For the meaning of "financing agency," see UCC 2–104(2).

[28] For the meaning of "overseas," see UCC 2–323(3).

[29] See Contracts, above, p. 67.

3. TITLE, CREDITORS, AND GOOD FAITH PURCHASERS

Title   Property is an interest in a thing, and one kind of property is title. We have already seen[30] that *an interest in goods can pass from one person to another only when the goods exist and are identified to the contract,* with the exception of a sale of a part interest in goods. If the goods are existing and are identified to the contract, there can be either a present sale or a contract to sell depending upon the intention of the parties; while if the goods are future goods, there can be only a contract to sell and title cannot pass until the goods become existing and are identified to the contract. The intention of the parties as expressed in their agreement determines when the title to the goods is to be transferred, limited only by the legal requirement that title to goods can be transferred only when they are existing and identified to the contract. Often the parties do not clearly express their intention as to when title is to be transferred. The Code[31] prescribes certain legal rules which are to apply, reflecting the implied intention of the parties concerning passage of title. Inasmuch as ignorance of the law is no excuse, if the parties do not express their intention concerning passage of title, then they impliedly intend the legal rules to apply. *Accordingly, the approach in determining who has title to goods is: first, are the goods, or have the goods become, existing and identified to the contract; next, what is the expressed intent of the parties regarding the passage of title; and lastly, in the absence of expressed intent, how do the legal rules regarding the passage of title apply?* First identification of existing goods to the contract will be discussed, and then the rules concerning passage of title in the absence of expressed intent by the parties.

Identification of Goods. *When particular existing goods are designated as the goods for a contract, such goods are then identified as the goods for that contract.* It is not relevant to identification whether the goods do or do not conform to the contract and that the buyer has a right to return or reject non-conforming goods. What is important is the identification of those particular goods to that contract. The parties by their agreement can determine how and when identification is to occur. In the absence of expressed intent, whether or not identification

---

[30] See above, p. 245.
[31] UCC 2–401.

occurs depends upon the kind of goods involved *at the time the contract is made. If already existing goods are designated for the contract,* they are identified. *If the goods are future goods other than future crops and unborn animals,* they are identified when they are later designated by the seller as goods to which the contract refers. *Such designation may occur by shipping, marking, or otherwise designating such goods as the goods to which the contract refers. If the future goods are crops to be grown under a contract for the sale of crops to be harvested within twelve months or the next normal harvest season after the contract was made, whichever is longer,* identification occurs when the crops are planted or otherwise become growing crops. While a crop of wool on an animal is a "growing" crop, nevertheless "the product of a lumbering, mining or fishing operation, though seasonal, is not within the concept of 'growing'. Identification under a contract for all or part of the output of such an operation can be effected early in the operation."[32] *If the future goods are unborn animals to be born within twelve months after the contract was made,* identification occurs when the young are conceived. *If the goods are an undivided share of existing goods,* such as an undivided share in a fungible mass, identification of the existing goods or of the mass is sufficient to identify the share therein to be sold. It is not necessary to identification that the goods be in a deliverable state or that the seller has not completed his contractual duties with respect to the goods; the seller bears the risk of loss for his non-completion of such duties even though the goods have been identified to the contract.

Identification of itself does not cause the title to pass to the buyer, although identification is one of the elements necessary for this to occur. However, identification does affect the rights of both the buyer and the seller. By identification, the buyer obtains a *special property* as well as an *insurable interest* in the goods. Generally, the buyer's special property consists of the buyer's right to recover the identified goods from the seller: on the seller's insolvency occurring within ten days after the buyer has made part or full payment;[33] or on the seller's repudiation or failure to deliver the identified goods.[34] Inasmuch as the buyer has such special property, he can insure the same against risk of loss; he has an insurable interest in the goods.[35] As for the seller, so long as he retains title to the goods or any security interest in the goods, he has property

---

[32] UCC 2–501, *Comment* 6.

[33] See below, p. 339.

[34] See below, p. 341.

[35] For insurable interests, see Insurance, below, pp. 879–80.

which he can insure against risk of loss; he too has an insurable interest in the goods. Identification of itself does not deprive the seller of his insurable interest in the goods, although it causes the buyer also to obtain an insurable interest in the goods. *It should be noted very carefully that, where the identification is by the seller alone, he may, until default or insolvency or notification to the buyer that the identification is final, revoke his identification and substitute other goods for those identified.*

Legal Rules for Passing of Title. There are only three limitations which the Code places on the transfer of title in a contract for the sale of goods, whether such transfer is by express agreement of the parties or otherwise:

1. *The goods must be existing and identified to the contract before title to them can pass,* with the exception of a sale of a part interest in existing and identified goods.[36]
2. *Title will pass to the buyer even though the seller reserves a security interest* [37] *in the goods.*
3. *Any attempted retention or reservation by the seller of title in identified goods shipped or delivered to the buyer is limited in effect to a reservation of a security interest in the goods.* Thus, if the goods are to be shipped, the transfer of title to the buyer is not affected by the fact that the goods were shipped with a reservation of a security interest in the seller, even though a document of title (e.g., bill of lading) is to be delivered at a time and place different from the goods, and despite any reservation of a security interest in the bill of lading.

Except as so prohibited by the Code, title to existing and identified goods passes from the seller to the buyer in any manner and on any conditions expressly agreed on by the parties. If the parties do not expressly agree on when title is to pass then, unless otherwise expressly agreed, under the Code[38] title will pass depending on whether the seller is to make a *physical delivery* of the goods or to make *delivery without moving the goods.*

If the seller is to make physical delivery of the goods then, unless otherwise expressly agreed, title passes when the seller completes his performance with respect to delivery of the goods pursuant to the contract. *If the contract requires or authorizes the seller to send the goods to the buyer but does not require him to deliver them at destination, title passes to the buyer at the time and place of shipment. But if*

---

[36] See above, p. 245.

[37] UCC 1–201(37): " 'Security interest' means an interest in personal property or fixtures which secures payment or performance of an obligation. . . ."

[38] UCC 2–401.

the contract requires delivery at destination, title passes on tender of delivery[39] *there.* For example, a purchase order providing for shipment "direct *to* (buyer's address)" without any other condition is merely a shipping direction, and title to the goods ordered passes *on their delivery to the carrier by the shipper.* However, while "delivery *at* (buyer's address)" without any other condition is also a shipping direction, title to the goods ordered passes only *on tender of the goods at the buyer's address.*

If the seller is to make delivery without moving the goods then, unless otherwise expressly agreed: *if the seller is to deliver a document of title, title passes at the time when and the place where he delivers such document; but if the goods are at the time of contracting already identified and no document is to be delivered, title passes at the time and place of contracting.* For example, the seller may have a bill of lading for goods being shipped to him and he contracts for the sale of such goods to the buyer, the agreement providing that the seller is to deliver the bill of lading to the buyer; title passes to the buyer when the seller delivers the bill of lading to the buyer at the proper time and place. Another example would be the buyer's contract to purchase and pick up a specific item in the seller's store; the title passes to the buyer at the time the contract is made.

In summary, goods must be existing and identified to the contract before title to them can pass in a contract for sale, with the exception of a sale of a part interest in existing and identified goods. The expressed intent of the parties concerning the transfer of title to goods when they are, or become, existing and identified to the contract for sale governs. *Except as prohibited by the Code, title to existing and identified goods passes to the buyer when, unless otherwise expressly agreed, the seller delivers the goods pursuant to the contract.* The reasoning is that the seller has finally committed himself with respect to the identified goods, and he is held to that commitment. If he is required or authorized to send the goods, then his commitment occurs when he has delivered the goods to the carrier. If the contract requires him to make delivery at destination, then his commitment occurs when he has done this. If no shipment is to occur, then his commitment is when he delivers the agreed document of title to the goods, or if no such document is to be delivered then his commitment is at the time the contract is made. Under the Code, *any* attempt by the seller to vary this result by reservation of title (e.g., bill of lading with seller as consignee)[40] is ineffective and results only in the

---

[39] For tender of delivery, see below, pp. 303 ff.

[40] For this effect irrespective of form of bill of lading, see below, p. 306.

creation of a seller's security interest in the goods. It should be noted carefully that a buyer's justified revocation of acceptance,[41] or his justified or unjustified rejection or other refusal to receive or retain the goods,[42] or his setting the transfer aside pursuant to any principle under the law of contracts[43] (e.g., fraud, duress, coercion, undue influence), revests title to the goods in the seller by operation of law, and such revesting is not itself a sale.

Rights of Seller's Creditors against Sold Goods   We have seen[44] that when existing goods are identified to the contract, the buyer acquires a special property in the goods consisting of the buyer's right to recover the identified goods from the seller under the conditions of the seller's insolvency or his repudiation or failure to deliver the identified goods. In the absence of the Code or state law to the contrary, the rights of *unsecured creditors* of the seller with respect to goods which have been identified to a contract for sale are subject to such buyer's rights. However, under the Code a creditor who has perfected his security interest has a right in the goods superior to that of the buyer.[45] If by state law where the goods are located retention of possession by the seller is fraudulent as to his creditors, the creditors may treat the sale or an identification of goods to a contract for sale as void.[46] However the Code modifies such state law to the extent that "retention of possession in good faith and current course of trade by a *merchant seller* for a commercially reasonable time after a sale or identification is not fraudulent." (Author's italics)[47] However, "Where identification to the contract for delivery is made not in current course of trade but in satisfaction of or as security for a pre-existing claim for money, security or the like and is made under

---

[41] See below, p. 319.

[42] See below, pp. 314–15.

[43] See above, pp. 43 ff.

[44] See above, p. 276.

[45] See below, p. 745.

[46] Whether or not retention by the seller is fraudulent as a matter of law as to the seller's creditors varies among the states. In most states, such retention raises a presumption of fraud which is rebuttable, as by the buyer showing he has not had a reasonable period of time in which to remove the goods because of their bulk or other meritorious reason. In the minority of states, the presumption is conclusive and the sale is void as to creditors. In some states, retention is presumptively or conclusively fraudulent only as to subsequent creditors, i.e., creditors who become such subsequent to the sale; while in other states, the presumption applies to existing creditors, i.e., creditors who were such at the time of the sale, as well as to subsequent creditors.

[47] UCC 2–402(2).

circumstances which under any rule of law of the state where the goods are situated"[48] would constitute the transaction a fraudulent transfer or voidable preference, the rights of the seller's creditors are preserved and are not impaired. If the retention is fraudulent in fact, i.e., made with an intent to hinder, delay, or defraud creditors, the sale is fraudulent as to the seller's creditors.

Good Faith Purchasers

In General. Under the Code, "A purchaser of goods acquires all title which his transferor had or had power to transfer except that a purchaser of a limited interest acquires rights only to the extent of the interest purchased. . . ."[49] Briefly, *the transferee gets only what the transferor has or has power to transfer.* (O owns a horse. If O sells it to B, B gets O's title to the horse. Instead, if T steals the horse from O and sells it to B, a good faith purchaser for value,[50] B gets what T his transferor had and, since there was no transfer from O to T, T got nothing from O and neither did B, T's transferee. O still has title to the horse.)

If the transferor does not have title to goods, his *power* to transfer a good title under certain circumstances becomes of utmost importance. Except for estoppel, Factors Acts, transfer of voidable title, and entrusting goods to a merchant, which will be discussed in that order, only the owner of an interest can transfer that interest. A person who is the owner of goods continues as such owner until he, or his authorized agent, transfers the title to the goods. A person who is not the owner of goods, and who has no authority to transfer title to such goods, can transfer no better title than the one he has. The English principle of "market overt," whereby a sale of goods on the open

---

[48] UCC 2–402(3)(b).

[49] UCC 2–403(1).

[50] The familiar term "bona fide purchaser for value" is a purchaser for value in good faith, without notice of any adverse claim. "Bona fide" means good faith. In the law of sales under the Code, he is called a "good faith purchaser for value."

Under UCC 1–201: "(33) 'Purchaser' means a person who takes by purchase"; "(32) 'Purchase' includes taking by sale, discount, negotiation, mortgage, pledge, lien, issue or re-issue, gift or any other voluntary transaction creating an interest in property"; "(44) 'Value'. Except as otherwise provided with respect to negotiable instruments and bank collections (Sections 3–303, 4–208 and 4–209) a person gives 'value' for rights if he acquires them

    (a) in return for a binding commitment to extend credit or for the extension of immediately available credit whether or not drawn upon and whether or not a charge-back is provided for in the event of difficulties in collection; or

    (b) as security for or in total or partial satisfaction of a pre-existing claim; or

    (c) by accepting delivery pursuant to a pre-existing contract for purchase; or

    (d) generally, in return for any consideration sufficient to support a simple contract."

market transfers a good title to a good faith purchaser for value, is not applicable in the United States. The buyer gets no better title than the title of the seller.

Transfer of Title by Estoppel. In our previous discussion of estoppel[51] we learned that when one person represents or "holds out" to another person a material fact and the other person changes his position materially to his prejudice in reasonable reliance on the holding out, the first person is prohibited in law or "estopped" to deny what he had asserted previously. The owner of goods may be precluded, i.e., estopped, from setting up his title to such goods because of his conduct, which has misled an innocent person to purchase the goods. (B asks O whether T is the owner of a certain horse in T's possession. O informs B that T is the owner, when in fact O is the owner. In reliance on the information received from O, B innocently purchased the horse from T. Although T did not have title to the horse or any authority to sell such horse and B would acquire only whatever title T had, nevertheless O has held out that T owned the horse and B has changed his position materially in reliance on the holding-out by purchasing the horse from T. T is the apparent owner and O, therefore, is estopped to set up his title as against B. If B had bought the horse from T *before* O had informed B that T was the owner, then, since B had not relied on O's statement, estoppel does not apply, and O retains title to the horse.)

Factors. A "factor" usually is a bailee in possession of goods with authority to sell them.[52] Under the laws in many of the states, called "Factors Acts," innocent persons who purchase goods from factors without knowledge of any violation of the authority of such factors obtain the title of the person who entrusted such goods to the factors.[53] Goods are sent to a factor "on consignment," signifying a bailment with authority to sell the goods, title remaining in the seller. This is not the same as a "sale on approval" contemplating later transfer of title to the buyer, and it is not the same as a "sale or return" whereby title thereby passes by sale to the buyer with the option in the buyer to revest title in the seller.[54]

Voidable Title. *When goods have been delivered under a transaction of purchase, the purchaser has the power to transfer a good title to the goods to a good faith purchaser for value.* It should be noted very carefully that the goods must be *delivered.* A "voidable title" is a title

---

[51] See above, p. 42.

[52] See below, pp. 509–10.

[53] See Agency, below, p. 561.

[54] See above, p. 262.

which is subject to a power of avoidance, and the sale of a voidable title to a good faith purchaser for value without notice of such power of avoidance terminates such power as against such purchaser. (S fraudulently induces O to sell goods to S, creating a voidable contract voidable at O's election. O delivers the goods to S, who then sells and delivers them to B, a good faith purchaser for value without notice of the fraud. B has O's title to the goods, and O cannot assert any power of avoidance as against B.)[55] Exercise of the power of avoidance *before* a subsequent sale to a good faith purchaser for value revests the title in the person exercising such power of avoidance and, therefore, there is no voidable title to transfer. (S fraudulently induces O to sell and deliver a horse to S. O avoids the contract and then S sells and delivers the horse to B, a good faith purchaser for value. Although the Code does not specifically provide for such a case, O probably has title to the horse because S has no voidable title to transfer. Note that, if O had delivered the horse to S who is a *merchant-dealer in horses,* B would acquire O's title to the horse under the rule concerned with entrusting goods to a merchant.[56] Note also that, if S is *not* a merchant-dealer in horses, if O had delivered the horse *and a bill of sale* to S and after avoidance S still possessed the horse *and* the bill of sale, S would be the apparent owner and title to the horse would be acquired by B.) It should be noted very carefully that a person with a voidable title has power to transfer a *good* title to a good faith purchaser for value. The Code[57] indicates the following ways by which a voidable title to goods may be created, although this does not preclude a power of avoidance arising by principles in other branches of the law (e.g., duress, coercion, undue influence in the law of contracts):

1. The transferor was deceived as to the identity of the purchaser. (O, the owner, sold and delivered his horse to B, who misrepresented that he was C. B then sold and delivered the horse to D, a good faith purchaser for value. D now has title to the horse.)
2. The delivery was in exchange for a check, which is later dishonored. (O, the owner, sold and delivered his horse to B, who gave O a check for the purchase price. B sold and delivered the horse to C, a good faith purchaser for value. B's check subsequently was dishonored. C has title to the horse.)
3. It was agreed that the transaction was to be a "cash sale." Under the former concept of "cash sale," the parties to the contract contemplated simultaneous transfer of title and possession in exchange for the price

---

[55] An infant's voidable contract for the purchase of goods is similarly affected under the law of contracts. See above, pp. 18–19.

[56] See below, pp. 283–84.

[57] UCC 2–403(1).

immediately, and title could not pass until both transfer of possession and payment of the purchase price occurred. Under the old law, if a check were given in payment pursuant to a bargain for a cash sale and the goods had been delivered to the buyer, the title did not pass to the buyer until the check was paid. (O sold and delivered goods to B in exchange for B's check in a cash sale. B subsequently sold and delivered the goods to C, a good faith purchaser for value. B's check was dishonored. Under the old law, O still had title to the goods. Under the Code, C acquires the title.)

4. The delivery was procured through fraud punishable as larcenous under the criminal law.

Entrusting Goods to a Merchant. In the absence of statute to the contrary, the mere entrusting of possession of goods by one person to a non-merchant without authority to sell such goods does not of itself give to the non-merchant any power to transfer the entruster's title to the goods. By "entrusting" is meant *any* delivery of goods and *any* acquiescence in retention of possession by another.[58] (A rents his electric saw to B. B sells the saw to C. C does not acquire A's title to the saw.) The mere entrusting without authority to deal with the goods is not such a sufficient representation of ownership or of authority as to mislead third persons that such ownership or authority exists.[59] However, "any entrusting of possession of goods to a *merchant who deals in goods of that kind* gives him *power* to transfer all rights of the entruster to a *buyer in ordinary course of business.*" (Author's italics)[60] A merchant-dealer has apparent ownership of, and inherent agency power[61] to sell, the kind of goods in his possession in which he is dealing, and any entrusting of that kind of goods to him places him in a position to mislead persons who buy in ordinary course from him. " 'A buyer in ordinary course of business' means a person who in good faith and without knowledge that the sale to him is in violation of the ownership rights or security interest of a third party in the goods *buys in ordinary course from a person in the business of selling goods of that kind* but does not include a pawnbroker. All persons who sell minerals or the like (including oil and gas) at wellhead or minehead shall be deemed to be persons in the business of selling goods of that kind. 'Buying' may be

---

[58] UCC 2–403(3): " 'Entrusting' includes any delivery and any acquiescence in retention of possession regardless of any condition expressed between the parties to the delivery or acquiescence and regardless of whether the procurement of the entrusting or the possessor's disposition of the goods have been such as to be larcenous under the criminal law."

[59] See Agency, below, pp. 560–561.

[60] UCC 2–403(2).

[61] See Agency, below, p. 561.

for cash or by exchange of other property or on secured or unsecured credit and includes receiving goods or documents of title under a pre-existing contract for sale but *does not include a transfer in bulk or as security for or in total or partial satisfaction of a money debt."* (Author's italics)[62] (O entrusts his watch for repair to J, a jewelry store which sells and repairs watches. J's sale of the watch to B, a buyer in ordinary course of business, transfers O's title to the watch to B, irrespective of whether J sells as the owner or as the agent of O.) (A buys an electric stove from D, a dealer in kitchen equipment, A to pick up the stove later. D sells and delivers the stove to B, a buyer in ordinary course of business. B has obtained A's title to the stove.) The rule extends even to a warehouseman of fungible goods, also in the business of buying and selling fungible goods, who unauthorizedly sells fungible goods entrusted to him for storage, even though a negotiable warehouse receipt is outstanding.[63] When other Articles of the Code are applicable to a transaction, they govern. Accordingly, the rights of other purchasers of goods and of lien creditors are governed by the Articles on Secured Transactions (Article 9), Bulk Transfers (Article 6) and Documents of Title (Article 7).

---

[62] UCC 1–201(9).

[63] UCC 7–205. See above, pp. 203–4.

Chapter VI

WARRANTIES

1. *IN GENERAL*

The Warranty **Meaning.** THE word "warranty" has a variety of meanings in the various branches of the law[1] and is one of the most difficult legal terms to define. In the law of sales, a warranty is essentially a party's assurance of fact, either expressly or impliedly in an agreement, concerning a state of goods and resulting in a contractual obligation of performance. An example is a statement that certain goods are or shall be of a certain kind. The warranty obligation springs from *the bargain in the agreement of the parties and it is a part of the basis for such bargain,* unless the parties lawfully disclaim the presence of such warranty obligation as not being a part of their agreement. The warranty term may be expressly or impliedly agreed to as a part of their agreement. A warranty expressly agreed to is called an "express warranty"; and a warranty impliedly agreed to is called an "implied warranty." However, the warranties of title and against infringement which would otherwise be considered as implied warranties are classified as express warranties in order that the Code rules of disclaimer applicable to implied warranties would not apply to them.[2]

The assurance of fact may occur at the time an agreement for the sale of goods is made, or subsequently as a modification of such prior agreement before the agreement is fully performed. As we have already seen,[3] a modification of a prior agreement may be made by a subsequent agreement or by course of performance, irrespective of the form of the original agreement, and need not be supported by consideration to be binding. (S and B contract for the sale of goods by S to B. Subsequently,

---

[1] See Samuel Williston, *The Law Governing Sales of Goods* (rev. ed.; New York: Baker, Voorhis & Co., 1948), Vol. I, sec. 181.

[2] UCC 2–312, *Comment 6.*

[3] See above, p. 252.

S warrants the quality of the goods. S's warranty is in modification of the original agreement and becomes a part of the contract.)

Caveat Emptor. The Common Law doctrine of *caveat emptor* does not exist under the Code. At Common Law, the seller was not responsible for the quality or condition of the goods under a contract for their sale, unless he had given an express warranty concerning them. Where the buyer had an opportunity to examine the goods and there was no fraud by the seller, the buyer took the risk of ascertaining that the goods were of the quality or condition that he expected them to be. This was the rule of *caveat emptor,* meaning "let the buyer beware." Later, by judicial decision, then by the Uniform Sales Act, and now by the Code various warranties are imposed by law in accord with the spirit of the bargain agreement between the parties. Warranties imposed by law are sometimes called "imposed" warranties, examples of which are the two express warranties of title and against infringement and the two implied warranties of merchantability and fitness for a particular purpose. Warranties arising expressly from the contract of the parties are sometimes called "contractual" warranties, examples of which are the five express warranties that goods will conform to an affirmation, promise, description, sample, or model.

	Contractual Warranties	*Imposed Warranties*
Express Warranties:	1. Goods shall conform to the affirmation.	1. Title.
	2. Goods shall conform to the promise.	2. Against infringement.
	3. Goods shall conform to the description.	
	4. Goods shall conform to the sample.	
	5. Goods shall conform to the model.	
Implied Warranties:		3. Merchantability.
		4. Fitness for a particular purpose.

First express warranties, then implied warranties, and finally enforceability of warranties will be discussed.

2. EXPRESS WARRANTIES

Express warranties may be imposed by law as a part of the agreement of the parties, or may be expressly agreed to in the agreement. First, express warranties imposed by law and then express warranties expressly agreed to by the parties will be discussed.

Express Warranty of Title. The Code recognizes
Imposed by   that, unless otherwise agreed and in the absence of
Law   circumstances to the contrary, the parties to a con-
                      tract for the sale of goods intend to transfer title to
the goods. The buyer wants, and in good faith expects, to acquire a good,
valid, clean title to the goods free from any lien or encumbrance of
which he has no knowledge at the time of contracting. The seller is held
to know this. Accordingly, *unless otherwise agreed and in the absence of
circumstances to the contrary, in every contract for the sale of goods
there is the following warranty by the seller:*

(a) *The title conveyed shall be good, and its transfer rightful; and*
(b) *The goods shall be delivered free from any security interest or other
lien or encumbrance of which the buyer at the time of contracting has
no knowledge.* (Authors' italics)[4]

It should be noted carefully that, with respect to (b) above, *at the time
the contract was made* the buyer must not have any *knowledge,* not
merely notice,[5] of any lien or encumbrance on the goods. A buyer is on
constructive notice of a recorded lien but, for the purpose of the warranty of title, he does not have *knowledge* of it and there is a breach of
the seller's express warranty of title. A contract for sale includes a
present sale and a contract to sell, and this express warranty occurs in
either transaction. It is unimportant whether or not the seller has
possession of the goods at the time of the contract for their sale. The
Code abolishes the implied warranty of quiet possession which existed
under the prior law; however, quiet possession is a part of what is
warranted under the warranty of title, and any disturbance of the
buyer's quiet possession of the goods is evidence of breach of the
warranty of title. Under the Code,[6] the Statute of Limitations begins to
run on a breach of warranty of title when tender of delivery of the
goods is made.

Exclusion or Modification of Warranty of Title. The warranty
of title may be excluded or modified "only by *specific language* of the
parties, or by *circumstances* which give the buyer reason to know that
the person selling does not claim title in himself or that he is purporting
to sell only such right or title as he or a third person may have."
(Author's italics)[7] A contract for the sale of goods "as is" or "with all

---

[4] UCC 2–312(1).
[5] For the difference between knowledge and notice, see UCC 1–201(25).
[6] UCC 2–725(2).
[7] UCC 2–312(2).

faults" does not disclaim this express warranty. A clause generally disclaiming "all warranties express or implied" is not sufficiently specific to exclude *any* warranty, express or implied. *The language must specifically exclude or modify with respect to title.* For example, "We assume no responsibility that the title conveyed shall be good or its transfer rightful or that the goods shall be delivered free from any security interest or rightful claim of any third person by way of infringement or otherwise"[8] excludes the express warranty of title as well as the express warranty against infringement. *The circumstance of persons selling goods by reason of their representative capacity does not impose a warranty of title by themselves personally.* Illustrations of such persons are: a sheriff, auctioneer, mortgagee, agent, executor, and broker. Such persons manifest to sell only what *they* have. Also, a contract for the sale of only what the *seller* has negates an express warranty of title.

Express Warranty against Infringement. A buyer of goods from a *merchant-dealer in goods of that kind* expects the goods not to be an infringement on the rights of third persons, such as their patent or trade-mark. Such an infringement would mar the buyer's title. A non-merchant seller is not in a position to learn whether or not such an infringement exists, but a merchant-dealer of such goods is in business and should be held to this responsibility. Accordingly, *unless otherwise agreed, in a contract for the sale of goods by a seller who is a merchant-dealer in goods of the kind sold, there is a warranty by the seller that the goods shall be delivered free of any infringement or the like of rights of third persons.* However, if the buyer orders goods by furnishing specifications prepared by himself, the buyer now is assuring or warranting to the seller that goods of such specifications would not infringe the rights of third persons; there is then no warranty against infringement by the seller, and the buyer must indemnify the seller for any loss suffered by him for infringement by his compliance with the buyer's specifications. The Code does not specify any particular way of excluding or modifying this warranty other than the buyer furnishing specifications.

Warranties Expressed in the Agreement

Express Warranties by Affirmation, Promise, Description, Sample, or Model. Warranty is a reflection of what the buyer desires and, accordingly, *what the seller has agreed to sell.* The *bargain* of the parties determines what is being sold and, therefore, warranted by the seller. The Code cuts through formal-

---

[8] William D. Hawkland, *Sales and Bulk Sales* (Philadelphia, Pa.: The American Law Institute, 1958), p. 49.

ity and concentrates on the *bargain*. It is for this reason that the bargain begets the seller's warranty and that clear proof must be given of the exclusion or modification of a seller's warranty. The parties' agreement consists of their bargain as found in their language or by implication from other circumstances, including course of dealing, usage of trade, or course of performance. When the seller expressly makes an affirmation or promise relating to the goods, gives a description of the goods, or uses a sample or model *as a part of the basis for the bargain,* this induces the buyer to rely on it in making the bargain, and the seller thereby has made five corresponding *express warranties* that:

1. The goods shall conform to the affirmation.
2. The goods shall conform to the promise.
3. The goods shall conform to the description.
4. The goods shall conform to the sample.
5. The goods shall conform to the model.

Form. It is not necessary that the seller use any special words, such as "warrant" or the often misused word "guarantee,"[9] or even that he intend to make an express warranty. Making the affirmation, promise, description, or using the sample or model as a basis for the bargain of itself assures and thereby warrants that performance in conformity will occur. An express warranty need not be in any special form, and it may be written or oral. "I promise the machine to be accurate" and "The machine is accurate" are express warranties. The first quotation is in the form of a promise. The second quotation is in the form of an affirmation of fact. An express warranty may be made for a future time, such as a promise that the machine will operate accurately for one year. The express warranty may occur in a present sale or in a contract to sell. The description need not be by language, but may be by a drawing, blueprint, map, design, or the like. Even a course of dealing of previous deliveries may expressly or impliedly constitute a description of quality. By "sample" is meant something drawn in good faith from a bulk, and by "model" is meant something illustrative but not drawn from a bulk. The affirmation, promise, description, sample, or model may be made at any time, and if made after the bargain it thereby becomes, without any requirement of consideration, a modification and part thereof. These five warranties are express warranties of quality and, since they were expressly made by the contract, are sometimes called "contractual warranties." In contrast, the express warranties of title and against infringement and the implied warranties of merchantability and fitness for a particular purpose are imposed by law.

---

[9] See Suretyship, below, p. 808.

The seller's affirmation, promise, description, sample, or model estab-lishes the respective corresponding warranty, and proof of reliance by the buyer on the seller's conduct is not required to establish such warranties. A seller's statement which becomes *part of the basis for the bargain* signifies that it induced the buyer to rely on such statement in entering into the bargain. *The seller's statement creates the warranty;* reliance on such statement by the buyer is presumed, and it is a *part of the bargain.* If the seller claims that none of these warranties exists, he must prove that his affirmation, promise, description, sample, or model was not a part of the bargain because the buyer did not rely on it. If the seller can prove that the buyer knew that the seller's affirmation, prom-ise, description, sample, or model is untrue, then it does not create a corresponding warranty in the bargain. The Code does not specifically state any requirement of inducement by the seller or reliance by the buyer on the seller's affirmation, promise, description, sample, or model; however, the Code's repeated use of the phrase "part of the basis for the bargain" is interpreted to presume such inducement and reliance. Reli-ance by the buyer occurs by his purchase of the goods, induced by the express warranty. The purpose of the express warranty is to induce the buyer to purchase the goods without making any examination of them, and the buyer's purchase without making any such examination in reliance on the express warranty excuses the buyer from sustaining the loss from any defects which such examination might have revealed. An express warranty does not cover any defect of which the buyer knows, or reasonably should know. The buyer's reliance must be a reasonable or justifiable reliance; he cannot reasonably rely on a seller's affirmation or promise of fact when he knows that such is false. A seller's express warranty may be general, such as that a horse is sound, and if the buyer knows that the horse is blind in one eye, the express warranty applies to the horse in every particular except the blindness in one eye.

Puffing. Courts permit sellers a great deal of latitude in praising and commending their wares, commonly called "puffing," in order to induce the buyer to purchase goods. Puffing and the use of words customarily used by honest traders and extravagant expressions regard-ing the goods that the buyer reasonably could understand to mean puffing do not constitute an express warranty. "The best car on the market" and "The best buy in toothpaste" are illustrations of puffing. Such puffing or sales talk is recognized by the public for what it is and, as really a representation of opinion only, it is not to be relied upon by a reasonable man *as a part of the basis for a bargain.*

Opinion. Under the Code, a statement purporting to be merely the seller's opinion or commendation of the goods, or the seller's affirmation merely of the value of the goods, does not create an express warranty.[10] A statement of value is a form of opinion, but a statement of the facts which determine the expressed value is an affirmation of fact and is an express warranty. "The goods are worth $100" is quite different from "The goods have a book value of $100"; the former is an expression of value and is not an express warranty, while the latter is a statement of fact and is an express warranty. "I have received two offers for this property at $500 each" is a statement of fact and is an express warranty; this is more than puffing. Similarly, a statement of the cost of the particular goods is a statement of fact and is an express warranty.

Exclusion or Modification. Under the Code: "Words or conduct relevant to the creation of an express warranty and words or conduct tending to negate or limit warranty shall be construed wherever reasonable as consistent with each other; but subject to the provisions of this Article on parol or extrinsic evidence (Section 2–202) negation or limitation is inoperative to the extent that such construction is unreasonable."[11] This Code provision seeks to protect the buyer and preserve the express warranties of conformity with affirmation, promise, description, sample, or model as a part of the basis for the bargain against a purported disclaimer that is not specific enough to dispel what the buyer bargained for. The disclaiming phrase excluding "all warranties express or implied" is not specific enough to exclude these express warranties.

3. IMPLIED WARRANTIES

Again, *the basis of the bargain* of the parties reflecting what goods the buyer expects from the seller and, therefore, *what the seller undertakes to supply* determines the warranties of the seller assuring the buyer with respect to such goods. The parties may *expressly* agree on warranties of merchantability and fitness for a particular purpose resulting in these two express warranties of quality. However, under certain circumstances these warranties of quality are *implied by law* in a con-

---

[10] Although the Code flatly so states, and the C.P.A. examiners have expected this as an answer, nevertheless mention should be made that a statement of opinion or of value may become an express warranty when the opinion or value is indicated as a fact and is made by an expert, or by someone who should know the correctness of the opinion or value, to a person who is ignorant of the correctness of the opinion or value. This could become a part of the basis for the bargain and an express warranty result.

[11] UCC 2–316(1).

tract for the sale of goods and, for this reason, they are sometimes called "imposed" warranties. Under the Code,[12] the serving for value of food or drink to be consumed either on the premises or elsewhere is a sale and, therefore, such food or drink can be the subject of the warranties of merchantability and fitness for a particular purpose imposed by law.

The warranties of merchantability and fitness for a particular purpose are easily distinguished from each other by their content. Under a warranty of merchantability, the goods are warranted *by a merchant in a given line of trade to be "of a quality comparable to that generally acceptable in that line of trade under the description or other designation of the goods used in the agreement"* (Author's italics)[13]—fit for the *ordinary* purposes for which such goods are used. Under a warranty of fitness for a particular purpose, the goods are warranted by the seller, whether a merchant or not, to be *fit for the known purpose of that particular buyer* who has relied on the seller's skill or judgment. The two warranties may exist at the same time, springing from the same transaction. First the implied warranty of merchantability and then the implied warranty of fitness for a particular purpose will be discussed.

Implied Warranty of Merchantability

An implied warranty of merchantability is implied by law if the seller is a merchant-dealer in goods of the kind being sold under the contract for sale. The merchant-dealer may be a grower or manufacturer of the goods. The buyer may order the goods by description, or he may specifically designate the goods he desires. The warranty of merchantability applies to a contract for second-hand goods, although such goods are in a different category of what is fit for the *ordinary* purposes for which such goods are sold. "Ordinary purposes" does not include the unusual use by a supersensitive or allergic buyer.

The Code clearly states when goods are merchantable and provides a standard for performance in conformity with the warranty:

(2) *Goods to be merchantable must be at least such as*
    (a) pass without objection in the trade under the contract description; and
    (b) in the case of fungible goods, are of fair average quality within the description; and
    (c) are fit for the *ordinary* purposes for which such goods are used; and

---

[12] UCC 2–314(1).
[13] UCC 2–314, *Comment 2.*

(d) run, within the variations permitted by the agreement, of even kind, quality and quantity within each unit and among all units involved; and

(e) are adequately contained, packaged, and labeled as the agreement may require; and

(f) conform to the promises or affirmations of fact made on the container or label if any. (Author's italics)[14]

Exclusion or Modification. The warranty of merchantability is commonly taken for granted, and its exclusion or modification in a contract for the sale of goods is so very unusual that it must be clearly brought to the buyer's attention and thereby prevent his unexpected and unbargained disclaimer. It is for this reason that the Code provides that, in order to exclude or modify the warranty of merchantability or any part of it:

1. The language of exclusion or modification *must specifically mention merchantability.*

2. *If* the exclusion or modification is contained *in a writing,* it *must be conspicuous therein.* "A term or clause is conspicuous when it is so written that a reasonable person against whom it is to operate ought to have noticed it. A printed heading in capitals (as: NON-NEGOTIABLE BILL OF LADING) is conspicuous. Language in the body of a form is 'conspicuous' if it is in larger or other contrasting type or color. But in a telegram any stated term is 'conspicuous.' Whether a term or clause is 'conspicuous' or not is for decision by the court."[15]

3. If the *"fit for the ordinary purposes" part* of the warranty of merchantability is to be excluded or modified, the exclusion or modification *must be in writing and be conspicuous.*

However, the circumstances surrounding the transaction may in themselves be sufficient to call the buyer's attention to the fact that no implied warranties are made or that a certain implied warranty is being excluded. Circumstances which do this and thereby exclude *any* implied warranty are:

1. The agreement is for the sale of goods "as is," "with all faults," or other similar language the common understanding of which has the same effect of calling to the buyer's attention that there is no such implied warranty.

2. Before entering into the contract: the buyer examined the goods, sample, or model as fully as he desired; or, after demand made by the seller to examine the goods fully, the buyer refused to do so. On such examination or refusal to examine, there is no implied warranty with regard to

---

[14] UCC 2–314(2).
[15] UCC 1–201(10).

defects which an examination ought in the circumstances to have revealed to him.[16]

3. Course of dealing, course of performance, or usage of trade may exclude an implied warranty.

4. The buyer's conduct may exclude an implied warranty. For example, where the buyer gives precise and complete specifications as to the goods, there is no implied warranty because the buyer expects to get only what he has specifically ordered and not merchantable goods. However, the precise description of the goods is a part of the basis of the bargain and, therefore, creates an express warranty that the goods shall conform to the description.[17] Also, inasmuch as the Code in its consideration of warranties is trying to reflect the reasonable expectations of the parties, if the buyer knows of a defect in the goods rendering them unmerchantable, a warranty of merchantability will not be implied.

Implied Warranty of Fitness for a Particular Purpose

An implied warranty that goods are fit for a *particular* purpose is imposed by law if two things occur:

1. *The buyer requires the goods for a particular purpose and is relying on the seller's skill or judgment to select or furnish goods suitable for that purpose;* and

2. *At the time the contract is made, the seller has reason to know of such particular purpose and of the buyer's reliance.* The buyer need not inform the seller of the particular purpose and reliance, although he can do so; what is important is that the seller has reason so to know at the time the contract is made, whether he was told by the buyer or the circumstances reasonably should so indicate to him.

An implied warranty of fitness for a particular purpose may arise in connection with a present sale or a contract to sell. The seller may be anyone, whether or not a manufacturer or grower and whether a merchant or a non-merchant, and the buyer may purchase for his own use or for resale.

A particular purpose means that the purpose is different from the ordinary purpose for which such goods are used. It is for some peculiar use by this buyer. If the goods are for ordinary use, then there is no implied warranty of fitness for a particular purpose, but there is an

---

[16] UCC 2–316, *Comment 8:* "The particular buyer's skill and the normal method of examining goods in the circumstances determine what defects are excluded by the examination. A failure to notice defects which are obvious cannot excuse the buyer. However, an examination under circumstances which do not permit chemical or other testing of the goods would not exclude defects which could be ascertained only by such testing. Nor can latent defects be excluded by a simple examination. A professional buyer examining a product in his field would be held to have assumed the risk as to all defects which a professional in the field ought to observe, while a nonprofessional buyer will be held to have assumed the risk only for such defects as a layman might be expected to observe."

[17] See the express warranty created by description, above, p. 289.

implied warranty of merchantability, because that warranty is for ordinary use. Both the warranties of fitness for a particular purpose and of merchantability may occur from the same transaction, the ordinary and particular purposes being present. (S contracts with B to supply and deliver to B a heater, which S knows B intends to use to heat B's house. There is an implied warranty of merchantability that the heater will heat, and there is an implied warranty of fitness for a particular purpose that the heater will heat B's house. If S had no reason to know of B's particular purpose of heating his house, then only the implied warranty of merchantability exists.)

The buyer must rely on the seller's skill or judgment. The buyer's selection of particular goods is in reliance on his own skill and judgment and not on that of the seller. (A picked out a TV set in S's retail TV store and bought it. There is no warranty of fitness for a particular purpose, although the implied warranty of merchantability is present.) The buyer need not give a description of the goods to the seller, although he may and often does so. However, the buyer's description may be so detailed a specification as to the goods that the buyer is not relying on the seller's skill or judgment, and there is no warranty of fitness for a particular purpose, nor of merchantability either,[18] although there will be an express warranty by the seller that the goods will conform with the description.[19] While prior to the Code the buyer's purchase of goods under its patent or trade name excluded any warranty of fitness for a particular purpose because the buyer thereby did not rely on the seller's skill or judgment, this is no longer true under the Code. The buyer's purchase of goods by patent or trade name does not *of itself* exclude the warranty of fitness for a particular purpose; it is no longer a conclusive fact of non-reliance but, rather, it is only one fact among others as evidence to prove that the buyer has not relied on the seller's skill or judgment. However, the buyer's *insistence* on a particular brand of goods may be such that he no longer relies on the seller's skill or judgment in supplying him with goods suitable for his particular purpose, and there is no implied warranty of fitness for a particular purpose.

Exclusion or Modification. It should be noted carefully that there are two warranties concerned with fitness for *a* purpose. One is the implied warranty of *fitness for a particular purpose.* The other is the implied warranty of *merchantability* which assures that the goods will

---

[18] See above, pp. 292–94.
[19] See above, p. 289.

be *fit for ordinary purposes.*[20] The Code provisions concerning exclusion or modification deal equally with the implied warranty of fitness for a particular purpose and with *only that part of the warranty of merchantability concerned with fitness for ordinary purposes.* Solely for the purpose of discussion under this paragraph heading, we will describe these two warranties concerned with fitness as "the two fitness warranties." The two fitness warranties may only be excluded or modified in any of the following five ways:

1. Except for 2, 3, 4, and 5 below, exclusion or modification *must be in writing and be conspicuous therein.* The language of exclusion or modification need not specifically refer to the two fitness warranties, but *may be general language* excluding both warranties. For example, "There are no warranties which extend beyond the description on the face hereof"[21] excludes the two fitness warranties.
2,3,4,5. These are the same as the four items on pages 293–94, above, in connection with exclusion or modification of the implied warranty of merchantability.

4. CUMULATION AND CONFLICT OF WARRANTIES

The intention of the contracting parties as disclosed by their agreement determines their respective contractual rights and obligations. Inasmuch as their contract is to be examined as a whole, reflecting all their intentions, if there is more than one warranty involved then *they are considered to be cumulative, and are to be construed as consistent with each other to the extent that this is possible.* If such construction is unreasonable, then recourse must be made to the intention of the parties to determine which of the conflicting warranties is to be dominant. The matter of the seller's good faith becomes important here. If the seller in good faith made warranties which subsequently are found to be inconsistent, then it must be determined which is to be dominant. However, if the seller has not acted in good faith and has misled the buyer by assuring him that the inconsistent warranties can be performed, then he is bound to perform *all* of them and he is estopped to assert their inconsistency. The Code establishes specific criteria to ascertain the intention of the parties as to which of inconsistent warranties is dominant:

(a) Exact or technical specifications displace an inconsistent sample or model or general language of description.

---

[20] See above, p. 292.
[21] UCC 2–316(2).

(b) A sample from an existing bulk displaces inconsistent general language of description.

(c) Express warranties displace inconsistent implied warranties other than an implied warranty of fitness for a particular purpose.[22]

5. ENFORCEABILITY OF WARRANTIES

Who May Enforce Warranties

By their *privity of contract,* the seller and buyer determine their respective contractual rights and obligations. Their rights and obligations derive from their contract and, unless otherwise agreed and in the absence of legislative provision or judicial decision to the contrary, a warranty in the contract is enforceable only against the person who made it and only by the person to whom it was made. In other words, the familiar rule in the law of contracts applies that only those parties who are in privity of contract may enforce the contract. It is their contract for them to agree upon as they please, but subject to any Code rules which reflect mandatory public policy. They may contract that the seller's warranties shall extend to third persons, who then can enforce such warranties directly against the seller as third party beneficiaries under the contract.[23] They may exclude all third persons from being beneficiaries under any *existing* warranties, but with one Code limitation. *To the extent that a warranty exists, it extends not only to the seller's buyer but also to natural persons in his buyer's family or household and to guests in his buyer's home whom the seller reasonably can expect to use, consume, or be affected by the warranted goods and who are injured in person by breach of such warranty.* (S sells goods to B, and C is injured by the goods, S having breached his warranty to B. If C is an employee of B, S is not liable to C. If B is a college and C is a student, C is not a member of B's household and, therefore, S is not liable to C. If C is a guest in B's home, S is liable to C. If S's contract with B provided that his warranty extended to all purchasers of such goods from B, then S is liable to C as a third party beneficiary of the contract between S and B. If B resold the goods to C with a warranty in favor of C, and D, a guest in C's home, is injured by use of the goods: B is liable to D on B's warranty to C; S is not liable to D on S's warranty to B because only B is S's buyer and D is not a guest in B's home. S is liable only to the beneficiary of *S's* buyer, namely B.) The seller cannot limit his warranty so as to escape this result. The purpose is to accord to such persons the same benefit of such

---

[22] UCC 2–317.

[23] See Contracts, above, p. 97.

warranty *as the buyer has* and not to limit their claim directly against the seller for breach of warranty because they were not in privity of contact with the seller.

Only to the above extent *under the Code* is the privity of contract rule broken. However, the Code does not preclude the enlargement or restriction of developing case law on the further invasion of the privity of contract rule, nor does the Code restrict or limit any right or remedy based on the tort of negligence. The Code limits its legislative invasion only to the extent indicated.

The Code compulsorily makes only those persons indicated above beneficiaries of a warranty; it does *not preclude* any other persons from being beneficiaries either by contractual provision of the parties or by the developing case law. The problem now being dealt with by developing case law is concerned with the status of sub-vendees or ultimate consumers. (M, manufacturer of foods, sells a can of beans to R, retailer of foods, who resells it to C, a consumer who is injured in eating the defectively processed beans. M has breached his warranty of merchantability to R and is liable to him under their contract. R has breached his warranty of merchantability to C and is liable to him under their contract. But should M be liable to C? Lack of privity of contract between M and C precludes C from asserting *any* warranty against M. But C may proceed against M for his tort of negligence, later discussed,[24] where no privity of contract is required.) Cases presenting this problem are often called "products liability" cases. Because of the obvious difficulty which a sub-vendee will have in proving negligence by a producer, in order to hold the producer liable for negligence some courts have sought to find a warranty from the producer to the sub-vendee and thereby ease the burden of the sub-vendee, who can then directly hold the producer liable for breach of warranty to him. Some of these courts have found such a warranty in the producer's method of advertising and distributing his goods through the distributor or retailer directly to the sub-vendee. A large number of courts have imposed strict liability on the producer of defective food and drink, irrespective of whether or not the producer was negligent, and some courts have extended strict liability to nonfood cases. Some courts which retain the privity of contract rule have resorted to the judicial expedient of permitting avoidance of legal circuity of action and, since the producer is liable to the retailer on the producer's warranty, and, in turn, the retailer is

---

[24] See below, pp. 299–301.

liable to the consumer on the retailer's warranty, the consumer has been permitted to shortcut and proceed directly against the producer. Some courts have resorted to the concept that the contract between the producer and middleman is a third party beneficiary contract in which the producer's warranty is for the benefit of the sub-vendee, who can enforce their contract by suing the producer directly on his warranty. A few courts have held the producer's disclaimer of liability to third parties, contained in his contract with a middleman, to be void as against public policy. The cases affording relief to the ultimate consumer directly against the producer are based either on tort or contract grounds. The dominant tendency appears to be in the direction of strict tort liability, although there is a wide difference of view as to who may hold whom liable for what!

Liability for Negligence In the law of torts certain duties are imposed upon a supplier of chattels which vary as the character of the supplier, the purpose of the chattel's use, and the gravity of harm to which the user is exposed. The supplier's negligent failure to comply with these duties which proximately causes harm causes the supplier to be liable for committing the tort of negligence, his liability extending to those persons who he reasonably can foresee will use the chattel or may be in the vicinity of its use for the purpose supplied. A person who, for any purpose and in any way, transfers his possession of a chattel for the use of others or permits others to use it, is a supplier. For example, a supplier may be a vendor, lessor, bailor, or donor. A supplier may supply a chattel to a user directly or indirectly through third persons, as, for example, a wholesaler may supply a chattel to a retailer who supplies it to a user (the consumer).

The supplier of a chattel which he *knows or has reason to know* is, or is likely to be, dangerous when used for the purpose supplied (e.g., chemicals) has a duty to exercise reasonable care to give warning of the danger to those persons who he can reasonably foresee will use the chattel, or may be in the vicinity of its use, for the purpose supplied, when he reasonably believes they are unlikely to discover and appreciate the danger. The chattel is *inherently dangerous for the use supplied*. The law with regard to the liability of a supplier to users other than his immediate transferee has developed greatly from no liability, when there was no privity of contract between the supplier and the remote users, to liability if the chattel is known to be inherently dangerous for the use supplied. Whether or not the supplier's warning to the person he supplied, on the assumption that the latter would warn subsequent transferees, is performance of the supplier's duty depends upon the gravity of the bodily harm threatened. If the danger is of slight bodily harm and the supplier has no reason to believe that the warning will not be communicated further, the supplier's warning is sufficient. If the danger is of death or serious bodily harm, the warning is insufficient if the supplier can utilize practicable and not unduly burdensome means of giving warning (e.g., the chattel bears its own warning, as by explanatory labels upon a container of poison or explosive). Also, one who supplies a chattel to a person who, the supplier knows or should know, is likely to use it so as to subject other persons than himself to an unreasonable risk of bodily harm, is liable to such persons for bodily harm thereby caused to them; this is knowingly supplying a chattel to a person incompetent to use it. A vendor other than a manufacturer who does not know, or has no reason for knowing, that the chattel is, or is likely to be, inherently dangerous has no duty to inspect the chattel, and he is not liable for bodily harm caused by the dangerous condition even though an inspection by him would have revealed the danger.

A manufacturer is liable not only as a supplier of chattels which he knows, or reasonably should know, to be inherently dangerous, but, by the famous case of *MacPherson* v. *Buick Motor Company*,[25] he is also liable to the same extent for the negligent manufacture of a chattel which he should realize, *if made negligently,* involves an unreasonable risk of *substantial* bodily harm in its use for the purpose manufactured. It is the risk of harm from imperfect manufacture of the chattel, and not the inherent danger in its use, that is important here. For example, a perfume or a coffee urn is not inherently dangerous, but its negligent manufacture involves an unreasonable risk of substantial bodily harm. This liability of the manufacturer is not affected by the fact that a person under a duty to the person injured to inspect the chattel would have discovered the danger if he had made the inspection. An independent contractor who negligently makes, rebuilds, or repairs a chattel of another has the same liability as that of a negligent manufacturer. A vendor who holds himself out as the manufacturer of a chattel which has been manufactured by another has the same liability as though he were the manufacturer. It should be noted that, if the supplier has

---

[25] 217 N.Y. 382, 111 N.E. 1050, L.R.A. 1916F, 696 (1916).

manufactured food which is in a sealed container, the container must not have been opened before acquisition by the remote consumer.

It should be noted very carefully that the supplier of chattels is liable to the remote consumer, and to those persons in the vicinity of the chattel's use, not on the ground of warranty but because of the commission of the tort of negligence.

PERFORMANCE AND BREACH OF CONTRACT

1. *PERFORMANCE OF THE CONTRACT*

EACH of the parties to a contract for the sale of goods has contractual rights and obligations to perform. Performance means complete performance; nonperformance means a failure of performance, whether in small or great degree. Performance or nonperformance by one party has an immediate legal effect on the rights and obligations of the other party. This chapter will discuss performance in the first section and nonperformance amounting to breach of contract in the second section.

Delivery and Payment

Obligations of the Parties. The seller's obligation is to transfer and deliver goods or a bill of lading, and the buyer's obligation is to accept and pay for such goods, in accordance with their contract. We have already seen[1] that the agreement of the parties determines their contractual rights and obligations and that an agreement consists of the bargain of the parties as expressly made, or as implied from other circumstances which include course of dealing, usage of trade, and course of performance. The Code fills in the omitted details of their bargain by reflecting commercial practice. The parties may agree that delivery of the goods or bill of lading by the seller and payment of the price by the buyer are to occur concurrently, or that payment is to precede or follow delivery. *Unless the parties otherwise agree, the seller's tender of delivery of the goods or bill of lading and the buyer's tender of payment of the price pursuant to the contract are concurrent conditions.* That is to say, unless otherwise agreed, the seller's tender of delivery in accordance with the contract is a condition to the buyer's duty to accept the goods or bill of lading and to pay for them, and the seller's tender entitles him to the buyer's acceptance of the goods and to the buyer's payment in accordance with the contract. Similarly, unless otherwise agreed, the buyer's tender of payment in

---

[1] See above, p. 247.

accordance with the contract is a condition to the seller's duty to tender and complete delivery of the goods or bill of lading, and the buyer's tender of payment entitles him to the seller's delivery of the goods or bill of lading in accordance with the contract. If the seller makes a conditional delivery to the buyer and demands payment, the buyer has no right with respect to the goods or document of title delivered to him until payment is made. Should the seller make conditional delivery and, on nonpayment by the buyer, fail to assert his right to repossession, the condition of payment is waived, it is a sale on credit, and the seller is merely a general creditor with no specific rights in the goods; although later discussion[2] will indicate that the seller has 10 days after such delivery in which to reclaim goods sold on credit to an insolvent buyer.

Effect of the Seller's Insolvency. The seller's insolvency materially affects the buyer's rights to identified goods. A person is insolvent "who either has ceased to pay his debts in the ordinary course of business or cannot pay his debts as they become due or is insolvent within the meaning of the federal bankruptcy law."[3] *After identification,* the buyer acquires a special property interest in the goods which includes the right to possession of the goods under certain conditions. If the *seller* identified goods to the contract and he becomes insolvent within 10 days after the buyer has paid either the full purchase price or the first installment of the purchase price, the buyer has the right to recover the identified goods from the seller, provided that if the full purchase price has not been paid the buyer make and keep good a tender of the unpaid portion of the purchase price. If the *buyer* made the identification, in addition to the above the identified goods must conform to the contract. The reason for this special provision when the buyer has made the identification is to preclude the buyer from getting goods greatly superior in quality or quantity to that called for by the contract.

The remainder of this section will consist of a discussion of delivery by the seller, payment by the buyer, and risk of loss in that order.

Delivery by the Seller

Seller's Tender of Delivery. Delivery means voluntary transfer of possession from one person to another. It may be made by one person through his authorized agent to another person through the latter's authorized agent. As we have seen,[4] delivery is important in the transfer of title. *Tender of delivery* is also important in connection with

---

[2] See below, p. 330.

[3] UCC 1–201(23).

[4] See above, pp. 277–79.

the buyer's duty to pay the price. *Tender of delivery by the seller occurs when the seller puts and holds conforming goods at the buyer's disposition and gives to the buyer any notification reasonably necessary to enable the buyer to take delivery.*[5] Unless otherwise agreed, it is the buyer's obligation to furnish facilities reasonably suited to the receipt of the goods. The contract of the parties determines the manner, time, and place for tender. Unless otherwise agreed, delivery may be tendered or demanded only at a reasonable hour, and if the tender is to be made of goods rather than of documents of title the goods must be kept available for the period reasonably necessary to enable the buyer to take possession. The seller's obligation may be to make a physical delivery of the goods, to make delivery without moving the goods, or to deliver documents, and his tender of delivery will vary accordingly.

Physical Delivery—Shipment. If the seller is to make physical delivery of the goods, normally he is only to *"ship,"* i.e., *send,* the goods to the buyer, although at times he is to *deliver them at a particular destination.* Each of these will be considered separately.

Under the Code,[6] when the seller is required or authorized to *send* the goods to the buyer then, unless otherwise agreed, in order to make a *tender of delivery* he must:

1. Put conforming goods in the possession of such a carrier and make such a contract for their transportation as may be reasonable having regard to the nature of the goods and other circumstances of the case; and
2. Obtain and promptly deliver or tender in due form any document which is necessary to enable the buyer to obtain possession of the goods or which is otherwise required by the agreement or by usage of trade; and
3. Promptly notify the buyer of the shipment.

The seller's failure to make a proper contract for the transportation of the goods as required in (1) above or to notify the buyer as in (3) above does not invalidate the seller's tender but, rather, is a ground for the buyer's rejection only if material delay or loss ensues. With respect to the seller's contract for transportation of the goods, if without the fault of either buyer or seller the agreed manner of delivery becomes commercially impracticable, as where there is a failure of facilities (e.g., the agreed berthing, loading, or unloading facilities fail), the Code permits substituted performance by the seller.[7] The seller has the obligation of making all necessary arrangements with the carrier which are reasonable under the circumstances, such as sending along any necessary

---

[5] UCC 2–503(1).

[6] UCC 2–504.

[7] UCC 2–614; see below, pp. 324–25.

help, refrigeration, watering of livestock. The seller's prompt notification to the buyer of shipment may be accomplished by the commercial practice of sending an invoice if it is an open credit shipment, or sending documents as provided in requirement (2). It should be noted that, unless otherwise agreed, since the seller has the right to demand payment on tender of delivery,[8] if the seller should so demand payment he must first permit the buyer to exercise his right to inspect the goods[9] so as not to impair his tender of delivery, unless the buyer's right of inspection has been precluded, such as by a C.I.F., C.O.D., or cash against documents contract.

If a seller is to *deliver goods at a particular destination,* he makes a *tender of delivery* if: he puts and holds conforming goods at the buyer's disposition at the destination; he gives to the buyer any notification reasonably required to enable the buyer to take delivery; and, if documents are involved, he tenders such documents as appropriate as indicated in the following two paragraphs where delivery occurs without moving the goods or the contract requires the seller to deliver documents.

Delivery without Moving the Goods. Where the goods are in the possession of a bailee (e.g., carrier, warehouseman, or other person not the seller), under the Code[10] the seller may make a *tender of delivery* in the following ways:

1. The seller may tender to the buyer a *negotiable* document of title covering the goods.
2. The seller may procure acknowledgment by the bailee of the buyer's right to possession of the goods.
3. The seller may tender to the buyer a *non-negotiable* document of title, subject to the buyer's seasonable objection.
4. The seller may tender to the buyer a written direction to the bailee to deliver the goods to the buyer, subject to the buyer's seasonable objection.

The first two methods of tender are proper and valid; but the buyer need not accept the third and fourth methods of tender, although his failure seasonably to object causes them to be valid. In connection with the fourth method of tender, receipt by the bailee of notification of the buyer's rights fixes those rights as against the bailee and all third persons. In connection with the third and fourth methods of tender, until the buyer has had a reasonable time to present the document of title to the bailee, the seller bears the risk of loss of the goods and the

---

[8] See above, pp. 303–4.

[9] See below, pp. 309 ff.

[10] UCC 2–503.

risk of any failure by the bailee to honor the non-negotiable document of title or to obey the direction to the bailee to deliver the goods to the buyer; a refusal by the bailee to honor the document or to obey the direction nullifies the tender.

Seller Required to Deliver Documents. Although it is extremely unusual, where the contract *requires* the seller to deliver documents instead of delivering goods, the seller is required to tender all such documents in correct form, except that with respect to bills of lading in a set under certain circumstances only one part of the bill of lading need be tendered.[11] Tender of documents through customary banking channels is sufficient, and dishonor of a draft[12] (i.e., bill of exchange) accompanying the documents constitutes non-acceptance or rejection by the buyer.[13]

Seller's Shipment under Reservation; Form of Bill of Lading. When goods are shipped by the seller, he will obtain a bill of lading from the carrier. The form of the bill of lading is irrelevant to the transfer of title to existing and identified goods which occurs when the goods have been delivered by the seller pursuant to the contract, irrespective of the seller's reservation of a security interest in the goods.[14] *Any attempted retention or reservation by the seller of title in identified goods shipped or delivered to the buyer is limited in effect to a reservation of a security interest in the goods.* However, the form of the bill of lading does affect the nature of the interests therein of the seller and buyer and their transferees, and the obligation of the carrier.

The bill of lading may be negotiable or non-negotiable. Under the Code,[15] where the seller has identified goods to the contract by or before shipment and has procured a *negotiable bill of lading,* irrespective of who the consignee named therein is, *the seller thereby acquires a security interest in the goods.* This is so even though the bill of lading is to the order of a financing agency[16] or of the buyer, which indicates that, in addition to the seller's security interest in the goods, the seller has the expectation of transferring that interest to that consignee. If the bill of lading is non-negotiable, then: if the *seller or his nominee*[17] is the

---

[11] See UCC 2–323(2) and 7–304.

[12] See UCC 3–104(2) (a).

[13] UCC 2–503(5) (b).

[14] See above, p. 277.

[15] UCC 2–505(1) (a).

[16] *Ibid.*

[17] The seller may find it convenient to have the goods sent to the order of his nominee, such as the bank extending credit to the seller or the financing agency to whom he intends to negotiate the bill of lading.

consignee, the seller's security interest is his *right to possession* of the goods as security; but if the *buyer* is the consignee, the seller has *no security interest in the goods* even though the seller retains possession of the bill of lading, and the buyer can rightfully obtain the goods from the carrier without surrendering any bill of lading to the carrier. As previously discussed,[18] the carrier's contract is to deliver possession of the goods to the consignee, or his known transferee, of a *non-negotiable* bill of lading without picking up the bill of lading; while if a *negotiable* bill of lading is outstanding, the carrier has the obligation of delivering the goods to the order of the consignee named in the bill, and the carrier cannot be compelled to deliver the goods to anyone without the surrender of the bill of lading. However, the seller consignee of a non-negotiable bill of lading still has the power, *as the unpaid seller of an insolvent buyer,* to stop the goods while they are in transit.[19] If the contract for sale provided that the seller had a right of payment against delivery of the goods, the seller could make an immediate demand for payment by the buyer and assert that his delivery of the goods to the carrier in exchange for a non-negotiable bill of lading *with the buyer as consignee* was a conditional delivery; but it should be noted carefully that, as previously discussed,[20] the buyer has the power to transfer title to the goods to a good faith purchaser for value or to a buyer in ordinary course of business, depending on the character of the latter's seller. It should be noted further that the shipping seller's reservation of a security interest in violation of the contract for sale is a breach of contract and is also an improper contract for transportation and, therefore, not a tender of delivery by the seller.[21] It should also be noted that a financing agency which has paid, or purchased for value, a draft which relates to a shipment of goods acquires to the extent of the payment or purchase: the rights of a holder of the draft;[22] the rights of a holder of any document of title securing the draft; the shipping seller's security rights in the goods (e.g., right to stop the goods while in transit if the buyer becomes insolvent); and the shipping seller's right to have the buyer honor the draft. When the financing agency has in good faith honored or purchased the draft under the commitment to or authority from the buyer, the agency has a right of reimbursement from the buyer, and this right is not impaired by subsequent discovery of defects

---

[18] See above, p. 220.

[19] See below, pp. 333–35.

[20] See above, pp. 281 ff.

[21] See above, pp. 303 ff.

[22] See Commercial Paper, below, pp. 418–21.

with reference to any relevant document which was apparently regular on its face.

Cure and Replacement. Sellers do not always tender or deliver conforming goods. As long as the time for a seller's performance under his contract has not expired, he may make other attempts to perform and cure the non-conformity. If the buyer rejects the seller's tender or delivery of non-conforming goods and the time for the seller's performance under the contract has *not expired,* the seller may make a delivery of conforming goods *provided he first seasonably notifies the buyer of his intention to cure his previous non-conforming tender or delivery.* If the buyer rejects a non-conforming tender *which the seller had reasonable grounds to believe would be acceptable,* and the time in which the seller was to perform *has expired,* nevertheless the seller may have a further reasonable time to substitute a conforming tender *provided he seasonably notifies the buyer of his intention to cure his previous nonconforming tender.*

Payment by the Buyer

Form of Payment. The price may be money or any other property or services, as previously discussed.[23] We have seen[24] that, unless the buyer and seller otherwise agree, the seller's tender of delivery and the buyer's tender of payment of the price pursuant to the contract are concurrent conditions. The parties may otherwise agree, as in a contract providing for credit to the buyer (which occurs in most commercial sales), in which case payment is to be made in accordance with such credit provision. Because tender of delivery and tender of payment are concurrent conditions unless otherwise agreed, and since the Code rules provide for the place of the seller's delivery if the parties have not otherwise agreed,[25] then the place and time of tender of payment by the buyer are determined by those Code provisions unless otherwise agreed.

Tender of payment is sufficient if made in the medium and manner agreed to by the parties. *Unless otherwise agreed, tender of payment is sufficient when made by any means or in any manner current in the ordinary course of business, which includes legal tender.*[26] However,

---

[23] See above, p. 264.

[24] See above, p. 302.

[25] See above, p. 269.

[26] Legal tender statutes prescribe the particular kind of money which an obligee is required to accept in discharge of an obligation. The term "money" includes, but is not limited to, legal tender. UCC 1–201(24): " 'Money' means a medium of exchange authorized or adopted by a domestic or foreign government as a part of its currency."

unless otherwise agreed, the seller has the right to payment in legal tender if he so desires to assert it. Because the buyer may be surprised at the time of the seller's performance by the seller's rightful demand for legal tender when the buyer may have contemplated payment in another manner, as by check, if the seller demands payment in legal tender he must also give any extension of time reasonably necessary for the buyer to procure it. The check[27] is a very widely used device to make payments and, if accepted by the seller, it is *conditional payment,* meaning that the check is accepted on the condition that it is paid. The buyer's contractual obligation to pay is not performed unless the check is honored. Meanwhile, the buyer's contractual obligation to pay the purchase price is suspended until the check's dishonor when duly presented for payment;[28] such dishonor nullifies the conditional payment by check. The seller's acceptance of a *credit* instrument from the buyer, such as the buyer's promissory note or his post-dated check, constitutes a delivery *on credit* as far as third parties are concerned, although as between the buyer and the seller the buyer's dishonor of the instrument affects the buyer's solvency and the seller's remedies therefor.[29] It should be noted carefully that we have considered only the *buyer's* check. Under the Code, if a *bank* is drawer, maker, or acceptor of the instrument delivered by the buyer to the seller in payment, the buyer has made full payment and his contractual obligation is discharged.[30] The reason is that such primary obligation of the *bank* is currently accepted in ordinary business as full payment.

It should also be noted that the seller may have obtained documents for goods shipped and may wish to draw a draft (i.e., bill of exchange) on the drawee (the person who is ordered to pay the instrument, e.g., buyer, financing agency financing the transaction) so as to be paid the purchase price on delivery of the documents to the drawee. Unless otherwise agreed, if the draft is payable *more than three days after presentment,* then the seller is to deliver the documents to the drawee on his "acceptance" (the drawee's signed engagement to honor the draft as presented)[31] of the draft; but if the draft is payable *earlier,* the drawee is to receive the documents only on the drawee's payment

Buyer's Right of Inspection. The buyer should have a reasonable opportunity to examine the goods being purchased in order to

---

[27] For definition of check, see below, p. 376.
[28] See Commercial Paper, below, pp. 451 ff.
[29] See below, p. 330.
[30] UCC 3-802(1), see below, p. 464.
[31] See UCC 3-410(1), below, p. 435.

determine whether they conform to the contract and whether he should make payment, unless the contract precludes it. Accordingly, under the Code,[32] *unless otherwise agreed, where goods are tendered or delivered or identified to the contract for sale, the buyer has a right before payment or acceptance to inspect them. He has this right even though:* the seller sent the goods under reservation of a security interest and tenders documents of title; the goods are sent under a C.I.F. contract which, however, *provides for payment on or after arrival,* although if the goods are lost delivery of the documents and payment are due when the goods should have arrived; the contract provides for payment against documents, *but also provides for payment due only after the goods become available for inspection.* Also, where there is casualty to identified goods resulting in partial loss to such goods or such deterioration in the goods as to cause them to become non-conforming, the buyer may demand an inspection.[33] However, *unless otherwise agreed, the buyer has no right of inspection if the contract provides:* for delivery C.O.D. or any other like terms; for payment against documents of title; for C.I.F. without any payment "on or after arrival" clause.

Unless otherwise agreed, the buyer's right is to inspect the goods at any reasonable place and time and in any reasonable manner. When the seller is required or authorized to send the goods to the buyer, the inspection may be after their arrival. The parties may, by their agreement, fix a place or method of inspection, and such place or method shall be presumed to be exclusive. If compliance with the agreed place or method of inspection becomes impossible, the intention of the parties becomes important. If the intention of the parties was that such compliance as agreed was an indispensable condition of the contract, then the contract is avoided. However, if this is not the intention of the parties, then the inspection shall be at any reasonable place and in any reasonable manner. The buyer bears the expense of inspection; however, if the goods are non-conforming and are rejected by the buyer, he may recover such expense from the seller. Where the contract requires the buyer to make payment before inspection, the buyer's payment does not constitute an acceptance of the goods or impair his right to inspect or any of his remedies. Under such a contract, the fact that the goods are non-conforming does not excuse the buyer from making the required payment, with two exceptions; the buyer is to pay first and, if the goods are non-conforming, litigate later. This is the intention of the parties,

---

[32] UCC 2–513.
[33] UCC 2–613.

and it is to be observed. However, the buyer is not required to make payment preceding inspection under such a contract if: the non-conformity of the goods appears without inspection; or, despite tender of the required documents, the circumstances would justify injunction against honor under UCC 5–114.

As can be expected, there are times when the parties disagree concerning the conformity or condition of the goods. In order to further the adjustment of any claim or dispute between them, the Code provides:

1. Either party on reasonable notification to the other and for the purpose of ascertaining the facts and preserving evidence has the right to inspect, test and sample the goods including such of them as may be in the possession or control of the other; and
2. The parties may agree to a third party inspection or survey to determine the conformity or condition of the goods and may agree that the findings shall be binding upon them in any subsequent litigation or adjustment.[34]

This provision lays the basis for amicable non-judicial adjustment, as by arbitration or otherwise.

Risk of Loss The parties to the contract determine who shall bear the risk of loss to the goods. If their agreement does not make provision for risk of loss, the Code provides that who bears the risk of loss depends primarily on whether or not there is a breach of contract by the seller or buyer.

Without Breach of Contract. *If there is no breach* then, unless otherwise agreed, *the risk of loss is on the seller until he completes his performance with respect to delivery of the goods pursuant to the contract by making physical delivery or by making delivery without moving the goods.*

1. Where the contract requires or authorizes the seller to *ship the goods by carrier:* if he is merely to *send* the goods, *the risk of loss passes to the buyer when the goods are duly delivered*[35] *to the carrier even though the shipment is under reservation;*[36] but if the contract requires the seller to *deliver the goods at a particular destination, the risk of loss passes to the buyer when delivery is tendered*[37] *to the buyer.*

---

[34] UCC 2–515.

[35] To be "duly delivered," the goods must be delivered to the carrier and a contract made for their transportation as may be reasonable, having regard to the nature of the goods and other circumstances of the case; and the seller must obtain a suitable document to enable the seller to tender delivery to the buyer. For tender of delivery, see above, pp. 303 ff.

[36] For shipment under reservation, see above, p. 277.

[37] For tender of delivery at destination, see above, pp. 303 ff.

2. Where the goods are *held by a bailee* (*not the seller*) *to be delivered without being moved, the risk of loss passes to the buyer:* on the buyer's *receipt* of a *negotiable* document of title covering the goods; or on *acknowledgment by the bailee* of the buyer's right to possession of the goods; or after the buyer's *receipt* of a *non-negotiable* document of title or other written direction to the bailee to deliver, *unless the buyer seasonably objects.*[38]

3. *In any case not within* (1) *or* (2) *above,* the risk of loss passes to the buyer on his *receipt* of the goods *if the seller is a merchant;* otherwise the risk passes to the buyer on *tender of delivery.* "The underlying theory of this rule is that a *merchant* who is to make physical delivery at his own place continues meanwhile to control the goods and can be expected to insure his interest in them. The buyer, on the other hand, has no control of the goods and it is extremely unlikely that he will carry insurance on goods not yet in his possession." (Author's italics)[39]

It should be noted that, as previously discussed,[40] in a sale on approval the risk of loss does not pass to the buyer until he accepts the goods. It should be noted further that if the seller is selling goods shipped prior to his contract with the buyer, as by the seller purchasing the goods already shipped by someone else, when the seller identifies such goods to the contract and the shipment of which is in conformity with the seller's contract with the buyer, the risk of loss then passes to the buyer *from that point* and not retroactively to the point of the initial shipment of such goods. The party who has caused loss to the goods should bear such risk of loss.

With Breach of Contract. *Until the seller performs the contract or the buyer accepts the goods, the seller bears the risk of loss; thereafter it shifts to the buyer.* If the seller's tender or delivery of the goods is non-conforming and the buyer has a right of rejection,[41] the seller bears the risk of loss until his cure of such improper tender or delivery[42] or until the buyer accepts the goods. However, where the buyer has accepted the goods but later rightfully revokes[43] his acceptance he may, to the extent that his effective insurance does not cover such loss, shift the risk of loss back to the seller as of the time the contract was made. Similarly, if the seller is still in possession of conforming goods identified to the contract and the buyer breaches the contract (e.g., repudiation) before the risk of loss passes to the buyer the seller may, to the extent that his effective insurance does not cover such loss, shift the risk

---

[38] See above, p. 305.

[39] UCC 2–509, *Comment 3.*

[40] See above, p. 262.

[41] See below, p. 314.

[42] See above, p. 352.

[43] As to when revocation of acceptance may occur, see below, p. 319.

of loss to the buyer for a commercially seasonable time. This means that the seller, provided he acts promptly, may procure insurance coverage to the extent of his non-coverage at the buyer's expense; any delay by the seller will cause him to waive his right so to act, and any subsequent loss to the extent of deficiency in his effective insurance coverage will be borne by the seller.

2. BREACH OF CONTRACT

In General
Under the law of contracts,[44] nonperformance of a contractual duty may or may not be a breach of contract, depending on whether or not such nonperformance is wrongful. A breach of contract is a wrongful nonperformance of a contractual duty. Failure to render performance when due without any legal justification or excuse for such nonperformance is wrongful and is a breach of contract. Repudiation when performance is due is a breach of contract; anticipatory repudiation before performance is due is an anticipatory breach of contract, which may be retracted under certain conditions.[45] The Code provisions on breach of contract in the law of sales reflect in large part the law of contracts, with adjustment to the sales transaction.

Under the Code,[46] the obligation of the seller is to transfer and deliver, and the obligation of the buyer is to accept and pay, in accordance with the contract. Improper delivery by the seller's failure to supply goods or to tender delivery in conformity with the contract,[47] or his failure to deliver the goods[48] constitutes a breach of contract. Wrongful rejection of goods by the buyer,[49] his wrongful revocation of his previous acceptance of the goods,[50] or his failure to make a payment when due on or before delivery[51] constitutes a breach of contract. Repudiation and anticipatory repudiation by either party is a breach of contract,[52] and failure to furnish specifications for performance or to cooperate in performance by either party may be treated by the other as a breach of contract, already discussed.[53] Most of these breaches will be

[44] See Contracts, above, pp. 126 ff.
[45] See above, p. 128.
[46] UCC 2–301.
[47] UCC 2–601.
[48] UCC 2–711(1).
[49] UCC 2–703.
[50] UCC 2–703.
[51] UCC 2–703.
[52] UCC 2–609, 610.
[53] UCC 2–311(3), see above, p. 268.

discussed later under Remedies.[54] The seller's nonperformance may be excused under certain circumstances[55] or may be waived by the buyer.[56] First improper delivery by the seller's failure to supply goods or to tender delivery in conformity with the contract, then repudiation, then substituted performance, and finally excused nonperformance will be discussed.

Improper Delivery Under the Code,[57] and subject to special Code provisions on breach in installment contracts,[58] contractual limitations of remedy,[59] and the seller's right to cure improper tender or delivery,[60] *if the goods or tender of delivery fail in any respect to conform to the contract, the buyer has the following rights: reject all the goods; accept all the goods; accept any commercial unit[61] or units and reject the rest.* Once a cause for rejection arises, the buyer acquires a remedy therefor, and the buyer's acceptance of a non-conforming tender or delivery does not deprive him of such remedy.[62] The buyer's right of rejection must be exercised in a certain manner, especially if he is a merchant; it is limited in installment contracts; it entails salvage of the rejected goods by the buyer; and it may be waived by the buyer's waiver of the breach of contract for wrongful delivery. These aspects of rejection will be discussed in that order.

Rightful Rejection. *Manner and Effect.* This discussion is confined to the buyer's rightful rejection. Should his rejection be wrongful, it would constitute a breach of contract with resulting legal rights and remedies in the seller.[63] The buyer may either reject or accept goods for nonconformity with the contract. Unless the buyer acts diligently to reject, his inactivity may constitute both a waiver of his right of rejection and an acceptance of the goods. The buyer may rightfully reject goods only in a proper manner and his subsequent conduct must not be inconsistent with his rejection. *The buyer may reject goods only within a reasonable time after their delivery or tender, and only if he season-*

---

[54] See below, pp. 329 ff.
[55] See below, p. 325.
[56] See below, p. 317.
[57] UCC 2–601.
[58] See below, p. 315.
[59] See below, p. 345.
[60] See above, p. 308.
[61] For definition of commercial unit, see above, p. 244.
[62] Remedies are discussed in Chapter VIII, below, pp. 329 ff.
[63] See below, pp. 329 ff.

ably notifies the seller of such rejection. What is a reasonable time depends on the circumstances and is directly affected by the buyer's right of inspection.[64] While the parties may expressly agree on the time for inspection or rejection, if such contractual provision is unconscionable because it does not afford the buyer a reasonable time to discover defects, the provision is void. Except for the buyer's limited obligation of salvage of the rightfully rejected goods, especially if he is a merchant, *the buyer has only two obligations with respect to rightfully rejected goods:*

1. He must not exercise ownership with respect to any commercial unit.
2. He must hold the goods with reasonable care at the seller's disposition for a time sufficient to permit the seller to remove them, if before rejection the buyer obtained physical possession of the goods in which he has no security interest.[65]

He is in effect an involuntary bailee for the seller. If negotiations are in process between the parties, of course the above discussion is appropriately limited or modified accordingly.

Installment Contracts. Often wrongful delivery occurs in connection with installment contracts. A contract which requires or authorizes delivery of goods in separate lots to be separately accepted is an installment contract. The parties cannot change this legal effect, even if the contract contains a clause "each delivery is a separate contract" or equivalent wording. Non-conformity by reason of a defect in *required documents* creates a right of rejection in the buyer; but if *goods* are non-conforming, the goods cannot be rightfully rejected unless the non-conformity *substantially* impairs the value of that installment *and* the non-conformity cannot be cured by the seller. However, if the non-conformity does not constitute a breach of the whole contract and if the seller gives adequate assurance of its cure,[66] the buyer *must* accept that installment. The reason for this is that the seller has the right to cure for improper delivery, and if the seller gives adequate assurance the entire contract can be saved. If the non-conformity or default in one or more installments substantially impairs the value of the *whole contract,* the whole contract is breached, although it may be reinstated by the aggrieved party's waiver of such breach. The test of substantial value is whether material inconvenience or injustice will result to the aggrieved party by the non-conforming installment. Waiver of the breach of the

---

[64] See above, pp. 309 ff.

[65] For the buyer's security interest in rejected goods, see below, p. 343.

[66] The seller's allowance against the price for a non-conforming installment often is a cure.

whole contract by the aggrieved party occurs by: his acceptance of a non-conforming installment without seasonably notifying the other party of cancellation; his bringing an action with respect only to past installments; or his demand of performance as to future installments. An installment agreement which expressly or impliedly requires accurate conformity in quality as a condition to acceptance in effect establishes the criterion of what is a substantial impairment of value impossible to cure.[67]

Salvage. Under the Code,[68] the rightfully rejecting buyer has a limited obligation of salvage of the rejected goods, especially if he is a merchant.

When the rightfully rejecting buyer is a *merchant,* under the Code[69] he has the following two obligations, in addition to the two indicated immediately above, subject to his security interest in the goods, *if the seller has no agent or place of business at the market where rejection occurred:*

1. The merchant buyer has a duty after rejection of goods in his possession or control to *follow any reasonable instructions received from the seller with respect to the goods.*
2. *In the absence of such instructions from the seller and if the goods are perishable or threaten to decline in value speedily,* the merchant buyer has the duty to *make reasonable efforts to sell them for the seller's account.*

Under (1), to be reasonable, the seller's instructions must, on the buyer's demand, include indemnity for expenses. Under (2), on such sale by the merchant buyer, he has a right of reimbursement from the seller or out of the proceeds for reasonable expenses of caring for and selling the goods, and if the expenses include no selling commission then to such commission as is usual in the trade or if there is none to a reasonable sum not exceeding 10 per cent on the gross proceeds. The merchant buyer is held only to good faith, and good faith conduct is neither acceptance on his part, conversion, nor the basis for any action for damages for errors in judgment.

---

[67] "Substantial impairment of the value of an installment can turn not only on the quality of the goods but also on such factors as time, quantity, assortment, and the like. It must be judged in terms of the normal or specifically known purposes of the contract. The defect in required documents refers to such matters as the absence of insurance documents under a C.I.F. contract, falsity of a bill of lading, or one failing to show shipment within the contract period or to the contract destination. Even in such cases, however, the provisions on cure of tender apply if appropriate documents are readily procurable." UCC 2–612, *Comment 4.*

[68] UCC 2–603.

[69] UCC 2–603.

When the buyer, *whether or not a merchant,* has rightfully rejected goods and the seller has given no instructions to him within a reasonable time after notification of rejection, the buyer has three options *which he may exercise if he wishes;* except, as indicated immediately above, if the buyer is a merchant and the goods are perishable he must make a reasonable effort to sell them for the seller's account. The options are: to store the rejected goods on the seller's account; to reship them to the seller; or to resell them for the seller's account, with reimbursement as in the case of a merchant buyer's sale of perishables. The buyer's exercise of an option is not an acceptance or conversion of the goods, and it does not impair his right of rejection.

Waiver of Breach by Buyer. *In General.* Either party may waive a breach of contract. The waiver may be without consideration and may be oral, by estoppel, or in the case of a disputed or alleged breach it must be in writing and signed and delivered by the aggrieved party to the other party. Course of performance is relevant to show a waiver of a contract term inconsistent with such course of performance,[70] although course of performance involves repeated occasions as contrasted with estoppel, which involves a single occasion. Our discussion will be concerned primarily with waiver on the single occasions of the buyer's failure to particularize defects and his acceptance of nonconforming goods, which will be discussed in that order. It should be noted however that, although the Code provides that in certain instances the buyer's remedies for defects survive his acceptance without being expressly claimed as long as he *notifies* the seller of such defects,[71] the Code also provides that, to be on the safe side, "A party who with explicit reservation of rights performs or promises performance or assents to performance in a manner demanded or offered by the other party does not thereby prejudice the rights reserved. Such words as 'without prejudice', 'under protest' or the like are sufficient."[72] A waiver of a breach of an executory contract may be retracted by reasonable notification *received* by the other party that strict performance will be required of any term waived, unless the retraction would be unjust in view of the other party's material change of position in reliance on the waiver. Unless a contrary intention by the parties clearly appears, expressions of "cancellation" or "rescission" of the contract or the like are not construed as a waiver, renunciation, or discharge of any claim in damages for an antecedent breach.

---

[70] See above, pp. 251–52.
[71] See below, p. 320.
[72] UCC 1–207.

Buyer's Failure to Particularize Defects. When the buyer has an opportunity to inspect the tendered *goods* to see if they are conforming, or to inspect tendered *documents* relating to the goods against which payment is required in order to see if the documents are correct on their face, the buyer may either reject or accept the goods, and he may pay or refuse to make payment against the documents.

In the case of goods, when both the seller and buyer are *not merchants,* if the buyer rejects the goods and the seller if seasonably notified by the buyer could have cured the defect,[73] then the buyer *must state in his rejection* particular defects which he could have ascertained by reasonable inspection. *If the buyer does not so particularize in his rejection such defects ascertainable by him, he is estopped to assert such ascertainable defects as a justification for his rejection or to establish breach of contract by the seller. The buyer has waived his right to resort to such defects.* If the defects were not ascertainable by the buyer on a reasonable inspection, there is no waiver by the buyer with respect to such non-ascertainable defects. However, if both the seller and buyer are *merchants,* after rejection the merchant seller *must* make a *written* request for a full and written statement of all defects on which the merchant buyer proposes to rely and, if the merchant buyer does not so comply with the seller's written request, *to the extent of particular defects ascertainable by him after a reasonable examination the merchant buyer is estopped to assert such defects as a justification for his rejection or to establish breach of contract by the seller.*

Where payment is required against documents, the buyer has the opportunity to inspect such documents to see if they are correct on their face, and *the buyer's payment without reservation of rights is an acceptance of such documents and he is estopped from recovering such payment because of the defects apparent on the face of the documents.* His acceptance of the documents does not constitute an acceptance of the goods nor does it impair his remedies for improper delivery of the goods by the seller.

Acceptance of Goods. The buyer has the obligation of accepting a proper delivery of goods conforming with the contract. *Acceptance is a manifestation of assent to become the owner of the identified goods* and may be made expressly, or impliedly as by his conduct or silence when he is to speak. The acceptance may be conditional on the conditions indicated in the acceptance; it may be qualified; and it may extend to part rather than all the tendered goods, except that acceptance cannot

---

[73] For cure, see above, p. 308.

be a part of a commercial unit[74] and a purported acceptance of a part of any commercial unit is an acceptance of that entire unit. The buyer expressly accepts the goods if, after he has had a reasonable opportunity to inspect the goods, he signifies to the seller that the goods are conforming or that he will take or retain them in spite of their non-conformity. Express words of acceptance are not required. Payment for the goods is a circumstance to prove acceptance, but it is not conclusive by itself. *The buyer must either accept or reject the goods, and his failure to effectively reject them after he has had a reasonable opportunity to inspect them constitutes an acceptance.* The buyer's conduct inconsistent with the seller's ownership is an acceptance. For example, the buyer's testing of an unreasonable quantity of the goods to determine their conformity with the contract is an acceptance of the goods. To the same effect is the buyer's use of the goods or his sale of the goods to another, although the buyer's conduct pursuant to his rights and duties concerning salvage[75] do not constitute acceptance or the tort of conversion. The buyer's act inconsistent with the seller's ownership of the goods but which is wrongful against the seller may, at the seller's option, be ratified by the seller and treated as an acceptance. It should be noted that, *once the buyer has effectively rejected the goods, he cannot thereafter accept them,* unless the seller has re-tendered the goods or has indicated that he is holding the tender open. Also, *once the buyer has accepted the goods he cannot revoke his acceptance,* except under the following circumstances, which he must meticulously observe:

1. The goods must be non-conforming.
2. Such non-conformity must substantially impair their value to the buyer.
3. The buyer accepted the goods on the reasonable assumption that their non-conformity would be cured, and they have not been seasonably cured; or he has accepted the goods without discovery of such non-conformity, his acceptance having been reasonably induced either by the difficulty of discovery before acceptance or by the seller's assurances.
4. Revocation must occur within a reasonable time after the buyer discovers or should have discovered the ground for it.
5. Revocation must occur before any substantial change occurs in the condition of the goods which is not caused by their own defects.
6. Revocation is not effective until the buyer notifies the seller of it.

While the agreement of the parties may limit the time for notification by the buyer, such provision must be in good faith and not unconscionable. Also, the buyer's revocation of his acceptance may be with respect

---

[74] For commercial unit, see above, p. 244.
[75] See above, p. 316.

to all the goods or to a lot or commercial unit. A buyer who has so revoked his acceptance has the same rights and duties with regard to the goods as if he had rejected them.[76] Reference should be made to previous discussion[77] concerning rightful rejection in installment contracts where breach of the whole contract could be waived by conduct of the aggrieved party in accepting a non-conforming installment.

While the buyer's acceptance of goods with knowledge of non-conformity precludes rejection and is non-revocable except under the conditions just discussed, *such acceptance does not of itself impair other remedies for non-conformity.* However, the buyer has the burden of establishing a breach of contract with respect to the goods accepted. When the buyer accepts a tender of delivery, within a reasonable time after he discovers or should have discovered any breach he must notify the seller of the breach; his failure to do so is a waiver barring him from any remedy for such breach. Also, where the buyer accepts a tender of delivery, the seller has breached his warranty against infringement,[78] and the buyer is sued as a result of such breach, the buyer must notify the seller within a reasonable time after he receives notice of the litigation; his failure to do so is a waiver barring him from any remedy against the seller for liability established by such litigation.[79] It should be noted in passing that the buyer has a duty to pay at the contract rate for any goods he accepts. Partial acceptance requires reasonable partial apportionment of the price if this can be accomplished.

Repudiation

Meaning. Repudiation[80] by a party of his duty to perform under his contract is wrongful and a breach of contract. Repudiation is a manifestation of an intention not to render substantial performance of a contractual duty. It may be made expressly, or impliedly from voluntary conduct which causes substantial performance to be either actually or apparently impossible. Unjustified repudiation may occur at the time when the duty is to be performed, and also prior to such time in which case it is called "anticipatory repudiation."

---

[76] See above, p. 314.

[77] See above, p. 315.

[78] See above, p. 288.

[79] See UCC 2–607(5) for the effect of seller participation or non-participation in a third party suit against the buyer for breach of warranty or other obligation for which the seller is answerable over to the buyer.

[80] See Contracts, above, p. 127.

Anticipatory Repudiation. Under the Code law of sales,[81] an anticipatory repudiation is characterized as *a party's repudiation of the contract with respect to a performance not yet due, the loss of which will substantially impair the value of the contract to the other.* Two things must occur: a party's repudiation of performance not yet due; and the loss of such performance will substantially impair the value of the contract to the other party. First, repudiation occurs by a party's expression, by statement or conduct, which either renders performance impossible or clearly indicates his intention not to perform the contract. While a party's demand for more than the contract provides is not in itself a repudiation, nevertheless if the demand reasonably indicates the demanding party's intention not to perform except on the condition that the other party perform in excess of what the contract provides, then such demand is a repudiation. The substantial impairment must be to the value of the contract *to the aggrieved party,* not to a reasonable man; this is a subjective test. "The most useful test of substantial value is to determine whether material inconvenience or injustice will result if the aggrieved party is forced to wait and receive an ultimate tender minus the part or aspect repudiated."[82]

When an anticipatory repudiation has occurred, the aggrieved party may do one of four things. *First,* he may, for a commercially reasonable time, await performance by the repudiating party. His inactivity and silence do not mislead the repudiating party. But he must not wait beyond a commercially reasonable time because, by doing so, he will not be able to recover resulting damages which he could have avoided on the expiration of the reasonable time; on breach, the aggrieved party has a duty to reduce or mitigate the damage caused by the repudiating party's breach. *Second,* he may resort to any remedy for breach even though he has notified the repudiating party that he would await the latter's performance and has urged retraction of the repudiation. His notification and urging of retraction do not prejudice his rights. *Third,* in addition to the first two courses of action, he may suspend his own performance. The anticipatory repudiation exposes the aggrieved party to a risk of nonperformance which he had not contemplated previously and, therefore, in all fairness to him he need not continue to perform his contractual promise if he so wishes. *Fourth,* if he is the seller he may decide not to suspend his own performance but, in addition to the first

---

[81] UCC 2–610.
[82] UCC 2–610, *Comment 3.*

two courses of action, exercise his seller's right to identify goods to the contract notwithstanding the breach or to salvage unfinished goods.[83]

Right to Adequate Assurance of Performance. Parties make a contract to obtain the performance agreed upon, and if one party's performance becomes reasonably uncertain to the other party, the latter should not be subjected to the hardship of continuing his performance while such uncertainty exists. If the initial willingness or ability of one party to perform *reasonably* appears to the other party to be *materially* reduced, reasonable uncertainty of performance exists causing understandable concern as to whether or not the due performance which was expected will occur and as to what should be done to minimize damage in the event due performance does not occur. The Code recognizes the well-established legal principle that *each contracting party has an obligation not to impair the other's expectation of receiving due performance,* and it provides: *"When reasonable grounds for insecurity arise with respect to the performance of either party the other may in writing demand adequate assurance of due performance and until he receives such assurance may if commercially reasonable suspend any performance for which he has not already received the agreed return."* [84]

Various elements are involved in this right to adequate assurance of due performance. *First,* the concerned party's expectation of receiving due performance must be impaired; he no longer has security of expectation. His insecurity must be based on reasonable grounds and be in conformance with his obligation to act in good faith; it must not be arbitrary or capricious. *As between merchants,* which is where this right becomes exceedingly important, the reasonableness of grounds for insecurity is determined according to commercial standards. Under commercial standards, insecurity may arise in various ways, only a few of which will be briefly considered. Anticipatory repudiation is a reasonable ground for insecurity. The ground for insecurity may arise because of the nature of the sales contract. For example, word to the buyer from a reliable source that the seller has shipped, or intends to ship, defective goods is a reasonable ground for the buyer's insecurity; although it should be noted that, if the contract was C.I.F. or cash against documents, the buyer must perform his contractual obligation to make payment before inspection of the goods, inasmuch as the risk of receiving defective goods after payment was assumed by the buyer and cannot be avoided on the ground of insecurity. The ground for insecurity need

---

[83] See below, p. 332.
[84] UCC 2–609(1).

not arise from the sales contract or even be related to it, but it may be based on other transactions. Examples are: the seller's insecurity caused by the buyer's failure to pay on other purchases from the same seller; the buyer's insecurity caused by hearing that the seller is supplying similar goods to other persons under their contracts and that such goods are defective. Another ground for insecurity is a party's repetition of occasions, such as breach of contract, which caused insecurity on those occasions. Similarly, a sudden expansion in the buyer's use of credit is a reasonable ground for the seller's insecurity. Rumors, even though false, of financial instability of a party to the sales contract are a reasonable ground for insecurity.

Second, what is adequate assurance of due performance depends objectively upon all the circumstances and upon the good faith of a reasonable man in the position of the aggrieved party, not on the *subjective* good faith of the aggrieved party; except that, as between merchants, the adequacy of assurance offered is determined according to commercial standards. A banker's good credit report on the party from whom assurance is due is usually adequate to dispel insecurity for suspected financial instability.

Third, when one party has reasonable ground for insecurity of due performance by the other, he *may* make a *written* demand for adequate assurance of due performance by the other. He need not make a demand, but if he does it must be in writing.

Fourth, until the aggrieved party receives adequate assurance of due performance from the other he may, if commercially reasonable, suspend any performance for which he has not already received the agreed return and also suspend preparation for such performance.

It should be noted very carefully that, if the demand for assurance is not pursuant to a reasonable ground for insecurity and therefore is unjustified, the aggrieved party's suspension of performance itself constitutes a reasonable ground for the other party's insecurity and justifies the *latter's* demand for assurance and. *his* suspension of performance. Also, the demanding party must not have already received what was due for that performance or part of performance which he intends to suspend; he has no insecurity for such performance inasmuch as he has already been paid therefor. However, acceptance of any improper delivery or payment by the aggrieved party does not prejudice his right to demand adequate assurance of future performance.

The party upon whom a justified demand has been made for adequate assurance of due performance has *a reasonable time not to exceed 30 days* after his *receipt* of the demand in which to provide such assurance, and his failure so to provide is a *repudiation* of the contract and a breach thereof. However, this, as well as any other, anticipatory repudiation may be retracted by the repudiating party, provided it is done before his performance is due and provided the aggrieved party has not indicated since the repudiation that he considers the repudiation as final. The aggrieved party's cancellation[85] or material change of position in reliance on the repudiation indicates that he considered the repudiation as final. Tender of assurance or of performance to the aggrieved party after such cancellation or material change of position is ineffectual to restore the aggrieved party's duty of performance under the contract; the latter's duty is discharged. Timely retraction of the repudiation may be made by any method which clearly indicates to the aggrieved party that the repudiating party intends to perform. However, to be effective, the retraction must include the adequate assurance of due performance justifiably demanded by the aggrieved party. An effective retraction restores the repudiating party to his status immediately prior to his repudiation. However, the repudiating party cannot profit from his own wrong and, therefore, his effective retraction of itself does not extend the time for his performance, although the *aggrieved* party receives due excuse and allowance for any delay caused by the repudiation.

Substituted Performance   When the parties cannot make delivery or payment *in the agreed manner,* substituted performance is permissible under certain conditions. It should be noted initially that, in the cases of casualty to identified goods[86] and failure of presupposed conditions,[87] discussed later, the failure or impossibility of performance is concerned with a basic assumption of the contract and goes to the essence of the contract, causing excuse and complete avoidance of the contract. In contrast, failure or impossibility to deliver or make payment *in the agreed manner* do not go to the essence of the contract, and an available commercially reasonable substitute must be made and the contract preserved.

If without the fault of either buyer or seller the agreed manner of delivery becomes commercially impracticable but a commercially reasonable substitute is available, the seller must tender and the buyer must accept such substitute. Failure of agreed facilities, such as berthing,

---

[85] Cancellation is the ending of a contract by one party because of the other party's breach. See above, p. 270, ftn. 19, for the distinction between cancellation and termination.

[86] See below, p. 325.

[87] See below, p. 326.

loading or unloading, or unavailability of an agreed type of carrier are illustrations of such commercial impracticability. The seller and buyer have no choice; the seller must tender and the buyer must accept an available commercially reasonable substitute. For example, when the contract provided for shipment of grain F.O.B. a named vessel place of shipment and the event of war compelled cancellation of shipment by that vessel, substituted delivery at the warehouse on the ship line's loading dock could be legitimately demanded by the buyer or tendered by the seller.

When the agreed *means or manner of payment* fails because of domestic or foreign governmental regulation, the effect depends upon whether or not the goods have already been delivered. If the goods have not been delivered, the seller may refuse delivery by withholding the goods or stopping their delivery en route; but if the buyer provides a means or manner of payment which is commercially a substantial equivalent of what was agreed to in the contract, the seller must accept the same and deliver the goods as agreed with reasonable allowance for any delay caused by the substitution of the equivalent manner or means of payment. If the goods were delivered before the governmental regulation and the regulation is not discriminatory, oppressive, or predatory (i.e., destructive), the buyer may tender and the seller must accept payment by the means or in the manner provided by the regulation; the buyer's obligation is discharged by such payment.

Excused Non-performance

Casualty to Identified Goods. *When the goods are identified at the time the contract for their sale is made and, before the risk of loss passes to the buyer,*[88] *the goods suffered casualty (i.e., destruction) without the fault of either party,* the effect of such casualty depends upon whether or not the loss is total. If the loss is total, the contract is avoided without any liability of either party to the other. If the loss is partial, or the goods have so deteriorated as no longer to conform to the contract, the buyer no longer has any obligation to perform unless he wishes to avail himself of the option to accept such goods. He can demand the opportunity to inspect the goods and at his option either treat the contract as avoided or accept the goods. If he accepts the goods, he is liable to the seller for the contract price less due allowance for the deficiency in quantity or deterioration, but with no other right against the seller. If the buyer has paid the full price to

---

[88] For risk of loss, see above, pp. 311 ff.

the seller in advance, the buyer's election to accept the goods entitles him to a reimbursement for the due allowance. It is irrelevant whether or not the contract is divisible. It should be noted that the identified goods may have so suffered before the contract was made without the knowledge of the parties as well as subsequent to the making of the contract. The above discussion is applicable, before the risk of loss passes to the buyer, in the case of a "no arrival, no sale" contract, when the seller has the obligation to ship conforming goods but he assumes no obligation that the goods will arrive, although he is not to interfere with their arrival.[89] The buyer has the above same option in the event of partial loss or deterioration of the goods, or their late arrival.

Failure of Presupposed Conditions. We have seen previously[90] under substituted performance that where, without the fault of either party, the agreed manner of delivery becomes commercially impracticable but a commercially reasonable *substitute is available,* the substitute must be tendered and accepted. We have also seen[91] under casualty to identified goods that the seller is *excused* to the extent of casualty to goods identified when the contract was made, the casualty having occurred without fault of either party and before the risk of loss has passed to the buyer. However, circumstances may arise which were *not previously contemplated* by the parties at the time their contract was made and a non-occurrence of which was a *basic assumption* on which the contract was made, making it *commercially impracticable to perform the contract as agreed* because of delay in delivery or non-delivery. Since the underlying basis for the contract is affected, the failure of delivery should not be a breach of contract and the seller should be *excused* for such delay or non-delivery. Accordingly, under the Code,[92] unless the seller has assumed a greater obligation under his contract[93] and except for the duty to make substituted performance, *the seller's delay in delivery or non-delivery whether in whole or in part is not a breach of contract if performance as agreed has become commercially impracticable because of unforeseen supervening circumstances not*

---

[89] See above, pp. 273–74.

[90] See above, p. 324.

[91] See above, p. 325.

[92] UCC 2–615.

[93] The seller's exemption does not apply "when the contingency in question is sufficiently foreshadowed at the time of contracting to be included among the business risks which are fairly to be regarded as part of the dickered terms, either consciously or as a matter of reasonable, commercial interpretation from the circumstances." UCC 2–615, *Comment 8.*

within the contemplation of the parties at the time their contract was made and the non-occurrence of which was a basic assumption at such time. There are two conditions to the seller not being held to a breach for such failure to make delivery as agreed. *First,* inasmuch as the excused seller should fulfill his contract to the extent that the supervening contingency permits, if only a part of the seller's capacity to perform is affected he *must allocate* production and deliveries among his customers in a fair and reasonable manner. He may at his option include among such customers his regular customers not then under contract as well as his own requirements for further manufacture in such allocation. His regular customers may be relying on making spot orders for supplies as they are needed. *Second,* the seller *must notify* the buyer seasonably of such delay in delivery or non-delivery and, when allocation of production and deliveries is being made, of the estimated quota that will be available for the buyer. Such unforeseen supervening circumstances are of great variety in business. While increased cost or the rise or fall of prices in the market place are not of themselves excuses for the seller's non-performance, nevertheless they could be if the circumstances causing them were unforeseen and their non-occurrence was a basic assumption of the contract.[94] It should be noted carefully that, if the agreed performance has become commercially impracticable, resulting in the seller's delay of delivery or non-delivery caused by an applicable foreign or domestic governmental regulation or order, whether or not later proved to be invalid, with which compliance has been made in good faith, the seller is similarly excused for such delay or non-delivery under the conditions discussed above and there is no breach of contract on his part.

---

[94] UCC 2–615, *Comments 4, 5:* "Increased cost alone does not excuse performance unless the rise in cost is due to some unforeseen contingency which alters the essential nature of the performance. Neither is a rise or a collapse in the market in itself a justification, for that is exactly the type of business risk which business contracts made at fixed prices are intended to cover. But a severe shortage of raw materials or of supplies due to a contingency such as war, embargo, local crop failure, unforeseen shutdown of major sources of supply or the like, which either causes a marked increase in cost or altogether prevents the seller from securing supplies necessary to his performance, is within the contemplation of this section. . . .

"Where a particular source of supply is exclusive under the agreement and fails through casualty, the present section applies rather than the provision on destruction or deterioration of specific goods. The same holds true where a particular source of supply is shown by the circumstances to have been contemplated or assumed by the parties at the time of contracting. . . . There is no excuse under this section, however, unless the seller has employed all due measures to assure himself that his source will not fail. . . . In the case of failure of production by an agreed source for causes beyond the seller's control, the seller should, if possible, be excused since production by an agreed source is without more a basic assumption of the contract. . . ."

While the seller is excused for his delay in delivery or non-delivery because of the failure of the presupposed conditions, the buyer is also affected by such failure of presupposed conditions. After the buyer has *received* the seller's notification of a material or indefinite delay in delivery or of a justified allocation, *the buyer may notify the seller in writing* that, with respect to the delivery in the seller's notice or with respect to the contract as a whole if such delivery substantially impairs the value of the whole contract: the contract is modified to the extent that the buyer acquiesces in the delay and agrees to take his available quota in substitution; or the contract is terminated and discharged as to any unexecuted portion thereof. The buyer's failure so to notify the seller within a reasonable time not exceeding 30 days after the buyer's *receipt* of the seller's notice causes the contract to be terminated and discharged as to any unexecuted portion thereof. Any contractual provision which seeks to vary the buyer's right so to notify the seller is void.

Chapter VIII

REMEDIES

---

1. SELLER'S REMEDIES

EACH of the parties to a contract for the sale of goods acquires rights and obligations of performance. The seller's obligation is to transfer and deliver the goods, and the buyer's obligation is to accept the goods and pay for them, in accordance with their contract. Each party has a right to the other party's performance of his obligation and, on his nonperformance, a right to pursue remedies for relief. "Right" includes "remedy," which means "any remedial right to which an aggrieved party is entitled with or without resort to a tribunal."[1] Most of the remedies of the seller or buyer are the result of breach of contract, although each party has certain remedies in the event of the other party's insolvency even though no breach of contract has occurred. The remedies provided by the Sales portion of the Code do not exclude or impair any other remedies for breach of any obligation or promise which is collateral or ancillary to a contract for the sale of goods. Thus, action may be brought on a dishonored check to pay for goods purchased and against a surety on the contract for sale. The seller's remedies will be discussed in Section 1, the buyer's remedies in Section 2, and miscellaneous remedies in Section 3.

In General

The seller's remedies arise either as the result of the buyer's insolvency or as the result of the buyer's breach of contract by his wrongful rejection, wrongful revocation of acceptance of goods, failure to make payment when due on or before delivery, or repudiation with respect to a part or the whole of the contract. First the seller's remedies on the buyer's insolvency will be discussed, and then his other remedies occasioned by the buyer's breach of contract.

---

[1] UCC 1–201(34)(36).

Prospective failure of consideration[2] occurs by the

Remedies on the Buyer's Insolvency

buyer's insolvency. "A person is 'insolvent' who either has ceased to pay his debts in the ordinary course of business or cannot pay his debts as they become due or is insolvent within the meaning of the federal bankruptcy law."[3] It is manifestly unfair for the buyer to hold the seller to his contractual obligation *to deliver* goods to the buyer when the buyer does not appear to be able to pay the price for such goods. Also, if the buyer misrepresents to the seller that he is solvent and the seller then *delivers* goods to the buyer, it would be unfair to permit the buyer to profit from his fraud and deny to the seller a reasonable opportunity to repossess such goods subject, of course, to the rights of intervening third parties. The buyer's misrepresentation of solvency may be made expressly, or impliedly by his receipt of goods while insolvent.

The Code precludes this injustice and deals with the seller's remedies with respect to goods not yet delivered and goods already delivered to an insolvent buyer.

Undelivered Goods. *As to goods not yet delivered to the buyer, when the seller discovers the buyer to be insolvent he has two remedies: refuse delivery except for cash, including payment for all goods theretofor delivered under the contract; and stop delivery of goods in transit or otherwise,* discussed later.[4] The seller's right so to withhold delivery exists irrespective of whether the buyer or seller has title to the goods.

Delivered Goods. *As to goods delivered to the buyer, when the seller discovers that the buyer has received goods on credit while insolvent, he has a right to reclaim the delivered goods: upon demand made within 10 days after the buyer's receipt of such goods; or at any time if the buyer has misrepresented his solvency in writing to the seller within three months before such delivery.* The seller is required to be very diligent within the 10-day period after a delivery of goods, or in order to avoid anxiety for such a short period he may obtain a written statement of solvency from the buyer addressed to him within three months prior to delivery. Of course, if the seller knew of the buyer's insolvency at the time of a delivery, the seller has no remedy to reclaim the goods delivered with such knowledge. It should be noted carefully that the seller's right is to *reclaim* the goods; a demand for their repossession is

---

[2] See Contracts above, p. 122.

[3] UCC 1–201(23). For the meaning of insolvency under the bankruptcy law, see below, p. 852.

[4] See below, p. 333.

sufficient, and physical repossession is not required. However, until the seller obtains physical repossession, his right to repossession is subject to the risk of intervening rights of third parties. We have already discussed: the good faith purchaser for value from a buyer with a voidable title;[5] the buyer in ordinary course of business from a merchant entrusted with possession of goods;[6] the lien creditors[7] of the buyer on consignment sales.[8] Inasmuch as the reclaiming creditor is given this preferential treatment over other creditors of the buyer, the seller's successful reclamation of goods excludes all other remedies with respect to such goods.

Remedies on the Buyer's Breach of Contract
In General. The seller acquires remedies also as a result of the buyer's breach of contract. Under the Code,[9] *where the buyer wrongfully rejects[10] or wrongfully revokes acceptance[11] of goods, or fails to make a payment due on or before delivery,[12] or repudiates with respect to a part or the whole of the contract,[13] then with respect to any goods directly affected and, if the breach is of the whole contract,[14] then also with respect to the whole undelivered balance, the aggrieved seller has the following remedies:* cancellation; withhold delivery of such goods; identify goods to the contract or salvage; stoppage of delivery in transit or otherwise; resale; recover damages for non-acceptance or repudiation; action for the price in a proper case; incidental damages. These remedies will be discussed in that order.

It should be noted very carefully that the Code provides that a *"person in the position of a seller"* acquires certain rights of that seller so as to protect himself with respect to the goods and the seller's rights against the buyer on the buyer's insolvency or breach. He may withhold delivery, stop the goods in transit or otherwise, resell, and recover

---

[5] See above, pp. 281–83.

[6] See above, pp. 283–84.

[7] UCC 9–301(3): "A 'lien creditor' means a creditor who has acquired a lien on the property involved by attachment, levy or the like and includes an assignee for benefit of creditors from the time of assignment, and a trustee in bankruptcy from the date of the filing of the petition or a receiver in equity from the time of appointment. . . ."

[8] See above, p. 264.

[9] UCC 2–703.

[10] See above, p. 314.

[11] See above, p. 319.

[12] See above, p. 310.

[13] For anticipatory breach, see above, p. 321.

[14] As to when a breach of the whole contract occurs, see above, pp. 315–16.

incidental damages. *A person in the position of a seller includes anyone who holds a security interest or other right in the goods similar to that of a seller.* He may be an agent who has authorizedly paid or become responsible for the price of goods on behalf of his principal and, therefore, has rights of reimbursement or indemnity against his principal;[15] and he may be a financing agency.[16]

Cancellation. The seller may cancel the contract. By cancellation a party puts an end to the contract because of the other's breach, all obligations which are still executory on both sides are discharged, and the cancelling party retains any remedy for breach of the whole contract or any unperformed balance.

Withhold Delivery. The buyer's breach of contract creates a right in the seller, or a person in the position of a seller, to withhold delivery of goods directly affected by the breach or, in the case of a breach of the whole contract, the whole undelivered balance of the goods. Withholding of delivery does not of itself cancel the contract; the parties may subsequently, in good faith, adjust their differences and the goods be delivered.

Identify Goods to the Contract or Salvage. On the buyer's breach of contract, the aggrieved seller may also deal with the goods so as to place him in the best position to recover the contract price and at the same time minimize the loss caused by the buyer's breach. What he may do depends upon whether or not the goods are finished and conforming to the contract.

Conforming Goods. When the goods conform to the contract, the seller may identify to the contract conforming goods not already identified if, at the time he learned of the breach, they are in his possession or control. In this way, on identification of conforming goods to the contract: the seller has a right of resale of the goods;[17] if resale is not practicable, the seller has a right to bring an action for the price of the goods.[18]

---

[15] See Agency, below, pp. 541–42, respectively.

[16] For definition of financing agency, see UCC 2–104(2). UCC 2–506: "(1) A financing agency by paying or purchasing for value a draft which relates to a shipment of goods acquires to the extent of the payment or purchase and in addition to its own rights under the draft and any document of title securing it any rights of the shipper in the goods including the right to stop delivery and the shipper's right to have the draft honored by the buyer.

(2) The right to reimbursement of a financing agency which has in good faith honored or purchased the draft under commitment to or authority from the buyer is not impaired by subsequent discovery of defects with reference to any relevant document which was apparently regular on its face."

[17] See below, pp. 335 ff.

[18] See below, p. 338.

Unfinished Goods. When the goods are unfinished, the seller may, in the exercise of reasonable commercial judgment for the purposes of avoiding and minimizing loss[19] *either: complete the manufacture of the unfinished goods and then wholly identify them to the contract,* thereby putting the seller in the same position as when he identified conforming goods to the contract, as discussed above; *cease manufacture and resell for scrap or salvage value the unfinished goods which have demonstrably been intended for the particular contract; or proceed in any other reasonable manner.*

Stoppage of Delivery in Transit or Otherwise. The seller, or a person in the position of a seller,[20] acquires the right to stop delivery of the goods to the buyer under the contract for their sale under certain conditions and with certain limitations on the quantity of goods which can be stopped.

When Created. The seller's remedy of stopping delivery arises on the following occasions: when the seller discovers the buyer's insolvency; the buyer's repudiation; the buyer's failure to make payment when due before delivery; when, for any other reason, the seller has a right to withhold or claim the goods. We have already discussed the various remedies which the seller may assert when the buyer becomes insolvent,[21] one of these remedies being the right to stop delivery. But the buyer's insolvency is only one of these occasions when the right to stop delivery arises. The quantity of goods which may be stopped depends upon the kind of occasion creating the right to stop delivery. *When the seller discovers the buyer to be insolvent,* he may stop delivery of goods in the possession of a carrier or other bailee, *regardless* of the quantity of goods involved. *When the buyer repudiates or fails to make a payment due before delivery, or if for any other reason the seller has a right to withhold or claim the goods,* he may stop delivery of *only* carload, truckload, planeload or larger shipments of express or freight. The reason for the difference in the quantity of goods that may be stopped is that stoppage in transit may impose a great burden on the carrier if it included small shipments, and so the right to stop for other than insolvency is limited in quantity to large shipments. If this fact should be of concern to the seller, he can agree to ship goods in smaller shipments C.O.D.

---

[19] For example, in the seller's reasonable commercial judgment, completion of manufacture of the goods would bring a better resale price resulting in an over-all reduction in loss which would otherwise occur by a resale for salvage.

[20] See above, p. 332.

[21] See above, p. 330.

How Exercised. In order that the seller may exercise this right of stoppage of delivery, he must do two things. *First, the seller must stop delivery to the buyer while the goods are still in the possession of the carrier or other bailee.* To the extent that goods have been delivered to the buyer by the carrier or other bailee, the seller has no right of stoppage of delivery with respect to such goods. *Delivery is made to the buyer,* and the seller's right of stoppage of delivery cannot be exercised, if: the buyer has *received* the goods; *the non-carrier bailee has acknowledged to the buyer* that he holds the goods for the buyer; *the carrier has acknowledged to the buyer* that he holds the goods for the buyer *by reshipment or as a warehouseman;* or a *negotiable* document of title (e.g., negotiable bill of lading or negotiable warehouse receipt) covering the goods has been *negotiated to the buyer.*[22] The buyer receives the goods either directly, or by his designated representative such as a subpurchaser to whom the seller has directly shipped the goods at the buyer's direction without the goods ever having been delivered directly to the buyer. The bailee's acknowledgment that the goods are held by him for the buyer causes the goods to have been delivered to the buyer through the bailee, who now holds the goods as the buyer's agent authorized to accept delivery. However, such an acknowledgment by a carrier must be by reshipment or by agreement to hold the goods as a warehouseman for the buyer.[23] Attachment or levy of execution upon the goods initiated by creditors of the buyer prior to the delivery of such goods to the buyer does not interrupt the status of the goods while in transit, nor is such action by the buyer's creditors effective when the goods are in the possession of a bailee other than a carrier who has not made acknowledgment to the buyer; the seller's right of stoppage of delivery is not cut off. In contrast, only the seller or a person in the position of the seller can exercise the right of stoppage of delivery.

Second, in order to stop delivery, the seller must so notify the bailee as to enable the bailee by reasonable diligence to prevent delivery of the goods. After such notification, the bailee must hold and deliver the goods according to the directions of the seller, who is liable to the bailee for any ensuing charges or damages. If a *negotiable* document of title

---

[22] See above, pp. 221 ff.

[23] UCC 2–705, *Comment 3:* "A diversion of a shipment is not a 'reshipment' . . . when it is merely an incident to the original contract of transportation. Nor is the procurement of 'exchange bills' of lading which change only the name of the consignee to that of the buyer's local agent but do not alter the destination of a reshipment.

"Acknowledgement by the carrier as a 'warehouseman' . . . requires a contract of a truly different character from the original shipment, a contract not in extension of transit but as a warehouseman."

has been issued for the goods, the bailee is not obliged to obey a notification to stop delivery until surrender of the document. The reason for this is that, since the bailee's agreement is to deliver the goods to the order of the consignee, the bailee has the obligation to hold the goods subject to such order, and should the negotiable document of title be duly negotiated to a holder, the latter would acquire title to the document and the bailee would be liable to him for the goods covered by the document.[24] If the carrier has issued a *non-negotiable* bill of lading, the carrier is obligated to obey the notification to stop delivery only when the notification is issued by the consignor. The carrier's contact is only with the consignor, and the carrier's obligation with respect to the goods is to him. It should be noted very carefully that, *as between the seller and the buyer,* the seller has the right to stop delivery of the goods, irrespective of whether or not the carrier is obligated to obey the stop order when a negotiable or a non-negotiable bill of lading is outstanding. So, if the carrier obeys the stop order, the buyer cannot complain; but the seller will be liable to the carrier for any ensuing charges or damages for following the seller's orders.[25]

Effect. Once delivery has been stopped, the seller is in the same position as though he had never made delivery to the carrier or other bailee for the buyer, and he re-acquires his seller's rights in the goods as though he had never made such delivery. Stoppage of delivery is not of itself a cancellation of the contract; the parties may subsequently, in good faith, adjust their differences and the goods be delivered. If the seller's stoppage of delivery is wrongful, it is a breach of contract on his part.

Resale. *On the buyer's breach of contract, the aggrieved seller or a person in the position of a seller*[26] *may resell the goods directly affected, or the whole undelivered balance of the goods if the whole contract is breached.* The remedy of resale is predicated on the seller acting in good faith and in a way that is commercially reasonable.

How. Unless otherwise agreed, resale may be by public or private sale, including sale by way of one or more contracts to sell or of identification to an existing contract of the seller. A public sale means a sale by auction. A private sale means a sale "effected by solicitation and negotiation conducted either directly or through a broker."[27] The resale

---

[24] See above, pp. 223–24.

[25] UCC 2–705(3) (b).

[26] See above, p. 332.

[27] UCC 2–706, *Comment 4* (continued) : "In choosing between a public and private sale the character of the goods must be considered and relevant trade practices and usages must be observed."

must be reasonably identified as referring to the broken contract. *The resale may be at any time and place and on any terms, but every aspect of the resale, including the method, manner, time, place, and terms must be commercially reasonable,* which also includes a resale within a reasonable time after the buyer's breach. Should the buyer demand an inspection pursuant to his right in connection with preserving evidence of goods in dispute,[28] the time may be extended appropriately. The resale may be as a unit or in parcels. In the event of an anticipatory breach, the goods may not be in existence nor any or all of them have been identified to the contract before the breach. *After the breach, the seller may exercise his right to identify conforming goods to the contract*[29] *and then resell them at a public sale.* Only identified goods may be sold at a public sale; however, if there is a recognized market for a public sale of futures in goods of the kind involved, then the unidentified goods can be sold as future goods at the public sale. *Where the resale is at a private sale,* the seller must give to the buyer reasonable notification of *his intention* to resell; the notice need not indicate the time and place of the resale.

Special additional rules govern a resale by public sale. The seller must give the buyer reasonable notice of the time and place of the public resale, except in the case of goods which are perishable or threaten to decline in value speedily, in which event no notice need be given. Such notice enables the buyer to attend and bid and, also, to induce others to do so. If the goods are not to be within the view of those attending the sale, the notification of sale must state the place where the goods are located and provide for their reasonable inspection by prospective bidders. *The seller may buy at the public resale.* After all, his power to sell is given by law, he sells in his own behalf, his opportunity to bid tends to increase the resale price, and he is selling as best he can to reduce the loss he may sustain and to mitigate the buyer's damages. The seller is to resell only at a usual place or market for public sale if one is reasonably available, which is a place where prospective bidders may reasonably be expected to attend.[30]

---

[28] See above, pp. 309 ff.

[29] See above, p. 332.

[30] UCC 2–706, *Comment 9:* "Such a market may still be 'reasonably available' . . . , though at a considerable distance from the place where the goods are located. In such a case the expense of transporting the goods for resale is recoverable from the buyer as part of the seller's incidental damages. . . . However, the question of availability is one of commercial reasonableness in the circumstances and if such 'usual' place or market is not reasonably available, a duly advertised public resale may be held at another place if it is one which prospective bidders may reasonably be expected to attend, as distinguished from a place where there is no demand whatsoever for goods of the kind."

Effect. A good faith purchaser for value at a resale takes the goods free of any rights of the original buyer, even though the seller fails to comply with one or more of the legal requirements for resale. The seller retains any profit on the resale. However, if the person reselling is a person in the position of a seller,[31] he may not keep any excess over his security interest and must account to the seller for such excess. The reason for resale by a person with a security interest is to obtain cash in satisfaction therefor, and this having been accomplished he has been made whole and should not be able to benefit any further. Where the resale is made in good faith and in a commercially reasonable manner, the seller may recover the difference between the resale price and the contract price together with any incidental damages allowed under the Code, but less expenses saved in consequence of the buyer's breach. When the seller has not conducted the resale properly, the measure of his damages is changed to that measure employed for non-acceptance or repudiation, which will now be discussed.

Seller's Damages for Non-acceptance or Repudiation. The buyer's obligation is to accept and pay for the goods. On the buyer's breach of contract by his non-acceptance of a proper tender of delivery or by repudiation, the seller has a right to damages therefor. The measure of damages is the difference between the market price[32] at the time and place of tender and the unpaid contract price together with any incidental damages,[33] but less expenses saved in consequence of the buyer's breach. If this measure of damages is "inadequate to put the seller in as good a position as performance would have done then the measure of damages is the profit (including reasonable overhead) which the seller would have made from full performance by the buyer, together with any incidental damages . . . , due allowance for costs reasonably incurred and due credit for payments or proceeds of resale."[34] The Code permits the recovery of lost profits in all appropriate cases. For example, if the seller is a dealer in goods similar to that contracted for and the market price is equal to or above the contract price, the seller's resale of the refused goods would not cause loss to him thereby, but it deprives the seller of making another sale of similar merchandise

---

[31] The person reselling may be a *buyer* who has rightfully rejected or justifiably revoked acceptance and is exercising his remedy of resale (see below, p. 387) of goods in his possession in order to recover on his security interest in the goods for payments made or expense incurred in connection with such goods.

[32] In the absence of a current market price at the time and place of tender, proof of a substitute market may be made under UCC 2–723, 724. See below, pp. 348–49.

[33] See below, p. 339.

[34] UCC 2–708(2).

to the purchaser who bought the refused goods, with a consequent loss of profit from the other possible sale. The buyer's breach has depleted the seller's sales from two to one, and the loss of profit from the lost sale should be a part of the seller's damages.

Action for the Price. *When the buyer fails to pay the price as it becomes due,*[35] *the seller may recover the contract price together with any incidental damages for:*

1. *Goods which have been accepted*[36] by the buyer and the acceptance has not been justifiably revoked.[37]
2. *Conforming goods* lost or damaged within a commercially reasonable time after risk of their loss has passed to the buyer.[38]
3. *Goods identified to the contract*[39] but which the seller is unable *after reasonable effort to resell at a reasonable price,* or the circumstances reasonably indicate that such effort will be unavailing.

It should be noted carefully that, *in the case of goods identified to the contract, the seller has a primary remedy of resale previously discussed,*[40] *and he must resort to it in order to be made whole before he can bring an action for the price of the identified goods. This requirement does not exist with respect to accepted goods and to conforming goods lost or damaged as indicated above.* It is irrelevant whether or not the title to the goods has passed to the buyer. If the seller *properly* sues for the price and still has in his possession or control goods identified to the contract, he must hold such goods for the buyer; but he has the privilege, but not the obligation, at any time after suit but prior to the collection of the judgment against the buyer to resell them for the price if a resale becomes possible. If such a resale occurs after suit and before collection of the judgment, the net proceeds therefrom must be credited to the buyer and payment of the judgment entitles the buyer to any goods not resold. The fact that the seller may not come within the above three occasions when he may sue for the price does not mean that he does not have any other remedies. After the buyer has wrongfully rejected or revoked acceptance of the goods or has failed to make a

---

[35] See above, p. 247.

[36] See above, p. 318.

[37] See above, p. 319.

[38] For risk of loss, see above, pp. 311–13.

[39] For goods identified to the contract without breach, see above, p. 275, and notwithstanding breach, see above, pp. 332–33.

[40] See above, pp. 335 ff.

payment due or has repudiated, a seller who is held not entitled to the price shall nevertheless be awarded damages for non-acceptance or repudiation, previously discussed.[41]

Seller's Incidental Damages. The seller is entitled to reimbursement from the buyer for expenses which he has reasonably incurred as a result of the buyer's breach, called "incidental damages." Incidental damages to the aggrieved seller include "any commercially reasonable charges, expenses or commissions incurred in stopping delivery, in the transportation, care, and custody of goods after the buyer's breach, in connection with return or resale of the goods or otherwise resulting from the breach."[42] The seller is not precluded by the Code from obtaining "consequential damages," although such damages are more frequently sustained by the buyer rather than by the seller and, for that reason, consequential damages are discussed later under the buyer's remedies.[43]

2. BUYER'S REMEDIES

In General

The obligation of the seller is to transfer and deliver the goods in accordance with his contract. The buyer has various remedies against the seller or against the goods which arise either as the result of the seller's insolvency or as the result of the seller's breach of contract. First the buyer's remedy on the seller's insolvency will be briefly restated, and then his other remedies occasioned by the seller's breach of contract will be discussed.

Remedy on the Seller's Insolvency

We have already discussed the buyer's right to goods on the seller's insolvency,[44] and we have seen that, after the seller has identified goods to the contract and the seller becomes insolvent within 10 days after the buyer has made a payment, the buyer has the right to recover from the seller the goods identified to the contract; but if the buyer, instead of the seller, identified the goods to the contract, the goods must also be conforming.

---

[41] See above, p. 337.

[42] UCC 2–710.

[43] See below, p. 344.

[44] See above, p. 303.

Remedies on the Seller's Breach of Contract **In General.** The buyer acquires remedies also as a result of the seller's breach of contract. Under the Code,[45] when the seller fails to make delivery[46] or repudiates,[47] or the buyer rightfully rejects[48] or justifiably revokes acceptance,[49] then with respect to any goods invo!ved, and with respect to the remaining unperformed part of the contract if the breach goes to the whole contract,[50] the aggrieved buyer has the following remedies: cancellation; recovery of the purchase price paid; and either cover and damages, or damages for non-delivery or repudiation. If the buyer receives non-conforming goods, the buyer may accept such goods and recover damages for non-conformity of tender. If the seller has breached the contract in any way, the buyer may accept the goods and deduct damages from the price due. If the seller fails to make delivery or repudiates, the buyer also has the remedies of specific performance or replevin in a proper case. On rightful rejection or justifiable revocation of acceptance, the buyer has the right of resale. The buyer also has remedies for incidental damages and, in a proper case, for consequential damages resulting from the seller's breach. These remedies will be discussed briefly in that order. However, *it should be recalled at the outset the seller has the right to cure his improper tender or delivery under certain conditions,*[51] *and the effect of cure of non-conformity in installment contracts.*[52]

Cancellation. The buyer may cancel the contract. By cancellation a party puts an end to the contract because of the other's breach, all obligations which are still executory on both sides are discharged, and the cancelling party retains any remedy for breach of the whole contract or of any unperformed balance.

Recovery of the Purchase Price Paid. Irrespective of whether or not the buyer cancels the contract, the buyer also has the right to recover so much of the purchase price as has been paid, together with damages as indicated in connection with either cover or non-delivery or repudiation, depending on which is applicable.

Cover. On the seller's failure to deliver or repudiation, or the buyer's rightful rejection or justifiable revocation of acceptance, then

---

[45] UCC 2–711.

[46] See above, pp. 303 ff.

[47] For anticipatory breach, see above, p. 321.

[48] See above, p. 314.

[49] See above, p. 319.

[50] As to when a breach of the whole contract occurs, see above, p. 315.

[51] See above, p. 308.

[52] See above, p. 315.

with respect to any goods involved, and with respect to the whole if the breach goes to the whole contract, the buyer may "cover," and his failure to cover does not bar him from any other remedy. *The buyer covers by making in good faith and without unreasonable delay any reasonable purchase of, or contract to purchase, goods in substitution for those due from the seller.* While the buyer is not required to cover and it is a matter of whether he wishes to avail himself of this remedy, nevertheless its exercise is important to the subjects of: consequential damages,[53] where recovery is limited to what could not reasonably have been prevented by cover; and replevin of identified goods,[54] where the buyer is unable to effect cover for such goods. The buyer may recover from the seller as damages the difference between the cost of cover and the contract price together with any incidental or consequential damages, but less expenses saved in consequence of the seller's breach.

Buyer's Damages for Non-Delivery or Repudiation. The seller's obligation is to transfer and deliver the goods. On the seller's breach of contract by his failure to make delivery or repudiation, the buyer has a right to damages therefor. The measure of damages is the difference between the market price[55] *at the time when the buyer learned of the breach* and the contract price together with any incidental and consequential damages,[56] but less expenses saved in consequence of the seller's breach. The place where the market price is to be determined *normally is the place of tender;*[57] but if the buyer has rightfully rejected or justifiably revoked his acceptance after arrival of the goods, the place where the market price is determined is *the place of arrival.* It should be noted that this right to damages for non-delivery or repudiation is alternative to the buyer's right to cover, just discussed, and cannot be utilized to the extent that the buyer has exercised cover.

Accept the Goods and Obtain Damages. We have already considered the buyer's acceptance of goods with proper notification to the seller of non-conformity of tender,[58] and we have seen that his failure to notify the seller would bar his right to reject and to recover damages for non-conformity. If the buyer has accepted and given proper notice of non-conformity of tender, and the time for revoca-

---

[53] See below, p. 344.

[54] See below, p. 343.

[55] In the absence of a current market price at the time and place of tender, proof of a substitute market may be made under UCC 2–723, 724. See below, pp. 348–49.

[56] See below, pp. 343–44.

[57] See above, pp. 303.

[58] See above, p. 320.

tion of acceptance has gone by, the damages which the buyer may recover depend upon whether or not it is a breach of warranty case. If it is not a breach of warranty, the buyer may recover as damages the loss resulting in the ordinary course of events from the seller's breach as determined in *any manner which is reasonable* and, in a proper case, any incidental and consequential damages. If it is a breach of warranty, the measure of the buyer's damages is *the difference at the time and place of acceptance between the value of the goods accepted and the value they would have had if they had been as warranted,* unless special circumstances show proximate damages of a different amount, and in a proper case any incidental and consequential damages.

Accept the Goods and Deduct Damages from the Price. If the buyer who has accepted the goods and properly notified the seller of the non-conforming tender has not yet paid the purchase price in full, he may recoup and not have to sue the seller to recover the purchase price, as just discussed. The buyer, on notifying the seller of his intention to do so, may deduct all or any part of the damages resulting from any breach of the contract from any part of the price still due under the same contract. It should be noted carefully that no general set-off is permitted here. The buyer may deduct from the purchase price of *that contract* the damages resulting from the seller's breach of *that contract.*

Specific Performance or Replevin. The buyer has two remedies available to him whereby he can proceed directly against the goods, namely specific performance of the contract and replevin for the goods. These will be considered briefly in turn.

Specific Performance. Specific performance means that, pursuant to court decree, the contract is to be performed as provided therein. It is an injunction to achieve as nearly as possible the contract effect. *The buyer may obtain a decree of specific performance only when the goods are unique or in other proper circumstances; the decree may include such terms and conditions as to payment of the price, damages, or other relief as the court may deem just.* Reference should be made to Contracts herein.[59] "Specific performance is no longer limited to goods which are already specific or ascertained at the time of contracting. The test of uniqueness . . . must be made in terms of the total situation which characterizes the contract. *Output and requirements contracts involving a particular or peculiarly available source or market present today the typical commercial specific performance situation,*

---

[59] See above, pp. 133–34.

as contrasted with contracts for the sale of heirlooms or priceless works of art, which were usually involved in the older cases. However, uniqueness is not the sole basis of the remedy . . . for the relief may also be granted 'in other proper circumstances' and *inability to cover is strong evidence of 'other proper circumstances.'*" (Author's italics)[60] Specific performance applies to any kind of goods.

Replevin. Replevin is a form of action to recover possession of specific chattels or goods. The right of replevin here is different from the buyer's right to recover possession of identified goods in the event of the seller's insolvency, previously discussed.[61] *Here, replevin is the buyer's right to sue for possession of goods: if after reasonable effort he is unable to effect cover for such goods, or the circumstances reasonably indicate that such effort would be unavailing; or if the goods have been shipped under reservation and satisfaction of the security interest in them has been made or tendered.* If a negotiable document of title representing the goods is outstanding, the buyer's right of replevin is directed to the document and not to the goods. It should be noted very carefully that, with respect to goods not shipped, the buyer cannot resort to replevin unless he has not been able to effect cover or the circumstances reasonably appear to preclude cover.

Resale. *When the buyer has rightfully rejected or justifiably revoked his acceptance, he has a security interest in goods in his possession or control for any payments made on their price and any expenses reasonably incurred in their inspection, receipt, transportation, care, and custody, and in order to recover such payments and expenses he has the right to hold such goods and resell them in like manner as an aggrieved seller.*[62] It should be noted that the buyer may not keep any profit which results from the resale; the profit goes to the seller. Also, payment includes not only cash but also acceptance of a draft or other time negotiable instrument, or the signing of a negotiable note.

Buyer's Incidental and Consequential Damages. The buyer is entitled to incidental damages and, in a proper case, consequential damages resulting from the seller's breach of contract.

Incidental Damages. "Incidental damages resulting from the seller's breach include expenses reasonably incurred in inspection, receipt, transportation and care and custody of goods rightfully rejected, any commercially reasonable charges, expenses or commissions in con-

---

[60] UCC 2–716, *Comment 2.*

[61] See above, p. 303.

[62] See above, pp. 335 ff.

nection with effecting cover and any other reasonable expense incident to the delay or other breach."[63]

Consequential Damages. It is but fair that the seller should be liable for loss which he reasonably could foresee would be a consequence of his failure to perform. This is particularly true in warranties. "One who warrants goods to possess a certain quality is held to an extensive liability for consequential damages for breach of the warranty. The nature of the warranty often gives notice to the seller of the probable consequences of a breach. He can more readily foresee injurious consequences from a breach of his obligation than an ordinary contractor."[64] However, the buyer has a duty to minimize damages, and his right of cover is one method of doing so. Accordingly, under UCC 2-715(2): "Consequential damages resulting from the seller's breach include (a) any loss resulting from general or particular requirements and needs of which the seller at the time of contracting had reason to know and which could not reasonably be prevented by cover or otherwise; and (b) injury to person or property proximately resulting from any breach of warranty."[65] A commonly occurring illustration of a buyer's consequential damages resulting from the seller's breach is the buyer's injury from the loss of a profitable resale of goods caused by the seller's failure to deliver them, provided the seller had reason to know at the time of contracting that the buyer was contemplating such resale, and provided also that the buyer could not reasonably have prevented the loss by cover or otherwise.

3. MISCELLANEOUS REMEDIES

Various miscellaneous remedies applicable to both parties to a contract for the sale of goods are covered in sections 2-718 through 2-725 of the Code. They deal with contractual provisions for damages and remedies, the effect of certain terms on remedies, remedies for fraud, remedies against third parties for injury to goods, determination of market price as a measure of damages, and a uniform Statute of Limita-

---

[63] UCC 2-715(1).

[64] Samuel Williston, *The Law Governing Sales of Goods* (rev. ed.; New York: Baker, Voorhis & Co., 1948) Vol. III, sec. 614.

[65] UCC 2-715, *Comment 5:* "Where the injury involved follows the use of goods without discovery of the defect causing the damage, the question of 'proximate' cause turns on whether it was reasonable for the buyer to use the goods without such inspection as would have revealed the defects. If it was not reasonable for him to do so, or if he did in fact discover the defect prior to his use, the injury would not proximately result from the breach of warranty."

tions applicable to contracts for the sale of goods. These will be considered briefly in turn. However, it should be recalled at this point that remedies for breach of any obligation or promise collateral or ancillary to a contract for the sale of goods are not impaired by the Sales part of the Code.

Contractual Provisions for Damages and Remedies The parties may provide in their contract for the liquidation or limitation of damages and return of deposit, and for modification or limitation of remedies, *as long as such contractual provisions are made in good faith[66] and are not unconscionable.[67]* Every contract or duty under the Code imposes an obligation of good faith in its performance or enforcement.

Liquidation or Limitation of Damages; Deposits. The parties' agreement may make provision for the liquidation of damages in the event of breach by either party. In this way certainty of reasonable compensation for loss caused by wrongful conduct is accomplished when it is difficult to determine the extent of such loss. The amount must not be a penalty to deter such conduct but, rather, it must be reasonably compensatory. *The liquidated amount must be reasonable in light of the anticipated or actual harm caused by the breach, the difficulties of proof of loss, and the inconvenience or nonfeasibility of otherwise obtaining an adequate remedy.* A provision fixing unreasonably large liquidated damages is void as a penalty, and a provision fixing unreasonably small liquidated damages is unconscionable and void.

When the buyer has made a payment or payments, either as a deposit or on the purchase price, and the seller justifiably withholds delivery of goods because of the buyer's breach, only a *reasonable* forfeiture can be imposed by the seller on the buyer. If their agreement provides for reasonable liquidated damages, then the seller is to make restitution to the buyer of any amount by which the sum of the buyer's payments exceeds the liquidated damages. If their agreement does not provide for reasonable liquidated damages, then the seller is to make restitution to the buyer of any amount by which the sum of the buyer's payments exceeds 20 per cent of the total performance for which the buyer is obligated under the contract, or $500, whichever is smaller. However, the amount which the seller is obligated to refund to the

[66] UCC 1–201(19), 1–203, 2–103(1)(b).
[67] See UCC 2–302.

buyer is subject to offset, or certain deductions which the seller may assert. He may deduct the amount of damages which he may properly claim under the Code, apart from the liquidated damages provided in their agreement. Also, he may deduct the amount or value of any benefits received by the buyer directly or indirectly by reason of the contract. If the buyer's payment was in the form of goods, the amount of such payment is the reasonable value of such goods or the proceeds from their resale in good faith and commercial reasonableness by the seller; except that if the seller has notice of the buyer's breach *before* such resale, his resale is governed by the rules applicable to an aggrieved seller's remedy of resale on the buyer's breach,[68] the seller is not required to resell the goods which he received as payment from the buyer, and in the absence of resale the reasonable value of the goods will determine the amount of the buyer's payment and the excess to be refunded by the seller to the buyer.

It should be noted in passing that, in furtherance of the adjustment of any claim or dispute between the seller and buyer, they may agree to a third party inspection or survey to determine the conformity or condition of the goods and may agree that the findings shall be binding upon them in any subsequent litigation or adjustment.[69]

Modification or Limitation of Remedies. The parties' agreement may also provide for remedies additional to, in substitution for, or in restriction of those remedies provided under the Code, and the parties may agree to limit or alter the measure of damages recoverable under the Code, *as long as such provisions are in good faith and are not unconscionable.* The parties should expect that each should have minimum adequate remedies available for breach of contractual obligation. Contractual provision limiting the buyer's remedies to return of the goods and repayment of the price or to repair and replacement of nonconforming goods or parts are reasonable provisions. When additional or substitutive remedies are provided, as a rule of construction it is deemed that such remedies are cumulative and optional rather than exclusive, unless a remedy is *expressly* agreed to be exclusive, in which case it is the sole remedy. Where circumstances cause an exclusive or limited remedy to fail of its essential purpose, the remedy or remedies available under the Code may be utilized.

The parties may limit or exclude consequential damages, unless the limitation or exclusion is unconscionable. *In the case of consumer goods,* which are goods used or bought for use primarily for personal,

---

[68] See above, pp. 335 ff.
[69] See UCC 2–513.

family, or household purposes, *it is prima facie unconscionable to limit consequential damages for injury to the person.* Limitation of consequential damages for commercial loss is not unconscionable. It should be recalled that remedies for breach of warranty can be limited and the seller can disclaim warranties, except that a seller cannot exclude or limit his liability to certain third party beneficiaries of his warranties.[70]

Effect of Certain Terms on Remedies
When an antecedent breach has occurred, rights accrue to the aggrieved party. Such rights are not to be impaired lightly and intended impairment must be clearly indicated. Such terms as "cancellation" or "rescission" or the like merely discharge contractual duty of *future* performance, but not of rights arising from previous nonperformance. As a rule of construction, "Unless the contrary intention clearly appears, expressions of 'cancellation' or 'rescission' of the contract or the like shall not be construed as a renunciation or discharge of any claim in damages for an antecedent breach."[71] A cancellation of a contract stating that it is "without reservation of rights" clearly renounces such rights.

Remedies for Fraud
Material misrepresentation or fraud in a contract for the sale of goods creates certain remedies in the aggrieved party, such as rescission or rightful rejection, but the existence of such remedies should not deprive the aggrieved party of those remedies available in non-fraudulent breach cases. Under the Code,[72] remedies for material misrepresentation or fraud include all remedies available under the Sales part of the Code for non-fraudulent breach. Neither recission nor a claim for rescission of the contract for sale, nor rejection nor return of the goods shall bar, or be deemed inconsistent with, a claim for damages or other remedy.

Remedies against Third Parties for Injury to Goods
A contracting party with an interest in the goods has a right against third parties who have damaged such interest. He is the real party in interest. Prior to identification of the goods to the contract, only the seller has an interest in the goods and only he can recover against wrongful third persons for injury to that interest. After identification of the goods to the contract, usually both the seller and buyer have interests in the goods which

[70] See above, p. 297.
[71] UCC 2–720.
[72] UCC 2–721.

may be injured by a third person. The interest may be the title to the goods, a security interest or a special property interest or an insurable interest in the goods. If the goods have been destroyed or converted[73] by a third person, the contracting party who bears the risk of loss under the contract for sale or who has assumed that risk after the injury occurred has the right to institute suit against the third person. The seller and buyer may agree that one of them may sue for the benefit of both or either of them as their interests may appear, or for the benefit of whom it may concern. If the parties have not so agreed and, at the time of injury, the party plaintiff did not bear the risk of loss as against the other party to the contract for sale, the plaintiff's suit or settlement is, subject to his own interest, as a fiduciary for the other party to the contract.

Determination of Market Price as a Measure of Damages
We have previously discussed the time and place when the market price is determined in connection with damages obtainable by the seller for non-acceptance or repudiation,[74] and damages obtainable by the buyer for non-delivery or repudiation.[75] However, if there has been an *anticipatory* repudiation and trial occurs before the time when performance was due for some or all of the goods, inasmuch as the market price cannot be ascertained at the time performance is due, damages based on the market price are determined according to the market price of the goods prevailing at the time when the aggrieved party learned of the repudiation. If evidence of the price prevailing at the times and places on the occasion of breach by the seller or buyer, whether anticipatory or not, is not readily available, "the price prevailing within any reasonable time before or after the time described or at any other place which in commercial judgment or under usage of trade would serve as a reasonable substitute for the one described may be used, making any proper allowance for the cost of transporting the goods to or from such other place."[76] When evidence of a relevant price prevailing at a time or place other than the one described in the Sales portion of the Code is offered by one of the parties, the evidence is not admissible unless and until the offering party has given to the other party such notice as the court finds sufficient to prevent unfair surprise.

---

[73] For conversion, see above, p. 193, ftn. 18.

[74] See above, p. 337.

[75] See above, p. 341.

[76] UCC 2–723(2).

In order to provide for the admissibility into evidence of market quotations, but without prescribing the weight to be given to such quotations, UCC 2–724 provides: "Whenever the prevailing price or value of any goods regularly bought and sold in any established commodity market is in issue, reports in official publications or trade journals or in newspapers or periodicals of general circulation published as the reports of such market shall be admissible in evidence. The circumstances of the preparation of such a report may be shown to affect its weight but not its admissibility."

Statute of Limitations Because the statutes of limitations for actions for breach of contract for the sale of goods differ in the various states, the Code has provided for a uniform Statute of Limitations. *An action for breach of contract for sale must be commenced within four years after the cause of action has accrued.* By their original agreement, the parties may shorten the period to not less than one year, but may not extend it beyond four years. When an action is timely commenced but has been so terminated that the plaintiff can institute another action for the same breach, he may commence the new action after the expiration of the time within which he could originally sue but only within six months after the termination of the first action. However, if the termination of the first action resulted from the plaintiff's voluntary discontinuance or from dismissal for failure or neglect to prosecute, then the plaintiff is limited solely to the time in which he originally could institute an action.

A cause of action accrues when the breach occurs, regardless of the aggrieved party's lack of knowledge of the breach. Ordinarily, a breach of warranty occurs when tender of delivery is made; however, where a warranty explicitly extends to *future* performance of the goods and discovery of the breach must await the time of such performance, the cause of action accrues when the breach *is, or should have been, discovered.*

It should be noted that the Code does not alter the law on tolling[77] of the Statute of Limitations, nor does it apply to causes of action which have accrued before the Code became effective.[78]

[77] See above, p. 148.
[78] UCC 2–725(4).

Chapter IX

BULK TRANSFERS

CONDUCT of a debtor which is not usual and which is not ordinarily associated with honest dealing is subject to the suspicion of fraud on creditors if creditors' rights are involved. Such conduct is often called a "badge of fraud," creating a presumption of a fraudulent conveyance. An illustration is a bulk transfer, dealt with in Article 6 of the Uniform Commercial Code. Two common illustrations of commercial fraud serve to indicate the need for remedial legislation. "(a) The merchant, owing debts, who sells out his stock in trade to a friend for less than it is worth, pays his creditors less than he owes them, and hopes to come back into the business through the back door some time in the future. (b) The merchant, owing debts, who sells out his stock in trade to any one for any price, pockets the proceeds, and disappears leaving his creditors unpaid."[1] While the first illustration is a form of fraudulent conveyance, no provision is made in the Uniform Fraudulent Conveyance Act[2] for any requirement of advance notice to the seller's creditors of the proposed sale so that they could investigate and decide whether or not to prevent the proposed sale from taking place. In the second illustration, if creditors of the seller had advance notice of the proposed sale, they could impound the sale proceeds and thereby protect themselves. *The requirement of adequate notice is the primary purpose of the Code's provisions covering bulk transfers.* While red tape and delay along with danger to an innocent purchaser are occasioned by the Code's provisions, nevertheless the necessary protection to creditors justifies such restrictions on certain kinds of bulk transfers. For a transfer to come within the Code's provisions on bulk transfers, it must be a *particular kind of transfer* in a *particular kind of enterprise* or business. Each of these will be considered in turn.

---

[1] UCC 6–101, *Comment 2.*
[2] See below, pp. 1173–74.

The Transfer *A bulk transfer is any transfer in bulk and not in the ordinary course of the transferor's business of a major part of the materials, supplies, merchandise, or other inventory of an enterprise covered by the Code.* Goods are " 'inventory' if they are held by a person who holds them for sale or lease or to be furnished under contracts of service or if he has so furnished them, or if they are raw materials, work in process or materials used or consumed in a business."[3] Equipment is not inventory; it is goods which are used or bought for use primarily in business, including farming or a profession, and which are not inventory, farm products, or consumer goods.[4] While a transfer of equipment is not of itself a bulk transfer, nevertheless a transfer of a substantial part of equipment of an enterprise included in the Code *in connection with* a bulk transfer of inventory is a bulk transfer. Since transfers of investment securities, money, accounts receivable, chattel paper, contract rights, negotiable instruments, and things in action generally are not believed to carry any major bulk sales risk, they are not included in the bulk transfer covered by this portion of the Code.[5] The Code enumerates certain types of transfers which come within the definition of a bulk transfer but which are specifically *excluded* from the provisions on bulk transfers because the major bulk sales risk to creditors is not present:

(1) Those made to give security for the performance of an obligation;
(2) General assignments for the benefit of all the creditors of the transferor, and subsequent transfers by the assignee thereunder;
(3) Transfers in settlement or realization of a lien or other security interest;
(4) Sales by executors, administrators, receivers, trustees in bankruptcy, or any public officer under judicial process;
(5) Sales made in the course of judicial or administrative proceedings for the dissolution or reorganization of a corporation and of which notice is sent to the creditors of the corporation pursuant to order of the court or administrative agency;
(6) Transfers to a person maintaining a known place of business in this State who becomes bound to pay the debts of the transferor in full and gives public notice of that fact, and who is solvent after becoming so bound;
(7) A transfer to a new business enterprise organized to take over and continue the business, if public notice of the transaction is given and the new enterprise assumes the debts of the transferor and he receives

---

[3] UCC 9–109(4).

[4] UCC 9–109(1): [Goods are] " 'consumer goods' if they are used or bought for use primarily for personal, family or household purposes."

[5] UCC 6–102, *Comment 3.*

nothing from the transaction except an interest in the new enterprise junior to the claims of creditors;

(8) Transfers of property which is exempt from execution.[6]

The Enterprise *The enterprise covered by the Code is one whose principal business is the sale of merchandise from stock, including one who manufacturers what it sells.* Such an enterprise does not include farming, contracting, professional services, nor businesses whose principal business is the sale of services and not merchandise. For example, restaurants and hotels are not included within such an enterprise.

Notice to Transferor's Creditors *A bulk transfer under the Code is ineffective as to every creditor of the transferor unless the transferee complies with the Code's provisions for notice to such creditors. First,* the transferee is to obtain from the transferor a written list, signed and either sworn to or affirmed by the transferor or his agent, containing the names and business addresses of all existing creditors of the transferor, with the amounts owed when known, together with the names of all persons who, the transferor knows, assert claims against him, even though such claims are disputed.[7] It should be noted *very* carefully that: *"Responsibility for the completeness and accuracy of the list of creditors rests on the transferor, and the transfer is not rendered ineffective by errors or omissions therein unless the transferee is shown to have had knowledge."* (Author's italics)[8] *Second,* the transferor and transferee are to prepare a schedule sufficient to identify the property to be transferred. *Third,* the transferee is to preserve the list and schedule for six months after the transfer has been made and permit any creditor of the transferor at all reasonable hours to inspect either or both and to copy therefrom, or he is to file the list and schedule if, and at the place, prescribed by state law. *Fourth, except in the case of a bulk transfer made by auction sale, at least 10 days before the transferee takes possession of the goods or pays for them, whichever happens first, the transferee is to give proper notice by personal delivery or by registered or certified mail to all persons shown on the list of creditors furnished by the transferor and to all other persons*

---

[6] UCC 6–103.

[7] UCC 6–104(2): "If the transferor is the obligor of an outstanding issue of bonds, debentures or the like as to which there is an indenture trustee, the list of creditors need include only the name and address of the indenture trustee and the aggregate outstanding principal amount of the issue."

[8] UCC 6–104(3).

who are known to the transferee to hold or assert claims against the transferor.[9] Creditors who are entitled to receive such notice are those who were creditors of the transferor *before* the bulk transfer and *before* the required notice to creditors was given. Those who became creditors thereafter are not entitled to such notice.

Under the Code:

(1) The notice to creditors . . . shall state:

    (a) that a bulk transfer is about to be made; and

    (b) the names and business addresses of the transferor and transferee, and all other business names and addresses used by the transferor within three years last past so far as known to the transferee; and

    (c) whether or not all the debts of the transferor are to be paid in full as they fall due as a result of the transaction, and if so, the address to which creditors should send their bills.

(2) If the debts of the transferor are not to be paid in full as they fall due or if the transferee is in doubt on that point then the notice shall state further:

    (a) the location and general description of the property to be transferred and the estimated total of the transferor's debts;

    (b) the address where the schedule of property and list of creditors . . . may be inspected;

    (c) whether the transfer is to pay existing debts and if so the amount of such debts and to whom owing;

    (d) whether the transfer is for new consideration and if so the amount of such consideration and the time and place of payment.[10]

It should be noted very carefully that, while a transferee's title to the property sold is defective because of *his* non-compliance with the Code's requirements, nevertheless *a good faith purchaser for value from such transferee without notice of such non-compliance takes the property free of such defect and acquires good title to the property.*

Special Code provisions govern a bulk transfer by sale at auction because of the presence of an auctioneer[11] and the uncertainty of the identity of the transferee, both of which facts require modification relative to the giving of notice and the effectiveness of the auction sale. Neither the price nor the transferee purchaser will be known until an auction sale has occurred. Also, the obligation to give notice to the transferor's creditors cannot be imposed on bidders at the auction, and

---

[9] The Code suggests additional provisions for those states which wish to impose additional duties on the transferee to assure that payment of new consideration will be applied to pay creditors of the transferor. See UCC 6–106, 6–107(2) (e), 6–108(3) (c), 6–109(2).

[10] UCC 6–107.

[11] UCC 6–108(3): "The person or persons other than the transferor who direct, control or are responsible for the auction are collectively called the 'auctioneer.' "

the auction sale must be effective. Accordingly, the Code requires an auctioneer: to obtain from the transferor the list of creditors described in "first" above; to assist the transferor in the preparation of the schedule of property described in "second" above; to preserve the list and schedule and make them available as described in "third" above; and at least 10 days before the auction occurs to give notice by personal delivery or by registered mail to all persons shown on the list of creditors furnished by the transferor and to all other persons who are known to the auctioneer to hold or assert claims against the transferor. *Failure of the auctioneer to perform any of these duties does not affect the validity of the sale or the title of the purchaser.* If the auctioneer did not know that the auction was a bulk sale, he is not liable to anyone for his non-compliance with the above four requirements. However, if he knew that it was a bulk sale, he is liable for his non-compliance to the transferor's creditors as a class for the sums owing to them by the transferor up to but not exceeding the net proceeds of the auction.

It should be noted in passing that the Code establishes a short-term Statute of Limitations of six months within which action may be brought or levy made after the date when the transferee took possession of the goods because of his non-compliance with the Code's requirements. However, if the transfer was concealed, action and levy may occur within six months after discovery of the concealed transfer.

APPENDIX TO PART THREE (C)

REFERENCES

1. Anderson, Ronald A. *Anderson's Uniform Commercial Code.* 2d ed. Rochester: Lawyers Cooperative Publishing Co., 1970.
2. Corman, Calvin W. "The Law of Sales under the Uniform Commercial Code," in *Uniform Commercial Code Handbook 21.* Chicago: American Bar Association, 1964.
3. Hawkland, William D. *A Transactional Guide to the Uniform Commercial Code.* Philadelphia: American Law Institute, 1964.
4. Lamey, William L. "How to Handle a Bulk Transfer," in *Uniform Commercial Code Handbook 165.* Chicago: American Bar Association, 1964.
5. *Uniform Laws Annotated,* Articles 2, 6, Uniform Commercial Code, 1962.

PROBLEMS

1. What is meant by the following:
   (a) Sale.
   (b) Present sale.
   (c) Contract to sell.
   (d) Future goods.
   (e) Fungible goods.

2. A orally contracted with B to sell B certain goods for $10,000. A tendered the goods, which B unjustifiedly refused to accept. A wrote a letter to B reciting the terms of the contract and inquiring the reasons for B's refusal. B's answering letter to A acknowledged receipt of A's letter and stated: "The goods which were the subject of the contract we made, as recited in your letter, no longer are desired by me."
   (1) Can A maintain an action against B for damages for non-acceptance of the goods?
   (2) Why?

3. A and B contracted whereby A agreed to sell and B agreed to buy two specific lots of merchandise, title to the first lot to be transferred together with delivery to B at the time the contract was made, and title to the second lot to be transferred together with delivery to B 30 days after the date of the contract—at which time B was to make payment for both lots. At the time the contract was made, the first lot had been partially de-

stroyed without the knowledge of the parties; subsequent to such contract but prior to the expiration of 30 days and prior to payment by B,
the second lot was partially destroyed without the fault of A or B. What
are the rights of the parties?

4. A delivered two machines to B, pursuant to an agreement between them
whereby B was to try out the machines for a week to see if they were
satisfactory and then either to keep one or both and pay A $500 for each
one kept by B or to return to A what he did not want.

   (1) During the week, damage was caused to one machine by B's negligence
   and, before the end of the week, this machine was returned to A. On
   the expiration of two weeks after receiving the machines, B tendered
   the return of the second machine, which A refused to accept. What
   are the rights of the parties?

   (2) In the absence of (1), what are the rights of B's creditors against the
   two machines during the one-week period? Explain.

   (3) In the absence of (1), what would be the legal effect of B's sale as
   owner and delivery of the two machines to C, a good faith purchaser
   for value during the one-week period? Explain.

   (4) In the absence of (1), A delivered five additional machines to B for
   repair. What would be the legal effect of B's sale as owner and delivery
   of three of these machines to X, a good faith purchaser in satisfaction
   of a past debt owed by B to X? Explain.

5. A orders goods by description from B, such goods to be sent to A, which
goods B delivers to a bailee for shipment to A.

   (1) Where is the title to the goods? Explain.

   (2) If, pursuant to the contract, the goods are to be sent C.O.D., where
   is the title? Explain.

   (3) If the bailee is a railroad and B obtains a bill of lading to B's order,
   where is the title to the goods? Explain.

   (4) If the bailee is a railroad and B obtains a straight bill of lading in
   favor of A, where is the title to the goods? Explain.

   (5) If B, pursuant to the contract, shipped the goods F.O.B. destination,
   how does this affect the transfer of title? Explain.

6. (a) A sold and delivered goods to B pursuant to B's fraudulent inducement.
   B sold and delivered the goods to C, a good faith purchaser for value
   without notice of B's fraud on A. A then discovers the fraud. Can A
   repossess the goods? Explain.

   (b) What is the effect of a seller's delivery to a buyer of:

      (1) A quantity of goods less than that provided in the contract?

      (2) A quantity of goods greater than that provided in the contract?

7. (a) B stole goods from A and pledged them with C, who was innocent of
   the theft, as security for a loan. On B's failure to repay the loan, C
   sold the goods to D at public auction.

      (1) Does A have any right to the goods? Explain.

      (2) Does D have any right against C? Explain.

   (b) X selected and purchased a washing machine from Y, a retailer of
   home appliances. The machine was delivered to X, who discovered
   that it was defective and would not function. What may X do?

8. A ordered goods by description from B to be sent to A, payment to be made in 30 days. B sent such goods to A by C, a carrier, from whom B obtained a negotiable bill of lading to the order of A and which was delivered to A. A sold, indorsed in blank, and delivered the bill of lading to D, a good faith purchaser for value. A became insolvent while the goods were being transported by C. Does B have any right to reacquire possession of the goods? Explain.

9. Allen, a manufacturer in Pittsburgh, sold to Burt, on credit, a carload of goods to be delivered at Jersey City at the Pennsylvania Railroad. The moment the car arrived at Jersey City the goods were levied on by the sheriff of Hudson County on an execution against Burt. Allen having learned of this and that Burt was insolvent gave notice of stoppage in transit to the railroad. Both Allen and the sheriff demanded possession. Who was entitled to it? Why? (Former C.P.A. Examination question)

10. (a) On January 7, 1972, S sold certain kitchen equipment and appliances for $5,000 to B, who paid $1,000 down and was to make four additional monthly payments before receiving possession of the goods. On January 12, 1972, S became insolvent. What may B do?

    (b) X sold goods to Y on credit on January 10, 1972. On January 15, Y became insolvent.
    (1) What may X do?
    (2) If Y had misrepresented to X on December 20, 1971, that he was solvent, how would this affect the answer to the problem?

11. A and B are merchants who, over the telephone, made an oral contract for the sale of goods by A to B for $10,000, delivery in two weeks when B would pick up the goods at A's store. A immediately sent a letter to B confirming the transaction which B received the next day. Two weeks later, B refused to pick up the goods or to acknowledge the transaction. Can A enforce the contract against B? Explain.

12. S, a merchant, offered in writing to sell certain goods to R for $1,000, the writing stating that the offer would be kept open for two months. After one month, R placed a written order with S for the goods on the terms stated in S's written offer. S refused to perform.
    (1) Can R enforce a contract against S? Explain.
    (2) Would it make any difference if the period of S's offer was five months and R placed his order with S at the end of four months? Explain.
    (3) Would it make any difference if S's offer was oral rather than in writing? Explain.
    (4) Would it make any difference if the form of written offer signed by S had been supplied by R? Explain.

13. X's letter offered to buy 10 horses from Z for a total purchase price of $20,000. Z's reply letter of acceptance contained additional and different terms.
    (1) Explain the legal effect of Z's additional and different terms.
    (2) Would it make any difference if X and Z were merchants? Explain.

14. A and B contracted for the sale of certain equipment by A to B over a period of six months.

(1) If A assigned "the contract" to C, who accepted it, what is the legal effect of such assignment?

(2) What is the effect of a clause in the contract between A and B "prohibiting assignment of the contract"?

15. (a) Name and classify, as express or implied, the warranties which may occur in a transaction for the sale of goods.

(b) In the event warranties on a sale of goods are in conflict, which warranties prevail?

16. S and B made a contract for the sale of goods by S to B which contained a clause disclaiming any liability by S to anyone except B for breach of warranty. Explain the effect of this clause.

17. (a) Before title can pass under a contract for sale, what basic legal requirement must occur?

(b) When a seller is required to send the goods to the buyer F.O.B. point of shipment, unless otherwise agreed how is the seller to make shipment?

18. As between the seller and the buyer, who bears the risk of loss to the goods when:

(1) The transaction is F.O.B. point of shipment?

(2) The transaction is F.O.B. destination?

(3) The goods are to be picked up by the buyer at the seller's establishment?

(4) The goods are held by a bailee and are to remain with the bailee after sale?

19. A and B contract for the sale of goods to be shipped by A to B. Before the date of A's performance, B wrote to A that he would not accept delivery. A then telephoned B and told him that, in light of B's letter, the contract was cancelled and he would sell the goods to C, a competitor of B. The next day, while A and C were negotiating for the sale of the goods by A to C, B telephoned A and told him he had changed his mind and that he would go through with the contract and accept the goods when delivered. A refused to deliver the goods to B and, instead, sold and delivered them to C. Is A liable to B? Explain.

20. What is meant by a "bulk transfer" and what is the purpose of Article 6 on Bulk Transfers under the Uniform Commercial Code?

SOME PREVIOUS C.P.A. LAW EXAMINATION QUESTIONS AND MODEL ANSWERS

MAY, 1971

No. 5 (Estimated time—20 to 25 minutes)

During the course of your examination of the financial statements of Grand Fashions, Inc. a retail dress merchant, you learned of the following transactions with wholesale dress merchants:

Transaction 1. The Corporation telephoned Stevens Company and ordered from Stevens' catalog 50 Junior Model dresses in assorted sizes for a total price of $300. The next day the Corporation received a written confirmation of the order from Stevens with a request that it sign and return the duplicate of the confirmation, which it did not do. A month later the Corporation sought to avoid the contract claiming that it was not liable since it did not sign the confirmation order.

Transaction 2. The Corporation placed a telephone order with Scott Company for ten dozen dresses for $1,000. The next day the Corporation received, inspected and accepted five dozen of the dresses. The Corporation refused to accept the balance when tendered and sought to return the other five dozen dresses claiming that it was not obligated.

Transaction 3. The Corporation purchased 25 dozen all-silk dresses from Lawrence Company after examining a sample dress made of all-silk that Lawrence Company submitted. The written confirmation received by the Corporation contained the words "as per sample submitted to the company." Upon delivery, inspection and testing the Corporation determined that the dresses were 65 percent silk and 35 percent dacron and immediately informed Lawrence Company that it wanted to return the dresses for full credit. Lawrence Company insisted that the Corporation take the dresses less a 25 percent discount, but the Corporation refused to do so.

Transaction 4. The Corporation executed a written contract with Roberts Company to purchase a miscellaneous collection of dresses for $5,000. A week before the agreed shipment date, Roberts called the Corporation and said "We cannot deliver at $5,000; unless you agree to pay $6,000, we will cancel the order." After considerable discussion the Corporation agreed to pay $6,000 if Roberts would ship as agreed in the contract. After the goods had been delivered and accepted by the Corporation, it refused to pay $6,000 insisting that it is legally obligated to pay only $5,000.

Discuss separately the validity of the contentions made by Grand Fashions, Inc. with respect to each of the four transactions.

Answer

Transaction 1. The Corporation is liable and its liability is enforceable by Stevens. The Corporation cannot successfully contend that it is not liable and that the contract is unenforceable. Under the Uniform Commercial Code on Sales, the seller offeree's written confirmation of the offer, sent within a reasonable time, is an acceptance. Here, the Corporation's telephonic order was an offer, and Stevens' confirmation received by the Corporation the next day was an acceptance resulting in a contract for the sale of the dresses. An oral contract for the sale of goods for $500 or more is within the Code's Statute of Frauds requiring a properly signed writing for its enforcement. Here, the price is less than $500 and, therefore, the contract is not within the Statute and is enforceable. The fact that the Corporation did not sign and return the duplicate of the confirmation does not affect the making of the contract nor its enforcement.

Transaction 2. The Corporation is liable for the purchase price of the 5 dozen dresses received and accepted by it, and its liability is enforceable by Scott. Under the Code on Sales, a contract for the sale of goods for $500 or more is within the Statute of Frauds and unenforceable unless there is a writing sufficient to indicate that a contract for sale has been made between the parties and the writing is signed by the party against whom enforcement of the contract is sought. Here, the contract for goods for $1,000 was oral and there is no such writing signed by the Corporation. However, if the buyer receives and accepts part or all of the sold goods, the contract is excluded from the Statute to the extent of the goods received and accepted by the buyer and to that extent it is enforceable although oral. Therefore, the contract can be enforced against the Corporation only for the 5 dozen dresses received and accepted by it; the remainder of the contract for the other 5 dozen dresses is still within the Statute and is unenforceable against the Corporation.

Transaction 3. The Corporation may reject the dresses and not be liable for the purchase price. When the buyer and seller of goods include as a part of the basis for their bargain a sample and description of the goods to be sold, there is an express warranty by the seller that the goods to be delivered to the buyer shall conform to the sample and the description. If the goods fail in any respect to conform to the contract, the buyer may rightfully reject the goods within a reasonable time after their delivery if he seasonably notifies the seller of such rejection. Here, the Corporation acted promptly in inspecting the goods and immediately notifying Lawrence of its rejection.

Transaction 4. The Corporation is liable for $6,000, and its liability is enforceable by Roberts. Under the Code on Sales, consideration is not required to make binding an agreement modifying the sales contract. Although an oral contract for the sale of goods for $500 or more is within the Statute of Frauds and unenforceable without a properly signed writing, nevertheless, to the extent of the goods received and accepted by the buyer, the contract is excluded from the Statute and enforceable although oral. Here, the contract as modified is now oral; but the Corporation received and accepted all the goods and, therefore, the entire oral modified contract for $6,000 is enforceable against the Corporation.

No. 6 (a. Estimated time—12 to 15 minutes)

a. During the examination of the financial statements of the Williams Watch Company the following problem was discovered.

On January 16, 1971, Crane, one of Williams' salesmen, called upon Parke, the vice president of purchasing for Carter Department Stores. He showed Parke the new line of mod watches with large, bright-colored faces. Parke ordered 150 watches costing from $5 to $20 with a total cost of $1,475. Delivery was to be made not later than March 15, 1971. Crane wrote the orders in his order book as Parke orally indicated the quantity of each watch he desired. Neither party signed anything.

Crane promptly submitted the Carter order to the sales department. The next day the order was recorded and a memorandum was sent to Carter Department Stores in care of Parke. The memorandum described the transaction indicating the number and prices of the watches purchased and was signed by S. A. Williams, vice president of marketing; however, the total price and delivery terms were excluded erroneously.

Parke received the memo on January 20. He read it and placed it in his goods on order file. On the 20th of February the market for mod watches collapsed and fair market value of the watches dropped to approximately $700. Parke promptly notified Williams Watch by phone that Carter Stores was not interested in the mod watches and would refuse delivery. Williams Watch filed suit for damages against Carter.

Will Williams Watch prevail in its suit against Carter Department Stores? State "yes" or "no" and discuss the relevant legal implications of the above facts.

Answer

a. Yes. The contract is enforceable by Williams against Carter. Under the Uniform Commercial Code on Sales, a contract for the sale of goods for $500 or more is within the Statute of Frauds and unenforceable unless there is a writing sufficient to indicate that a contract for sale has been made between the parties and the writing is signed by the party against whom enforcement of the contract is sought or by his agent. Here, the contract for the sale of goods for $1,475 is within the Statute and oral. The writing must indicate that a contract for sale of goods has been made, specify a quantity of goods, and be signed as indicated. It is not insufficient because it omits to state the price and delivery terms. When the transaction is between merchants, a merchant's written memorandum of the contract which is sufficient to make the contract enforceable against him will also be sufficient as a written memorandum against the merchant recipient if he received the writing within a reasonable time after the transaction was made, he had reason to know its contents, and he did not give to the sender written notice of his objection to the contents within ten days after he received the written memorandum. Here, Williams and Carter are merchants and Williams' written memorandum became that also of Carter sufficient to satisfy the Statute and to prove the oral contract which is now enforceable by Williams against Carter.

NOVEMBER, 1970

No. 2B

(This question was included in the questions on Contracts, inasmuch as both the law of Contracts and of Sales is involved. See the question and answer there, pp. 156–60.)

No. 3 (Estimated time—20 to 25 minutes)

Each of the following numbered sentences states a legal conclusion relating to the lettered material. You are to determine whether the legal conclusion is true or false according to the *Uniform Commercial Code and general principles of sales law*. Write on a separate sheet whether each conclusion is true or false. Your grade will be determined from your total of correct answers less a penalty for your incorrect answers; an omitted answer will not be considered an incorrect answer.

A. Archer, a farmer, wrote Nevins, a tractor dealer, as follows:

> Confirming telephone conversation of today, please ship me one Centipede Model 2 tractor at $3,500, COD.
>
> *Archer*

Nevins failed to deliver the tractor to Archer who thereafter bought one elsewhere for $5,000.

61. Archer has a valid cause of action on a contract of sale against Nevins.

62. The answer to the preceding question would be different if Archer's letter had been accompanied by a $3,500 check which Nevins cashed.

63. Assume that 15 days after receiving and reading Archer's letter, Nevins wrote Archer advising that the price for the tractor was $4,000 and that he would not sell for $3,500. In such a case, Archer would have a valid cause of action against Nevins for breach of contract.

64. The answer to the preceding question would be the same if both Archer and Nevins were tractor dealers.

65. Assume that promptly upon receipt of Archer's letter, Nevins shipped the tractor and Archer refused to pay $3,500 on delivery. In such a case, Archer may successfully defend Nevins' action for breach of contract on the basis that no enforceable contract existed.

B. In connection with his examination of the financial statements of the Commonwealth Boiler Company for the year ended March 31, 1970, a CPA is concerned about the legal implications of the following situation: Commonwealth Boiler Company agreed in a contract of sale made on January 2, 1970, to sell and deliver nine boilers to Osgood Contracting Corporation, three boilers to be delivered on or about February 1, three on or about March 1 and the remaining three on or about April 1. Payment of the price, plus interest, was to be made by Osgood in six monthly installments commencing May 1. In negotiating the contract on January 2 Osgood falsely represented its solvency to Commonwealth in writing. On March 15, after timely delivery of the first six boilers, Commonwealth learns of Osgood's insolvency. No payment of any part of the price of the boilers has been made by Osgood.

66. Commonwealth may legally refuse to deliver the remaining three boilers unless Osgood pays the price therefor in cash on delivery.

67. Before it is obligated to deliver the remaining three boilers, Commonwealth may demand immediate cash payment for the six boilers previously delivered.

68. If the remaining three boilers have been shipped but not yet delivered, Commonwealth may stop delivery in transit.

69. If, immediately upon discovery of Osgood's insolvency, Commonwealth demands return of all boilers previously delivered, its rights therein would be superior to those of other general creditors of Osgood even though it had no perfected security interest in the boilers.

70. On the basis of the facts set forth in item 69, Commonwealth could reclaim the six boilers from Dunkins, even though Dunkins had acquired them from Osgood in good faith and for value.

C. Ace Equipment Company delivered a printing press to Green Printers, Inc. The written agreement between Ace and Green provided that the press could be returned after a reasonable trial period if it did not satisfy Green's needs. Payment was to be made upon Green's acceptance. One week after delivery of the press, Green is adjudicated a bankrupt. Ace Equipment's CPA is discussing with the credit manager the amounts, if any, to be included in the financial statements for this transaction.

71. This was a sale-or-return transaction.
72. The answer to item 71 would be different if Green was in the business of selling printing presses for its own account.
73. Risk of loss on the press was upon Ace after the delivery to Green.
74. Ace could successfully repossess the printing press from Green's trustee in bankruptcy.
75. Assuming that the agreement between Ace and Green providing for the return of the press was not written, Ace could not repossess the press from Green's trustee in bankruptcy.

D. Pursuant to a written contract of sale Falmouth Ltd., a British manufacturer, agreed to sell and deliver 15 electric generators to Harris & Co., an American equipment dealer located in St. Louis, terms $150,000, C.I.F. New York. In connection with his effort to secure a proper cut-off of inventory transactions at the balance sheet date, several legal questions have come to the attention of Harris' CPA regarding the contract with Falmouth.

76. The price to Harris included the cost of the goods, freight to New York and insurance for Harris' account.
77. Harris is required to pay the price upon tender to it of proper documents although the goods have not yet arrived in New York.
78. Assuming Falmouth properly discharges all of its obligations under the contract, risk of loss of the goods at sea is upon Harris.
79. If Falmouth had neglected to effect insurance for Harris' account, the answer to the preceding questions would be the same.
80. If the contract had specified "C & F" terms, risk of loss at sea would be upon Falmouth.

E. Ingram, a do-it-yourself type, decided to paint the exterior of his house with the new Excello All Purpose brand of paint which was advertised to be "no-chipping or peeling and absolutely weatherproof" for five years. Ingram purchased the Excello paint from Collins' paint store. Shortly after painting the house, Ingram discovered that the paint had blistered and was peeling in several places and that his paint job had not stood up well in a mild rain storm.

81. Since Ingram bought the paint from Collins by trade name, no implied warranty by Collins attached to the sale.
82. In selling the paint to Ingram, Collins impliedly warranted its merchantability.
83. Advertising claims such as those made by Excello have been held to be express warranties.
84. If Ingram advised Collins of his intended use for the paint and Collins suggested the Excello All Purpose brand, Collins warranted the fitness for use by Ingram.
85. If Collins sold the paint to Ingram with a written warranty that it was suitable for exterior use, there could be no implied warranties in connection with the sale.

F. Dexter Company, a clothing manufacturer, purchased goods from Johnson Fabrics, Inc. The contract specified 100 bolts of a 50 percent wool, 50 percent acetate fabric in a particular color. Only 75 bolts were delivered by Johnson and 25 of these were not of the color specified in the contract.

86. Dexter may reject the entire shipment.
87. Dexter may accept the 50 bolts of the proper color and reject the remainder of the shipment.
88. Assume Dexter accepted the entire shipment and later discovered, on testing, that the goods were only 25 percent wool. In such a case, Dexter is bound by its acceptance.
89. If the goods were shipped F.O.B. Johnson's plant, risk of loss was upon Dexter and it could not reject the goods.
90. Assume that Johnson became insolvent before delivery but after identification to the contract and that Dexter paid for the goods upon execution of the contract and seven days before Johnson's insolvency. In such a case, Dexter could recover the goods from Johnson's creditors.

Answer

61. False	67. True	73. True	79. False	85. False
62. True	68. True	74. True	80. False	86. True
63. False	69. True	75. False	81. False	87. True
64. False	70. False	76. True	82. True	88. False
65. False	71. False	77. True	83. True	89. False
66. True	72. True	78. True	84. True	90. True

No. 7 (Estimated time—25 to 30 minutes)

a. In your examination of the financial statements of the Terminal Ice Company for the year ended September 30, 1970, you discover correspondence relating to a dispute concerning the transferability to Igloo Ice Cream Company of Terminal's contract with The Polar Bear Ice Cream Company. Polar Bear had been purchased by Igloo. A synopsis of the facts follows.

Terminal made a contract to deliver ice to Polar Bear. Before the contract expired, Polar Bear assigned the contract to Igloo. Terminal refused to deliver ice to the assignee and was threatened by Igloo with legal action for recovery of damages for the alleged breach.

The contract obligated Terminal to sell and deliver to the loading platform of Polar Bear up to 250 tons of ice per week for $23.25 a ton. The contractual rights of Terminal were (a) to be paid every Tuesday for all ice purchased by Polar Bear during the week ending at midnight of the preceding Saturday; (b) to require Polar Bear neither to buy nor accept ice from any source other than Terminal, except for amounts needed in excess of the weekly maximum of 250 tons. The contract was for a period of three years with an option that permitted Polar Bear to renew for an additional three years. Polar Bear renewed for three years.

Before the first year of the renewal contract had expired, without the consent or knowledge of Terminal and for a valuable consideration, Polar Bear executed and delivered to Igloo on August 15, 1970, a written assignment of its agreement with Terminal. The assignment was part of the purchase transaction by which Igloo acquired "the plant, equipment, rights, credits, choses in action, goodwill, contracts and trade, custom and patronage rights" and any other assets of Polar Bear's ice cream business. The purchaser took full possession and continued the former business carried on by Polar

Bear which was to be operated as a separate division engaged in the ice cream business serving the same area as before the purchase. Igloo was prepared to pay cash for all ice delivered under the contract.

Igloo is a much larger company than Polar Bear and serves an area contiguous to Polar Bear's. Igloo's plants are more efficient and have sufficient capacity to supply the markets of both companies during most of the year; thus, Igloo would probably buy ice from Terminal only when there was a price advantage in doing so.

As soon as Terminal learned of this purported assignment and the acquisition of Polar Bear by Igloo, it notified Polar Bear that the contract was terminated and declined to deliver any ice to Igloo. Obligations between the original parties were fully performed and discharged to the date of assignment.

(1) What are the legal problems and implications of the above facts? Discuss.

(2) What is the effect of these legal problems and implications on the financial statements of Terminal Ice Company for the year ended September 30, 1970? Discuss.

b. In the course of the examination of the financial statements of Williams Watch Company for the year ended October 31, 1970, the following situation was discovered during a review of correspondence included in the purchase orders outstanding file.

[A letter addressed to Williams]

> October 12, 1970. Gentlemen: We offer a once in a lifetime sale of gold filled expansion watch bands, catalogue #426, at $7.26 each. Minimum order 500, maximum order 1,000. Acceptance by October 15, 1970. Delivery F.O.B. Buffalo by the end of the month, 2/10, net/30.
>
> Very truly yours,
> Jackson Watch Band Co.

[To this Williams replied by mail]

> October 15, 1970. Gentlemen: We accept. Please rush shipment of 500. We can use them immediately. Ship draft against bill of lading inspection allowed.
>
> Williams Watch Co.

[Jackson sent Williams the following letter]

> October 17, 1970. Gentlemen: Sorry your acceptance did not arrive until October 16 and was improper in several respects. We regret we cannot accept your counteroffer because the price on the item has risen to $8.75 each. We will be happy to receive an order at this price.
>
> Very truly yours,
> Jackson Watch Band Co.

Further review disclosed that on October 15, 1970, Williams Watch made a firm contract to sell Promotions, Inc. 500 gold filled expansion watch bands identified as #426 at $8.00 each. Williams Watch has been unable to find another supplier who would provide 500 watch bands of a quality comparable to #426 at a unit price of less than $8.75.

(1) What are the legal problems and implications of the above facts? Discuss.

(2) What is the effect of these legal problems and implications on the financial statements of Williams Watch Company for the year ended October 31, 1970? Discuss.

Answer

a. (1) One legal problem is whether the contract between Terminal and Polar Bear was assignable. Another legal problem is whether Polar Bear could delegate its duty to pay for the ice to be supplied by Terminal.

Under the Uniform Commercial Code on Sales, all contract rights of either the seller or the buyer can be assigned except where the assignment would materially change the duty of the other party, increase the burden or risk imposed on him by his contract, or impair his chance of obtaining return performance. Here, the contract between Terminal and Polar Bear is a requirements and exclusive dealings contract obligating Terminal to supply ice to Polar Bear according to its particular requirements up to a 250 tons weekly maximum, and obligating Polar Bear to buy its initial weekly 250 tons exclusively from Terminal. Terminal has supplied ice to Polar Bear for over 3 years, establishing a supply pattern to which Terminal has adjusted its business operation. The contract renewal obligated Terminal to continue for 2 more years. These facts themselves tend to indicate that the contract is of a non-assignable character. However, when to this is added the facts that Igloo is larger than Polar Bear, can supply all of its plants including Polar Bear with ice, can react to market price variations on the price of ice and buy from Terminal only when price increase in ice makes this more desirable and thereby vary materially Terminal's ice product supply to Igloo, it would seem that the assignment of the contract would so vary the seller's (Terminal) obligation under its contract as to materially change his duty and increase his risk. Therefore, the contract is impliedly non-assignable by Polar Bear to Igloo.

The contract provided for sale on credit by Terminal to Polar Bear, which would usually cause this contract duty not to be delegable. However, Igloo agreed with Polar Bear to pay cash, and this would eliminate this factor, not impair Terminal's chance of being paid for the ice supplied, and thereby not preclude the delegation as a part of the assignment.

(2) I would obtain an opinion letter from legal counsel concerning the resolution of these legal points and include a footnote to Terminal's financial statements reflecting such legal opinion.

b. (1) The question raises the following legal problems: was the Williams' letter an acceptance by being mailed on October 15; did that letter reject the Jackson offer and constitute a counter offer; if a contract was formed between Williams and Jackson, was it enforceable and what remedies are available to Williams for its breach by Jackson; and can Jackson be compelled to specifically perform its contract?

Under the Uniform Commercial Code on Sales, if the offer does not indicate otherwise, acceptance may occur in any manner and by any medium reasonable in the circumstances. Here, Jackson's letter did not indicate otherwise and, therefore, Williams' prompt use of the mails caused his letter to be an acceptance when mailed.

If the offeree's expression of acceptance states terms altering the offer, this does not prevent the expression from being an acceptance of those terms in the offer with which it conforms. As between merchants, such additional terms become part of the contract unless they materially alter it or the offeror notifies the offeree of his objection to them within a reasonable time. Here, Williams' letter is an acceptance of Jackson's offer, and while the additional terms therein did not materially alter the offer nevertheless Jackson's second letter was a timely objection to them.

Although the contract was for the sale of goods for over $500 and, under the Code's Statute of Frauds, would be unenforceable without a proper writing, the first two letters between the parties here constituted the written contract and the contract is, therefore, enforceable.

Jackson's refusal to perform the contract on October 31 is an anticipatory breach, and under the Code the aggrieved buyer (Williams) may: for a commercially reasonable time, await performance by the seller; suspend his own performance; cancel the contract; cover, by purchasing substitute goods and holding the seller liable for the difference in price ($8.75 and $7.26); or recover damages for the difference between the market price ($8.75) and the contract price ($7.26) including consequential damages.

The remedy of specific performance under the Code is not available if the goods are unique or the buyer can cover, which he can do here since the same goods are available at a higher price ($8.75).

(2) The opinion of legal counsel should be sought and a footnote to Williams' financial statements should indicate these contracts in detail and reflect counsel's opinion. Provision should be made for any loss that may occur because of the Promotions contract.

NOVEMBER, 1969

No. 6 (a. Estimated—7 to 8 minutes)

a. Several large creditors of the now defunct Valvo Plumbing Corporation have written letters to Sanitary Plumbing Corporation demanding the purchase price or the return of large quantities of plumbing supplies the creditors sold to Valvo on account. Sanitary Plumbing had purchased all of Valvo's assets, which consisted almost exclusively of its stock in trade (plumbing supplies), office equipment, and fixtures. The purchase was privately negotiated and notice was not given by Sanitary to Valvo's creditors. The owners of Valvo have disappeared without paying their trade creditors.

What liability, if any, does Sanitary Plumbing have as a result of the above facts? Explain.

Answer

a. Sanitary is liable to the creditors, at their election, for either the return of the property to them or the value of such property in order to satisfy their claims. Under the Uniform Commercial Code on Bulk Transfers, a bulk transfer is ineffective as to every creditor of the transferor unless the transferee complies with the Code's provisions for notice to such creditors. A bulk transfer is any transfer in bulk and not in the ordinary course of the transferor's business of a major part of the inventory of a business engaged in the sale of merchandise from stock. The transferee is to obtain from the transferor a proper list of creditors of the transferor and, within 10 days before the transferee takes possession of the goods or pays for them, properly notify the creditors on the transferor's list or known as such to the transferee. Here, Sanitary privately purchased all of Valvo's inventory without giving any notice to Valvo's creditors. This was a bulk transfer ineffective as to the creditors who can resort to the sold property or its value in order to satisfy their claims.

PART FOUR

COMMERCIAL PAPER

Chapter I

INTRODUCTION

Historical Background   THE LAW of negotiable instruments had its beginnings in the customs of merchants in commercial transactions, called the "Law Merchant," several centuries ago. The Law Merchant was well known among merchants and almost universally applied in England and in Europe. The Law Merchant developed apart from the early Common Law and was applied in special mercantile courts which had jurisdiction over commercial paper. First the bill of exchange, and then the promissory note by the Statute of Anne in 1704, payable to order or bearer, were recognized as being negotiable in character and assignable. In 1882 the English Bills of Exchange Act was enacted, and in 1896 the Uniform Negotiable Instruments Act was proposed in the United States, both codifying the Law Merchant regarding negotiable instruments. Today, the Uniform Commercial Code is the latest codification of the law of negotiable instruments in the United States, repealing the Uniform Negotiable Instruments Act.

Article 3 of the Code is entitled "Commercial Paper" and is concerned with four negotiable instruments: the draft (formerly called "bill of exchange"), the check, the certificate of deposit, and the promissory note. Bonds, documents of title (e.g., bills of lading, warehouse receipts), and money are excluded from Article 3.[1] However, Article 3 also applies to any instrument whose terms do not preclude transfer and which would be negotiable except for the fact that it is not payable to order or to bearer; *but no one can be a holder in due course of such an instrument.* Since the rights acquired by a holder in due course are much greater than those acquired by one not a holder in due course, and since the instrument must be negotiable in order for a person to become a holder in due course of the instrument, it is understandable why the

---

[1] Bonds are included in Investment Securities under Article 8, and documents of title are included in Article 7. Traders may acquire bonds knowing that, as bona fide purchasers for value, their ownership and status will not be adversely affected by the fact that the bonds are overdue or that default has occurred.

status of a holder in due course is so desirable and at the heart of Article 3, and why it is of the utmost importance to determine whether an instrument is negotiable. It is for this reason that, under the Code and throughout Part Four of the book, unless otherwise indicated *the word "instrument" means a negotiable instrument.*

It should be noted that the Law Merchant is not dead and, under the Code,[2] unless displaced by the Code, it supplements the Code. It should be noted also that bank deposits and collections are included under Article 4 and letters of credit are included under Article 5 of the Code. Some sections of Article 4 are discussed later in Chapter VIII of this part of the book. Inasmuch as negotiable instruments are the subject of collection by banks and are also used as collateral under Article 9 of the Code on Secured Transactions, Article 3 on Commercial Paper will apply to negotiable instruments as involved under Articles 4 and 9, unless inconsistent therewith, in which case Articles 4 and 9 will prevail, because they are concerned with the *use* of such instruments.[3]

Purpose of Negotiable Instruments

A "negotiable instrument" is a formal writing containing a contractual obligation or chose in action, payable in money, and with certain unusual effects on its transfer. The purpose of the negotiable instrument is to provide a simple, easy method of transferring a credit device or substitute for money, assuring to the holder of the instrument that he will receive the money as indicated on the instrument. The transfer of tangible property and the assignment of a chose in action[4] at Common Law caused the transferee to acquire no better title to the property than that of the transferor[5] and the assignee to acquire no better title to the chose in action than the assignor had.[6] However, by the Law Merchant, the delivery of a properly indorsed negotiable instrument to a bona fide purchaser for value, without notice of any defect of title or infirmity in the instrument (called a "holder in due course"), transferred to such purchaser a valid title to the negotiable instrument and to the claim or chose in action represented thereby. In other words, such a transfer of a negotiable instrument cut off all equities or claims to the instrument, and the transferee obtained a valid title. (B steals A's horse and sells it to C, a bona fide purchaser for

---

[2] UCC 1–103.

[3] UCC 3–103(2).

[4] For a discussion of "chose in action," see above, pp. 169–70.

[5] See above, p. 280.

[6] See above, pp. 102–3.

value without notice of the theft. The transferee, C, obtained only what his transferor, B, had, and since A never had made any transfer to B, then A may regain his horse. C would have a right of action against B for breach of express warranty of title.[7] The same effect would result if S fraudulently induced R to buy goods from S and S assigned to T his claim against R for the purchase price. S's fraud caused his contract with R to be voidable by R, and the assignee, T, acquired only what his assignor, S, had. R may avoid the contract, and T cannot enforce his claim against R. T would have a right of action against S for breach of implied warranty.[8] However, if P fraudulently induced D to draw a check payable to the order of P which P indorsed with solely his signature on the back of the check, and X stole the check from P and sold and delivered it to Z, who is a bona fide purchaser for value without notice of the theft, Z would have title to the instrument which P could not regain and which D would have to pay.) Such protection to the transferee of the negotiable instrument, resulting in ready acceptance of such an instrument by merchants, was the objective of the Law Merchant.

In order to achieve this result the instrument had to be negotiable and the transferee had to obtain the instrument under circumstances making him a "holder in due course." *Basically, a study of negotiable instruments is a study of the character of the instrument to determine whether it is negotiable, and a determination of the character of the transferee to determine whether he is a holder in due course.* Article 3 is concerned basically with negotiable instruments and its provisions generally deal with: the formal requisites of negotiable instruments; the negotiation of such instruments; the holder in due course; the liabilities of the parties on such an instrument; the presentment of such instrument for payment or acceptance, notice of dishonor and protest; and the discharge of the parties from liability on the instrument. The subject of Commercial Paper will be discussed in this order after a brief, preliminary examination of the kinds of negotiable instrument and of the parties thereto.

Classification There are four kinds of negotiable instrument: the draft (formerly called "bill of exchange"), the check, the certificate of deposit, and the promissory note. Examples of these instruments follow on pages 376–77. They are distinguishable from each other in the following ways: the draft is a

---

[7] See Sales, above, p. 287.

[8] See above, p. 104 for implied warranties in an assignment.

written order drawn by one person and directing another person to pay to the order of the person indicated in the draft or to bearer; the check is a draft of a special kind in which the order is directed to a bank and the instrument is payable on demand; the certificate of deposit is a bank's written acknowledgment of a receipt of money and its promise to repay it; and the note is a written promise other than a certificate of deposit by one person to pay to the order of the person indicated in the note or to bearer.

The above four negotiable instruments are used in a variety of ways and, because of this, particular names often are given to such instruments indicating the use to which they have been put.

Bank Draft. A check drawn by a bank on another bank commonly is called a "bank draft."

Cashier's Check. A "cashier's check" is a check drawn by a bank on itself and payable to the order of the person named as payee in the cashier's check, as illustrated on page 378.

Traveller's Check. What is called a "traveller's check" is a check on which there is no payee's name at the time of its issuance, the person drawing the instrument and the person required to pay it often

DRAFT

CHECK

being the same person, the latter having accepted (i.e., assenting to pay it) the instrument in advance. When the instrument is not drawn on a bank it is a draft and not a check. The purchaser of the instrument signs his name on the instrument at the time of its issuance to him, and when he wishes to cash it he writes the name of the payee in the space provided and he signs the instrument.

Certified Check. A "certified check" is a check which has been accepted by the bank on which it is drawn. (See illustration, page 378.)

Banker's Acceptance. A "banker's acceptance" is a draft which has been drawn on a bank and which has been accepted by that bank.

Letter of Credit. A "letter of credit" is not a negotiable instrument; however, it is considered at this time in order to distinguish it from a negotiable instrument. Generally, it is a written promise or authorization to honor drafts or other demands for payment to be drawn on the promissor by the person named and pursuant to the terms stated therein.[9]

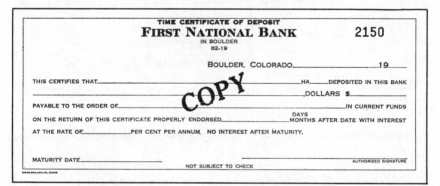

CERTIFICATE OF DEPOSIT

PROMISSORY NOTE

---

[9] See UCC 5–103(1)(a) and 2–325(3).

CASHIER'S CHECK

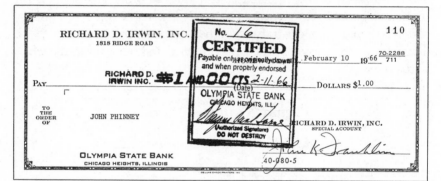

CERTIFIED CHECK

TRADE ACCEPTANCE

No.					19
TO (Buyer)		(CITY OF DRAWER)		(DATE)	
(NAME OF DRAWEE)		(ADDRESS OF DRAWEE)			
ON (DATE OF MATURITY) PAY TO THE ORDER OF					
		(NAME OF PAYEE)			
		DOLLARS, ($)			

THE TRANSACTION WHICH GIVES RISE TO THIS INSTRUMENT IS THE PURCHASE OF GOODS BY THE ACCEPTOR FROM THE DRAWER. THE DRAWEE MAY ACCEPT THIS BILL PAYABLE AT ANY BANK, BANKER OR TRUST COMPANY IN THE UNITED STATES WHICH SUCH DRAWEE MAY DESIGNATE.

ACCEPTED AT _____ ON _____ 19 ____
   (CITY)   (DATE)

PAYABLE AT _____
  (NAME OF BANK)

LOCATION _____   (Seller)
             (SIGNATURE OF DRAWER)

No. 29 (Buyer)   BY _____
(SIGNATURE OF ACCEPTOR)

TRADE ACCEPTANCE

Trade Acceptance. A "trade acceptance" is a draft which is drawn by a seller on the buyer to whom he has sold goods and which is accepted by the buyer. (See above illustration.)

Parties   The parties to an instrument have definite names in order to facilitate immediate comprehension of their status.

Maker. A "maker" is the person who executes or makes a certificate of deposit or a note and who thereby promises to pay the same. When two or more persons execute a certificate of deposit or note, each is called a "co-maker."

Drawer. A "drawer" is the person who executes or draws a draft or a check ordering the drawee to pay the same.

Drawee. A "drawee" is the person on whom a draft or a check is drawn and who is ordered to pay the same.

Payee. A "payee" is the person to whose order an instrument is drawn.

Bearer. A "bearer" is the person in possession of an instrument which is either payable to bearer or indorsed in blank.

Indorser. An "indorser" is the person who places his signature on an instrument other than as a maker, drawer, or acceptor and who does not indicate any intention to be bound in any other capacity.

Indorsee. An "indorsee" is the person to whom an indorser by his indorsement makes the instrument payable.

Acceptor. An "acceptor" is the drawee who has properly manifested his written assent to the order of the drawer and thereby agreed to pay the draft.

Holder. A "holder" is the payee or indorsee of an instrument who is in possession thereof, or who is a bearer. In short, he is within the tenor of the instrument and is in possession of it.

Holder in Due Course. A "holder in due course" is a special kind of holder. He is a person who became a holder of an instrument for value, in good faith, and without notice that it is overdue or has been dishonored or of any defense against, or claim to, it on the part of any person.

Several of these parties are visually presented in the previous illustrations of instruments. On the check Ruth Donaldson is the drawer, Olympia State Bank is the drawee, and Francis Poore is the payee. On the certified check the Olympia State Bank, and on the trade acceptance the buyer drawee, is the acceptor. On the note Ralph Mahn is the maker and John Purvis is the payee. The following indorsements on the back of the check, now possessed by Frank Fay, visually present the remain-

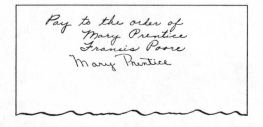

ing parties. In the illustration on page 379, Mary Prentice is an indorsee by reason of the indorsement of Francis Poore who now is an indorser, and Mary Prentice's subsequent signature is a blank indorsement causing her to be an indorser. The last indorsement being in blank, the instrument is now payable to bearer. Since Frank Fay possesses the bearer instrument he is the bearer and, thus, a holder.

Primary and Secondary Liability. The parties to an instrument may be classified in accordance with their liability as parties primarily liable and parties secondarily liable. The person primarily liable on an instrument is the person who, by the terms of the instrument, is absolutely required to pay the same. All other parties are liable on the instrument on a condition, and they are secondarily liable. On a certificate of deposit or a note the maker is the party primarily liable. On a draft or a check the acceptor is the party primarily liable. Until the drawee of a draft or a check accepts the same he is not liable on the instrument; he is under no contractual obligation to the holder to pay the instrument. On acceptance, the acceptor becomes absolutely liable on the instrument. The drawer and indorsers are secondarily liable on an instrument, and they are called "secondary" parties.[10] It is important to note the distinction between parties primarily and secondarily liable, inasmuch as parties secondarily liable have recourse against parties primarily liable for whatever loss they have sustained on the instrument.

---

[10] UCC 3–102(1) (d).

Chapter II

FORMAL REQUISITES OF NEGOTIABLE INSTRUMENTS

1. SPECIFIC REQUISITES

For All Negotiable Instruments
THE SAME specific requisites apply to all four negotiable instruments, whether a draft, check, certificate of deposit, or note, except that, inasmuch as these instruments differ in purpose, the specific requisites for each differ only to the following extent: the draft contains an order on a drawee to pay; the check is a draft drawn on a bank and payable on demand; and the certificate of deposit and the note contain a promise to pay.

The specific requisites of a negotiable instrument are:

1. A writing signed by the maker or drawer containing
2. An unconditional promise or order to pay (and no other promise, order, obligation, or power given by the maker or drawer except as authorized by Article 3)
3. A sum certain in money
4. Payable on demand or at a definite time
5. Payable to order or to bearer.

The fifth requisite contains the key words of negotiability; without them the writing is merely a contract, assignable without the effects of negotiability, and there cannot be a holder in due course of a nonnegotiable instrument.

It is of the utmost importance to remember that *"the negotiability of an instrument is always to be determined by what appears on the face of the instrument alone."*[1]

For Particular Negotiable Instruments
Draft. A draft must comply with the above requisites except for the deletion of the word "maker" in the first requisite and the word "promise" in the second requisite. Under the Code,[2] an instrument which complies with the above requisites is a "draft" ("bill of exchange") if it is an order.

---

[1] UCC 3–119, *Comment 5*.
[2] UCC 3–104(2) (a).

Check. A check must comply with the same requisites as a draft, indicated above; and, in addition, the instrument must be drawn on a bank and payable on demand. Its purpose is immediate collection. Under the Code,[3] an instrument which complies with the above requisites is a "check" if it is a draft drawn on a bank and payable on demand.

Certificate of Deposit. A certificate of deposit must comply with the above requisites except for the deletion of "drawer" in the first requisite and "order" in the second requisite. Under the Code,[4] an instrument which complies with the above requisites is a "certificate of deposit" if it is an acknowledgment by a bank of receipt of money with an engagement to repay it.

Note. A negotiable promissory note must comply with the above requisites except for the deletion of "drawer" in the first requisite and "order" in the second requisite. Under the Code,[5] an instrument which complies with the above requisites is a "note" if it is a promise other than a certificate of deposit.

2. INTERPRETATION OF FORMAL REQUISITES

General Rule of Form

It is not essential to a negotiable instrument that any particular language be used; it is sufficient if the writing manifests an intention to comply with the formal requisites of a negotiable instrument and, in fact, so does comply. The words "I undertake" instead of "I promise," or "Pay to holder" instead of "Pay to bearer," would not be sufficient cause to prevent negotiability.[6]

Writing Signed by Maker or Drawer

An instrument must be in writing; it may be written in pencil or ink, and may be "printing, typing, or any other intentional reduction to tangible form."[7] An instrument must be signed by the maker or drawer. *Only persons whose signatures are on an instrument are liable thereon.* An undisclosed principal whose signature is not on an instrument is not liable thereon.[8] It should be noted very carefully that, under the Code,[9] a person is liable for his negligence

---

[3] UCC 3–104(2) (b).

[4] UCC 3–104(2) (c).

[5] UCC 3–104(2) (d).

[6] UCC 3–104, *Comment 5*.

[7] UCC 1–201(46).

[8] See Agency, below, pp. 566, 549.

[9] UCC 3-406. See below, p. 432.

which substantially contributes to his unauthorized signature, e.g., a person's negligence in not properly caring for a signature stamp or other similar device. He is precluded from asserting the alteration or lack of authority against a holder in due course or against a drawee or other payor who pays the instrument in good faith and in accordance with the reasonable commercial standards of the drawee's or payor's business.

The maker's or drawer's signature may appear anywhere on the instrument and need not be in any particular form. A maker's or drawer's signature usually appears on the face of the instrument in the lower right-hand portion thereof. The signature may be placed anywhere on the instrument, so long as it is indicated as being the signature of the person as a maker or as a drawer. A maker or drawer is not required to "subscribe" to the instrument; the signature does not have to be at the end of the instrument. The signature may be written, printed, engraved, or stamped; may be made with pencil or pen; and may be made in a trade name, assumed name, or by mark (e.g., an "X" or a thumb print), so long as the intent of the maker or drawer is to make it his signature. The signature may even appear in the body of the instrument, as "I, Frank Fay, promise to pay," etc.

A negotiable instrument may be signed by one or more persons or by their authorized agents. The signature may be by two or more persons acting jointly, severally, jointly and severally, or by an incorporated or an unincorporated association. An agent's authority to sign a negotiable instrument on behalf of his principal is not required to be in writing. The same is true of an agent's signature on behalf of any other party to the instrument. An authorized agent who signs a negotiable instrument, indicating his representative capacity and disclosing the identity of his principal, is not liable as a party to the instrument. However, under the Code, an authorized representative who signs his own name to an instrument is, except as otherwise established between the immediate parties, "personally obligated if the instrument names the person represented but does not show that the representative signed in a representative capacity, or if the instrument does not name the person represented but does show that the representative signed in a representative capacity."[10] For example, if the instrument is signed

Peters
Anderson

it can be shown *only as between Peters and Anderson* that Peters was the principal and Anderson the agent signing for him. In litigation

---

[10] UCC 3–403 (2) (b).

between the immediate parties, eg., Peters and Anderson, the parol evidence rule permits the introduction of parol evidence to prove a signature as having been made by an agent in a representative capacity.[11]

Unconditional Promise or Order to Pay   An instrument must contain an unconditional promise or order to pay the amount of money indicated in the instrument. First the promise or order and then the unconditional character will be considered.

The Promise or Order. The promise or order must be stated expressly on the face of the negotiable instrument. The exact terms of "promise" or "order" are not required; any words of like import are sufficient if they can be interpreted as manifesting an intent to promise or to order payment.

The Promise. Under the Code,[12] a promise is an undertaking to pay and must be more than an acknowledgment of an obligation. An acknowledgment of a debt, in the form of an I.O.U. or a due bill or otherwise, may raise an implied promise imposing a contractual obligation under the law of contracts, but such expressions are insufficient as a promise which is requisite for a negotiable instrument. However, under judicial decisions prior to the Code, an acknowledgment of a debt accompanied by such words as "payable on demand" or similar words which could be interpreted as indicating an intent to pay such debt, constituted a promise sufficient for a negotiable instrument. Similarly, instruments containing words of the following nature contain an express promise sufficient for a negotiable instrument: "due John Jones on demand," "due John Jones or bearer," "I.O.U. $100 payable on demand," "I.O.U. $100 payable 30 days from date." It would seem that this would still be the result under the Code.

The Order. An order to pay directs and requires payment; it is imperative. Under the Code,[13] an order is a direction to pay and must be more than an authorization or request. An authorization to the addressee to pay an instrument is not an order, because it does not *require* the addressee to pay. An order to pay is not qualified by words of courtesy such as "please" or "kindly." However, "I wish you would pay" is not an order. A draft or check does not contain the word "order" in directing the drawee to pay, as "I order you to pay"; instead, the word "pay" is used to order the drawee to make such payment. In the phrase

[11] UCC 3–403, *Comment 3.*
[12] UCC 3–102(c).
[13] UCC 3–102(b).

"pay to the order of," the word "pay" is the order or direction to the drawee, while the words "order of" relate to the payee and mean that the drawee is to pay as the payee may direct. The order must identify the person to pay with reasonable certainty, and it may be addressed to one or more such persons jointly or in the alternative but *not in succession.* Often, a firm may have accounts with more than one bank in the same city or different cities, and for commercial convenience it should be able to issue checks with various drawees, e.g., to pay indebtedness and dividends to corporate shareholders. However, drawees in succession is prohibited so that the payee should not be required to make more than one presentment for payment.[14]

Unconditional. The promise or order must be payable absolutely, unqualifiedly, and in any event; there must not be any uncertainty regarding such payment at the time indicated by the instrument. Whether or not the promise or order is unconditional is determined *solely from the instrument itself;* any separate agreement apart from the instrument does not affect its negotiability. However, if the instrument states that it is subject to, or governed by, any other agreement, it is conditional on that agreement and, therefore, it is non-negotiable. Thus, a note which promises to pay *subject to* the conditions as stated in the mortgage security for the note is non-negotiable, because the promise is conditional on such mortgage terms. Similarly, a promise to pay *subject to* the terms of a particular contract is conditional, and performance is dependent on such contract terms. However, the promise or order is unconditional if the instrument: "states its consideration, whether performed or promised, or the transaction which gave rise to the instrument, or that the promise or order is made or the instrument matures in accordance with or 'as per' such transaction."[15] For example, the instrument may refer to, or state that it arises out of, a separate agreement, or it may refer to a separate agreement for rights as to prepayment or acceleration; or it may state that it is drawn under a letter of credit. Similarly, the promise or order is unconditional if the instrument states that it is secured, whether by mortgage, reservation of title, or otherwise. To the same effect, the instrument may indicate the source or fund from which *reimbursement* of the money is to be made, e.g., as by debiting a particular reimbursing account, or by specifying a particular sinking fund, road tolls, or special taxes as a source of reimbursement.

---

[14] See below, p. 454, indicating that presentment may be made to any one of various drawees.

[15] UCC 3–105(1) (b).

But, with two exceptions, a promise or order to pay *only out of* a particular source or fund limits the promise to that source or fund and makes it conditional on sufficient money being in that source or fund. Thus, a promise to pay "on account of" or "as per" a particular contract does not promise to pay out of a particular fund, but a promise to pay out of the proceeds of such contract is conditional. *The first exception* to the rule that a promise or order to pay only out of a particular fund or source is conditional precluding negotiability is when the promise or order is contained in an instrument issued by a government or governmental agency or unit. This exception "is intended to permit municipal corporations or other governments or governmental agencies to draw checks or to issue other short-term commercial paper in which payment is limited to a particular fund or to the proceeds of particular taxes or other sources of revenue"[16] and is intended not to disappoint the public in its acquisition of such instruments in reliance on their negotiability. *The second exception* is an instrument which limits payment only out of the entire assets of a partnership, unincorporated association, trust, or estate by, or on behalf of, which the instrument is issued. It should be noted carefully that this exception is concerned only with the negotiability of an instrument and is not meant to have any effect on the law of any state concerned with limitation of liability of a partner, association member, trustee, or the representative of an estate. It should be noted also that an instrument which is subject to "implied or constructive conditions" does not cause the promise or order to be conditional. Conditions must be apparent on the instrument itself, and a recital in an instrument that it is given in exchange for an executory promise that some obligation will be performed does not of itself imply that the instrument will be paid only on the condition that such performance occurs. Unless otherwise indicated on the instrument, such a recital merely refers to the consideration or to another agreement, without any inference of a condition.

Sum Certain in Money

The instrument to be negotiable must promise or order to pay a sum certain in money. First money, and then a sum certain, will be discussed.

Money. A negotiable instrument cannot be made payable in anything but money at the time the instrument is made. By money is meant a medium of exchange authorized or adopted by a domestic or foreign government as a part of its currency.[17] However,

---

[16] UCC 3–105, *Comment 6.*
[17] UCC 1–201(24).

money does not mean "any medium of exchange current and accepted in the particular community, whether it be gold dust, beaver pelts, or cigarettes in" an occupied country.[18] Money is not limited to legal tender. The unusual instruments payable in "current funds" or in "currency" are payable in money. Under the Code: "A promise or order to pay a sum stated in a foreign currency is for a sum certain in money and, unless a different medium of payment is specified in the instrument, may be satisfied by payment of that number of dollars which the stated foreign currency will purchase at the buying sight rate for that currency on the day on which the instrument is payable or, if payable on demand, on the day of demand. If such an instrument specifies a foreign currency as the medium of payment the instrument is payable in that currency."[19] Fluctuation in the exchange value of foreign currency does not affect the sum as being certain in money.

Sum Certain. The money payable under a negotiable instrument must be a sum certain in amount as determined from the instrument, including any necessary computation which can be made from the instrument itself. A promise to pay taxes, and a promise to pay income if earned, are not negotiable because of uncertainty in amounts; the promise to pay income if earned also is not an unconditional promise because payment of income is not absolute but is subject to the condition that income is earned. Although the principal sum payable is certain in amount, nevertheless, additional provisions in the instrument may cause uncertainty in connection with interest to be paid, discounts or additions, acceleration or extension[20] clauses, payment in exchange, or collection costs and attorney's fees on default in payment of principal or interest. The Code[21] removes from these additional provisions this uncertainty in amount by providing that the sum payable is certain in such instances. Thus, provisions for the payment of collection costs and attorney's fees upon default in the payment of principal or interest give to the instrument greater security, enhance its attractiveness, and encourage more ready negotiation. Also, the sum payable is certain even though the instrument provides for a stated discount or addition of money if the instrument is paid before or after the date fixed for payment, as long as the computation can be made from the instrument itself. Similarly, the amount may be payable with exchange or less exchange, whether at a fixed rate or at the current rate.

---

[18] UCC 3–107, *Comment 1.*

[19] UCC 3–107(2).

[20] Extension is discussed later under "Definite Time," below, pp. 389 f.

[21] UCC 3–106.

A sum payable with interest is certain in amount. The interest may be computed easily when payment is to be made. A promise that, on default in payment at maturity, a different rate of interest will be paid before or after default or a specified date does not affect the certainty of the sum to be paid. However, it should be noted carefully that, if such interest is to be increased and begin from the date of the instrument or a specified date before maturity rather than solely from the date of maturity, the increased rate from such date is a sum certain, although by local law such antedating of increased interest may be illegal as a forfeiture. The Code's rules regarding a sum certain are concerned only with the negotiability of an instrument and are not intended to validate any term which is otherwise illegal, e.g., as constituting usury under state law. The instrument may provide for a *stated* interest; or it may provide for payment "with interest" without specifying the rate, in which event interest is at the judgment rate[22] at the place of payment from the date of the instrument, or if it is undated from the date of its issue.[23]

Under the Code, words control figures except that if the words are ambiguous figures control. Thus, where the sum payable is expressed in words and also in figures and there is a discrepancy between the two, the sum denoted by the words is the sum payable; but if the words are ambiguous, then the figures control and fix the amount payable.

A sum, whether principal or interest, payable in stated installments is certain in amount. The sum payable is certain although the instrument contains an acceleration clause providing that the whole amount shall mature and become due on the default of an installment of principal or of interest, or providing that the instrument as one of a series of instruments is subject to acceleration on default of one of the instruments in the series.

Payable on Demand or at a Definite Time

A negotiable instrument must be payable at a time certain to arrive, otherwise the instrument would not circulate freely. The time is certain when it is payable on demand or at a definite time.

On Demand. An instrument is payable on demand when it so states, when it is payable at sight or on presentation, or when no time for payment is stated on the instrument.

Definite Time. If not payable on demand, the instrument must be payable at a definite time in order to be negotiable. "The time of payment is definite if it can be determined from the face of the instru-

---

[22] For contracts other than commercial paper which provide for interest but do not specify the rate, the legal rate applies. See above, p. 132.

[23] UCC 3–102: "'Issue' means the first delivery of an instrument to a holder or a remitter."

ment."[24] An instrument which is not dated but which is payable "thirty days after date" is not payable at a definite time because the time of payment cannot be determined from the face of the instrument. However, such an instrument is an incomplete instrument and, when completed later with a date, will state a definite time. Similarly, an instrument which by its terms is otherwise payable only upon an act or event uncertain as to time of occurrence is not payable at a definite time even though the act or event has occurred.[25] Examples are: a post-obituary promise payable on the death of a specified person; a promise to pay on the completion of a specified building; a promise to pay a specified person on his attainment of a stated age; and a promise to pay on the marriage of a specified person.[26] The occurrence of the particular event does not make definite the time when payment is to be made and, therefore, the instrument is not negotiable.

An instrument is payable at a definite time if, by its terms, it is payable:

(a) on or before a *stated date* or at a fixed period after a *stated date;* or
(b) at a fixed period after sight; or
(c) at a *definite* time subject to any *acceleration;* or
(d) at a *definite* time subject *to extension* at the option of *the holder,* or *to extension* to a further *definite* time at the option of *the maker or acceptor or automatically upon or after a specified act or event.* (Author's italics)[27]

Often the maker or drawer may wish to have the opportunity to pay before the stated date and the insertion of "on or before" the stated date states a definite time when the instrument is payable under (a) above.

Acceleration and Extension Clauses. Acceleration and extension clauses under (c) and (d) above are basically the same in that they vary the time of payment from the stated time. A note payable in two years but providing that the maker may pay it after one year involves *acceleration* in payment time. A note payable in two years but providing that the maker may extend the time of payment one year involves an *extension* in payment time. It should be noted carefully that, in any event, the instrument must state a definite time which is subject to such acceleration or extension. The instrument may provide for acceleration at the option of the maker, the holder, or automatically

---

[24] UCC 3–109, *Comment 2.*

[25] UCC 3–109(2).

[26] It should be observed that an acceleration clause might be so used as to accomplish what is otherwise prohibited, e.g., acceleration to a specific point of time in the event of death, non-payment of taxes, etc., if as a matter of judicial interpretation such a clause is not deemed to constitute an evasion of pertinent Code provisions.

[27] UCC 3–109(1).

upon the occurrence of an event; and if the acceleration clause is so uncertain as to be of no effect, the instrument is payable at the definite time.[28] The possibility of abuse of an acceleration term by whim and caprice does not affect the definite time and the negotiable character of the instrument.[29]

While a definite time is subject to *any* acceleration, it should be noted carefully that this is not true of an extension of a definite time. Every holder of an instrument has the legal right to extend the definite time when it is payable, and the Code merely recognizes this right. However, a holder may not exercise his option to extend an instrument over the objection of a maker or acceptor or other party who properly tenders full payment[30] when the instrument is due.[31] The extension clause at the option of the holder need not indicate a time limit. However, if the extension is at the option of the maker, acceptor, or automatically upon or after a specified act or event, then the clause must indicate a definite time limit to such extension or the time of payment would be uncertain and the instrument not be negotiable. Unless otherwise specified, consent to extension authorizes a single extension for not longer than the original period. A consent to extension, expressed in the instrument, is binding on secondary parties and accommodation makers.[32] An illustration of such an extension clause is "The makers and indorsers of this note consent that it may be extended without notice to them."

Payable to Order or to Bearer

A negotiable instrument must contain words of negotiability. The usual words are "to order" and "to bearer."

To Order. An instrument is payable to order when it specifies a person therein with reasonable certainty as the payee and makes the instrument payable to the payee's order. The phraseology may be either "to the order of" the payee, or to the payee "or his order"; e.g., "pay to the order of John Jones,"

---

[28] UCC 3–109, *Comment 4.*

[29] UCC 1–208 deals with abuse in the exercise of an acceleration term in a *time* instrument: "A term providing that one party or his successor in interest may accelerate payment or performance or require collateral or additional collateral 'at will' or 'when he deems himself insecure' or in words of similar import shall be construed to mean that he shall have power to do so only if he in good faith believes that the prospect of payment or performance is impaired. The burden of establishing lack of good faith is on the party against whom the power has been exercised."

[30] For tender of payment, see below, p. 468.

[31] UCC 3–118(f).

[32] *Ibid.*

and "pay to John Jones or his order." An instrument payable to a specified payee without containing the words "order of" or their equivalent is not a negotiable instrument payable to order, with two exceptions. The first exception is an instrument payable "to the assigns" of a specified payee, without using the words "to the order"; the instrument is payable to order. The second exception is an instrument which has conspicuously[33] designated on its face that the instrument is "exchange" or the like and names a payee; the instrument is payable to order, reflecting international usage.

An instrument payable to order may be made payable to the order of:

1. The maker or drawer.
2. The drawee.
3. A payee who is not a maker, drawer or drawee.
4. Two or more payees together or in the alternative. The Code does not use the word "jointly" here; this is deliberately done so as to preclude any possible implication of a right of survivorship, unless otherwise expressly indicated on the instrument. An instrument payable to "A and B" is payable to A and B as tenants in common, without any right of survivorship. An instrument payable to "A or B" is payable to either of them. An instrument payable to "A and/or B" is payable to either A or B or to both of them together as tenants in common.
5. An estate, trust or fund, in which case it is payable to the order of the representative of such estate, trust or fund or his successors. It is not necessary that the reasonably identified payee be a legal entity. "The Community Chest" or "The Community Fund" are sufficient to identify the payee.
6. An office, or an officer by his title as such, in which case it is payable to the principal, but the incumbent of the office or his successors may act as if he or they were the holder.[34] For example, an instrument payable to the order of the "Italian Consulate" or to the order of the "Treasurer of the City of Denver" is payable to the incumbent of that office or his successors.
7. A partnership or unincorporated association, in which case it is payable to the partnership or association and may be indorsed or transferred by any person thereto authorized. The payee is not required to have a legal entity. The instrument may be payable to the order of a partnership or a labor union. The authorized representative of the partnership or

---

[33] UCC 1–201 (10): " 'Conspicuous': A term or clause is conspicuous when it is so written that a reasonable person against whom it is to operate ought to have noticed it. A printed heading in capitals (as: NON-NEGOTIABLE BILL OF LADING) is conspicuous. Language in the body of a form is 'conspicuous' if it is in larger or other contrasting type or color. But in a telegram any stated term is 'conspicuous.' Whether a term or clause is 'conspicuous' or not is for decision by the court."

[34] For a discussion of instruments payable to a named payee with the addition of words describing him, see below, pp. 387 f.

association payee may indorse or transfer the instrument in the name of such partnership or association payee.[35]

When an instrument is made payable both to order and to bearer, it is payable to order; however, if the bearer words are handwritten or typed, the instrument is payable to bearer. Normally, people specifying a payee on an instrument mean to make the instrument payable to the order of that payee and not to bearer, even though the printed words "or bearer" appear on the instrument—which words the signer may not have noticed. Accordingly, only if a person writes or types "or bearer" is such construed to signify that he intended to have it payable to bearer and not to order. Thus, an instrument reading "Pay to the order of Frank Fay or bearer" is payable to the order of Frank Fay, unless the words "or bearer" are handwritten or typed, in which case the instrument is payable to bearer.

To Bearer. An instrument not payable to order must be payable to bearer in order to be negotiable. While an order instrument must specify a payee with reasonable certainty, a bearer instrument does not specify any particular payee. An instrument is payable to bearer only when, *by its terms,* it is payable to either: bearer or to the order of bearer; or a named person or bearer; or "cash" or to the order of "cash"; or any other indication which does not purport to designate a specific payee.[36] Thus, an instrument reading "Pay to the order of————" is not a bearer instrument but, rather, an incomplete order instrument. Similarly, the fact that the instrument is made payable to the order of a specified unnamed officer of a specified association, such officer not existing, does not cause the instrument to be payable to bearer; it is an order instrument. It should be noted carefully that an instrument payable to order and indorsed in blank becomes payable to bearer and continues to be a bearer instrument until it is specially indorsed, at which time it no longer is a bearer instrument.[37]

Terms and Omissions Not Affecting Negotiability

Date, Antedating, Postdating. Where an instrument or any signature thereon is dated, the date is presumed to be correct. The negotiability of an instrument is not affected by the fact that it is undated, antedated or postdated.

Undated. The lack of a date on an instrument causes the instrument to be incomplete, but the date may or may not

---

[35] See UCC 3–110(1).

[36] UCC 3–111.

[37] See below, p. 407.

be essential to the instrument. If the date is not essential, the instrument is not incomplete in any *necessary* respect and it is negotiable and enforceable, e.g., an undated check. If the date is essential, the instrument is incomplete in a necessary respect and, therefore, is neither negotiable nor enforceable until subsequently dated. For example, an undated instrument payable "thirty days after date" is incomplete in a necessary respect and, therefore, is incomplete and unenforceable.

Antedating and Postdating. If an instrument is signed January 5 but dated January 3 it is antedated, and if dated January 7 it is postdated. Whether or not such antedating or postdating is made for a fraudulent or illegal purpose is a matter of defense, but does not affect the negotiability of the instrument, which is determined from its face. Thus, a note signed and delivered January 5, 1971, promising to pay interest at 6 per cent per annum on a loan then made and payable January 4, 1972, as stated on the instrument, but which is antedated to January 5, 1970, may be illegal and void as evidencing an usurious loan, but the instrument on its face states a definite time when it is payable and it is negotiable *on its face.* Where an instrument is antedated or postdated, the time when it is payable is determined by the stated date if the instrument is payable on demand, or at a fixed period after date. It is possible for an antedated instrument to be due prior to its issue.[38] The person to whom an antedated or postdated instrument is delivered acquires the title thereto as of the date of such delivery.

Seal. An instrument otherwise negotiable is negotiable even though it is under seal.

Omission of Stated Consideration and Where Drawn or Payable. The negotiability of an instrument is not affected by the omission of a statement of any consideration or of the place where the instrument is drawn or payable.

Collateral. The negotiability of an instrument is not affected by a statement that collateral has been given to secure obligations either on the instrument or otherwise of an obligor on the instrument, or that in case of default on those obligations the holder may realize on, or dispose of, the collateral. Also, the instrument may state a promise or power to maintain or protect collateral, or to give additional collateral; e.g., the holder is "to pay taxes" on the collateral of the note. Often, instruments containing the latter terms will provide for acceleration in the event of

---

[38] In such a case, an indorsement already on the instrument would be thereon after maturity and the indorser would not be entitled to presentment, notice of dishonor or protest in order to be charged with liability on the instrument. See below, p. 451.

non-compliance with such terms, which is permissible as discussed previously under definite time.[39]

Confession of Judgment. The negotiability of an instrument is not affected by a term authorizing a confession of judgment[40] on the instrument if it is not paid when due. Whether or not such a confession of judgment is legal is irrelevant to the matter of the instrument being negotiable. A note with such a term is called a "cognovit note."

Waiver of Statutory Benefits. The negotiability of an instrument is not affected by a term purporting to waive the benefit of any law intended for the advantage or protection of any obligor. Again, whether or not such a waiver is legal is irrelevant to the matter of the instrument being negotiable.

Indorsement of Full Satisfaction. The negotiability of an instrument is not affected by a term in a draft providing that the payee by indorsing or cashing it acknowledges full satisfaction of an obligation of the drawer.

Draft in a Set of Parts. The negotiability of an instrument is not affected by a statement in a draft drawn in a set of parts[41] to the effect that the order is effective only if no other part has been honored.

Construction of Ambiguous Terms

The Code establishes fixed rules for construing ambiguous terms in an instrument in order to encourage freer circulation of an instrument without the necessity of having to resort to the parol evidence rule for protection. Several have been discussed.[42]

---

[39] See above, p. 390, ftn. 29.

[40] By confession of judgment is meant a person's consent to the jurisdiction of a court and to a judgment against him without the trial of any issues between the parties. Under U3C, sec. 2.415: "Authorization to Confess Judgment Prohibited. A buyer or lessee may not authorize any person to confess judgment on a claim arising out of a consumer credit sale or consumer lease. An authorization in violation of this section is void."

[41] UCC 3–801: "Drafts in a Set. (1) Where a draft is drawn in a set of parts, each of which is numbered and expressed to be an order only if no other part has been honored, the whole of the parts constitutes one draft but a taker of any part may become a holder in due course of the draft.

"(2) Any person who negotiates, indorses or accepts a single part of a draft drawn in a set thereby becomes liable to any holder in due course of that part as if it were the whole set, but as between different holders in due course to whom different parts have been negotiated the holder whose title first accrues has all rights to the draft and its proceeds.

"(3) As against the drawee the first presented part of a draft drawn in a set is the part entitled to payment, or if a time draft to acceptance and payment. Acceptance of any subsequently presented part renders the drawee liable thereon under subsection (2). With respect both to a holder and to the drawer payment of a subsequently presented part of a draft payable at sight has the same effect as payment of a check notwithstanding an effective stop order (Section 4–407).

"(4) Except as otherwise provided in this section, where any part of a draft in a set is discharged by payment or otherwise the whole draft is discharged."

[42] Conflicting words and figures, above, p. 388, judgment rate of interest applicable

Draft or Note? When the appearance of an instrument, as by phrasing or by form, is such that there is doubt whether the instrument is a draft or a note, the holder may treat it as either at his election. The instrument must be ambiguous in its appearance; an instrument unambiguous in its appearance but lacking in essential requisites may not be treated as another instrument at the election of the holder. For example, an instrument in the form of a draft but with the drawee omitted thereon cannot be treated as a draft or a note; it is an incomplete instrument and neither negotiable nor enforceable until subsequently completed. Holders are on notice of the omission and of the apparent intent to make the instrument a draft. The purported draft without a drawee does not contain an express unconditional promise to pay and cannot be a note and, inasmuch as it does not have a drawee, it cannot be a draft. A draft drawn on the drawer is effective as a note, e.g., a draft drawn by a corporation on its treasurer; the drawer is liable as the maker.

Conflicting Handwritten, Typewritten, and Printed Terms. Handwritten terms control typewritten and printed terms, and typewritten terms control printed terms.

Co-signers. Often two or more persons sign in the same capacity, e.g., as co-makers. When co-signers indicate their capacity, it is in that capacity that they are liable to all subsequent parties on the instrument. However, unless they indicate otherwise, are they jointly, severally, or jointly and severally liable thereon? Under the Code, unless the instrument otherwise specifies, two or more persons who sign as maker, acceptor, drawer, or indorser and *as a part of the same transaction* are jointly and severally liable thereon. Such liability is not altered if the instrument contains the words "I promise to pay." This rule of construction applies only where the parties sign in the same capacity as a part of the same transaction. Successive indorsers do not sign as a part of the same transaction and, therefore, are liable only severally.

Incomplete
Instruments
 Whether or not a paper is, or may become, a negotiable instrument is determined at the time it is signed. If the contents of the paper at the time of signing do not indicate that it was intended to be, or to become, a negotiable instrument, it cannot then or later be or become a negotiable instrument. For example, a blank paper with a

---

to an instrumental providing for interest without specifying the rate, above, p. 388; and consent to an extension of time when an instrument is payable, and the holder's exercise of his option to extend, above, p. 390.

signature is not, and after being filled in subsequently cannot become, a negotiable instrument. A "complete writing which lacks an essential element of an instrument and contains no blanks or spaces or anything else to indicate that what is missing is to be supplied,"[43] is not an incomplete instrument; it is not meant to be a negotiable instrument at all. However, a person can, apart from the Code rule, authorize another to fill in a negotiable instrument on the blank paper above the first person's signature and thereby cause such paper to become a negotiable instrument. This would then be a matter of proving such authority under the law of agency.

When a paper whose contents at the time of signing show that it is intended to become an instrument is signed while still incomplete in any necessary respect, it is an incomplete instrument under the Code and cannot be enforced until subsequently completed.[44] If the omission is not of a necessary element, e.g., the instrument is not dated and does not require it to make the time definite when the instrument is payable, the instrument is negotiable, as previously discussed under definite time[45] and undated instruments.[46] The date of issue of an instrument is not essential, unless it is necessary to fix the date when the instrument is payable, in which event the omitted date is a necessary element and the instrument is incomplete. An illustration is an instrument payable at a fixed time after such date, e.g., an undated instrument payable "thirty days after date." However, the omission may be of an essential element, one which is necessary to a complete instrument, e.g., the promise or order, the amount payable, a specified payee. When a blank is left for the insertion of a time when the instrument is payable, a necessary element is missing and the instrument is incomplete; but where it is clear that no time is intended to be stated, the instrument is complete and is payable on demand.[47]

The authorized completion of an incomplete instrument makes the instrument effective as completed. The unauthorized completion of an incomplete instrument is a material alteration and, as later discussed,[48] such lack of authority can be asserted as a defense against anyone except a holder in due course, or holder or transferee properly claiming through a holder in due course, who may enforce the instrument as completed

---

[43] UCC 3–115, *Comment 2.*
[44] UCC 3–115(1).
[45] See above, pp. 388 f.
[46] See above, pp. 392 f.
[47] See above, p. 388.
[48] See below, p. 433.

even though the instument was never delivered by the maker or drawer. The completion of an instrument is presumed authorizedly done, and the burden of establishing that any completion is unauthorized is on the party so asserting.

Instruments Payable to Two or More Persons.
Miscellaneous   An instrument may be made payable to the order of two or more persons; this occurs frequently. If the instrument is payable in the alternative, e.g., "A or B," it is payable to any one of them, and it may be negotiated or enforced by any one of them who has possession of it. However, if the instrument is not payable in the alternative, e.g., "A and B," it is payable to all of them, and it may be negotiated or enforced only by all of them. An instrument payable to "A and/or B" is payable in the alternative to A or B and it is also payable to A and B together; it may be negotiated or enforced by either of them or by all of them.

Named Payee with Description. We have seen from previous discussion[49] that an instrument may be made payable to the order of a named officer by his title. When an instrument is made payable to a named person with the addition of words describing him, such words may describe him as a particular kind of a fiduciary, as a general kind of fiduciary, and in any other manner. The kind of description is important for the purposes of determining who the payee is, who may act as the holder, and the effect of such person's indorsement with respect to subsequent parties.

Particular Kind of Fiduciary. If the words describe the named person as an agent or officer of a specified person, the instrument is payable to his specified principal. However, the agent or officer may act as if he were the holder. Illustrations are: "John Smith, President of Utopia Corporation"; "Frank Fay, Mayor of the City of Boulder"; and "Joseph Kane, agent of Neil Duncan." It is commercially understood in such cases that the instrument was made to be paid to the principal and that the agent was named only to convenience the principal, so that the named agent could cash the instrument for him. It should be noted carefully that an instrument made payable to a person as agent or officer without specifying the principal, e.g., "John Jones, agent," does not come within the Code rule, and it is payable to him as payee and not to his principal.

General Kind of Fiduciary. If the words describe the named

---

[49] See above, p. 391.

person as a fiduciary, other than an agent or officer, for a specified person or purpose, the instrument is payable to the payee and may be negotiated or enforced by him. Illustrations are: "Frank Smith, Trustee of Franklin Trust"; "James King, Administrator of the Estate of Roland Calhoun"; and "Charles Dunn, Executor of the Will of Fanny Kellogg." Of course, the payee is liable for breach of his fiduciary obligation, and, while subsequent holders of the instrument are on notice of the payee's fiduciary character, they are not precluded from becoming holders in due course unless they have notice of his breach of fiduciary obligation. It should be noted carefully that an instrument made payable to a person without specifying the interest or purpose for which he is a fiduciary does not come within the Code rule, and the instrument is payable to him as payee for all purposes as far as subsequent third parties dealing with the instrument are concerned.

Any Other Manner. If the words describe the named person in any other manner than a particular or general kind of fiduciary for a specified person or purpose, it is payable to the payee unconditionally, and the additional words are without effect on subsequent parties. Illustrations are: "Joseph Lang, Attorney"; "Bernard Jones, agent"; "Mary King, 945 Spring Street"; "Charles Doe, Treasurer." Whether or not the payee meets the description is irrelevant as far as third parties are concerned.

Other Writings Affecting an Instrument. Several writings may be executed as a part of the same transaction, such as a note and a security agreement providing for a security interest in connection with the sale of goods or the lending of money (e.g., a note secured by a real property mortgage). Under the familiar law of contracts, the writings are to be read and construed together as a part of the agreement. However, what is the effect of an additional writing on the negotiability of an instrument in the same transaction, and on the original parties to the instrument and subsequent transferees thereof? First the effect of an additional writing on the negotiability of an instrument, both of which are executed as a part of the same transaction, will be discussed and then the effect of the additional writing on the rights and obligations of the original parties and subsequent transferees of the instrument.

The mere fact that there is a separate agreement, apart from the instrument but part of the same transaction, does not of itself affect the negotiability of the instrument. "The negotiability of an instrument is always to be determined by what appears on the face of the instrument alone, and if it is negotiable in itself a purchaser without notice of the separate writing is in no way affected by it. If the instrument itself states that it is subject to or governed by any other agreement, it is not negotiable . . . ; but if it merely refers to a separate agreement or states that it arises out of such an agreement, it is negotiable."[50]

As between the original parties to the instrument and subsequent transferees thereof, the terms of the instrument may be modified or affected by the additional writing, except to the extent that a transferee is a holder in due course without notice of any limitation of his rights on the instrument. A purchaser of the instrument may or may not know of the additional writing and may or may not know of the terms of such additional writing. If he takes the instrument without knowledge of the additional writing, he may become a holder in due course. If he takes the instrument with knowledge of the additional writing but without notice of any defense or claim arising from the terms of such additional writing, he may become a holder in due course; but if he has notice of any such defense or claim, he cannot be a holder in due course. If he takes the instrument with knowledge of the additional writing and with notice of a limitation in the additional writing, such limitation not itself giving notice of any present defense or claim (e.g., a limitation that the note shall be extended one year under certain conditions), he can be a holder in due course although he takes the instrument subject to such limitation. In the latter case, if he has no notice of such limitation at the time he took the instrument, he does not take the instrument subject to such limitation.

A person has "notice" of a fact when
(a) he has actual knowledge of it; or
(b) he has received a notice or notification of it; or
(c) from all the facts and circumstances known to him at the time in question he has reason to know that it exists.

A person "knows" or has "knowledge" of a fact when he has actual knowledge of it. "Discover" or "learn" or a word or phrase of similar import refers to knowledge rather than to reason to know. The time and circumstances under which a notice or notification may cease to be effective are not determined by this Act.[51]

Instruments "Payable through" a Bank. Often a firm will issue checks "payable through" another bank specified in the check. An instrument which states that it is "payable through" a bank or the like designates that bank as a collecting bank to make presentment but does not of itself authorize the bank to pay the instrument.[52] The through

---

[50] UCC 3–119, *Comment 5.*
[51] UCC 1–201(25).
[52] UCC 3–120.

bank is not a drawee and is not authorized or directed to pay the instrument.

Instruments Payable at a Bank. There is a strong difference of view among the various states concerning the effect of a note or acceptance payable at a bank. The commercial and banking practice of New York and its surrounding states causes such states to treat such a note or an acceptance as the equivalent of a draft on the bank, ordering it to pay the instrument when it falls due and without consultation out of the account of the maker or acceptor. Western and southern states treat such a note or acceptance as merely designating a place of payment, the bank to notify the maker or acceptor of presentment of the instrument and to ask for instructions; the instrument is not, of itself, an order or authorization to the bank to pay it. Because uniformity on this matter appears to be unattainable, and inasmuch as most of such instruments are notes not really requiring uniformity, the Code provides for two alternatives, the eastern view or the western and southern view, either of which may be adopted by a state.

Accrual of Cause of Action **Maker and Acceptor.** These parties are primarily liable on the instrument and a cause of action accrues against them: on *time* instruments, on the day after maturity; on *demand* instruments, on the date stated on the instrument or, if no date is stated, on the date of issue.[53] No demand for payment is required of the maker and acceptor because, being primarily liable on the instrument, presentment of the instrument to them for payment is not necessary in order to cause them to be liable thereon. However, an exception is made in the case of the maker obligor of a certificate of deposit. Because certificates of deposit are taken with the expectation of holding them for a considerable time, whether they are demand or time certificates, and with the bank's expectation that the holder will demand payment when he wants it, a cause of action accrues against the obligor only upon demand, which can be made only after the maturity date in the case of a time certificate of deposit.

Drawer and Indorser. The drawer of a draft, including a check, and an indorser on any instrument are parties secondarily liable. Under their contract on an instrument,[54] they engaged to pay the instrument on its dishonor and on any necessary notice of dishonor or protest. These

---

[53] For date of issue, see above, p. 388, ftn. 23.
[54] See below, p. 440.

are the conditions which must occur before they can be charged with payment on the instrument. A notice of dishonor to the drawer or an indorser is a demand for payment. Accordingly, a cause of action accrues against them when the instrument is dishonored *and* a demand upon them has been made. However, if no notice of dishonor or protest is necessary, e.g., it has been waived or excused, after dishonor a demand for payment is not necessary, and the holder of the instrument has an immediate right of recourse against them, the cause of action accruing solely on dishonor of the instrument. It should be noted that, as discussed later,[55] neither presentment, nor notice of dishonor, nor protest is necessary in order to charge an indorser who has indorsed an instrument after maturity.

Interest. The terms of an instrument determine the interest to be paid thereon. As previously discussed,[56] if an instrument provides for interest but does not specify the rate or time when it runs, the judgment rate applies from the date of the instrument or, if the instrument is undated, from the date of issue. However, if the instrument is silent on the matter of interest, unless the instrument otherwise provides, interest at the judgment rate runs from the date of the accrual of a cause of action, with one exception. The exception is that on a demand instrument the interest runs only from the date of actual demand.

---

[55] See below, p. 451.
[56] See above, p. 388.

Chapter III

NEGOTIATION

1. GENERAL CONCEPT

AN INSTRUMENT is a contract which is revocable and of no effect until it has been issued by delivery to the first holder. Once issued, it may be negotiated by the holder to another holder, who may negotiate it to other holders. Negotiation includes issue,[1] which is the first negotiation of the instrument.

Definition

"Negotiation" consists of the delivery of an instrument to a person who thereby becomes a holder. A "holder" is a person who has possession of an instrument and who is within the tenor thereof either as the payee, indorsee, or bearer.[2] An "indorsee" is a person to whom an instrument has been indorsed. Accordingly, in every negotiation an instrument is delivered to either a payee, indorsee, or bearer. Inasmuch as instruments are most frequently made payable to the order of a payee rather than to bearer, the subsequent negotiation by the payee of an instrument requires delivery *and* his indorsement. First delivery and then indorsement will be considered, after distinguishing negotiation from transfer.

Distinguished from Transfer

A careful distinction should be made between the words "negotiation" and "transfer." "Negotiation" is used only in connection with negotiable instruments, while "transfer" is used in connection with either negotiable instruments or non-negotiable instruments. "Negotiation" and "negotiable instrument" are words used by the Code, and under it an instrument is *negotiated* by its delivery to a holder. A non-

---

[1] Frederick K. Beutel, *Beutel's Brannan Negotiable Instruments Law* (7th ed.; Cincinnati: W. H. Anderson Co., 1948), p. 591.

[2] UCC 1–201(20): "'Holder' means a person who is in possession of a document of title or an instrument or an investment security drawn, issued or indorsed to him or to his order or to bearer or in blank."

negotiable instrument is *transferred* by its delivery to a transferee. A delivery of a negotiable instrument to one not a holder is also a transfer. A transferee, like an assignee, acquires only the rights of his transferor, which may be subject to some defense precluding payment of the instrument. A holder may, either as a holder in due course or by claiming through a previous holder who was a holder in due course, acquire the right to payment on the instrument, and what are often called "personal defenses" may not be asserted against him.

2. DELIVERY

Requirement and Presumption of Delivery   Until a negotiable instrument is delivered with the intent to transfer the rights in the instrument, the instrument is of no effect *between the immediate parties*. When a *holder* possesses an instrument, a valid delivery has been made to him unless the defendant establishes otherwise. Although, as later discussed,[3] the personal defense of non-delivery cannot be asserted against a holder in due course. (D makes a check or note payable to the order of P, which is stolen by P. As between D and P, D can prove that he never delivered the instrument to P and that P never obtained any property rights in the instrument because of such non-delivery, and D would thereby avoid liability to P on the instrument. If P had indorsed and delivered the instrument to H, a holder in due course, D would be liable to H because the personal defense of non-delivery cannot be asserted against a holder in due course. As between D and H, D made the instrument and took the risk of its being negotiated without his consent to a holder in due course.)

Intent to Transfer Title by Delivery   *As between the immediate parties to a delivery,* the transferor may prove that the parties did not intend that the property in the instrument was to be transferred by such delivery, but as against a subsequent holder in due course, such a personal defense cannot be established.[4] (M made a note to the order of P and delivered it to P on condition that P deliver certain goods to M before the note matured. P did not deliver the goods. As between M and P, M may prove that delivery was made with the intention of making M liable on

---

[3] See below, p. 425.
[4] *Ibid.*

the instrument only when P had delivered the goods, and that M is not liable thereon to P. If P had indorsed and delivered the instrument to H, a holder in due course, M would be liable to H.)

3. *INDORSEMENT*

Nature of Indorsement   An "indorsement" is a signature[5] of a person other than as maker, drawer, or acceptor, made alone or with written words qualifying the effect of such signature, and made on the instrument itself or on a paper so firmly affixed thereto as to become a part thereof. Such affixed paper is called an "allonge." The person making the indorsement is the "indorser" and, if the indorsement is made to a specified person, such specified person is the "indorsee." An indorsement of an instrument which is delivered so as to constitute a negotiation has a twofold effect: title to the instrument is transferred to the holder, and liability is imposed on the indorser according to the terms of his indorsement, discussed later.[6] *Unless the instrument clearly indicates that a signature is made in some other capacity, it is an indorsement.* The character of a signature on an instrument is to be determined solely from the face of the instrument itself.[7]

Words often accompany an indorsing signature and are a part of the indorsement. While they may qualify the legal *effect* of the indorsement, they do not qualify the nature of a *signature itself as an indorsement.* Thus, words of assignment (e.g., "I hereby assign all my right, title and interest in the within note"), condition (e.g., "Pay A on the completion of the building"), waiver (e.g., "I waive notice of dishonor and protest"), guaranty (e.g., "I guarantee payment"), limitation or disclaimer of liability ("without recourse") and the like accompanying an indorsement do not affect its character as an indorsement.[8] The liability of the indorser on the instrument may be affected by additional words, but his signature is an indorsement.

---

[5] For a discussion of what constitutes a signature, see above, p. 383.

[6] See below, pp. 440.

[7] UCC 3–402, *Comment:* "The indication that the signature is made in another capacity must be clear without reference to anything but the instrument. *It may be found in the language used.* Thus, if John Doe signs after 'I, John Doe, promise to pay', he is clearly a maker; and 'John Doe, witness' is not liable at all. *The capacity may be found in any clearly evidenced purpose of the signature,* as where a drawee signing in an unusual place on the paper has no visible reason to sign at all unless he is an acceptor. *It may be found in usage or custom.* Thus by long established practice judicially noticed or otherwise established a signature in the lower right hand corner of an instrument indicates an intent to sign as the maker of a note or the drawer of a draft." (Author's italics)

[8] UCC 3–202(4).

An indorsement is effective for negotiation only when it conveys the entire instrument or any unpaid residue thereof. If the indorsement purports to be of less, it operates only as a partial assignment and is not effective for negotiation. Consequently, no subsequent person can become a holder. An illustration of such an indorsement is "Pay John Jones one-half." The reason for this is that the maker or drawer would be subjected to a multiplicity of actions on the instrument by more than one person in the event of the dishonor of the instrument, which was a risk that the obligor did not intend to assume. The splitting of a cause of action is prohibited.

When Indorsement Required Only the person to whom the instrument is payable, either as payee or indorsee, is required to indorse the instrument in order to transfer the title thereto. An instrument payable to bearer requires no indorsement, and title is transferred by delivery of the instrument with the intent thereby to transfer title to such instrument. However, the transfer of title to an instrument payable to the order of a specified person either as a payee or indorsee, requires the indorsement of such person and the delivery of the instrument with the intent thereby to transfer title to such instrument. If an instrument is delivered *for value* with such an intent but without a proper indorsement, the transferee has the right to obtain the transferor's indorsement[9] in order to effect a negotiation of the instrument to him. An accommodation party may be an indorser, as well as a maker, drawer, or drawee, but such accommodation indorsement is not necessary to transfer title to the instrument and is placed on the instrument solely for the purpose of giving additional security to the instrument by subjecting the accommodation indorser to liability thereon in the event the instrument should be dishonored.

The Indorser An instrument payable to the order of a specified person must be indorsed by such person,[10] and an instrument indorsed to a specified person must be indorsed by such indorsee. When an instrument is made payable to the order of two or more persons jointly—e.g., "A and B"—the instrument must be indorsed by all such payees, unless one of them is authorized to sign for the others. The signature of an indorser, or any party to the instrument, may be made by an authorized agent; authority to do so is

---

[9] See above, p. 404.

[10] For impostors and negligence contributing to unauthorized signatures, see below, pp. 507–8.

not required to be in writing or in any particular form. As discussed previously,[11] an instrument made payable to a named person with the addition of words describing him as agent or officer of a specified person is payable to his principal, but the agent or officer may act as if he were the holder. Thus, an instrument payable to the order of, or indorsed to, a "cashier" of a specified bank or corporation is deemed payable to the bank or corporation, but the instrument may be negotiated by the indorsement either of the cashier or of the bank or corporation.

An indorsement is effective as such even though rescindable, even if it imposes no liability on the indorser, and even if its character causes the transaction itself to be rescindable or void. *It is an indorsement,* quite distinct from legal remedies and other legal effect. Thus, the indorsement of an infant or a corporation acting *ultra vires*[12] is effective to transfer the title to the instrument, regardless of whether or not such indorsement imposes any liability upon the indorser. An instrument, whether a note or draft, payable to the order of the maker or drawer must be indorsed by the payee maker or drawer. The indorsement does not enlarge the maker's or drawer's liability on the instrument but is merely a step in the negotiation of the instrument, effected by the delivery of the instrument so indorsed to a holder. Further, negotiation is effective to transfer the instrument although the negotiation is: (1) made by an infant, a corporation exceeding its powers, or any other person without capacity; or (2) obtained by fraud, duress or mistake of any kind; or (3) part of an illegal transaction; or (4) made in breach of duty.[13] Except as against a subsequent holder in due course, the negotiation by items (1) through (4) is, in an appropriate case, subject to rescission, the declaration of a constructive trust, or any other remedy permitted by law.

It often occurs that the payee's name is misspelled or improperly designated by a name other than his own. He may indorse in such name or his own, or both. While the indorsement of such a payee in the misspelled or improperly described name, or in his own true name, will transfer his interest in the instrument and can be negotiated by subsequent delivery, nevertheless this is not commercially desirable. The proper and desirable form of indorsement consists of indorsements in both names, and a person paying or giving value for the instrument has a right to require this.

---

[11] See above, p. 391.

[12] See below, p. 680.

[13] UCC 3–207(1).

Kinds of Indorsement

There are three kinds of indorsement: special, in blank, and restrictive.[14] None of these destroys the negotiable character of an instrument. An instrument which is negotiable continues to be negotiable; it continues to be negotiable even after maturity.

Special Indorsement. A special indorsement is an indorsement specifying the person to whom, or to whose order, it makes the instrument payable, e.g., "Pay A," or "Pay to the order of A." *Any* instrument specially indorsed becomes payable to the order of the special indorsee and may be further negotiated only by his indorsement. For example, if an instrument payable to the order of A is indorsed in blank by A, the instrument thereby becomes payable to bearer and may be negotiated by A's delivery of the instrument to B. If B indorses the instrument "Pay to C (signed) B," the instrument is no longer a bearer instrument, and C's indorsement is necessary for its further negotiation. The owner of an instrument has the right to direct its subsequent payment as he wishes, as long as his direction is not violative of the Code. The rule applies to an instrument originally issued payable to bearer, which may be specially indorsed and thereby no longer be a bearer instrument. For example, an instrument drawn "Pay to bearer" is indorsed by A, the holder, "Pay to B." B's indorsement is necessary for further negotiation of the instrument.

Indorsement in Blank. An indorsement which does not specify any particular indorsee is an indorsement in blank or "blank indorsement." Such an indorsement causes the instrument to be payable to bearer, and it then may be negotiated solely by delivery; however, should a special indorsement be made subsequently, the instrument ceases to be a bearer instrument. The holder may convert a blank indorsement into a special indorsement by writing over the signature of the indorser in blank any contract consistent with the character of the indorsement. This is commonly done by the holder inserting words above the blank indorsement making the instrument payable to him or to his order. For example, an instrument drawn payable to the order of A is indorsed by A in blank and delivered to B, who inserts above A's blank indorsement the words "Pay to B." However, the insertion of words which unauthorizedly vary the contract of the blank indorser constitutes a material alteration of the blank indorsement, and, if made with a fraudulent purpose, thereby discharges the blank indorser from liability on the instrument, except as to a subsequent holder in due

---

[14] For what is often called a "qualified indorsement," see below, pp. 441, 444.

course. Illustrations are: "Without recourse" and "Protest waived."

Restrictive Indorsement. Often indorsements are accompanied by words which seek to prohibit further transfer or negotiation of the instrument. Under the Code this cannot be done. Such an indorsement is called a "restrictive indorsement." An indorsement is restrictive if the additional words: are conditional; purport to prohibit further transfer of the instrument; include the words "for collection," "for deposit," "pay any bank," or like terms signifying a purpose of deposit or collection; or otherwise state that the indorsement is for the benefit or use of the indorser or of another person.[15] Examples are: conditional, "Pay A on his twenty-first birthday"; prohibiting further transfer, "Pay A only"; for benefit or use, "Pay A for the benefit of B," which is a trust indorsement, A being a trustee for B.

A restrictive indorsement has various legal effects. *First,* as already indicated, a restrictive indorsement cannot prevent further transfer or negotiation of the instrument. Because of this, the indorsee or any holder from him can become a holder in due course. *Second,* a restrictive indorsement does not, of itself, give notice to subsequent parties of any defense or claim of the indorser. *Third,* an intermediary bank,[16] or a payor bank[17] which is not the depositary bank,[18] is neither given notice nor otherwise affected by a restrictive indorsement of any person except the bank's immediate transferor or the person presenting the instrument for payment. "Such banks ordinarily handle instruments, especially checks, in bulk and have no practicable opportunity to consider the effect of restrictive indorsements."[19] With the exceptions indicated, such banks may disregard any restrictive indorsement. *Fourth,* when the indorsement is conditional or includes the words "for collection," "for deposit," "pay any bank," or like terms signifying a purpose of deposit or collection, any transferee except an intermediary bank must pay or apply any value given by him for or on the security of the instrument consistently with the indorsement, and to the extent that he does so he becomes a holder for value. In addition, if he otherwise complies with the requirements of being a holder in due course, he is a holder in due course. *Fifth, the first taker* under an indorsement for the benefit or use

---

[15] UCC 3–205.

[16] UCC 4–105(c): " 'Intermediary bank' means any bank to which an item is transferred in course of collection except the depositary or payor bank."

[17] UCC 4–105(b): " 'Payor bank' means a bank by which an item is payable as drawn or accepted."

[18] UCC 4–105(a): " 'Depositary bank' means the first bank to which an item is transferred for collection even though it is also the payor bank."

[19] UCC 3–206, *Comment 3.*

of the indorser or of another person must pay or apply any value given by him for or on the security of the instrument consistently with the indorsement, and to the extent that he does so he becomes a holder for value. In addition, such taker is a holder in due course if he otherwise complies with the requirements on what constitutes a holder in due course. A *later* holder for value is neither given notice nor otherwise affected by such restrictive indorsement, unless he has *knowledge* that a fiduciary or other person has negotiated the instrument in any transaction for his own benefit or otherwise in breach of duty.[20]

Reacquisition An instrument may be returned to, or reacquired by, a prior party. For example, M's note to P may be subsequently negotiated by P to A, A to B, and finally B to P. It is unimportant whether the instrument is negotiated or just transferred to the prior party; he does not have to be a holder on reacquisition. When such reacquisition occurs, intervening parties are discharged as against the reacquiring party and as against subsequent holders who are not holders in due course. Thus, in the above illustration, A and B are discharged from liability to P on the instrument. Otherwise, P would have an action against B and A who, in turn, would have an action back against P on the instrument. Such a discharge by reacquisition precludes such circuity of action. However, intervening parties are not discharged as against a holder in due course subsequent to the reacquiring party if he should reissue or further negotiate the instrument. In the above illustration, if P should negotiate the note to X, a holder in due course, A and B would still be secondarily liable on the instrument to X. P may prevent this and discharge the liability of A and B to X by cancelling the indorsements of A and B. The reacquiring party owns the instrument and has the right to relieve any indorser from liability on the instrument and, therefore, he has the right to cancel intervening indorsements. However, he must be careful not to cancel any indorsement necessary to his title.

---

[20] UCC 3–206, *Comment 6:* "But trustees commonly and legitimately sell trust assets in transactions entirely outside the bank collection process; the trustee therefore has power to negotiate the instrument and make his transferee a holder in due course. . . . payment to the trustee or to a purchaser from the trustee is 'consistent with the terms' of the trust indorsement."

Chapter IV

THE HOLDER IN DUE COURSE

1. REQUISITES

A DISTINCTION must be drawn between a holder and a holder in due course because the rights of each, and the rights which each may transfer, differ greatly. A holder in due course is a *holder* to whom an instrument has been *negotiated* under circumstances which make him so *innocent* a purchaser for *value* as to merit his obtaining complete title to the instrument subject to no claims by anyone, and subject to no so-called "personal defenses" by anyone a party thereto with whom he has not dealt. The elements constituting a holder in due course are very simple:

1. He is a holder of the instrument.
2. He takes the instrument:
   (a) for value,
   (b) in good faith,
   (c) without notice that the instrument is overdue or has been dishonored or of any defense against, or claim to, the instrument on the part of any person.

A payee may be a holder in due course.

However, it should be carefully noted at the outset that, although a person satisfies the above requisites, under the Code he cannot become a holder in due course of an instrument:

   (a) *by* purchase of it at judicial sale or by taking it under legal process; or
   (b) *by* acquiring it in taking over an estate; or
   (c) *by* purchasing it as part of a bulk transaction not in regular course of business of the transferor.[1] (Author's italics)[2]

---

[1] Examples of bulk purchases lying outside of the ordinary course of business of the seller are: a new partnership taking over for value all of the assets of an old one after a new member has entered the firm; a reorganized or consolidated corporation taking over in bulk the assets of a predecessor; the purchase by one bank of a substantial part of the paper held by another bank which is threatened with insolvency and seeking to liquidate its assets. UCC 3–302, *Comment 3.*

[2] UCC 3–302(3).

The reason is that, in these particular circumstances, he has taken the instrument under unusual circumstances not in due course of trade,[3] indicating that he is merely a successor in interest to the prior holder and, therefore, should acquire only the rights of his transferor. Note that he cannot become a holder in due course *by* acquiring the instrument in such a manner, but he can be a holder in due course if his transferor was, or could claim through a prior transferor as, a holder in due course.

The above requisites for becoming a holder in due course will be considered in the order stated.

Holder   A holder of an instrument is a person in possession of the instrument which is issued or indorsed to his order, to bearer, or in blank.[4] The payee can be a holder. The forged indorsement of a specified person to whom the instrument is payable, either as payee or indorsee, precludes any person subsequent to the forgery from being a holder.[5] There is a gap in the chain of indorsements, and the person in possession is not within the tenor of the instrument; it has never been properly indorsed to him. The person asserting that he is a holder has the burden of proving it.

When a person is a holder of an instrument, he may recover on the instrument as a holder in due course, unless the defendant establishes a defense. The burden of going forward and proving that the holder is a holder in due course is satisfied by proof of the status of being a holder. Until a defense is raised, there is no issue of whether or not he is a holder in due course. After it is shown that a defense exists, a person claiming the rights of a holder in due course has the burden of establishing that he, or some person under whom he claims, is in all respects a holder in due course. (D drew a check to the order of P for $1,000 and delivered it to P on P's promise to deliver certain goods to D. P negotiated the check to H and never delivered the goods to D. H sues D for payment of the check. H proves he is a holder. D proves failure of consideration for the check by P's non-delivery of the promised goods. H *now* has the burden of going forward and proving that he is a holder

---

[3] Leary, Jr., "Commercial Paper," in *Uniform Commercial Code Handbook* 87 (Chicago: American Bar Association, 1964), pp. 109–110: "It is just that these transactions are not in the due course of trade, and the concept of negotiability cutting off defenses, is to foster the due course of trade, and is not to be extended to such transactions of an extraordinary and non-trade nature."

[4] UCC 1–201(20).

[5] William E. Britton, *Handbook of the Law of Bills and Notes* (St. Paul: West Publishing Co., 1961), sec. 139.

in due course and, if he so proves, D must pay H.) The holder can prove either that he is a holder in due course, or that he acquired the rights of a prior holder in due course.

For Value

For a holder to acquire the status of a holder in due course, he must take the instrument for value. The Code distinguishes between "value" and "consideration." *Value is either: what a person parts with,* e.g., the payee pays money, surrenders a claim, gives a negotiable instrument or makes an irrevocable commitment to a third person in exchange for the instrument which he thereby acquires; *or an antecedent claim,* whether or not the claim is due, e.g., M gives P his note as security for an antecedent debt owing to P. The presence of value by the holder justifies, in exchange, his acquisition of an interest in an instrument. *For a person to have a contractual obligation to perform his promise,* either: someone must have furnished *consideration,* i.e., *what the promisor requested* and which the party rendering it was under no previous legal obligation to do; or there is an *antecedent claim* against the promisor or anyone else supporting the promise. (M promises to pay P $100 if P will sell and deliver certain goods to M. P sells and delivers the goods to M, and M's promise now is a contract with an obligation to pay. P's sale and delivery of the goods to M was what M's promise requested and, when performed by P, is the consideration for M's promise. If M gave P his note for such goods, and P never delivered the goods, M's promise on the note is not a contractual obligation to pay and such defense may be asserted against P, but not against a holder in due course or a transferee or holder under the shelter of a holder in due course.) So when we say "value," we are thinking of *what a holder paid* (or an antecedent claim) in order to see if he is a holder in due course with his superior status. When we say "consideration," we are thinking of *what an obligor on an instrument has requested and whether it was rendered* (or an antecedent claim); if it was not rendered, he has a personal defense of failure of consideration. Usually the value and the consideration in a transaction are the same thing. (M's note to the order of P is for the purchase price of goods to be sold and delivered by P to M. P cannot become a holder in due course until he gives value, i.e., he sells and delivers the goods to M. M cannot be held liable to P on M's promise to pay in the note until the consideration, namely the sale and delivery of the goods to M, has occurred. If M delivered his note to P, who never delivered the goods to M but, rather, negotiated the note to H, a holder in due course for $100, H is a holder in due course having paid value, and M has a personal defense of failure of consideration assertable against P but not against H.) Thus, under the Code, a holder takes the instrument for value:

(a) to the extent that the agreed consideration has been performed or that he acquires a security interest in or a lien on the instrument otherwise than by legal process; or

(b) when he takes the instrument in payment of or as security for an antecedent claim against any person whether or not the claim is due; or

(c) when he gives a negotiable instrument for it or makes an irrevocable commitment to a third person.[6]

Examples of a holder taking an instrument under the above circumstances may be helpful. The following two illustrations are concerned with (a) above. (1) D draws and delivers to P a check in payment for the goods sold and delivered to him by P; P took the instrument for value, namely the goods, which he delivered as the agreed consideration. (2) M made a note to P who pledged it to B bank as security for a loan then made to P; B has a security interest in, and lien on, the instrument for the money loaned to P. If, in the latter illustration, B had instead levied execution and thereby acquired the note from P, B would not have taken the instrument for value. The following illustration is concerned with (b) above. The debtor, D, owes C bank money, which debt is due and unpaid, and D delivers to C, either as security for the debt or in payment therefor, a note made by M to D. In either case, the antecedent debt serves as the basis for the use of the instrument for payment or security, and C takes M's note for value. The following two illustrations are concerned with (c) above. (1) P delivers to B a note, previously made by M to P, in exchange for B's check drawn by B to the order of P; P took the check for value, namely, M's note. (2) D is in debt to C and S later becomes a surety for such debt, D delivering to S D's check as compensation for S becoming a surety. S took D's check for value, namely, S's irrevocable commitment to C to be liable as a surety for D.

It should be noted carefully that under (a), the holder must actually render the consideration for there to be value. An executory promise to give value is not itself value, except as indicated in (c) above. *Performance* of the executory promise is value. It is for this reason that a bank's credit to a depositor's account of an item to be collected *without a right to draw against it until collected*[7] is, in effect, a promise by the bank to

---

[6] UCC 3–303.

[7] If the depositor has the right of immediate withdrawal before collection, see below, p. 480, and UCC 4–208(1), 209 for collecting bank's security interest.

pay the amount to the depositor and, as such, the promise does not constitute value; only to the extent that the depositor actually withdraws some or all of the amount of the credit is there value and the bank becomes to that extent a holder for value. It should be noted that, if the bank takes the item in partial or complete satisfaction of an antecedent debt, the bank becomes a holder for value for the full amount of the item. In determining when the depositor has drawn on the credit established by the bank in connection with a collectible item, under the Code the "first money in is the first money out."[8]

A holder in due course purchaser of a limited interest in an instrument becomes a holder in due course only to the extent of the interest purchased. "A purchaser of a limited interest—as a pledgee in a security transaction—may become a holder in due course, but he may enforce the instrument over defenses only to the extent of his interest, and defenses good against the pledgor remain available insofar as the pledgor retains an equity in the instrument."[9] (C lends D $1,000 and receives D's note for that amount, secured by D's pledge of M's note payable to D for $5,000 which D indorsed in blank and delivered to C. D had fraudulently induced M to issue his note to D, of which C was innocent. C is a holder in due course of the M note only to the extent of D's debt to C. On maturity of both notes and on D's default on his note to C, C can overcome M's personal defense of fraud on his note to D and recover from M *only the amount of D's debt to C,* because C is a holder in due course for value only to that extent. Anything beyond that amount on M's note is subject to M's defense thereon.)

In Good Faith   The holder must take the instrument in good faith. Under the Code, " 'Good faith' means honesty in fact in the conduct or transaction concerned."[10] The test of good faith is a subjective one—did the holder know facts at the time he took the instrument which *caused him to believe* that any defense against, or claim to, the instrument existed on the part of any person? If he did, then he took the instrument dishonestly and not in good faith, but rather in bad faith. Good faith is the converse of bad

---

[8] See UCC 4–208, and below, pp. 480 f.

[9] UCC 3–302, *Comment 4.*

[10] UCC 1–201(19). Under U3C, sec. 2.403: "Certain Negotiable Instruments Prohibited. In a consumer credit sale or consumer lease, other than a sale or lease primarily for an agricultural purpose, the seller or lessor may not take a negotiable instrument other than a check as evidence of the obligation of the buyer or lessee. A holder is not in good faith if he takes a negotiable instrument with notice that it is issued in violation of this section."

faith. It is the holder's state of mind which is the measure of good faith, and not what the facts and circumstances *should have* caused him to believe. Persons differ in their astuteness and have different beliefs based upon the same facts and circumstances. What may be bad faith for one holder may not be bad faith for another holder. An instrument is taken in good faith when *in fact* it is taken honestly, whether or not it is taken negligently or imprudently. Mere knowledge of suspicious circumstances is not bad faith per se, i.e., in and of itself, although it is evidence of bad faith. Bad faith must be proved as a fact and is a question of fact for the jury. It has been well stated:

> Merely suspicious circumstances sufficient to put a prudent man on inquiry, or even gross negligence on the part of plaintiff, at the time of acquiring the note, are not sufficient of themselves to prevent recovery unless the jury finds from the evidence that plaintiff acted in bad faith. . . . But failure of the holder to make inquiry such as a reasonable man would have made may properly be submitted to the jury as evidence of bad faith. . . . The existence of suspicious circumstances does not necessarily spell bad faith. Negligence is not a synonym for bad faith, and failure to make inquiries does not compel a finding of bad faith; yet as the question is one of honesty and good faith it is competent to show these facts and it then becomes the province of the jury to say whether the person taking the instrument was guilty of bad faith.[11]

The purchase of an instrument at a heavy discount is evidence of bad faith, but is not bad faith per se. If the holder can prove that he made all reasonable inquiry prior to his purchase of the instrument in order to determine whether anything was wrong with the instrument or with the title of the person negotiating it to him, there would be no bad faith.

Without Notice of Certain Facts A holder may have taken the instrument in good faith but still not be a holder in due course because the Code also requires that he take the instrument *without notice:* (1) that the instrument was overdue; (2) that it has been dishonored; (3) of any defense against, or claim to, it on the part of any person. Notice of such facts, therefore, becomes extremely important in determining whether a holder is a holder in due course. Under the Code,[12] a person has notice of a fact when: (1) he has actual knowledge of it; or (2) he has received a notice or notification of it; or (3) from all the facts and circumstances known to him at the time in question, he has reason to know that it exists.

---

[11] Frederick K. Beutel, *Beutel's Brannan Negotiable Instruments Law* (7th ed.; Cincinnati: W. H. Anderson Co., 1948), pp. 772, 774, 776.

[12] UCC 1–201(25).

It should be noted carefully that, just as the status of a good faith purchaser for value is determined at the time of the purchase and not subsequent to such purchase, so the status of a holder in due course is determined as of the time the instrument was negotiated to the holder. One who is a holder in due course does not lose such status because of his *subsequent* notice of facts which would have precluded him from being a holder in due course if he had had such notice at the time the instrument was negotiated to him. If an instrument is negotiated to a holder who pays part of the value agreed upon and, in all other respects, is a holder in due course, he is a holder in due course only to the extent of what he has paid, and he can recover only that amount. Should he obtain notice of a defense against, or claim to, the instrument on the part of any person prior to his payment of the remaining amount, he is not a holder in due course as to such additional payment. (A note for a face amount of $200 is negotiated to H for $150, H paying $100 down and the remaining $50 to be paid in 30 days. Prior to the expiration of the 30 days H learns of a defense against the instrument. H is a holder in due course only for the amount of $100.) If an instrument subject to defenses is pledged as security for value extended by the pledgee, and the pledgee is a holder in due course, he is a holder in due course with a lien on the instrument for the face amount of the instrument to the extent necessary to satisfy the obligation.

Notice that Instrument Is Overdue. The purchaser has notice that an instrument is overdue if he has reason to know any of the following:

1. That any part of the principal amount is overdue.
2. That there is an uncured default in payment of another instrument of the same series.
3. That the instrument has been accelerated.
4. That he is taking a demand instrument after demand has been made.
5. That he is taking a demand instrument after demand has been made or more than a reasonable length of time after its issue. A reasonable time for a check drawn and payable within the states and territories of the United States and the District of Columbia is presumed to be 30 days.[13]

Notice of a Claim or Defense. The holder must take the instrument without notice of any defense against, or claim to, the instrument on the part of any person. The purchaser[14] of the instrument has notice of a claim or defense if:

---

[13] But see UCC 3–503(2) and below, p. 454, regarding a reasonable time for presentment of an uncertified check.

[14] See UCC 3–304(1).

1. *On its face,* the instrument is so incomplete, bears such visible evidence of forgery or alteration, or is otherwise so irregular as to call into question its validity, terms or ownership or to create an ambiguity as to the party to pay.[15]
2. The purchaser has notice that the obligation of any party is voidable in whole or in part.
3. The purchaser has notice that all parties on the instrument have been discharged.[16]

The purchaser has notice of a claim against the instrument when he has *knowledge* that a fiduciary has negotiated the instrument in payment of, or as security for, his own debt or in any transaction for his own benefit or otherwise in breach of duty.

Facts Not Constituting Notice of Claim or Defense. Knowledge of the following facts does not of itself give the purchaser notice of a claim or defense:

1. That the instrument is antedated or postdated.
2. That the instrument was issued or negotiated in return for an executory promise or accompanied by a separate agreement, unless the purchaser has notice that a defense or claim has arisen from the terms thereof.
3. That any party has signed for accommodation.
4. That an incomplete instrument has been completed, unless the purchaser has notice of any improper completion. Any person in possession of an instrument has prima facie authority to complete the instrument by filling in the blanks thereon.[17]
5. That any person negotiating the instrument is, or was, a fiduciary. The purchaser's payment to the fiduciary for the instrument is not in itself notice of impropriety or breach of fiduciary obligation.
6. That there has been default in payment of interest on the instrument or in the payment of any other instrument, except one of the same series. This is a reflection of banking and commercial practice recognizing the great frequency of delayed interest payments.

It should be noted that the filing or recording of a document does not of itself constitute notice within the provisions of the Commercial Paper portion of the Code to a person who would otherwise be a holder in due

---

[15] UCC 3–304, *Comment 2:* "An instrument may be blank as to some unnecessary particular, may contain minor erasures, or even have an obvious change in the date, as where 'January 2, 1948,' is changed to 'January 2, 1949,' without even exciting suspicion. *Irregularity is properly a question of notice to the purchaser of something wrong, and is so treated here.*" (Author's italics)

[16] UCC 3–304, *Comment 4:* "Notice that one party has been discharged is not notice to the purchaser of an infirmity in the obligation of other parties who remain liable on the instrument. A purchaser with notice that an indorser is discharged takes subject to that discharge as provided in the section on effect of discharge against a holder in due course (Section 3–602) but is not prevented from taking the obligation of the maker in due course."

[17] See UCC 3–406 and 3–407; and below, pp. 432 f.

course. Also, to be effective, notice must be received at such time and in such manner as to give a reasonable opportunity to act on it. Thus, "a notice received by the president of a bank one minute before the bank's teller cashes a check is not effective to prevent the bank from becoming a holder in due course."[18]

2. RIGHTS AND DEFENSES

Rights   The rights of parties seeking to enforce an instrument vary according to their status. First the rights of a person who is not a holder in due course will be discussed and then the rights of a holder in due course.

Person Not a Holder in Due Course. A transferee and a holder who is not a holder in due course individually have certain rights solely because of the status of each, and both together with all other persons have certain rights because they are not holders in due course. The rights of these persons will be discussed in that order.

Transferee. A transferee of an instrument *payable to the order of* his transferor and delivered unindorsed to the transferee *for value* acquires the title to the instrument and has the specifically enforceable equitable right to have the instrument *unqualifiedly indorsed* by his transferor,[19] Unless the transferor and the transferee have agreed to the contrary.[20] Until the transferor indorses, the transferee is not a holder because he is not within the tenor of the instrument, i.e., he is not a payee, an indorsee, or bearer. Negotiation is completed and takes effect by such indorsement, and the time for determining whether the transferee is a holder in due course is when he becomes a holder, which is when the negotiation is completed. (An instrument is delivered unindorsed by the payee to H for value, without notice of a defense against the instrument. However, at the time H obtains the payee's subsequent indorsement, H has notice of the defense. H is not a holder in due course.) The transferee must prove that he is the lawful owner of the instrument, and until negotiation takes effect there is no presumption that he is the owner of the instrument.

When the transferee proves the transfer, he is entitled to the presumption of ownership of the instrument and of the rights of a holder

---

[18] UCC 3–304, *Comment 12*, also, see UCC 1–201(27) regarding notice to an organization.

[19] See above, p. 405.

[20] UCC 3–201, *Comment 6:* "The agreement for the transferee to take less than an unqualified indorsement need not be an express one, and the understanding may be implied from conduct, from past practice, or from the circumstances of the transaction."

of it. Until then he has rights similar to those of an assignee of a chose in action or of a non-negotiable instrument, namely *only the rights of his transferor subject to whatever defenses were available against his transferor on the instrument.* If his transferor was a holder in due course, the transferee has the rights of a holder in due course, with one very important exception. *A transferee who has himself been a party to any fraud or illegality affecting the instrument, or who as a prior holder had notice of a defense or claim against it, cannot improve his position by taking from a later holder in due course.*[21] (P fraudulently induced M to make an instrument payable to the order of P. If P negotiates the instrument to H, a holder in due course who delivers it to X who has notice of the fraud, X is not a holder in due course but, as the transferee of H, he acquires H's rights on the instrument free of M's defense of fraud. If P had repurchased the instrument from H, he would not acquire H's rights as a holder in due course free of M's defense of fraud but, instead, he would take the instrument subject to the defense. If P had negotiated the instrument to A, who had notice of the fraud, A then negotiated the instrument to H, a holder in due course, and H then resold the instrument to A, A would not acquire H's rights as a holder in due course free of M's defense of fraud but, instead, he would take the instrument subject to the defense. In the last illustration, if A had no notice of the fraud when the instrument had been negotiated to him as a holder but, before he had delivered the instrument to H, he had such notice, the same result would follow.)

It should be noted that the transfer of a limited interest in the instrument, e.g., a security interest in the instrument, passes only the transferor's rights in the instrument to the extent of such interest. If the interest transferred is a security interest, then the transaction comes under Article 9 of the Code on Secured Transactions.[22]

Holder. A person may be a holder but fail to comply with the requisites of being a holder in due course. (P fraudulently induces M to make and deliver his note to P, who then negotiates the note to H, indorsee, as a gift. H is a holder, since he is an indorsee, but he is not a holder in due course because he did not take the note for value.) As previously discussed,[23] until a defense is raised by the defendant, there is no issue of whether or not a holder is a holder in due course and, therefore, payment is to be made to him. After it is shown that a defense exists, a person claiming the rights of a holder in due course has the bur-

---

[21] UCC 3–201.

[22] See below, pp. 727–79.

[23] See above, p. 411.

den of establishing that he, or some person under whom he claims, is in all respects a holder in due course.

The holder of an instrument, whether or not he is the owner (e.g., finder of a bearer instrument is holder but not owner), may transfer or negotiate the instrument,[24] and he has the right to recover on the instrument unless the defendant establishes a defense.[25] To the extent that a party liable on the instrument makes payment or satisfaction to the holder, the liability of such party is discharged, with three exceptions, later discussed.[26] If an instrument has been transferred to a holder, the holder is also a transferee within the tenor of the instrument and, as such, he has the right of a transferee and acquires the rights of his transferor, as discussed above under the rights of a transferee. A holder may improve his position by taking the instrument from a prior holder in due course, subject to the limitations already discussed under the rights of a transferee.

By operation of law the holder's rights and title to an instrument may vest in another. The death of the holder causes the title to vest in the legal representative of his estate. The bankruptcy of the holder causes the title to vest in the trustee in bankruptcy. When there is more than one payee as tenants in common, the death of one payee causes his title to vest in the representative of his estate.

Any Person Not a Holder in Due Course. All persons not holders in due course acquire an instrument subject to all valid claims to it by any person and subject to the so-called "personal defenses" and "real defenses," to be discussed shortly.[27] If the person acquiring the instrument is a transferee, and a holder can be a transferee, the transferee acquires the rights of his transferor. This means that, with the limitations discussed previously under the rights of a transferee,[28] the latter can improve his position and acquire the rights of a previous holder in due course. (P fraudulently induces M to make and deliver his note to P, who negotiates the note to H, a holder in due course. H then negotiates the note to B, a purchaser for value, with notice that the note is overdue. B is not a holder in due course, because he took the note with

---

[24] UCC 3–301.

[25] UCC 3–307(2).

[26] The three exceptions are: an adverse claimant to the instrument either posts indemnity or restrains payment by legal process, or payment in bad faith involving theft of the instrument by the holder or one through whom the holder claims, or payment to the holder not in accordance with the restrictively indorsed instrument possessed by the holder. These are discussed below, pp. 466–68.

[27] See below, pp. 422–427.

[28] See above, p. 419.

notice that it was overdue. However, B acquires the rights of his transferor, H, and since H is a holder in due course B therefore acquires the rights of a holder in due course, even though he himself is not a holder in due course.)

We have learned that a holder has a right to recover on the instrument unless the defendant establishes a defense. *The obligor's contract on an instrument is to pay the holder of the instrument.* If other persons have claims to the instrument, that is not the concern of the obligor whose obligation is to perform his contract on the instrument. It is for this reason that the obligor is neither required nor permitted to assert any such claim adverse to the holder and, with certain exceptions,[29] he is discharged to the extent of payment to the holder. Besides, the obligor may not be certain of the validity of the adverse claim and not wish to take the risk or time to refuse payment of the instrument. *Accordingly, for the protection of both the obligor and the holder, under the Code,[30] the claim of any third person to the instrument is not otherwise available as a defense to any party liable thereon, unless the third person himself defends the action for such party.* (D drew a check to the order of P and delivered it to P. A fraudulently induced P to negotiate the check to A, who then negotiated it to H, a holder, after maturity. D cannot assert against H P's defense of fraud against A, and D must pay H on the check.)

Holder in Due Course. A holder in due course has the right to enforce the instrument according to its terms at the time it was negotiated to him. He takes the instrument free from all claims to it by any person, free from the so-called "personal defenses," but subject only to the so-called "real defenses," about to be discussed. In contrast, a holder and a transferee take the instrument subject to all valid claims to it by any person, subject to all personal defenses except as the holder or transferee acquires the rights of a previous holder in due course, and subject to real defenses available on the instrument against their respective transferors.

Defenses   Although the Code does not use the terms "real defense" and "personal defense," under the prior law these terms were used extensively, "personal defenses" to describe those defenses which were effective against everyone except a holder in due course or a transferee or holder properly claiming through a holder in due course, and "real defenses" to describe

---

[29] See above, p. 420, ftn. 26, and below, pp. 466–68.

[30] UCC 3–306(d).

those defenses which were effective against everyone, including a holder in due course. There is no reason to believe that the courts will not continue to use these terms in this context, and they are used here for that purpose. A negotiation of an instrument to a holder in due course cuts off personal defenses but not real defenses. Accordingly, it becomes very important to distinguish between real and personal defenses.

Real or absolute defenses are readily distinguishable from personal defenses, which include Common Law as well as equitable defenses. Defenses which successfully attack the inherent validity or continuing existence of an instrument *as a contract binding on the defending party* are real defenses. Personal defenses do not question the inherent validity or continuing existence of the instrument as a contract binding on the defending party but, rather, seek to *avoid* the instrument and liability thereon. First real defenses will be discussed and then personal defenses.

Real Defenses. Under the Code,[31] to the extent that a holder is a holder in due course, he takes the instrument free from all claims to it on the part of any person, and free from all defenses of any party to the instrument with whom the holder has not dealt, except the following real defenses: incapacity, in the case of the limited incapacity of an infant to the extent that infancy is a defense to a simple contract, or because of no capacity to contract at all; such duress or illegality of the transaction as precludes the creation of a contractual obligation; fraud in the procurement; discharge in insolvency proceedings. Also a material alteration of a negotiable instrument is, with certain exceptions, a real defense. These will be considered in turn, except for material alteration, which is considered later.[32]

Incapacity—Limited Capacity and Lack of Capacity. The Code distinguishes between the *limited capacity* of an infant to make a contract and *lack of capacity* of a person to make any contract.

1. Infancy. *To the extent that infancy is a defense to a simple contract,* it is a real defense by an infant party to an instrument, personal only to him, and assertable against everyone, including a holder in due course. An infant has a limited capacity to contract and, therefore, may issue an instrument; but should the infant exercise his power of avoidance, he no longer is liable as a party on the instrument. The law of a particular state may impose conditions upon an infant in the exercise of his power of avoidance, e.g., he is to return the considera-

---

[31] UCC 3–305.

[32] See below, pp. 432 ff. UCC 9–206 prohibits waiver by buyer or lessee, as against an assignee, or real defenses in a security agreement for consumer goods; see below, p. 740–42.

tion as a condition precedent to avoidance, or preclude the infant from exercising such right, e.g., estoppel as by his misrepresentation of his age. It is for this reason that, only to the extent that an infant may assert infancy as a defense to the contract on the instrument, infancy is a real defense. The law of the local state governs.

2. Lack of Capacity. *Lack of capacity to contract precludes the creation of a contract* and, therefore, of a contractual obligation on an instrument. "It covers mental incompetence, guardianship, ultra vires acts or lack of corporate capacity to do business, any remaining incapacity of married women, or any other incapacity apart from infancy. Such incapacity is largely statutory. Its existence and effect is left to the local state. If under the local law the effect is to render the obligation of the instrument entirely null and void, the defense may be asserted against a holder in due course. If the effect is merely to render the obligation voidable at the election of the obligor, the defense is cut off."[33] Thus, a corporation[34] and a nontrading partnership[35] without authority to issue negotiable instruments are not bound by their issue of such instrument; their defenses are real. However, although they have no contractual liability on an instrument, nevertheless title to the instrument can pass through them to a subsequent holder in due course.

Duress Precluding Contract. Duress may either preclude the formation of a contract or render a contract voidable at the election of the wronged party.[36] *To the extent that duress precludes the formation of a contract,* the party upon whom duress has been imposed has no contractual liability and, therefore, is not liable as a party to an instrument. Such duress is a real defense, assertable against everyone, including a holder in due course. Local law governs the effect of duress. Duress which may render a contract voidable at the election of the wronged party is a personal defense and is not assertable against a holder in due course.

Illegality Precluding Contract. An agreement is illegal when its formation or performance is contrary to law by being opposed to statute, or to public policy as declared by the courts.[37] While, generally, illegal agreements are void by either statute or judicial decision and create no contractual obligation, nevertheless in some instances illegality causes an agreement to be voidable and not void. Although the

[33] UCC 3–305, *Comment 5.*
[34] See below, p. 678.
[35] See below, p. 624.
[36] See Contracts, above, p. 49.
[37] See Contracts, above, pp. 89–90.

issuance of an instrument or the transaction giving rise to the instrument may be illegal, nevertheless, they are not void unless made void by statute or judicial decision. Accordingly, mere illegality in connection with the issuance of an instrument is a personal defense, not assertable against a holder in due course; but if, *by law, the illegality nullifies or precludes any contractual obligation on the instrument,* the illegality is a real defense and assertable against everyone, including a holder in due course. The effect of illegality is a matter of local state law, e.g., a state statute declaring void an instrument given in settlement of a gambling debt.

Fraud in the Procurement. Fraud may either preclude the formation of a contract or render a contract voidable at the election of the person wronged, depending on the type of fraud which occurs.[38] *Fraud in the procurement* (also called "fraud in the factum," "fraud in the execution," "fraud in the inception," or "fraud in the essence") *precludes the formation of a contract.* The Code describes fraud in the procurement as "such misrepresentation as has induced the party to sign the instrument with neither knowledge nor reasonable opportunity to obtain knowledge of its character or its essential terms."[39] (P misrepresents to M that a paper is a receipt when, in fact, it is a form of note. M, with neither knowledge nor reasonable opportunity to obtain knowledge of the character of the paper or its essential terms, signs the paper. M is not liable on any contractual obligation on the instrument.) Fraud in the procurement is a real defense assertable against everyone, including a holder in due course. In contrast, fraud in the inducement (also called "fraud in the treaty") causes the resulting contract to be voidable at the election of the party wronged and is a personal defense assertable against everyone except a holder in due course or a transferee or holder properly claiming through a holder in due course. (P intentionally misrepresented his financial solvency to M and induced M to enter into a contract to buy goods from P. M made a note payable to the order of P for the purchase price. M may avoid the sales contract and assert the fraud as a personal defense against P on the note.) It should be noted that *when the word "fraud" is used without qualification, it signifies fraud in the inducement.*

Discharge in Insolvency Proceedings.[40] The discharge in bank-

---

[38] See Contracts, above, pp. 45–46.

[39] UCC 3–305(2) (c).

[40] UCC 1–201(22) : " 'Insolvency proceedings' includes any assignment for the benefit of creditors or other proceedings intended to liquidate or rehabilitate the estate of the person involved."

ruptcy or other insolvency proceedings of a party to an instrument terminates his contractual obligation thereon and, therefore, is a real defense assertable against everyone including a holder in due course.

The discharge of a party *other than* in bankruptcy or other insolvency proceedings is a *personal defense* which is assertable against anyone except a holder in due course without notice of such discharge at the time he took the instrument. As indicated previously,[41] a purchaser of an instrument has notice of a claim or defense if he has notice that *all* the parties on the instrument have been discharged, but "notice of any discharge which leaves other parties liable on the instrument does not prevent the purchaser from becoming a holder in due course. The obvious case is that of the cancellation of an indorsement, which leaves the maker and prior indorsers liable. As to such parties the purchaser may be a holder in due course, but he takes the instrument subject to the discharge of which he has notice. If he is without such notice, the discharge is not effective against him."[42]

Personal Defenses. *Personal defenses may be asserted against everyone except a holder in due course and a transferee or holder claiming through a holder in due course, except a transferee or holder who has himself been a party to any fraud or illegality affecting the instrument or who, as a prior holder, had notice of a defense or claim against it.*[43] All defenses which are not real are personal. The Code succinctly sums up the rights of one not a holder in due course, indicating the nature of the personal defenses assertable against him:

Unless he has the rights of a holder in due course any person takes the instrument subject to
(a) all valid claims to it on the part of any person; and
(b) all defenses of any party which would be available in an action on a simple contract; and
(c) the defenses of want or failure of consideration, nonperformance of any condition precedent, non-delivery, or delivery for a special purpose (Section 3–408); and
(d) the defense that he or a person through whom he holds the instrument acquired it by theft, or that payment or satisfaction to such holder would be inconsistent with the terms of a restrictive indorsement. The claim of any third person to the instrument is not otherwise available as a defense to any party liable thereon unless the third person himself defends the action for such party.[44]

---

[41] See above, p. 417.
[42] UCC 3–305, *Comment 9.*
[43] See above, p. 419.
[44] UCC 3–306.

It may be helpful to give an explanation or illustrations of the items indicated above. Under (a) above, there is included "not only claims of legal title, but all liens, equities, or other claims of right against the instrument or its proceeds. It includes claims to rescind a prior negotiation and to recover the instrument or its proceeds."[45] Under (b) above, the person who takes the instrument takes it as though it were non-negotiable and, therefore, acquires only the rights of his transferor. Defenses available against his transferor are also available against him. (P fraudulently induced M to issue his note to P, who indorsed it in blank and delivered it to H after maturity. H is not a holder in due course because he took the instrument after maturity and also without value. H cannot improve his position by claiming through P as a holder in due course, because P is not a holder in due course by reason of his lack of good faith and notice of M's defense on the instrument for fraud. Since H got what P, his transferor, had, and P is subject to M's personal defense of fraud, H takes the instrument subject to that defense also.) Under (c) above, want of consideration exists when an instrument is given without any expectation of consideration in return. (D draws and delivers to his son a check for $2.00 as a gift. D may assert want of consideration as a personal defense against his son on the check.) Failure of consideration exists when the consideration bargained for is not received. (D draws and delivers to P a check in payment of the purchase price for goods sold and to be delivered by P to D, which goods are never delivered to D. D may assert failure of consideration as a personal defense against P on the check.) An illustration of nonperformance of a condition precedent is M's issuance of his note payable to P in payment of the purchase price of property bought by M from P on approval, the note to be returned to M if M did not elect to take the property. If M did not elect to take the property, the condition precedent for M's note has not occurred, and M can assert non-purchase of the property as a personal defense against P on the note. An illustration of non-delivery is where D drew a check to the order of P, lost it, and P found it. D may assert non-delivery as a personal defense against P on the check. An illustration of delivery for a special purpose is where D drew a check to the order of P, delivered it to S, D's secretary, and asked her to hold it. Instead, S delivered the check to P. D has a personal defense of unauthorized delivery against P on the instrument. Item (d) indicates that, with two exceptions, a defendant party liable on an instrument cannot assert as a defense the claim of a

---

[45] UCC 3–306, *Comment 2.*

third person to the instrument unless the third person himself defends the action for the defendant party. The first exception is that the defendant may assert as a defense that the holder claimant, or a person through whom he holds the instrument, acquired it by theft from a third person. "The exception made in the case of theft is based on the policy which refuses to aid a proved thief to recover, and refuses to aid him indirectly by permitting his transferee to recover unless the transferee is a holder in due course."[46] (D's check to the order of P and delivered to P is indorsed by P in blank and stolen by A. D stops payment on the check, and A sues to enforce the check against D. While A is a holder, nevertheless D can assert P's defense that the check belongs to P. If A had negotiated the check to B after maturity thereby precluding B from being a holder in due course, D could also assert the defense against B. But if A had negotiated the check to H, a holder in due course, H would take the check free of such defense. If H had negotiated the check to C after maturity thereby precluding C from being a holder in due course, nevertheless C would acquire H's rights and, therefore, take the check free of the defense.) The second exception is that payment or satisfaction to such holder would be inconsistent with the terms of a restrictive indorsement.[47]

It should be noted that, while want or failure (in whole or in part) of consideration is a personal defense unavailable against a holder in due course, nevertheless "no consideration is necessary for an instrument or obligation thereon given in payment of or as security for an antecedent obligation of any kind."[48] Thus, where the debtor (or a third person) gives to his creditor a note or draft, or indorses either, as payment or as security for the debt, the new obligation does not fail for want of consideration. The antecedent obligation provides the basis for the new obligation being effective as such.

Establishing Signatures and Burden of Proof. Under the Code,[49] when a party brings an action to recover on an instrument, each signature thereon is admitted as effective, unless specifically denied in the pleadings. When the effectiveness of a signature is put in issue, the party claiming under the signature has the burden of establishing it. He is assisted in his burden by a legal presumption that a signature is

---

[46] UCC 3–306, *Comment 5.*

[47] See above, p. 408.

[48] UCC 3–408; (continued) : "Nothing in this section shall be taken to displace any statute outside this Act under which a promise is enforceable notwithstanding lack of failure of consideration."

[49] UCC 3–307.

presumed to be genuine or authorized, except where the action is to enforce the obligation of a purported signer who has died or become incompetent before proof is required. When signatures on an instrument have been admitted or established, production of the instrument by the holder entitles him to recover on the instrument unless the defendant establishes a defense. After it is shown that a defense exists, a person claiming the rights of a holder in due course has the burden of establishing that he or some person under whom he claims is a holder in due course.

Chapter V

LIABILITY OF PARTIES

---

1. IN GENERAL

Signature Required AN INSTRUMENT is a formal contract, and no person is liable *on the instrument* unless his signature appears thereon. " 'Signed' includes any symbol executed or adopted by a party with present intention to authenticate a writing."[1] An allonge[2] with an indorsement is part of the instrument to which it is affixed. A principal is not liable *on an instrument* signed by his agent without the principal's name appearing on the instrument, irrespective of whether or not the payee knew of the principal's identity. However, a person not liable on an instrument because his signature does not appear thereon may have liability arising from circumstances outside of the instrument. For example, a person may be liable on an obligation pursuant to which the instrument was issued, e.g., the buyer is liable on his contract of purchase even though he did not sign the instrument executed by someone else to pay the purchase price. Or, a person may be liable for payment of the instrument by estoppel, e.g., D erroneously tells H that a signature on the instrument is D's, and H justifiably then purchases the instrument from P, causing D to be estopped to deny that it is his signature. Local state law governs any requirement and method of authentication of a signature on an instrument, e.g., witnessing or acknowledging a signature by mark (X).

The signature on an instrument determines the status of the signing party and, therefore, the extent of his liability. The face of the instrument alone determines the character of a signature thereon and, *unless the instrument clearly indicates that a signature is made in some other capacity, it is an indorsement.* Parol evidence is not admissible to prove such a signature in any other capacity, except as local law permits for the purpose of reformation. *"The indication that the signature is made in another capacity must be clear without reference to anything but the*

---

[1] UCC 1–201(39).

[2] See above, p. 404.

instrument. It may be found in the language used. Thus if John Doe signs after 'I, John Doe, promise to pay,' he is clearly a maker; and 'John Doe, witness' he is not liable at all. *The capacity may be found in any clearly evidenced purpose of the signature,* as where a drawee signing in an unusual place on the paper has no visible reason to sign at all unless he is an acceptor. *It may be found in custom or usage.* Thus, by long established practice judicially noticed or otherwise established, a signature in the lower right hand corner of an instrument indicates an intent to sign as the maker of a note or the drawer of a draft." (Author's italics)[3]

A person's signature on an instrument may be made by another person, either with or without authority to do so. A signature may be made by an authorized representative, whether an agent or other representative, e.g., corporate officer, trustee, executor. The representative's authority so to sign may be established as in other cases of representation. The authority need not be in writing, and no particular form of appointment is necessary in order to establish such authority. An authorized representative who signs his own name to the instrument is personally obligated on the instrument as a party thereto, unless the instrument names the person represented *and* shows that the representative signed in a representative capacity, in which case the representative is not obligated on the instrument; either one without the other is insufficient to relieve the representative from being personally obligated on the instrument. Thus, if Arthur Anderson is the authorized representative and Peter Pan is the principal, what would be the legal effect of the following signatures appearing on an instrument:

(1) "Arthur Anderson";
(2) "Arthur Anderson, agent";
(3) "Peter Pan";
(4) "Peter Pan
         Arthur Anderson";
(5) "Peter Pan by Arthur Anderson, agent"?

The representative is personally obligated on the instrument in (1), (2), and (4), but not in (3) and (5). The principal is bound on the instrument in (3), (4), and (5). Except as otherwise established, the name of an organization preceded or followed by the name and office of an authorized individual is a signature made in a representative capac-

---

[3] UCC 3–402, *Comment.*

ity. For example, "Peter Pan Corporation by Arthur Anderson, President," or "Arthur Anderson, President, Peter Pan Corporation."

An *unauthorized* signature is wholly inoperative as that of the person whose name is signed. " 'Unauthorized' signature or indorsement means one made without actual, implied or apparent authority and includes a forgery."[4] However, *the unauthorized signature operates as the signature of the unauthorized signer in favor of any person who, in good faith, pays the instrument or takes it for value.* (P forged M's signature as maker of a note payable to the order of P, indorsed it in blank and delivered it to H, who took it for value in good faith without notice of the forgery. The purported signature of M is treated as the signature of P, who is liable as a maker to H on the instrument.) *The person whose name was unauthorizedly signed may ratify the unauthorized signature or, by reason of estoppel, be precluded from denying the signature as his.* Ratification may be expressed, or implied from the conduct of the ratifying party, as by his retention of what he received from the transaction with knowledge of the unauthorized signature. The law of agency on ratification is applicable.[5] Ratification of the signature is retroactive in effect, authenticating the signature at the time it was made as though it had been authorized. Ratification causes the ratifying party to be bound by such signature as though authorizedly made and, since the signature on the instrument is now that of the ratifying party and not of the unauthorized signer, the latter is no longer liable *on the instrument.* However, ratification does not relieve the unauthorized signer from criminal liability, particularly if it is a forgery, nor does it relieve him of civil liability for loss caused to the ratifying party. Estoppel occurs when the person whose name was unauthorizedly signed represents to another person that the signature is genuine and the latter, in reliance thereon, subsequently purchased the instrument.

An instrument may be issued to a payee who is intended not to have any interest in the instrument. The person who intends that the payee is not to have any interest in the instrument may be: the maker or drawer; one signing for them; the agent of the maker or drawer who supplied the name of the payee to the latter who signed the instrument; or any impostor who, impersonating as the payee face to face with the maker or drawer or by the use of the mails, persuaded the maker or drawer to issue the instrument to him or his confederate in the name of the payee.

---

[4] UCC 1–201(43).
[5] See below, pp. 530 ff.

Since the instrument on its face is payable to the order of a named payee, it is not payable to bearer and, therefore, must be indorsed in the payee's name so that the chain of continuity from maker or drawer through the payee as indorser is not broken. Since the payee is not intended to have any interest in the instrument, an indorsement by him is not required but may be made by *any person* in the name of such payee. Although such an indorsement and delivery of the instrument is effective to negotiate the instrument, the local state criminal law is not affected thereby, and prosecution for any crime involved may occur.

The Code imposes a duty of care upon anyone handling an instrument not to act *negligently* and thereby *substantially contribute* to a material alteration of the instrument or to the making of an unauthorized signature. The negligent party is not made liable in tort but, instead, is precluded or estopped from asserting the alteration or lack of authority against a holder in due course or against a drawee or other payor who pays the instrument in good faith and in accordance with the reasonable commercial standards of the drawee's or payor's business. The party must be *negligent,* and his negligence must *substantially contribute* to the *material alteration* of the instrument or the making of an *unauthorized signature.* Negligence is a question of fact for the jury, or the judge if there is no jury. The negligence must afford an opportunity of which advantage may be taken. Leaving spaces in the body of an instrument so that words or figures could be inserted has been held to be such negligence. "The most obvious case is that of the drawer who makes use of a signature stamp or other automatic signing device and is negligent in looking after it. The section extends, however, to cases where the party has notice that forgeries of his signature have occurred and is negligent in failing to prevent further forgeries by the same person. It extends to negligence which contributes to a forgery of the signature of another, as in the case where a check is negligently mailed to the wrong person having the same name as the payee."[6]

Alteration It is very important to understand the effect of an alteration of an instrument under the Code.[7] The alteration may be material or not material. *It is material if it thereby changes the contract of any party to the instrument in any respect.* Illustrations are a change in: the number or

---

[6] UCC 3–406, *Comment 7.*
[7] UCC 3–407.

relations of the parties;[8] an incomplete instrument, by completing it otherwise than as authorized; the writing as signed, by adding to it or by removing any part of it. *If an alteration is both fraudulent and material* and is made *by a holder,* except as against a subsequent holder in due course *it discharges* any party to the instrument whose contract is thereby changed, unless that party assents or is precluded from asserting the defense. If an alteration is *not* both fraudulent and material, and *irrespective of by whom made,* except as against a subsequent holder in due course it does *not* discharge any party to the instrument, which may be enforced according to its original tenor or, as to incomplete instruments, according to the authority given. In contrast, a subsequent holder in due course may, in all cases, enforce the instrument according to its original tenor, except that if an incomplete instrument has been unauthorizedly completed he may enforce it as completed.[9]

Several aspects of alteration should be particularly noted. *For discharge of a party to occur, the alteration must be both fraudulent and material.* By fraudulent is meant intentionally altering unjustly a contractual obligation. "A material alteration does not discharge any party unless it is made for a fraudulent purpose. There is no discharge where a blank is filled in the honest belief that it is as authorized; or where a change is made with a benevolent motive, such as a desire to give the obligor the benefit of a lower interest rate. Changes favorable to the obligor are unlikely to be made with any fraudulent intent; but if such an intent is found the alteration may operate as a discharge."[10] The material and fraudulent alteration must be made by the holder (personally or through his agent), and not by a meddler who is a stranger to the instrument, in order for a discharge to occur. Only the party on the instrument whose contract thereon is changed by a holder's fraudulent and material alteration can assert the defense of discharge; the defense is personal to him and cannot be asserted by anyone else. It should be

---

[8] Any change in the number or relations of the parties is material "only if it changes the contract of one who has signed. The addition of a co-maker or a surety does not change in most jurisdictions the contract of one who has already signed as maker and should not be held material as to him. The addition of the name of an alternative payee is material, since it changes his obligation." UCC 3–407, *Comment 1.*

[9] Paralleling the protection given to a subsequent holder in due course, UCC 4–401(2) provides: "A bank which in good faith makes payment to a holder may charge the indicated account of its customer according to
(a) the original tenor of his altered item; or
(b) the tenor of his completed item, even though the bank knows the item has been completed unless the bank has notice that the completion was improper."

[10] UCC 3–407, *Comment 3b.*

noted in passing that a purchaser who takes a materially altered instrument with notice of such,[11] takes with notice of a defense against the instrument and cannot be a holder in due course.[12]

2. CONTRACTUAL OBLIGATIONS OF PARTIES TO AN INSTRUMENT

An instrument is a contract and the parties thereto have certain contractual obligations thereon and make various warranties on its presentment for payment or acceptance and on its transfer. This Section will consider their contractual obligations, and Section 3 will consider their warranties. First parties primarily liable will be considered, then parties secondarily liable, followed by the accommodation party and lastly by the guarantor.

Parties Primarily Liable

In General. Parties on a negotiable instrument who, by the terms thereof, are absolutely required to pay it are parties primarily liable; all other parties on the instrument are secondarily liable. "Absolutely" liable means "unconditionally" liable, as distinguished from the conditional liability of parties secondarily liable. The absolute liability of parties primarily liable does not mean that real and personal defenses are unavailable to them; such defenses may be asserted by them. The only parties who are primarily liable are a maker of a note and an acceptor of a draft or a check.

Neither demand nor presentment for payment is necessary in order to charge a party primarily liable on the instrument. The liability of the maker is fixed and absolute the moment the instrument is issued and that of the acceptor is fixed and absolute the moment he accepts the instrument. If the party primarily liable tenders the full amount to a holder when or after it is due and such tender is improperly refused, the familiar effect of an improper refusal of a valid tender of payment prevails: the debt is not discharged; costs of collection on the instrument are borne by the party wrongfully refusing the tender; interest stops running on the instrument from that date; and the lien on the collateral security for payment of the instrument is discharged. Under the Code, "Where the maker or acceptor of an instrument payable otherwise than on demand is able and ready to pay at every place of payment specified in the instrument when it is due, it is equivalent to

---

[11] For notice of defense, see above, p. 416.

[12] For holder in due course, see above, p. 411.

tender."[13] It should be observed that, for this rule to apply, the instrument must be payable at a specified place. If the instrument is payable at more than one specified place, the maker or acceptor must be able and ready to pay the instrument at each of such specified places.

Maker. As a party primarily liable on the note made by him, *the maker engages that he will pay the note according to its tenor at the time he signed it, or as later completed either authorizedly*[14] *or unauthorizedly,*[15] *and he admits as against all subsequent parties the existence of the payee and his then capacity to indorse the note.* The maker, therefore, is estopped to assert against a subsequent party that the purported signature of the payee is not that of the payee because he does not exist, and that the payee was an infant who avoided his indorsement or a foreign corporation which could not contract by its indorsement because it did not comply with state statutes for the regulation of foreign corporations doing business in that state. However, if the issuance of the note is void (not voidable) for illegality, the real defense of illegality may be asserted by the maker against all subsequent parties, including a holder in due course.

Acceptor. *No person is liable on an instrument until his signature appears thereon.*[16] A check or other draft does not of itself operate as an assignment of any funds in the hands of the drawee available for its payment, and the drawee is not liable on the instrument until he accepts it.[17] *Acceptance is the drawee's signed engagement to honor the draft as presented.* It *must* be written on the draft, and may consist of his signature alone.[18] Writing "Accepted" on the instrument is not necessary, but if written it is ineffective until accompanied by the drawee's signature. Where the draft is payable at a fixed period after sight, e.g., payable "30 days after sight," if the acceptor fails to date his acceptance the holder may complete it by supplying a date in good faith. The reason for this is that such an undated acceptance is incomplete until dated. The acceptance may be anywhere on the draft, either front or back, although it is usually written vertically across the face of the instrument. It is not an acceptance if accompanied by words refusing to honor the draft as presented. A draft may be accepted although it has

---

[13] UCC 3–604(3).

[14] For incomplete instruments, see above, p. 396.

[15] See alteration, above, p. 432.

[16] UCC 3–401(1).

[17] UCC 3–409(1). This does not affect any liability in contract, in tort or otherwise which may arise *apart* from the instrument itself, as from a separate letter of credit or other obligation or representation which is not an acceptance.

[18] UCC 3–410(3).

not been signed by the drawer, or is otherwise incomplete, or is overdue, or has been dishonored. An acceptance becomes operative when completed by delivery or notification to the holder or pursuant to his instructions. This is an exception to the rule that an obligation on the instrument is effective only on delivery. Usually the instrument is forwarded to the drawee for his acceptance; sometimes, instead, the holder relies on a separate written obligation, e.g., letter of credit, which cannot be an acceptance because the drawee's signature is on it and not on the instrument itself.

Certification of a check is acceptance. (See illustration on page 378.) Where a *holder* procures certification, the drawer and all prior indorsers are discharged. It should be noted carefully that if, instead of the holder, the *drawer* procures the certification, the drawer is not discharged from liability on the instrument. Also, if an indorsement is placed on the instrument after certification, the indorsement is effective as such. Unless otherwise agreed, a bank has no obligation on the check to certify it; it is a demand instrument calling for payment rather than acceptance, and also, until it is accepted, the drawee has no obligation thereon. However, the bank may be liable for breach of a contract separate from the check, made with a person, e.g., the drawer, holder, or any other person, that the bank would certify the check.

A holder is entitled to have the draft honored by being accepted in accordance with the terms of the draft. While a draft not honored as presented is dishonored, nevertheless, if the drawee's proffered acceptance in any manner varies the terms of the draft, the holder has an election. He may treat the draft as dishonored, in which case the drawee is entitled to have his acceptance cancelled. Or, he may assent to the proffered acceptance varying the terms of the draft, in which case each drawer and indorser who does not *affirmatively* assent is discharged from liability on the draft. There is no implied assent by the silence of such a drawer and indorser; their assent must be made expressly in order to preclude such discharge. Illustrations of a proffered acceptance which varies the terms of the draft are when the proffered acceptance: is to pay part only of the amount for which the draft is drawn; qualifies the time as expressed in the draft in which it is to be paid after acceptance; is by some one or more of the drawees but not all of them; is payable on the fulfillment of a condition not expressed in the draft. The terms of the draft are not varied by an acceptance to pay at any particular bank or place in the United States, but they are varied if the acceptance states that the draft is to be paid *only* at such bank or place.

As a party primarily liable on the instrument (draft or check) accepted by him, *the acceptor engages that he will pay the instrument according to its tenor at the time of his acceptance, or as later completed either authorizedly*[19] *or unauthorizedly,*[20] *and he admits as against all subsequent parties the existence of the payee and his then capacity to indorse the instrument.* If the instrument was altered *prior* to acceptance, the acceptance applies to the instrument as altered and not to its original tenor.[21] The effect of alteration of the instrument *after* an acceptance is governed by the rules on alteration.[22] The acceptor, therefore, is estopped to assert against a subsequent party that the purported signature of the payee is not that of the payee because he does not exist, and that the payee was an infant who avoided his indorsement or a foreign corporation which could not contract by its indorsement because it did not comply with state statutes for the regulation of foreign corporations doing business in that state. However, if the issuance of the instrument is void (not voidable) for illegality, the real defense of illegality may be asserted by the acceptor against all subsequent parties, including a holder in due course.

Finality of Payment or Acceptance. *Payment or acceptance of an instrument is final in favor of a holder in due course, a transferee with the rights of a holder in due course, or a person who has, in good faith, changed his position in reliance on the payment, with two exceptions.* First, the rule is subject to the warranties made by a person who obtains payment or acceptance, discussed later.[23] Second, the rule is subject to the right of a payor bank, which has not made final payment,[24] to recover a payment improperly paid if it returns the item or sends notice of dishonor within the limited time provided in UCC 4–301.[25] Thus, under this rule of finality of payment or acceptance, if the drawee accepts or pays an instrument on which the drawer's signature was forged, the acceptor is bound by his acceptance and the drawee cannot recover the money paid. A paying maker and a paying or accepting drawee are responsible; they are in a better position to determine the genuineness of the maker's or drawer's signature than anyone else, and they should bear the loss for such payment or acceptance. In the case of a paying maker, he certainly ought to recognize his own signature, and in the

---

[19] See above, p. 396.

[20] See above, p. 432.

[21] For warranty of no material alteration of an instrument prior to acceptance, made by the person obtaining acceptance, see below, p. 449.

[22] See above, pp. 432 ff.

[23] See below, pp. 447 ff.

[24] See UCC 4–213.

[25] See below, p. 1075.

case of a paying or accepting drawee, he has the drawer's signature available to him for examination. Similarly, if an instrument is accepted or paid by a drawee when the funds of the drawer are insufficient, the acceptor is liable on his acceptance and is estopped to assert insufficiency of the drawer's funds as a defense to payment, nor can the drawee recover the money paid. By accepting the instrument the acceptor, and by paying on the instrument the drawee, admit that the drawer's funds are sufficient to permit payment of the instrument, and they are estopped from later denying such sufficiency. They are responsible for knowing the state of the drawer's account with them before the instrument is accepted or before the money is paid. It should be noted carefully that finality of payment and acceptance applies only to a holder in due course; a transferee, under the shelter of a holder in due course, who has the rights of a holder in due course; and a person who has, in good faith, changed his position in reliance on the payment. A holder who is neither a holder in due course nor under the shelter of a holder in due course and *who has not given value,* loses nothing by being denied any right to enforce the acceptance or by being compelled to return the money paid. He should not profit at the expense of the drawee. Nor should the result be any different in the case of forgery of the accepted instrument if such a holder gave an executory promise or credit, because he cannot be compelled to perform it after discovery of the forgery.

Conversion of the Instrument. An instrument is property belonging to the holder and, like other chattels, is subject to conversion by a wrongdoer. The tort of conversion has been discussed at length previously,[26] but briefly it involves interference with possession of a chattel inconsistent with another person's right to its immediate possession and inconsistent with his right to control and dominion over the chattel. The Code lists, but does not limit conversion to,[27] three ways by which an instrument may be converted:

(a) a drawee to whom it is delivered for acceptance refuses to return it on demand; or

(b) any person to whom it is delivered for payment refuses on demand either to pay or to return it; or

(c) it is paid on a forged indorsement.[28]

Several aspects should be noted particularly. Since an instrument is voluntarily delivered for payment or acceptance, its detention by the recipient is not wrongful until demand has been made, either expressly

---

[26] See above, p. 193, ftn. 18.

[27] See UCC 1–103, and above, p. 5.

[28] UCC 3–419(1).

or impliedly, for its return. " 'Refuses' is meant to cover any intentional failure to return the instrument, including its intentional destruction. It does not cover a negligent loss or destruction, or any other unintentional failure to return. In such a case the party may be liable in tort for any damage sustained as a result of his negligence, but he is not liable as a converter"[29] under the Code. Also, in an action for conversion under any of the above three ways *against the drawee,* the drawee's liability *is* the face amount of the instrument; as *against anyone else,* the measure of liability is *presumed* to be the face amount of the instrument.[30] The reason for the presumption as against anyone other than the drawee is that evidence may show that the obligation on the instrument is of no value or worth less than the face amount, as by a condition of insolvency. As an exception to the conversion rule, a representative, including a depositary[31] or collecting[32] bank, who has in good faith and in accordance with the reasonable commercial standards applicable to the business of such representative dealt with an instrument or its proceeds on behalf of one who was not the true owner, is not liable in conversion or otherwise to the true owner beyond the amount of any proceeds remaining in his hands.[33] Refusal by the representative to turn over the proceeds still in his possession to the true owner is a conversion of such proceeds. If the representative still has possession of the instrument, he can be compelled to turn it over to the true owner. An intermediary[34] bank, or a payor bank which is not a depositary bank, is not liable in conversion *solely* by reason of the fact that proceeds of an item indorsed restrictively are not paid or applied consistently with the restrictive indorsement of an indorser other than its immediate transferor.[35]

Parties Secondarily Liable

The drawer and indorsers are secondarily liable on an instrument and, therefore, are called "secondary parties."[36] They are liable on a condition and have recourse against parties primarily liable thereon for whatever loss they have sustained on the instrument. Each will be considered briefly.

---

[29] UCC 3–419, *Comment 2.*

[30] UCC 3–419(2).

[31] UCC 4–105(a): " 'Depositary bank' means the first bank to which an item is transferred for collection even though it is also the payor bank."

[32] UCC 4–105(d): " 'Collecting bank' means any bank handling the item for collection except the payor bank."

[33] UCC 3–419(3).

[34] UCC 4–105(c): " 'Intermediary bank' means any bank to which an item is transferred in course of collection except the depositary or payor bank."

[35] See UCC 3–205, 3–206, below, p. 1047; see above, p. 408.

[36] UCC 3–102(1) (d).

Drawer. As a party secondarily liable on the instrument, *the drawer engages that, upon dishonor of the draft and any necessary notice of dishonor or protest, he will pay the amount of the draft to the holder or to any indorser who takes it up.*[37] (D draws a check on E payable to P, who negotiates it to H. On H's presentment of the check to E for payment it is dishonored. D is liable to H as holder of the instrument. If H had recovered from P on his indorsement, D would be liable to P as an indorser.) The drawer may disclaim this liability by drawing the instrument without recourse. *By drawing an instrument, the drawer admits as against all subsequent parties, including the drawee, the existence of the payee and his then capacity to indorse.* It should be noted very carefully that the drawer's liability on the instrument is conditional upon dishonor of the instrument and any necessary notice of dishonor or protest. *Failure* to give necessary notice of dishonor or protest discharges the drawer *from liability on the instrument.* However, as discussed later,[38] unexcused *delay* in giving such notice of dishonor discharges the drawer *only to the extent of loss sustained by him through the drawee's supervening insolvency during the delay.* The drawer, therefore, is estopped to assert against a subsequent party that the purported signature of the payee is not that of the payee because he does not exist, and that the payee was an infant who avoided his indorsement or a foreign corporation which could not contract by its indorsement because it did not comply with state statutes for the regulation of foreign corporations doing business in that state. However, if the drawing of the instrument is void (not voidable) for illegality, the real defense of illegality may be asserted by the drawer against all subsequent parties, including a holder in due course.

Indorser. Every indorser is a party secondarily liable on the instrument and engages that, unless the indorsement otherwise specifies, upon dishonor of the instrument and any necessary notice of dishonor and protest he will pay the instrument according to its tenor at the time of his indorsement to the holder or to any subsequent indorser who takes it up, even though the indorser who takes it up was not obligated to do so. (M issues a note payable to P, who indorses and delivers it to A, who negotiates it to H. The note is dishonored. Since P and A are indorsers and H is the holder, H can recover from A or P, and if H recovers from A then A in turn can recover from P.) It should be noted very carefully that, similar to acceptance of a draft, the indorser conditionally engages

---

[37] UCC 3–413(2).
[38] See below, p. 452.

to pay the instrument *according to its tenor at the time of his indorsement.* If the instrument was altered *prior* to an indorsement, that indorsement applies to the instrument as altered and not to its original tenor. The effect of alteration of the instrument *after* an indorsement is governed by the rules on alteration, previously discussed.[39]

An indorser can disclaim, or qualify, his contractual liability as an indorser on the instrument only by *specifying the disclaimer in the indorsement itself;* the disclaimer cannot be proved by parol evidence. Such an indorsement often is called a "qualified indorsement" because it qualifies the indorser's liability on the instrument. The liability of an unqualified indorser is very different from that of an assignor who merely assigns what he has and is not liable for the value thereof. An indorsement *assigning* the title to the instrument limits the indorser's liability and does not preclude either the further negotiation of the instrument or subsequent holders from being holders in due course. "Without recourse" or words of similar import clearly indicate that the indorser merely assigns the title to the instrument and that no recourse is to be made against the indorser for non-payment of the instrument.[40] Prior to the Code there was conflict but, by the majority view, words of assignment in an indorsement did not qualify the indorsement and were mere surplusage; the intent to qualify an indorser's liability had not been sufficiently expressed. An example is an indorsement, "I hereby assign this instrument." The Code does not seem to have resolved this controversy. Qualified indorsements usually are made by persons acting in a representative capacity, such as attorneys, trustees, and executors, so as to exclude personal liability.

Accommoda-tion Party   An accommodation party is one who signs the instrument in any capacity for the purpose of lending his name to another party to it. He may be an accommodation maker, acceptor, drawer, or indorser. (H will extend credit to P to purchase goods only if M signs a note to pay the price. M issues a note to the order of P, who negotiates it to H. M is an accommodation maker for P. If M had wanted to purchase the goods from H but needed P's signature on the note as security, M's issuance of the note to the order of P, who negotiated it to H, causes P to be an accommodation indorser for M.) An accommodation party is a

---

[39] See above, pp. 432 ff.

[40] "Apart from such a disclaimer all indorsers incur this liability, without regard to whether or not the indorser transferred the instrument for value or received consideration for his indorsement." UCC 3–414, *Comment 1.*

surety for the party accommodated, and his signature is placed on the instrument solely for the purpose of giving additional security to the instrument by subjecting the accommodation party to liability thereon in the event that the instrument should be dishonored. It is immaterial whether or not the accommodating party has received value therefor, i.e., whether he is a paid or a gratuitous surety. It is important, however, that *value be given before the instrument is due*[41] *by the person who took the instrument,* irrespective of whether he gave value before or after the accommodation party signed the instrument. Only when this occurs is the accommodation party liable on the instrument in the capacity that he signed, even though the taker knew of the accommodation. Except as against a holder in due course without notice of the accommodation, parol evidence that a party signed for accommodation is admissible to give the accommodation party the benefit of discharges dependent on his character as such. It should be noted that an indorsement which shows that it is not in the chain of title is notice of its accommodation character. (M issues his note payable to P to pay for goods sold by P to M. The note made and delivered to P has A's blank indorsement on the back. P indorses the note in blank and delivers it to H. P and H are on notice by the first indorsement of A that A is an accommodation indorser for M.)

An accommodation party is not liable to the party accommodated, and if he pays the instrument he has a right of recourse on the instrument against such party. (M is an accommodation maker for P on a note held by H. The note is dishonored and H recovers on it against P. P cannot recover on the note against M, who accommodated P. If H had recovered from M instead of P on the note, M has a right of recourse on the note against P.)[42]

Guarantor The addition of words of guaranty to a signature on an instrument has a meaning and effect varying as such words. If words of guaranty accompany an indorsement, they do not affect its character as an indorsement.[43] When words of guaranty are used, presentment, notice of dishonor and protest are not necessary to charge the user; he has waived them as a

---

[41] Under UCC 3–415, *Comment 3,* the limitation that value must be given before the instrument is due "is one of suretyship law, by which the obligation of the surety is terminated at the time limit unless in the meantime the obligation of the principal has become effective."

[42] M is a surety for P and his right of recourse is based on the rights of reimbursement and subrogation under the law of suretyship, see below, pp. 826 ff, 829 ff.

[43] UCC 3–202(4).

condition to liability on the instrument. Inasmuch as a sole maker or sole acceptor on an instrument is primarily and absolutely liable on the instrument, words of guaranty added to the signature of either do not affect his liability thereon. However, words of guaranty added to the signature of one of two or more makers or acceptors create a presumption that the signature is for the accommodation of others. When words of guaranty accompanying a signature do not otherwise specify (e.g., "Guaranteed"), they guarantee payment of the instrument. A guaranty of payment, e.g., "payment guaranteed" or equivalent words, added to a signature means that the signer engages that if the instrument is not paid when due he will pay it according to its tenor without resort by the holder to any other party. But a guaranty of collection, e.g., "collection guaranteed" or equivalent words, added to a signature means that the signer engages that, if the instrument is not paid when due, he will pay it according to its tenor only: (1) after the holder has reduced his claim against the maker or acceptor to judgment and execution has been returned unsatisfied; or (2) after the maker or acceptor has become insolvent or it is otherwise apparent that it is useless to proceed against him. Any guaranty written on the instrument is enforceable notwithstanding any statute of frauds.[44]

3. WARRANTIES ON PRESENTMENT AND TRANSFER OF AN INSTRUMENT

The Code provides for warranties in connection with commercial paper and distinguishes warranties on transfer of an instrument from warranties on presentment resulting in payment or acceptance of an instrument. These warranties will be considered in that order after a brief examination of principles applicable to all of these warranties.

In General　　Initially it should be observed that these warranties are important to all parties who have dealt with the instrument. The warranties are concerned with: title to the instrument; the genuineness of signatures and authority to sign for another; material alteration; and defenses to liability on the instrument. Some of these warranties are applicable to parties who have transferred the instrument merely by delivery without their signature

---

[44] The reason for this is that, while some statutes require the written proof of the guaranty to state the consideration for the promise of guaranty, generally they are not held applicable to a written guaranty on a negotiable instrument because it is unusual for such a guaranty to state the consideration therefor.

appearing thereon, e.g., the transfer of a bearer instrument. Unless disclaimer of warranty is prohibited by law, warranties may be disclaimed by the parties to a transaction. Under the law on commercial paper, the warranties imposed by the Code may be disclaimed by the immediate parties as between themselves, e.g., the payee orally disclaiming warranties to the maker on taking the maker's note from him; but a disclaimer of warranties by an indorser is ineffective unless the words of disclaimer *specifically* accompany, or appear in the form of, his indorsement on the instrument. For example, the payee's indorsement on a note "Without recourse. (signed) John Jones" is effective to disclaim certain warranties which the payee would otherwise be held to as an indorser of the instrument. When there is reliance in good faith on a warranty, various remedies become available for breach of warranty, e.g., rescission of the transaction and an action for damages. Lastly, the liability on these warranties of a selling agent or broker (but not an agent for collection), representing another, who transfers an instrument or obtains payment or acceptance of it depends upon whether or not he has disclosed his status. If he has, he warrants only his good faith and authority; if he has not, the warranties apply to him.

Warranties on Transfer

In General. The warranties on transfer are *in addition* to contractual liability on the instrument, previously discussed.[45] It may be that a holder may prefer to rescind or bring action immediately for breach of contract rather than wait until the instrument becomes due and then assert his rights against parties secondarily liable on the instrument. Or, if the holder is unable to enforce such secondary liability, as by his having failed to comply with the requisites of presentment, notice of dishonor or protest, or because of a qualified indorsement or lack of an indorsement, the remedies for breach of warranty are his only source of relief.

Unless otherwise properly disclaimed, there are five warranties (discussed below) given by *any* person who *transfers* an instrument and *receives consideration.* It should be noted carefully that the transferor's warranty must be supported by consideration, which may be consideration sufficient to support a simple contract or an antecedent obligation of any kind.[46] Also, the transfer may be by negotiation or by assignment. *If the transfer is by indorsement,* the transferor makes these warranties

---

[45] See above, pp. 434–42.
[46] UCC 3–408; also above, p. 412.

to his *immediate transferee* and to any subsequent *holder* who takes the instrument *in good faith. If the transfer is without indorsement,* the transferor makes these warranties *only to his immediate transferee.* (M makes a note payable to P and delivers it to P. P indorses it in blank and delivers it to A, who indorses it in blank and delivers it to B, who delivers it without indorsement to C, who delivers it without indorsement to H, who takes it in good faith. P's warranties are to A, B, C, and H. A's warranties are to B, C, and H. B's warranties are only to C, and C's warranties are only to H.)

Warranty of Title or Authority. *The transferor of an instrument for consideration received warrants that (1) he has good title to the instrument or is authorized to obtain payment or acceptance on behalf of one who has a good title, and (2) the transfer is otherwise rightful.* A transferee expects to acquire a good title to the instrument from his transferor, safe against the claim of any true owner and, when he presents the instrument for payment or is paid, safe against any defense that he lacks good title and will not be paid or a claim that he must refund the money. The transfer of an instrument with a forged required indorsement in the chain of title precludes any subsequent transferee from acquiring title to the instrument and, therefore, there is a breach of warranty of title by the transferor. It should be noted that the transferor of a bearer instrument found or stolen by him is the bearer but he does not have title, and while his transfer of the instrument to a holder in due course is a breach of warranty of title, nevertheless the holder in due course does acquire title. The holder in due course may wish to rescind the transfer rather than risk the inconvenience of having to sue to enforce the instrument, or defending against a claim to the instrument, and establishing that he is a holder in due course in order to overcome the claim or defense.

Warranty of Signatures as Genuine or Authorized. *The transferor of an instrument for consideration received warrants that all signatures are genuine or authorized.* "Genuine" means free of forgery or counterfeiting.[47] An "unauthorized" signature means one made without actual, implied, or apparent authority, and includes a forgery.[48] The transfer of an instrument with a forged required signature in the chain of title is a breach of warranty of genuine signature and also a breach of warranty of title. A transferee expects to acquire not only title to the instrument but also freedom from concern that he may not be able to

---

[47] UCC 1–201(18).
[48] UCC 1–201(43).

hold a purported party on the instrument secondarily liable, and that he may become liable for breach of warranty of genuine signature if he transfers the instrument to his transferee.

Warranty against Material Alteration. *The transferor of an instrument for consideration received warrants that the instrument has not been materially altered.* A transferee expects to acquire an instrument without a material alteration thereon, which would either limit the liability of previous parties on the instrument who became such prior to such alteration or discharge them entirely.

Warranty of No Good Defense. *The transferor of an instrument for consideration received warrants that no defense of any party is good against him.* A transferee expects to acquire an instrument capable of being enforced. While this warranty may be breached and, nevertheless, the transferee become a holder in due course so that personal defenses are cut off against him as a holder in due course, he may not wish to take on a lawsuit in order to enforce the instrument and have to establish his status as a holder in due course. It should be noted very carefully that a transfer "without recourse" changes this warranty of the transferor to be a warranty that he has *no knowledge* of any defense of any party good against him. As previously discussed,[49] the words "without recourse" in an indorsement also effectively disclaim the *contractual* obligation of that indorser on the instrument.

Warranty of No Knowledge of Insolvency Proceedings. *The transferor of an instrument for consideration received warrants that he has no knowledge of any insolvency proceeding instituted with respect to the maker, acceptor, or the drawer of an unaccepted instrument.* The transferor of an instrument does not warrant the credit risk or solvency of any party on the instrument; this is a matter for the buyer of the instrument to determine for himself. However, the Code imposes a duty upon a transferor of an instrument who knows that such insolvency proceedings have been instituted to disclose this information to his transferee prior to such transfer. The transferor's concealment of this very important fact is a fraud on the transferee buyer. A transferee of an instrument expects to acquire an instrument which will be paid when due. The institution of insolvency proceedings against one of the parties expected to pay the instrument puts such payment in jeopardy; also, should the transferee in turn transfer the instrument, there is a greater risk that he may be held to his secondary liability on the instrument if dishonored.

---

[49] See above, p. 441.

Warranties on Obtaining Payment or Acceptance

We have already observed[50] that, with two exceptions, *payment or acceptance of an instrument is final in favor of a holder in due course* (or a transferee with rights of a holder in due course), *or a person who has in good faith changed his position in reliance on the payment.* The two exceptions are concerned with recovery of bank payments under Article 4 of the Code on Bank Deposits and Collections[51] and with liability for breach of *warranty on presentment* for payment or acceptance, now about to be discussed.

When an instrument is presented for payment or acceptance, the person who obtains payment or acceptance, and any prior transferor, makes three warranties. If any of these warranties is breached, the payment or acceptance is not final and the payment may be recovered or the acceptance rescinded. These warranties are: warranty of title or authority to obtain payment or acceptance; warranty of no knowledge of unauthorized signature of maker or drawer; warranty of no material alteration. It is expected that the person presenting an instrument for payment or acceptance does so in good faith that he is the owner of the instrument, that he has no knowledge that the signature of the maker or drawer is unauthorized, and that the instrument has not been materially altered. The holder in due course so acts and, because of his superior status, these warranties are applicable to him to a very limited extent. These warranties are imposed upon any person who obtained payment or acceptance, and any prior transferor, for the benefit of the person who *in good faith* paid or accepted. If payment or acceptance was not made in good faith, they were made without reliance on the presentment as being in good faith and, therefore, there is no breach of these warranties.

Warranty of Title or Authority. *Only the person with good title to the instrument, or his authorized representative, has the right to obtain payment or acceptance of the instrument.* While the drawee can verify the drawer's signature by comparing the drawer's signature on the instrument with that in his records, the drawee usually has no opportunity to verify the *indorsements* on the instrument. It is for this reason that the party who pays or accepts an instrument does not thereby admit the genuineness of the indorsements thereon and, if they are not genuine, can recover the money paid to the person presenting

---

[50] See above, p. 437.
[51] See UCC 4-301 and 4-213.

the instrument or rescind his acceptance. The party who presented the instrument did not have good title. *In effect, therefore, this warranty by the presenting party includes the genuineness of the required indorsements.* (D drew a check on E bank payable to the order of P. A stole the check from P, forged P's blank indorsement and delivered it for value to H who took the check in good faith. H presented the check to E, who paid it in good faith. H has breached his warranty of title, E may recover the money from H, who does not have good title to the instrument, and D is still liable to P, the owner of the check even though P does not have possession of the check. If, before E had demanded repayment or attempted to rescind his acceptance, H had meanwhile, in good faith, changed his position in reliance on the payment, under the rule of finality of payment E could not recover the money from H.)

Warranty of No Knowledge of Unauthorized Signature of Maker or Drawer. Any person who obtains payment or acceptance, and any prior transferor, warrants to a person who in good faith pays or accepts that he has *no knowledge that the signature of the maker or drawer is unauthorized,* with certain limitations as to a holder in due course. It should be noted that in the warranty of title or authority the warranty included that *all required indorsements were genuine,* while this warranty is that the presenting party has *no knowledge* that the signature of the maker or drawer is unauthorized and not genuine.

A holder in due course had no notice of any defense to the instrument *at the time he took the instrument as a holder,* but he may learn of the unauthorized signature of the maker or drawer of the instrument *thereafter and before presenting the instrument for payment or acceptance.* If this should occur, since he has not acted in good faith the warranty should apply to him and the maker recover the money or the acceptor rescind his acceptance. However, if this did not occur, then the warranty should not apply to him and recovery be denied the maker or rescission be denied the acceptor. The reason for this result is that the maker ought to recognize his own signature, and the drawee is in a superior position to verify the drawer's signature with a copy in his possession. If payment or acceptance is made mistakenly by them, as between them and the holder in due course who acted *in good faith,* they must bear the loss. Thus, the Code provides:

> . . . except that this warranty is not given by a holder in due course acting *in good faith*
>> (i) to a maker with respect to the maker's own signature; or
>> (ii) to a drawer with respect to the drawer's own signature, whether or not the drawer is also the drawee; or

(iii) to an acceptor of a draft if the holder in due course took the draft after the acceptance or obtained the acceptance without knowledge that the drawer's signature was unauthorized; . . .
(Author's italics)[52]

Warranty of No Material Alteration. Any person who obtains payment or acceptance, and any prior transferor, warrants to a person who in good faith pays or accepts that *the instrument has not been materially altered,* with certain limitations as to a holder in due course. The paying or accepting party is not obliged to be contractually liable for other than the tenor of the instrument as originally drawn and can recover money paid or rescind an acceptance for more than that amount on a materially altered instrument, except as to a holder in due course of an instrument materially altered *by unauthorized completion.*[53]

A holder in due course had no notice of any defense to the instrument *at the time he took the instrument as a holder,* but he may learn of the material alteration *thereafter and before presenting the instrument for payment.* If the holder in due course *in good faith* presents the materially altered instrument for payment or acceptance, and payment or acceptance is given, the warranty should not apply to him, and such payment cannot be recovered and the acceptance cannot be rescinded. If the instrument is a draft and if the holder in due course took the *previously* materially altered draft *after* the acceptance, the warranty should not apply to him even though the acceptance provided "payable as originally drawn" or equivalent terms. If legal effect were given to such words in the acceptance, they would defeat the entire purpose of making an acceptance, which is to obtain a definite obligation of the drawee to honor a definite instrument.[54] If the draft was materially altered *after* acceptance and the holder in due course *in good faith* presented it for payment, the warranty should not apply to him, and the acceptor should be denied recovery of the money. The acceptor can easily verify the accuracy of the draft as accepted with information in his possession. Thus, the Code provides:

. . . except that this warranty is not given by a holder in due course acting *in good faith*
(i) to the maker of a note; or
(ii) to the drawer of a draft whether or not the drawer is also the drawee; or
(iii) to the acceptor of a draft with respect to an alteration made prior to

---

[52] UCC 3–417(1)(b).

[53] See above, p. 433.

[54] UCC 3–417, *Comment 5.*

the acceptance if the holder in due course took the draft after the acceptance, even though the acceptance provided "payable as originally drawn" or equivalent terms; or

(iv) to the acceptor of a draft with respect to an alteration made after the acceptance.

(Author's italics)[55]

---

[55] UCC 3–417(1) (c).

Chapter VI

PRESENTMENT, NOTICE OF DISHONOR, AND PROTEST

---

1. *REQUIREMENTS AND LEGAL EFFECT*

Purpose   PRESENTMENT is *a demand for acceptance or payment* made upon the maker, acceptor, drawee or other payor by, or on behalf of, the holder. Presentment is *not* necessary in order to fix the liability of the *maker or acceptor as a party primarily liable* on the instrument; his absolute contractual obligation is to pay the instrument according to its tenor.[1] However, the contractual obligation of the *drawer and indorser as secondary parties* on an instrument is that *upon dishonor and any necessary notice of dishonor and protest* he will pay the instrument to the holder or to any subsequent indorser who takes it up. It becomes important, therefore, whether presentment for acceptance or payment, notice of dishonor, and protest are necessary in order to charge secondary parties, i.e., hold them liable on the instrument. First we will consider when presentment for acceptance and payment, notice of dishonor, and protest are necessary; then, in order, the elements of presentment for acceptance and payment, notice of dishonor, protest, evidence of dishonor, and notice of dishonor, and finally when presentment, notice of dishonor, and protest are waived or excused.

When   Presentment, notice of dishonor, and protest are
Necessary necessary in certain instances and not in others. When they are not necessary, the secondary parties remain liable on the instrument for the statute of limitations period, just as do primary parties. Presentment, notice of dishonor, and protest are not necessary in order to charge an indorser who has indorsed an instrument after maturity.

---

[1] UCC 3–122(2) makes an exception and *requires* demand by presentment of a *demand or time certificate of deposit* on or after the date of maturity in order for a cause of action to accrue against the obligor thereon at the time of such demand.

Presentment for Acceptance or Payment. *Presentment for Acceptance.* Unless excused,[2] presentment for acceptance is *necessary* in order to charge the drawer and indorsers of a *draft* where the draft: (1) so provides; or (2) is payable elsewhere than at the residence or place of business of the drawee; or (3) its place of payment depends upon such presentment, e.g., a draft payable after sight. A holder *may*, at his option, present for acceptance *any other* draft payable at a stated date.

Presentment for Payment. Unless excused,[3] presentment for payment is *necessary* in order to charge: (1) any indorser; (2) any drawer; (3) the acceptor of a draft payable *at a bank;* (4) the maker of a note payable *at a bank.* Presentment for payment is *not necessary* in order to charge an acceptor of a draft or maker of a note payable other than at a bank.

Failure to Present when Necessary. Where, without excuse, any necessary presentment is delayed beyond the time when it is due, the following parties are discharged fully, with one limitation: (1) any indorsers; (2) any drawer; (3) the acceptor of a draft payable at a bank; (4) the maker of a note payable at a bank. The limitation applies to the last three parties, each of whom is discharged *only to the extent that he has been deprived of funds if:* (1) he maintained with the drawee or payor bank sufficient funds to cover payment of the instrument; (2) the drawee or payor bank became insolvent during the delay causing the party to be deprived of such funds; *and* (3) the party makes a written assignment to the holder of his rights against the drawee or payor bank in respect of such funds. The holder's delay caused such loss of funds, and the party is discharged, but only to the extent of such loss.

Notice of Dishonor. Unless excused,[4] notice of dishonor is *necessary* in order to charge: (1) any indorser; (2) any drawer; (3) the acceptor of a draft payable *at a bank;* or (4) a maker of a note payable *at a bank.* Where, without excuse, any necessary notice of dishonor is delayed beyond the time when it is due, any indorser is discharged fully; and the drawer, the acceptor of a draft payable at a bank, and the maker of a note payable at a bank are discharged *only to the extent of the deprived funds as indicated in the preceding paragraph.*

---

[2] See below, p. 462.

[3] *Ibid.*

[4] *Ibid.*

Protect. Unless excused,[5] protest of any dishonor is *necessary* in order to charge the drawer and indorsers of any draft which *on its face* appears to be *drawn or payable outside of the states and territories of the United States and the District of Columbia.* This is an "international" or "foreign" draft and, because protest of any dishonor of such a draft is generally required by foreign law, the necessity of protest under the Code is retained. For his convenience, a holder *may,* at his option, make protest of any dishonor of *any other* instrument and, in the case of a foreign draft, may on insolvency of the acceptor before maturity make protest for better security.[6] Where, without excuse, a necessary protest is delayed beyond the time when it is due, any drawer or indorser is *completely discharged.*

Presentment

Time When Made. If the instrument states a time when presentment is to be made, that time governs. The times for presentment for acceptance and payment differ.

Presentment for Acceptance. Unless a different time is expressed in the instrument, the time for presentment for acceptance is determined as follows:

1. *Instrument payable at, or a fixed period after, a stated date.* Any presentment for acceptance must be made on or before the date it is payable.
2. *Instrument payable after sight.* It must either be presented for acceptance or negotiated within a reasonable time after date, or issue, whichever is later.
3. *Any other instrument.* With respect to the liability of any *secondary party,* presentment for acceptance is due within a reasonable time after such party becomes liable thereon.

Presentment for Payment. Unless a different time is expressed in the instrument, the time for presentment for payment is determined as follows:

1. *Instrument payable at stated date.* Presentment for payment is due on that date.
2. *Accelerated instrument.* Presentment for payment is due within a reasonable time after the acceleration.
3. *Any other instrument.* With respect to the liability of any *secondary party,* presentment for payment is due within a reasonable time after such party becomes liable thereon.[7]

---

[5] *Ibid.*

[6] UCC 3–501(3).

[7] See UCC 3–503(1).

Reasonable Time. A reasonable time for presentment is determined by the nature of the instrument, any usage of banking or trade, and the facts of the particular case. If the instrument is an *uncertified check which is drawn and payable within the United States and which is not a draft drawn by a bank,* the following are presumed to be reasonable periods within which to present for payment or to initiate bank collection:

1. With respect to the liability of the *drawer, 30 days after date, or issue, whichever is later.*
2. With respect to the liability of an *indorser, seven days after his indorsement.*

The drawer's liability is for a reasonably longer time than that of an indorser. "The drawer, who has himself issued the check and normally expects to have it paid and charged to his account, is reasonably required to stand behind it for a longer period, especially in view of the protection now provided by Federal Deposit Insurance. The thirty days specified coincides with the time after which a purchaser has notice that a check has become stale. . . ."[8] The indorser, who has normally merely received the check and passed it on, and does not expect to have to pay it, is entitled to know more promptly whether it is to be dishonored, in order that he may have recourse against the person with whom he has dealt."[9]

Time of Day and Day. Presentment to be sufficient must be made at a reasonable hour and, if at a bank, during its banking day. Where any presentment is due on a day which is not a full business day for either the person making presentment or the party to pay or accept, presentment is due on the next following day that is a full business day for both parties.

How Made. *The Demand.* Presentment is a *demand* for payment or acceptance. The demand itself is presentment, and the instrument *need not be exhibited,* although the party to whom presentment is made may properly require its exhibition. A demand is made *by,* or on behalf *of,* the holder. Presentment may be made *to:* (1) any one of two or more makers, acceptors, drawees, or other payors, irrespective of whether or not they are partners or one has authority to act for the other; or (2) any person who has authority to make or refuse the acceptance or payment.

---

[8] See above, p. 416, in connection with notice to a purchaser that an instrument is overdue, precluding him from becoming a holder in due course.

[9] UCC 3–503, *Comment 3.*

Method and Place.[10] Presentment may be made in the following ways and places:

1. By mail, in which event the time of presentment is determined by the time of receipt of the mail.
2. Through a clearing house, in which event the time of presentment is the time when it reaches the obligor.
3. At the place of acceptance or payment specified in the instrument, or if there be none at the place of business or residence of the party to accept or pay. If neither the party to accept or pay, nor anyone authorized to act for him, is present or accessible at such place, presentment is excused.

A draft accepted, or a note made payable, at a bank in the United States *must* be presented at such bank.

Rights of Party to Whom Presentment Made. Presentment is merely a demand for acceptance or payment. While refusal of the demand dishonors the instrument, nevertheless the party to whom presentment is made has the right to protect himself from making improper payment or acceptance by making reasonable demands upon the presenting party without thereby dishonoring the instrument. The Code[11] permits him to require the presenting party: to exhibit the instrument; reasonably to identify himself and prove his authority if he is acting for another; to produce the instrument at the proper place, which is that specified in the instrument or, if not so specified, at any place reasonable under the circumstances;[12] to sign a receipt on the instrument for partial or full payment; to surrender the instrument if full payment is made. The party to whom presentment is made must not demand more than is permitted by the Code nor be unreasonable in connection with any permitted demand. For example, if he knows the presenting party, it would be unreasonable for him to require identification by the presenting party. If the demand by the party to whom

---

[10] UCC 4–210. **"Presentment by Notice of Item Not Payable by, Through or at a Bank; Liability of Secondary Parties.** (1) Unless otherwise instructed, a collecting bank may present an item not payable by, through or at a bank by sending to the party to accept or pay a written notice that the bank holds the item for acceptance or payment. The notice must be sent in time to be received on or before the day when presentment is due and the bank must meet any requirement of the party to accept or pay under Section 3–505 by the close of the bank's next banking day after it knows of the requirement.

"(2) Where presentment is made by notice and neither honor nor request for compliance with a requirement under Section 3–505 is received by the close of business on the day after maturity or in the case of demand items by the close of business on the third banking day after notice was sent, the presenting bank may treat the item as dishonored and charge any secondary party by sending him notice of the facts."

[11] UCC 3–505.

[12] UCC 4–204(3): "Presentment may be made by a presenting bank at a place where the payor bank has requested that presentment be made."

presentment has been made is unreasonable, the instrument is thereby dishonored. The presenting party's failure to comply with a reasonable demand invalidates the presentment. However, the time for presentment is extended for a reasonable time in which the presenting party may comply with the demand. The time for acceptance or payment runs from the time of such compliance. If the presenting party should fail to comply with the demand within a reasonable time, the effect is as though a presentment had never been made.

Time Allowed for Acceptance or Payment. The party to whom presentment is made must act promptly in deciding whether or not to accept or pay the instrument. The short times allowed for acceptance and payment differ. *If the instrument is presented for acceptance,* the party to whom presentment is made may, without dishonor, defer acceptance until the close of the next business day following presentment. The holder also may, in a good faith effort to obtain acceptance and without either dishonor of the instrument or discharge of secondary parties, allow postponement of acceptance for an additional business day. *If the instrument is presented for payment,* payment of the instrument may be deferred without dishonor pending reasonable examination to determine whether it is properly payable; but, with two exceptions, payment must be made in any event before the close of business on the day of presentment. The first exception is that payment may be made at any earlier time if agreed to by the party to pay. Under the second exception, a longer time may be allowed for payment in the case of documentary drafts[13] drawn under a letter of credit.[14]

---

[13] UCC 4-104(1)(f): " 'Documentary draft' means any negotiable or non-negotiable draft with accompanying documents, securities or other papers to be delivered against honor of the draft."

[14] UCC 5-112. **"Time Allowed for Honor or Rejection; Withholding Honor or Rejection by Consent; 'Presenter.'** (1) A bank to which a documentary draft or demand for payment is presented under a credit may without dishonor of the draft, demand or credit

(a) defer honor until the close of the third banking day following receipt of the documents; and

(b) further defer honor if the presenter has expressly or impliedly consented thereto. Failure to honor within the time here specified constitutes dishonor of the draft or demand and of the credit [except as otherwise provided in subsection (4) of Section 5-114 on conditional payment].

"Note: *The bracketed language in the last sentence of subsection (1) should be included only if the optional provisions of Section 5-114(4) and (5) are included.*

"(2) Upon dishonor the bank may unless otherwise instructed fulfill its duty to return the draft or demand and the documents by holding them at the disposal of the presenter and sending him an advice to that effect.

"(3) 'Presenter' means any person presenting a draft or demand for payment for honor under a credit even though that person is a confirming bank or other correspondent which is acting under an issuer's authorization."

UCC 5-114: "[(4) When a credit provides for payment by the issuer on receipt of

Dishonor. Dishonor of an instrument may occur when presentment is necessary or optional, or when presentment is excused. *When a necessary or optional presentment is duly made,* the instrument is dishonored if: due acceptance or payment is refused or cannot be obtained within the prescribed time; or, in the case of bank collections, the instrument is seasonably returned by the midnight deadline.[15] *When*

notice that the required documents are in the possession of a correspondent or other agent of the issuer

(a) any payment made on receipt of such notice is conditional; and

(b) the issuer may reject documents which do not comply with the credit if it does so within three banking days following its receipt of the documents; and

(c) in the event of such rejection, the issuer is entitled by charge back or otherwise to return of the payment made.]

[(5) In the case covered by subsection (4) failure to reject documents within the time specified in sub-paragraph (b) constitutes acceptance of the documents and makes the payment final in favor of the beneficiary.]

"**Note:** *Subsections (4) and (5) are bracketed as optional. If they are included the bracketed language in the last sentence of Section 5-112(1) should also be included.*"

[15] UCC 4-301. "**Deferred Posting; Recovery of Payment by Return of Items; Time of Dishonor.** (1) Where an authorized settlement for a demand item (other than a documentary draft) received by a payor bank otherwise than for immediate payment over the counter has been made before midnight of the banking day of receipt the payor bank may revoke the settlement and recover any payment if before it has made final payment (subsection (1) of Section 4-213) and before its midnight deadline it

(a) returns the item; or

(b) sends written notice of dishonor or nonpayment if the item is held for protest or is otherwise unavailable for return.

"(2) If a demand item is received by a payor bank for credit on its books it may return such item or send notice of dishonor and may revoke any credit given or recover the amount thereof withdrawn by its customer, if it acts within the time limit and in the manner specified in the preceding subsection.

"(3) Unless previous notice of dishonor has been sent an item is dishonored at the time when for purposes of dishonor it is returned or notice sent in accordance with this section.

"(4) An item is returned:

(a) as to an item received through a clearing house, when it is delivered to the presenting or last collecting bank or to the clearing house or is sent or delivered in accordance with its rules; or

(b) in all other cases, when it is sent or delivered to the bank's customer or transferor or pursuant to his instructions.

UCC 4-302. "**Payor Bank's Responsibility for Late Return of Item.** In the absence of a valid defense such as breach of a presentment warranty (subsection (1) of Section 4-207), settlement effected or the like, if an item is presented on and received by a payor bank the bank is accountable for the amount of

(a) a demand item other than a documentary draft whether properly payable or not if the bank, in any case where it is not also the depositary bank, retains the item beyond midnight of the banking day of receipt without settling for it or, regardless of whether it is also the depositary bank, does not pay or return the item or send notice of dishonor until after its midnight deadline; or

(b) any other properly payable item unless within the time allowed for acceptance or payment of that item the bank either accepts or pays the item or returns it and accompanying documents."

UCC 4-213: "(1) An item is finally paid by a payor bank when the bank has done any of the following, whichever happens first:

(a) paid the item in cash; or

presentment is excused,[16] the instrument is dishonored if it is not duly accepted or paid. The return of an instrument for lack of proper indorsement is not a dishonor.

We have seen previously[17] that a bank may certify a check before returning it for lack of a proper indorsement; by doing so, the drawer is discharged. A draft or an indorsement thereon may provide a stated time within which re-presentment of the instrument may be made in the event the draft is dishonored by non-acceptance if a time draft or by non-payment if a sight draft. The holder of a draft with such a provision may, at his option, waive the dishonor and present it again within the stated time without affecting the liability of any secondary party who is bound by the provision.

We have seen[18] that the contractual obligations of a drawer of a draft and, unless the indorsement otherwise specifies, of every indorser on an instrument is that, upon dishonor of the instrument and any necessary notice of dishonor and protest, he will pay the amount of the instrument to the holder or to any subsequent indorser who takes it up. Thus on dishonor of an instrument and subject to any necessary notice of dishonor and protest,[19] the holder has an immediate right of recourse against the drawer and indorsers. It should be recalled that, as previously discussed,[20] a cause of action against a drawer of a draft or an indorser of any instrument accrues *upon demand* following dishonor of the instrument. *Notice of dishonor is a demand.*

Notice of Dishonor

By Whom. Usually notice of dishonor is given by the holder or by an indorser who has himself received notice. Notice of dishonor may be given by any party who may be compelled to pay the instrument to any party who may be liable on the instrument. Thus, notice

---

(b) settled for the item without reserving a right to revoke the settlement and without having such right under statute, clearing house rule or agreement; or

(c) completed the process of posting the item to the indicated account of the drawer, maker or other person to be charged therewith; or

(d) made a provisional settlement for the item and failed to revoke the settlement in the time and manner permitted by statute, clearing house rule or agreement.

Upon a final payment under subparagraphs (b), (c), or (d) the payor bank shall be accountable for the amount of the item."

[16] See below, p. 462.

[17] See above, p. 436.

[18] See above, p. 440.

[19] See above, pp. 452–53.

[20] See above, p. 400.

may be given by, or on behalf of, the holder or any party who has himself received notice. In addition, an agent or bank in whose hands the instrument is dishonored may give notice to his principal or customer or to another agent or bank from which the instrument was received. Notice operates for the benefit of all parties who have rights on the instrument against the party notified. Thus, it is sufficient if a party is notified of dishonor *once;* his liability is fixed and so he need not receive additional notice. (D draws a check on E payable to P and delivers it to P, who indorses it in blank and delivers it to A. A indorses it in blank and delivers it to B, who indorses it in blank and delivers it to H. H presents it to E for payment, and it is dishonored. H gives notice of dishonor to B, A, P, and D. It is not necessary for B to give A, P, and D notice again. Their liability is fixed as secondary parties by H's previous notice of dishonor.)

Time. Any necessary notice given by a person other than a bank must be given *before midnight of the third business day after dishonor or receipt of notice of dishonor.* (The drawer of a check is D, and the indorsers in order are P and A. H is the holder. On dishonor, H gives A notice of dishonor. A must give notice of dishonor to P and D before midnight of the third business day after *he* received notice of dishonor from H. If A gives notice of dishonor only to P, P in turn must give notice of dishonor to D before midnight on the third business day after *he* received notice of dishonor from A.) A bank must give any necessary notice of dishonor before its midnight deadline.

Method. Notice may be given in any reasonable manner. It may be oral or written and in any terms which identify the instrument and state that it has been dishonored. A misdescription which does not mislead the party notified does not cause the notice to be insufficient. Sending the instrument bearing a stamp, ticket, or writing stating that acceptance or payment has been refused, or sending a notice of debit with respect to the instrument, is sufficient. Written notice is given when *sent,* although it may not be received.

To Whom. We have just observed that an agent or bank in whose hands the instrument is dishonored may give notice of dishonor as indicated. Notice to one partner is notice to each partner, although the firm may have been dissolved. When any party is in insolvency proceedings instituted after the issue of the instrument, notice may be given either to the party or to the representative of his estate. When any party is dead or incompetent, notice may be sent to his last-known address or given to his personal representative.

Protest

Protest of dishonor is necessary only for a draft which, *on its face,* appears to be drawn or payable outside of the states and territories of the United States and the District of Columbia. Such a draft is sometimes called a "foreign" or "international" draft.[21] Unless excused,[22] protest of any dishonor is necessary in order to charge the drawer and indorsers of such a draft. The purpose of protest is to preserve proof of presentment and dishonor in a form recognized and given credence universally. Protest is required *in addition* to presentment, dishonor, and notice of dishonor as a condition precedent to the exercise of the holder's right of recourse against the drawer and indorsers.

A protest is a certificate of dishonor made under the hand and seal of a United States consul or by a vice-consul or a notary public or other person authorized to certify dishonor by the law of the place where dishonor occurs. It may be made upon information satisfactory to such person, and he need not certify as to his own knowledge. The protest need not be in any particular form, but it must: (1) identify the instrument; (2) certify either that due presentment has been made or the reason why it is excused; and (3) certify that the instrument has been dishonored by non-acceptance or non-payment. The protest need not be annexed to the instrument, and it may be forwarded separately.

---

[21] The Code clarifies the status of a "letter of advice" in connection with international sight drafts. "1. Checks drawn by one international bank on the account it carries (in a currency foreign to itself) in another international bank are still handled under practices which reflect older conditions, but which have a real, continuing reason in the typical European rule that a bank paying a check in good faith and in ordinary course can charge its depositor's account notwithstanding forgery of a necessary indorsement. To decrease the risk that forgery will prove successful, the practice is to send a letter of advice that a draft has been drawn and will be forthcoming. Subsection 3 recognizes that a drawer who sends no such letter forfeits any rights for improper dishonor, while still permitting the drawee to protect his delinquent drawer's credit.

"2. Subsection (2) clears up for American courts, the meaning of another international practice: that of charging the drawer's account on credit of the letter of advice. This practice involves no conception of trust or the like and the rule of Section 3–409(1) (Draft not an assignment) still applies. *The debit has to do with the payment of interest only.* The section recognizes the fact." UCC 3–701, *Comments 1, 2.* (Author's italics)

UCC 3–701. **"Letter of Advice of International Sight Draft.** (1) A 'letter of advice' is a drawer's communication to the drawee that a described draft has been drawn.

"(2) Unless otherwise agreed when a bank receives from another bank a letter of advice of an international sight draft the drawee bank may immediately debit the drawer's account and stop the running of interest pro tanto. Such a debit and any resulting credit to any account covering outstanding drafts leaves in the drawer full power to stop payment or otherwise dispose of the amount and creates no trust or interest in favor of the holder.

"(3) Unless otherwise agreed and except where a draft is drawn under a credit issued by the drawee, the drawee of an international sight draft owes the drawer no duty to pay an unadvised draft but if it does so and the draft is genuine, may appropriately debit the drawer's account."

[22] See below, p. 462.

Protest usually certifies, although it is not required to do so, that notice of dishonor has been given to all parties or to specified parties. Usually, protest is forwarded together with the notice of dishonor and, with one exception, necessary protest is due at the time that notice of dishonor is due. Under the exception, if, before protest is due, an instrument has been noted for protest by the officer to make protest, the protest may be made at any time thereafter as of the date of the noting. It should be observed that, where protest is not necessary but merely optional with the holder, it may be made at any time before it is used as evidence.[23]

Evidence of Dishonor and Notice of Dishonor

There are three kinds of evidence which are admissible to prove dishonor and notice of dishonor. Each kind creates a presumption of dishonor and notice of dishonor if shown therein. The obligor can overcome the presumption by evidence that dishonor did not occur, that notice of dishonor was not given, and that protest is not valid. The first kind of evidence is the protest itself; it is authentic. The second kind of evidence is the purported stamp or writing of the drawee, payor bank or presenting bank on the instrument or accompanying it stating that acceptance or payment has been refused for reasons consistent with dishonor. The following reasons are satisfactory evidence of dishonor: "Not sufficient funds"; "Account garnished"; "No account"; "Payment stopped."[24] The third kind of evidence is any book or record of the drawee, payor bank, or any collecting bank kept in the usual course of business which shows dishonor, even though there is no evidence of who made the entry.

Waiver and Excuse

Under certain circumstances *delay* in presentment, notice of dishonor, or protest is *excused,* and in other circumstances presentment, notice of dishonor, or protest are *entirely excused.* In some instances they are *waived.* First their waiver will be considered and then their excuse.

Waiver. Where a waiver of presentment or notice of dishonor or protest is embodied in the instrument itself, it is binding on all parties; but where it is written above the signature of an indorser it binds him only. *A waiver of protest is also a waiver of presentment and of notice of dishonor,* even though the protest is not required, e.g., "protest waived" on an instrument.

---

[23] UCC 3–509, *Comments 4, 5, 7.*
[24] UCC 3–510, *Comment 2.*

Excuse. *Delay Excused.* *Delay* in making presentment, notice of dishonor, or protest is excused when the party to make it is without notice that the instrument is due, or the delay is caused by circumstances beyond his control and he exercises reasonable diligence after the cause of the delay ceases to operate. Illustrations are where the instrument has been accelerated without his knowledge, or demand has been made by a prior holder immediately before his purchase.[25]

Entirely Excused. *Presentment or notice of dishonor or protest,* as the case may be, *is entirely excused* under the following circumstances:

1. The party to be charged has expressly or impliedly waived presentment or notice of dishonor or protest. The waiver may be oral or in writing and may be made either before or after it is due.
2. The party to be charged has no reason to expect, or right to require, that the instrument be accepted or paid. Illustrations are: he himself has dishonored the instrument, or countermanded payment as by a stop order on the drawee bank on a check; the drawee of a check has no funds or insufficient funds of the drawer party to be charged.
3. Presentment or protest cannot be made or notice of dishonor given by the exercise of reasonable diligence. For example, after the exercise of reasonable diligence presentment for payment cannot be made because the maker's whereabouts cannot be ascertained.

Presentment is also *entirely excused* when: (1) the maker, acceptor or drawee of any instrument, except a documentary draft,[26] is dead or in insolvency proceedings instituted after the issue of the instrument; or (2) acceptance or payment is refused but not for want of proper presentment. The reason for (1) is that, in such instances, immediate payment or acceptance is impossible or unlikely so that the holder cannot reasonably be expected to make presentment. He is permitted, instead, to have his *immediate* recourse against the drawer or indorser.[27] The reason for (2) is that, since the purpose of presentment is to ascertain whether or not the maker, acceptor, or drawee will pay or accept the instrument, respectively, if a refusal to do so is given without a presentment having been made, then there is no sense in requiring presentment for a purpose which has already been refused.

If a draft has been previously dishonored by non-acceptance, later

---

[25] UCC 3–511, *Comment 2.*

[26] "The exception for the documentary draft is to preserve any profit on the resale of goods for the creditors of the drawee if his representative can find the funds to pay." UCC 3–511, *Comment 6.*

[27] UCC 3–511, *Comment 6.*

presentment for payment, notice of dishonor, and protest for non-payment are excused entirely. However, if the previous dishonor by non-acceptance is followed by an acceptance, then necessary presentment for payment, notice of dishonor, and protest for non-payment are not excused.

Chapter VII

DISCHARGE

ANY PARTY, as distinct from *all parties,* on an instrument may be discharged from liability thereon in various ways. The instrument is a paper evidencing the contractual obligations of the parties thereon; it is not the liability itself and, therefore, cannot as such be discharged. Often an instrument is given in payment of an obligation. It is usually said that a check or other instrument given in payment of an obligation is "conditional payment," meaning that the underlying obligation for which the instrument is given is not thereby discharged but, rather, cannot be enforced by suit until the instrument is due. Does the instrument discharge the underlying obligation for which it was issued, or is it solely conditional payment suspending enforcement of the underlying obligation until the due date of the instrument? The agreement of the parties governs, and in the absence of agreement the effect will depend upon the type of instrument given. *Unless otherwise agreed, where an instrument is taken for an underlying obligation, the obligation is completely discharged if a bank is drawer, maker or acceptor of the instrument, and there is no recourse on the instrument against the underlying obligor.* Thus, the debtor's delivery to the creditor of a cashier's check with the creditor as payee and not indorsed by the debtor causes the debtor to be discharged immediately from his underlying obligation. Since his signature is not on the cashier's check, he is not liable thereon. However, usually the debtor will give his own check or other instrument in payment. *Unless otherwise agreed, where an instrument is taken for an underlying obligation in any case other than that stated in italics above, the underlying obligation is suspended completely until the instrument is due or, if it is payable on demand, until its presentment.* If the instrument is dishonored, action may be taken on *either* the instrument or the obligation; discharge of the underlying obligor on the instrument also discharges him on the obligation. It should be recalled that, as discussed previously,[1] if the *holder* of a check

---

[1] See above, p. 436.

causes it to be certified, the drawer as well as all prior indorsers on the check are thereby discharged.

It should be noted that the taking in good faith of a check does not of itself so extend the time on the original obligation as to discharge a surety, as long as the check is not postdated. This is in accord with the law of suretyship.[2] The check is taken as a means of immediate payment; the 30-day period for presentment, previously discussed,[3] does not affect the surety's liability.[4]

First the discharge from liability of *any party* on an instrument will be discussed and then the discharge of *all parties* from liability on an instrument.

Discharge of Any Party On an Instrument

Any party may be discharged from his liability on an instrument in any of the following ways:

1. Payment or satisfaction.
2. Tender of payment.
3. Cancellation or renunciation.
4. Impairment of right of recourse or of collateral.
5. Reacquisition of the instrument by a prior party (previously discussed).[5]
6. Fraudulent and material alteration (previously discussed).[6]
7. Certification of a check (previously discussed).[7]
8. Acceptance varying a draft (previously discussed).[8]
9. Unexcused delay in presentment or notice of dishonor or protest (previously discussed).[9]

Any party is also discharged from his liability on an instrument to another party by any other act or agreement with such party which would discharge his simple contract for the payment of money. Discharge may also occur by additional ways provided by statute, e.g., federal bankruptcy discharge, and state statutes concerning negotiable instruments negotiated in furtherance of gambling transactions; the Code is not intended to preclude discharge arising apart from it.

Before considering these various methods of discharging a party

---

[2] See below, pp. 821 ff.

[3] See above, p. 454.

[4] UCC 3–802, *Comment 4.*

[5] See above, p. 409.

[6] See above, p. 433.

[7] See above, p. 436.

[8] *Ibid.*

[9] See above, p. 452.

from liability on an instrument, it should be recalled very carefully that *no discharge of any party other than a discharge in insolvency proceedings is effective against a subsequent holder in due course unless he has notice thereof when he takes the instrument.* Any such discharge of a party is a personal defense which is cut off, and cannot be asserted, against a holder in due course who took the instrument without notice of any defense to the instrument.[10] He takes the instrument free of all defenses of any party to the instrument with whom he has not dealt,[11] with certain exceptions, one of which is any discharge other than a discharge in insolvency proceedings of which the holder has notice when he took the instrument. (H is a holder in due course of a note made by M. When H took the note he knew that A, one of the indorsers, had been released from liability on the note. On dishonor of the instrument, H cannot recover against A, but he can recover against the other indorsers and M on the note.)

Payment or Satisfaction. We have seen[12] that the holder of an instrument, whether or not he is the owner, has the right to recover on the instrument unless the defendant establishes a defense. *The liability of any party to the instrument is discharged to the extent of his payment or satisfaction to the holder, with three exceptions.*

First Exception. If the payment or satisfaction is made to the holder *with knowledge* of a claim of another person to the instrument, *the payor is discharged by such payment or satisfaction unless, prior to such payment or satisfaction, the adverse claimant either:* supplies indemnity deemed adequate by the payor; or enjoins payment or satisfaction by court order in an action in which the adverse claimant and the holder are parties.[13] On notification of an adverse claim to the instrument, the payor usually is unable to ascertain whether or not the adverse claim is valid. The paying obligor's contractual obligation on the instrument is to "pay the holder of the instrument, and he performs it by making such payment. Except in cases of theft or restrictive

---

[10] See above, pp. 416 f., 425.

[11] See above, p. 410.

[12] See above, p. 411.

[13] UCC 3–803. "**Notice to Third Party.** Where a defendant is sued for breach of an obligation for which a third person is *answerable over* under this Article he may give the third person written notice of the litigation, and the person notified may then give similar notice to any other person who is answerable over to him under this Article. If the notice states that the person notified may come in and defend and that if the person notified does not do so he will in any action against him by the person giving the notice be bound by any determination of fact common to the two litigations, then unless after seasonable receipt of the notice the person notified does come in and defend he is so bound." (Author's italics)

indorsement there is no good reason to put him to inconvenience because of a dispute between two other parties unless he is indemnified or served with appropriate process."[14] If the adverse claimant posts indemnity or restrains payment or satisfaction by legal process, the party seeking to make payment or satisfaction on the instrument is not to do so, and should he do so he will not be discharged from liability on the instrument to such adverse claimant.

Second Exception. A party who, *in bad faith,* pays or satisfies the holder who acquired the instrument *by theft or who* (unless having the rights of a holder in due course) *holds through one who so acquired it, is not discharged from liability on the instrument.* The policy of the law here refuses to aid a thief directly, or indirectly by aiding his transferee, unless the latter is a holder in due course or a holder or transferee claiming through a holder in due course with his rights. (M's note to the order of P and delivered to P is indorsed by P in blank and stolen by A. A presented the note to M, who paid it, and P sues M on the note. While A is the holder, nevertheless, whether or not M is discharged depends upon whether M paid A in bad faith, knowing that A was a thief. If M paid in *bad faith,* he is not discharged; if M paid in *good faith,* he is discharged. If A had negotiated the note to B after maturity, thereby precluding B from being a holder in due course, whether or not M's payment to B would discharge M from liability on the note again depends on M's good or bad faith. However, if A had negotiated the note to H, a holder in due course, M's payment to H would discharge M, irrespective of whether or not he paid in bad faith. H would take the note free of the defense of theft. If H had negotiated the note to C after maturity, thereby precluding C from being a holder in due course, M's payment to C would discharge M from liability on the note. C would acquire H's rights and, therefore, take the note free of the defense of theft.)

Third Exception. A party, *other than* an intermediary bank[15] or a payor bank which is not a depositary bank,[16] who pays or satisfies the holder of an instrument which has been restrictively indorsed *in a manner not consistent with the terms of such restrictive indorsement, is not discharged from liability on the instrument.* The effect of restrictive indorsements has been discussed previously.[17] (M is the maker of a note restrictively indorsed by P, the payee, to A, an indorsee for collection. If

---

[14] UCC 3–603, *Comment 3.*

[15] See below, p. 475.

[16] *Ibid.*

[17] See above, p. 408.

M pays A, M is discharged since, by his indorsement, P desired such payment to occur and it has occurred consistent with such indorsement. However, if M had credited *A's personal account,* M has not paid consistently with such indorsement, and he is not discharged.) *If the indorsee, or transferee of the indorsee, of a restrictively indorsed note is a holder in due course, then the maker's payment to him discharges the maker from liability on the note.* With respect to banks, *an intermediary bank or a payor bank which is not the depositary bank is neither given notice nor otherwise affected by a restrictive indorsement of any person except the bank's immediate transferor or the person presenting the instrument for payment.* (D is the drawer of a check on E bank restrictively indorsed for deposit by P, the payee, and delivered by P to X for safekeeping. X deposited the check with A bank. A forwarded it for collection to B bank, who obtained collection from E. E paid B, who paid A, and X then withdrew the money from his account with A. P can recover on the check from A, which is a depositary bank not paying consistently with the terms of the restrictive indorsement—for the deposit to *P's* account. B is an intermediary bank and E is a payor bank which is not the depositary bank, and so they are not liable to P.) The depositary bank is bound by all prior indorsements and, if the instrument is restrictively indorsed, becomes a holder in due course if payment is made to the holder consistently with the restrictive indorsement.

Two additional points should be noted carefully. First, if the holder *accepts* any other satisfaction instead of payment of the instrument, the party rendering such satisfaction is discharged from liability on the instrument. Secondly, payment or satisfaction may be made with the *consent of the holder* by *any* person, including a stranger to the instrument. Surrender of the instrument to such a person gives him the rights of a transferee.[18]

Tender of Payment. Any party making tender of full payment to a holder when or after it is due is discharged *only to the extent* of all subsequent liability for interest, costs, and attorney's fees. He is still liable on the instrument for the face amount thereof up to the time of tender. He has made the money available to the holder and should not be penalized because the money is not accepted. *The holder's refusal of such tender wholly discharges any party who has a right of recourse against the party making the tender.* (M is the maker of a note, P is the payee, and the order of blank indorsements is P, A, B. H is the holder.

---

[18] See above, p. 418.

On the due date P tenders the full amount of the note to H, who refuses it. B and A are completely discharged from liability on the instrument, and P is discharged to the extent of all subsequent liability for interest, costs, and attorney's fees. B and A would have had recourse against P in the event that they had to pay the note on dishonor. They should not now continue to be liable to H on the note when the proffered full payment by P was made available to H.) Where the maker or acceptor of an instrument payable otherwise than on demand is able and ready to pay at every place of payment specified in the instrument when it is due, it is equivalent to tender.

Cancellation and Renunciation. The *holder* may discharge any party from his liability on the instrument, without any requirement of consideration, by cancellation or renunciation. Neither cancellation nor renunciation affects the title to the instrument as long as the holder does not surrender it. *Cancellation is made by the holder in any manner apparent on the face of the instrument or the indorsement,* as by *intentionally cancelling* the instrument or the party's signature by destruction or mutilation, or by *striking out* the party's signature. *Renunciation occurs by the holder renouncing his rights by a writing signed and delivered, or by the surrender of the instrument, to the party to be discharged.*

Impairment of Recourse or of Collateral. Under the law of suretyship, the creditor's release of the principal debtor discharges the debt and, since there is no debt for which there can be security, the surety as security for such debt is also discharged and the lien on any property as security is also terminated. If the creditor releases the principal debtor but *reserves his rights against the surety,* his release is construed as a covenant not to sue the principal debtor and, since the principal debtor is not discharged, the surety is not discharged and has rights against the principal debtor in the event that the creditor enforces his suretyship obligation on the principal debtor's default. To the extent that the principal debtor's contract with the creditor is modified by the creditor without the consent of the surety so as to create a possibility that the surety's risk will be increased thereby, the surety is thereby discharged. A common illustration is the creditor's binding agreement with the principal debtor extending the time of payment by the principal debtor to the creditor without the surety's consent and without reserving the creditor's rights against the surety. Also, to the extent that the creditor, *with knowledge of the suretyship relationship,* surrenders or impairs the security, the creditor makes it unavailable to the surety for recourse in the event that the creditor enforces his suretyship obligation on the principal debtor's default. All this is discussed later under Suretyship.[19] If the surety *consents* to these actions of the creditor, he is not discharged.

The Code reflects these elements of suretyship in connection with a party's discharge in Commercial Paper. Thus, the holder of an instrument may, without a party's consent, by his conduct toward another party on the instrument or a person off the instrument cause the discharge of the party on the instrument. (M is the maker of a note with P as the payee, who negotiated it to A, who indorsed it in blank and delivered it to B, who indorsed it in blank and delivered it to H. (a) Without the consent of P, A, and B, H released M. P, A, and B are discharged, because they have been deprived of recourse against M. (b) Without the consent of A and B, H released P. A and B are discharged because they have been deprived of recourse against P. (c) Without the consent of A and B, H released P, reserving his rights against A and B, and H promptly notified A and B. Nobody is discharged on the note, although H cannot recover against P on the note. (d) H releases P, A, and B, knowing that M is an accommodation maker. Not only are P, A, and B discharged, but M is discharged also because he has been deprived of recourse against P in the event M should be held liable on the note. If H did not know of M's accommodation status, M would not be discharged.) Consent by parties on the instrument to such conduct by a holder which would otherwise constitute suretyship defenses against the holder may be given in advance or after such conduct, although it very frequently is written on the instrument itself and is binding on the parties subject to it. No consideration is required for such consent.

We can now better understand the Code's provision on impairment of recourse or of collateral:

(1) The holder discharges any party to the instrument to the extent that without such party's consent the holder

   (a) *without express reservation of rights* releases or agrees not to sue any person against whom the party has *to the knowledge of the holder* a right of recourse or agrees to suspend the right to enforce against such person the instrument or collateral or otherwise discharges such person, except that failure or delay in effecting any required presentment, protest or notice of dishonor with respect to any such person does not discharge any party as to whom presentment, protest or notice of dishonor is effective or unnecessary; or

   (b) unjustifiably impairs any collateral for the instrument given by or

---

[19] See below, pp. 818–24.

on behalf of the party or any person against whom he has a right of recourse.

(2) By *express* reservation of rights against a party with a right of recourse the holder preserves

  (a) all his rights against such party as of the time when the instrument was originally due; and

  (b) the right of the party to pay the instrument as of that time; and

  (c) all rights of such party to recourse against others. (Author's italics) [20]

Perhaps a brief comment would be helpful with respect to the provision in (1) (a) above regarding presentment, protest, or notice of dishonor. The failure of a holder to make necessary presentment or protest or to give notice of dishonor discharges liability *to him* by the party who was entitled to have such occur, but it has no effect on the other parties to the instrument. (M is the maker of a note with P as the payee, indorsed in order by P, A, and B. H, the holder, gives only A necessary notice of dishonor. B and P are discharged from their secondary liability *to H* as indorsers under their engagement that they would be liable only if necessary notice of dishonor was given to them.[21] A can give P notice of dishonor within the proper time[22] and thereby recover from P—as well as from M as a party primarily liable—on the instrument.)

By Any Other Act or Agreement. Any party is also discharged from his liability on an instrument to another party by any other act or agreement with such party which would discharge a simple contract for the payment of money. This includes accord and satisfaction, novation, mutual rescission, and the other methods of discharge discussed previously under "Contracts."[23]

Although discharge by payment means that money has been paid, it is commonplace to refer to discharge by payment when, instead of the payment of money, new instruments are issued to the creditor discharging the obligation of a party or parties liable on the old instrument. Actually, such new instruments are forms of accord and satisfaction or of novation, and discharge is occurring by that method. It is important to determine when newly issued instruments do, and do not, effect a discharge of the obligation of a party or parties liable on the old instrument. Most of the cases are concerned with promissory notes. The agreement of the parties controls, and if the new note is issued solely as

[20] UCC 3–606.
[21] See above, p. 440.
[22] See above, p. 459.
[23] See above, pp. 139 ff.

security for the old note, there is no accord and satisfaction or novation and the obligation of a party or parties liable on the old note is not discharged. When, pursuant to agreement, the new note is issued to the creditor as a *renewal* of the old note which the creditor is to *retain* along with the new note, in the absence of agreement to the contrary and by the majority view it is presumed that the obligation of a party or parties liable on the old note is not discharged. However, if the renewal note is issued to the creditor *in exchange* for the surrender of the old note, in the absence of agreement to the contrary it is presumed that the obligation of a party or parties liable on the old note thereby is discharged.

Discharge of All Parties on the Instrument
All the parties to an instrument are discharged when no party is left with rights against any other party on the paper.[24] As stated previously, the instrument is a paper evidencing the contractual obligations of the parties thereon; it is not the liability itself and, therefore, cannot as such be discharged. Accordingly, under the Code[25] the liability of all parties is discharged when any party who has himself no right of action or recourse on the instrument either: (1) reacquires the instrument in his own right; or (2) is discharged under any provision of the Article on Commercial Paper, except as otherwise provided with respect to discharge for impairment of recourse or of collateral. The instrument still exists and may be reissued or renegotiated. If it subsequently is taken by a holder in due course, we have seen[26] that no discharge of any party on an instrument other than a discharge in insolvency proceedings is effective against a subsequent holder in due course unless he has notice thereof when he takes the instrument .

Lost, Destroyed, or Stolen Instruments
The loss, destruction, or theft of an instrument does not, of itself, discharge the obligations of the parties thereon, and the owner may recover on the instrument. Under the Code,[27] the owner of an instrument which is lost, whether by destruction, theft, or otherwise, may maintain an action in his own name and recover from any party liable thereon upon due proof of (1) his ownership, (2) the facts which prevent his production of the instrument, and

---

[24] UCC 3–601, *Comment 3.*
[25] UCC 3–601(3).
[26] See above, p. 425.
[27] UCC 3–804.

(3) its terms. The court *may* require security indemnifying the defendant against loss by reason of further claims on the instrument. The circumstances may be such, as by lapse of considerable time, that there is so little doubt about destruction of the instrument and about its ownership that the court may not require any indemnity. The matter is left to judicial discretion.

Chapter VIII

THE RELATIONSHIP BETWEEN A PAYOR BANK AND ITS CUSTOMER

1. *IN GENERAL*

**Code Articles
4 and 5**

ARTICLE 3 of the Code is concerned with Commercial Paper, Article 4 with Bank Deposits and Collections, and Article 5 with Letters of Credit. Although various provisions in Articles 4 and 5 tie in with Commercial Paper either directly or indirectly, nevertheless because of the specialized nature of these two Articles they are treated separately under the Code. Because of their specialized nature and because, with the exception of Part 4 of Article 4, they are not of such pressing importance with respect to the function of this book as to merit analysis here, these two Articles will not be discussed. However, because of their pertinency, their provisions are included at the end of this portion of the book on Commercial Paper. Part 4 of Article 4 deals with the relationship between payor bank and its customer and, because it is very closely aligned with Commercial Paper, it will be considered briefly here.

It should be noted initially that, to the extent that items[1] in Article 4 are also within the scope of Articles 3 on Commercial Paper and 8 on Investment Securities, they are subject to those Articles. In the event of conflict, the provisions of Article 8 govern over 4, and those in Article 4 govern over 3.[2] Also, the liability of a bank for action or non-action with respect to any item handled by it for purposes of presentment, payment, or collection is governed by the law of the place where the bank is located. In the case of action or non-action by or at a branch or separate office of a bank, its liability is governed by the law of the place where the branch or separate office is located.[3]

---

[1] UCC 4–104(1)(g): "'Item' means any instrument for the payment of money even though it is not negotiable but does not include money."

[2] UCC 4–102.

[3] UCC 4–102.

Kinds of Bank

It is important to understand the various kinds of bank which may be involved with an item which the customer has deposited with his bank for collection. Under the Code:

(a) "Depositary bank" means the first bank to which an item is transferred for collection even though it is also the payor bank;
(b) "Payor bank" means a bank by which an item is payable as drawn or accepted;
(c) "Intermediary bank" means any bank to which an item is transferred in course of collection except the depositary or payor bank;
(d) "Collecting bank" means any bank handling the item for collection except the payor bank;
(e) "Presenting bank" means any bank presenting an item except a payor bank;
(f) "Remitting bank" means any payor or intermediary bank remitting for an item.[4]

Legal Status of Bank and Customer Relationship

In General. The relationship between the bank and its customer is the result of their agreement. Their agreement is usually in the form of the signature card on which the customer agrees to be bound by the rules of the bank, which are usually stated on the deposit receipt or on a separate paper or card. Under the Code,[5] *unless a contrary intent clearly appears, and prior to the time that a settlement given by a collecting bank for an item is or becomes final,[6] the bank is an agent or subagent of the owner of the item, and any settlement given for the item is provisional.* This applies regardless of the form of indorsement or lack of indorsement, and even though credit given for the item is subject to immediate withdrawal as of right or is in fact withdrawn.

Bank's Duty of Care in the Collection Process. The bank and the customer each has a duty of care with respect to the other. Under the Code,[7] *the effect of the provisions under Article 4 may be varied by agreement, except that no agreement can disclaim a bank's responsibility for its own lack of good faith[8] or failure to exercise ordinary care, nor can it limit the measure of damages for such lack or failure.*

---

[4] UCC 4–105.
[5] UCC 4–201.
[6] UCC 4–211(3), 4–212, 4–213.
[7] UCC 4–103.
[8] UCC 1–201(19): "'Good faith' means honesty in fact in the conduct or transaction concerned."

However, the parties may by agreement determine the standards by which such responsibility is to be measured if such standards are not manifestly unreasonable. Inasmuch as the agreement between the bank and customer is in light of banking activity, there is included in their agreement, whether or not specifically assented to by all parties interested in the items handled, Federal Reserve regulations and operating letters, clearing house[9] rules, and the like. Action or non-action approved by Article 4 or pursuant to Federal Reserve regulations or operating letters constitutes the exercise of ordinary care and, in the absence of special instructions, action or non-action consistent with clearing house rules and the like or with a general banking usage not disapproved by Article 4 prima facie constitutes the exercise of ordinary care. The measure of damages for failure to exercise ordinary care in handling an item is the amount of the item reduced by an amount which could not have been realized by the use of ordinary care, and where there is bad faith it includes other damages, if any, suffered by the party as a proximate consequence.[10]

A collecting bank has the duty to exercise ordinary care in the collection process. However, except for its duty of care in the selection of properly qualified intermediary banks and giving to them proper instructions, the bank is not liable for the insolvency, neglect, misconduct, mistake, or default of another bank or person, or for loss or destruction of an item in transit or in the possession of others. A collecting bank must use ordinary care in: (1) presenting an item or sending it for presentment;[11] (2) sending notice of dishonor or nonpayment, or returning an item other than a documentary draft[12] to the bank's transferor, after learning that the item has not been paid or accepted, as the case may be; settling[13] for an item when the bank receives final settlement; making or providing for any necessary protest; and notifying its transferor of any loss or delay in transit within a reasonable time after discovery thereof. A collecting bank acts seasonably if it takes proper action before its midnight deadline[14] following

---

[9] UCC 4–104(1)(d): " 'Clearing house' means any association of banks or other payors regularly clearing items."

[10] UCC 4–103(5).

[11] As previously discussed, above, p. 455, presentment may be made by a presenting bank at a place where the payor bank has requested that presentment be made.

[12] See UCC 4–104(1)(f).

[13] UCC 4–104(1)(j): " 'Settle' means to pay in cash, by clearing house settlement, in a charge or credit or by remittance, or otherwise as instructed. A settlement may be either provisional or final."

[14] UCC 4–104(1)(h): " 'Midnight deadline' with respect to a bank is midnight on its next banking day following the banking day on which it receives the relevant item or notice or from which the time for taking action commences to run, whichever is later."

receipt of an item, notice, or payment. Taking proper action within a reasonably longer time may be seasonable, but the bank has the burden of so establishing.

Delays will occur in the collection process. Under the Code,[15] unless otherwise instructed, a collecting bank in a good faith effort to secure payment may, in the case of specific items and with or without the approval of any person involved, waive, modify or extend time limits imposed or permitted by Article 4 for a period not in excess of an additional banking day without discharge of secondary parties and without liability to its transferor or any prior party. Delay by a collecting bank or payor bank beyond time limits prescribed or permitted by Article 4, or by instructions, is excused if caused by interruption of communication facilities, suspension of payments by another bank, or emergency conditions or other circumstances beyond the control of the bank, provided it exercises such diligence as the circumstances require.

In order to establish ground rules among collecting banks as to the source of authority of each in the collection process, the Code provides[16] that, subject to Code provision in Articles 3 and 4 on conversion of instruments[17] and restrictive indorsements,[18] *only a collecting bank's transferor* can give instructions which affect the bank or constitute notice to it; a collecting bank is not liable to prior parties for any action taken pursuant to such instructions or in accordance with any agreement with its transferor.

Deposits and Issuance of Checks

In General. When the customer makes a deposit of cash, or he has deposited checks drawn by others for collection and his account has been credited on their final settlement, the relationship between the bank and the customer is debtor-creditor. The money deposited or collected became a part of the bank's funds. The customer's issuance of a check is not an assignment of funds in the bank, and the holder of the check has no recourse against the bank. Until the bank's signature appears on the check, it is not liable thereon.[19] The bank's obligation is to its customer for violation of its contract to pay pursuant to the customer's order. The holder's only recourse is against the parties liable on the instrument issued by the customer. A deposit of money in a bank is final when made but, subject to any right of the bank to apply

---

[15] UCC 4–108.

[16] UCC 4–203.

[17] See above, p. 438.

[18] See above, p. 408, and below, p. 478.

[19] See above, pp. 429, 435.

the deposit to any obligation of the customer, the deposit becomes available for withdrawal as of right at the opening of the bank's next banking day following receipt of the deposit.

While the bank is not required to certify a check,[20] banks are usually willing to certify, at the customer's request, checks drawn by him. They are not so willing to do so at the request of a *holder* of a check. By certification of a check, the bank has accepted the instrument and now is a party primarily liable thereon. There are many occasions (as when a relatively large amount of money is involved) when the parties to a transaction feel that a certified check is more desirable than an uncertified check with the risk of its dishonor. When certification of a check is procured by the *holder,* the drawer and all indorsers are discharged; when procured by the *drawer,* only the indorsers are discharged, the drawer remaining secondarily liable on the instrument.

Often a customer may not have indorsed an item to be deposited in his account at the bank. A depositary bank which has taken an item for collection may supply an indorsement of the customer which is necessary to title, unless the item contains the words "payee's indorsement required" or the like. *In the absence of such a requirement, a statement placed on the item by the depositary bank to the effect that the item was deposited by a customer or credited to his account is effective as the customer's indorsement.* As discussed previously,[21] an intermediary bank, or payor bank which is not a depositary bank, is neither given notice nor otherwise affected by a restrictive indorsement of any person except the bank's immediate transferor.

Warranties of Customer and Collecting Bank concerning Items. We previously discussed[22] under Commercial Paper the warranties made by a person who obtains payment or acceptance of an instrument, and any prior transferor, to a person who in good faith pays or accepts the instrument, and those made to his transferee by a person who transfers an instrument and receives consideration and, if the transfer is by indorsement, those made to any subsequent holder who takes the instrument in good faith. Under the Code,[23] in general, identi-

---

[20] See above, p. 436.

[21] See above, p. 408.

[22] See above, pp. 444–450.

[23] UCC 4–207. **"Warranties of Customer and Collecting Bank on Transfer or Presentment of Items; Time for Claims.** (1) Each customer or collecting bank who obtains payment or acceptance of an item and each prior customer and collecting bank warrants to the payor bank or other payor who in good faith pays or accepts the item that

   (a) he has a good title to the item or is authorized to obtain payment or acceptance on behalf of one who has a good title; and

   (b) he has no knowledge that the signature of the maker or drawer is unauthorized,

cal warranties are made by: each customer or collecting bank who obtains payment or acceptance of an item, and each prior customer and collecting bank, to the payor bank or other payor who in good faith pays or accepts the item; and by each customer and collecting bank who transfers an item and receives a settlement or other consideration for it made to his transferee and to any subsequent collecting bank who takes the item in good faith. *Reference should be made to the previous discussion under Commercial Paper.*

However there are a few differences from the warranty provisions under Commercial Paper. First, in the warranties on transfer, the distinction between transfer without indorsement to a transferee and with indorsement to a subsequent holder does not exist here. Second, no qualification is made here for any warranty "without recourse" nor for a

except that this warranty is not given by any customer or collecting bank that is a holder in due course and acts in good faith

    (i) to a maker with respect to the maker's own signature; or

    (ii) to a drawer with respect to the drawer's own signature, whether or not the drawer is also the drawee; or

    (iii) to an acceptor of an item if the holder in due course took the item after the acceptance or obtained the acceptance without knowledge that the drawer's signature was unauthorized; and

    (c) the item has not been materially altered, except that this warranty is not given by any customer or collecting bank that is a holder in due course and acts in good faith

    (i) to the maker of a note; or

    (ii) to the drawer of a draft whether or not the drawer is also the drawee; or

    (iii) to the acceptor of an item with respect to an alteration made prior to the acceptance if the holder in due course took the item after the acceptance, even though the acceptance provided 'payable as originally drawn' or equivalent terms; or

    (iv) to the acceptor of an item with respect to an alteration made after the acceptance.

    "(2) Each customer and collecting bank who transfers an item and receives a settlement or other consideration for it warrants to his transferee and to any subsequent collecting bank who takes the item in good faith that

    (a) he has a good title to the item or is authorized to obtain payment or acceptance on behalf of one who has a good title and the transfer is otherwise rightful; and

    (b) all signatures are genuine or authorized; and

    (c) the item has not been materially altered; and

    (d) no defense of any party is good against him; and

    (e) he has no knowledge of any insolvency proceeding instituted with respect to the maker or acceptor or the drawer of an unaccepted item.

In addition each customer and collecting bank so transferring an item and receiving a settlement or other consideration engages that upon dishonor and any necessary notice of dishonor and protest he will take up the item.

    "(3) The warranties and the engagement to honor set forth in the two preceding subsections arise notwithstanding the absence of indorsement or words of guaranty or warranty in the transfer or presentment and a collecting bank remains liable for their breach despite remittance to its transferor. Damages for breach of such warranties or engagement to honor shall not exceed the consideration received by the customer or collecting bank responsible plus finance charges and expenses related to the item, if any.

    "(4) Unless a claim for breach of warranty under this section is made within a reasonable time after the person claiming learns of the breach, the person liable is discharged to the extent of any loss caused by the delay in making claim."

selling agent or broker. However, there are included here some things not under the warranty provisions under Commercial Paper. Each customer and collecting bank transferring an item and receiving a settlement or other consideration engages that, upon dishonor and any necessary notice of dishonor and protest, he will take up the item. Also, these warranties by customer and collecting bank on payment or acceptance and on transfer arise notwithstanding the absence of indorsement or words of guaranty or warranty in the transfer or presentment, and a collecting bank remains liable for their breach despite remittance to its transferor. Damages for breach of such warranties or engagement to honor shall not exceed the consideration received by the customer or collecting bank responsible plus finance charges and expenses (e.g., ordinary collection expenses) related to the item, if any. Lastly, unless a claim for breach of warranty is made within a reasonable time after the person claiming learns of the breach, the person liable is discharged to the extent of any loss caused by the delay in making claim.

Bank As a Holder in Due Course. A bank may become a holder in due course if it complies with the requirements for such status.[24] One of the ways that the Code says a bank has given value for an item is the extent that the bank has a security interest in such item.

Security Interest of Collecting Bank in Items, Accompanying Documents, and Proceeds. The Code specifies when a collecting bank has a security interest in an item and any accompanying documents or the proceeds of either, how the security interest is spread over various items, and for self-liquidation of the bank's security interest:

(1) A bank has a security interest in an item and any accompanying documents or the proceeds of either
   (a) in case of an item deposited in an account to the extent to which credit given for the item has been withdrawn or applied;
   (b) in case of an item for which it has given credit available for withdrawal as of right, to the extent of the credit given whether or not the credit is drawn upon and whether or not there is a right of chargeback; or
   (c) if it makes an advance on or against the item.[25]
(2) When credit which has been given for several items received at one

---

[24] See above, p. 410.

[25] "Subsection (1) does not derogate from the banker's general common-law lien or right of set-off against indebtedness owing in deposit accounts. See Section 1–103. Rather subsection (1) specifically implements and extends the principle as a part of the bank collection process." UCC 4–208, *Comment 1.* See below, p. 790, "General Liens."

time or pursuant to a single agreement is withdrawn or applied in part the security interest remains upon all the items, any accompanying documents or the proceeds of either. For the purpose of this section, credits first given are first withdrawn.

(3) Receipt by a collecting bank of a final settlement for an item is a realization on its security interest in the item, accompanying documents and proceeds. To the extent and so long as the bank does not receive final settlement for the item or give up possession of the item or accompanying documents for purposes other than collection, the security interest continues and is subject to the provisions of Article 9 except that

(a) no security agreement is necessary to make the security interest enforceable (subsection (1) (a) of Section 9–203); and

(b) no filing is required to perfect the security interest; and

(c) the security interest has priority over conflicting perfected security interests in the item, accompanying documents or proceeds.[26]

When Bank May Charge Customer's Account. A draft, including a check, is an order to make payment and, as against its customer, *a bank drawee may charge against his account any item which is otherwise properly payable from that account, even though the charge creates an overdraft.* The draft implies a promise to reimburse the bank for an overdraft. The bank has no obligation to pay an overdraft, although banks generally do extend this courtesy to some of their customers depending upon various factors, e.g., the size of the overdraft and the credit standing of the customer.

The item drawn by the customer and paid by the bank may have been altered by unauthorized completion or otherwise. We have seen[27] that: a holder's fraudulent, material alteration of an instrument discharges any party on the instrument whose contract thereon is changed without his assent; and any other alteration does not discharge any party but, rather, the instrument may be enforced according to its original tenor, or as to incomplete instruments unauthorizedly completed enforced according to the authority given. Also, if the altered instrument is negotiated to a holder in due course, he may enforce the instrument according to its original tenor if it was complete when issued, and as completed if it was incomplete when issued and subsequently unauthorizedly completed. As between the customer drawer and bank drawee, should the drawer be discharged by the fraudulent, material alteration and the bank be unable to charge the customer's account and have to

---

[26] UCC 4–208.

[27] See above, pp. 432 ff.

look to the holder who has been paid? Under the Code,[28] *a bank which, in good faith, makes payment to a holder may charge the indicated account of its customer according to:* (1) *the original tenor of his altered item; or* (2) *the tenor of his completed item, even though the bank knows the item has been completed as long as the bank does not have notice that the completion was improper.*

Bank's Liability to Customer for Wrongful Dishonor. The obligation of the bank is to honor an item of its customer if the item is in proper form, e.g., properly indorsed, and sufficient funds of the customer are available on deposit. *In the event the payor bank wrongfully dishonors an item, it is liable to its customer for damages proximately caused by such wrongful dishonor.* If the wrongful dishonor occurs through the bank's *mistake,* the bank's liability is limited to *actual* damages which are proved. The actual damages may include *consequential* damages, such as damages for the arrest or prosecution of the customer or damages for injury to his reputation, provided the damages are proximately caused by the wrongful dishonor. Proximate cause is a question of fact and not of law.

Customer's Right to Stop Payment. A customer sometimes has occasion to stop the payment of an item which he has drawn. For example, he may have made a mistake in its amount or issuance, or the party to whom he issued the item has defrauded him or failed to render the agreed consideration. While having the bank stop payment on the item is an inconvenience to the bank, nevertheless this is a service which the bank must render to its customer. Accordingly, *a customer has the right to order his bank to stop payment of any item payable from his account.* However, the order must be received by the bank at such a time and in such a manner as to give the bank a reasonable opportunity to act on it before it has taken any of the following action on the item which would preclude the stop payment order from being effective:

(a) accepted or certified the item;

(b) paid the item in cash;

(c) settled for the item without reserving a right to revoke the settlement and without having such right under statute, clearing house rule or agreement;

(d) completed the process of posting the item to the indicated account of the drawer, maker or other person to be charged therewith or otherwise has evidenced by examination of such indicated account and by action its decision to pay the item; or

(e) become accountable for the amount of the item under subsection (1)

---

[28] UCC 4–401(2).

(d) of Section 4–213[29] and Section 4–302[30] dealing with the payor bank's responsibility for late return of items.[31]

Only the customer can stop payment, with the exception of an interested party stopping the bank from paying after the customer's death.[32]

Usually the order to stop payment will be given hastily, and normally it is done over the telephone. Because of the haste, the oral stop payment order should exist for only a short time and then be put in writing to be effective for a longer time and also for the protection of both the customer and the bank. Accordingly, under the Code,[33] *an oral order is binding upon the bank only for fourteen calendar days, unless confirmed in writing within that period. A written order is effective for only six months, unless renewed in writing.*

The bank's payment in violation of a valid stop payment order is improper and subjects the bank to liability for loss resulting therefrom. It is inevitable that mistakes will be made by a bank in failing to comply with a stop payment order, but this is a part of the overhead expense in the operation of the banking business. We have already seen[34] that no agreement between bank and customer can disclaim the bank's responsibility for its own failure to exercise ordinary care nor can it limit the measure of damages for such failure. The customer has the burden of establishing the fact, and amount, of loss resulting from the payment of an item contrary to a binding stop payment order. However, the bank has a right of subrogation to prevent unjust enrichment by the bank's payment, now to be discussed.

Payor Bank's Right to Subrogation on Improper Payment. The effect of the stop payment order is to retain in the customer's account the amount of the item. Should the bank fail to comply with a

---

[29] "(1) An item is finally paid by a payor bank when the bank has done any of the following, whichever happens first:

(d) made a provisional settlement for the item and failed to revoke the settlement in the time and manner permitted by statute, clearing house rule or agreement." UCC 4–213.

[30] UCC 4–302. **"Payor Bank's Responsibility for Late Return of Item.** In the absence of a valid defense such as breach of a presentment warranty (subsection (1) of Section 4–207), settlement effected or the like, if an item is presented on and received by a payor bank the bank is accountable for the amount of

(a) a demand item other than a documentary draft whether properly payable or not if the bank, in any case where it is not also the depositary bank, retains the item beyond midnight of the banking day of receipt without settling for it or, regardless of whether it is also the depositary bank, does not pay or return the item or send notice of dishonor until after its midnight deadline; or

(b) any other properly payable item unless within the time allowed for acceptance or payment of that item the bank either accepts or pays the item or returns it and accompanying documents."

[31] UCC 4–303(1).

[32] See below, p. 485.

[33] UCC 4–403(2).

[34] See above, p. 475.

stop payment order, it will have to reimburse the customer's account. However, the bank must be able to be made whole to the extent possible; it cannot profit from the occasion. Thus, the bank has: a right of subrogation; a possible defense that the customer, by conduct in recognizing the bank's payment, has ratified such payment over the stop payment order; the right to recover money paid under a mistake.[35]

The bank's right of subrogation places the bank in a position to have the rights of the person to whom payment is made as against the customer, and the rights of the customer against the person paid. If the person paid is a holder in due course and the customer's defenses are not assertable against him, the bank, by being subrogated to the rights of the holder in due course, can charge the customer. Often customers erroneously believe that all that need be done to avoid liability on an item is to stop payment thereon. (D draws a check on E payable to P for goods that P never delivers to D. D issues a stop payment order to E. P negotiates the check to H, a holder in due course, who presents the check to E, who dishonors it. H can recover against D on the check because the personal defenses of P's fraud and failure of consideration are cut off as to a holder in due course. If E had wrongfully paid the check over the stop payment order, E would be subrogated to H's rights on the instrument and, therefore, would be able to recover the money from D, its customer.) Accordingly, under the Code:[36]

> If a payor bank has paid an item over the stop payment order of the drawer or maker or otherwise under circumstances giving a basis for objection by the drawer or maker, to prevent unjust enrichment and only to the extent necessary to prevent loss to the bank by reason of its payment of the item, the payor bank shall be subrogated to the rights
> (a) of any holder in due course on the item against the drawer or maker; and
> (b) of the payee or any other holder of the item against the drawer or maker either on the item or under the transaction out of which the item arose;[37] and
> (c) of the drawer or maker against the payee or any other holder of the item with respect to the transaction out of which the item arose.[38]

---

[35] UCC 4–403, *Comment 8;* UCC 4–407, *Comment 5.*

[36] UCC 4–407.

[37] "It may well be that the payee is not a holder in due course but still has good rights against the drawer. These may be on the check but also may not be as, for example, where the drawer buys goods from the payee and the goods are partially defective so that the payee is not entitled to the full price, but the goods are still worth a portion of the contract price. If the drawer retains the goods he is obligated to pay a part of the agreed price. If the bank has paid the check it should be subrogated to this claim of the payee against the drawer." UCC 4–407, *Comment 2.*

[38] "If, for example, the payee was a fraudulent salesman inducing the drawer to issue his check for defective securities, and the bank pays the check over a stop order but reimburses the drawer for such payment, the bank should have a basis for getting the money back from the fraudulent salesman." UCC 4–407, *Comment 3.*

Payment of Stale Checks. By banking and commercial practice, checks outstanding for a period of more than six months are considered stale. Prior to the Code, while banks could pay such checks, by many state statutes they were not compelled to do so. Reflecting this practice and concern, under the Code[39] *a bank is under no obligation to its customer having a checking account to pay his uncertified check if presented more than six months after its date.* However, the bank may, if it wishes and provided it acts *in good faith,* pay the stale check and charge the customer's account therefor. For example, the drawee bank knows that its drawer corporate customer will want to have its outstanding dividend checks paid even though they are presented more than six months after date. Certified checks are excluded because the customer's account has been charged on certification and the certified check is now a primary obligation of the bank to the holder.

Death or Incompetence of Customer. Although under the law of agency[40] the supervening death or adjudication of incompetency of the principal immediately and without notice terminates the agency relationship, the unique position of a bank payor or a collecting bank justifies a modification in the law based on the bank's knowledge of such state of facts in connection with its authority to pay or collect items. The very large volume of items handled in the collection process and the bank's difficulty in learning of the death or adjudication of incompetence of its customer make a change in the law necessary. *Accordingly, neither death nor incompetence of a customer revokes the authority of a payor or collecting bank to accept, pay, collect an item or to account for proceeds of its collection until the bank knows of such death or adjudication of incompetence and has a reasonable opportunity to act on it.* Also, such authority is not affected by the customer's incompetency at the time the item is issued or its collection undertaken if the bank does not know of an adjudication of incompetence. It should be noted carefully that only actual knowledge, and not constructive notice, is the criterion.

Under the Code *a bank, even with knowledge of its customer's death, may, for 10 days after the date of death, pay or certify checks drawn on or prior to that date, unless ordered to stop payment by a person claiming an interest in the account.* The reason for this is "to permit holders of checks drawn and issued shortly before death to cash them without the necessity of filing a claim in probate. The justification is that such checks normally are given in immediate payment of an

---

[39] UCC 4–404.
[40] See below, p. 583.

obligation, that there is almost never any reason why they should not be paid, and that filing in probate is a useless formality, burdensome to the holder, the executor, the court, and the bank."[41] Examples of a person claiming an interest in the account are a surviving relative or creditor of the decedent, or the person named in the decedent's will as executor or legatee even though the will has not yet been admitted to probate.

It should be noted in passing that the gift of a check is not a gift of the amount indicated on the check until the drawee has paid or certified the check, and should the drawer die before payment or certification, the gift is incomplete and the holder has no claim against either the drawee or the estate of the drawer. The protection given to a bank who pays without knowledge of the death of its drawer customer or within 10 days after death with knowledge thereof is solely to relieve the payor bank of liability for such payments; it has no effect upon the validity of the claims of recipients of payment nor upon the right of an executor or administrator of the decedent's estate to reclaim money paid to the holders.

Customer's Duty to Discover and Report Unauthorized Signature or Alteration. Generally a bank makes available to its customers a periodic statement of account accompanied by items, e.g., cancelled checks, paid in good faith in support of the charges against their accounts. This may be done either by: sending the statement and items to the customer; or holding the statement and items available to the customer pursuant to his request or instructions; or otherwise in a reasonable manner making them available to the customer. *The customer has a duty to exercise reasonable care and promptness to examine the statement and items to discover his unauthorized signature or any alteration on any item, and to notify the bank promptly after discovery thereof.* The customer's failure so to comply with his duty of reasonable care, promptness, and notification has a twofold effect. *First,* the customer is precluded or estopped from asserting against the bank his unauthorized signature or any alteration if the bank establishes that it suffered a loss by reason of the customer's failure. It should be noted that the bank has the burden of establishing both the customer's failure and that it suffered loss by reason thereof in order to preclude the customer. *Second,* if the statement and an item with an unauthorized signature or alteration are made available to the customer, the customer does not notify the bank of such unauthorized signature or alteration within a reasonable period not exceeding 14 calendar days, and before

---

[41] UCC 4–405, *Comment 3.*

notification concerning the item the bank in good faith pays another item unauthorizedly signed or altered by the *same wrongdoer,* the customer is precluded from asserting such additional unauthorized signature or alteration against the bank. Again, the bank has the burden of establishing the customer's failure to comply with his duty of reasonable care, promptness, and notification. However, even if the bank proves such failure by the customer, the customer is not precluded in the above two instances if the customer establishes lack of ordinary care on the part of the bank in paying the item or items. Examples of the latter are: the bank's payment or acceptance of an item which has been altered and which alteration the bank could have detected by the exercise of ordinary care in the examination of the item; and the bank's payment or acceptance of an item on which the customer's signature has been forged. The customer has the burden of proving the bank's lack of ordinary care.

Irrespective of care or lack of care of either the customer or the bank, the customer has a limited time within which to assert a claim against the bank for payment of an item with his unauthorized signature, alteration, or unauthorized indorsement, after which time he is precluded from asserting such claim. After the statement and item are made available to the customer, he must discover and report: *his unauthorized signature or any alteration* on the face or back of the item *within one year thereafter; any unauthorized indorsement within three years thereafter.* The reason for the difference in times is that it will probably take a longer time for the customer to learn of a forged indorsement. Reference should be made to previous discussion[42] concerning negligence that contributed to an alteration or unauthorized signature, which is a protection to the bank against its customer.

A payor bank cannot waive its defense or fail to assert a defense to the prejudice of a collecting bank. Accordingly, under the Code, "If under this section a payor bank has a valid defense against a claim of a customer upon or resulting from payment of an item and waives or fails upon request to assert the defense the bank may not assert against any collecting bank or other prior party presenting or transferring the item a claim based upon the unauthorized signature or alteration giving rise to the customer's claim."[43]

[42] See above, p. 432.
[43] UCC 4–406(5).

APPENDIX TO PART FOUR

REFERENCES

1. Anderson, Ronald A. *Anderson's Uniform Commercial Code,* 2d ed. Rochester, N.Y.: Lawyers Cooperative Publishing Co., 1970.
2. Clarke, Bailey III, and Young, Jr. *Bank Deposits and Collections under the Uniform Commercial Code.* Philadelphia, Pa.: American Law Institute, 1963.
3. Hawkland, William D. *A Transactional Guide to the Uniform Commercial Code.* Philadelphia, Pa.: American Law Institute, 1964.
4. Huggins, Rollin C., and Phemister, Dean B. "Bank Deposits and Collections," in *Uniform Commercial Code Handbook 129.* Chicago: American Bar Association, 1964.
5. Leary, Fairfax, Jr. "Commercial Paper," in *Uniform Commercial Code Handbook 87.* Chicago: American Bar Association, 1964.
6. Mentschikoff, Soia. "Letters of Credit under the Uniform Commercial Code," in *Uniform Commercial Code Handbook 153.* Chicago: American Bar Association, 1964.
7. *Uniform Laws Annotated,* Articles 3–5, Uniform Commercial Code, 1962.

PROBLEMS

1. (a) Differentiate draft, check, certificate of deposit, and note.
   (b) Is a bond a note?
   (c) What is meant by the following:
       (1) Cashier's check?
       (2) Certified check?
       (3) Trade acceptance?

2. Enumerate the requisites of a negotiable instrument.

3. (a) John Jones orally authorized Peter Poe to execute and issue a note in the name of John Jones. In accordance with this authority, Peter Poe executed and issued a writing, signing it in pencil as follows:

   John Jones
   by P. P., agent.

   (1) What is the effect of this signature on the negotiability of an otherwise negotiable promissory note?
   (2) Why?
   (b) M executed a writing containing the following words: "This note is

488

given in payment for a refrigerator sold by P to M this date, possession to be delivered to M when this note has been paid."

   (1) What is the effect of these words on an otherwise negotiable promissory note?

   (2) Why?

4. (a) What is the effect of the following provisions in an otherwise negotiable promissory note, and explain why:

   (1) The writing promised to pay "$1,000 or, at the holder's election, to deliver 100 shares of common stock of X corporation."

   (2) The writing promised to pay $10,000 in installments of $1,000 each and provided that, on default in the payment of an installment, the whole amount would become due at the holder's option.

   (3) The writing promised to pay interest but did not state the amount or percentage.

   (4) The writing provided that, on default, the interest should be increased from 4 per cent to 6 per cent, the increased rate to be retroactively effective as from the date of the instrument.

   (5) The writing provided for collection costs and attorney's fees if the instrument were dishonored.

  (b) How are the following ambiguities in a negotiable instrument resolved:

   (1) Where the sum payable is expressed in words and also in figures and there is a discrepancy between the two.

   (2) Where the instrument provides for the payment of interest, without specifying the date from which interest is to run.

   (3) Where the instrument is not dated.

   (4) Where there is a conflict between the handwritten, typewritten, and printed provisions.

5. (a) Frank Fay executed and delivered the following writing to Peter Poe:
Pay to Peter Poe or bearer $1,000.

     To: John Jones   (signed) Frank Fay
          1405 Pearl Street,
          Boulder, Colorado.

   (1) Is this a negotiable instrument?

   (2) Why?

   (3) When does a cause of action accrue against Frank Fay?

  (b) When does a cause of action accrue on a certificate of deposit?

6. (a) A negotiable promissory note in the amount of $1,000 payable to the order of "A and B," who were not related to each other in any way, was indorsed by A to C for $500 and to D for $500.

   (1) What was the effect of this indorsement?

   (2) Why?

  (b) A check was payable to the order of "John Jarson," an infant whose proper name is "John Larson." The infant indorsed the check "John Larson" and delivered it to another person, who subsequently negotiated it to a holder in due course. The infant then disaffirmed all liability on the instrument.

(1) What was the effect of the infant's indorsement?
(2) Why?

7. What is meant by, and what is the effect of, each of the following indorsements? Give an example of each.
   (1) Special indorsement.
   (2) Indorsement in blank.
   (3) Restrictive indorsement.

8. (a) Define the following:
      (1) Holder.
      (2) Holder in due course.
   (b) Briefly explain the difference between "value" and "consideration" and explain how they are applicable to commercial paper.

9. B sold goods to A for $200, taking A's note in payment, with the agreement that B would deliver the goods immediately. B sold and indorsed the note to C, an innocent party, for $100, of which $50 was paid in cash and $50 was to be paid in 10 days. B did not deliver the goods, for which the note had been given, before the 10 days expired, and A so informed C. C sued A for $200 on the note.
   (1) Can C recover?
   (2) Why? (Former C.P.A. Examination question)

10. P fraudulently induced D to issue his check to P, who two days later indorsed it in blank and delivered it for value to A, who knew of the fraud. Two weeks later, A indorsed the check in blank and delivered it for value to H, who took it in good faith without notice of the fraud. A week later, H in good faith negotiated the check to A for value. Can A enforce the check against D? Explain.

11. M issued a note to the order of P who changed the face amount of the note from $1,000 to $10,000. Before maturity P indorsed and delivered the note for value to H, who did not know of, and reasonably could not discern, the change in amount. The note was dishonored subsequently.
   (1) Does H have any right against M on the note?
   (2) Why?
   (3) Would the result have been any different if, instead of P's changing the face amount of the note, M had issued the note with the amount blank and instructed P to fill in the amount for $1,000, but P filled it in for $10,000? Explain.

12. A stole goods from B, misrepresented to M that A was B, sold and delivered the goods to M, and received from M a negotiable promissory note payable to the order of B. Before maturity of the note, A forged B's signature as an indorsement in blank and sold and delivered the note for value to C, who was innocent of what had occurred previously. The note was dishonored subsequently.
   (1) Does C have any right against M on the note?
   (2) Why?

13. P was general manager of M's large firm. It was part of P's job to prepare the payroll list every week with the names of the firm's employees and

the weekly compensation due each employee. Unknown to M, over a period of months P included in the payroll list the names of many former employees, and M innocently prepared and signed checks for them drawn on E bank, delivering the checks to P for distribution among the employees each week. P forged the blank indorsements of the former employee payees on the checks and cashed them through the various banks where P had checking accounts. M now discovers the facts.

(1) Can M compel E to recredit his account for the checks drawn to such former employees and paid by E?

(2) Explain.

14. (a) Allen, without receiving any consideration, and for the accommodation of Brown, signs a note payable to the order of Brown, who indorses and delivers it for value to Cox before due. When Cox took the note he knew that Allen received no value and was only an accommodation party. Brown is irresponsible, and Cox sues Allen on the instrument.

(1) Can Cox recover from Allen? Explain.

(2) If Cox had released Brown from liability on the note, could Cox now recover from Allen on the note? Explain.

(b) Amos, who was 17 years old, gave a note in payment for goods to Blue, who indorses it to Coty for value before maturity. The note is not paid at maturity. Coty sues Amos and Blue. Both Amos and Blue set up the infancy of Amos as a defense. Can Coty recover from Amos, or Blue, or both, or neither? Explain. (Former C.P.A. Examination question)

15. On January 9, 1972, D issued to the order of P a check drawn on E in the amount of $1,000. On the same day the check was negotiated by P to A; and on January 19 it was negotiated to B, who immediately presented it to E for payment. The check was dishonored for insufficient funds, the account never having had more than $200 on deposit. Notice of dishonor was given immediately to P and A.

(1) Does B have any rights against D, P, or A?

(2) Why?

16. P forged D's signature as drawer to a check on E bank payable to the order of P. P indorsed the check in blank and sold and delivered it for value to H who was unaware of the forgery. Later that day, H telephoned D and, after accurately describing the check to D, he asked D if it was a check signed and issued by D. D said "Yes, and I will stand behind it." Two days later, D stopped payment on the check, which was dishonored when presented for payment the next day by H to E. Can H recover the amount of the check from:

(1) D? Explain.

(2) P? Explain.

17. (a) What is an acceptance?

(b) What is required for an acceptance?

(c) Give one instance when presentment for acceptance must be made.

(d) Does a holder of a draft or a check have a right to present the instrument for acceptance and to have it accepted?

(e) What is the effect of certification of a check?

(f) What is the effect of a qualified acceptance?

18. M is the maker of a note and P is the payee holder. A stole the note from P, forged P's blank indorsement, indorsed the note in blank, and sold and delivered it for value to H, who took the note in good faith and without notice of the theft and forgery. At maturity, H presented the note to M, who paid it in good faith without notice of the theft and forgery.

(1) Does P have any rights against M on the note? Explain.

(2) Does M have any rights against H? Explain.

19. Allen drew his check to the order of Burt upon the Yanktown Bank. Burt duly presented the check at the bank for payment. Though the bank at the time had funds of Allen more than sufficient to pay the check, it refused to pay it. Can Burt maintain an action against the bank? (Former C.P.A. Examination question)

20. On a Monday afternoon X signed a check for $7,000 and delivered it to P, the payee, as a gift. On the next day, X was killed in an accident. The bank learned of X's death that day. Two weeks later, P cashed the check at the bank on which it was drawn, P not knowing of X's death.

(1) Can X's estate recover from the bank the amount of the check?

(2) Can the legal representative of X's estate recover the amount of the check from P? Explain.

21. State the contractual obligations on an instrument of:

(a) The maker and acceptor. (b) The drawer. (c) An indorser.

22. (a) When are presentment for payment and acceptance necessary?

(b) What is the effect of unexcused failure to make a necessary presentment?

(c) When is protest necessary?

(d) When is notice of dishonor necessary?

23. On the maturity date of his note, M paid the note to H, the holder but not a holder in due course. Is M discharged from liability on the note, indorsed in blank by P, the payee, if:

(1) The note had been stolen from P by A who then negotiated the note to H? Explain.

(2) If A, the thief, had negotiated the note to B, a holder in due course, who later negotiated it to H? Explain.

24. P fraudulently induced D to issue a check on E to the order of P. D later discovered the fraud and orally told the president of E to stop payment on the check. Ten minutes later E mistakenly paid P on his presentment of the check. D demands that E reimburse his account for the amount of the check. Will he succeed?

25. A certified public accountant who had completed his professional work for an out-of-town corporate client delivered his report to the president of the corporation in the latter's office. The president thereupon told him that the corporation's check for his fee would be given to him in half an hour and that the accountant could have it certified on his way to the railroad station,

or, if the accountant preferred, a check already certified would be given to him in three quarters of an hour. Disregarding entirely all matters of personal convenience, which offer should the accountant accept? (Former C.P.A. Examination question)

SOME PREVIOUS C.P.A. LAW EXAMINATION QUESTIONS AND MODEL ANSWERS

NOVEMBER, 1970

No. 8 (Estimated time—20 to 25 minutes)

a. Joseph Martin persuaded his employer, Robert Franklin, to issue a check payable to the order of Milton Small in the amount of $1,000. Martin represented to Franklin that Small was entitled to a refund of $1,000 for merchandise returned that day by Small. Franklin delivered the check to Martin and instructed him to mail it to Small.

   Martin's statement was false. He did not know any person called Milton Small. When Martin received the check intended for Small, he indorsed the check in the name of Milton Small and delivered it to Arthur Smith, a holder in due course. Martin absconded and when Franklin discovered what had happened he stopped payment on the check. Smith sues Franklin.

   (1) Was the check bearer paper or order paper at the time of issue? Explain.

   (2) Was Martin's indorsement effective to negotiate the check? Explain.

   (3) May Smith recover from Franklin? Explain.

b. Lawrence executed and delivered a check for $1,000 payable to the order of Evans. Lawrence used due care in preparing the check. However, Evans (by methods best known to forgers) raised the amount to $10,000 and negotiated the check for value to Mark who took the check in good faith without notice of the alteration. When Mark presented the check for payment it was returned marked "insufficient funds." Mark then sued Lawrence. In connection with his examination of Lawrence's financial statements, a C.P.A. is attempting to determine the liability and related loss on this item, if any.

   (1) Can Mark recover? Explain.

   (2) If so, how much? Explain.

c. In the course of his examination of Smith's financial statements, a C.P.A. learns that Smith drew a check on the State Bank payable to the order of Paul N. Hodys in the sum of $500 and delivered it to Hodys for goods sold and delivered. Morris stole the check from Hodys, indorsed Hodys' name and delivered the check to Parks who took the check for value in good faith and deposited the check in his account in the National Bank. National Bank collected the amount of the check from State Bank who in turn charged Smith's account in the sum of $500.

(1) What are the rights of Smith against State Bank? Explain.

(2) What are the rights of Hodys against State Bank? Explain.

(3) What are the rights of State Bank against National Bank? Explain.

Answer

a. (1) Order paper. Under the Uniform Commercial Code on Commercial Paper, a check payable to the order of a named payee is order paper, even though the payee is not intended to have any interest in the check.

   (2) Yes. Under the Code, when the payee of a check is not intended to have any interest in tl e check, an indorsement by him is not required but may be made by any person in the name of the payee. Here, Martin's indorsement of tl.e check in Small's name and delivery to Smith constituted a negotiatic n to Smith.

   (3) Yes. Martin's negotiation of the check to Smith as a holder in due course transferred the title to the check to Smith. Under the Code, the fraud by Martin on Franklin is a personal defense to Franklin not assertable against a holder in due course.

b. (1) Yes. Under the Code, a fraudulent material alteration of a negotiable instrument made by a holder discharges any prior party to the instrument, except that such discharge is not effective as against a subsequent holder in due course. Here, Evans intentionally raised the amount of the check, which was fraudulent. An alteration is material if it changes the contract of any party to the instrument in any respect, so the alteration here was material. Mark is a holder in due course and Lawrence is not discharged as to him.

   (2) $1,000. The holder in due course can recover on such an altered instrument only for the original tenor, unless the drawer was negligent in drawing it thereby facilitating the alteration. Here, Lawrence was not negligent and Mark can recover only $1,000 from Lawrence.

c. (1) Smith has a right against State Bank for $500. Under the Code, a drawee bank can charge its drawer customer's account only if it, in good faith, pays the holder. A holder is the payee or indorsee in possession of the instrument. Here, the payee, Hodys, never indorsed the check and, therefore, no subsequent person could be a holder. Therefore, Parks was not a holder and State Bank could not charge Smith's account.

   (2) Hodys, as the owner of the check, has a right against State Bank for $500, the face amount of the check, for the bank's tort of conversion by paying the check on a forged indorsement.

   (3) State Bank has a right against National Bank for $500 under the Code for breach of its implied warranties of title and that the indorsements are genuine. Such warranties are made by the transferor of a check to his transferee who pays him. The warranty of title is also made by any person who presents a check for payment and who is paid.

MAY, 1970

No. 6 (Estimated time—25 to 30 minutes)

Arthur purchased securities from William, giving William his check payable to William's order and drawn on Produce Bank in payment. At William's insistence, the check was indorsed by Arthur's friend, Gregory, before it was delivered. William then indorsed the check to the order of Robert, "without recourse," and it was accepted by Robert in payment of a debt owed him by William. Robert indorsed the check in blank and delivered it to his son, Charles, as a birthday gift. Arthur has discovered that the securities sold him by William are worthless and has directed Produce Bank to stop payment.

a. Identify the status of all parties to the check described above at each step in its negotiation, explaining such identifications.

b. When Produce Bank refuses to pay Charles on the check and Charles sues Arthur, may Arthur assert the defense of failure of consideration against Charles? Explain.

c. Assuming Charles knew Gregory signed the check as an accommodation to William and received no value for his accommodation, may Charles nevertheless recover from Gregory on the Bank's failure to honor the check? Explain.

d. Assume Arthur has no defense on the check and is insolvent, that Charles took the check from Robert for value, and that the Bank refused to pay the check for lack of funds in Arthur's account. Discuss the rights and liabilities of Charles, Robert, William, and Gregory.

Answer

a. *Arthur* is the drawer, directing the drawee bank to pay to the order of the payee. *Gregory* is an accommodation indorser having indorsed to accommodate William.

William is the payee to whose order the check is drawn and payable. He is also an indorser by signing as payee, making a special qualified indorsement to the order of Robert. William negotiated the indorsed check when he delivered it to Robert.

Robert became a holder in due course when William negotiated the check to him. Under the Code, a past debt is value. He is a holder because he is the indorsee in possession of the check, and having taken it for value, in good faith, before its dishonor, and without notice of any defense thereon. He also became an indorser when he indorsed it in blank, causing the check to be payable to bearer. He negotiated the indorsed check when he delivered it to Charles.

Charles is the bearer holder of the check. However, he is not a holder in due course, since he paid no value for the check. But he has all the rights of Robert, who is a holder in due course.

b. No. Failure of consideration is a personal defense which cannot be asserted against a holder in due course or a holder claiming through a holder in due course. Here, Charles claims through Robert, a holder in due course.

c. Yes. Gregory became an accommodation indorser in order to be liable as a surety for Arthur in the event of dishonor of the check. Notice of accommodation does not preclude a holder from enforcing the liability of the accommodation indorser.

d. Charles is a holder in due course having taken the check as a holder, for value, in good faith, before dishonor, and without notice of any defense on the check. Since indorsers who do not otherwise qualify their liability on the check engage that on its dishonor and any necessary notice of dishonor they will pay the check, Robert and Gregory are liable to Charles for the amount of the check. William was a qualified indorser and not liable on the check's dishonor here to subsequent holders. As between Robert, William, and Gregory, Robert and Gregory are liable to each other in the order in which they indorsed the check. William is a qualified indorser and is not liable to anyone. Accordingly, Charles can recover from Robert, who can then recover from Gregory.

MAY, 1969

No. 3 (Estimated time—20 to 25 minutes)

Each of the following numbered phrases or clauses states a legal conclusion as it completes the related lettered material. You are to determine whether each of the legal conclusions is true or false according to the provisions of Article 3 (Commercial Paper) and Article 4 (Bank Deposits and Collections) of the Uniform Commercial Code. Write on a separate answer sheet whether each conclusion is true or false. Your grade will be determined from your total net score obtained by deducting your total of incorrect answers from your total of correct answers; an omitted answer will not be considered an incorrect answer.

A. James Clemens purchased an automobile from Charles Dunlop. As consideration Clemens executed and delivered the following instrument to Dunlop:

> New York, N.Y., May 2, 1969
> For value received, I promise to pay to the order of Charles Dunlop, ONE THOUSAND DOLLARS ($1,000) payable at my principal place of business on May 1, 1970. If at any time the holder of this instrument shall deem himself insecure, he may declare the instrument due and payable immediately.
>
> *James Clemens*

61. The instrument is a trade draft.
62. The instrument is a bearer instrument.
63. The language "For value received" is unnecessary to satisfy the requirements of negotiability.
64. The acceleration clause destroys negotiability.
65. Clemens has negotiated the instrument to Dunlop.

B. Henry Fenimore had a negotiable draft in his possession. The draft was originally payable to the order of Walter Barnes. The back of the instrument contained the following indorsements:

(1) *Arthur Thomas*

(2) *Walter Barnes*

(3) Pay to the order of Frank Small,
    Donald Keith

(4) Pay to Henry Fenimore, without recourse,
    Frank Small

(5) For deposit,
    Henry Fenimore

66. If Thomas signed as an accommodation indorser, he did not make any warranties to Fenimore.

67. The instrument was bearer paper when it contained only the signature of Thomas and Barnes.

68. Small has no warranty liability on the instrument since he signed "without recourse."

69. The last indorsement is a restrictive indorsement.

70. The last indorsement prohibits any further negotiation.

C. Harper fraudulently misrepresented the value of oil stock he knew to be worthless and received a negotiable check for $9,000 from Goodwin in exchange for the worthless stock. Harper promptly cashed the check at the Acme Finance Company, paying off a loan of $1,000 and receiving the balance in cash. Harper's indorsement was "without recourse."

71. The fraudulent misrepresentation constitutes a real defense.

72. Acme Finance only gave value to the extent that it paid Harper cash.

73. Acme Finance cannot qualify as a holder in due course because of Harper's indorsement "without recourse."

74. Even if Acme Finance is a holder in due course a timely stop order will eliminate Goodwin's liability on the check.

75. If the drawee bank arbitrarily refused to cash the check Acme Finance could sue the bank and recover any loss resulting from the bank's arbitrary action.

D. The following handwritten instrument was negotiated by Elmer Dodd for value to Jane Maples:

Toronto, Canada, May 5, 1969
Sixty days after date pay to the order of Elmer Dodd, one hundred and fifty dollars ($150), payable at New National Bank, U.N. Plaza, New York, N.Y. Value received and charge the trade account of Olympia Sales Corporation, New York, New York.

W. Stark

76. The instrument is a negotiable foreign time draft.

77. In the event of dishonor a formal protest is required to hold secondarily liable parties.

78. A timely presentment for payment can be made at any time within a week following the expiration of 60 days from the date of issue (May 5, 1969).

79. Olympia Sales has primary liability on the instrument.

80. In the event Olympia Sales is insolvent and cannot pay, W. Stark will be liable to Jane Maples if she has complied with the proper procedural steps and sues him.

E. Hills issued a check to the order of Lewis on April 3, 1969. It was postdated May 6, 1969. Lewis negotiated the check to Gordon. On May 6 Gordon had the check certified by the drawee, Wilson National Bank.

81. At the time of issue the instrument was not negotiable because it was postdated.
82. At the time of issue Hills was primarily liable on the instrument.
83. A refusal to certify the check at Gordon's request would have constituted a dishonor by the bank.
84. Upon certification the bank became primarily liable on the instrument.
85. Upon certification Hills and all indorsers were discharged from liability.

F. Barnaby's Department Store drew a refund check to the order of Flynn for $100 on Merchant Bank. The check was stolen from Flynn's mail box. The thief forged Flynn's signature and raised the amount to $400. James, a subsequent holder in due course, presented the check for payment and the bank paid him $400, charging Barnaby's account. Barnaby's promptly discovered the alteration and forgery and immediately notified the bank.

86. Barnaby's has a right to have Merchant Bank credit its account for $400.
87. Flynn will not be able to collect the $100 from anyone except the thief.
88. James is entitled to keep the $400 if the bank seeks to collect it from him.
89. If the bank had dishonored the check James could recover from any prior indorser.
90. The forged indorsement and the raised amount constitute real defenses.

Answer

61. False	67. True	73. False	79. False	85. True
62. False	68. False	74. False	80. True	86. True
63. True	69. True	75. False	81. False	87. False
64. False	70. False	76. True	82. False	88. False
65. True	71. False	77. True	83. False	89. True
66. True	72. False	78. False	84. True	90. True

PART FIVE

AGENCY

Chapter I

CONCEPT OF AGENCY

1. *NATURE AND SCOPE*

THE subject of agency is concerned with the legal effect of the acts of one person who represents another. It is an old legal maxim that he who acts through another acts himself. The law of agency developed for the most part during the nineteenth century, influenced in large part by the great expansion in business and in business organization. Today the law of agency is to be found everywhere in business, whether the businesses are large or small. The discussion of agency will consider: the concept of agency; how a person can become a representative to act on behalf of another; the extent of the representative's authority to act; the effect of the representative's acts; and, finally, the termination of the agency.

Definition *"Agency" is a legal relationship between two persons who agree that one is to act on behalf of the other, subject to the latter's control.* The party manifesting consent to have the other act on his behalf is called a "principal," and the party who consents to act on his behalf is called an "agent." (P asks A to sell P's horse, and A consents to do so. P is a principal, and A is an agent.) The two focal elements of agency are: the agreement that one is to act on behalf of another; and the principal's right of control over the agent's acts. The agent's consent to the principal's manifestation must be given as required in such manifestation. The manifestation may require a written or oral consent to be communicated to the principal, or performance of the act requested in reliance on the manifestation. (P writes A asking him to sell P's horse. A, in reliance thereon, sells P's horse. A has consented to the manifestation, and agency has been created. If A, ignorant of P's writing, had sold P's horse for P, the sale would not be binding on P because there was no agency. P's manifestation had not been communicated to A, and A had not consented thereto in reliance thereon.) The principal's right to control performance of the

501

agency is essential, and without it agency cannot exist. *A person is responsible only for the instruments he employs and over which he has the right of control.*

Agency Distinguished

Agency should be distinguished from other legal relationships which are similar to, but different from, agency.

Trust. A "trust" is similar to agency in that a person called a "trustee" acts on behalf of a person called a "beneficiary." They differ in that the trustee has title to the property held in trust, while the agent usually does not have title to any property; the trustee does not have authority to make his beneficiary a party to a contract with anyone, while an agent usually has authority to bind his principal by contract; the trustee acts in his own name as trustee, while the agent usually acts in the name of his principal; and the trust is not revocable by the trustee, while an agency usually is revocable by the agent or the principal.

Lien. A person having a lien—i.e., a legal right in the property of another as security for the performance of an obligation—has certain powers exercisable on default of the obligation secured. The existence of the powers inherent in a seller's lien, a pledge, or a mortgage, which are exercisable on the obligor's default, does not constitute an agency relationship between an obligor and obligee because neither the seller, pledgee, nor mortgagee is to act on behalf of the obligor, but rather on his own behalf. In agency the agent acts on behalf of his principal. A "lienor" is the person who has a lien, while a "lienee" is the person against whose property there is a lien.

Family Relationships. It is sometimes said that the purchase of necessaries by a spouse or an infant subjects the other spouse or the parent to liability for the purchase because there is authority implied by law to make such purchase and the person bound is a principal. This is not an agency relationship because the person liable has not manifested consent to another's acting for him; and the obligation to pay for the reasonable value, rather than the contract price, of such purchases is based on a quasi-contractual liability imposed by law. Similarly, the liability imposed on an owner of an automobile for damage caused to third persons and to their property by the negligence of one to whom the owner has entrusted the automobile for his own pleasure, usually a member of the owner's family, is based on statute and not on any agency relationship. Marriage or consanguinity does not of itself create agency. The elements of the definition of agency must be present.

Bailment. When goods are delivered to an agent with authority to dispose of the goods as directed by the principal, the agent is a bailee with authority to sell. Bailment differs from agency in that a bailment may be solely for the purpose of holding goods for the bailor with no duty to act otherwise for the bailor, while in agency the agent has a duty of loyalty and obedience to his principal.

Independent Contractor Compared

An independent contractor is not an agent. He is a person who contracts to render an agreed performance for another, called an "employer," does not act on his employer's behalf, has no authority to deal with third persons or to affect the employer's contractual relations with third persons, and whose manner of performance is not subject to any right of control by the employer. Builders, engineers, public accountants, plumbers, electricians, masons, carpenters, and supervisors of construction are illustrations of an independent contractor. The independent contractor exercises some independent calling, usually supplies his own labor and materials, and often is paid in a lump sum or on a cost-plus basis. He contracts to render an end result. Generally,[1] the employer is not liable to third persons for the acts of the independent contractor employed.

While ordinarily it is easy to distinguish an independent contractor from a servant because of the lack of a fiduciary relationship and no right of control, nevertheless, at times it is difficult to distinguish between them. In a way, the independent contractor and the servant produce an end result, but the principal's right of control differs. A plumber or electrician usually is an independent contractor, but the principal's right of control over his performance may be such that he has the status of a servant to the person for whom he is doing the job. The terms of their agreement and the surrounding circumstances must be considered in determining the relationship. One's right to object to materials to be used or to supervise performance through the architect does not disturb the status of an independent contractor. However, the right to authorize the purchase of certain materials or to employ certain labor, together with employment by the day, probably would cause the relationship to be one of master and servant. Household employees are servants, and skilled employees are servants of their employers although

---

[1] While an employer generally is not liable for the wrongful conduct of an independent contractor working for him, nevertheless, there are exceptions when the employer is liable, as when the work is intrinsically dangerous or the responsibility is nondelegable from the employer to the independent contractor.

they may be independent contractors as to third persons. An example of the latter is a plumber who is a skilled servant of the firm employing him, but an independent contractor to the third person for whom he is rendering service.

Chapter II

CREATION OF AGENCY

---

1. PARTIES

Principal   THE principal and the agent are the only parties to
an agency. A principal may be any person who has
legal capacity to authorize another to act for him and who has legal capacity to be bound by the authorized transaction between the agent and
the third person. A person can do through another whatever he can do
himself.[1] If the principal enters into a contract of agency with his agent,
the principal must have legal capacity to contract. If the principal authorizes one to act as his agent without any contract of agency, the principal need have only the legal capacity to authorize an agent to act for
him. Persons with limited capacity may be principals, such as infants and
the insane; but if the agency is one of contract, then such contract is
voidable at the election of the principal and the law of contracts applies.
In some states an infant cannot act through someone else, and his attempt to do so is legally void. Partnerships and corporations, if acting
within the scope of their authority, and joint, joint and several, and
several, persons, may be principals and may be agents.

Anyone may be an agent, except a person who physi-
Agent   cally or mentally cannot act.[2] The agent usually does
not become a party to the transaction which he nego-
tiates between his principal and a third person, so that there is no problem of his legal capacity to act for himself. An infant may be an agent. A
husband and wife may act as agent or principal for each other, but not
because of their marital relationship. A person with interests adverse to
another may, nevertheless, act as an agent for the other, although he has
a duty to inform the other of his adverse interest. If the agent does not
disclose his adverse interest, then the remedies available to the principal
depend upon the nature of the transaction. If the transaction is *solely between the principal and the agent,* it is voidable at the election of the

---

[1] But see "Illegality," below, pp. 512 f.

[2] An act is a person's affirmative physical manifestation of his will. Every act, therefore, is voluntary.

principal. (P authorizes A to buy certain securities on the market. A had the same securities and sold them to P at the market price without informing P. The transaction between P and A is voidable by P.) If the agent does not disclose to his principal that he represents a third person whose interests are adverse to the principal, the principal may avoid the transaction *with the third person,* provided such third person knew of such adverse interests at the time of the transaction; but if the third person did not have such knowledge, the transaction is not voidable by the principal against the third person.[3] If the agent discloses to his principal his adverse interest and the principal consents to it, or the agent discloses to his principal and to the third person the adverse interests of the principal and the third person, both of whom the agent is representing, and the principal and third person consent to his representation of both, then neither the third person nor the principal may avoid the transaction.

Master and Servant. The law of agency has developed greatly from its beginnings in the law of "Master and Servant," as it was called prior to the 19th century, when the word "agent" rarely occurred. Brokers, factors, and attorneys at law were called by those names and were not known as "special agents" as they are today. Beginning with the 19th century, it was recognized that there were two types of person acting for others, "servants" who performed manual services and "agents" who dealt in business transactions for others, they being distinguished from each other by their functions. Inasmuch as both types of person acted for others, it was later realized that the same rules with respect to their creation, operation, and the legal effect of their relationship with others should apply to both "servant" and "agent." These terms were consolidated, and today the word "agent" includes these two types of person with such functions, and the same rules of agency apply to each, with one extremely important difference, the effect of control.

Control. Under the law, one who has control or the right to control an activity becomes subject to liability for the improper exercise of control over that activity. Since an agent's conduct is subject to the principal's control, the principal is subject to liability for the agent's conduct while acting on behalf of his principal. However, the principal has a varying degree of control over the conduct of his agents; he has the right to control the physical conduct or movements of some agents but not of others. *Only to the extent that the principal has control over,*

---

[3] See the example on p. 545.

or the right to control, the physical conduct of his agent should the principal be liable therefor. Accordingly, solely in order to distinguish the two types of agent over whose physical conduct the principal does or does not have the right of control and for which he is or is not liable, the term "servant" has been retained to indicate the agent whose physical conduct is subject to the principal's control. The person served by the servant is called a "master." Accordingly, we can define a servant as an agent employed to render services for his master and whose physical conduct in the rendition of such services is controlled, or is subject to the right to control, by the master. A master may be defined as a principal who has employed an agent to render services on his behalf and who controls or has the right to control the agent's physical conduct in the rendition of such services. *Unless otherwise indicated, everything that is said in this book about principal and agent applies also to master and servant.*

Liability. The master's liability for the conduct of the servant is the same as the principal's liability for the conduct of a non-servant agent, only *in addition,* the master is liable for the *tortious physical* harm caused by the servant to third persons while the servant is acting within the "scope of his employment" and in certain special instances when he is acting outside the scope of his employment. Also, the master being an employer and the servant being an employee, certain duties and immunities are imposed because of this relation. Today, the term "employee" as generally used in statutes[4] and in court decisions means a servant, although some statutes[5] are interpreted to give the term "employee" a wider meaning.

Distinguished. As we have observed, an agent may be a servant or a non-servant agent. If we look to the closeness of the relationship between the agent and his principal, we can more readily determine whether or not he is a servant.[6] Since a servant renders services, sells his time, and is subject to his master's control, he is an integral part of the

---

[4] For example, Employer's Liability Acts, Workmen's Compensation Acts, social security, and unemployment insurance.

[5] For example, minimum wage and fair labor statutes.

[6] "The relation of master and servant is indicated by the following factors: an agreement for close supervision or *de facto* close supervision of the servant's work; work which does not require the services of one highly educated or skilled; the supplying of tools by the employer; payment by hour or month; employment over a considerable period of time with regular hours; full time employment by one employer; employment in a specific area over a fixed route; the fact that the work is part of the regular business of the employer; the fact that the community regards those doing such work as servants; the belief by the parties that there is a master and servant relation; an agreement that the work cannot be delegated." American Law Institute, *Restatement: Agency 2d,* 1958, sec. 220, *Comment h.*

establishment; although he need not necessarily be physically located at the business plant or office, he generally is. A non-servant agent is not a part of the establishment and his physical movements or conduct are not subject to control by the business, although he assists in its operations. For example, the business manager and other officers of a business, store salesmen along with the typists, secretaries, and other such non-officer personnel are servants. A travelling salesman may or may not be a servant. Many cases are concerned with the independent contractor, the question to be resolved being whether the independent contractor has become a servant, thereby subjecting his master to liability by his conduct. Where a railroad company's contract with a construction company provided that the latter was to construct a temporary place for war materials in the railroad's yards and that, among other details for performance of the work, the railroad's superintendent was to select the time and place of loading and approve of purchases and costs, the court held that the construction company was not an independent contractor but, rather, a servant of the railroad and that the railroad was liable for injuries to employees of the construction company, even though the contract provided that the construction company was an independent contractor for performance of the work.[7]

General and Special Agents. Agents may be classified as "special agents" and "general agents." The distinction is important because of the difference in their authority, apparent authority, the liability of the principal for their conduct, and the termination of their authority and apparent authority. They may be distinguished by their *continuity of service.* "(1) A general agent is an agent authorized to conduct a series of transactions involving a continuity of service. (2) A special agent is an agent authorized to conduct a single transaction or a series of transactions not involving continuity of service."[8] As the number of transactions to be performed, the number of persons to be dealt with, and the time required to perform the job increase, the agent tends to become a general agent. Most general agents are servants, such as sales clerks and managers of businesses. An agent employed to deliver a truck is a special agent, although he may also be the sales clerk and therefore a general agent to sell the store's merchandise. Look to see whether there is a continuity of service with respect to the particular transaction he is to perform. It is often said erroneously that a general agent has wide general discretion, while a special agent does not. Each job to be performed has its own degree of discretion, but this has nothing to do

---

[7] *Cimorelli* v. *N.Y. Central Railroad Co.*, 148 F. 2d 575, 577 (1945).

[8] American Law Institute, *Restatement: Agency 2d*, 1958, sec. 3.

with continuity of service. An agent authorized to purchase a truck, or a broker or an attorney, as special agents, may have more discretion than a sales clerk general agent. Sometimes a professional independent contractor, such as a broker, factor, auctioneer, or attorney at law, who is employed as a special agent, is called a "professional agent."

Four common types of special agent are attorneys at law, auctioneers, brokers, and factors. They are independent contractors, but when employed they become special agents for that employment only. While they exercise discretion in the manner of their performance, nevertheless, the principal has the right to give them lawful directions which they are under a duty to obey; and they have the authority to affect the principal's contractual relations in their dealings with third persons.

Attorney at Law. An attorney at law is a lawyer licensed by a state to engage in legal proceedings and legal functions. The word "attorney" means "agent" or "representative." An "attorney in fact" is not a lawyer but is one who has authority to perform acts of a nonlegal nature, his authority being in writing and called a "letter of attorney" or "power of attorney"; although, in a larger sense, attorney in fact includes all such persons with authority irrespective of whether or not the authority is in writing.

Auctioneer. An auctioneer is a person authorized or licensed by law to sell property for another at a public sale. He is the agent of the person making the sale and has authority to accept bids and to sell for cash. On the acceptance of a bid, unless the parties indicate to the contrary, he is the agent of the buyer and of the seller to sign a memorandum of the sale. In the absence of any express authority to the contrary, an auctioneer has implied authority to fix the terms of the sale, to receive the price, to deliver possession of the property to the buyer on receiving the price, and to sue the buyer for the price in his own name. He also has apparent authority to do this. An auctioneer has no implied or apparent authority to: sell at a private sale; sell on credit; delegate his authority to another; deliver possession to the buyer before he has received payment; give an express warranty regarding the property; modify or cancel the sales contract.

Broker. A broker is a person engaged in the *negotiation* of contracts for the sale of property on behalf of others. He usually does not have possession of the property and does not act in his own name but rather in the name of the person he is representing. Examples are stockbrokers, insurance brokers, and real estate brokers.

Factor. A factor is a person who is authorized to buy goods or to sell goods in his possession, on behalf of another, and who buys or sells, usually in his own name, for a commission called a "factorage." He is often called a "commission merchant" or "commission agent." He has a lien on the goods or proceeds for his compensation. A del credere agent is a factor who sells goods on credit and, for a higher commission, guarantees to his principal performance of the sales contract by the buyer. Such a promise is made primarily for the benefit of the del credere agent (promisor) and not for the benefit of the buyer (debtor) and is not within the statute of frauds.[9] The del credere agent is liable to his principal on the guaranty.

2. METHOD

Appointment **By Contract and Gratuitously.** Agency is a consensual and voluntary relationship between principal and agent. Agency may be created by appointment in two ways: by a contract, which is the usual method; and without a contract—e.g., gratuitous agency. If agency is created without a contract, then the law of contracts does not apply, except to the extent of promissory estoppel.[10] Agency usually is created by a contract between the agent and the principal, and the law of contracts applies in the formation, interpretation, and enforcement of such a contract. Just as in contracts the offeror's manifestation is tested by what a person in the offeree's position reasonably could understand from it, so in the law of agency the principal's manifestation is tested by what a person in the agent's position reasonably could understand the principal's expression to mean. If the agent reasonably can understand that the principal's manifestation indicated an intent to authorize the agent, and the agent assents thereto, then the relationship of agency exists. If the principal's manifestation indicates an intent to have a contract of agency, then there is no agency until a contract is formed between the agent and the principal.

Application of Estoppel and Ratification Inasmuch as estoppel and ratification have, to a large extent, the same effect as the creation and operation of agency by appointment and by contract, it is often said that an agency may be created by ratification and by estoppel. Although they do not create agency *because there has been no manifestation of consent by a principal to an agent to act on behalf of the principal,* nevertheless, the frequency of the assertion that they are methods of creating agency requires their

---

[9] See above, pp. 109 f., and below, pp. 814.

[10] See above, pp. 87 ff.

mention at this point. The application and effect of estoppel[11] and ratification[12] will not be considered at this time but rather under the discussion of authority in the next chapter.

3. FORM

The principal's manifestation creating the agency may be in writing, oral, or by any other conduct, unless required to be in a certain form by law. The principal's silence may be a manifestation of authority if it is usual for one in the principal's position to speak and dissent to unauthorized acts and the principal does not manifest dissent, causing the agent reasonably to believe that he is authorized. An illustration of silence creating authority is a prior course of unauthorized action by a person to which the principal did not object.

In Writing It is often said that if the authorized act that is to be performed must be in writing or under seal, then, for the act to have any legal effect, the authority must be of the same stature or formality as the act to be performed. This is not true, generally. The statute of frauds provides that, to be enforceable, a contract to convey land or an interest therein and a contract not performable within one year after the making thereof must be in writing, or a note or memorandum thereof must be in writing. Most states require the authority to sell, i.e., to convey an interest in, land to be in writing to be enforceable. Inasmuch as most real estate brokers usually have only the authority to find a person who is ready, willing, and able to buy, the broker's authority does not have to be in writing. By statute in some states, the authority of an agent to execute a contract not performable within one year from the making thereof must be in writing. The Code[13] provides that a person may sign a negotiable instrument by his authorized agent and does not require such authority to be in writing. An agent's execution of a sealed instrument on behalf of the principal, made outside of the principal's presence, is of no legal effect unless the agent is authorized by a sealed writing, or a statute removes the Common Law effect of a seal.

4. PROOF

The burden of proving an agency is on him who asserts or alleges such agency; it may be the principal, the agent, or the third person. An

---

[11] See below, pp. 527–30.

[12] See below, pp. 530–39.

[13] UCC 3–403 (1).

agent may testify as to facts in order to prove or disprove agency. For example, the agent may testify as to the words spoken to him by the principal; these are facts proving agency. If the agency is by written authority, then the writing is the best evidence of the agency. An agent's statements of his authority or of the extent of his authority, made prior to a trial, are admissible against the agent to show that he purported to act as an agent for a principal or that he purported to act for himself. However, such statements are inadmissible as proof of agency unless it is shown that the agent had authority to make such statements. The agent's statement that "P authorized me to tell you" is not admissible by itself to prove agency; but if it can be shown that the principal informed the third person that the agent would tell him of the agent's authority, then the agent's statement is admissible to prove agency.

5. ILLEGALITY

An agency agreement must be legally valid in its formation and in its purpose and is subject, generally, to the principles of the law of contracts regarding illegality. Agency agreements which are contrary to statute or to public policy as declared by the courts are illegal. Statutes provide that certain acts are of such a personal character that their performance cannot be delegated to someone else. Illustrations are the right to vote in a public election, the execution of an affidavit, and the essential duties to be performed by the holder of a public office. Statutes provide that only specific persons may perform particular acts. Illustrations are a broker in real estate transactions, an attorney at law for the practice of law, and a doctor for the practice of medicine; these people must be licensed in order to perform the acts essential to their profession. Illustrations of agency agreements contrary to public policy as declared by the courts are agency agreements to restrain trade unreasonably or to commit a crime or a tort.

While generally an illegal agency agreement is of no legal effect, there are instances where it does have a legal effect. *As between the principal and the agent,* the legal effect of the agency agreement is determined by the law of contracts, previously discussed,[14] to which reference should be made at this time. *As between the principal and the third person,* the agent's performance of the illegal agreement may cause the principal, as well as the agent, to be responsible criminally for

---

[14] See above, pp. 89 ff.

the agent's commission of the crime and to be liable civilly for the agent's commission of the tort, contemplated by the agency agreement. Generally, a principal is not responsible for the criminal acts of his agent. However, a principal who authorizes, participates in, aids, procures, or approves of the commission of a crime by his agent is responsible therefor. Also, by statute in specific instances criminal responsibility may be imposed vicariously upon the principal for his agent's criminal acts, e.g., the agent's violation of pure food laws.

Chapter III

AUTHORITY

1. ACTUAL AUTHORITY

Interpretation　　AGENCY is essentially a matter of authority. *Author-ity is the power of an agent to affect his principal's legal relations by acting in accordance with the principal's manifestation of consent to him.*[1] The nature and extent of authority is a matter of interpretation of the principal's manifestations. The rules of interpretation in the law of contracts are applicable to the law of agency. *What can a person in the position of the agent reasonably understand the principal's manifestation to him to mean?* Authority is created by a principal's manifestation, made and communicated to an agent, which the agent reasonably can understand to mean that he is empowered to act on the principal's behalf and is subject to the principal's control in accordance with such manifestation. Authority is his power to act in accordance with such interpretation. The authority of the agent is to affect the principal's relations with third persons. It is the principal's manifested intent to authorize another, and not the principal's unexpressed intent, which is important. As in the law of contracts, an offer can be accepted only by the offeree's knowledge of the offer and his assent thereto, so in the law of agency the agent's act must be in reliance on, and in compliance with, the principal's manifestation of authority. (P sends A written authority to buy a horse for P. A buys the horse for P without knowledge of the written authority. There was no agency because P's manifestation had not been received by A and A had not consented to it. A had no authority to make such purchase for P because he was not acting in reliance on, and in compliance with, the written authority.)

The principal's manifestation of a desire for agency must be communicated to the agent and the agent's consent given in order to create the agency. The principal's manifestation usually indicates what the agent is to do, which is the agent's authority or power to act for his prin-

---

[1] American Law Institute, *Restatement: Agency 2d,* 1958, sec. 7.

cipal. Subsequent manifestations by the principal may direct how performance is to occur and these constitute authority also. Authority is power to act as directed and in reliance thereon, and acts not so done are not authorized.

Express and Implied Authority   The authority received by the agent is called *"actual authority"* because that is the authority he actually has. The authority specifically expressed in the principal's manifestation is called *"express authority."*

Often, the performance of the express authority requires the agent to do something not included in the express authority. It is implied from the principal's manifestation that the agent has authority to do that which is reasonably required to perform the express authority, and such is called *"implied authority"* or *"inferred authority."* "Implied authority" and "inferred authority" are different ways of expressing the same authority; the manifestation implies, and the agent infers from the manifestation, such authority. Implied authority is that authority which the agent reasonably may understand is implied from the principal's manifestation of express authority in light of the circumstances under which the manifestation was made. Implied authority is in furtherance, and is not in contradiction, of such express authority, except in the case of implied authority by emergency,[2] or for the protection of the agent's security interest.[3] Accordingly, actual authority is that express and implied authority deriving from the principal's manifestation as reasonably interpreted by the agent.

General Implied Authority. Unless his express authority indicates to the contrary, an agent generally has implied authority to act primarily and only on behalf of his principal. In dealing with third persons, A normally would be expected to disclose that he is an agent, who his principal is, and to disclose the extent and proof of his authority, unless P has expressly or impliedly indicated otherwise to him; accordingly, A has implied authority to do these things. "The authorized disclosure would not, however, include statements of matters commonly not revealed to third persons, such as the maximum price authorized to be paid for a specified article or conditions to which the principal is willing to accede, but which he hopes will not be required."[4] *Since A is authorized to disclose that he has authority, his disclosure is therefore a manifestation by P to T creating apparent authority.* It should be

---

[2] See below, pp. 517–18, 546–47.

[3] See below, pp. 546–47.

[4] American Law Institute, *Restatement: Agency 2d,* 1958, sec. 46, *Comment a.*

noted carefully that A's authority is to act on behalf of P and that his implied authority is to disclose that he has authority to act for P and that he is acting for P; however, *if A does not intend to act for P he has no implied authority to disclose that he has authority to act in the particular transaction, because he is not acting for P.* For example, P authorizes A to borrow money from T for P. A, intending to act for P, has implied authority to represent to T that he is P's agent to borrow for P, and the subsequently accomplished loan binds P. However, if A intended to borrow the money in P's name and to keep it for himself, A has neither authority to borrow in P's name nor implied authority to represent to T that he is P's agent to borrow for P; A's unauthorized disclosure of authority does not create apparent authority.[5]

There are other instances of general implied authority commonly occurring in business. Ordinarily, previously hired employees may assume that they are authorized to continue to do what they have been doing and new employees may assume that they have the authority of their predecessors, in the absence of P's manifestation or circumstances to the contrary. Usually, directions to a general agent are construed as suggestions or advice and not as limitations on his authority, and directions to a servant are construed usually as limitations on his authority. Unless indicated to the contrary, the manifestations of two or more principals to an agent to act for them jointly does not imply authority to act for them severally. For example, if X and Y are partners in a partnership that owns land, X and Y individually also owning separate pieces of land, their joint authority to A to sell "their land" implies authority to sell only their partnership land.

Extent of Implied Authority

Generally, unless the principal has expressed an intent to the contrary, an agent has implied authority: to disclose the indicia of his authority; to act only for the benefit of his principal; to act jointly if he is jointly authorized with others; to act as an agent only so long as his authority exists; to disclose the identity of his principal; and to interpret his express authority in light of what is incidental to such express authority, of custom and usage, of previous course of dealing between him and his principal, of an emergency, and of what he reasonably can interpret the principal's manifestation to mean. In general, it may be said that there are the following kinds of implied authority: incidental, by custom and usage, by course of dealing, and by emergency.

---

[5] However, this is one of the instances of inherent agency power, discussed on pages 559–60, when liability would be imposed upon P by A's unauthorized borrowing.

Incidental Authority. *Incidental authority* is implied authority to do that which is incidental to the performance of what has been expressly authorized. An agent authorized in writing to sell land has incidental authority to sign a contract for the sale and to sign a deed; a manager of a store has the incidental authority to hire salesmen; and authority to sell has the incidental authority to receive payment in cash. A general agent has broad incidental authority, while a special agent has a narrow incidental authority. The nature and extent of incidental authority will vary with the circumstances.

By Custom and Usage. A principal is presumed to know the custom and usage in his own locality and that custom and usage prevail in other communities and throughout the United States.[6] Accordingly, his manifestation, as interpreted under the circumstances, implies authority to comply with custom and usage which are not contrary to the express authority in carrying out such express authority. Custom and usage do not enlarge or limit the express authority, but authority is implied to comply with such custom and usage as is reasonably necessary to the performance of the express authority.

By Course of Dealing. *Silence implies authority only when there is a duty to speak and the principal's silence reasonably leads one to believe that the principal intends assent by such silence.* Authority to perform one act does not imply authority to continue to perform similar acts, but, as the number of similar acts authorized increases, authority reasonably may be implied that similar acts are to be performed in the future. Accordingly, authority to do an act may be implied by course of dealing.

By Emergency. An agent has implied authority by emergency, sometimes called "by necessity," to act as he believes reasonably necessary under the circumstances in the event of an emergency exposing the principal to loss, provided the agent reasonably believes: that the emergency was caused by an event not anticipated by the principal; that it is impracticable or impossible under the circumstances for him to communicate the fact to his principal; that action contrary to, or in excess of, his actual authority is necessary to protect his principal's interests; and that his principal under the circumstances would have authorized him so to act. (P in California ships oranges to A, his factor, to sell in New York. While the oranges are in transit, the market price drops severely in New York and sale of P's oranges there will result in loss to P. A

---

[6] Usage is an habitual or customary practice. Generally, the words "custom" and "usage" are used synonymously. The circumstances surrounding a transaction are considered in interpreting the manifestations which occurred. Custom and usage are a part of the circumstances. For "usage of trade" under the Code, see UCC 1–205(2).

cannot communicate with P. A reroutes the oranges for sale in Philadelphia where the market price is higher. A had implied authority by emergency so to reroute reasonably under the circumstances.)

Specific Instances. It may be helpful to discuss briefly some specific instances of implied authority in common transactions and forms of business. Authority cannot be implied contrary to the express authority, except in the case of implied authority by emergency, or for the protection of the agent's security interest.[7]

Authority to Buy or Sell. Authority is implied to buy or sell on behalf of the principal when such sale or purchase is either: incidental to the performance of the authorized transaction; implied by custom and usage; or implied by emergency. The express authority "to buy" or "to sell" is ambiguous, requiring interpretation under the circumstances. Such authority may mean to find a willing purchaser or seller, or to make a contract to buy or sell, or to transfer or receive title. The subject matter and the form of the transaction of purchase or sale are helpful in determining the intention of the principal. If the sales transaction must be in writing in order to be enforceable—e.g., to sell land—then the authority is interpreted to mean that the agent is to produce a willing buyer or seller. If the transaction is not required to be in writing in order to be enforceable, then the nature of the subject matter becomes important. When personal property is the subject matter of the transaction, the nature of the authority depends upon whether or not it is usual for the agent to have possession of the property. It is usual for an agent with authority to transfer title to have possession of the personal property, unless it is too bulky to handle, in which case the problem of interpretation becomes more difficult. *If the agent has possession with the authority to sell, his authority is to transfer title. If the agent does not have possession of personal property which is not bulky, the agent's authority is interpreted as merely to solicit orders for the purchase of the property and to obtain willing buyers.*

It is important to determine whether the implied authority of an agent is to produce a willing buyer or seller, or whether his authority is to transfer or acquire title. When the agent's express or implied authority is to transfer title to the principal's property, or to acquire title to property on behalf of the principal, the agent has the following implied authority: to fix the terms of the sale or purchase; to make or receive the warranties usually given or which are required in connection with such transaction; to execute the necessary papers in connection with

---

[7] See below, pp. 546–47.

such transaction; to pay or to receive payment; and to deliver or to receive possession of the subject matter or documents of title. If the authority is to produce a willing buyer or seller, authority is implied: to describe the subject matter of the transaction; to explain the principal's terms; and to solicit offers to buy or sell. Authority to purchase implies authority to purchase at a private or public sale, while authority to sell implies authority to sell only at a private sale.

Usually the manifestation of express authority to buy or sell indicates the price. Unless the circumstances surrounding the manifestation of such authority indicate to the contrary, the agent has implied authority to sell or buy at a price most favorable to the principal but not in excess of the express authority. (P authorizes A to purchase a certain horse for $100. A has the implied authority to purchase the horse for $90.) The agent's knowledge that his principal has a fixed price policy is an illustration of circumstances which preclude any implied authority to deviate from the fixed price. In the absence of any indicated price in the authority to buy or sell, there is implied authority to buy or sell at the market price or, if there is no market price, at a reasonable price.

An agent with authority to sell personal property, but who does not have possession of such property, has no implied authority to receive the purchase price; if he is in possession, he has the implied authority to receive the purchase price. An agent with authority to buy personal property but with no authority to receive possession of such property has no implied authority to pay the purchase price. If the express authority prescribes the terms of the transaction in which the agent is to engage, the agent has implied authority to comply with such terms at the time of the transaction. For example, if the terms provide that payment is to be made or received, or that possession is to be transferred or received, at the time of the transaction, the agent has the implied authority to do those particular things at that time.

Authority to sell implies authority to sell only for cash, except that a factor has implied authority to sell also on credit; however, authority to sell on credit usually implies authority also to sell for cash, unless the circumstances preclude such an implication. Authority to buy implies authority to buy only for cash if the principal has advanced the money to the agent; otherwise, authority is implied to buy only on the principal's credit.

Authority to buy or sell implies authority to give or receive only those warranties usually accompanying such a transaction, either in connection with the subject matter of the transaction or in connection with the credit of the principal if it is a sale to the principal on credit. Although there is a conflict of authority on whether or not there is implied authority to give a warranty of quality, most courts hold that such authority may be implied.

Authority to buy or sell does not imply authority to modify or rescind a completed transaction; except that an agent with authority to buy has implied authority to have the contract corrected to state the terms properly, and to return the purchase price if the agent has made material misrepresentations to the seller with or without the principal's authority.

It should be noted that, in the absence of agreement to the contrary, authority to act for two or more principals jointly does not include authority to act for them severally. (A and B authorize C to sell their land. C sells A's land. C has no authority to do this inasmuch as his authority is to represent *them* and not *each* separately.) (A and B authorize C to sign a contract for them with D. C signs a contract for A with D. C does not have authority to represent A; his authority is to represent A and B.)

Authority to Borrow. An agent's authority to borrow in his principal's name is not implied readily. Such authority is implied only when performance of the express authority otherwise cannot occur, or it is implied by emergency. Authority to borrow implies the pledging of the principal's credit only to the extent reasonably required under the circumstances.

Authority to Receive Payment. Authority to receive payment may be implied from the express authority if the circumstances permit. Such authority to receive payment implies authority to receive only full payment when due, in cash, and to give receipts and other necessary papers in exchange therefor. Today as a general practice checks are given and received only as conditional payment and, should they be dishonored, the debtor is liable on the original debt. An agent to receive payment has implied authority to receive checks as conditional payment and, should the check be to the agent's order and paid, such payment to the agent is payment to the principal. He also has implied authority to receive a bank draft, certified check, or a Post Office money order as well as a check as conditional payment.

Authority regarding Commercial Paper. Authority to *issue* negotiable instruments usually is not incidental to performance of the authorized acts and, therefore, it is not implied readily. Authority to borrow implies authority to issue negotiable instruments in the name of the principal for the amount authorized to be borrowed. When the agent's position in the management of a principal's business is such that it is absolutely necessary to the operation of such business that the agent issue commercial paper, he has implied authority to draw on the principal's bank account for such purposes. Such authority may be implied also by emergency only when it is necessary to avoid any extremely substantial loss to his principal. Authority *to indorse* commercial paper in the name of a principal is not implied readily, except for deposits in the principal's account, in which case it is readily implied.

Where there is implied authority to issue or indorse negotiable instruments, the agent's wrongful use of such implied authority subjects the principal to liability to an innocent purchaser of the instrument for value, called a "holder in due course,"[8] as though the agent had acted properly.

This is as good a place as any to emphasize the rule, to be discussed later,[9] that when an agent with authority to contract in P's name and for P's benefit acts for his own benefit or for other improper purpose, P is subject to liability to third persons who are innocent of A's improper purpose. P gave A the authority and placed A in a position where third persons could trust to P's selection of a reliable agent and, therefore, P assumes the risk of liability to innocent third persons for A's conduct with an improper purpose.

Authority to Manage a Business. Authority to manage a business implies authority to do what is reasonably required to operate the business, such as to employ help, to buy or sell depending on the nature of the business, and to obtain supplies and equipment. Similarly, authority to manage or take care of property implies authority to do what is reasonably required in order to preserve and maintain such property.

Authority to Delegate and to Appoint Others. An agent may not delegate authority to perform his authorized acts if he has no implied authority to do so. An agent has a fiduciary duty to act on behalf of his principal, and, usually, he has discretion, special skill, or judgment in the performance of the expressly authorized act. For this reason authority to perform, usually being of a personal character, cannot be delegated by the agent to someone else. However, delegation to a subagent of the authority to perform all or an incidental part of the authorized act is permitted as an exception to the rule if the agent's discretion, special skill, or judgment is not required for such performance, such as performance of an act of a mechanical or ministerial character. (P authorizes A, a real estate broker, to procure a willing purchaser of P's land, or to sell the land at a fixed price. A's discretion, special skill, or judgment is not required to perform the authorized act,

---

[8] See UCC 3–302, and above, p. 410.

[9] See below, pp. 559–60.

and A may delegate the authority to perform to B. If P had authorized A to sell the land, leaving to A the discretion of fixing the price or selling at the best price obtainable, authority to delegate performance would not be implied.) Authority to buy or sell is not impliedly delegable, and authority to settle claims is not impliedly delegable to an arbitrator, because the agent's discretion, special skill, or judgment is involved in the performance of such authorized acts. When the agent's discretion, special skill, or judgment is required for the performance of the authorized act, the agreement between the agent and the principal is a personal agreement, and the legal principles governing assignments in the law of contracts are applicable regarding nondelegation of duties in personal contracts.[10] First the appointment of other agents will be discussed, then the appointment of subagents, and finally the appointment of subservants.

1. *Appointment of Other Agents.* Unless otherwise manifested by P, authority is implied to appoint other agents of P if A's business position or operation of the business reasonably so requires or such authority is implied by usage or emergency. Thus, the general manager of a store has implied authority to hire sales and other necessary personnel for operation of the store. A bank that has received from a depositor a check for collection from a bank in another locality has implied authority to appoint a bank in the other locality as the depositor's agent for collection and to forward the check to it. There are many cases involving perishables in which it has been held that A had implied authority to appoint other agents for P to help preserve the perishables in an emergency.

It should be noted carefully that when an agent appoints *another agent* pursuant to his authority, the other agent is solely the agent of P and is not the agent of the appointing agent. The diagram would be:

$$P$$
$$|$$

(Appointing agent)   A₁——A₂   (Appointed agent)

The fact that the appointed agent is subject to the orders of the appointing agent, as a salesman appointed by the general manager of a store takes orders from the latter, does not cause the appointed agent to be a subagent of the appointing agent. *The authorized appointment of another agent places the latter in the same relationship with P as though P had made the appointment himself.* The appointing agent or the appointee, or both, may be non-servant agents or servants. Since the

---

[10] See above, pp. 104–5.

appointee is not an agent of the appointing agent, the latter is not responsible to P for the appointee's conduct. Should A *unauthorizedly* appoint another agent for P, the appointee does not become the agent of P, who is not liable for the appointee's acts; the appointing agent is in the position of being a principal toward the appointed agent, and the latter has the power to subject the appointing agent to liability with third persons.

2. *Appointment of Subagents.* We have seen that the authorized appointment of *another agent* causes the appointee to be *solely the agent of P.* However, if an agent's authority is to conduct a transaction or perform an act himself or have another person do it for P, if the agent appoints another to do it for P, the appointee to be the agent of the appointing agent and the appointing agent to be responsible to P for the conduct of the appointee, then the appointee is a subagent. He is "sub," under the appointing agent; and because the appointee is an agent of the appointing agent, the latter is a principal as to the appointee and responsible for his conduct. The appointee has two principals, the appointing agent's principal and the appointing agent himself. The Restatement of Agency defines a subagent as "a person appointed by an agent empowered to do so, to perform functions undertaken by the agent for the principal, *but for whose conduct the agent agrees with the principal to be primarily responsible.*"[11] The diagram would be:

$$P$$
$$|$$
$$(\text{Appointing agent}) \quad A$$
$$|$$
$$(\text{Subagent}) \quad SA$$

For example, the bank teller who has the responsibility for collecting notes for depositors is the servant agent of the bank principal and the subagent for the depositors as principals. An insurance company's general agent, responsible for a specified territory with authority to open offices within that territory and who appoints insurance agents in such offices, causes such appointees to be subagents—agents under the general agent and working as agents for the company in selling insurance.

Unless otherwise manifested by P, authority is implied to an agent, who is to conduct a transaction for P, to appoint a subagent to do so only if A reasonably can believe that P is willing for A to have someone

---

[11] American Law Institute, *Restatement: Agency 2d,* 1958, sec. 5(1). (Author's italics.)

else do it. A reasonably can so believe if: A is an organization, such as a corporation or a partnership, which acts through its employees; it is either impracticable or illegal for A to perform; or usage or emergency so permits. Thus, an agent with authority to act for P may not be licensed by law so to act and would have to appoint licensed subagents to perform, such as a lawyer to sue, an auctioneer to auction, or a real estate broker to sell land. Also, it is usual for brokers, attorneys at law, and factors to have implied authority to act through their employees as subagents of the principal. It should be noted carefully that, should an agent *unauthorizedly* appoint a subagent of P, the appointee does not become a subagent of P and P is not liable for his acts; the appointing agent is in the position of being a principal toward the subagent, and the latter has the power to subject the appointing agent to liability to third persons.

3. *Appointment of Subservants.* We have learned that an agent may be either a servant or a non-servant agent, such as a professional special agent (e.g., broker, attorney at law, factor). *While an agent may appoint a subagent, only a servant can appoint a subservant.* As discussed previously,[12] the only reason for distinguishing a servant from a non-servant agent is that the master controls or has the right to control the physical conduct of the servant agent and, therefore, he is subject to liability to third persons for the physical acts of the servant. Since the principal does not have such control, he is not liable for the physical conduct of his non-servant agent. *Thus, the servants of a non-servant agent are not servants of the principal.* When, pursuant to authority, a servant appoints another servant to perform the first servant's duties for his master, *the master and first servant to control the physical conduct of the appointed servant,* the appointee is both a servant of the first servant and a subservant of the master, *for whose conduct the first servant is responsible to the master.* In other words, the appointee has two masters, the appointing servant and the latter's master. The Restatement of Agency defines a subservant as "a person appointed by a servant empowered to do so, to perform functions undertaken by the servant for the master and subject to the control as to his physical conduct both by the master and by the servant, *but for whose conduct the servant agrees with the principal [master] to be primarily responsible.*"[13] The diagram would be:

---

[12] See above, pp. 506–7.

[13] American Law Institute, *Restatement: Agency 2d,* 1958, sec. 5(2). (Author's italics and brackets.)

```
                          P
                          |
(Servant)                 S
                          |
(Subservant)              SS
```

When a servant is paid by the job and is authorized to employ his own assistants who, it is agreed between the master and the servant, are to be subject to the control of the servant and subject to the superior control of the master, such assistants are subservants. For example, where a company's branch manager has authority to hire, pay, and control his employees, the company having the right to control both the manager and the employees, such employees are subservants with the power to subject the company and the manager to liability for their conduct, but for which the manager is ultimately liable to the company as an indemnitor. *If the company did not retain the right to control the manager's employees, they would be the servants solely of the manager and only the manager would be liable for their physical conduct.* They would be subagents but not subservants of the company. *It is the element of control over physical conduct that is the key to servant status and concomitant liability.* If a company master wants control over the servants of an employee servant, then the company must pay the price in terms of risk of loss therefor.

The section which follows considers the subject of apparent authority. *The above discussion of the extent of implied authority is applicable to apparent authority, in determining the extent of such apparent authority.* Information available to the agent and not to the third person may cause the agent's implied authority to be different from his apparent authority. (P appoints A as general manager of P's large retail store, but without authority to hire sales personnel. T knows that A is the general manager of P's store. While A has no *implied* authority to hire sales personnel, nevertheless, since T reasonably can believe that A as general manager has authority to hire sales personnel, A has *apparent* authority to do so.)

2. *APPARENT AUTHORITY*

Interpretation   A person is responsible for the reasonable interpretation put upon his utterances and acts by persons to whom they have been directed. In the law of contracts if a person in the position of an addressee reasonably could interpret the manifestation made to him as an expression of an intent to contract with him, the manifestation is an offer to him which he may accept and thereby form a contract. Similarly, in the law of agency if the addressee reasonably can interpret the manifestation made to him as an expression of an intent to have him act on behalf of the utterer and subject to the latter's control, and he consents thereto, agency has been created. The extent of the *agent's* authority again is the *agent's* reasonable interpretation of the principal's manifestation made *to him.* If a person's manifestation is made to a *third person* which the *third person* reasonably can interpret as creating an agency in, and as conferring authority on, another, the latter is an "apparent agent" with "apparent authority" to act on behalf of the first person as his "apparent principal." The third person may rely justifiably on the manifestation of the apparent principal and deal with the apparent agent with the same effect as though agency and actual authority existed. (P informs T that A is his agent with certain authority. A has apparent authority to act as P's agent to the extent as manifested by P to T.) Apparent authority often is called "ostensible authority."

Principles Applicable

The principles applicable to the creation, interpretation, and operation of agency and authority are equally applicable to apparent agency and apparent authority. Just as an agent's reasonable interpretation of the principal's manifestation to him is the measure of his authority, so the third person's reasonable interpretation of the principal's manifestation to him is the measure of the apparent authority of the apparent agent. Similarly, to the third person the manifestation of the apparent principal may *imply* authority in the apparent agent. (P tells T that A is authorized to sell P's horse in A's possession. T reasonably can believe that A has implied authority to deliver the horse to T and to receive payment at the time of the sale.)

Apparent authority exists whether or not there is any actual authority.[14] (P tells T that A has authority to sell P's horse. P tells A that he is authorized to sell the horse for $100. A has apparent authority to sell the horse at a reasonable price. If P had told T that A could sell only for $100, the extent of the actual and apparent authority would have been the same.) It is the apparent principal's manifestation to the third person, not the principal's manifestation to his agent, which is the source of apparent authority.

---

[14] American Law Institute, *Restatement: Agency 2d*, 1958, sec. 8, *Comment a.*

An apparent principal's manifestation to a third person may be made orally, in writing, or by other conduct. If the manifestation is in writing intended for the third person's examination, and the third person knows this, apparent authority is limited by the contents of the writing. The manifestation may be made by the appointment of a general agent whose status is known to the third person. (P appoints A as general manager of P's store. P has held A out to the public as a general manager, and this manifestation creates apparent authority to act as a general manager with all the authority implied from that position.) Just as silence at times may be interpreted reasonably by a person as a manifestation of intent to authorize him to perform as an agent, so a third person may interpret silence as creating apparent authority. (In P's presence and hearing, A represents to T that he has authority to sell P's horse, when he had no such authority, and the horse is sold to T by A acting on P's behalf. P remained silent. A had *apparent authority* to sell P's horse. P's silence *under the circumstances,* when he reasonably should speak, is a manifestation *to T* that A had authority to sell the horse. Note that A also has *authority* here because A reasonably could so believe from P's manifestation of silence *to A* under the circumstances.)

It should be noted very carefully that A's disclosure of his agency and authority to T pursuant to his express or implied authority to do so on P's behalf creates apparent authority to the extent of such disclosure. However, A's misrepresentation of his authority, or his disclosure of authority for an improper purpose and not on P's behalf, is unauthorized and does not create apparent authority. P is not manifesting through A when the latter occurs.

3. APPLICATION OF ESTOPPEL

In General   *Estoppel* is a principle of law which prevents a person from asserting the reverse of what he has represented previously if, meanwhile, the addressee has changed his position materially in reasonable reliance on the previous representation.[15] (T asks P if the signature on a certain check is P's signature. P says it is, when in fact it is not his signature. T then buys the check and pays for it. P refuses to honor the check on the ground that it was not signed by him. P is liable on the check and is estopped to deny the signature as his own.) In the above illustration of forgery, P did not actually or appar-

---

[15] See above, pp. 42–43 ff.

ently authorize anyone to sign for him. T did not rely on anyone doing an act in compliance with any assertion by P, but he did rely on P's assertion itself, and the principle of estoppel was applicable. (T asks P if A is authorized to sign a check for P, and P says A is authorized, when A is not authorized. A signs a check for P and delivers it to T, who delivers value to A for it. P is bound because A had apparent authority. Estoppel does not apply.) Apparent authority causes P and T to have mutuality of agreement, each manifesting assent to each other through A, and a contract results from this manifestation of mutual assent. In estoppel there is no such mutuality or element of agreement. Neither P nor T is manifesting assent to each other directly or through an intermediary; there is no mutuality of agreement and, therefore, no basis for contract between P and T.

If an apparent principal is bound by the apparent authority of his apparent agent, there is no room for the use of the principle of estoppel. The utterer (apparent principal) is bound without the use of estoppel. It should be observed that, while reliance on apparent authority binds the apparent principal and the third person to the transaction as parties thereto, the application of estoppel does not do this. By estoppel the third person can enforce the transaction against the utterer, but the utterer may not enforce the transaction against the third person. Thus, when the circumstances permit application of the principle of apparent authority, this principle becomes more desirable than the principle of estoppel, which then becomes inapplicable.

The Holding Out   *Estoppel occurs when two elements are present: a holding out to another of something other than authority; and a material change of position by the other in reasonable reliance on the holding out.* P's holding out or manifestation may be in any form. It may be oral, in writing, and even silence under circumstances in which P has reason to know that A is misrepresenting that he has authority to act for P or that he owns property belonging to P, and P does not take reasonable steps to notify T of the facts. (P knows that A is stating to T that A is P's agent with authority to sell P's goods. P does nothing and T buys the goods and pays A the purchase price. There is no authority because P has not manifested to A that he has authority, and there is no apparent authority because P has not manifested to T that A has authority. P is estopped to deny A's authority and he loses his interest in the goods to T. The same result would occur under these circumstances if A had misrepresented to T that A owned the goods.) This is but another illustration of the fundamental principle discussed previously[16] that silence under circumstances when a person has a duty to speak and dissent is an assent to the transaction that occurs, and responsibility is imposed for such silence.

Material Change of Position in Reliance   While a third person need only rely on the apparent authority, in estoppel a third person must change his position materially in reliance on the holding out so that it would be to his detriment or damage to permit the utterer to deny the truth of his previous assertion.

The third person's making a contract with A is reliance but is not a material change of position. (P informs T that A is authorized to sell P's horse, P knowing A has no such authority. T relies on P's statement and contracts with A to buy P's horse. Immediaely after the contract was made but before anything was done thereunder T learned that A did not have authority to sell the horse. Under the principle of apparent authority, T's reliance was sufficient and P is bound by the contract. Under the principle of estoppel, T's reliance was not a material change of position because he will not suffer any damage if the transaction is treated as a nullity; T was not bound to P and all that T had done was to make a promise which is not binding on him. If T had paid the purchase price to A before he knew of A's lack of authority, such payment would be a material change of position. However, inasmuch as P is bound by the principle of apparent authority the principle of estoppel is unnecessary.)

Apparent Authority versus Estoppel   The unnecessary confusion between apparent authority and estoppel may be traced to a change in the law of contracts. At one time it was the view that a contract could not be formed without a "meeting of the minds"—i.e., that the actual mental intents of the parties were in agreement. This was the subjective view of contracts. Accordingly, when a principal represented, or permitted his agent to represent, to a third person that the agent had authority and, in reasonable reliance thereon, the third person dealt with the agent, but the agent did not comply exactly with his authority, the principal could not be bound by the transaction. He did not intend to be bound by a transaction other than one made in exact compliance with the agent's authority. (P informed T that A had authority to sell

---

[16] See above, p. 511.

P's horse. P told A that he was not to give a warranty that the horse was sound, although such a warranty usually is given. A sells the horse to T with a warranty of soundness. Under the subjective view of contracts, P was not bound by any contract.) The principle of estoppel was utilized to impose liability on the principal so that the third person who reasonably relied on a principal's representation of authority could enforce the transaction against the principal who was estopped to deny the authority of the agent.

In its development the law of contracts changed so that today the objective view is applied in the formation of contracts. A contract is formed by the *manifestation* of mutual assent, regardless of the mental intents of the parties. It is the addressee's reasonable interpretation of an expression uttered to him which is important and not the unexpressed mental intent of the utterer. Accordingly, a principal who represents an agent as having authority is manifesting an intent to be bound by the agent's exercise of the authority which the third person reasonably can understand him to have. If the third person relies on this manifestation, even though the agent acted unauthorizedly, the principal is *bound by the contract*. In the horse illustration in the paragraph above, P would be bound by the contract. Therefore, where a principal holds out another as his agent with apparent authority, the principal is *bound* by the agent's exercise of such apparent authority, and the artificial device of estoppel is unnecessary.

4. *APPLICATION OF RATIFICATION*

Definition   Often a person, A, professes to act on behalf of another, P, but, because of his lack of authority so to act, the other is not bound by such act. However, the other may wish to be bound by such act to the third person, T, with whom A had dealt on P's behalf. In order to give effect to what both parties desire without having to go through the throes of making a new contract, the law permits the alleged principal to consent to the transaction and thereby to cause the transaction to be binding upon both parties as of the time the transacion occurred, as though it had been authorized. When this occurs it is called "ratification." *Accordingly, ratification may be defined as a person's manifestation of consent to a previously unauthorized act not binding on him, made either by one who purported to act on the first person's behalf or by one who rendered services purporting or intending to act on the first person's behalf, which has an effect as though such act were authorized by the first person previously. (A* unauthorizedly, and in P's name, sells P's horse to T. P later learns of the sale and tells T that he approves of the transaction. P and T are bound to each other by contract as of the time when A originally acted.) The word "affirmance" is used in this book when discussing ratification to indicate P's manifestation of consent to the unauthorized act on P's behalf. Ratification is not authority, because authority is the power *to act* in compliance with the principal's manifestation, while ratification is concerned with an unauthorized act which has *already occurred*. However, ratification has the effect of authority and relates back to the time of the occurrence of the transaction. The elements of ratification will be discussed separately.

Previous Transaction Not Other- wise Binding on Ratifying Party	The purpose of ratification is to overcome the effect of a transaction not authorized. If the transaction bound the principal either because of actual or apparent authority, or otherwise, ratification cannot occur.

Inasmuch as ratification relates back to the time of the occurrence of the transaction, the principles applicable to the creation of agency and of authority are applicable to ratification. A transaction which could not have been authorized at the time of its occurrence because of incapacity of the parties, illegality, or other reason precludes ratification. A person cannot ratify an act that he could not have authorized at the time of its occurrence because he was not in existence at that time. (For example, when promoters of a corporation to be formed make a contract in the corporation's name with a third person, on its creation, the corporation cannot ratify the contract.)[17] An exception is made in the case of legal representatives, whose appointments are made effective as of a previous time; they may ratify acts that they could have authorized if they had been appointed at the earlier time. Examples are trustees in bankruptcy, executors and administrators, and assignees. Ratification by a person with limited capacity—e.g., an infant—subjects the ratification to possible avoidance by such person subsequently. Only the principal on whose behalf the agent purported to act may ratify the transaction. The principal's identity need not be known to the third person. A

Authority Previously Possible (margin heading)

---

[17] While the courts are in conflict on this phase of agency and corporate law, nevertheless, the legal concepts of adoption, novation, and continuing offer are employed by dissenting courts to accomplish the same result as ratification. See below, pp. 675-76.

transaction which was illegal at the time of its occurrence cannot be ratified, but a transaction which was legal at the time of its occurrence and subsequently became illegal may be ratified, provided the statute making such transaction illegal is not retroactive.

Purporting to Act for the Principal

Ratification is to authenticate the transaction. Ratification gives legal effect to the intentions of the parties to an unauthorized consensual transaction not binding on them by binding the parties to each other. They intended to deal with each other, T at the time the unauthorized transaction occurred when A purported to be acting for P, and P when he subsequently manifested his consent to the transaction. P's affirmance gives to T what he desired, namely P as a party to the transaction with T. If A had not purported to be acting on P's behalf, T would not have intended to deal with P but rather with A. (A, without authority and in P's name, sold P's goods to T. P affirmed the sale. P is bound to T. If A had misrepresented to T that the goods belonged to A, the contract would have been between A and T since T intended to deal only with A and, inasmuch as A had not purported to act for P, P cannot ratify the sale.) It would be contrary to T's manifested intent to permit P, a party with whom T did not intend to contract, to make himself a party to an unauthorized transaction in which A did not purport to act for anyone but himself.[18] It is the manifested intent of the parties that is being furthered by ratification so as to achieve the effect of an agreement, usually a contract, properly entered into by the manifesting parties. A's motive is of no importance; what is important are the manifested intentions of P and T to make an agreement between themselves, although indirectly through A.

"Purporting" here is a professing or manifesting by A that he is acting on behalf *of another*. It is not necessary for A to identify P to T, although he usually does. A need only indicate that he is acting for another and then, unless otherwise indicated by T, T's intent is to deal with that other person as represented to him by A. If A identifies P to T, then P is the person with whom T wished to deal. If A describes P without identifying him, for example as "my principal" or "the abutting landowner," then affirmance can be made only by the person complying with that description. If the description applies equally to two or more

---

[18] It is for this reason that an undisclosed principal cannot ratify the unauthorized act of his agent not binding on him and thereby become bound as a party to the contract; A does not purport to represent anyone but himself. However, he may be liable to the third person for restitution of the reasonable value of what he has received. See American Law Institute, *Restatement: Agency 2d,* 1958, sec. 104, *Comment d.*

persons, then it seems but logical that affirmance can be made only by the one on whose behalf A intended to act. A need not even indicate that he is authorized, although A is impliedly so warranting unless he has otherwise indicated,[19] nor need T even believe that A has authority so to act. For example, A may tell T that he is not sure that he is authorized so to act, or that he is not authorized but that P will probably affirm A's conduct in acting on P's behalf in dealing with T. *It is T's intent to deal with P that controls;* if T intends to deal with P through A, even though T may believe A is not authorized so to act and can merely hope that P will affirm, the law deems T's intent to deal with P sufficient for the purpose of ratification.

Forgery. The courts have not been in accord on whether or not a forgery can be ratified. The Code permits ratification of a forged signature on a negotiable instrument, reflecting the trend to permit ratification of a forged signature on other instruments as well as negotiable instruments. *The Restatement of Agency permits ratification of any simulated signature by the person whose signature it has been purported to be:* "However, if one impersonates another, thereby purporting to act as another, or executes or delivers an instrument purportedly signed by another, the rationale of ratification is applicable and the act or transaction can be ratified by affirmance if it does not involve an illegal agreement. . . . In no event, however, is a ratification effective in favor of one who obtained it by promising not to prosecute the forger."[20] It should be noted carefully that liability for a forged signature may also be imposed by estoppel. (A forged P's signature to a check. P told T that it was his signature and T, in reliance thereon, took the check in exchange for merchandise then sold to A. P is estopped to deny the signaure as his and he is liable on the check.)

A's Rendition of Services. Thus far we have been discussing consensual transactions with third persons, conducted by A when A has purported to T that he was acting on P's behalf. However, there are situations not involving a consensual transaction with third persons when A is rendering *services* intending them to be on P's behalf and either purporting or not purporting to third persons that he is acting on P's behalf in rendering such services. (P has a retail store. A, without P's authority, takes and drives P's truck, delivering P's merchandise to customers to whom sales have been made. A drives negligently and injures T.) Some courts have extended the rationale of ratification and

---

[19] For A's express and implied warranties of authority, see below, p. 577.

[20] American Law Institute, *Restatement: Agency 2d,* 1958, sec. 85, *Comment b.*

have permitted P to affirm A's conduct, thereby causing the relationship between P and A to be master and servant with consequent liability on P for the tortious physical conduct of his servant, A, while acting within the scope of his employment. It should be noted carefully that A must be rendering *services,* and *either* intending or purporting to be acting on P's behalf in the rendition of such services for ratification to be possible. Thus, in this type of case, P may be liable to T even though A did not purport to T that he was acting on behalf of P. In the example given, P may affirm A's conduct and thereby become liable to T for A's negligence.

The Principal's Consent

The principal must consent to the previous unauthorized transaction in order for ratification to occur. His manifestation of consent is proof of his intent to consent to the transaction, and may be in writing, oral, or implied from his conduct. The form of his consent must be the same as that required in order to create an agency to engage in that transaction. An *oral* consent to an agent's contract to sell the principal's land is ineffective as a ratification. The principal's expression or conduct must manifest his intent to make the transaction his own.

P's manifestation of consent is not required to be communicated to anyone in order for it to be effective in producing a ratification. All that is required is that P manifest an intent to make the transaction his own or to adopt another's conduct; the manifestation is merely proof of P's intent. P's manifestation is proof of such intent if made to A or T, but is not proof if made to someone not a party to the transaction and who is not expected to act on P's manifestation. (P, with knowledge of A_1's unauthorized conduct in making a contract in P's name with T, tells A_2 to inform A_1 that A_1 did a good job. P has manifested assent and the transaction is ratified.) However, if T without knowledge of P's affirmance changes his position so that it would be inequitable to permit ratification, T may avoid P's subsequent affirmance.

There are various ways by which P may manifest his consent. Although P's affirmance may be oral, written, or any other conduct of his indicating his consent, inasmuch as ratification relates back to the time of A's unauthorized act, if it was required that authority to do the unauthorized act be made with a specified formality, e.g., under seal or in writing, then P's manifestation of consent must also be in that form. P's conduct other than an express manifestation may imply consent.

P's Silence with Knowledge. *P's silence with knowledge of an unauthorized transaction under circumstances in which P would be* *expected to repudiate the unauthorized transaction and dissent to it* may be an affirmance resulting in ratification. (P learns of A's previous unauthorized contract to purchase goods in P's name and does nothing. P's silence is an affirmance resulting in ratification.) (A unauthorizedly makes a contract in P's name and either A or T telegraphs P to inquire if it is all right. P does not reply; his silence is an affirmance resulting in ratification.)

P's Receipt of Benefits with Knowledge. *P's receipt of the benefits of an unauthorized transaction with knowledge of all the facts, and not for any reason other than the transaction itself,* is an affirmance, even though P received the benefits under a mistake of law. Thus, if A has authority to contract in P's name with T, A unauthorizedly included additional terms in the contract not binding on P, and A receives the benefits of the contract, which he then turns over to P, who knows of all the facts, P's *receipt of such benefits with knowledge* is an affirmance resulting in ratification of the transaction. (P authorizes A to sell merchandise to T for $100. A unauthorizedly sells the merchandise to T for $80 and delivers the money to P, who knows all the facts. P's *receipt of the money with knowledge* is an affirmance resulting in ratification.) If P should receive the benefits with knowledge of all the facts but at the same time *repudiate* the unauthorized transaction, T has an election either to treat the transaction as ratified or to rescind it. On the other hand, P's receipt of the benefits of the unauthorized transaction with knowledge of all the facts but for a reason other than the transaction itself, for example, belief that he is entitled to such benefits irrespective of the unauthorized transaction, is not an affirmance, irrespective of whether or not he is right in his belief. (P is fraudulently induced by X to sell his horse to T, a good faith purchaser for value, who thereby obtains title to the horse. A, unauthorizedly and in P's name, purchases the horse from T and delivers it to P, who knows all the facts but believes that the horse is still his because of the fraud. P's receipt is not an affirmance because he claimed the horse not by reason of A's unauthorized transaction but, rather, because he believed he had never lost title to the horse because of the fraud.) Obviously, if P is actually entitled to such benefits irrespective of the unauthorized transaction, of course, his receipt of them is not an affirmance. (A_1 steals P's goods and sells them as the owner to T. A_2, without authority and in P's name, purchases the goods from T and delivers them to P, who knows all the facts. P's receipt is not an affirmance because he never lost title to the goods.) If P should receive benefits from an unauthorized transaction without knowledge of the facts, there is no affirmance, unless P assumes the risk of his lack of knowledge and receives the benefits not caring what the facts are.

P's Retention of Benefits with Knowledge. *P's retention of the benefits of an unauthorized transaction, with knowledge of all the facts and before P has changed his position and not for any reason other than the transaction itself* is an affirmance. In the previous paragraph we considered P's *receipt with knowledge* as an affirmance. Here, we are concerned with P's *retention with knowledge* as an affirmance, P not having knowledge when he received the benefits. If P has received the benefits and then learns of all the facts, he is then in the same position as when a principal receives the benefits with knowledge of all the facts, and the rules applicable in the latter instance as discussed previously apply with respect to retention with knowledge. The difference occurs if P has changed his position *before* learning of all the facts. If P has so changed his position *without* knowledge of all the facts so that it would be inequitable to require P to return what he has innocently received from the unauthorized transaction, then P will not be required to return what he has received and his retention is not an affirmance, although P may be liable to T restitutionally for that which T has parted with and P has received.

P's change of position before learning of all the facts precluding retention as an affirmance may occur in a variety of ways: P may, as a good faith purchaser for value, obtain title to the property unauthorizedly acquired by A in P's name; P may have so mixed the property with P's own property or something else as to make the original property inseparable or no longer individually distinguishable; or P's own situation may have so changed as to make it inequitable to require P to return what he has received from the unauthorized transaction. (A, husband, unauthorizedly and in the name of his wife, P, purchased from T an automobile on P's credit. A delivered the automobile to P as a gift, P not knowing the facts. P continued to drive the automobile *after* she had learned of what A had done. P has affirmed the transaction and is liable to T for the same.) (A unauthorizedly and in P's name purchased building materials from T and delivered them to P's workmen who included them in the building construction. After the building was built, P learned all of the facts. P's retention of the materials is not an affirmance, and no ratification results.) (A unauthorizedly took P's goods and, stating that the goods were his own, sold them to T who paid by giving to A his check payable to A's order. A indorsed the check in blank and delivered it to P in exchange for cash in the face amount of the check. P then learned of all the facts. P's retention of the check is not an affirmance and no ratification results, because P validly obtained title to the check as a holder in due course when he innocently purchased it from A.) (A, a special agent, with authority to sell P's corporate shares, unauthorizedly agrees with a purchaser, T, that, at T's election, P will repurchase the shares after a lapse of three years at a higher amount per share. A delivers the purchase price to P who, without knowledge of the unauthorized additional terms, places the money in the business. If T exercises his option at the end of three years, P's retention of the money is not an affirmance and no ratification results.)

P's Assertions in a Legal Action. *P's assertion of a claim or a defense in a legal action, based upon A's unauthorized transaction in P's name as though it were authorized, made with knowledge of the facts,* is an affirmance. (A, unauthorizedly and in the name of P, an ice manufacturer, made a contract to sell ice to T. P, without knowledge of the facts, delivered only some of the ice to T. T sued P for damages for breach of contract and P, with knowledge of what A had done, asserted a counterclaim for the price of the ice already delivered to T. P has affirmed and is liable on the contract for its breach by P.) P's assertion of a claim or a defense in an action with T or A, P not believing T's statement that A has unauthorizedly inserted additional terms in the agreement between T and A in P's name, is not an affirmance of the unauthorized additional terms.

P's Ignorance of Material Facts. There is a wide difference of view among the courts as to whether or not P's ignorance of a material fact precludes affirmance.[21] The Restatement of Agency holds to the preferred view that ignorance of a material fact involved in an unauthorized transaction made by A in P's name does not prelude P's affirmance and resulting ratification. However, since P's ignorance existed also at the time of the unauthorized transaction, the transaction is thereafter *voidable by P provided T, meanwhile, has not changed his position in reliance on the ratification.* (P authorizes A to sell P's goods, which A does in P's name but unauthorizedly misrepresents the goods to T_1, the buyer. A tells P of the sale without informing P of the misrepresentation, and P innocently affirms the transaction. Later P learns of the misrepresentation. P can rescind his affirmance. However, if T_1 had innocently resold the goods to T_2 prior to P's attempted rescission of his affirmance, P cannot rescind his affirmance because of

---

[21] See extensive *Reporter's Notes,* American Law Institute, *Restatement: Agency 2d,* 1958, Appendix, sec. 91.

T_1's change of position.)[22] *A fact is material if it would so substantially affect the existence or extent of the liabilities of the parties to a transaction as to be important to a reasonable person's decision of whether or not to become a party to the transaction or to affirm previous conduct.*[23] Of course, if P assumes the risk of his ignorance of material facts and consents to an unauthorized transaction in his name, not caring to investigate when, in the light of his knowledge, a normally prudent man would make inquiry, then P's affirmance cannot be avoided for ignorance of material facts. (P authorizes A to sell P's goods, which A does in P's name but unauthorizedly misrepresenting the goods to T, the buyer. P is informed of the transaction and, ignorant of the details of the transaction including the misrepresentation, P states that he will stand by A in whatever he has done. P cannot avoid his affirmance.) P's affirmance with ignorance of the material fact of *T's* fraud or duress in inducing *A* to make the unauthorized transaction in P's name is voidable by P. Also, T's inducement of P's affirmance by fraud or duress causes the affirmance to be voidable by P.

Third Person's Withdrawal Precludes Ratification

Lack of authority on the part of the purported agent causes the transaction not to be binding on the third person. The third person is then in a position similar to that of an offeror who may withdraw his offer at any time prior to acceptance. Accordingly, the third person may manifest his withdrawal from the transaction at any time prior to ratification. Once ratification occurs, the transaction has the same effect as though it had been authorized previously. The third person's manifestation of withdrawal may be any expression or conduct which reasonably can be understood as indicating his intent not to continue with the transaction, and it is effective as a withdrawal regardless of his reason and regardless of his knowledge or ignorance of the purported agent's lack of authority. The commencement of an action by the third person against the agent for damages for breach of warranty implies his intent to withdraw. If, prior to any attempt to withdraw, the principal first repudiates the transaction and then ratifies the transaction, the third person cannot withdraw, unless the third person had acted in reliance on the repudiation prior to the attempted ratification.[24]

---

[22] Under UCC 2–403, when the seller of goods has a voidable title that has not been avoided at the time the goods are sold to a good faith purchaser for value, the latter acquires the title free of the power of avoidance.

[23] See above, p. 44.

[24] See "Anticipatory Breach," above, pp. 127 ff.

**Ratification
of Entire
Transaction**

Ratification is of the entire transaction and cannot be confined to a part of such transaction. If there are several independent unauthorized transactions, the principal may ratify one or several but need not ratify all.

**Change of
Situation**

The situation subsequent to the occurrence of the unauthorized transaction may so change as to make it inequitable to permit ratification to occur. (A, without authority and purporting to act on behalf of P, sold P's valuable race horse to T, the price to be paid in 30 days. Three days thereafter the horse died without the fault of anyone. P will not be permitted to ratify the transaction.) A common illustration is the attempt of the owner of a building, after a fire has occurred, to ratify the issuance of a fire insurance policy on such building obtained previously by a person without authority and purporting to act on behalf of the owner.

Chapter IV

OPERATION OF AGENCY

---

1. DUTIES AND LIABILITIES BETWEEN PRINCIPAL AND AGENT

THE DUTIES of the parties to an agency are determined, expressly or impliedly, by the terms of the appointment of agency. In the absence of any manifested intent to the contrary, the law fixes certain duties between the principal and the agent. Duties on the part of either reflect correlative rights of the other.

Principal to Agent A principal has, essentially, four duties to his agent: compensation, reimbursement, indemnity, and performance according to the terms of the agency. These will be considered in turn.

Compensation. Unless the terms of the agency are to the contrary, a principal is under an obligation to compensate his agent for performance in accordance with the terms of the agency. A gratuitous agency creates no obligation of compensation. If there is no express contract of agency, rendition of performance by an agent at the request of his principal implies a promise on the part of the principal to pay the reasonable value of such services. A request for performance is implied by a person's knowing acceptance of performance which he reasonably can understand was rendered with the expectation of compensation, such as where payment is usual, especially in a business or profession. In the absence of anything to the contrary, performance rendered by near relatives does not imply any expectation of compensation. Ratification of an unauthorized act may create a duty to compensate the agent, because ratification relates back to the time when the unauthorized act was performed and validates such act as though it had been authorized.

Compensation is due when the agent has performed under the terms of the agency and is in such amount as agreed therein. If the amount of compensation has not been specified under the terms of the agency, then the market rate prevails, or, if there is no market rate, then a reasonable rate. Unless provided to the contrary, a drawing account, in effect, is a salary and is not a loan or advance. A salesman on commission with a drawing account has no obligation to return or to pay for what he draws.

P's Competition with A. It is important to distinguish between an exclusive agency and an exclusive sale. Unless otherwise agreed, an exclusive agency to deal with particular property is generally interpreted as precluding P from employing another agent but not precluding P from competing with A to accomplish the particular result, although an exclusive agency to sell a manufacturer's or dealer's product in a specified locality generally is interpreted to preclude P's competition. An exclusive sale contract generally is interpreted to mean that A has the exclusive power to sell. All of this is a reflection of the larger rule that, unless otherwise provided, P's contract to compensate for A's accomplishment of a particular result does not preclude P from competing with A either personally or through another agent.

Indemnity and Reimbursement. The word "indemnity" connotes a legal assurance by one person to another of payment to the other for his appropriate expense and loss sustained. Part of this duty of indemnity is concerned with payment to the other for *authorized payments* that he has made out of his own pocket, which we will call "reimbursement." Payment to the other for *expense and loss* sustained by the other *as a result of acting within the scope of his authority*, we will call "indemnity." These terms will be used in this sense.

Reimbursement. Unless otherwise agreed, P has a duty to pay A for payments made by A *pursuant to his authority*. A's right to such payment is called the "right of reimbursement." If such expenditures were made at the actual request of the principal, there is express authority to make such expenditures; if such expenditures are incurred in performing an authorized act reasonably requiring such expenditures, a request to make the same is implied, creating implied authority to make such expenditures. Authority to perform an act requiring travel by the agent implies authority to incur reasonable travel expense. However, if A's compensation depends upon his accomplishing a particular result, such as a broker with authority to sell land, unless otherwise agreed, P has no duty to reimburse A for the expense he incurs in endeavoring to accomplish the result, such as if in his search for potential purchasers he incurs advertising expense in listing the land for sale and expense in driving potential purchasers to the land. A cannot make a profit by reimbursement; he is made whole.

Indemnity. Unless otherwise agreed and in the absence of statute to the contrary, P has a duty to compensate A for expense and loss sustained without A's fault *while acting within the scope of his author-ity*. Thus, a right of indemnity arises from A's payment on contracts that he authorizedly made for P, as by becoming a party to the contract and becoming liable thereon. If such performance is not obviously illegal, and the agent is ignorant of the illegality, the principal has the duty to indemnify his agent for any loss or damage caused thereby. If such performance is obviously illegal, then there is no such obligation on the part of the principal.

Performance. Either P or A has the power to terminate agency at any time because the relation exists only by the *continuing* consent of P and A. There is a duty on the part of the principal, as well as on the part of the agent, not to breach a contract of agency. If the agreement is terminable at will, the agency agreement may be terminated with impunity, although the principal is liable for compensation due at the time of the termination. If the agency is one of contract, the principal has no right to terminate such contract except for cause—e.g., the agent's violation of his duty thereunder. Should a principal breach a contract of agency, the law of contracts is applicable. Immediately on such breach, the agent has three remedies. First, he may sue for damages for breach of contract immediately on the occurrence of such breach. Second, if it is an anticipatory breach, he may bring an action for damages immediately, or he may wait until the arrival of the time when the principal was under a duty to perform under the contract and then sue for damages. If he waits until such time, he has a duty to mitigate, and not to enhance, damages and he must make a reasonable effort to secure similar employment elsewhere. His third remedy is to rescind the contract and to assert his right to restitution for the reasonable value of the services he has rendered, less what he has been paid already under the contract.

The principal is not liable for damage proximately caused by his justifiable termination, although the agent may be able to obtain restitution for the reasonable value of the services he has rendered, less the damage caused to the principal by his wrongful conduct. Similarly, when termination occurs by operation of law, such as by the death of the principal or agent, there is no right of action for any damage caused by such termination inasmuch as it is not a breach of contract, although compensation may be due for services already rendered under such a contract.

If the agent has acted adversely to his principal in the transaction without the knowledge and consent of his principal, or if the agent has acted for more than one principal with adverse interests in the same transaction and without the knowledge and consent of both, the agent has no right to compensation for such services rendered. If the principal had knowledge of the agent's adverse interests and had consented to the agent's performance of the authorized act, or if both the principals with adverse interests had knowledge of the circumstances and had consented thereto, the agent then has a right of compensation for the services he has rendered to the consenting principal. An agent has a duty of loyalty and may not profit from his disloyalty in performance of the agency.

Unless otherwise agreed, an agent has a possessory lien by law on the principal's property in the agent's possession as security for reimbursement and indemnity for expense incurred in connection with that property under the terms of the agency. The lien is a specific lien and not a general lien (except that factors, bankers, and attorneys at law also have a general lien) and applies only to the particular property on which the expenditures were made; it is not a lien on all of the principal's property. An attorney at law has such a lien on his client's papers to secure the payment of fees owing in connection with those papers. Similarly, a factor has a lien on the principal's goods in his possession for advances made, or expenses incurred, in connection with such goods. Agents who, pursuant to authority, buy goods on behalf of the principal and advance their own money or pledge their own credit in connection with such purchases, have a security interest in such goods and a right to retain such goods in their possession. The lien cannot be exercised by the sale of such property, except in the case of a factor's lien, when sale may be made on default as provided by law. The privilege of the lien is to retain the property until the debt has been paid.

An agent who, pursuant to authority, has purchased goods for his principal in his own name and has paid for such purchase and shipped the goods to the principal, may retain a security interest in such goods and cause the issuance of a bill of lading in favor of himself. Should conditions occur which create a seller's right of stoppage in transit,[1] such an agent may exercise this same right in furtherance of his right of lien.

When Relationship Is Master and Servant. When the agency relationship is one of master and servant,[2] the master's duties to his servant are, to a large extent, fixed by statute. At Common Law the master had the duty: to provide reasonably safe conditions for work; to

---

[1] An unpaid seller's right of stoppage in transit is the right to stop and regain possession of goods while they are in transit to the buyer if the buyer is insolvent. See above, pp. 333 ff.

[2] For a discussion of servant, see above, pp. 506 ff.

provide reasonably safe tools and equipment; to exercise reasonable care in the selection of adequate, competent, fellow servants; and to exercise reasonable care in the operation of the business and in the formulation of reasonable operating rules. The master was liable to the servant for damage caused to him by negligence on the part of the master in the performance of his duties, except when such damage was caused: by the negligence of a fellow servant; by the servant's contributory negligence; or by known risks of the business voluntarily assumed by the servant. These three exceptions were often referred to, respectively, as the fellow-servant rule, the servant's contributory negligence rule, and the assumption-of-risk rule.

Today, under workmen's compensation statutes, society has imposed upon industry as an overhead operating expense the risk of personal injury to employees arising out of, and in the course of, employment. Employers are required to make adequate financial provision in order to assure payment for such damage. Usually the employer is required to take out insurance, either under a state insurance fund or with an insurance company; or the employer may self-insure by providing proof of financial ability to pay the compensation himself and depositing adequate securities with the state workmen's compensation commission. Essentially, the purpose of such statutes is to assure indemnity to employees in business for personal injuries arising out of, and in the course of, employment. Domestic servants and farm laborers usually are excluded from protection under such statutes. Generally, compensation is not allowed for self-inflicted injury or if the injured employee was intoxicated. The law in some states gives to business the election of coming within the terms of a workmen's compensation statute. In other states there are compulsory workmen's compensation laws in which industry must participate.

It should be noted that, in the absence of agreement to the contrary, the inventions and discoveries of a servant employee belong to him, irrespective of whether they were made before, during, or after the termination of his employment. However, if an employee on his employer's time or by the use of his employer's facilities and materials invents or discovers a new process, inasmuch as the time, facilities, or materials involved were at the employer's expense, the employer acquires, in the absence of agreement to the contrary, a limited shop right to the use of such invention or discovery without any obligation to pay the employee therefor. In effect, the employer's right is a free, nonexclusive, irrevocable, nonassignable license to use the invention or discovery under the equitable principle called the "shop right" doctrine.

Agent to Principal
The duties of an agent to his principal may be described as: to be loyal to his principal; to give obedience in complying with the terms of the agency; to exercise reasonable care in performance of the agency; to account to his principal for what he has received under such agency; and to perform his agency obligations.

Loyalty. An agent has a fiduciary duty of loyalty and trust toward his principal because he is authorized to act on his principal's behalf and is trusted by him. An agent may act for another whose interests are *not adverse* to that of his principal in the performance of the agency. A carrier of goods sent C.O.D. is the agent of the consignee for the purpose of transportation and is also the agent of the consignor for the purpose of collecting the purchase price. An agent authorized to produce a buyer ready, willing, and able to purchase may also act as the agent of a willing buyer in procuring a sale to him;[3] there is no discretion in A which he can use to the disadvantage of either P or T. In each of these two instances the two principals do not have adverse interests; the consignee is interested in transportation and the consignor is interested in payment, while the seller of the property is interested only in the procurement of a willing buyer and the willing buyer is interested in obtaining the property, respectively.

An agent with interests adverse to his principal, and an agent representing a third person with interests adverse to those of his principal, may be, and act as, an agent, but he has a duty to disclose the facts to his principal and to such third person. (P authorizes A to sell P's land on a commission basis. T authorizes A to purchase such land on a commission basis. P is interested in selling his land at as high a figure as possible and has entrusted this discretion to A. T is interested in purchasing the land for as low a price as possible and has entrusted this discretion to A. P and T have adverse interests and A should not represent both without their mutual knowledge and consent. If A acts representing both, without their mutual knowledge and consent, the transactions between *P and A* and between *A and T* are voidable at the election of P or T and, if avoided, A is not entitled to compensation.)[4]

---

[3] In the law governing real estate brokers, adversity of interest has been defined generally to include representing the buyer as well as the seller in the same transaction; also, it is unethical and illegal by statute in many states for a broker to represent both the buyer and the seller without their knowledge of, and consent to, this fact.

[4] As between *P and T*, if P and T are ignorant of such adverse interests, neither can avoid against the other, although each may avoid against A; while if either P or T is not ignorant of such adverse interests, the innocent party may avoid against the knowing party. See above, pp. 505 f.

An agent may act for himself in dealing with his principal regarding the subject matter of the agency only with his principal's knowledge and consent. Without the principal's knowledge and consent the transaction is voidable at the election of the principal, regardless of the benefit or loss derived by the principal from the transaction.

The agent has a duty to notify his principal of all material facts of which he has notice in connection with the agency. He should notify his principal of the adverse interests of himself or of other agents of the principal, or of threatened loss to the principal's interests. Notice to the agent is notice to his principal, unless a third person knows, or has reason to know, that the agent would not communicate such information to his principal. An agent would not be expected to communicate information to his principal under the following circumstances: when the agent is under a duty to another not to disclose the information to his principal; when the agent is known to be acting adversely to his principal, either on his own or on another's behalf; and when information is given by a third person to an agent, both of whom collude to defraud the principal. An agent has the duty not to disclose during, or after termination of, the agency confidential information which he acquired during such agency when such disclosure would be to the principal's disadvantage or prejudice. After the agency has been terminated, the agent may use the names of customers and methods of operation of the principal's business as he remembers them; but he cannot make use of such information if he obtained the information in violation of his agency.

Obedience. An agent has the duty of obeying all reasonable instructions of his principal in the performance of the agency. *The agent is absolutely liable for loss proximately caused to his principal by his disobedience.* Selling goods for less than the authorized price; selling for credit when authorized to sell only for cash, resulting in loss caused by the debtor's default; and the agent's failure to comply with instructions to sell at the market price, believing that the market will go up in price when the market in fact goes down, causing loss to the principal, are illustrations of disobedience causing loss for which the agent is liable to the principal. The good faith of the agent, intending and purporting to act on behalf of the principal, is no excuse. The principal's ratification of the unauthorized act discharges the agent from the liability for loss caused to the principal by his disobedience.

An agent may justifiably disobey his principal's instructions in only two instances. The first is where authority to disobey is implied by emergency. The second is where the agent has a security interest in the property and obedience of the principal's instructions would endanger such security interest. An agent who has authorizedly advanced money on the security of the principal's property in the agent's possession may justifiably disobey the principal's instruction to sell the property, as such sale would endanger the agent's security interest.

Reasonable Care. An agent has the duty to exercise the care of a reasonable, prudent person in the position of the agent, in the performance of the agency, and is liable to the principal for any loss proximately caused by his negligence in failing to exercise such care. An agent professing to have abilities or special skill has the duty of care of a person with such abilities or special skill. Liability is imposed upon the agent only for his negligence. An agent with authority to insure has the duty of exercising reasonable care in the selection of a competent insurance company, and he is not liable for loss caused to his principal by subsequent insolvency of such a company if the agent has used reasonable care in its selection. A collection agent is not liable for his failure to effect collections, provided he was not negligent in his efforts to make such collections. An agent with authority to sell on credit is not liable for loss caused to the principal by the debtor's default if the agent has exercised reasonable care in selling to a financially responsible buyer. An agent also has the duty to exercise reasonable care in his conduct toward, and transactions with, third persons in the performance of the agency so as not to subject his principal to liability for his torts.

To Account. An agent is under a duty to account to his principal for all money and property which he has received and which belong to his principal. He may not secretly profit from his agency, and, in the absence of agreement to the contrary, *any* profit he acquires as a result of any transaction in which he has engaged on behalf of his principal, and *any* profitable use of the principal's property or of confidential information received during the course of the agency, he holds in trust for the principal. The agent is under a duty to keep the funds and property of his principal separate from his own, and failure to do so may result in liability for any loss caused to the principal. If the principal's funds are intermingled with the funds of the agent in a bank account, and the bank should fail, the agent is liable for any loss which the principal suffers by such failure. Similarly, if the agent mixes the principal's property with his own so that separation is impossible, the principal is entitled to the entire mass.

Performance. An agent has a duty to perform a contract of agency, but no duty to perform an agency of a noncontractual nature. However, once an agent begins performance of a noncontractual agency and the principal relies on his acts, the principle of equitable estoppel[5] applies and the agent is liable to the principal for damages caused by the agent's nonperformance or his negligent performance. If the agent breaches a contractual agency, the agent is liable for damages for breach of contract. The agent is also liable in conversion for the reasonable value of the principal's goods if they are used by the agent in a manner or for a purpose not authorized. Further, the principal may have a right of action in replevin for repossession of the goods while they are still in the possession of the agent.

2. DUTIES AND LIABILITIES BETWEEN PRINCIPAL AND THIRD PERSON

A principal's manifestations expose him to liability for the authorized acts of his agent and for the unauthorized acts of his apparent agent. Third persons expose themselves to liability by their dealings with an agent or an apparent agent. This liability between principal and third persons may be in contract or in tort. First their duties and liabilities in contract will be discussed and then their duties and liabilities in tort.

Contracts

A discussion of the contractual duties and liabilities of a principal and third person will be divided into two parts—namely, when the principal is disclosed or partially disclosed, and when the principal is undisclosed. Under each part will be discussed the effect of the authorized and unauthorized acts of an agent or apparent agent.

Disclosed Principal. In the absence of a manifested intent by the principal to the contrary, an agent has implied authority to disclose his agency and the identity of his principal, unless such disclosure would adversely affect the interests of his principal, in which case such authority is not implied. However, agents with or without authority often do not disclose their agency, or if they do disclose their agency they do not disclose the identity of their principals. Whether or not a principal is *disclosed, partially disclosed,* or *undisclosed* depends on the knowledge of the third person at the time of the transaction between the agent and

---

[5] Under the principle of equitable estoppel, one person whose voluntary conduct causes another person materially to change his position in reliance thereon precludes the first person from asserting rights which he otherwise might have; e.g., when, under a gratuitous agency, the agent begins to perform and the principal relies on such beginning of performance, the agent is estopped to assert as against his principal that there is no contract between them.

such third person. If the third person knows, or reasonably should know, that the agent is acting as an agent for a principal known to such third person, the principal is a disclosed principal. If the third person knows, or reasonably should know, that the agent is, or may be acting as, an agent for a principal but he does not know the principal's identity, the principal is a partially disclosed principal. If the third person does not know, or reasonably should not know, that the agent is an agent acting for a principal, the principal is an undisclosed principal. Unless otherwise indicated, use of the term "disclosed principal" includes a partially disclosed principal.

Parties. A disclosed principal may become a party to a contract by the authorized act of his agent. It is for the agent and the third person to decide who are the parties to the contract; whether the contract is between the principal and the third person, between the agent and the third person, or between the principal and agent and the third person. Inasmuch as the principal has been disclosed, it is implied that the third person desires the principal, and not the agent, as a party to the contract, unless the agent and the third person manifest an intent to the contrary.

A disclosed principal is presumed to be a party to every contract authorizedly made by his agent and a third person, whether or not the principal is described therein, with the following three exceptions when he is not a party:

1. If the contract is under seal in a state where the Common Law effect of the seal exists and the principal is not described as a party thereto.
2. If the contract is in the form of a negotiable instrument and the principal's name does not appear thereon. Although the principal is not a party to the negotiable instrument he is a party to the contract under which the negotiable instrument was issued. However, if the principal's name appears anywhere on the instrument, evidence is admissible to show that the intent of the agent and third person was to include the principal as a party to the contract.
3. If *the contract,* whether written or oral, *specifically* excludes the principal as a party. The contract definitely must exclude the principal as a party. If the contract is signed by the agent indicating his status as agent but not identifying his principal, while the agent and the third person are parties to the contract, nevertheless, such a contract does not specifically exclude the principal as a party, and evidence may be introduced to prove the intent of the agent and the third person to have the principal as a party.

The parties to a contract may be the disclosed principal and third person, the agent and third person, or all three. *Unless an intent is manifested to the contrary, only the disclosed principal and the third person are parties to the contract.*

Although, as discussed thus far in this section, extrinsic evidence may be utilized to prove that a disclosed principal is a party to a simple written contract, nevertheless, *on the face of the contract,* that is, by the appearance and wording, is P a party? If the written instrument or a series of written instruments when considered as a whole indicate that an agent was acting as such for a principal *disclosed in the instrument,* then, unless the parties have manifested to the contrary therein, the instrument is considered that of the principal and not of the agent. All printing and other writing on the instrument, the heading, salutation, body, signature, etc., the language used, and the form of the instrument, are considered in order to interpret who were meant to be the parties. Thus, checks with P's name printed on them and containing blanks to be filled in, and stationery with P's name printed on it, when filled in and signed by an agent, are considered to be that of P. If the signature on the instrument contains both P's name and A's name, indicating that he is an agent of P, the instrument is interpreted to be that of P and not of A. The signature may be: "P, by A"; "P, by A, agent"; "A, agent for P"; "P, by A, President". But if the instrument is signed simply "A, agent" then, unless otherwise manifested in the instrument, on the face of the instrument A is a party to the instrument; although, as stated above, extrinsic evidence is admissible to prove that P is also a party, or that P and not A was to be the party to the contract. If the contract is not in writing, and in the absence of manifestation therein to the contrary, the known fact that A is acting for the disclosed principal is enough to cause the contract to be between P and T, without A being a party. An agent should be careful to sign an instrument clearly to preclude his being a party thereto by having the signature contain P's name and A's name, followed by his office or status.

Although a note or memorandum of a transaction within the statute of frauds is not a contract, nevertheless, the above principles apply, and the authorized signature by an agent acting on behalf of his principal, but not identifying the principal in the note or memorandum, is binding upon the principal as though he had signed such note or memorandum himself.

Liability by Actual and Apparent Authority. Agency is a method of becoming a party to a contract through the authorized act of another. If the agent's contractual act on behalf of his principal is unauthorized, the principal is not a party to the contract and is not bound thereby, unless the principal has created apparent authority and the agent's acts were within the scope of such apparent authority. If an apparent agent acts within the scope of his apparent authority, his acts have the same effect in binding his apparent principal to a third person relying on such apparent authority as though the apparent agent had been authorized and had acted within the scope of his actual authority.

A principal may create apparent authority by his manifestation made to third persons. The principal may make such manifestation to a third person himself or he may place his agent in a position where the principal knows, or reasonably should know, that the agent will represent him to third persons. Appointment of a general agent creates apparent authority in the agent to do what a person in such position apparently has the authority to do. A limitation on his actual authority does not affect his apparent authority if the third person does not know, or reasonably should not know, of such limitation. (P appoints A general manager of his store but instructs A that he has no authority to hire personnel or to purchase goods for the store. A, purporting to act as P's agent, contracts with T for the purchase of goods for the store, and hires S as a salesman. P is bound as a party to the contracts with T and S because of A's apparent authority and the reliance of T and S thereon. While A had no implied authority so to act because of P's instructions, yet he had apparent authority so to act because T and S reasonably can interpret A's position as implying such authority.) The principal's limitation may be on his agent's express or implied authority, but if the principal manifests to a third person that another has authority, such other is an apparent agent with apparent authority. The above example illustrates the principal's limitation on an agent's implied authority.

Duty of Third Persons to Ascertain Agency and Authority. It is the duty of third persons to ascertain the existence, nature, and extent of an agent's authority. Third persons deal at their peril with a person who purports to be an agent of someone. Third persons cannot rely solely on the agent's statements of authority. Authority originates in the principal, and a third person must make sure that such authority has been given by the principal. Where a principal manifests to a third person that another is his agent, the principal's manifestation creates apparent authority, making it unnecessary for the third person to make further inquiry regarding such authority.

If authority is dependent upon the occurrence of a contingency, a third person has the duty to ascertain whether or not such contingency has occurred, unless knowledge of such occurrence is peculiarly that of the agent and the third person cannot ascertain easily, if at all, whether the contingency has occurred, in which case the third person justifiably may rely on the agent's representation regarding the occurrence of the contingency. (T knows that P has authorized A to sell goods shipped to P by X, but A is to sell such goods only on the arrival of the ship. A represents to T that the ship has arrived. T cannot rely on A's statement but must ascertain such arrival for himself.) If the agent of a common carrier unauthorizedly and wrongfully issues a negotiable bill of lading without first having received the goods for which the bill was issued, a third person without knowledge of the carrier's nonreceipt of the goods may rely on the agent's representation by his issuance of such bill that the goods have been received by the carrier because the third person cannot ascertain this fact for himself. Another illustration is a bank cashier's certification of a check when the drawer has insufficient funds.

A principal may give an agent express authority subject to certain limitations which are to remain secret as between the principal and agent. While the agent's express authority is narrowed by the secret limitations, nevertheless, the secret limitations are not binding on a third person who is ignorant of them because he cannot ascertain them for himself. (P authorized A to sell P's chattel for not less than $100 but not to reveal this price limitation. A sells the chattel in P's name for $90 to T, who does not know of P's instructions. P is bound by the sale.) The principal, by his conduct, has held out his agent as having authority without such secret limitations, and such conduct in conjunction with A's representation to T that A is acting for P creates apparent authority in the agent not limited by the secret instructions. The express and apparent authority differ, and the principal is bound by the third person's reliance on the apparent authority.

When an agent's authority is in writing and this is known to the third person, or if the agent's authority to be legally effective and to create an agency must be in writing or under seal, the agent's actual and apparent authority is limited by the authority as expressed in the writing or the writing under seal. The third person is under a duty to examine what is in writing or under seal, as that is the only manifestation from the principal on which the third person may rely. If the writing is not meant to be available for examination by third persons, then the third persons are not limited by the contents of such writing.

When a third person is on notice that the acts or interests of a purported agent are adverse to the interests of the principal whom he purports to represent, the third person is under a duty to examine and question whether or not the agent has the authority he alleges he has. Under such circumstances, many courts hold that there is a presumption that no agency exists.

Notice. Notice to an agent is notice to his principal if the agent had actual or apparent authority to receive such notice or, in the case of an undisclosed principal, if the agent had acted within his powers until the principal is disclosed. If a third person knows, or reasonably should know, that the agent would not communicate such information to his principal, notice to the agent is not notice to his principal.[6]

Liabilities of P and T for A's Unauthorized Conduct. Thus far we have considered the liabilities of a disclosed or partially disclosed principal and a third person as parties to contracts *authorizedly* and purportedly made by A for P. Many times in business transactions, the agent varies from his authority and, because of the social desirability of imposing liability upon P rather than upon an innocent T *in certain particular instances only,* A's unauthorized conduct in such situations is binding upon a disclosed or partially disclosed principal with the same effect between P and T as though A were authorized so to act. *Liability is imposed upon the disclosed or partially disclosed P not because of A's authority but because of apparent authority or because of A's inherent power, springing from the agency relation alone.* These instances are very important in business because they provide to P judicial guidelines of his potential liability for A's unauthorized conduct, on the basis of which P can pattern his business organization and conduct more clearly and provide for adequate insurance protection against such liability.

There is no problem about apparent authority, the rules discussed previously with respect to whether or not a disclosed or partially disclosed P is a party to a contract being equally applicable to apparent principals and with the same effect as when the agent is authorized. The discussion that follows concerning the effect of unauthorized conduct on the part of A applies to both disclosed and partially disclosed principals as well as to apparent principals. In many of the following instances where liability has been imposed upon P for A's unauthorized conduct, apparent authority has been present and P could be bound on that basis. When apparent authority is not present, the rules in the following instances apply to bind P irrespective of any apparent authority. For the most part, these rules are illustrations of inherent agency power, which binds P in the absence of authority and apparent authority, although many courts inappropriately apply the rule of apparent authority instead of these rules.[7] As time goes on, more of the courts will utilize these rules, not previously crystallized and established as such, as reflective of the trend of decisions in order to attain the results desired.

---

[6] See above, p. 546.

[7] See Judge Learned Hand's comment in *Kidd* v. *Thomas A. Edison, Inc.,* 239 F. 405 (D.C.N.Y. 1917), affirmed 242 F. 923 (2d Cir.).

Special principles of agency apply inherent agency power subjecting disclosed and partially disclosed principals to liability for A's unauthorized conduct. It should be recalled that an agent's power to affect his principal's legal relations by acting *in accord* with the principal's manifestation to the agent is called "authority." The power of an agent to affect his principal's legal relations *without acting in accord* with P's manifestation to the agent is called "inherent agency power."[8] Some of these special principles will be discussed.

1. *Unauthorized Party to the Contract.* A may have been authorized to make the contract in P's name and A *makes the authorized contract but in A's, instead of P's, name.* The contract, nevertheless, is binding on P because, as discussed previously,[9] when P is a disclosed or partially disclosed principal, he is presumed to be a party to the contract, unless the contract is under seal, a negotiable instrument, or it specifically excludes him. If A's authority was to make the contract in A's name and not to disclose his agency or P's identity and A *makes the authorized contract but discloses his agency or P's identity,* since P got essentially what he desired, namely the contract, even though his existence was disclosed, he is bound as a presumed party to it.

2. *A's Negligent Ascertainment of Facts for Authority.* When A has authority only if certain facts exist, *if A reasonably but negligently determines that such facts exist,* then A has authority and P is bound as though such facts did exist. If A is unreasonable, then A does not have authority.

3. *Unauthorized Amount or Separable Part of Contract.* Although an unauthorized contract made by A does not bind his disclosed or partially disclosed principal, nevertheless, *if the only difference between the unauthorized contract and the contract as it would be if it were authorizedly made is in the amount involved or in the exclusion or inclusion of a separable part, P is bound on the contract as it was authorized to be made, provided that, before P changes his position in reliance on the unauthorized contract, T manifests assent to the contract as it was authorized to be made.* (P authorizes A to sell P's land without warranties. A, in P's name, sells the land to T_1 with warranties. If P, on learning of what A has done, sells the land to T_2, P is not bound on the unauthorized contract with T_1. If, before P has sold the land to T_2, T_1 tendered P the money and offered to take the land *without any warranties,* P is bound to T_1.) It seems most equitable that T should be able to hold P to what he authorized A to do if the unauthorized part is easily

---

[8] American Law Institute, *Restatement: Agency 2d,* 1958, sec. 8A.
[9] See above, p. 549.

and clearly separable and if P has not yet done anything to prejudice his position in reliance on the unauthorized transaction. Thus, by various cases: where A's authority was to guarantee payment of $22,000 and A unauthorizedly, in the same contract by a separate clause, guaranteed $40,000 more, T could hold P for $22,000; where A's authority was to borrow at 7 per cent interest and A unauthorizedly borrowed at 8 per cent, T could hold P to the loan at 7 per cent; where A made a contract unauthorizedly adding a settlement clause, T could enforce the contract if he did not insist on the settlement clause; where A's authority was to borrow $75 and he unauthorizedly borrowed $150, T could enforce the loan against P for only $75, since A could have borrowed on two separate items of $75 each.

4. *T's Reliance on A's Unauthorized Representations Pursuant to P's Invitation.* A disclosed or partially disclosed principal is not bound by A's false representations of the existence and extent of his authority or the facts on which it depends. (P authorized A to buy certain corporate stocks when the market price reaches a certain point, and P tells this to T. A misrepresents to T that the market price has reached the specified point and T, relying on A's statement as being true, makes a contract with P through A to sell P the stock. P is not bound. *It should be noted carefully that P did not invite T to rely upon A's statement as to when the specified point had been reached.*) Nevertheless, there are occasions when P's conduct so causes T reasonably to rely on A's representations that P is bound by them even though made unauthorizedly, of which T does not have notice. Three such occasions will be discussed.

First, when P manifests to T that A is P's agent with *authority to disclose the terms* on which he is authorized to deal with T and *P invites T to rely on A's statement regarding such terms,* if A discloses terms that are not authorized and of which T has no notice of their being unauthorized, P is bound by such terms. (P hires A as a sales clerk in P's store. T asks A what the price of a sweater is and A misreads the cyphered price on the sweater and sells it for a slightly lower price than marked. P is bound. T can rely on A's statement of the price.) This seems but fair, since P has invited T to rely on A's statement of the terms.

Second, if P manifests to T that A is P's agent with *authority to begin on the occurrence of a specified event and P invites T to deal with A,* not when the event occurs, but *when A tells T that the event has occurred,* T is justified in reasonably relying on A's statement that the event has occurred and P is bound even if A was untruthful. (P informs T that when the road gravel bed has been levelled by A, P's foreman, A will inform T and order the concrete for the roadbed from T. A tells T that the roadbed has been levelled and, in P's name, orders the concrete from T, who reasonably relies on A's statement which, unknown to T, is untrue. P is bound to T.)

Third, if P manifests to T that A is his *general agent with authority to make a contract in P's name when a particular event occurs, its occurrence being within the peculiar knowledge of A,* then if A misrepresents to T that the event has occurred and T reasonably relies on A's statement and contracts with A for P, P is bound to T. A's *general agency status,* indicating that he is a part of P's business establishment and conducting multiple transactions, is more readily to be relied upon by T in this type of situation than that of a special agent, although P can manifest to T regarding a special agent instead of a general agent with the same result, as, for example, where P's special accreditation of A[10] to T is to buy a particular machine and T can rely on A's statement that A has not as yet bought such a machine.

5. *Certain Unauthorized Acts of General Agents.* This element of general agency status is very important in T's dealing with A for P because it connotes reliability and trust placed in A by P, on which T may justifiably rely and, in certain instances, it causes P to be bound to T even though A has acted unauthorizedly. In addition to the last instance stated, there are other occasions reflecting this concept. Three such occasions will be discussed.

First, when P appoints A *as a general agent in a position where, as a part of his regular employment, he is to issue commercial documents representing chattels or choses in action*[11] *only when certain facts exist or on the occurrence of a certain event, such facts or event being within the peculiar knowledge of the general agent,* if A issues such commercial documents unauthorizedly and they are *purchased by innocent persons for value without notice of A's impropriety,* P is bound by A's conduct as though A had acted authorizedly. Examples are: the agent of a common carrier or of a warehouseman with authority to issue bills of lading or warehouse receipts on receipt of goods for carriage or storage; a corporate stock transfer agent with authority to issue new certificates of stock in place of cancelled certificates; and a cashier of a bank with authority to certify checks of depositors who have sufficient funds in

---

[10] See below, p. 585.

[11] By "commercial documents representing chattels or choses in action" are meant documents that carry with them the owner's interests in things or rights, which are transferred by transfer of the document. Examples are bills of lading, warehouse receipts, certificates of stock.

their accounts to pay for such checks when they are presented for payment. Should the agent issue a bill of lading or a warehouse receipt without receiving the goods or the cashier certify the check when the drawer of the check does not have an account with the bank or, if he is a depositor, there are insufficient funds in his account, P as the common carrier, warehouseman, or bank is liable to an innocent purchaser for value of the bill of lading, warehouse receipt, or certified check as though A were authorized so to act.

Second, when P employs A *as a general agent in a position where it is usual for A to issue (to sign and deliver) negotiable instruments,* should A issue a negotiable instrument for an unauthorized purpose and *the instrument be acquired by a holder in due course,*[12] P is liable to him on the instrument as though A had acted authorizedly.[13] This often occurs in trading partnerships, where a partner unauthorizedly issues a firm check for his private purpose. (A, of the trading partnership consisting of A, B, and C, and engaged in retail men's clothing, buys a wrist watch for his own use and unauthorizedly draws a check in the partnership name payable to V, the vendor. Although the partnership, P, is not liable to V on the check if V is deemed on notice of A's unauthorized act, if V purchases supplies from H and negotiates the check to H in payment, H not having notice of A's unauthorized conduct, the partnership, P, is liable to H on the check.)

The importance of this rule to businessmen cannot be overemphasized, and adequate office administration and insurance coverage should be considered. Under this rule, a general agent in such a position has the *power to issue* a check in P's name to the order of a person not intended to have any interest in the instrument and by indorsing the check in the payee's name to cause it to be cashed, the principal being none the wiser until the fateful day when he discovers the fraud of his agent. Under the law of agency, the knowledge of the agent here is the knowledge of his principal. The Code[14] reflects this and provides that when an instrument is drawn and signed by the general agent for his maker or drawer principal, naming as payee a person not intended to have any interest in the instrument, an indorsement by *any* person in the name of the named payee is effective and the instrument can be negotiated to a holder in due course who can enforce the instrument against the maker or drawer principal. It should be noted carefully that the same result occurs when

---

[12] A holder in due course is the familiar innocent purchaser for value, to whom the instrument has been negotiated. See UCC 3–302.

[13] See UCC 3–305.

[14] See UCC 3–405.

a general agent without authority or inherent agency power *to issue* a negotiable instrument *prepares for P's signature* a negotiable instrument naming as payee a person not intended by the agent, and therefore by his principal, to have any interest[15] in the instrument, and the principal innocently signs the instrument. Such conduct by the agent has caused the so-called "padded payroll cases."

Third, a general agent with authority to conduct transactions subjects his disclosed principal to liability to a third person for his unauthorized acts on his principal's behalf, which usually accompany or are incidental to such transactions, if the third person reasonably believes that the agent is authorized to do them and has no notice that he is not so authorized.[16] This is one of the most important illustrations of inherent agency power binding P for the unauthorized acts of A, his general agent. This often occurs when P places A in a position of managing the business of P, a disclosed or partially disclosed principal, and A deals with third persons contrary to A's authority but in conformity with what is usual in such business, T not having notice of the impropriety of A's conduct. (P appoints A as the manager of P's textile manufacturing business with authority to buy raw materials only from T_1. A buys raw materials from T_2, who has no notice of A's lack of authority to deal with him. P is bound to T_2. If T_2 did not know of A's status as manager, A would not have apparent authority and P is bound to T_2 only by reason of this special agency power. If T_2 knew of A's status as manager, then A would have apparent authority so to act and P could be bound to T_2 on the basis of *either* inherent agency power or apparent authority.) Although it is true that in many of the cases apparent authority is present and they can be decided on that basis, *there are many other cases where A's status as a general agent is not known to T and P's liability can be predicated only on the basis of this inherent agency power rule;* many courts, however, still reach the same result by inappropriately asserting that P is liable on the basis of apparent authority when apparent authority is not present. It should be noted very carefully that it is the status of a general agent under the circumstances indicated in the rule here that is important, *irrespective of whether or not T knows of such status* in his dealing with A.

Although the above rule illustrates inherent agency power in connection with general agents, it should be remembered that inherent agency power exists also in connection with special agents. Thus far we

---

[15] *Ibid.*

[16] See American Law Institute, *Restatement: Agency 2d,* 1958, sec. 161, and Appendix, *Reporter's Notes,* sec. 161.

have discussed inherent agency power rules that, unless indicated as applicable only to general agents, apply equally to all agents irrespective of whether they are general or special agents. *The following discussion, unless otherwise indicated, applies to special and general agents.* It should be noted that a general agent, because of his position, has broad inherent agency power to bind P in instances where a special agent cannot do this. The special agent, generally, is pretty much limited to authority and apparent authority to bind P, although as we have seen and will see the special agent as well as the general agent can, in certain instances, bind P by inherent agency power.

Illustrative of the force of inherent agency power are the following two particular instances concerned with unauthorized representations made by A and A's improper purposes or motives.

6. *Unauthorized Untruthful Misrepresentations of What A Has Been Authorized to Represent Truthfully.* When a disclosed or partially disclosed P authorizes *A to make a contract and A has authority or apparent authority to make true representations other than of his authority with respect to incidents in connection with the contract,* if A should make untrue representations with respect to such incidents in connection with the authorized contract and T is not on notice of A's lack of authority or of their untruthful nature, P is liable to T *in an action on the contract or for its rescission* for such representations *as though A were authorized so to represent.* (P appoints A as his sales clerk in P's store. A misrepresents the cotton and wool content of an article and sells it to T, who reasonably relies on A's untruthful statement without notice of its falsity. T can rescind the contract or sue P for breach of contract.) Misrepresentations by a bank cashier to a customer purchaser of discounted notes of the financial condition of the makers, by a automobile salesman to a customer purchaser of an automobile concerning the parts of the automobile, and by a salesman of securities to a customer purchaser concerning the assets, liabilities, and personnel management of a corporation whose securities are bought by the customer, are other examples of situations where P is liable for A's misrepresentations and T, the customer, can rescind or sue P for breach of the contract.

7. *Authorized Conduct with an Improper Purpose by A.* When a disclosed or partially disclosed P authorizes A to make a contract for P's benefit and *A makes the authorized contract in P's name but for an improper purpose,* as for the benefit of A or someone other than P, and T is not on notice of A's improper purpose, *P is liable on the contract as though A had acted for an authorized purpose.* It is P's responsibility to select agents to contract for him on whose fiduciary sense of loyalty he can rely. Third persons cannot question the purposes or motives of an agent and, unless they have notice from the circumstances that A's purpose is, improperly, not to act for P's benefit, as between T and P it is P who must be bound by A's conduct for an improper purpose as though A's purpose had been proper. (P authorizes A, in P's name and for P's benefit, to borrow money from T. A does so with the intent to embezzle the funds. P is bound to T.) *It should be noted very carefully that, although A has apparent authority to state to T that he has authority to do that which he was authorized to do for P's benefit, he does not have apparent authority to state to T that he has authority when he does not intend to act for P's benefit.*[17] In the example given, A's improper purpose precluded any apparent authority to state that he had authority to borrow. *Thus, when A's improper purpose is present, if P has not manifested to T that A has authority, there cannot be authority or apparent authority, and P's liability to T is based solely on inherent agency power.* The impact of this rule on business transactions is extremely important. Thus, an agent with authority to issue and to indorse checks in P's name and for P's benefit has *power* to do so for his own purposes, causing P to be liable on the signature to a holder in due course and permitting P's bank innocently to rely on the signature to a negotiable instrument and charge P's account for the same. The door of legal liability is wide open for P by the authorized acts of his agent performed for an improper purpose.

8. *A's Unauthorized Acts with Chattels and Instruments Entrusted to Him by P.* When P entrusts to A a chattel, a commercial document, a negotiable instrument, or a document with blank spaces, and A acts unauthorizedly in connection with it, whether or not P is bound by A's unauthorized conduct depends on the authority given by P to A and to whom the item was entrusted. Seven situations will be discussed.

First, if P entrusts to A possession of a chattel, other than a commercial document representing a chattel or chose in action, but with no authority to affect P's interest in the chattel, A's unauthorized act to transfer P's interest in the chattel does not bind P, *in the absence of statute to the contrary.* Thus, the bailment[18] of a chattel without authority in the bailee agent to sell it, or to display it for sale, or otherwise to affect P's interest in it, does not subject P to liability or loss of interest in

---

[17] See above, p. 527.

[18] Bailment is a legal relationship that occurs when chattels or goods are delivered by one person, called a bailor, to another person, called a bailee, pursuant to an agreement whereby the goods are to be returned to the bailor or pursuant to his direction in accordance with the bailment agreement.

the bailed chattel by the bailee agent's unauthorized conduct with the goods. Examples are: the garage to whom P has delivered his automobile for repair or storage has no power to sell or encumber P's automobile; the bailee of hogs or cattle for fattening them or having them on the ranch for feed has no power to sell them. Mere entrusting of possession of a chattel without authority to deal with it is not such a sufficient representation of ownership or authority over it as to cause P to be deprived of an interest in it by a bailee's unauthorized disposition of it. Even if the bailee has authority to use the chattel, such as to demonstrate it to induce persons to purchase an article similar to it, the bailee cannot unauthorizedly deprive P of his interest in it. However, the Code, Section 2–403(2), provides: "Any entrusting of possession of goods to a merchant who deals in goods of that kind gives him power to transfer all rights of the entruster to a buyer in ordinary course of business." (P delivers his watch for repair to A, a jeweler, who repairs and sells watches. A's sale of the watch unauthorizedly and in P's name to T, an innocent customer, does not deprive P of his title; however, under the Code T obtains P's title.)

Second, if P entrusts to A possession of a chattel, other than a commercial document representing a chattel or chose in action, with authority to deal with it in a specified manner, A's unauthorized act dealing with the chattel *in a different manner than authorized* does not affect P's interest in the chattel, *in the absence of statute to the contrary.* By statute in many states, called Factors Acts, it is provided, generally, that P's delivery of chattels to a mercantile agent for disposition of a particular interest therein *empowers* the agent to dispose of *any* interest of P in the chattel, whether or not it is the interest authorized by P, to a good faith purchaser for value in the regular course of trade. Thus, consignees and factors have power to pledge goods delivered to them for sale. Accordingly, it is of utmost importance that the statutes in each state be consulted to determine the extent of inherent agency power in A to act unauthorizedly and thereby to affect P's interests in chattels entrusted to A. For example: P entrusts an automobile to A, an automobile dealer, to sell and A, in P's name, creates a security interest in it, such interest is ineffective as to P; P delivers a watch to A, a watch dealer, to sell it, and A in P's name exchanges it for a ring, the exchange is ineffective as to P. In these examples, many current statutes would cause P to lose the interest in the chattel unauthorizedly disposed of by A.

Third, if P entrusts to A possession of a chattel, other than a commercial document representing a chattel or chose in action, with authority to deal with it in a specified manner, and A deals with it in the same manner as authorized but not in accord with other parts of his authority, P's interests in the chattel are affected if T reasonably believes A to be authorized so to act and T pays value. Thus, P's authority to A to sell, pledge, or otherwise deal with a chattel at a specified price and on other terms *empowers* A to do these things at a different price and on different terms and thereby affects P's interests in the chattel.

Fourth, if P entrusts to *a dealer* possession of a chattel *with authority to exhibit it for sale or to sell it but only with P's consent, or to other than a specified person, or for a specified price,* and A sells the chattel, in accord with normal business practice but not in accord with the conditions in his authority, to T, who reasonably believed A to be authorized so to act, P is bound by the transactions as though A were authorized so to act. The Code, Section 2–403(2), quoted previously[19] is applicable. (P delivers a horse to A, *a horse dealer,* with authority to find a willing purchaser and to inform P. A unauthorizedly sells the horse to T, who reasonably believes that A has authority to do so. P is bound to T. If P had delivered the horse to A for sale for $1,000 and A had sold it to T for $900, P would be bound to T, both by this "dealer" rule and also by the *third* rule above.) *More than one of these rules may apply concurrently to a particular transaction.*

Fifth, if P entrusts to A possession of a commercial document representing a chattel or chose in action, which is in such form that its possessor is commonly regarded as having a power to dispose of it, and P gives to A a limited authority to deal with the document, A's unauthorized disposal of the document to an innocent purchaser without notice of A's lack of authority causes P's interests in the document to be thereby affected. A commercial document was described previously.[20] (P delivers a warehouse receipt to A with authority to obtain the goods in the warehouse and to store them elsewhere. A, in P's name, unauthorizedly sold the warehouse receipt to T, an innocent purchaser without notice of A's lack of authority. Whether or not T obtains title to the warehouse receipt depends upon its form. If the warehouse receipt is in favor of P and P indorsed it in blank, T gets title to it. If the warehouse receipt has not been properly indorsed by P, then P still has title to it.)[21]

Sixth, if P entrusts to A possession of a negotiable instrument not

---

[19] See above, p. 561.

[20] See above, p. 556, ftn. 11.

[21] In connection with the preceding first through fifth rules, see American Law Institute, *Restatement: Agency 2d,* 1958, Appendix, *Reporter's Notes,* sec. 174.

payable to bearer and not indorsed to A, and A unauthorizedly transfers the instrument or collects the claim on it, P's interests in the instrument are not affected. Although the Code[22] provides that a holder in due course of a negotiable instrument takes it free from all claims, with exceptions not material here, in order to be a holder in due course the instrument must be properly indorsed so as to read in favor of the possessor. For example, a check payable to the order of P, the payee, may be indorsed: by P in blank with just his signature, thereby making the instrument payable to bearer; or by P in favor of X, who on receiving it in good faith and for value can enforce it. Until the instrument has been indorsed by the payee in blank or in favor of the possessor, it cannot be negotiated further and, since all persons are on notice of this, the rule described above concerning negotiable instruments precludes any unauthorized person from affecting the interests of the person in whose favor the instrument reads. (P has a check payable to his order, and he entrusts it to A to hold for him. A cannot collect it or dispose of it unauthorizedly and thereby affect P's interest in the check.) It should be noted that apparent authority to collect on the instrument or to dispose of it may be created by the appointment of A to a position in P's business where he would have apparent authority so to act, as, for example, by appointment as general manager in charge of an investment business, or by authorization on previous occasions so to act, and third persons have notice of this fact but not of the limitation on A's authority.

Seventh, if P entrusts to A a document executed by P and containing blanks with authority to complete the blanks in a particular manner and A completes the blanks in an unauthorized manner and, in P's name, transfers the document to T, an innocent purchaser for value, P is liable on the document only if T had no notice that the document had blanks when delivered to A. P has placed within A's power the opportunity to mislead innocent third persons that the document was completed properly and, accordingly, P exposes himself to possible liability by entrusting such a document to A. This rule is in accord with the Code where the maker of a negotiable instrument with blanks that are unauthorizedly filled in by another is liable to a holder in due course of the instrument.[23] It should be noted that this rule applies to non-negotiable, as well as to negotiable, instruments. Also, if A were a general agent he would come under not only this rule but also under the rule discussed

---

[22] UCC 3–305.
[23] See UCC 3–115, 3–407.

previously[24] concerning the unauthorized acts of a general agent incidental to transactions that he is authorized to conduct.

9. *A's Unauthorized Acts in the Payment or Collection of Debts.* Often an agent authorized to pay debts of his principal or to collect debts due to his principal acts unauthorizedly, either mistakenly or deliberately. *If P authorizes A to pay P's debt and A does so but in a mistaken amount, P is bound to the creditor by A's conduct as though A were authorized so to act.* Although restitutional remedies may become available for overpayment by P, depending on the innocence of the creditor and his change of position, P is bound by A's act. If P authorizes A to inform the debtor of what he owes to P when the creditor ordinarily computes the amount, A's unauthorized misrepresentation to the debtor of a larger amount owing, which the debtor pays to A, binds P to T as though A were authorized so to act. (A, pursuant to authority from P, a gas utility, reads a gas meter and informs T, the gas user, of the amount owing, unauthorizedly stating a larger amount than what is actually due, which T pays, A keeping the excess over the correct amount due. P is bound to T, who may obtain restitution of the excess amount from P.) *This rule applies to situations where P usually obtains and computes the amount due and often employs an agent to do this.* The rule does not usually apply in the case of fixed amounts owing under a contract and, P's collecting agency not normally being directed to state such amounts to the debtor, P is not bound by A's unauthorized erroneous representation to the debtor. If A were a general agent under these rules, he would come under not only these rules but also under the rule discussed previously[25] concerning the unauthorized acts of a general agent incidental to transactions that he is authorized to conduct.

Defenses. Rights and duties between the contracting parties may be in existence at the time the contract is made, may arise out of the transaction, or may occur subsequent to the contract's formation. Whether or not they can be asserted as between P and T depends upon the time of their occurrence. Each of these will be considered in turn.

1. *Defenses Existing When Contract Is Made.* Rights and liabilities between the disclosed or partially disclosed principal and A and between T and A, *existing at the time a contract is made* binding P and T, do not affect the rights and liabilities of P and T with respect to each other, unless otherwise agreed. (P authorizes A to *sell* a typewriter to T for $500, which A does in P's name. If A owed T $100 at the time the

---

[24] See above, p. 558.
[25] See above, pp. 558–59.

contract was made, T cannot set off against P the $100 claim that T has against A; T owes P $500. Similarly, if A's authority had been to *buy* the typewriter for $500 and T owed A $100 at the time the contract was made, P could not set off against T the $100 claim that A has against T; P owes T $500.)

2. *Defenses Arising out of the Transaction.* However, all defenses *arising out of the transaction between A and T* are available to the contracting parties, *except that defenses which are personal to A,* such as infancy, bankruptcy discharge, and set-off of personal debts owing to A, are not available to P. Thus fraud, duress, or coercion perpetrated by T on P through A or upon P by collusion between A and T, may be asserted by P as a defense against T; and, similarly, if such has been perpetrated by A on T, then T can assert it as a defense against P. If P is not a party to the contract, either because he has been specifically excluded or the contract is under seal or in the form of a negotiable instrument and P's name does not appear therein, then, since the contract cannot be enforced by T or P against the other, such defenses are unavailable to them against each other.

3. *Defenses Arising After the Contract Is Made.* When T is paid what is owing to him by P, T's claim against P is discharged. This is obviously true if A and P are joint contracting parties on the contract with T, because payment by one joint contracting party, such as A, discharging the debt, operates to discharge all the joint contracting parties on the debt to T. This raises the matter of indemnity as between A and P, previously discussed.[26] P's settlement with A for expenses authorizedly incurred by A in P's name for which P is liable to T, but for which expenses P indemnifies A without notice that A has not paid T, does not relieve P of his liability to T for such expenses, unless P has relied on T's conduct misleading P that A's account with T has been paid by A and which conduct by T has not been fraudulently induced by A. The courts are not in accord here, except that they are in accord when T misleads P and P relies thereon without any inducing misrepresentations by A to T. (A authorizedly ships P's goods and obtains a paid receipt from the railroad without having paid for the transportation charges. A misrepresents to P that A has paid the charges and delivers the railroad paid receipt to P, and P in reasonable reliance thereon pays A the amount of such charges. P is no longer liable to T for such charges. If A had fraudulently induced the railroad to issue the receipt, P is still liable to the railroad for such charges.)

---

[26] See above, pp. 541–42.

The Undisclosed Principal. An undisclosed principal is a principal of whose existence T is unaware. As previously defined,[27] if T has no notice that A is acting for a principal, the principal is undisclosed. Often P wishes A to act for P without disclosing his agency status. This section will discuss, in the following order: the parties to a contract made for an undisclosed principal; T's election when he later learns of P's identity; the liabilities between P and T; and, finally, the defenses of P and T against the claim of the other.

Parties. Inasmuch as P is undisclosed, any contract made by A with T would have only A and T as the parties thereto. Although P is not a party to the contract, he obtains the benefit of the contract authorizedly made by A, who holds the contract on P's behalf; also, T's assets are available to A and, through A, to P for T's breach of the contract, while only A's assets are available to T for A's breach. Because of this imbalance, the courts have caused P to become liable as a party to any contract authorizedly, and in some instances unauthorizedly,[28] made by A for an undisclosed P from which P is not excluded either by the contract being under seal or in the form of a negotiable instrument, or by the contract specifically excluding P or any undisclosed principal as a party to it.[29] *By law, therefore, P is made a contracting party,* quite contrary to the law of contracts where only the manifested intentions of the parties determine who are the parties to the contract. In effect, therefore, *T has two rights, one against A and one against P,* although the English courts hold that T has only one alternative right against either A or P between whom T must elect. It is not unusual outside of the law of contracts for one person to have two rights, one against each of two different persons originating from one transaction; for example, a pedestrian negligently struck by A, P's truck driver, authorizedly delivering merchandise for P, has a claim against A as the wrongdoer and a claim against P as a master responsible for the torts of his servants while acting within the scope of their employment. If, as indicated previously, P is excluded from the contract, then the law will not impose P as a party upon the contracting parties, A and T, who emphatically do not desire P as a party to the contract. P is bound by A's exercise of his authority, and the previous discussion of authority[30] is applicable here. Apparent authority is inapplicable to a discussion of

---

[27] See above, p. 549.

[28] See below, pp. 568–71.

[29] See above, p. 549.

[30] See above, pp. 514–39.

undisclosed principals because A is not an apparent agent for any principal.

T's Election. T's discovery of P's identity is of legal importance in two ways. First, thereafter, in T's dealings with A, T is dealing with A on behalf of a disclosed principal and the previous discussion concerning disclosed and partially disclosed principals[31] is applicable. Secondly, T can continue to look to P and A as severally liable on the contract or make a choice between them, the choice being irrevocable and discharging the party not selected. Since P and A are severally liable to T, T is not required to make any choice between them. If T elects to choose between them, *he can make a choice in only one way. After T learns of P's identity, if T obtains a judgment against either P or A for breach of contract,* the party against whom the judgment was *not* obtained is discharged from liability on the contract. Although there is conflict, by the majority view, satisfaction of a judgment is not necessary to the election; by the minority view, satisfaction is necessary, thereby permitting two judgments by T against A and P, respectively, in order to satisfy T's claim on the contract. If T obtains judgment against A *before* he learns of P's identity, T has not made an election and he can still obtain a judgment against P to the extent that T's claim has not yet been satisfied against A on that judgment. The courts are in accord on this. T's *commencement* of an action against P or A is not election by T.

After T learns of P's identity, T does not make an election thereby discharging P by continuing to look only to A for performance of the contract. For example, T's billing A for payment or T's proving his claim in bankruptcy against A's bankrupt estate after T learns of P's identity do not cause T to lose his right against P on the contract.

Liabilities between P and T. We have found that, when an agent acts within the scope of his authority, the agent's conduct binds his principal. If the agent's authority was to make a contract for his disclosed or partially disclosed principal with a third person and the agent does this, his principal is bound to the third person as parties to the contract. The fact that P is an undisclosed principal does not preclude his becoming a party to the contract by operation of law.[32] This being so, *the legal rules applicable to disclosed and partially disclosed principals, insofar as they can be applied with the same legal effect, should govern the liabilities of the undisclosed principal in his relations with third persons with whom his agent has dealt.*

---

[31] See above, pp. 549–65.

[32] See above, p. 566.

The discussion thus far about undisclosed principals has been concerned with whether an undisclosed principal can be a party to the contract *authorizedly* made by his agent. Since he can be a party, then his liability on the contract is like that of the disclosed or partially disclosed principal on contracts *authorizedly* made for them. However, so that the rights and liabilities of the undisclosed P and T may be equitably balanced against each other, with respect to such rights and liabilities P is put in the position substantially of an assignee. *P takes the contract as it existed before T learned of P's identity.* There is no real problem in fixing the rights and liabilities of P and T as of that time if the contract between them was *authorizedly* made. However, the same problem posed for disclosed and partially disclosed principals is posed for undisclosed principals, namely, to what extent is the undisclosed P bound by A's *unauthorized* conduct? The following discussion will consider this problem.

The liability of the undisclosed principal for the *unauthorized* acts of his agent is an example of inherent agency power. Some of the instances where such liability is imposed will be discussed.

1. *Unauthorized Acts of General Agents.* With respect to *general agents,* the previous discussion of a general agent's unauthorized conduct on behalf of a disclosed or partially disclosed principal[33] is applicable here. Briefly, *a general agent with authority to conduct transactions subjects his undisclosed P to liability to a third person for his unauthorized acts on P's behalf, which usually accompany or are incidental to such transactions, if the third person reasonably believes that the agent is authorized to do them and has no notice that he is not so authorized.* This often occurs when the undisclosed P places his agent in charge of P's business as the apparent owner of it and A acts contrary to his authority but in conformity with what is usual in such business. (P authorizes A to manage P's men's retail clothing store and to represent that it belongs to A, but not to pay more than $40 for suits for resale. A buys suits for $50 from T, a clothing manufacturer who does not know of A's status as an agent and believes A to be the owner. P is liable to T for the sale.) However, P's liability is limited to the assets of the business and to the benefits P received.

There are many other situations where, whether the agent be a general agent or a special agent, an undisclosed P is liable for A's unauthorized conduct. These situations will be discussed briefly.

2. *Unauthorized Untruthful Misrepresentations of What A Has*

<hr>

[33] See above, pp. 556–58.

Been Authorized to Represent Truthfully. An undisclosed P is liable in an action on the contract or for its rescission not only for A's authorized representations in connection with the authorized contract, but also for *A's unauthorized representations with respect to incidents in connection with the otherwise authorized contract if A had authority to make true representations with respect to such incidents and T has no reason to know that such representations are untrue.* (A is P's agent with authority to sell P's goods in A's name but not to expressly warrant the goods. A sells the goods with an express warranty to T, who believes that A owns the goods and who relies on A's express warranty. P is bound to T on the sale and on the warranty.)

3. *Authorized Conduct with an Improper Purpose by A.* Unlike the case of disclosed and partially disclosed principals where P is liable for A's authorized act for an improper purpose,[34] *an undisclosed P is not liable for A's making the authorized contract without an intent to act for P.* (P authorizes A to buy goods from T. A makes a contract with T to buy the goods but with the intent to resell the goods as his own and to keep the proceeds for himself. T does not know of A's agency nor of A's intent. P is not bound on the contract with T. (However, if *A intends to act for P but he has an improper motive,* such as the purchase by A, an apparent store owner, of inferior goods so as to disparage P's reputation, P is bound by A's conduct. The mere fact of agency is not enough to justify an inherent agency power in A to make P liable for A's conduct when A does not intend to act for P, although inherent agency power is present to make P liable for A's improper motive.

4. *Unauthorized Nondisclosure of P.* *A's unauthorized nondisclosure of the existence or identity of his P causes P to be liable on the otherwise authorized contract with T, if T has no reason to know of P's existence and if P is not excluded as a party to the contract* because the contract either is under seal, in the form of a negotiable instrument, or it specifically excludes P. As indicated later,[35] the fact that P did not seek to conceal his existence affects T's right of set-off against P's enforcement of the contract against T.

5. *Unauthorized Amount or Separable Part of Contract.* The same rule[36] applies to an undisclosed principal as to a disclosed or partially disclosed principal that, although an unauthorized contract made by A does not bind his undisclosed P, nevertheless, *if the only difference*

---

[34] See above, pp. 559–60.

[35] See below, p. 572.

[36] See above, pp. 554–55.

between the unauthorized contract and the contract as it would be if it were authorizedly made is in the amount involved or in the exclusion or inclusion of a separate part, P is bound on the contract as it was authorized to be made, provided that, before P changes his position in reliance on the unauthorized contract, T manifests assent to the contract as it was authorized to be made. (P authorizes A to sell P's goods in A's name as the owner for $1,000. A makes a contract in his own name to sell the goods to T for $850. P informs T that A was acting for him, but unauthorizedly as to the price, and P refuses to deliver the goods to T. T may assent to the contract and hold P liable for damages for breach of the contract. If P should change his position in reliance on the contract made by A, as by selling the goods to another before T assents to the contract, the contract cannot be enforced by T against P.)

6. *A's Unauthorized Acts with Chattels and Instruments Entrusted to Him by P.* Generally, the same rules apply to an undisclosed principal as to a disclosed or partially disclosed principal with respect to A's unauthorized acts with chattels and instruments entrusted to him by P, as previously discussed,[37] and reference should be made to that material for explanation, examples, and the impact of statutes. Those rules, changed to fit the undisclosed principal, are as follows:

First, if P entrusts to A possession of a chattel, other than a commercial document representing a chattel or chose in action, but with no authority to affect P's interest in the chattel, A's unauthorized transaction with respect to the chattel with T, who believes A to be the owner of the chattel, does not bind P, *in the absence of statute to the contrary.*

Second, if P entrusts to A possession of a chattel, other than a commercial document representing a chattel or chose in action, with authority to deal with it in a specified manner, A's unauthorized act dealing with the chattel *in a different manner than authorized* does not affect P's interest in the chattel, *in the absence of statute to the contrary.*

Third, if P entrusts to A possession of a chattel, other than a commercial document representing a chattel or chose in action, with authority to deal with it in a specified manner and A deals with it in the usual and ordinary course of business *in the same manner as authorized but not in accord with other parts of his authority,* P's interests in the chattels are affected if T reasonably believes A to be the owner and T pays value.

Fourth, if P entrusts to a dealer possession of a chattel with authority to exhibit it for sale or to sell it but only with P's consent, or to other

---

[37] See above, pp. 560–64.

than a specified person, or for a specified price, and A sold the chattel, in accord with normal business practice but *not in accord with the conditions in his authority,* to T who reasonably believed A to be the owner, P is bound by the transaction as though A were the owner.

Fifth, if P entrusts to A possession of a commercial document representing a chattel or chose in action, which is in such form that its possessor is commonly regarded as having a power to dispose of it, and P gives to A a limited authority to deal with the document, A's unauthorized disposal of the document to an innocent purchaser who believes that A is the owner causes P's interests in the document to be thereby affected.

7. *A's Unauthorized Transfer of Title Entrusted to Him by P. If an undisclosed P entrusts to A title to something, A has power to transfer the title to T who has no notice of P's interests and who either pays value or changes his position in reliance thereon.* A becomes a trustee of the legal title; and a good faith purchaser for value of the title, whether from A or from A's transferee who has notice of A's lack of authority, acquires the title. (A, pursuant to his authority and acting on behalf of his undisclosed P, purchases a horse from T_1 in A's name. P tells A to hold the horse and the bill of sale in A's name. A, unauthorizedly and in his own name, sells the horse to T_2, who paid the purchase price to A and who believes that A is the owner without notice of A's lack of authority. T_2 owns the horse.) A's transfer of the title to T, who knows of A's violation of his authority or who is a donee who has not changed his position in reliance on A's ownership without notice of A's lack of authority, can be set aside. The title may be to intangibles, such as accounts receivable, as well as to land and chattels.

Defenses. P and T can enforce against each other the contract made by A only if P is a party to it. If P is not a party to the contract because he was excluded from it, either because the contract was under seal or in the form of a negotiable instrument or it specifically excluded him as a party, then neither P nor T can enforce the contract against each other. Various situations affect P's and T's defenses.

1. *Multiple Ps.* If A is authorized by multiple undisclosed Ps *individually* to make a contract on their behalf and A, without their consent, combines all their orders into one contract, the undisclosed Ps are not parties to the contract with T.[38] However, since A holds the combined contract in trust for the Ps individually, all the Ps

---

[38] The same result is applicable to disclosed principals.

can, as the beneficial owners of the contract between A and T, combine and sue T on the contract.

2. *Misrepresentation that P Is Not a Principal.* Although an undisclosed P is a party to the contract made by A with T, if A misrepresents to T that he is not acting for a principal, A or P having notice that T would not have dealt with P, and thereby induces T to make the contract, the contract is voidable by T. The mere fact that A did not disclose to T that he was acting for an undisclosed P does not of itself cause the contract to be voidable. It is well known that agents often represent undisclosed principals and there is no duty to disclose the agency status, unless such status is material to T and A or P knows this; then the duty to disclose arises. Although there is conflict, this is the great majority view and tendency among the courts.

3. *Set-Off.* Whether or not P has authorized A to misrepresent to T about P's existence determines to what extent T may set off against P any claim that T had against A before T learned of P's existence. If A's authority was to conceal P's existence, then P gets only what A could enforce against T and, therefore, T can set off against P any claim T had against A before T learned of P's existence. If A's authority was to disclose P and A did not do so, then, since P did not want T to be misled as to whom he was dealing with, T cannot set off against P any claim T has against A, unless P has entrusted the chattels to A and thereby misled T to extend credit to A on the basis of such chattels. (A, pursuant to authority for his undisclosed P, made a contract in his own name to sell P's horse to T for $600. A owed T $100 at the time the contract was made. When P sued T on the contract, T could set off $100 against P's claim of $600. If P had authorized A to disclose P's identity and A did not do so, then T cannot so set off against P. If P had authorized A to disclose P's identity and had delivered the horse to A and A did not disclose P's identity, T can set off against P.) The reason for the distinctions here is that, although P is an undisclosed principal and should be bound by A's inherent agency power, there should be a limit to such power where P is trying to be forthright with T. Thus, if P intends to be disclosed, then only binding P on the contract should be enough and T cannot set off against P T's claim against A; but if P intends to conceal his existence or entrusts chattels to A, thereby more forcibly inducing T to deal with A as not representing anyone, then the full force of the inherent agency power is employed, and T can set off against P T's claim against A.

4. *A's Knowledge and Notice.* Before T knows of the existence of an undisclosed P, T is dealing only with A and A is, with P's knowl-

edge, dealing with T. Before P's existence is known to T, P is charged with knowledge or notice acquired by himself or through A, and this may affect P's liability to T; after P's existence is disclosed, P becomes a disclosed or partially disclosed principal from that point on and the rules concerning notice to the principal through his agent become applicable.[39]

5. *A's Conduct after Contract's Formation.* If A had made a contract binding on his undisclosed P, A has the *power* to perform or to receive performance or to rescind the contract, or to modify the contract if the modified contract would have been binding upon P initially. After P's existence is known to T, from that point on A has only the power of an agent for a disclosed or partially disclosed P.[40]

6. *P's Contract Rights Similar to Those of Assignee. The undisclosed P's position in the enforcement of the contract made by A and binding P as a party is substantially that of an assignee. P takes the contract as it exists before T learns of P's identity.* T has all the defenses that he would have had if the transaction had been made by P instead of by A. Thus, if A had not performed the contract or had practiced fraud, duress, or coercion on T, these defenses could be asserted by T against P in his action to enforce the contract against T. Similarly, P has all the defenses arising out of the transaction that A had against T, and which are not personal to A.

A's personal defenses are infancy, bankruptcy discharge, and set-off against T in the absence of contract provision to the contrary. (A, an infant, pursuant to authority from his undisclosed P, made a contract with T. When T tries to enforce the contract against P, P could not assert A's infancy as a defense and thereby avoid the contract.)

T should not be exposed to a greater obligation than that provided for by the contract and, therefore, performance or tender of performance by P is proper unless it is substantially different from that which the contract requires, in which event there is nonperformance by P and A. If the contract called for the rendition of personal services by A, since the contract is of a personal nature A's contractual duties are nondelegable and P cannot render the performance required by the contract. (A, pursuant to authority from his undisclosed P, made a contract with T to sell P's land with a warranty deed to T. P tendered his own warranty deed to the land. P has not performed.) If A has performed or tendered performance of his contractual obligation, P can

---

[39] See above, pp. 546, 553.
[40] See above, pp. 549–64.

enforce the contract against T irrespective of A's personal service already rendered or tendered. Similarly, P can compel T to perform the contract to P instead of to A, unless T's services to be rendered to A are personal in nature or performance by T to P would impose upon T a performance substantially different from that required by the contract. (Under the terms of the contract for the sale of goods by T to A, who is acting authorizedly for an undisclosed P, T extends credit to A personally. A becomes insolvent. P cannot enforce the contract against T.)

7. *P's Discharge by T's Conduct.* P can assert the following as good defenses to an action by T on the contract made by A and binding P, his undisclosed principal, as a party to it.

First, T's Election to Hold A on the Contract. As discussed previously,[41] after T learns of P's identity, if T should obtain a judgment against A for breach of contract, by the majority view P is discharged from liability on the contract.

Second, Satisfaction of T's Claim against A. Satisfaction of T's claim against A discharges P as well as A from further liability to T on the contract. Since P's liability is based on A's contract with T, if the contract out of which T's claim arose is discharged, then there is no further basis for P's liability to T. Satisfaction may occur by: performance of the contract; mutual agreement between T and A discharging the contract, such as by mutual rescission, accord and satisfaction, novation, release; and by satisfaction of a judgment obtained by T against A.

Third, P's Settlement of Accounts with A in Reliance on T's Misleading Conduct. P's settlement of accounts with A on the contract with T, without notice that the contract has not been performed but made in reliance on T's conduct misleading P that the contract has been discharged, T's conduct not having been fraudulently induced by A, discharges P from liability on the contract with T. This was discussed previously in connection with contracts of disclosed and partially disclosed principals.[42]

Torts

By Servants. The master is liable for loss or harm caused to third persons by the tortious physical acts of his servants while acting within the scope of their employment, but, generally, not while they are acting outside the scope of their employment. Whether or not a servant was acting within the scope of his employment is a question of fact. The purpose and nature

---

[41] See above, p. 567.
[42] See above, p. 565.

of the servant's act, and the time, place, and manner of its performance all are considered in determining whether or not the act was performed within the scope of the employment. A servant is acting within the scope of his employment if he is performing acts of the same kind as he was authorized to perform, not unreasonably outside the time or area when such performance was to occur, and with the purpose of serving his master. Slight deviations in the manner of performance or in the time or place of such performance do not cause such performance to be outside the scope of the servant's authority. (P authorizes S to serve food up until 2:00 P.M. S serves food until 2:07 P.M. S was acting within the scope of his employment.) A servant's unauthorized use of equipment different from that authorized, but not substantially different, is conduct occurring within the scope of the servant's employment. Loss or damage caused to third persons by a servant's negligent use of equipment entrusted to him while acting within the scope of his employment subjects his master to liability therefor. A servant acting with an intent not to serve his master is not acting within the scope of his employment. The reason why a master is liable for loss or damage caused by the tortious physical acts of the servant while acting within the scope of his employment is that the master has a right of control over the physical acts of such servant and should be responsible for the acts of such servants.

By Non-Servant Agents. Inasmuch as the principal has no right of control over the physical acts of non-servant agents, as distinguished from servants, the principal is not liable for loss or damage caused by the tortious physical acts of such agents, unless they were acting as authorized by the principal and the principal had a duty to use care in the performance of such acts. Misrepresentations made by an agent with authority, apparent authority, or in connection with a transaction of the kind authorized, which a third person reasonably believes to be true and made with authority, causes the principal to be liable for such misrepresentations. (P appoints A as general manager of P's store. A gossips with B and slanders C. P is not liable to C for the slander. If A had fraudulently induced B, a customer, to buy goods by making intentional misrepresentations regarding the goods, P would be liable to B for the tort of deceit.[43] B could also rescind the transaction.)

Non-physical torts committed by an agent within the scope of his apparent authority subject the principal to liability therefor. (P appoints A, his agent, to send out bills to P's customers each month and to

[43] See above, p. 44, ftn. 29.

collect on the same. A pads a bill to C, a customer, who pays such bill, and A keeps the padded excess. P is liable for A's tort in obtaining the excess amounts.) A principal is not liable for torts of apparent agents or servants unless third persons rely on the apparent authority and are injured by torts committed by the apparent agent or servant occurring during such reliance. (P appoints A as manager of P's store, but A is not to demonstrate machines for sale, although it is incidental to the duties of a manager to do so. A demonstrates a machine to B, a customer. During the demonstration B is injured by the negligent demonstration. P is liable, as B has relied on A as acting within his apparent authority as manager of the store.) It is for this reason that an undisclosed principal is not liable for loss or damage caused by his agent acting as apparent owner of a business; the principal being undisclosed there is no apparent authority.

3. DUTIES AND LIABILITIES BETWEEN AGENT AND THIRD PERSON

Contracts   As discussed previously,[44] an agent may become a party to a contract with a third person, or with the third person and his principal. In the absence of agreement to the contrary, a person making or purporting to make a contract with a third person as an agent for a fully disclosed principal is not a party to the contract, while he is a party to the contract if his principal is partially disclosed. An agent acting for an undisclosed principal but purporting to contract for himself is a party to the contract with the third person. An agent is not a party to a contract under seal in a state where the Common Law effect of the seal exists if he is not described as a party thereto; nor is he a party to a contract in the form of a negotiable instrument on which his name does not appear. A person who purports to make a contract for a nonexistent principal, such nonexistence being known to the third person who is the other party to the contract, makes the agent a party to the contract with the third person. (A, acting as a promoter for a corporation to be formed, enters into a contract in the name of such unborn corporation with T, who knows of the nonexistence of the corporation. The contract is between A and T.) An agent who is not a party to the contract cannot maintain an action thereon in the name, and on behalf, of his principal; but if he is a party he can sue thereon in his own name on behalf of his principal. Factors often are

---

[44] See above, pp. 549–50.

parties to the contract along with the principal and the third person and can sue thereon in their own names.

A person who purports to act as an agent impliedly warrants that he has authority so to act and is liable for breach of such warranty, regardless of his good faith, to a third person reasonably believing him to have such authority. If the agent intentionally deceived a third person as to his authority, the agent is liable also in tort for deceit. The principal's ratification of the agent's unauthorized acts discharges the agent from liability for breach of warranty or misrepresentation. If an agent's disclosed principal has limited capacity to make the contract, the agent is not liable for damage caused to the third person by his principal's failure to perform the contract, unless the agent knows of the third person's ignorance of such limited capacity and he does not inform the third person, or the agent expressly warrants in the contract that the principal has full capacity to make the contract. An agent does not impliedly warrant that his principal has full capacity to contract, but, if the agent knows of the third person's ignorance of his principal's limited capacity to contract, he is under a duty to disclose this fact to the third person. When the agent fails in his duty to disclose such fact in his dealings with a third person, there is an implied warranty by law that the agent's principal has full capacity to contract and the agent is liable to the third person for damages for breach of such implied warranty if the principal should disaffirm the transaction.

Defenses. When an agent is a party to a contract with a principal and a third person, the agent may assert those defenses created by the contract and also his personal defenses against the third person. As a surety for his principal, the agent has the defenses available to a surety, which will be discussed subsequently under Suretyship.[45] An illustration of such a defense is performance by the principal which discharges the contract and discharges the agent from any liability thereon. If the agent and principal are not jointly liable on the contract, the third person has contract rights against each, and a judgment obtained by the third person against either one does not discharge the other unless the judgment is satisfied. When the principal is undisclosed and the third person, with subsequent knowledge of the principal's identity, obtains judgment against the principal, by the majority view, the agent is discharged by the third person's election to hold the principal liable for performance of the contract.

---

[45] See below, pp. 818 ff.

The third person may assert against an agent who is suing on the contract in his own name on behalf of his principal all the defenses which he could have asserted against the principal if the latter were the plaintiff. The third person can set off all claims he could have set off against the principal. The third person also may assert as a defense that the agent had no authority to bind the principal and did not bind him to any contract with the third person.

Torts
An agent who commits a tort, whether within or without the scope of his authority, is liable to the third person for such tort perpetrated upon him, regardless of whether or not the principal also is liable for the tort. (A, P's truck driver, negligently injures T while driving the truck delivering P's merchandise. A is liable as the wrongdoer, and P is liable for A's physical tort while acting within the scope of his employment as P's servant.) Similarly, a third person is liable to an agent for torts committed against the agent, regardless of whether or not the agent was acting within or without the scope of his authority. Some of the common torts committed by agents are deceit, negligence, and conversion.

Although an agent is liable to third persons for damage caused to them by his active misconduct, commonly called "misfeasance," nevertheless, an agent generally is not liable to third persons for his failure to act, commonly called "nonfeasance." The reason for this result is that a person who acts has a duty to act reasonably, while a person without any duty to act violates no duty by his inaction, and he commits no wrong. Although an agent has a duty to his principal to perform his contract of agency, generally an agent has no duty to third persons so to perform. However, once an agent begins to perform he has a duty to act reasonably. Also, if an agent undertakes with his principal to perform an act which he should realize, under the circumstances, is necessary to the safety of a third person or his property, thereby causing the third person or the principal to rely upon performance by the agent, a duty is imposed upon the agent to exercise reasonable care to perform his undertaking. The agent's failure to take affirmative action in accordance with his duty subjects him to liability for damage proximately caused thereby.

An agent who has the duty to exercise control over the acts of other agents or servants of his principal must exercise due care in performing his duty, and he is liable for his negligence in not exercising such care. If he exercises reasonable care and other agents or servants commit torts on third persons, causing injury to them, the agent is not liable; only the principal is liable to the third persons. However, if the principal is undisclosed to the other agents or servants, the agent with authority to supervise the other agents or servants is liable for their torts as though he were a principal; this does not exclude the undisclosed principal from liability therefor if the tort occurred during the performance of authorized acts.

Chapter V

TERMINATION OF AGENCY

1. TERMINATION OF ACTUAL AUTHORITY

AGENCY may be terminated by the act of the parties or by operation of law. Apparent agency may be terminated by notice to third persons of the cessation of actual authority. The termination of actual and apparent authority will be discussed in turn.

By Act of the Parties
Express or Implied Terms of the Agency. The relationship of agency terminates when the agency agreement expressly or impliedly so provides. The agreement may specify that, on the accomplishment of the object to be performed, on the expiration of a certain period of time, on the occurrence of a particular event, or at the will of either party if it is an agency terminable at will, the agency is to terminate. It is implied that, if the agreement does not specify when it is to terminate, the agency is meant to terminate on the expiration of a reasonable period of time under the circumstances. Conditions may so change as impliedly to cause the agency to terminate. If the agent reasonably can believe from the change in conditions that the principal no longer would desire the agency to continue, the agency is terminated.

Mutual Rescission. Agency, by definition, is created by mutual consent and is a continuing, legal relationship until such mutuality of consent is terminated. The principal and agent consented to the creation of the agency, and it is their right to agree to rescind the agency.

Revocation or Renunciation. Either the principal or the agent individually may terminate the agency. The principal's withdrawal of his consent is called "revocation," and the agent's withdrawal of his consent is called "renunciation." The principal has the power to revoke an agency although his wrongful termination of a contract of agency subjects him to liability to the agent for damages for breach thereof. Similarly, the agent may renounce the agency and, if the agency is one of contract, the agent exposes himself to liability to his principal for damages for breach thereof. Any provision in the agency contract that the contract is irrevocable does not prevent revocation or renunciation of the contract, but merely indicates that breach of the contract will impose liability therefor. Unless otherwise agreed, a party's revocation or renunciation must be *actually received* by the other party either from the one revoking or renouncing, or by his knowledge of facts which would lead him reasonably to believe that the agency has been revoked or renounced. Revocation or renunciation is effective as such only if the addressee reasonably could understand such manifestation to be a revocation or renunciation. Agency under seal may be revoked by parol. Revocation or renunciation of the agency for cause does not constitute a breach and does not impose liability for termination.

"Irrevocable Agency." It is often said that there are two so-called exceptions to the rule that agency is revocable, namely, *authority given as security* (consideration is given by the power holder), and *authority coupled with an interest in the subject matter* (title is transferred to the power holder). These two instances do not involve authority but, rather, they are non-agency power situations. Authority may be revoked or renounced, as discussed previously, and on its termination all agency power, all inherent agency power, and agency itself are terminated. With these distinctions in mind, let us examine these two types of power.

1. *Authority Given as Security.* If the principal *contracts* (not merely agrees) with his agent, whereby the agent renders the performance requested by the principal who, in return, *promises authority to the agent as security for the principal's performance of an obligation* (often payment of his indebtedness) to the agent, such authority is irrevocable. *It is the fact that the principal's promise of authority to secure performance of his obligation is supported by sufficient consideration which causes the contract to be made and the authority to be irrevocable.* (P and A *contract* whereby A lends $1,000 to P, who agrees to repay the same on a certain date and, *as security for the payment of such debt, P authorizes A* to sell P's horse if P defaults on such payment. P does not deliver the horse to A. P's promise of authority for the purpose of security to A is supported by sufficient consideration, namely A's loan to P, and such authority therefore is irrevocable.) If the principal's promise of authority to A for the purpose of security is not supported by sufficient consideration, there is no contract but merely an agreement, and P's promise is unenforceable and revocable. (P owes A $1,000. P authorizes A to sell P's horse for $2,000, to retain $1,000 in satisfaction of the debt and to account to P for the balance. P does not deliver the

horse to A. P's promise of authority is not supported by sufficient consideration and, therefore, it is revocable.) This irrevocable authority is called *authority given as security.* Authority given as security is irrevocable during the lifetime of the principal and, although there is conflict among the courts, by the better view it is also irrevocable on the death of the principal. At Common Law there was a failure to distinguish between a security power and the fiduciary power contained in authority. The death of the principal does not terminate any authority here because there is no agency nor authority but, instead, a security power and the power holder as such is not an agent for the purpose of the power.

It should be noted carefully that while an agent may have an interest in performing his authority and thereby earn the agreed compensation for such performance, e.g., a commission for the sale of merchandise, nevertheless, such an interest is not sufficient to cause the authority to be irrevocable, even if the principal agreed not to revoke such authority. This authority is not given as *security.* This interest of the agent in compensation solely *for the exercise of authority* is a normal part of agency and, for the principal's failure to perform, the agent has the remedy of an action for breach of contract.

2. *Authority Coupled with an Interest in the Subject Matter.* If the principal *transfers to his agent a property interest* (e.g., title) in the principal's property *to secure performance of the principal's obligation* owing by the principal to the agent, *together with authority* to dispose of such property on the principal's default on his obligation, the agent's *authority is coupled with an interest in the subject matter* (the principal's property) and is irrevocable by the principal and by his death. No contract is required between the principal and the agent with respect to such authority. All that is necessary is such transfer and such authority for the purpose of security. (P owes A $1,000. P delivers to A title to P's horse with authority to sell the horse for $2,000 on P's default, to retain $1,000 in satisfaction of the debt, and to account to P for the remainder. The authority to sell on default is coupled with an interest in the subject matter, namely, the title to the property, and is irrevocable by P or by P's death.)

Authority coupled with an interest in the subject matter is irrevocable by the principal's death because the agent may proceed against the property in his own name. It is unimportant whether or not consideration is given for the property interest, as long as the property interest is created.

Death. Inasmuch as the agency relation is consensual and personal in character, the death of the principal or of the agent terminates the agency, unless the agency is so-called irrevocable. Notice to the surviving agent o˙ principal is not required. Termination in this matter does not constitute a breach of any agency contract, and the estate of the decedent is not liable for damages for such termination. The death of one or more joint principals or joint agents has the same effect. Although P's death immediately terminates authority without notice, business convenience and necessity require that, in certain cases, A should still have a *power* to bind P's estate when A, without notice of P's death, does what he was authorized to do. This need is reflected by the Code, which provides that the death or incompetence of a customer does not revoke the bank's authority to accept, pay, or collect items issued by the principal depositor, or to account for proceeds of collection on them, until the bank knows of the fact of death or of an adjudication of incompetence and has reasonable opportunity to act on it. The Code also provides that, even with knowledge, a bank may for 10 days after the date of death pay or certify checks drawn on or prior to that date, unless ordered to stop by a person claiming an interest in the account.

By Operation of Law

Insanity. Insanity of the principal or of the agent terminates the agency, unless the agency is so-called irrevocable. Notice to the principal or the agent of the other's insanity is not required. The insanity of one or more joint principals or joint agents has the same effect.

Bankruptcy. The effect of the principal's bankruptcy upon the agent's authority depends upon the transactions in which the agent is to engage, except that so-called irrevocable agency is not affected by such bankruptcy. On bankruptcy, a trustee in bankruptcy is appointed and the bankrupt's nonexempt property passes to him for distribution among the bankrupt's creditors. With respect to such nonexempt property, the agent's authority is terminated without any notice to the agent. With respect to exempt property and with respect to an agent's authority to bind the principal personally, the agent's authority does not terminate until he receives notice of the principal's bankruptcy. On receiving such notice, if the agent reasonably can believe from such a change in the principal's financial condition that the principal no longer would desire the agency to continue, the agency impliedly is terminated, as stated previously.[1] Usually the bankruptcy of the agent also will

---

[1] See above, p. 580.

terminate the agency, although if his bankruptcy will not in any way affect his performance of authorized acts, his bankruptcy does not terminate the agency.

Change of Law.   Generally, a change of law causing the agency to be illegal, or causing performance of the act authorized to be illegal and entirely ineffective, terminates the agent's authority without notice to the agent.

Destruction of Subject Matter.   Generally, the loss or destruction of the particular subject matter which is the object of the agency terminates the agent's authority without notice to the agent.

The above discussion of termination of authority either by the acts of P and A or by the occurrence of subsequent events applies to the termination of the authority of subagents (which includes sub-servants), making allowance for their "sub" status. This, since subagency involves relations between P and A as the result of P's manifestation of consent to A, between A and SA (subagent) as a result of A's manifestation of consent to SA, and between P and SA as a result of P's manifestation of consent to SA through A, the withdrawal of either P's consent to A or A's consent to SA terminates the subagency. However, SA may still have apparent authority to bind P or A. *Accordingly, termination of the relation between P and A or between A and SA terminates the subagency but not necessarily SA's apparent authority.* When notice of termination is not required for termination of authority, SA's authority ceases immediately without notice; when such notice is required, notice to SA accomplishes this result, but if the notification of P's termination of his relation to A is received only by A, SA's authority does not terminate until A has had a reasonable time to communicate the notice of termination to SA.

2. TERMINATION OF APPARENT AUTHORITY

Notice to T, When Required   Apparent authority is created by P's manifestation to T that A has authority to act as P's agent. Apparent authority is A's power to affect P's legal relations with T by acting in accordance with P's manifestation to T just as though A were P's agent. Since apparent authority is concerned with T's belief from P's manifestation to him that A has authority to act as P's agent, termination of apparent authority does not occur until T no longer reasonably has this belief. The supervening death or loss of capacity of P or A,[2] or supervening impossibility by change of law or

---

[2] See above, p. 583.

destruction of subject matter,[3] terminates authority and apparent authority immediately and without notice to anyone. However, with these three exceptions, termination of authority does not of itself terminate apparent authority. Termination of apparent authority can occur only by proper notice to T. *It is only to those third persons to whom the agent has apparent authority that the principal must give notice of the termination of the agency in order to terminate such apparent authority.*

General and Special Agents. *General Agents.* Because general agents are authorized to conduct a series of transactions involving a continuity of service, it is considered a reasonable interpretation of a principal's appointment of a general agent that third persons are to continue to deal with a general agent until notified to the contrary or until lapse of time should cause third persons to realize that authority has been terminated. *Accordingly, unless otherwise manifested by P to T, notice to T is required in order to terminate the apparent authority of a general agent.*

Special Agents. However, in the case of a special agent, who is authorized to conduct a single transaction or a series of transactions not involving continuity of service, it is considered a reasonable interpretation of a principal's appointment of a special agent that third persons should realize that his authority may terminate without notice to third persons. *Accordingly, unless otherwise manifested by P to T, termination of authority of a special agent immediately terminates his apparent authority, without notice to T, with four exceptions when apparent authority exists and, unless otherwise manifested by P, when notice to T is required.* The exceptions follow.

1. *A specially accredited agent* is an agent whom P has indicated to T has been specially selected to deal with T and whose authority T reasonably can believe is to continue unless P notifies T of its modification or termination. A general, as well as a special, agent may be a specially accredited agent; consequently, *unless otherwise manifested by P, notice to T is required to terminate the authority of a specially accredited agent.*

2. *A has begun to deal with T, of which P has notice.* T can reasonably expect that if, with P's knowledge, A is dealing with T on P's behalf as his agent, P would notify T of the termination of A's authority. It is deemed but reasonable that P should be required to respect T's expectation. The agent may be a special or a general agent.

---

[3] See above, p. 584.

So, *unless otherwise manifested by P, notice to T is required to terminate the authority of an agent who, known to P, has begun to deal with T.*

3. *When P entrusts to A written authority intended for exhibition to third persons, as to third persons to whom the writing is exhibited and who do not know of termination of A's authority, the apparent authority of A cannot be terminated without notice to them of such termination.* The agent may be a special or a general agent.

4. *When P manifests to T that A's authority terminates on the occurrence of a specified event and that A has authority to represent when the event has occurred, T is justified in relying on the truth of A's statement concerning the occurrence or non-occurrence of the specified event, and the occurrence of the event without notice to T does not terminate A's apparent authority.* P's manifestation to T that A has authority to represent when the event has occurred may be made expressly, or may be made impliedly when knowledge of the event's occurrence is peculiarly, but not necessarily exclusively, within the knowledge of a general agent or when it is within the exclusive knowledge of a special agent. (P authorizes A to buy a horse and P tells T_1 that A has such authority and that A is coming over to look at T_1's horse. A, authorizedly and in P's name, buys a horse from T_2, without the knowledge of P and T_1. A then looks at T_1's horse, misrepresents to T_1 that he had not yet purchased a horse for P, and contracts in P's name with T_1 for the purchase of his horse, T_1 reasonably believing A. P is bound to T_1. A is a special agent with exclusive knowledge of the occurrence of the event of the purchase of a horse and with apparent authority to represent its non-occurrence to T_1.) (P appoints A as general manager of P's retail men's clothing store with instructions that he is not to have more than 500 shirts in stock for sale at any time, a fact which T, a shirt manufacturer, knows. A has 350 shirts in stock, but he tells T that there are only 200 shirts in stock. T reasonably believes A and he contracts with A in P's name to sell to P 300 more shirts. P is bound to T. A is a general agent.)

Kinds of Notice to T

Two kinds of notice are involved in the termination of apparent authority, namely actual notice and reasonable notice. The kind of notice of termination of authority that T is to receive in order to terminate apparent authority depends upon the kind of agent and prior credit transactions between T and P through A.

Actual Notice. *T must receive actual notice of termination of authority in all of the following cases,* the last three of which have just been discussed:

1. When T previously has either extended credit to P, or received credit from P, through A in reliance on P's manifestation of A's continuing authority.
2. A is a specially accredited agent to T.
3. A has begun to deal with T, of which P has notice.
4. A has exhibited to T, who reasonably can rely on A's exhibit, P's written indicia of authority, which P has entrusted to A.

Actual notice to T occurs when:

1. P has actually told T, or
2. A reasonable period of time has elapsed after P's written notice of termination of authority has been delivered by P either:
   a. To T personally, or
   b. To a person with authority or apparent authority to receive communications for T either:
      (1) At T's place of business, or
      (2) At the place that T has designated as one where his business communications are received, or
      (3) At "a place which, in view of the business customs or relations between the parties is reasonably believed to be the place for the receipt of such communications by" T.[4]

Reasonable Notice. *All other third persons to whom A has apparent authority are entitled to reasonable notice by either:* "(a) advertising the fact in a newspaper of general circulation in the place where the agency is regularly carried on; or (b) giving publicity by some other method reasonably adapted to give the information to such third person."[5] Of course, if they receive actual notice of termination this would be sufficient notice also. Those third persons as to whom A has apparent authority and who are entitled to receive such reasonable notice are: those who have dealt previously with P through A on a *cash basis;* and those who have never dealt previously with P through A but who knew of A's authority either directly from P or through A's reputation as P's agent, *irrespective of whether they learned of A's apparent authority either before or after the termination of A's authority.* It should be noted that, after A's authority has been terminated, A does not have authority to represent to third persons with whom A is dealing for the *first* time that he has authority, and such wrongful

---

[4] American Law Institute, *Restatement: Agency 2d,* 1958, sec. 136 (1) (b) (iv).
[5] *Ibid.,* sec. 136 (3) (a) (b).

misrepresentation by A to T does not thereby create apparent authority.

It should be noted that the previous discussion of the termination of an agent's apparent authority applies also to the termination of the apparent authority of a subagent, which includes a subservant.

APPENDIX TO PART FIVE

REFERENCES

1. American Law Institute. *Restatement: Agency 2d.* 1958.
2. Frascona, Joseph L. *Agency.* Englewood Cliffs, N.J.: Prentice-Hall, Inc., 1964.
3. Mechem, Floyd R. *Outlines of the Law of Agency.* 4th ed., Philip Mechem. Chicago: Callaghan & Co., 1952.
4. Mechem, Floyd R. *A Treatise on the Law of Agency.* 2d ed. Chicago: Callaghan & Co., 1914.
5. Seavey, Warren A. *Handbook of the Law of Agency.* St. Paul, Minn.: West Publishing Co., 1964.

PROBLEMS

1. (a) What is the meaning of the following:
   (1) Agency.
   (2) Servant.
   (3) Independent contractor.
   (4) Special agent.
   (5) General agent.
   (6) Del credere agent.
   (b) Who may be a principal and who an agent?
2. (a) P wrote to A authorizing him to purchase a truck. A, without knowledge of P's written authorization and without any other authority from P, represented to T that he was authorized by P to purchase a truck; and he purchased a truck from T in P's name. T did not know of P's written authorization. P refused to accept the truck and refused to pay for it.
   (1) Is P liable to T for such purchase? Why?
   (2) Is A liable to T for such purchase? Why?
   (b) P orally authorized A to mortgage P's land. Although he didn't tell A, P had meant that A was to mortgage only X land; instead, A executed and delivered to T a mortgage on P's Y land. P refused to recognize the mortgage as valid.
   (1) Is the mortgage valid?
   (2) Why?

3. A certified public accountant was making a balance sheet audit of a coal dealer's business and the accountant, at his own expense, engaged an engineer to survey coal piles and to report to the accountant the quantity in each pile. The engineer in the due performance of his work purchased necessary supplies for which he did not pay. Has the vendor of these supplies an enforceable claim against the accountant? (Former C.P.A. Examination question)

4. (a) P authorized A to sell 1,000 barrels of oil in P's possession. A, in P's name, sold the oil to T, who paid A the purchase price. A absconded with the proceeds. P refused to deliver the oil to T until T had paid P the purchase price.
   (1) Has T a right to possession of the oil without paying P the purchase price?
   (2) Why?
   (b) P authorized A to sell certain goods. After A, in P's name, had sold such goods to T, A and T agreed to rescind the sale. P refused to recognize the rescission, tendered the goods, and demanded the purchase price.
   (1) Was the rescission binding on P?
   (2) Why?
   (c) P delivered goods to A and authorized him to sell them. A, in P's name, sold the goods to T and received T's check for the purchase price.
   (1) Is the transaction binding on P?
   (2) Why?

5. Jones, an orange grower, ships oranges to his factor in New York. Twenty hours before they are due to arrive the factor learns that in New York, due to excessive arrivals, oranges will not bring enough to satisfy freight charges, but if diverted to a factor in Philadelphia, they will bring a much larger price at no greater freight cost. He cannot communicate with Jones in time to make the change. The factor reroutes the oranges to Philadelphia, where they are destroyed by flood.
   (1) Did the factor have authority to reroute the shipment of oranges?
   (2) Is he liable for the loss?
   (3) Explain. (Former C.P.A. Examination question)

6. P authorized A to purchase two used tractors at the lowest possible price. A delegated to B the authority to purchase one tractor, and B purchased a tractor from T in P's name. A agreed to purchase another tractor from X at an agreed price; and A authorized C to sign the contract in P's name, which C did. P disclaims any liability for both purchases for lack of authority and refuses to accept the tractors.
   (1) Who is bound by these transactions?
   (2) Why?

7. P appointed A general manager of P's large department store and informed him that he had no authority to buy goods for sale in the store nor any authority to sell any goods himself. A fired B, a salesman, and employed C to take B's place. In P's presence, A made an excellent sale of merchandise to D, P remaining silent throughout the transaction. A also purchased merchandise from E and in P's name for sale in the store. Only P and A knew of P's limitation on A's authority.

(1) Is P bound by these transactions?

(2) Why?

8. (a) P authorized A in writing to sell and transfer title to certain merchandise for $10,000 and directed A to show the writing to anyone interested in the purchase. P told T that A had authority to sell the merchandise and that A's authority was contained in a writing possessed by A and available for T's examination. T did not examine the writing and, ignorant of A's limitation of authority to sell only for $10,000, purchased the merchandise from A for $9,000. P refused to accept the $9,000 and refused to deliver the merchandise, claiming that the transaction was not binding upon him.

(1) Is P bound?

(2) Why?

(b) In the above problem, would the result have been any different if P had directed A not to disclose the $10,000 limitation and T had been ignorant of the written authorization and of its $10,000 limitation? Why?

9. A misappropriated merchandise from P's warehouse and, representing that the merchandise belonged to A, sold and delivered it to T—intending to pocket the proceeds payable in 30 days. T did not know that the merchandise belonged to P until P informed T that he ratified the transaction and demanded the purchase price at the end of the 30 days. T then informed P of his withdrawal from the transaction and tendered the return of the merchandise, which P refused.

(1) Does P have a right against T for the purchase price?

(2) Why?

10. A traveling salesman, authorized to contract to sell certain securities at par, reported to his principal that he had contracted to sell a large quantity at 1 per cent below par. The principal withheld action upon the report for one month and then notified the vendee that the contract was repudiated. Is the principal bound by the contract? (Former C.P.A. Examination question)

11. (a) P authorized A to travel to X, examine two dozen typewriters for sale, and—if satisfactory to A—to purchase them for cash. A paid the travel charges and advanced the purchase price for the typewriters, which were delivered to A. P demands the typewriters, which A refuses to deliver until the travel costs and advance of purchase price have been paid.

(1) May A so refuse?

(2) Why?

(b) P authorized A to obtain a ready, willing, and able purchaser of P's land for $10,000, A to receive a 5 per cent commission for doing so. T offered A a 5 per cent commission if A could get P to sell his land to T for $10,000. T is such a ready, willing, and able purchaser, whom A introduced to P as willing to buy the land for $10,000. Just before the sale was about to be made P learned of the agreement for a commission between A and T, and P refused to sell the land to T.

(1) Does A have a right against P for the commission promised him by P?

(2) Why?

12. An infant, 20 years of age, authorized his agent to purchase certain bonds, the agent knowing the infancy of his principal. The agent purchased the bonds, disclosing the name of his principal but not disclosing the fact of infancy. The vendor did not know that the principal was an infant, and the agent had every reason to believe that the vendor was ignorant of this fact. Upon reaching the age of 21, the infant disaffirmed the purchase, returned the bonds and all interest received thereon, and was reimbursed for the purchase price. Is the agent legally responsible to the vendor? (Former C.P.A. Examination question)

13. (a) P authorized A to purchase a particular lot of goods if it was satisfactory to A and to resell it at the highest price possible. A examined the lot, purchased it in his own name and with his own funds, sold it at a profit, and kept the proceeds. A misrepresented to P that the lot was unsatisfactory to A. P later learned of A's acts.

(1) Does P have any right against A?

(2) Why?

(b) P authorized A to purchase certain goods at a specified price. A learns that the goods are deteriorating in quality but, without telling P of such deterioration, bought the goods. P did not know of the deterioration until he received the goods and thereby suffered loss.

(1) Is A liable to P for such loss?

(2) Why?

14. P authorized A, an infant, to purchase on 30 days credit certain goods from T but not to disclose P's identity to T. T refused to sell the goods to A if he was representing P and A misrepresented that he was purchasing the goods for himself. Relying on this, T subsequently sold the goods to A on 30 days credit, taking A's negotiable promissory note therefor. On A's failure to pay the note when due, T sued A on the note and obtained judgment. A has no assets. T then learned of P's identity and demanded the purchase price from him.

(1) Is P liable to T for the purchase price?

(2) Why?

15. P owed A $5,000 and delivered his horse to A with authority to sell the horse, retain $5,000 in satisfaction of the debt, and to pay P the remainder. P died and E, the executor of P's estate, demanded the return of the horse from A. A refused to deliver the horse to E.

(1) Does E have a right to possession of the horse?

(2) Why?

16. P authorized A to buy merchandise for P's store when A considered such purchases necessary. A, in P's name, made various purchases from different wholesalers, including T, over a period of years. P always paid for such purchases. P sent A a letter revoking A's authority; but, after the letter was sent and before A had received it, A purchased merchandise from T for P. P also had sent a letter to T stating that A's authority had been revoked;

but T never received the letter, nor did T know of such revocation. After A had received P's letter, A made a second purchase from T in P's name and absconded with the goods.

(1) Is P bound by A's first purchase from T? Why?

(2) Is P bound by A's second purchase from T? Why?

(3) What should P do immediately?

17. An agent sent an order in the name of his principal, by mail the day before the death of the principal, to a merchant with whom he had a general arrangement for goods to be supplied on order during the year. The merchant, who was ignorant of the principal's death, filled the order within a reasonable time. The principal's executor refused to pay for the goods. Can the merchant recover? (Former C.P.A. Examination question)

18. A drew a check payable to his own order, forged P's signature to it, and indorsed and sold it to T, who was innocent of the forgery. T subsequently telephoned P and asked him whether the signature on the check was his and whether A was P's agent to buy goods for P. P mistakenly believed it was his signature and that A was his agent and answered "Yes," when in fact A was not his agent. A then contracted in P's name with T for the purchase of goods for the reasonable value of $1,000 and A drew a check to T's order for the purchase price, signing it in P's name by A.

(1) Is P liable to T on the forged check?

(2) Is P liable to T on the contract for the purchase of the goods from T?

(3) Is P liable to T on the check for the purchase price?

19. P innocently purchased stolen goods belonging to O. P's agent, A, without notice of the theft and pursuant to his authority, sold the goods to B. A paid O $500 in reasonable compromise of O's claim against A for conversion of the goods. Does A have any right against P for $500?

SOME PREVIOUS C.P.A. LAW EXAMINATION QUESTIONS AND MODEL ANSWERS

MAY, 1971

No. 8 (Estimated time—20 to 25 minutes)

a. In the course of your examination of the financial statements of Prince Realty Corp. for the year ended March 31, 1971, you learned of the following: Prince orally employed Baker, 20 years old, to manage an apartment house that it owned. Prince Realty instructed Baker not to contract for any repair work without its prior approval. Prince Realty also instructed Baker to collect in person the monthly rent from the 100 tenants. Contrary to these instructions Baker contracted with Trinity Plumbing Company to repair some plumbing for $200 and a bill for the services rendered has been submitted to Prince Realty for payment. In addition Corbin, a tenant, asserted a claim against Prince Realty alleging that he was assaulted by Baker who was attempting to collect past due rent. Although Baker was discharged after managing the apartment house for three months, he collected the rent for the fourth month on all apartments and absconded. After learning this Prince Realty has billed the tenants for the fourth month's rent.

   (1) Is Prince Realty liable to Trinity Plumbing? State "yes" or "no" and discuss.
   (2) Is Prince Realty liable to Corbin? State "yes" or "no" and discuss.
   (3) Can Prince Realty recover from the tenants for the fourth month's rent? State "yes" or "no" and discuss.
b. In the course of your examination of the financial statements of Higgins Electronics, Inc. for the year ended March 31, 1971, you learned of a claim for $75,000 that James Ladd had made against the Company. Your investigation disclosed that the Company wanted to purchase some valuable used electronic equipment from Ladd, a competitor. The Company hired Lemmon to make the purchase in his name and instructed him not to disclose that he was acting for the Company. Lemmon signed a contract in his own name to purchase the equipment from Ladd for $75,000 with delivery and payment to be made 30 days later. Before the payment date the Company learned of a major technological breakthrough in electronic equipment and decided to buy new equipment which incorporated the discovery. Lemmon was instructed immediately to neither pay nor accept delivery of the used equipment. When Ladd learned subsequently that the Company was Lemmon's principal he sued the Company for breach of contract. The Company defended contending that it was not liable to Ladd because (1) Ladd intended to contract with Lemmon only and (2) recovery was barred because Ladd discovered the identity of the Company after the contract was executed.
   (1) Discuss the validity of each defense asserted by your client, Higgins Electronics, Inc.
   (2) Discuss the extent of Lemmon's liability to Ladd.

Answer

a. (1) Yes. Under the law of agency, a principal is liable for the acts of his agent while acting within the scope of his apparent authority. In most states an infant may be an agent. A principal's appointment of a general agent whose status is known to third persons is a manifestation to them of such agency and creates apparent authority to do what third persons reasonably can believe such apparent agents in that position may do. Here, Baker is an agent with actual and apparent authority to manage the building, although he did not have authority to contract for repair work. Trinity reasonably could believe that Baker, as manager, could contract for repair work to the building. Accordingly, although Baker did not act within the scope of his authority, he did act within the scope of his apparent authority thereby binding Prince to Trinity by contract. Since Prince was a disclosed principal, the agent Baker is not a party to the contract and an infant's power to avoid his contract is personal to him.

   (2) Yes, if Baker did assault Corbin. A principal is liable for the conduct of his agent-servant for his physical torts while acting within the scope of his employment. A servant is an agent employed to render services for his master and whose physical conduct is subject to his master's control. Here, Baker is a servant who, while acting within the scope of his employment collecting rents for Prince, assaulted Corbin, a tenant.

Baker was not acting on his own behalf. Therefore Prince is liable to Corbin for the assault.

(3) No. Apparent authority is terminated only if notice is given by the principal to third persons who know of the continuing apparent agency that the agency no longer exists. Here, although Prince terminated Baker's authority to collect the fourth month rents, the tenants did not receive any notice of this. Therefore, Baker's apparent authority continued to exist and he acted within its scope thereby binding Prince by his conduct.

b. (1) The first defense is not valid. An undisclosed principal by operation of law, along with his agent and the third person, is a party to a contract made by his agent within the scope of his authority. Here, Lemmon acted authorizedly and, therefore, the Company is bound to Ladd and liable for its breach of the contract.

The second defense is not valid. The third party may enforce the contract against the party with whom he has contracted. Here, the Company is a party, and the fact that Ladd learned of the Company's identity after the contract was made does not preclude Ladd from recognizing the agency and holding the Company liable as the principal.

(2) Since Lemmon is a party to the contract, Ladd may hold him liable for its breach. The Company as an undisclosed principal, and his agent, are both parties to the contract and severally liable thereon to the third party, who may sue either one.

NOVEMBER, 1969

No. 1 (Estimated time—20 to 25 minutes)

Each of the following numbered sentences states a legal conclusion as it relates to the preceding related lettered fact situation. You are to determine whether each of the legal conclusions is true or false and write on a separate answer sheet whether each conclusion is true or false. Your grade will be determined from your total net score obtained by deducting your total of incorrect answers from your total of correct answers; an omitted answer will not be considered an incorrect answer.

Write on a separate answer sheet whether the following numbered sentences are true or false according to the *general principles of agency law.*

A. The Gordon Company, a manufacturer of cosmetics, employed Wood as its agent to promote its products. Under the terms of the contract signed, the agency is to last one year and is renewable at the Company's option. The contract provides that Wood is to be paid a 1 per cent commission on gross sales of the Company. In addition, the Company is to provide $100,000 to Wood to be used over the year to advertise the Company's products. Wood made no promise to work a specific amount of time during the year for the Company. Wood started to place advertising for the Company and to arrange promotional events. Three months after entering into the contract the Company marketed a new type of cosmetic. Marketing studies conducted by an independent firm engaged by the Company indicate that the new product will sell so well without any promotion that gross sales of the Company should more than triple, but that the product will not sell any better if it is promoted. The Company has notified Wood his contract is being terminated early.

1. Wood has no rights under the contract because all contracts of agency are terminable at will.
2. Wood has no rights under the contract because he has not given any consideration in return for the Company's promise to employ him.
3. The Company is not free to terminate the contract on the grounds that the marketing of the new product is an unexpected development which substantially changes the relationship of the parties.
4. The contract must remain in force, but Wood will not be entitled to commissions on the sale of the new product.
5. Wood may recover damages in a suit against the independent firm that studied the market for the new product for interfering with his contract with the Company.

B. Charles Jackson borrowed $20,000 from the Morgan Loan Company. He executed a note and a real property mortgage on his land and factory to secure payment of the loan. Subsequently, Jackson defaulted on the loan and authorized the Morgan Loan Company in writing to sell the factory on his behalf and retain an amount sufficient to satisfy the debt.

6. Unless the Morgan Loan Company filed the mortgage on the property it will be unable to enforce against Jackson.
7. The mortgage did not include the inventory stored in the factory.
8. Jackson can terminate the agency relationship with Morgan at any time prior to the consummation of the sale of the land and factory.
9. The death of Jackson would terminate the agency relationship but would not affect Morgan's rights on the mortgage.
10. Morgan has an agency coupled with an interest.

C. Philip Star was a car salesman employed by the Modern Motor Company. The Company instructed Star not to sell an antique car belonging to the Company which was kept on the Company's premises. When Roger Bloom came to purchase a car and expressed an interest in the antique car, Star informed Bloom that the car belonged to him personally and that he would sell it for $500 although it was worth $2,000. Bloom agreed and paid Star $500 cash and received a bill of sale. Star then disappeared.

11. Bloom is entitled to the antique car since he dealt with an authorized agent of Modern Motor Company.
12. When Bloom entered the Modern Motor Company showroom, he could properly assume that any car salesman was authorized to sell any new car on the premises.
13. When Bloom paid Star $500 cash for the antique car, Bloom could not properly assume that Star had apparent authority as an agent to sell the car.
14. Modern Motor Company must pay Bloom $500 because the Company was negligent in failing to place a sign on the antique car which stated "This car is not for sale."
15. Modern Motor Company must pay Bloom $500 because as a principal it

is responsible for the wrongful acts of its agent done in the course of his employment.

D. John James, a local jobber, purported to act as the agent for Fairway Department Store when he in fact had no authority to bind Fairway. James made a contract in Fairway's name with Frank Williams to purchase 100 desk lamps at $4.75 each. James did this with the expectation of receiving a commission from Fairway because he believed the 100 lamps were a bargain at $475.

16. James would be personally liable on the contract if Fairway refuses to purchase the lamps.

17. Williams would not be liable to anyone if he repudiated the contract prior to any action by Fairway.

18. If Fairway learned of the transaction and affirmed the contract prior to any action by Williams, Fairway may enforce the contract against Williams.

19. If the contract were consummated and Fairway made a large profit on the lamps, Fairway must pay James a commission.

20. Since James committed a fraud at the initial stage of the contract, it was void at the inception.

E. Majestic Merchandise Mart employed Paul to deliver merchandise purchased by its customers and provided Paul with a light truck to make deliveries. Paul was told not to drive over 35 miles per hour, which was 5 miles less than the speed limit. Paul, while making his deliveries, drove at 40 miles per hour and hit and injured Elaine. Paul was also injured.

21. Paul would be entitled to worker's compensation even if he were shown to have been negligent.

22. If Paul were negligent, Majestic may be held liable for Paul's action only if Majestic were negligent in its hiring of Paul.

23. Majestic could not be held liable even if Paul were negligent since he disobeyed company instructions.

24. If Elaine sued and recovered from Paul, she could not recover from Majestic also.

25. If Paul were held liable to Elaine, he could obtain indemnification from Majestic since he was acting as an agent for and on behalf of his principal when the accident occurred.

F. Michael Evans was employed as the purchasing agent for Restaurant Corporation. He purchased goods on credit for the Corporation in his own name from the Martin Food Supply Company. Martin Food Supply did not know that Evans was acting as an agent when he purchased the goods. The goods were used by the Corporation. When Martin Food Supply attempted to collect the cost of the goods from Evans, Evans informed Martin that he (Evans) was an employee and had purchased the goods for Restaurant Corporation's account. Later, Owens, who was the sole stockholder of Restaurant Corporation, sold all of his shares of stock to Diamond.

26. Prior to the sale of the Restaurant Corporation shares to Diamond, the Corporation was responsible to Martin Food Supply for the goods Evans bought as purchasing agent.

27. As sole stockholder of the Corporation, Owens would be personally

responsible to satisfy the claim of Martin Food Supply if Restaurant Corporation were liable and did not have sufficient assets to meet the obligation.

28. Evans's liability for the cost of the goods purchased did not end after the fact that he was an agent became known.

29. Owens was not an undisclosed principal of either Restaurant Corporation or Evans and therefore had no liability to Martin.

30. After the purchase of the Restaurant Corporation shares by Diamond, a defense which would preclude liability on the part of the Corporation would be that Diamond was unaware of the debt owed to Martin Food Supply when he purchased the shares of stock.

Answer

1. False	7. True	13. True	19. False	25. False
2. False	8. False	14. False	20. False	26. True
3. True	9. False	15. False	21. True	27. False
4. False	10. True	16. True	22. False	28. True
5. False	11. False	17. True	23. False	29. True
6. False	12. True	18. True	24. True	30. False

NOVEMBER, 1963

No. 6

a. Acme Manufacturing Company wished to acquire a site for a warehouse. Knowing that if it negotiated directly for the purchase of the property the price would be substantially increased, it employed Anson, an agent, to secure lots without disclosing that he was acting for Acme. Anson's authority was evidenced by a writing signed by the proper officers of Acme Company. Anson entered into a contract in his own name to purchase Thomas' lot, giving Thomas a negotiable note for $1,000, signed by Anson, as first payment. Believing that Stuart would succeed better with Davis for the purchase of Davis' property, Anson employed Stuart for that purpose, giving him written authorization. Stuart signed a contract in his own name to buy a lot owned by Davis. Davis' lot was not within the area of the proposed site and therefore not within the actual authority given by Acme to Anson. Unaware that the lot was not a part of the site, Acme wrote both Anson and Stuart approving their individual purchases. Acme's identity as principal became known to Thomas and Davis.

(1) Is the Acme Company liable to Thomas on the note? Explain.

(2) Is the Acme Company liable to Davis on the contract to buy Davis' lot? Explain.

(3) Could Davis hold Stuart personally liable on their contract? Explain.

b. Brian purchased an electric typewriter from Robert under a written contract by which Robert reserved the title until the purchase price was fully paid and reserved the right to repossess the typewriter if Brian failed to make any of the required ten payments. Arthur, an employee of Robert, was instructed to repossess the machine on the ground that Brian had defaulted in making the third payment. Arthur took possession of the typewriter and delivered it to Robert. It was then discovered that Brian was not in default.

(1) May Brian recover damages from Arthur? Explain.

(2) May Brian recover damages from Robert? Explain.

(3) Assuming that Brian recovers damages from Arthur, does Arthur have the right of indemnification from Robert? Explain.

Answer

a. (1) No. An undisclosed principal is not a party to a written contract which is a negotiable instrument on which his name does not appear. This is not changed when the third person later learns of the principal's identity. Therefore the Company is not liable on the note signed by Anson.

(2) No. An undisclosed principal is not liable to a third person on a contract made by his agent without authority. An agent does not have implied authority to delegate his discretionary authority to another. Here, Anson was to purchase lots and at a price within his discretion. Anson's delegation of such authority to Stuart to purchase the Davis lot was in excess of his authority. Also the Davis lot was not within the area of the proposed site and Anson did not have authority to purchase that lot. Therefore, the Company is not liable on the contract to buy Davis' lot.

It should be noted that an undisclosed principal cannot ratify the unauthorized act of his agent not binding on him and thereby become bound on a contract with a third party, and, therefore, the Company could not ratify the conduct of Anson and Stuart in making a contract to buy the Davis lot. Also, a principal's ratification is voidable by him if, at the time of ratification, he was ignorant of material facts. The Company did not know that the Davis lot was outside the proposed site area.

(3) Yes. A contract is enforceable by the parties to it. A contract made by an agent for an undisclosed principal causes the agent to be a party thereto. Therefore Stuart is liable to Davis on their contract which, being for land, is specifically performable.

b. (1) Yes. The fact that the wrongdoer is an agent of a principal is irrelevant to his liability for tort to a third person. Here, Arthur committed the tort of conversion by repossessing the typewriter and, therefore, he is liable to Brian.

(2) Yes. The principal is liable for his agent's torts committed pursuant to authority. Therefore, Robert is liable to Brian for conversion of the typewriter.

(3) Yes. A principal has a duty to idemnify his agent for loss sustained without his fault or misconduct, while acting pursuant to his authority. If the agent's performance is not obviously illegal, and the agent is ignorant of the illegality, he has a right of indemnity against his principal. Since that was the case here, Arthur may assert his right of indemnity against Robert and recover damages.

PART SIX

BUSINESS ORGANIZATIONS

A. PARTNERSHIPS

Chapter I

NATURE OF PARTNERSHIP

---

1. GENERAL CONCEPT

**A Form of
Business
Organization**
PARTNERSHIP is a very old form of business organization and originally was regulated by the customary law of merchants called "Law Merchant." The law of partnership subsequently became a part of the Common Law and, today, it has become crystallized with modern innovations into what is now known as the "Uniform Partnership Act." Throughout this Part, references to the Uniform Partnership Act will carry the abbreviation of U.P.A.

A choice of sole proprietorship, corporation, or partnership as a form of business organization depends upon the business needs and purposes of the particular enterprise in which the organization is to engage. Each has its advantages and disadvantages, and some of the factors which are considered in making this choice are: the expense and complexity of creation, method of operation, credit, liability, risk of loss, and duration.

Definition
Under U.P.A., sec. 6, "A partnership is an association of two or more persons to carry on as co-owners a business for profit." The word "partnership" designates a legal relationship of persons called "partners," or "co-partners" as they are sometimes termed. There is considerable dispute as to whether or not a partnership is a legal entity separate and distinct from its members. For some purposes it is, and for others it is not, a legal entity. A partnership consists of persons in a certain relationship and, under U.P.A., a partnership is an entity, as for the purpose of holding property. However, under U.P.A., a partnership also comprises the members thereof, as is indicated by their respective liabilities.

2. THE GENERAL PARTNERSHIP DISTINGUISHED FROM OTHER FORMS OF BUSINESS ORGANIZATION

Corporation
A partnership may be distinguished from a corporation in its creation, as a legal entity, and in its liabil-

ity, operation, and duration. A partnership is formed by the voluntary agreement between the partners, while a corporation is formed only pursuant to statutory authority. A partnership is a legal entity in some respects and not in others and, in the absence of statute to the contrary, can sue and be sued only in the names of the individual partners. A corporation is a legal entity, separate and distinct from the shareholders, and can sue and be sued only in the corporate name. Each and every partner is liable for the partnership debts, while the shareholders are not liable for the corporate debts. A partnership acts through its partners, while a corporation acts through its elected or appointed officials. Partners control a partnership, while shareholders have an exceedingly small degree of control over the corporation. The death, bankruptcy, or withdrawal of a partner, or the admission of a new partner, dissolves the partnership, while such occurrences with reference to a shareholder or a director have no effect on the continuance of the corporation.

Business Trust   A business trust is a form of association created by owners of interests in property transferring such interests to trustees in exchange for certificates of interests or shares in the property, the trustees to manage the business or enterprise. There is a split of the legal and equitable title to property. Whether or not a business trust is a partnership depends upon the right of control which the certificate holders have over the trustees in the management of the business. If the certificate holders have no control, it cannot be a partnership; if they do have control, it is a partnership. *Usually a business trust is not a partnership.* In a partnership the partners have full control in the management of the business, while in a business trust the certificate holders do not have any control. In a partnership the partners are liable for partnership obligations, while in a business trust the certificate holders have no liability to creditors of the business. The death, bankruptcy, or withdrawal of a partner dissolves a partnership, while such occurrences do not affect the continuance of a business trust. A business trust has many of the characteristics of a corporation and it attempts to acquire the benefits of a partnership and of a corporation. It is sometimes referred to as a "Massachusetts Trust."

Joint Adventure   A joint adventure, often called a "joint venture," is a form of business organization which is not called a partnership but, because of its similarity to a "general" or an "ordinary" partnership, many of the principles of partnership law are applied to it. Joint adventure differs from a general partnership in its purpose and duration. The joint adventure usually is formed for a single undertaking which does not require the full attention of the members thereof. While a general partnership may be formed for a single undertaking, nevertheless, this is unusual. Inasmuch as the members of a joint adventure have control over their activities they are liable for the debts of the joint adventure. Members of a joint adventure usually have very limited powers to affect the contractual relations of each other, and there is no mutual agency as in a general partnership. An example of a joint adventure is where two parties agree to sell their individual properties together for the highest price.

Unusual Types of Partnership The general partnership should be distinguished from certain unusual types of associations which are essentially partnerships but which are not called such, except for the "limited partnership." Only the limited partnership and joint stock company will be considered briefly here.

Limited Partnership. Limited partnership is a form of partnership not very extensively used in the United States. With a few exceptions it has all the characteristics of a general partnership. It exists only by compliance with statutory authority. Limited partners cannot participate in the management and control of the partnership and, consequently, are not individually liable for partnership obligations. The death, bankruptcy, or withdrawal of a limited partner in no way affects the continuance of the limited partnership, unless no limited partner remains in the partnership. The subject of limited partnership will be considered separately later.[1]

Joint-Stock Company. A joint-stock company is a form of partnership in which the members have shares in the company which are transferable without affecting the continued existence of the company. Authority to manage the company's affairs is concentrated in the representatives of the members of the company, but because the members of the company have power to control the conduct of their representatives, they are personally liable for the debts of the company. A joint-stock company has many of the characteristics of a corporation.[2]

---

[1] See below, pp. 638–43.
[2] See below, p. 657, ftn. 1.

Classification
of Partners

In a general partnership the partners may be classified as: ostensible, secret, dormant, nominal, retiring, incoming, surviving, or continuing. In a limited partnership the partners are classified as general or limited.

Ostensible Partner. An ostensible partner, sometimes called a "public" partner, is a partner who holds himself out publicly as such and usually engages actively in the partnership business. If he does not take an active part in the business, he is sometimes called a "silent" partner.

Secret Partner. A secret partner is a partner who actively participates in the business but is not known to the public as a partner.

Dormant Partner. A dormant partner is a partner who is not known to the public as such and who does not actively participate in the partnership business.

Nominal Partner. A nominal partner is not a partner at all but is a person who holds himself out, or permits others to hold him out, as a partner.

Retiring Partner. A retiring partner is a partner who leaves a partnership.

Incoming Partner. An incoming partner is a partner who has come into an existing partnership.

Surviving Partner. A surviving partner is a partner surviving after the death of another partner.

Continuing Partner. A continuing partner is a partner continuing the business after the partnership has been dissolved.

General and Limited Partners. A limited partnership has one or more general partners and one or more limited partners. A general partner is an ordinary partner, as in a general partnership, while a limited partner is a partner with no control in the management of the partnership, who is not personally liable for the partnership obligations. A limited partner is sometimes called a "special" partner.

Chapter II

CREATION OF PARTNERSHIP

1. *PARTIES*

THE parties to a partnership enter into an agreement, usually a contract and in written form. The law of contracts is applicable in determining those who may be parties to a partnership agreement. All persons who have capacity to contract may be partners. Under U.P.A., sec. 2, a person "includes individuals, partnerships, corporations, and other associations." Infants, insane persons except those adjudicated to be insane, married women, and aliens who are not enemy aliens may be partners. Infant or insane partners have the power of avoidance or rescission as they do in contract. Rescission may occur also for fraud and material misrepresentation practiced by one partner on another in inducing him to become a partner. A corporation has capacity to contract and, therefore, can be a partner, but it may not become a partner unless the corporation has been expressly authorized to do so by statute or by charter. In a majority of states a corporation may be a partner.

2. *METHOD, FORM, AND ILLEGALITY*

Method   Partnership is a voluntary business association of persons, formed pursuant to an agreement, usually in the form of a written contract. The agreement of the parties manifests their intention and, if it contains those elements requisite to the formation of a partnership, the legal relationship of partnership has been created. Just as the manifestations of the parties had a particular significance in the law of contracts and of agency in creating those legal relationships, so is it true in the law of partnership. The agreement of the parties may expressly or impliedly create a partnership.

Express Agreement. The agreement of the parties is usually a contract, although not necessarily so, expressly providing for the formation of a partnership. It usually is in writing and is called "articles of partnership." An agreement of the parties contemplating the formation of a partnership and using the terms "partnership" and "partners" does not

607

of itself create a partnership. Partnership is a legal relationship which exists if the elements of a partnership exist; the parties' intention to create a partnership and the use of the words "partnership" and "partners" are not sufficient in themselves to create a partnership. *A partnership is an association of two or more persons to carry on as co-owners a business for profit.* It is a question of law whether or not the agreement creates a partnership. A partnership may occur even if the agreement between the parties expressly excludes their relationship as partners.

Implied Agreement. The manifestation of the parties is the basis for a determination of whether or not a partnership has been formed. When the parties do not manifest any express intent to create a partnership, their manifestation in the form of a written or oral expression or other conduct must be interpreted to determine their intentions and whether or not a partnership exists. If their manifestations comply with the requisites of partnership, then it is implied that their intention was to create a partnership and a partnership is formed. The test of partnership is whether or not the elements in the definition of partnership exist.

Application of Estoppel. A partnership is formed by agreement among the parties and only those parties are partners. A person cannot become a partner in any other way and, therefore, a person cannot become a "partner by estoppel." U.P.A., sec. 7 (1), provides, "Except as provided by section 16 persons who are not partners as to each other are not partners as to third persons." Section 16 deals with estoppel and provides for the *liability* of one who is estopped to deny that he is a partner. If a person holds himself out, or consents to another holding him out, as a partner to a third person, when he is not a partner, and the third person changes his position materially in reasonable reliance on the holding out by extending credit to the purported partnership, he is a nominal partner and cannot deny later that a partnership exists of which he is a member and he is liable for such representation or holding out. Although it is commonly said that the person so holding out is a "partner by estoppel," he actually is not a partner because he is not a party to the agreement. However, as far as third persons are concerned, he is liable to third persons as a partner. A person who holds himself out as a partner may be enjoined from continuing to do so.

For the principle of estoppel to apply there must be a holding out of one's status as a partner *and* a material change of position in reliance on the holding out. The holding out may occur by a writing, words, or other conduct to which he consents, made by the purported partner or by someone else. Although there is conflict, by the better view a person who learns that he has been held out by another as a partner has a duty to dispel the impression of his status as a partner. His silence with knowledge, coupled with a duty to speak, is the equivalent of consent to the holding out. He must take reasonable steps to do this depending upon the circumstances of such holding out; usually publication in the proper newspapers in the proper place is sufficient to dispel the impression of partnership.

The person who has been held out as a partner is estopped to deny his status as a partner only as against persons to whom such holding out was made and who relied thereon. (A permits B to represent to C that A and B are partners, when they are not partners. D, unaware of the holding out, advances credit to the purported partnership of A and B. A is not estopped to deny that he is a partner. If C had extended credit in reliance on B's representation, A would be estopped.) It is significant to note that, under U.P.A., sec. 16(1), if the holding out was made in a public manner, the person so held out as a partner is liable to third persons who subsequently dealt with the purported partnership, regardless of whether or not such third persons had knowledge of the holding out or representation.

Form   No particular form of partnership agreement is necessary, although it is most desirable to have the agreement in writing so as to preclude future uncertainty regarding the terms thereof. Some provisions of the partnership agreement may come within the statute of frauds and, if so, they are unenforceable unless they have complied with requirements of the statute. A partnership agreement not to be performed within one year from the making thereof is within the statute. A partnership agreement to *transfer* an interest in real property to a partner also *is* within the statute, although a partnership agreement *to engage* in the real estate business is *not* within the statute. While there is some conflict regarding the application of the statute to a promise made by an incoming partner to assume partnership obligations, by the better view such a promise is not within the statute inasmuch as it is made to the debtors[1]—namely, the partners in the existing partnership, and not to the creditors of the partnership. However, it should be noted that such a promise creates a third party creditor beneficiary contract which is enforceable by the creditor.[2]

The articles of partnership usually contain the following information: names of the partners; purpose of the partnership; name of the partnership; duration of the partnership; location of the partnership business; the capitalization or contributions of the partners; how the

[1] See above, p. 109.

[2] See above, pp. 97 ff.

profits and losses are to be shared; a system of accounts and provision for the time when the partnership books are to be closed and the individual partners' accounts credited or debited; salary and withdrawals of each partner; the amount of time which each partner is to devote to the business; duties and authority of each partner; restrictions on the authority of each partner; and the method and priority of distribution of assets among the partners on dissolution. Sometimes a partnership has by-laws to implement the articles of partnership.

A partnership may use any name it wishes, provided it complies with whatever statute is in effect regarding such names. Often statutes provide that a person who is not a partner may not have his name in the partnership name; or that "& Co." must not be used to mislead the public into believing that the business is a corporation, but this phrase may be used to indicate that there are partners in the partnership other than the one whose name appears in the partnership name. Statutes usually require that partnerships must record a certificate indicating the name of the partnership, its location, the names of the partners and their addresses, and other information. If the statute is not complied with regarding the recording of such a certificate, the partnership will not be permitted to sue.

Illegality The law of contracts applies in connection with the legality of partnership agreements and, if the agreement is contrary to statute or to public policy as declared by the courts in its purpose or formation, it is illegal and the agreement is void. No partnership results from an illegal agreement, unless the illegal matter can be separated from the legal matter, in which event the partnership exists only for the legal purposes. If the agreement is illegal, the courts usually leave the parties where they find them and give no relief to any party to the agreement. *The partnership just does not exist.* (A and B agree to be a partnership to carry on a business unlawful by statute, e.g., to commit a crime. There is no partnership for this purpose.)

3. THE PURPOSE OF THE ASSOCIATION

A partnership occurs when there is a voluntary association for the purpose of carrying on as co-owners a business for profit. There is no partnership until the parties by their agreement expressly or impliedly intend to become partners. An agreement to become partners at a future time does not create a partnership at the time the agreement is formed.

Partnership occurs at the moment when the parties by their agreement intend their status to be that of partners.

Carrying on a Business for Profit

It is essential to a partnership that the parties be carrying on a business for profit. By "business" is meant the carrying on of a series of commercial transactions as an enterprise. U.P.A., sec. 2, describes business as including "every trade, occupation, or profession." A business in the mercantile sense is carried on for the purpose of making a profit and is to be distinguished from fraternal or other nonprofit associations which are not partnerships. Although members of nonprofit associations are not partners, nevertheless, they may expose themselves to liability under the law of agency if they authorize others to affect their contractual relations with third persons. A business is "carried on" when it is being conducted in a continuing manner.

Co-owners of a Business for Profit

Partners are *co-owners* of a *business* for profit. Co-ownership of property does not, of itself, create a partnership, but it is a factor for consideration in connection with other circumstances in determining whether or not a partnership exists. U.P.A., sec. 7(2), lists various forms of co-ownership of *property* which, in themselves, are insufficient to establish a partnership. Joint tenancy, tenancy in common, tenancy by the entirety, joint property, common property, and part ownership in property do not make a *business for profit* and, even though the co-owners share in the profits made from the use of their property, there is no partnership. Co-ownership of property is not necessary for a partnership; partners may own property individually which they have contributed to the partnership only for use in the partnership business. If to the fact of co-ownership of property is added the right to share in gross returns, this also is insufficient evidence to establish co-ownership of the business, although it is some evidence of such.

Co-ownership of a business means that the parties have a *mutual interest* in carrying on the business for profit. Co-ownership of property, control over the management of the business, and the sharing of losses constitute evidence to prove co-ownership of the business. However, the sharing of profits is sufficiently *strong* evidence to prove co-ownership of a business; and a person receiving such profits is prima facie a co-owner of, and a partner in, the business carried on for a profit. The presumption of co-ownership of the business is rebuttable by proof that, although profits are shared, the person receiving such profits has no *mutual interest* in the carrying on of the business and, therefore, is not a partner. The receipt of profits as payment of a debt, for wages or rent, as an annuity to a widow or representative of a deceased partner, as interest on a loan, or as consideration for the sale of partnership property rebuts the presumption of co-ownership of the business and the recipient is not a partner. If, in these instances when the *receipt of profits alone* does not create co-ownership, there is added the element of control in the management of the business, the two factors of *sharing in the profits and the right of control* constitute sufficiently strong evidence to prove co-ownership of the business and to make such person a partner. Each of the above instances will be considered briefly.

Payment of a Debt. A creditor has no mutual interest in the carrying on of the business; his interest is solely in the profits for the purpose of paying his debt. Often creditors agree to run a failing business in order to produce enough partnership profit to pay their claims. Such creditors are not partners inasmuch as they have no mutual interest in the carrying on of the business; their interest is in the payment of their claims, they do not own the property interest in the business, and they merely operate the business on behalf of the debtor. Profits earned by the partnership business carried on by the creditors belong to the partnership, although such profits are to be made available to the creditors.

Wages or Rents. The payment of wages to an employee, or of rents to a landlord, out of profits does not create that co-ownership of the business necessary to a partnership and, therefore, wage earners are not partners with their employers and landlords are not partners with their tenants. The fact that their wages or rents may vary as the profits vary is irrelevant. A wage earner may, in addition to his share in the profits as compensation, have the right to exercise a control over the management of the business, which makes him a co-owner of the business and, therefore, a partner. A landlord who shares in the gross receipts from the use of land or chattels is not a co-owner of the business to which such property is put. The rental of land for a percentage of the crops does not make the landlord a partner.

Annuity to Widow or Representative. On the death of a partner it is often agreed between the remaining partners and the widow or representative of the estate of the decedent that the business will be continued by the surviving partners and a share in the profits will be paid to the widow or representative in lieu of liquidation and payment of the decedent's interest in the partnership. Such payments are in the form of an annuity, but the recipient is not a co-owner of the business and is not a partner therein. Should the recipient of such payment have the right to participate in the control of the management, then the combination of the receipt of profits and the right of control in the management of the business creates co-ownership of the business and, therefore, the recipient is a partner.

Interest on a Loan. A person advancing a loan to a business, the interest on which is to be paid out of the profits, is an investor and is not a co-owner of the business. He has no mutual interest in the carrying on of the business for profit; he is concerned solely with the acquisition of interest on the loan from the profits. Often investors wish to supervise the management of the business with little, if any, control therein. Supervision, and no affirmative control, over the business does not make the investor a co-owner of the business. However, an investor's degree of control over the business may be such that, in conjunction with his receipt of a share of the profits, it is sufficient to make him a co-owner of the business and, therefore, a partner.

Consideration for Sale of Partnership Property. The terms of sale of tangible or intangible property of a business may provide that the sales price is to be paid by a share in the profits. This interest in the profits is insufficient to make the seller a co-owner of the business. There is no *mutual interest* in the carrying on of the business for profit.

Chapter III

PARTNERSHIP PROPERTY

---

1. *NATURE AND ACQUISITION OF PARTNERSHIP PROPERTY*

Nature   PARTNERSHIP property consists of all that real or personal property acquired by the partnership at the time of its formation or subsequently, regardless of the method of acquisition. Such property may be an original or subsequent contribution by the partners, or it may be property created by the use of partnership property or of property belonging to the partners. The property may be intangible, such as the firm's interest in an insurance policy taken out by the firm on the life of a partner, the premiums having been paid by the firm. A partnership may have the right to use certain property which is still owned individually by the partners.

Acquisition   Partnership property usually is acquired by contributions of such property by the partners or by the use of partnership funds in the purchase of such property. Under U.P.A., sec. 8(2), "Unless the contrary intention appears, property acquired with partnership funds is partnership property." The intention of the parties determines the ownership of the property. (A and B are partners who agree to buy a horse from partnership funds, such horse to be a part of B's share in the profits, or as an advance to B. The horse is the property of B. If the horse had been purchased without such agreement, it would be partnership property.) When property is purchased by individual partners out of their own funds the property is owned by the individual partners, unless the bill of sale, deed of the property, or agreement between the parties indicates to the contrary. Similarly, if partners owning property as tenants in common use such property in the partnership business, such property still belongs to the individual partners as tenants in common, the partnership having merely the right of use.

614

2. *TITLE TO PARTNERSHIP PROPERTY*

Title to partnership property may be in the name of one or more partners, individually, who hold the same for the partnership and, under U.P.A., such property may be held in the partnership name, regardless of whether it is real or personal property. The extent of a partnership's interest in real property is entire, as though the partnership were a legal person; even words of inheritance are unnecessary. In the absence of U.P.A., although personal property may be held in the name of the partners individually or in the name of the partnership, nevertheless, there is conflict on whether the partnership can hold real property in the partnership name. At Common Law the grantee of real property had to be a natural or legal person. Courts of equity, and subsequently many courts of law, first held that if the name of a partner was included in the partnership name title vested in that partner for the benefit of the partnership; subsequently such courts held that title vested in the partnership even though the partnership name did not contain the name of any partner. U.P.A., sec. 8(3), resolved this difficulty.

Transfer of Partnership Property Personal property of the partnership may be transferred by any partner with actual or apparent authority to do so. The manner of conveying real property of the partnership depends upon the terms of the conveyance to the partnership. Title in the name of the partnership can be conveyed only in the partnership name. Any partner can convey the title to *real property in the partnership name* by executing a *conveyance in the partnership name.* However, the partnership can recover the property, unless either the conveying partner had actual or apparent authority so to convey, or the property subsequently was conveyed to a bona fide purchaser for value without notice of the partner's lack of authority, in which case the partnership cannot recover the property. A partner's execution of a *conveyance of real property in his own name* when the *real property is in the name of the partnership,* passes equitable title to the grantee if it is within the actual or apparent authority of the partner. Since the grantee can, in a court with equity powers, compel the partnership to convey the legal title, the grantee has what is called "equitable title." If the real property of the partnership is *in the name of one or more but not all of the partners individually,* and the record does not disclose the interest of the partnership, only such partners have legal title to the property and they can convey title to the property by a conveyance in their own names. However, the partnership can recover the property, unless either the conveying partners had actual or apparent authority so to convey, or the grantee or his assignee is a bona fide purchaser for value without knowledge of the partner's lack of authority, in which case the partnership cannot recover the property. If the real property of the partnership is in the names of all of the partners individually, only the partners have legal title to the property and a conveyance executed by all of them passes all their rights in the property.

Individual Partner's Interest Therein
A partner has a property right in the specific property of the partnership and is a co-owner of such property with the other partners. He is called a "tenant in partnership." A tenancy in partnership is very different from a tenancy in common, joint tenancy, and other interests in real property held by more than one person. The partner's right in specific partnership property cannot be transferred by him unless all the other partners join in such transfer of the same property; it is not subject to legal process—e.g., attachment or execution—by his *personal* creditors; and it is not subject to dower or curtesy, which are common law interests in real property. *Each partner has a right to possess specific partnership property for partnership purposes, unless the partners agree to the contrary.*

A decedent partner's interest in partnership *personal property* passes to the surviving partners or partner or, if there are none, to the legal representative of his estate, who possesses the property solely for partnership purposes. Although a decedent's interest in *real property* descends to his heirs, this is not so in the case of a decedent partner's interest in specific partnership real property held in the partnership name. Such interest in real property is considered in equity as personal property for the purpose of liquidating the partnership assets and of winding up the partnership affairs and passes to the surviving partners for such purpose. The principle of equity converting partnership realty into personalty for partnership purposes is called the "doctrine of equitable conversion." All partnership property remaining after partnership obligations have been satisfied is personal property for the purpose of distribution. If partnership real property is held in the name of a decedent partner then, inasmuch as he had legal title in trust for the partnership, the legal title vests in his heirs or devisees, who hold the same in trust for the partnership.

Chapter IV

RIGHTS AND DUTIES OF PARTNERS AMONG THEMSELVES

---

1. *RIGHTS*

ARTICLES of partnership usually specify the rights and duties of the various partners in connection with the carrying on of the partnership business. When the parties fail to make such express provision, it is implied that their intention is to comply with ordinary mercantile rules in effect. The rules to be discussed apply unless the parties have provided to the contrary in their agreement. First the rights, then the duties, and then the enforcement of such rights and duties of the partners, will be discussed.

In Partnership Operation

Management of Partnership. *Unless the partners agree to the contrary,* all partners have equal rights in the management and operation of the partnership business, regardless of the nature and extent of the partners' contributions.

Majority Vote. U.P.A., sec. 18(h), provides, "Any difference arising as to ordinary matters connected with the partnership business may be decided by a majority of the partners; but no act in contravention of any agreement between the partners may be done rightfully without the consent of all the partners." Majority rule applies to the ordinary, internal affairs of the partnership. "It is clear, however, that no majority however large can, against the dissent of the minority, change the essential nature or extent of the partnership business as originally agreed upon, as, for example, to alter or amend the articles, reduce or increase the capital, embark upon a new business, change its agreed location, alter the share of a partner, admit a new member, and the like. If they attempt to do so, the dissenting partners will not be bound."[1]

---

[1] Floyd R. Mechem, *Elements of the Law of Partnership* (2d ed.; Chicago: Callaghan & Co., 1920), sec. 281.

Reimbursement and Indemnity. A partner has the right to be reimbursed and indemnified for any expenditures or losses which he reasonably incurred while acting within his authority in carrying on the business in a proper way. A partner has a right of contribution from other partners to the extent that he has paid more than his share of the partnership obligations. A partner has no right of reimbursement or indemnity for expenditure or loss caused by the partner's negligence or bad faith.

Compensation. Unless the partners agree to the contrary, a partner is not entitled to any additional compensation for his services rendered to the partnership. His right to share in the profits is deemed to be adequate compensation. If the illness of one partner causes the other partners to carry a heavier load in operating the partnership business, such partners are not entitled to any extra compensation. Many partnership agreements, however, provide for special duties to be performed by a partner and specify that he is to receive compensation therefor. A partner may be the manager of the partnership business and obtain, in addition to his share in the profits, a specified salary for his services as manager. Although at one time a surviving partner was not entitled to any compensation for his services in winding up the partnership affairs, nevertheless, today, in the absence of any agreement to the contrary, a surviving partner is entitled to compensation for such services.

Advances. Advances by partners which are not additions to their capital contributions are loans to the partnership. Advances cannot be made contrary to the partnership agreement. In the absence of agreement to the contrary, the partner making such advance is entitled to interest thereon from the date such advance was made and is entitled to be repaid such advance when due. If the partnership assets are insufficient to make such repayment, then all the partners have a duty to contribute to the extent of their respective shares of such deficiency.

Capital. Property contributed by partners for use and risk in the carrying on of the partnership business is capital. On dissolution, or as otherwise agreed by the partners, after partnership liabilities have been satisfied, each partner's capital contribution is to be returned to the partner. In the absence of agreement to the contrary, a partner is not entitled to interest on such capital except from the date when repayment should have been made

Profit and Loss. In the absence of agreement to the contrary, partners have the right to share in partnership profits and surplus *equally,* and have the duty to share in partnership losses, whether capital or otherwise, in the same ratio as they share the profits. (A contributed $10,000, B contributed $7,000, and C contributed $4,000 to the partnership business, making a total capital investment of $21,000. On dissolution the firm suffered a loss of $15,000. A, B, and C each are to contribute $5,000 toward this loss. Therefore, A receives $5,000 and B receives $2,000 as the remainder of their capital contributions, and C contributes $1,000 to make up his deficiency.) Although the capital contributions vary, nevertheless, in the absence of agreement to the contrary, losses are shared as profits are shared. Whether the profits are to be retained in the business as additions to the capital contribution of each partner, or are to be made available for distribution, depends upon the terms of the partnership agreement.

New Partners. A partnership is a voluntary association and, in the absence of agreement to the contrary, a person cannot become a member of a partnership without the consent of all the partners.

Partnership Books. Unless the partners agree to the contrary, partnership books are to be kept at the principal place of the partnership business, and the partners have a right to inspect and make copies of such books at all times.

Continuation of Partnership. A partnership may continue in business even though the agreed time of its duration has expired and, if there is no express agreement regarding such continuance, it is a partnership at will. A continuation of a partnership business by the partners without liquidation or settlement is prima facie evidence that the partnership is being continued. The rights and duties of the partners remain the same as they were at the time when the partnership was to have expired by its terms.

Accounting. A formal account of partnership affairs is inconvenient and costly and, inasmuch as the partnership accounts are available for examination by the partners, a partner is not entitled to a formal account prior to dissolution, with certain exceptions. As exceptions, a partner has a right to an accounting without dissolution: when he has been wrongfully excluded from participation in the partnership business; when the partnership agreement so provides; when a partner has acquired secret profits from his participation in the partnership business and has not accounted to the partnership for them; and whenever other circumstances are such that it would be just and reasonable to require an accounting.[2]

Property Rights   Under U.P.A., sec. 24, a partner has three property rights: "(1) his rights in specific partnership property, (2) his interest in the partnership, and (3) his right to participate in the management." A partner's

---

[2] 7 *Uniform Laws Annotated*, Uniform Partnership Act, 1914, sec. 22.

rights in specific partnership property and his right to participate in the management of the partnership business have been discussed already.[3] A partner's interest in the partnership consists of his interest in profits and surplus, and this property right is personal property. Of these three property rights, a partner individually may assign only one—namely his interest in the partnership. Such assignment does not dissolve the partnership, but if the partner also ceases to be engaged in the carrying on of the partnership business then the partnership is dissolved. The assignee acquires only the assigning partner's rights to surplus and profits to the extent as provided in the assignment. On dissolution the assignee has the right to the assigning partner's interest in the partnership and the right to an accounting from the date of the last accounting agreed to by all the partners.

Charging Order. An unpaid judgment creditor of an individual partner may obtain a court order charging the debtor partner's interest in the partnership and directing that the payment of surplus and other moneys due the debtor partner by the partnership be paid to a receiver, appointed by the court for this purpose. Payments made to the receiver are, in turn, paid to the judgment creditor until the judgment has been satisfied. The interest charged may be redeemed by the debtor partner at any time prior to foreclosure, and foreclosure and sale of the debtor partner's interest in the partnership does not cause the partnership to be dissolved.

2. DUTIES

To Perform Partnership Agreement A partner has the duty to comply with the partnership agreement, which usually provides specific duties for various partners. A partner's failure to observe and perform his partnership duties subjects him to liability for loss caused to the partnership by such failure. The cost of employing others, whether partners or not, to perform the delinquent partner's duties is borne by such delinquent partner. Conduct by a partner in violation of his partnership duties causing loss to the partnership subjects him to liability for such loss.

Good Faith A partner is a fiduciary and owes his complete loyalty to the partnership. He has a duty to act for the best interests of the partnership and not for himself alone. A partner cannot retain for himself, and he must account to the partnership for, any benefit or profit which he has acquired in any transaction performed in connection with the partnership. All profits and benefits so acquired belong to the partnership, and the partner holds them in trust

---

[3] See above, pp. 616, 617 ff.

for the partnership. Each partner has a duty to make full disclosure to the other partners of all transactions in connection with the partnership business. Dealings between a partner and the partnership without the knowledge and consent of the partnership are voidable at the election of the partnership.

Unless the partners agree to the contrary, each partner has the duty of devoting his entire attention, time, skill, and efforts to the partnership business. However, a partner may engage in a noncompeting business elsewhere so long as the small amount of time required by the other business and the nature of the other business are not to the prejudice of the partnership business. Articles of partnership usually provide for the amount of time which partners are to devote to the partnership business and also provide that partners are not to engage in any other business competing with the partnership. A partner's devotion of excessive time elsewhere and his participation in a business competing with the partnership not only are grounds for dissolution, but the partner must account to his partnership for the benefits he received thereby and turn them over to the partnership. These same duties apply to a representative of a deceased partner winding up the partnership affairs.

Care and Skill   Each partner has the duty to exercise reasonable care and skill in transacting the partnership business, and he is liable personally to the partnership for loss proximately caused by his failure to do so. He is not liable for loss caused by his honest mistakes and errors of judgment. A partner who is also at fault in the same matter cannot complain to his co-partner at fault.

Keep Accounts   Each partner has the duty to keep a record of the partnership transactions in which he has engaged. Usually the duty of keeping accounts for the entire partnership is entrusted to one of the partners. Each partner has the right to examine any partnership transaction engaged in by any other partner.

Disclosure of Partnership Information   Each partner has a duty to disclose partnership information when demanded by other partners. He also has the duty to make voluntary disclosure of important partnership matters and to consult with his other partners.

3. REMEDIES

The proper legal forum for the settlement of disputes regarding partnership affairs is the equity court or a court with equity powers. The disputes may be between a partnership and a partner, or may be among partners. Such disputes are resolved in connection with an accounting or dissolution of the partnership. At law, in the absence of a statute to the contrary, a partnership cannot sue, nor be sued by, a partner because, inasmuch as a partnership sues and is sued in the names of the partners, in effect the partnership would be suing, or would be sued by, itself. It is for this reason that, at law, a partnership cannot sue a partner and cannot be sued by a partner, nor can a partnership sue another partnership when both partnerships have a partner in common.

Partners cannot sue each other at law regarding partnership rights and duties in connection with partnership affairs, with certain exceptions; the proper forum is a court of equity or a court with equity powers in a proceeding for an accounting or on dissolution. There are exceptions to this rule which permit such actions when the subject matter is not related to partnership affairs or when nothing remains to be done but to pay an amount owing on liquidation of partnership affairs.

> The general rule is that one partner cannot sue another partner at law until there has been a complete settlement of the partnership affairs and a balance struck. . . .
> There are, however, well-established exceptions to the general rule. A partner may maintain an action at law against his co-partner upon claims growing out of the following state of facts:
> (1) Claims not connected with the partnership.
> (2) Claims for an agreed final balance.
> (3) Claims upon express personal contracts between the partners.
> (4) Failure to comply with an agreement constituting a condition precedent to the formation of the partnership.
> (5) Where the partnership is terminated, all debts paid, and the partnership affairs otherwise adjusted, with nothing remaining to be done but to pay over the amount due by one to the other, such amount involving no complicated reckoning.
> (6) Where the partnership is for a single venture or special purpose which has been accomplished, and nothing remains to be done except to pay over the claimants share.
> (7) When the joint property has been wrongfully destroyed or converted.
> (8) When one partner has been guilty of fraud in contracting the debt or in incurring the obligation or by concealing the property or by other device defeating the rights of the complaining party. . . .[4]

---

[4] *Pugh* v. *Newbern,* 193 N.C. 258, 260 f., 136 S.E. 707, 708 f. (1927).

Chapter V

AUTHORITY AND APPARENT AUTHORITY OF PARTNERS

1. ACTUAL AUTHORITY

EACH partner is an agent of the partnership *for the purpose of carrying on the partnership business in the usual way of that particular partnership and of partnerships similar to the particular partnership.* Every partner has such actual authority, express and implied, unless the partnership agreement provides to the contrary, and he also has such apparent authority by reason of his status as a partner. Each partner is both a principal of, and an agent for, the other partners.[1] The principles of the law of agency are applicable.

Express Authority   A partner's express authority to act for the partnership is found in the partnership agreement, which is the manifestation of the partners concerning their relationship.

Implied Authority   Unless the partnership agreement provides to the contrary, the nature and extent of a partner's implied authority depends upon the character of the partnership business. For the purpose of determining the character of a business, partnerships are classified as "trading partnerships" and "nontrading partnerships." A trading partnership is one which is engaged in the business of buying and selling property; it does not include a partnership engaged in selling services. A partnership engaged in the manufacture or retailing of goods is an example of a trading partnership. A partnership of public accountants, lawyers, or doctors is an illustration of a professional nontrading partnership.

The implied and apparent authority of a partner to buy and sell, to borrow money, and to execute and indorse negotiable instruments on

---

[1] Floyd R. Mechem, *Elements of the Law of Partnership* (2d ed.; Chicago: Callaghan & Co., 1920), sec. 234.

behalf of the partnership is different in trading and nontrading partnerships. The implied and apparent authority of a partner to employ personnel, to pay partnership debts, to mortgage partnership property, to settle and compromise claims for and against the partnership, to receive payment of obligations owing to the partnership, to receive partnership information and to make representations on behalf of the partnership generally is the same in trading and nontrading partnerships. Such implied and apparent authority of partners in trading and nontrading partnerships will be discussed briefly.

To Buy and Sell. Partners in a trading partnership have implied authority to buy and sell property in which the partnership business is engaged, and to make contracts therefor, when it is reasonably necessary to do so in order to carry on the partnership business. A partner does not have implied authority to sell property other than the property in which the partnership is engaged. Partners in a nontrading partnership may have implied authority by necessity, or by custom and usage in that or similar partnerships, to purchase property reasonably necessary for use in the partnership business. The authority of an accountant to purchase working papers for his public accounting firm, and the authority of a lawyer to purchase law books for his firm, is implied by necessity.

To Borrow Money. A partner in a trading partnership has implied authority to borrow money in the name of the partnership, if it is reasonably necessary in order to carry on the partnership business. The amount borrowed must be reasonable for the purpose. A partner in a nontrading partnership does not have this implied authority, except when implied by necessity or by custom and usage.

Regarding Negotiable Instruments. A partner in a trading partnership has implied and apparent authority to execute and indorse negotiable instruments in the partnership name, if such is reasonably necessary in order to carry on the partnership business. Should a partner so act when it was not reasonably necessary in order to carry on the partnership business, the partnership is not bound by such action unless the instrument has been negotiated to a "holder in due course,"[2] who is in effect a bona fide purchaser for value without notice of the wrongfulness of the partner's conduct. The partnership is bound to the holder in due course and to holders who properly claim through him.[3] A partner in a nontrading partnership does not have this implied and apparent authority, except when implied by necessity or by custom and usage. The

---

[2] See UCC 3–302, and above, p. 410.
[3] See above, pp. 419, 425.

execution or indorsement of a negotiable instrument in the partnership name by a partner with no implied or apparent authority is not binding on the partnership, even as to a holder in due course.

Regarding Personnel. A partner has implied authority to employ personnel whose services are reasonably necessary in order to carry on the partnership business. He has implied authority to make reasonable contracts for a reasonable salary.

To Pay Partnership Debts. A partner has implied authority to pay the firm's debts and to satisfy the firm's obligations out of partnership funds. However, a partner has no implied authority to use partnership funds or property to pay or secure his personal debts.

To Mortgage. A partner has implied authority to mortgage the partnership property, whether or not the property is for sale in the partnership business, in order to provide security for partnership obligations or to borrow, when expressly or impliedly authorized, on behalf of the partnership.

To Settle, Compromise, and Receive Payment. A partner has implied authority to settle and compromise claims for and against the partnership. A partner also has implied authority to receive payments due the partnership and to execute proper papers, such as receipts, in connection therewith.

To Receive Partnership Information. A partner has implied authority to receive partnership notices, and such notice and his knowledge is notice to, and knowledge of, the partnership. U.P.A., sec. 12, provides, "Notice to any partner of any matter relating to partnership affairs, and the knowledge of the partner acting in the particular matter, acquired while a partner or then present to his mind, and the knowledge of any other partner who reasonably could and should have communicated it to the acting partner, operate as notice to or knowledge of the partnership, except in the case of a fraud on the partnership committed by or with the consent of that partner."

To Make Representations. A partner has implied authority to make admissions and representations in connection with partnership affairs if it is for the purpose of carrying on the partnership business in the usual way. Such admissions or representations are, in effect, those of the partnership.

Authority Not Implied. A partner does not have implied authority to perform certain acts in the partnership name because they are not for the carrying on of the partnership business in the usual way. U.P.A., sec. 9(3), enumerates instances when there is no such implied authority:

(3) Unless authorized by the other partners or unless they have abandoned the business, one or more but less than all the partners have no authority to:

    (a) Assign the partnership property in trust for creditors or on the assignee's promise to pay the debts of the partnership,

    (b) Dispose of the good-will of the business,

    (c) Do any other act which would make it impossible to carry on the ordinary business of a partnership,

    (d) Confess a judgment,

    (e) Submit a partnership claim or liability to arbitration or reference.

The first three instances illustrate lack of implied authority to prevent the partnership business from continuing to function. The last two instances illustrate a lack of implied authority to delegate the performance of an act which requires the partner's special skill, judgment, or discretion. In addition to these instances, a partner does not have implied authority to make the partnership a surety or guarantor of another's obligation, although the partnership business may be such that this authority is implied. An illustration is a partnership engaged in the business of buying and selling securities, where signatures to such securities would have to be guaranteed. A partner does not have implied authority to use partnership funds for the purchase of corporate capital stock, although, again, the partnership business may be such that this authority is implied. A partner does not have implied authority to do business gratuitously on behalf of the partnership, although he can do so on his own behalf; a partnership business is carried on for profit.

2. *APPARENT AUTHORITY*

Regardless of whether or not a partner has actual authority, a partner has *apparent authority to carry on the partnership business in the usual way.* Transactions between a partner without actual authority but with apparent authority for the apparent purpose of carrying on the partnership business, and a third person who reasonably believes that the partner has such authority and enters the transaction in reliance thereon, are binding on the partnership. Under U.P.A., sec. 9(1):

Every partner is an agent of the partnership for the purpose of its business, and the act of every partner, including the execution in the partnership name of any instrument, for apparently carrying on in the usual way the business of the partnership of which he is a member binds the partnership, unless the partner so acting has in fact no authority to act for the partnership in the particular matter, and the person with whom he is dealing has knowledge of the fact that he has no such authority.

A partner does not have apparent authority if the third person knows, or reasonably should know, that the partner has no authority to make the particular transaction in the name of the partnership. Without any actual or apparent authority a partner cannot bind the partnership in transactions with third persons. A partner has no apparent authority to buy horses for a jewelry business; to buy a refrigerator for a clothing business; to borrow an obviously unreasonable amount; or to employ personnel at an obviously unreasonable salary. A partner has no apparent authority to act on behalf of a partnership if the third person is aware of the partner's adverse interest to the partnership. A partner with actual authority to act in the partnership name, but with no apparent authority, binds the partnership if he acts in accordance with his actual authority.

Chapter VI

PARTNERSHIP LIABILITY

---

1. *NATURE OF LIABILITY*

Liability of Partnership PARTNERSHIP liability begins at the moment the partnership is formed. The partnership is liable for all contracts made on its behalf by partners with actual or apparent authority. The partnership is also liable for damage caused to third persons by the torts of partners while carrying on the partnership business in the usual way and, under the law of agency, for the torts of its employees while acting within the scope of their employment. Negligence and fraud are frequent sources of partnership liability. Willful torts usually are outside the scope or ordinary course of the partnership business, but not necessarily so. The person's intent, whether to act for himself or for the partnership, is an important factor. Acts by partners overzealous in their devotion to partnership affairs do not cause such acts to be out of the ordinary course of partnership business. U.P.A., sec. 14, provides, "The partnership is bound to make good the loss: (a) Where one partner acting within the scope of his apparent authority receives money or property of a third person and misapplies it; and (b) Where the partnership in the course of its business receives money or property of a third person and the money or property so received is misapplied by any partner while it is in the custody of the partnership." The partnership is not liable to partners who have experienced injury or loss by the tort of another partner acting within the ordinary course of the partnership business.

Liability of Partners The partnership consists of the partners within it, and the liability of the partnership is a liability of the partners. Partners are liable jointly and severally for partnership torts and only jointly for partnership contracts. Although in some states liability is made joint and several and, in some instances, specifically includes partnerships, some courts refuse to interpret general statutes to this effect as applying to partnerships. An agreement between the partners providing for their respective shares of partnership liability is binding on the partners but the agreement is not binding on third persons, even though they have knowledge of such provisions. (Partners A and B agree that A alone will be liable for all partnership contracts. This agreement is not binding on C, a partnership creditor, who can hold A and B liable personally on his contract with the partnership.)

An infant partner has the power to avoid his partnership contract, just as he can any other contract, and thereby avoid personal liability to his co-partners and to partnership creditors, in the absence of statute to the contrary. However, in weighing between the equities of an infant and those of a third person who has dealt with the partnership relying on the availability of its joint property and who has become a creditor of a partnership, the courts recognize the superiority of such creditor's equities and cause the infant's capital contribution to be available to such creditor. In most states the infant partner's capital contribution is made available also to the claims of those of his co-partners who have not fraudulently induced the infant to become a partner.

Under U.P.A., secs. 17 and 36, specific provision is made for the liability of an incoming partner, liability of the estate of a deceased partner, the effect of dissolution on a partner's liability, and for the discharge of a partner's liability. *An incoming partner is liable for partnership obligations incurred prior to his admission, but such liability shall be satisfied only out of partnership property.* Partnership creditors may not resort to his personal estate to satisfy such liability. The estate of a decedent partner is liable for partnership obligations after his individual creditors have been provided for. Dissolution of the partnership does not discharge the partners from their liability for partnership obligations. On dissolution, a novation may occur between the partnership creditor, the partners continuing the partnership business, and the particular partner who is to be discharged. Release by a partnership creditor of a partner from a partnership obligation for which he is jointly liable discharges all the partners jointly liable. However, a partnership creditor may contract not to sue a partner on a partnership obligation, reserving his rights against the other partners; this does not affect the joint liability of the other partners for the partnership obligation.

2. ENFORCEMENT OF PARTNERSHIP LIABILITY

Nature of Action   Partners who are liable severally, or jointly and severally, may be sued individually. However, when the partnership obligation is joint, in the absence of a statute to the contrary, a partnership can be sued and can sue only in the names of its partners. In many states a partnership can be sued and can sue in its firm name. An action against a partnership must join all the partners, and all available solvent partners must be served personally with process. Partners being sued may object to the nonjoinder of all the available solvent partners. Should no objection be made to the nonjoinder of all such partners, a judgment obtained against the partnership is effective only against the partnership property and against the property of those partners who were served personally with process or who appeared in the action. The claim against the partnership is merged in the judgment. Accordingly, no action may be brought subsequently against the other partners not joined in the previous action. "When the contract is joint, and not joint and several, the entire cause of action is merged in the judgment. The joint liability of the parties not sued with those against whom the judgment is recovered, being extinguished, their entire liability is gone. They cannot be sued separately, for they have incurred no several obligation; they cannot be sued jointly with the others, because judgment has already been recovered against the latter, who would otherwise be subjected to two suits for the same cause."[1] In some states this rule is changed by statute, sometimes called "joint debtor statutes," which provide that when service is made on some of the parties jointly liable and judgment is obtained against them, the cause of action against the parties not served and who have not appeared is not merged in the judgment, and they may be sued subsequently on the original cause of action. (In state X, C is an unpaid creditor of the partnership of A and B. C sued the partnership, served process only on A, and obtained a judgment. Since the partnership property and A's assets are insufficient to satisfy C's judgment, C now wishes to sue B. He cannot do so, unless X is a joint debtor state, in which event he can.)

Satisfaction of Judgment   A judgment creditor of a partnership may satisfy his judgment only out of the property of the partnership and of the judgment debtors who were served personally with process in the action or who appeared therein. The judgment creditor of a partnership may obtain a writ of execution against the partnership property and the property of the partners who were so served. In some states he cannot proceed against the property of the individual partners until he has exhausted the partnership property in satisfaction of the judgment. In contrast with a judgment creditor of a partnership, a judgment creditor of an

---

[1] *Mason* v. *Eldred*, 6 Wall. 231, 238 (U.S. 1867).

individual partner for his individual obligations first must resort to the property of the individual partner, and then he may charge[2] the individual partner's interest in the partnership.

Marshaling of Assets. At law, in the absence of a statute to the contrary, a judgment creditor of a partnership has the right to satisfy his judgment out of an individual partner's estate without first resorting to partnership property, thereby depriving such individual partner's creditors of that property in satisfaction of their claims. The rule is different in courts of equity, or courts with equity powers in cases of an equitable nature, and in bankruptcy courts where the doctrine of "marshaling of assets" is applied. Under this doctrine, each individual partner's estate is made available first to his individual creditors, and any surplus remaining is made available to partnership creditors; while partnership property is made available first to partnership creditors, and any surplus remaining is distributed among the partners and, as a part of an individual partner's estate, is made available to the creditors of each of the individual partners. U.P.A., sec. 40(h), provides, "When partnership property and the individual properties of the partners are in possession of a court for distribution, partnership creditors shall have priority on partnership property and separate creditors on individual property, saving the rights of lien or secured creditors as heretofore." Secured creditors, of course, have priority over all other creditors to the security on their obligations.

---

[2] See Charging Order, above, p. 620.

Chapter VII

DISSOLUTION AND WINDING UP

---

1. *CAUSES OF DISSOLUTION*

A PARTNERSHIP is formed for the purpose of carrying on as co-owners a business for profit. When a partner ceases to be associated in the carrying on of a partnership business, the partnership is dissolved. Dissolution does not terminate the partnership, however, and it continues in existence until its affairs have been settled. The settling of such affairs is called the "winding up" of the partnership. The winding up begins with dissolution and ends with termination of the partnership. The three terms of "dissolution," "winding up," and "termination" should not be confused.

Dissolution may occur by the act of the partners, by operation of law, and by the decree of a court ordering dissolution; they will be discussed in this order.

By Act of Partners Dissolution usually occurs by the acts of the partners. When dissolution occurs without violation of the partnership agreement, there is no breach of contract and, therefore, no liability for such dissolution. If the partnership is terminable at will, any partner may dissolve the partnership at any time. If the partnership was formed for a particular period or for the accomplishment of a particular objective and such time has expired or the objective has been accomplished, the partnership dissolves by the terms of the partnership agreement. All the partners created the partnership and it is their privilege to dissolve the partnership; however, those partners who have assigned their interests in the partnership or whose interests have become subject to a charging order have no voice in the decision of the remaining partners to dissolve. A partnership agreement may specify causes for the expulsion of a partner and, in accordance with such provisions, a partner may be expelled for cause and the partnership dissolved thereby. A partnership agreement is not irrevocable and may be dissolved by the wrongful act of a partner at

632

any time. Such partner is liable for damages for breach of contract and may be sued at law or his account charged therefor. The admission of an incoming partner dissolves the partnership and creates a new partnership.

By Operation of Law A partnership is dissolved immediately and automatically by the death of a partner, the bankruptcy of a partner or of the partnership, and by a change of law causing the partnership to be illegal. A partner's death interrupts the relationship of the association in carrying on the partnership business. The bankruptcy of a partner deprives him of association in the carrying on of the partnership business, and the partnership is dissolved. If the partnership itself becomes bankrupt, the partnership property is transferred to the trustee in bankruptcy, and the partnership business cannot be carried on any longer by the partners. A partnership may become an involuntary bankrupt, but a partnership *cannot* become a voluntary bankrupt unless: either the partnership is insolvent—i.e., the firm assets, together with the assets of the general partners available after allowance for their individual creditors, are insufficient to pay the firm debts; or the solvent partners consent to the partnership being adjudged a bankrupt. A change of law may occur causing the partnership to be illegal and dissolved.

By Court Decree Dissolution by the decree of a court is, essentially, dissolution by operation of law, but it is considered separately at this point for emphasis. A judicial determination is necessary in many instances to determine whether or not the circumstances are such that, on the application of a partner, the partnership should be dissolved. A court of equity, or a court with equity powers, has jurisdiction over such proceedings. If the circumstances are such that the carrying on of the partnership business is seriously prejudiced, the court has discretion to decree dissolution. Grounds for dissolution by decree of a court are as follows:

Incapacity of Partner. A partner may be adjudicated to be insane, he may be of unsound mind without any adjudication of insanity, or for some other reason he may be incapable of performing his part of the partnership agreement. However, such incapacity may be temporary or partial and, in the discretion of the court, the carrying on of the partnership business may not be affected for the time being and dissolution be denied.

Misconduct of Partner. A partner's misconduct, either in the carrying on of the partnership business or otherwise, may so prejudice or make impracticable the carrying on of the partnership business as to justify dissolution of the partnership. Bitter disagreements, or a rupture in working relationship, among the partners seriously affecting the carrying on of the partnership business justify dissolution; ordinary disputes among the partners are usually insufficient. Petition for dissolution may not be made by the delinquent partner.

Operation Only at a Loss. The purpose of a partnership is to earn profits and, if it can operate only at a loss, the partnership may be ordered dissolved.

Equitable Necessity. Circumstances may exist which equitably justify dissolution. An illustration is the occurrence of fraud in the creation of the partnership.

By Partner's Assignee under Certain Circumstances. An assignee of a partner's interest in the partnership may obtain a decree of dissolution at any time if the partnership was terminable at will or on the expiration of the agreed duration of the partnership either in time or in objective.

2. EFFECT OF DISSOLUTION

Dissolution does not terminate the partnership but causes its affairs to be settled preliminary to its termination. Dissolution has an important effect on the authority of the partners, has a limited effect on the liability of the partners as among themselves, and involves rights and powers in connection with the winding up of the partnership business. These effects will be considered in turn.

Authority of Partners Dissolution operates to terminate the authority of the partners to act on behalf of the partnership, except to the extent necessary in order to wind up the partnership affairs. In the absence of agreement to the contrary, partners who have not wrongfully caused dissolution of the partnership or the legal representative of the last surviving partner, not bankrupt, have implied authority to participate in the winding up of the partnership; in a proper case a court has power to wind up a partnership on application by a proper party. Partners, nevertheless, have apparent authority to carry on the partnership business with third persons who knew of the partnership prior to dissolution but who are unaware of such dissolution, and all partners have apparent authority to wind up the partnership affairs in dealing with third persons who are unaware of the ineligibility of certain partners to engage in the winding up. Accordingly, proper notice must be given to third persons in order to terminate the apparent authority of partners.[1]

The apparent authority of partners to carry on the partnership business may be terminated by giving proper notice of the dissolution to third persons who knew of the partnership prior to dissolution but had no knowledge or notice of such dissolution. If such third persons *had extended credit to the partnership prior to dissolution,* they are to be given *actual notice,* i.e., they are to *actually receive* notice of dissolution; sending such notice is not enough. If such third persons *had not extended credit to the partnership prior to dissolution,* they are to be given *general notice,* as by newspaper publication or otherwise in the place or places where the partnership business was carried on. Similar notice to such third persons must be given regarding the ineligibility of certain partners to participate in the winding up of the partnership business. In the event that such notice is not given or otherwise received by such third persons, the partnership will be bound by the acts of the partners pursuant to their apparent authority to carry on the partnership business or to wind up a dissolved partnership. However, under U.P.A., sec. 35(3), a partnership is not liable to third persons for the unauthorized act of a partner after dissolution if notice of dissolution has not been given to such third persons, "(a) Where the partnership is dissolved because it is unlawful to carry on the business, unless the act is appropriate for winding up partnership affairs; or (b) Where *the* partner has become bankrupt; . . ." (Author's italics).

Liability of Partners

Dissolution does not affect the liability of partners to third persons for partnership obligations,[2] but it does affect the liabilities of the partners among themselves.

Where dissolution has occurred by the act of a partner or by the death or bankruptcy of a partner but a partner, not having knowledge of the dissolution caused by the partner's act or not having knowledge or notice of the dissolution caused by a partner's death or bankruptcy, enters a transaction on behalf of the partnership, each of the partners has an obligation to contribute his share of any liability caused by such transaction.

---

[1] If a dormant partner retires, no such notice is necessary to third persons who did not know that he was a partner; but notice must be given to those who knew he was a partner. See Alan R. Bromberg, *Crane and Bromberg on Partnership* (St. Paul, Minn.: West Publishing Co., 1968), p. 466.

[2] However, see U.P.A., sec. 35(2), concerning a dormant partner's liability after dissolution. Also see ftn. 1 above.

Although a change in partnership personnel causes dissolution of the partnership, nevertheless, the partnership business may be carried on without liquidation of the partnership affairs. Under U.P.A., sec. 41, extensive provision is made for protection of the creditors of the dissolved partnership in the event the partnership business is continued without liquidation. Under this section creditors of the dissolved partnership are also creditors of the person or partnership carrying on the partnership business. This section should be examined carefully. When a partnership is dissolved by a partner's death or retirement and the partnership business is continued without the settlement of accounts between the partnership and the retiring partner or the legal representative of the deceased partner, such partner or representative of a deceased partner has the right to an accounting of the value of the partner's interest in the partnership at the time of dissolution and the partner or representative is entitled to such interest as a creditor of the person or partnership continuing the business. The continued use of the surname of a deceased or retired partner does not of itself make the estate of the decedent or the retired partner liable for partnership obligations.

3. WINDING UP

Nature and Authority   The winding up of a partnership business involves the liquidation of partnership assets and the settlement of partnership affairs with partnership creditors and among the partners themselves, and precludes taking on new business for the partnership. U.P.A., sec. 35(1)(a), provides that a partner has authority to perform ". . . any act appropriate for winding up partnership affairs or completing transactions unfinished at dissolution. . . ." The partners have the authority to liquidate the assets, receive payment of debts due the partnership and to execute proper receipts therefor, pay the partnership debts, distribute to the various partners their interests in the partnership, and to do any other appropriate acts in effecting the winding up of the partnership affairs. In the absence of agreement to the contrary, partners who have not wrongfully caused dissolution of the partnership or the legal representative of the last surviving partner, not bankrupt, have implied authority to wind up the partnership affairs.

Rights of Partners. Every partner has a right to an accounting for his interest in the dissolved partnership, to receive the advances he has made to the partnership and his capital contribution, and to participate in the surplus and profits as against the partners winding up the partnership affairs or as a creditor of the partnership continuing the business.

Distribution. The settlement of accounts between the partners after dissolution, in the absence of agreement to the contrary, is governed by U.P.A., sec. 40. Under section 40(b):

> The liabilities of the partnership shall rank in order of payment, as follows:
>
> I. Those owing to creditors other than partners,
> II. Those owing to partners other than for capital and profits,
> III. Those owing to partners in respect of capital,
> IV. Those owing to partners in respect of profits.

Partnership liabilities are satisfied first by resorting to the partnership property and then to the contributions by the individual partners in the ratio that they share profits, unless they have provided to the contrary. The estate of a decedent partner is liable for contribution of his share to such liabilities. The estate of a bankrupt partner is liable first to the individual creditors of the bankrupt partner, then to the partnership creditors, and finally to his other partners by way of contribution. If any partner has paid more than his share of such liabilities, he is entitled to contribution from the remaining partners for such excess.

Chapter VIII

LIMITED PARTNERSHIP

---

1. *PURPOSE*

THE PURPOSE of a limited partnership is to have an association of partners, one or more of whom will not be liable for partnership obligations, and one or more of whom will be so liable. Those not so liable are "limited partners," inasmuch as they are liable only to the partnership and only for their contribution of cash or other property in accordance with their partnership agreement. The general partners are liable for the partnership obligations and may be contributing solely their skill and services. Statutes now exist in all the states permitting the formation of a limited partnership, although similar legislation did not occur in England until 1907. The Uniform Limited Partnership Act has been adopted in the majority of states. Comments will be made here on a few of the more salient provisions. Throughout this chapter, references to the Uniform Limited Partnership Act will carry the abbreviation of U.L.P.A.

2. *LIMITED PARTNERSHIP DISTINGUISHED FROM GENERAL PARTNERSHIP*

Definition   *A "limited partnership" is a partnership of one or more general partners and one or more limited partners formed in compliance with U.L.P.A.* There are only two kinds of partner in a limited partnership, namely, general partners who are the same as partners in a general partnership, and limited partners who have limited liability and interests in the limited partnership. Limited partners are sometimes called "special partners."

A limited partnership exists only by virtue of its compliance with the statute creating it. Failure to comply with the statute often results in the association becoming a general partnership. Under U.L.P.A., sec. 2, the partners must

Formation

638

sign and swear to a certificate containing detailed information regarding: the name, character, and location of the principal place of business; the names and addresses of each of the limited and general partners, their status as such being indicated; the cash or other property contributed by each limited partner; how each limited partner is to share in the profits of the partnership; and other information. This certificate must be filed in the proper place as provided in each state. A limited partnership may be formed by exact compliance with the statutory requisites regarding the details of the certificate, or by substantial compliance in good faith with such requirements.

Contributions   A limited partner's contribution to the partnership may be only cash or other property, but not services.
A general partner may contribute to the limited partnership just as he could to any general partnership. Under the U.L.P.A., sec. 12:

(1) A person may be a general partner and a limited partner in the same partnership at the same time.
(2) A person who is a general, and also at the same time a limited, partner shall have all the rights and powers and be subject to all the restrictions of a general partner; except that, in respect to his contribution, he shall have the rights against the other members which he would have had if he were not also a general partner.

**Partnership
Name**   A limited partner's surname may not appear in the name of the partnership unless it is the same name as that of a general partner, or his name was included in the partnership name before he became a limited partner. Failure of a limited partner to comply with this requirement exposes him to liability as a general partner to partnership creditors who have extended credit to the partnership without knowing that he was not a general partner.

**Participation
in Management**   A limited partner may not participate in the control of the limited partnership, and if he does participate he is liable as a general partner to partnership creditors. Only the general partners of the limited partnership may participate in the management or control of the partnership business.

Death, Assignment, New Partners
The partnership is not dissolved by the death of *a* limited partner, by *a* limited partner's assignment of his interest in the partnership, or by the admission of *a* new limited partner. In the latter instance, the certificate of limited partnership must be amended in order to include the information regarding the new limited partner. All partners must sign the amendment for admission of a new partner. However, the retirement, death, or insanity of a general partner dissolves the partnership unless the partnership is continued by the remaining general partners pursuant to the terms of the certificate or with the consent of all the partners.

Rights of Limited Partner
A limited partner's interest in the partnership is personal property. Under U.L.P.A., sec. 10:

(1) A limited partner shall have the same rights as a general partner to

(a) Have the partnership books kept at the principal place of business of the partnership, and at all times to inspect and copy any of them.

(b) Have on demand true and full information of all things affecting the partnership, and a formal account of partnership affairs whenever circumstances render it just and reasonable, and

(c) Have dissolution and winding up by decree of court.

(2) A limited partner shall have the right to receive a share of the profits or other compensation by way of income, and to the return of his contribution as provided in sections 15 and 16.

Compensation of Limited Partner. Under U.L.P.A., sec. 15:

A limited partner may receive from the partnership the share of the profits or the compensation by way of income stipulated for in the certificate; provided, that after such payment is made, whether from the property of the partnership or that of a general partner, the partnership assets are in excess of all liabilities of the partnership except liabilities to limited partners on account of their contributions and to general partners.

Withdrawal or Reduction of Limited Partner's Contribution. Under U.L.P.A., sec. 16:

(1) A limited partner shall not receive from a general partner or out of partnership property any part of his contribution until

(a) All liabilities of the partnership, except liabilities to general partners and to limited partners on account of their contributions, have been paid or there remains property of the partnership sufficient to pay them,

(b) The consent of all members is had, unless the return of the contribution may be rightfully demanded under the provisions of paragraph (2), and

(c) The certificate is cancelled or so amended as to set forth the withdrawal or reduction.

(2) Subject to the provisions of paragraph (1) a limited partner may rightfully demand the return of his contribution

(a) On the dissolution of a partnership, or

(b) When the date specified in the certificate for its return has arrived, or

(c) After he has given six months' notice in writing to all other members, if no time is specified in the certificate either for the return of the contribution or for the dissolution of the partnership,

(3) In the absence of any statement in the certificate to the contrary or the consent of all members, a limited partner, irrespective of the nature of his contribution, has only the right to demand and receive cash in return for his contribution.

(4) A limited partner may have the partnership dissolved and its affairs wound up when

(a) He rightfully but unsuccessfully demands the return of his contribution, or

(b) The other liabilities of the partnership have not been paid, or the partnership property is insufficient for their payment as required by paragraph (1a) and the limited partner would otherwise be entitled to the return of his contribution.

Loans and Other Business Transactions with Limited Partner. Under U.L.P.A., sec. 13:

(1) A limited partner also may loan money to and transact other business with the partnership, and, unless he is also a general partner, receive on account of resulting claims against the partnership, with general creditors, a pro rata share of the assets. No limited partner shall in respect to any such claim

(a) Receive or hold as collateral security any partnership property, or

(b) Receive from a general partner or the partnership any payment, conveyance, or release from liability, if at the time the assets of the partnership are not sufficient to discharge partnership liabilities to persons not claiming as general or limited partners,

(2) The receiving of collateral security, or a payment, conveyance, or release in violation of the provisions of paragraph (1) is a fraud on the creditors of the partnership.

Liability of Limited Partner   *Limited partners as such are not bound by the obligations of the partnership.* Under U.L.P.A., sec. 17:

(1) A limited partner is liable to the partnership

(a) For the difference between his contribution as actually made and that stated in the certificate as having been made, and

(b) For any unpaid contribution which he agreed in the certificate to make in the future at the time and on the conditions stated in the certificate.

(2) A limited partner holds as trustee for the partnership

(a) Specific property stated in the certificate as contributed by him, but which was not contributed or which has been wrongfully returned, and

(b) Money or other property wrongfully paid or conveyed to him on account of his contribution.

(3) The liabilities of a limited partner as set forth in this section can be waived or compromised only by the consent of all members; but a waiver or compromise shall not affect the right of a creditor of a partnership who extended credit or whose claim arose after the filing and before a cancellation or amendment of the certificate, to enforce such liabilities.

(4) When a contributor has rightfully received the return in whole or in part of the capital of his contribution, he is nevertheless liable to the partnership for any sum, not in excess of such return with interest, necessary to discharge its liabilities to all creditors who extended credit or whose claims arose before such return.

Authority
In general, the authority of a general partner is the same as that of a partner in a general partnership.

A limited partner does not have any authority to act on behalf of the partnership.

Litigation
A limited partner is not required to be a party in actions for or against the limited partnership, unless the limited partner is asserting a right against the partnership or the partnership is asserting a right against the limited partner. Only the general partners are proper parties.

Distribution
On dissolution of a limited partnership the assets are distributed among various persons in the following priority of liabilities, as provided under U.L.P.A., sec. 23:

(a) Those to creditors, in the order of priority as provided by law, except those to limited partners on account of their contributions, and to general partners,

(b) Those to limited partners in respect to their share of the profits and other compensation by way of income on their contributions,

(c) Those to limited partners in respect to the capital of their contributions,

(d) Those to general partners other than for capital and profits,

(e) Those to general partners in respect to profits,

(f) Those to general partners in respect to capital.

Cancellation or Amendment of Certificate
U.L.P.A. requires that the certificate of limited partnership be cancelled or amended in certain specified instances. Under sec. 24:

(1) The certificate shall be cancelled when the partnership is dissolved or all limited partners cease to be such.

(2) A certificate shall be amended when

(a) There is a change in the name of the partnership or in the amount or character of the contribution of any limited partner,

(b) A person is substituted as a limited partner,

(c) An additional limited partner is admitted,

(d) A person is admitted as a general partner,

(e) A general partner retires, dies or becomes insane, and the business is continued under section 20,

(f) There is a change in the character of the business of the partnership,

(g) There is a false or erroneous statement in the certificate,

(h) There is a change in the time as stated in the certificate for the dissolution of the partnership or for the return of a contribution,

(i) A time is fixed for the dissolution of the partnership, or the return of a contribution, no time having been specified in the certificate, or

(j) The members desire to make a change in any other statement in the certificate in order that it shall accurately represent the agreement between them.

APPENDIX TO PART SIX (A)

REFERENCES

1. Bromberg, Alan R. *Crane and Bromberg on Partnership.* St. Paul, Minn.: West Publishing Co., 1968.
2. Mechem, Floyd R. *Elements of the Law of Partnership.* 2d ed. Chicago: Callaghan & Co., 1920.
3. 8 *Uniform Laws Annotated,* Uniform Limited Partnership Act, 1916.
4. 7 *Uniform Laws Annotated,* Uniform Partnership Act, 1914.

PROBLEMS

1. (a) Define a partnership.
   (b) Distinguish a partnership from:
       (1) A corporation.
       (2) A business trust.
   (c) What is meant by:
       (1) Ostensible partner?
       (2) Dormant partner?
       (3) General partner?
       (4) Special partner?
   (d) Can a corporation be a partner? Explain.
2. (a) A learned that B has held himself out to the public as being a partner of A when no such partnership existed. What should A do and why?
   (b) What information does a partnership agreement usually contain?
3. Two men were legally engaged in an unincorporated business under the duly recorded assumed name of The Atlantic Company without any written agreement, and it became necessary to determine whether they were partners. One had invested cash in the business and the other had lent his credit to it and had assisted in the management of it. What documents would you examine and for what other facts would you inquire as apt to have significant bearing on the question? (Former C.P.A. Examination question)
4. (a) A owns a small business and pays a share of the profits to B and C, his employees, as compensation for their services and pays a share of the profits to D, his landlord, as rent. Such compensation and rent fluctuate as the profits fluctuate.
       (1) Is this a partnership?
       (2) Why?

(b) X, Y, and Z are creditors of A, whose business is failing. They all agree that X, Y, and Z are to help A to operate the business and X, Y, and Z are to share in the profits until their claims are satisfied.
(1) Is this a partnership?
(2) Why?

5. (a) The real and personal property of the partnership of A and B is held in the name of A. A conveyed part of the partnership realty to C in violation of the partnership agreement. C conveyed it to D, a bona fide purchaser for value without notice of such violation. Can the partnership reacquire the title to the property? Why?

(b) X, Y, and Z are partners, the firm property being held in the firm name.
(1) C, a judgment creditor of X, caused a levy of execution on the partnership property. Could such property be sold to satisfy the judgment? Why?
(2) Y died leaving a widow. Who is entitled to the partnership realty and personalty? Why?

6. In a partnership of A, B, and C:
(a) A and B purchased merchandise for the carrying on of the partnership business in the usual way over the objection of C who refused to be bound by the purchase. Is C, together with A and B, liable for the purchase? Why?
(b) Do A and B have the right to amend the Articles of Partnership over C's objection? Why?
(c) C became ill, temporarily causing A and B to do extra work in operating the partnership business. Are A and B entitled to compensation for such additional work? Why?

7. (a) A contributed $5,000, B $10,000, and C $15,000 to the partnership of ABC, but no provision was made in the partnership agreement for the sharing of profits and losses. At the end of the year the firm had a loss of $6,000.
(1) How will the loss be shared?
(2) Why?
(b) When does a partner have a right to a formal accounting of partnership affairs prior to dissolution?

8. A, B, and C were partners under a written agreement made in 1950 that it should continue for 10 years. During 1957 C being indebted to X sold and conveyed his interest in the partnership to X. A and B paid X $5,000 as C's share of the profits for the year 1957, but refused X permission to inspect the books or to come into the managing office of the partnership. X brings an action setting forth the above facts and asks for an accounting and an order to inspect the books and to participate in the management of the partnership business.
(1) Does C's action dissolve the partnership?
(2) To what is X entitled with respect to (a) partnership profits, (b) inspection of partnership books, (c) accounting by the partnership, and (d) participation in the partnership management?

(3) In case of a dissolution, to what is X entitled with respect to C's interest and accounting? (Former C.P.A. Examination question)

9. On May 2, 1961, the three partners in the firm of A, B, & C signed a dissolution agreement whereby the firm's affairs were to be liquidated as of the following June 30th. On May 15th, B without the knowledge or consent of A or C procured for himself a five-year lease of the premises occupied by the firm to run from the following July 1st, and on July 1st B sold this lease at a profit. Have A and C a legal right to share in B's profit? (Former C.P.A. Examination question)

10. (a) Why is it that, with certain exceptions and in the absence of statute to the contrary, a partnership cannot sue a partner nor be sued by a partner at law?
    (b) What is the nature of the exceptions?
    (c) What is the nature and effect of a charging order?
    (d) What is meant by a trading partnership and a nontrading partnership? Give an illustration of each, and explain why the distinction between them is important.

11. A, B, and C are partners in a large retail furniture business and operate a large store for this purpose under the firm name of ABC. In the absence of express authority, of any custom and usage, and of unusual circumstances, which of the following acts by A are binding on the firm? *If the act is binding, state "Yes"; and if not binding, state "No."*
    (1) A bought furniture for sale in the store.
    (2) A paid for such purchase of furniture by executing and delivering a check in the firm name.
    (3) A bought a suit of clothes and an automobile for himself in the firm name.
    (4) A paid for the purchase of the clothes and automobile by executing and delivering a check in the firm name, such check subsequently being held by a holder in due course.
    (5) A borrowed money in the firm name and used it to pay for a firm purchase of furniture and thereby obtained a cash discount.
    (6) A mortgaged the firm personal property as security for the money borrowed in (5) above.
    (7) A assigned the firm property in trust for creditors.
    (8) A received payment for an obligation owing to the firm and executed a receipt therefor.
    (9) A employed a salesman to work in the store.
    (10) A compromised and settled a claim against the firm and paid the settled amount out of the firm funds.
    (11) A submitted to arbitration a claim against the firm.
    (12) A sold the firm goodwill.

12. It was provided in the partnership agreement between A, B, and C, that A would not be liable for partnership obligations. An employee of the firm negligently injured X while driving the firm truck on firm business. The firm failed to perform a contractual obligation owing to Y. Subsequently D was admitted to the partnership.

(a) Are the partners who are liable for the claims of X and Y liable jointly, severally, or jointly and severally? Explain.

(b) Is A liable for the claims of X and Y? Why?

(c) Is D liable for the claims of X and Y? Why?

(d) If X and Y obtained judgments on their claims, how may such judgments be satisfied?

(e) If the partners liable have individual creditors:

   (1) Does this fact affect X and Y in the satisfaction of their judgments? Why?

   (2) Would it make any difference if the firm of A, B, C, and D were dissolved subsequent to the judgments obtained by X and Y but prior to any attempt to satisfy such judgments? Why?

13. Jock and Kilroy, partners, took Lee in as a partner. At the time of Lee's admittance, the partnership liabilities were $10,000. One year after Lee's admittance the liabilities were $15,000 and the assets $6,000. The partners decided then to dissolve. What is the liability of each partner under the Uniform Partnership Act? (Former C.P.A. Examination question)

14. The copartnership articles of Alden and Bruer stipulated that Alden should furnish all the capital and that Bruer should manage the business but without any liability for firm debts. Connors, knowing of these provisions, sold goods on credit to the firm.

(1) Who is liable? Alden, or Bruer, or both Alden and Bruer?

(2) What would your answer be if the copartnership articles further stipulated that Bruer was a limited partner? (Former C.P.A. Examination question)

15. (a) Distinguish dissolution, winding up, and termination of a partnership.

(b) Name two ways by which a partnership may be dissolved under each of the following methods:

   (1) By act of the partners.

   (2) By operation of law.

   (3) By the decree of a proper court.

(c) Which partners may and may not participate in the winding up?

16. A, B, and C are partners in a retail rug business which has just been dissolved pursuant to mutual agreement. While the firm was being wound up, A purchased additional rugs from D who had never heard of the firm previously, from E who had known of the firm previously but had never dealt with it, and from F who had dealt with the firm previously. All of A's transactions were in the firm name and neither D, E, nor F knew of the dissolution.

(1) Is the firm bound by these transactions?

(2) Why?

17. Holland, Jones, and Kerr were partners doing business as note brokers under the name of Holland & Co. The partnership was duly dissolved May 1, 1972, Kerr being named as liquidating partner. On May 20, 1972, Kerr procured and sold to Martin a note purporting to be made by the Acme Corporation and dated May 19, 1972. This transaction was conducted in the name of Holland & Co. and Martin, who had no actual knowledge that

the partnership had been dissolved, gave Kerr a check to the order of Holland & Co. in payment of the purchase price and accepted from Kerr a guaranty of the signature on the note signed "Holland & Co." Kerr indorsed the check in the name of Holland & Co. and deposited it in his own bank account. The Acme Corporation note proved to be a forgery. Against whom has Martin any rights? (Former C.P.A. Examination question)

18. X, Y, and Z are partners. X contributed $10,000, Y $20,000, and Z $30,-000 to the partnership. X had loaned the firm $5,000; the firm owes R, a creditor, $7,000; and the firm has assets of $94,000 at the time of dissolution. In the absence of any provisions in the partnership agreement for the sharing of profits and losses and for distribution of the partnership's assets on dissolution, how should assets be distributed and in what priority?

19. X and Y are partners. Z is an incoming partner who orally promises X and Y to assume the partnership obligations existing prior to his entry into the partnership. Is Z's promise enforceable? Explain.

20. A is an incoming partner of a partnership, the latter's debts amounting to $10,000. A year later these debts are still unpaid, and the new partnership has incurred $5,000 of additional debts. What is A's liability for all these debts? Explain.

SOME PREVIOUS C.P.A. LAW EXAMINATION QUESTIONS AND MODEL ANSWERS
MAY, 1970

No. 3 (Estimated time—20 to 25 minutes)

Each of the following numbered statements states a legal conclusion relating to the lettered material. You are to determine whether each of the legal conclusions is true or false according to the *Uniform Partnership and Limited Partnership Acts*. Write on a separate answer sheet whether each conclusion is true or false. Your grade will be determined from your total net score obtained by deducting a weighted total for your incorrect answers from your total of correct answers; an omitted answer will not be considered an incorrect answer.

A. Vaughn is a limited partner in the Maxwell, Wallace, and Grand Limited Partnership, a real estate syndication. He purchased his interest for $5,000 when the partnership was created. Subsequently he loaned the Partnership $8,000 for five years at 6 percent interest. The Partnership has prospered, and Vogel has offered to buy Vaughn's limited partnership interest for $6,-500. The general partners are opposed to the sale because they dislike Vogel.
    61. A limited partnership is formed by compliance with state statutory requirements; it is not recognized at common law.
    62. As a limited partner Vaughn would only have personal liability after the Partnership assets and the assets of the general partners have been used to satisfy creditors.
    63. Active participation in the management of the Partnership would impose personal liability as a general partner on Vaughn.
    64. Vaughn could only sell his limited partnership interest with the consent of the general partners.

65. Assuming a valid sale of Vaughn's entire limited partnership interest to Vogel, Vogel would automatically become a substituted limited partner.

66. Since Vaughn is both a creditor and a partner of the Partnership, his loan would rank behind outside creditors upon dissolution.

67. The death of Vaughn would cause a dissolution of the limited partnership.

68. Vogel would have the right to be admitted as a general partner upon purchase of Vaughn's limited partnership interest.

69. Vaughn's limited partnership interest is real property since the Partnership is a real estate venture.

70. Vaughn would have the same rights as a general partner to inspect the Partnership books.

B. Franklin, an accountant, has been retained by the creditors of the Wade Limited Partnership to prepare a balance sheet. There are three general partners, two of whom are hopelessly insolvent and one general partner, Sampson, who has $10,000 in assets and $8,000 in debts. There are 25 limited partners, all of whom are solvent. The Partnership has $8,000 in assets and $40,000 of liabilities. Each limited partner contributed $2,000 for his limited partnership interest with the exception of Wilson who agreed to contribute $2,000 but who only contributed $1,000.

71. The Partnership creditors would be able to obtain $2,000 from Sampson.

72. The limited partners would receive nothing in return for their capital contribution.

73. The partnership creditors could obtain $1,000 from Wilson.

74. If Wilson had permitted his surname to be used in the partnership name, i.e., Wade & Wilson, he would be liable to any partnership creditor who extended credit to the partnership without actual knowledge of the fact that he was not a general partner.

75. The Partnership creditors could validly assert claims against the property owned by the wives of the two insolvent general partners.

C. The Viking Partnership consisted of seven equal partners. Wells, one of the partners, purchased six shares of the Azuma Dairy Farm Corporation stock. He used partnership funds to purchase the stock. Subsequently another share was purchased and each partner's capital account was debited for an amount equal to one-seventh of the total purchase price. Furthermore, Wells had indicated that each partner owned one share.

76. There is a presumption that the stock is Partnership property in that Partnership funds were used.

77. If the property is Partnership property, an individual partner has no right to one of the shares.

78. In the event of insolvency, the various firm and personal creditors would be interested in the question of the ownership of the property.

79. Partnerships are precluded from investing in corporate stock.

80. The stock in question would be held to belong to the individual partners and not the Partnership.

D. Adams, Webster, and Coke were partners in the construction business. Coke decided to retire and found Black who agreed to purchase his interest. Black was willing to pay Coke $20,000 and promise to assume Coke's share of all firm obligations.

81. Unless the partners agree to admit Black as a partner, he could not become a member of the firm.
82. The retirement of Coke would cause a dissolution of the firm.
83. The firm creditors are third party beneficiaries of Black's promise to Coke.
84. Coke would be released from all liability for firm debts if his interest were purchased by Black and Black promised to pay Coke's share of firm debts.
85. If the other partners refused to accept Black as a partner, Coke could retire, thereby causing a dissolution and winding up.

E. Carson, Crocket, and Kitt were partners in the importing business. They needed additional capital to expand and located an investor named White who agreed to purchase a one-quarter interest in the Partnership by contributing $50,000 in capital to the Partnership. At the time he became a partner there were several large creditors who had previously loaned money to the Partnership. The Partnership subsequently failed and the creditors are attempting to assert personal liability against White.

86. White is personally liable on all firm debts contracted subsequent to his entry into the firm.
87. Creditors of the first partnership automatically become creditors of the new partnership continuing the business.
88. Creditors of the old firm which existed prior to White's entry cannot assert rights against his capital contribution.
89. White has no personal liability for firm debts existing prior to his entry into the firm.
90. If White agreed to pay the individual creditors at the time he entered the partnership, a novation would have occurred.

Answer

61. True	67. False	73. True	79. False	85. True
62. False	68. False	74. True	80. True	86. True
63. True	69. False	75. False	81. True	87. True
64. False	70. True	76. True	82. True	88. False
65. False	71. True	77. True	83. True	89. True
66. False	72. True	78. True	84. False	90. False

MAY, 1968

No. 1 (Estimated time—20 to 25 minutes)

Each of the following numbered phrases or clauses states a legal conclusion as it completes the related lettered material. You are to determine whether each of the legal conclusions is true or false according to the Uniform Partnership Act. Write on a separate answer sheet whether each conclusion is true or false. Your grade will be determined from your total net score obtained by deducting your total of incorrect answers from your total of correct answers; an omitted answer will not be considered an incorrect answer.

A. Edward and Arnold, two brothers, inherited their deceased father's factory under the provisions of his will. The will provided that the brothers were to own the factory jointly and run it as partners. Edward and Arnold decided, however, that they did not wish to be partners. Instead, it was agreed between them that Edward, the older brother, would employ Arnold and pay him a portion of the profits from the business as a salary. Later Edward and Arnold decided that a partnership would be better and they orally agreed to be partners. A lawyer later drew a formal partnership agreement for the brothers. After executing the partnership agreement and leaving the lawyer's office Edward and Arnold orally agreed to change the terms of the agreement.

1. Edward and Arnold became partners when their father's will took effect at his death.
2. Edward and Arnold became obligated at the time their father executed his will to become partners upon his death.
3. The arrangement for Edward to employ Arnold did not constitute a partnership.
4. A partnership was created prior to the execution of the written partnership agreement by the oral agreement between Edward and Arnold.
5. The written partnership agreement could not be orally modified.

B. Five individuals gathered one evening to discuss the formation of an investment club to provide for joint stock investments. The suggestion was made that the investment club be formed as a partnership and this suggestion was unanimously adopted. Then other ideas were discussed.

It would be possible to have a partnership even if it was also decided that

6. The investment club is to be a nonprofit organization donating all of its income to charity.
7. The investment club is to be a profit-making organization and the gains on the sale of stocks are to be divided unequally among only three members with all dividends received going to the other two members.
8. Only four of the individuals will make capital contributions.
9. The investment club is not to employ any personnel on a salary basis.
10. The investment club is not to be held out as a partnership to the public.

C. The partners in a partnership composed of seven members have differing views on several partnership issues. If the partnership agreement makes no provision for the number of partners required to decide particular issues, the necessary authority would exist

11. To require the discharge of a clerk accused of stealing if only two partners are in favor.
12. To cause the dissolution of the partnership if only three partners are in favor.
13. To require the change of the partnership business from a wholesale to a retail operation if only four partners are in favor.
14. To require the submission of a partnership claim to arbitration if only five partners are in favor.
15. To submit to a confession of judgment on behalf of the partnership if only six partners are in favor.

D. Alvin, Barry, and Charles are in business together as partners. Alvin is the active manager of the business. Barry and Charles are wealthy and do not work in the business. Although the partnership is a financial success, Alvin has personal losses and an involuntary bankruptcy petition was filed against him by his individual creditors. Daniel offered to purchase Alvin's interest and to enter the partnership either as a working partner or as a nonworking partner.

16. Alvin's individual creditors may not force the partnership into bankruptcy to gain access to Alvin's interest in the partnership.

17. After being adjudicated a bankrupt, Alvin retains full power to deal with third persons and to bind the partnership so long as he acts in good faith.

18. After Alvin is adjudicated a bankrupt, Barry and Charles may not continue to operate as a partnership without a dissolution even if a satisfactory agreement is reached to pay the value of Alvin's interest to the trustee in bankruptcy.

19. Daniel may not enter the partnership as a nonworking partner because the partnership must have at least one member working in the business in a managerial capacity.

20. If Daniel purchases Alvin's interest and enters the partnership as an active partner, Daniel will not be personally liable for partnership debts incurred while Alvin was a member of the partnership.

E. Frank, Gerald, and James are partners in an insurance brokerage firm. Their partnership agreement states that "profits earned by them are to be shared equally." Frank's father is a well-known insurance broker and Frank, without his father's knowledge, often represents to clients that his father is associated with the firm. Gerald, to make extra money, sells real estate on weekends over the objection of his fellow partners who feel that this part-time activity damages the image of the partnership. They informed Gerald that if he continues to sell real estate his profits from real estate sales must be turned over to the partnership. James was named as an executor in a will and is now administering the estate.

21. Frank's father may be found to be a partner by estoppel.

22. Gerald is violating his duty to the partnership by selling real estate.

23. If Gerald continues to sell real estate he need not share his profits from real estate sales with his partners.

24. James must share any income earned as executor with his partners.

25. Each partner is free to render insurance brokerage services to nonpartnership clients after normal working hours and need not inform his partners of this or bring these clients to the partnership so long as he does not handle these matters during the normal working day or use partnership supplies.

F. Jane, Carol, Edith, and Alice formed a partnership. Capital contributions were: Jane, $13,000; Carol, $10,000; Edith, $5,000; and Alice made no capital contribution. There was no provision for sharing profits or losses in the partnership agreement. The partnership owes Jane $6,000 for a loan which has not been repaid. The assets of the partnership are worth $20,000 and the partnership owes $26,000 to trade creditors. The partners decide to terminate the partnership, and Edith agrees to take charge of the liquidation. Upon liquidation

26. Each partner must contribute an additional $1,500.

27. Jane may demand interest on the loan she made to the partnership in the absence of any provision in the partnership agreement.

28. Carol will not be required by the partners to make an additional contribution to the partnership to cover losses.
29. The partners can agree that Edith will receive additional compensation for her work in liquidating the partnership.
30. Unpaid creditors may not sue the individual partners while the partnership continues to remain in existence.

Answer

1. False	7. True	13. False	19. False	25. False
2. False	8. True	14. False	20. True	26. False
3. True	9. True	15. False	21. False	27. True
4. True	10. True	16. True	22. False	28. True
5. False	11. False	17. False	23. True	29. True
6. False	12. True	18. False	24. False	30. False

MAY, 1966

No. 6 (Estimated time—20 to 25 minutes)

A, B, and C formed the ABC Company, a partnership, with A contributing $12,000 of capital, B contributing $8,000 and C contributing $6,000. In their partnership agreement, A, B, and C provided that the partnership was to exist for twenty years, but the partners made no provision as to the proportions in which profits and losses were to be shared. During the course of operating the partnership, A made a loan of $1,000 to the partnership which has not been repaid and the partnership also owes outside creditors additional amounts which exceed the value of partnership assets by $3,000.

a. Under the Uniform Partnership Act, in absence of a specific agreement between the parties, how is the compensation and profit for each partner determined during the course of operating the partnership?
b. Under the Uniform Partnership Act
   (1) If A wishes to terminate the partnership but B and C do not, does A have the right to withdraw from the partnership? Explain.
   (2) If A, B, and C agree to terminate the partnership, how will losses be divided?
c. Discuss
   (1) The rule of marshaling of assets.
   (2) The distinction between the "dissolution" of the partnership and the "winding up" of partnership affairs.
d. If D becomes a partner in ABC Company and replaces A, what is D's liability with respect to obligations arising before his admission to the partnership?

Answer

a. Under the Uniform Partnership Act, unless the partners agree to the contrary, a partner is not entitled to any additional compensation for his services rendered to the partnership. His right to share in the profits is deemed to be adequate compensation, with one exception. A surviving partner is entitled to compensation for his services in winding up partnership affairs. In the absence of agreement to the contrary, partners have the right to share in partnership profits equally.

b. (1) Yes. Any partner may withdraw from a partnership, but if such withdrawal is wrongful he will be liable for damages for breach of contract. Here, the partnership agreement is for twenty years, and if A's withdrawal is before the twenty years have expired his withdrawal is a breach of contract.

(2) $10,000 each by A, B, and C. In the absence of agreement to the contrary, partners have the duty to share in partnership losses, whether capital or otherwise, in the same ratio as they share the profits. Here, the partners did not agree on how the profits and losses were to be shared and, inasmuch as the profits are then shared equally, the losses are to be shared equally. The partnership loss is $30,000, consisting of $3,000 owed to outside creditors, $1,000 owed to A, and $26,000 owed to capital. Therefore, each partner will bear $10,000 of that loss. Thus, A will receive $3,000 after deducting $10,000 from his $13,000 consisting of $1,000 loan repayment and $12,000 capital contribution. B will contribute $2,000 resulting from deducting his $8,000 capital contribution from the $10,000 loss borne by him. C will contribute $4,000 resulting from deducting his $6,000 capital contribution from the $10,-000 loss borne by him. The $6,000 contributed by B and C as their shares of the loss will pay $3,000 to the firm's outside creditors and $3,000 to A.

c. (1) Marshaling of assets is an equitable doctrine. As applied to partnerships, each individual partner's estate is made available first to his individual creditors, and any surplus remaining is made available to partnership creditors; while partnership property is made available first to partnership creditors, and any surplus remaining is distributed among the partners and, as a part of an individual partner's estate, is made available to the creditors of each of the individul partners.

(2) Dissolution of a partnership occurs when a partner ceases to be associated in the carrying on of the partnership business. Dissolution does not terminate the partnership, which continues in existence until its affairs have been settled. The settling of such affairs is called the "winding up" of the partnership. The winding up begins with dissolution and ends with termination of the partnership.

d. D, as an incoming partner, is liable for partnership obligations incurred prior to his admission, but such liability may be satisfied only out of partnership property.

B. CORPORATIONS

Chapter IX

A FORM OF BUSINESS ORGANIZATION

---

1. A LEGAL ENTITY

Definition   A "CORPORATION" may be defined as *an association of persons carrying on an enterprise or activity and clothed with a legal personality by compliance with a statute creating it.* The business corporation, as distinguished from other types of corporation, developed in response to a need for a form of business organization with certain attributes not available in any other form of business organization. The great expansion of business in the last 175 years has accelerated the growth and development of the corporation. Today corporations are everywhere, and participation in business requires a knowledge of this form of business organization.

      The choice of sole proprietorship, partnership,[1] or

Desirability   corporation as the form of business organization depends upon which is best suited to the needs of the particular enterprise or activity. Among the outstanding advantages of the corporate form are perpetual existence, ease of transfer of corporate interest, centralization of management, and its legal entity. Its disadvantages are the expense in its creation and maintenance; the burden of double taxation, first by the corporation and then by the shareholder on

---

[1] Although the general characteristics of a joint-stock association were discussed previously (see above, p. 605) under Partnerships, its resemblance to and its distinction from a corporation should be noted here. The joint-stock association resembles a corporation in the following respects: (1) it can have perpetual existence; (2) it issues shares of stock which are transferable; and (3) it is operated by directors and officers of the association. It differs from a corporation in the following respects: (1) it is not a legal entity, as is a corporation; (2) it is created by agreement among its members, while a corporation is created by state statute; (3) property of the association is acquired and conveyed only in the names of its members individually, while acquisition and conveyance is in the corporate name; (4) it can sue and be sued only in the names of its members, while the corporate name is used in corporations; (5) its members are personally liable for the association's debts, while the shareholders of a corporation are not liable for corporate obligations; and (6) it may be dissolved without state approval, while corporate dissolution requires state approval.

his income received as dividends; and the inconvenience of governmental supervision.

Perpetual Existence. A corporation may, unless it is provided in the charter to the contrary, continue perpetually. Unlike partnership, it is not dissolved by a change in the relation among the associates, caused by one of them ceasing to be associated in the carrying-on of the business. Perpetual existence makes for business stability; and, in the case of large business organizations, it is the only form of organization suitable.

Transferability of Interest. Shares or interests in the corporation are transferable easily without affecting the continuation of the organization's existence. This facilitates the acquisition of corporate capital.

Centralization of Management. The management and control of the corporation is concentrated or centralized in a small group, the board of directors, who are fiduciaries of the property of the corporation for the benefit of the shareholders and who owe a duty to the corporate creditors not to dissipate the corporate property.

Legal Entity. The corporation is a juristic person, separate and distinct from its shareholders; holds property in the corporate name; is sued and sues in the corporate name; and does business in the corporate name. A corporation retains its separate legal entity and personality even though one person may be the sole owner of all the shares in the corporation. (A wrongfully acquires possession of corporate property without corporate consent, and B, a sole shareholder, seeks to dispossess A of the property. B cannot succeed because the property belongs to the corporation.) Under the corporate form of organization a shareholder has no right to participate in its management and operation and is not liable for the obligations of the corporation. The shareholder has a limited amount of control but not such as to impose liability upon him for corporate obligations. This fact is of great importance in the acquisition of corporate capital.

Disregard of Legal Entity Courts do not go beyond the corporate entity as an association of persons with a legal personality unless the association is formed, or is being conducted, for an improper or illegal purpose. Courts will not permit utilization of the legal cloak of a corporate entity to permit the perpetration of fraud or illegality and will disregard the corporate form and hold the individuals in the association liable personally. (A corporation is engaged in the manufacture of beer and is controlled by the same shareholders who control B corporation, which is engaged in the solicitation of freight for railroads. B did not solicit freight from businesses other than A and obtained so-called commissions from the railroad on the freight routed to them. In effect, the purported commissions were rebates going to A in violation of law, and such practice is illegal. Courts would look beyond the corporate entity because of the illegal purpose and operation of B corporation.)

2. CLASSIFICATION OF CORPORATIONS

Corporations may be classified as profit and nonprofit, in accordance with their purpose; as private, public, and quasi-public, depending upon the interests to be served; as stock and nonstock, if the corporation is divided into shares of interest; and as domestic and foreign, depending upon the place of incorporation. For convenience of discussion, corporations will be classified as public and private, stock and nonstock, and domestic and foreign.

Public Corporations

Public corporations are corporations created and controlled by a state or the federal government to administer governmental functions. The Federal Deposit Insurance Corporation is an illustration of a federal corporation, and a municipal corporation is an illustration of a state corporation. Municipal corporations are political subdivisions of a state which are incorporated for the better administration of governmental functions. Incorporated cities and towns are illustrations of municipal corporations. The term "quasi-corporation" often is used to describe local governmental bodies, such as counties and school districts; it is not a corporation but, inasmuch as it has some corporate functions and attributes, it is treated like a corporation. A "quasi-public corporation" is commonly known as a "public-service corporation." It is not organized by the federal or state government and is not for any governmental purpose; but it provides services in which the public has an interest and, for this reason, is subject to greater governmental regulation than private corporations. Electric light corporations, gas corporations, railroad corporations, and water corporations are illustrations of public-service corporations. They operate by virtue of a franchise from the state and have special powers.

Private Corporations

Private corporations are composed of, and controlled by, private persons with no governmental functions or duties. They may be conducted for profit or be nonprofit. The private business corporation is organized for the purpose of engaging in business for profit and often is called a "business corporation." Nonprofit corporations are not engaged in business with the purpose of making a profit but exist for the mutual benefit of the members. If they are formed for charitable or benevolent purposes they are often called "eleemosynary." Hospitals, educational institutions, and fraternal organizations are illustrations of nonprofit corporations. The principles of the law of agency apply in the operation of nonprofit corporations, and those consenting to action to be taken by the association or corporation are bound as principals for such authorized acts.

Stock and Nonstock Corporations

A stock corporation is one in which the interests in the corporation are divided into shares of stock representing rights of participation in the limited control of the corporation, in its surplus or profits, and in the distribution of assets on dissolution. Such shares are evidenced by certificates of stock. The stock corporation is the form of corporate organization utilized by business. A nonstock corporation is a corporation in which the rights and liabilities of the members are determined by the corporation agreement without the creation of any shares of interest. Fraternal organizations are illustrations of nonstock corporations.

Domestic and Foreign Corporations

Domestic Corporations. A corporation is a domestic corporation in the state in which it was formed; in all other states and countries it is a foreign corporation. A corporation is a person and is a citizen of the state in which it was created. The use of the word "person" in statutes and constitutions is construed to include corporations, unless the statute or constitution provides to the contrary. Accordingly, corporations are included in the use of the term "person" in the Fifth and Fourteenth Amendments to the United States Constitution, respectively, which provide: ". . . nor shall any person . . . be deprived of life, liberty, or property, without due process of law; . . . ," and ". . . nor shall any State deprive any person of life, liberty, or property, without due process of law; nor deny to any person within its jurisdiction the equal protection of the laws." A corporation is not entitled to the equal protection of the laws, however, until it has been permitted to do business in the particular state. Corporations are not included within the term "citizen" as used in Article 4, section 2, and the Fourteenth Amendment to the Constitution of the United States which provide, respectively, that citizens of each state shall be entitled to all the privileges and immunities of citizens in the several states, and that no state shall make or enforce any law which shall abridge the privileges or immunities of citizens of the United States.

Foreign Corporations. A foreign corporation is permitted to do business in all the states subject to its compliance with reasonable statutory restrictions and regulations on their doing business therein. It is unconstitutional for states to enact unreasonable and arbitrary discriminatory legislation against foreign corporations. In general, such regulations have as their purpose the protection of those resident persons who may deal with such foreign corporations. Statutes usually provide: that a certified copy of the certificate of incorporation is to be filed with the Secretary of State; a filing and license fee is to be paid; the Secretary of State is to be appointed as an agent of the foreign corporation for the service of process; the proposed location of its office in the state and the names and addresses of its directors are to be disclosed; and it is not unusual for the state to require security of some kind. Failure to comply with these requirements has an effect which varies among the states. The corporation may be ejected, civil liability or criminal punishment may be imposed on its members severally, the corporation may be deprived of the right to use the state courts for suit on its contracts, its contracts may be declared to be void, and the shareholders may be exposed to liability for corporate debts.

"Doing Business." There is much uncertainty regarding the meaning of the phrase "doing business" in a state by foreign corporations. A corporation is doing business in a state when it is carrying on an enterprise in a substantial and continuous manner, as contrasted with isolated or casual transactions. The following corporate conduct in a state does not constitute "doing business" in that state: the operation of an office as a headquarters for salesmen to solicit orders for goods to be sold and supplied from outside the state by the corporation that is to accept such orders; the doing of a mail-order business in the state; engaging in acts which are concerned with the management of the corporation, such as holding corporate meetings and transferring corporate stock; the performance of a single transaction without intent of continuity. However, the installation of permanent corporate facilities in a state has been held to be doing business in that state.

Corporate Acts Subject to State Court Jurisdiction. While a foreign corporation doing business in a state can be compelled by that state to qualify formally as a foreign corporation doing business therein, there is the question of whether the state has *in personam* (personal) jurisdiction over a foreign corporation not doing business in the state for a corporate act within the state. For example, a foreign corporation outside the state sent a contract to a resident in the state for his execution and return to the foreign corporation. Irrespective of whether or not a foreign corporation is "doing business" within a state, the United States Supreme Court has held[2] that the state acted within the federal due process and interstate commerce clauses when it asserted *in personam* jurisdiction over a foreign corporation for its acts in the state where the corporation has certain *minimum contacts* with the state and suit would not offend "traditional notions of fair play and substantial justice." The foreign corporation obtains a benefit from the state's protection and may not complain about the reasonable burden imposed upon it by being amenable to the jurisdiction of the state's courts for its acts within the state. As a consequence, many state statutes now extend the long arm of the state's jurisdiction over a foreign corporation for acts imputable to it within the state without having to rely on the concept of the corporation "doing business" therein;[3] although many states still rely on the "doing business" test as the basis of state *in personam* jurisdiction in an action against a foreign corporation for an activity within the state. Today, it can be said that a state has *in personam* jurisdiction over a foreign corporation for any activity within a state even though the corporation may not be doing business therein.

---

[2] *International Shoe Co.* v. *State of Washington*, 326 U.S. 310, 66 S.Ct. 154, 90 L.Ed. 95, 161 ALR 1057 (1945); *McGee* v. *International Life Insurance Co.,* 355 U.S. 220, 78 S.Ct. 199, 2 L.Ed.2d 223 (1957).

[3] See 26 Corp. Journal 75 (1970). Also see U3C, sec. 1.203.

Chapter X

FORMATION OF THE CORPORATION

1. INCORPORATION REQUIREMENTS

INCORPORATION may occur solely pursuant to federal or state law. At one time corporations were created individually by legislative enactment. The great increase in the number of corporations being formed, the desire to standardize incorporation procedure, and the inconvenience of separate legislative enactment for the creation of each corporation caused the states to formulate general corporation laws, and corporations were formed by complying with such laws. The issuance of a charter by a state to the incorporators pursuant to their request creates a contract between the state and the corporation which, under the United States Constitution, is irrevocable by the state except for cause through the proper exercise of its police power or except as the terms of such contract permit. In order to utilize the latter exception, state statutes usually contain a provision reserving to the state the power to repeal, amend, or modify its corporate law, such provision constituting a part of the contract between the state and the corporation.

Mandatory and Directory Requirements As a condition precedent to the formation of a corporation, it is necessary for the incorporators to comply with the statutory requirements. Some of the statutory provisions are *mandatory* and some are *directory*. Corporate existence is dependent upon substantial compliance with the mandatory provisions of the statutes. Directory provisions are not essential to the formation of a corporation, and noncompliance with such provisions is an irregularity not affecting the formation of a corporation. Careful examination of the general corporation laws is necessary in order to determine the legislative intent regarding the mandatory or directory character of statutory provisions. In general, these mandatory provisions may be described as the preparation of articles of incorporation or of an application for incorporation, and the filing of such articles or application and the payment of fees in connection therewith as required by the statute. These two factors will now be considered.

Articles of Incorporation. The articles of incorporation constitute a proposal to incorporate and, when properly filed, are an acceptance of the state's offer to incorporate; on creation of the corporation, they form a contract between the corporation and the subscribing shareholders and also between the corporation and the state. The state's written approval of such articles of incorporation constitutes a charter which creates the corporation. The state's approval also is necessary for amendment of the charter and amendment is governed by statute. The terms of the charter consist of the provisions contained therein and, whether expressly or impliedly indicated, the laws of the state. Statutes prescribe in detail the data to be included in such articles of incorporation and an examination will be made of these requirements.

Name. A corporate name is necessary to identify the corporate entity. In general, any name may be chosen, subject to legal restriction. Such restriction may be in statutory form requiring the use of "Corporation," "Incorporated," or "Inc." to appear at the end of the corporate name so that the public can recognize the corporate nature of the organization. In some instances "Company" or "Co." are permitted at the end of the corporate name. Because certain types of corporation are governed by special statute—e.g., insurance and banking corporations —statutes usually provide that the following words are not permitted to be included in a corporate name: "bank," "trust," "safe deposit," "savings," "insurance," "guaranty," "title," "casualty," "benefit," and "cooperative." Use may not be made of names which all persons may lawfully use, such as geographical names; and names the same as, or deceptively similar to, those of other corporations or unincorporated associations may not be used. The reasons for the latter are to prevent unfair competition and to protect the goodwill of the names used by other businesses.

Object. The object of the corporation must be expressly stated. A corporation may be formed for any lawful object in which a natural person could engage, provided it is expressly permitted by a valid statute and is not contrary to law. The object of the corporation must be clearly stated in the articles of incorporation in order to determine whether or not it is sanctioned by statute and to determine the extent of the express corporate authority. If part of the object or purpose is unauthorized and part is authorized, the corporation may be formed for the authorized object and the unauthorized object will be surplusage and of no effect. Generally, a corporation may have more than one object and diverse objects if permitted by statute.

Duration. Generally, statutes require the duration of the corporation to be expressed in the articles of incorporation. A corporation has perpetual existence, unless the statute or the articles of incorporation provides to the contrary.

Place of Business. Statutes usually require the articles of incorporation to give the location of the principal office or place of business of the corporation.

Incorporators. Incorporators are those persons who sign the articles of incorporation; on formation of the corporation they become shareholders and cease to be incorporators. The charter is issued by the state to the incorporators authorizing them to do business as a corporation. Most statutes provide for a minimum number of incorporators, usually three. Usually the statutes require the incorporators to be natural persons, and in many states a certain number of the incorporators must be either citizens or residents of the United States or of the state of incorporation. Inasmuch as incorporation is contractual in nature, the incorporators must have legal capacity to contract. In most states infants, however, cannot be incorporators. Married women may be incorporators. Unless a statute expressly authorizes a corporation to be an incorporator, the corporation is incapable; usually corporations are excluded. Often incorporators are dummies in the sense that they represent other people and, on incorporation, transfer their shares to others; in this way corporations can, in effect, create other corporations. The names and addresses of the incorporators must be stated in the articles of incorporation. A "closed corporation" exists when the shares of stock are held by a limited number of persons; and if such persons are members of the same family, there is a "family corporation."

Capitalization. In order to discuss capitalization, various terms should be defined. The Model Business Corporation Act,[1] section 2, provides:

(d) "Shares" means the units into which the proprietary interests in a corporation are divided.

(e) "Subscriber" means one who subscribes for shares in a corporation, whether before or after incorporation.

(f) "Shareholder" means one who is a holder of record of shares in a corporation.

---

[1] ABA—ALI Model Business Corporation Act, Revised (1966).

(j) "Stated capital"² means, at any particular time, the sum of (1) the par value of all shares of the corporation having a par value that have been issued, (2) the amount of the consideration received by the corporation for all shares of the corporation without par value that have been issued, except such part of the consideration therefor as may have been allocated to capital surplus in a manner permitted by law, and (3) such amounts not included in clauses (1) and (2) of this paragraph as have been transferred to stated capital of the corporation, whether upon the issue of shares as a share dividend or otherwise, minus all reductions from such sum as have been effected in a manner permitted by law.

Statutes require that the articles of incorporation state: the authorized total amount of the capital stock; the number of shares into which it is to be divided; the different classes of stock and the number of shares in each class; the relative rights and preferences of each class of stock; and the names and addresses of all the original subscribers to the capital stock, with the amounts subscribed indicated opposite each name.

Directors and Officers. In those states where a certain amount of organization is required as a condition precedent to incorporation, it is sometimes required that the names of the members of the first board of directors and the officers be stated. In those states where no such pre-incorporation organization is required, such names are not to be stated in the articles of incorporation.

Execution. Statutes require that the articles of incorporation be signed and sealed by the incorporators and, in some instances, that the original subscribers sign such articles. Although each signature is to be accompanied by a seal of the signatory, nevertheless, this requirement is usually deemed to be directory. Usually statutes require that such signatures be acknowledged before one authorized to administer oaths.

Filing and Recording. The articles of incorporation are to be filed in the office of a state official, usually the Secretary of State. If the articles are satisfactory, the Secretary files and records such articles and issues a certificate of incorporation together with an indorsement of approval on copies of the articles, called the charter. One copy of the charter is then filed in the county where the corporation's principal place of business is located, usually in the office of the county clerk. A fee for such filings is to be paid by the incorporators. The filing or recording of a corporate charter is not notice to third persons of the contents thereof but is made for convenient reference when desired.

---

² The term "stated capital" has, in general, the same meaning as the commonly used term "capital stock."

2. DEFECTIVE INCORPORATION

De Facto
Corporations
A corporation which has complied completely or substantially with all the mandatory statutory requirements for its creation is a *"de jure* corporation." It has been held that the omission of the incorporators to seal the articles of incorporation was unimportant and that substantial compliance with the statutory requirements had occurred. The status of a *de jure* corporation cannot be questioned by anyone.

However, frequently incorporators fail to comply, completely or substantially, with the mandatory statutory provisions. In such an event, the status of the incorporators may be either a *"de facto* corporation" or a partnership. Courts have attempted to avoid the harshness of exposing incorporators to liability as partners when they have honestly tried but failed to comply substantially with the mandatory statutory requirements of incorporation, and have created the *de facto* doctrine. Under this doctrine, an association of incorporators may be recognized as, in effect, having all the attributes, rights, and liabilities of a corporation, subject to the power of the state in a direct proceeding, called a "quo warranto" proceeding, to question the existence of the purported corporation and to enjoin its continuance as such. For all practical purposes, therefore, a *de facto* corporation has the same status in business as a *de jure* corporation, except for the right of the state to question its existence.[3] In order for a *de facto* corporation to exist four things are necessary:

1. A valid statute under which such association could have become a *de jure* corporation.
2. An honest attempt to comply with the statutory provisions concerning incorporation. The attempt must be an honest one, bona fide; an intent not to comply with the statute precludes the creation of a *de facto* corporation.
3. Colorable compliance with the statute. This does not mean that substantial compliance with the mandatory provisions is necessary; if this were so, the association would have become a *de jure* corporation. However, if compliance with a mandatory provision is absolutely essential to the creation of a corporation, noncompliance with such a provision does not create a *de jure* or a *de facto* corporation.
4. Corporate user. If the associates have not begun to carry on any corporate business, no harm will come to them if their status as a *de facto* corporation is denied. However, if they have used the corporate entity in carry-

---

[3] It should be noted that a *"de facto* officer" or a *"de facto* director" does not mean that he is an officer or a director of a *de facto* corporation. He is holding such office colorably as legally elected to it but, because of some irregularity, he has not been regularly so elected and, therefore, he is not a *de jure* officer or director.

ing on corporate business, harm will result and, accordingly, a *de facto* status is accorded to them. The extent of what is required for corporate user varies among the states. Generally, the courts do not require much evidence of corporate user, as long as some transactions or acts have occurred in the corporate name.

Application of Estoppel

When third persons innocently *deal* with an association as a corporation, the members of which innocently believe that they have a corporate status, in the absence of a statute to the contrary most courts hold that both the association and such third persons are estopped to deny the status of the association as a corporation for the purpose of that particular deal or transaction, regardless of whether or not the association is a *de facto* corporation. However, a person who knows that the association is not a corporation cannot estop the other party from denying that the association is a corporation, because there has been no material change of position in reasonable reliance upon the misrepresentation made to him and, accordingly, third persons or members of the association who know that no corporation exists cannot assert estoppel. (A, B, and C represent to D that they are a corporation and induce D to contract with them as a corporation. If A, B, and C, and also D, are unaware that there is no corporation *de jure* or *de facto,* all are estopped to deny that there is a corporation. If only D knew that there was no corporation, A, B, and C are not estopped to deny that there is a corporation; if only A, B, and C so knew, D is not estopped to deny that there is a corporation.) The application of the principle of estoppel does not make the association a corporation, although it is commonly called a "corporation by estoppel"; it precludes a denial of corporate status in the *particular transaction* which has occurred.

Liability of Members of an Association Not a De Jure Corporation

A *de facto* corporation has the status of a *de jure* corporation in the carrying-on of its business, and the members are liable only for their subscriptions for the purchase of corporate shares. When the association is not a *de facto* corporation and corporate estoppel is applicable, by the majority view the members of the association are not liable individually; only the association is liable as a corporation. However, if the third person is not estopped to deny the corporate status of the association—e.g., fraud perpetrated on the third person by members of an association holding out that they are a corporation—then the members of the association are liable as partners in most jurisdictions. Other courts hold either: that those members representing the association as a corporation are liable for damages for breach of implied warranty of authority, under the principles of the law of agency when there is no principal and no authority; or that those members actively participating in dealings with third persons as representatives of a corporation are individually liable, and that innocent passive members are not liable individually. When a statute expressly imposes personal liability on members of a defectively formed association holding itself out as a corporation, the principle of estoppel is inapplicable and the members are liable as provided by the statute.

3. CAPITALIZATION

In many states, perhaps a majority, it is not required that any minimum amount of capital be acquired either prior to incorporation or subsequent to incorporation but before doing business. A corporation is capitalized—i.e., financed—by the issuance of membership shares in the corporation[4] and by borrowing on the credit of the corporation and issuing bonds therefor. First the issuance of shares of stock and then the issuance of bonds will be considered.

Issuance of Shares A share of stock is intangible personal property consisting of a person's share or interest in the corporation and is owned by a "shareholder" or "stockholder." The share of stock is also a contract between the corporation and the shareholder. A certificate of stock is a writing issued by the corporation through its proper officer evidencing that the person named in such certificate is the registered owner of such shares. It contains: the name of the corporation; the state of incorporation; the name of the person to whom issued; the number and class of shares represented by the certificate; the par value of each share or a statement that the shares are without par value; and the signature of the corporation through its proper officers. Shares may be purchased for money, labor or services, or property actually received by the corporation. Such labor or services, or property, must have a fair value, although in the minority of states they must have a true value—i.e., a cash value equal to the value placed upon such labor or services or property.[5] The

---

[4] For the securities laws regulating the sale and transfer of corporate securities, see below, p. 674.

[5] For a discussion of the two tests of the value of services or property exchanged for shares, see below, p. 706.

corporation has a lien on those shares which have not been paid for fully.[6]

Kinds of Shares. Shares of stock may be classified basically as either common or preferred, or par value or no-par value. Common shares or common stock contain the ordinary rights of a shareholder to participate in the control of the corporation, in the surplus and profits, and in the distribution of corporate assets on dissolution. Below and on

Number		Shares
100		

Incorporated under the laws of the State of Illinois

——————— **Publishing Company**

This Certifies that,————————————————————————

is the owner of ——————————————————————— fully paid and non-assessable shares without par value of the Common Capital Stock of the ——————— Publishing Company, transferable on the books of the corporation in person or by duly authorized attorney upon surrender of this Certificate properly endorsed. A statement of the preferences, qualifications, limitations, restrictions and special or relative rights in respect of the shares as set forth in the corporation's Articles of Incorporation, appears on the reverse side of this Certificate.

IN WITNESS WHEREOF the said company has caused this Certificate to be signed by its duly authorized officers and its corporate seal to be hereunto affixed this ——————day of ————————————, A. D. 19———.

——————— PUBLISHING COMPANY

ATTEST: By————————————
                                                        President

——————————
Secretary

CERTIFICATE OF COMMON STOCK (*front*)

the next page is reproduced a certificate of common stock. Preferred stock is stock which has some preference over the common stock, such as: preference in the payment of dividends; a fixed cumulative or noncumulative dividend; or a preferential priority on distribution of corporate assets on dissolution. Par value stock has a certain minimum nominal price issue, such price or "par value" fixing the pro rata interest of the share in the corporation. The par value of a share does not reflect the true value of such share but furnishes the basis for the extent of contribution to, and participation in, the corporation. No-par stock has

——————

[6] See UCC 8–103, and below, p. 698.

STATEMENT OF PREFERENCES, QUALIFICATIONS, LIMITATIONS, RESTRICTIONS, AND SPECIAL OR RELATIVE RIGHTS OF THE COMMON SHARES OF THE CORPORATION AS SET FORTH IN ITS ARTICLES OF INCORPORATION.

The holders of the Common Shares will have no preemptive or other prior right to subscribe for any shares of the Company of any class or any securities of the Company of any kind convertible into shares of the Company of any class or any warrants or other instruments issued by the Company carrying the right to purchase shares of the Company of any class, which may be issued at any time hereafter and whether now or hereafter authorized.

For value received, _____ hereby sell, assign and transfer unto

_____

please print or typewrite name and address of assignee

_____

_____ Shares of the
Capital Stock represented by the within Certificate and do hereby irrevocably constitute and appoint _____
Attorney, to transfer the said stock on the books of the within-named Corporation, with full power of substitution in the premises.

DATED_____

In presence of:

_____

NOTICE: The signature to this assignment must correspond with the name as written upon the face of the certificate, in every particular, without alteration or enlargement, or any change whatever.

CERTIFICATE OF COMMON STOCK (*back*)

no nominal or par value indicated on the face of the certificate of such stock, and it may be issued for such consideration as is determined by the board of directors or the shareholders, as provided by statute or charter.

672 · C.P.A. LAW REVIEW

"Authorized shares" are those shares which the corporation is authorized to issue under its charter. Until the shares have been issued they are called "unissued shares"; once issued they are called "issued" or "outstanding" shares. The issued shares reacquired by a corporation are called "treasury stock."

Subscriptions. Persons may indicate their desire to purchase shares by subscribing for the purchase of such shares. They subscribe to the purchase of shares by indicating on a subscription list the number of shares each subscriber desires to purchase. A subscription agreement to purchase shares is to be distinguished from an underwriting agreement wherein a person, called an "underwriter," contracts that he will purchase the shares which he is unable to sell to the public. A subscription agreement is also distinguishable from a "stock warrant" which is not a share of stock but is an agreement on the part of the corporation to permit the holder of the stock warrant to subscribe to shares of stock. By the majority view a subscription agreement is not within the statute of frauds, unless the subscription agreement is not to be performed within a year from the making thereof, and may be in any form whatsoever. However, today by statute in some states subscription agreements are required to be in writing.

Preincorporation Subscriptions. Subscriptions may be made before incorporation, called "preincorporation subscriptions," or may be made after the corporation has been formed, called "postincorporation subscriptions." Preincorporation subscriptions are usually in the nature of continuing offers to purchase by subscribers and, being subject to the law of contracts, may be withdrawn or expire—e.g., by the subscriber's death—at any time before such subscription has been accepted by the corporation. Restrictions on withdrawal are imposed in some states and under the Model Business Corporation Act. By statute in many states, ". . . the persons who subscribe to the articles of incorporation automatically become shareholders upon incorporation."[7] Generally, express conditions in preincorporation subscriptions render the agreement void. In some states only the express condition is void and the remainder of the subscription agreement is valid. However, noncompliance with the offer contained in the subscription agreement, as by the formation of a different kind of corporation than that provided for in the subscription agreement, precludes enforcement of the subscriber's promise to purchase, inasmuch as his offer has never been accepted. Similarly, if the

---

[7] Robert S. Stevens, *Handbook on the Law of Private Corporations* (2d ed.; St. Paul: West Publishing Co., 1949), p. 384. See also Henry W. Ballantine, *Ballantine on Corporations* (rev. ed.; Chicago: Callaghan & Co., 1946), secs. 190, 190a. In some states the corporation is to act affirmatively to accept preincorporation subscription offers.

articles of incorporation which were made prior to the subscription were substantially changed subsequent to such subscription, the subscriber's offer cannot be enforced.

Postincorporation Subscriptions. A postincorporation subscription in response to a corporate offer to sell shares creates a contract immediately, making the subscriber a shareholder. However, infrequently the postincorporation subscription is not made in response to a corporate offer and is an offer to the corporation; a contract occurs only when the corporation subsequently accepts such subscription and, on such acceptance, the subscriber becomes a shareholder. Issuance of a certificate and payment for such shares are not conditions precedent[8] to the subscriber becoming a shareholder if a contract has been formed. A distinction is drawn at times between a subscription and a contract to purchase shares. Under a contract to purchase shares the purchaser does not become a shareholder until a certificate of stock has been issued to him. The problem is one of interpretation of the agreement to determine whether the intention of the parties was to subscribe or to purchase. Postincorporation subscriptions may have express conditions and, until such conditions are satisfied, the subscriber is under no liability if such conditions were conditions precedent. If the condition is a condition subsequent,[9] the subscriber becomes a shareholder when the contract is formed and has a right of action for damages against the corporation for breach of contract. Where there is doubt whether the conditional subscription contained a condition precedent or a condition subsequent, the subscription is construed as a condition subsequent.

Issuance of Bonds

The capitalization or financial structure of a corporation is dependent upon its issuance of bonds and debentures, as well as capital stock.[10] When a corporation borrows on its credit it usually executes two instruments, a bond and a mortgage. The bond, essentially, is the corporate promise to pay the indebtedness, and is secured by the mortgage. The mortgage is a lien on corporate property as security for performance of the bond. The mortgagee is a trustee holding the lien for the benefit of the bondholders, who are creditors. A "debenture" is an unsecured written corporate promise, often called a bond because, while it is not secured by any specific property, it is backed by the general credit of the corporation. A "convertible bond" is a bond with

---

[8] See above, p. 117.

[9] See above, p. 118.

[10] Corporate bonds are included under Article 8, Investment Securities, of the Code rather than under Commercial Paper.

the privilege of its conversion into shares of stock at the option of the bondholder. An "income bond" is a bond on which the interest is payable only if earned and out of such earnings and after the interest on prior mortgages has been paid during a specified period. A "collateral trust bond" is a bond which is secured by miscellaneous pledged securities (e.g., stocks, bonds) owned by the issuing corporation. A "participating bond," also called a "profit-sharing bond," is a bond with a fixed rate of interest and with the right to participate with shareholders in corporate earnings to the extent as provided in the bond. The interest on a participating bond is a fixed charge and must be paid irrespective of earnings, and it differs in this respect from the income bond.

Securities Laws   Laws have been enacted by the various states and by the federal government regulating the sale and transfer of securities, including corporate securities. State laws commonly are called "blue-sky laws," and the best-known federal laws are the Securities Act of 1933 and the Securities Exchange Act of 1934. The state laws are concerned with intrastate transactions and the federal laws are concerned with interstate transactions. The purpose of these state and federal laws is to prevent fraud on investors and purchasers by requiring full public disclosure of all information relating to the securities being offered or sold and by regulation of dealers and brokers engaged in the sale and marketing of securities. A registration statement containing certain specified information regarding the securities to be sold, together with a prospectus or circular containing information to be made available to purchasers and investors, is to be filed with the state commission or, in the case of the federal government, with the Securities and Exchange Commission. The Securities Exchange Act is concerned with the registration and regulation of national security exchanges and of brokers and dealers, and with other pertinent information. The necessity for federal regulation supplementing state regulation through federal jurisdiction over interstate commerce and the mails was emphasized by the financial collapse in the 1920's.[11]

4. PROMOTION

The Promoter   "Promoters" are persons who undertake, further, originate, and organize the formation of a corpora-

---

[11] See below, pp. 970–76, for excerpts from various federal statutes affecting an accountant's legal responsibility.

tion. They have a fiduciary duty to act on behalf of the corporation and of the incoming shareholders. The fiduciary duties of agents, in general, are applicable to promoters. Promoters organize corporations with the expectation of receiving promotion profits of some kind.

Preincorpora-tion Contracts Promoters may enter into preincorporation contracts of various kinds on behalf of the corporation. The promoter is a party to such contracts, inasmuch as the unborn corporation is incapable of being a party, and is liable on such contracts, unless the parties provide to the contrary. Illustrative contracts are employment contracts, brokerage contracts, and purchase options on property to be used by the corporation when it comes into existence. The principles of the law of contracts are applicable to these preincorporation contracts. If a preincorporation agreement contemplates perpetration of a fraud on the corporation when formed, the agreement is illegal and void. (P, promoter, agrees with V, vendor, that V is to sell certain property to the corporation and, on such sale, V is to pay P a commission or a part of the sales price without informing the corporation of such compensation to P. Such an agreement is void.) A promoter's contract with a third person may provide that, on the creation of the corporation, the corporation is to undertake the performance of the contract and, for corporate failure to do so, the promoter is to be discharged from any liability on such contract. As a party to a preincorporation contract, the promoter may enforce such contract against the other party thereto and, in turn, may be sued thereon by the other party, unless the contract provides to the contrary.

Theories of Corporate Liability. The creation of a corporation does not automatically make it a party to a preincorporation contract created by a promoter on its behalf, nor is the corporation liable for its performance. However, a corporation may become bound *by the terms* of a promoter's preincorporation contract, but there is much difference of judicial opinion as to how this result may be accomplished. Adoption, novation, continuing offer, and ratification are the theories utilized in order to accomplish this result. *Adoption* occurs when the corporation undertakes to perform the promoter's contract. Adoption does not discharge the promoter from any liability under the terms of the contract, and the corporation thereby does not become a party to the contract. If the promoter assigns the contract to the corporation, the promoter still is liable as a party to the contract and the corporation thereby does not become a party to it, although by assuming performance of the contract the corporation thereby becomes obligated to render such performance to the third person as a third party beneficiary of the contract between the promoter and the corporation. *Novation* is the method most frequently used in order to discharge the promoter from any liability under the preincorporation contract and, by the new contract, to substitute the corporation as a party to the same terms as those in the preincorporation contract. The *continuing offer* theory is that a preincorporation agreement, such as a subscription agreement, is a continuing offer to the corporation and, when accepted by the corporation, a contract is formed between such offerors and the corporation. A corporation cannot *ratify* a preincorporation contract because it was not in existence at the time the contract was made and had no legal capacity to make such a contract.[12]

In the absence of statutory provision to the contrary, a corporation is not liable for the expenses of its incorporation. Statutes in some states provide that corporations have a quasi-contractual obligation to pay for the reasonable value of such incorporation services. In most states, only an express corporate promise to pay for a promoter's organizational expense will be enforced.

Fraudulent Promotion

A promoter has a fiduciary duty to the corporation to be created to act solely on its behalf and for its benefit. A promoter who derives benefit by defrauding the corporation or by making secret profits can be compelled to disgorge such benefits and secret profits. Promoters often acquire property or options prior to incorporation which, subsequent to incorporation, are sold to the corporation at an inflated price, resulting in a profit to the promoter. Unless the promoter has made full disclosure of the material facts of such a transaction, he cannot retain the benefits and he may be compelled to deliver them to the corporation. Such property having been acquired by him as a promoter on behalf of the corporation, the promoter cannot profit therefrom without the consent of the corporation. If the promoter acquires property prior to his becoming a promoter, he may sell such property to the corporation without any duty of disclosure and he may make a fair and reasonable profit from such sale. For a promoter to retain the profits made from the sale of property to the corporation which he acquired while a promoter, he must do one of four things:

---

[12] For ratification in the law of agency, authority must have been previously possible; see above, p. 531.

1. Make full disclosure to an independent board of directors not under the control of the promoter. Should the board of directors approve of the transaction, then the contract is binding on the corporation and on the promoter, who may retain his profits.
2. Make full disclosure to all the original subscribers of corporate shares.
3. Make full disclosure to the existing shareholders at a shareholders' meeting and obtain ratification of the transaction by a majority vote at such meeting.
4. Subscribe to all of the shares involved in the corporate transaction. Inasmuch as the corporation really consists of the shareholders, if all the shareholders have knowledge of the transaction there is no secret profit and the promoter or promoters may retain such profits. Subsequent purchasers of the corporate stock purchase at their own risk; they have the burden of ascertaining the value of the property being purchased.

Chapter XI

OPERATION OF THE CORPORATION

---

1. *CORPORATE AUTHORITY*

Actual
Authority

Express Authority. CORPORATE authority is the lawful power of a corporation to affect its legal relations with third persons. A corporation is a creature of statute and derives its authority to exist and to act from statute. The corporate charter is the state's assent to the creation of the corporation and contains the authority to act pursuant to the corporate object indicated therein. Accordingly, all corporate authority derives from statute and from the charter. Corporate authority may be express or implied, the express authority being indicated in the charter and the statute, and the implied authority consisting of that reasonably required for carrying out the express authority. Corporate transactions made pursuant to corporate express or implied authority are binding on the corporation.

Implied Authority. A corporation has implied authority to do those acts which are reasonably incidental to the carrying on of the corporate business and to do that which is usual in similar corporations. A corporation has certain implied authority, in the absence of any statutory or charter provision or circumstances to the contrary, which will be discussed briefly.

Perpetual Succession. A corporation has implied authority to continue to do business during the period for which the corporation has been formed. If there is no fixed period, then the corporation has implied authority to continue for an indefinite period of time.

Corporate Name. A corporation has implied authority to sue and to be sued in the corporate name, and to acquire, hold, and transfer property in the corporate name.

Corporate Seal. Most states do not require a corporation to have a corporate seal; and, in the absence of statute to the contrary, a corporation has implied authority not to use a corporate seal, except when it is required of a natural person, in which case it may use or adopt any seal as its own for the purpose of the transaction.

Bylaws. A corporation has implied authority to enact bylaws for the implementation of its charter and the regulation of its corporate internal affairs. The power to make bylaws rests primarily in the shareholders, unless delegated to the directors by statute or charter.

Property. A corporation has implied authority to acquire, hold, and dispose of real or personal property reasonably incidental to carrying on the corporate business. It has implied authority to sell its property to satisfy, and to mortgage or pledge its property as security for, corporate obligations.

Stock. In most states corporations have implied authority to reacquire their own corporate stock, unless such reacquisition would be unfair to shareholders or to corporate creditors. By statute in most states corporations are permitted to acquire stock in other corporations provided it is incidental to carrying on the corporate business and, in many of these states, the acquired stock must be in corporations with objects similar to that of the acquiring corporation. In those states which do not have such statutory permission, most of them do not imply any corporate authority to acquire stock in other corporations unless such stock was acquired incidentally. An illustration of the latter is where a corporation takes the corporate stock of another corporation as security for debts due to the corporation, and, on default, the corporation thereby acquires such stock.

Make Contracts. A corporation has implied authority to make contracts in order to carry out its express and implied authority.

Borrow Money. A corporation has implied authority to borrow on the credit of the corporation if it is reasonably incidental to carrying on the corporate business.

Negotiable Instruments. A corporation, especially a trading corporation, has implied authority to issue and indorse negotiable instruments when it is *reasonably incidental* to carrying on the corporate business. If a corporation issues a negotiable instrument but such an instrument is not issued for a corporate purpose, the corporation is not bound by the issuance of such an instrument unless the instrument is held by a "holder in due course,"[1] who is in effect a bona fide purchaser for value without notice; the corporation is bound to the holder in due course and to holders who properly claim through him.[2] A corporation does not have implied authority to act as an accommodation indorser on a negotiable instrument for a noncorporate purpose but, inasmuch as the corporation has implied authority to indorse negotiable instruments for

---

[1] See UCC 3–302, and above, p. 410.

[2] See above, pp. 419, 425.

a corporate purpose, the corporation is bound on such an instrument only to a holder in due course and to holders who properly claim through him. The corporation is not bound to a third person who knew that the corporation had acted in excess of its implied authority at the time such instrument was negotiated to him.

Bonds. Inasmuch as a corporation has implied authority to borrow on corporate credit and to pay corporate debts, it has implied authority to issue bonds, which are promises to pay the debt incurred.

Suretyship and Guaranty. A corporation has no implied authority to act as a surety or guarantor unless it is reasonably incidental to the corporate business.

Partnership. Unless the statute or charter expressly permits, a corporation has no power and no implied or apparent authority to become a member of a partnership. The fixing of policy and the management of the corporation by the board of directors would be subject to interference by the other members of the partnership and, in this way, the board of directors and shareholders could lose control over the corporation. For this reason there is no such implied authority. Further, the liability of shareholders is limited to the purchase price of their shares. Today, in a majority of states a corporation may be a partner.

Charitable Contributions. A corporation has no implied authority to make contributions to charity; however, there is a tendency on the part of the courts to countenance the expenditure of corporate funds when such expenditures are incidental to employee betterment, as for the erection of hospitals or lodging for employees.

Ultra Vires   The acts of a corporation within the scope of its authority are called *intra vires* acts; if the acts are outside the scope of the corporate authority, they are called *ultra vires* acts. A corporation is bound by *intra vires* acts, but there is conflict regarding the liability of a corporation for *ultra vires* acts. The courts will not enforce an executory *ultra vires* contract and will not interfere in an *ultra vires* executed contract but will leave the parties as it finds them. A majority of the courts will enforce an *ultra vires* contract which has been partially executed—i.e., it has been executed on one side but not on the other—in an action brought by the party who has fully performed his side of the contract. (C corporation makes an *ultra vires* contract with A to supply A with iron rails. C supplied the iron rails to A and A refused to pay the contract price. C may enforce the contract against A.) The reason for the enforcement of partially executed *ultra vires* contracts is that injustice otherwise would result. Shareholders may enjoin the threatened commission of an *ultra vires* act, and creditors may object on the ground that their security is being jeopardized.

Just as *ultra vires* is no defense to an action on a contract which has been partially executed by the plaintiff, so *ultra vires* is no defense and a corporation is liable for damage caused by torts committed during the authorized performance of an *ultra vires* corporate transaction. (C corporation without authority hired a truck to engage in the trucking business. While the truck was being driven in performance of an *ultra vires* corporate transaction, the driver negligently injured a pedestrian. The corporation is liable to the pedestrian for the tort of its driver during the performance of the *ultra vires* transaction.) Any other result would be obviously unjust.

2. *CORPORATE MANAGEMENT*

A corporation is an association of shareholders with a legal interest in the corporation and it operates on behalf of all of such shareholders. A corporation is a juridical person and can act only through its agents. The shareholders have the right, at a legal shareholders' meeting, to elect directors to the board of directors. The board of directors establishes corporate policy and manages the corporation. Although the shareholders are the owners of the corporation, nevertheless, they may not participate directly in the establishment of corporate policy and in managing the corporation. Shareholders have indirect control by their right to elect directors and to ratify voidable corporate transactions. Shareholders may act only at legal corporate meetings.

Corporate Meetings

The action taken by shareholders at corporate meetings is binding on the corporation. Such meetings must be legal in the sense that they have been properly held; otherwise action taken at such meetings is of no effect.

Time. The time when regular meetings, and the occasion when special meetings, are to occur are fixed by statute, charter, or bylaws. Notice of regular meetings usually is not required. However, notice usually is required for special meetings. The charter or bylaws usually contain special provisions regarding the number of shareholders or the percentage of the voting power which is necessary to require a special meeting. Notice of such special meeting must indicate the date, time, place, and nature of the business to be transacted, and must be given within a reasonable period of time prior to such meeting.

Place. In the absence of statute to the contrary, the corporate meetings must be held within the state of incorporation. The exact place of the meeting either is specified in the charter or bylaws, or is left to the discretion of the board of directors.

Quorum. A quorum is that number of persons required to be present at a meeting in order to transact business. A quorum of the shareholders is necessary in order to have a corporate meeting. At Common Law and in the absence of statute to the contrary, any number of shareholders, not less than two, who appear at the meeting constitute a quorum. Today, by statute, charter, or bylaws, a quorum is determined by specific provision, often by a percentage of the voting power or a specific number of the holders of corporate shares. Once a quorum is present and a corporate meeting begun, the meeting can continue and transact corporate business even though less than a quorum is present because some of the shareholders have left the meeting.

Voting. Only those shareholders registered on the corporate books as of the date when such books were closed in anticipation of the corporate meeting have the right to vote at such meeting. A shareholder who has pledged his shares has the right to vote, in the absence of agreement to the contrary. Shares held by the issuing corporation—e.g., treasury shares—have no voting rights and are not counted as part of the voting power. At Common Law a shareholder had to appear personally in order to vote. Today, by statute, charter, or bylaws, shareholders have the right to authorize other persons to vote for them and in their stead. Such authorization is called a "proxy," which is in the form of an informal writing. A proxy can be given only by the legal owner of corporate shares. A proxy is revocable, regardless of the terms therein, unless coupled with an interest in the share. Revocation may be express or implied; the transfer of shares implies revocation of the proxy. The word "proxy" is used also to describe the person who has written authority to vote for a shareholder.

Unless there is charter or statutory provision to the contrary, each share has one vote. Statutes in most states permit cumulative voting solely in connection with the election of the directors. The charter or bylaws may permit cumulative voting. The purpose of cumulative voting is to enable minority shareholders to obtain representation on the board of directors. Under the cumulative voting method, a shareholder has a number of votes equal to the number of directors to be elected, multiplied by the number of shares which he has, which he may distribute among the candidates as he wishes. For example, if four directors are to be elected and a shareholder has one hundred shares, he has four hundred votes, which he may distribute among the candidates as he wishes; he may cast all the votes for one candidate. (Three directors are to be elected. A has 90 shares and B has 40 shares. By ordinary voting, A would elect all three directors by casting 90 votes for each of his three nominees. B would be unable to elect any director because his 40 votes for his nominee would be insufficient. By cumulative voting, A would have 270 votes which he would use by casting 90 for each of his three nominees. B would have 120 votes and would cast them all for his nominee. A would elect two directors and B would elect one director.) In some states, cumulative voting is mandatory by law.

Voting Trusts. A shareholder may participate in a voting trust without any requirement of corporate authority. A voting trust is created by the transfer of shares by shareholders to a trustee or trustees for the purpose of voting all such shares in a block and thereby retaining control of corporate management. The title to the corporate shares is transferred to trustees, who then have the right to vote such shares at corporate meetings and who hold such shares in trust for the members of the voting trust. The trustees issue to such members voting trust certificates which are transferable in the same manner as certificates of stock. Voting trusts are valid in the majority of states provided they are not contrary to statute or public policy. If the purpose of the voting trust is to avoid the anti-trust laws, or to perpetrate a fraud on the minority shareholders, or is for an unreasonable length of time, the voting trust is void.

Majority Rule. In the absence of statute, charter, or bylaws to the contrary, a majority of the shares voting at a legal corporate meeting is the will of the meeting, if the transactions are within the scope of the corporate business. The majority cannot make fundamental changes in the corporate business, such as a change in the capital stock, the nature of the corporate business, or the charter. Fundamental changes in the corporate structure require the unanimous consent of all the shareholders, unless statute, charter, or bylaws provide to the contrary. Usually it is provided that a specified large percentage of the holders of shares of corporate stock is required for fundamental changes. The majority may not exploit the corporation or oppress the minority shareholders. The majority may not, over the opposition of the minority, carry out *ultra vires* transactions.

Board of Directors All corporate authority to act on behalf of a corporation is centered in the corporate board of directors. The board of directors is the agent of the corporation. The authority of the board of directors is derived from statute, charter, and bylaws. The acts of the board of directors within the scope of its corporate authority are binding on the corporation. The board of directors has the primary function of establishing corporate policy and managing the corporation. The board of directors does not have the authority to make fundamental changes in the corporate structure without the consent of the shareholders—e.g., dissolve the corporation, amend the charter, increase or decrease capital stock, sell the corporate assets, merge or consolidate the corporation with other corporations.

Eligibility. The number, qualifications, term of office, and method of election of directors are governed by statute, charter, and bylaws. In the absence of any provision to the contrary, anyone, including infants and persons who are not shareholders, may become directors.

Duty and Standard of Care. The board of directors is a fiduciary with the duty to act on behalf of the corporation, and also, by the minority but preferred view, on behalf of the shareholders. Directors have a duty to exercise "that degree of care and diligence which an ordinary prudent director reasonably could be expected to exercise in a like position under similar circumstances."[3] A director is not liable for honest errors of judgment in the exercise of his discretion on behalf of the corporation. As a fiduciary, a director must make full disclosure of all material facts regarding any transaction made between himself and the corporation for his own benefit.

Meetings. The directors may act only as a board at a legal meeting. Usually notice of a regular meeting is not required to be given, but notice of a special meeting must be given unless it is impossible or impracticable or otherwise useless to give such notice. Failure to give proper notice causes the meeting to be illegal, and business transacted at such a meeting is not the act of the board of directors. A majority of the board of directors constitutes a quorum, in the absence of statute, charter, or bylaws to the contrary. A vacancy on the board is counted in determining the existence of a quorum. A majority vote of the quorum is the will of the board. Meetings of the board of directors may be held within or outside of the state of incorporation, in the absence of statute, charter, or bylaw to the contrary.

Dealings between Director and Corporation. A director who has a personal interest in the action to be taken by the board of directors should not participate in a vote on the matter because of the conflict of

---

[3] Henry W. Ballantine, *Ballantine on Corporations* (rev. ed.; Chicago: Callaghan & Co. 1946), sec. 63. *Cf.* the duty of care required of a trustee under an express trust; see below, pp. 954 ff. Also *cf.* the duty of care required of a corporate director with that required of a trustee, below, p. 954.

his fiduciary duty to the corporation and his own self-interest. If his presence is necessary for a quorum of the board, or if his vote is necessary in order to pass a resolution regarding the transaction, his participation makes the action taken voidable at the election of the corporation. By the majority view, although a director with a personal interest is disqualified from participating in any action by the board regarding the particular transaction in which he is interested, nevertheless, if his presence was not necessary to constitute a quorum and his vote was not necessary for passage of the resolution, the action taken by the board is valid. A director dealing with the corporation on his own behalf has a fiduciary duty to make full disclosure of all material facts pertinent to the transaction, and his failure to do so renders the transaction voidable at the election of the corporation. Action taken at an improperly held meeting of the board of directors may be ratified subsequently by a proper meeting of the board. The shareholders at a corporate meeting also may ratify improper action by the board of directors if such action was within the authority of the board but was not exercised properly.

Compensation. A director is not entitled to compensation for his services rendered to the corporation as a director in the absence of any provision in the charter or bylaws to the contrary or in the absence of a contract for such services. The shareholders at a corporate meeting, or the board of directors if specifically authorized, may pass a resolution awarding compensation for such services. Should a director perform special services either outside of the ordinary services to be rendered as a director or as an officer of the corporation, a corporate promise is implied by law to pay for the reasonable value of such services. An officer who is also a director may receive a salary for his services as an officer, but may not receive any for his ordinary services as a director. The compensation of corporate officers is fixed by the board of directors.

Delegation. The board of directors has implied, if not express, authority to delegate to others some of its authority and discretion to manage and carry on the corporate business. Such authority is delegated to officers of the corporation who are elected by the board of directors. While the board of directors may delegate much of its authority, it may not delegate the authority to supervise and control the operation and management of the corporation. It is for this reason that a director may not vote by proxy at a meeting of the board of directors because he has no express or implied authority to delegate his special skill, judgment, and discretion, which he has a duty to exercise at a meeting of the board. The board of directors is the fountainhead of corporate authority, and it may delegate such authority not only to corporate officers but also to committees of directors, in order to accomplish some of the many duties of the board. As long as the board of directors retains the right to supervise and control all activities, whether on the part of its committees or by corporate officers, the board has not exceeded its express or implied authority so to delegate its authority.

Corporate Officers

Corporate bylaws usually provide expressly for the number of corporate officers to be appointed by the board of directors, their qualifications and terms of office, and their duties. Corporate officers usually consist of a president, one or more vice-presidents, a secretary, a treasurer, and a cashier if the corporation is a bank. The authority of corporate officers is limited to that given to it by the board of directors and by the charter and bylaws. Their function is to operate the corporate business within the scope of their authority. Corporate officers are agents of the corporation, and the principles of the law of agency are applicable to their actions. As fiduciaries, corporate officers have the duty to act on behalf of the corporation. Corporate officers have the duty to exercise the diligence and care which a reasonable, prudent person in their position would exercise under the circumstances. They are not liable for honest errors of judgment in the exercise of their discretion. Their compensation usually is determined by the board of directors at a directors' meeting, although the bylaws may fix their compensation.

Corporate Torts and Crimes

A corporation is liable, just like any other principal, for damage caused by the torts of its agents while acting within the scope of their authority. The corporation is liable for such torts even though they were committed during the course of an *ultra vires* transaction, so long as the agent was acting within the scope of the authority accorded to him. Similarly, criminal responsibility may be imputed to a corporation for the crime committed by its agents while acting within the scope of the authority given to them. Whether the corporation may be guilty of a criminal offense depends upon the expressed intention of the legislature in the state statutes. Corporations do not come within the purview of criminal statutes which provide punishments which are inapplicable to corporations, such as imprisonment, or which prescribe elements of the crime which are inapplicable to corporations, such as murder which involves the killing of one human being by another human being. Generally, criminal statutes apply to corporations as well as to natural persons, unless the statute expressly or impliedly excludes corporations. Inasmuch as injunctions may be issued against corporations, it follows that corporations may be punished for civil or criminal contempt of court, as that is the only way that the injunctions may be enforced.

Chapter XII

SHAREHOLDERS' RIGHTS AND LIABILITIES

---

1. SHAREHOLDERS' RIGHTS

OWNERS of shares have various rights as shareholders in the corporation. Among these rights are the following: the right to vote at corporate meetings; the right to share in the profits of the corporation; preemptive rights; the right to share in the surplus (i.e., net corporate assets) on dissolution of the corporation; the right to inspect corporate books; rights in connection with certificates of stock and transfer of stock; and the right legally to enjoin improper corporate action. These rights will be examined briefly in turn.

Right to Vote A shareholder has the right to attend corporate meetings and to vote at such meetings, unless his shares are nonvoting shares. Only the shareholders, and not the board of directors, may vote at corporate meetings on proposed fundamental changes in the corporate structure. The right to vote is a source of great protection to shareholders and gives to such shareholders a limited degree of control over the corporation.

Right to Dividends Shareholders have the right to participate in corporate profits in the form of dividends in the proportion that their holdings bear to the number of shares outstanding which are also entitled so to participate. The corporate profits or surplus set aside for, or distributed to, shareholders by a corporation pursuant to a declaration of its board of directors is called a "dividend." Dividends may be in the form of cash, stock dividend, or other property—e.g., securities of other corporations, personal or real property, scrip. One of the usual preferences of preferred stock is priority in dividends. Preferred stock may be cumulative in that a certain amount of dividends is to be paid each year and to accumulate over the years, with priority over dividends to be paid to holders of common stock; and it may be noncumulative so that the holders of preferred stock are entitled only to a priority of dividends declared each year. Dividends on preferred shares are impliedly cumulative. Preferred stock also may be participating or nonparticipating. Participating preferred stock is that stock which is entitled to participate along with the common stock in any surplus available for dividends remaining after dividends have been paid on the preferred stock. Nonparticipating preferred stock is that stock which cannot so participate in such surplus.

Declaration of Dividends and Effect. Dividends are distributed only within the discretion of the board of directors. A dividend is declared when the board of directors has passed a resolution approving of a dividend and such dividend has been announced. The shareholders become general creditors of the corporation and, should the corporation subsequently become insolvent prior to distribution of dividends, the shareholders would be general creditors of the corporation to the extent of the dividends due them. It is not necessary that funds be set aside in order to make the dividend effective. However, once funds have been set aside for the purpose of paying such dividends, such funds represent a trust fund in favor of the shareholders, and corporate creditors cannot proceed against such funds.

Whether or not a declaration of dividends is revocable by the corporation, through its board of directors, depends upon the nature of the dividend. If it is a cash dividend, it is irrevocable because a debtor-creditor relationship has been created between the corporation and the shareholders, with exceptions. The *ultra vires* declaration of an illegal cash dividend is revocable, as when there is no corporate surplus from which a dividend could be paid. The declaration of an interim dividend, which is a payment on account of the next forthcoming dividend, may be revoked at any time before it becomes payable where adverse change in corporate circumstances makes it advisable to do so. Where a resolution has been passed approving of a dividend and it has not been made public or communicated to the shareholders and no fund therefor has been set aside, the resolution may be rescinded. The declaration of a stock dividend does not create a debtor-creditor relationship, and, accordingly, it is revocable at any time prior to issuance of such stock. The declaration of a dividend payable in scrip certificates, which are convertible into cash, stock, or interest-bearing obligations, may be revoked before the scrip is issued if adverse change in corporate circumstances makes it advisable to do so, even though enough surplus remains to satisfy the dividend.

Equitable Relief. Courts are very reluctant to interfere in the internal management of the corporation or to interfere with the discretion of the board of directors. However, if the board of directors has abused its discretion in not declaring dividends when it should have done so, the shareholders may obtain a court decree compelling the corporation through the board of directors to declare and distribute dividends. It is not an abuse of discretion to set aside reasonable funds for reasonable corporate expansion and for adequate safety margins. Courts will not compel a corporation to borrow money in order to pay dividends.

Effective Date. A proper declaration of dividends is irrevocable, and the dividends belong to the holders of the shares at the time such dividend is effective. A dividend may be declared on one day, effective on another day, and payable on still another day. However, a corporation ignorant of a transfer of shares prior to the effective date is protected if it distributes dividends to the owner of the shares who is registered on the books of the corporation on the effective date. Dividends are payable to a pledgee of shares of stock, if the pledgee is registered on the corporate books or the corporation otherwise has notice of such pledge, and such dividend is to be applied by the pledgee in reduction of the pledgor's debt, in the absence of pledge agreement to the contrary.

Source of Dividends. In almost all states cash and property dividends can be payable only out of surplus, often called "net profits," and are not payable out of capital because the return of capital to shareholders would prejudice corporate creditors. Excess of net assets over net liabilities including capital stock is surplus, which may be either earned surplus or capital surplus—e.g., paid-in surplus consisting of the consideration paid for par value shares in excess of such par value or of that portion of the amount received as consideration for no-par value shares not allocated to capital stock. However, unrealized appreciation of the value of fixed assets is not, and realized appreciation thereof is, surplus available for distribution as cash dividends in almost all states. In some states a stock dividend may be declared out of a surplus from such unrealized appreciation, because no assets are being withdrawn from the corporation and creditors are not prejudiced. The illegal distribution of dividends out of capital is recoverable by the corporation, except as against shareholders innocent of the illegality who may retain the dividends received by them. If the corporation is insolvent at the time of such illegal distribution, even innocent shareholders must return the dividends received by them. The directors who voted the illegal dividend are liable personally to the corporation therefor.

Pre-emptive Rights   At Common Law a shareholder had the right to subscribe to an increase in the capital stock of the corporation to the proportionate extent of his holdings in the corporation. This right is called a "pre-emptive right" and exists today in the absence of statute, charter, or bylaw to the contrary. This right exists only in connection with a *newly authorized* issue of stock, and it does not apply to the corporate sale of shares previously issued and reacquired by the corporation (treasury stock) or to unissued shares from an existing authorized issue. The purpose of this right is to permit shareholders to retain their relative interest in the corporation.

Rights on Dissolution Each shareholder has the right, on corporate dissolution, to receive his proportionate share of corporate assets remaining after corporate obligations have been satisfied. Usually the remaining assets are liquidated and distribution is made in money. Distribution may also be made in securities or in kind. If the corporation is in reorganization proceedings, whether under the Bankruptcy Act or not, the expense of a sale may not be necessary in order to determine the value of the corporate property and the value of the shares owned by dissenting shareholders.

Inspection of Corporate Books Shareholders are the owners of the corporation and have a right to be informed regarding the corporate business. Shareholders, and their representatives, have the right to examine the corporate books and to make copies thereof provided it is exercised at reasonable times, at the proper place, and for a proper purpose. Similarly, shareholders have the right to request and receive corporate information from officers and directors of the corporation, especially in connection with dealings between shareholders and such officers, directors, or the corporation.

A corporation should keep essential corporate books and records, whether or not required by statute. Such books and records are:

1. Charter.
2. Bylaws.
3. Minute books of the meetings of the board of directors and of the shareholders.
4. Subscription book.
5. Subscribers ledger.
6. Stock certificate book.
7. Stockholders ledger.

Corporate books and records are admissible in evidence if it is shown that they have been kept in the regular course of business and are properly authenticated. They represent prima facie evidence of their contents and the corporate transactions contained therein. For the admission of such records into evidence the following steps must be taken:

(1) identification of the records by their custodian; (2) proof that the entries were made in the regular course of business; (3) proof that the entries were made at or near the time the transactions occurred; (4) proof that the entrant had personal knowledge of the facts recorded, or the data were furnished to him by those who had personal knowledge; (5) testimony regarding the entries must be given by the entrant, or, if he be dead, outside the state, or unavailable, then the official custodian must testify that such entries were made in the regular course of business.

Transfer of Shares

In General. *Certificate of Stock under the Code.* Article 8 of the Uniform Commercial Code governs the transfer of investment securities, called "security" for short under the Code. A security includes certificates of stock, stock warrants, bonds, and anything which securities markets are likely to regard as suitable for trading.[1] Money is not included in the term security. A security, and therefore *a certificate of stock, is an instrument of a negotiable character,*[2] and a "bona fide purchaser" of a security will acquire more rights under the security than would a mere "purchaser" of a security, a transferee of a chattel, or an assignee of a contract right. A purchaser is a person who takes by purchase, which "includes taking by sale, discount, negotiation, mortgage, pledge, lien, issue or re-issue, gift or any other voluntary transaction creating an interest in property."[3] *A bona fide purchaser "is a purchaser for value in good faith and without notice of any adverse claim who takes delivery of a security in bearer form or of one in registered form issued to him or indorsed to him or in blank."*[4] A certificate of stock "is in 'bearer form' when it runs to bearer according to its terms and not by reason of any indorsement."[5] A certificate of stock is in "registered form" when it runs to a person named therein.

Statute of Frauds. A contract for the sale of a certificate of stock and the shares represented thereby, irrespective of the price, is within the statute of frauds and is unenforceable unless proved in any *one* of

---

[1] UCC 8-102, *Comment.* "The validity of a security and the rights and duties of the issuer with respect to registration of transfer are governed by the law (including the conflict of laws rules) of the jurisdiction of organization of the issuer." UCC 8-106.

[2] A security is even called a "negotiable instrument" under this portion of the Code, although a security as a particular kind of negotiable instrument is governed only by Article 8, and not by Article 3, which is concerned with Commercial Paper—negotiable instruments payable in money.

[3] UCC 1-201(32),(33).

[4] UCC 8-302. (Author's italics)

[5] UCC 8-102(1)(d).

five ways. To the extent possible, the statute of frauds provisions under Article 8 are similar to the statute of frauds provisions under the Sales portion of the Code. Reference should be made to the full discussion there[6] in amplification of the requirements of the statute of frauds provisions discussed briefly here under Article 8. The *first* way is a *writing* indicating that (1) a contract had been made for the sale (2) of a stated number of shares of a particular stock (3) at a defined or stated price, and the writing has been *signed* by the party against whom enforcement of the contract is sought or by his authorized agent or broker. *Second, delivery* of a certificate of stock has been made and accepted, but the contract is enforceable only to the extent of the certificate so delivered. *Third,* a *payment* has been made, but the contract is enforceable only to the extent of such payment. *Fourth,* within a reasonable time after the contract was made, a *written confirmation* of the contract made by one of the parties to the contract, sufficient against the sender under "First" above, was received by the other party, who then failed to send a written objection to its contents within 10 days after his receipt. The recipient has a duty to manifest his objection to the sender's timely erroneous confirmation, and his failure to do so soon is an admission that the confirmation is correct and he thereby makes it a written manifestation of his own. *Fifth,* the party against whom enforcement is sought *admits* in his pleading, testimony or otherwise in court that a contract was made for sale for a stated number of shares of a particular stock at a defined or stated price.

Restrictions on Transfer. An issuing corporation may, and usually does, require that the transfer of shares be recorded on the corporate books in order that the corporation may treat the registered owner as the owner of such shares for the purpose of dividends, voting at corporate meetings, and as liable for calls and assessments on the shares. However, the corporation cannot require such registration as a condition precedent to the transfer of title to the certificate of stock or to the shares represented thereby. Any lawful corporate restriction on the transfer of a certificate or the shares represented thereby must be *noted conspicuously*[7] *on the certificate* in order to be effective notice as to everyone except a person with actual knowledge of it, who obviously does not require such additional notice. The corporate bylaws or the contract for sale of such shares may provide that the corporation or other shareholders shall have a pre-emptive or prior right to the pur-

---

[6] See above, pp. 255–260.

[7] For conspicuously, see above, p. 391, ftn. 33.

chase of corporate shares; this is a reasonable and permissible restriction on the transfer of such shares, provided it is noted conspicuously on the certificate. The requirement of conspicuous notation is to provide notice of the restriction, and this can be accomplished without the notation stating the full text of the restriction. It should be noted that the Code law on restrictions deals only with restrictions imposed by the corporation issuing the stock certificate. It does not alter prevailing case law recognizing the freedom to transfer stock as an inherent right in stock ownership; it does not affect restrictions imposed by statute; nor does it deal with private agreements among shareholders containing restrictive covenants as to the sale of the certificate and the shares represented thereby.[8]

Method of Transfer. A certificate of stock and the shares represented thereby can be transferred only when two things occur. *First,* if the certificate is in registered form or has been specially indorsed, the "appropriate person's" indorsement, either special or in blank, must be made on the certificate or on a separate document. *Secondly,* the certificate so indorsed, or the certificate and the separate document with the indorsement, must be delivered. First indorsement and then delivery will be discussed.

Indorsement. An indorsement is a person's signature made alone or with other words on the issued certificate of stock or on a separate document. The indorsement may be complete or partial and is effective to the extent of the indorsement. If the certificate of stock is in registered form, an indorsement of the certificate is made when an appropriate person signs on it or on a separate document an assignment or transfer of the certificate or the shares represented thereby or a power so to assign or transfer, or when the signature of such person is written without more upon the back of the certificate. If the certificate is in bearer form, no indorsement is required, but if the certificate is indorsed the indorsement does not otherwise affect any right to registration which the holder may possess. An indorsement may be in blank or special. An indorsement in blank consists only of the signature of the person signing; it includes an indorsement to bearer. A special indorsement specifies the person to whom the certificate is to be transferred, or who has power to transfer it ("to John Smith. [signed] Frank Fay"). A holder[9] may convert a blank indorsement into a special indorsement, as

---

[8] UCC 8–204, *Comments 3, 4.*

[9] UCC 1–201(20): " 'Holder' means a person who is in possession of a document of title or an instrument or an investment security drawn, issued or indorsed to him or to his order or to bearer or in blank."

by the insertion of the name of a person above the blank indorsement. The indorsement must be made by an "appropriate person," who is:

(a) the person specified by the security or by special indorsement to be entitled to the security; or

(b) where the person so specified is described as a fiduciary but is no longer serving in the described capacity,—either that person or his successor; or

(c) where the security or indorsement so specifies more than one person as fiduciaries and one or more are no longer serving in the described capacity,—the remaining fiduciary or fiduciaries, whether or not a successor has been appointed or qualified; or

(d) where the person so specified is an individual and is without capacity to act by virtue of death, incompetence, infancy or otherwise,—his executor, administrator, guardian or like fiduciary; or

(e) where the security or indorsement so specifies more than one person as tenants by the entirety or with right of survivorship and by reason of death all cannot sign,—the survivor or survivors; or

(f) a person having power to sign under applicable law or controlling instrument; or

(g) to the extent that any of the foregoing persons may act through an agent,—his authorized agent.[10]

The purchaser of a certificate of stock has a specifically enforceable right to have any necessary indorsement supplied. Unless otherwise agreed, the transferor of the certificate must, on due demand, supply his purchaser "with any proof of his authority to transfer or with any other requisite which may be necessary to obtain registration of the transfer of the security but if the transfer is not for value a transferor need not do so unless the purchaser furnishes the necessary expenses. Failure to comply with a demand made within a reasonable time gives the purchaser the right to reject or rescind the transfer."[11] Each signature in a necessary indorsement is presumed genuine (i.e., free of forgery or counterfeiting) or authorized, but if the effectiveness of a signature is put in issue, then the burden of establishing it is on the party claiming under the signature. When an indorsement is admitted or established, production of the certificate entitles the holder to recover on it unless the defendant establishes a defense or a defect going to the validity of the certificate, in which event the plaintiff has the burden of establishing that he or some person under whom he claims is a person against whom the defense or defect is ineffective.[12] It should be noted very carefully that "Failure of a fiduciary to comply with a controlling

---

[10] UCC 8–308(3).

[11] UCC 8–316.

[12] UCC 8–105.

instrument or with the law of the state having jurisdiction of the fiduciary relationship, including any law requiring the fiduciary to obtain court approval of the transfer, does not render his indorsement unauthorized for the purposes of this Article."[13] When an indorsement is unauthorized,[14] unless the owner has ratified the unauthorized indorsement or is otherwise precluded from asserting its ineffectiveness:

(a) he may assert its ineffectiveness against the issuer or any purchaser other than a purchaser for value and without notice of adverse claims who has in good faith received a new, reissued or re-registered security on registration of transfer;[15] and

(b) an issuer who registers the transfer of a security upon the unauthorized indorsement is subject to liability for improper registration (Section 8–404).[16]

(T steals O's certificate of stock issued by C in registered form in O's name, forges O's blank indorsement on the certificate, and sells and delivers it to P, a purchaser for value in good faith without notice of O's adverse claim. O can reclaim the certificate from P. However, if P had delivered the certificate to C in exchange for a new certificate on registration of transfer, O could not reclaim the new certificate and would have only a right to damages against C.) Unless otherwise agreed, the indorser by his indorsement assumes no obligation that the certificate will be honored by the issuing corporation.

Delivery. If a sale of a certificate of stock and the shares represented thereby is made other than through brokers,[17] then, unless otherwise agreed, the transferor of a certificate under a contract for sale has a duty to deliver the certificate by placing it, in a form to be negotiated by the purchaser, in the possession of the purchaser or of a person designated by him or, at the purchaser's request, by causing an acknowledgment to be made to the purchaser that it is held for him.[18] Delivery to a purchaser occurs when:

---

[13] UCC 8–308(7).

[14] UCC 1–201(43): "'Unauthorized' signature or indorsement means one made without actual, implied or apparent authority and includes a forgery." Unless a required indorsement is valid, a purchaser is not a bona fide purchaser. See above, p. 692.

[15] UCC 8–311, *Comment 1:* "Since the bulk of present day security purchases is made through brokers, the purchaser who normally receives and sees only a certificate registered in his own name cannot realistically be held to have notice of or to have relied upon a forged or unauthorized indorsement on the original security transferred. A bona fide purchaser holding a new, reissued or re-registered certificate is therefore protected."

[16] UCC 8–311.

[17] For delivery in a sale through brokers, see UCC 8–314(1).

[18] UCC 8–314(2).

(a) he or a person designated by him acquires possession of a security; or

(b) his broker acquires possession of a security specially indorsed to or issued in the name of the purchaser; or

(c) his broker sends him confirmation of the purchase and also by book entry or otherwise identifies a specific security in the broker's possession as belonging to the purchaser; or

(d) with respect to an identified security to be delivered while still in the possession of a third person when that person acknowledges that he holds for the purchaser; or

(e) appropriate entries on the books of a clearing corporation are made under Section 8–320.[19]

Effect of Transfer. The purchaser of a certificate of stock and the shares represented thereby acquires rights against the corporation which issued the certificate and against his transferor. Each will be considered briefly in turn.

Purchaser's Rights against the Issuing Corporation. The issuing corporation has a duty, under certain conditions,[20] on request to register transfer of a certificate of stock which is in registered form and properly indorsed and which has been presented to it. If the certificate presented for transfer was *issued with an unauthorized*[21] *signature,* such signature is ineffective, with one exception. If the unauthorized signature was made by a person with inherent agency power,[22] as to a purchaser for value in good faith without notice of the lack of authority such signature is effective and binding on the issuing corporation as though it were validly made. When the certificate contains the signatures necessary to its issue or transfer but is *incomplete in any other respect,* any person may complete it by filling in the blanks as authorized; and if the blanks are incorrectly filled in, the certificate as completed is enforceable by a purchaser who took it for value and without notice of such incorrectness. However, if completion of the blank for an incorrect number of shares resulted in an overissue of the corporate shares, meaning that the corporation will have issued a number of shares in excess of the amount which the corporation has corporate power to issue, the corporation cannot be compelled to issue a certificate for such excess. Although the person with a certificate which, if enforced against the issuing corporation, would result in an overissue cannot compel such overissue, nevertheless he may compel the corpora-

---

[19] UCC 8–313(1).

[20] UCC 8–401.

[21] For meaning of unauthorized, see above, p. 696, ftn. 14.

[22] The unauthorized signing is done by a person entrusted with the signing, preparation, or responsible handling of the certificate. See UCC 8–205; also Agency, above, pp. 556–58.

tion to purchase and deliver an identical certificate for the proper number of shares on the surrender of the original certificate, if the identical certificate does not constitute an overissue and is reasonably available for purchase; or if such an identical certificate is not so available for purchase, he may recover from the corporation the price he or the last purchaser for value paid for the original certificate with interest from the date of his demand. *Improper alteration of a complete certificate,* even though done fraudulently, is ineffective, and the certificate remains enforceable only according to its original terms. All the terms of the certificate must be stated on the certificate; however, the terms of the certificate include not only those stated on the certificate but also those made part of the certificate by reference to other instruments and records and which are not in conflict with the stated terms on the certificate.[23] "Such a reference does not of itself charge a purchaser for value with notice of a defect going to the validity of the security even though the security expressly states that a person accepting it admits such notice."[24] A lien on a certificate of stock or the shares represented thereby in favor of the issuing corporation must be noted conspicuously on the certificate in order to give notice of such lien to purchasers of the certificate and, therefore, to be effective as to them. If a certificate is required to be presented or surrendered for exchange, the purchase of the certificate more than two years[25] after the date when such surrender or presentation was to be made causes the purchaser, by law, to have notice of any defect in its issue or defense of the issuing corporation. The issuing corporation's defense of non-delivery and conditional delivery, as by theft or unauthorized delivery by the person to whom the certificate was entrusted, of a certificate effective against the corporation, is ineffective against a purchaser for value without notice of the particular defense.

Purchaser's Rights against Adverse Claims. The status of a purchaser of a certificate of stock and the shares represented thereby determines to what extent adverse claims to the certificate and such shares may be asserted against him. An adverse claim "includes a claim that a transfer was or would be wrongful or that a particular adverse person is the owner of or has an interest in the security."[26] A purchaser is different from a bona fide purchaser for value, and the rights acquired

---

[23] The certificate may refer to another instrument, indenture, or document or to a constitution, statute, ordinance, rule, regulation, order, or the like.

[24] UCC 8–202(1).

[25] Under UCC 8–203(1)(a) the time is reduced to one year under certain circumstances.

[26] UCC 8–301(1).

by each differ. Upon delivery of a certificate to a purchaser, he acquires the rights in the certificate and the shares represented thereby which his transferor had or had authority to convey, with one exception. The exception is that "a purchaser who has himself been a party to any fraud or illegality affecting the security or who as a prior holder had notice of an adverse claim cannot improve his position by taking from a later bona fide purchaser."[27] *In contrast with a purchaser, a bona fide purchaser acquires both the rights of a purchaser and also the certificate and the shares represented thereby free of any adverse claim.* It should be recalled carefully that, under Article 8 of the Code, a bona fide purchaser "is a purchaser for value in good faith and without notice of any adverse claim who takes delivery of a security in bearer form or of one in registered form issued to him or indorsed to him or in blank."[28] Accordingly, a purchaser cannot be a bona fide purchaser if the delivered certificate does not have a necessary indorsement; but when the purchaser does acquire that necessary indorsement, the transfer is *then* complete as of that time and, *as to all persons other than his transferor,* whether or not he is a bona fide purchaser is determined as of that time. However, *as between the transferor and the purchaser,* the transfer is complete upon delivery, although the purchaser has a specifically enforceable right to have any necessary indorsement supplied. (O owns a certificate of stock in registered form in O's name. (1) T steals the certificate, forges O's blank indorsement on the certificate, and sells and delivers it to P, a purchaser for value in good faith without notice of the theft and forgery. Since O's required indorsement has not occurred, P is not a bona fide purchaser. (2) If O indorsed the certificate in blank and T stole, sold, and delivered the certificate to P, a purchaser for value in good faith without notice of the theft, P is a bona fide purchaser. However, if P then sold and delivered the certificate to R for value, R having notice of the theft, while R's notice precludes him from being a bona fide purchaser, nevertheless, as P's transferee, R acquires whatever rights P had, which was a valid title to the certificate and to the shares represented thereby. (3) A fraudulently induced O to indorse the certificate in blank and deliver it to A, who then sold and delivered it to P, a bona fide purchaser, who in turn later resold the certificate to A. Since A knew of O's adverse claim at the time he purchased the certificate from P he is not a bona fide purchaser; and since he was a party to the fraud on O, he cannot assert against O that he has O's title to the certificate. A cannot claim title through P.)

Whether or not the owner of a certificate of stock may recover

---

[27] *Ibid.*

[28] UCC 8-302.

possession of the certificate and title to the shares represented thereby after a transfer which is wrongful as to him, depends upon why the transfer was wrongful, the owner's conduct with respect to the wrongful transfer, and the status of the person presently in possession of the certificate. *If the transfer was wrongful because of an unauthorized indorsement,* the owner may recover the original certificate or new certificate from *anyone,* unless the owner has ratified the unauthorized indorsement, the owner is otherwise precluded from asserting its ineffectiveness, or the other person is a purchaser for value without notice of adverse claims who has in good faith received a new, reissued or re-registered certificate on registration of transfer.[29] *If the transfer is wrongful for any reason other than an unauthorized indorsement,* the owner may, as against anyone except a bona fide purchaser, reclaim possession of the original or new certificate or obtain damages. The right to obtain or reclaim possession of a certificate may be specifically enforced and its transfer enjoined and the security impounded pending the litigation.

A purchaser who has notice[30] of an adverse claim at the time a certificate is transferred to him cannot be a bona fide purchaser of such certificate. The notice may come from the certificate itself as well as from circumstances apart from the instrument. If the certificate, whether in bearer or registered form, has been indorsed for a purpose not involving transfer, as "for surrender," a purchaser (including a broker for the seller or buyer but excluding an intermediary bank) of the certificate is on notice of an adverse claim. Similarly, such a purchaser has notice of an adverse claim if a certificate in bearer form has on it an unambiguous statement that it is the property of a person other than the transferor. The mere writing of a name on a certificate is not such a statment.[31] If a certificate is required to be presented or surren-

---

[29] See UCC 8–315, 8–311. The issuing corporation is liable to the rightful owner of the original certificate and must issue an identical certificate to him unless such issuance would result in an overissue.

[30] UCC 1–201(25) : "A person has 'notice' of a fact when

(a) he has actual knowledge of it; or

(b) he has received a notice or notification of it; or

(c) from all the facts and circumstances known to him at the time in question he has reason to know that it exists.

"A person 'knows' or has 'knowledge' of a fact when he has actual knowledge of it. 'Discover' or 'learn' or a word or phrase of similar import refers to knowledge rather than to reason to know. The time and circumstances under which a notice or notification may cease to be effective are not determined by this Act."

[31] UCC 8–304(1) (b). Also, the "fact that the purchaser (including a broker for the seller or buyer) has notice that the security is held for a third person or is registered in the name of or indorsed by a fiduciary does not create a duty of inquiry into the rightfulness of

dered for exchange, the purchase of the certificate more than one year[32] after the date when such surrender or presentation was to be made causes the purchaser, by law, to have notice of adverse claims.

Warranties on Presentment and Transfer. The Code specifies in detail the warranties made by a person on presentation of a certificate to the issuing corporation for registration of transfer, by a purchaser for value without notice of adverse claims who receives a certificate from the corporation, by a person transferring a certificate to a purchaser for value, by an intermediary, by a pledgee or other holder for security, and by a broker.

(1) A person who presents a security for registration of transfer or for payment or exchange warrants to the issuer that he is entitled to the registration, payment or exchange. But a purchaser for value without notice of adverse claims who receives a new, reissued or re-registered security on registration of transfer warrants only that he has no knowledge of any unauthorized signature (Section 8–311) in a necessary indorsement.

(2) A person by transferring a security to a purchaser for value warrants only that
  (a) his transfer is effective and rightful; and
  (b) the security is genuine and has not been materially altered; and
  (c) he knows no fact which might impair the validity of the security.

(3) Where a security is delivered by an intermediary known to be entrusted with delivery of the security on behalf of another or with collection of a draft or other claim against such delivery, the intermediary by such delivery warrants only his own good faith and authority even though he has purchased or made advances against the claim to be collected against the delivery.

(4) A pledgee or other holder for security who redelivers the security received, or after payment and on order of the debtor delivers that security to a third person makes only the warranties of an intermediary under subsection (3).

(5) A broker gives to his customer and to the issuer and a purchaser the warranties provided in this section and has the rights and privileges of a purchaser under this section. The warranties of and in favor of the broker acting as an agent are in addition to applicable warranties given by and in favor of his customer.[33]

It should be noted carefully that, under the second sentence of the first paragraph quoted, the purchaser for value without notice of adverse

---

the transfer or constitute notice of adverse claims. If, however, the purchaser (excluding an intermediary bank) has knowledge that the proceeds are being used or that the transaction is for the individual benefit of the fiduciary or otherwise in breach of duty, the purchaser is charged with notice of adverse claims." UCC 8–304(2).

[32] Under UCC 8–305(b) the time is reduced to six months under certain circumstances.

[33] UCC 8–306.

claims warrants no "knowledge" as distinguished from "notice," which affords him real protection against a claim of a forged indorsement.

Effect of Certificate Outstanding. Once a certificate of stock is issued and outstanding, no attachment or levy may be made upon the certificate or the shares represented by such certificate unless either: the certificate is actually seized by the officer making the attachment or levy; the certificate is surrendered to the corporation which issued it; or the transfer of the certificate by the holder is enjoined by court order. Also, the corporation cannot be compelled to issue a new certificate of stock for such shares unless the certificate outstanding is surrendered to the corporation.

If a certificate has been lost, apparently destroyed or stolen, the status of such certificate and of a new certificate in its place, the rights and liabilities of the owner of the old certificate and the purchasers of the original and new certificates are materially affected. When an owner claims that a certificate has been lost, destroyed, or wrongfully taken, the issuing corporation *must* issue a new certificate in place of the original certificate if the owner complies with the following conditions: the owner must request a new certificate before the corporation has notice that the certificate has been acquired by a bona fide purchaser; the owner files with the corporation a sufficient indemnity bond; and the owner satisfies any other reasonable requirements imposed by the corporation. The corporation may voluntarily issue a replacement certificate without any necessity for a court order, although a court may compel a corporation wrongfully refusing to issue a new certificate to do so. If a new certificate is issued and a bona fide purchaser of the original certificate presents it for registration of transfer, the corporation must register the transfer, unless such registration would result in an overissue, in which event the corporation's liability is that previously discussed under overissue.[34] However, the owner of a certificate which has been lost, apparently destroyed or wrongfully taken has a duty to notify the issuing corporation of that fact within a reasonable time after he has notice of it. If the corporation, without notice of an adverse claim and without violation of its duty to inquire into adverse claims, registers a transfer of a properly indorsed certificate before receiving notice from the owner of its loss, destruction or wrongful taking and after a reasonable time has expired in which the owner could have notified the corporation, the owner is precluded from asserting any claim against the

---

[34] See above, pp. 697–98.

corporation for so registering and from asserting any claim to a new certificate from the corporation.

Right to Sue A share of stock represents a contract between the corporation and the shareholder. Shareholders have the right to redress for loss caused by impairment of the value of their shares by wrongful conduct. When a shareholder sustains injury individually, as distinct from injury sustained by all shareholders because of a wrong done to the corporation, the individual shareholder has a right of action against the wrongdoer. The injury has been personal to the shareholder. The shareholder has the right to institute an action in his own name against the corporation or the director or directors who caused such injury. An individual shareholder has a right of action against the corporation for breach of the contractual relation and may either enforce the contract or bring an action for damage caused thereby, in the following illustrative instances: improper refusal to declare dividends; refusal to permit a shareholder to exercise his right to vote at corporate meetings; refusal to permit a shareholder to make a proper inspection of corporate books; and refusal to permit a shareholder to exercise his pre-emptive right. In dealings between a shareholder and a director of a corporation, misrepresentation, or in a minority of states non-disclosure, of material facts by the director to the shareholder causing loss to the shareholder creates a right of action in such shareholder against such director for the loss caused by the director's wrongful conduct. If more than one shareholder has been individually injured by wrongful conduct, one of such shareholders may institute an action on behalf of all the other injured shareholders; this is called a class or representative suit. A class or representative suit also may be instituted by one shareholder on behalf of all the other shareholders if the wrong has been done *to the corporation;* however, in this instance, shareholders cannot sue in their own names, but can sue derivatively on behalf of the corporation.

Derivative Suits. When a wrong has been done to the corporation, only the corporation as a legal entity may bring an action therefor. Individual shareholders may not sue in their own names as they could in actions where they were individually wronged and injured. The right of action is that of the corporation, which may be asserted by the board of directors. Inasmuch as the corporation consists of all the shareholders in it, the shareholders should have an opportunity to consider the matter. Injuries caused to the corporation by mismanagement or wrongful conduct on the part of the board of directors is an illustration of a corporate injury with a corporate right of action for damages therefor. Courts are very reluctant to interfere in the internal management of a corporation and to interfere with the discretion of those who are responsible for such management. However, if a wrong has been caused to the corporation and there is an abuse of discretion or wrongful conduct in not asserting a proper claim for such wrong, the courts will interfere and grant relief.

A complaining shareholder first must exhaust his internal corporate remedies before he may, on behalf of the corporation, institute an action for a wrong done to the corporation. The shareholder must request the board of directors to take proper action or show cause why it would be futile to make a request of the board of directors. If a majority of the board of directors is involved in the particular wrong or is prejudiced, recourse need not be made to the board of directors. Similarly, the minority shareholders must request the shareholders at a corporate meeting to take proper action regarding the wrong to the corporation, unless such recourse is futile. An illustration of such futility would be that a majority of the shareholders is involved in the wrong or is prejudiced in the matter, or that such biased shareholders have a sufficient number of shares to control corporate meetings in general. A shareholder's suit on behalf of the corporation is defective unless such internal corporate remedies have been exhausted or resort to them excused. Although there is conflict, by what appears to be the preferable view, a shareholder is disqualified from instituting such a suit unless he was a shareholder at the time the wrongful transaction occurred or he became a shareholder subsequently by operation of law. Shareholders who acquiesced in the particular wrong also are disqualified from instituting a shareholder's suit therefor.[35]

2. *SHAREHOLDERS' LIABILITIES*

The corporate entity, being separate and distinct from the shareholders, precludes shareholder liability for corporate obligations, whether in contract or tort. Whatever shareholder liability exists is predicated, essentially, on the shares issued to him or his contracts made for the acquisition of shares. At one time shareholders were under extensive statutory liability for corporate obligations, measured by their

---

[35] The corporation becomes a nominal party defendant to the action and, since the shareholders are suing on behalf of the corporation, the proceeds of a successful action generally inure to the corporation's benefit. In some instances the proceeds inure to the benefit of shareholders. See note, *Individual Pro Rata Recovery in Stockholders' Derivative Suits*, 69 Harv. L. Rev. 1314 (1956).

capital contributions. This was true especially in the case of bank shares, and the shareholders were liable to the extent of their capital contributions in addition to such contributions already made. Beginning in 1933 and ending in 1953, the additional liability of holders of shares in national banks was abolished and, with few exceptions, state statutes have followed this pattern in relieving holders of shares of state banks from any additional liability. Shareholders still are exposed to liability as partners in the event of a defectively organized corporation which does not have a *de jure* or a *de facto* status and when the doctrine of estoppel is inapplicable. Also, in the case of illegal dividends, those shareholders are liable for the return of such dividends who received such dividends with notice of the illegality or who received dividends declared by an insolvent corporation. Corporate creditors may enforce the above instances of shareholder liability.

Subscription Liability
Shareholders are liable to the corporation for the unpaid portion of their subscription contracts for corporate shares. The right to such payments is a corporate asset. Corporate creditors may not proceed against shareholders for such unpaid subscription price until they have first exhausted their legal remedies in resorting to other corporate assets. It is only then that creditors, by a creditors' bill in equity or in a court with equity powers, may proceed against such shareholders. In most states subscriptions fraudulently induced are voidable at the election of the shareholders who, on avoidance, are not liable to corporate creditors on such subscriptions.

Watered Stock
Creditors can proceed against the *corporate assets* and, through a creditors' bill, proceed against shareholders for *their liability to the corporation.* However, if shares are issued to a shareholder gratuitously, called "bonus stock" or "bonus shares," there is no shareholder liability *to the corporation* and there is, therefore, no such corporate asset available to corporate creditors. Similarly, if shares are issued to shareholders for labor or services, or for property, at a known overvaluation, the asset available *to the corporation,* and therefore to the corporate creditor, is solely the property exchanged for the shares. However, such shareholders may be liable to corporate creditors for fraud on them.[36]

Methods of Watering. Par value shares issued as fully paid when no consideration has been paid or agreed to be paid, or the consideration

---

[36] See below, pp. 706–7.

paid or agreed to be paid is much less than the par value of the shares issued, is watered to the extent of such deficiency. The capital stock and, therefore, the value of the shares is diluted or watered, from which the phrase "watered stock" originates. Shares may be watered in the following ways: issuance of shares in exchange for services or property which are knowingly overvalued and worth less than the par value of the shares; shares issued for payment in money less than the par value; shares issued as stock dividends without transfer of any surplus to capital; shares issued as a bonus either to induce the purchase of preferred shares or bonds, or gratuitously. The capital stock is watered to the extent the shares are issued for less than their par value. This is unfair to creditors who rely on the corporate assets, including capital contributions by shareholders on their shares, from which the creditors' claims are to be satisfied. In many states an exception is made in the case of a corporation in financial difficulties, which may issue par value shares below the par value for the highest price it can obtain in order to rehabilitate the corporation's financial position.

Tests of Value. There are two tests of the value of services or property exchanged for shares, the "good-faith" rule which prevails in the majority of states, and the "true-value" rule which prevails in the minority of states. Under the good-faith rule, the value is adequate if it was fixed by the corporation through its board of directors in good faith and without fraud. If the value fixed was honestly and reasonably believed to be the fair value, then such value is adequate and the shareholders are not liable for any deficiency between the value fixed in good faith and the actual value of the services or property. Overvalue, by itself, is insufficient to make the value inadequate. Under the true-value rule, good faith is disregarded and the actual value of the services or property is the test. If the actual value is less than the par value of the shares received in exchange for such services or property, the shareholders of such shares are liable to corporate creditors for the deficiency in making full payment. Under state blue-sky laws, state boards or commissions are set up to determine the adequacy of the consideration to be exchanged for the issuance of shares and to permit such issuance only when the value is adequate. Under the federal Securities Act, the Securities and Exchange Commission has the function of determining the relative adequacy of the consideration to be exchanged for the shares to be issued and requires full disclosure of all material facts.

Watering, a Wrong to Corporate Creditors. The issuance of watered shares is a wrong to corporate creditors in that the represented capital is not available as a part of the assets to satisfy the creditors' claims. Corporate creditors may recover from the shareholders of watered stock the deficiency in value for the par value shares issued to them. Each shareholder is liable to corporate creditors only to the extent of his pro rata portion of the amount due such creditors, but not in excess of the deficient amount due on such shares. Creditors first must proceed against corporate assets and, if such assets are insufficient to satisfy their claims, creditors may then proceed in equity or in a court with equity powers under a creditors' bill against the shareholders of the watered shares. The amounts owing by shareholders under subscription contracts with the corporation are available to creditors as a corporate asset. Any further liability of the shareholders is to the creditors and not to the corporation, by reason of their wrong perpetrated on such creditors. Inasmuch as the right to recover from shareholders of watered shares belongs to the corporate creditors and is not a corporate asset, the receiver or trustee in bankruptcy of an insolvent corporation cannot assert this right.

The corporation and the shareholders of the watered shares have committed the tort of fraud or deceit on corporate creditors by misrepresenting to such creditors that the capital stock outstanding represents an amount of capital paid, or agreed to be paid, to the corporation. In order for a creditor to recover for fraud, it is necessary for him to show that he has relied upon such misrepresentation. It is deemed that reliance has occurred if the creditor became such subsequent to such misrepresentation; however, if a subsequent creditor had knowledge of the misrepresentation at the time he became a creditor, there is no reliance on the misrepresentation and he cannot recover. Accordingly, only subsequent creditors without notice may recover from shareholders of watered shares; prior creditors, and subsequent creditors with notice of such misrepresentation, cannot recover.

Nonliability of Certain Shareholders. The shareholder to whom watered shares have been issued may not avoid his liability to corporate creditors by transferring such shares to a bona fide purchaser. Bona fide purchasers of watered shares for value in good faith and without notice of their watered character are not liable for the previous watering and deficiency. Shareholders of treasury stock and shareholders of no-par shares have no liability except for the *agreed* purchase price of their shares. Treasury shares may be sold at any price and need not be sold for the par value.

Chapter XIII

CORPORATE DISSOLUTION AND WINDING UP

A CORPORATION is an entity created by law and can be dissolved only by law. Insolvency of a corporation, lack of corporate assets, or temporary cessation of corporate activities does not constitute a dissolution of the corporation. Liquidation of the corporate assets and distribution to creditors and shareholders does not dissolve the corporation. Dissolution means termination of the corporate entity by legal authority, and may occur by: expiration of the corporate charter; legislative repeal of the corporate charter; surrender of the corporate charter; forfeiture of the corporate charter; order of a court of equity, or a court with equity powers, in some instances; and merger or consolidation. Each of these will be considered briefly in turn.

Expiration of Corporate Charter
A corporation's right to perpetual succession does not mean that it is to exist forever, but rather that the corporation as a legal entity shall continue uninterruptedly for its duration as provided in the corporate charter. It is not usual today to incorporate for a fixed term but when this occurs the corporation automatically dissolves on the expiration of such term and no further action is required.

Legislative Repeal of Corporate Charter
A corporate charter issued by a state constitutes authority for the creation of the corporation for the purposes indicated therein and is a contract between the state and the corporation. The United States Constitution, Article I, section 10, provides that no state shall pass any law impairing the obligation of contract. Accordingly, a state may not alter or repeal the corporate charter without the consent of the corporation. Today most states reserve the right to alter or repeal corporate charters; however, under the Fourteenth Amendment to the United States Constitution, no state shall deprive any person of property without due process of law. There is no violation of the due process clause if the state validly exercises its police power and legislatively repeals or modifies the corporate charter.

Surrender of Corporate Charter

Inasmuch as a corporate charter is issued on the application of persons desiring to incorporate, the state of incorporation will dissolve such corporation on the application of the shareholders. In the absence of a statute to the contrary, the consent of all the shareholders is required for corporate dissolution, unless the corporation is insolvent; in the event of corporate insolvency a majority of the voting power and, in some states, merely a vote of the board of directors, is sufficient to constitute corporate action. Today, statutes in the various states specify what is necessary for voluntary dissolution. In most states a large majority of the voting power—e.g., two-thirds—is required. If the corporation has been adjudicated a bankrupt, then a majority of the voting power and the resolution of the board of directors are sufficient to constitute corporate action. In a few states only the resolution of the board of directors is sufficient. Although corporate insolvency by itself does not constitute dissolution, yet in some states by statute it does.

Involuntary Dissolution by Forfeiture of Corporate Charter

The state of incorporation has the right, through its attorney general, to institute quo warranto proceedings requesting a court decree to dissolve a corporation. A court will decree dissolution only for cause. Improper corporate acts—e.g., fraud—seriously affecting the public constitute sufficient cause. *Ultra vires* acts by themselves usually are insufficient for forfeiture, although the state may either: through quo warranto proceedings oust the corporation from further exercise of the unauthorized powers; or, by suit in a court with equity powers, obtain an injunction against the *ultra vires* act. Dissolution lies within the court's discretion, and a court may decree dissolution or it may permit the corporation to continue in existence but punish it by fine and enjoin continuance of such wrongful conduct. A state statute may provide for automatic forfeiture of a corporate charter by a corporation's noncompliance with statutory requirements, such as by nonpayment of taxes or failure to make corporate reports. Automatic forfeiture and dissolution by such noncompliance does not occur unless the statute expressly permits.

Involuntary Dissolution by Court Decree on Request of Minority Shareholders

There is conflict regarding the authority of a court of equity or a court with equity powers, in the absence of statute to the contrary, to dissolve a corporation at the request of minority shareholders. The growing tendency is that courts of equity have such power. Today, by statute in many states, courts of equity or courts with equity powers are given the authority to dissolve and wind up a corporation at the request of minority shareholders under certain circumstances. Courts of equity or courts with equity powers will grant such relief only when there is fraud or serious mismanagement by the board of directors or the majority of shareholders; an additional ground is that the corporation cannot be operated except at a loss.

Merger or Consolidation
A corporation may sell its assets and discontinue doing any business as a corporation without thereby causing corporate dissolution, although usually a dissolution occurs soon thereafter. By statute today a prosperous corporation may sell all of its corporate assets and business on approval by the board of directors and a large majority of the voting shareholders, and a failing corporation may make such sale on approval by the board of directors and a majority of the voting shareholders. Such assets and business usually are sold to another corporation in exchange for the other corporation's shares of stock. Dissenting shareholders may cause their shares to be appraised and receive payment in cash for their fair value. Today, reorganization of a failing corporation usually is administered under the Bankruptcy Act as amended.[1] Such a sale must not be contrary to the corporate charter or to public policy or law, and it must not be in fraud of corporate creditors.

Often such sale is a part of a merger or consolidation of corporations. In a merger one corporation is absorbed by another corporation, while in a consolidation various corporations are unified and are absorbed into a newly created corporation. Statutes provide for merger and consolidation and, on their occurrence, the old corporation is dissolved. Statutes require that corporate assent to merger or consolidation be given by the board of directors and by a large majority of the holders of outstanding voting shares. Creditors of the merged or consolidated corporation are creditors of the remaining or new corporation, respectively, unless the transfer of such corporate assets and business constitutes a fraudulent conveyance, in which case the creditors can set aside such conveyance. It is not often that dissenting shareholders take advantage of statutory provision for appraisal of the fair value of their old shares, because of the considerable expense involved in an appraisal proceeding.

Effect of Corporate Dissolution
Dissolution terminates the corporate entity, and the corporate property then belongs to the shareholders subject to the rights of corporate creditors. Dissolution may occur before or after winding up of the cor-

---

[1] See below, pp. 866 f.

porate affairs. Winding up consists of liquidating the corporate assets and making distribution first to corporate creditors and then to shareholders. By statute in a few states winding up must precede dissolution. If dissolution precedes winding up, by statute in many states the members of the former corporation may sue and be sued as a corporate entity *solely* for the purpose of winding up the corporate affairs. To this extent the corporate personality continues in existence until the board of directors as trustees for corporate creditors and shareholders has wound up the corporation. If winding up proceedings are under judicial supervision, the court may appoint a receiver for this purpose.

APPENDIX TO PART SIX (B)

REFERENCES

1. American Bar Association—American Law Institute. *Model Business Corporation Act* (Revised), 1966.
2. Anderson, Ronald A. *Anderson's Uniform Commercial Code.* 2d ed. Rochester: Lawyers Cooperative Publishing Co., 1970.
3. Ballantine, Henry W. *Ballantine on Corporations.* Rev. ed. Chicago: Callaghan & Co., 1946.
4. Fletcher, William M. *Cyclopedia of the Law of Private Corporations.* Rev. & per. ed. Chicago: Callaghan & Co., 1971.
5. Hawkland, William D. *A Transactional Guide to the Uniform Commercial Code.* Philadelphia: American Law Institute, 1964.
6. Israels, Carlos L. "Investment Securities as Commercial Paper; How to Handle Transfers of Stocks, Bonds and Other Investment Securities; Stop-Transfer Procedures and the Securities Act of 1933—Addendum to Uniform Commercial Code—Article 8," in *Uniform Commercial Code Handbook 211, 229, 247,* Chicago: American Bar Association, 1964.
7. Stevens, Robert S. *Handbook on the Law of Private Corporations.* 2d ed. St. Paul: West Publishing Co., 1949.
8. *Uniform Laws Annotated,* Article 8, Uniform Commercial Code, 1962.

PROBLEMS

1. (a) State three advantages and three disadvantages of the corporate form of business organization.
   (b) When will courts disregard the corporate entity?
   (c) What is meant by a foreign corporation and when is it "doing business" in a state?

2. On May 28, 1972, the Benjamin Corporation procured a policy of fire insurance and the property covered thereby was destroyed by fire on June 25, 1972. Upon refusal of the insurer to pay this loss, the corporation sued the insurance company. The latter defended on the ground that on December 15, 1971, the corporate existence of the Benjamin Corporation was terminated by proclamation under a statute of its state of incorporation because of its failure to pay its franchise tax. This statute provided that the corporate existence of a tax-delinquent corporation "shall immediately cease

712

and shall be deemed dissolved without further legal proceedings" upon the publication of such a proclamation.

(a) Is the insurance company's defense valid?

(b) Would it have been valid if the action had been brought by a receiver duly appointed to wind up the corporation's affairs?

(Former C.P.A. Examination question)

3. What is meant by the following and how does each occur:

(a) *De jure* corporation.

(b) *De facto* corporation.

(c) "Corporation by estoppel."

4. F, G, and H on March 15, 1972, agree orally to begin business in corporate form on May 1, 1972, and they retain a lawyer who prepares the certificate of incorporation which they execute on April 3, 1972. On April 10, 1972, F takes this certificate for delivery to the lawyer, but he inadvertently fails to deliver it. During the month of April, 1972, G and H sign a lease for office space and make various other contracts, all in the name of the proposed corporation. The lawyer inferred that the matter of the proposed incorporation had been dropped and he did nothing further with respect to it. Can F, G, and H be held personally liable on the lease and the other contracts made in April? If so, would they be held jointly, severally, or jointly and severally liable? (Former C.P.A. Examination question)

5. (a) A, B, and C subscribed to purchase shares of stock in a corporation to be formed. Prior to incorporation A died and B informed the promoter and other interested persons of the withdrawal of B's subscription. The corporation was formed and it demanded of A's estate, of B, and of C payment of the amounts of their respective subscriptions. All refused to make any payment and C informed the corporation that he thereby withdrew his subscription.

(1) Are A's estate, B, and C liable to the corporation for their respective subscription amounts?

(2) Why?

(b) If the corporation was formed for a purpose different from that described in the subscription agreement, would the liability of any of the parties have been affected thereby? Why?

(c) Would the result have been any different in "(a)" above if the subscriptions had been made after the corporation had been formed? Why?

6. A, B, and C were promoters engaged in the formation of X corporation and they acquired land and machinery for $50,000 expecting to sell this property to X at a profit. The corporation was created and the property sold to it for $150,000.

(1) Can the corporation compel the promoters to return $100,000 to the corporation?

(2) Why?

7. (a) A contracted to sell to X corporation 100 shares of stock in X corporation and 100 shares of stock in Y corporation. X was engaged in the manufacture of refrigerators and Y was an automobile manufacturer.

A refused to perform the contract.
(1) Can X enforce the contract?
(2) Why?

(b) P, president of R corporation engaged in the retailing of home appliances, had authority to issue corporate checks for corporate purposes. Without authority, P purchased an automobile for himself and issued a check in R's name for the purchase price.
(1) Is R liable on the check?
(2) Why?

8. (a) A corporation engaged in mining contracted with B corporation to manufacture and sell to it a specified quantity of explosives, which A was not authorized to do by its charter. A manufactured and delivered the explosives to B, who subsequently refused to pay for it on the ground that A had acted *ultra vires*.
(1) Can A enforce the contract against B?
(2) Why?

(b) P, a pedestrian, was negligently injured by one of A's trucks hauling explosives manufactured by A under its contract with B in "(a)" above.
(1) Is A liable for such injury?
(2) Why?

9. The officers of a manufacturing corporation, by authority of the directors, indorsed, in the corporate name, a note for the accommodation of an allied corporation. The note was discounted by a bank on the faith of the indorsement, and with knowledge that it was indorsed for accommodation.
(1) May the corporation do this? Why?
(2) Was the bank a holder in due course? Why?
(3) May the bank recover upon the indorsement? Why?
(Former C.P.A. Examination question)

10. (a) Answer the following "Yes" or "No"; reasons are not required:
(1) In the absence of statute, corporate meetings may be held outside of the state of incorporation.
(2) A corporate meeting begun with a quorum may continue to transact corporate business even though a quorum does not continue to be present.
(3) Shares held by an issuing corporation have voting rights and are counted as part of the voting power.
(4) A shareholder's proxy is revocable, regardless of its terms, unless coupled with an interest in the share of stock.
(5) Cumulative voting is not permitted in most states.
(6) Voting trusts are valid in most states.
(7) A director may not vote by proxy at a meeting of the board of directors.

(b) Give three instances of what a majority at a corporate meeting may not do.

11. (a) D, a director of X corporation, learned of facts which would cause certain corporate property to become very valuable if the facts were known. D did not disclose this information to other directors who were ignorant of it and contracted with the corporation for his purchase of

the property. The other directors then learned the facts and refused to transfer the property to D.

    (1) Is the contract enforceable against X?

    (2) Why?

  (b) A director has a personal interest in action to be taken by the board of directors.

    (1) Should he vote on the matter?

    (2) Why?

12. You are called upon to audit the books of a corporation for 1971 and you find, among other things, the following: The corporation is on a calendar-year basis. In December, the corporation paid to each of its five directors a salary of $2,000 and to the treasurer, who was not a director, $12,000, for their services during 1971 as such officials.

    (1) Were these payments proper as to (a) the directors, and (b) as to the treasurer? Why?

    (2) Where would you look for authority to make these payments? (Former C.P.A. Examination question)

13. Under the bylaws of a corporation, the term of office of president was one year. Defendants and plaintiff together owned a majority of the voting stock and constituted a majority of the board of directors. They made a written contract, with consideration, which provided that plaintiff was to be annually elected president during a period of three years. Upon what ground, if any, could this contract be held invalid? (Former C.P.A. Examination question)

14. (a) X corporation had a large surplus at the end of its first year of operation which the directors reasonably believed should be used for expansion of the corporate plant.

    (1) Can the shareholders compel the board of directors to declare a dividend?

    (2) Why?

  (b) A corporate board of directors declared a dividend.

    (1) What is the status of the shareholders?

    (2) If specific funds for the payment of such dividend had been set aside solely for this purpose, could corporate creditors proceed against such funds? Why?

    (3) Is a proper declaration of corporate dividends revocable?

    (4) If the corporation had notice that a share of stock had been pledged, is the dividend to be paid to the pledgor or to the pledgee?

15. A corporation has realized an operating profit and has a balance in its surplus account, but because of additions to fixed capital assets it has no cash beyond its requirements for working capital.

  (a) Can this corporation legally declare a dividend (not a liquidating one)?

  (b) On the assumption that such a dividend can legally be declared, how can payment of it be arranged? (Former C.P.A. Examination question)

16. A certified public accountant, in his examination of a wholly owned subsidiary corporation, finds that its board of directors has declared a dividend in

excess of the amount of surplus at the beginning of the year plus the net profit for the year, and that this dividend has been paid to the parent corporation. What should the accountant do with respect to this situation? (Former C.P.A. Examination question)

17. (a) What is meant by a shareholder's pre-emptive right?
    (b) To what extent does a shareholder have any right to examine corporate books?
    (c) X corporation issued its shares of stock as a bonus to its shareholders. May corporate creditors recover the par value of such shares? Explain fully.

18. (a) B fraudulently induced A to deliver to him A's certificate of stock representing 1,000 shares in X corporation. B forged A's signature in blank on the certificate and sold and delivered it to C, a purchaser for value without notice of B's fraud and forgery. C delivered the certificate to X who issued a new certificate of stock to C for 1,000 shares in X.
    (1) Does A have any rights?
    (2) Why?
    (b) O is the owner of a certificate of stock representing 9,000 shares in Z corporation, the certificate being indorsed in blank by O. T stole the certificate from O and delivered it to C in satisfaction of T's debt to C. C did not know of the theft.
    (1) Does O have a right to the certificate?
    (2) Why?

19. (a) Distinguish merger from consolidation.
    (b) Name three other methods by which a corporation may be dissolved.
    (c) Explain the effect of corporate dissolution.

20. P, the president of a corporation engaged in selling machinery, had authority to issue corporate checks for corporate purposes. P purchased furniture for his home and drew a corporate check, which he delivered to V, the vendor, in payment of the purchase price.
    (1) Is the corporation liable to V on the check?
    (2) If V negotiated the check to H, a holder in due course without notice of P's wrongful conduct, is the corporation liable to H on the check?
    (3) If H negotiated the check to R who knew of P's wrongful conduct, is the corporation liable on the check to R?

21. (a) Explain when a shareholder has a right to sue:
    (1) In his own name against the corporation or a director. Give an illustration of an instance.
    (2) Derivatively on behalf of the corporation.
    (b) What is meant by the phrase watered stock, and how, in general, does this watering occur?
    (c) To what extent, if any, are shareholders of watered stock liable to corporate creditors?

SOME PREVIOUS C.P.A. LAW EXAMINATION
QUESTIONS AND MODEL ANSWERS

MAY, 1971

No. 1 (Estimated time—20 to 25 minutes)

Each of the lettered statements of facts below is followed by numbered sentences that state legal conclusions relating to those facts. You are to determine whether each legal conclusion is true or false according to the *general principles of corporation and securities law*. Use a soft pencil, preferably #2, to blacken the appropriate space on the separate printed answer sheet to indicate your answer. Your grade will be determined from your total of correct answers less a penalty of approximately one half for each of your incorrect answers; an omitted answer will not be considered an incorrect answer.

A. Morgan Corporation was incorporated in the State of Delaware in 1962 and it operated exclusively in Delaware until 1969. Since then it has been increasing the scope of its operations and now has substantial sales and servicing activities in southern New Jersey. Clearview Corporation of New Jersey, a competitor, is seeking to prevent Morgan from continuing its selling activities in New Jersey. Morgan has not qualified to do business in New Jersey.
   1. Morgan is a foreign corporation in New Jersey.
   2. Morgan does not have to qualify to do business in New Jersey unless it maintains permanent facilities there.
   3. Clearview's best legal recourse is to file a complaint with the Attorney General of New Jersey since he is the proper person to proceed against Morgan.
   4. Since interstate commerce is involved in some of Morgan's operations, federal law has preempted the field and New Jersey is precluded from interfering with or restricting any of Morgan's operations there.
   5. If Morgan had done all of its business in New Jersey at the time that it was incorporated, it could not have been incorporated in Delaware.

B. Black Corporation has made several attempts to purchase the Blue Corporation. After Blue rejected the offers by Black, it was decided that the best way to consummate the transaction was to form a new corporation, the Black and Blue Corporation, which would be the successor to both corporations. All assets belonging to the two corporations would be transferred to Black and Blue in exchange for Black and Blue common stock. These shares then would be exchanged for those in the combining corporations after which Black Corporation and Blue Corporation would be completely liquidated. There are minority stockholders in both corporations who vehemently oppose this proposed action.
   6. This transaction is a statutory merger.
   7. Approval by at least a two-thirds vote of the stockholders of each corporation will be required.
   8. Dissenting stockholders have the right to receive an appraisal and payment in cash for their shares.
   9. In the appraisal proceeding the dissenting stockholders will receive for their stock an amount equal to the Corporation's book value per share.

    10. Creditors of the liquidated corporations automatically have rights against the Black and Blue Corporation.

C. Sigma Corporation, a publicly held corporation, has outstanding 100,000 shares of 6 percent, $90 par value preferred stock each of which was originally issued at $100, is callable at $102 and is currently selling at $78. The board of directors decided to reacquire 40,000 of these shares in the open market and to hold them as treasury stock for eventual use in an acquisition. Vandergrift, a minority stockholder and creditor, has objected to the use of corporate funds for such a purpose.

    11. The board of directors must submit the question of reacquiring the preferred stock to a vote by the common stockholders.

    12. Vandergrift has a valid objection if Sigma's stated capital was impaired by the reacquisition of the shares.

    13. Treasury stock validly acquired constitutes an asset of the corporation.

    14. If the Sigma preferred is reacquired and then reissued to acquire another corporation, the value of the property received must equal or exceed $90 per share.

    15. If it decides to reissue this amount of its stock, Sigma would be required to file a registration statement with the Securities and Exchange Commission.

E. Carter was the president and a member of the board of directors of the Fairway Construction Corporation. Carter recommended that Fairway purchase the assets of the Hale Corporation. He did not disclose that he would receive a 10 percent finder's fee from the owners of Hale if the transaction were consummated. The board, including Carter, unanimously approved the transaction. In addition, Carter bought a tract of land which Fairway would need to go ahead with its plans to construct and own a suburban shopping center.

    21. In this situation Carter has violated his fiduciary duty to the stockholders.

    22. If the board refuses to take action, a stockholder derivative action may be brought by Fairway stockholders to recover the 10 percent finder's fee.

    23. Fairway could compel Carter to convey the tract of land to the Corporation.

    24. Carter's actions would justify his removal for cause as president and a member of the board.

F. Harding was a promoter in the formation of the Majestic Corporation. Prior to Majestic's incorporation, Harding, for and on behalf of Majestic, made several contracts in the name of the Corporation. After interviewing several applicants, he selected and signed Johnson to a one-year contract as Majestic's plant manager. Johnson received a better offer elsewhere and promptly notified Harding he would not perform. The future directors of Majestic were informed of this prior to incorporation.

    Next, Harding on behalf of the Corporation rented one floor in a new office building for two years to be utilized as the Corporation's home office. The board of directors neglected to adopt this contract due to an oversight. However, they promptly moved into the office space and have been there for two months. They are unhappy about the rental price and have refused to pay the price agreed to by Harding.

    Finally, Harding signed an agreement for one year with JCN Computer to lease one of its latest model computers. At its meeting immediately following incorporation the board decided that another type of computer was needed and rejected the contract made by Harding with JCN.

25. Prior to incorporation Harding was an agent for a nonexistent principal.
26. The Corporation can recover against Johnson for breach of contract.
27. Harding has a right to compensation for services rendered to the Corporation prior to its incorporation.
28. By implication Majestic has adopted the rental price for the lease of the office space.
29. JCN has no rights against Majestic Corporation.
30. Harding is liable to JCN on the computer leasing contract.

Answer

1. True	6. False	11. False	21. False	26. False
2. False	7. True	12. True	22. True	27. False
3. True	8. True	13. False	23. True	28. True
4. False	9. False	14. False	24. True	29. True
5. False	10. True	15. True	25. True	30. True

NOVEMBER, 1968

No. 1 (Estimated time—20 to 25 minutes)

Each of the following numbered phrases or clauses states a legal conclusion as it completes the related lettered material. You are to determine whether *each* of the legal conclusions is true or false according to *general principles of corporation law*. Write on a separate answer sheet whether each conclusion is true or false. Your grade will be determined from your total net score obtained by deducting your total of incorrect answers from your total of correct answers; an omitted answer will not be considered an incorrect answer.

A. Frank, Mark, and John joined together to promote the formation of Eagle Corporation to construct houses. The promoters contracted with Frank's brother-in-law, George, that the Corporation would purchase a tract of land owned by George for $100,000 to be paid six months after the Corporation was formed. The contract specifically provided that Frank, Mark, and John would not incur any liability as promoters. After executing the contract the promoters completed incorporation through the purchase of stock at par for cash by the promoters and several of their friends and relatives. Mark and his three sons were elected as directors and hired as officers. The Corporation then had the land surveyed, had building plans drawn, and tendered $100,000 to George for the land.

1. Prior to the incorporation the promoters had no fiduciary duties.
2. Upon incorporation the promoters could satisfy any obligation to make a full disclosure of their activities to the Corporation by making such a disclosure to the board of directors.
3. The agreement made by the promoters with George did not constitute an enforceable contract at the time it was executed.
4. The Corporation could be regarded as a third party beneficiary of the contract between the promoters and George.
5. The actions of the officers of the Corporation would constitute an

adoption of the contract between George and the promoters which would bind both George and the Corporation to the contract.

B. You have been the auditor of Cybul Corporation for the three years it has been in existence. Upon incorporation 1,000 shares of $50 par value common stock authorized by the articles of incorporation were sold for cash to the public. The Corporation was very profitable and the board of directors, which has as its members all of the officers of the Corporation, to reward management for outstanding work, has increased the salary of each officer by $5,000. The Corporation plans to expand its production facilities and issue more stock to obtain additional capital. To date the Corporation has paid no dividends.

    6. The directors breached their duty to the shareholders by not declaring a dividend.

    7. The directors must obtain shareholder approval to amend the certificate of incorporation prior to issuing additional shares of stock.

    8. The directors may not effectively agree to raise the officers' salaries.

    9. The directors may legally agree to allow themselves to have the first opportunity to subscribe to the additional shares of stock to be issued.

    10. The general investing public must be offered a reasonable opportunity to purchase shares of the new stock to be issued when present shareholders are given an opportunity to purchase such shares.

C. David and Sidney each own 50 percent of the capital stock of Diamond Corporation. They are unrelated and have no other business relationship. They entered into a shareholders' agreement which provided that upon the death of either, the survivor would purchase the other's stock in the Corporation at book value with the book value to be determined annually by a C.P.A. The book value of each party's stock interest as determined by a C.P.A. on the date of the execution of the agreement was $20,000. David and Sidney plan to purchase life insurance on each other so that funds will be available to meet their obligations under the agreement.

    11. The shareholders' agreement cannot remain valid for more than ten years unless it is renewed.

    12. The shareholders' agreement may remain in effect even if David and Sidney fail to have a C.P.A. annually review the book value of their stock interests.

    13. If the premium to be paid by Sidney on the insurance policy he takes out on David's life is higher than the premium David must pay, Sidney is entitled to reimbursement for the additional cost from the Corporation.

    14. If David should die the insurance proceeds Sidney collects would constitute a dividend.

    15. If David and Sidney both sell their stock they could not take out additional insurance on each other's lives.

D. Your client, Plywood Corporation, a manufacturer, has consistently operated at a loss since its incorporation three years ago. Plywood is now insolvent and owes twenty creditors a total of more than $50,000. Stanley is a stockholder of Plywood and Walter owns bonds issued by Plywood which are now due. Most bondholders will not demand payment until conditions improve. Stanley demands that Plywood purchase his stock at his cost and Walter demands payment for his bonds. Each threatens to force Plywood into bankruptcy if his demand is not met. Stanley also owns stock in Hardwood Corporation, a very successful enterprise, and Hardwood has offered to purchase its own stock from Stanley at a price in excess of the market price of the stock.

16. Plywood may not repurchase Stanley's stock because it has a deficit balance in its legal capital.

17. Walter cannot alone file a petition for the involuntary bankruptcy of Plywood if Plywood refuses to retire Walter's bonds.

18. If Plywood repurchases Walter's bonds and immediately files a voluntary petition in bankruptcy, the trustee in bankruptcy may be able to claim that Walter received a preference.

19. Hardwood's stock would be "watered stock" if Hardwood should repurchase its own stock from Stanley for more than the market price.

20. Hardwood would commit an *ultra vires* act by repurchasing its own stock from Stanley.

E. Alan is chairman of the board of directors of Shipping Corporation, one of your clients. The bylaws of the Corporation provide for a seven-man board of directors, one of whom has just died. The bylaws have no provision for filling a vacancy and Alan would like to appoint his brother. Alan has also learned that two ships, the Nina and the Pinta, are available for purchase. Alan would like to purchase the Nina himself and attempt to sell it for profit and he thinks the Corporation should purchase the Pinta.

Alan attempted to telephone the other directors and inform them of what he learned and what he would like to do. He contacted two directors who agreed by telephone to all of his plans. A third director could not be reached. The fourth director agreed to Alan's plans on behalf of himself and the fifth director, who had given his proxy to the fourth director. The substance of the telephone calls was not reduced to writing.

21. Alan did not hold a valid director's meeting.

22. Alan, as chairman of the board of directors, does not have implied power to fill a vacancy on the board of directors.

23. Alan was free to purchase the Nina without disclosing his plans.

24. The director who could not be contacted will be strictly accountable for any wrong done by his fellow directors even though he was unaware of what was happening.

25. Directors have power to vote by proxy to the same extent as shareholders.

F. Evan and Norman each own 50 percent of the capital stock of Eian Corporation. They arranged a conference with their lawyer and their accountant to agree on the terms of a stockholders' agreement. If agreed upon by both stockholders the following provisions could be properly adopted as a part of the stockholders' agreement.

26. The stockholders' agreement is to terminate if the Corporation's stock should be sold to the investing public.

27. The Corporation can be dissolved without court approval if the stockholders disagree.

28. A stockholder wishing to sell all or part of his stock in the Corporation must first offer the stock to the other stockholder at a price to be determined by an independent appraisal.

29. The sale of stock is to be restricted.
30. The activities in which the Corporation may engage under the terms of its charter are to be increased.

Answer

1. False	7. True	13. False	19. False	25. False
2. False	8. True	14. False	20. False	26. True
3. True	9. False	15. True	21. True	27. True
4. True	10. False	16. True	22. True	28. True
5. True	11. False	17. True	23. False	29. True
6. False	12. True	18. True	24. False	30. False

MAY, 1965

No. 7 (Estimated time—25 to 30 minutes)

The Cover Manufacturing Corporation was formed on January 1, 1964, for the purpose of manufacturing and selling umbrellas. You are engaged in the examination of its financial statements as of December 31, 1964.

a. Discuss the legal status of each of the following expenses and name all of the documents or records that you might examine for authorization of each.
   (1) Directors' compensation.
   (2) Officers' salaries.
   (3) Promoters' organization expenses.

b. During your examination you discovered that the president of the Corporation, who is also the principal stockholder, had committed the Corporation to a partnership agreement with Harry Gore. The partnership, formed for the purpose of importing and selling umbrellas, began operation on April 1, 1964.

   Discuss the legal significance of your discovery.

c. Your examination of the account, Stock Subscriptions Receivable, disclosed that the account included amounts applicable to some subscriptions made before and some made after the Corporation was formed. You examined correspondence received from both types of subscribers in which it was requested that subscriptions be cancelled. No action has been taken to cancel or to collect these subscriptions.

   Discuss the balance sheet presentation of the subscriptions that the subscribers have requested be cancelled; include a discussion of the legal status of the subscriptions.

Answer

a. (1) A director is not entitled to compensation for his services rendered to the corporation as a director in the absence of any provision in the charter or bylaws to the contrary or in the absence of a contract for such services. The shareholders at a corporate meeting, or the board of directors if specifically authorized, may pass a resolution awarding compensation for such services. Should a director perform special services either outside of the ordinary services to be rendered as a director or as an officer of the corporation, a corporate promise is implied by law to pay for the reasonable value of such services. An officer who is also a director may receive a salary for his services as an officer, but he may not receive any salary for his ordinary services as a director. The compensation of corporate officers is fixed by the board of directors. I would examine the charter, bylaws, and the minutes of the directors' meetings and shareholders' meetings for authorization for directors' compensation.

(2) Corporate officers are appointed by the corporate board of directors and their compensation usually is fixed by the board of directors at a directors' meeting, although the bylaws may fix their compensation. I would examine the bylaws and the minutes of the directors' metings.

(3) In the absence of statutory provision to the contrary, a corporation is not liable for the expenses of its incorporation. Statutes in some states provide that corporations have a quasi-contractual obligation to pay for the reasonable value of such incorporation services. In most states, only an express corporate promise to pay for a promoter's organizational expense will be enforced. I would examine the bylaws, the minutes of the first shareholders' meeting and the minutes of the first several directors' meetings.

b. Unless a statute or the corporate charter expressly permits, a corporation has no power and no implied or apparent authority to become a member of a partnership. If not so permitted, the corporate agreement and any contracts of the purported partnership would be *ultra vires* as to the corporation, and the president of the corporation will be liable for any damage thereby caused to the corporation.

c. Preincorporation stock subscriptions are usually offers to purchase corporate shares made by subscribers and may be revoked at any time prior to acceptance by the later formed corporation. By statute in many states, the subscribers automatically become shareholders upon incorporation. In such states, these subscriptions would be shown on the corporate balance sheet as current assets if they had not been revoked prior to incorporation. By statute in some states restrictions on withdrawal of subscriptions before incorporation will prevent revocation. Also, by statute in some states the corporation is to act affirmatively to accept the subscription offers, thereby allowing more time for subscribers to revoke their subscriptions. If that should be the case, such revoked subscriptions should not be shown on the balance sheet.

Postincorporation subscriptions may be offers by the corporation to sell corporate shares to persons who, on signing the subscription, become shareholders. The corporate balance sheet should then reflect these subscriptions as current assets. However, postincorporation stock subscriptions may also be offers to the corporation to subscribe for corporate shares which, on acceptance by the corporation, cause the subscribers to become shareholders. The corporate balance sheet should then reflect these subscriptions as current assets. If a subscriber revokes his subscription offer before its acceptance, such revoked subscriptions should not be shown on the balance sheet.

PART SEVEN

SECURITY

A. PROPERTY SECURITY TRANSACTIONS

Chapter I

CONSENSUAL PROPERTY SECURITY TRANSACTIONS

1. CONCEPT OF SECURITY

Purpose of Security   THE WORD "security" has a broad, general, well-recognized meaning; it also has a narrow, technical meaning under Article 8 of the Uniform Commercial Code on Investment Securities. Under Article 8 of the Code, security is an "investment security," an instrument traded on the securities markets, e.g., a certificate of stock or bond, previously discussed.[1] Throughout this book, except in the portion on Investment Securities under the transfer of corporate shares in the law of corporations, such an instrument is described by its full name as an "investment security." In the broad, general, and well-recognized sense *the word "security" is the name for the creditor's interest in specific property, or in the obligation of a third person, as assurance for the performance of the debtor's obligation.* The purpose of security for the performance of an obligation, whether for the payment of a debt or otherwise, is to provide a specific source from which the creditor or obligee will obtain performance of the obligation, or payment for loss sustained by the obligee, in the event of the obligor's failure to perform. Essentially, the purpose is to obtain *priority* over other obligees of the obligor in resorting to a particular source. (A delivers his horse to B as security for B's loan of money to A. B has security against which he has the prior right to resort in the event of A's default.) A "secured creditor" has security for the obligation owing to him, while an "unsecured creditor" has no such security. The security may be in the form of property or in the form of a third person's contract to perform the debtor's obligation in the event of his default, called "suretyship." Accordingly, the entire subject of Security will be divided into two parts, namely Property Security Transactions and Suretyship, and will be considered in that order.

---

[1] See above, p. 692.

Kinds of Property Security Transaction

Property security transactions may be consensual or nonconsensual. In consensual transactions the parties *agree* to create the security for an obligation, as A's delivery of a horse as security for a loan. In nonconsensual transactions the parties *do not agree* to any property as security for the performance of an obligation but, by statute or Common Law, a security interest in specific property is created, e.g., the right of a mechanic to retain an automobile that he has repaired at the request of the owner as security for the payment of such repairs. When the lien is created by statute, it is called a "statutory lien." Consensual property security transactions may involve personal or real property. Accordingly, in this chapter, Section 2 will consider secured transactions involving personal property and fixtures, Section 3 will consider the real property mortgage; Chapter II will consider nonconsensual property security transactions.

2. *PERSONAL PROPERTY AND FIXTURES*

Introduction

In General. Article 9 of the Uniform Commercial Code on Secured Transactions is concerned with all *consensual* security interests in personal property and fixtures, with a few exceptions. It simplifies and unifies in a single structure security devices dealing with such property, removing many of the complexities in security financing which have grown up during a long period of time in a vastly expanding economy. *There is only one security device,* namely the "security agreement," which is "an agreement which creates or provides for a security interest."[2] A "security interest" is "an interest in personal property or fixtures which secures payment or performance of an obligation. . . . The term also includes any interest of a *buyer* of accounts or chattel paper which is subject to Article 9."[3] *The Article applies to any transaction (regardless of its form) which is intended to create a security interest in personal property or fixtures, and also to sales of accounts or chattel paper.* It should be noted very carefully that the Article applies to security interests created by a contract which *intended* to create such security interest, as well as to *sales* of accounts and chattel paper. Accordingly, *statutory* liens are excluded from the Article, except for a provision with respect to priorities, discussed later.[4]

---

[2] UCC 9–105(1)(h). The term "security agreement" replaces various terms, such as "chattel mortgage," "conditional sale," "trust receipt," "assignment of accounts receivable."

[3] UCC 1–201(37).

[4] See below, p. 756.

A security interest in property is a *"lien," which is a legal right in the property of another as security for the performance of an obligation.* Some liens are possessory, in that they include the right to possess specific property, e.g., the pledge;[5] while other liens are non-possessory, in that they do not include such right to possession, e.g., the security interest in an automobile possessed by the owner.[6] The fact that the security interest is in an obligation itself secured by a transaction or interest to which the Article does not apply does not exclude such security interest from the Article.[7]

Various types of transaction are excluded from the Article because primarily they are not security transactions, and also because they are either the subject of federal statute or of such local social concern that they are more properly within the purview of state statute rather than a uniform law. The Article does not apply:

(a) to a security interest subject to any statute of the United States to the extent that such statute governs the rights of parties to and third parties affected by transactions in particular types of property; or

(b) to a landlord's lien; or

(c) to a lien given by statute or other rule of law for services or materials except as provided in Section 9–310 on priority of such liens; or

(d) to a transfer of a claim for wages, salary or other compensation of an employee; or

(e) to a transfer by a government or governmental subdivision or agency; or

(f) to a sale of accounts or chattel paper as part of a sale of the business out of which they arose, or an assignment of accounts or chattel paper which is for the purpose of collection only, or a transfer of a right to payment under a contract to an assignee who is also to do the performance under the contract or a transfer of a single account to an assignee in whole or partial satisfaction of a preexisting indebtedness; or

(g) to a transfer of an interest or claim in or under any policy of insurance, except as provided with respect to proceeds (Section 9–306) and priorities in proceeds (Section 9–312); or

---

[5] "A pledge is a security interest in a chattel or in an intangible represented by an indispensable instrument, the interest being created by a bailment for the purpose of securing the payment of a debt or the performance of some other duty." American Law Institute, *Restatement: Security,* 1941, sec. 1.

[6] Formerly called a "chattel mortgage."

[7] UCC 9–102, *Comment 4:* "The owner of Blackacre borrows $10,000 from his neighbor, and secures his note by a mortgage on Blackacre. This Article is not applicable to the creation of the real estate mortgage. . . . However, when the mortgagee pledges the note to secure his own obligation to X, this Article applies to the security interest thus created, which is a security interest in an instrument even though the instrument is secured by a real estate mortgage."

(h) to a right represented by a judgment (other than a judgment taken on a right to payment which was collateral); or

(i) to any right of set-off; or

(j) except to the extent that provision is made for fixtures in Section 9–313, to the creation or transfer of an interest in or lien on real estate, including a lease or rents thereunder; or

(k) to a transfer in whole or in part of any claim arising out of tort; or

(l) to a transfer of an interest in any deposit account (subsection (1) of Section 9–105), except as provided with respect to proceeds (Section 9–306) and priorities in proceeds (Section 9–312).[8]

Security interests arise under the Sales portion of the Code, e.g., the seller may reserve a security interest in shipped goods, and they come within the purview of Article 9. However, they are exempted from certain provisions of the Article under certain conditions. While a security interest arising *solely* under the Sales portion of the Code is under Article 9, nevertheless to the extent that, and so long as, the debtor does not have or does not lawfully obtain *possession* of the goods: no security agreement is necessary to make the security interest enforceable; no filing is required to perfect the security interest; and the rights of the secured party on default by the debtor are governed by the Sales portion of the Code.[9] However, if the debtor lawfully obtains *possession* of the goods under a sales transaction, the secured party must comply with the provisions of Article 9 in order to obtain security protection thereunder against third parties. It should be noted in passing that the creation of a security interest is not a bulk transfer under the Bulk Transfers portion of the Code.[10]

Terminology. It is important to understand the terminology employed by the Article. Some basic terms will be considered at this time. The "security agreement" and "security interest" terms have already been defined. The parties to the security agreement are the "debtor" and the "secured party." A debtor is "the person who owes payment or other performance of the obligation secured, whether or not he owns or has rights in the collateral, and includes the seller of accounts or chattel paper."[11] A secured party is "a lender, seller or other person in whose favor there is a security interest, including a person to whom accounts

---

[8] UCC 9–104.

[9] UCC 9–113.

[10] See above, pp. 350 ff.

[11] UCC 9–105(1)(d); (continued): "Where the debtor and the owner of the collateral are not the same person, the term 'debtor' means the owner of the collateral in any provision of the Article dealing with the collateral, the obligor in any provision dealing with the obligation, and may include both where the context so requires."

or chattel paper have been sold."[12] By the security agreement, the secured party acquires a security interest in "collateral," which is "the property subject to a security interest, and includes accounts and chattel paper which have been sold."[13] An "account debtor" is "the person who is obligated on an account, chattel paper or general intangible."[14] A security interest is called a "purchase money security interest" *to the extent that it is:* taken or retained by the seller of the collateral to secure all or part of its price; or taken by a person who, by making advances or incurring an obligation, gives value to enable the debtor to acquire rights in or the use of collateral if such value is in fact so used.[15] It should be noted very carefully that *a security interest taken as security for, or in satisfaction of, a pre-existing claim or antecedent debt does not qualify as a purchase money security interest.*

The Collateral

Tangibles and Intangibles. The security interest is in personal property or fixtures under Article 9, which are called "collateral." *Collateral means the property subject to a security interest, and includes accounts and chattel paper which have been sold.* Collateral consists of tangible and intangible personal property. First tangibles consisting of goods and fixtures will be discussed, then intangibles consisting of those represented by indispensable paper and those not evidenced by any instrument or document, and lastly after-acquired collateral.

Tangibles—Goods, Fixtures. Tangible personal property consists of goods. Goods includes all things which are movable at the time the security interest attaches or which are fixtures. Goods includes the unborn young of animals, growing crops, and standing timber which is to be cut or removed under a conveyance or contract for sale. Goods does not include money, documents, instruments, chattel paper, accounts, general intangibles, or minerals, oil, gas, or the like before extraction. There are four classes of goods, namely, consumer goods, equipment, farm products, and inventory. While most of the Article's sections apply to all kinds of goods, there are some sections which have

---

[12] UCC 9–105(1)(m); (continued): "When the holders of obligations issued under an indenture of trust, equipment trust agreement or the like are represented by a trustee or other person, the representative is the secured party."

[13] UCC 9–105(1)(c).

[14] UCC 9–105(1)(a).

[15] UCC 9–107, *Comment 1:* ". . . a seller has a purchase money security interest if he retains a security interest in the goods; a financing agency has a purchase money security interest when it advances money to the seller, taking back an assignment of chattel paper, and also when it makes advances to the buyer (e.g. on chattel mortgage) to enable him to buy, and he uses the money for that purpose."

rules applicable only to a particular kind of goods. It is very important that the *nature* and *use* of these different kinds of goods be understood inasmuch as failure to comply with the particular sections applicable to each of them may preclude the perfection[16] of a security interest in them. Goods are *consumer goods* "if they are used or bought for use primarily for personal, family or household purposes."[17] For example, a refrigerator used in a home is consumer goods. Goods are *equipment* "if they are used or bought for use primarly in business (including farming or a profession) or by a debtor who is a non-profit organization or a governmental subdivision or agency or if the goods are not included in the definitions of inventory, farm products or consumer goods."[18] For example, a refrigerator used in a store to hold perishable foods for sale is equipment. Goods are *inventory* "if they are held by a person who holds them for sale or lease or to be furnished under contracts of service or if he has so furnished them, or if they are raw materials, work in process or materials used or consumed in a business. Inventory of a person is not to be classified as his equipment."[19] For example, a refrigerator for sale in a kitchen appliance store is inventory. Difficulty in distinguishing goods as inventory rather than equipment can be resolved by applying the principal test, are the goods held for immediate or ultimate sale? If they are, they are inventory.[20] Goods are *farm products* "if they are crops or livestock or supplies used or produced in farming operations or if they are products of crops or livestock in their unmanufactured states (such as ginned cotton, wool-clip,

---

[16] By perfection is meant compliance with the Article's provisions in order to obtain maximum priority for a security interest in collateral as against third persons. See below, p. 745.

[17] UCC 9–109(1).

[18] UCC 9–109(2).

[19] UCC 9–109(4).

[20] In discussing the meaning of inventory, UCC 9–109, *Comment 3:* "Implicit in the definition is the criterion that the prospective sale is in the ordinary course of business. Machinery used in manufacturing, for example, is equipment and not inventory even though it is the continuing policy of the enterprise to sell machinery when it becomes obsolete. Goods to be furnished under a contract of service are inventory even though the arrangement under which they are furnished is not technically a sale. When an enterprise is engaged in the business of leasing a stock of products to users (for example, the fleet of cars owned by a car rental agency), that stock is also included within the definition of 'inventory'. It should be noted that one class of goods which is not held for disposition to a purchaser or user is included in inventory: 'Materials used or consumed in a business'. Examples of this class of inventory are fuel to be used in operations, scrap metal produced in the course of manufacture, and containers to be used to package the goods. In general it may be said that goods used in a business are equipment when they are fixed assets or have, as identifiable units, a relatively long period of use; but are inventory, even though not held for sale, if they are used up or consumed in a short period of time in the production of some end product."

maple syrup, milk and eggs), and if they are in the possession of a debtor engaged in raising, fattening, grazing or other farming operations. If goods are farm products they are neither equipment nor inventory."[21]

Under the Article, security interests may be acquired in fixtures. The Article defines a fixture in very broad terms as goods which "become so related to particular real estate that an interest in them arises under real estate law,"[22] *with the legal effect that interests in the goods as chattels become subordinate to real estate interests*—except for priorities of interests in the fixture as established by the Code. It is for this reason that the Code provides for "fixture filing," i.e. recording in real estate records (where real estate mortgages are filed or recorded) in order to acquire priority against real estate interests. The Article leaves to local law the determination of when a chattel becomes a fixture because of its integral incorporation into the real estate, except that the Article precludes ordinary building materials incorporated into an improvement on land from becoming fixtures. Glass, lumber, bricks, tile, cement, and network are examples of such a kind of building materials.[23]

Intangibles. Intangible personal property consists of intangibles represented by indispensable paper, and intangibles not evidenced by any instrument or chattel paper. Intangibles are rights. Intangibles may be represented by indispensable paper, i.e., paper the possession of which is essential to the enjoyment, transfer, or enforcement of the intangible. Such indispensable paper consists of documents, instruments, and chattel paper. By document is meant a document of title, which is a document "which in the regular course of business or financing is treated as adequately evidencing that the person in possession of it is entitled to receive, hold and dispose of the document and the goods it covers."[24] Examples are bills of lading and warehouse receipts, previously discussed under Documents of Title.[25] By instrument is meant a negotiable instrument[26] or an investment security[27] "or any other writing which evidences a right to the payment of money and is not itself a security agreement or lease and is of a type which is in ordinary course

---

[21] UCC 9–109(3).

[22] UCC 9–313(1)(a).

[23] See UCC 9–313(1)(2); and below, pp. 758–60, 904.

[24] UCC 1–201(15).

[25] See above, pp. 200 ff.

[26] See above, p. 381.

[27] See above, p. 692.

of business transferred by delivery with any necessary indorsement or assignment."[28] Examples of a negotiable instrument are checks, negotiable promissory notes, and drafts; and examples of a security investment are certificates of stock and bonds. By chattel paper is meant "a writing or writings which evidence both a monetary obligation and a security interest in or a lease of specific goods. . . . When a transaction is evidenced both by such a security agreement or a lease and by an instrument or a series of instruments, the group of writings taken together constitutes chattel paper."[29] For example, the former conditional sales contract, whereby the buyer acquires a refrigerator but the seller reserves a security interest in the refrigerator, evidences both the buyer's debt to the seller of the balance of the unpaid purchase price and also that the seller has a security interest in the refrigerator to assure payment of the debt. The conditional sales contract is the security agreement and, should the seller wish to borrow money on the contract and his security interest in the refrigerator, he may refinance by using the contract representing his security interest in the refrigerator as security for his refinancing. The conditional sales contract is the chattel paper and the collateral for such refinancing.

Intangibles may not be evidenced by any instrument or document. Such intangibles are accounts and general intangibles. An account is "any right to payment for *goods sold or leased* or for *services rendered* which is not evidenced by an instrument or chattel paper, whether or not it has been earned by performance." (Author's italics.)[30] This is the usual account receivable. (S orally sells and *delivers* goods to B for $100 on 30 days credit. S has an account receivable of $100.) General intangibles "means any personal property (including things in action) *other than* goods, accounts, chattel paper, documents, instruments, and money." (Author's italics.)[31] Examples are goodwill, rights to performance, patents, and copyrights. General intangibles is a catchall term including miscellaneous types of right included in the Article but not included in account or the rights represented by instruments, documents, and chattel paper. An illustration may help to clarify some of these terms. "A dealer sells a tractor to a farmer on conditional sales contract or purchase money security interest contract. The conditional sales contract is a 'security agreement', the farmer is the 'debtor', the dealer is the 'secured party' and the tractor is the type of 'collateral'

---

[28] UCC 9–105(1)(i).

[29] UCC 9–105(1)(b).

[30] UCC 9–106.

[31] *Ibid.*

defined in Section 9–109 as 'equipment'. But now the dealer transfers the contract to his bank, either by outright sale or to secure a loan. Since the conditional sales contract is a security agreement relating to specific equipment, the conditional sales contract is now the type of collateral called 'chattel paper'. In this transaction between the dealer and his bank, the bank is the 'secured party', the dealer is the 'debtor', and the farmer is the 'account debtor'.[32]

It should be noted that the collateral subject to a security interest may be owned by a person other than the debtor. The Article fixes the legal status of such owner, unless otherwise agreed, with respect to his right to receive from the secured party any surplus resulting after the claim of the secured party has been enforced and satisfied, the owner not being liable for the debt or for any deficiency after resale of the collateral.[33]

After-Acquired Collateral. The secured party may wish to acquire a security interest in personal property to be later acquired by the debtor.[34] It becomes very important whether such a security interest is acquired as security for an antecedent debt or as security for new value given, because if no new value is given the acquisition of the additional security interest may have an important effect in federal bankruptcy or state insolvency proceedings. The Article specifies that a security interest in after-acquired collateral is acquired for new value and not as security for an antecedent debt if two things occur. *First,* the secured party must give new value, which occurs if he makes an advance, incurs an obligation, releases a perfected security interest, or otherwise gives new value. *Secondly,* the debtor acquires rights in the after-acquired collateral either in the ordinary course of his business, or under a contract of purchase made pursuant to the security agreement within a reasonable time after new value is given. A purchase money security interest is also new value.[35]

Conflict of Laws Rules concerning Perfection of Security Interests in Multiple State Transactions. The state where the col-

---

[32] UCC 9–105, *Comment 4.*

[33] UCC 9–112: [Such owner also] "has the same right as the debtor

(a) to receive statements under Section 9–208;

(b) to receive notice of and to object to a secured party's proposal to retain the collateral in satisfaction of the indebtedness under Section 9–505;

(c) to redeem the collateral under Section 9–506;

(d) to obtain injunctive or other relief under Section 9–507(1); and

(e) to recover losses caused to him under Section 9–208(2)."

[34] See below, pp. 757 f., for details regarding after-acquired property clause coverage.

[35] For the definition of value, see below, p. 744, ftn. 52.

lateral is located has jurisdiction over it and has legal power to declare not only its legal status, but also whether perfection of a security interest in the collateral has occurred and the legal effect of perfection or non-perfection of a security interest in the collateral. The state in which the collateral is located must, however, consider comity with other state jurisdictions with respect to tangible collateral which has come from another jurisdiction and with respect to the location of intangible collateral, such as an account or general intangible. While the Article's provisions apply as the law of the state in which the collateral is located, nevertheless special rules in the Article apply to: accounts, general intangibles, and mobile goods; documents, instruments, and ordinary goods; certificate of title; chattel paper; and minerals. Before considering each of these in the order indicated, it should be recognized at the outset that the Article's provisions apply to rights, obligations, and remedies regardless of the location of title to the collateral, whether it is in the secured party or in the debtor.

Accounts, General Intangibles, and Mobile Goods. Each state has laws for the filing of assignment of accounts so that creditors of the debtor-assignor in each particular state will have constructive notice of such assignment and of the security interest in the account. There are similar state laws for general intangibles and mobile goods. The Article has special rules with respect to accounts, general intangibles, and mobile goods of a type which are normally used in more than one jurisdiction (such as motor vehicles, trailers, rolling stock, airplanes, shipping containers, road building and construction machinery, and commercial harvesting machinery, and the like) if such goods are classified as equipment or classified as inventory by reason of their being leased or held for lease by the debtor to others, and are not covered by a certificate of title. The place where creditors of a debtor will most probably look to see if he has made an assignment and thereby created a security interest in his accounts, and the place where creditors of a debtor will most probably look to see if any other creditors have perfected a security interest in the debtor's general intangibles or such mobile goods, is the place where the debtor is located. Accordingly, *the Article provides that the law of the jurisdiction where the debtor is located will govern the perfection and the effect of perfection or nonperfection of a security interest with regard to accounts, general intangibles, and mobile goods of a type which are normally used in more than one jurisdiction if such goods are classified as equipment or classified as inventory by reason of their being leased or held for lease by the debtor to others.* The debtor is considered to be located at "his place of business if he has one, at his chief executive office if he has more than one place of business, otherwise at his residence."[36]

Documents, Instruments, and Ordinary Goods. Tangible collateral may be subject to a security interest before coming into a state. The state into which the collateral has come has jurisdiction to determine its legal status. Several rules under the Article[37] become pertinent. First, for the purpose of determining whether perfection of a security interest has occurred, and the legal effect of perfection or non-perfection of a security interest, of collateral consisting of documents, instruments, and ordinary goods, the governing law is that of the jurisdiction *where the collateral was located at the time when the last act necessary to such alleged perfection or non-perfection has occurred.* It is the law of the place of the collateral's location at that time which governs. Thus, with respect to a refrigerator located in state A where a financing statement is filed, the law of state A governs the perfection of the security interest in the refrigerator, and any security interest so perfected in state A will continue to be effective in state B into which the refrigerator is brought subsequently. Second, if a *purchase money* security interest *in goods* is created, and the parties creating such security interest understood at the time that the security interest *attached* that the goods would be kept *permanently* in another jurisdiction, then the law of the latter jurisdiction governs from the time the security interest attaches until thirty days after the debtor receives possession of the goods. If a filing and perfection occur in the latter jurisdiction, and the goods arrive in that jurisdiction within the thirty day period, the perfection continues to be effective without any interruption. Thus, in the refrigerator illustration just mentioned, if at the time the security interest attached to the refrigerator the debtor-owner of the refrigerator and the secured party knew that the debtor-owner planned to move his residence to state B, and the debtor-owner brought the refrigerator into state B within thirty days after the security interest attached to the refrigerator, then the law of state B governs the perfection and the effect of perfection or non-perfection of the security interest. *Third,* if the security interest was already perfected under the law of the jurisdiction from which the collateral was removed before being brought into the state where the collateral now is, the security interest continues perfected

---

[36] (continued) "If, however, the debtor is a foreign air carrier under Federal Aviation Act of 1958, as amended, it shall be deemed located at the designated office of the agent upon whom service of process may be made on account of the foreign air carrier." UCC 9–103(3)(d).

[37] UCC 9–103 (1).

in the state where the collateral now is for four months and also thereafter, if within the four-month period it is perfected in the state where the collateral now is. However, if the period of perfection effectiveness in the state from which the collateral comes is less than four months, then the security interest becomes unperfected at the end of that shorter period, rather than at the end of a four-month period. Thus, secured parties from other jurisdictions have a reasonable time in which to trace the collateral subject to their security interest, and purchasers in the state into which the collateral has come can deal with the debtor-owner of the collateral with assurance that, on the expiration of the reasonable time, there is no perfected security interest in the collateral. On the expiration of the four-month period, the secured party's security interest is treated as unperfected, and it then becomes subject to defeat by those persons who will have priority in the collateral over an unperfected security interest therein, as determined by the law of the state in which the collateral is located. However if, *within* the four-month period, the secured party perfects his security interest anew in the state where the collateral is now located, his original perfected security interest continues through the new perfection, without gap in time. While the security interest may be perfected in the state where the property is located *after* the expiration of the four-month period, nevertheless perfection dates from the time of perfection in the state where the collateral is located. It should be noted that these rules concerned with collateral subject to a security interest being brought into a state do *not* apply to collateral moved from one filing district to another *within the same state,* but only to collateral being brought *into* the state from another jurisdiction.

Certificate of Title to Goods. If the collateral is covered by a certificate of title issued under a statute of a jurisdiction which requires indication on the certificate of title of any security interest in the collateral as a condition of perfection, then the perfection and the effect of perfection or non-perfection are governed by *the law of the jurisdiction which issued the certificate.* An automobile certificate of title is a good example. However, if the goods are removed from that jurisdiction, then the law of that jurisdiction no longer governs after the four months or the surrender of the certificate, and the goods are no longer covered by the certificate. For further details, see UCC 9–103 (2) (c) (d).

Chattel Paper. Security interests in chattel paper may be possessory or non-possessory. If the security interest is possessory, the rules under "Documents, Instruments, and Ordinary Goods" apply. If the security interest is non-possessory, the rules under "Accounts, General Intangibles, and Mobile Goods" apply.

Minerals. The law of the jurisdiction where the wellhead or mine-head is located governs the "perfection and the effect of perfection or non-perfection of a security interest which is created by a debtor who has an interest in minerals or the like (including oil and gas) before extraction and which attaches thereto as extracted, or which attaches to an account resulting from the sale thereof at the wellhead or mine-head."[38]

Creation and Attachment of a Security Interest

There are three steps to perfection of a security interest: (1) the security interest must be created; (2) it must attach to collateral; and lastly (3) it must be perfected either by the filing of a financing statement[39] or by the secured party acquiring possession of the collateral, as required by the Article. However, some security interests may be perfected without compliance with the third step, from which they are exempted, e.g., a purchase money security interest in consumer goods.[40] These three steps will be considered in that order.

Creation. Possessory and Non-possessory Security Interests. Except for those security interests arising under the Code in connection with a collecting bank[41] and under Sales,[42] *a security interest will not be recognized as enforceable against the debtor or third parties with respect to the collateral, and it does not attach to collateral, unless either the collateral is in the possession of the secured party or the debtor has signed a security agreement.* A security agreement is an agreement which creates or provides for a security interest. It need only be in writing, signed by the debtor, and contain a description of the collateral or kinds of collateral. Any description of personal property or real property is sufficient, whether or not it is specific, as long as it reasonably identifies what is described. However, if the security interest covers crops, growing or to be grown, or timber to be cut, a description of the land is to be included in the security agreement. These are the simple formal requisites of the security agreement, although in commercial practice it may generally include much more information.

---

[38] UCC 9–103(5).

[39] For the formal requisites of a financing statement, see below, pp. 764–65.

[40] See below, p. 748.

[41] See above, pp. 480–81.

[42] See above, p. 730.

These formal requisites constitute a statute of frauds with respect to security agreements. The Article does not intend to invalidate *regulatory* statutes, particularly in the field of consumer finance (e.g., small loan acts, retail installment acts and the like) *which will prevail over the Article's provisions,* except as they provide for filing, default, etc., in which case the Article governs. Thus, an enforceable security interest may be either possessory, or non-possessory and created by a security agreement.

Validity. A non-possessory security interest is not invalid or fraudulent as to creditors because the debtor has unfettered dominion or control over the collateral.[43] The former requirement by judicial decision of policing the conduct of the debtor is no longer required as a matter of law, although the debtor and secured party may, for business reasons, agree to strict accountability, etc., by the debtor. Thus, the "floating lien" or floating charge or lien on a shifting stock of goods is validated by the Article. Unless otherwise agreed, the debtor may use, commingle, or dispose of all or part of the collateral (including returned or repossessed goods); collect or compromise accounts or chattel paper; accept the return of goods or make repossessions; use, commingle, or dispose of the proceeds; and do all this without accounting for the proceeds or replacing the collateral.[44] Where the security interest is possessory, perfection of the security interest depends upon possession of the collateral by the secured party or by a bailee, e.g., a field storage warehouseman,[45] and the freedom of the debtor is limited only by the necessity that the collateral remain in the possession of the secured party or a bailee.

Also, with certain limitations, the validity of a security agreement is not affected by a provision therein that the buyer or lessee will not assert against an assignee of the seller or lessor secured party defenses which the buyer or lessee may have against the seller or lessor. Such a waiver of defenses is enforceable by an assignee for value, in good faith and without notice of a claim or defense. There are three limitations on the validity of such a waiver. *First,* the waiver is valid as to buyers and lessees of *consumer* goods only if no statute or judicial decision establishes a different rule. There is much controversy concerning the valid-

---

[43] See UCC 9–205, *Comment 1.*

[44] UCC 9–205.

[45] Pledge has already been defined; see above, p. 729, ftn. 5. Under the increasingly prevalent device of field storage warehousing, the pledgor does not have possession of the pledged chattels which are warehoused convenient to the pledgor's temporary and limited use from time to time, and the pledgee has sufficient control and possession of the chattels so that third persons have notice of the pledgee's interest therein.

ity of such waivers in the consumer goods field,[46] and the Article takes no position in that area. *Second,* defenses which could be asserted against a holder in due course of a negotiable instrument[47] and thereby cancel the obligation of the buyer or lessee may not be waived by the buyer or lessee in a security agreement and, as to such defenses, the waiver clause is illegal and void. *Third,* purchase money security trans-

---

[46] Because of a sharp irreconcilable difference among the states as to whether or not an assignee of rights in a consumer credit sale or consumer lease takes the assigned rights subject to the buyer's or lessee's claims and defenses against the seller or lessor arising out of the sale or lease, and whether that portion of an agreement between the parties waiving such claims or defenses is valid, U3C Sec. 2. 404 provides alternative provisions.

"Alternative A: **Assignee Subject to Defenses.**

With respect to a consumer credit sale or consumer lease, other than a sale or lease primarily for an agricultural purpose, *an assignee of the rights of the seller or lessor is subject to all claims and defenses of the buyer or lessee against the seller or lessor arising out of the sale or lease notwithstanding an agreement to the contrary,* but the assignee's liability under this section may not exceed the amount owing to the assignee at the time the claim or defense is asserted against the assignee. Rights of the buyer or lessee under this section can only be asserted as a matter of defense to or set-off against a claim by the assignee.

Alternative B: **When Assignee Not Subject to Defenses.**

(1) With respect to a consumer credit sale or consumer lease, other than a sale or lease primarily for an agricultural purpose, *an agreement by the buyer or lessee not to assert against an assignee a claim or defense arising out of the sale or lease is enforceable only by an assignee not related to the seller or lessor who acquires the buyer's or lessee's contract in good faith and for value, who gives the buyer or lessee notice of the assignment as provided in this section and who, within 3 months after the mailing of the notice of assignment, receives no written notice of the facts giving rise to the buyer's or lessee's claim or defense. This agreement is enforceable only with respect to claims or defenses which have arisen before the end of the 3-month period after notice was mailed.* The notice of assignment shall be in writing and addressed to the buyer or lessee at his address as stated in the contract, identify the contract, describe the goods or services, state the names of the seller or lessor and buyer or lessee, the name and address of the assignee, the amount payable by the buyer or lessee and the number, amounts and due dates of the instalments, and contain a conspicuous notice to the buyer or lessee that he has 3 months within which to notify the assignee in writing of any complaints, claims or defenses he may have against the seller or lessor and that if written notification of the complaints, claims or defenses is not received by the assignee within the 3-month period, the assignee will have the right to enforce the contract free of any claims or defenses the buyer or lessee may have against the seller or lessor which have arisen before the end of the 3-month period after notice was mailed.

(2) An assignee does not acquire a buyer's or lessee's contract in good faith within the meaning of subsection (1) if the assignee has knowledge or, from his course of dealing with the seller or lessor or his records, notice of substantial complaints by other buyers or lessees of the seller's or lessor's failure or refusal to perform his contracts with them and of the seller's or lessor's failure to remedy his defaults within a reasonable time after the assignee notifies him of the complaints.

(3) To the extent that under this section an assignee is subject to claims or defenses of the buyer or lessee against the seller or lessor, the assignee's liability under this section may not exceed the amount owing to the assignee at the time the claim or defense is asserted against the assignee and rights of the buyer or lessee under this section can only be asserted as a matter of defense to or set-off against a claim by the assignee." (Author's italics.)

[47] UCC 3–305(2). See above, pp. 422–25.

actions are sales of goods and the Sales portion of the Code governs the sale and any disclaimer, limitation, or modification of the seller's warranties.[48]

Duties of the Secured Party. The secured party may acquire possession of collateral as a pledgee before the debtor's default, or he may take possession of the collateral after the debtor's default. In either case, *the secured party's possession of the collateral imposes upon him a duty of reasonable care in the custody and preservation of the collateral.* If the collateral is an instrument or chattel paper, reasonable care includes taking necessary steps to preserve rights against prior parties, unless otherwise agreed. *The duty of care imposed by the Article cannot be disclaimed by agreement between the parties,*[49] although they may agree on reasonable standards as to what shall constitute reasonable care. The secured party's failure to exercise reasonable care will subject him to liability for any loss caused thereby, but he does not lose his security interest. The secured party may either notify the debtor of anything that is to be done in connection with the secured party's exercise of his care and let the debtor do it, or the secured party can do it himself. Unless otherwise agreed, when collateral is in the secured party's possession:

(a) reasonable expenses (including the cost of any insurance and payment of taxes or other charges) incurred in the custody, preservation, use or operation of the collateral are chargeable to the debtor and are secured by the collateral;

(b) the risk of accidental loss or damage is on the debtor to the extent of any deficiency in any effective insurance coverage;

(c) the secured party may hold as additional security any increase or profits (except money) received from the collateral, but money so received, unless remitted to the debtor, shall be applied in reduction of the secured obligation;

(d) the secured party must keep the collateral identifiable but fungible collateral may be commingled;

(e) the secured party may repledge the collateral upon terms which do not impair the debtor's right to redeem it.[50]

Also, a "secured party may use or operate the collateral for the purpose of preserving the collateral or its value or pursuant to the order of a

---

[48] See above, pp. 285 ff.
[49] UCC 1–102(3).
[50] UCC 9–207(2).

court of appropriate jurisdiction or, except in the case of consumer goods, in the manner and to the extent provided in the security agreement."[51] Subsection (a) above is applicable in connection with the expense incurred in such use or operation.

It is but reasonable for the debtor to verify the status of his account with the secured party. The Article recognizes a right in the debtor to demand a statement of account or of collateral and imposes a duty on the secured party reasonably to comply with such demand. The debtor may make, sign, and send to the secured party a *written* statement of what he believes to be the unpaid indebtedness as of a specified date, requesting that the statement be approved or corrected and returned to him. When the security agreement or any other record kept by the secured party identifies the collateral, the debtor may also submit a list of the collateral to the secured party and request him to approve or correct the list. The secured party must comply with such request within two weeks after its receipt. The secured party's failure without reasonable excuse to comply with such request makes him liable for any loss caused *to the debtor thereby;* and also, if the debtor has properly included in his request a good faith statement of the obligation or a list of the collateral or both, the secured party may claim a security interest *only as shown in the statement against persons misled by his failure to comply.* In order to be proper, the secured party's reply must contain a *written* correction or approval of the debtor's statement of account and of the list of collateral if that is also included in the debtor's request. However, if the secured party claims a security interest in all of a particular type of collateral owned by the debtor, he may indicate that fact in his reply and need not approve or correct the debtor's itemized list of such collateral. If the secured party no longer has an interest in the obligation or collateral at the time he received the request, because of assignment or otherwise, his reply must state the name and address of any successor in interest known to him, and his failure so to indicate makes him liable for any loss caused to the debtor thereby. A successor in interest of the secured party has no obligation to reply to a debtor's request for approval or correction until he receives such a request. A debtor is entitled to such a statement from the secured party without charge once every six months. The secured party may require payment of a charge not exceeding $10 for each additional statement furnished. Unless otherwise agreed, when a secured party knows that collateral is

---

[51] UCC 9–207 (4).

owned by a person who is not the debtor, the owner of the collateral has the same right as the debtor to receive the above statements from the secured party.

Attachment of the Security Interest. A security interest is created by the security agreement and is effective according to its terms. However, the security interest must attach to collateral in order to be an interest therein and for the secured party to acquire rights in the collateral *as against the debtor.* Attachment is different from perfection of a security interest in that perfection is concerned with the maximum extent of the rights of the secured party in the collateral *as against other creditors of, and purchasers from, the debtor.* By perfection, the secured party acquires the maximum rights in the collateral which he can acquire under the law of secured transactions, although they may not necessarily be supreme and accord to him top priority over the rights of other persons in the same collateral.

In the absence of explicit agreement to the contrary postponing the time of attaching, *a security interest attaches to collateral when three things occur, irrespective of the order of their occurrence:* (1) *there is a security agreement that the security interest attach, or the collateral is in the possession of the secured party pursuant to agreement;* (2) *value has been given; and* (3) *the debtor has rights in the collateral.* The interest of a secured party is in what is owned by the debtor in collateral, and until the debtor acquires rights in the collateral the security interest cannot attach to the collateral to the extent of such rights of the debtor. The value to be given is generally consideration sufficient to support a simple contract or an antecedent or pre-existing debt.[52] The security agreement may provide that a security interest will attach to collateral not yet owned by the debtor. The Article makes specific provision as to when a debtor acquires rights in certain kinds of future collateral. A security agreement may contain an after-acquired property clause by providing that collateral, *whenever acquired,* with one exception, shall secure all obligations covered by the security agreement.

---

[52] UCC 1–201(44): " 'Value.' Except as otherwise provided with respect to negotiable instruments and bank collections (Sections 3–303, 4–208 and 4–209) a person gives 'value' for rights if he acquires them

(a) in return for a binding commitment to extend credit or for the extension of immediately available credit whether or not drawn upon and whether or not a charge-back is provided for in the event of difficulties in collection; or

(b) as security for or in total or partial satisfaction of a pre-existing claim; or

(c) by accepting delivery pursuant to a pre-existing contract for purchase; or

(d) generally, in return for any consideration sufficient to support a simple contract."
For the meaning of charge-back, see below, pp. 770–71.

This, when combined with the debtor's right to use and deal freely with the collateral in his possession and proceeds therefrom, validates the floating lien or floating charge or lien on a shifting stock of goods. The obligations covered by a security agreement may include future advances or other value whether or not the advances or value are given pursuant to commitment. However, the security interest in future advances may be subordinated to a conflicting purchase money security interest in the same collateral.[53] The one exception to "whenever acquired" in connection with an after-acquired property clause has a definite limitation in the time in which a security interest may attach to after-acquired collateral. No security interest attaches under an after-acquired property clause to consumer goods, other than accessions,[54] when given as additional security *unless the debtor acquires rights in them within ten days after the secured party gives value.*

Perfection of the Security Interest

Meaning. We have seen that a security interest attaches when the collateral becomes subject to the security interest. The reason for a secured party perfecting his security interest is to obtain the maximum priority for his security interest in collateral which cannot be defeated in insolvency proceedings or, in general,[55] by other creditors of, or transferees from, the debtor. *A security interest is perfected when the security interest has attached and the secured party has complied with all of the Article's requirements for perfection of the security interest.* The order of occurrence is unimportant. Thus, if the various steps required for perfection occur before the security interest attaches to the collateral, the security interest is perfected when it attaches. For example, the financing statement may have been filed before value has been given or before the debtor has acquired rights in the collateral; the later giving of value or the debtor's subsequent acquisition of rights in the collateral causes the security interest to attach and the security interest to become perfected. *If a security interest is perfected in one way and subsequently, without an intermediate period when it is unperfected, it is perfected in another way under the Article, it is perfected continously from the time of its original perfection.* Failure to perfect a security interest causes it to be subordinate to the

---

[53] See below, pp. 757–58.

[54] For accessions, see UCC 9–314.

[55] Some interests have priority even over perfected security interests. See UCC 9–312, and also below, pp. 755 ff.

rights of certain persons who have a limited priority over the unperfected security interest. They are:

(a) persons entitled to priority under Section 9–312;

(b) a person who becomes a lien creditor[56] before the security interest is perfected;

(c) in the case of goods, instruments, documents, and chattel paper, a person who is not a secured party and who is a transferee in bulk[57] or other buyer not in ordinary course of business[58] or is a buyer of farm products in ordinary course of business, to the extent that he gives value and receives delivery of the collateral without knowledge of the security interest and before it is perfected;

(d) in the case of accounts and general intangibles, a person who is not a secured party and who is a transferee to the extent that he gives value without knowledge of the security interest and before it is perfected.[59]

It should be noted very carefully that a purchase money security interest, discussed previously,[60] relates to the time when the security interest attaches and has a limited priority over rights during the intervening period between the time of the filing of a financing statment and when the security interest attaches. Thus, if the secured party of a purchase money security interest files his financing statement before or within ten days after the debtor receives possession of the collateral, the secured party takes priority over only the rights of a transferee in bulk or of a lien creditor which arise between the time the security interest attaches and the time of filing.[61]

Methods of Perfecting. *Filing Required.* The filing of a financing statement[62] is the basic requirement of the Article in order to perfect a security interest. *Unless otherwise provided by the Article, perfection of a security interest can be made only by filing.*

---

[56] UCC 9–301(3): "A 'lien creditor' means a creditor who has acquired a lien on the property involved by attachment, levy or the like and includes an assignee for benefit of creditors from the time of assignment, and a trustee in bankruptcy from the date of the filing of the petition or a receiver in equity from the time of appointment."

[57] A transferee in bulk is not in the ordinary course of business. For bulk transfer, see above, p. 351.

[58] UCC 1–201(9): " 'Buyer in ordinary course of business' means a person who in good faith and without knowledge that the sale to him is in violation of the ownership rights or security interest of a third party in the goods buys in ordinary course from a person in the business of selling goods of that kind but does not include a pawnbroker. 'Buying' may be for cash or by exchange of other property or on secured or unsecured credit and includes receiving goods or documents of title under a pre-existing contract for sale but does not include a transfer in bulk or as security for or in total or partial satisfaction of a money debt."

[59] UCC 9–301(1).

[60] See above, p. 731.

[61] UCC 9–301(2).

[62] For the formal requisites of a financing statement, see below, pp. 764–66.

Filing Not Required. There are eight transactions which are exempted from the Article's requirement of filing a financing statement in order to perfect a security interest in collateral.

First, possession by the secured party of goods, instruments, money, negotiable documents, chattel paper, or letters and advices of credit[63] *perfects his security interest in such collateral without filing.* It should be noted very carefully that not all kinds of collateral are included. Accounts and general intangibles are excluded. This method of perfection by possession reflects the Common Law of pledge, the secured party's possession of the collateral being notice to all persons of an interest therein, so that filing to give notice of such security interest thus becomes unnecessary. Possession of the collateral may be by the secured party himself or by his agent on his behalf. The security interest is perfected by possession from the time possession is taken and continues only so long as possession is retained, except as otherwise provided in the Article. However, if the collateral, except for goods covered by a negotiable document, is in the possession of a bailee, the secured party is deemed to have possession from the time the bailee receives notification of the secured party's interest in the collateral and, therefore, the time of perfection of the secured interest is when the bailee receives such notification. It is no longer necessary for a bailee to inform the secured party or acknowledge that he holds the collateral for the secured party. Perfection by the secured party's possession of the particular collateral does not preclude perfection before or after possession in any other way permitted by the Article.

Second, a security interest in instruments or negotiable documents is perfected without filing or the taking of possession of such instruments or negotiable documents for a period of 21 days from the time it attaches to the extent that it arises for new value given under a written security agreement. This is a temporary perfection which expires at the end of the 21-day period unless perfected as required by the Article within that period, in which event the security interest continues uninterruptedly from the time of its original perfection at the beginning of the 21-day period.

Third, a secured party's perfected security interest in collateral continues as a perfected security interest in the proceeds resulting from disposition of the collateral. However, if the proceeds are received by the debtor, the security interest continues to be perfected for only 10 days after the debtor's receipt of the proceeds, when perfection then

---

[63] See UCC 5–116(2)(a).

ceases unless the proceeds from the original collateral are identifiable cash proceeds, or the security interest in the proceeds is perfected by filing a financing statement or by acquiring possession of the proceeds before the expiration of the 10-day period.[64]

Fourth, a purchase money security interest in consumer goods is perfected without filing; but filing is required for a motor vehicle required to be registered, and for fixtures for priority over conflicting interests in fixtures. This is the only transaction where filing is not required when the goods subject to the security interest are in the debtor's possession.

Fifth, while a filing is necessary to perfect a security interest in accounts, nevertheless no filing is necessary to perfect a security interest on the assignment of accounts which does not transfer, either alone or in conjunction with other assignments to the same assignee, a significant part of the outstanding accounts of the assignor. This is meant to cover casual or isolated assignments; however, any person who regularly takes assignments of any debtor's accounts should file.[65] It should be recalled that the Article does not apply "to a sale of accounts or chattel paper as part of a sale of the business out of which they arose, or an assignment of accounts or chattel paper which is for the purpose of collection only, or a transfer of a right to payment under a contract to an assignee who is also to do the performance under the contract, or a transfer of a single account to an assignee in whole or partial satisfaction of a preexisting indebtedness."[66]

Sixth, no filing is required in order to perfect a security interest of a collecting bank in items, accompanying documents and proceeds therefrom,[67] *or a security interest arising solely under the Article on Sales as long as the debtor does not have or lawfully obtain possession of the goods.*[68]

Seventh, no filing is required for a security interest created by an assignment of a beneficial interest in a trust or a decedent's estate.[69]

Eighth, also no filing is required for an assignment for the benefit of all the creditors of the assignor, and subsequent transfers by the assignee thereunder. This obviously is not a financing transaction.[70]

---

[64] For further discussion of perfecting a security interest in proceeds, see below, pp. 751–52.

[65] UCC 9–302, *Comment 5.*

[66] UCC 9–104(f).

[67] UCC 4–208.

[68] UCC 9–113.

[69] UCC 9–302(1)(c).

[70] UCC 9–302 (1)(g).

Often the secured party will assign his perfected security interest. Since the security interest has been perfected and is effective against the *debtor's* creditors and transferees, it continues to be so perfected in the hands of the assignee and no filing is required in order to continue the perfected status of the security interest against creditors of, and transferees from, the *original debtor.* However, if the assignment was intended as security from the assignor to the assignee, or it was a sale of accounts or chattel paper,[71] the assignee will have to comply with the requirements of the Article in order to perfect his security interest in the collateral against the *assignor's* creditors and transferees.

The filing provisions of the Article are not necessary to perfect a security interest in property subject to: a federal statute or treaty which provides for a national or international registration, or a national or international certificate of title, or which specifies a place of filing different from that specified in this Article for filing of the security interest; a certificate of title statute of another jurisdiction requiring indication of a security interest on the certificate as a condition of perfection.[72]

The Article makes special provisions for the perfection of a security interest in instruments, documents and goods covered by documents, and also for a secured party's rights on disposition of collateral. These will be considered in that order.

Perfection of Security Interest in Instruments, Documents, and Goods Covered by Documents. We have seen that a security interest in instruments, negotiable documents, and chattel paper may be perfected by possession in the secured party. However, a security interest in *negotiable documents and chattel paper* may also be perfected by *filing;* but, except for temporary perfection, a security interest *in instruments* (other than instruments which constitute part of chattel paper) and money can be perfected *only* by the secured party taking *possession* of the instruments and money, except for the proceeds of collateral which is discussed later.[73] In normal commercial practice, the secured party has possession of instruments and negotiable documents, and their possession is sufficient to alert creditors and transferees of the debtor of the existence of a security interest therein. However, chattel paper often is assigned and possession is left in the hands of the assignor for the purpose of collection, in which case the assignee can

---

[71] Under UCC 9–102(1)(b) the Article applies to any sale of accounts or chattel paper.

[72] UCC 9–302(3)(a).

[73] See below, pp. 751–53.

perfect his security interest against the assignor's creditors and transferees by filing a financing statement.

A distinction is drawn between negotiable and non-negotiable documents because title to the covered goods is deemed tied into a negotiable
document, but not into a non-negotiable document. Inasmuch as the
way to deal with goods covered by a negotiable document is through the
negotiable document, perfection of a security interest in the document is
automatically perfection of a security interest in the covered goods.
Also, any other security interest perfected in the covered goods while a
negotiable document is outstanding is subject to the perfected security
interest in the negotiable document. If goods are in the possession of a
bailee who has not issued a negotiable document therefor, a security
interest in the goods is perfected by either of three ways: issuance of a
document in the name of the secured party, e.g., as consignee of a
straight bill of lading or as the person to whom delivery would be made
under a non-negotiable warehouse receipt; the bailee's receipt of notification of the secured party's interest in the goods, which is the equivalent of the secured party's obtaining possession of the goods; or by filing
as to the goods. The Article also recognizes that commercial practice
often requires the temporary surrender of the possession of goods,
documents, and instruments to the debtor. For example, the goods or
documents representing the goods may be made available to the debtor
for the purpose of ultimate sale or exchange or for the purpose of
dealing with them in a manner preliminary to their sale or exchange,
such as loading, unloading, storing, shipping, transshipping, manufacturing, processing; and an instrument may be delivered to the debtor
for the purpose of ultimate sale or exchange or of presentation, collection, renewal, or registration of transfer. Accordingly, the Article provides for temporary perfection without filing by, or possession in, the
secured party. In the case of a *non-perfected* security interest in *instruments,* or *negotiable documents,* the secured interest is perfected without filing or the taking of possession for a period of 21 days from the
time it attaches to the extent that it arises for *new value* given under a
written security agreement. In the case of *an already perfected security
interest* in *goods, negotiable document, or instrument* in the possession
of a bailee who has not issued a negotiable document therefor, the
security interest remains perfected for a period of 21 days without filing
only if the secured party makes available to the debtor the goods or
documents, or he delivers the instrument to the debtor, for any of the
purposes as respectively indicated immediately above. On the expiration
of the 21-day period in the last two paragraphs, the temporary perfec-

tion is ended unless, meanwhile, the security interest has been perfected as otherwise provided by the Article.

Disposition of Collateral. The collateral or proceeds may be disposed of by sale, exchange, collection, or otherwise, and whatever is received therefrom is called "proceeds." When the proceeds·are in the form of money, checks, deposit accounts, and the like, it is called "cash proceeds"; all other proceeds are "non-cash proceeds." *A filing as to collateral is now considered to be an automatic filing as to the proceeds from such collateral;* no further indication need be given on the financing statement in order to accomplish this automatic effect. Except as the Article otherwise provides, when collateral is disposed of without authority from the secured party, the latter's security interest continues in the collateral and also in any *identifiable* proceeds therefrom, including collections received by the debtor. However, if the secured party authorized such disposition of the collateral, his security interest in the collateral is terminated but his security interest continues in the *identifiable* proceeds therefrom. In other words, if the secured party can trace the proceeds, his security interest in them survives. If the security interest of the secured party in the original collateral was perfected, then the security interest in the proceeds therefrom is a continuously perfected security interest. However, if the proceeds are received by the debtor, the security interest continues to be perfected *for only 10 days after the debtor's receipt of the proceeds,* when perfection then ceases, unless the proceeds from the original collateral are identifiable cash proceeds, or the security interest in the proceeds is perfected by filing a financing statement or by acquiring possession of the proceeds before the expiration of the 10-day period, as discussed previously.[74] It should be observed carefully that, although a perfected security interest in collateral continues therein when unauthorizedly disposed of, some purchasers of such collateral take free of the security interest. This is discussed later.[75]

The institution of insolvency proceedings[76] does not affect the secured party's security interest in proceeds, and a secured party with a perfected security interest in proceeds has a perfected security interest:

---

[74] See above, pp. 747–48.

[75] See below, pp. 753–55.

[76] UCC 1–201(22), (23): " 'Insolvency proceedings' includes any assignment for the benefit of creditors or other proceedings intended to liquidate or rehabilitate the estate of the person involved. A person is 'insolvent' who either has ceased to pay his debts in the ordinary course of business or cannot pay his debts as they become due or is insolvent within the meaning of the federal bankruptcy law."

(a) in *identifiable non-cash proceeds and in separate deposit accounts containing only proceeds;*
(b) in *identifiable cash proceeds in the form of money* which is *neither* commingled with other money nor deposited in a deposit account prior to insolvency proceedings;
(c) in *identifiable cash proceeds in the form of checks and the like* which are *not* deposited in a deposit account prior to the insolvency proceedings; and
(d) in all *cash and deposit accounts* of the debtor, *in which proceeds have been commingled with other funds,* but the perfected security interest under this paragraph (d) is
  (i) subject to any right of set-off; and
  (ii) limited to an amount not greater than the amount of any cash proceeds received by the debtor within ten days before the institution of the insolvency proceedings less the sum of
    (I) the payments to the secured party on account of cash proceeds received by the debtor during such period and
    (II) the cash proceeds received by the debtor during such period to which the secured party is entitled under paragraphs (a) through (c) of this subsection (4). (Author's italics.)[77]

When previously sold collateral is returned to the debtor seller, questions arise as to who have security interests in the collateral and of priorities among secured parties. If a sale of goods results in an account or chattel paper which is transferred by the seller to a secured party, and if the goods are returned to, or are repossessed by, the seller or the secured party, various rules determine the priorities of competing secured parties to the goods. *First,* the goods may have been collateral for the seller's debt at the time of the sale, and the secured party is still unpaid at the time of their return to, or repossession by, the seller. In this event, as between the debtor and the secured party, the original security interest attaches again to the goods and continues as a perfected security interest if it was perfected at the time when the goods were sold. Whether or not the security interest continues to be perfected after reattachment depends upon the method used to perfect it originally. If it was originally perfected by a filing which is still effective, nothing further is required to continue the perfected status; however, in any other case, the secured party must take possession of the returned or repossessed goods or must file a financing statement. *Second,* the seller of goods that are subject to a security interest of a secured party may sell such goods to a buyer who executes chattel paper in favor of the seller. The seller transfers the chattel paper as security for the seller's debt to the transferee. When the goods are returned to, or

---

[77] UCC 9–306(4).

repossessed by, the seller, the unpaid transferee of chattel paper has a security interest in the goods *against the transferor*. However, his security interest is subordinate to the security interest of the original secured party, except as the transferee is entitled to priority as a purchaser of the chattel paper under certain conditions, discussed later.[78] *Third,* the seller of goods, which are subject to a security interest of a secured party, may sell such goods to a buyer who now owes part or all of the purchase price. The seller transfers the "account" as security for the seller's debt to the transferee. When the goods are returned to, or repossessed by, the seller, the unpaid transferee *of the account* has a security interest in the goods *against the transferor*. However, such security interest is subordinate to the security interest of the original secured party. It should be noted very carefully that the security interest of an unpaid transferee of chattel paper or of an account must be perfected in order to protect it against creditors of the transferor and purchasers of the returned or repossessed goods.

Rights of Third Parties. Often there is conflict between a secured party on the one hand and a purchaser of the collateral on the other hand, and also between secured parties in the same collateral. First, purchasers of collateral will be discussed and then priorities among conflicting security interests.

Purchasers of Collateral. We have already seen that certain purchasers of collateral take free of an *unperfected* security interest therein.[79] Here we are concerned with whether, and to what extent, if any, purchasers take free of *perfected* security interests in the collateral purchased. The collateral purchased may be the goods themselves, or other collateral such as chattel paper, negotiable instruments, negotiable documents, and investment securities. These will be discussed briefly in that order.

Goods subject to a security interest may be sold with or without the authority[80] of the secured party. If sold with authority, the purchaser takes the goods free of the security interest. *If sold without authority, only a buyer in ordinary course of business,*[81] *other than a person buying farm products from a person engaged in farming operations, takes free of a security interest created by his seller even though the security*

---

[78] See below, pp. 754 f.

[79] See above, pp. 745–46.

[80] Under the Article "authority" means consent. Under the law of agency, authority is an agent's power to act in accord with his principal's manifestation to him. See Agency, above, p. 514.

[81] See above, p. 746, ftn. 58.

interest is perfected and even though the buyer knows of its existence.
Such a buyer purchases *inventory* from a merchant.[82] Also, such a buyer
purchases in good faith and without knowledge that the sale to him is *in
violation* of the ownership rights or security interest of a third party in
the goods. A buyer's knowledge of a security interest does not mean that
he knows that the sale is in violation of the security agreement. (For
example, if a secured party files a financing statement of a security
interest in inventory consisting of refrigerators in the dealer's showroom, and a buyer in ordinary course of business purchases one of the
refrigerators knowing that it is subject to a security interest, the buyer
takes the refrigerator free of the security interest.) However, in the case
of *consumer goods* the manner of perfecting the security interest, the
buyer's knowledge of the security interest at the time of the sale, and the
purpose of the purchase become important. If the secured party has filed
a financing statement before the sale, the buyer takes subject to the
security interest. If perfection occurred in any other way and the buyer
purchased without knowledge of the security interest, for value and for
his own personal, family, or household purposes, the buyer takes free
of the security interest. Although a secured party with a purchase
money security interest in consumer goods need not file a financing
statement in order to perfect the security interest,[83] nevertheless he
should do so in order that all *buyers* will take subject to his security
interest. Conflicting security interests in fixtures are discussed later.[84]

The purchase may be of chattel paper or negotiable instruments.
First let us consider chattel paper. The security interest in chattel paper
of a secured party may be a specific interest acquired by his giving new
value against the paper or merely a claim to proceeds therefrom. We
have seen that possession of chattel paper by the secured party perfects
his security interest without filing.[85] He may also perfect his security
interest in the chattel paper by permissive filing,[86] which he may wish
to do if he permits the chattel paper to be possessed by the debtor.
Commercial practice varies as to whether the debtor seller who acquires chattel paper from the buyer will be permitted by the secured
party to retain possession of the chattel paper and make collections
thereon from the buyer. If chattel paper is permitted to remain in the

---

[82] For the effect of entrusting goods to a merchant who sells them to a buyer in
ordinary course of business, see Sales, above, p. 283.

[83] See above, p. 748.

[84] See below, pp. 758–60.

[85] See above, p. 747.

[86] See above, pp. 750–51.

seller's possession, purchasers of such chattel paper would take subject to a prior perfected security interest, except for a certain kind of purchaser who would have priority. If the purchaser of chattel paper gives *new value* and *takes possession* of it in the ordinary course of *his* business and *without knowldege* that the specific paper is subject to a security interest, he has priority over a security interest which has been perfected by permissive filing or has temporary perfection. If such a purchaser of chattel paper *has knowledge* that the specific paper is subject to a security interest, nevertheless he has priority over a security interest in chattel paper which is *claimed merely as proceeds of inventory* subject to a security interest.

The purchase may be of negotiable paper, namely a negotiable instrument,[87] a negotiable document of title,[88] or an investment security.[89] We have already discussed the paramount position of certain purchasers of such negotiable paper, and nothing in the Article limits the rights of a holder in due course of a negotiable instrument,[90] a holder to whom a negotiable document of title has been duly negotiated,[91] or a bona fide purchaser of an investment security.[92] Such holders or purchasers take priority over an earlier security interest, even though perfected, and filing under the Article does not constitute notice of the security interest to them.

Priorities among Conflicting Security Interests. We have already considered priorities in mentioning the security interest of collecting banks in items being collected, accompanying documents and proceeds,[93] and in discussing: the rights to which an unperfected security interest is subordinate;[94] goods covered by documents;[95] proceeds and repossessions;[96] buyers of goods;[97] possessory against non-possessory interests in chattel paper or negotiable instruments;[98] and security interests in negotiable instruments, negotiable documents of title, and investment securities, immediately above. We will now consider: priori-

[87] See above, p. 381.
[88] See above, p. 201.
[89] See above, p. 692.
[90] See UCC 3–305, and also Commercial Paper, above, p. 410.
[91] See UCC 7–501, and also Documents of Title, above, p. 224.
[92] See UCC 8–301, and also Investment Securities, above, p. 699.
[93] See above, pp. 480–81, 748.
[94] See above, pp. 745–46.
[95] See above, pp. 749–51.
[96] See above, pp. 751–53.
[97] See above, pp. 753–54.
[98] See above, pp. 754–55.

ties between perfected security interests and liens by operation of law; conflicting security interests in crops; the priority of a purchase money security interest; priorities in cases for which the Article has not otherwise provided; security interests in fixtures as against interests in real estate; security interests in accessions as against interests in goods; conflicting security interests where goods lose their identity or become part of a product; and contractual subordination.

Often there is conflict for priority between earlier perfected security interests and later Common Law or statutory liens for materials and services rendered to the collateral, called an artisan's lien at Common Law. Inasmuch as such materials and services rendered in the ordinary course of business are intended to preserve or enhance the value of the collateral, it is but just that the liens for them should have priority, unless state public policy by statute is to the contrary. Accordingly, under the Article, when a person *in the ordinary course of his business* furnishes services or materials with respect to goods subject to a security interest, a lien upon goods *in the possession of such person* given by statute or rule of law for such materials or services takes priority over a perfected security interest; however a state statute to the contrary on this will prevail over the Article.

It is not unusual for a debtor to have an interest, whether legal title or an equity, in collateral. Previous conflicts as to whether the security agreement legally could prohibit the debtor's transfer of his rights in the collateral and whether the debtor's creditors could proceed by judicial process against his rights, such as by attachment, levy, or garnishment, are resolved in favor of voluntary and involuntary alienability of the debtor's rights in the collateral. Accordingly, *the debtor's rights in collateral may be voluntarily or involuntarily transferred notwithstanding a provision in the security agreement prohibiting any transfer or making the transfer constitute a default.*

Conflict between security interests in crops as the result of a *current* crop production loan is resolved on the length of time of such loan relative to the time when the collateral became growing crops. A perfected security interest in crops securing obligations *due more than six months before* the crops became growing crops by planting or otherwise is subordinate to a later perfected security interest in the crops which (1) is for new value (2) to enable the debtor to produce the crops during the production season and (3) *given not more than three months before* the crops became growing crops by planting or otherwise. Such later security interest has priority even though the secured party giving new value had knowledge of the earlier security interest.

Reference should be made to previous discussion concerning the extent to which a security interest attaches to collateral other than crops under an after-acquired property clause.[99]

Conflicts of priority often arise in the same collateral between purchase money security interests and non-purchase money security interests, which are interests arising mainly under after-acquired property clauses. Under certain conditions the purchase money security interest will have priority. It should be recalled that, while a security agreement may provide that collateral, whenever acquired, shall secure all obligations covered by the security agreement, nevertheless no security interest attaches under an after-acquired property clause to consumer goods, other than accessories, when given as additional security unless the debtor acquires rights in them within 10 days after the secured party gives value.[100] The rules for priority distinguish between purchase money security interests in non-inventory collateral and in inventory collateral. *With respect to non-inventory collateral,* a purchase money security interest in non-inventory collateral has priority over a conflicting security interest in the same collateral or its proceeds if the purchase money security interest is perfected (by filing or temporarily) *at the time the debtor receives possession* of the collateral *or within 10 days thereafter.* "The perfection requirement means that the purchase money secured party either has filed a financing statement before that time or has a temporarily perfected interest in goods covered by documents . . . (which is continued in a perfected status by filing before the expiration of the twenty-one day period . . .)."[101] *With respect to inventory collateral,* a perfected purchase money security interest in inventory collateral has priority over a conflicting security interest in the same collateral and also has priority in identifiable cash proceeds received on or before the delivery of the inventory to a buyer only if the following conditions occur:

1. The purchase money security interest is *perfected at the time the debtor receives possession* of the collateral inventory.
2. The holder of the purchase money security interest has given written notice of his purchase money security interest to any secured party whose security interest is *known* to him, or to a secured party who has *filed* a financing statement covering the same items or type of inventory either *before* the purchase

---

[99] See above, pp. 744–45.

[100] *Ibid.*

[101] UCC 9–312, *Comment 3.* For a temporary perfected interest in goods covered by documents, see above, pp. 750–51.

money secured party filed his financing statement, or *before* the beginning of the 21 day period where the purchase money security interest is temporarily perfected without filing or possession.

3. The secured party with the non-purchase money security interest has *received* such written notice within five years *before* the debtor has received *possession* of the inventory covered by the purchase money security interest.

4. Such notice states that the person giving the notice has or expects to acquire a purchase money security interest in inventory of the debtor, describing such inventory by item or type.[102]

Unless otherwise provided by specific rules, the Article establishes catchall provisions for the resolution of conflicting security interests in the same collateral in all other cases. The date of filing or perfection with respect to the collateral is also the date of filing or perfection as to its proceeds. "If future advances are made while a security interest is perfected by filing or the taking of possession, the security interest has the same priority . . . with respect to the future advances as it does with respect to the first advance. If a commitment is made before or while the security interest is so perfected, the security interest has the same priority with respect to advances made pursuant thereto. In other cases a perfected security interest has priority from the date the advance is made."[103]

Security interests may be acquired in fixtures, which are goods that "become so related to particular real estate that an interest in them arises under real estate law,"[104] *with the legal effect that interests in the goods as chattels become subordinate to real estate interests.* The concept of fixtures and the law applicable have been discussed previously.[105] For the purpose of financing interests in goods, the exact character and legal status become very important. Some goods are not affixed to

---

[102] See UCC 9–312, *Comment 3:* "The reason for the additional requirement of notification is that typically the arrangement between an inventory secured party and his debtor will require the secured party to make periodic advances against incoming inventory or periodic releases of old inventory as new inventory is received. A fraudulent debtor may apply to the secured party for advances even though he has already given a security interest in the inventory to another secured party. The notification requirement protects the inventory financer in such a situation: if he has received notification, he will presumably not make an advance; if he has not received notification (or if the other interest does not qualify as a purchase money interest), any advance he may make will have priority. Since an arrangement for periodic advances against incoming property is unusual outside the inventory field," no such notification is required for non-inventory collateral.

[103] UCC 9–312(7).

[104] UCC 9–313(1)(a).

[105] See above, p. 733. For a further discussion, see below, p. 904.

realty and thus they retain their character and legal status as chattels; some goods become construction materials and, when affixed to realty, become such an integral part of the realty as to lose their character and legal status as chattels for the purpose of chattel financing; and other goods, although affixed to the realty, retain their legal character and status as chattels and become fixtures for the purpose of chattel financing. Inasmuch as state real estate law can create an encumbrance or lien on fixtures, when this occurs a conflict may be created regarding priority of security interests in such fixtures. Security interests may be created in goods before they become fixtures as well after they become fixtures. Priority in time of filing, or recording of a real estate interest, governs the priority of dominance of a particular interest here.[106] Thus, a perfected security interest in fixtures has priority over a conflicting interest of an encumbrancer or owner of the real estate where the security interest is perfected by a "fixture filing"[107] before the interest of the encumbrancer or owner is of record, the debtor has an interest of record in the real estate or is in possession of the real estate, and the security interest has priority over any conflicting interest of a predecessor in title of the encumbrancer or owner. However, if the security interest in the fixture is a *purchase money security interest,* the interest of the encumbrancer or owner arises before the goods become fixtures, the debtor has an interest of record in the real estate or is in possession of the real estate, and the security interest is perfected by a fixture filing before the goods become fixtures or within ten days thereafter, then the perfected security interest in the fixtures has priority. This priority of the purchase money security interest in fixtures is subordinate, however, to a construction mortgage recorded before the goods become fixtures if the goods become fixtures before the completion of the construction. To the extent that a mortgage is given to refinance a construction mortgage, the mortgage has the same priority as that of the construction mortgage. If the fixtures are readily removable factory or office machines or are readily removable replacements of domestic appliances which are consumer goods, and the security interest in the goods is perfected by any method permitted by the Article before the goods become fixtures, the security interest in the fixtures has priority. Also, the security interest in a fixture perfected by any method permitted by the Article has priority over a conflicting interest in real estate which was obtained by legal or equitable proceedings after the security interest in the fixtures was perfected. Of course, if the en-

---

[106] UCC 9–313(4).
[107] See above, p. 733.

cumbrancer or owner has consented in writing to the security interest in fixtures or has disclaimed an interest in the goods as fixtures, or if the debtor has a right to remove the goods as against the encumbrancer or owner, the security interest in fixtures, irrespective of whether or not perfected, has priority. If the debtor's right to remove the goods terminates, the priority of the security interest in fixtures continues for a reasonable time. In all other instances of conflicting security interests in fixtures, the security interest in fixtures is subordinate to the conflicting interest of an encumbrancer or owner of the real estate who is not the debtor. A secured party with priority over the claims of all persons who have interests in the real estate may, on default, remove his collateral from the real estate. However, he has a duty to reimburse any encumbrancer or owner of the real estate who is not the debtor, and who has not otherwise agreed, for the cost of repair of any physical injury, but not for any diminution in the value of the real estate caused by the absence of the goods removed or by necessity for replacing them. A person entitled to reimbursement may refuse permission to remove the fixture until the secured party gives adequate security for the performance of his obligation of reimbursement.

Accession to goods subject to a security interest is a normal, everyday occurrence. Accession means augmentation, addition. In the law of secured transactions, *accession means goods which have been so added to other goods as to become a permanent part thereof*—for example, the addition of component parts into a machine, as a new muffler in an automobile, a new generator in a power plant, a new engine in a truck. A security interest may attach to goods before or after they become accessions. A security interest in goods either before or after they become accessions is *subordinate* to the interests of the following persons who acquired their interests *after* the security interest in the accessions was acquired, *without knowledge* of the security interest, and *before it was perfected:* a subsequent purchaser for value of any interest in the whole; a creditor with a lien on the whole subsequently obtained by judicial proceedings; a creditor with a prior perfected security interest in the whole to the extent that he makes subsequent advances. *Except as just indicated,* a security interest in goods which attaches *before* they are installed in or affixed to other goods takes priority as to the goods installed or affixed over the claims of all persons to the whole. However, if the accession has become part of a product or mass and is so manufactured, processed, assembled, or commingled that its identity is lost in the product or mass: the security interest continues in the product or mass; and the security interest ranks equally without priority with other security interests in the product or mass according to the ratio that the cost of the goods to which each interest originally attached bears to the cost of the total product or mass. If a financing statement covering the accession also covered the product into which it was manufactured, processed, or assembled, while the security interest continues in the product or mass, nevertheless no separate security interest in that part of the accession which has been manufactured, processed, or assembled into the product may be claimed. Also *except as just indicated,* a security interest which attaches to accessions *after* they become part of a whole is valid and takes priority against all persons subsequently acquiring interests in the whole, except that it is invalid as against any person with an interest in the whole at the time the security interest attached to the accession who has not *in writing consented* to the security interest or disclaimed an interest in the accession as part of the whole. A purchaser of the whole at a foreclosure sale other than the holder of a perfected security interest purchasing at his own foreclosure sale is a subsequent purchaser of an interest in the whole, just discussed. A secured party with priority over the claims of all persons who have interests in the whole may, on default, remove his collateral from the whole. However, he has a duty to reimburse any encumbrancer or owner of the whole who is not the debtor and who has not otherwise agreed for the cost of repair of any physical injury, but not for any diminution in the value of the whole caused by the absence of the accessions removed or by any necessity for replacing them. A person entitled to reimbursement may refuse permission to remove the accession until the secured party gives adequate security for the performance of his obligation of reimbursement.

It should be noted that the owner of a security interest with a priority may waive, and agree to waive, such priority either completely, or partially by subordinating it to a particular claim or interest. It should be noted further that a secured party is not vicariously liable in contract or tort for the debtor's acts or omissions merely because of the existence of the security interest or because the secured party authorized (consented) the debtor to dispose of or use the collateral.

Assignment of Accounts. The law under the Code favors freely the assignment of accounts and the creation of a security interest in a general intangible for money due or to become due. A term is ineffective in any contract between an account debtor and an assignor if the term prohibits assignment of an account or prohibits creation of a security interest in a general intangible for money due or to become due, or requires the account debtor's consent to such assignment or security interest.[108] *With certain limitations, as discussed previously,*[109] an account debtor's security agreement may validly provide that the account debtor will not assert against an assignee of the secured party assignor defenses which the account debtor may have against the assignor. If the account debtor has not agreed to waive his defenses, the rights of an assignee are subject to all the terms of the contract between the account debtor and assignor and any defense or claim arising therefrom, and any other defense or claim of the account debtor against the assignor which accrues *before* the account debtor receives notification of the assignment. The account debtor and secured party assignor may modify their contract or make a substitute contract without the consent of the assignee, even though the account debtor has notice of the assignment, under certain conditions. Such modification or substitution is effective against an assignee who acquires corresponding rights under the modified or substituted contract. *First,* the contract between the account debtor and secured party assignor must not prohibit such modification or substitution. Although no such prohibition is present, the contract between the *assignor and the assignee* may properly provide that such modification or substitution is a breach of contract by the assignor. If modification or substitution is made in violation of a contract prohibition against it, such modification or substitution may be binding on the parties to it but it is not effective as to the assignee. *Second,* such modification or substitution is *effective* against an assignee only if the assignor has *not already fully earned* the right to part or full payment by his performance of his contract with the account debtor. To the extent that the assignor *has earned* the right to part or full payment, such modification or substitution is *ineffective* against the assignee. This occurs when the work or goods have been rendered by the assignor in accordance with the contract and payment then becomes due. *Third,* such modification or substitution must be made in good faith and in accordance with reasonable commercial standards.

The account debtor's contractual obligation is to pay the assignor the amount due or to become due. The account debtor's receipt of notice that the amount due or to become due has been assigned does not, of itself, vary his obligation; *the account debtor must also receive notice that payment is to be made to the assignee. On his receipt of such notice of assignment and that payment is to be made to the assignee, the account debtor's obligation is to make payment only to*

---

[108] See UCC 9–318.
[109] See above, pp. 740–41.

the assignee.[110] The notice must reasonably identify the rights assigned, or it is ineffective. The account debtor has the right to request that the assignee furnish him with reasonable proof that the assignment has been made. The assignee has the duty to comply with such request, and his failure so to comply permits the account debtor to make payment to the assignor.

Filing. *Purpose.* The purpose of filing a financing statement is to give public notice of a security interest in collateral. As we have already seen,[111] filing is required in order to perfect a security interest, with several exceptions.

Place. The Article[112] provides for local filing, which is usually in the Office of the County Clerk and Recorder, and for central filing, which is usually in the Office of the Secretary of State. Provision is also made for double filing, both local and central. Inasmuch as it was not expected that uniformity among the various states could be attained as to the place of filing, three alternatives are presented by the Article. *One* is central filing for all transactions except for timber to be cut, minerals or the like (including oil and gas) and an account resulting from their sale after extraction at the wellhead or minehead, and fixtures, which is local filing. The *second* is local filing for transactions of essentially local concern, including fixtures, and central filing for all other transactions. The *third* is the same as the second except that it provides for double filing in the case of a debtor who has only one, or no, place of business in the state. A filing which has been made in good faith, but in an improper place or not in all of the places required, is effective insofar as it was properly filed and it is also effective for the collateral covered by the financing statement against any person who knows the contents of such filing statement. The Article provides two alternatives in the case of a change in the county of the debtor's residence, place of business, or location of the collateral or its use. *One alternative* does not require any new filing in the county to which the collateral has been removed; the place of the original proper filing continues effective. Under the *second alternative,* the original filing is effective for four months after the change, but is ineffective thereafter

---

[110] "So long as the assignee permits the assignor to collect accounts or leaves him in possession of chattel paper which does not indicate that payment is to be made at some place other than the assignor's place of business, the account debtor may pay the assignor even though he may know of the assignment. In such a situation an assignee who wants to take over collections must notify the account debtor to make further payments to him." UCC 9–318, *Comment 3.* Also see U3C sec. 2.412.

[111] See above, pp. 746 ff. Also, see UCC 9–302.

[112] UCC 9–401.

unless a copy of the financing statement signed by the secured party is filed in the new county *within* the four-month period, in which case perfection continues uninterruptedly from the date of the original filing. Under the second alternative, perfection in the new county *after* the expiration of the four-month period dates from the time of such perfection in the new county. The rules with respect to collateral brought into the state from another jurisdiction have been discussed previously.[113] The residence of an organization is its place of business if it has one, or its chief executive office if it has more than one place of business.

The Financing Statement. The document filed in order to perfect a security interest is called a "financing statement." Financing statement means the original financing statement and any amendments thereto, except that if the amendment adds collateral it is effective as to the added collateral only from the filing date of the amendment. A financing statement substantially complying with the Article's requirements is effective even though it contains minor errors which are not seriously misleading. A financing statement is sufficient if it: (1) is signed by the debtor (and the secured party where required by state law), (2) gives an address of the secured party from which information concerning the security interest may be obtained, (3) gives a mailing address of the debtor, (4) contains a statement indicating the types, or describing the items, of collateral. When the financing statement covers crops growing or to be grown, the statement must also contain a description of the real estate concerned. When the financing statement covers timber to be cut, minerals or the like (including oil and gas) or an account resulting from their sale after extraction at the wellhead or minehead, or fixtures, the statement must also show that it covers this type of collateral, must recite that it is to be filed for record in the real estate records, and must contain a description of the real estate. If the debtor does not have an interest of record in the real estate, the financing statement must show the name of the record owner. A copy of the security agreement is sufficient as a financing statement if it contains the above information and is *signed by the debtor* (or both parties where required by state law). A reproduction of a security agreement or a financing statement is sufficient as a financing statement if the security agreement so provides or if the original has been filed in the same state where the reproduction is being filed.

The reason for the required filing of the financial statement is to

---

[113] See above, pp. 735–39.

give notice to everyone of its contents. It is "constructive notice." It can be readily understood, therefore, why this system of filing such a simple and uncomplicated document is called "notice filing." The financing statement merely indicates that the secured party has an interest in the collateral described, and anyone who desires details may obtain them by inquiry from the parties at their addresses as shown on the financing statement. It should be noted that the financing statement is not required to be witnessed or acknowledged. A suggested form of financing statement is provided by the Article.[114] When the filing is concerned with a security interest in collateral which is already subject to a security interest in another jurisdiction and the collateral is now located in the state of filing, or when the debtor's location is changed to the latter state, the financing statement must state that the collateral was brought into the state or that the debtor's location was changed to the state under such circumstances. When the filing is concerned with a security interest in proceeds[115] and the security interest in the original collateral was perfected, the financing statement must describe the original collateral. In the two cases described in the two preceding sentences, or if the financing statement is to perfect a security interest in collateral as to which the filing has lapsed, or if collateral is acquired after a change of name, identity or corporate structure of the debtor, the financing statement is deemed sufficient[116] if it is *signed only by the secured party instead of the debtor* and is otherwise in compliance with the Article's requirements. When the name, identity, or corporate structure of a debtor is so changed that a filed financing statement becomes seriously misleading, the filing is not effective to perfect a security interest in collateral acquired by the debtor more than four months after the change, unless a new appropriate financing statement is filed before the expiration of that time. It should be noted carefully that the Article now permits a mortgage of real estate which describes goods which are, or are to become, fixtures to be effective as a financing statement filed as a fixture filing if the goods are described by item and type, the mortgage complies with the requirements for a financing statement, and the mortgage is duly recorded.

---

[114] UCC 9–402(3).

[115] For proceeds, see above, pp. 747–48, 751–52.

[116] The reason for dispensing with the debtor's signature in these two cases is that the necessity for refiling arises from actions of the debtor (in moving his place of business or residence, or the collateral, or disposing of it), which may have been unauthorized or fraudulent. "The secured party should not be penalized for failing to make a timely filing by reason of difficulty in procuring the signature of a possibly reluctant or hostile debtor." UCC 9–402, *Comment 4*.

A reservation of title under a lease or consignment of goods is not a security interest, unless intended to be such.[117] If it is so intended, the lessor or consignor may file a financing statement using the terms "consignor," "consignee," "lessor," and "lessee," instead of "secured party" and "debtor," and the security interest of the lessor or consignor which attaches to the goods is perfected by such filing.

Method and Duration of Filing. Filing occurs by presentation for filing of a financing statement and tender of the filing fee, or by acceptance of the financing statement by the filing officer. *Constructive notice of the filing runs from the time of presentation of the financing statement and tender of the filing fee.*

The filing period is for five years, except for a real estate mortgage effective as a fixture filing, and it is effective from the date the financing statement was filed. The effectiveness of a filed financing statement lapses on the expiration of such five-year period, unless a continuation statement is filed prior to the lapse. Upon such lapse, the security interest becomes unperfected, unless it is perfected without filing. Upon unperfection by such lapse, the security interest is deemed to have been unperfected as against a person who became a purchaser or lien creditor *before* lapse. Upon timely filing of the continuation statement, the effectiveness of the original statement is *continued* for five years after the last date to which the filing was effective, whereupon it lapses unless another continuation statement is filed prior to such lapse. Succeeding continuation statements may be filed in the same manner to continue the effectiveness of the original statement. A continuation statement may be filed by the secured party within six months prior to the expiration of the five-year period. A continuation statement must identify the original statement by file number, state the original statement is still effective, and be signed by the secured party except that a continuation statement signed by a person other than the secured party of record must be accompanied by a separate written statement of assignment signed by the secured party of record. A filing officer marks each statement with a file number and with the date and hour of filing, indexes the statements according to the name of the debtor, notes in the index the file number and the address of the debtor given in the statement, and holds the statement for public inspection. A financing statement filed as a fixture filing, or covering timber to be cut, minerals or the like (including oil and gas) and an account resulting from their sale after extraction at the wellhead or minehead, is indexed under

_____

[117] UCC 1-201(37).

the names of the debtor and any owner of record shown in the financing statement in the same fashion as if he were the mortgagor in a mortgage of the real estate described and, where the state law provides for indexing of mortgages under the name of the mortgagee, under the name of the secured party as if he were the mortgagee thereunder.

Termination Statement. A procedure is established under the Article for giving public notice that the secured obligation is discharged and the financing transaction is terminated. This is done by means of a termination statement. The termination statement simply states that the secured party no longer claims a security interest under the financing statement which is identified by file number, and it is signed by the secured party. A termination statement signed by a person other than the secured party of record must include or be accompanied by the assignment or a statement by the secured party of record that he has assigned the security interest to the signer of the termination statement. *When a financing statement covers consumer goods,* and there is no outstanding secured obligation and no commitment to make advances, incur obligations or otherwise give value, *within one month* or within *ten days following written demand by the debtor* the secured party must *file with each filing officer* with whom the financing statement was filed a termination statement to the effect that he no longer claims a security interest under the financing statement, identified by file number. *If the financing statement covers other than consumer goods,* whenever there is no outstanding secured obligation and no commitment to make advances, incur obligations or otherwise give value, the debtor *may* make a *written demand* on the secured party for a statement that he no longer claims a security interest under the financing statement. The secured party must comply with the latter request *within ten days after demand,* by *sending to the debtor* a termination statement for each filing officer with whom the financing statement was filed. Failure by the secured party to send such termination statements or to file them as prescribed, makes him liable to the debtor for $100 and, in addition, for any loss caused to the debtor by such failure. On presentation of the termination statement to the filing officer, he notes it in the index.

Assignment of Security Interest. The secured party may assign all or a part of his security interest in collateral either before or after filing the financing statement. However, to be effective against persons *other than the secured party,* the assignment should be made a matter of record. If the assignment is made *before* filing, the financing statement may disclose the amount of the security interest in the collateral described in the statement by an indication in the statement of the name and address of the assignee or by the assignment itself or a copy thereof on the face or back of the statement. The assignment may occur *after* filing, and it is made a matter of record by the filing, in the place where the original financing statement was filed, of a separate written statement of assignment signed by the secured party of record and setting forth the name of the secured party of record and the debtor, the file number and the date of filing of the financing statement, the name and address of the assignee, and a description of the collateral assigned. A copy of the assignment is sufficient as a separate statement if it complies with the preceding sentence. An assignment of record of a security interest in a fixture contained in a mortgage effective as a fixture filing may be made only by an assignment of a mortgage as prescribed by state law other than Code provision.

Release of Collateral. A secured party of record may, by his signed statement, release all or part of any collateral described in a filed financing statement. The statement of release is sufficient if it contains a description of the collateral being released, the name and address of the debtor, the name and address of the secured party, and the file number of the financing statement.

Information from the Filing Officer. If the person filing any financing statement, termination statement, statement of assignment, or statement of release furnishes the filing officer a copy thereof, on request the filing officer will note upon the copy the file number and date and hour of the filing of the original and deliver or send the copy to such person. Upon the request of any person, the filing officer will issue his certificate showing whether there is on file on the date and hour stated therein, any presently effective financing statement naming a particular debtor and any statement of assignment thereof and, if there is, giving the date and hour of filing of each such statement and the names and addresses of each secured party therein.

Default

In General. The rights of a secured party in the collateral after the debtor's default is the heart of a security transaction. Such rights, duties, and remedies distinguish a secured creditor from an unsecured or general creditor. When a debtor is in default under a security agreement, the secured party and also the debtor have various rights, remedies, and duties. The secured party has the rights and remedies provided by the Article and, unless contrary to the Article, those provided in the security agreement. The secured party's rights are cumulative, and he may exercise any of them. The secured party may reduce his claim to judgment and have it satisfied. The secured party in possession of the collateral has various rights, remedies, and duties, already discussed.[118] After default, the debtor also has the rights and duties provided by the Article, those provided in the security agreement and, as already discussed,[119] those where the secured party is in possession of the collateral. The Article provides that the parties may not waive or vary certain rights of the debtor and duties of the secured party under some of the sections on default, but does permit waiver or variation in connection with compulsory disposition of collateral and redemption of collateral. However, where waiver or variance is prohibited, the parties may, by agreement, determine the *standards* by which the fulfillment of these rights and duties is to be measured if such standards are not manifestly unreasonable. It should be noted that, if the security agreement covers both real and personal property, the secured party may proceed under the Article provisions on default as to the personal property or he may proceed as to both the real and the personal property in accordance with his rights and remedies in respect of the real property (outside the Code), in which case the default provisions do not apply.

The following rights and duties will be discussed in the order indicated: the secured party's rights to judgment and execution sale; the secured party's collection rights; the secured party's right to take possession after default; the secured party's right to dispose of collateral after default; the debtor's right to redeem collateral; the secured party's liability for failure to comply with the Article's requirements.

Judgment and Execution Sale. On the debtor's default, the secured party may bring an action against the debtor, reduce his claim to judgment, and foreclose[120] or otherwise enforce the security interest by any available judicial procedure. If the collateral is documents, the secured party may proceed either as to the documents or as to the goods covered thereby. When a secured party has reduced his claim to judgment and levy is made upon the collateral by virtue of execution based upon the judgment, the resulting lien upon the collateral relates back to the date of the perfection of the security interest in such collateral. A judicial sale, pursuant to such execution, is a foreclosure of the security interest by judicial procedure within the meaning of the Article, and

---

[118] See above, pp. 742–43.

[119] *Ibid.*

[120] By foreclosure is meant the termination of the debtor's right to redeem the collateral.

the secured party may purchase at the sale and thereafter hold the collateral free of any other requirements of the Article.

Collection Rights of the Secured Party. Among the advantages to an assignee in financing by assignment of intangibles (accounts, general intangibles, chattel paper, instruments) is the fact that the collateral is a highly liquid asset, may be utilized with a minimum of interference with the operation of the debtor's business, and does not have the complexities on default inherent in other kinds of financing.[121] The security agreement may provide for either direct collection, where payment is made *directly* by the account debtor to the assignee of the collateral, called "notification financing" because the account debtor is to receive notice of the assignment of his obligation and is to pay to the assignee, or indirect collection, where payment is made *indirectly* by the account debtor to the assignor and by the assignor to the assignee, called "non-notification financing." If the security arrangement is non-notification financing, on default the secured party acquires the same rights as in notification financing, namely to notify an account debtor or the obligor on an instrument to make payment to him whether or not the assignor was theretofor making collections on the collateral, and also to take control of any proceeds[122] to which he is entitled.

There are two forms of account financing concerned with the credit risk: one in which the assignee assumes the credit risk without any right of recourse or charge-back against the assignor if the account is uncollectible; the other in which the assignee does not assume the credit risk and has a right of full or limited recourse or charge-back if the account is uncollectible. (S sells goods to B and sells and assigns B's chattel paper to C. B defaults on his contract of purchase and has insufficient assets to pay C's claim against him. If the assignment provided for charge-back, C could charge back to S and recover the deficiency from S. If it did not provide for charge-back, C could not recover the deficiency from S.) A secured party who by agreement is entitled to charge back uncollected collateral or otherwise to full or limited recourse against the debtor and who undertakes to collect from the account debtors or obligors must proceed in a *commercially reasonable manner* and may deduct his reasonable expenses of realization from the collections. Dumping accounts receivable, "if the result will be to increase a pos-

---

[121] UCC 9–502, *Comment 1.*

[122] For a discussion of proceeds, see above, pp. 747–48, 751–52.

sible deficiency claim or to reduce a possible surplus"[123] is not commercially reasonable. *If the security agreement secures an indebtedness* (collateral assigned as security for a loan), the secured party must account to the debtor[124] for any surplus, and, unless otherwise agreed, the debtor is liable for any deficiency. But, *if the underlying transaction was a true sale* of accounts or chattel paper, the debtor is not entitled to any surplus and is not liable for any deficiency unless the security agreement so provides.

Secured Party's Right to Take Possession after Default. Unless otherwise agreed, on default a secured party has the right to take possession of the collateral. Of course, if the secured transaction was possessory, i.e., a pledge in which the secured party had possession under the security agreement before default, he has no problem about acquiring possession on default. In taking possession on default, a secured party may proceed without judicial process if this can be done in accordance with procedural due process of law[125] and without breach of the peace, or he may proceed by action.[126] However, removal of the collateral from the debtor's premises may not be economically feasible or practicable. For example, the collateral may be heavy equipment in the debtor's plant or storage, and removal would be very expensive if not impracticable. For this reason, if the collateral is equipment, a secured party may repossess the equipment without removing it from the debtor's premises, render it unusable, and dispose of collateral on the debtor's premises. Also, the collateral possessed by the debtor may be in different places and be difficult or expensive for the secured party to gather it together in one place. For this reason, *if the security agreement so provides,* the secured party may require the debtor to assemble the collateral and make it available to the secured party at a place to be designated by the secured party which is reasonably convenient to both parties. The secured party must act in a *commercially reasonable manner* inasmuch as every aspect of the exercise of the secured party's right

---

[123] UCC 9–502, *Comment 2; 3:* "If the 'charge-back' provisions of the assignment arrangement provide only for 'charge-back' of bad accounts against a reserve, the debtor's claim to surplus and his liability for a deficiency are limited to the amount of the reserve."

[124] See above, pp. 743 f., for secured party's duties when he knows that the collateral is owned by a person who is not the debtor.

[125] Procedural due process of law is concerned with reasonable notice and opportunity to appear and to be heard. Important case law is occurring on this point in connection with pre-judgment repossession on default. See below, p. 847.

[126] Replevin is the form of action to recover possession of specific chattels.

to disposition of the collateral must be in a commercially reasonable manner.

Secured Party's Right to Dispose of Collateral after Default. After default, a secured party may sell, lease, or otherwise dispose of any or all of the collateral in its then condition or following any commercially reasonable preparation or processing. Any sale of *goods* is subject to the Code provisions on Sales, previously discussed.[127]

(3) Disposition of the collateral may be by public or private proceedings and may be made by way of one or more contracts. Sale or other disposition may be as a unit or in parcels and at any time and place and on any terms but every aspect of the disposition including the method, manner, time, place and terms *must be commercially reasonable.*[128] Unless collateral is perishable or threatens to decline speedily in value or is of a type customarily sold on a recognized market, reasonable notification of the time and place of any public sale or reasonable notification of the time after which any private sale or other intended disposition is to be made shall be sent by the secured party to the debtor, if he has not signed after default a statement renouncing or modifying his right to notification of sale. In the case of *consumer goods* no other notification need be sent. *In other cases* notification shall be sent to any other secured party from whom the secured party has received (before sending his notification to the debtor or before the debtor's renunciation of his rights) written notice of a claim of an interest in the collateral. The secured party may buy at any public sale and if the collateral is of a type customarily sold in a recognized market or is of a type which is the subject of widely distributed standard price quotations he may buy at private sale. (Author's italics.)[129]

The proceeds of the disposition must be distributed in a prescribed order of priority. *First* are the reasonable expenses for retaking, holding, preparing for sale or lease, selling, leasing, and the like and, to the extent provided for in the security agreement and not prohibited by law, the reasonable attorneys' fees and legal expenses incurred by the secured party. *Second* is payment of the debt secured by the security interest under which the disposition was made. *Third* is payment of debts secured by subordinate security interests in the collateral, only if written notification of demand therefor is received before distribution of the proceeds is completed. The secured party has the right to request the holder of a subordinate security interest to seasonably furnish reasonable proof of his interest, and if he fails to do so the secured party need not comply with his demand. If the security interest secures

---

[127] See above, pp. 335–37, for a discussion of the seller's right of resale.

[128] For what is commercially reasonable, see below, p. 775.

[129] UCC 9–504(3).

an indebtedness, the secured party must account to the debtor[130] for any surplus, and, unless otherwise agreed, the debtor is liable for any deficiency. But if the underlying transaction was a true sale of accounts or chattel paper, the debtor is not entitled to any surplus and is not liable for any deficiency unless the security agreement so provides.

When collateral is disposed of by a secured party after default, the disposition transfers to a purchaser for value all of the debtor's rights in such collateral, discharges the security interest under which it was made and any subordinate security interest or lien. *The purchaser takes free of all such rights and interests even though the secured party failed to comply with the requirements of the Article for disposition or of any judicial proceedings as long as the purchaser acted in good faith.* The purchaser acted in good faith at a *public sale* if he had no knowledge of any defects in the sale and he did not buy in collusion with the secured party, other bidders, or the person conducting the sale. A person who is liable to a secured party under a guaranty, indorsement, repurchase agreement, or the like, and who receives a transfer of collateral from the secured party or is subrogated to his rights, has thereafter the rights and duties of the secured party. Such a transfer of collateral is not a sale or disposition of the collateral under the Article.[131]

On the debtor's default, the secured party is not required to take possession of the collateral subject to the security interest. However, if the secured party does take possession, he may make disposition of it or, under certain conditions, retain it in satisfaction of the secured obligation. *When the transaction involves consumer goods:* if the secured party has either a purchase money security interest in such goods, or has a non-purchase money security interest in such goods to secure a loan; the debtor has paid 60 per cent of the cash price or 60 per cent of the loan, respectively; and the debtor has not, after default, signed a statement renouncing or modifying his rights under the Default part of the Article, the secured party *must* make disposition of the collateral within 90 days after he takes possession of the collateral. His failure so to dispose of the collateral subjects him to liability for conversion of the collateral at the option of the debtor. *In any other case involving consumer goods or any other collateral,* the secured party in possession of the collateral is not required to sell it but may retain it in satisfaction of the secured obligation. However, in order to do so, he must send a written notice of his intention to the debtor if the debtor has not, after

---

[130] See above, pp. 745 f., for secured party's duties when he knows that the collateral is owned by a person who is not the debtor.

[131] UCC 9–504(5).

default, signed a statement renouncing or modifying his rights in this connection. *If consumer goods are involved, no other notice* need be given; but *in the case of other kinds of goods,* the secured party *must send notice* to any other secured party from whom he has received (before sending his notice to the debtor or before the debtor's renunciation of his rights) *written* notice of a claim of an interest in the collateral. If the secured party does *not* receive written objection from a person entitled to receive notification within twenty-one days *after the notice was sent,* the secured party may retain the collateral in satisfaction of the debtor's obligation. However, if he receives such written objection, then he *must* dispose of the collateral.

Debtor's Right to Redeem Collateral. Except in the case of consumer goods, just discussed, and apart from the requirement that all aspects of the secured party's disposition of the collateral on the debtor's default must be in a commercially reasonable manner, the Article does not require the secured party who has possession to dispose of the collateral within a prescribed period of time. Meanwhile, the debtor,[132] or any other secured party, has a right to redeem after the debtor's default. Redemption may be made (1) after the debtor's default, (2) before the secured party has disposed of the collateral or entered into a contract for its disposition, and (3) before the obligation has been discharged by the secured party's retention of possession in satisfaction of the secured obligation. Unless otherwise agreed in writing after the debtor's default, redemption of the collateral may be made by tendering fulfillment of all obligations secured by the collateral as well as the expenses reasonably incurred by the secured party in retaking, holding, and preparing the collateral for disposition, in arranging for the sale and, to the extent provided in the agreement and not prohibited by law, his reasonable attorneys' fees and legal expenses.[133]

Secured Party's Liability for Failure to Comply with the Article. As we have seen in previous discussion under Default, the buyer's default on his secured obligation imposes various duties on the secured party. If it is established that the secured party is not complying with

---

[132] See above, pp. 745 f., for secured party's duties when he knows that the collateral is owned by a person who is not the debtor.

[133] UCC 9–506, *Comment:* " 'Tendering fulfillment' obviously means more than a new promise to perform the existing promise; it requires payment in full of all monetary obligations then due and performance in full of all other obligations then matured. If unmatured obligations remain, the security interest continues to secure them as if there had been no default.

"Under Section 9–504 the secured party may make successive sales of parts of the collateral in his possession. The fact that he may have sold or contracted to sell part of the collateral would not affect the debtor's right under this Section to redeem what was left. In such a case, of course, in calculating the amount required to be tendered the debtor would receive credit for net proceeds of the collateral sold."

such duties, he may be restrained by court order. Disposition of the collateral may be ordered or restrained. If disposition has occurred, the debtor or any person entitled to notification[134] or whose security interest has been made known to the secured party prior to the disposition, has a right to recover from the secured party any loss caused by a failure to comply with the provisions of the Article. If the collateral is consumer goods, the debtor has a right to recover in any event an amount not less than the credit service charge plus 10 per cent of the principal amount of the debt or the time price differential plus 10 per cent of the cash price.[135]

The Article[136] establishes criteria of disposition of collateral in a commercially reasonable manner. A secured party has sold collateral in a commercially reasonable manner if:

1. He sells the collateral in the usual manner in any recognized market therefor.
2. He sells at the price current in such market at the time of his sale.
3. He has otherwise sold in conformity with reasonable commercial practices among dealers in the type of property sold.

Any other disposition in compliance with these criteria is commercially reasonable. A disposition which has been approved in any judicial proceeding or by any bona fide creditors' committee or representative of creditors is conclusively commercially reasonable. The fact that a better price could have been obtained by a sale at a different time or in a different method from that selected by the secured party is not of itself sufficient to establish that the sale was not made in a commercially reasonable manner.

The Code revision of the law on secured transactions is a remarkable improvement and is in keeping with modern commercial practice. It is clear, comprehensive, very usable by businessmen, and is so designed as to allow room for development in the law along with development in commerce. It should stand the buffeting of time very well.

Pledge   Although pledge as a security interest is included under the Secured Transactions portion of the Code, nevertheless its distinctiveness and wide application in business transactions justify a closer examination of its elements.

---

[134] See above, pp. 745 f., for secured party's duties when he knows that the collateral is owned by a person who is not the debtor.

[135] UCC 9–507(1).

[136] UCC 9–507(2).

Definition. A bailment of chattels as security for the performance of an obligation creates a right in the bailee to retain possession of such property as security and, on default of the obligation, to deal with the property in a certain way—e.g., sell it and apply the proceeds on the obligation in default. The security interest so created is a property interest in the bailed chattels. *This security interest in chattels created by a bailment for the purpose of security is called a "pledge" or "pawn"* —"A security interest in a chattel or in an intangible represented by an indispensable instrument, the interest being created by a bailment for the purpose of securing the payment of a debt or the performance of some other duty."[137] The person creating the pledge is the "pledgor," and the person acquiring the pledge is the "pledgee."

Only chattels are the subject of pledge. In the law of security, as in the law of bailments, chattels include documents representing goods (e.g., bills of lading and warehouse receipts) and instruments representing intangibles (e.g., certificates of stock representing shares in a corporation, and negotiable and non-negotiable instruments representing rights of action, such as checks, promissory notes, insurance policies, and savings bank books.) When the chattel bailed as security is a negotiable document of title, the security interest is in the document and in the goods it represents; and when the chattel is an "indispensable instrument"[138] (meaning an instrument representing an intangible, possession of the instrument being essential to the enjoyment, transfer, or enforcement of the intangible), such as a certificate of stock and the other instruments representing intangibles described immediately above, the security interest is in the instrument and in the intangible it represents. In the absence of agreement to the contrary and unless the pledgee has waived it, the secured interest is also in the increase or profits occurring from the bailed chattels, such as interest or dividends on bailed securities and the young born of bailed animals. It is for this reason that, in the absence of agreement to the contrary, the pledgee has the privilege, in order conveniently to obtain such increase or profits from bailed securities when he is entitled to it, to cause the pledged securities to be registered in his own name.[139] The pledgee's failure so to register is evidence of a waiver of this privilege, permitting the pledgor to retain the increase or profits which he receives. The pledgee must account to the pledgor for any such increase or profits received by him and is to apply it in accordance with the pledge agreement.

---

[137] American Law Institute, *Restatement: Security,* 1941, sec. 1.

[138] *Ibid.,* sec. 2.

[139] See above, p. 690.

A pledge is one of various types of lien. A lien may be defined as a legal right in the property of another as security for the performance of an obligation. Some liens include the right to possess specific property —e.g., the pledge—while other liens do not include such right to possession—e.g., security interest in an automobile still in the debtor's possession. The lien of pledge also includes the power to sell on defualt of the obligation for which it is security. A "lienor" is the person who has a lien, while a "lienee" is the person against whose property there is a lien.

Delivery. It is of the essence of pledge that a bailment, involving a delivery of chattels, occur with the intent to make such chattels security for the performance of an obligation.

Delivery may be actual or symbolical. Actual delivery may occur by the pledgor's physical delivery of the chattels to the pledgee, by the pledgee's retention of chattels previously in his possession, or by a third person already in possession of chattels for the pledgor continuing in such possession for the benefit of the pledgee pursuant to the bailment agreement *and after having been notified so to do.* (A holds chattels of B. B and C agree to a pledge of such chattels to C. A pledge is effected when A is notified by B or C of such bailment agreement.) Another illustration of the latter requirement of notice is where a straight bill of lading or a non-negotiable warehouse receipt has been delivered by one person to another, and the carrier or warehouseman, on being notified of such delivery, retains possession of the bailed goods for the benefit of the holder of the document. Notification to the carrier or warehouseman is necessary in order to create such a pledge in the case of a non-negotiable document of title because, as between the consignee of a non-negotiable document of title and the bailee, the consignee has the right to acquire possession of such chattels without production of the document.[140] A transferee of such a document must notify the carrier or warehouseman of such transfer to him in order to acquire the bailee's obligation to hold the chattels for him.[141]

Symbolical delivery occurs by delivery of the means by which access may be made to the particular chattel—e.g., delivery of keys to a strongbox thereby accomplishing delivery of the contents thereof—or by the pledgee's manifested assumption of control over identified chattels which can be moved only with difficulty—e.g., bulky goods, as metal in a heap.

---

[140] See above, p. 220.
[141] *Ibid.*

Pledgee's Right to Possession. A contract *of* pledge is not required to be in writing, and the terms of the contract determine the rights of the parties thereto. In the absence of agreement certain rights are created and certain duties are imposed by law.[142] The pledgee has the right to retain possession of the pledged chattel until the obligation for which the pledge occurred has been performed. The pledgee may bring an action against the pledgor who has wrongfully dispossessed the pledgee or who refuses to return to the pledgee the pledged chattels temporarily returned to the possession of the pledgor. Such action may be for damages for breach of contract, replevin for recovery of the chattel, or conversion of the chattel to the extent of the value of the pledgee's interest therein. Similarly, the pledgee may bring an action against third persons who wrongfully have acquired possession of the chattel without the consent of the pledgee. Such action may be in replevin for repossession of the chattel, in trespass for damage to the pledgee's interest in the chattel, or in conversion for the value of the chattel (which includes trespassory damage to the pledgor's reversionary interest in the chattel).

Where the pledgor transfers a pledged chattel to a third person, the transferee acquires the pledgor's interest in the chattel but the transferee's interest is subject to the interest of the pledgee unless the transferee is a:

(a) good faith purchaser for value from a pledgor who is in possession with the consent of the pledgee and the purchaser has relied upon the pledgor's possession,[143] or

(b) holder in due course of a negotiable instrument[144] or a holder to whom a negotiable document of title has been duly negotiated.[145]

A pledgee can assign his claim against the pledgor and, inasmuch as the pledge follows the claim, the pledge can be assigned also. The pledgee has the duty of care of a reasonably careful man required of a bailee in a mutual-benefit bailment and has a right of reimbursement against the pledgor for reasonable expense incurred in the care, maintenance, and preservation of the security. The pledgee's interest in the security has priority over the claims of all other creditors of the pledgor.

Pledgor's Rights in the Chattel. The pledgor retains title to the pledged chattel and may sell such chattel subject to the pledge of the pledgee. When a purchaser authorizes a broker to purchase securities on

---

[142] The pledgee's rights on the debtor's default have already been discussed. See above, pp. 768 ff., and UCC 9–501. For the pledgee's duties, see above, pp. 742–43.

[143] See above, pp. 740, 746. But note carefully pp. 750–51.

[144] American Law Institute, *Restatement: Security,* 1941, sec. 16. See above, pp. 410, 421.

[145] See above, pp. 223 ff.

margin, the broker's purchase of such securities causes the purchaser to obtain title thereto and to be a pledgor of the securities to the pledgee, who may have these securities (and other securities pledged as security for the securities purchased on margin) registered in the pledgee's name to facilitate their sale on the pledgor's default on his obligation; also, the pledgee may sell and repledge such securities to secure advances made by him. The pledgor has a cause of action against the pledgee for loss caused to the pledged chattel by the negligent or willful misconduct of the pledgee, and a cause of action against the pledgee in conversion for the value of his interest if the pledgee has used the pledged chattel other than for its care and preservation. The pledgor also has a cause of action against third persons for their wrongful trespassory damage to the pledgor's reversionary interest in the pledged chattel, unless the pledgee already has obtained a judgment against the third person therefor.

Termination. A pledge is dependent upon the pledgee's right of retention of possession of the pledged chattel. The pledgee's voluntary surrender of the pledged chattel to the pledgor terminates the pledge, but: "A pledge is not terminated by delivery of the chattel to the pledgor for a temporary and limited purpose relating to the maintenance of the value of the pledgee's interest and having to do with the protection, improvement or sale of the chattel, or where the chattel is an instrument or document, its handling or collection."[146] Under the increasingly prevalent device of field storage warehousing, the pledgor does not have possession of the pledged chattels which are warehoused convenient to the pledgor's temporary and limited use from time to time, and the pledgee has sufficient control and possession of the chattels so that third persons have notice of the pledgee's interest therein. The pledge is not disturbed by the wrongful dispossession of the pledgee without his authority, and the pledgee can recover possession of the pledged chattel. Performance of the obligation for which the chattel has been pledged, as well as tender of such performance, terminates the pledge. A pledgee's improper refusal or failure to return the pledged chattel to the pledgor constitutes a conversion which terminates the pledge. Similarly, the pledgee's unauthorized use of the pledged chattel constitutes a conversion and terminates the pledge.

3. THE REAL PROPERTY MORTGAGE

Nature   The real property mortgage is a widely used credit device. It is the non-possessory interest in real property transferred by one called the "mortgagor" to another called

---

[146] American Law Institute, *Restatement: Security,* 1941, sec. 11(2). But note carefully pp. 750–51.

the "mortgagee" for the purpose of securing the performance of an obligation owing to the mortgagee, usually the payment of money. It is a lien[147] on the property, with no right to possession of such property, but with a right to have such property sold on default of the obligation and to use the proceeds to satisfy the creditor's claim. A mortgage is the security for the claim and, on transfer of the claim, accompanies such claim. It is easily distinguishable from the pledge, which is predicated on possession of the chattel; the mortgage does not usually include possession and is on real property. A "purchase-money mortgage" is a mortgage on real property given by the purchaser to the seller at the time of the conveyance of the property to the purchaser as security for the unpaid portion of the purchase price. A contract to give a mortgage does not create a mortgage but creates an equitable lien on specific property, and the creditor has the right to enforce such contract specifically. A mortgage on specific property with an after-acquired property clause, whereby the mortgagor agrees that the mortgagee will have a mortgage on any future property acquired by the mortgagor, does not create a mortgage on such future property until it has been acquired and, in that event, the mortgagee has an equitable mortgage or lien on such after-acquired property.

Deeds as Mortgages

Any such conveyance of property for the above-described purpose is a mortgage of such property. A trust deed or "deed of trust," whereby a debtor party conveys title to the property to a trustee to hold such title as security for the performance of the debtor's obligation to a creditor, is in effect a mortgage, and such is its status. The temptation to creditors to insist on receiving title to property as security and, on default of the debtor, to keep such title—thereby masking the transaction as a transfer of title rather than a mortgage—and defeat the debtor's right to redeem, causes the courts to make an exception to the parol evidence rule so that the true nature of the transaction may be proved, the conveyance treated as a mortgage, and injustice prevented.

The Contract of Mortgage

The contract creating a real property mortgage, often called "the mortgage," is within that provision of the statute of frauds providing that a contract for the sale of land or of an interest therein is unenforceable unless it is in writing, or there is a note or memorandum in

---

[147] A "lien" is a legal right in the property of another as security for the performance of an obligation. A "lienor" is the person who has a lien, while a "lienee" is the person against whose property there is a lien.

Recorded at...................o'clock...........M., ...

Reception No.................. ....Recorder.

THIS INDENTURE, Made this   day of   Recorder's Stamp
in the year of our Lord one thousand nine hundred and
between

of the   County of
and State of   , of the first part, and

of the   County of
and State of   , of the second part,

WITNESSETH:
    That the said part   of the first part, for and in consideration of the sum of
                        Dollars, to   in hand paid by the said part   of the second part, the receipt
whereof is hereby acknowledged, do   hereby grant, bargain, sell and convey unto the said part   of the second
part   heirs and assigns, the following described lot   or parcel   of land situate, lying and being in
the   County of   and State of Colorado, to-wit:

    TO HAVE AND TO HOLD the same, together with all and singular the privileges and appurtenances there-
unto belonging forever; Provided always, that if the said part   of the first part,   heirs, executors
or administrators, shall pay or cause to be paid to the said part   of the second part,   heirs, executors,
administrators or assigns the said above mentioned sum, according to the tenor and effect of   promissory
note   of even date herewith, payable to the order of the said part   of the second part,

after the date hereof with interest at the rate of   per cent per annum, interest payable
and shall in the meantime keep and perform the covenants and agreements herein contained, then these presents
shall be null and void, otherwise remain in full force and effect.
    That the said part   of the first part, for   sel   heirs, executors and administra-
tors, for the consideration aforesaid, covenant   and agree   to and with the said part   of the second part,
              heirs, executors, administrators and assigns, that   hold   the said premises by
title in fee simple; that the same are free and clear of all liens and encumbrances, except

that   will pay in due season all taxes and assessments levied on said premises, and will keep the
buildings now and hereafter erected thereon insured, for the benefit of the said part   of the second part,
heirs, executors, administrators and assigns; that   will pay the costs and attorney's fees incurred by said
part   of the second part,   heirs, executors, administrators and assigns in any foreclosure action, other
suit or proceeding, by reason hereof; and that upon default in the payment of said note   or any part thereof, or
any of the interest thereon, or upon the breach of any of the covenants or agreements herein contained; this mortgage may be forthwith foreclosed.
    IN WITNESS WHEREOF, The said part   of the first part ha   hereunto set   hand   and
seal   the day and year first above written.

Signed, Sealed and Delivered in the Presence of

....[SEAL]

....[SEAL]

        STATE OF COLORADO   }ss.
            County of   }
    The foregoing instrument was acknowledged before me this   day of
A. D. 19   , by
    My commission expires   , 19   . Witness my hand and official seal.

....
                                    Notary Public.

REAL PROPERTY MORTGAGE

writing of the agreement signed by the party to be charged or by his authorized agent.[148] A contract of mortgage does not create a mortgage until it has been delivered by the mortgagor to the mortgagee and the mortgagee has accepted it. A contract of mortgage contains the names

[148] See above, pp. 110 f.

of the parties, the consideration, words of conveyance, a description of the property mortgaged, any covenants which may be involved, a defeasance clause, and the signature under seal of the mortgagor. In most states the seal does not have its common law effect, and its absence does not affect the validity of the mortgage.

Notice to Third Persons   As between the mortgagor and the mortgagee, the latter has a mortgage, but as between the mortgagee and third persons ignorant of the mortgage, no mortgage appears to be outstanding against the property[149] of the mortgagor, who has title to the mortgaged property and is in possession thereof. A sale of the property by the mortgagor to an innocent third person, or a levy on such property by a creditor of the mortgagor, is valid, and the interest of such a party is superior to the mortgage of the mortgagee. The reason for this result is that the failure of the mortgagee to give notice of such mortgage to third persons would make it possible to defraud such third persons in their innocent dealings with the mortgagor. Today, statutes provide that a mortgage which is valid as between the mortgagor and the mortgagee is void as to all innocent third persons unless it has been recorded in the proper place, which is usually in the county clerk's office in the county where the property is located. Prompt recording by the mortgagee is essential in order to protect the mortgage as against innocent creditors and innocent third persons who subsequently may deal with the mortgagor. Third persons who are on notice of such mortgage, whether by reason of the recording or otherwise, and who subsequently acquire any interests in the mortgaged property, acquire interests which are subject to the priority of the mortgage.

The Right to Redeem   **The Common Law Right of Redemption.** A mortgagor always has had the right to redeem his property, which is the right to have the title to property which is security for performance of an obligation restored free of the mortgage lien. At Common Law a contract of mortgage conveyed title to the property to the mortgagee, subject to the common law right of the mortgagor to perform his obligation *when due* and thereby to reacquire the title to the property. This is called the "title theory" of mortgages because the title passed to the mortgagee, subject to the condition subsequent of defeasance by the mortgagor's performance of his obligation. The mortgagor had a common law right

---

[149] For security interests in fixtures, see above, pp. 733, 758–60.

to redeem by performing his obligation on the due date and thereby reacquire the title. Immediately on the mortgagor's default, the mortgagee kept the title absolutely and the mortgagor no longer had any right to redeem. The mortgagor's default caused undue hardship to the mortgagor when the value of the mortgaged property was in excess of the obligation secured by the mortgage.

The Equitable Right of Redemption. The English Court of Chancery created the mortgagor's equitable right to redeem, often called the "equity of redemption," whereby, *after default,* the mortgagor was accorded a reasonable period of time within which to perform the obligation and thereby acquire the right to get back his title. After the mortgagor's default, the mortgagee could petition the equity court for a decree fixing the period of time within which the mortgagor could redeem; and on the expiration of such time, the mortgagor's right to redeem was ordered cut off or "foreclosed," and the mortgagee kept the title to the property. Although the mortgagor acquired the equitable right to redeem, he still suffered the undue hardship of losing the title to mortgaged property which was of greater value than the obligation for which the mortgage was given as security. Chancery later recognized this injustice and the "lien theory" of mortgages came into existence. Under the lien theory the contract of mortgage, although stating that it conveyed title to the mortgagee subject to defeasance by the mortgagor's performance, was construed as conveying solely a security interest in the property which constituted a lien without the right to possession but with the right in the mortgagee to proceed against the property on the mortgagor's default. The mortgagor retained the title and possession of the property with the right to perform his obligation when due and to redeem. Inasmuch as the mortgagee acquired solely a security interest in the mortgaged property, on the foreclosure sale of the property after the mortgagor's default the proceeds were applied in satisfaction of the obligation secured by the mortgage and to legal costs, and any surplus remaining belonged to the mortgagor. Today the majority of states are lien states with respect to real property mortgages.

The Statutory Right of Redemption. The last broad step in the development of the right of redemption occurred when, by statute, the mortgagor was accorded the right to redeem within a statutory short period of time *after his equity of redemption had expired* by foreclosure sale. The time in which to redeem after foreclosure sale usually is six months to a year.

Exercise of the Right to Redeem. Either the mortgagor or any person claiming through the mortgagor—e.g., an assignee of the right of redemption, the legal representative of the deceased mortgagor, or a judgment creditor of the mortgagor—may exercise the mortgagor's right of redemption, as provided by statute. The person exercising the equity of redemption before sale must pay to the mortgagee the mortgage obligation, the interest thereon, and the expenses incurred by the mortgagee, including costs. After sale, the person redeeming must pay to the purchaser at the sale, or to the sheriff or other proper public official, the price at which the property was sold and, on such payment, a certificate of redemption or its equivalent is issued to the mortgagor, which he may record, thereby giving notice that the title has been redeemed. The effect of redemption after sale is to nullify such sale and to revest in the mortgagor the title to the property, subject to the liens thereon at the time of the sale.

Foreclosure   The mortgage is enforceable after the mortgagor has defaulted in the performance of his obligation. Default occurs when the mortgagor has failed to perform his obligation for which the mortgage is security, or to perform some other obligation contained in the mortgage contract—e.g., to pay taxes on the mortgaged property or to insure the same. A mortgage contract may provide that, on the mortgagor's default in the payment of principal or interest, the whole principal shall become due; such provision is an acceleration clause. Such non-payment does not necessarily mean that the entire principal is due and payable automatically and that the mortgage is enforceable. Unless the mortgage contract expressly provides that acceleration will occur automatically on default in payment, the acceleration clause is interpreted to mean that acceleration may occur only at the option of the mortgagee. The mortgagor cannot force the mortgagee to accelerate payment of the principal by the mortgagor's default.

The mortgagee's right to enforce the mortgage by the sale of the mortgaged property, to cut off or to foreclose the mortgagor's equity of redemption, and to apply the proceeds to satisfy his claim against the mortgagor is called the mortgagee's equitable "right to foreclose." Although the sale itself foreclosed the mortgagor's equity of redemption, by statute today there is a right of redemption in the case of real property mortgages which may be exercised up until the expiration of a specified period of time after the sale.

Kinds of Foreclosure. Statutes in the various states prescribe how foreclosure may be accomplished. There are four statutory methods: by entry and by writ of entry; by strict foreclosure; by suit for foreclosure and sale; and by foreclosure by sale pursuant to a power of sale. The first two methods apply to mortgages in only a few states. Foreclosure by entry and by writ of entry are substantially the same, foreclosure being accomplished after the mortgagor's default by entering into possession of the property; after the expiration of the statutory period of time, the mortgagee obtains absolute title.

Strict Foreclosure. Strict foreclosure occurs on the mortgagor's default by the decree of foreclosure providing that, if the mortgagor does not perform his obligation within a specified period of time after such default, the mortgagee acquires absolute title to the property. Because of the harshness of strict foreclosure, this method of foreclosure is used infrequently, except when the mortgaged property is worth less than the mortgage obligation, the mortgagee is willing to accept the property in satisfaction of the mortgage obligation, or the mortgagor is insolvent. Strict foreclosure is prohibited in some states.

Suit for Foreclosure and Sale. The usual method of foreclosure is by suit for foreclosure and sale. On the mortgagor's default of his obligation the mortgagee institutes a proceeding in a court of equity, or a court with similar powers, asking for an adjudication and judgment for the amount due and for a decree directing the sale of the mortgaged property. Notice of the proposed sale is given to the public and to all interested parties whose rights will be affected by the foreclosure. The court may order the sale of only part of the mortgaged property if it appears that the proceeds therefrom would be sufficient to satisfy the mortgagee's claim. The property is sold at public auction to the highest bidder, and the mortgagee may bid at such sale. All other liens on the property inferior to the mortgage being foreclosed are extinguished by such sale, except to the extent that they have a right to share in any surplus remaining after the mortgagee's claim has been satisfied. If the sale has been conducted properly by the official responsible therefor, the sale will be confirmed by the court, the court will issue a deed to the property in favor of the purchaser, and the proceeds will be applied in the following order of priority: to pay the expense of sale and court costs; to satisfy the mortgage debt; and to satisfy other creditors of the mortgagor having liens on the mortgaged property; any surplus remaining belongs to the mortgagor. If the proceeds are insufficient to satisfy the mortgagee's claim, a deficiency judgment for the amount still owing is rendered in favor of the mortgagee. Where, by statute, the right of redemption may be exercised within a specified period of time after the foreclosure sale, a deed to the property is not delivered to the purchaser at the sale until the expiration of such period of time. It often occurs that there are various liens on property with varying priorities. In the event of foreclosure by an inferior lien—e.g., a second mortgage—the property is sold subject to all liens superior to the lien being foreclosed —e.g., a first mortgage.

Sale Pursuant to a Power. In order to avoid the expense of a judicial proceeding by suit for foreclosure and sale, mortgage contracts frequently provide that the mortgagee has a power of sale in the event of default by the mortgagor. Although such a provision is prohibited in some states, nevertheless, it is valid in most. This is a power coupled with an interest in the subject matter and, therefore, is irrevocable by the mortgagor or by the death of the mortgagor or mortgagee. In the absence of the usual statute requiring public sale under a power of sale, the mortgagee may sell at a public or private sale. In the absence of the mortgagor's express consent or statutory sanction, the mortgagee may not purchase the property at the sale. The proceeds of the sale are held in trust by the mortgagee and, after deducting what is necessary in order to satisfy his claim against the mortgagor, he must account to the mortgagor for any surplus. If the proceeds are insufficient to satisfy the mortgagee's claim, he may bring an action against the mortgagor for the deficiency and obtain a judgment therefor.

Marshaling of Assets. The equitable doctrine of marshaling of assets is applicable in the foreclosure of mortgages. This doctrine applies when there are two classes of creditors, one class having recourse to more than one asset while the other class has recourse to only some but not all of those assets. Under the doctrine, creditors are to resort first to those assets not available to other creditors and then to the other assets available to the other creditors. Thus, when a creditor holds a first mortgage on two parcels of the debtor's land and another creditor holds a second mortgage on one of those two parcels, on the debtor's default on his debt to the first mortgagee the second mortgagee can compel the first mortgagee seeking to foreclose to proceed first against the parcel unencumbered by the second mortgage.

Rights and Duties of the Mortgagor
The mortgagor and the mortgagee have various rights and duties in connection with the mortgage. The mortgagor has the right to exercise his equity of redemption within the prescribed period of time. Inasmuch as the mortgagor retains title in most states, he may convey title to the property *subject to* the mortgage and, similarly, a creditor of the mortgagor may levy upon and sell the mortgaged property subject to the mortgage. The mortgagor is liable

for the mortgage debt, and the property is subject to the mortgage. Accordingly, any transfer of the property by the mortgagor does not cause the transferee to become personally liable on the mortgagor's debt. The transferee acquires the mortgagor's title to the property *subject to* the mortgage of the mortgagee. However, if the transferee *assumes* payment of the mortgagor's obligation, a change occurs in the relationship between the mortgagor and the transferee and in the relationship between the transferee and the mortgagee. The mortgagor cannot escape liability on his obligation by transferring the property to another and, accordingly, the mortgagor remains liable to the mortgagee thereon. However, as between the mortgagor and the assuming transferee, the transferee is ultimately liable for the performance of the mortgagor's obligation, and the mortgagor becomes a surety for the transferee.[150] By contracting to assume the mortgagor's obligation, the transferee becomes personally liable to the mortgagee, who is a third party creditor beneficiary[151] of the contract between the mortgagor and the transferee, and the mortgagee may enforce the contract against the transferee. Although the mortgagor is liable for the payment of taxes on the mortgaged property, if the mortgagor fails to make such payment, the mortgagee may do so and add such expense to the mortgage debt. Regardless of whether the mortgagor or the mortgagee is in possession of the mortgaged property, the one in possession may not waste such property, and he must exercise reasonable care in its preservation. The mortgagee has a right of reimbursement against the mortgagor for expenses reasonably incurred in the preservation of the mortgaged property.

---

[150] See below, p. 810.

[151] See above, pp. 97 ff.

Chapter II

NONCONSENSUAL PROPERTY SECURITY TRANSACTIONS

1. COMMON LAW LIENS

Nature AT COMMON LAW various liens[1] on personal property could be acquired without the consent of the owner of such property, but not on real property. Common law liens were called "possessory liens" because the liens consisted only of the right to possess the property; they contained no power to foreclose or to sell such property. In the latter respect, common law liens differed from the pledge, which also existed at Common Law as a lien. Such liens were accorded to those persons engaged in a public calling, for the improvement of another's property at his request, and pursuant to mercantile custom.

Specific Liens The innkeeper, common carrier, and public warehouseman were engaged in businesses of a public calling and, because they had the duty of serving the public generally, the law accorded to them a lien on the property which they served. The innkeeper had an innkeeper's lien on the goods of each guest as security for the payment of the cost of lodging. The common carrier had a carrier's lien on the goods transported and stored in connection with such transportation for the charges therefor. Similarly, the public warehouseman had a warehouseman's lien on the goods stored with him as security for the payment of storage charges. A lien was accorded to persons who improved the property of another at the latter's request. The lien on such property, called an "artisan's lien," was security for the payment of proper charges therefor. These liens are *specific liens* because they are only on the specific property for services rendered to such property. The lien did not extend to other property of the debtor

---

[1] A "lien" is a legal right in the property of another as security for the performance of an obligation. A "lienor" is the person who has a lien, while a "lienee" is the person against whose property there is a lien.

in the creditor's possession on which services had not been rendered. (A delivers a bureau to B for repair and later delivers a chair to B for repair. After making such repairs, B has a lien on the chair for the repairs made to it, and a separate lien on the bureau for the repairs made to it. If B delivers the bureau to A without receiving payment, B does not have a lien on the chair for the cost of repairs to the bureau and to the chair. B has a common law artisan's lien on the chair only for the repairs made to it. B's delivery of the bureau to A caused B to lose his lien on the bureau.)

General Liens

A *general lien* is a lien on property other than that on which services have been rendered. A general lien will not be created except either by express agreement between the parties concerned or by mercantile custom. Mercantile liens are general liens arising from mercantile custom. An illustration of a mercantile lien which is a general lien is a banker's lien on the funds and securities of a depositor as security for a debt of the depositor to the bank. However, the delivery of property to another for a special purpose excluding a lien thereon as inconsistent with such purpose, precludes any lien from attaching to such property. The deposit of money in a trust account, or the delivery of securities or other property in trust, does not permit the creation of a lien on such property in favor of the person in possession as security for a debt owing by the person who has delivered such property.

Extinguishment of Liens

Common law liens carry only the right to possess the particular property; they are possessory liens and exist only so long as the creditor retains the right to possession. The creditor's loss of possession without his consent or authority, as by theft, does not terminate the lien, and he has the right to reacquire possession. The creditor's voluntary relinquishment of possession to the debtor for a temporary and limited purpose, or pursuant to the debtor's fraudulent inducement to part with such possession, does not terminate the lien. The creditor's voluntary surrender of possession to the debtor extinguishes the lien, and the debtor's subsequent return of possession to the creditor does not re-establish the lien. Payment of the debt owing to the creditor, or a valid tender of such payment, discharges the lien and, on the creditor's refusal to return possession to the debtor, the debtor may bring an action in replevin for such possession or an action in conversion for the reasonable value of the property.

2. *STATUTORY LIENS*

Today statutes in the various states have expressly included many of the common law liens and have created new liens. The Code provides for carriers' liens and warehousemen's liens.[2] Some of the new liens refer to personal property—e.g., landlord's liens and finder's liens—and some refer to real property, the most important of which are the mechanics' liens.

Mechanics'
Liens
Mechanics' liens are accorded to those persons who, pursuant to contract with the owner of real property or his agents or independent contractors, have rendered labor, services, or material for the improvement of such property; the lien is security for payment for such labor, services, or material. Contractors, subcontractors, laborers, and materialmen benefit from such a lien. In some states the lienor—i.e., the one who has the lien—has a lien on the property only to the extent of what is owing by the owner to the contractor, while in other states the lien extends to the real property regardless of the amount owing by the owner to the contractor. In order to establish their liens, lienors must file a notice of lien within a specified period of time after the last of such labor, services, or materials has been furnished. Such liens must be foreclosed within a specified period of time or the lien is lost. Foreclosure proceedings are the same as for foreclosure of a real estate mortgage. The mechanic's lien does not disturb prior liens on the property, but such prior liens are superior only to the extent of the value of the property in its unimproved state. The mechanic's lien has priority to the extent that improvement has been made, if this can be ascertained.

---

[2] UCC 7–307, 7–209.

APPENDIX TO PART SEVEN (A)

REFERENCES

1. American Law Institute. *Restatement: Security.* 1941.
2. Anderson, Ronald A. *Anderson's Uniform Commercial Code.* 2d ed. Rochester, N.Y.: Lawyers Cooperative Publishing Co., 1970.
3. Coogan, Peter F.; Hogan, William E.; and Vagts, Detlev F. *Secured Transactions under the Uniform Commercial Code.* New York: Matthew Bender & Company, Inc., 1963.
4. Gilmore, Grant. *Security Interests in Personal Property.* Boston, Mass.: Little, Brown and Co., 1965.
5. Hawkland, William D. *A Transactional Guide to the Uniform Commercial Code.* Philadelphia, Pa.: American Law Institute, 1964.
6. Osborne, George E. *Handbook on the Law of Mortgages.* 2d ed. St. Paul, Minn.: West Publishing Co., 1970.
7. Spivack, Oscar. *Secured Transactions under the Uniform Commercial Code.* Philadelphia, Pa.: American Law Institute, 1963.
8. *Uniform Commercial Code Handbook 257–550,* American Bar Association, Chicago, 1964.
9. *Uniform Laws Annotated,* Uniform Commercial Code, 1962.

PROBLEMS

1. Explain what is meant by the following terms under Article 9 on Secured Transactions under the Uniform Commercial Code:
   (a) Security agreement.
   (b) Security interest.
   (c) Secured party.
   (d) Collateral.
   (e) Purchase money security interest.
   (f) Chattel paper.
   (g) Perfection of a security interest.
2. Is Article 9 on Secured Transactions under the Code applicable to:
   (a) Statutory liens? Explain.

(b) A pledged note secured by a real property mortgage? Explain.

(c) Accounts and chattel paper? Explain.

(d) A security interest arising under the Sales portion of the Code? Explain.

3. (a) Explain the meaning of each of the four classes of goods under Article 9 on Secured Transactions under the Code.

(b) Without explaining, indicate the class of goods of each of the following:

(1) Refrigerator in a home.

(2) Refrigerator for fish in a retail fish business.

(3) Refrigerator for sale by a retailer of electrical appliances.

(4) Cattle raised for sale.

(5) Materials used up or consumed in a business.

4. Sam sold goods to Bob for $1,000. Under Article 9 on Secured Transactions under the Code, does Sam have an "account" against Bob? Explain.

5. Name the three things which must occur for each of the following:

(a) Perfection of a security interest.

(b) A security interest to attach to collateral.

6. Name six transactions where a security interest in collateral may be perfected without the normal requirement of filing a financing statement under Article 9 on Secured Transactions under the Code.

7. If a secured party with a perfected security interest assigns it, how does such assignment affect the perfected security interest?

8. B contracts with S to buy a refrigerator from S, B to pay for the same in installments.

(a) What is the effect of a clause in the contract prohibiting S from assigning this account against B?

(b) If S had defrauded B in the transaction, may B assert such fraud against X, S's assignee of the account? Explain.

(c) If S assigns the account to E, may B and S subsequently modify the terms of the sales contract without E's consent? Explain.

(d) If S delivers the refrigerator to B, S then assigns the account to Z who notifies B of the assignment, and B then makes an installment payment to S, does Z have a right against B for payment to Z of that installment? Explain.

9. (a) What is the purpose and nature of a financing statement?

(b) Explain fully how the length of the filing period is determined.

(c) What is the purpose and nature of a continuation statement?

(d) If a security interest is assigned, explain fully what the assignee should do in order to make it effective against persons other than the secured party assignor.

10. A delivered his automobile for repair to B, an automobile repair shop. B redelivered the automobile to A without collecting the $100 charges due for the repairs. One month later A again delivered his automobile to B for additional repairs amounting to $50. A tendered $50 to B, but B now refuses to redeliver the automobile to A until A has paid the $150 repair charges.

(a) Does B have a right to retain possession of the automobile?

(b) Why?

11. As between bank and depositor:

   (a) What are the rights of set-off of matured debts of a depositor to a bank in a deposit and checking account?

   (b) What are a bank's rights of set-off of an immature note from a depositor? (Former C.P.A. Examination question)

12. (a) Allen delivered silver to Burt, a jeweler, to be made into a medallion. Burt was to receive $50 for his work, 30 days after the delivery of the medallion. After the completion of the medallion Burt refused to deliver it except upon the payment of the $50, claiming a workman's lien. Was Burt justified in his refusal?

   (b) Allen delivered woolen cloth to Williams to be made into ladies' suits, agreeing to pay him $20 for each suit. After the suits were finished and before they had been paid for, Fredericks levied upon them under a judgment recovered against Williams. Was the levy good? (Former C.P.A. Examination question)

SOME PREVIOUS C.P.A. LAW EXAMINATION QUESTIONS AND MODEL ANSWERS

MAY, 1971

No. 2 (Estimated time—20 to 25 minutes)

Each of the lettered statements of facts below is followed by numbered sentences that state legal conclusions relating to those facts. You are to determine whether each legal conclusion is true or false according to *Article 9 of the Uniform Commercial Code (Secured Transactions)*. Use a soft pencil, preferably #2, to blacken the appropriate space on the separate printed answer sheet to indicate your answer. Your grade will be determined from your total of correct answers less a penalty of approximately one half for each of your incorrect answers; an omitted answer will not be considered an incorrect answer.

A. Owens, an automobile dealer, had an inventory of 30 passenger cars and 5 trucks. He financed the purchase of this inventory with State Bank under an agreement dated January 5 which gave the bank a security interest in all vehicles on Owens' premises, all future acquired vehicles and the proceeds thereof. On January 5 State Bank properly filed a financing statement which identified the collateral in the same way that it was identified in the agreement. On April 1 Owens sold a passenger car to Cobb for his family use and a truck to Stanton Company for its hardware business.

   31. The security agreement may not provide for a security interest in future acquired vehicles even if the parties agree.

   32. The passenger car sold by Owens to Cobb continues to be subject to the security interest of the State Bank.

   33. The signatures on the financing statement must be notarized or witnessed.

34. If Owens retained a security interest in the passenger car sold to Cobb until it was paid for, this would be included in the inventory class of collateral under the security agreement with the bank.

35. The security interest of the State Bank includes the proceeds from the sale of the truck to Stanton Company.

B. Dr. Bell, a physician, bought an X-ray machine from Medical Equipment Corporation for use in his practice which he conducted in his home. At the time of purchase Dr. Bell signed a security agreement which provided that he pay the purchase price by making 36 monthly installments of $500.

36. The collateral was consumer goods since it was used by Dr. Bell in his home.

37. If Medical Equipment Corporation transferred the security agreement to a bank as collateral for a loan made by the bank to the Corporation, the security agreement would be chattel paper.

38. If Dr. Bell defaults, the Corporation may take possession of the machine if it can do so without breach of the peace.

39. If repossessed by the Corporation after Dr. Bell's default, the machine must be sold at a public auction.

40. The Corporation may purchase the machine at public auction if it is the highest bidder.

C. Time and Chimes, Inc., a manufacturer of clocks, shipped $100,000 in merchandise to various customers on credit with payment due in 60 days. As soon as the goods were shipped, the company sold and assigned the accounts to Factors, Inc. which purchased them for $95,000 pursuant to a written agreement. Factors, Inc. paid the company and took possession of the duplicate invoices covering the goods shipped. The original of each invoice was stamped: "This invoice has been assigned to Factors, Inc." Factors, Inc. did not file a financing statement. A month later Norton, a judgment creditor of Time and Chimes, levied on the accounts.

41. Factors, Inc. will prevail over Norton since it perfected its security interest in the particular accounts receivable by taking possession of the assigned invoices.

42. If Factors, Inc. properly had filed a financing statement pursuant to an oral security agreement, its security interest would be enforceable against the Company and third parties.

43. A security interest in collateral can never be perfected unless a financing statement is properly filed.

44. If a filed financing statement does not state a maturity date, it is effective for a period of three years from the date of filing.

45. A security agreement may be filed as a financing statement if it complies with all the requirements applicable to a financing statement.

D. Beautiful Dolls, Inc., a doll manufacturer, borrowed $300,000 from First Bank and executed a security agreement which provided that the Company granted a security interest to the bank in all of its accounts receivable, inventory and equipment and the proceeds of all such collateral. The company defaults.

46. After default the bank at any time lawfully may notify all of the com-

pany's account debtors of the security interest it has in the accounts receivable and demand that payment be made directly to the bank even if the company objects.

47. After default the bank lawfully may demand that the company assemble all the equipment in one empty storage building owned by the company and convenient to both parties.

48. The bank lawfully may retain any surplus realized from the disposition of the collateral if the security agreement is silent as to which party is entitled to the surplus.

49. The bank lawfully may retain any surplus realized from the disposition of the collateral if the security agreement so provides.

50. The security interest in inventory includes not only finished inventory but also raw materials and work in process.

E. National Bank loaned $25,000 to Knitwear Manufacturing Corporation under a written security agreement which provided that the corporation was to use the money to purchase three looms. The corporation purchased the looms with the borrowed money and took possession of them on July 9. The bank did not file a financing statement covering the transaction until July 15. On July 10 Seaver, a judgment creditor of the corporation, levied on the looms. Seaver contends that his levy is superior to the bank's security interest since the levy occurred before the bank filed and he had no knowledge of the bank's security interest.

51. Seaver's contention is correct.

52. The bank had a purchase money security interest.

53. The bank could have filed a financing statement before a security agreement was executed or before the corporation came into possession of the looms.

54. Even if the bank had not filed a financing statement, it would prevail over Seaver.

55. To be legally effective the financing statement must identify each loom by serial number.

F. Elegant Manufacturing Corporation owned 30 sewing machines which it used in its business of manufacturing fancy tablecloths. The corporation borrowed $3,000 from Albert Bank under a security agreement dated December 1 which provided that the corporation give the bank a security interest in the 30 machines and all other machines thereafter acquired. The bank filed a financing statement on December 2 in the proper office. Later, on January 21 the corporation bought 20 additional sewing machines from Green Machine Company under a written agreement to pay for the machines in monthly installments and to give Green Machine Company a security interest in the 20 sewing machines until the purchase price is paid. The machines were delivered to the corporation on January 28. On January 30 the corporation defaulted on its indebtedness to Albert Bank and the bank immediately seized all 50 sewing machines. On February 2 Green Machine Company properly filed a financing statement covering the 20 machines and then claimed that its security interest in these machines prevailed over that claimed by the Albert Bank.

56. Green Machine Company is correct.
57. To be enforceable the security agreement between Green Machine Company and Elegant Manufacturing Corporation must be signed by both parties regardless of the amount involved.
58. If Albert Bank and the corporation agreed, Green Machine Company could have lawfully taken a second security interest in the 30 machines already subject to the security interest of the bank.
59. Green Machine Company always will prevail over the security interest claimed by the bank in these 20 machines regardless of when it files a financing statement.
60. The bank perfected its security interest on December 1, the date of the security agreement.

Answer

31. False	37. True	43. False	49. False	55. False
32. False	38. True	44. False	50. True	56. True
33. False	39. False	45. True	51. False	57. False
34. False	40. True	46. True	52. True	58. True
35. True	41. False	47. True	53. True	59. False
36. False	42. False	48. False	54. False	60. False

No. 3A (Estimated time—4 to 5 minutes)

Each of the lettered statements of facts below is followed by numbered sentences that state legal conclusions relating to those facts. You are to determine whether each legal conclusion is true or false according to the *general principles of real property law*. Use a soft pencil, preferably #2, to blacken the appropriate space on the separate printed answer sheet to indicate your answer. Your grade will be determined from your total of correct answers less a penalty of approximately one half for each of your incorrect answers; an omitted answer will not be considered an incorrect answer.

A. Brown wished to raise some additional capital for his manufacturing business. Ames, his accountant, suggested that he mortgage his estate, Longacre. Brown then did this, receiving a $10,000 loan from Central Bank and giving his mortgage bond in that amount. Brown neglected to advise either Ames or the bank that he previously had mortgaged Longacre to Collins who failed to record the mortgage. The bank promptly recorded its mortgage. In anticipation of his son Henry's wedding to Helen Smith, Brown deeded Longacre as a wedding gift to Henry Brown and Helen Smith. Henry and Helen recorded the deed and were married.
61. Collins' mortgage is prior in time and would take priority over that of the Bank.
62. Henry and Helen's deed would not be subject to the lien of Collins' mortgage.

63. Henry and Helen's deed would not be subject to the lien of the Bank's mortgage.
64. If the deed to Henry and Helen stated that it was subject to the bank's mortgage, Henry and Helen could be called upon personally to pay any deficiency on foreclosure by the bank.
65. If Henry and Helen had assumed the bank mortgage, the answer to item 64 would be different.
66. On foreclosure Brown could be called upon to pay the bank any deficiency.

Answer

61. False	63. False	65. True
62. False	64. False	66. True

NOVEMBER, 1969

No. 3 (Estimated time—10 to 12 minutes)

Each of the following numbered sentences states a legal conclusion as it relates to the preceding related lettered fact situation. You are to determine whether each of the legal conclusions is true or false according to the *Uniform Commercial Code* and write on a separate answer sheet whether each conclusion is true or false. Your grade will be determined from your total net score obtained by deducting your total of incorrect answers from your total of correct answers; an omitted answer will not be considered an incorrect answer.

A. Charles purchased a power saw for use in his home from Herman's Hardware Store for $500, payable $100 "down" and the balance in specified monthly installments. This purchase was covered by a conditional sales contract (security agreement) which gave Herman a valid security interest in the saw to secure payment of the full purchase price. The contract further prohibited Charles from disposing of the saw so long as any part of the purchase price remained unpaid. No financing statement was filed for this transaction. Peter subsequently offered to purchase the saw from Charles.
61. Herman has a perfected security interest in the saw.
62. If Charles defaults after having paid $150 of the price, Herman must resell the saw within a stated period of time after repossessing it unless, after default, Charles waives his right to require such resale in writing.
63. If Charles had purchased the saw for use in his cabinet making business, Herman would be required to file a financing statement to perfect his security interest.
64. Unless Herman waives the prohibition contained in the contract, Charles may not transfer a valid title to the saw to Peter.
65. If Charles sells the saw to Peter after Herman files a financing statement and Peter pays value without knowledge of Herman's security interest therein, Peter will take the saw free of the security interest.
B. Baker Loan Company made secured loans to Smith, Jones, and Roe. Smith

gave Baker a security interest in his household furniture. Jones delivered to Baker his rare coin collection as a pledge. Roe's loan is evidenced by his promissory note, is repayable over three years in monthly payments, and is secured by a security interest in the inventory of Roe's Clothing Store, a sole proprietorship owned by Roe. Proper security agreements were made and financing statements were duly executed and filed with respect to all of these transactions on the dates of the transactions.

66. The filing of a financing statement was required to perfect the security interest in Smith's household furniture.

67. Baker's security interest in Jones' coin collection was perfected before a financing statement was filed.

68. On filing a financing statement covering Roe's inventory, Baker's security interest therein was perfected, but only for a maximum period of two years.

69. The financing statement for Roe's inventory must include a detailed itemization and valuation of the inventory if the financing statement is to be valid.

70. Baker's security interest in Roe's inventory is superior to the rights of any customer of Roe's who purchases items therefrom in the ordinary course of business with actual knowledge of the security interest.

C. Ace Motor Sales, a corporation engaged in selling motor vehicles at retail, borrowed money from Star Finance Company and gave Star a properly executed security agreement in its present and future inventory and in the proceeds thereof to secure the loan. Star's security interest was duly perfected under the laws of the state where Ace does business and maintains its entire inventory. However, through error, the financing statement filed by Star did not include the proceeds received from the sale of Ace's inventory. Thereafter, Ace sold a new pick-up truck from its inventory to Albert and received Albert's certified check for the full price in payment therefor. Albert then resold the truck to Roger, a resident of the state, for use by Roger in a laundry business carried on by him in the state. Roger duly gave Albert a valid security interest in the truck to secure payment of the balance of the purchase price and the security interest was duly perfected under the laws of the state. Six months after purchasing the truck from Albert, Roger moved himself and his business and property to an adjoining state.

71. Star must file an amendment to the financing statement every time Ace receives a substantial number of additional vehicles from the manufacturer if Star is to maintain a valid security interest.

72. Star had a perfected security interest in Albert's certified check for 10 days after Ace's receipt of the check.

73. The security agreement between Ace and Star could include a provision which would give Star a valid security interest in Ace's inventory without further filing if Star advanced additional money.

74. Albert's security interest in the truck he sold to Roger would be perfected in the adjoining state by virtue of being perfected in Albert's home state, but only for a limited period of time.

75. If Albert's security interest had not been perfected under the laws of his home state prior to removal of the truck to an adjoining state, the security interest may not thereafter be perfected in the adjoining state.

Answer

61. True	64. False	67. True	70. False	73. True
62. False	65. False	68. False	71. False	74. True
63. True	66. True	69. False	72. True	75. False

B. SURETYSHIP

Chapter III

NATURE OF SURETYSHIP

1. GENERAL

Background   SURETYSHIP arose because of the need for shifting risks in the doing of business—the desire for security against loss from nonperformance of an obligation owing.[1] (D desires to purchase goods on credit from C, who requires some security that D will pay for such goods if they are sold to him. S agrees that, if C sells such goods to D and D does not pay therefor, S will make such payment. Pursuant to this agreement C sells the goods to D. C's risk of loss from D's nonperformance of his obligation is now shifted to S. C now has two persons to whom he may resort for performance of D's obligation.) In the illustration, S is called the surety, D is called the principal debtor, and C is called the creditor. The surety undertakes to perform specific *obligations of a third person,* then existing or which may occur in the future, owing to the creditor on the default of such third person. It is readily apparent that suretyship is both a credit device to the principal debtor and a risk-bearing device to the creditor. Suretyship is widely used in business today as a security device.

"Suretyship" is a particular kind of legal relationship
Definition   involving three parties, used for the purpose of security. It may be defined as a relationship in which one person called a "surety" and another person called a "principal debtor" are obligated to perform the same obligation for a person called a "creditor" who is entitled to only one performance, and as between the surety and principal debtor the latter is to perform the obligation and is ultimately liable therefor. (S contracts with C that, if C will extend credit to D, S will pay the amount owing by D on D's default. Both D and S are under the same obligation to pay C the amount, although S's obligation is not performable until D defaults, while D's obligation is performable on the day the debt matures. C is entitled to but one payment. As be-

---

[1] See above, p. 727.

tween S and D, D is to pay and will be ultimately liable to S for S's payment to C on the obligation; it is for this reason that D is called a *principal* debtor.) Essentially, a surety makes his credit or his property available to the creditor for the benefit of the principal debtor.

Suretyship is the relation among the three parties of surety, creditor, and principal debtor, and is created by the suretyship contract. The suretyship contract may include all three parties, only the surety and the creditor (which is a very common occurrence), or only the surety and the principal debtor for the benefit of the creditor. The consent or knowledge of the principal debtor is not necessary to the suretyship contract between the surety and the creditor. The suretyship contract relates to the obligation of the principal debtor, and although the obligation of the principal debtor, as well as the obligation of the surety under the suretyship contract, usually is a contract obligation, it may be an obligation arising from a tort. (S contracts with C that D's obligation to pay the damage D caused to C's property will be performed.) Further, the respective obligations of the surety and of the principal debtor may not be coextensive. (S contracts with C to pay for all the merchandise that D purchases from C not in excess of $10,000 on D's failure to make such payment. D purchases merchandise costing $15,-000 from C. D is liable to C for $15,000 while S is liable only to the extent of $10,000 if D defaults.) The surety's obligation is fixed by the suretyship contract, and the obligation of the principal debtor is fixed by his contract or tort.

Contract of Indemnity Distinguished

A contract of suretyship should be distinguished carefully from a contract of indemnity because the statute of frauds is applicable to a suretyship contract (except a contract for strict suretyship) but not to an indemnity contract.[2] An important difference is that the indemnity contract does not promise to answer for the *debt, default, or miscarriages of the promisee's* (creditor's) *obligor* (principal debtor), while a suretyship contract (except a contract for strict suretyship) does. A contract of indemnity is made by an indemnitor with an indemnitee whereby the indemnitor assures the indemnitee that any loss he sustains will be paid by the indemnitor, *regardless of the liability of any third person therefor*. Such a contract contemplates loss for which third persons may not be involved or liable; a contract of suretyship contemplates loss caused by the *default* or *wrongs* of the promisee's obligor. (A contracts with B to pay B for any damage B sustains by the use of

---

[2] This is the reason why, in the absence of statute to the contrary, life and fire insurance contracts being for indemnity are not within the statute of frauds. See below, p. 883.

B's automobile. B damages his automobile. This is a contract of indemnity and A is liable to B for such damage.) (X contracts with Y whereby X is to pay Y for any defalcations of his employees; or X contracts with Y whereby X is to pay Y for any defaults of customers of Y in paying their debts. These are contracts of suretyship and X is liable to Y for such defalcations or defaults.) A contract of indemnity may later give rise to a suretyship relation. (A contracts with B to pay B for any damage B sustains by the use of B's automobile. This is a contract of indemnity. C wrongfully damages B's automobile thereby causing C to be liable to B. A and C are liable on the same obligation to B for which C is ultimately liable. The relation is suretyship, A being the surety, B the creditor, and C the principal debtor.)

2. CLASSIFICATION

The terms of the suretyship contract between the surety and the creditor determine the obligation of the surety. Because the nature of the surety's obligation varies according to the terms of each particular contract, specific names are given to various types of suretyship contract, which are classified according to the nature of the surety's obligation. The following classifications will be discussed: strict surety, absolute guaranty, conditional guaranty, continuing guaranty, unlimited guaranty, limited guaranty, general guaranty, special guaranty, and the position of a general indorser on a negotiable instrument.

Strict Suretyship

A "strict surety" is a surety who is a *co-debtor* with the principal debtor for the same obligation owing to the creditor. He is a surety because: he and the principal debtor are liable to the creditor for the same obligation; the creditor is entitled to only one performance of the obligation; and as between the surety and the principal debtor the latter is ultimately liable for performance of the obligation. It is the nature of the surety's obligation as a co-debtor which characterizes this special type of suretyship and distinguishes it from all others, where the obligation of the surety is so very different. For example, S and M are co-makers of a promissory note, S being a surety for M. Since S and M are co-debtors on the note, S is a strict surety.

Guaranty

Guaranty is a type of suretyship in which the surety is called a "guarantor,"[3] the suretyship contract is called a "guaranty," and the person to whom the guaranty is made is called a "guarantee," and in which the verb "guar-

---

[3] UCC 1–201(40): " 'Surety' includes guarantor."

antee" is used. Guaranty differs from strict suretyship in the nature of the surety's obligation. The strict surety has a primary liability to the creditor in that his obligation is to perform as co-debtor the same obligation as the principal debtor. In contrast, the guarantor has a liability secondary or collateral to the obligation of the principal debtor; the guarantor's obligation is to perform the principal debtor's obligation only when the principal debtor has defaulted or when something else has occurred—e.g., the creditor cannot make collection on the principal debtor's obligation. Further, the contract of strict suretyship is not, while the contract of guaranty is, within the statute of frauds.

Guaranty and warranty often are used interchangeably but they should be distinguished because of their different meanings. A warranty is a promise or affirmation of fact relating to certain property which induces the buyer to purchase such property—e.g., warranties of title or quality; a guaranty is not concerned with the attributes of property but, rather, with security for performance of an obligation. A warranty involves two, while a guaranty involves three, persons. A warranty is not necessarily, while a guaranty is, within the statute of frauds.

Absolute Guaranty. An "absolute guaranty" is an absolute or unconditional contract to perform another's obligation *on his default*. A common example is the *guaranty of payment* whereby the guarantor guarantees payment to the creditor *when* the principal debtor fails to pay him; "I guarantee payment of the within obligation" are words indicating such a guaranty. Such a guaranty is enforceable only on the principal debtor's default. A promise performable only after the lapse of a certain period of time is an absolute promise. There are no conditions to its immediate performance; the law does not consider a lapse of time as a condition.

Conditional Guaranty. A guaranty which is not absolute is conditional. Any contract of guaranty which undertakes to perform the obligation, usually to pay a debt, of the principal debtor on a contingency or a condition is a conditional guaranty. It is a contract to pay *"if."* A common illustration is the *guaranty of collection,* which undertakes to pay the debt of the principal debtor if the creditor is unable to collect it. The liability of a guarantor of collection is contingent and is not enforceable until the creditor has exercised due diligence in collecting the debt and the result has been no recovery or incomplete recovery thereof. The creditor must bring an action against the principal debtor promptly, obtain a judgment, attempt to levy execution, the writ of execution must be returned unsatisfied, and the creditor must notify the guarantor within a reasonable time of his failure to effect collection.

Continuing Guaranty. A "continuing guaranty" contemplates a series of transactions and undertakes to guarantee their payment or collection. "I guarantee payment for all of the merchandise A may buy from you" is an illustration of a continuing guaranty contemplating a series of purchases of merchandise. "I'll be responsible and answer for all the horses bought by A up to $10,000" is a continuing guaranty, effective so long as A's purchases of horses do not exceed $10,000. If A's purchases reach $10,000 and then A pays $5,000 of the debt, the guaranty continues in effect up to the original amount of $10,000.

Unlimited Guaranty. An "unlimited guaranty" is a guaranty unlimited in time and in amount. "I guarantee payment for all the goods A buys from you" is an illustration.

Limited Guaranty. A "limited guaranty" is a guaranty limited in time or amount. "I guarantee payment for all the goods A buys from you up to $10,000," and "I guarantee payment for all the goods A buys from you from January 2 through June 30, 1965," are illustrations. Similarly, a guarantor may limit his liability to particular property, as by his pledging securities with the creditor for the principal debtor's obligation or by his lending the securities to the principal debtor so that he may pledge them as security for credit extended to him.

General Guaranty. A "general guaranty" is a guaranty made to the public generally and is not addressed to any particular person. A guaranty addressed to all the merchants of a particular area—e.g., a city—is a general guaranty.

Special Guaranty. A "special guaranty" is a guaranty addressed to a designated person or persons, and only such person or persons may rely on the guaranty. A general or special guaranty is, in effect, a letter of credit which is acted upon by the addressee. A guaranty may be of one or more of the several guaranties just discussed. "John Jones. I guarantee payment of all the merchandise you may sell to John Smith not in excess of $10,000 (signed) John Doe," if relied on by John Jones, is an absolute, continuing, limited, special guaranty. The various types of guaranty are named for the particular suretyship obligation involved.

Indorser on a Negotiable Instrument. An indorser is a special kind of guarantor, and his liabilities as such are fixed by the Commercial Paper portion of the Code. Unless the indorsement otherwise specifies, an indorser on a negotiable instrument is a secondary party liable thereon, engaging that upon dishonor and any necessary notice of dishonor and protest he will pay the instrument. On his payment of the instrument, he has a right against the maker or acceptor of the instrument for whom he was a guarantor, and a right against those secondary parties liable on the instrument prior to him on their guaranty to him. The liability of an indorser developed mostly under the Law Merchant rather than under the Common Law and an indorser's guaranty, therefore, differs from that of other guaranties under the law of suretyship.

3. THE SURETYSHIP CONTRACT

General   The suretyship contract between the surety and the creditor may be made at the same time as the contract between the principal debtor and the creditor, and both obligations may be contained in the same instrument or in different instruments. (In one writing, S contracts as an absolute guarantor, C contracts to sell goods to D, and D contracts to buy the goods from C. Or, S and C may contract in one writing and C and D may contract in another writing.) The two obligations may occur at different times. (D contracts to purchase goods from C, and subsequently S contracts with C as an absolute guarantor for D.) A contract between the surety and the principal debtor for the benefit of the creditor may create the suretyship relation, but the creditor is not affected by the suretyship relation until he has knowledge of it.[4] (S owns land which he has mortgaged to C. S contracts with D whereby the land is sold to D and D assumes payment of the mortgage debt. C is a third party creditor beneficiary of the contract and, inasmuch as S and D are both liable to C on the same obligation for which one payment may be made, there is a suretyship relation. As between S and D, D now is the principal debtor and S is his surety. If S is required to pay the debt, S has a right of reimbursement against D. If mortgaged land is sold to the purchaser subject to the mortgage—i.e., the purchaser does not assume the mortgage—the land is still subject to the same obligation as is the mortgagor; the purchaser being liable *only to the extent of the land for the same obligation as the mortgagor,* the relation of suretyship is created in which the purchaser is a surety to the extent of the land and the mortgagor is the principal debtor. If the mortgage is foreclosed and the land sold, the previous purchaser whose land was sold is entitled to reimbursement from the mortgagor.)

**Surety as   Any person with capacity to contract may contract
a Party   to become a surety.

---

[4] See the legal effect of the creditor's lack of such knowledge when he surrenders or impairs the security, below, p. 823.

Manifestation of Mutual Assent
A suretyship contract is governed by the law of contracts, except as otherwise modified by the law of suretyship; reference should be made to the law of contracts regarding the formation of contracts.[5]

Accordingly, manifestation of mutual assent, which is concerned with offer and acceptance, is governed by the law of contracts.

Offer. Only the offeree can accept the offer to contract as a surety. (S offers to C to become a surety for D. Only C can accept S's offer.) A continuing offer of suretyship may be made, and each compliance with the offer in reliance thereon constitutes an acceptance creating a contract; if more than one acceptance occurs, then more than one contract is formed. (G offers to guarantee to C the payment by D for all merchandise bought by D from C. In reliance on G's offer, C sells goods to D on three different occasions. There are three contracts of suretyship between G and C. G's offer is an offer of a continuing guaranty of payment, unlimited in amount, addressed to C.)

An offer is revocable by the offeror, or it may terminate, by operation of law, at any time prior to acceptance. Revocation by the offeror is ineffective until the offeree has actually received notice of such revocation. An offer may be terminated by operation of law—e.g., death of the offeror—and no notice to the offeree of such termination is required. In the case of a continuing offer of suretyship, the acceptances which have already occurred created contracts of suretyship, but a revocation of the continuing offer precludes any future acceptances. Any attempt to accept subsequent to revocation of the offer is of no effect because there is no offer to accept.

Acceptance. An offer to contract as a surety may be unilateral or bilateral. If the offer is for a bilateral contract of suretyship, acceptance must be made as required by the offer. Unless the offer provides to the contrary, acceptance by the use of the same means of communication as used for the transmission of the offer, or whatever channel is customarily used for transactions of that nature at the place where the offer is received, is proper and effective to create a contract, even though the acceptance is never received by the offeror.[6] If the offer is for a unilateral contract of suretyship, the offeree is not required to give the offeror notice of his acceptance, unless the offeree has reason to know that the offeror will not receive notice of acceptance with reasonable promptness

---

[5] See "Contracts," Chapter II, pp. 18 ff.

[6] For the general rule of the acceptable channel of communicating an acceptance when the offer does not expressly prescribe it, see above, p. 40.

in the ordinary course of affairs, in which case, by the majority view, the offeree has the duty to notify the offeror of performance of the unilateral act requested within a reasonable time thereafter.[7] Failure to notify the offeror when required does not affect the formation of the unilateral contract, which occurred when the act requested was performed, but it does *discharge* the offeror from the duty of performing under the contract. (G offers to guarantee to C the payment by D for all merchandise bought by D from C. On each occasion when C extends credit to D for purchases in reliance on the offer, C has the duty of informing G of such purchases within a reasonable time after each purchase. Failure to do so discharges G from liability as a guarantor on each such contract.)

Sufficient Consideration
A suretyship contract requires sufficient—i.e., valuable—consideration. The focal point of attention is the consideration requested by the offer to contract as a surety. If that consideration is rendered, and the other elements of a contract are present, a contract of suretyship is formed. If the offer requests an act—e.g., extension of credit to the principal debtor or the formation of a contract between the principal debtor and the creditor—the performance of the act creates a unilateral contract.

The suretyship contract may occur at the same time as the principal debtor's obligation is created, or subsequently. (G, D, and C all contract together that C will sell goods to D on credit, D will buy such goods, and G guarantees to C payment by D for such purchases. C's contract with D is the consideration for G's promise to guarantee, thereby creating a contract between G and C. G's promise does not become enforceable until C extends credit to D who defaults in payment therefor.) If the suretyship contract occurs subsequently, consideration must be present. (C advanced credit to D. G subsequently promises C to guarantee payment of the debt by D. G's promise is unenforceable—i.e., there is no contract—because no consideration is present. If C had paid G for his promise, then a suretyship contract would have been formed.)

Legally Valid Transaction
The requirement under the law of contracts that the transaction be legally valid is applicable to contracts of suretyship.

---

[7] See above, pp. 41–42.

Statute of Frauds

A common provision in the statute of frauds in effect throughout the various states is that a promise to answer for the debt, default, or miscarriages of another person (construed to mean the promisee's obligor) is unenforceable unless the contract is in writing or there is a note or memorandum in writing of the contract signed by the party to be charged or by his lawfully authorized agent.[8]

Contracts of Strict Surety and Guarantor. The suretyship contract of a strict surety is not, while that of a guarantor is, within the statute of frauds. The suretyship contract of a strict surety is not within the statute because the strict surety does not promise to answer for the obligation of *another*. The strict surety has assumed the principal debtor's obligation as his own and is a co-debtor with the principal debtor on the same obligation owing to the creditor. In contrast, the suretyship contract of a guarantor is within the statute because it undertakes to answer for the *principal debtor's obligation.*

Promisee Must Be Creditor. It should be observed very carefully that the statute has been construed to refer only to such promises *made to the person to whom the principal debtor's obligation is owing*— namely, the creditor. (For sufficient consideration G orally promises X to guarantee payment to C of D's debt to C. G's promise is not within the statute because the promisee is not the person to whom D's obligation is owing; G's promise is enforceable. If G's oral promise had been made to C, the promise would be within the statute and unenforceable.) A promise to the principal debtor to guarantee payment of his obligation to his creditor is not within the statute, although it creates a suretyship relation if it is supported by sufficient consideration. (G orally contracts with D to guarantee payment by D of his obligation owing to C. The contract is not within the statute of frauds and is enforceable; however, G is liable to C as a third party creditor beneficiary[9] of the contract between G and D and, therefore, the relation of suretyship exists.) A promise of suretyship is not within the statute if no principal obligation is owing to the promisee. (G contracts with C whereby C is to deliver goods to G, the cost is to be charged to D, and G guarantees payment by D. G had no authority to order these goods on D's account and, inasmuch as D is under no obligation to C, G's promise is not within the statute of frauds.)

---

[8] See discussion above, pp. 108 ff. The statute makes the contract unenforceable and not void, although in a few states the statute is construed as making the agreement void.

[9] See above, pp. 97 ff.

Simultaneous Promises for Benefit of One Promisor. If promises are made by two or more persons to the same promisee for the same obligation in return for consideration for the sole benefit of only one of the promisors, the promise of the one not benefited is within the statute of frauds, unless the promises were made jointly or unless the promisee did not have knowledge that the consideration was for the sole benefit of only one promisor. The reason for this is that when only one of two promisors receives a benefit the other is deemed to be a surety for him.[10] However, if the promises are joint only, and not joint and several or several, the promises can be treated only as a unit and, inasmuch as *both* promises are not made for the purpose of being sureties, neither promise is within the statute. If the promises are not joint and are for the benefit of only one promisor and the promisee has no reason for knowing that the benefit is for only one of them, the promisee should not be subjected to possible loss in not being able to enforce the contract because of his ignorance of their true relationship. The promisee's delivery of goods or benefits to one of the promisors is not notice to him that the benefit is to inure to only one of them.

Promise of Suretyship for Promisor's Benefit. The promise to answer for another's obligation is a benefit to the principal debtor and, therefore, is within the statute of frauds. If the promise appears to be of suretyship and for another's benefit, but really is for the *primary* benefit of the promisor in that the consideration for his promise is primarily for himself, the promise is not within the statute.[11] This is sometimes called the "main purpose" rule because the *main* purpose of the promise is to benefit the promisor and not the principal debtor. The fact that the promisor derives an incidental benefit from the consideration rendered by the promisee does not bring it within the main purpose rule. (S and C are creditors of D. C is about to attach D's property. S is afraid that such attachment will ruin D and thereby jeopardize S's collection of the debt owing to him by D, and S *orally* promises C that if C will not attach the property for one month, S will guarantee payment of D's debt to C if D does not pay by that time. C, in reliance on S's promise, forbears from attaching the property. S's promise is not within the statute and is enforceable because it was made solely for his own benefit and not for D's benefit. If S were not a creditor of D and had made the promise as a friend of D, S's promise would be within the statute and, being oral, would be unenforceable.) The promise of a del credere

---

[10] American Law Institute, *Restatement: Contracts,* 1932, sec. 181, *Comment a.*
[11] See above, pp. 109–10.

agent—i.e., a factor who for consideration in the form of a higher commission guarantees to his principal that the purchaser of goods from the agent will pay for the same—is not within the statute because his promise is made primarily for his own benefit.[12] However, the promise of a *paid surety*[13] is within the statute of frauds if the only consideration received by the *surety* is a premium of insurance that the principal debtor's obligation will be performed.[14] The reason for this exception to the "main purpose" rule is that the purpose of the statute was to include this type of promise irrespective of premium benefit to the promisor *surety.* The distinction between a paid *surety* and a paid *indemnitor* should be noted carefully again.[15]

---

[12] See above, p. 510.

[13] A paid surety, or compensated surety as he is often called, is "a person who engages in the business of executing surety contracts for a compensation called a premium, which is determined by a computation of risks on an actuarial basis. Compensated sureties are generally incorporated. . . . .

"It is important to distinguish between compensated and other sureties because the rules of suretyship, notably those relating to the defenses of the surety, are not in all respects alike for the two classes. The basis for the distinction is that one engaged in the business of executing surety contracts can be expected to have contemplated and taken account of, in the premium charged, certain elements of risk which are not considered to have been assumed by other sureties." American Law Institute, *Restatement: Security,* 1941, sec. 82, *Comment i.*

[14] American Law Institute, *Restatement: Contracts,* 1932, sec. 93.

[15] See above, pp. 806–7.

Chapter IV

DEFENSES OF THE SURETY

1. RIGHTS OF THE CREDITOR

**Against the
Surety**
THE creditor has the right to proceed against the surety on his obligation when the surety's promise is enforceable according to its terms. The strict surety's promise is enforceable on the due date of the obligation, while the enforcement of the guarantor's promise is dependent on the type of guaranty—the absolute guaranty being enforceable on default by the principal debtor and the conditional guaranty being enforceable on the occurrence of the condition (e.g., a guaranty of collection is enforceable after the creditor has exercised reasonable diligence in his unsuccessful attempt to effect collection from the principal debtor). When the principal debtor has defaulted on his obligation, the creditor has the right, at his election, to proceed: against the principal debtor, or against the surety when the surety's obligation is enforceable according to its terms, or both; or against the property held as security for performance of the principal debtor's obligation. The principal debtor's waiver or extension of the statute of limitations in favor of the creditor on the principal debtor's obligation has no effect on the statute as running on the creditor's claim against the surety on his obligation; and similarly, such waiver or extension by the surety does not affect the principal debtor's obligation to the creditor. The creditor is not required to give to the surety notice of the principal debtor's default, except when the suretyship contract provides to the contrary, although the creditor must give a guarantor of collection reasonable notice of his failure to collect on the principal debtor's obligation. The creditor may delay in taking any action after the principal debtor's default, except that in the case of a guaranty of collection the creditor is required to exercise reasonable diligence in attempting to make collection. Except for such guaranty of collection, the creditor is not unlike any other creditor with a right against his surety debtor which he may assert when and if he wishes to do so.

816

Against the Security

A creditor has a security interest in any property delivered to the creditor or to the surety[1] as security for performance of the principal debtor's obligation.

On the principal debtor's default, the creditor can proceed against such security or, at his election, proceed against the surety. The creditor has the right to recover on the obligation owing to him, without delay, and is not required to resort to the security. However, if by doing so the surety will suffer undue hardship, *and* if postponement of the creditor's right to proceed against the surety before resorting to the security will not prejudice the creditor, the surety may obtain a court decree compelling the creditor to resort first to the security. The reason that, except in such case of undue hardship to the surety, the surety cannot compel the creditor to proceed *first* against the security as an application of the doctrine of marshaling of assets is that the surety can protect himself by paying the creditor's claim against the debtor on which the surety is bound and thus become subrogated to the creditor's rights in such security, which he then can use to reimburse himself for what he has paid to the creditor.

Application of Payment by Principal Debtor to Creditor

Payment by the principal debtor to the creditor on his obligation is applied to such obligation. If the principal debtor has obligations to the creditor other than the one on which the surety is bound, such payment is to be applied on the particular obligation as indicated by the principal debtor. If the principal debtor does not indicate, then the creditor may, at his election, apply it to any of the obligations within a reasonable time after he has received such payment. If neither the principal debtor nor the creditor indicates his intention as to how the payment is to be applied, it will be applied in the manner most favorable to the creditor, unless such application would be inequitable under the circumstances (e.g., application of the doctrine of marshaling of assets if other persons are affected by the application of the payment). The source of the funds for such payment is unimportant, except that if the funds originate from the surety as security for performance of the principal debtor's obligation and *the creditor knows this,* then such payment must be applied to the obligation on which the surety is bound regardless of the principal debtor's instructions to the creditor to the contrary.[2]

---

[1] See equitable subrogation, below, p. 830.
[2] American Law Institute, *Restatement: Security,* 1941, sec. 142.

2. DEFENSES AVAILABLE TO THE SURETY

Defenses in   The principal debtor and the surety each may have
General   defenses to the creditor's claims on their respective
obligations. Some of the defenses available to the
principal debtor are personal only to him, while the others are available
to the surety as well as to the principal debtor. The surety has, in
addition to defenses which are not personal to the principal debtor,
defenses which are available only to the surety. Some of the defenses
available to the surety completely discharge him from his obligation,
while others discharge him only to the extent of the loss he has sustained or to the extent that he has been prejudiced. First the defenses
available to the principal debtor, and then the defenses available to the
surety, will be enumerated briefly; then the defenses which completely
discharge the surety will be examined, and finally the defenses partially
discharging the surety will be considered.

Defenses Available to Principal Debtor. The defenses available to the principal debtor against the creditor on the principal debtor's
obligation are as follows: (1) discharge of the principal debtor by
performance of his obligation; (2) tender of performance of the principal debtor's obligation by either the principal debtor or the surety; (3)
the creditor's release of the principal debtor from his obligation; (4)
fraud or duress perpetrated by the creditor on the principal debtor;
(5) by operation of law; (6) material nonperformance of the creditor's promise not justified by any conduct of the principal debtor; (7)
the creditor's material alteration of the written contract between him
and the principal debtor; (8) and the principal debtor's power of
avoidance because of his infancy or insanity. Only the principal debtor's
discharge in bankruptcy—i.e., by operation of law—and the last defense
are personal to him and may be exercised solely by him.

Defenses Available to Surety. Defenses available to the surety
against the claim of the creditor on the surety's obligation, as well as
those defenses available to the principal debtor and not personal to him,
are as follows: the surety's power of avoidance because of his infancy;
by operation of law; the creditor's nondisclosure of material facts bearing on the surety's risk and unknown to the surety; modification of the
principal debtor's contract by the principal debtor and the creditor
without the consent of the surety; the creditor's surrender or impairment of security received from the principal debtor; the creditor's release of a co-surety without the other surety's consent; inability of the

creditor to make collection because of his delay in enforcing a guaranty of collection; and failure of the creditor to give a guarantor of collection reasonable notice of the creditor's inability to effect collection, to the prejudice of the guarantor.

Complete Defenses Those defenses which completely discharge the surety may occur by performance of the principal debtor's obligation, by reason of the surety's lack of capacity or limited capacity to contract, by operation of law, and by the conduct of the creditor.

Performance of Principal Debtor's Obligation. Performance of the principal debtor's obligation, either by the principal debtor or by someone on his behalf, discharges the principal debtor and the surety.

Surety's Capacity to Contract. A person who has no capacity to contract cannot be a party to a suretyship contract. An infant has limited capacity to contract and may become a surety; however, he may avoid liability as a surety by exercising his power to avoid the contract.

Operation of Law. The surety is completely discharged if the statute of limitations has run against the creditor on the surety's obligation or the surety has been discharged in bankruptcy. Impossibility of performance by the principal debtor or illegality of such performance also completely discharges the surety, in the absence of a contrary provision in the contract between the surety and the creditor.

Conduct of Creditor. Most of the instances where the surety is completely discharged occur by reason of the conduct of the creditor. Several of these instances will be considered.

Release of Principal Debtor. The creditor's release of the principal debtor from his obligation discharges the surety, unless the creditor has reserved his rights against the surety or the surety consents to such release. The principal debtor's obligation has been terminated, and there is no reason for any further liability of the surety as security for the performance of the terminated obligation. An additional reason for the surety's discharge is that such release deprives the surety of the creditor's right against the principal debtor, to which the surety would have been subrogated on his performance of his suretyship obligation to the creditor. When the principal debtor has been discharged from his obligation under a composition agreement, the surety on such obligation is discharged because the creditor has voluntarily agreed to the discharge of the principal debtor. However, such release does not extinguish the creditor's interest in any security which the surety may be holding for performance of the principal debtor's obligation. It may have been because of such security that the creditor released the principal debtor.

It should be noted that, should a surety be discharged by reason of performance by the principal debtor or on his behalf and subsequently the creditor is legally compelled to surrender what he has received from the principal debtor, on such surrender the surety's suretyship obligation is revived. An illustration is an insolvent principal debtor's payment to his creditor, set aside subsequently as a voidable preference in a bankruptcy or an insolvency proceeding against the principal debtor, and the creditor is compelled to return such preference; on the creditor's return of such preference the surety's suretyship obligation is revived.

The creditor's reservation of his rights against the surety is construed as a covenant not to sue the principal debtor, and the principal debtor is not discharged from the performance of his obligation to the creditor. The effect of this is that, on the creditor's recovery against the surety on his suretyship obligation, the surety acquires the rights of reimbursement, and of subrogation to whatever security the creditor may have, for performance of the principal debtor's obligation. If it were not for such reservation of rights, the creditor's release of the principal debtor would discharge the principal debtor and would deprive the surety of his rights of reimbursement and of subrogation because the principal debtor is no longer liable on any obligation and, therefore, the surety is discharged.

Refusal of Proper Tender. The creditor's improper refusal of a proper tender of performance of the principal obligation by the principal debtor or by the surety, *with knowledge of the suretyship relation,* discharges the surety. (S and D contract with C for the purchase of goods for $900. C does not know that S is a surety for D. When D tendered $900 on the due date, C mistakenly refused the money. Neither S nor D is discharged of the debt.)

Creditor's Fraud on Principal Debtor. When the creditor has perpetrated fraud or duress on the principal debtor in inducing him to become obligated to the creditor, the principal debtor's defense of such fraud or duress is, by the majority view, also available to the surety. The surety may assert the defense regardless of whether or not the principal debtor has done so. The creditor may not profit from his fraud by obtaining the obligation of a surety as security for a voidable obligation of the principal debtor.

Creditor's Fraud on Surety. The creditor's fraudulent inducement of the surety to become such causes the contract of suretyship to be voidable at the surety's election. *Prior* to formation of the suretyship contract, the creditor has a duty to disclose to the surety all material facts which increase the surety's risk, which are known to the creditor, which the creditor reasonably believes are unknown to the surety, and which are unknown to the surety. The creditor's failure to observe this duty is a fraud on the surety. *After* the suretyship contract is formed, the creditor has no duty to inform the surety of material facts of which he learns subsequently, unless the contract of suretyship provides to the contrary, or the contract of suretyship is terminable by the surety at any time as in the usual type of fidelity bond, or if it is a continuing suretyship. In a continuing suretyship the surety makes a continuing offer to contract as a surety, and the creditor has a duty to make disclosure to the surety, inasmuch as the latter's liability will be increased by his ignorance of such material facts. Fidelity bonds usually provide for termination of the bond on the occurrence of conditions indicated therein, and the creditor's failure to make proper disclosure to the surety of facts which would permit the surety to terminate his bond discharges the surety from liability thereon. (S contracts with C, an employer, as surety for C against the defalcations of his employees. X, an employee of C, embezzles money from C, who does not inform S, who is ignorant of what has occurred. X again embezzles money from C. S is not liable for the second embezzlement.)

Although a principal debtor's exercise of his power of avoidance of his obligation on the ground of his infancy does not discharge the surety, except to the extent of the consideration returned by the principal debtor to the creditor, however, if the creditor knew of such infancy at the time the suretyship contract was made and he reasonably believed that the surety was unaware of it at that time, the creditor had a duty to disclose this material fact of infancy to the surety at that time. The creditor's failure so to disclose is a fraud on the surety and causes the suretyship contract to be voidable at the election of the surety. Nondisclosure of the principal debtor's infancy increases the surety's risk of performance because of the increased possibility of the principal debtor's default on his obligation by the exercise of his power to disaffirm the obligation.

Modification of Principal Debtor's Contract. Whether or not modification of the principal debtor's contract by the principal debtor and the creditor without the surety's consent will result in discharging the surety depends upon such modification. If the modification (1) increases the possibility of the surety's risk and (2) is binding on the modifying parties, the surety is discharged. Each of these will be considered in turn.

If the modification can be only beneficial to the surety, by the majority view the surety is not discharged; however, *if there is any possibility that the surety's risk will be increased, the surety is discharged.* A *contract* between the creditor and the principal debtor for the reduction of the rate of interest payable on the obligation does not discharge the surety because there is no possibility that the surety's risk will be increased and also because, in effect, it constitutes a reduction of the indebtedness. The substitution of a new obligation of the principal debtor to the creditor, or a material change in the principal debtor's obligation, discharges the surety. The surety never agreed to be liable for such a modified obligation of the principal debtor. While there is conflict, by the better view[3] a paid surety is not discharged if his risk is increased slightly; he is discharged only to the extent of any loss caused to him by the modification of the principal debtor's contract. The basis for this exception is that the paid surety should anticipate small changes affecting his risk slightly and take this into consideration in fixing his premiums.

If the creditor makes a *binding agreement* with the principal debtor extending the time of payment by the principal debtor, without the surety's consent and without reserving his rights against the surety in the agreement, the surety is discharged.[4] The surety is discharged because of the possibility of an increase in the surety's risk. The surety is deprived of his privilege, at the time his obligation to the creditor matures, to perform the obligation himself and thereby become entitled to reimbursement by the principal debtor and become subrogated to the creditor's rights against the principal debtor *immediately.* The binding agreement between the creditor and the principal debtor postpones this right of the surety, which is prejudicial to the surety, adversely affecting his risk. *Unless the extension agreement is binding, the obligation of the principal debtor is not modified.* The agreement must be supported by sufficient consideration.[5] The creditor's gratuitous promise to extend the time of payment is not enforceable for want of consideration, and the surety is not discharged. If the surety consents to a binding extension agreement between the creditor and the debtor, the surety's express or implied promise to continue to be bound is enforceable without consideration as an exception to the consideration rule.[6] Although there is

---

[3] *Ibid.,* sec. 128.

[4] For the application of this rule to commercial paper, see above, p. 469.

[5] For extension of an interest-bearing obligation *as a contract,* see above, p. 66.

[6] See above, pp. 86–87. Also, see above, p. 470.

conflict, by the better view[7] a paid surety is discharged only to the extent that he has been prejudiced by such extension of time. The discharge of a nonpaid surety by such an extension agreement does not disturb the creditor's interest in security held by the surety for performance of the principal debtor's obligation.

Creditor's Material Nonperformance. Unexcused failure of consideration by the creditor—i.e., material nonperformance without justification[8]—discharges the principal debtor's obligation to perform and thereby increases the risk of the principal debtor's nonperformance of his obligation and increases the surety's risk of loss on the suretyship contract. It is for this reason that the surety is discharged completely. However, should the principal debtor elect to treat the creditor's material nonperformance as an immaterial nonperformance or to waive it, the surety's risk has not been increased and, therefore, the surety is not discharged.

Creditor's Material Alteration of Written Contract. As discussed previously in Contracts,[9] a material alteration of a written contract discharges such contract. The alteration must be made to the instrument containing the contractual obligation. When this is done by the creditor, the surety is discharged as well as the principal debtor.

Partial Defenses The creditor's conduct may cause a reduction in the security available to the surety or otherwise prejudice the surety's position in the event of the principal debtor's default, justifying the surety's discharge *only to the extent of such loss of security or prejudice.* A few of the ways by which the surety's partial discharge may occur will be examined briefly.

Creditor's Surrender or Impairment of Security. A creditor who *has knowledge* of the suretyship relation and who surrenders to the principal debtor, or negligently or willfully impairs the value of, security received from the principal debtor thereby causes the surety to be discharged to the extent of the security surrendered or impaired by the creditor. Should the creditor subsequently proceed against the surety on the surety's obligation, the surety would be deprived of the opportunity to have recourse against the security so surrendered or impaired and, rather than cause the surety to suffer to such extent, the surety is partially discharged.

---

[7] American Law Institute, *Restatement: Security,* 1941, sec. 129.

[8] See above, pp. 121–22.

[9] See above, p. 146.

Creditor's Release of Co-surety. Unless the creditor reserves his rights against the remaining co-sureties, the creditor's release of one of two or more co-sureties causes the co-sureties not released to be deprived of the contributive share of the released co-surety in the event of the principal debtor's nonperformance of his obligation, and the co-sureties not released are discharged to the extent of such contributive share at the time of their performance of their obligations. The contributive share of the released co-surety is measured as of the time when the co-sureties not released are entitled to such contributive share, which occurs at the time they are compelled to perform their suretyship obligations. If the released co-surety is insolvent or unavailable *at that time,* the remaining co-sureties are not discharged to any extent.

Creditor's Conduct if Guaranty of Collection. A guarantor of collection engages that the principal debtor's obligation is collectible and, if not, that he will pay it. Before the guarantor's promise is enforceable the creditor has two duties to perform. He must act with reasonable promptness to enforce collection of the obligation of the principal debtor and, on failure to effect collection, he must give to the guarantor notice of such failure within a reasonable time thereafter. The guarantor is discharged to the extent that the creditor's failure to act promptly to enforce collection caused him not to effect collection, and the guarantor is also discharged to the extent that he has been prejudiced by the creditor's failure to give notice to the guarantor of the creditor's inability to effect collection.[10]

It should be noted carefully that, if the guaranty of collection is on *commercial paper,* under the Code:

> "Collection guaranteed" or equivalent words added to a signature mean that the signer engages that if the instrument is not paid when due he will pay it according to its tenor, but only after the holder has reduced his claim against the maker or acceptor to judgment and execution has been returned unsatisfied, *or after the maker or acceptor has become insolvent or it is otherwise apparent that it is useless to proceed against him.* (Author's italics)[11]

Surety's Right of Setoff. A surety has the right to set off against the creditor any claims against the creditor which are available to the surety whether or not arising out of the suretyship transaction. A claim of the principal debtor against the creditor is not available to the surety unless the principal debtor has assented thereto.

---

[10] American Law Institute, *Restatement: Security,* 1941, secs. 130, 137.

[11] UCC 3–416(2); also see above, p. 443.

Chapter V

REMEDIES OF THE SURETY

1. EXONERATION

WHEN the principal debtor has failed to perform his obligation and the surety's obligation becomes enforceable, the surety has various remedies: exoneration, reimbursement, subrogation, and contribution. Exoneration is a remedy available to the surety *before* the surety has performed his obligation. Reimbursement is a remedy available to the surety *after* the surety has performed *part* or *all* of his obligation. Subrogation and contribution are remedies available to the surety *after* the surety has performed his obligation *completely.* These remedies will be considered in turn.

Nature
A surety's right of exoneration is an equitable right *springing from the principal debtor's duty to the surety* to perform his obligation to the creditor and thereby spare the surety loss and inconvenience in the performance of his suretyship obligation. The principal debtor's duty originates in his promise *to the surety* to perform his obligation to the creditor and, in the event of his nonperformance, to make the surety whole for the surety's performance of his suretyship obligation. The principal debtor's promise may be express and contained in a contract between the principal debtor and the surety, or may be implied from the principal debtor's request to the surety. Accordingly, on the principal debtor's nonperformance of his obligation to the creditor and when the surety's obligation *becomes enforceable,* the surety has the right to be exonerated from the performance of his suretyship obligation by obtaining a court decree compelling the principal debtor to perform in accordance with his promise to the surety. The surety's right to such equitable relief is called the "right of exoneration."

Exercise
The surety may assert this right before, or at the same time as, the creditor seeks recovery against the surety on his suretyship contract. Although a surety cannot obstruct the right of the creditor to recover against him, nevertheless, the

surety can join the principal debtor as a party to the action by the creditor and have the principal debtor compelled to perform his obligation to the extent that he can do so. If the principal debtor has a defense to the performance of his obligation to the creditor, the surety has no right of exoneration. If the surety has a defense to the creditor's claim —e.g., the statute of limitations bars enforcement of the creditor's claim—then since the surety is not exposed to any loss the surety has no right of exoneration.

Co-sureties who become such *at the request of each other* owe to each other the duty to contribute their respective shares of the liability imposed upon them by the principal debtor's nonperformance of his obligation. A surety has the right of exoneration to the extent of the contributive share of each co-surety when the suretyship obligation matures and is enforceable against him. He need not wait until the creditor seeks to enforce his obligation.

2. REIMBURSEMENT OR INDEMNITY

The terms "reimbursement" and "indemnity" often are used interchangeably as describing a right which one person, the surety, has against another, the principal debtor, for the surety's performance of his obligation by his partial or complete performance of the principal debtor's obligation. Inasmuch as the surety's right of indemnity against the principal debtor is limited to reimbursement for the expenditure of the surety in the performance of his obligation, the term "reimbursement" will be used.

Nature A surety has the right to receive from the principal debtor, on the latter's failure to perform his obligation, whatever reasonable outlay the surety has made pursuant to his suretyship obligation to the creditor. This right is the surety's "right of reimbursement." Such outlay may reduce or discharge the principal debtor's obligation to the creditor and, although the surety may make such outlay prior to, as well as after, the date when the principal debtor's obligation is enforceable, the surety has no right of reimbursement until the principal debtor's obligation matures.[1] (D's contract with C provides for D's payment on a certain date. S, surety for D, pays D's obligation to C prior to that date. S has no right of reimbursement against D until the date when D was to perform. The statute of limitations does not begin to run on the surety's right of reimbursement

---

[1] American Law Institute, *Restatement: Restitution*, 1937, sec. 77.

against the principal debtor until the surety acquires such right.) The surety need not pay the principal debtor's obligation in full in order to acquire a right of reimbursement against him; an outlay which reduces the principal debtor's obligation gives rise to the surety's right of reimbursement. If the surety's outlay does not reduce or discharge the principal debtor's obligation to the creditor but was reasonably made while acting as a surety, the surety has a right of reimbursement for this outlay also.

Extent The extent of a surety's right of reimbursement depends upon whether or not the surety became such *at the principal debtor's request* because the surety's right of reimbursement originates in the principal debtor's duty to reimburse the surety. If the principal debtor requested the surety to be such then, either because the surety's right of reimbursement is expressed in the contract or is implied in the contract from the principal debtor's request of the surety to be such, the surety has a contract right of reimbursement for his reasonable outlay, whether or not it reduced the principal debtor's obligation to the creditor. The surety reasonably may have defended an action brought by the creditor against the surety on the surety's obligation for the principal debtor's failure to perform his obligation, which action the principal debtor has refused to defend. The surety has the right to be reimbursed by the principal debtor for the expense of his reasonable defense of such action, as well as for his payment to the creditor discharging the principal debtor's obligation to him. If the surety has become such by contract with the creditor *without the consent of the principal debtor,* the surety is entitled equitably to his outlay *only* to the extent that it discharged or reduced the principal debtor's obligation to the creditor because only to that extent has the principal debtor become *unjustly enriched at the surety's expense.* It is essential to the right of reimbursement that the outlay be made by a person under a suretyship obligation for performance of the principal debtor's obligation; a person who is not under a suretyship obligation and who makes such outlay is a volunteer with no right of reimbursement against the principal debtor.

Surety Cannot Profit. The surety cannot profit from the suretyship relation at the expense of the principal debtor. The purpose of a surety is security for the performance of the principal debtor's obligation, and the purpose of the surety's right of reimbursement against the principal debtor is to make whole the surety for his reasonable outlay on the principal debtor's behalf. If the surety settles with the creditor for less than the obligation of the principal debtor who is thereby *discharged,* the surety has a right of reimbursement only for his reasonable outlay, consisting of the amount paid by the surety to the creditor and the surety's reasonable settlement expenses, if any. If the surety elects to perform the specific obligation of the principal debtor on the latter's failure to perform, the surety cannot profit from such performance. (S is surety for D's performance of his contract with C to construct a building. On D's failure to do so, S completes the building and, pursuant to the contract between C and D, S receives from C an amount thereunder greater than S's expense in making such completion. S must account to D for the excess. If S had received an amount less than his expense in constructing the building, S would have a right of reimbursement for such deficiency.)

Effect of Defenses When defenses against the creditor's claim are available to the principal debtor, to the surety, or to both, the possibility of a surety's right of reimbursement is seriously affected. A surety is not required to assert his *own* defense to the creditor's claim against him on his suretyship obligation, and the principal debtor cannot require the surety to assert such defense. The surety's failure to assert such a defense does not affect his right of reimbursement. (S is surety for D's payment to C. The statute of limitations runs on C's claim against S but not on C's claim against D. S pays C. S has a right of reimbursement against D.) However, a surety cannot disregard a defense of the *principal debtor* because, to the extent of such defense, the principal debtor is not liable to the creditor and the surety has no right of reimbursement to that extent.

In the above illustration, if the statute of limitations had run on C's claim against D but not on C's claim against S, S's failure to assert D's defense and S's payment to C do not cause S to acquire any right of reimbursement against D. The surety is security for performance of the principal debtor's obligation and, on the surety's performance of his obligation, he has a right of reimbursement only to the extent that he has performed the principal debtor's obligation. (S, without D's consent, became a surety on D's obligation to pay C $1,000. D has a partial defense to C's claim to the extent of $400 of which S is ignorant. S pays C $1,000 on D's default. S has a right of reimbursement against D only to the extent of $600. D has been unjustly enriched only to the extent of $600, for which S has the right of reimbursement.) If the surety knows of defenses of the principal debtor which are also available to the surety, the surety should assert them in any claim made by the creditor against the surety. If the surety is ignorant of such defenses and performs his suretyship obligation to the creditor, the surety has no right of reimbursement against the principal debtor to the extent of such defenses, unless the principal debtor has failed in his duty to disclose such defenses to the surety.

Principal Debtor's Duty of Disclosure. A principal debtor has the duty to disclose *only to a surety whom he has requested to be such,* those defenses of the principal debtor which are also available to the surety; he has no duty to inform the surety of the principal debtor's discharge from his obligation to the creditor. Should the principal debtor fail in his duty to make such disclosure to the surety and the surety perform his obligation to the creditor ignorant of such defenses, the surety has a right of reimbursement therefor against the principal debtor. A defense against the creditor which is personal to the principal debtor[2] cannot be asserted by the surety, but defenses not personal to the principal debtor and which are available to the surety may be asserted by the surety against the creditor. If the surety knows of defenses of the principal debtor which are available to the surety, the surety may assert them and give the principal debtor an opportunity to defend against the claim asserted by the creditor in an action against the surety; should the principal debtor refuse to defend the action and the surety satisfies a judgment obtained by the creditor against the surety, the latter has a right of reimbursement therefor.

3. SUBROGATION

Nature A surety's recovery on his right of reimbursement against the principal debtor is assisted materially by the right of subrogation, which arises when the principal debtor's obligation *to the creditor* is *discharged.* To the extent that the surety has contributed to such discharge by performance of his suretyship obligation, the surety acquires an equitable right to occupy the creditor's position immediately on such discharge of the principal debtor. This right is available to the surety by operation of law, independent of any contract, although it may be provided for by contract. The surety is subrogated to: (1) the creditor's rights against the principal debtor; (2) the creditor's interests in property held as security for performance of the principal debtor's obligation; (3) the creditor's rights against third persons who are also liable to the creditor on the principal debtor's

---

[2] For the principal debtor's personal defenses, see above, p. 812.

obligation; and (4) to the creditor's rights against co-sureties and security held by them for the principal debtor's nonperformance of his obligation.[3] If the creditor has a preferred claim against the principal debtor, the surety acquires the creditor's preference of such claim. If the creditor's claim is a secured claim, the surety acquires the security for such claim. The surety's right to be placed in the creditor's position on the discharge of the principal debtor's obligation, to the extent that the surety's property has been used to satisfy the creditor's claim and to effect such discharge, is called the surety's "right of subrogation."

Equitable Subrogation Distinguished

The surety's right of subrogation should be distinguished carefully from the creditor's right of equitable subrogation. On the principal debtor's default the creditor has the right to resort to any security which has been deposited by the debtor *with the surety*. The creditor is subrogated to the surety's right against the property of the principal debtor. This right of the creditor to reach such security is called the "right of equitable subrogation." Until the principal debtor's default, the surety has the obligation to preserve the security.

Proof of Claim When Debtor Is Bankrupt

When the principal debtor is adjudicated a bankrupt, the creditor's claim must be proved against the bankrupt's estate within a specified period of time if it is to be allowed. If the creditor does not prove his claim within such time and the bankrupt is discharged from his provable debt, the creditor no longer has any claim against the bankrupt. However, the creditor can recover from the surety for the principal debtor on his suretyship obligation to the creditor. The principal debtor's discharge in bankruptcy is a defense personal to the principal debtor and is not available to the surety, who remains liable to the creditor on his suretyship obligation. On payment to the creditor, the surety has no right of reimbursement against the discharged bankrupt, and he is not subrogated to any right of the creditor, because the principal debtor's obligation has been discharged. In order to avoid such loss to the surety by the creditor's failure to prove his claim against the bankrupt's estate, the Bankruptcy Act, section 57i, provides that where the creditor does not prove his claim the surety may prove it in the creditor's name. Now the creditor will receive some payment on the bankrupt's obligation, and the surety is liable to the creditor only for the deficiency. Should the surety prove the creditor's claim in the creditor's

---

[3] American Law Institute, *Restatement: Security*, 1941, sec. 141.

name and then pay the creditor on the bankrupt's obligation, to the extent of such payment the surety is subrogated to the creditor's claim.

4. CONTRIBUTION

Nature Co-sureties are sureties for performance of the same obligation of a principal debtor and may contract together, or on different contracts, as co-sureties. When a surety has performed his suretyship obligation to the extent that he has paid more than his proportionate share of the principal debtor's obligation on the principal debtor's default, he has a right against his co-sureties on their suretyship obligations for their respective contributive shares for such excess. Such right is called the "right of contribution." The statute of limitations begins to run against a surety's right of contribution as soon as the surety acquires such right. A surety's right of contribution does not arise until the principal debtor has defaulted, the surety has paid more than his proportionate share of the principal debtor's obligation, and the obligations of the co-sureties have matured. A surety's negotiable promissory note made by the surety and delivered to the creditor, who accepts it in discharge of the creditor's claim against the surety, has the effect of payment and creates an immediate right of contribution in the surety against his co-sureties.

Duty to Disclose Defenses Co-sureties who have become such *with the consent of each other* have the duty to disclose to each other whatever defenses they may have against the creditor. Failure to disclose such defenses to a surety who paid the creditor in ignorance of them subjects the co-sureties to liability for their contributive shares. If such defenses are disclosed, the paying surety must assert such defenses against the creditor or the paying surety will not have any right of contribution to the extent of such defenses. Co-sureties who have become such *without the consent of each other* have no duty to disclose to each other defenses available to them.

Amount of Contributive Share The amount contributed by each co-surety depends on whether or not the co-sureties became such by mutual assent. *If there is mutual assent,* then the co-sureties share in all expenses incurred by a particular surety, regardless of whether or not the surety's expense reduced or discharged the liability of each co-surety—e.g., cost of reasonably defending an action brought against one surety by the creditor. *If there is no mutual assent* among the co-sureties, then the contributive share of each co-surety is limited only to the extent that his respective liability to the creditor has been reduced or discharged. Inasmuch as the right of contribution is an equitable right, contribution is to be made among the *available, solvent co-sureties.* (S₁ discharges D's obligation by paying C $1,000. There are five co-sureties. S₁ has a right of contribution against his four co-sureties for $200 each. If S₂ is insolvent, S₃ is outside the state, and S₄ is an infant who has avoided his suretyship contract, S₁ has a right of contribution against S₅ for $500.) Co-sureties may not profit at the expense of each other and must share the loss caused to any of them and, accordingly, if one of them has settled and discharged the creditor's claim against the principal debtor *and* the co-sureties for less than the amount due the creditor, the co-sureties are liable only for their respective contributive shares of such reduced payment. Once final settlement has been determined among co-sureties and their respective contributions made, if one of them should be reimbursed subsequently by the principal debtor or any person on his behalf, the other former co-sureties have no right to share in such reimbursed amount.

When one of several co-sureties has security or other benefit for the performance of the principal debtor's obligation, whether or not his co-sureties have any proportionate rights in such security depends upon the reason for delivery of the security, the agreement if any among the co-sureties, the consent of the other co-sureties, who gave the security, and when the security was given. Also, the extent of the right of contribution of the co-surety who has the security against his co-sureties depends upon what he did with the security. Any agreement among the co-sureties regarding such security is, of course, determinative of their rights. In the absence of agreement to the contrary, however, various equitable principles control. As a general rule, co-sureties are entitled to share proportionately in any security or other benefit received by a co-surety from the principal debtor in assurance of the latter's performance on which they are co-sureties. The reason for this principle is that the resources of the principal debtor are assets to which the co-sureties would have recourse if and when they were entitled to proceed against the principal debtor on his default, and any diminution of such resources to a co-surety as security for his own suretyship obligation, without the consent of the other co-sureties, would be inequitable to the other co-sureties and a breach of good faith on the part of such co-surety receiving the security. If such security should emanate from a third person or from another co-surety, the reason for the rule ceases to exist and the other co-sureties have no right to participate in the security. The gen-

eral rule that all co-sureties share proportionately in the security received from the principal debtor applies only when the recipient of the
security is a co-surety. Therefore, if the recipient receives such security
for his sole benefit at or before the time he became a co-surety, the general rule does not apply. Also, when the various co-sureties have paid
their respective contributive shares and thereby become independent
creditors of the principal debtor, their relationship of co-suretyship
ceases, and any subsequent reimbursement by the principal debtor to
one of them for his sole benefit does not enure to the benefit of the
others.

A co-surety who receives security from the principal debtor, in
which, under the general rule stated above, his co-sureties have rights
proportionate to their liability on the principal debtor's default, has a
right of contribution against his co-sureties when he has paid more than
his proportionate share of the principal debtor's obligation on the latter's default, irrespective of such security. His right of contribution has
matured and he can enforce it; but he may do so only if he shares the
security with his co-sureties and accounts to them therefor. The extent
of his right of contribution is reduced proportionately by his impairment or surrender of the security and by the amount he has received
from its proper and careful disposal. His right of contribution is affected further by his expense incurred in connection with the creation,
preservation, or enforcement of such security, which entitles him to reimbursement therefor, and by income which he has received from the
security, which reduces what he otherwise should receive.

Co-sureties are liable to each other for their contributive shares according to whether there is a contract among them providing for such
liability or, in the absence of such a contract, by the terms of their respective contracts of suretyship. In the absence of a contract among
them, the contributive share of each co-surety is determined according
to his maximum liability under his suretyship contract. When the co-
sureties are all liable for the same maximum amount, the liability of
each co-surety to the one who has paid the entire amount is measured
by dividing such amount paid by the number of co-sureties who are *solvent and available.* (If there are four co-sureties, each liable for a maximum amount of $1,000, and one pays the creditor the $1,000 owing by
the principal debtor to the creditor in discharge of the liability of the
principal debtor and the co-sureties, each of the three other co-sureties
is liable to the payor for $250.) When the co-sureties are not liable in
the same maximum amount on their respective suretyship contracts, the

contributive share of each co-surety is determined by the proportion that his maximum liability under his contract bears to the total of the maximum liability of all of them. (S_1's liability on his suretyship contract is \$10,000, S_2's is \$15,000, and S_3's is \$20,000. S_1 paid the entire debt of the principal debtor amounting to \$9,000. S_1's share is $\dfrac{10,000}{45,000}$ of \$9,000—namely, \$2,000. S_2's share is $\dfrac{15,000}{45,000}$ of \$9,000—namely, \$3,000. S_3's share is $\dfrac{20,000}{45,000}$ of \$9,000—namely, \$4,000. Accordingly, S_1 has a right of contribution of \$3,000 from S_2 and \$4,000 from S_3.)

Contribution Affected by a Surety's Conduct

Just as a creditor's conduct may affect his right of recovery against a surety, so the conduct of a surety may affect his right of contribution against his co-sureties after he has paid more than his proportionate share of the principal debtor's obligation. A surety's *binding* agreement with the principal debtor to extend the time within which he may make reimbursement discharges the nonpaid co-sureties from their duty to make contribution, unless the paying surety reserves his rights against the co-sureties. A paid surety is discharged only to the extent that he has been prejudiced by such extension of time. If the paying surety releases the principal debtor from his duty to make reimbursement, or surrenders or impairs the security which he has for the performance of the principal debtor's obligation, the co-sureties are discharged from their duty to make contribution to the extent that such release, surrender, or impairment is in excess of the proportionate share of the payor. The reason for such partial discharge of the co-sureties is that, on payment of their respective contributive shares, they become subrogated to the paying surety's right of reimbursement against the principal debtor or against the particular security and, to the extent that such right of reimbursement from the principal debtor or from the security has been reduced, the co-sureties are discharged.

APPENDIX TO PART SEVEN (B)

REFERENCES

1. American Law Institute. *Restatement: Contracts.* 1932.
2. American Law Institute. *Restatement: Restitution.* 1937.
3. American Law Institute. *Restatement: Security.* 1941.
4. Simpson, Laurence P. *Handbook on the Law of Suretyship.* St. Paul, Minn.: West Publishing Co., 1950.

PROBLEMS

1. (a) What is suretyship?
   (b) Distinguish a contract of suretyship from a contract of indemnity, and indicate why this distinction is important.
   (c) S orally contracted with C to be liable with D on D's debt to C.
      (1) Is the contract enforceable?
      (2) Why?
   (d) Distinguish a guaranty from a warranty.
2. A promised B that, if B sold goods to C and C did not pay therefor, then A would pay B. D also promised B that, if B sold goods to C and B could not recover the money from C, then D would pay B. In reliance on these promises B sold goods to C, who failed to pay for them.
   (1) Does B have any rights against A and D?
   (2) Why?
3. A mortgaged his land to B as security for payment of A's mortgage debt to B. A then sold and conveyed the land to C.
   (1) If C purchased the land subject to the mortgage, explain the relationship among the parties.
   (2) If C purchased the land and assumed the mortgage, explain the relationship among the parties.
4. A, in one state, promised B, in another state, that he would be liable for all of C's purchases of merchandise from B up to $10,000 if C did not pay therefor. In reliance thereon B sold merchandise to C on three different occasions, the purchase price totaling $15,000. A did not know of such sales by B to C. A died. C paid B $10,000 on the debt. B was ignorant of A's death and sold $5,000 of additional merchandise to C. C then failed to pay the $10,000 owing to B.

(1) Does B have any right against A's estate?

(2) Why?

5. A guaranteed payment by B to C for merchandise to be sold by C to B on credit, in reliance on which C sold merchandise to B. B gave C his negotiable promissory note for the purchase price, payable in 90 days at 6 percent interest per anum.

    (1) If B defaulted on his note, what would be the effect on A's liability of an agreement between B and C for the extension of time within which B could pay the debt? Why?

    (2) What would be the effect on A's liability of a contract between B and C to reduce the interest rate from 6 percent to 5 percent? Why?

    (3) What would be the effect on A's liability of C's release of B from the debt? Why?

6. Explain the meaning of the following:

    (a) Exoneration.

    (b) Reimbursement.

    (c) Subrogation.

    (d) Contribution.

7. Allen was the guarantor for the payment of rent by Burt under a lease from Carr. The lease was for two years. There was a clause in the lease to the effect that at the expiration of the lease the lessee had the privilege to renew upon 30 days' notice or, if he remained in possession after the expiration, it was agreed that the lease was to continue for two years more. There was a default in the payment of rent for the extended time and Carr sues Allen on the guaranty. Allen contends that he was liable only for the term of the lease and not for the extended term. Who should receive judgment, Allen or Carr? On what principle? (Former C.P.A. Examination question)

8. A surety company duly guaranteed the honesty of X's cashier. Thereafter, the cashier embezzled X's funds, which X discovered, but X did not discharge the cashier nor did X notify the surety company. Still later, the cashier committed a further embezzlement, whereupon X discharged him and notified the surety company. Is the surety company liable to X for either part or both of these thefts? (Former C.P.A. Examination question)

9. Allen and Bell are co-sureties on a debt of Covey to Dixon for $12,000. Covey fails to pay. Allen is compelled to pay Dixon $8,000 in partial payment of the debt. Allen sues Bell, his co-surety, for $4,000 contribution. Can Allen recover $4,000 from Bell? State your reason. (Former C.P.A. Examination question)

10. (a) S is surety on one of D's obligations to C. D paid C but did not specify to which of his obligations the payment was to be applied.

    (1) May C apply the payment to obligations of D other than the one on which S is a surety?

    (2) If S had advanced the money to D which he had paid to C, would this affect the answer to (1) above?

  (b) C knew, and reasonably believed that S did not know, that D was an infant at the time S became bound as a surety for performance of D's obligation to C. S did not know of D's infancy at that time. Do these facts affect S's suretyship obligation to C?

(c) How is a surety's obligation affected by the creditor's surrender to the principal debtor of security held by the creditor as assurance of performance by the principal debtor?

(d) S_1, S_2, S_3, and S_4 are co-sureties on an obligation owing by D to C. C released S_1 from his suretyship obligation to C. How are the suretyship obligations of S_2, S_3, and S_4 affected by such release?

11. S had a contract with D to make repairs and additions to S's house, in which S was residing. D purchased lumber from C, as he needed it for the work on S's house. D was in arrears on payments for the lumber and C refused to extend further credit to D. S orally promised C that, if C would continue to extend credit to D, S would guarantee payment by D. In reliance thereon, S extended further credit to D who, after purchasing more lumber from C for S's house, defaulted in making any further payments to C. Can C recover from S as a surety the money owing by D to C for lumber purchased by D and used in S's house? Explain.

SOME PREVIOUS C.P.A. LAW EXAMINATION QUESTIONS AND MODEL ANSWERS

MAY, 1971

No. 7 (Estimated time—20 to 25 minutes)

During the course of your examination of the financial statements for the year ended March 31, 1971, for Finest Fashions, Inc., a company with a dozen retail stores specializing in the sale of exclusive maxi coats and dresses, you learned of a claim of $50,000 asserted against the company by Fancy Fabrics. Upon investigation you learned that the company purchased most of its merchandise from Terry Knitting Mills, a large manufacturer. Several months ago when Terry was in financial difficulty and could no longer purchase raw materials from Fancy Fabrics on credit, Terry asked the company and Grand Gowns, Inc. to sign as co-sureties its purchase order to Fancy Fabrics for raw materials costing $50,000. Both companies did so on the same day that Terry signed the purchase order. When Terry did not pay on the due date, Fancy Fabrics did not notify either surety. However, 15 days later the company received a demand for payment of the entire purchase price of $50,000 from Fancy Fabrics. The company has refused to pay contending that its contract as surety was unenforceable because (1) it did not receive any consideration, (2) it received no notice of default, and (3) its maximum liability, if any, is $25,000.

a. Discuss the validity of each defense asserted by your client, Finest Fashions, Inc.

b. If Finest Fashions pays $50,000 to Fancy Fabrics, what would be its rights against Grand Gowns? Explain.

c. If Finest Fashions pays $50,000 to Fancy Fabrics, what would be its rights against Terry? Explain.

d. If Fancy Fabrics extended Terry's time for payment for another six months without Finest Fashions' consent, what would be the legal effect on the company's obligation? Explain.

Answer

a. (1) The first defense of no consideration is invalid. A suretyship contract requires sufficient consideration. If the suretyship contract occurs at the same time as the principal debtor's obligation is created, the creditor's contract with the principal debtor is the consideration for the surety's promise to be a surety, thereby creating a contract between the surety and the creditor.

   (2) The second defense of no notice of default is also invalid. When the principal debtor defaults, the creditor may enforce the surety's contractual obligation to perform. The creditor is not required to give notice of such default to the surety, unless the suretyship contract provides to the contrary, which is not the case here.

   (3) The third defense of $25,000 maximum liability is also invalid. Unless co-sureties have agreed to the contrary, each is liable for the entire amount as specified in his suretyship contract. Here, the liability is for $50,000, and the creditor can enforce the suretyship contract against either co-surety or both for the entire amount until he is paid that amount.

b. Finest Fashions may recover $25,000 from Grand Gowns. When a surety has performed his suretyship obligation to the extent that he has paid more than his proportionate share of the principal debtor's obligation on the latter's default, he has a right of contribution against his co-surety on the co-surety's suretyship obligation for his contributive share. Here, since each co-surety was liable for $50,000, the contributive share of each is $25,000.

c. Finest Fashions may recover $50,000 from Terry. When a surety has fully performed his principal debtor's obligation pursuant to his suretyship contract, he has a right of reimbursement and a right of subrogation against the principal debtor for his outlay.

d. The answer depends upon whether the extension of time was a contract binding on Fancy Fabrics. If it was, Finest Fashions is discharged of its suretyship contract. If it was not, then the suretyship contract of Finest Fashions is not affected. When the creditor makes a *binding* agreement with the principal debtor extending the time of payment by the principal debtor, without the surety's consent, the surety is discharged. The creditor's promise of extension is binding upon him only if it was supported by sufficient consideration. The problem does not state facts on whether or not sufficient consideration is present.

NOVEMBER, 1969

No. 3 (Estimated time—10 to 12 minutes)

   Each of the following numbered sentences states a legal conclusion as it relates to the preceding related lettered fact situation. You are to determine whether each of the legal conclusions is true or false according to the *general principles of suretyship law* and write on a separate answer sheet whether each conclusion is true or false. Your grade will be determined from your total net score obtained by deducting your total of incorrect answers from your total of correct answers; an omitted answer will not be considered an incorrect answer.

D. Humbolt Hardware Company (a partnership which manufactures hardware), Charles, and Williams have each duly become co-sureties of a $12,000 loan made to Francis by Richards.

77. If none of the co-sureties had known of the others at the time they made their respective suretyship agreements, the relationship of co-suretyship would not exist among them.

78. If Richards should fully release Francis without reserving his rights against Humbolt, Charles, and Williams, they would also be fully released.

79. If Francis should default on repayment of the loan, Richards may recover only $4,000 from Humbolt.

80. If, on Francis' default, Williams should pay Richards the full $12,000, Williams would be entitled to recover $4,000 each from Charles and Humbolt.

E. Davidson purchased Backacre (improved real property) with funds obtained by a first mortgage loan made to him by Zeno Bank. Davidson thereafter sold Backacre to Harvey subject to Zeno's first mortgage which Harvey duly assumed. To finance the purchase from Davidson, Harvey obtained a loan from Yellowstone Bank and gave Yellowstone a second mortgage on Backacre to secure the mortgage. Irving guaranteed repayment of Harvey's loan from Yellowstone.

81. Davidson is a surety on the first mortgage debt assumed by Harvey.

82. Davidson and Irving are co-sureties for Harvey's obligations for the purchase of Backacre.

83. If Harvey should default on the second mortgage, Yellowstone Bank may not collect the debt from Irving if Harvey has filed a voluntary bankruptcy petition in Federal Court.

84. If Harvey should default on both mortgages, the banks must first foreclose the mortgages on Backacre before proceeding against Davidson or Irving.

85. If Harvey had previously defaulted on several other loans made to him by Yellowstone and Yellowstone willfully failed to advise Irving of this at the time it obtained his guaranty, Irving may assert such failure as a defense in an action against him on the guaranty by Yellowstone.

F. Franklin Corporation borrowed money from the Lifetime Insurance Company and gave Lifetime a nonnegotiable promissory note for the amount of the loan. Lifetime insisted that Walter Williams, the president of Franklin, sign the note as co-maker. In addition, Lifetime insisted that Franklin pledge 1,000 shares of stock that Franklin owned in a subsidiary corporation.

86. Williams is liable as a surety on the loan by Lifetime to Franklin.

87. If Lifetime should assign the notes and collateral to a third party, Williams would be released.

88. If Franklin should default and Williams should pay the loan, Williams would be entitled to Lifetime's rights in the pledged stock.

90. If Franklin should default and Lifetime should thereafter sell the pledged stock for an amount in excess of the debt, Lifetime may retain the profit.

Answer

77. False	80. True	83. False	86. True	90. False
78. True	81. True	84. False	87. False	
79. False	82. False	85. True	88. True	

NOVEMBER, 1964

No. 5

a. On January 1, 1963, Leonard loaned Bert $1,000. Upon receipt of the $1,000, Bert gave Leonard a signed nonnegotiable promissory note which acknowledged the debt and included a promise to repay the $1,000 plus 4 percent interest one year from date. As part of this transaction, Bert gave to Leonard, as security for the loan, certain stocks, properly indorsed, then having a market value of $1,300.

On June 10, 1963, the market value of the stock had fallen to $800, and Leonard demanded of Bert further security for the loan. Pursuant to this demand Bert requested his friend Stewart to sign the nonnegotiable note of January 1 as surety. When Stewart signed the note as surety, he received no consideration therefor and was unaware that Leonard was then holding the stock as security for Leonard's loan to Bert.

On January 1, 1964, Leonard demanded payment of the note from Bert and, failing to collect from him, he demanded payment from Stewart, who paid $1,000 to Leonard. A few days later, Stewart learned that Leonard was holding Bert's stocks as security for the loan and demanded these stocks from Leonard.

(1) State and explain the right upon which Stewart as a surety is basing his demand on Leonard that he be given Bert's stocks.

(2) On the facts as stated above, is Stewart entitled to the stocks? Explain.

b. Paul obtained a loan of $1,000 from Charles on January 1, 1962, payable on April 15, 1962. At the time of the making of the loan, Stanley became a noncompensated surety thereon by written agreement. On April 15, 1962, Paul was unable to pay and wrote to Charles requesting an extension of time. Charles made no reply, but did not take any immediate action to recover. On June 30, 1962, Charles demanded payment from Paul and, failing to collect from him, proceeded against the surety, Stanley. Stanley claims that as Charles had allowed Paul more time than the agreement had called for, he has been discharged as surety thereby.

Is Stanley's claim valid? Explain.

c. David desired to establish credit with Carl, but the latter required a surety to protect himself from loss. At David's request, Sam and Seth wrote letters to Carl in which Sam guaranteed David's credit up to $10,000, and Seth guaranteed it up to $20,000, both guaranties being continuous in character. Sam and Seth were aware of each other's guaranty.

(1) David became insolvent when he was indebted to Carl to the extent of $9,000. Sam was compelled to pay the full amount. To what extent may Sam obtain contribution from Seth? Explain.

(2) If Sam is in possession of collateral worth $3,000 given by David to

protect Sam against loss from his guaranty, how would this affect your answer to (1) above? Explain.

Answer

a. (1) The right of subrogation. This is the surety's right to be placed in the creditor's position on the discharge of the principal debtor's obligation to the creditor to the extent that the surety's property has been used to satisfy the creditor's claim and to effect such discharge. Subrogation enitles the surety to the collateral held by the creditor as security on the principal debtor's obligation.

(2) No. Suretyship arises only as the result of a contract, which requires sufficient consideration. Here, there was no consideration for Stewart's promise to pay on the Bert note. The loan had been made to Bert prior to Stewart's signing the note as a purported surety. Therefore, Stewart is not a surety and has no right of subrogation, even when he paid $1,000 to Leonard. Also, the right of subrogation arises when the debt is paid in full, and here $40 in interest is still unpaid.

b. No. If the creditor makes a binding agreement with the principal debtor extending the time of payment by the principal debtor, without the surety's consent and without reserving his rights against the surety in the agreement, the surety is discharged. Here, Charles did not make any agreement with Paul to extend the time of payment. A creditor may assert his claim at any time within the period covered by the statute of limitations. Therefore, Stanley is not discharged as a surety and Charles may proceed against him.

c. (1) $6,000. When co-sureties have not contracted among themselves for their contributive shares and they are not liable in the same maximum amount on their respective suretyship contracts, the contributive share of each co-surety is determined by the proportion that his maximum liability under his contract bears to the total of the maximum liability of all of them. Here, Sam's maximum liability is $10,000, or ⅓ of the $30,000 total combined maximum liability of Sam and Seth. Therefore, ⅔ of $9,000 is $6,000, which is Seth's share of the loss and to which Sam has a right of contribution against Seth.

(2) Sam has a right of contribution against Seth for $4,000. Co-sureties are entitled to share proportionately in any security or other benefit received by a co-surety from the principal debtor in assurance of the latter's performance on which they are co-sureties. Here, the $3,000 collateral reduces the loss to $6,000, Sam's share being one third, or $2,000, and Seth's share being two thirds, or $4,000.

PART EIGHT

BANKRUPTCY

Chapter I

NATURE OF BANKRUPTCY

---

1. *CREDITORS' RIGHTS IN GENERAL*

BANKRUPTCY is a specialized branch of the law concerned with the rights and duties of debtors and creditors. Before beginning a discussion of bankruptcy a brief survey of creditors' rights in general should be made, in order to become familiar with the underlying concepts of the debtor-creditor relationship and the methods of enforcing creditors' rights.

Property Available to Creditors   All property of a debtor, except as otherwise provided by statute, is available to his creditors for utilization in satisfaction of their claims when such claims are in the form of judgments. Such property may be legal or equitable and includes real and personal property. By statute in the various states, certain property is exempted and is made unavailable to creditors, such as a homestead and a certain portion of a debtor's salary.

Fraudulent Conveyances. Should the debtor attempt to make any of his property unavailable to his creditors, the latter may utilize various legal remedies which preclude the successful conclusion of such an attempt and which permit recovery of property fraudulently conveyed or transferred. In most states, a conveyance or transfer of property by a debtor without a fair consideration in exchange creates a presumption of fraud on existing creditors, rebuttable by the debtor's proof that sufficient assets remain available to satisfy the claims of his creditors. If insufficient assets remain available, the debtor is insolvent because, under the Uniform Fraudulent Conveyance Act, sec. 2(1), ". . . the present fair salable value of his assets is less than the amount that will be required to pay his probable liability on his existing debts as they become absolute and matured. . . ."

845

Ordinary Creditors' Remedies

The process by which a creditor may enforce his debtor's obligation and utilize the debtor's assets in satisfaction of his claim is fixed by statute in each state. The creditor cannot simply seize his debtor's property; he must follow the method outlined by the statute.

Execution. The creditor usually first brings an action[1] against his debtor and reduces his claim to a judgment. After a judgment has been obtained, the creditor is called a "judgment creditor" and the debtor is called a "judgment debtor." If the judgment debtor does not satisfy the judgment, the judgment creditor has a right to obtain a "writ of execution" issued by the court through the clerk of court directing the sheriff (or marshal, if a federal court) to levy upon and seize so much of the property of the judgment debtor as is necessary in order to satisfy the judgment, sell it at public sale, deliver to the judgment creditor, or to the court where so required, the proceeds in an amount sufficient to satisfy the judgment, and deliver the surplus to the judgment debtor. It is usually provided that docketing of the judgment causes the judgment to become a lien on any real property of the judgment debtor located in the particular county in which the judgment has been docketed, thereby precluding the subsequent creation of any interest in such property superior to the lien of the judgment creditor. Such property is available for sale under the writ of execution. The judgment debtor usually has a statutory right of redemption (right to redeem) in real property so sold, which must be exercised within the period of time specified by the statute.

Garnishment after Judgment. The writ of execution normally cannot reach debts owed by third persons to the judgment debtor or chattels of the judgment debtor lawfully possessed by third persons. Generally, in the absence of statute to the contrary, such assets of the judgment debtor are not available in satisfaction of the judgment until the writ of execution has been returned unsatisfied to the issuing court, and an affidavit has been made to the effect that no other property of the judgment debtor is deemed available to satisfy the judgment and designating third persons who are believed to be indebted to the judgment debtor or who are in possession of his chattels. An order is issued by the court through the clerk of court directing the third person, called a

---

[1] *"Lis pendens"* means that a suit is pending. A notice of *lis pendens* is a warning to all persons that the property involved in the suit is subject to a judgment affecting it. The *lis pendens* is made a matter of public record by filing in the official public place of record.

"garnishee," to appear in court and to answer questions regarding such indebtedness or property. If, after examination of the garnishee, it is found that he owes money to the judgment debtor or is in possession of the judgment debtor's chattels in which the garnishee has no property interest, the court may order that such money or chattels be made available for use in satisfaction of the judgment. The judgment creditor is proceeding against the interest owned by the judgment debtor and cannot obtain more than such interest. Accordingly, if the judgment debtor's interest is a debt owing by the garnishee to the judgment debtor and if the garnishee has a claim or "setoff" against such debt, the judgment creditor can garnish such debt less the setoff. Or if the garnishee has a possessory lien (a right to possession) on a chattel of the judgment debtor as security for a claim of the garnishee against the judgment debtor, the judgment creditor may garnish the chattel subject to the lien of the garnishee.

Attachment.   Attachment is an extraordinary remedy and is statutory. Its purpose is to cause property of a specified person or persons to be levied upon and seized before judgment is rendered in favor of the plaintiff and to utilize such property to satisfy the anticipated judgment when rendered. The plaintiff is required to post a bond to protect the defendant debtor from loss he may sustain by being deprived of the use of his property pending trial and for court costs in the event that the plaintiff is unsuccessful in his action. The grounds for attachment are enumerated by statute and are, generally: that the defendant debtor is a nonresident of the state or is a foreign corporation; or that he is concealing himself, or that he has been absent from the state for a prescribed period of time, so that service of process cannot be made upon him; or that his whereabouts have been unknown for a prescribed period of time; or that he has made, or is about to make, a fraudulent conveyance; or that he has concealed, or is about to conceal, his property; or that he has removed, or is about to remove, his property from the state.

Attachment is begun by an affidavit of the plaintiff which states his cause of action against the defendant—e.g., the indebtedness by the defendant to the plaintiff—and which states a legal ground for attachment. On the filing of the affidavit and bond, the court issues a writ of attachment directing the proper public officer, usually the sheriff or constable (or marshal, if a federal court), to levy upon and to seize the defendant debtor's property to the extent necessary to satisfy the plaintiff's demand. If the plaintiff is successful in the action, the property is sold and the proceeds used to satisfy the plaintiff's judgment. Attachment process must be in accordance with "due process of law," and generally must be preceded by notice and hearing so that the debtor defendant will have the opportunity to appear and to be heard before his property is seized.

Garnishment under Attachment. Garnishment is a statutory remedy. The nature and principles of garnishment are the same whether begun under attachment before judgment or begun after judgment. Its function is to reach property of the debtor not available under a writ of attachment or under a writ of execution, respectively. When garnishment is used as a species or type of attachment, it is subject to the same requirements as for attachment and, in general, has the same effect.

Special Statutory Limitations on Garnishment. One federal law and one uniform state law impose limitations on garnishment before and after judgment.

Federal Consumer Credit Protection Act (1968). Section 303(a) provides for the maximum part of the aggregate disposable earnings of an individual for any workweek which may be subjected to garnishment. It may not exceed "(1) 25 per centum of his disposable earnings for that week, or (2) the amount by which his disposable earnings for that week exceed *thirty* times the Federal minimum hourly wage prescribed by section 6(a) (1) of the Fair Labor Standards Act of 1938 in effect at the time the earnings are payable, whichever is less. . . ." (author's italics). Section 304(a) prohibits an employer from discharging "any employee by reason of the fact that his earnings have been subjected to garnishment for any *one* indebtedness" (author's italics). Section 305 provides that the Secretary of Labor, who is charged with enforcement of this law, may by regulation exempt from the provisions of section 303(a) "garnishments issued under the laws of any State if he determines that the laws of that State provide restrictions on garnishment which are substantially similar to those provided in section 303(a)." Section 307 provides that this law "does not annul, alter, or affect, or exempt any person from complying with, the laws of any State (1) prohibiting garnishments or providing for more limited garnishments than are allowed under this title, or (2) prohibiting the discharge of any employee by reason of the fact that his earnings have been subjected to garnishment for more than one indebtedness."

Uniform Consumer Credit Code (1969). Section 5.104 prohibits a creditor from garnishment of his debtor's unpaid earnings *before obtaining a judgment* for a debt *arising from a consumer credit sale, a consumer lease, or a consumer loan.* Section 5.105 provides for the maximum part of the aggregate disposable earnings of an individual for any workweek which may be subjected to garnishment to enforce payment of a *judgment* arising from a *consumer credit sale, consumer lease, or consumer loan.* It may not exceed "(2) (a) 25 per cent of his disposable earnings for that week, or (b) . . . *forty* times the Federal minimum hourly wage. . . ." (Author's italics) Section 5.106 prohibits an employer from discharging an employee "for the reason that a creditor of the employee has subjected or attempted to subject unpaid earnings of the employee to garnishment or like proceedings directed to the employer for the purpose of paying a judgment arising from a consumer credit sale, consumer lease, or consumer loan." Section 5.106 prohibits employment discharge for *any* such garnishment, whether one or more.

2. THE BANKRUPTCY ACT

Background   The rigors of business competition and economic fluctuation have their effect in causing some businessmen to succumb, financially. While creditors have their usual remedies,[2] nevertheless, society is strongly of the opinion that these remedies alone are insufficient under such circumstances to assist creditors and failing debtors adequately. The Bankruptcy Act is an additional recourse available to creditors to ensure equitable distribution of all the debtor's nonexempt assets among themselves, except for secured creditors and creditors with claims with priority status; and it also is a boon to honest debtors, making it possible for them to begin anew unencumbered by many debts. In essence, this is the purpose of the Bankruptcy Act today.

Under the United States Constitution, Article I, section 8(4), Congress has the sole power to establish ". . . uniform Laws on the subject of Bankruptcies throughout the United States"; the states do not have this power. Congress passed and repealed three bankruptcy laws before the fourth law was passed in 1898. This law exists today with many amendments.

Judges and Referees   Under the Bankruptcy Act, original and exclusive bankruptcy jurisdiction is vested in the United States District Courts, which are made bankruptcy courts; the United States Courts of Appeals are invested with appellate jurisdiction; and the Supreme Court of the United States is

---

[2] See above, pp. 840 ff.

vested with jurisdiction to review the action taken by the United States Courts of Appeals. The judges in the United States District Courts have authority to appoint referees in bankruptcy to assist them in bankruptcy proceedings, and to remove such referees. Referees have judicial duties and have the following jurisdiction: to consider all bankruptcy petitions and to take action thereon; to administer oaths and examine witnesses, but not to commit for contempt of court, which power is reserved to the judge; to exercise the powers of the judge in connection with the bankrupt's property when the judge is unavailable; to grant, deny, or revoke discharges of bankrupts, determine the dischargeability of debts, and render judgment thereon; to confirm or set aside arrangements or wage-earner plans; and to authorize the employment of stenographers during bankruptcy proceedings, such expense to be chargeable to the bankrupt's estate. The duties of a referee are: to give notice to all parties in interest concerning bankruptcy proceedings and creditors' meetings; to see that schedules of property are prepared and filed properly; to furnish parties in interest information concerning bankruptcy proceedings pursuant to their request; to declare dividends on all allowed claims; and to handle the administrative details for the preservation of evidence and of records.

Outline of Procedure
The bankruptcy proceeding is initiated by the filing of a petition in bankruptcy, either by the debtor or by his creditors, requesting that the debtor be adjudicated a bankrupt. In involuntary proceedings, the debtor is given an opportunity to answer the petition and, if such answer denies any allegation of insolvency or the allegation that an act of bankruptcy has occurred, the debtor is entitled to a trial on such issues. If the debtor is adjudicated to be a bankrupt, meetings of creditors are called and the bankrupt's accounts examined. A trustee in bankruptcy is appointed to collect the bankrupt's property, reduce it to money and to disburse the money to the creditors pursuant to court order. The creditors are given an opportunity to object to the bankrupt's application for discharge, and either the bankrupt is discharged from his provable debts with certain exceptions, or a discharge is denied to him. The bankrupt's estate is wound up, the trustee is discharged, and the bankruptcy proceedings terminated. This is a brief outline of the procedure which will now be examined in detail.

Chapter II

PROCEEDINGS IN BANKRUPTCY

1. *WHO MAY BECOME BANKRUPT*

Bankrupt Defined

UNDER the Bankruptcy Act, section 1(4), the term "bankrupt" is defined to "include a person against whom an involuntary petition or an application to revoke a discharge has been filed, or who has filed a voluntary petition, or who has been adjudged a bankrupt." The word "person" includes a partnership and a corporation.

Kinds of Bankrupt

There are two kinds of bankrupt: "voluntary," and "involuntary."

Voluntary Bankrupt. A voluntary bankrupt may be any person except a building and loan association, or a municipal, railroad, insurance, or banking corporation. It should be noted that, except for partnership, the Act does not require a voluntary bankrupt to be insolvent; however, he must owe debts. He cannot petition bankruptcy for the purpose of perpetrating fraud.

Involuntary Bankrupt. An involuntary bankrupt may be any natural person, except a wage earner or farmer, and any moneyed, business, or commercial corporation, except a building and loan association and a municipal, railroad, insurance, or banking corporation, owing debts to the amount of $1,000 or over. Under the Bankruptcy Act, section 1(32), a wage earner is "an individual who works for wages, salary, or hire, at a rate of compensation not exceeding $1,500 per year." Under the Act, section 1(17), a farmer is "an individual personally engaged in farming or tillage of the soil. . . ."

Partnerships. Although a partnership *may* become an involuntary bankrupt, a partnership *cannot* become a voluntary bankrupt unless: either the partnership is insolvent—i.e., the firm property, together with the assets of the general partners available after allowance for their individual creditors, are insufficient to pay the firm debts; or the solvent partners consent to the partnership being adjudged a bankrupt. As long as one general partner remains solvent the partnership cannot, without his consent, be a voluntary bankrupt because the partnership is not insolvent. If the solvent partner does not consent to the partnership property being administered in bankruptcy, he is required to settle the partnership business as quickly as possible and to account to the trustee in bankruptcy for the interest of the partner or partners adjudged bankrupt.

2. ACTS OF BANKRUPTCY

Involuntary bankruptcy cannot occur unless the bankrupt has committed an act of bankruptcy; voluntary bankruptcy may occur without an act of bankruptcy. An involuntary petition must be filed by the creditors *within four months after an act of bankruptcy has been committed,* otherwise they may not assert it as a basis for their petition.

The six acts of bankruptcy consist of active or passive conduct on the part of the debtor *causing his assets to be unavailable for equitable distribution among his creditors.* Under the Bankruptcy Act, section 3a:

> Acts of bankruptcy by a person shall consist of his having (1) concealed, removed, or permitted to be concealed or removed any part of his property, with intent to hinder, delay, or defraud his creditors or any of them, or made or suffered a transfer of any of his property, fraudulent under the provisions of section 67 or 70 of this Act; or (2) made or suffered a preferential transfer as defined in subdivision *a* of section 60 of this Act; or (3) suffered or permitted, while insolvent, any creditor to obtain a lien upon any of his property through legal proceedings or distraint and not having vacated or discharged such lien within thirty days from the date thereof or at least five days before the date set for any sale or other disposition of such property; or (4) made a general assignment for the benefit of his creditors; or (5) while insolvent or unable to pay his debts as they mature, procured, permitted, or suffered voluntarily or involuntarily the appointment of a receiver or trustee to take charge of his property; or (6) admitted in writing his inability to pay his debts and his willingness to be adjudged a bankrupt.

It is to be observed that insolvency is not required for all of the acts of bankruptcy. A person is insolvent under the Bankruptcy Act whenever his property, exclusive of property fraudulently transferred or concealed, has a fair value which is insufficient in amount to pay his debts. This definition of insolvency under the Bankruptcy Act should be distinguished carefully from the meaning of insolvency as used elsewhere. Insolvency does not mean that the debtor is unable to pay his debts as they mature but means that the aggregate of his assets is less than his debts. Under UCC 1–201 (23) : "A person is 'insolvent' who either has ceased to pay his debts in the ordinary course of business or cannot pay his debts as they become due or is insolvent within the meaning of the federal bankruptcy law." It is a defense to any proceedings under the first act of bankruptcy that the bankrupt was solvent at the time such act was committed. Section 3a of the Bankruptcy Act should be examined carefully in a study of the acts of bankruptcy.

3. THE PROCEEDINGS

Initiation Bankruptcy proceedings are initiated by the filing of a petition in the bankruptcy court, either by a debtor petitioning for voluntary bankruptcy, or by creditors petitioning for an involuntary bankruptcy on the ground that a debtor has committed an act of bankruptcy. A creditor is any person who has a claim provable in bankruptcy. A petition for involuntary bankruptcy must be filed within four months after the particular act of bankruptcy has been committed by the debtor. Under the Bankruptcy Act, section 59 :

a. Any qualified person may file a petition to be adjudged a voluntary bankrupt.
b. Three or more creditors who have provable claims not contingent as to liability against a person, amounting in the aggregate to $500 in excess of the value of any securities held by them, or, if all of the creditors of the person are less than twelve in number, then one or more of the creditors whose claim or claims equal that amount, may file a petition to have him adjudged a bankrupt; . . . .

Bankruptcy proceedings are not abated by the death or insanity of the bankrupt. In the event of the bankrupt's death, the bankrupt's right to the exemption of certain property from bankruptcy proceedings is preserved to his estate. Similarly, the death or removal of a receiver or trustee in bankruptcy does not abate any action or proceeding in which he was engaged.

Trial Unless the judge directs otherwise, the clerk of the court refers the bankruptcy proceeding to a referee. The judge may transfer a bankruptcy proceeding from one referee to another at any time. A person against whom an involuntary petition has been filed has the right to a trial on the issues of insolvency and of the commission of an act of bankruptcy. He also has the right to a trial by jury on these issues if he makes application within the time in which he could have filed his answer to the petition. When there is an issue of the debtor's insolvency or of his inability to pay his debts as they mature, the debtor must appear in court, produce his books, records, and accounts, and testify concerning the matter; his failure to do so causes him to have the burden of proof of solvency or of ability to pay his debts as they mature. Under the Bankruptcy Act, section 21, *l,* "In any proceeding under this Act against a bankrupt for an accounting by him for his property or the disposition thereof, or to compel a turn-over of property by him, if his books, records, and accounts shall fail to disclose the cost to him of such property sold by him during any period under consideration, it shall be presumed, until the contrary shall appear, that such property was sold at a price not less than the cost thereof to him."

Receivers and Trustees in Bankruptcy

Receivers and trustees in bankruptcy are officers of the court—i.e., the judge or a referee—with specific functions to be performed in connection with the bankrupt's property. After a petition for involuntary bankruptcy has been filed, and *pending the adjudication of the debtor as a bankrupt and the subsequent appointment of a trustee in bankruptcy,* the creditors may desire the appointment of an officer in order to receive and take charge of the debtor's property. An application is made to the court for the appointment of such an officer, the applicant posts a bond to indemnify the debtor for any loss or expense he may sustain by the detention of his property in the event he subsequently is adjudicated not to be a bankrupt, and the court, within its discretion, makes the appointment. The appointee is called a "receiver." The receiver must post a bond conditioned on his faithful performance of his official duties. The debtor may file a counter-bond conditioned on his making his property or its value in money available to the trustee, which releases the property from possession of the receiver. The receiver must account to the court for all property received by him, and he cannot make disbursements from such property without the authority of the court.

A trustee in bankruptcy is an officer appointed by the creditors and approved by the court, or appointed by the court on the failure of the creditors to appoint a trustee or on the failure of the appointee to qualify as trustee, at the first meeting of creditors *after the debtor has been adjudicated to be a bankrupt.* If a receiver has been appointed pending the adjudication of bankruptcy and the appointment of a trustee, on the appointment of the trustee the receiver accounts to the court for the debtor's property in his possession and the receiver then is discharged from his duties. The receiver subsequently may become the trustee. The trustee is required to post a bond similar to that required of a receiver. The duties of a trustee may be summarized, generally, as follows:

1. To collect all the assets of the bankrupt and to reduce them to cash.
2. To deposit the money in designated depositories.
3. To make disbursements only pursuant to the direction of the court and only by check or draft on such depositories.
4. To keep accounts of all property received by him and to set aside the bankrupt's property which is entitled to exemption.
5. To examine the bankrupt at all creditors' meetings and on the hearings for objection to the bankrupt's discharge.
6. To examine all proofs of claim and to object to the allowance of improper claims.
7. To oppose the bankrupt's discharge when deemed advisable.
8. On request, to make available to parties in interest information concerning the administration of the bankrupt's estate.
9. To distribute dividends pursuant to the order of the referee.
10. To account to the court and to the creditors regarding the administration of the bankrupt's estate.

The court may order the receiver or trustee to defend any suits pending against the bankrupt, or to continue as receiver or trustee any suits begun by the bankrupt. If, pursuant to the court's direction, the receiver or trustee commences any suits, such suits must be brought only in the courts where the bankrupt might have brought them. Pursuant to the court's direction, a receiver or trustee may submit to arbitration any controversy arising in the settlement of the bankrupt's estate or compromise any controversy arising in the administration of the bankrupt's estate.

Chapter III

ADMINISTRATION OF ESTATES IN BANKRUPTCY

1. MEETINGS OF CREDITORS

When Held IT HAS been aptly stated[1] that "Promptness is an essential feature of any efficient system of bankruptcy administration, whether one considers primarily the interest of the creditors, or of the debtor, or of the community." Immediately after the adjudication of bankruptcy, the administration of the bankrupt's estate is required to proceed expeditiously. Not less than 10 and not more than 30 days after the adjudication, as fixed by the court, the first meeting of creditors must occur. The importance of this first meeting is illustrated by the fact that: at such meeting the trustee is appointed; the six-month period within which creditors may prove their claims begins to run from the date of such meeting; the time when objections to the bankrupt's discharge may be filed must be not less than 30 days nor more than 90 days after the first date set for the first meeting of creditors; and the bankrupt's unexcused failure to appear at such meeting is deemed to be a waiver of his right to a discharge and an order is entered to that effect. At the first meeting the judge or referee presides and, after allowing or disallowing claims of creditors, he publicly examines the bankrupt and may permit creditors to examine the bankrupt. The court is required to call additional meetings of creditors whenever one-fourth or more of those creditors who have proved their claims so request and, of its own motion, the court may call a special meeting whenever it is deemed necessary. When the bankrupt's estate is about to be closed, a final meeting of creditors must be called, unless there are no assets available, in which case no final meeting is required.

Voting Only those creditors whose claims have been allowed and who are present may vote at creditors' meetings. Secured creditors and creditors who have priority are

---

[1] William M. Collier, *The Collier Bankruptcy Manual* (edited by F. Kelliher; New York: Matthew Bender & Co., 1948), p. 556.

not entitled to vote at creditors' meetings, except to the extent that, in the opinion of the court, their claims are in excess of the value of their securities or priorities. Action may be taken at such meetings by a majority vote in number and amount of claims of all creditors whose claims have been allowed and who are present. Creditors may vote by proxy.

Notices   All notices to the trustee, creditors, and the bankrupt, and all public notices, are given by the referee, unless otherwise ordered by the judge. Parties entitled to notice may waive the same. All required notices are given by mail. All creditors are to receive notice by mail at least 10 days before each examination of the bankrupt, each meeting of creditors, each proposed sale of bankrupt property, the filing of accounts of the receiver and trustee for which confirmation is asked, and the proposed compromise of any controversy. In addition to notice of the first meeting of creditors sent to the creditors as listed in the bankrupt's schedules, notice of such first meeting may be published on court order.

Duties of Bankrupt   The bankrupt has various duties. Within five days after his adjudication if an involuntary bankrupt, and with his petition if a voluntary bankrupt, he is required: to file a schedule of all his property, its location and value; to file a list of all his creditors, their addresses if known to him, the amount due and the security held by them; and to file a claim for his property exempted from bankruptcy. The bankrupt must appear at the first meeting of creditors, as well as at the meeting on objections to his discharge and at such other times as the court may order. He is required to submit to examination concerning his bankruptcy, the administration and settlement of his estate in bankruptcy, and his discharge. The bankrupt has the duty of examining all proofs of claim and reporting to the trustee concerning their correctness, and to inform the trustee of any attempts made by anyone to evade the provisions of the Bankruptcy Act. And finally, he must comply with all lawful orders of the court.

2. PROOF AND ALLOWANCE OF CLAIMS

Provable Claims   Provable claims consist of any debt, demand, or claim which, with but few exceptions, could be asserted against the debtor in bankruptcy at the time the petition was filed. Provable claims may be summarized, generally, as consisting of:

1. Fixed liabilities evidenced by a judgment or written instrument and absolutely owing at the time the petition in bankruptcy was filed, whether then payable or not.
2. Costs taxable to the bankrupt in a proceeding instituted by the bankrupt pending at the time the petition was filed and which the trustee does not wish to continue.
3. An open account, or a contract express or implied.
4. A provable debt reduced to judgment after the petition had been filed and before the consideration of the bankrupt's application for a discharge.
5. A workman's compensation award for an injury which occurred prior to the bankrupt's adjudication.
6. The right to recover damages in an action for negligence instituted prior to and pending at the time the petition in bankruptcy was filed.
7. Contingent debts and contingent contractual liabilities.[2]
8. Claims for anticipatory breach of contracts, including unexpired leases of property, except that a landlord's claim for damages under an unexpired lease rejected by the trustee is limited to the amount owing for unpaid rent up to the time that the leased premises are surrendered to the landlord, or when he has re-entered thereon, whichever first occurs, plus one year's rent thereafter.

A claim which is contingent or unliquidated and which has been proved but has not been allowed because it has not been liquidated or the amount thereof has not been estimated, is not a provable claim.

Proof and Allowance

All provable claims must be proved within six months after the date of the first meeting of creditors in order to be allowed, except that: the rights of infants and insane persons without guardians, who have no notice of the bankruptcy proceedings, may continue for six months longer; and the court, for cause shown, may extend the time within which claims of the United States or of a state or any subdivision thereof may be filed. Under the Bankruptcy Act, section 57a, "A proof of claim shall consist of a statement, in writing and signed by a creditor, setting forth the claim; the consideration therefor; whether any and, if so, what securities are held therefor; and whether any and, if so, what payments have been made thereon; and that the claim is justly owing from the bankrupt to the creditor." When a claim is based upon a written instrument, such instrument must be filed with the proof of claim, unless the instrument has been lost or destroyed, in which case a sworn statement of such loss or destruction must be filed

---

[2] They are "contingent" because they are not certain of occurrence and depend, in turn, upon the occurrence of an uncertain future event.

with the claim. The fact that a claim has been duly proved does not mean that it will be allowed. All claims which have been duly proved are allowed, unless there is objection to their allowance, or an unliquidated or contingent claim has not been liquidated or the amount thereof estimated within the time directed by the court. Objections to claims are heard by the court, and a decision rendered regarding their allowance. Under section 57g, "The claims of creditors who have received or acquired preferences, liens, conveyances, transfers, assignments or encumbrances, void or voidable under this Act, shall not be allowed unless such creditors shall surrender such preferences, liens, conveyances, transfers, assignments, or encumbrances."

Set-off. Under the Bankruptcy Act, section 68a, "In all cases of mutual debts or mutual credits between the estate of a bankrupt and a creditor the account shall be stated and one debt shall be set off against the other, and the balance only shall be allowed or paid." A claim may be set off against property of the debtor in the hands of the creditor. A bank may set off against a debtor depositor's account its claim against the depositor.[3] A claim which is absolutely owing at the time the petition was filed but which is not yet due or which is unliquidated, may be set off against a claim of the bankrupt. However, under section 68b, a claim may not be set off against the bankrupt's estate which was not provable and allowable in bankruptcy or which was acquired ". . . after the filing of the petition or within four months before such filing, with a view to such use and with knowledge or notice that such bankrupt was insolvent or had committed an act of bankruptcy." The right of set-off does not apply to joint debts and credits. The creditor cannot set off against the bankrupt a debt due from the bankrupt who was jointly liable thereon with others; nor may a bankrupt set off a claim against the creditor on which the creditor was jointly liable with others.

Secured Claims. Claims may be secured or unsecured. Under the Bankruptcy Act, section 1 (28), " 'Secured creditor' shall include a creditor who has security for his debt *upon the property of the bankrupt* of a nature to be assignable under this Act or who owns such a debt for which some indorser, surety, or other person secondarily liable for the bankrupt has such security *upon the bankrupt's assets*" (author's italics).[4] A creditor who holds security which is not a part of the bankrupt's property is not a secured creditor. A secured creditor is not required to prove his claim in order to preserve his lien on the security.

---

[3] See General Liens, above, p. 792.

[4] Various types of security were considered previously, above, pp. 727–87.

The secured creditor may prove his secured claim, have the worth of the security determined in terms of money and applied against the claim, and the unsecured portion of the claim is then provable as a claim in bankruptcy. The surety of a creditor of the bankrupt may file and prove the creditor's claim if the creditor should fail to do so and, if the surety partially or completely performs his suretyship obligation to the creditor, the surety is "subrogated" to the creditor's rights to the extent of such performance.

3. THE BANKRUPT'S ESTATE

Nature   The bankrupt's estate consists of all the bankrupt's nonexempt property. Property of the bankrupt which is exempted from utilization in satisfaction of a judgment by the laws of the United States or of the state[5] in which the bankrupt was domiciled during the six months prior to the filing of the petition in bankruptcy or for a longer portion of such six months than in any other state is exempted from inclusion in the bankrupt's estate for distribution to creditors under the Bankruptcy Act. The trustee of the bankrupt's estate is vested with the title of the bankrupt to all nonexempt property as of the date the bankruptcy petition was filed. He also has the rights and powers of a creditor with a judgment or lien as a result of an action, whether or not such a creditor existed. Generally, the trustee has 60 days after the bankrupt's adjudication, or 30 days after his qualification as trustee, whichever is later, within which to reject or assume any executory contract of the bankrupt and contracts not assumed within that time are deemed rejected. Rejection of such contracts may give rise to provable claims for damages for the breach thereof. All the bankrupt's defenses against third persons are available to the trustee. Liens obtained on property of the bankrupt by legal proceedings[6] within four months before the petition in bankruptcy had been filed are void if, at the time the lien was obtained, the debtor was insolvent or the lien was acquired fraudulently under the Bankruptcy Act. However, statutory liens[7] which arise within four months prior to the filing of the petition in bankruptcy, even while the debtor is insolvent, are valid. Under the Bankruptcy Act, section 70d:

After bankruptcy and either before adjudication or before a receiver takes possession of the property of the bankrupt, whichever first occurs—

---

[5] Concerning the exemption of the bankrupt's life insurance, see below, p. 892.

[6] E.g., attachment liens, judgment liens, execution liens, garnishment liens.

[7] E.g., wage liens, mechanics' liens, landlords' liens, tax liens.

(1) A transfer of any of the property of the bankrupt, other than real estate, made to a person acting in good faith shall be valid against the trustee if made for a present fair equivalent value or, if not made for a present fair equivalent value, then to the extent of the present consideration actually paid therefor, for which amount the transferee shall have a lien upon the property so transferred;

(2) A person indebted to the bankrupt or holding property of the bankrupt may, if acting in good faith, pay such indebtedness or deliver such property, or any part thereof, to the bankrupt or upon his order, with the same effect as if the bankruptcy were not pending.

Preferences
One of the basic principles of the Bankruptcy Act is that there must be an equitable distribution of the bankrupt's assets among his unsecured creditors, except for exempt property and creditors with priority. Any transfer of a debtor's property to or for the benefit of a creditor, for or on account of an antecedent debt, made or suffered by such debtor while insolvent and within four months prior to the filing of a voluntary or an involuntary petition in bankruptcy and which has the effect of such creditor being enabled to receive a greater precentage of payment on his debt than another creditor of the same class, is a *preference.* Such a preference is voidable by the trustee in bankruptcy only if the creditor had reasonable cause to believe that the debtor was insolvent at the time of such transfer. If it is a voidable transfer, the trustee may recover the property transferred or, if it has been converted, bring an action in conversion for the reasonable value of such property. However, under section 60b, the trustee's power to avoid a preferential transfer cannot be exercised against a ". . . bona fide purchaser from or lienor of the debtor's transferee for a present fair equivalent value: *Provided, however,* That where such purchaser or lienor has given less than such value, he shall nevertheless have a lien upon such property, but only to the extent of the consideration actually given by him. . . ."

4. DISTRIBUTION

Dividends
The assets of the bankrupt's estate are liquidated and distributed among those creditors whose claims have been proved and allowed, pursuant to court order. After first setting aside sufficient assets to pay the claims of secured creditors to the extent of the security surrendered and to pay creditors whose claims have priority in payment, the remaining assets are distributed among the unsecured creditors. Such distribution is called a "dividend." Dividends or other monies which remain unclaimed for 60 days after the

final dividend has been declared and distributed are paid into the bankruptcy court and, if not claimed for at least five years, are deposited in the United States Treasury subject to withdrawal by a claimant pursuant to court order.

Marshaling of Assets
The Bankruptcy Act provides for the marshaling of assets in connection with the bankruptcy of a partnership.[8] Each individual partner's estate first is made available to his individual creditors, and any surplus remaining is made available to partnership creditors; partnership property first is made available to partnership creditors, and any surplus remaining is distributed among the partners and is made available to the creditors of each of the individual partners.

Priorities
The Bankruptcy Act, section 64, specifies certain claims which are entitled to priority and payment in full. Such claims are listed in the order of their priorities among themselves and may be summarized, generally, as follows:

First priority. The expenses of: preserving the bankrupt's estate; recovering the bankrupt's property which has been fraudulently transferred or concealed; and administration—e.g., fees of an accountant retained by the trustee pursuant to court order, fees of the referee.

Second priority. Wages and commissions due to workmen, servants, clerks, and traveling or city salesmen on a salary or a commission basis, not exceeding $600 for each claimant, which were earned within three months before the petition in bankruptcy was filed; traveling or city salesmen include all such salesmen, whether or not they are independent contractors selling the products or services of the bankrupt on a commission basis, with or without a drawing account or formal contract. The assignment of a wage claim with priority transfers to the assignee the claim and its priority of payment.

Third priority. The reasonable expenses of creditors: in successfully defeating confirmation of an arrangement or wage-earner plan, or in preventing the bankrupt's discharge; and in procuring evidence causing the conviction of a person for violation of the provisions of the Bankruptcy Act.

Fourth priority. Taxes due and owing by the bankrupt to the United States or any state or subdivision thereof which are not released by a discharge in bankruptcy.

---

[8] For the pertinent text of the Bankruptcy Act, see sec. 5g, below, p. 1175.

Fifth priority.   Debts which, by the laws of the United States, are entitled to priority, or rent owing to a landlord who is entitled to priority by state law; such rent must have been for actual use and occupancy of the premises which accrued within three months immediately prior to filing of the petition in bankruptcy.

5. DISCHARGE OF THE BANKRUPT

Nature of Discharge   The primary benefit derived by a bankrupt from the Bankruptcy Act is his discharge in bankruptcy which, with few exceptions, releases him from all of his debts which are provable in bankruptcy, whether allowable in full or in part. The adjudication of a debtor as a bankrupt operates automatically as an application for a discharge, except that a corporation must file an application for discharge within six months after it has been adjudicated a bankrupt. The court must make an order fixing a time for the filing of objections to the bankrupt's discharge which must be not less than 30 days nor more than 90 days after the first date set for the first meeting of creditors. Notice of the court's order must be given to all parties in interest. Upon the expiration of such time or court extension thereof, the court holds a hearing on the objections filed or, if no objections have been filed, it discharges the bankrupt, provided the filing fees required by the Bankruptcy Act have been fully paid.

When Granted or Denied   A bankrupt has a right to a discharge if he has complied with the requirements of the Bankruptcy Act. The court—i.e., the judge or the referee—is required to grant a discharge unless the bankrupt has waived his right to a discharge or, by his conduct in not complying with the Bankruptcy Act, he does not have such right.

Waiver.   Under the Bankruptcy Act, section 14e, "If the bankrupt fails to appear at the hearing upon the objections to his application for a discharge, or having appeared refuses to submit himself to examination, or if the court finds after hearing upon notice that the bankrupt has failed without sufficient excuse to appear and submit himself to examination at the first meeting of creditors or at any meeting specially called for his examination, he shall be deemed to have waived his right to a discharge, and the court shall enter an order to that effect."

Denial.   Under the Bankruptcy Act, section 14c, a bankrupt is denied a discharge if he has committed any of various acts, which may be summarized, generally, as follows:

1. Committed an offense punishable by imprisonment for concealment of assets, false oaths and claims, or bribery, as provided under title 18, United States Code, section 152.
2. Destroyed, mutilated, falsified, concealed, or failed to keep or preserve books of account or records, from which his financial condition and business transactions might be ascertained, unless in the discretion of the court such acts or failure were justified under all the circumstances of the case.
3. While engaged in business as a sole proprietor, partnership, or as an executive of a corporation, obtained such business money or property on credit, or obtained an extension or renewal of credit, by a materially false written statement respecting his financial condition.
4. Within twelve months immediately preceding the filing of the petition in bankruptcy, transferred, removed, destroyed, or concealed, or permitted to be removed, destroyed, or concealed, any of his property, with the intent to hinder, delay, or defraud his creditors.
5. In a proceeding under the Bankruptcy Act commenced within six years prior to the date of the filing of the petition in bankruptcy, had been granted a discharge, or had a composition or an arrangement by way of composition or a wage earner's plan by way of composition confirmed under the Bankruptcy Act.
6. Refused to obey any lawful order of, or to answer any material question approved by, the court during a proceeding under the Bankruptcy Act.
7. Failed to explain satisfactorily any losses of assets or deficiency of assets to meet his liabilities.
8. Failed to pay in full the filing fees required to be paid under the Act.

Under the Bankruptcy Act, section 17a:

Effect of Discharge   A discharge in bankruptcy shall release a bankrupt from all of his provable debts, whether allowable in full or in part, except such as (1) are taxes which became legally due and owing by the bankrupt to the United States or to any State or any subdivision thereof within three years preceding bankruptcy . . . except that a discharge in bankruptcy shall not release or affect any tax lien; (2) are liabilities for obtaining money or property by false pretenses or false representations, or for obtaining money or property on credit or obtaining an extension or renewal of credit in reliance upon a materially false statement in writing respecting his financial condition made or published or caused to be made or published in any manner whatsoever with intent to deceive, or for willful and malicious conversion of the property of another; (3) have not been duly scheduled in time for proof and allowance, with the name of the creditor, if known to the bankrupt, unless such creditor had notice or actual knowledge of the proceedings in bankruptcy; (4) were created by his fraud, embezzlement, misappropriation or defalcation while acting as an officer or in any fiduciary capacity; (5) are for wages and commissions to the extent they are entitled to priority under subdivision "a" of section 64 of this Act; (6) are due for moneys of an employee received or retained by his employer to secure the faithful performance by such employee of the terms of a contract of employment; (7) are for alimony due or to become due, or for maintenance or support of wife or child, or for seduction of an unmarried female, or for breach of promise of marriage accompanied by seduction, or for criminal conversation; or (8) are liabilities for willful and malicious injuries to the person or property of another other than conversion as excepted under clause (2) of this subdivision.

The bankrupt's discharge does not alter the liability of a person who is a co-debtor or surety for the bankrupt. Nor does such discharge preclude the court, within one year after the discharge has been granted, from revoking it if: it was obtained by the bankrupt's fraud and the facts did not warrant the granting of a discharge; the bankrupt fraudulently failed to report or deliver to the trustee property properly a part of the bankrupt estate; or during such proceeding for revocation the bankrupt refused to obey any lawful order of the court or to answer any material question approved by the court.

Chapter IV

COMPOSITIONS

Nature   A COMPOSITION outside of bankruptcy is an agreement whereby an insolvent or financially embar-
rassed debtor agrees with some or all of his creditors that, on his immediate payment to each of them a part of his indebtedness to each,
each will discharge the debtor.[1] Under the Bankruptcy Act a composition is permitted between a debtor and his creditors with the approval
of the court, and the debtor is discharged from liability for such debts.
Various types of composition are provided for under the Bankruptcy Act,
including corporate reorganizations, arrangements, real property arrangements by persons other than corporations, and wage-earners'
plans.

Agricultural   Agricultural compositions and extensions between a
Compositions   farmer who is insolvent or unable to meet his debts
and Extensions   as they mature and his creditors for all practical purposes no longer is included in the Bankruptcy Act.

                    Corporate reorganizations are initiated by the filing
Corporate Re-   of a petition by the corporation, or by three or more
organizations   creditors with claims totaling $5,000 or more which
                    are liquidated as to amount and not contingent as to
liability. The petition may be filed in a pending bankruptcy proceeding
either before or after the adjudication of a corporation. The petition
must state: (1) that the corporation is insolvent or unable to pay its
debts as they mature; (2) the applicable jurisdictional facts; (3) the

---

[1] See above, p. 68.

nature of the business of the corporation; (4) the assets, liabilities, capital stock, and financial condition of the corporation; (5) the nature of all pending proceedings affecting the property of the corporation known to the petitioner or petitioners and the courts in which they are pending; (6) the status of any plan of reorganization, readjustment, or liquidation affecting the property of the corporation, pending either in connection with or without any judicial proceeding; (7) the specific facts showing the need for relief, and why adequate relief cannot be obtained under Arrangements; and (8) the desire of the petitioner or petitioners that a plan be effected. A plan of reorganization is formulated and, on approval by creditors holding two-thirds in amount of the claims filed and allowed in each class of creditors, and, if the debtor is solvent, on written approval by shareholders holding a majority of the stock filed and allowed of each class, the court will confirm the plan of reorganization if: the plan complies with the requirements of the Bankruptcy Act; the plan is fair, equitable and feasible; the plan has been proposed and accepted in good faith; and all payments made or promised have been fully disclosed to the court and are reasonable.

Arrangements   A debtor who is insolvent or unable to pay his debts as they mature and who could become a bankrupt, may file a petition for confirmation of a plan for the settlement, satisfaction, or extension of the time of payment of his unsecured debts, called an "arrangement." Under the arrangement the rights of unsecured creditors are modified or altered upon any terms or for any consideration. On the written acceptance by all the creditors affected by the arrangement, and the debtor's deposit of the agreed amount in the proper depository, the court will confirm the arrangement if it is satisfied that the arrangement has been made and accepted in good faith. If all the creditors affected thereby have not accepted the arrangement, the court may confirm the arrangement if: a majority in number of the creditors affected, whose claims have been proved and allowed, representing a majority in amount of such claims have accepted it in writing; the debtor has deposited the agreed amount in the proper depository; it is for the best interests of the creditors; it is feasible, and the debtor has not been guilty of any of the acts, or failed to perform any of the duties, which would be a bar to the discharge of a bankrupt; and the proposal and its acceptance are in good faith. The effect of confirmation is to discharge the debtor from all of his unsecured debts and liabilities provided for in the arrangement; however, the debtor is not discharged from provable claims not dischargeable in bankruptcy.

Real Property Arrangements and Wage-earner Plans

Real property arrangements by persons other than corporations are concerned with arrangements between a debtor, other than a corporation, who could become a bankrupt and who is the legal or equitable owner of real property or a chattel real which is security for any debt, and his creditors. Wage-earners' plans are concerned with plans for a composition or extension, or both, of payment of claims by a wage earner, who is defined as an individual whose principal income is derived from wages, salary, or commissions.

APPENDIX TO PART EIGHT

REFERENCES

1. Collier, William M. *Collier on Bankruptcy.* 14th ed. New York: Matthew Bender & Co., 1965.
2. Laube, William T. *Collier Pamphlet Edition, Bankruptcy Act.* 1971 ed. New York: Matthew Bender & Co., 1971.
3. The Bankruptcy Act, *United States Code,* Title 11.

PROBLEMS

1. Explain the meaning and application of the following remedies available to creditors:
   (a) Attachment.
   (b) Execution.
   (c) Garnishment.
2. (a) In general, what is the purpose of the Bankruptcy Act?
   (b) Who is a referee in bankruptcy and how is he appointed?
   (c) Who may become:
      (1) Voluntary bankrupts?
      (2) Involuntary bankrupts?
   (d) What is a wage earner?
3. A receiver in bankruptcy employs a public accountant to examine and report on the accounts of the bankrupt.
   (1) May the receiver do this?
   (2) What is required?
   (3) How is the compensation for the accountant's services determined? (Former C.P.A. Examination question)
4. (a) A, B, and C are partners. A and B become insolvent.
      (1) Can the partnership become an involuntary bankrupt? Why?
      (2) Can the partnership become a voluntary bankrupt? Why?
   (b) D has various creditors and gratuitously transfers some of his assets to his friends with the intent to hinder, delay, or defraud his creditors. D is still solvent.
      (1) Has D committed an act of bankruptcy? Why?
      (2) Can D be adjudicated a bankrupt? Why?
5. (a) Enumerate the six acts of bankruptcy.
   (b) What is meant by insolvency under the Bankruptcy Act?

6. (a) A owed $900 and made an assignment for the benfit of all of his creditors, who totaled 11 in number. B, one of A's creditors, had a claim against A for $600, and he filed a petition to have A adjudicated an involuntary bankrupt.
    (1) Can A be adjudicated an involuntary bankrupt?
    (2) Why?
  (b) X owed his 15 creditors $10,000 and committed an act of bankruptcy. Five months later all of his creditors decided to petition to have him adjudicated an involuntary bankrupt.
    (1) Can X be adjudicated an involuntary bankrupt?
    (2) Why?
  (c) What is the effect of the death of a debtor during proceedings to have him adjudicated an involuntary bankrupt?

7. (a) Distinguish a receiver in bankruptcy from a trustee in bankruptcy.
  (b) Explain the importance of the first meeting of creditors after the adjudication of bankruptcy.

8. (a) Name three types of provable claim.
  (b) Within what period of time must a provable claim be proved?
  (c) What is a proof of claim and what does it contain?

9. The Amalgo company holds a note of the Crockett company for $2,500. This note is secured by collateral worth $1,800. The Crockett company goes into bankruptcy. The trustee expects to pay creditors 40 cents on the dollar. How much is this note held by the Amalgo company worth? (Former C.P.A. Examination question)

10. The partnership firm of Altman, Berkley, & Calvert became bankrupt. Among the claims presented was an unpaid income tax due the United States by a partner, Altman. The tax was based on income he had received from the partnership business. Is the United States entitled to payment out of the firm estate in priority to firm creditors? (Former C.P.A. Examination question)

11. A person occupying premises under a lease files a petition in bankruptcy four years prior to the termination of the lease and immediately vacates the premises. What are the landlord's rights and what should he do to protect them? (Former C.P.A. Examination question)

12. D is insolvent and transferred to C, one of his creditors, $1,000 in satisfaction of C's claim against D for the same amount. Within four months thereafter D's creditors filed a petition to have D adjudicated an involuntary bankrupt and D was so adjudicated.
  (a) Does the trustee in bankruptcy have any rights against C? Why?
  (b) If D had conveyed to C realty worth $1,000 instead of cash and C then had sold the realty to E, a bona fide purchaser, for $1,000, would the trustee in bankruptcy have any rights against E? Why?
  (c) In (b) above, if, instead of C's selling the realty to E, C mortgaged the realty to F as security for a loan of $500 then advanced to C, would the trustee in bankruptcy have any rights against F or the realty? Why?

13. (a) What property of a bankrupt is exempted from inclusion in his estate for distribution to creditors under the Bankruptcy Act?
  (b) What claims have priority in the distribution of the bankrupt's estate?

14. What rights does a trustee in bankruptcy take in the bankrupt's life insurance policies—(1) in policies payable to his estate, and (2) in policies payable to third party beneficiaries? (Former C.P.A. Examination question)

15. (a) List three instances when a bankrupt may be denied a bankruptcy discharge.
    (b) List three provable debts from which a bankrupt is not discharged.
    (c) S is a guarantor of a debt of D to C. D is adjudicated an involuntary bankrupt. C did not prove his claim. After D had obtained a discharge in bankruptcy C demanded from S the amount owed by D for which S was surety.
      (1) Does C have any right against D or S? Why?
      (2) Does S have any right against D? Why?

SOME PREVIOUS C.P.A. LAW EXAMINATION QUESTIONS AND MODEL ANSWERS

MAY, 1970

No. 7 (Estimated time—20 to 25 minutes)

Zeta Corporation is insolvent. It has 20 unsecured creditors and three creditors who have liens on its assets. Zeta, while insolvent, paid $20,000 to Jones, one of its unsecured creditors, in partial payment of goods sold and delivered by Jones to Zeta six months earlier. Adams, one of the secured creditors, loaned Zeta funds ten months ago and, two months ago, when he knew Zeta was insolvent, obtained from Zeta a security interest in the company's accounts receivable which he duly perfected under applicable state law. Collins, another of the secured creditors, sold Zeta some machinery six months ago and obtained a security interest therein which he has neglected to perfect. Barton, the remaining secured creditor, holds a mortgage on Zeta's plant which he obtained two years ago and which is duly filed and recorded under applicable state law.

a. Has Zeta committed an act of bankruptcy? Explain.

b. Assuming Zeta has committed an act of bankruptcy, how many of its creditors must join in an involuntary petition in bankruptcy? How much in provable claims must such petitioning creditors have? Explain.

c. Assume an involuntary petition has been filed against Zeta and Zeta has been adjudicated bankrupt, all other facts recited above remaining the same. Discuss the rights of Adams, Collins, and Barton in relation to Zeta's trustee in bankruptcy.

d. Assuming Jones received a preference, might the trustee be able to recover the $20,000 from Jones? Explain.

Answer

a. Yes. The federal Bankruptcy Act lists various acts of bankruptcy. One is the debtor's preferential transfer of his property to a creditor on account of an antecedent debt, made while he was insolvent, and which has the effect of such creditor being enabled to receive a greater percentage of payment on his debt than another creditor of the same class. Here, Zeta while insolvent preferred Jones by paying him $20,000, and also preferred Adams by giving him a security interest in the company's accounts receivable. An involuntary petition in bankruptcy will have to be filed within four months of the commission of an act of bankruptcy.

b. At least three of Zeta's creditors whose provable claims total at least $500. Under the Act, three or more creditors with provable claims not contingent as to liability, amounting to a total of $500 in excess of any securities held by them, may file an involuntary petition in bankruptcy.

c. Under the Act, if the preferential transfer occurred within four months before a petition in bankruptcy is filed, and if a preferred creditor had reasonable cause to believe that the debtor was insolvent at the time of such transfer, the preference is voidable by the trustee in bankruptcy. Since Adams knew of Zeta's insolvency at the time of the lien transfer to him, the trustee can avoid the transfer to Adams, who then becomes an unsecured creditor. Collins did not perfect his security interest in the machinery acquired more than four months before the petition was filed, and since the trustee becomes a lien creditor the lien of Collins is subordinate to the trustee's lien. Barton's mortgage lien was obtained more than four months before the petition was filed and was duly filed and recorded. Therefore the mortgage lien is not voidable by the trustee. If the foreclosure of Barton's lien results in a surplus, it will become available to pay Zeta's other creditors. If it results in a deficiency, then Barton becomes an unsecured creditor in that amount.

d. The answer depends on whether Jones had reasonable cause to believe that Zeta was insolvent at the time of the preferential transfer. If Jones had such cause, it is a voidable preference as defined in "c" above, and the trustee in bankruptcy can recover the $20,000. If Jones did not have such cause, there is no voidable preference and the trustee cannot recover the money.

MAY, 1969

No. 2 (Estimated time—20 to 25 minutes)

Each of the following numbered statements states a legal conclusion. You are to determine whether *each* legal conclusion is true or false according to *general principles of bankruptcy law*. Write on a separate answer sheet whether each conclusion is true or false. Your grade will be determined by deducting your total of incorrect answers from your total of correct answers; an omitted answer will not be considered an incorrect answer.

A. Richardson owns all of the stock of Richardson Corporation. Recently the firm has been unprofitable. A supplier who in the past sold to the Corporation on credit now demands cash on delivery because he believes the Corporation is becoming insolvent.

    31. The Corporation is insolvent in the equity sense if it is unable to meet its debts as they mature.

    32. The Corporation is insolvent in the bankruptcy sense if its assets valued on the basis of a voluntary sale are less than its liabilities.

    33. The Corporation cannot be considered insolvent so long as Richardson has adequate funds which he can donate to the Corporation.

    34. Proof of insolvency is itself an act of bankruptcy.

    35. If an involuntary petition in bankruptcy should be filed against Richardson charging him with concealing his assets with intent to defraud his

creditors, proof by Richardson that he was solvent at the time the petition was filed would be a complete defense to the action.

B. Harris, while he was insolvent and within four months of filing a petition in bankruptcy, transferred property to Michael, a creditor of his for an antecedent debt. The effect of the transfer was to enable Michael to obtain a greater percentage of his debt than Harris's other creditors of the same class.

36. Harris's action will not bar him from obtaining a discharge in bankruptcy.

37. Michael need not return the payment he received if he did not know that Harris was insolvent when the transfer was made.

38. The transfer of property from Harris to Michael constitutes a preference.

39. Harris's action will bar him from filing a voluntary petition in bankruptcy.

40. Harris's action constitutes an act of bankruptcy.

C. Anderson conveyed all of his property to Barker to escape the unfair demands of Collins. Anderson instructed Barker to sell the property and pay the proceeds to all of Anderson's creditors except Collins.

41. Anderson committed an act of bankruptcy.

42. Solvency would not be a valid defense to an involuntary petition filed in bankruptcy by Collins.

43. The conveyance of the assets to Barker was a preferential transfer.

44. A trustee in bankruptcy would seek to set aside such a conveyance.

45. If Anderson had not excluded Collins from participation in the distribution of the proceeds from the sale of the property by Barker, Collins would be barred from filing an involuntary petition in bankruptcy.

D. John Mitchell, an employee of the Sampson Aircraft Company, earns $120 per week. He has amassed $5,000 of unpaid bills which are payable to nine creditors who wish to have him declared a bankrupt.

46. To place Mitchell into involuntary bankruptcy at least three of his creditors with claims aggregating at least $500 over the value of any security they hold must file a petition for involuntary bankruptcy against him.

47. To place Mitchell into involuntary bankruptcy he must have committed an act of bankruptcy within four months of the filing of a petition against him.

48. If Mitchell is adjudged a bankrupt he will be assured of obtaining a discharge.

49. If Mitchell obtains a discharge in bankruptcy he will be automatically and unqualifiedly relieved of all his debts.

50. If Mitchell is declared a bankrupt and obtains a discharge he may not incur any credit obligations for six months after his discharge unless he informs his potential creditor that he was recently a bankrupt.

E. Thomas Serota owns a shop in which he repairs electrical appliances. Jones Company left a machine with Serota for repair. Electrical Supply Company sold Serota a machine on credit three months ago for testing electrical appliances and has a perfected security interest as security for payment of the unpaid balance due. Serota's creditors have now filed an involuntary petition in bankruptcy against him.

51. Jones Company should file a creditor's claim with the trustee in bankruptcy to obtain the return of their machine.
52. Jones Company will be entitled to share in any pro rata distribution of assets made to the creditors of Thomas Serota.
53. Electrical Supply Company must turn its perfected security interest over to the trustee in bankruptcy and share as a general creditor of the bankrupt's estate.
54. If the trustee desires to do so he may successfully claim that Electrical Supply Company's perfected security interest constitutes a preference which is voidable.
55. Electrical Supply Company is a secured creditor which is free to repossess the electrical testing machine sold to Serota and satisfy the obligation by properly disposing of the collateral.

F. Wood and Small are partners who wish to file for voluntary bankruptcy.

56. Wood and Small may be adjudged bankrupt as individuals separately from the partnership.
57. The partnership cannot be adjudged a bankrupt.
58. A voluntary bankrupt may not be adjudicated a bankrupt until a trustee in bankruptcy is appointed.
59. A creditor who wishes to file a claim against the bankrupts must be present or represented at the first creditors' meeting.
60. The marshalling of assets doctrine will apply if the partnership and both partners are insolvent.

Answer

31. True	37. True	43. True	49. False	55. True
32. True	38. True	44. True	50. False	56. True
33. False	39. False	45. False	51. False	57. False
34. False	40. True	46. False	52. False	58. False
35. True	41. True	47. True	53. False	59. False
36. True	42. False	48. False	54. False	60. True

PART NINE

INSURANCE

Chapter I

THE INSURANCE CONTRACT

---

1. *NATURE OF INSURANCE*

**Concept of
Insurance**   THE subject of insurance is concerned with the shifting of risk of loss. Risk is the likelihood of the occurrence or nonoccurrence of a specified event. Risk of loss is inherent in business, and it is socially desirable to effect the transfer of risk of loss, except where it is contrary to public policy. Insurance is a risk-bearing device whereby risk of loss is shifted from one person and spread among many. It is a method of indemnity against loss by widespread assumption of the risk of loss by many persons. It is in this respect that insurance is distinguished from a wager, which is contrary to public policy in most states. By means of insurance, persons seek to shift the risk of loss occurring by chance, while in a wager persons seek to make a profit by chance. By insurance loss is avoided, while by a wager gain and loss are created. By insurance an existing risk of loss is shifted, while immediately before a wager is made there is no risk of loss to shift, and the risk of loss is created by the wager itself.

**Insurance
Contract**   Although the risk of loss may be shifted by operation of law—e.g., workmen's compensation statutes—ordinarily insurance is created by contract. A contract of insurance is a contract whereby one party for a consideration called a "premium" assumes the risk of loss borne by another party and agrees to indemnify the latter for loss caused by a specified contingency, the assumed risk to be distributed among a group of persons. There are many forms of the insurance contract varying according to the risk assumed, such as life, fire, marine, health, accident, and a host of others. First an examination of the fundamental principles underlying the concept of the insurance contract as a contract of indemnity, and then an examination of fire and life insurance, will be made.

As a Contract of Indemnity. While the subject of insurance includes both contracts of indemnity and contracts of suretyship, *throughout this discussion of insurance and unless otherwise indicated only insurance as a contract of indemnity will be considered.* When the insurer is a surety the rules of suretyship apply; these rules have been discussed previously[1] and a contract of indemnity was distinguished from a contract of suretyship.[2] Briefly, in a contract of indemnity the indemnitor assures the indemnitee that any loss he sustains will be paid for by the indemnitor, *regardless of the liability of any third person therefor;* e.g., fire insurance and life insurance contracts. While in a suretyship contract the surety engages to be *liable for the fault of a third person;* e.g., S's contract with C assuring him that if C will extend credit to D and D doesn't pay, S will pay C.

2. FORMATION OF THE INSURANCE CONTRACT

Parties   The principles of the law of contracts are applicable to the insurance contract, commonly called a "policy." One of the essential elements in the formation of an insurance contract is that the parties have capacity to contract. The party who assumes the risk is called the "insurer," and the party whose risk has been assumed is called the "insured" or "assured." Although natural persons may, in the absence of statute to the contrary, act as insurers, nevertheless, most insurers are corporations.

Insurance companies may be stock, mutual, or mixed. A stock company has capital which is divided into shares of stock; the shareholders have no relation to the insured. Mutual companies do not issue shares of stock, and the members thereof are both insurers and the insured, the company contracting to indemnify each member. In mutual companies a fixed advanced premium is paid and a fund is accumulated to indemnify for loss sustained; profits are shared by the members. Mixed companies have characteristics of both the stock and mutual companies, a small amount of stock being issued entitling shareholders to dividends thereon, and all policyholders becoming members with beneficial interests as in a mutual company.

Infants have limited capacity to contract[3] and, except as otherwise provided by statute, they may be parties to contracts of life insurance and may exercise their power to avoid such contracts. While there is

---

[1] See above, pp. 805–34.

[2] See above, pp. 806–7.

[3] See above, pp. 18 ff.

conflict, by the majority view if an infant is the insured, on his disaffirmance of his life insurance contract he may recover all premiums paid by him; the insurance contract is not one for necessaries. Statutes in many states permit infants above a specified age to procure life insurance with certain specified persons as beneficiaries (e.g., mother, father, brother, sister) but deprive infants of power to avoid such insurance contracts. In most instances a parent, rather than the infant, procures the contract of life insurance on the infant's life and the parent then is the insured and the contracting party with the insurer.

Insurable Interest

An insurance contract is concerned with the assumption of a risk of loss. A person who is exposed to a risk of loss has an insurable interest in the object of the risk. It is essential that the insured have an insurable interest in the subject matter insured; otherwise there is no contract of insurance and the transaction is a wager. A person has an insurable interest in property or life when he will benefit by the continued existence, or suffer loss by the destruction, of such property or life.

A person has an *insurable interest in property* if he will suffer pecuniary loss by its destruction or impairment, or benefit from its preservation. Examples of persons with an insurable interest in particular property are: mortgagor and mortgagee in the mortgaged property, tenant in the rented property, partner in the partnership property, bailee in the bailed property, stockholder in the corporate property, and a person with a legal or equitable title in property. A secured creditor has an insurable interest in the security to the extent of the obligation owing to him, while a general creditor does not have an insurable interest in his debtor's property, although he does have an insurable interest in his debtor's life. Risk of pecuniary loss fixes the insurable interest.

Inasmuch as it is impossible to determine the value of a person's life, precluding any estimation of the loss caused by his death, the test of the risk of pecuniary loss in a determination of insurable interest cannot be applied to life insurance. Accordingly, an *insurable interest in life* is determined by the relationship existing between the insured and the person whose life is insured. If the relationship is such that the insured has a reasonable expectation of deriving a benefit by the continuance of the life insured or of suffering loss by its termination, the insured has an insurable interest in the life insured. Blood, marital, and commercial relationships in which this expectation of benefit or loss is present create an insurable interest. Examples of a person who has an insurable interest in the life of another are: parents and children; brothers and sisters;

husband and wife; business associates in the lives of each other—e.g., partners and officers or directors of a corporation or other "key personnel"; and a creditor's interest in the life of his debtor. It is obvious that a person has an insurable interest in his own life.

There are three important distinctions to be observed between an insurable interest in property and an insurable interest in life. First, an insurable interest in property is predicated upon some legal or equitable interest in property, the impairment or destruction of which will cause pecuniary loss; while an insurable interest in life is not predicated necessarily upon any legal or equitable interest in life or upon pecuniary loss by termination of that life. Second, in property insurance the insured must have an insurable interest only *at the time of loss*,[4] provided the parties to the contract intend that the insurer's risk is to attach to property of the insured then, or subsequently to be, acquired, although there is much apparently obsolete dicta and a minority view which requires that the insured have an insurable interest also at the time the contract was made.[5] In life insurance the insured must have an insurable interest in the life insured only *at the time the contract of insurance was made.* Third, recovery on property insurance is limited to the extent of pecuniary loss to the insurable interest, while recovery on life insurance is for the face value of the policy.

Consideration A contract of insurance requires consideration. The money paid by the insured, pursuant to the terms of the insurance contract, is called a "premium." In a contract for property insurance the insurer's promise to insure and the insured's promise to pay premiums, or his payment of premiums, constitute consideration for each other.

The consideration is different in a life insurance contract. The insurer promises to insure the insured who promises to pay only the first premium; he does not promise to pay any other premiums. The contract of life insurance does not exist until the insured has paid, or has promised to pay, the first premium and the insurer has agreed to insure the insured. The insurer is bound to keep the insurance contract alive as long as the premiums are paid and, on the nonpayment of a premium when due, the contract of insurance is discharged. It is really a contract

---

[4] In marine insurance, the insured must have an insurable interest at the time the contract of insurance is made and, by the majority view, at the time of loss, except for "lost or not lost" insurance coverage when no insurable interest is required.

[5] William R. Vance, *Handbook on the Law of Insurance* (3d ed., Buist M. Anderson; St. Paul: West Publishing Co., 1951), sec. 30.

subject to discharge by the occurrence of a condition subsequent—namely, failure to pay the premiums when due. The insured is not liable for his failure to pay any premiums after the first premium.

The payment of premiums is to be made as specified in the contract of insurance. Usually such premiums are required to be paid in money, but the insurer may expressly or impliedly waive such right and accept payment by check. The insurer's acceptance of a check in payment of premiums is a waiver of its right to receive only money. Similarly, the insurer may waive its right to receive payment at the place indicated in the contract.

Legally Valid Transaction
The contract of insurance must be for a legally valid transaction. Noncompliance by the insurer with statutory requirements has a varying effect among the states. In most states such agreements to insure are void. In states where such an agreement is not expressly made void, the contract is not enforceable by the insurer, but it is enforceable by the insured. An agreement to insure for loss caused by the willful commission of a crime or a tort is void.

Manifestation of Mutual Assent
Offer and acceptance constituting a manifestation of mutual assent is essential to a contract of insurance. Usually an offer is made by the person desiring insurance on an application form provided by the particular insurer and addressed to the insurer. On the insurer's acceptance of such application, the contract of insurance is created. Usually by the terms of the insurance policy representing the contract of the parties, the policy becomes effective only on its delivery and payment of the first premium. However, this may be varied by the terms of the policy. If these are different from the terms included in the application, there is no contract of insurance until the insured accepts the policy according to its terms. Delivery of a life insurance policy may be actual or constructive. While most jurisdictions would hold that delivery of the policy by the insurer to the broker would be a constructive delivery to the insured, a constructive delivery to the insured exists when the policy is mailed to the insured.

In the case of property insurance, a contract of insurance may be in effect without the delivery of the policy and the payment of the first premium. Pending consideration by the insurer of an application for property insurance and pending issuance of a formal policy, a temporary contract of property insurance may be made orally and evidenced by a written memorandum of the contract, called a "binder," made by the insurer, often through its agent.[6]

Misrepresentation. Material misrepresentation, whether fraudulent or innocent, in the inducement of a contract of insurance causes the contract to be voidable at the election of the party to whom the misrepresentation was made. A misrepresentation is material when knowledge of the fact misrepresented would have been likely to have influenced the conduct of a reasonable man. The problem of material misrepresentation usually arises in connection with false statements made by the applicant for insurance on the application form. If the applicant's misrepresentation is material, the contract represented by the policy is voidable at the election of the insurer. Courts more readily interpret intentional misrepresentations of fact as material than they do misrepresentations of fact which were made innocently. Although formerly a misrepresentation of age in a life insurance policy caused the policy to be voidable by the insurer, today in most states the policy is not voidable on this ground and payment is made by the insurer on death in an amount of what coverage the premium paid would provide for the person on the basis of his correct age.

Warranties. While a misrepresentation must be material in order to create the power of avoidance, a warranty is not required to be material, and a breach of the warranty justifies rescission of the contract. It is important, therefore, to distinguish between representations and warranties. A representation is a statement of fact made to induce formation of the insurance contract and is not included in the contract. A warranty is a statement of fact contained in the contract, or included therein by reference, the truth of which is a condition to the insurer's liability under the contract. Breach of warranty justifies rescission of the contract, regardless of any consideration of the materiality of the breach, while a misrepresentation of fact must be material in order to justify rescission. Breach of warranty, therefore, justifies an insurer in declaring the contract rescinded and forfeited. Inasmuch as the law abhors forfeitures, statements of fact made by the insured are interpreted as representations rather than as warranties, unless the parties clearly indicate that such statements constitute warranties. Warranties, therefore, are distinguished from representations in the following ways: warranties are part of a contract and essential to it, while representations are not part of the contract and are made to induce formation of the

---

[6] An insurance binder is a written memorandum of an oral, temporary contract of property insurance, issued by the insurer to evidence such contract pending consideration and issuance of a formal policy.

contract; warranties always are material to the contract, while representations may or may not be material; breach of warranty by the insured justifies the insurer in rescinding the contract and declaring it forfeited, while the representation must be false and must be material in order to create the power to avoid or rescind the contract.

Concealment. In the law of contracts, failure to disclose material facts in violation of a duty to make such disclosure constitutes a material misrepresentation, regardless of whether such nondisclosure was intentional or innocent, and any contract so made is voidable at the election of the party to whom such disclosure should have been made. If such nondisclosure was intentional, it constitutes fraud; if it was innocent, it constitutes solely a material misrepresentation. In the law of insurance, innocent material misrepresentation by nondisclosure is insufficient as a ground for rescission of the contract. *The concealment, or nondisclosure, must have been fraudulent in order to justify rescission;* except in the case of marine insurance where, following the law of England, innocent material misrepresentation is sufficient. *An applicant for a contract of insurance has a duty to make disclosure of all material facts to the insurer,* and fraudulent concealment of material facts causes the contract induced thereby to be voidable at the election of the insurer.

Statute of Frauds The statute of frauds is inapplicable to contracts of insurance, unless otherwise provided by statute. It is not a contract to answer for the debt, default, or miscarriages of another; it is a contract of indemnity,[7] to pay for loss. Further, a contract of insurance is not within that part of the statute of frauds which provides for contracts which are not to be performed within the space of one year from the making thereof; the contract is *performable* within the space of one year should the insured event occur within that time. Although oral contracts of insurance are enforceable in the absence of statute to the contrary, nevertheless, most contracts of insurance are in writing. Often statutes provide for standard forms of insurance policies.

Waiver and Estoppel Waiver and estoppel often are confused; their distinction is important in determining the rights of the parties, inasmuch as waiver and estoppel mean different things.

Waiver. *A waiver is the insurer's manifestation of intent to give up a known defense to recovery on the contract of insurance or to give*

---

[7] See above, pp. 877–78.

up its right to rescind the contract. An illustration is the insurer's acceptance of a premium with knowledge that the insurance contract has been materially breached by the insured. Although the *act* of an insurer in recognizing the insurance contract as still in force even though there has been a breach of condition or warranty justifying its forfeiture constitutes a waiver of such defense, the insurer's *silence* after he has acquired knowledge of such fact justifying forfeiture of the policy does not of itself constitute a waiver of such forfeiture, unless there was a duty to speak when he learned of such fact. The insurer's silence with knowledge that premiums have not been paid does not waive the insurer's right to declare the contract forfeited, unless the insurer has waived such right by a previous course of dealings between the parties. If the ground of forfeiture is other than for nonpayment of premiums and the insurer learns of such fact prior to the occurrence of the insured event, the insurer has the *duty* to notify the insured of his exercise of his right of forfeiture within a reasonable period of time after he has acquired knowledge of such fact; his failure to give such notice constitutes a waiver of such forfeiture.[8] Waivers made prior to, or at the time of, the formation of the contract of insurance are inadmissible as evidence because of the parol evidence rule. Waivers which occur after the contract of insurance has been formed are admissible in evidence. Any right acquired by the contract may be waived, unless such waiver would be contrary to public policy. An illustration is an insurer's inability to waive the legal requirement that the insured have an insurable interest.

Estoppel. *Estoppel occurs when a material fact has been misrepresented with knowledge of its falsity in order to induce reliance thereon, and the addressee reasonably relies thereon by changing his position materially;* the utterer is estopped to deny what he previously had asserted. The insurer's representation that a contract of insurance is enforceable when the insurer knows of a defense to the enforcement of the policy, if relied on by the applicant, estops the insurer from asserting his defense subsequently. It is essential to estoppel that the addressee of the misrepresentation be ignorant of the falsity thereof and reasonably rely thereon.

---

[8] Vance, *op. cit.,* p. 493.

Chapter II

OPERATION OF THE INSURANCE CONTRACT

---

1. NATURE OF FIRE AND LIFE INSURANCE

Fire Insurance   A FIRE insurance contract is a contract of indemnity, insuring against property loss proximately caused by a hostile fire. The character of the insured is a material consideration in determining the risk of the insurer and, accordingly, *a contract of fire insurance is a personal contract.*

There are various kinds of fire insurance contract, each kind varying according to the risk assumed. Among the more common types of fire insurance contract are valued and open policies, blanket and specific policies, and floating policies. In a *valued policy* a specific value is placed upon the insured property so that, in the event of its total destruction or loss, the extent of such loss is fixed and cannot be questioned by the parties. An *open policy* does not specify the value of the insured property but establishes a fixed maximum liability of the insurer for loss or damage to such property. The value of the property is left open for determination at the time of loss. The total destruction of the insured property under an open policy, in the absence of statute or contract provision to the contrary, does not entitle the insured to the maximum amount as fixed by the policy. It can be shown that the loss was less than the maximum amount of the policy. In a *blanket policy* several items of property are insured with a fixed maximum over-all liability for loss or damage to the property, but the value of each item and the maximum liability of the insurer on each item are not specified. A *specific policy* specifically indicates the maximum liability of the insurer on each item. In a *floating policy* the insured property is of such a nature that it is constantly changing and is transitory—e.g., a merchant's stock in trade—and the policy applies to the particular property as it comes within the terms of the policy.

Life Insurance   Technically, a contract of life insurance is not a contract of indemnity because it is impossible to determine the value or extent of the particular loss of life.

886 · *C.P.A. LAW REVIEW*

It is a contract to pay a specified amount in the event the life insured is terminated. The insurer builds up a reserve from each premium paid by the insured in order to accumulate the amount payable on the maturity of the policy and, for that reason, a life insurance contract often is considered as a form of investment. The life insured may be either that of the insured, or that of a person other than the insured if the insured has an insurable interest therein at the time the insurance contract is made.

There are various kinds of life insurance contract, the most common of which are: ordinary life, limited payment life, term, and endowment insurance contracts. *Ordinary life insurance,* or "straight" life insurance as it is often called, provides for a fixed payment to the beneficiary of the contract at the time of the termination of the life insured in return for the payment of premiums during the entire lifetime of the life insured. *Limited payment life insurance* provides for a limited number of payments of premiums during a specified period and, after having made such payments, the insured is protected for the rest of the life insured, as well as the period during which such payments were made. *Term insurance* provides for a fixed premium for a specified term during which term only is the insurer liable for the termination of the life insured. There usually is no accumulation of any reserve. In term insurance the insurer is subjected to a risk of loss which may or may not happen during the period of the term, as contrasted with ordinary life and limited payment life insurance when the insured event—namely the termination of the life insured—is certain to happen during the life of the policy. *Endowment insurance* provides for the payment of fixed premiums for a specified period of time and, on the expiration of such time, a fixed amount is to be paid to the insured or to his beneficiary. The sum is payable at a fixed period of time if the insured is still alive or, on his death, at the time of his death. This form of policy represents a combination of term and annuity insurance.

2. *RIGHTS AND LIABILITIES UNDER THE INSURANCE CONTRACT*

Fire Insurance   The liability of the insurer is determined by the occurrence of the insured event and the terms of the policy fixing the extent of such liability. In a fire insurance contract the insured event is the destruction or impairment of property proximately caused by a hostile fire. By fire is meant actual ignition. It is the fire which must begin the chain of causation leading to loss, although the actual loss may not be by direct contact with the fire. The fire must be hostile and not friendly. A fire is hostile when it is burning in a place where it was not intended to burn. A fire in a fireplace where it was intended to burn is a friendly fire, but if it should extend beyond the fireplace to where it was not intended it becomes a hostile fire. Fire proximately causes loss if it is a substantial factor in causing such loss. Loss caused by actual contact of the insured property with the hostile fire, by smoke from the fire, by falling walls caused by the fire, by the use of water in extinguishing the fire, or by the occurrence of theft of the insured property while being rescued from the fire, is proximately caused by the fire. The insurer is not liable for loss specifically excluded by the terms of the policy. The insurer is liable for loss irrespective of the negligence of the insured, but he is not liable for loss intentionally caused by the insured.

Extent of Insurer's Liability. The extent of the insurer's liability for property loss is determined by the terms of the insurance contract.[1] This involves a determination of whether the loss was total or partial, the measure of the loss, and whether the policy has any coinsurance or pro rata provisions. Loss is total or partial; it is total if there is nothing left to use in the restoration of the property to the purpose for which it was used at the time of the loss; otherwise it is partial. If there is a total loss, the policy should be examined to see whether or not it is a valued or open insurance policy. If it is a valued policy, then the insurer must pay the fixed amount as specified in the policy. If it is an open policy, then the extent of the actual loss must be determined, and the insurer is liable for such loss not in excess of the maximum amount as specified in the policy. If it is a total loss under an open policy, the measure of the loss is the actual cash value of the insured property at the time of the loss. If it is a partial loss, the measure of the loss is the cost of repair in order to restore the property to its original condition—i.e., replacement cost. In order to protect the insurer against an unfair valuation of loss and against unfair proofs of loss, fire insurance policies usually provide that the insurer has the option to restore the damaged property to its condition at the time of the loss. It should be noted in passing that the insurer of property is subrogated to the insured's rights against a wrong-

---

[1] It should be noted that, in one form or another, a policy of fire insurance may provide that any change in the interest, title, or possession of the subject matter insured which increases the risk to the insurer terminates the policy of fire insurance. There is conflict concerning the effect of a partner's transfer of his partnership interest when the partners are jointly insured. Generally, in the absence of contract provision to the contrary: a partner's transfer of his interest in the partnership (i.e., his interest in profits and surplus) to another partner or to one not a partner, does not affect insurance; a partner's retirement from the partnership does not affect the insurance; but *the admission of a new partner terminates the insurance.*

doer who caused damage to, or loss of, the insured property for which the insurer has paid under the policy.

Coinsurance Clause. Because fires usually do not result in a total loss of the property, owners insure their property for less than its full value. In order to induce owners to insure their property against loss by fire for a higher percentage of the property's value, coinsurance clauses are often included in fire insurance contracts. The theory of coinsurance is that if the insured does not insure his property up to a certain percentage of its fair value, the insured shares with the insurer in the risk of loss to the extent of the deficiency between the face amount of the policy and the amount of insurance which should have been carried on the property. (The coinsurance clause in a fire insurance policy provided that the owner was to carry insurance for 80 per cent of the fair value of the property. The property was worth $10,000 at the time of loss to such property of $4,000. The owner had a fire insurance policy on the property for $6,000. To the extent that the owner failed to carry insurance in the amount of 80 per cent of the fair value of the property, the insured is to participate in such loss.

$$\frac{\$6,000 \ (\text{policy})}{\$8,000 \ (80\% \ \text{of} \ \$10,000)} \times \$4,000 \ [\text{loss}] = \$3,000 \ [\text{owner's re-}$$

covery]. He has shared in the loss to the extent of his failure to carry insurance to the extent of 80 per cent of the fair value of the property.) A coinsurance clause in a fire insurance policy is not applicable to total losses. A coinsurance clause is implied by law in marine insurance policies.

Pro Rata Clause. Fire insurance contracts often contain a pro rata clause which provides that, if there is more than one insurer on the same risk, any loss will be apportioned among them in the ratio that the amount of insurance issued by each insurer bears to the total amount of the insurance on the risk, and each is liable to the insured for his pro rata share of such loss.

Notice and Proof of Loss. The requirement in fire insurance contracts for notice of loss and proof of loss is a condition subsequent after the insurer's liability for loss has become fixed by the occurrence of loss. Because the law does not favor forfeitures unless the parties specifically so provide in their contract, failure to give the notice or proof of loss as required by the contract does not cause the contract to be forfeited, unless there is an express contract provision to the contrary. If the policy provides for an immediate notice of loss, the word "immediate" is interpreted to mean a reasonable period of time after the loss has occurred by the exercise of due diligence. Such notice of loss must indicate the nature and extent of such loss. The purpose of notice of loss is to inform the insurer of the loss so that he may protect the property from further loss; and the purpose of proof of loss is to inform the insurer of the extent of his liability on such loss and to give him an opportunity to ascertain the correctness of the loss alleged. In most courts, the requirement of notice and proof of loss is not considered to be a condition subsequent causing forfeiture for their nonobservance. This discussion of notice and proof of loss is applicable equally to life insurance.

Beneficial Interests. The insured of a fire insurance policy is entitled to the proceeds on the occurrence of loss, provided he has an insurable interest in the property insured at the time of the loss. On the issuance of a mortgage it is usual to provide that the mortgagor must insure the mortgaged property for the benefit of the mortgagor and the mortgagee. Fire insurance policies contain one of two types of mortgage clause. Under the type which designates the mortgagee as the payee as his interest may appear, sometimes called an "open mortgage" or "loss payable" clause, the mortgagee is merely a beneficiary of the policy; he is not a party to the insurance contract and the continuance of his interest in the policy depends upon the performance or default of the mortgagor insured. Under the other type, often known as a "standard" or "union" mortgage clause, a contract is created between the insurer and the mortgagee whereby the policy will not lapse by reason of the mortgagor's default but the mortgagee can pay the premium; most courts hold the mortgagee is under no obligation so to pay, while other courts hold the mortgagee is obligated so to pay, the premium. In both types of mortgage clause, the mortgagee is a third party creditor beneficiary of the insurance contract and he can recover on the same.[2] Fire insurance policies with a mortgage clause usually provide that, in the event of loss, the proceeds will be applied first to the mortgagee in satisfaction of the mortgage debt and any surplus will be paid to the owner of the property. If the policy does not provide for payment to the mortgagee, the mortgagee has no interest in the policy; however, the mortgagee may become a judgment creditor and then be able to reach the proceeds owing to the mortgagor under the policy. If the mortgagee carries fire insurance on the mortgaged premises, the insurer's payment to the mortgagee for loss that has occurred subrogates the insurer to the mortgagee's claim against the mortgagor. The right of subrogation does not exist in accident or life insurance.

---

[2] See above, pp. 97 ff.

Assignment. Whether or not a fire insurance *contract* is assignable depends upon the terms of the contract and when, and to whom, assignment is to be made. Assignment may occur before or after loss covered by the policy has occurred. Because a fire insurance contract is a *personal contract* between the insurer and the insured, whether or not it is assignable *before loss* depends upon to whom assignment is to be made. Assignment *before loss* cannot be made to a purchaser of the entire insurable interest of the insured in the subject matter covered by the contract without the consent of the insurer. Consent by the insurer creates a novation, the new contract having the insurer and the assignee (thereafter he is the insured) as parties and containing the same terms as the old contract. Assignment before loss for the purpose of security to an assignee with an insurable interest in the property insured (e.g., assignment of the contract to a mortgagee of the insured property) may be made without the consent of the insurer, as long as the insured retains an insurable interest in the property insured. *After loss,* the contract claim for the loss may be assigned without the consent of the insurer, just as any other chose in action may be assigned.

If the fire insurance contract is assigned and the insurer does not consent to the assignment when such consent is required, the insured is entitled to a refund of the unearned premium, the insurer retaining the customary short rate of insurance premium for the period during which the insurance was in effect. It is for this reason that vendors of insured property acquire the consent of the insurer to the assignment of the policy to the vendee, so that the lower rate of insurance for the longer period of time will result in a more favorable adjustment in the purchase price in favor of the vendor when the sale takes place.

Cancellation. Fire insurance policies usually provide for a few days' advance notice of the intention of a party to cancel the policy. Such notice may be waived by either party. On cancellation, the unearned portion of the premium paid is to be returned to the insured after the insurer has retained the customary short rate of insurance premium.

Life Insurance The liability of the insurer is determined by the termination of the life insured and by the terms of the policy fixing the extent of the insurer's liability. Life insurance contracts exclude insurer liability for termination of the life insured in but few instances, such as: death caused by the commission of a crime; death caused by, or while in, military service in time of war; execution as punishment by the state or federal government; suicide within the period of time specified in the policy; and death caused by an airplane in which one is a passenger under the circumstances specified in the contract. The occurrence of death during the commission of a crime, or while in military service during time of war (if the contract excludes death *caused by,* but does not exclude death *while in,* military service), but not caused by *such* fact does not exempt the insurer from such liability under the policy for such death. Life insurance policies usually exclude liability for death caused by suicide within a specified period of time. Such suicide clauses are interpreted by most courts to mean that the insurer is liable if the person was insane at the time of such suicide; suicide while insane is a risk not excluded from the policy. In the absence of any clause in a policy excluding liability for death by suicide, in most states suicide is included as one of the insurer's risks. It should be noted in passing that subrogation is inapplicable to life insurance because no accurate valuation can be placed on human life.

Incontestable Clause. It is usual for life insurance policies to include an *incontestable clause* which provides that after the expiration of a certain period of time the policy is incontestable, except as otherwise provided therein. The purpose of such a clause is to induce people to acquire life insurance policies and thereby be relieved of the fear that the policy will be avoided on the termination of the life insured or that payment thereon will be contested. Unless the defense of suicide is expressly reserved and excepted from the incontestable clause, such clause includes suicide. Defenses which are not excluded by the incontestable clause are: those so stated in the policy; lack of an insurable interest on the part of the insured; failure to give proof of loss as provided in the policy; and the loss was a risk excepted from the terms of the policy.

Beneficiary. The beneficiary of a life insurance contract may be the insured or some other person. The beneficiary is not required to have an insurable interest in the life insured if the insured had an insurable interest at the time the contract was made; it is not necessary that the insured's insurable interest exist at the time of the policy's maturity. A common example is the issuance of life insurance to a partnership or a corporation on the life of a partner or of an officer or director in the corporation and, at the time of death, the insured did not have his previous business status. A beneficiary has a vested interest in a life insurance policy if the insured has not reserved the right to change the beneficiary. However, if such right has been reserved, the beneficiary is an expectant beneficiary whose rights under the contract may be terminated at the will of the insured.

Assignment. Unlike a fire insurance contract, a life insurance contract is assignable without the consent of the insurer. If the beneficiary is the insured or his estate, or if the beneficiary is a third person and the insured has reserved the right to change the beneficiary, such insurance contract may be assigned without any difficulty. However, if the beneficiary is a third person and the insured has not reserved the right to change the beneficiary, the beneficiary has a vested interest in the insurance contract which cannot be assigned without his consent. In the absence of statute to the contrary, a beneficiary with a vested interest in the insurance contract may assign his interest. An assignment of the insurance contract or of an interest therein must be accomplished as provided by the terms of the insurance contract. Life insurance contracts usually provide that the insurer is not affected by an assignment of the insurance contract until the insurer receives notice of the assignment.

Creditors. Creditors of the insured may, on obtaining judgment, resort to the assets of the insured in satisfaction of their claims. The insured's interest in a life insurance contract is an asset. However, under the law of insurance, if the beneficiary is a third person and the insured has reserved the right to change the beneficiary, by state statute the creditors cannot reach this power or right and cannot cause the beneficiary to be changed so that the proceeds of the policy will be made available to them. Under the Bankruptcy Act, the insured's right to change the beneficiary passes to the trustee in bankruptcy; but, inasmuch as a bankrupt's assets exempted from inclusion in his estate available to creditors by state law is exempt from inclusion in his estate in bankruptcy and, therefore, is unavailable to the trustee in bankruptcy, almost all states by statute have exempted all or part of the proceeds from life insurance contracts as unavailable to creditors, with the result that, to such extent, the trustee in bankruptcy also cannot reach the exempted proceeds. If the right to change the beneficiary has not been reserved, there is no interest of the bankrupt in the policy available to the creditors. The insured's fraudulent transfer of his interest in a life insurance policy may be set aside by his creditors, just as any other transfer fraudulent as to creditors.

When premiums are paid by the insured from embezzled funds, there is a constructive trust of the proceeds of the policy in favor of the person from whom the funds were embezzled. However, the extent of the interest of such person depends upon whether all the premiums were paid with such embezzled funds or whether the first premium at least was paid by the insured without embezzled funds. In the former instance, the beneficiary is a constructive trustee of the proceeds in favor of the person from whom such funds were embezzled. In the latter instance, there is conflict on whether there is a constructive trust of the proceeds only to the extent of the amount embezzled (with interest) and used to pay the premiums, or to the extent that the embezzled money contributed to the proceeds of the policy. By statute in most of the states, the proceeds of a life insurance policy in a reasonable amount on which the premiums were paid by an insolvent debtor husband, the beneficiary being the insured's wife or children, are exempt from his creditors, unless there was actual fraud on the part of the insured. If actual fraud is shown, then the creditors have an interest in the proceeds of the policy to the extent of the amount of the premiums paid while insolvent or such premiums and interest thereon.

Cancellation. Although the insured may cancel or surrender the policy, nevertheless, the insurer cannot do so. On the surrender of a life insurance policy, there is a reserve fund which has been accumulated from the premiums paid on the policy. The surrender value of the policy is determined by this reserve less a handling charge. Such surrender value is often called the "cash surrender value." In order to avoid forfeiture of policies for nonpayment of premiums, many policies include clauses which provide for the utilization of the cash surrender value to purchase paid-up insurance, or extended insurance (which is term insurance) in the same amount as the original policy for a period of time dependent upon the amount of the cash surrender value.

APPENDIX TO PART NINE

REFERENCES

1. Appleman, John A. *Insurance Law and Practice.* St. Paul, Minn.: West Publishing Co., 1965.
2. Keeton, Robert E. *Basic Text on Insurance Law.* St. Paul, Minn.: West Publishing Co., 1971.
3. Vance, William R. *Handbook on the Law of Insurance.* 3d ed., Buist M. Anderson. St. Paul, Minn.: West Publishing Co., 1951.

PROBLEMS

1. (a) A mortgaged his realty to B as security for the payment of A's debt to B.
   (1) Does B have an insurable interest in the mortgaged property? Why?
   (2) Does B have an insurable interest in the rest of A's property? Why?
   (3) Does B have an insurable interest in A's life? Why?
   (b) X, Y, and Z are partners. The partnership applied for and obtained life insurance on the life of Y, the policy naming the partnership as beneficiary. Later Y withdrew from the partnership but X and Z continued as partners and maintained the policy of insurance until Y's death.
   (1) Does the partnership have a right to the proceeds of the policy on Y's death?
   (2) Why?

2. (a) A insured his house against loss by fire, naming himself as beneficiary. A's house was mortgaged to B as security for the payment of A's debt to B. A sold the house to C and assigned his fire insurance policy to C without the consent of the insurance company. Subsequently, the house was damaged by fire.
   (1) Who has a right to enforce the policy?
   (2) Why?
   (b) Would the result have been any different if the sale and assignment had taken place subsequent to the fire? Why?

3. (a) What is a "binder"?
   (b) Distinguish a warranty from a representation.

894

(c) Distinguish insurance from wager.
(d) X failed to disclose material facts to Y Insurance Company in applying for a policy of life insurance. Y was ignorant of such material
facts and issued a policy of life insurance to X. A few months later
Y learned of such facts and declared that it avoided the policy.
(1) Is the policy voidable by Y?
(2) Why?
4. A fraudulently misrepresented to B Insurance Company that he had an insurable interest in certain property and obtained a policy of fire insurance
on the property from B. B subsequently learned of the fraud but continued
to receive the payment of premiums from A. The property was destroyed
by fire.
(a) Is B liable to A on the policy?
(b) Why?
5. (a) What is meant by the following kinds of insurance policies:
(1) Valued policy.
(2) Open policy.
(3) Blanket policy.
(4) Specific policy.
(5) Floating policy.
(b) X Insurance Company issued to B a policy insuring B's property from
loss by fire. Fire occurred damaging B's property.
(1) How is it determined whether the loss is total or partial?
(2) If it is an open policy, how is the extent of loss measured?
6. A has a policy of fire insurance on his property for $10,000. The policy con-
tained an 80 percent coinsurance clause. A's property was worth $20,000 at
the time it was damaged by fire to the extent of $8,000.
(a) How much can A recover under the policy?
(b) Explain your answer.
7. (a) What is meant by a pro rata clause in a fire insurance policy?
(b) Does failure to give notice or proof of loss as required by a fire insurance policy cause the policy to be forfeited? Why?
(c) Why should a vendor of property obtain the insurer's consent to assignment to the vendee of the policy of fire insurance on the property?
(d) Is it necessary that the beneficiary of an insurance policy have an insurable interest in the property or life insured? Why?
8. A obtained a policy of insurance on his life in which someone other than
the insured or his estate was named as the beneficiary.
(a) Does A have the right to assign such policy? Why?
(b) Does a creditor of A have a right to resort to the policy in order to
satisfy his claim?
(c) If A had embezzled funds from B and used them to pay premiums
on the policy and then A had died, does B have any right to the proceeds? Why?
(d) If A had paid premiums on the policy while he was insolvent, do A's
creditors have any rights against the proceeds of the policy on A's
death? Why?
(e) Can A or the insurer cancel or surrender the policy? Why?

SOME PREVIOUS C.P.A. LAW EXAMINATION
QUESTIONS AND MODEL ANSWERS

NOVEMBER, 1970

No. 1 (Estimated time—20 to 25 minutes)

Each of the following numbered sentences states a legal conclusion relating to the lettered material. You are to determine whether the legal conclusion is true or false according to the *general principles of insurance and property law.* Write on a separate sheet whether each conclusion is true or false. Your grade will be determined from your total of correct answers less a penalty for your incorrect answers; an omitted answer will not be considered an incorrect answer.

A. Mortimer, a C.P.A., was a sole public accounting practitioner. He applied for and obtained a $100,000 malpractice insurance policy from the Faithful Insurance Company.

    1. If Mortimer sells his practice, he may transfer to the buyer the insurance policy in exchange for the premium applicable to the unexpired portion of the policy.

    2. If Mortimer intentionally issues an unqualified auditor's opinion on financial statements he knows to be false, the insurance company will not be liable under the policy.

    3. If Mortimer admits a junior partner, the policy will automatically cover the new partnership.

    4. In the event the insurance company has to pay a claim to one of Mortimer's clients for Mortimer's negligence, the insurance company will be subrogated to the client's rights against Mortimer.

B. Williamson, Johnson, and Fox were partners in a public accounting firm. The firm purchased a $50,000 life insurance policy on the life of each of its partners to provide funds to purchase the partnership interest of a deceased partner. The partnership was named as the beneficiary and paid all premiums.

    5. Each partner owns the individual policy covering his life.

    6. The partnership has a valid insurable interest in the lives of its partners.

    7. The individual partners have an insurable interest in the lives of their partners.

    8. The voluntary withdrawal of one of the partners would require the partnership to surrender the policy for its cash surrender value.

    9. In the event of financial stress, the partnership could assign its interest in the policies to its creditors.

    10. If the firm went bankrupt, its creditors would have a prior claim to the insurance policies over the claims of creditors of the individual partners.

C. A C.P.A.'s client, Granite Flexible Tube Corporation, entered into a sale-and-leaseback agreement with the Greenleaf Foundation. The C.P.A.'s examination revealed the following: Under the terms of the contract Greenleaf purchased Granite's plant and warehouse for $750,000. Granite received $450,000 in cash, and Greenleaf assumed a $300,000 mortgage on the plant and warehouse held by the First State Bank. In addition, Granite obtained a 30-year lease on the property at an annual rental of $25,000.

    11. Granite has an insurable interest in the plant and warehouse.

12. Greenleaf has an insurable interest in the plant and warehouse.
13. First State Bank has an insurable interest in the plant and warehouse.
14. If Granite retained the same amount of fire insurance (full coverage) that it had prior to the sale of the plant and warehouse, it would not be entitled to recover more than the fair market value of its interest in the property at the time of destruction.

D. On January 1, 1967, Wilson Packing Company insured its plant, which had a fair market value of $220,000, with the Miracle Insurance Company for $200,000 on a standard fire insurance policy that included a 90 percent coinsurance clause. On the night of December 28, 1969, a fire started in an adjoining building, which was owned by the Star Chemical Company. The fire spread to Wilson Packing and partially destroyed the plant. The extent of the damage was determined to be $80,000, and the fair market value of the plant at the time of the loss was $240,000. In his examination of Wilson's financial statements for the year ended December 31, 1969, a C.P.A. is considering the effects of the fire and various related insurance aspects.

16. The coinsurance clause will not prevent Wilson from recovering the full amount of the loss ($80,000).
17. Assuming the building had been totally destroyed, Wilson could have recovered $180,000 from Miracle Insurance.
18. Assuming Wilson does not fully recover its loss from Miracle Insurance, it can recover from Star Chemical if Star's negligence caused the fire.
19. Wilson may not assign its right of recovery under the Miracle policy to its creditors.
20. Miracle, to the extent it pays Wilson under the Wilson policy, will be subrogated to Wilson's rights against any third party who may have wrongfully caused the fire.
21. If the fire had been caused by the negligent maintenance of Wilson's heating and electrical equipment, Miracle would not have been obligated to pay on the policy.
22. If Wilson negotiated a partial settlement with Star Chemical and gave Star a complete release from liability, Miracle would not be obligated to pay on the policy.
23. To avoid the operation of the coinsurance clause, periodic valuations of the insured property should be made and the insurance coverage increased accordingly.

E. Warren applied for $50,000 of life insurance with the Gem Life Insurance Company. He filled in the application and arranged for a physical examination. The application contained a clause which stated:
Coverage of the insured will begin only upon delivery of the policy to the applicant in good health.

24. Even without the above clause, physical delivery of the policy is a prerequisite to the making of a contract of insurance.
25. Such clauses have been held invalid as against public policy by the majority of states.
26. Receipt of the policy by Warren while suffering from a common cold would not bar recovery, even though the cold developed into pneumonia which caused Warren's death.

27. If Warren died in an auto accident before delivery of the policy, there would be no recovery against Gem on the policy.

F. Marshall owned a seven-story office building. He occupied one floor and rented the remaining floors. He originally insured the property against fire with the Superior Fire and Casualty Company for $200,000. Subsequently he took out another policy with the Freedom Fire Insurance Company for the same amount. The property was totally destroyed by fire and it has been agreed by all parties that at the time of the loss the fair market value of the building was $300,000. Both policies contained the standard pro rata liability clause. Marshall's C.P.A. is studying the policies in order to prepare himself for a discussion with his client and his client's attorney.

28. Marshall will collect a total of $300,000.

29. Superior will be liable for $200,000 since it was the original insurer.

30. In the event that Superior was insolvent and unable to pay more than $100,000 on the Marshall policy, Freedom would be obligated to pay $200,000.

Answer

1. False	7. True	13. True	20. True	26. True
2. True	8. False	14. True	21. False	27. True
3. False	9. True	16. False	22. True	28. True
4. False	10. True	17. False	23. True	29. False
5. False	11. True	18. True	24. False	30. False
6. True	12. True	19. False	25. False	

MAY, 1965

No. 5

a. C Corporation owned two pieces of realty known respectively as Blackacre and Whiteacre. C Corporation concluded an oral contract for the sale of Blackacre with building to Byer. The closing date was set ninety (90) days after the agreement; at that time the purchase price and deed were to be exchanged. Immediately upon concluding the oral contract, Byer paid to G Fire Insurance Company the premium on a standard fire insurance policy covering the Blackacre building. Twenty days later the Blackacre building was completely destroyed in a fire of unknown origin. Byer duly notified the insurance company of the loss.

Can Byer recover from the insurance company? Explain.

b. C Corporation procured from E Life Insurance Company a $20,000 policy on the life of its president, Bilder, whose annual compensation averaged $30,000. Bilder stated in the application that his age was 40 years when in fact he was 47 years old. Three months later Bilder left the employment of the Corporation. Two months following his termination of employment, he died.

Is the Corporation entitled to collect on the policy held on Bilder's life? Explain.

c. Arthur carries two policies with the X Insurance Company. One is upon his life; the other is upon his home. His next door neighbor was burning trash and negligently left the fire unattended and improperly safeguarded. The fire passed over to Arthur's property and destroyed his home. In trying to put out the fire, Arthur lost his life. The Insurance Company paid the decedent's estate the amount of the two policies and seeks to hold the neighbor liable for such payments on the ground of subrogation.

Will it succeed? Explain.

d. Roger owned the manuscript of a famous author's book that he insured with the Z Insurance Company against loss, including "all direct loss or damage by fire." In the course of rearranging his library, Roger negligently placed the manuscript with some magazines he intended to burn. The manuscript and magazines were thrown by Roger into a trash burner and were completely destroyed by the fire. Roger seeks to collect the proceeds from the insurance policy covering the manuscript.

Will he succeed? Explain.

Answer

a. No. It is essential to a contract of fire insurance that the insured have an insurable interest in the property. A person has an insurable interest in property if he will suffer pecuniary loss by its destruction or impairment, or benefit from its preservation. A person has an equitable interest in land which is the subject of an enforceable contract for its sale to him. A contract for the sale of land is unenforceable unless there is a writing. Here, the contract for the sale of Blackacre to Byer was oral and there was no written memorandum thereof. Since the contract is unenforceable, Byer has no insurable interest. Therefore, the purported contract of fire insurance is void and Byer cannot recover on it.

b. Yes, but not the face amount. It is essential to a life insurance contract that the insured have an insurable interest in the life insured. An insurable interest in life is determined by the relationship existing between the insured and the person whose life is insured. If the relationship is such that the insured has a reasonable expectation of deriving a benefit by the continuance of the life insured or suffering loss by its termination, the insured has an insurable interest in the life insured. Here, at the time the insurance was taken out, the C Corporation had an insurable interest in the life of its president because it would benefit from his existence, and suffer loss by his death in loss of time, effort and money in obtaining a replacement. It is unimportant that the insurable interest does not exist at the time of death; it must exist only at the time the contract of insurance was made. The premium was paid at the time of Bilder's death, so the insurance is in effect at the time of Bilder's death and the corporation can recover on it.

Although formerly a misrepresentation of age caused the policy to be voidable by the insurer, today in most states the policy is not voidable on this ground and payment is made by the insurer on death in an amount of what coverage the premium paid would provide for the person on the basis of correct age. This would be the extent of the corporation's recovery on the policy here, on Bilder aged 47.

c. Yes, in connection with the property insurance; no, in connection with the life insurance. The insurer of property is subrogated to the insured's rights against a wrongdoer who caused the loss of the insured property for which the insurer has paid under the policy. Here, the neighbor's negligence proximately caused the fire and loss of Arthur's insured house and, therefore, on payment to Arthur for such loss the insurance company is subrogated to Arthur's claim against his neighbor.

However, subrogation is inapplicable to life insurance because no accurate valuation can be placed on human life. But Arthur's estate can recover not only on the life insurance policy but also against the wrongful neighbor for Arthur's death.

d. No. A contract of fire insurance insures only against loss caused by a hostile fire. A fire is hostile when it is burning in a place where it was not intended to burn. Here, the fire was friendly and not hostile in that it was burning where it was intended to burn, the trash burner. Since the insured manuscript was not destroyed by a hostile fire, there is no loss covered by the policy and the insurance company is not liable.

PART TEN

REAL PROPERTY

I. *Nature and Transfer of Interests in Land* (903–920)
  1. *Nature of interests in land* (903–904)
    a. *Concept of property* (903)
      (1) *Interests* (903)
      (2) *Land* (904)
        (a) *Fixtures* (904)
    b. *Estates in land* (904)
      (1) *Interests which are estates in land* (904–905)
        (a) *Freehold estates* (905)
        (b) *Nonfreehold estates* (905)
      (2) *Some interests which are not estates in land* (905–907)
        (a) *Easements* (906)
        (b) *Covenants running with the land* (907)
        (c) *Natural rights* (907)
    c. *Rights of each estate* (907–912)
      (1) *Estate in fee simple* (907)
      (2) *Life estates* (907)
      (3) *Estate for years* (908)
      (4) *Tenancy at will* (911)
      (5) *Tenancy from period to period* (911)
      (6) *Tenancy at sufferance* (912)

  2. *Transfer of ownership* (912–920)
    a. *Forms of ownership* (912–915)
      (1) *Severalty* (912)
      (2) *Joint tenancy* (912)
      (3) *Tenancy in common* (913)
      (4) *Tenancy by entirety* (914)
      (5) *Community property* (914)
    b. *Methods of transferring ownership* (915–920)
      (1) *By agreement* (915–917)
        (a) *Kinds of deed* (916)
        (b) *Contents of deeds* (917)
      (2) *On death, by will or by intestacy* (917)
      (3) *By adverse possession* (917)
      (4) *By judicial process* (920)
      (5) *By eminent domain* (920)

NATURE AND TRANSFER OF INTERESTS IN LAND

1. *NATURE OF INTERESTS IN LAND*

Concept of Property   **Interests.** THE different concepts of the word "property," to which reference should be made at this time, have been discussed previously.[1] Usually, the word "property" is used in the sense of describing some thing, such as a tangible thing (e.g., land, chattels) or an intangible thing (e.g., a right, as a contract right). For example, a person may claim that a horse is his property, meaning that the horse is property. Technically, property describes an interest in some thing; the thing is the object of property. For example, a person may claim that he has title to a horse, meaning that he owns the full or general interest in the horse. Under this concept of property, an owner of property is a person who has an interest in some thing. Because the word "property" usually is used to describe a thing rather than an interest in a thing, throughout this book the word "property" refers to a thing rather than to an interest in a thing, except when otherwise indicated. In the law of real property, however, *the word "property" is used in its technical sense as an interest in land,* and, accordingly, it is used in this sense *throughout this chapter.*

The broadest classification of property is "real property" and "personal property." The term "real property" describes a particular kind of interest in land called a "freehold," which is an interest in land for a period of time the termination of which cannot be measured or computed exactly in terms of years, months, and days, and which is not terminable at the will of the transferor.[2] An interest in land which is not a freehold is called a "chattel real," e.g., a tenant's interest in land by reason of his lease. All chattels real and all interests in movables—i.e., tangible things other than land and intangible things—are called "personal property."

---

[1] See above, pp. 170 f.

[2] American Law Institute, *Restatement: Property,* 1936, sec. 8.

Land. Land means the surface of the earth (whether soil or water) and that which is affixed to it permanently, that which is below it, and the space above it, in the absence of statute or judicial decision to the contrary.

Fixtures. A fixture is a chattel which has been so annexed to the land that it becomes a permanent part thereof.[3] Whether or not a chattel is a fixture is determined generally by the following tests: Is the chattel so physically attached to the land or of such a nature as an improvement that it is permanently a part of the land, and removal of the fixture would materially damage the land or a structure which is a part thereof; and is it the intention of the annexor, i.e., the party affixing the chattel, that it is to be a permanent part of the land? If the tenant annexes a chattel to the land and its removal would not substantially damage the land or destroy the chattel, generally as between the tenant and the landlord the chattel is not permanently annexed to the land and is not a fixture. This type of chattel formerly was called a "trade fixture" and, like a "domestic fixture," is removable by the tenant. Inasmuch as fixtures constitute a part of the land, they are not removable by the tenant without the consent of the landlord; and their improper removal damages the reversion of the landlord. If the duration of the lease is definite, the tenant must exercise whatever right he has to remove fixtures before the expiration of the term but no later than his surrender of possession of the premises. If the duration of the lease is indefinite, the tenant has a reasonable time after its termination in which to remove the fixtures. The landlord may cause fixtures to become chattels by his severance of them from the land. Until such severance, they are a part of the land, except that a contract for their sale contemplates severance and, for the purpose of the contract, they are considered as personal property.[4]

Estates in Land   Interests in land are distinguished from each other by whether or not they are estates in land. An estate in land is an interest in land which is, or may become, possessory and which is measured by duration of time.[5] Some interests in land are estates in land, while others are not. First those interests in land which are estates in land, and then a few common illustrations of interests in land which are not estates in land, will be considered.

Interests Which Are Estates in Land. Interests in land which are

---

[3] See above, pp. 733, 758–60.

[4] See above, p. 169.

[5] See American Law Institute, *Restatement: Property,* 1936, sec. 9.

estates in land vary, principally, as to their duration. A freehold estate is for a period of time the termination of which cannot be measured or computed exactly in terms of years, months, and days, and it is not terminable at the will of the transferor. An estate less than a freehold exists for an ascertainable period of time or is terminable at the will of the transferor.

Freehold Estates. Freehold estates may be divided into those estates which pass to the owner's heirs or devisees,[6] called "estates of inheritance," and those estates which are not inheritable. The usual type of inheritable freehold estate is the "estate in fee simple." There are two kinds of freehold estates which are not inheritable. One is an estate for the life of the owner of the estate who is called a "life tenant." (A owns land and conveys the land to B for the life of B.) The other is an estate *"pur autre vie,"* which is for the life or lives of a person or persons other than, or in addition to, the life tenant. (A owns land and conveys the land to B for the life of C and D, or A conveys the land to B for the life of B and C.) A life estate, whether for the life of the tenant or *pur autre vie,* may be created in two ways. One way is by the act of the owner of the land, e.g., his delivery of a deed to the grantee, in which case it is called a "conventional life estate." Another way is by operation of law, e.g., the estates of dower and of curtesy, in which case it is called a "legal life estate." An estate of dower is the widow's life estate in a portion of the land of her deceased husband. An estate of curtesy is the surviving husband's life estate in the land of his deceased wife. Today, by statute, dower and curtesy are largely abolished and, in their place, provision is made for statutory interests of husband and wife in each other's estates.

Nonfreehold Estates. Estates less than a freehold estate are often called "tenancies." Such tenancies may be an estate or tenancy for years, a tenancy at will (meaning that it is terminable at the will of the landlord or of the tenant), a tenancy from period to period, or a tenancy at sufferance.[7]

Some Interests Which Are Not Estates in Land. Easements, covenants running with the land, natural rights of a landowner, and

---

[6] "Devisees" are those persons to whom a freehold estate in land passes on the death of the owner as provided in the decedent owner's will. "Heirs" has two meanings. The older meaning refers to those persons to whom a freehold estate in land passes directly on the death of the owner by operation of law and not by the decedent owner's will. Today, under statutes of descent and distribution in connection with decedents' estates, "heirs" refers to those persons to whom property, whether real or personal, passes on the death of the owner by operation of law and not by the decedent owner's will.

[7] Herbert T. Tiffany, *A Treatise on the Modern Law of Real Property* (New abridged ed., Carl Zollman; Chicago: Callaghan & Co., 1940), sec. 31.

liens on land (e.g., real property mortgages) are illustrations of interests in land which are not estates in land. A brief discussion of the first three of these interests may be helpful.

Easements. An easement is an interest in adjoining land without any right of profit in such adjoining land. The land with the interest is called the "dominant tenement," and the land subject to the easement is called the "servient tenement." An example is a right of way over the servient tenement as a means of access to, and egress from, the dominant tenement. *An easement is a right inherent in ownership of the dominant tenement and passes with the dominant tenement on the transfer of such ownership.* A purchaser of the servient tenement becomes the owner thereof subject to the easement. An easement is distinguishable from a license, which is a permission to use or possess land but which is not an interest in the land and which is revocable at any time by the landowner, who is called a "licensor"; the person to whom the license has been given is called the "licensee." If the license is coupled with an interest, it is irrevocable; e.g., a license to deposit chattels upon the licensor's land gives to the licensee the irrevocable right to enter upon the land and remove the chattels. The license is a privilege personal to the licensee; it cannot be assigned by him, and it is not inheritable.

An easement may be created in various ways. An easement may be created expressly or impliedly[8] by the owner of the servient tenement. It may be created also by "prescription," which is the name given to the acquisition of an incorporeal hereditament—i.e., an intangible inheritable interest in land—by open and continuous possession and use of land under a claim of right to such for a statutory period of time.

An easement may be terminated in various ways: the cessation of the purpose of the easement; the merger of the ownership of the dominant and servient tenements; the release of the easement by the owner of the dominant tenement to the owner of the servient tenement; abandonment of the easement; prescription by the use of the servient

---

[8] An easement by necessity is an illustration of an implied easement. The circumstances under which a conveyance of one piece of land out of another piece of land are such as to create the implication that the former owner's right of use of both pieces of land as a unit was intended to continue in the conveyee who may exercise such right of user in the land not conveyed to the extent justified by the circumstances. Public policy favoring land utilization is the most important factor causing implication of an easement by necessity when land cannot be used effectively without such easement. Only as the conveyance expressly denies such an implication is the easement precluded. (O possesses a parcel of land contiguous to a highway and he conveys a part of the land to A, retaining a piece of the land completely enclosing the portion conveyed to A. Nothing in the deed refers to easements. A has an easement by necessity over O's land in order to reach the highway.)

tenement adversely to the easement; conveyance of the dominant tenement without a reservation of the easement, because an easement appurtenant to land cannot be separated from the dominant tenement; and purchase of the servient tenement without the purchaser's actual notice, or constructive notice by recording, of the easement.

Covenants Running with the Land. A "covenant" was a promise under seal at Common Law; but today, because the Common Law effect of the seal does not exist in most of the states, it also may be a promise not under seal. A "real covenant" is a covenant running with the land and is an obligation for the benefit of specific land which becomes one of the rights of ownership of that land and inures to each subsequent landowner; it runs with the land. For example, a clause in a deed provides that the premises shall not be used for a specified purpose. There must be privity of estate between the convenantor and the covenantee—e.g., mortgagor and mortgagee of the land under a mortgage creating an easement. A "personal covenant" is not concerned with land and is personal as between the covenantor and the covenantee. Examples of a personal covenant are the lessee's covenants to pay rent and to repair.

Natural Rights. A landowner has the right to have adjoining property used in a natural way so as not to interfere with his right of enjoyment of his land. Such a right is called a "natural right." He has no right to the passage of air or light, nor the right to a view; but he does have the right to have the air which comes to him be unpolluted. He also has the right to make reasonable use of water flowing on, through, or along the borders of, his land—such rights being relative to the rights of riparian owners. A landowner has the right to have his land remain in its natural state and to have lateral support by adjoining land, called the right to "lateral support."

Rights of Each Estate

Estate in Fee Simple. The owner of an estate in fee simple has all the property (often called "title") in the land. It is the largest and most comprehensive estate in land, and the owner may use and dispose of it as he wishes, provided he does not act contrary to law. The owner's property is subject to the rights of the state, which may sell it for unpaid taxes or which may exercise its right of eminent domain and thereby acquire the land for public use.

Life Estates. The life estates of curtesy and dower, created by operation of law, were described previously. Other life estates may be created by grant, i.e., by deed, or they may be created by will, i.e., by devise. The life tenant has the exclusive right to possession of the land and may institute possessory actions for interference with his right to exclusive possession. He is entitled to make reasonable use of the land and to retain the profits therefrom. However, he cannot injure the inheritance by the commission of "waste," which is the result of unreasonable use of the land. Timber on the land may be used for the repair and improvement of the property on the land and for firewood. The life tenant is entitled to the crops growing upon the land. He also has the right to assign all or any part of his estate. A life estate is an asset of the life tenant; and his creditors may proceed against it, sell it, and apply the proceeds in satisfaction of their claims. The life tenant has the duty of paying current taxes and his share of taxes for permanent improvements to the land, and he also has the duty to pay interest on encumbrances on the land. The life tenant is not required to make improvements to the property; but he is required, at his own expense, to make ordinary repairs to the property.

Estate for Years. An estate for years is an estate for any fixed period of time, the beginning and ending of which must be specified and certain—e.g., an estate for five years. The estate may be for one day or for one hundred years, as long as it has a specified beginning and ending. An estate for years is created by a conveyance called a "lease," which creates the relationship of lessor and lessee, or landlord and tenant. The interest of the lessee is for the duration of the estate; thereafter, possession reverts to the lessor, whose interest in the residue on termination of the estate is called a "reversion." If, after the termination of a preceding estate, the residue of an estate returns to the grantor, the interest in such an estate is a reversion; however, if the interest passes to someone other than the grantor, it is called a "remainder" and the owner of the remainder is called a "remainderman."

An estate for years is created by a "lease." "Lease" is an *inter vivos* conveyance of an estate in land, usually for years, for a term less than that held by the lessor, and is also referred to as the contract for such conveyance. An ordinary lease contains the names of the parties, a description of the premises, the estate term, provisions for the payment of rent, convenants and conditions, and the signatures of the parties; in states where the Common Law effect of the seal continues, the signatures must be under seal. A lease may be oral or in writing but, inasmuch as it conveys an interest in land, by statute in the various states a lease of an interest in land for more than a specified minimum period of time is within the statute of frauds, requiring a written contract of lease or a note or memorandum of the lease in writing signed by the party to be charged.

Rights and Duties—Possession and Enjoyment. The rights and duties of the lessor and lessee are determined by the lease. A lessee has the right to exclusive possession and quiet enjoyment of the premises. A provision in the lease that a party is to do or to refrain from doing something is a covenant, and a lessor impliedly covenants that he has title to the premises and that the lessee will have quiet enjoyment of them. Under the covenant of quiet enjoyment, the lessee has the right of noninterference with his possession by the lessor during the lessee's estate and by any third persons with title paramount to that of the lessor. The lessor does not undertake the duty to prevent interference with the lessee's possession by third persons who do not have a title paramount to the lessor. The lessee has the right to institute possessory actions for interference with his possession, and the lessor has the right to damages from third persons for their damage to his reversion. The lessor has the right to enter upon the premises in order to determine whether or not waste by the lessee has occurred and also for the purpose of making repairs.

The lessee takes the premises as he finds them, in the absence of an express covenant to the contrary. On the expiration of the term, the lessee's duty is to return such premises in the same condition as they were received, except for reasonable wear and tear. He is liable for use of the premises in an unreasonable manner causing waste. The lessor has the duty to inform the lessee of hidden dangers on the premises of which the lessor knows, or reasonably should know, at the time of the lease. His failure to do so, which causes harm or loss to the lessee, subjects the lessor to liability therefor.

Repairs. Unless the lease provides to the contrary, the lessee has the duty to make ordinary repairs to the premises and to keep them in good condition so that he may return them to the lessor in the same condition as when he received them. The lessor does not have the duty to make such repairs, unless he covenants to the contrary;[9] and he is not liable to third persons for injuries caused to them because of the lessee's negligence in failing to keep the premises in proper repair. If the lessor has convenanted to make repairs, he is then liable to third persons for any injuries to them caused by his failure to make proper repairs. If the lessor retains control over any part of the premises, whether used by the

---

[9] This principle of law is presently being questioned; e.g., whether a tenant has the right to withhold rent for the landlord's failure to repair.

lessor or by both the lessor and the lessee, the lessor has the duty of repair for such part and he is liable for injury caused by his failure to do so. If the lessor has covenanted to make repairs and has failed to do so, the lessee may: make such repairs and assert a right of reimbursement against the lessor; sue the lessor for damages caused by such failure; or, if such failure is substantial, he may treat the lessor's neglect as an eviction discharging the lessee from his duties under the lease. In the absence of a provision to the contrary in the lease, neither the lessor nor the lessee has the duty to make improvements on the premises, and the lessor is to pay the taxes on the premises.

Rent. The lessee covenants in a lease to pay a specified rent for the use and possession of the leased premises. The lessor's breach of his covenant of quiet enjoyment discharges the lessee from his duty to pay rent. The lessee's failure to pay the rent when due is a breach of covenant creating a right in the lessor to dispossess the lessee.

Assignment and Subletting. The lessee may assign his interest in the lease or sublet the premises, unless the lease expressly prohibits such assignment or sublease, and the lessor may assign his reversion. *By an assignment the lessee transfers his entire term to the assignee, while in a sublease the lessee transfers to the sublessee a part of his term.* Each assignee of the lessor and the lessee, respectively, acquires the rights and duties of his assignor and may enforce the covenants running with the land and conditions of the lease. An involuntary assignment of the lease may occur by operation of law—e.g., the bankruptcy or death of the lessee. The trustee in bankruptcy acquires the rights of the lessee and, an estate for years being personal property, the legal representative of the decedent lessee's estate acquires the benefit of the lease. Neither the lessor nor the lessee by assignment may avoid liability to each other under the lease. *When the lessee parts with only a portion of his estate so that he has a reversion for the remainder, the transaction is a sublease.* A prohibition against assignment of the lease does not prohibit subletting unless it, too, is expressly prohibited. Similarly, a prohibition against subletting of the lease does not prohibit assignment unless it, too, is expressly prohibited. The sublessee is a tenant of the lessee and has no contractual obligations to the lessor, unless a novation[10] has occurred. No rights or duties are owing between the lessor and the sublessee. However, subletting does not release the lessee from his duties to the lessor nor is the lessor precluded from asserting his rights; e.g., the lessor may dispossess or evict the sublessee for nonpayment of rent due and unpaid by the lessee.

---

[10] For a discussion of novation, see above, pp. 144–45.

Termination. An estate for years may be terminated in a variety of ways. The expiration of the term terminates the estate. If the lease expressly provides for forfeiture for breach of a specified covenant or condition, then the occurrence of such breach terminates the term by forfeiture. The lease may provide for termination of the estate on the occurrence of a contingency—e.g., the death of a particular person or the bankruptcy of the lessee. The lessee's surrender of his lease to the remainderman or to the owner of the reversion, which is accepted by such person, terminates the lease. The termination of the lessor's term terminates the lease, inasmuch as the lessor cannot create a term greater than that which he has. Neither the death of the lessor nor of the lessee terminates the lease, unless the lease provides to the contrary. The reversion is acquired by the heirs or devisees of the lessor as real property if it is an inheritable estate, or by the legal representative of the lessor's estate as personal property if it is not an inheritable estate; and the residue of the term is acquired by the legal representative of the lessee's estate as personal property. By statute in many states the rule of the Common Law has been changed, and the accidental destruction of the premises without the fault of the lessee gives to the lessee the right to surrender or abandon the lease.

An actual eviction is the physical ouster of the tenant by the landlord from full or partial possession of the rented premises. A constructive eviction is the nonphysical ouster of the tenant by the landlord by means of conditions controlled by the landlord which make continuance of the tenancy undesirable, difficult, uncomfortable, or unpleasant, and otherwise contrary to the purpose for which the lease was acquired.

Tenancy at Will. A tenancy at will is an estate in which the lessee acquires possession of land with the consent of the lessor, terminable at the will of the lessor or the lessee and which is not for any specified or certain period of time. The lessee is called a "tenant at will" because he is a tenant only so long as it is the will of the lessor. A tenancy at will may be terminated by the lessor or the lessee at any time. (A conveys land to B "to hold at the will of A." Either A or B may terminate the tenancy.) The tenant at will has the right to the reasonable use and occupation of the premises. In the absence of statute, no notice of termination of a tenancy at will is necessary. The death of either the lessor or the lessee terminates such tenancy.

Tenancy from Period to Period. A tenancy from period to period is an estate with no definite duration of time and in which rent is agreed to be paid from one period to another. It may exist from year to year, month to month, day to day, or any other period to period of time.

It commonly is a tenancy from year to year because, usually, the rent is payable from year to year; however, it may be payable from month to month or day to day. (A owns land and leases it to B for one year. At the end of the year, B continues in possession of the land *with A's consent* but without any agreement as to the duration of B's occupancy. B is a tenant from year to year.) A tenancy from period to period is terminable by the lessor or by the lessee *giving to the other proper notice of his intent to terminate the estate;* state statutes usually prescribe the manner and time of such notice.

Tenancy at Sufferance. A tenancy at sufferance is an estate which is created by a tenant holding over after the termination of his previous tenancy *without the consent of the lessor.* It differs from a tenancy at will because no consent of the lessor is required in a tenancy at sufferance. The landlord has the option to treat the tenant either as a trespasser or as a tenant from period to period on the terms of the previous tenancy which has terminated.

2. TRANSFER OF OWNERSHIP

Land may be owned, and ownership of it may be transferred, in various ways. First the various forms of ownership, and then some methods of transferring ownership, will be discussed.

Forms of Ownership   Land (also chattels and intangibles) may be owned in severalty, or concurrently with other persons by joint tenancy, tenancy in common, tenancy by entirety, or as community property. These will be considered briefly.[11]

Severalty. When an estate in land is owned by one person alone, it is owned in "severalty."

Joint Tenancy. Joint tenancy is a form of ownership of one estate in land by two or more persons as a unit and as one tenant. The persons or tenants in such a tenancy are called "joint tenants." *They have a unity of interest, title, time, and possession;* that is, they have an interest of the same duration which vested in them at the same time,

---

[11] It should be noted in passing that the need for co-ownership of housing in a multi-unit structure or plan of buildings with community living has been reflected in the co-operative plan of owning real estate and in the condominium. In the co-operative, the property is usually owned by a corporation with unit owners having stock or a membership and a lease of units. In the condominium, each member owns a unit in fee and is a tenant in common with the other members of the commonly used areas. State horizontal property acts regulate the legal status of the condominium.

and they all share in undivided possession. (A owns land and delivers to B and C a deed conveying the land "to B and C as joint tenants and not as tenants in common.") During their existence, joint tenants share the profits, use, and possession of the land. *The outstanding characteristic of joint tenancy is the right of survivorship,* so that on the death of a joint tenant the estate survives *as a unit* to the remaining joint tenants until only one tenant survives; and, on the latter's death, the estate passes either to his heirs or devisees if it is an inheritable estate, or to the legal representative of his estate if it is not inheritable. The destruction of one of the four unities of joint tenancy destroys the tenancy. Thus, the conveyance by one of three joint tenants of his interest to a fourth person has the following effect: the joint tenancy among the three joint tenants is terminated; the other two joint tenants continue to hold their interest by joint tenancy; and the fourth person becomes a tenant in common with the two joint tenants. If one of two joint tenants conveys his interest to a third person, the joint tenancy is terminated and the other former joint tenant and the third person become "tenants in common" in possession of the land. Inasmuch as the Common Law reason favoring joint tenancy as a form of ownership does not exist today, by legislation and by judicial decision *a conveyance or devise of an estate in land to two or more persons is construed, generally, to be a tenancy in common and not a joint tenancy, in the absence of a manifested intent to the contrary.* By statute, some states have abolished the right of survivorship and some states have abolished joint tenancy as a form of ownership.

Tenancy in Common. Tenancy in common is a form of ownership by more than one person who own various estates in the same land (e.g., one has a fee simple, another has a life estate), all of the tenants having a unity of possession. Each tenant owns a separate estate, but all the tenants have an undivided interest in the possession of the same land. The unity of interest, title, and time required for a joint tenancy is not required for a tenancy in common. Each tenant in common has the same interest as a tenant in severalty, except for the interest of possession which they all share. Conveyance by one tenant in common of his estate causes his grantee to become a tenant in common with his former tenants in common. There is no element of survivorship in a tenancy in common as there is in a joint tenancy, and, on the death of a tenant in common, the decedent's share in possession passes to his heirs or devisees, or to the legal representative of his estate, depending on whether or not his estate is inheritable. Inasmuch as each tenant has an undivided share in the possession, the tenancy is terminable either: by partition, whereby each tenant in common acquires the right to possess a separate portion of the land, each tenant becoming an owner in severalty; or by uniting all the interests in possession in one person, who thereby becomes an owner in severalty.

Tenancy by Entirety. Tenancy by entirety is a form of ownership by husband and wife who, but for their marital relationship, would be joint tenants. The Common Law concept of husband and wife as one person in law caused a conveyance or devise to them while they are husband and wife to vest the entire estate in them as one person. All the characteristics of a joint tenancy are present, except that the conveyance of either spouse alone to a third person cannot deprive the other spouse of the right of survivorship. A judgment creditor of one spouse alone cannot reach the judgment debtor's interest in the tenancy, but a judgment creditor of both spouses can reach their combined interests in the tenancy. Tenancy by entirety can be terminated by divorce or annulment of the marriage, which causes the parties to be either joint tenants or tenants in common; partition then is possible. Today, some states by statute have abolished tenancy by entirety as a form of ownership.

Community Property. The marital relationship has created another form of ownership by statute in several southwestern and western states, called "community property." This concept of ownership originated in the civil law and, as modified by the Common Law and by statute, exists today in those states and, in part, in the federal system of income taxation as applied to husband and wife. Under this concept, the property of spouses is either community property or the separate property of each. Husband and wife have a community of interest in property acquired during their marriage by their joint efforts, in the income and profits from that property, and in property exchanged for it, whether real or personal property. Such property is called "community property." Property acquired after marriage is presumed to be community property, unless shown to be separate property of either spouse, and all property not separate property is community property. Property acquired by either spouse before marriage, property acquired by either spouse after marriage by gift, will, or intestacy, and that property which is acquired by the exchange of such property, is separate property. Except for a few of these states, separate property includes the income and profits acquired during marriage from separate property.

The termination of the tenancy of community property and the transfer of interests in community property present difficulties. Community property cannot be partitioned, just as in tenancy by entirety, but divorce terminates the tenancy and partition then is possible. The extent to which community property and separate property are available to judgment creditors of either husband or wife, and the extent of the husband's control over community property, are complex and vary among the community property states. The death of either spouse causes the survivor to acquire at least half of the community property, the remaining half passing by the will or by the intestacy of the decedent, except as otherwise provided by statute in a few of these states.

Methods of Transferring Ownership Ownership of land may be transferred in various ways, of which the following will be considered: by agreement; on death, by will or intestacy; by adverse possession; by prescription; by judicial process; and by eminent domain.

By Agreement. Ownership of land may be transferred pursuant to an agreement between the parties, and it occurs by the delivery of a deed by the grantor to the grantee and by the grantee's acceptance of the deed. A deed is a signed writing under seal transferring ownership of land. Today, in most states, a deed is effective without a seal.

Delivery of the deed by the grantor to the grantee *and* acceptance of the deed by the grantee are absolutely necessary to effect a conveyance of ownership. Death of the grantor prior to delivery renders the deed inoperative. Delivery of the deed by the grantor to a third person for delivery to the grantee may be an absolute delivery or a delivery in escrow, depending on the terms of the delivery. If delivery is to be made by the third person to the grantee unconditionally and immediately on the expiration of a specified period of time or on the occurrence of an event which is certain to happen, the delivery is absolute; the deed is irrevocable by the grantor and by his death. If delivery is to be made by the third person (called an "escrow holder") to the grantee on the occurrence of a condition (e.g., payment by the grantee), it is a delivery in escrow; on failure of the condition the grantor is entitled to the return of the deed; but, pending such failure, the deed is irrevocable by the grantor or by his death, or by the death of the grantee. It should be noted that a purchaser, before finally closing the transaction with the seller, usually has his lawyer examine the abstract of title to ascertain the title of the seller. An abstract of title is a legal instrument describing, in chronological order, the history of ownership of particular land. Among the items found in an abstract are deeds, mortgages, and judgments. An abstract of title should not be examined by an accountant for the purpose of giving an opinion regarding the same, and an examination for this purpose should be made only by a lawyer. When a title search is made, the public records are searched carefully to determine who is the record owner of the land, all interests therein, and all encumbrances and restrictions thereon. Often the buyer of land obtains "title insurance," which is a contract of indemnity against loss or damage caused by defect or failure of title.

The delivery and acceptance of a deed is effective to create a conveyance as between the parties but, by statute in the various states, such a conveyance is void as to subsequent purchases for value without notice of the conveyance unless the deed was recorded in the proper place—usually the county clerk's office in the county where the land is located. While the statutes differ in the various states regarding the effect on creditors of a nonrecorded deed, nevertheless, in most states such a conveyance is void as to innocent judgment creditors or lien creditors; in some states it is void as to all innocent creditors. Under the "Torrens System" of registering titles in some states, a certificate of title issued pursuant to a court decree is conclusive concerning title and eliminates the necessity of the usual method of recording the deed. Liens and encumbrances are noted upon the certificate, and title is subject only to them. There is much dispute concerning the desirability of using the Torrens System.

Kinds of Deed. At Common Law, deeds of conveyance were either by "deed poll" or "deed indenture." The deed poll is executed only by the grantor and is the type of deed commonly used today. A deed indenture is a deed executed by both the grantor and the grantee. Three of the most common types of deed in common use today are the quitclaim deed, the bargain and sale deed, and the warranty deed. A quitclaim deed purports to convey whatever title the grantor has and contains no covenants by the grantor. Its purpose is to divest the grantor of any interest he might have and to clear title to a particular estate. A bargain and sale deed is a deed for a valuable consideration, although the consideration need not be stated in the deed. It conveys title but does not contain any covenants, or warranties. A warranty deed is a deed which conveys title and contains covenants and warranties by the grantor; following are five usual covenants found in a warranty deed: that the grantor has title to the estate; that the grantor has the right to convey the estate; that the estate is free from encumbrances, except those named in the deed, if any; that the grantee shall have quiet enjoyment; that the grantor will warrant and defend the title to the estate. The first three are personal covenants and do not run with the land, while the last two are covenants which run with the land and may be enforced by all subsequent grantees.

Contents of Deeds. A deed consists of the following parts: the premises, habendum clause, terms and conditions, covenants, words indicating the execution of the deed and the date, the signature and seal (in the few states where required) of the grantor, and the signatures of the witnesses attesting to the grantor's signature. The premises include: the names of the parties, namely, the grantor and grantee;[12] an explanation for the conveyance, if any; the consideration for the conveyance and an acknowledgment of its receipt;[13] the words of conveyance or the granting clause; and, lastly, a description of the land conveyed. The habendum clause defines and limits the estate conveyed and usually begins with the words "To have and to hold." The terms and conditions include any reservations, called a "reddendum," to the grantor and any conditions to the conveyance, e.g., a condition on which the estate shall terminate. The covenants may be of various kinds, e.g., covenant of quiet enjoyment or covenant against encumbrances. The deed is followed by a certificate of acknowledgment signed by some proper public officer with authority to take acknowledgments, which is a statutory requirement in many of the states. The acknowledgment authenticates the deed and, in many states, is required in order to have the deed recorded.

On Death, by Will or by Intestacy. As distinguished from a transfer between living persons—i.e., *inter vivos*—ownership may be transferred on the death of the owner. Transfer may be effected either by will of the owner or, in the absence of any will, by operation of law. By his will the owner, called the "testator" if a man or "testatrix" if a woman, devises his ownership of land to a person called a "devisee," effective on the owner's death. The maker of a will may revoke it at any time prior to his death; a will is ambulatory and operative only at the time of his death. A person who dies without a will has died "intestate." Ownership of inheritable real property is transferred by intestacy in accordance with the statutes of descent and distribution in each state, and it passes to the intestate's heirs in the order as provided by statute. In contrast, personal property passes to the legal representative of the intestate.

By Adverse Possession. Ownership or title to land may be acquired by actual, exclusive, and continuous possession of land under claim of right adverse or hostile to the true owner in an open and notorious manner for the statutory period of time, which varies among

---

[12] Misspelling of the grantee's name or the absence of required federal revenue stamps on a deed conveying real property does not invalidate the deed.

[13] If the consideration was not paid, nevertheless, the deed is valid.

Recorded at................o'clock........M., ...

Reception No............................. ....Recorder.

Recorder's Stamp

THIS DEED, Made this   day of

19   , between

of the   County of   , State of
Colorado, of the first part, and

of the   County o·   and State of
Colorado, of the second part:

WITNESSETH, That the said part   of the first part, for and in consideration of the sum of

DOLLARS

to the said part   of the first part in hand paid by the said parties of the second part, the receipt whereof is hereby confessed and acknowledged, ha   remised, released, sold, conveyed and quit claimed, and by these presents do   remise, release, sell, convey and quit claim unto the said parties of the second part, their heirs and assigns forever, not in tenancy in common but in joint tenancy, all the right, title, interest, claim and demand which the said part   of the first part ha   in and to the following described lot   or parcel   of land situate, lying and being in the County of   and State of Colorado, to-wit:

TO HAVE AND TO HOLD the same, together with all and singular the appurtenances and privileges thereunto belonging or in anywise thereunto appertaining, and all the estate, right, title, interest, and claim whatsoever of the said part   of the first part, either in law or equity, unto the said parties of the second part, their heirs and assigns forever, not in tenancy in common but in joint tenancy.

IN WITNESS WHEREOF, The said part   of the first part ha   hereunto set hand   and seal   the day and year first above written.

Signed, Sealed and Delivered in the presence of

....[SEAL]

....[SEAL]

....[SEAL]

STATE OF COLORADO,
            County of   } ss.

The foregoing instrument was acknowledged before me this   day of
19   , by

My commission expires

WITNESS my hand and official seal.

....

Notary Public.

No. 962 QUIT CLAIM DEED.—To Joint Tenants.—Bradford-Robinson Printing Company, 1824-46 Stout Street, Denver, Colorado

QUITCLAIM DEED

Recorded at................................o'clock................M., ...

Reception No..........................   ....Recorder.

RECORDER'S STAMP

THIS DEED, Made this   day of
19   between

of the   County of   and State of
Colorado, of the first part, and

of the   County of   and State of Colorado, of the second part:
WITNESSETH, that the said part   of the first part, for and in consideration of the sum of
DOLLARS,

to the said part   of the first part in hand paid by the said parties of the second part, the receipt whereof is
hereby confessed and acknowledged, ha   granted, bargained, sold and conveyed, and by these presents do
grant, bargain, sell, convey and confirm unto the said parties of the second part, their heirs and assigns forever, not
in tenancy in common but in joint tenancy, all the following described lot   or parcel   of land, situate, lying and
being in the   County of   and State of Colorado, to-wit:

TOGETHER with all and singular the hereditaments and appurtenances thereunto belonging, or in anywise
appertaining, the reversion and reversions, remainder and remainders, rents, issues and profits thereof; and all the
estate, right, title, interest, claim and demand whatsoever of the said part   of the first part, either in law or equity,
of, in and to the above bargained premises, with the hereditaments and appurtenances.
TO HAVE AND TO HOLD the said premises above bargained and described, with the appurtenances, unto the said
parties of the second part, their heirs and assigns forever. And the said part   of the first part, for   sel
heirs, executors, and administrators do   covenant, grant, bargain and agree to and with the said parties
of the second part, their heirs and assigns, that at the time of the ensealing and delivery of these presents
well seized of the premises above conveyed, as of good, sure, perfect, absolute and indefeasible estate of inheritance, in
law, in fee simple, and ha   good right, full power and lawful authority to grant, bargain, sell and convey the same in
manner and form aforesaid, and that the same are free and clear from all former and other grants, bargains, sales, liens,
taxes, assessments and encumbrances of whatever kind or nature soever,

and the above bargained premises in the quiet and peaceable possession of the said parties of the second part, their heirs
and assigns, against all and every person or persons lawfully claiming or to claim the whole or any part thereof, the said
part   of the first part shall and will WARRANT AND FOREVER DEFEND.
IN WITNESS WHEREOF the said part   of the first part ha   hereunto set   hand   and
seal   the day and year first above written.

Signed, Sealed and Delivered in the Presence of

....[SEAL]

....[SEAL]

....[SEAL]

STATE OF COLORADO, } ss.
County

The foregoing instrument was acknowledged before me this   day of
19   , by*

My commission expires   19   Witness my hand and official seal.

....
Notary Public.

No. 921. WARRANTY DEED—To Joint Tenants.—Bradford-Robinson Printing Company, 1824-46 Stout Street, Denver, Colorado

WARRANTY DEED

the states. The acquisition of title to land by this method is called a transfer by "adverse possession." Title to incorporeal hereditaments (e.g., a right of way)[14] may be acquired in the same manner as adverse possession, except that the possession is not required to be exclusive; it is sufficient if the user of the land asserts the rights as his own. The acquisition of title to incorporeal hereditaments in this manner is called a transfer by "prescription."

By Judicial Process. Title to land may be transferred by reason of a judicial proceeding. Under the Bankruptcy Act, the trustee in bankruptcy acquires title to the bankrupt's property as of the date of the filing of the petition in bankruptcy. A sale of land pursuant to the levy of a writ of execution, issued at the instigation of the judgment creditor, and the issuance of a deed by the sheriff or other proper public official conveys the title to the purchaser. A court decree in a proper legal proceeding effectively transfers title to land.

By Eminent Domain. A state has the power to appropriate land from private persons for public use on payment of proper compensation therefor, called the "right of eminent domain," and the exercise of this power transfers title to such land to the state. The proceedings by which this right is exercised are called "condemnation proceedings."

---

[14] See above, pp. 906–7.

APPENDIX TO PART TEN

REFERENCES

1. American Law Institute. *Restatement: Property.* 1936.
2. Burby, William E. *Handbook of the Law of Real Property.* 3rd ed. St. Paul, Minn.: West Publishing Co., 1965.
3. Thompson, George W. *Thompson on Real Property.* Indianapolis, Ind.: The Bobbs-Merrill Co., Inc., 1965.
4. Tiffany, Herbert T. *A Treatise on the Modern Law of Real Property.* New abridged ed., Carl Zollman. Chicago: Callaghan & Co., 1940.

PROBLEMS

1. (a) What is the meaning of "property"?
   (b) Distinguish real property from personal property.
   (c) What is the meaning of "chattel real"?
   (d) What is meant by a conventional life estate?
   (e) What is meant by "dower" and "curtesy"?
2. A is a life tenant of land.
   (a) If A is unlawfully dispossessed by someone other than the remainderman, does the life tenant have the right to a possessory action for such dispossession? Why?
   (b) Does A have the right to crops or timber growing on the land?
   (c) May A assign his entire life estate? Why?
   (d) May A's creditors proceed against his life estate in satisfaction of their claims? Why?
   (e) Does A have the duty to pay for the following, do not explain:
      (1) Current taxes on the land?
      (2) Permanent improvements to the land?
      (3) Interest on encumbrances on the land?
      (4) Ordinary repairs to the land?
3. (a) Distinguish reversion from remainder.
   (b) What is an "estate for years"?
   (c) What are the contents of a lease?
4. (a) A leases land to B, who is unlawfully dispossessed by C, who causes damage to the land. What rights do A and B each have against C?
   (b) X leases land to Y and fails to inform Y of a hidden danger on the premises known to X but unknown to Y, which causes injury to Y.

      (1) Does Y have any right against X?

      (2) Why?

    (c) The lessor covenanted to make repairs to the leased premises and failed to make necessary repairs. What are the rights of the lessee?

5. Write the numbers 1 to 10 in a column and write opposite each number the word *"True"* if the statement is true and *"False"* if the statement is not true. Reasons are *not* to be given.

    (1) The assignment of a lease of premises is not the same as subletting such premises.

    (2) A lessor may assign his reversion.

    (3) A lessee has the right to assign his lease without the consent of the lessor, unless the lease provides to the contrary.

    (4) An assignee of a lessor or lessee acquires the rights and duties of his assignor and may enforce the covenants running with the land and conditions of the lease.

    (5) Termination of the lessor's term terminates the lease.

    (6) Neither the death of the lessor nor of the lessee terminates the lease, unless the lease provides to the contrary.

    (7) Death of one of three joint tenants terminates the joint tenancy.

    (8) On the death of one tenant in common his interest in land passes to the surviving tenants in common.

    (9) Tenancy in common is terminable by agreement among the tenants.

    (10) A joint tenancy is terminable by a joint tenant disposing of his interest during his lifetime.

6. (a) What is a fixture, and what tests are used to determine if there is a fixture?

    (b) Distinguish an easement from a license.

    (c) Enumerate three ways by which ownership of land may be transferred.

    (d) How do a quitclaim deed, a bargain and sale deed, and a warranty deed differ from one another?

7. (a) A executed a deed conveying ownership of his land to B and delivered the deed to B, who accepted it and placed it in his safe-deposit box. If A then executed another deed to the property in favor of C and delivered it to C, is it possible for C to divest B of his title to the land? Explain.

    (b) Enumerate the contents of a deed.

    (c) What is meant by "eminent domain"?

SOME PREVIOUS C.P.A. LAW EXAMINATION QUESTIONS AND MODEL ANSWERS

MAY, 1971

No. 3 (Estimated time—16 to 20 minutes)

Each of the lettered statements of facts below is followed by numbered sentences that state legal conclusions relating to those facts. You are to determine whether each legal conclusion is true or false according to the *general principles of real property law*. Use a soft pencil, preferably #2, to blacken the appropriate space on the separate printed answer sheet to indicate your answer. Your grade will be determined from your total of correct answers less a penalty of approximately one half for each of your incorrect answers; an omitted answer will not be considered an incorrect answer.

A. Brown wished to raise some additional capital for his manufacturing business. Ames, his accountant, suggested that he mortgage his estate, Longacre. Brown then did this receiving a $10,000 loan from Central Bank and giving his mortgage bond in that amount. Brown neglected to advise either Ames or the bank that he previously had mortgaged Longacre to Collins who failed to record the mortgage. The bank promptly recorded its mortgage. In anticipation of his son Henry's wedding to Helen Smith, Brown deeded Longacre as a wedding gift to Henry Brown and Helen Smith. Henry and Helen recorded the deed and were married.

67. The deed to Henry and Helen created a tenancy by the entirety.

68. If Henry and Helen were married at the time they received the deed, the answer to item 67 would be different.

69. Either Henry or Helen may dispose of his or her interest in Longacre without the consent of the other.

70. If Henry and Helen were tenants by the entirety in Longacre and Helen dies first, Henry automatically becomes the owner of the entire estate even if Helen's will provides otherwise.

B. The Western Lumber Company owns a large tract of timberland. Unknown to Western, Skidmore has enclosed part of Western's tract with a fence, built a cabin upon it and plans to farm the land commercially. The applicable prescription period under local law is 15 years. Skidmore mistakenly believes that the land in question is part of the adjacent tract which he owns.

71. At the end of the prescription period, Skidmore will obtain title by adverse possession against Western.

72. If Skidmore should die before the end of the prescription period, his heirs must hold adversely against Western for an additional 15 years in order to acquire title by adverse possession.

73. If Skidmore merely occupies the land in question, but acknowledges that it is owned by Western, he cannot acquire title by adverse possession against Western.

C. Parker contracts to purchase Greenacre from Archer as a site for his factory. Prior to closing Parker discovers that there are liens for unpaid taxes against the property, that the property is subject to an easement of right of way and that the property is zoned for residential use. The contract of sale does not mention any of the foregoing.

74. Parker may decline to close the sale unless Archer pays and discharges the tax liens.

75. Parker must accept title subject to the easement of right of way.

76. Parker must accept title subject to the zoning restriction on the property.

77. If Parker accepts title without knowledge of the above facts and receives a full warranty deed from Archer, upon learning the facts he would have grounds for an action against Archer because of defects in the title.

78. If Parker took a quitclaim deed from Archer, the answer to item 77 would be the same.

D. Church and Jasper, C.P.A.s wish to relocate their offices. The lease on their present offices is for five years with three years to run and it contains a survival clause which provides that the tenant's liability shall survive the landlord's termination of the lease for a breach by the tenant. Their landlord is not agreeable to canceling the lease which also prohibts a sublease without the landlord's consent. Church and Jasper have a financially responsible and respectable prospective subtenant but have reason to believe that the landlord will not consent to a sublease.

79. If Church and Jasper sublease the premises without the landlord's consent, they will breach their lease and entitle the landlord to terminate the lease.

80. If the landlord terminates the lease under the circumstances described in item 79, Church and Jasper would not be liable to the landlord for any deficiency in rent for the balance of the term of their lease.

81. Regardless of the prohibition against subletting in their lease, Church and Jasper may assign their lease to a third party without breaching the lease.

82. Assuming that Church and Jasper are free to assign their lease, they will not be liable to the landlord under the lease for the performance of all of their obligations as tenants.

83. If the landlord consents to a subletting, the mere giving of such consent will relieve Church and Jasper of any further obligations under the lease.

84. If the landlord consents to a subletting, he may collect the rent due under the lease directly from the subtenant.

85. If Church and Jasper assign their lease, the landlord may not collect the rent due directly from the assignee.

E. Assume Church and Jasper have decided to remain in their present quarters until their lease expires on June 1. On May 15 they entered into a two-year lease for new office space with Bolt Realty Corporation to commence June 1. On May 25 Church and Jasper discover that the occupant of their new space, whose lease expires on May 31, has not vacated and does not plan to do so until June 15.

86. If the lease is silent on the point, Bolt Realty will not be liable to Church and Jasper for damages if Bolt is unsuccessful in evicting the old tenant before June 1.

87. If Bolt Realty takes no action against the old tenant and does not deliver possession on June 1, Church and Jasper are free to terminate the lease without liability to Bolt.

88. If Bolt Realty neglected to sign the lease but Church and Jasper had signed it, it would be enforceable against Bolt.

89. If Church and Jasper retain their old offices until June 15, their old landlord may elect to hold them as holdover tenants for an additional year.

90. In the circumstances described in item 89, the old landlord may evict Church and Jasper.

Answer

67. False	72. False	77. True	82. False	87. True
68. True	73. True	78. False	83. False	88. False
69. True	74. True	79. True	84. False	89. True
70. True	75. False	80. False	85. False	90. True
71. True	76. True	81. True	86. True	

MAY, 1962

No. 5

a. Mr. Lawrence rented an apartment in the Regency House. He was an elderly gentleman and felt the heat very badly. His apartment was fully air-conditioned and in this way he was able to stand the otherwise unbearable heat of the summer. The landlord was dissatisfied with the current rental and, although the lease had a year to run, insisted that Mr. Lawrence agree to an increase. Mr. Lawrence refused. In fact, he was desirous of leaving the Regency House but did not want to abandon the premises because he feared he would be liable for the balance of the term of the lease. The landlord attempted to force Mr. Lawrence to pay the increase by turning off the electricity and thereby stopping the apartment's air-conditioners. He also sent up heat on the hot days. After one week of such treatment Mr. Lawrence, claiming he had been evicted, moved out.

   (1) What is the difference between an actual and constructive eviction?

   (2) In this case, has there been an eviction? Explain.

b. George signed a two-year lease which contained a clause which expressly prohibited subletting. After six months George asked the landlord for permission to sublet the apartment for one year. The landlord refused. This angered George and he immediately assigned his rights under the lease to William. William was a distinguished gentleman and George knew that everyone would consider him a desirable tenant.

   (1) What is the difference between an assignment of a lease and a sublease?

   (2) Can George validly assign his lease of the apartment to William? Explain.

c. Henry leased an apartment for one year. The landlord sought an increase over the prior rental but the negotiations broke down. The year expired and Henry did nothing. He remained on the premises in the hope that he could continue under the old rental. There is no emergency rent law in force.

   (1) What is the type of tenancy under which Henry is currently occupying the premises?

   (2) What optional remedies does the landlord have in respect to Henry's occupancy of the premises?

Answer

a. (1) An actual eviction is the physical ouster of the tenant by the landlord from full or partial possession of the rented premises. A constructive eviction is the nonphysical ouster of the tenant by the landlord by means of conditions controlled by the landlord which make continuance of the tenancy undesirable, difficult, uncomfortable or unpleasant. For the tenant to claim a constructive eviction it is necessary that the tenant quit the premises promptly.

(2) Yes. Deprivation of electricity and, therefore, stopping the apartment's air-conditioners so essential to Lawrence's comfort under the circumstances, and forced heat in the room on hot days, both controlled by the landlord, together with Lawrence's prompt moving out after one week of such conditions, constituted a constructive eviction of Lawrence.

b. (1) By an assignment the lessee transfers his entire term to the assignee, while in a sublease the lessee transfers to the sublessee a part of his term and has a reversion for the remainder. Also, in a sublease the sublessee is a tenant of the lessee and has no contractual obligations to the lessor landlord, unless a novation has occurred. No rights and duties are owing between the lessor and sublessee.

(2) Yes. A prohibition against subletting of a lease does not prohibit assignment unless it, too, is expressly prohibited.

c. (1) Tenancy at sufferance.

(2) The landlord has the following optional remedies:
   (a) Treat the tenant as a trespasser.
   (b) Treat the tenant as a tenant from period to period, here from year to year under the terms of the expired lease.

PART ELEVEN

WILLS AND DECEDENTS' ESTATES

Chapter I

THE WILL

---

1. FORMAL REQUIREMENTS

THE transfer of ownership of property may occur during the lifetime of the owner and on his death. The law reflects the desire of society to be able to effect a transfer of ownership at the time of a person's death in accordance with the wishes of the deceased and provides the method of a "will." Failure to execute a will causes the decedent's real property (in the sense of its being an inheritable freehold estate in land) to vest in his heirs,[1] and his personal property (in the sense of its being an interest in a thing other than a freehold estate in land)[2] to be transferred to his legal representative for distribution, according to the laws of descent and distribution as provided by statute in each particular state. A person who executes a will is called a "testator," if it is a man, and a "testatrix," if it is a woman; and a person with a will dies "testate," while a person without a will dies "intestate."

Definition of a Will A "will" is a person's expression in proper legal form of his desires and directions concerning the distribution of his property at the time of his death. It often is called a "testamentary disposition" of his property. The following elements in the formation of a will are to be considered: the law applicable; the capacity of the testator; the testamentary intent of the testator; the writing; the testator's signature; and attestation.

Law Applicable The requirements for making a will are prescribed specifically by statute in each state and absolute compliance therewith is necessary. The law applicable to the making of a will is the law of the place where the testator was domiciled at the time of his death, except that, in the case of an interest in land being transferred under a will, the law of the place where the land is situated governs.

---

[1] For definition of "heirs" see above, p. 905, ftn. 6.

[2] For the concept of real and personal property, see above, p. 903.

929

Capacity of Testator

Any person with mental capacity and who is above the statutory age, usually 21 years or 18 years, has legal capacity to make a will. A person has mental capacity to make a will when he has the *ability* to understand and comprehend the nature and extent of his property, the disposition he is making of his property, and to remember his relatives.

Testamentary Intent

The contents of a will consist of any written (except for nuncupative wills) manifestation of the testator's intent thereby to make a will and to dispose of his property. His expression is not required to be in any particular form and may be very informal. Although the writing may manifest such testamentary intent, nevertheless, after the testator's death it may be proved that the testator did not have such intent (e.g., because of fraud, undue influence, mistake) thereby disproving such writing as his will.

The Writing

A will must comply with statutory requirements in order to be effective as such. Statutes require wills to be in writing, with the exception of the oral or "nuncupative" will which is permitted only under certain circumstances. A nuncupative will is valid if: it was made during the last sickness of the testator; it was made in the testator's home or in the house where the testator died; the testator intended that his words constitute his will; the testator has published to the required number of witnesses, present at his request as witnesses, that his words were intended to be his will; and the witnesses have committed the will to writing within a specified number of days after the making thereof. Statutes in the various states make provision for soldiers' and sailors' nuncupative wills while soldiers are in actual service and sailors are at sea. A nuncupative will can transfer only personal property. With the exception of nuncupative wills, all wills must be in writing.

The writing may be made with ink or pencil, it may be typewritten or printed, and it may be a combination of these. A will which is entirely in the testator's handwriting, including his signature, is called a "holographic" will. The writing may be on one page of paper or on several pages if they clearly are a part of one instrument. In most states a will may include as a part thereof papers not attached to it but which are clearly described therein and which were in existence at the time the will was executed by the testator, even though such papers are not of the requisite formality of a will. Such doctrine of inclusion is called "incorporation by reference." The will must indicate an intention on the part of the testator to include such papers, which were not present at the time of the execution of the will, as a part of the will.

Testator's Signature

It is necessary that the testator's signature appear on the instrument to authenticate it as his will. His signature may be made by himself or, in most states, by another person at his request and direction and in his presence as his proxy. In most states the testator's signature is not required to be made at the end of the instrument, although usually it is placed there, but it may be placed anywhere on the instrument. An instrument on which the testator's signature must appear at the end must be "subscribed" by the testator. The signature may be made in ink or pencil, printed or stamped, and made by initials or any mark or device which is intended by the testator to be his signature.

Attestation

The signature of the testator, or his acknowledgment of a signature as his own, must be witnessed, called "attested," by the required number of witnesses, who are such pursuant to the testator's request. Most states require only two witnesses, although many require three. Witnesses must be competent to be such at the time of the execution of the will, and their subsequent incompetency does not cause the will to be invalid. They must be competent to testify concerning the facts surrounding the execution of the will and concerning the mental capacity and testamentary intent of the testator to execute the will. In most states the interest of a person as a beneficiary under the will does not disqualify him from being a witness thereto; however, if his testimony is necessary in order to prove the will, although the witness may testify as such, he thereby loses his right to any interest under the will, except to the extent of his intestate share if there were no will. A person who has an indirect interest under a will —e.g., a member of an association, church, or club which is a beneficiary under the will—is not an interested party; only a person who is a direct beneficiary under the will is an interested party.

After the testator has executed the instrument in their presence, the witnesses are required to sign their names as attesting witnesses anywhere upon a paper attached to the will and usually at the end of the will, although signing at the end is not required in most states. Statutes in most states do not require the witnesses to be present at the same time nor to sign in the presence of each other. Usually an attestation clause follows immediately at the end of the will, but this is not required by statute in most of the states. An attestation clause describes the formalities which were observed at the time of the execution of the will, is an excellent method of proving the will, and is helpful to witnesses in recalling such execution. By statute in many states, a holographic will does not require any attesting witnesses. In most states, publication of the will by the testator—i.e., the testator's declaration to the witnesses that the instrument is his last will and testament—is not required. In no state is it necessary that the witnesses know the contents of the will.

2. REVOCATION

By Act of Testator   A will may be revoked by the act of the testator or by operation of law. The will is ambulatory and speaks as of the time of death and, until that event, the testator may revoke his will even though he has executed a contract not to do so. Revocation is accomplished by the expressed intent of the testator thereby to revoke the will and, in order to prove such revocation, statutes require that revocation be either: by a subsequent writing of the testator expressly or impliedly revoking a previously executed will; or by the testator's physical act to the instrument.

By Subsequent Writing. In most states, the testator's subsequent writing is required to be executed with the same formality as the will itself; however, in some states, a testator's alteration in his own hand of a holographic will revokes the portion altered. A will executed in the ordinary way is not revoked by a subsequent nuncupative will. The subsequent writing may be a new will or a "codicil." It may expressly or impliedly revoke a prior will. An express clause of revocation in a subsequent will or codicil may revoke a part of a prior will or codicil. A prior will may be revoked impliedly by a subsequent will which makes such a change in the terms of the prior will as to indicate the testator's intent to revoke the prior will. Inasmuch as a codicil is a part of a will, an expression of revocation of an entire will extends also to the codicil or codicils. A codicil is an instrument executed by the testator subsequent to the execution of his will with the same formality as is required for the execution of a will, changing or adding to the will, and constituting a supplementary part of the will. The loss of a will does not cause its revocation if it can be proved satisfactorily that the will had been executed properly. If the lost will contained an express clause of revocation of a prior will, such clause is effective to accomplish the revocation of the prior will.

By Act to the Instrument. Generally, the testator's mutilation of a will with the intent thereby to revoke such will effectively revokes the same, although the wording of the statutes varies among the states and the requirements for this method of revocation are different. The physical acts to the instrument may be done by the testator or by someone at his request and in his presence. Whether the revocation of the will by act to the instrument also revokes the codicil depends upon the testator's intent at the time the act occurred. In the absence of proof of intent to revoke the codicil also, the codicil is not revoked.

By Operation of Law When a material change in the circumstances of a testator or a testatrix occurs which would have caused the testator or the testatrix to revoke the will, such change revokes the will by operation of law. Although in most states in the absence of statute a marriage subsequent to the will does not revoke the will, nevertheless, by statute in many states such marriage does effect a revocation unless the will was made in contemplation of such marriage or the will made provision for the widow or widower, respectively, thereby indicating an intent that such marriage was not to constitute a revocation of the will. However, in the absence of statute to the contrary, a will is revoked by a subsequent marriage *and* the subsequent birth of a child because the occurrence of both constitute a material change which would have caused the testator or testatrix to revoke the will.

In most states, a will by a *married* person is not revoked by the subsequent birth of a child from the marriage because the fact of marriage must have caused the testator or the testatrix to contemplate the possibility of having a child from the marriage and, the will having been made in the light of such contemplation, the subsequent birth is not such a change in circumstances implying an intention to revoke. However, the desire of society not to disinherit the after-born child when the will did not provide for it has caused almost all states by statute to accord to the child his intestate share as though there were no will, which is in effect a partial revocation of the will to such extent; but in almost all states the child does not acquire his intestate share if the child is provided for, or even merely mentioned, in the will because such provision or mention manifests a contemplation of the birth by the testator or testatrix precluding any implication of revocation by such birth.

In most states in the absence of statute, a divorce without a property settlement does not revoke a prior will of a former spouse or a provision in the will for a former spouse. However, in most states a divorce accompanied by a property settlement between the parties impliedly revokes that portion of the will providing for the other party.

3. BENEFICIARIES

By the Will A "beneficiary" under a will is a person named in the will who is to receive property thereunder as a gift. The beneficiary of real property is called a "devisee," and the beneficiary of personal property is called a "legatee." A "legacy" is the name of the bequest of personal property, and "devise" describes the gift of real property. The interest of a beneficiary is a property interest which is available to his creditors. Legacies may be general, specific, or demonstrative. Today, devises may be general or specific. A "general legacy" is payable out of the general assets of the estate and does not require the delivery of any specific property. ("I give and bequeath to my sister, Anne Jones, the sum of $1,000, if she survives me.") A "specific legacy" is a gift of specific personal property. ("I give and bequeath to my brother, John Jones, if he survives me, the gold horse tie pin which I inherited from my father.") A "demonstrative legacy" is a gift of personal property, the testator having indicated a particular source of such gift but not having restricted the gift to such source in the event that the source is unavailable or inadequate. The demonstrative legacy is a charge on the source named and is payable in any event, unless the estate is inadequate after satisfying the specific legacies and devises.

By Intestacy State statutes of descent and distribution prescribe the beneficiaries of the property of a decedent who died intestate, predicated upon their marital or blood relationship to the intestate. The word "descent" refers to real property descending and passing directly from the intestate to beneficiaries called "heirs," and the word "distribution" refers to the transfer of personal property from an intestate to the latter's legal representative and distributed by him to beneficiaries called "distributees," under the statutes of descent and distribution. Today the majority of state statutes of descent and distribution provide for the same persons as beneficiaries of real property and personal property of an intestate, and, accordingly, the word "heirs" refers, generally, to those persons to whom property, whether real or personal, passes by intestacy under these statutes.

Marital Relationship with Intestate. While statutes of descent and distribution differ among the various states, they do follow a general pattern. A spouse who survives the intestate generally receives a specified fractional share of the intestate's estate, and often the extent of the share is dependent upon whether or not there are surviving children or other specified heirs and their number. If children or other specified heirs survive, the surviving spouse shares in the estate with them and, generally, has a one-third or a one-half share. If no children or other specified heirs survive, the surviving spouse usually takes the entire estate. In community property states the statutes vary, separate and community property often not passing in the same manner. By statute in most states a surviving spouse has a right, subject to limitation and variation among the states, to elect to disregard the provisions of the will of the decedent spouse and to take against the will, meaning an election to receive his or her intestate or fractional share as prescribed by statute.

Blood Relationship with Intestate. Blood relatives of the intestate may be lineal (by direct line) and be either descending (e.g., the intestate's children) or ascending (e.g., the intestate's parents), or the blood relatives of the intestate may be collateral, meaning they are of a common ancestor (e.g., first, brothers and sisters of the intestate and their descendants; second, uncles and aunts of the intestate and their descendants; and so on). The line of inheritance first descends for the purpose of intestate succession, and the children of the intestate have priority as beneficiaries, irrespective of the order of their birth and of their sex. If the intestate is survived by his only child, the latter takes the entire estate. If the intestate has more than one child, all the children share equally, and the issue (children) of the intestate's children who predeceased the testator take the share of their parent by representation (they representing their parent) and share equally among themselves. (A has three children, B, L, and W, each of which has three children: B having C, D, and E; L having M, N, and O; and W having X, Y, and Z. On A's death, there survive: B and all his children; L and all his children; and X, Y, and Z. A's estate is distributed: ⅓ to B; ⅓ to L; and ⅑ to each of X, Y, and Z.) If no children of the intestate survive the intestate, but their issue survive, the grandchildren of the intestate are in equal lineal degree of relationship with the intestate and in the majority of states they share *per capita,* while in a minority of states they share *per stirpes. Per capita,* signifying "by heads," means that all persons who stand in the same degree of relationship to the intestate share equally in the estate without consideration of any right of representation. *Per stirpes,* signifying "by stocks" or "by roots," is the antithesis of *per capita* and means that the survivors of their parent represent their parent and take his share by such representation for division among themselves; it is a right by representation. Thus, in the above illustration, if A's three children did not survive him but A was survived by B's three children, two of L's children, and one of W's children: if the grandchildren share *per capita,* each of the grandchildren would have an equal share in the estate; but if the grandchildren share *per stirpes,* B's three children take B's ⅓ share equally and each of them receives ⅑ of A's estate, L's two children take L's ⅓ share equally and each of them receives ⅙ of A's estate, and W's child takes W's ⅓ share of A's estate.

In the absence of a surviving spouse and of lineal descendants, the line of intestate succession ascends and, in most states, the parents of the intestate surviving the intestate share equally and a surviving parent takes the entire estate. If the intestate is survived only by brothers and sisters of the intestate, brothers and sisters are next in line, sharing equally; and when some of the brothers and sisters have predeceased the intestate but have left issue surviving, such issue share in like manner by representation as the surviving issue of children of the intestate share with surviving children of the intestate, as previously discussed. This process of priorities and sharing in intestate succession continues at great length and is prescribed by statute in each state.

Chapter II

PROBATE AND ADMINISTRATION

---

1. PROBATE

Nature   PROBATE means proof and is the term applied to the procedure of proving to a proper court that an instrument is the last will and testament of a decedent. Until the testator dies and the will subsequently is probated, the will lies dormant and does not have legal status or effect as such. Certain courts in each state have jurisdiction to handle the probate of wills, sometimes called "probate courts" and "surrogate courts." A will is probated in the state and county in which the testator was domiciled at the time of his death. If the testator has property located in other states, the will would be admitted to probate in such states; however, once a will is probated in one state, the probate is effective in all states, except in those states where land in which the testator has an interest is located, the law of the latter states governing the validity of the will. A petition for probate may be filed in the proper court by any interested person, although the executor usually makes the petition. After a petition has been filed for probate of a will, all interested parties notified, and the will admitted to probate, the will is certified by the court as the will of the testator; the legal representative, often called the "personal representative," then is appointed by the court.

The Legal Representative   The legal representative of the decedent is appointed by the court. An "executor" is the person named by the testator in his will and appointed by the court to represent the testator in the administration of his estate by carrying out his desires as provided in his will. If the testator's appointee is a woman, she is an "executrix." The legal representative of an intestate appointed by the court is called an "administrator," or an "administratrix" if a woman. If the person named in the will as an executor predeceases the testator or for some other reason is unavailable

937

or cannot qualify as an executor, the legal representative of the testator is appointed by the court and is called an "administrator (or administratrix) with the will annexed." If an administrator or an executor has been unable to administer the estate completely, the person appointed by the court in his place is called an "administrator (or administratrix) *de bonis non,*" who is an administrator of the property of the estate not administered previously. Generally, the title to all of the decedent's personal property vests in the legal representative of the decedent's estate, and the title to all of the decedent's real property vests in the testator's devisees or the intestate's heirs, as of the time of the decedent's death.

2. ADMINISTRATION

Function and Duties of the Legal Representative

Function. The function of the legal representative of a decedent is: to collect all the assets of the decedent's estate; to pay the debts of the estate and the administration expenses; and to distribute the remaining assets to the beneficiaries of the estate either pursuant to the direction of the testator as provided in his will, or pursuant to the statute of descent and distribution in the case of intestacy, under the court's supervision. This procedure is called "administration."

Duties. The legal representative has the duty to exercise that degree of care in administering the estate which would and should be exercised by a reasonable prudent person in his position in handling his own affairs. The legal representative's duties are confined to the conservation and distribution of the estate. He should maintain detailed accounts of his receipts and disbursements and, in the event that he is a trustee as well as a legal representative, he should keep separate trust accounts. He should use due care in selecting a proper depository for the funds of the estate and deposit the funds in the name of the estate; such funds should not be mixed with his own personal funds nor deposited in an account in his own name. He has the duty to collect assets of the estate and to sue for their collection if necessary; to discharge claims and, pursuant to court order as required in some states, to compromise claims against the estate; and to sell personal property of the estate pursuant to any express power of sale contained in the will or, in the absence of any such power, to sell either with or without court order depending upon the law of the state in which the estate is being administered. The legal representative has the duty to pay taxes and to pay all claims which must be presented within the time prescribed by law, regardless of whether or not they are mature or immature. A secured creditor is not required to prove his claim in order to recover against his security. Claims for the decedent's nonperformance of nonpersonal contracts made with the decedent may be asserted against the legal representative. (A's promissory note to B for $500 is overdue and unpaid. On A's death, B has a claim against A's estate for $500.) In any contract made by the legal representative pursuant to authority, the legal representative personally is a party to such contract, which may be asserted against him personally. In the latter case, the legal representative has a right of reimbursement against the estate for his outlay. The legal representative may not continue the business of the decedent unless the authority for temporary operation of such business in order to preserve the assets of the estate or to realize thereon is given expressly by the will, by the consent of interested parties in the estate, or by court order.[1] He has no power to bind the estate by the issue or indorsement of negotiable instruments. In most states he is to resort first to the personal property of the estate to pay its debts and, should that be insufficient, he then may resort to the real property either pursuant to testamentary power of sale contained in the will or pursuant to court order. Devisees and heirs take the decedent's real property subject to this testamentary power of sale and the authority of the court to order its sale.

Final Settlement

On the expiration of the statutory period of time within which claims against the estate may be presented and after payment by the legal representative of such claims as have been presented, the legal representative has the duty to render to the court a final account of his administration of the estate. This is the last of several periodic accounts which may be required of the legal representative. Notice of the submission of the final account to the court is required to be given to all interested parties so that they may have an opportunity to object to it. After a court hearing, the final account is judicially allowed constituting a judicial approval and adjudication of such account, called a "decree of final settlement." A court order or decree of distribution then is rendered which specifies the persons to whom distribution is to be made and which orders such distribution. If the testator has created a trust in his will, called a "testamentary trust," the property of the trust is transferred at this point to the trustee, called a "testamentary trustee," to be held and administered by him in accordance with the terms of the testamentary trust. After distribution is made pursuant to the court decree, the legal representative is discharged and the estate is closed.

---

[1] Thomas E. Atkinson, *Handbook of the Law of Wills* (2d ed.; St. Paul: West Publishing Co., 1953), sec. 121.

APPENDIX TO PART ELEVEN

REFERENCES

1. Atkinson, Thomas E. *Handbook of the Law of Wills.* 2d ed. St. Paul, Minn.: West Publishing Co., 1953.
2. Bowe, William J., and Parker, Douglas H. *Page on the Law of Wills.* Cincinnati, Ohio: The W. H. Anderson Co., 1962.
3. Rollison, W. D. *The Law of Wills.* Chicago: Callaghan & Co., 1939.
4. *Uniform Probate Code,* 1969. St. Paul, Minn.: West Publishing Co.

PROBLEMS

1. (a) When does a person die "testate" and when "intestate"?
   (b) How is property transferred when a person dies:
       (1) Testate.
       (2) Intestate.
   (c) Who are the following:
       (1) Testator.
       (2) Executor.
       (3) Administrator.
       (4) Administrator with the will annexed.
       (5) Devisee.
       (6) Legatee.
       (7) Heir.
2. (a) The law of what place is applicable to the making of a will?
   (b) What is meant by the following in the law of wills:
       (1) A will.
       (2) A codicil.
       (3) "Incorporation by reference."
   (c) Name the essential elements of a will.
   (d) What is a nuncupative will, and when is it permitted?
   (e) What is a holographic will?
   (f) May a will be written in pencil? Answer "Yes" or "No."
3. (a) Must the testator's actual signature appear on his will?
   (b) Are a testator's initials sufficient as a signature to his will?
   (c) What is the purpose of witnesses to a will?
   (d) A and B are witnesses to T's will. Subsequently A and B became incompetent to be such witnesses.

941

   (1) Is the instrument invalid as a will because of such incompetency?
   (2) Why?
   (e) What is the effect of a beneficiary under a will also being a witness thereto?
   (f) Is it necessary that a witness to a will know the contents thereof? Answer "Yes" or "No."

4. (a) What is the effect of a testator's writing expressing an intent thereby to revoke his previously made will?
   (b) How may a testator revoke his will other than by a subsequent writing?
   (c) What is the effect of the following on a previously made will:
      (1) The testator's marriage.
      (2) The birth of the testator's child.
      (3) The testator's divorce from his wife.

5. (a) When does a will have any effect?
   (b) When a legal representative of a testator's estate has been appointed:
      (1) In general, what are his functions?
      (2) Describe five of his specific duties.
      (3) When may he continue the testator's business?
      (4) When may he bind the estate by his issuance of a negotiable instrument?

SOME PREVIOUS C.P.A. LAW EXAMINATION QUESTIONS AND MODEL ANSWERS

MAY, 1966

No. 3

Each of the following numbered phrases or clauses states a legal conclusion as it completes the related lettered material. You are to determine whether each of the legal conclusions is true or false according to the general principles of estate law. Blacken the appropriate space on the separate answer sheet to indicate whether each conclusion is true or false. Your grade will be determined from your total net score obtained by deducting your total of incorrect answers from your total of correct answers; an omitted answer will not be considered an incorrect answer.

A. X may effectively dispose of his interest in the following property by will:
   121. Property he owns as a joint tenant.
   122. Property he owns as a tenant by the entirety.
   123. Property he owns as a tenant in common.
   124. Insurance proceeds payable to his estate.
   125. X's life estate in real property.
B. X may effectively
   126. Make a contract to make a particular provision in his will.
   127. Make a holographic will with his wife.
   128. Orally revoke his will.
   129. Execute a new will which does not revoke a prior will.
   130. Amend a prior will by executing an unwitnessed codicil.

C. In his will X may not effectively
    131. Revoke his prior will if he does not have capacity to execute a new will.
    132. Revive an old will after it has been revoked.
    133. Designate a particular fund in his will from which transfer and estate taxes are to be paid.
    134. Appoint a guardian for his minor children.
    135. Establish a trust to run as long as any of his descendants are living.
D. X may effectively condition a bequest made in his will by requiring the legatee
    136. To survive X for six months.
    137. To attend X's funeral service.
    138. To refrain from attacking X's will.
    139. To commit a crime.
    140. To be under the age of twenty-one at X's death.
E. After X's death, the executor named in X's will
    141. Must, under all circumstances, offer the will for probate.
    142. May refuse to serve because he is too busy.
    143. Will receive letters of administration to evidence his appointment.
    144. Must offer X's will for probate in the state in which the will was drawn.
    145. Will be required to post a bond if the will does not relieve him of this obligation.
F. After X's death, his personal representative will have the implied power
    146. To pay X's funeral expenses and debts.
    147. To erect a suitable gravestone on his grave.
    148. To use estate funds to continue to maintain and expand X's business.
    149. To use estate funds to invest in a new business.
    150. To continue to administer the estate for as long a time as the majority of beneficiaries wish him to do so.

Answer

121. False.	127. True.	133. False.	139. False.	145. True.
122. False.	128. False.	134. False.	140. True.	146. True.
123. True.	129. True.	135. True.	141. False.	147. True.
124. True.	130. False.	136. True.	142. True.	148. False.
125. False.	131. True.	137. True.	143. False.	149. False.
126. True.	132. False.	138. True.	144. False.	150. False.

PART TWELVE

TRUSTS

Chapter I

NATURE OF A TRUST

"A TRUST is one of several juridical devices whereby one person is enabled to deal with property for the benefit of another person."[1] Its distinguishing characteristics are: the separation of the legal title to property from the beneficial equitable interest in the property; the flexibility of use of the trust device in a variety of transactions to which it is peculiarly suitable; the fiduciary relationship between the trustee and beneficiary; and a method of transferring property. There are three kinds of trust—namely, "express," "resulting," and "constructive." The ordinary kind of trust is the express trust, and this part of the book is concerned mainly with it. First the three kinds of trust will be distinguished briefly from each other, and the express trust distinguished from a few other legal relationships; and then the creation, administration, modification, and termination of the express trust will be discussed.

Kinds of Trust

Express Trust. An express trust is a fiduciary relationship between persons in connection with property whereby one person called the "settlor" by his manifestation of intention causes property to be held by a person called the "trustee" for the benefit of a person called a "beneficiary" or *"cestui que trust,"* the trustee being under a duty so to deal with the property.[2] The fiduciary relationship of trust is between the trustee and the beneficiary. The property held in trust is called "trust property." An express trust may be private or charitable, the latter distinguished mainly by its charitable purpose. *Unless otherwise indicated in this portion of the book, the term "trust" refers solely to an express trust.*

Resulting Trust. It is of the essence of an express trust that the settlor manifest an intent to transfer the beneficial interest as well as the title to trust property for the benefit of someone. If title alone is transferred and an intent to transfer the beneficial interest has not been expressed and cannot be implied, there is no express trust. Accordingly,

---

[1] American Law Institute, *Restatement: Trusts 2d,* 1959, Introductory Note, p. 1.
[2] See *ibid.,* sec. 2.

when the owner of property transfers title thereto without consideration and without intending to transfer the beneficial interest therein and the beneficial interest is not transferred to anyone else, there is no express trust and the person holding the title is a trustee of such title for the transferor by operation of law. Such trust is a resulting trust, resulting in the transferor being entitled to the return of the title to the property.

A resulting trust arises:

1. When an express trust fails, thereby causing the transferee to hold the trust property for the transferor under a resulting trust, in the absence of the transferor's manifestation of intent to the contrary; or

2. When some portion of the trust property remains after an express trust has been performed, thereby causing the trustee to hold the excess for the settlor under a resulting trust, in the absence of the settlor's manifestation of intent to the contrary; or

3. When property is purchased by one person and the seller delivers the property to a third person pursuant to the direction of the purchaser, it being presumed that, in the absence of the purchaser's manifestation of intent to the contrary, the purchaser does not intend a gift of the property to the transferee third person and, therefore, that the transferee holds the property for the purchaser under a resulting trust.

In all of these situations, inasmuch as there is no implication of an intent by the person causing the transfer of the property that the transferee of the title also is to have the beneficial interest, there is a resulting trust.

Constructive Trust. A constructive trust, like the resulting trust, is created by operation of law and arises regardless of the intention of the parties. A constructive trust is imposed by law in order to prevent unjust enrichment to the party with the title to the trust property. "A constructive trust arises where a person who holds title to property is subject to an equitable duty to convey it to another on the ground that he would be unjustly enriched if he were permitted to retain it."[3] (A fraudulently induced B to convey the title to B's land to A. A holds the title under a constructive trust for B, who is entitled to restitution of the land.)

Trust Distinguished There are other legal relationships in which one person deals with property for the benefit of another which should be distinguished from a trust. Only bailment, agency, and sale of goods will be considered

---

[3] Austin W. Scott, *The Law of Trusts* (3d ed.; Boston: Little, Brown & Co., 1967), Vol. V, p. 3413; also see American Law Institute, *Restatement: Restitution,* 1937, sec. 160 and *Comment.*

here. A bailment is concerned only with goods, is predicated on possession of such property, and the bailee does not have title to the property;
in contrast, a trust may be concerned with real or personal property, and
the trustee has title to the property. Agency is distinguishable from a
trust, in that the agent usually does not have title to the property, he is
subject to the control of his principal, his death terminates the agency,
and he can subject his principal to liability to third persons; in contrast, a
trustee has title to the property and is not subject to anyone's control,
although the beneficiary can compel him to perform his trust duties, the
trustee's death does not terminate the trust, and the trustee cannot subject
the beneficiary to any liability. A sale of goods consists in the passing of
title from the seller to the buyer for a price. A trust relationship consists
of the transfer of legal title to any kind of property to a trustee to hold,
use, and manage for the benefit of a beneficiary who has an equitable
interest in the property. The subject of the sale can be only tangible,
movable personal property; for a trust, it may be tangible or intangible
personal or real property. In sale, the legal title is transferred; in trust,
the title is split into legal title and a beneficial equitable title. In sale,
the buyer can do with his property as he wishes; in trust, the trustee and
beneficiary are limited by the terms of the trust.

Chapter II

THE EXPRESS TRUST

---

1. *CREATION OF AN EXPRESS TRUST*

Methods   THE Restatement of Trusts, section 17, describes various ways by which an express trust may be created:

A trust may be created by
(a) a declaration by the owner of property that he holds it as trustee for another person; or
(b) a transfer inter vivos by the owner of property to another person as trustee for the transferor or for a third person; or
(c) a transfer by will by the owner of property to another person as trustee for a third person; or
(d) an appointment by one person having a power of appointment to another person as trustee for the donee of the power or for a third person;[1] or
(e) a promise by one person to another person whose rights thereunder are to be held in trust for a third person.

Capacity of Settlor. The settlor must have legal
Requirements   capacity to create a trust and any person who can transfer title to property can create a trust, which is essentially a transfer of property for the purpose of benefiting someone. If a person has legal capacity to make an *inter vivos* transfer, he has legal capacity to create a trust; if he has legal capacity to make a testamentary transfer, he has legal capacity to create a testamentary trust.

Manifestation of Settlor's Intent to Create a Trust. The settlor must make a proper manifestation of his intent *thereby* to create a trust. His manifestation of an intent to create a trust other than at the time of the manifestation is ineffective to create a trust. Also, the settlor must manifest an intent to impose legally enforceable duties on the trustee.

Statute of Frauds. The settlor's manifestation of intent to create a trust may be written or oral, in the absence of statute to the contrary,

---

[1] E.g., A conveys land to B for B's life, the remainder to be determined by B. B creates a trust of the remainder for the benefit of D, naming C as trustee.

and any words may be used which manifest such intent. The statutes of frauds in most states follow the pattern of the English Statute of Frauds requiring that all declarations or creations of trusts of any interest in land shall be manifested and proved by some writing signed by the party who is by law enabled to declare such trust, or by his last will in writing, or else they are void and of no effect. The statute is satisfied if the signed memorandum specifies the trust property, the purpose of the trust, and the beneficiary. Express trusts of personal property, and resulting and constructive trusts, are not within the purview of the statute. Except for nuncupative wills, statutes require a will to be in writing and, accordingly, a testamentary trust must be in writing.

Testamentary Trust. A testamentary trust is a trust created by a will which arises on the death of the testator. It is a testamentary disposition and, therefore, is governed by the law concerning wills. A will is ambulatory and speaks as of the time of the testator's death. An *inter vivos* disposition which does not transfer the beneficial interest to the property and which is not to take effect until the death of the settlor is ineffective to create a trust and is a testamentary disposition which must comply with the law concerning wills. A transfer *inter vivos* of the beneficial interest in trust, the enjoyment of which is postponed until the settlor's death, is effective to create a nontestamentary disposition. (A conveys property to B in trust for the benefit of C, who is to receive the trust property on A's death.)

No Notice or Acceptance Required. A trust may be created without any notice to the trustee or beneficiary and without their acceptance. Disclaimer by the trustee does not terminate the trust; its effect is to cause the title to the trust property to be transferred back to the settlor who then holds the property as a constructive trustee with the obligation to appoint another trustee and transfer the property to him. If one of several trustees disclaims, the title passes to those who did not disclaim. However, disclaimer by the beneficiary terminates the trust; and, if the settlor has declared himself as trustee, he holds the property free from the trust, while, if the settlor has transferred the title to another in trust, the trustee holds the title in a resulting trust for the settlor.

No Consideration Required. Consideration is not required as an ingredient in the creation of a trust and is not necessary in exchange for the settlor's declaration. However, a promise to create a trust is unenforceable unless it is supported by sufficient consideration, as required by the law of contracts.

Legality. The purpose of the trust must be legal; and a purported trust, or a provision in an otherwise valid trust, for an illegal purpose is void. If only a provision in the trust is illegal, only that provision is void and the trust remains otherwise unaffected, unless the separation of the illegal provision would defeat the trust purpose in which event the purported trust is void.

Transfer of Property. A trust involves the transfer of title and the beneficial interest in property, so that the trustee has the title for the benefit of the beneficiary. A person may transfer the property to another as trustee, or he may declare himself as trustee and thereby transfer the property to himself as trustee (e.g., the settlor's deposit of money in a bank account in the settlor's name as trustee for another, in the absence of any evidence to indicate to the contrary, creates a revocable trust, revocable at the election of the depositor settlor). Failure to effect such a transfer precludes the creation of a trust.[2]

The Trust Property. The trust property must be specific, in existence, and capable of being transferred by the owner, at the time the trust is created. An interest in intangibles—e.g., a debt—and equitable as well as legal interests can be trust property.

The Trustee. Any person who has legal capacity to take, hold, and administer property if it were his own has legal capacity to be a trustee of such property. Infants, juristic persons (e.g., corporations), the beneficiary, or the settlor may be trustees. The death of a trustee does not terminate the trust, and the death of one of several trustees causes the title to vest in the surviving trustees. In the absence of statute to the contrary, the death intestate of a sole trustee causes the title to vest, subject to the trust, in his heirs if the trust property is real property and in his legal representative if it is personal property.

A trustee is removable pursuant to the terms of the trust or by a proper court. The appointment of a trustee is made in the same manner in the event that there is no trustee or one of several trustees has ceased to be a trustee. A trustee cannot resign a trust he had accepted previously, except either in accordance with the terms of the trust, with the consent of all the beneficiaries if they are capable of consenting, or by an order of a proper court.

Identifiable Beneficiary. Only those persons to receive beneficial interests as indicated by the settlor's manifested intention are beneficiar-

---

[2] As an exception, a trust is created if the attempted transfer to another as trustee is ineffective *solely* because the trustee is not named in the instrument of conveyance (e.g., deed) or the named trustee is incapable of taking title to such property. The beneficiary may, by court order, compel the settlor to dispose of such property pursuant to such order. See American Law Institute, *Restatement: Trusts 2d,* 1959, sec. 32.

ies. Persons who benefit incidentally from a trust are not beneficiaries. Any person who has legal capacity to take and hold particular property can be a beneficiary of a trust of such property. The beneficiary may be a natural person or a juristic person and must be identifiable at the time that the trust is created, or identifiable within the period of the rule against perpetuities,[3] i.e., in most states a period for the life of a person or persons in existence at the time the trust is created and 21 years after the death of such person or persons. A definite class of persons may be a beneficiary, provided that the members of the class are identifiable at the time of the creation of the trust or within the period of the rule against perpetuities. There may be more than one beneficiary, and the settlor himself may be a beneficiary. A beneficiary's interest is personal property if the trust property is personal property, and it is real property if the trust property is real property, except for the principle of equitable conversion. Under this principle:

(1) If real property is held in trust and by the terms of the trust a duty is imposed upon the trustee to sell it and hold the proceeds in trust or distribute the proceeds, the interest of the beneficiary is personal property.

(2) If personal property is held in trust and by the terms of the trust a duty is imposed upon the trustee to expend it or its proceeds for the purchase of real property, the interest of the beneficiary is real property unless it is so limited in duration that if it were a legal interest it would be personal property.[4]

2. ADMINISTRATION OF AN EXPRESS TRUST

Duties and Powers of Trustee

Duties. A trustee has the duty to act in accordance with the terms of the trust except for impossibility or illegality of performance. If the circumstances unknown to the settlor and not anticipated by him so change that compliance with the terms of the trust would defeat its purpose or substantially impair its implementation, a proper court may authorize or direct the trustee to act contrary to the terms of the trust. The trustee owes a duty of loyalty to the beneficiary to administer the trust properly for the sole benefit of the beneficiary and to observe the fiduciary relationship between them in his dealings with the beneficiary for his personal gain. The trustee has the duty, on request, to furnish to the beneficiary all information regarding the administration of the trust and to make all records available to the beneficiary for his examination.

---

[3] American Law Institute, *Restatement: Trusts 2d,* 1959, sec. 112. Generally, the rule against perpetuities does not apply to charitable trusts.

[4] *Ibid.,* sec. 131.

The trustee has the duty to administer the trust in a reasonable manner. He is to exercise that care which would be exercised by a reasonable, prudent man in the care of *his own property* under the circumstances.[5] He may not delegate trust duties which he reasonably can do personally. He is required to control and preserve the trust property, collect on claims which he holds in trust, defend actions which subject the trust estate to loss when such defense appears to be reasonable, cause the trust property to produce returns when feasible, keep the trust property separate from his own property and make deposits of trust monies in a separate trust bank account, and keep accounts of the administration of the trust.

Powers. The powers of a trustee in administering the trust may be express or implied. A trustee has implied power to do only that which is reasonably necessary in order to execute the purpose of the trust and which is not prohibited by the terms of the trust. A trustee has implied power to incur reasonable expense in doing that which is reasonably necessary to administer the trust and not prohibited by the terms of the trust, and he has a right of reimbursement therefor. Although a trustee has implied power to sell trust property when reasonably required and not prohibited by the terms of the trust, he does not have any implied authority to mortgage or pledge trust property nor to borrow on the credit of the trust estate. In order to fulfill his duty to make the trust property productive, he has implied authority reasonably to lease the trust property, in the absence of any provisions to the contrary in the terms of the trust. He has implied power to exercise his reasonable discretion in compromising, arbitrating, or abandoning claims in connection with the trust estate and, in the absence of terms of the trust to the contrary, to vote and exercise those other powers inherent in shares of stock which are a part of the trust property. If there is more than one trustee and the terms of the trust are not to the contrary, trust action is taken only by their unanimous consent; in charitable trusts, a majority of the trustees is sufficient.

In carrying out his functions of preserving the trust property and of causing such property to produce returns, the trustee has the duty to exercise proper care in the investment of trust property not contrary to the terms of the trust. The trustee should make a reasonable distribution of the risk of loss by diversification of investment and dispose of improper investments in existence at the time of his appointment as trustee

---

[5] *Cf.* the duty of care required of a trustee with that required of a corporate director, above, p. 684.

and of proper investments which subsequently become improper. Because of the trustee's duty to make the trust property productive, if certain of such property is unproductive it should be sold. Similarly, if some of the property is subject to depletion, i.e., wasting property—e.g., leaseholds, patents, copyrights—the trustee should sell the same or amortize the depreciation. It should be noted carefully that, in the absence of trust provision to the contrary, there is a conflict of view[6] on whether or not a trustee is permitted to amortize the depreciation or obsolescence of a building.

The trustee has the duty to make proper allocations and charges to the principal and income accounts, and his failure to do so resulting in loss subjects him to liability therefor. The *trustee's* purchase of investments at a premium requires amortization of the premium out of the income from the investment, such amortization fund being principal and not income. However, the *settlor's* purchase of investments at a premium does not require amortization of the premium by the trustee, in the absence of trust provision to the contrary, and all income is available for distribution to the income beneficiary pursuant to the terms of the trust. Where trust investments are acquired at a discount, the benefit of such discount usually is considered as principal and is available to the principal beneficiary. Ordinary current administrative and operative expense is chargeable to income—e.g., ordinary taxes, water rates, premiums on trustee's bond, insurance on the trust property, interest on a mortgage on trust property, and ordinary repairs to trust property. Other than ordinary current expense is chargeable to principal—e.g., the cost of purchasing or selling investments, the expense of litigation in protecting the trust property, the cost of setting up the trust, and the cost of permanent improvements. Under the Uniform Principal and Income Act, sec. 10, when trust property is subject to depletion: if the trustee is under a duty to sell it, and in the absence of trust provision to the contrary, a statutory annual percentage of its value is income and the remainder is principal; while if the trustee has no duty to sell, and in the absence of trust provision to the contrary, the full return from the property is income.

While income is allocated to the income account and made available to the income beneficiary and increase in principal is allocated to the principal account, nevertheless, there often is difficulty in ascertaining whether receipts from shares of stock are principal or income. Although

---

[6] See Austin W. Scott, *The Law of Trusts* (3d ed.; Boston: Little, Brown & Co., 1967), Vol. III, sec. 239.4.

there are different rules in various states, under the Restatement of Trusts, section 236:

Except as otherwise provided by the terms of the trust, if shares of stock of a corporation are held in trust to pay the income to a beneficiary for a designated period and thereafter to pay the principal to another beneficiary, the following rules are applicable:

(a) Except as stated in Clauses (e) and (f), dividends payable in cash or in property other than in shares of the declaring corporation, including ordinary and extraordinary dividends, are income, if payable to shareholders of record on a designated date which is within the period; or, if no such date is designated, if declared at a date within the period.

(b) Dividends payable in shares of the declaring corporation are principal.

(c) If the trustee has the option of receiving a dividend either in cash or in shares of the declaring corporation, the dividend is income irrespective of the choice made by the trustee.

(d) Rights to subscribe to the shares or other securities of the declaring corporation and the proceeds of any sale of such rights are principal, but rights to subscribe to the shares of other corporations are income.

(e) Upon the total or partial liquidation of the corporation during the period, amounts paid as cash dividends declared before such liquidation occurred or as arrears of preferred or guaranteed dividends are income; all other amounts paid upon corporate shares on distribution of the corporate assets to the shareholders are principal.

(f) A distribution by a corporation which is a return of capital and not a distribution of earnings is principal.

(g) The earnings of a corporation not distributed by the corporation during the period are not income.

Liability of Trustee

A trustee is liable to the beneficiary for his breach of trust and ". . . he is chargeable with (a) any loss or depreciation in value of the trust estate resulting from the breach of trust; or (b) any profit made by him through the breach of trust; or (c) any profit which would have accrued to the trust estate if there had been no breach of trust."[7] The beneficiary's consent to the trustee's breach of trust, either before or at the time of such breach, or his affirmance or release of such breach discharges the trustee from any liability to the beneficiary therefor. A trustee may incur personal liability to third persons while properly administering the trust, but this does not permit the claimants to proceed against the trust property in satisfaction of their claims. The trustee has a right of exoneration[8] against the trust property just as he has a right

---

[7] American Law Institute, *Restatement: Trusts 2d,* 1959, sec. 205.

[8] This is the trustee's right to have the trust property used to discharge his personal liability and thereby relieve him of the necessity of discharging the liability with his own property.

of reimbursement for his expenditures. The trustee is liable to third persons on his contracts, as well as for his torts, which have occurred while he was administering the trust.

3. MODIFICATION AND TERMINATION OF AN EXPRESS TRUST

A settlor may not modify or revoke a trust unless the terms of trust so permit or the settlor has reserved such power. The reason for this is that the beneficial interest in the trust property has been transferred to the beneficiary and he cannot be deprived of such interest without his consent. In the absence of any evidence to indicate to the contrary, the power of the settlor to revoke is implied in a trust created by the settlor's deposit of money in a bank account in the settlor's name as trustee for another person. If a trust is created by a writing and the settlor intended to reserve a power to modify or to revoke the trust but, by mistake, this power was omitted from inclusion in the writing, the settlor has the right to have the writing reformed so as to include this power. Also, the settlor has a right to rescind a trust or to have it reformed on the same grounds which permit any other transfer of property to be rescinded or reformed—e.g., fraud, undue influence, or mistake.

A trust may terminate in various ways. It may expire according to its terms.[9] If the circumstances unknown to the settlor and not anticipated by him so change that compliance with the terms of the trust would defeat its purpose or substantially impair its implementation, a court may order the termination of the trust. Impossibility of performance of the trust or supervening illegality are grounds for judicial termination of the trust. The consent of all the beneficiaries, if they are capable of consenting, may compel the termination of the trust, except when "the continuance of the trust is necessary to carry out a material purpose of the trust. . . ."[10] A spendthrift trust[11] is an illustration of a trust with a ma-

---

[9] *Cy pres* means as nearly as possible. *Cy pres* is an equitable doctrine of construction of instruments whereby the charitable intention of the settlor of a charitable trust is carried out as nearly as possible when circumstances prevent its being carried out exactly. It is applicable where the settlor's manifested intent indicates a particular, as well as a general, charitable purpose and the *particular* charitable purpose cannot, but the *general* charitable purpose can, be carried out. For example, if the settlor's manifested general intention was to improve medical facilities in a community and, in his will, he bequeathed property in trust for the establishment of a hospital in the community, and at the time of his death a hospital had been established in the community, a court could apply *cy pres* and direct that the trust property be applied in other ways to provide for the ill people in that community in furtherance of the settlor's general charitable purpose.

[10] American Law Institute, *Restatement: Trusts 2d*, 1959, sec. 337.

[11] A trust which, by statute or by valid trust provision, restrains the voluntary or involuntary transfer of the beneficial interest of the trust by the beneficiary or by his creditors

terial purpose precluding termination by the consent of all the beneficiaries. However, if the settlor and all beneficiaries consent to the termination of the trust, then the trust is terminable even though there was a material purpose. The merger of the beneficial interest with the legal title to the trust property in one person terminates the trust.

---

is called a "spendthrift trust." Its purpose is to protect the beneficiary from his improvidence.

APPENDIX TO PART TWELVE

REFERENCES

1. American Law Institute. *Restatement: Restitution.* 1937.
2. American Law Institute. *Restatement: Trusts 2d.* 1959.
3. Scott, Austin Wakeman. *The Law of Trusts.* 3d ed. Boston: Little, Brown & Co., 1967.

PROBLEMS

1. (a) What is meant by the following:
    (1) Settlor.
    (2) *Cestui que trust.*
    (3) Trust property.
   (b) Enumerate the requisites of an express trust of personal property.
   (c) A orally declared to B that, beginning from that moment, A held certain specified personal property of A in trust for B.
    (1) Has a trust been created?
    (2) Why?
2. (a) Who may create a trust?
   (b) A promised B to create a trust of certain specified personal property of A for B.
    (1) Did A's promise create a trust? Why?
    (2) Is A's promise enforceable? Why?
   (c) X declared a trust of certain specified personal property of X for Y and named Z as trustee.
    (1) What is the effect of Z's refusal to act as trustee?
    (2) What is the effect of X's declaration if X was ignorant of the fact that Z was not alive at the time it was made?
   (d) R delivers his property to S in trust for T. What is the effect of T's disclaimer of the trust?
3. (a) What is a testamentary trust?
   (b) May an *inter vivos* trust be created under the terms of which enjoyment of the trust by the beneficiary can be postponed until after the settlor's death? Why?
   (c) Can a trust of intangible personal property be created? Answer "Yes" or "No."

(d) When must the beneficiary of a trust be identifiable?

(e) What is the effect of the death of one of several trustees of a trust?

4. (a) Describe the relationship between the trustee and the beneficiary of a trust.

(b) Describe the duties of a trustee.

(c) May a trustee delegate trust duties? Explain.

(d) How must the trustee allocate trust principal and income for trust expense and for investments of trust property acquired at a premium?

SOME PREVIOUS C.P.A. LAW EXAMINATION QUESTIONS AND MODEL ANSWERS

MAY, 1965

No. 2

Each of the following numbered phrases or clauses states a legal conclusion as it completes the related lettered material. You are to determine whether *each* of the legal conclusions is true or false according to the *general principles of trust law*. Write on a separate answer sheet whether each conclusion is true or false. Your grade will be determined by deducting your total of incorrect answers from your total of correct answers; if you omit an answer it will not affect either total.

A. The creation of an express trust consisting of real property
61. Must be evidenced by a writing to satisfy the Statute of Frauds.
62. Requires consideration to be effective.
63. Can be done by a minor.
64. Is subject to the rule against perpetuities.
65. Requires that the subject matter be definite and specific.

B. The trustee of a legally effective trust
66. Can be anyone legally capable of dealing with property.
67. Must exercise a high degree of loyalty toward the creator of the trust.
68. Must be specifically named by the creator of the trust.
69. Is an insurer against loss of trust property.
70. Is, in effect, the agent of the beneficiary.

C. The beneficiary of a legally effective trust
71. Must be specifically identified by name or by designation of the class to which he belongs.
72. May be a judicially declared incompetent.
73. May ordinarily transfer or assign his interest in the trust.
74. May be legally protected from having his creditors reach his interest in the trust by the donor's creation of a spendthrift trust.
75. Will be presumed to have accepted the trust in the absence of an express disclaimer.

D. A charitable trust
76. May be created solely for philanthropic purposes.
77. May be created to aid individual but unascertained students.
78. Is not affected by the rule against perpetuities.

79. May have its purpose changed by application of the *cy pres* doctrine.
80. Must have as trustee some corporate body to assure continuity of existence.

E. An implied trust
   81. Is created by equity to prevent injustice.
   82. Can take the form of a constructive or charitable trust.
   83. May be expressly created by the parties involved or may be inferred from their conduct.
   84. That takes the form of a resulting trust imposes no duties of performance upon the trustee.
   85. Is not subject to the Statute of Frauds.

F. A spendthrift trust
   86. Is one which provides a fund for the maintenance of an improvident person.
   87. Cannot prohibit the beneficiary from selling his interest in the trust.
   88. Can prohibit the beneficiary from subjecting the distributed trust income to the claims of his creditors.
   89. Can be created by a person for his own benefit to immunize himself against the claims of his creditors.
   90. Is often prohibited as contrary to public policy in thwarting the just claims of creditors.

Answer

61. True	67. False	73. True	79. True	85. True
62. False	68. False	74. True	80. False	86. True
63. False	69. False	75. True	81. True	87. False
64. True	70. False	76. False	82. False	88. False
65. True	71. True	77. True	83. False	89. False
66. True	72. True	78. True	84. True	90. True

NOVEMBER, 1961

No. 7

a. Thomas transferred his transistor manufacturing business to the X Trust Company in trust for the benefit of his son, Peter, for life, with the remainder to go to Peter's son James. The X Trust Company insured the business with the Y Insurance Company by taking out two policies. The first policy was a standard fire insurance policy covering the building, equipment, etc. The other policy was secured to cover the loss of income during any period that the business was inoperable as a result of tornado, earthquake or fire. The buildings and equipment were subsequently destroyed by fire and the Y Insurance Company paid the proceeds to the X Trust Company. Both Peter and James claim the entire proceeds of the insurance policies. What disposition should the X Trust Company make of the entire proceeds under the terms of the trust? Explain.

b. In December 1958 Howard transferred 1,000 shares of Z Company stock to the X Trust Company in trust for the benefit of his wife for life with the remainder to go to his son. The Z Company declared a noncash dividend in

1960 of 10 shares of stock of the M Company for each 100 shares of Z Company stock. The M Company stock had been bought by Z Company as an investment. The son claims that this dividend should be added to the corpus (principal) whereas the wife claims that she is entitled to the dividend. How should the trust company treat the dividend? Explain.

c. Same facts as above except that in 1960 the Z Company split-up its stock 2-for-1. Subsequently, the trustee sold one half of the 2,000 shares of the Z Company stock at a profit and the son and wife both claim the proceeds. How should the trust company treat the stock split-up and the proceeds from the sale? Explain.

d. X, as trustee for the benefit of Y, the life beneficiary, received the $1,000 annual cash dividends on the stock which made up the corpus of the trust. Y was abroad at the time of receipt and X in good faith and with complete honesty deposited the money in his own (X's) bank account. Before Y returned X's bank failed and the dividend in bankruptcy will only amount to fifty cents on the dollar. Y claims that X must make up the difference. Is X liable? Explain.

Answer

a. The X Trust Company should retain all the proceeds as the trust property. That portion of the proceeds resulting from the policy to cover loss of income will be treated as income and will be distributed to Peter, the life beneficiary. That portion of the proceeds resulting from the fire insurance policy will be treated as principal, to be distributed to James, the remainderman.

b. Unless otherwise provided in the trust agreement, the dividend is income and should be distributed to the wife, life tenant. Dividends payable in cash or property other than in shares of the declaring corporation are income, with exceptions inapplicable here.

c. Unless otherwise provided in the trust agreement, the stock split-up and proceeds from the sale should be treated as principal. Dividends payable in shares of the declaring corporation are principal. Profits from the sale of the additional shares are, therefore, principal also.

d. Yes, for $500. A trustee has the duty to keep the trust property separate from his own property and to make deposits of trust monies in a separate trust bank account. Any loss to trust property by the trustee commingling trust funds with his own funds causes him to be liable for such loss.

PART THIRTEEN

ACCOUNTANT'S LEGAL RESPONSIBILITY

Chapter I

RESPONSIBILITY TO CLIENT AND THE PUBLIC

ANY brief discussion of the status, duties, and liabilities of a public accountant must, of necessity, be limited to the high points and matters of dominant concern in this connection. First the status of a public accountant and then his duties and liabilities to his client and to third persons will be discussed.

Status of the Public Accountant
An accountant has been well defined as a person "competent to design and control the systems of accounts required for records of multifarious transactions of business, trade, and finance."[1] If he serves more than one employer as an independent contractor, he is a public accountant. If he has been certified as a certified public accountant by a state regulatory body, usually an administrative board, he has such status.

The public accountant is a professional person and an independent contractor, except as he changes his status. An independent contractor is a person who contracts to render an agreed performance for another called an employer, does not act on his employer's behalf, has no authority to deal with third persons or to affect the employer's contractual relations with third persons, and whose manner of performance is not subject to any right of control by the employer. A public accountant renders professional services of a specialized nature involving the exercise of judgment not subject to his client's control, and he comes within the class of an independent contractor. However, if a public accountant should be hired and paid a salary as an employee, he is an agent of his employer principal. To the extent that a public accountant is retained for a fee to render an accounting service, he is an independent contractor; to the extent that he also has authority to contract in the name of his client, he is an agent of his client as a principal. The relationship

---

[1] I Am. Jur., *Accountants,* sec. 2 (1962).

between a public accountant and his client is of a personal character[2] and, therefore, the death or serious physical disability of the public accountant or the death of the client discharges the contract by operation of law because of impossibility of performance.[3]

Duties and Liabilities of the Public Accountant   The activities of a public accountant are the result of his relationship with his client and often affect third persons. First the public accountant's duties and liabilities with respect to his client, and then with respect to third persons, will be discussed.

To His Client. *Not to Practise Law.* A public accountant is not licensed to practise law. However, he must be knowledgeable of the legal significance of the transactions and activities of his client so that he may properly reflect their nature and materiality in his audit, reports, and other accounting services rendered to his clients. It has been well stated that: "An accountant may apply legal knowledge and answer legal questions in connection with the practice of his ordinary work in the keeping of books and records and the preparation of tax returns and advising with respect to such matters, but where he undertakes to give legal advice and answer legal questions completely disconnected with such ordinary work in keeping and auditing books and preparing tax returns, he is guilty of practising law without a license."[4]

Generally. The public accountant's legal responsibility to clients is: to possess that ability and competence which a member of that profession and status professes to have and does have; to use the care, skill, and diligence of a reasonable man who is a public accountant; and to use his best prudence, discretion, and judgment as a public accountant. The professional man is an expert in the area of his profession and the layman retaining his services does not have (and cannot be expected to have) the knowledge to appraise properly the quality of the professional work being done. The client relies on the professional man's superior knowledge in such area and trusts in him. Accordingly, the law imposes a special duty upon a professional man. The public accountant's legal responsibility is to ascertain the facts pertinent to the performance required of him, to act reasonably in properly utilizing such facts in such performance, and to use reasonable care in com-

---

[2] See above, pp. 101–2, 105.
[3] See above, pp. 149–50.
[4] I Am. Jur., *Accountants,* sec. 9 (1962).

municating the performance to his client so that the client may understand and properly utilize such performance.

Communication to His Client. Numerous lawsuits against public accountants are based upon the premise that there has been a failure to communicate the information obtained in an audit to non-accountant laymen suitable, in content and terminology, to their needs as the users of such information. Generally, at the present time, it is not sufficient that the public accountant has complied with "generally accepted accounting principles," but he must inform the layman user of what *he* needs to know in terms that *he* reasonably can understand. Only then is there a full, fair, and complete disclosure consistent with the public accountant's responsibility to his client. If he fails to do this and has made a misrepresentation, he is negligent and liable for damage proximately caused by his negligence. At the present time, it appears that whether or not there has been a fair disclosure will be determined by a layman's standard established by the jury, namely, has there been a disclosure of information adequately meaningful to the particular user?

Quality of Work. A public accountant has the legal duty toward his client to exercise reasonable care, in good faith, without fraud or collusion, and to follow standard accounting practices. Except as otherwise provided by law, he exercises reasonable care when he employs that knowledge, skill, judgment, and discretion usually employed by public accountants in that particular locality under similar circumstances. Since he is in privity of contract with his client, the public accountant is liable to his client for damages for breach of contract and for loss proximately caused to his client by his ordinary negligence. However, he is not an insurer against damage to his client, and is not liable for small inaccuracies and errors of judgment. Inaccuracies of a serious character constitute a material breach of contract and preclude compensation for his services. A public accountant is to perform his work within the time expressly provided by the contract with his client, or in a reasonable time if the contract has not expressly so provided. Failure to perform within such time precludes any right to compensation for such services, unless delay is waived or excused by his client or his client's conduct caused such delay.

Payment and Lien. The contract normally fixes the fee or compensation to be paid to the public accountant. In the absence of any express provision, it is implied that his compensation will be for what his services are reasonably worth under the particular circumstances of that employment. He does not have a Common Law lien on his client's materials in his possession, but he may well acquire a statutory lien for services rendered on his client's materials (books, etc.) by their improvement.

Since a public accountant is an independent contractor employed to render accounting services, he owns and may retain his own copies of his client's books and records, copies of tax returns and working papers, in the absence of agreement to the contrary. Also, a public accountant may require his working papers and copies should his performance be questioned later, and such papers should be in his possession. He also owns the originals of letters written to him in connection with his work, copies of letters written by him, analyses, computations, and other such materials. Inasmuch as such materials contain data which are the subject of a confidential relationship between the public accountant and his client, their transfer or disclosure by the accountant without the client's permission would be improper as a violation of their confidential relationship and is not ethically or legally sanctioned. Of course, papers, records and other materials loaned by the client are the property of the client and are to be returned to him by the public accountant. It should be noted that if a public accountant becomes an employee and, therefore, an agent, the working and other papers belong to his employer principal.

Privileged Communications. Because of the confidential relationship existing between the public accountant and his client, communications between them in connection with the employment are confidential and *ethically* are not to be disclosed by the public accountant without his client's permission. However, unless such communications are recognized and privileged by statute, the public accountant can be compelled to testify in court concerning such communications. Such communications were not privileged at Common Law. A communication is privileged when, by statute, it is recognized as a confidential communication of such a nature as to be precluded from admission into evidence in court without the utterer's consent. The purpose of according a statutory privilege to communications between public accountant and his client is to encourage free discussion and exchange of information between the parties, even at the expense of making such communications unavailable in court under the rules of evidence. Today, most of the statutes which provide that communications between a public accountant and his client are privileged do not limit the privilege with respect to any particular proceedings; in some states the privilege is inapplicable in matters involving criminal law. When a statute causes communications between public accountant and his client to become privileged, the public accountant has a *legal* duty not to disclose such communications without his client's consent. The privilege is for the benefit of his client, and only the client can waive it. By statute, the client's permission to the accountant to testify is a waiver of the client's privilege and the accountant is relieved of his obligation not to testify. Although not a matter of specific statutory provision, it would seem that the client had waived his privilege if he sued the accountant on a privileged matter or if the client had published the otherwise privileged matter, especially if it were published to a third person who was suing the accountant in connection with such matter.

To Third Persons. While a public accountant has duties towards his client because of their privity of contract, since no such privity of contract exists between the public accountant and third persons there is no duty of care owing to them, with one exception. When the public accountant has reason to believe that his accounting services which he has rendered to his client (e.g., a certified balance sheet) will be made available by his client to third persons, then a legal duty of care is imposed upon the public accountant. The extent of this duty of care depends upon whether the public accountant knows the specific identity of the third person and that he intends to rely upon the public accountant's professional opinion.[5] If the specific identity of the third person is known to the public accountant, then the latter has the same duty of care toward such identified third person as he has to his client, and he is liable for damage caused to such third person by his ordinary negligence. However, if the public accountant does not know the specific identity of the third person to whom his professional opinion is to be made available, then his liability to such third person is only for actual fraud, or for gross negligence amounting to constructive fraud. It should be noted that actual fraud exists when there is present an actual intent to mislead, legally called "scienter"; while constructive fraud exists when there is no such actual intent but there is reckless disregard for the truth. "A mere mistake in the balance sheet which is the result of negligence only is not ordinarily a basis for recovery by a third person, but a representation certified as true to the knowledge of the accountant when there is no knowledge, a reckless misstatement, or an opinion based on grounds so flimsy as to lead to the conclusion that there is no genuine belief in its truth, is a sufficient basis for liability."[6] In other words, a misrepresentation made recklessly, careless whether the matter misrepresented be true or false, is made without belief in its

---

[5] William L. Prosser, *Handbook of the Law of Torts* (5th ed.; St. Paul, Minn.: West Publishing Co., 1971), pp. 718, 721–28.

[6] I Am. Jur., *Accountants,* sec. 19 (1962).

truth. A person's misrepresentation which expressly or impliedly asserts a particular basis for his knowledge or belief, such as his actual knowledge of the matter misrepresented or his personal investigation of it, when there is no such basis for his professed knowledge or belief, is made fraudulently.

Federal Statutes. An increasing amount of recent civil litigation and criminal prosecution involving public accountants should alert the accounting profession to the serious exposure of public accountants to federal and state *statutory* civil and criminal[7] liability for fraudulent and negligent misrepresentations made in the practice of accountancy. Of particular importance are the federal: Securities Act of 1933; Securities Exchange Act of 1934; Internal Revenue Code; False Statements Act; Mail Fraud Act; and Conspiracy Statute. These should be very carefully examined, particularly regarding negligent and fraudulent misrepresentations made in various statements, e.g., registration, financial, and accompanying documents. Pertinent excerpts from these statutes are reproduced here for guidance.

Each state has a legal right, in exercise of its police power, to prevent "speculative schemes which have no more basis than so many feet of blue sky." Such state laws requiring securities registration are usually licensing laws. Full disclosure about the securities being offered for purchase by investors does not of itself entitle the securities to be registered. The state administrator of blue-sky laws still must pass upon the speculative character of the securities and what is reasonably necessary to protect the public, e.g., the issuer posting a bond, before permitting registration. In contrast, the federal government *supplements* state blue-sky laws by the federal Securities Act of 1933, which requires securities registration, and the Securities Exchange Act of 1934. The primary purpose of the 1933 Act is full disclosure about the securities being offered for purchase by investors and, on such disclosure, the securities are registered irrespective of how speculative they may be.

Federal Securities Act of 1933. The federal Securities Act of 1933, U.S. Code, Title 15, Chapter 2A, provides for civil liability of independent accountants in connection with a false registration statement:

§ 77k. Civil liabilities on account of false registration statement

(a) In case any part of the registration statement, when such part became effective, contained an untrue statement of a material fact or omitted to state a

---

[7] For an excellent article, see "Criminal Liability of Accountants: Sources and Policies," by Thomas W. Dunfee and Irvin N. Glein, 9 *American Business Law Journal*, Spring, 1971, pp. 1–20.

material fact required to be stated therein or necessary to make the statements therein not misleading, any person acquiring such security (unless it is proved that at the time of such acquisition he knew of such untruth or omission) may, either at law or in equity, in any court of competent jurisdiction, sue—

. . . . . .

(4) every accountant, engineer, or appraiser, or any person whose profession gives authority to a statement made by him, who has with his consent been named as having prepared or certified any part of the registration statement, or as having prepared or certified any report or valuation which is used in connection with the registration statement, with respect to the statement in such registration statement, report, or valuation, which purports to have been prepared or certified by him;

(5) every underwriter with respect to such security.

If such person acquired the security after the issuer has made generally available to its security holders an earning statement covering a period of at least twelve months beginning after the effective date of the registration statement, then the right of recovery under this subsection shall be conditioned on proof that such person acquired the security relying upon such untrue statement in the registration statement or relying upon the registration statement and not knowing of such omission, but such reliance may be established without proof of the reading of the registration statement by such person.

(b) Notwithstanding the provisions of subsection (a) of this section no person, other than the issuer, shall be liable as provided therein who shall sustain the burden of proof—

(1) that before the effective date of the part of the registration statement with respect to which his liability is asserted (A) he had resigned from or had taken such steps as are permitted by law to resign from, or ceased or refused to act in, every office, capacity, or relationship in which he was described in the registration statement as acting or agreeing to act, and (B) he had advised the Commission and the issuer in writing that he had taken such action and that he would not be responsible for such part of the registration statement; or

(2) that if such part of the registration statement became effective without his knowledge, upon becoming aware of such fact he forthwith acted and advised the Commission, in accordance with paragraph (1) of this subsection, and, in addition, gave reasonable public notice that such part of the registration statement had become effective without his knowledge; or

(3) that (A) as regards any part of the registration statement not purporting to be made on the authority of an expert, and not purporting to be a copy of or extract from a report or valuation of an expert, and not purporting to be made on the authority of a public official document or statement, he had, after reasonable investigation, reasonable ground to believe and did believe, at the time such part of the registration statement became effective, that the statements therein were true and that there was no omission to state a material fact required to be stated therein or necessary to make the statements therein not misleading; and (B) as regards any part of the registration statement purporting to be made upon his authority as an expert or purporting to be a copy of or extract from a report or valuation of himself as an expert, (i) he had, after reasonable investigation, reasonable ground to believe and did believe, at the

time such part of the registration statement became effective, that the statements therein were true and that there was no omission to state a material fact required to be stated therein or necessary to make the statements therein not misleading, or (ii) such part of the registration statement did not fairly represent his statement as an expert or was not a fair copy of or extract from his report or valuation as an expert; and (C) as regards any part of the registration statement purporting to be made on the authority of an expert (other than himself) or purporting to be a copy of or extract from a report or valuation of an expert (other than himself), he had no reasonable ground to believe and did not believe, at the time such part of the registration statement became effective, that the statements therein were untrue or that there was an omission to state a material fact required to be stated therein or necessary to make the statements therein not misleading, or that such part of the registration statement did not fairly represent the statement of the expert or was not a fair copy of or extract from the report or valuation of the expert; and (D) as regards any part of the registration statement purporting to be a statement made by an official person or purporting to be a copy of or extract from a public official document, he had no reasonable ground to believe and did not believe, at the time such part of the registration statement became effective, that the statements therein were untrue, or that there was an omission to state a material fact required to be stated therein or necessary to make the statements therein not misleading, or that such part of the registration statement did not fairly represent the statement made by the official person or was not a fair copy of or extract from the public official document.

(c) In determining, for the purpose of paragraph (3) of subsection (b) of this section, what constitutes reasonable investigation and reasonable ground for belief, the standard of reasonableness shall be that required of a prudent man in the management of his own property.

.   .   .   .   .

(e) The suit authorized under subsection (a) of this section may be to recover such damages as shall represent the difference between the amount paid for the security (not exceeding the price at which the security was offered to the public) and (1) the value thereof as of the time such suit was brought, or (2) the price at which such security shall have been disposed of in the market before suit, or (3) the price at which such security shall have been disposed of after suit but before judgment if such damages shall be less than the damages representing the difference between the amount paid for the security (not exceeding the price at which the security was offered to the public) and the value thereof as of the time such suit was brought: *Provided,* That if the defendant proves that any portion or all of such damages represents other than the depreciation in value of such security resulting from such part of the registration statement, with respect to which his liability is asserted, not being true or omitting to state a material fact required to be stated therein or necessary to make the statements therein not misleading, such portion of or all such damages shall not be recoverable. . . .

.   .   .   .   .

(f) All or any one or more of the persons specified in subsection (a) of this section shall be jointly and severally liable, and every person who becomes liable to make any payment under this section may recover contribution as in cases of contract from any person who, if sued separately, would have been liable to make the same payment, unless the person who has become liable was, and the other was not, guilty of fraudulent misrepresentation.

(g) In no case shall the amount recoverable under this section exceed the price at which the security was offered to the public.

. . . . .

§77m. Limitation of actions

No action shall be maintained to enforce any liability created under section 77k or 77*l* (2) of this title unless brought within one year after the discovery of the untrue statement or the omission, or after such discovery should have been made by the exercise of reasonable diligence, or, if the action is to enforce a liability created under section 77*l* (1) of this title, unless brought within one year after the violation upon which it is based. In no event shall any such action be brought to enforce a liability created under section 77k or 77*l* (1) of this title more than three years after the security was bona fide offered to the public, or under section 77*l* (2) of this title more than three years after the sale.

. . . . .

§77x. Penalties

Any person who willfully violates any of the provisions of this subchapter, or the rules and regulations promulgated by the Commission under authority thereof, or any person who willfully, in a registration statement filed under this subchapter, makes any untrue statement of a material fact or omits to state any material fact required to be stated therein or necessary to make the statements therein not misleading, shall upon conviction be fined not more than $5,000 or imprisoned not more than five years, or both.

The Act does not define "material fact," but the Securities and Exchange Commission has held that a material fact is "a fact which if it had been correctly stated would have deterred or tended to deter the average prudent investor from purchasing the securities in question."

Federal Securities Exchange Act of 1934. The federal Securities Exchange Act of 1934, U.S. Code, Title 15, Chapter 2B, provides in part:

§78r. Liability for misleading statements

(a) Any person who shall make or cause to be made any statement in any application, report, or document filed pursuant to this chapter or any rule or regulation thereunder or any undertaking contained in a registration statement as provided in subsection (d) of section 78*o* of this title, which statement was at the time and in the light of the circumstances under which it was made false or misleading with respect to any material fact, shall be liable to any person (not knowing that such statement was false or misleading) who, in reliance upon such statement, shall have purchased or sold a security at a price which was affected by such statement, for damages caused by such reliance, unless the person sued shall prove that he acted in good faith and had no knowledge that such statement was false or misleading. A person seeking to enforce such liability may sue at law or in equity in any court of competent jurisdiction. In any such suit the court may, in its discretion, require an undertaking for the payment of the costs of such suit, and assess reasonable costs, including reasonable attorneys' fees, against either party litigant.

· · · · ·

(c) No action shall be maintained to enforce any liability created under this section unless brought within one year after the discovery of the facts constituting the cause of action and within three years after such cause of action accrued.

· · · · ·

§78ff. Penalties

(a) Any person who willfully violates any provision of this chapter, or any rule or regulation thereunder the violation of which is made unlawful or the observance of which is required under the terms of this chapter, or any person who willfully and knowingly makes, or causes to be made, any statement in any application, report, or document required to be filed under this chapter or any rule or regulation thereunder or any undertaking contained in a registration statement as provided in subsection (d) of section 78o of this title, which statement was false or misleading with respect to any material fact, shall upon conviction be fined not more than $10,000, or imprisoned not more than two years, or both, except that when such person is an exchange, a fine not exceeding $500,000 may be imposed; but no person shall be subject to imprisonment under this section for the violation of any rule or regulation if he proves that he had no knowledge of such rule or regulation.

· · · · · ·

Internal Revenue Code. The federal Internal Revenue Code, Chapter 75, provides in part:

§7206. Fraud and false statements

Any person who—

(1) *Declaration under penalties of perjury.*—Willfully makes and subscribes any return, statement, or other document, which contains or is verified by a written declaration that it is made under the penalties of perjury, and which he does not believe to be true and correct as to every material matter; or

(2) *Aid or assistance.*—Willfully aids or assists in, or procures, counsels, or advises the preparation or presentation under, or in connection with any matter arising under, the internal revenue laws, of a return, affidavit, claim, or other document, which is fraudulent or is false as to any material matter, whether or not such falsity or fraud is with the knowledge or consent of the person authorized or required to present such return, affidavit, claim, or document; or

(3) *Fraudulent bonds, permits, and entries.*—Simulates or falsely or fraudulently executes or signs any bond, permit, entry, or other document required by the provisions of the internal revenue laws, or by any regulation made in pursuance thereof, or procures the same to be falsely or fraudulently executed, or advises, aids in, or connives at such execution thereof; or

(4) *Removal or concealment with intent to defraud.*—Removes, depos-

its, or conceals, or is concerned in removing, depositing, or concealing, any goods or commodities for or in respect whereof any tax is or shall be imposed, or any property upon which levy is authorized by section 6331, with intent to evade or defeat the assessment or collection of any tax imposed by this title; or

(5) *Compromises and closing agreements.*—In connection with any compromise under section 7122, or offer of such compromise, or in connection with any closing agreement under section 7121, or offer to enter into any such agreement, willfully—

(A) *Concealment of property.*—Conceals from any officer or employee of the United States any property belonging to the estate of a taxpayer or other person liable in respect of the tax, or

(B) *Withholding, falsifying, and destroying records.*—Receives, withholds, destroys, mutilates, or falsifies any book, document, or record, or makes any false statement, relating to the estate or financial condition of the taxpayer or other person liable in respect of the tax;

shall be guilty of a felony and, upon conviction thereof, shall be fined not more than $5,000, or imprisoned not more than 3 years, or both, together with the costs of prosecution.

§7207. Fraudulent returns, statements, or other documents

Any person who willfully delivers or discloses to the Secretary or his delegate any list, return, account, statement, or other document, known by him to be fraudulent or to be false as to any material matter, shall be fined not more than $1,000, or imprisoned not more than 1 year, or both. Any person required pursuant to sections 6047(b) or (c), 6056, or 6104(d) to furnish any information to the Secretary or any other person who willfully furnishes to the Secretary or such other person any information known by him to be fraudulent or to be false as to any material matter shall be fined not more than $1,000, or imprisoned not more than 1 year, or both.

Federal Fraud and False Statements Act. The federal Fraud and False Statements Act, U.S. Code, Title 18, Chapter 47, sec. 1001, on statements or entries generally, provides:

Whoever, in any matter within the jurisdiction of any department or agency of the United States knowingly and willfully falsifies, conceals or covers up by any trick, scheme, or device a material fact, or makes any false, fictitious or fraudulent statements or representations, or makes or uses any false writing or document knowing the same to contain any false, fictitious or fraudulent statement or entry, shall be fined not more than $10,000 or imprisoned not more than five years, or both.

Federal Mail Fraud Act. The federal Mail Fraud Act, U.S. Code, Title 18, Chapter 63, provides in part:

§1341. Frauds and swindles

Whoever, having devised or intending to devise any scheme or artifice to defraud, or for obtaining money or property by means of false or fraudulent pretenses, representations, or promises, or to sell, dispose of, loan, exchange, alter, give away, distribute, supply, or furnish or procure for unlawful use any counterfeit or spurious coin, obligation, security, or other article, or anything represented to be or intimated or held out to be such counterfeit or spurious article, for the purpose of executing such scheme or artifice or attempting so to do, places in any post office or authorized depository for mail matter, any matter or thing whatever to be sent or delivered by the Postal Service, or takes or receives therefrom, any such matter or thing, or knowingly causes to be delivered by mail according to the direction thereon, or at the place at which it is directed to be delivered by the person to whom it is addressed, any such matter or thing, shall be fined not more than $1,000 or imprisoned not more than five years, or both.

. . . . .

§1343. Fraud by wire, radio, or television

Whoever, having devised or intending to devise any scheme or artifice to defraud, or for obtaining money or property by means of false or fraudulent pretenses, representations, or promises, transmits or causes to be transmitted by means of wire, radio, or television communication in interstate or foreign commerce, any writings, signs, signals, pictures, or sounds for the purpose of executing such scheme or artifice, shall be fined not more than $1,000 or imprisoned not more than five years, or both.

Federal Conspiracy Act. The federal Conspiracy Act, U.S. Code, Title 18, Chapter 19, sec. 371, provides:

§371. Conspiracy to commit offense or to defraud United States

If two or more persons conspire either to commit any offense against the United States, or to defraud the United States, or any agency thereof in any manner or for any purpose, and one or more of such persons do any act to effect the object of the conspiracy, each shall be fined not more than $10,000 or imprisoned not more than five years, or both.

If, however, the offense, the commission of which is the object of the conspiracy, is a misdemeanor only, the punishment for such conspiracy shall not exceed the maximum punishment provided for such misdemeanor.

Professional Ethics

The American Institute of Certified Public Accountants is a national association serving certified public accountants and assisting in the maintenance of high professional standards. It publishes a "Code of Professional Ethics and Interpretive Opinions" which is kept continually current, reflecting the standards of conduct expected of certified public accountants. Examination of this publication reflects, among other things, that a certified public accountant will hold the affairs of his clients in strict confidence, and in expressing an opinion on representations in financial statements which he has examined he or an associate may be held guilty of an act discreditable to the profession if:

(a) he fails to disclose a material fact known to him which is not disclosed in the financial statements but disclosure of which is necessary to make the financial statements not misleading ;or

(b) he fails to report any material misstatement known to him to appear in the financial statement; or

(c) he is materially negligent in the conduct of his examination or in making his report thereon; or

(d) he fails to acquire sufficient information to warrant expression of an opinion, or his exceptions are sufficiently material to negative the expression of an opinion; or

(e) he fails to direct attention to any material departure from generally accepted accounting principles or to disclose any material omission of generally accepted auditing procedure applicable in the circumstances.[7]

The publication also states in Opinion No. 3, "Member selling accounting practice should not give the purchaser access to working papers, income tax returns, and correspondence pertaining to accounts being sold without first obtaining permission of client."[8] Such ethical concepts and the law are in accord. Public accountants should be guided in their conduct by standards as expressed by legislation, judicial decisions, and standards established by the profession.

---

[7] *Code of Professional Ethics and Interpretive Opinions,* American Institute of Certified Public Accountants, December 30, 1969, pp. 3–4.

[8] *Ibid.,* p. 12.

APPENDIX TO PART THIRTEEN

SOME PREVIOUS C.P.A. LAW EXAMINATION QUESTIONS AND MODEL ANSWERS

MAY, 1971

No. 4 (Estimated time—25 to 30 minutes)

Part a. Risk Capital Limited, a Delaware corporation, was considering the purchase of a substantial amount of the treasury stock held by Florida Sunshine Corporation, a closely held corporation. Initial discussions with the Florida Sunshine Corporation began late in 1969.

Wilson and Wyatt, Florida Sunshine's accountants, regularly prepared quarterly and annual unaudited financial statements. The most recently prepared financial statements were for the year ended September 30, 1970.

On November 15, 1970, after protracted negotiations, Risk Capital agreed to purchase 100,000 shares of no par, Class A Capital Stock of Florida Sunshine at $12.50 per share. However, Risk Capital insisted upon audited statements for calendar year 1970. The contract specifically provided:

Risk Capital shall have the right to rescind the purchase of said stock if the audited financial statements of Florida Sunshine for calendar year 1970 show a material adverse change in the financial condition of the Corporation.

The audited financial statements furnished to Florida Sunshine by Wilson and Wyatt showed no such material adverse change. Risk Capital relied upon the audited statements and purchased the treasury stock of Florida Sunshine. It was subsequently discovered that, as of the balance sheet date, the audited statements were incorrect and that in fact there had been a material adverse change in the financial condition of the Corporation. Florida Sunshine is insolvent and Risk Capital will lose virtually its entire investment.

Risk Capital seeks recovery against Wilson and Wyatt.
(1) Discuss each of the theories of liability that Risk Capital will probably assert as its basis for recovery.
(2) Assuming that only ordinary negligence is proven, will Risk Capital prevail? State "yes" or "no" and explain.

Part b. Wells and White, the accountants for the Allie Corporation, provided various professional services for Allie over 15 years under annual retainer agreements. The services included tax return preparation, special cost analyses, and the preparation of the Corporation's audited and unaudited financial statements.

The relationship had been quite harmonious until the retirement of Roberts, the president and founder of Allie Corporation. His successor, Strong, was a very aggressive, expansion-oriented individual who lacked the competence and personal attraction of his predecessor. Two years after Roberts' retirement the unbroken record of increases in annual earnings was in jeopardy.

Strong realized that a decrease in earnings would have an unfavorable impact on his image and on his plans to merge with a well known conglomerate. He called Wells, the senior partner of Wells and White, and demanded that the method of computing and reporting the current year's earnings be changed in a way that would preserve the upward trend in earnings.

Although the proposed method would be within the realm of generally accepted accounting principles, Wells subsequently told Strong that, in the exercise of its professional judgment, the firm could not agree to such a change. Strong promptly dismissed the firm and refused to pay the final billing of $1,750 for services rendered to the date of dismissal under its agreement with Wells and White.

Wells and White have brought suit against Allie Corporation for the $1,750. Allie Corporation responded by denying liability on the ground that the firm's refusal to cooperate constituted a breach of contract which precluded recovery. Allie also counterclaimed by demanding the return of all audit working papers, correspondence and duplicate tax returns and supporting explanations pertaining to Allie Corporation.

(1) Is the Wells and White account receivable valid and enforceable against the Allie Corporation? State "yes" or "no" and explain.

(2) Will Allie Corporation prevail on its counterclaim demanding return of the audit working papers, correspondence and tax returns? State "yes" or "no" and explain.

Part c. Continuing the situation described in Part "b" above: Strong was unable to find other accountants who approved of the proposed change in the method of computing and reporting earnings, so he abandoned this demand and then engaged new accountants, Bar & Cross. Income continued to decrease in the next two quarters and Strong became convinced that the cause of this must be due to defalcations by some dishonest employee. Therefore, he engaged Bar & Cross to make a special study to discover the guilty person. After several months of intensive work Bar & Cross were able to discover minor defalcations of $950. Of this amount, $600 was stolen during the last two years while Wells and White were Allie Corporation's accountants. Allie Corporation sues Wells and White for the loss.

Will Allie Corporation recover the loss from Wells and White? State "yes" or "no" and explain.

Answer

a. (1) The first theory of liability is that Wilson and Wyatt were ordinarily negligent in their audit and liable to Risk Capital for its consequent loss. Although there is no privity of contract between the accountant and third persons and, therefore, there is no duty of care owing by him to third persons, nevertheless there is an exception. Only if the accountant has reason to believe that his accounting services which he has rendered to his client will be made available by his client to third persons will a legal duty of care be imposed upon him. If he knows the specific identity of the third person and that he intends to rely upon the accountant's professional opinion, then he has the duty to exercise reasonable care, and he is liable for his ordinary negligence which proximately causes damage to the third person. Here, Risk Capital will assert that Wilson and Wyatt knew of Risk Capital's identity and that it intended to rely upon the audit. Risk Capital will then assert that Wilson and Wyatt were ordinarily negligent in that they failed to exercise reasonable care in their examination, and that their failure to comply with generally accepted accounting principles indicated negligence.

The second theory of liability is that Wilson and Wyatt were guilty of actual or constructive fraud in their audit and therefore liable to Risk Capital for its consequent loss. If an accountant does not know the specific identity of the third person to whom his professional opinion is to be made available, then his liability to such third person is only for actual fraud, or for gross negligence amounting to constructive fraud. Actual fraud exists if there is an actual intent to mislead. Constructive fraud exists if there is no actual fraud but, rather, a reckless disregard for the truth. Risk Capital would have to prove actual or constructive fraud by Wilson and Wyatt.

(2) No. Ordinary negligence is not enough for fraud; and it is not enough by itself without a reasonable belief by Wilson and Wyatt that their audit would be made available by their client to Risk Capital for its reliance thereon.

b. (1) Yes. The accountant is an independent contractor whose obligation is to render an agreed end performance and whose manner of performance is not subject to any right of control by his client employer. While he is to follow standard accounting practices and to comply with generally accepted accounting principles, nevertheless the manner and end result of his performance are within his sole prerogative. Therefore, Wells and White have a valid and enforceable account receivable against Allie for their services rendered.

(2) No. Inasmuch as the accountant is an independent contractor, the audit working papers, correspondence, and tax returns belong to him, in the absence of agreement to the contrary.

c. No. There is no proof of ordinary negligence by Wells and White in their audit. The usual audit function does not include special search for defalcations. Bar and Cross did not discover the minor defalcations in their audits until engaged to make a special study for that purpose, and then only after several months of intensive study. Also, the defalcations were of a minor nature. These facts would prove no negligence by Wells and White.

NOVEMBER, 1970

No. 5 (Estimated time—20 to 25 minutes)

Part a. The Chriswell Corporation decided to raise additional long-term capital by issuing $3,000,000 of 8 percent subordinated debentures to the public.

May, Clark & Co., C.P.A.s, the company's auditors, were engaged to examine the June 30, 1970, financial statements which were included in the bond registration statement.

May, Clark & Co. completed its examination and submitted an unqualified auditor's report dated July 15, 1970. The registration statement was filed and became effective on September 1, 1970. Two weeks prior to the effective date one of the partners of May, Clark & Co. called on Chriswell Corporation and had lunch with the financial vice president and the controller. He questioned both officials on the company's operations since June 30 and inquired whether there had been any material changes in the company's financial position since that date. Both officers assured him that everything had proceeded normally and that the financial condition of the company had not changed materially.

Unfortunately the officers' representation was not true. On July 30, a substantial debtor of the company failed to pay the $400,000 due on its account receivable and indicated to Chriswell that it would probably be forced into bankruptcy. This receivable was shown as a collateralized loan on the June 30 financial statements. It was secured by stock of the debtor corporation which had a value in excess of the loan at the time the financial statements were prepared but was virtually worthless at the effective date of the registration statement. This $400,000 account receivable was material to the financial condition of Chriswell Corporation, and the market price of the subordinated debentures decreased by nearly 50 percent after the foregoing facts were disclosed.

The debenture holders of Chriswell are seeking recovery of their loss against all parties connected with the debenture registration.

Is May, Clark & Co. liable to the Chriswell debenture holders? Explain.

Part b. Meglow Corporation manufactured ladies' dresses and blouses. Because its cash position was deteriorating, Meglow sought a loan from Busch Factors. Busch had previously extended $25,000 credit to Meglow but refused to lend any additional money without obtaining copies of Meglow's audited financial statements.

Meglow contacted the C.P.A. firm of Watkins, Winslow & Watkins to perform the audit. In arranging for the examination, Meglow clearly indicated that its purpose was to satisfy Busch Factors as to the Corporation's sound financial condition and thus to obtain an additional loan of $50,000. Watkins, Winslow & Watkins accepted the engagement, performed the examination in a negligent manner and rendered an unqualified auditor's opinion. If an adequate examination had been performed, the financial statements would have been found to be misleading.

Meglow submitted the audited financial statements to Busch Factors and obtained an additional loan of $35,000. Busch refused to lend more than that amount. After several other factors also refused, Meglow finally was able to persuade Maxwell Department Stores, one of its customers, to lend the additional $15,000. Maxwell relied upon the financial statements examined by Watkins, Winslow & Watkins.

Meglow is now in bankruptcy and Busch seeks to collect from Watkins, Winslow & Watkins the $60,000 it loaned Meglow. Maxwell seeks to recover from Watkins, Winslow & Watkins the $15,000 it loaned Meglow.

(1) Will Busch recover? Explain.

(2) Will Maxwell recover? Explain.

Answer

a.   Yes. Under the federal Securities Act of 1933, privity of contract between an accountant and third persons is not required as a basis of liability on the part of the accountant to third party investors for an untrue statement of a material fact or an omission to state a material fact required to be stated in a registration statement. Here, the $400,000 account receivable, later shown to have been worthless, was material to the financial condition of the Corporation. Accordingly, the financial statements included in the bond registration statement contained either a false statement or a material omission. However, an accountant may avoid liability if he can prove that he had made a reasonable investigation and had reasonable ground to believe and did believe that, at the time the registration statement became effective, the statements therein were true and that there was no omission to state a material fact. Here, the C.P.A. firm failed to make a reasonable investigation to verify the validity of the financial statements as of the effective date. Reliance upon the assurances of the Corporation's officers was insufficient. Therefore, the C.P.A. firm will be liable to the debenture holders.

b. (1) Yes, but only $35,000. The original $25,000 loan was made by Busch before the C.P.A. firm had rendered any opinion which, therefore, was not a cause for any loss to Busch in connection with that loan. Although there is no privity of contract between an accountant and third persons and, therefore, there is no duty of care owing by him to third persons, nevertheless there is an exception. Only if the accountant has reason to believe that his accounting services which he has rendered to his client will be made available by his client to third persons will a legal duty of care be imposed upon him. If he knows the specific identity of the third person and that the latter intends to rely upon the accountant's professional opinions, then he has the duty to exercise reasonable care and he is liable for his ordinary negligence which proximately caused damage to the third person. Here, the C.P.A. firm knew of Busch's identity and that it intended to rely upon the audit. Since the C.P.A. firm was negligent which caused the loss to Busch, the C.P.A. firm is liable for such loss.

(2) No. Since the C.P.A. firm did not know of Maxwell's identity and that its accounting services rendered to its client would be made available by its client to Maxwell, it has no duty of ordinary reasonable care to Maxwell and is not liable to Maxwell for ordinary negligence.

MAY, 1970

No. 1 (Estimated time—13 to 17 minutes)

Each of the following numbered statements states a legal conclusion relating to the lettered material. You are to determine whether each of the legal conclusions is true or false according to *general principles of accountants' legal responsibility*. Write on a separate answer sheet whether each conclusion is true or false. Your grade will be determined from your total net score obtained by deducting a weighted total for your incorrect answers from your total of correct answers; an omitted answer will not be considered an incorrect answer.

A. Marshall, Clay, Henry and Company is a brokerage firm which deals in over-the-counter stocks and commodities. The brokerage firm engaged the accounting firm of Smith and Wilson to examine quarterly financial statements. Smith and Wilson performed the audit for three years (1966–68) and the business appeared to be prosperous. Early in 1969 Baron, a trusted employee in charge of the commodities department, confessed to fraud after an office investigation by Marshall, Clay, Henry and Company. As a result it was learned that Baron had stolen over one million dollars during the four-year period preceding his confession. Baron had falsified the books of the firm to avoid detection. Marshall, Clay, Henry and Company has sued the accounting firm.

  1. The accounting firm is liable for the loss for breach of contract in that the standard audit contract guarantees the discovery of defalcations.
  2. The standard of care that must be used in the audit is the care which a reasonably prudent and skillful accountant would use under like circumstances.
  3. If it can be shown that the brokerage firm failed to exercise reasonable care and thus contributed to Baron's continued defalcations, the accountants will not be liable for the losses.
  4. In the event a surety paid the brokerage firm for a portion of the defalcations under a blanket fidelity bond which covered Baron, the surety company could obtain reimbursement from the accountants if they were negligent in performing any of the audits.
  5. If the audit contract were not in writing, the accountants could plead the Statute of Frauds and avoid liability.

B. Watts and Williams, a firm of certified public accountants, audited the accounts of Sampson Skins, Inc., a corporation that imports and deals in fine furs. Upon completion of the examination the auditors supplied Sampson Skins with 20 copies of the certified balance sheet. The firm knew in a general way that Sampson Skins wanted that number of copies of the auditor's report to furnish to banks and other potential lenders.

The balance sheet in question was in error by approximately $800,000. Instead of having a $600,000 net worth, the Corporation was insolvent. The management of Sampson Skins had "doctored" the books to avoid bankruptcy. The assets had been overstated by $500,000 of fictitious and non-existing accounts receivable and $300,000 of nonexisting skins listed as inventory when in fact Sampson Skins had only empty boxes. The audit failed to detect these fraudulent entries. Martinson, relying on the certified balance sheet, loaned Sampson Skins $200,000. He seeks to recover his loss from Watts and Williams.

  6. If Martinson alleges and proves negligence on the part of Watts and Williams, he would be able to recover his loss.
  7. If Martinson alleges and proves constructive fraud, i.e., gross negligence on the part of Watts and Williams, he would be able to recover his loss.

8. Martinson is not in privity of contract with Watts and Williams.

9. Unless actual fraud on the part of Watts and Williams could be shown, Martinson could not recover.

10. Martinson is a third party beneficiary of the contract Watts and Williams made with Sampson Skins.

C. The Dandy Container Corporation engaged the accounting firm of Adams and Adams to examine financial statements to be used in connection with a public offering of securities. The audit was completed and an unqualified opinion was expressed on the financial statements which were submitted to the Securities and Exchange Commission along with the registration statement. Two hundred thousand shares of Dandy Container common stock were offered to the public at $11 a share. Eight months later the stock fell to $2 a share when it was disclosed that several large loans to two "paper" corporations owned by one of the directors were worthless. The loans were secured by the stock of the borrowing corporation which was owned by the director. These facts were not disclosed in the financial report. The director involved and the two corporations are insolvent.

11. The Securities Act of 1933 applies to the above described public offering of securities in interstate commerce.

12. The accounting firm has potential liability to any person who acquired the stock in reliance upon the registration statement.

13. An insider who had knowledge of all the facts regarding the loans to the two "paper" corporations could nevertheless recover from the accounting firm.

14. An investor who bought shares in Dandy Container would make a prima facie case if he alleges that the failure to explain the nature of the loans in question constituted a false statement or misleading omission in the financial statements.

15. The accountants could avoid liability if they could show they were neither negligent nor fraudulent.

16. Accountants' responsibility as to the fairness of the financial statements is determined as of the date of the auditor's report and not beyond.

17. The accountants could avoid or reduce the damages asserted against them if they could establish that the drop in price was due in whole or in part to other causes.

18. The Dandy investors would have to institute suit within one year after discovery of the alleged untrue statements or omissions.

19. It would appear that the accountants were negligent in respect to the handling of the secured loans in question—if they discovered the facts regarding the loans to the "paper" corporations and failed to disclose them in their financial statements.

20. The Securities and Exchange Commission would defend any action brought against the accountants in that the SEC examined and approved the registration statement.

Answer

1. False	3. True	5. False	7. True	9. False
2. True	4. True	6. False	8. True	10. False

11. True	13. False	15. True	17. True	19. True
12. True	14. True	16. False	18. True	20. False

MAY, 1964

No. 6

a. Peter is a certified public accountant and Frank is one of his clients. Frank was sued and Peter was called as a witness by the opposing party. After being sworn in, Peter was asked certain questions which related to confidential business matters of Frank which came to Peter's attention in his professional accounting capacity. Frank's attorney immediately objected to the questions, claiming that the admission of such evidence would be violative of the "privileged communication" rule.

(1) Explain the meaning of the term privileged communication.

(2) What is the policy factor which has led to the recognition of privileged communication as a valid reason for the exclusion of evidence?

(3) Indicate the most common types of relationships that give rise to privileged communication.

(4) Based upon the attorney's objection, what will the result be in the above fact situation according to the common law rule? Explain.

Answer

a. (1) A communication is privileged when, by statute, it is recognized as a confidential communication of such a nature as to be precluded from admission into evidence in court without the utterer's consent.

(2) The purpose of according a statutory privilege to communications is to encourage free discussion and exchange of information between the parties, even at the expense of making such communications unavailable in court under the rules of evidence.

(3) Husband and wife, attorney and client, physician and patient, priest and penitent, accountant and client.

(4) Peter will be compelled to testify and answer the questions. Under the Common Law, communications between accountant and client were not privileged. In those states where the Common Law rule has been changed and communications between accountant and client are privileged, Peter could not be compelled to testify and answer the questions.

PART FOURTEEN

PUBLIC LAW REFERENCES AND QUESTIONS

DISCUSSION

THE 1970 edition of "Information for CPA CANDIDATES," published by the American Institute of Certified Public Accountants, indicates three topics in the area of public law which are new to the Business Law section of the Uniform C.P.A. Examination and "may be expected in the *November 1972 and subsequent examinations.*" They are: antitrust, federal securities regulation, and regulation of the employer and employee relationship.

Public law is that part of the law concerned with the creation and operation of government in a politically organized society. The topic of antitrust is primarily concerned with the preservation of competition in business. The major sources of law on this topic are the Sherman, Clayton, Robinson-Patman, and Federal Trade Commission Acts. The publication of the Institute indicates that the questions on the examination "will cover matters such as monopolization; price fixing and other cooperative matters among competitors; resale price maintenance; boycotts; exclusive dealing and tying restrictions; mergers; and price discrimination."

The topic of federal securities regulation is concerned with the federal Securities Act of 1933 and Securities and Exchange Act of 1934, briefly discussed previously.[1] The publication of the Institute further states: "Included are the scope of the 1933 Act's registration requirements, exempt securities, exempt transactions, and the liability of the various parties involved in making a public offering of securities. Included within the coverage of the 1934 Act are the application of the Act's rules to both listed and unlisted corporations, corporate reporting requirements, antifraud provisions and disclosure of insider information, and short-swing profits."

---

[1] See above, pp. 674, 970–74.

The topic of regulation of the employer and employee relationship is concerned with the impact on employer-employee relationships of the federal Fair Labor Standards Act and Social Security Act, and state workmen's compensation laws.

While these three topics under public law are not included to any great extent, if at all, in courses in business law, nevertheless they are included in courses on government regulation of business. Because of limitations in academic time, C.P.A. candidates should examine the various laws indicated above so as to be prepared for questions on their coverage. Copies of these laws should be available through any public library. A few of the recent questions in the area of public law are given as illustrations of what has been asked on two of these topics.

APPENDIX TO PART FOURTEEN

SOME PREVIOUS C.P.A. LAW EXAMINATION QUESTIONS

MAY, 1971

No. 1 (Estimated time—3 to 4 minutes)

Each of the lettered statements of facts below is followed by numbered sentences that state legal conclusions relating to those facts. You are to determine whether each legal conclusion is true or false according to the *general principles of corporation and securities law*. Use a soft pencil, preferably #2, to blacken the appropriate space on the separate printed answer sheet to indicate your answer. Your grade will be determined from your total of correct answers less a penalty of approximately one half for each of your incorrect answers; an omitted answer will not be considered an incorrect answer.

D. Marvel Corporation has decided to make an offering of its securities to raise additional capital. It plans to issue 30,000 shares of its common stock at $20 a share and to restrict the offer to its existing stockholders, customers, employees, retired employees, and relatives of such people. The securities will be offered to fewer than 500 people and it is expected that only 300 people will actually make purchases. The Marvel Corporation does business in a tri-state area.

16. A registration statement need not be filed with the Securities and Exchange Commission because the amount of the transaction is less than $1,000,000.

17. No registration is required because the number of people who will purchase the shares is small and select.

18. If interstate commerce were not involved, the offer would be exempt.

19. If the 30,000 shares are treasury stock for which a registration statement previously had been filed, no additional registration is required.

20. Although the corporation files a registration statement, state blue sky laws are applicable.

MAY, 1970

No. 2 (Estimated time—7 to 8 minutes)

Each of the following numbered statements states a legal conclusion. You are to determine whether each legal conclusion is true or false according to the *general principles of corporation law.* Write on a separate answer sheet whether each conclusion is true or false. Your grade will be determined from your total net score obtained by deducting a weighted total for your incorrect answers from your total of correct answers; an omitted answer will not be considered an incorrect answer.

C. Dodson, an accountant, performed services in connection with the organization of Beta Corporation for which he was issued shares of Beta's common stock as compensation. Three years later Dodson decided to sell his Beta stock and took an ad in a nationally distributed newspaper offering to sell the stock to the highest bidder. Dodson had performed no services for Beta other than those described above and his Beta stock represented less than 1 percent of Beta's issued and outstanding common stock.

41. Dodson violated the Securities Act of 1933.
42. If Dodson sells his Beta stock to members of the public using instrumentalities of interstate commerce, he would violate the Securities Act of 1933.
43. The answer to the preceding two questions would be different if Dodson's stock represented more than 50 percent of Beta's issued and outstanding common stock.
44. In the circumstances described in the preceding question, Dodson would be considered the "issuer" of the Beta stock he owned for purposes of the Securities Act of 1933.
45. If Dodson had acquired his Beta stock under the facts in item 43 intending to resell it to the public in interstate commerce, he would be deemed an "underwriter" of the stock by the Securities Act of 1933.

D. Bancroft and Davis are directors and substantial shareholders of Gotham Corporation, a large publicly held corporation whose securities are listed on a national securities exchange. Making use of information known only to Gotham's management, Bancroft made a large profit trading in Gotham stock. Five months ago Davis purchased additional Gotham stock on the market, which he now proposes to sell at a profit.

46. Bancroft may have incurred liability to members of the public dealing with him in his transactions with Gotham stock.
47. Davis, who had no knowledge of the insider information, may be liable to Gotham for any profit realized by him on the sale of his additional Gotham shares within six months from the date of purchase.
48. The answer to the preceding two questions would be different if Gotham's stock were not listed on a national exchange but were traded "over-the-counter."
49. If Davis should sell the remaining shares of his Gotham stock in a regular exchange transaction without first registering such stock under the Securities Exchange Act of 1933, he might violate the Act.
50. The answer to the preceding question would be different if Davis should sell his stock to Jones, a stockbroker, who bought for his own account for investment.

NOVEMBER, 1969

No. 4 (Estimated time—12 to 15 minutes)

Andrews, a director of Omega Corporation, learned of a very valuable mineral discovery on certain land which could be acquired at a bargain price. Without revealing this information to Omega, Andrews, acting through his brother-in-law, acquired the mineral rights for the property and resold them to Omega at a large profit.

b. At the meeting of Omega's board of directors which approved purchase of these mineral rights, the board also decided to raise $1,500,000 in capital to exploit such rights by selling some of Omega's common stock (then held as treasury stock) to Smith for $500,000 and by a public sale in interstate commerce of newly authorized common stock. Smith attended the board meeting, was a sophisticated businessman who was thoroughly familiar with Omega's operations, and represented that he would acquire such stock on his own account for investment.

Immediately following the board meeting and before any public announcement of Omega's acquisition of the mineral rights was made, Baxter, one of Omega's directors, purchased a large block of Omega stock through his broker.

After a press release describing the acquisition of the mineral rights by Omega, Jones, another Omega director, purchased Omega stock through a broker and resold the stock five months thereafter at a large profit.

At all pertinent times, Omega was a large, publicly owned corporation whose stock was listed on a national securities exchange.

(1) Discuss the application of the Federal Securities Act to the sales of Omega's common stock to Smith and to the public.

(2) If Smith purchased the Omega stock intending to resell it immediately to the public in interstate commerce and Omega knew of this intention, is Omega obligated to register the stock with the Securities and Exchange Commission? Explain.

(4) Would Baxter be liable to members of the public whose stock he purchased under the circumstances described above? Explain.

(5) Could Omega recover from Jones the profit he made on the resale of the Omega stock he purchased? Explain.

MAY, 1968

No. 7 (Estimated time—15 to 19 minutes)

b. The Jason Corporation sold various interrelated products which it manufactured. One of the items was manufactured almost exclusively by Jason Corporation. It was sold throughout most of the United States. The Corporation realized the importance of the product to its purchasers and decided to capitalize on the situation by requiring all purchasers to take at least two other Jason products in order to obtain the item over which it had almost complete market control.

At the spring sales meeting the president of Jason Corporation informed the entire sales force that they were to henceforth sell only to those customers who agreed to take the additional products. He indicated that this was a great opportunity to substantially increase sales of laggard items.

The plan was adopted and gross sales of the additional items more than doubled and were in excess of one million dollars.

You are the auditor examining the financial statements of Jason Corporation and upon inquiry as to the reason for the great spurt in sales of certain items the above facts came to light.

(1) Discuss the legal problems created by the above set of facts.

(2) What are the probable legal actions by customers, competitors and the United States government which Jason Corporation may face as a result of the above facts? Explain.

NOVEMBER, 1967

No. 3 (Estimated time—2 minutes)

Each of the following numbered phrases or clauses states a legal conclusion as it completes the related lettered material. You are to determine whether each of the legal conclusions is true or false according to the *general principles of corporation law*. Write on a separate answer sheet whether each conclusion is true or false. Your grade will be determined from your total net score obtained by deducting your total of incorrect answers from your total of correct answers; an omitted answer will not be considered an incorrect answer.

F. "Blue Sky Laws"

146. Refer to outdated statutes regulating the incorporation of corporations.

147. Need not be complied with if the stock of a corporation is publicly traded on an exchange.

148. Refer to state statutes regulating the issuance and sale of securities.

149. Are administered by the Securities and Exchange Commission.

150. Refer to federal statutes regulating corporations.

STATUTES

UNIFORM COMMERCIAL CODE, AS AMENDED 1962 OFFICIAL TEXT

ARTICLE 1

GENERAL PROVISIONS

PART 1

SHORT TITLE, CONSTRUCTION, APPLICATION AND SUBJECT MATTER OF THE ACT

Section 1-101. Short Title.

This Act shall be known and may be cited as Uniform Commercial Code.

Section 1-102. Purposes; Rules of Construction; Variation by Agreement.

(1) This Act shall be liberally construed and applied to promote its underlying purposes and policies.

(2) Underlying purposes and policies of this Act are

  (a) to simplify, clarify and modernize the law governing commercial transactions;

  (b) to permit the continued expansion of commercial practices through custom, usage and agreement of the parties;

  (c) to make uniform the law among the various jurisdictions.

(3) The effect of provisions of this Act may be varied by agreement, except as otherwise provided in this Act and except that the obligations of good faith, diligence, reasonableness and care prescribed by this Act may not be disclaimed by agreement but the parties may by agreement determine the standards by which the performance of such obligations is to be measured if such standards are not manifestly unreasonable.

(4) The presence in certain provisions of this Act of the words "unless otherwise agreed" or words of similar import does not imply that the effect of other provisions may not be varied by agreement under subsection (3).

(5) In this Act unless the context otherwise requires

  (a) words in the singular number include the plural, and in the plural include the singular;

  (b) words of the masculine gender include the feminine and the neuter, and when the sense so indicates words of the neuter gender may refer to any gender.

Section 1-103. Supplementary General Principles of Law Applicable.

Unless displaced by the particular provisions of this Act, the principles of law and equity, including the law merchant and the law relative to capacity to contract, principal and agent, estoppel, fraud, misrepresentation, duress, coercion, mistake, bankruptcy, or other validating or invalidating cause shall supplement its provisions.

Section 1–104. Construction Against Implicit Repeal.

This Act being a general act intended as a unified coverage of its subject matter, no part of it shall be deemed to be impliedly repealed by subsequent legislation if such construction can reasonably be avoided.

Section 1–105. Territorial Application of the Act; Parties' Power to Choose Applicable Law.

(1) Except as provided hereafter in this section, when a transaction bears a reasonable relation to this state and also to another state or nation the parties may agree that the law either of this state or of such other state or nation shall govern their rights and duties. Failing such agreement this Act applies to transactions bearing an appropriate relation to this state.

(2) Where one of the following provisions of this Act specifies the applicable law, that provision governs and a contrary agreement is effective only to the extent permitted by the law (including the conflict of laws rules) so specified:

Rights of creditors against sold goods. Section 2–402.

Applicability of the Article on Bank Deposits and Collections. Section 4–102.

Bulk transfers subject to the Article on Bulk Transfers. Section 6–102.

Applicability of the Article on Investment Securities. Section 8–106.

Perfection provisions of the Article on Secured Transactions, Section 9–103.

Section 1–106. Remedies to Be Liberally Administered.

(1) The remedies provided by this Act shall be liberally administered to the end that the aggrieved party may be put in as good a position as if the other party had fully performed but neither consequential or special nor penal damages may be had except as specifically provided in this Act or by other rule of law.

(2) Any right or obligation declared by this Act is enforceable by action unless the provision declaring it specifies a different and limited effect.

Section 1–107. Waiver or Renunciation of Claim or Right After Breach.

Any claim or right arising out of an alleged breach can be discharged in whole or in part without consideration by a written waiver or renunciation signed and delivered by the aggrieved party.

Section 1–108. Severability.

If any provision or clause of this Act or application thereof to any person or circumstances is held invalid, such invalidity shall not affect other provisions or applications of the Act which can be given effect without the invalid provision or application, and to this end the provisions of this Act are declared to be severable.

PART 2

GENERAL DEFINITIONS AND PRINCIPLES
OF INTERPRETATION

Section 1–201. General Definitions.

Subject to additional definitions contained in the subsequent Articles of this Act which are applicable to specific Articles or Parts thereof, and unless the context otherwise requires, in this Act:

(1) "Action" in the sense of a judicial proceeding includes recoupment, counterclaim, set-off, suit in equity and any other proceedings in which rights are determined.

(2) "Aggrieved party" means a party entitled to resort to a remedy.

(3) "Agreement" means the bargain of the parties in fact as found in their language or by implication from other circumstances including course of dealing or usage of trade or course of performance as provided in this Act (Sections 1–205 and 2–208). Whether an agreement has legal consequences is determined by the provisions of this Act, if applicable; otherwise by the law of contracts (Section 1–103). (Compare "Contract".)

(4) "Bank" means any person engaged in the business of banking.

(5) "Bearer" means the person in possession of an instrument, document of title, or security payable to bearer or indorsed in blank.

(6) "Bill of lading" means a document evidencing the receipt of goods for shipment issued by a person engaged in the business of transporting or forwarding goods, and includes an airbill. "Airbill" means a document serving for air transportation as a bill of lading does for marine or rail transportation, and includes an air consignment note or air waybill.

(7) "Branch" includes a separately incorporated foreign branch of a bank.

(8) "Burden of establishing" a fact means the burden of persuading the triers of fact that the existence of the fact is more probable than its non-existence.

(9) "Buyer in ordinary course of business" means a person who in good faith and without knowledge that the sale to him is in violation of the ownership rights or security interest of a third party in the goods buys in ordinary course from a person in the business of selling goods of that kind but does not include a pawnbroker. All persons who sell minerals or the like (including oil and gas) at wellhead or minehead shall be deemed to be persons in the business of selling goods of that kind. "Buying" may be for cash or by exchange of other property or on secured or unsecured credit and includes receiving goods or documents of title under a pre-existing contract for sale but does not include a transfer in bulk or as security for or in total or partial satisfaction of a money debt.

(10) "Conspicuous": A term or clause is conspicuous when it is so written that a reasonable person against whom it is to operate ought to have noticed it. A printed heading in capitals (as: NON-NEGOTIABLE BILL OF LADING) is conspicuous. Language in the body of a form is "conspicuous" if it is in larger or other contrasting type or color. But in a telegram any stated term is "conspicuous". Whether a term or clause is "conspicuous" or not is for decision by the court.

(11) "Contract" means the total legal obligation which results from the parties' agreement as affected by this Act and any other applicable rules of law. (Compare "Agreement".)

(12) "Creditor" includes a general creditor, a secured creditor, a lien creditor and any representative of creditors, including an assignee for the benefit of creditors, a trustee in bankruptcy, a receiver in equity and an executor or administrator of an insolvent debtor's or assignor's estate.

(13) "Defendant" includes a person in the position of defendant in a cross-action or counterclaim.

(14) "Delivery" with respect to instruments, documents of title, chattel paper or securities means voluntary transfer of possession.

(15) "Document of title" includes bill of lading, dock warrant, dock receipt, warehouse receipt or order for the delivery of goods, and also any other document which in the regular course of business or financing is treated as adequately evidencing that the person in possession of it is entitled to receive, hold and dispose of the document and the goods it covers. To be a document of title a document must purport to be issued by or addressed to a bailee and purport to cover goods in the bailee's possession which are either identified or are fungible portions of an identified mass.

(16) "Fault" means wrongful act, omission or breach.

(17) "Fungible" with respect to goods or securities means goods or securities of which any unit is, by nature or usage of trade, the equivalent of any other like unit. Goods which are not fungible shall be deemed fungible for the purposes of this Act to the extent that under a particular agreement or document unlike units are treated as equivalents.

(18) "Genuine" means free of forgery or counterfeiting.

(19) "Good faith" means honesty in fact in the conduct or transaction concerned.

(20) "Holder" means a person who is in possession of a document of title or an instrument or an investment security drawn, issued or indorsed to him or to his order or to bearer or in blank.

(21) To "honor" is to pay or to accept and pay, or where a credit so engages to purchase or discount a draft complying with the terms of the credit.

(22) "Insolvency proceedings" includes any assignment for the benefit of creditors or other proceedings intended to liquidate or rehabilitate the estate of the person involved.

(23) A person is "insolvent" who either has ceased to pay his debts in the ordinary course of business or cannot pay his debts as they become due or is insolvent within the meaning of the federal bankruptcy law.

(24) "Money" means a medium of exchange authorized or adopted by a domestic or foreign government as a part of its currency.

(25) A person has "notice" of a fact when

    (a) he has actual knowledge of it; or

    (b) he has received a notice or notification of it; or

    (c) from all the facts and circumstances known to him at the time in question he has reason to know that it exists.

A person "knows" or has "knowledge" of a fact when he has actual knowledge of it. "Discover" or "learn" or a word or phrase of similar import refers to knowledge rather than to reason to know. The time and circumstances under which a notice or notification may cease to be effective are not determined by this Act.

(26) A person "notifies" or "gives" a notice or notification to another by taking such steps as may be reasonably required to inform the other in ordinary course whether or not such other actually comes to know of it. A person "receives" a notice or notification when

   (a) it comes to his attention; or
   (b) it is duly delivered at the place of business through which the contract was made or at any other place held out by him as the place for receipt of such communications.

(27) Notice, knowledge or a notice or notification received by an organization is effective for a particular transaction from the time when it is brought to the attention of the individual conducting that transaction, and in any event from the time when it would have been brought to his attention if the organization had exercised due diligence. An organization exercises due diligence if it maintains reasonable routines for communicating significant information to the person conducting the transaction and there is reasonable compliance with the routines. Due diligence does not require an individual acting for the organization to communicate information unless such communication is part of his regular duties or unless he has reason to know of the transaction and that the transaction would be materially affected by the information.

(28) "Organization" includes a corporation, government or governmental subdivision or agency, business trust, estate, trust, partnership or association, two or more persons having a joint or common interest, or any other legal or commercial entity.

(29) "Party", as distinct from "third party", means a person who has engaged in a transaction or made an agreement within this Act.

(30) "Person" includes an individual or an organization (See Section 1–102).

(31) "Presumption" or "presumed" means that the trier of fact must find the existence of the fact presumed unless and until evidence is introduced which would support a finding of its non-existence.

(32) "Purchase" includes taking by sale, discount, negotiation, mortgage, pledge, lien, issue or re-issue, gift or any other voluntary transaction creating an interest in property.

(33) "Purchaser" means a person who takes by purchase.

(34) "Remedy" means any remedial right to which an aggrieved party is entitled with or without resort to a tribunal.

(35) "Representative" includes an agent, an officer of a corporation or association, and a trustee, executor or administrator of an estate, or any other person empowered to act for another.

(36) "Rights" includes remedies.

(37) "Security interest" means an interest in personal property or fixtures which secures payment or performance of an obligation. The retention or reservation of title by a seller of goods notwithstanding shipment or delivery to

the buyer (Section 2–401) is limited in effect to a reservation of a "security interest". The term also includes any interest of a buyer of accounts or chattel paper which is subject to Article 9. The special property interest of a buyer of goods on identification of such goods to a contract for sale under Section 2–401 is not a "security interest", but a buyer may also acquire a "security interest" by complying with Article 9. Unless a lease or consignment is intended as security, reservation of title thereunder is not a "security interest" but a consignment is in any event subject to the provisions on consignment sales (Section 2–326). Whether a lease is intended as security is to be determined by the facts of each case; however, (a) the inclusion of an option to purchase does not of itself make the lease one intended for security, and (b) an agreement that upon compliance with the terms of the lease the lessee shall become or has the option to become the owner of the property for no additional consideration or for a nominal consideration does make the lease one intended for security.

(38) "Send" in connection with any writing or notice means to deposit in the mail or deliver for transmission by any other usual means of communication with postage or cost of transmission provided for and properly addressed and in the case of an instrument to an address specified thereon or otherwise agreed, or if there be none to any address reasonable under the circumstances. The receipt of any writing or notice within the time at which it would have arrived if properly sent has the effect of a proper sending.

(39) "Signed" includes any symbol executed or adopted by a party with present intention to authenticate a writing.

(40) "Surety" includes guarantor.

(41) "Telegram" includes a message transmitted by radio, teletype, cable, any mechanical method of transmission, or the like.

(42) "Term" means that portion of an agreement which relates to a particular matter.

(43) "Unauthorized" signature or indorsement means one made without actual, implied or apparent authority and includes a forgery.

(44) "Value". Except as otherwise provided with respect to negotiable instruments and bank collections (Sections 3–303, 4–208 and 4–209) a person gives "value" for rights if he acquires them

  (a) in return for a binding commitment to extend credit or for the extension of immediately available credit whether or not drawn upon and whether or not a charge-back is provided for in the event of difficulties in collection; or

  (b) as security for or in total or partial satisfaction of a pre-existing claim; or

  (c) by accepting delivery pursuant to a pre-existing contract for purchase; or

  (d) generally, in return for any consideration sufficient to support a simple contract.

(45) "Warehouse receipt" means a receipt issued by a person engaged in the business of storing goods for hire.

(46) "Written" or "writing" includes printing, typewriting or any other intentional reduction to tangible form.

Section 1–202. Prima Facie Evidence by Third Party Documents.

A document in due form purporting to be a bill of lading, policy or certificate of insurance, official weigher's or inspector's certificate, consular invoice, or any other document authorized or required by the contract to be issued by a third party shall be prima facie evidence of its own authenticity and genuineness and of the facts stated in the document by the third party.

Section 1–203. Obligation of Good Faith.

Every contract or duty within this Act imposes an obligation of good faith in its performance or enforcement.

Section 1–204. Time; Reasonable Time; "Seasonably".

(1) Whenever this Act requires any action to be taken within a reasonable time, any time which is not manifestly unreasonable may be fixed by agreement.

(2) What is a reasonable time for taking any action depends on the nature, purpose and circumstances of such action.

(3) An action is taken "seasonably" when it is taken at or within the time agreed or if no time is agreed at or within a reasonable time.

Section 1–205. Course of Dealing and Usage of Trade.

(1) A course of dealing is a sequence of previous conduct between the parties to a particular transaction which is fairly to be regarded as establishing a common basis of understanding for interpreting their expressions and other conduct.

(2) A usage of trade is any practice or method of dealing having such regularity of observance in a place, vocation or trade as to justify an expectation that it will be observed with respect to the transaction in question. The existence and scope of such a usage are to be proved as facts. If it is established that such a usage is embodied in a written trade code or similar writing the interpretation of the writing is for the court.

(3) A course of dealing between parties and any usage of trade in the vocation or trade in which they are engaged or of which they are or should be aware give particular meaning to and supplement or qualify terms of an agreement.

(4) The express terms of an agreement and an applicable course of dealing or usage of trade shall be construed wherever reasonable as consistent with each other; but when such construction is unreasonable express terms control both course of dealing and usage of trade and course of dealing controls usage of trade.

(5) An applicable usage of trade in the place where any part of performance is to occur shall be used in interpreting the agreement as to that part of the performance.

(6) Evidence of a relevant usage of trade offered by one party is not admissible unless and until he has given the other party such notice as the court finds sufficient to prevent unfair surprise to the latter.

Section 1–206. Statute of Frauds for Kinds of Personal Property Not Otherwise Covered.

(1) Except in the cases described in subsection (2) of this section a contract for the sale of personal property is not enforceable by way of action or defense beyond five thousand dollars in amount or value of remedy unless there is some writing which indicates that a contract for sale has been made between the parties at a defined or stated price, reasonably identifies the subject matter, and is signed by the party against whom enforcement is sought or by his authorized agent.

(2) Subsection (1) of this section does not apply to contracts for the sale of goods (Section 2–201) nor of securities (Section 8–319) nor to security agreements (Section 9–203).

Section 1–207. Performance or Acceptance Under Reservation of Rights.

A party who with explicit reservation of rights performs or promises performance or assents to performance in a manner demanded or offered by the other party does not thereby prejudice the rights reserved. Such words as "without prejudice," "under protest" or the like are sufficient.

Section 1–208. Option to Accelerate at Will.

A term providing that one party or his successor in interest may accelerate payment or performance or require collateral or additional collateral "at will" or "when he deems himself insecure" or in words of similar import shall be construed to mean that he shall have power to do so only if he in good faith believes that the prospect of payment or performance is impaired. The burden of establishing lack of good faith is on the party against whom the power has been exercised.

ARTICLE 2

SALES

PART 1

SHORT TITLE, GENERAL CONSTRUCTION AND
SUBJECT MATTER

Section 2–101. Short Title.

This Article shall be known and may be cited as Uniform Commercial Code—Sales.

Section 2–102. Scope; Certain Security and Other Transactions Excluded From This Article.

Unless the context otherwise requires, this Article applies to transactions in goods; it does not apply to any transaction which although in the form of an unconditional contract to sell or present sale is intended to operate only as a security transaction nor does this Article impair or repeal any statute regulating sales to consumers, farmers or other specified classes of buyers.

Section 2–103.   Definitions and Index of Definitions.

(1) In this Article unless the context otherwise requires
   (a) "Buyer" means a person who buys or contracts to buy goods.
   (b) "Good faith" in the case of a merchant means honesty in fact and the observance of reasonable commercial standards of fair dealing in the trade.
   (c) "Receipt" of goods means taking physical possession of them.
   (d) "Seller" means a person who sells or contracts to sell goods.

(2) Other definitions applying to this Article or to specified Parts thereof, and the sections in which they appear are:

"Acceptance". Section 2–606.
"Banker's credit". Section 2–325.
"Between merchants". Section 2–104.
"Cancellation". Section 2–106(4).
"Commercial unit". Section 2–105.
"Confirmed credit". Section 2–325.
"Conforming to contract". Section 2–106.
"Contract for sale". Section 2–106.
"Cover". Section 2–712.
"Entrusting". Section 2–403.
"Financing agency". Section 2–104.
"Future goods". Section 2–105.
"Goods". Section 2–105.
"Identification". Section 2–501.
"Installment contract". Section 2–612.
"Letter of Credit". Section 2–325.
"Lot". Section 2–105.
"Merchant". Section 2–104.
"Overseas". Section 2–323.
"Person in position of seller". Section 2–707.
"Present sale". Section 2–106.
"Sale". Section 2–106.
"Sale on approval". Section 2–326.
"Sale or return". Section 2–326.
"Termination". Section 2–106.

(3) The following definitions in other Articles apply to this Article:
"Check". Section 3–104.
"Consignee". Section 7–102.
"Consignor". Section 7–102.
"Consumer goods". Section 9–109.
"Dishonor". Section 3–507.
"Draft". Section 3–104.

(4) In addition Article 1 contains general definitions and principles of construction and interpretation applicable throughout this Article.

Section 2–104.   Definitions: "Merchant"; "Between Merchants"; "Financing Agency."

(1) "Merchant" means a person who deals in goods of the kind or otherwise by his occupation holds himself out as having knowledge or skill peculiar to the practices or goods involved in the transaction or to whom such knowledge or skill may be attributed by his employment of an agent or broker or other intermediary who by his occupation holds himself out as having such knowledge or skill.

(2) "Financing agency" means a bank, finance company or other person who in the ordinary course of business makes advances against goods or documents of title or who by arrangement with either the seller or the buyer intervenes in ordinary course to make or collect payment due or claimed under the contract for sale, as by purchasing or paying the seller's draft or making advances against it or by merely taking it for collection whether or not documents of title accompany the draft. "Financing agency" includes also a bank or other person who similarly intervenes between persons who are in the position of seller and buyer in respect to the goods (Section 2–707).

(3) "Between merchants" means in any transaction with respect to which both parties are chargeable with the knowledge or skill of merchants.

Section 2–105. Definitions: Transferability; "Goods"; "Future" Goods; "Lot"; "Commercial Unit".

(1) "Goods" means all things (including specially manufactured goods) which are movable at the time of identification to the contract for sale other than the money in which the price is to be paid, investment securities (Article 8) and things in action. "Goods" also includes the unborn young of animals and growing crops and other identified things attached to realty as described in the section on goods to be severed from realty (Section 2–107).

(2) Goods must be both existing and identified before any interest in them can pass. Goods which are not both existing and identified are "future" goods. A purported present sale of future goods or of any interest therein operates as a contract to sell.

(3) There may be a sale of a part interest in existing identified goods.

(4) An undivided share in an identified bulk of fungible goods is sufficiently identified to be sold although the quantity of the bulk is not determined. Any agreed proportion of such a bulk or any quantity thereof agreed upon by number, weight or other measure may to the extent of the seller's interest in the bulk be sold to the buyer who then becomes an owner in common.

(5) "Lot" means a parcel or a single article which is the subject matter of a separate sale or delivery, whether or not it is sufficient to perform the contract.

(6) "Commercial unit" means such a unit of goods as by commercial usage is a single whole for purposes of sale and division of which materially impairs its character or value on the market or in use. A commercial unit may be a single article (as a machine) or a set of articles (as a suite of furniture or an assortment of sizes) or a quantity (as a bale, gross, or carload) or any other unit treated in use or in the relevant market as a single whole.

Section 2–106. Definitions: "Contract"; "Agreement"; "Contract for Sale"; "Sale"; "Present Sale"; "Conforming" to Contract; "Termination"; "Cancellation".

(1) In this Article unless the context otherwise requires "contract" and "agreement" are limited to those relating to the present or future sale of goods.

"Contract for sale" includes both a present sale of goods and a contract to sell goods at a future time. A "sale" consists in the passing of title from the seller to the buyer for a price (Section 2–401). A "present sale" means a sale which is accomplished by the making of the contract.

(2) Goods or conduct including any part of a performance are "conforming" or conform to the contract when they are in accordance with the obligations under the contract.

(3) "Termination" occurs when either party pursuant to a power created by agreement or law puts an end to the contract otherwise than for its breach. On "termination" all obligations which are still executory on both sides are discharged but any right based on prior breach or performance survives.

(4) "Cancellation" occurs when either party puts an end to the contract for breach by the other and its effect is the same as that of "termination" except that the cancelling party also retains any remedy for breach of the whole contract or any unperformed balance.

Section 2–107. Goods to Be Severed From Reality: Recording.

(1) A contract for the sale of minerals or the like (including oil and gas) or a structure or its materials to be removed from realty is a contract for the sale of goods within this Article if they are to be severed by the seller but until severance a purported present sale thereof which is not effective as a transfer of an interest in land is effective only as a contract to sell.

(2) A contract for the sale apart from the land of growing crops or other things attached to realty and capable of severance without material harm thereto but not described in subsection (1) or of timber to be cut is a contract for the sale of goods within this Article whether the subject matter is to be severed by the buyer or by the seller even though it forms part of the realty at the time of contracting, and the parties can by identification effect a present sale before severance.

(3) The provisions of this section are subject to any third party rights provided by the law relating to realty records, and the contract for sale may be executed and recorded as a document transferring an interest in land and shall then constitute notice to third parties of the buyer's rights under the contract for sale.

PART 2

FORM, FORMATION AND READJUSTMENT
OF CONTRACT

Section 2–201. Formal Requirements; Statute of Frauds.

(1) Except as otherwise provided in this section a contract for the sale of goods for the price of $500 or more is not enforceable by way of action or defence unless there is some writing sufficient to indicate that a contract for sale has been made between the parties and signed by the party against whom enforcement is sought or by his authorized agent or broker. A writing is not insufficient because it omits or incorrectly states a term agreed upon but the contract is not enforceable under this paragraph beyond the quantity of goods shown in such writing.

(2) Between merchants if within a reasonable time a writing in confirmation of the contract and sufficient against the sender is received and the party receiving it has reason to know its contents, it satisfies the requirements of

subsection (1) against such party unless written notice of objection to its contents is given within ten days after it is received.

(3) A contract which does not satisfy the requirements of subsection (1) but which is valid in other respects is enforceable

(a) if the goods are to be specially manufactured for the buyer and are not suitable for sale to others in the ordinary course of the seller's business and the seller, before notice of repudiation is received and under circumstances which reasonably indicate that the goods are for the buyer, has made either a substantial beginning of their manufacture or commitments for their procurement; or

(b) if the party against whom enforcement is sought admits in his pleading, testimony or otherwise in court that a contract for sale was made, but the contract is not enforceable under this provision beyond the quantity of goods admitted; or

(c) with respect to goods for which payment has been made and accepted or which have been received and accepted (Sec. 2–606).

Section 2–202. Final Written Expression: Parol or Extrinsic Evidence.

Terms with respect to which the confirmatory memoranda of the parties agree or which are otherwise set forth in a writing intended by the parties as a final expression of their agreement with respect to such terms as are included therein may not be contradicted by evidence of any prior agreement or of a contemporaneous oral agreement but may be explained or supplemented

(a) by course of dealing or usage of trade (Section 1–205) or by course of performance (Section 2–208); and

(b) by evidence of consistent additional terms unless the court finds the writing to have been intended also as a complete and exclusive statement of the terms of the agreement.

Section 2–203. Seals Inoperative.

The affixing of a seal to a writing evidencing a contract for sale or an offer to buy or sell goods does not constitute the writing a sealed instrument and the law with respect to sealed instruments does not apply to such a contract or offer.

Section 2–204. Formation in General.

(1) A contract for sale of goods may be made in any manner sufficient to show agreement, including conduct by both parties which recognizes the existence of such a contract.

(2) An agreement sufficient to constitute a contract for sale may be found even though the moment of its making is undetermined.

(3) Even though one or more terms are left open a contract for sale does not fail for indefiniteness if the parties have intended to make a contract and there is a reasonably certain basis for giving an appropriate remedy.

Section 2–205. Firm Offers.

An offer by a merchant to buy or sell goods in a signed writing which by its terms gives assurance that it will be held open is not revocable, for lack of consideration, during the time stated or if no time is stated for a reasonable time, but in no event may such period of irrevocability exceed three months; but any such term of assurance on a form supplied by the offeree must be separately signed by the offeror.

Section 2–206.   Offer and Acceptance in Formation of Contract.

(1) Unless otherwise unambiguously indicated by the language or circumstances

(a) an offer to make a contract shall be construed as inviting acceptance in any manner and by any medium reasonable in the circumstances;

(b) an order or other offer to buy goods for prompt or current shipment shall be construed as inviting acceptance either by a prompt promise to ship or by the prompt or current shipment of conforming or nonconforming goods, but such a shipment of non-conforming goods does not constitute an acceptance if the seller seasonably notifies the buyer that the shipment is offered only as an accommodation to the buyer.

(2) Where the beginning of a requested performance is a reasonable mode of acceptance an offeror who is not notified of acceptance within a reasonable time may treat the offer as having lapsed before acceptance.

Section 2–207.   Additional Terms in Acceptance or Confirmation.

(1) A definite and seasonable expression of acceptance or a written confirmation which is sent within a reasonable time operates as an acceptance even though it states terms additional to or different from those offered or agreed upon, unless acceptance is expressly made conditional on assent to the additional or different terms.

(2) The additional terms are to be construed as proposals for addition to the contract. Between merchants such terms become part of the contract unless:

(a) the offer expressly limits acceptance to the terms of the offer;

(b) they materially alter it; or

(c) notification of objection to them has already been given or is given within a reasonable time after notice of them is received.

(3) Conduct by both parties which recognizes the existence of a contract is sufficient to establish a contract for sale although the writings of the parties do not otherwise establish a contract. In such case the terms of the particular contract consist of those terms on which the writings of the parties agree, together with any supplementary terms incorporated under any other provisions of this Act.

Section 2–208.   Course of Performance or Practical Construction.

(1) Where the contract for sale involves repeated occasions for performance by either party with knowledge of the nature of the performance and opportunity for objection to it by the other, any course of performance accepted or acquiesced in without objection shall be relevant to determine the meaning of the agreement.

(2) The express terms of the agreement and any such course of performance, as well as any course of dealing and usage of trade, shall be construed whenever reasonable as consistent with each other; but when such construction is unreasonable, express terms shall control course of performance and course of performance shall control both course of dealing and usage of trade (Section 1–205).

(3) Subject to the provisions of the next section on modification and waiver, such course of performance shall be relevant to show a waiver or modification of any term inconsistent with such course of performance.

Section 2–209. Modification, Rescission and Waiver.

(1) An agreement modifying a contract within this Article needs no consideration to be binding.

(2) A signed agreement which excludes modification or rescission except by a signed writing cannot be otherwise modified or rescinded, but except as between merchants such a requirement on a form supplied by the merchant must be separately signed by the other party.

(3) The requirements of the statute of frauds section of this Article (Section 2–201) must be satisfied if the contract as modified is within its provisions.

(4) Although an attempt at modification or rescission does not satisfy the requirements of subsection (2) or (3) it can operate as a waiver.

(5) A party who has made a waiver affecting an executory portion of the contract may retract the waiver by reasonable notification received by the other party that strict performance will be required of any term waived, unless the retraction would be unjust in view of a material change of position in reliance on the waiver.

Section 2–210. Delegation of Performance; Assignment of Rights.

(1) A party may perform his duty through a delegate unless otherwise agreed or unless the other party has a substantial interest in having his original promisor perform or control the acts required by the contract. No delegation of performance relieves the party delegating of any duty to perform or any liability for breach.

(2) Unless otherwise agreed all rights of either seller or buyer can be assigned except where the assignment would materially change the duty of the other party, or increase materially the burden or risk imposed on him by his contract, or impair materially his chance of obtaining return performance. A right to damages for breach of the whole contract or a right arising out of the assignor's due performance of his entire obligation can be assigned despite agreement otherwise.

(3) Unless the circumstances indicate the contrary a prohibition of assignment of "the contract" is to be construed as barring only the delegation to the assignee of the assignor's performance.

(4) An assignment of "the contract" or of "all my rights under the contract" or an assignment in similar general terms is an assignment of rights and unless the language or the circumstances (as in an assignment for security) indicate the contrary, it is a delegation of performance of the duties of the assignor and its acceptance by the assignee constitutes a promise by him to perform those duties. This promise is enforceable by either the assignor or the other party to the original contract.

(5) The other party may treat any assignment which delegates performance

as creating reasonable grounds for insecurity and may without prejudice to his rights against the assignor demand assurances from the assignee (Section 2–609).

PART 3

General Obligation and Construction of Contract

Section 2–301.   General Obligations of Parties.

The obligation of the seller is to transfer and deliver and that of the buyer is to accept and pay in accordance with the contract.

Section 2–302.   Unconscionable Contract or Clause.

(1) If the court as a matter of law finds the contract or any clause of the contract to have been unconscionable at the time it was made the court may refuse to enforce the contract, or it may enforce the remainder of the contract without the unconscionable clause, or it may so limit the application of any unconscionable clause as to avoid any unconscionable result.

(2) When it is claimed or appears to the court that the contract or any clause thereof may be unconscionable the parties shall be afforded a reasonable opportunity to present evidence as to its commercial setting, purpose and effect to aid the court in making the determination.

Section 2–303.   Allocation or Division of Risks.

Where this Article allocates a risk or a burden as between the parties "unless otherwise agreed", the agreement may not only shift the allocation but may also divide the risk or burden.

Section 2–304.   Price Payable in Money, Goods, Realty, or Otherwise.

(1) The price can be made payable in money or otherwise. If it is payable in whole or in part in goods each party is a seller of the goods which he is to transfer.

(2) Even though all or part of the price is payable in an interest in realty the transfer of the goods and the seller's obligations with reference to them are subject to this Article, but not the transfer of the interest in realty or the transferor's obligations in connection therewith.

Section 2–305.   Open Price Term.

(1) The parties if they so intend can conclude a contract for sale even though the price is not settled. In such a case the price is a reasonable price at the time for delivery if

    (a) nothing is said as to price; or

    (b) the price is left to be agreed by the parties and they fail to agree; or

    (c) the price is to be fixed in terms of some agreed market or other standard as set or recorded by a third person or agency and it is not so set or recorded.

(2) A price to be fixed by the seller or by the buyer means a price for him to fix in good faith.

(3) When a price left to be fixed otherwise than by agreement of the parties fails to be fixed through fault of one party the other may at his option treat the contract as cancelled or himself fix a reasonable price.

(4) Where, however, the parties intend not to be bound unless the price be fixed or agreed and it is not fixed or agreed there is no contract. In such a case the buyer must return any goods already received or if unable so to do must pay their reasonable value at the time of delivery and the seller must return any portion of the price paid on account.

Section 2–306. Output, Requirements and Exclusive Dealings.

(1) A term which measures the quantity by the output of the seller or the requirements of the buyer means such actual output or requirements as may occur in good faith, except that no quantity unreasonably disproportionate to any stated estimate or in the absence of a stated estimate to any normal or otherwise comparable prior output or requirements may be tendered or demanded.

(2) A lawful agreement by either the seller or the buyer for exclusive dealing in the kind of goods concerned imposes unless otherwise agreed an obligation by the seller to use best efforts to supply the goods and by the buyer to use best efforts to promote their sale.

Section 2–307. Delivery in Single Lot or Several Lots.

Unless otherwise agreed all goods called for by a contract for sale must be tendered in a single delivery and payment is due only on such tender but where the circumstances give either party the right to make or demand delivery in lots the price if it can be apportioned may be demanded for each lot.

Section 2–308. Absence of Specified Place for Delivery.

Unless otherwise agreed
  (a) the place for delivery of goods is the seller's place of busines or if he has none his residence; but
  (b) in a contract for sale of identified goods which to the knowledge of the parties at the time of contracting are in some other place, that place is the place for their delivery; and
  (c) documents of title may be delivered through customary banking channels.

Section 2–309. Absence of Specific Time Provisions; Notice of Termination.

(1) The time for shipment or delivery or any other action under a contract if not provided in this Article or agreed upon shall be a reasonable time.

(2) Where the contract provides for successive performances but is indefinite in duration it is valid for a reasonable time but unless otherwise agreed may be terminated at any time by either party.

(3) Termination of a contract by one party except on the happening of an agreed event requires that reasonable notification be received by the other party and an agreement dispensing with notification is invalid if its operation would be unconscionable.

Section 2–310. Open Time for Payment or Running of Credit; Authority to Ship Under Reservation.

Unless otherwise agreed
- (a) payment is due at the time and place at which the buyer is to receive the goods even though the place of shipment is the place of delivery; and
- (b) if the seller is authorized to send the goods he may ship them under reservation, and may tender the documents of title, but the buyer may inspect the goods after their arrival before payment is due unless such inspection is inconsistent with the terms of the contract (Section 2–513); and
- (c) if delivery is authorized and made by way of documents of title otherwise than by subsection (b) then payment is due at the time and place at which the buyer is to receive the documents regardless of where the goods are to be received; and
- (d) where the seller is required or authorized to ship the goods on credit the credit period runs from the time of shipment but post-dating the invoice or delaying its dispatch will correspondingly delay the starting of the credit period.

Section 2–311. Options and Cooperation Respecting Performance.

(1) An agreement for sale which is otherwise sufficiently definite (subsection (3) of Section 2–204) to be a contract is not made invalid by the fact that it leaves particulars of performance to be specified by one of the parties. Any such specification must be made in good faith and within limits set by commercial reasonableness.

(2) Unless otherwise agreed specifications relating to assortment of the goods are at the buyer's option and except as otherwise provided in subsections (1) (c) and (3) of Section 2–319 specifications or arrangements relating to shipment are at the seller's option.

(3) Where such specification would materially affect the other party's performance but is not seasonably made or where one party's cooperation is necessary to the agreed performance of the other but is not seasonably forthcoming, the other party in addition to all other remedies
- (a) is excused for any resulting delay in his own performance; and
- (b) may also either proceed to perform in any reasonable manner or after the time for a material part of his own performance treat the failure to specify or to cooperate as a breach by failure to deliver or accept the goods.

Section 2–312. Warranty of Title and Against Infringement; Buyer's Obligation Against Infringement.

(1) Subject to subsection (2) there is in a contract for sale a warranty by the seller that
- (a) the title conveyed shall be good, and its transfer rightful; and
- (b) the goods shall be delivered free from any security interest or other

lien or encumbrance of which the buyer at the time of contracting has no knowledge.

(2) A warranty under subsection (1) will be excluded or modified only by specific language or by circumstances which give the buyer reason to know that the person selling does not claim title in himself or that he is purporting to sell only such right or title as he or a third person may have.

(3) Unless otherwise agreed a seller who is a merchant regularly dealing in goods of the kind warrants that the goods shall be delivered free of the rightful claim of any third person by way of infringement or the like but a buyer who furnishes specifications to the seller must hold the seller harmless against any such claim which arises out of compliance with the specifications.

Section 2–313. Express Warranties by Affirmation, Promise, Description, Sample.

(1) Express warranties by the seller are created as follows:
- (a) Any affirmation of fact or promise made by the seller to the buyer which relates to the goods and becomes part of the basis of the bargain creates an express waranty that the goods shall conform to the affirmation or promise.
- (b) Any description of the goods which is made part of the basis of the bargain creates an express warranty that the goods shall conform to the description.
- (c) Any sample or model which is made part of the basis of the bargain creates an express warranty that the whole of the goods shall conform to the sample or model.

(2) It is not necessary to the creation of an express warranty that the seller use formal words such as "warrant" or "guarantee" or that he have a specific intention to make a warranty, but an affirmation merely of the value of the goods or a statement purporting to be merely the seller's opinion or commendation of the goods does not create a warranty.

Section 2–314. Implied Warranty: Merchantability; Usage of Trade.

(1) Unless excluded or modified (Section 2–316), a warranty that the goods shall be merchantable is implied in a contract for their sale if the seller is a merchant with respect to goods of that kind. Under this section the serving for value of food or drink to be consumed either on the premises or elsewhere is a sale.

(2) Goods to be merchantable must be at least such as
- (a) pass without objection in the trade under the contract description; and
- (b) in the case of fungible goods, are of fair average quality within the description; and
- (c) are fit for the ordinary purposes for which such goods are used; and
- (d) run, within the variations permitted by the agreement, of even kind, quality and quantity within each unit and among all units involved; and
- (e) are adequately contained, packaged, and labeled as the agreement may require; and

(f) conform to the promises or affirmations of fact made on the container or label if any.

(3) Unless excluded or modified (Section 2–316) other implied warranties may arise from course of dealing or usage of trade.

Section 2–315. Implied Warranty: Fitness for Particular Purpose.

Where the seller at the time of contracting has reason to know any particular purpose for which the goods are required and that the buyer is relying on the seller's skill or judgment to select or furnish suitable goods, there is unless excluded or modified under the next section an implied warranty that the goods shall be fit for such purpose.

Section 2–316. Exclusion or Modification of Warranties.

(1) Words or conduct relevant to the creation of an express warranty and words or conduct tending to negate or limit warranty shall be construed wherever reasonable as consistent with each other; but subject to the provisions of this Article on parol or extrinsic evidence (Section 2–202) negation or limitation is inoperative to the extent that such construction is unreasonable.

(2) Subject to subsection (3), to exclude or modify the implied warranty of merchantability or any part of it the language must mention merchantability and in case of a writing must be conspicuous, and to exclude or modify any implied warranty of fitness the exclusion must be by a writing and conspicuous. Language to exclude all implied warranties of fitness is sufficient if it states, for example, that "There are no warranties which extend beyond the description on the face hereof."

(3) Notwithstanding subsection (2)

(a) unless the circumstances indicate otherwise, all implied warranties are excluded by expressions like "as is", "with all faults" or other language which in common understanding calls the buyer's attention to the exclusion of warranties and makes plain that there is no implied warranty; and

(b) when the buyer before entering into the contract has examined the goods or the sample or model as fully as he desired or has refused to examine the goods there is no implied warranty with regard to defects which an examination ought in the circumstances to have revealed to him; and

(c) an implied warranty can also be excluded or modified by course of dealing or course of performance or usage of trade.

(4) Remedies for breach of warranty can be limited in accordance with the provisions of this Article on liquidation or limitation of damages and on contractual modification of remedy (Sections 2–718 and 2–719).

Section 2–317. Cumulation and Conflict of Warranties Express or Implied.

Warranties whether express or implied shall be construed as consistent with each other and as cumulative, but if such construction is unreasonable the intention of the parties shall determine which warranty is dominant. In ascertaining that intention the following rules apply:

(a) Exact or technical specifications displace an inconsistent sample or model or general language of description.

(b) A sample from an existing bulk displaces inconsistent general language of description.

(c) Express warranties displace inconsistent implied warranties other than an implied warranty of fitness for a particular purpose.

Section 2–318. Third Party Beneficiaries of Warranties Express or Implied.

A seller's warranty whether express or implied extends to any natural person who is in the family or household of his buyer or who is a guest in his home if it is reasonable to expect that such person may use, consume or be affected by the goods and who is injured in person by breach of the warranty. A seller may not exclude or limit the operation of this section.

Section 2–319. F.O.B. and F.A.S. Terms.

(1) Unless otherwise agreed the term F.O.B. (which means "free on board") at a named place, even though used only in connection with the stated price, is a delivery term under which

(a) when the term is F.O.B. the place of shipment, the seller must at that place ship the goods in the manner provided in this Article (Section 2–504) and bear the expense and risk of putting them into the possession of the carrier; or

(b) when the term is F.O.B. the place of destination, the seller must at his own expense and risk transport the goods to that place and there tender delivery of them in the manner provided in this Article (Section 2–503);

(c) when under either (a) or (b) the term is also F.O.B. vessel, car or other vehicle, the seller must in addition at his own expense and risk load the goods on board. If the term is F.O.B. vessel the buyer must name the vessel and in an appropriate case the seller must comply with the provisions of this Article on the form of bill of lading (Section 2–323).

(2) Unless otherwise agreed the term F.A.S. vessel (which means "free alongside") at a named port, even though used only in connection with the stated price, is a delivery term under which the seller must

(a) at his own expense and risk deliver the goods alongside the vessel in the manner usual in that port or on a dock designated and provided by the buyer; and

(b) obtain and tender a receipt for the goods in exchange for which the carrier is under a duty to issue a bill of lading.

(3) Unless otherwise agreed in any case falling within subsection (1)(a) or (c) or subsection (2) the buyer must seasonably give any needed instructions for making delivery, including when the term is F.A.S. or F.O.B. the loading berth of the vessel and in an appropriate case its name and sailing date. The seller may treat the failure of needed instructions as a failure of cooperation under this Article (Section 2–311). He may also at his option move the goods in any reasonable manner preparatory to delivery or shipment.

(4) Under the term F.O.B. vessel or F.A.S. unless otherwise agreed the buyer must make payment against tender of the required documents and the seller may not tender nor the buyer demand delivery of the goods in substitution for the documents.

Section 2–320.   C.I.F. and C. & F. Terms.

(1) The term C.I.F. means that the price includes in a lump sum the cost of the goods and the insurance and freight to the named destination. The term C. & F. or C.F. means that the price so includes cost and freight to the named destination.

(2) Unless otherwise agreed and even though used only in connection with the stated price and destination, the term C.I.F. destination or its equivalent requires the seller at his own expense and risk to

- (a) put the goods into the possession of a carrier at the port for shipment and obtain a negotiable bill or bills of lading covering the entire transportation to the named destination; and
- (b) load the goods and obtain a receipt from the carrier (which may be contained in the bill of lading) showing that the freight has been paid or provided for; and
- (c) obtain a policy or certificate of insurance, including any war risk insurance, of a kind and on terms then current at the port of shipment in the usual amount, in the currency of the contract, shown to cover the same goods covered by the bill of lading and providing for payment of loss to the order of the buyer or for the account of whom it may concern; but the seller may add to the price the amount of the premium for any such war risk insurance; and
- (d) prepare an invoice of the goods and procure any other documents required to effect shipment or to comply with the contract; and
- (e) forward and tender with commercial promptness all the documents in due form and with any indorsement necessary to perfect the buyer's rights.

(3) Unless otherwise agreed the term C. & F. or its equivalent has the same effect and imposes upon the seller the same obligations and risks as a C.I.F. term except the obligation as to insurance.

(4) Under the term C.I.F. or C. & F. unless otherwise agreed the buyer must make payment against tender of the required documents and the seller may not tender nor the buyer demand delivery of the goods in substitution for the documents.

Section 2–321.   C.I.F. or C. & F.: "Net Landed Weights"; "Payment on Arrival"; Warranty of Condition on Arrival.

Under a contract containing a term C.I.F. or C. & F.

(1) Where the price is based on or is to be adjusted according to "net landed weights", "delivered weights", "out turn" quantity or quality or the like, unless otherwise agreed the seller must reasonably estimate the price. The payment due on tender of the documents called for by the contract is the amount so estimated, but after final adjustment of the price a settlement must be made with commercial promptness.

(2) An agreement described in subsection (1) or any warranty of quality or condition of the goods on arrival places upon the seller the risk of ordinary deterioration, shrinkage and the like in transportation but has no effect on the place or time of identification to the contract for sale or delivery or on the passing of the risk of loss.

(3) Unless otherwise agreed where the contract provides for payment on or after arrival of the goods the seller must before payment allow such preliminary inspection as is feasible; but if the goods are lost delivery of the documents and payment are due when the goods should have arrived.

Section 2–322. Delivery "Ex-Ship".

(1) Unless otherwise agreed a term for delivery of goods "ex-ship" (which means from the carrying vessel) or in equivalent language is not restricted to a particular ship and requires delivery from a ship which has reached a place at the named port of destination where goods of the kind are usually discharged.

(2) Under such a term unless otherwise agreed

    (a) the seller must discharge all liens arising out of the carriage and furnish the buyer with a direction which puts the carrier under a duty to deliver the goods; and

    (b) the risk of loss does not pass to the buyer until the goods leave the ship's tackle or are otherwise properly unloaded.

Section 2–323. Form of Bill of Lading Required in Overseas Shipment; "Overseas".

(1) Where the contract contemplates overseas shipment and contains a term C.I.F. or C. & F. or F.O.B. vessel, the seller unless otherwise agreed must obtain a negotiable bill of lading stating that the goods have been loaded on board or, in the case of a term C.I.F. or C. & F., received for shipment.

(2) Where in a case within subsection (1) a bill of lading has been issued in a set of parts, unless otherwise agreed if the documents are not to be sent from abroad the buyer may demand tender of the full set; otherwise only one part of the bill of lading need be tendered. Even if the agreement expressly requires a full set

    (a) due tender of a single part is acceptable within the provisions of this Article on cure of improper delivery (subsection (1) of Section 2–508); and

    (b) even though the full set is demanded, if the documents are sent from abroad the person tendering an incomplete set may nevertheless require payment upon furnishing an indemnity which the buyer in good faith deems adequate.

(3) A shipment by water or by air or a contract contemplating such shipment is "overseas" insofar as by usage of trade or agreement it is subject to the commercial, financing or shipping practices characteristic of international deep water commerce.

Section 2–324. "No Arrival, No Sale" Term.

Under a term "no arrival, no sale" or terms of like meaning, unless otherwise agreed,

(a) the seller must properly ship conforming goods and if they arrive by any means he must tender them on arrival but he assumes no obligation that the goods will arrive unless he has caused the non-arrival; and

(b) where without fault of the seller the goods are in part lost or have so deteriorated as no longer to conform to the contract or arrive after the contract time, the buyer may proceed as if there had been casualty to identified goods (Section 2–613).

Section 2–325. "Letter of Credit" Term; "Confirmed Credit".

(1) Failure of the buyer seasonably to furnish an agreed letter of credit is a breach of the contract for sale.

(2) The delivery to seller of a proper letter of credit suspends the buyer's obligation to pay. If the letter of credit is dishonored, the seller may on seasonable notification to the buyer require payment directly from him.

(3) Unless otherwise agreed the term "letter of credit" or "banker's credit" in a contract for sale means an irrevocable credit issued by a financing agency of good repute and, where the shipment is overseas, of good international repute. The term "confirmed credit" means that the credit must also carry the direct obligation of such an agency which does business in the seller's financial market.

Section 2–326. Sale on Approval and Sale or Return; Consignment Sales and Rights of Creditors.

(1) Unless otherwise agreed, if delivered goods may be returned by the buyer even though they conform to the contract, the transaction is

(a) a "sale on approval" if the goods are delivered primarily for use, and

(b) a "sale or return" if the goods are delivered primarily for resale.

(2) Except as provided in subsection (3), goods held on approval are not subject to the claims of the buyer's creditors until acceptance; goods held on sale or return are subject to such claims while in the buyer's possession.

(3) Where goods are delivered to a person for sale and such person maintains a place of business at which he deals in goods of the kind involved, under a name other than the name of the person making delivery, then with respect to claims of creditors of the person conducting the business the goods are deemed to be on sale or return. The provisions of this subsection are applicable even though an agreement purports to reserve title to the person making delivery until payment or resale or uses such words as "on consignment" or "on memorandum". However, this subsection is not applicable if the person making delivery

(a) complies with an applicable law providing for a consignor's interest or the like to be evidenced by a sign, or

(b) establishes that the person conducting the business is generally known by his creditors to be substantially engaged in selling the goods of others, or

(c) complies with the filing provisions of the Article on Secured Transactions (Article 9).

(4) Any "or return" term of a contract for sale is to be treated as a separate contract for sale within the statute of frauds section of this Article

(Section 2–201) and as contradicting the sale aspect of the contract within the provisions of this Article on parol or extrinsic evidence (Section 2–202).

Section 2–327. Special Incidents of Sale on Approval and Sale or Return.

(1) Under a sale on approval unless otherwise agreed

    (a) although the goods are identified to the contract the risk of loss and the title do not pass to the buyer until acceptance; and

    (b) use of the goods consistent with the purpose of trial is not acceptance but failure seasonably to notify the seller of election to return the goods is acceptance, and if the goods conform to the contract acceptance of any part is acceptance of the whole; and

    (c) after due notification of election to return, the return is at the seller's risk and expense but a merchant buyer must follow any reasonable instructions.

(2) Under a sale or return unless otherwise agreed

    (a) the option to return extends to the whole or any commercial unit of the goods while in substantially their original condition, but must be exercised seasonably; and

    (b) the return is at the buyer's risk and expense.

Section 2–328. Sale by Auction.

(1) In a sale by auction if goods are put up in lots each lot is the subject of a separate sale.

(2) A sale by auction is complete when the auctioneer so announces by the fall of the hammer or in other customary manner. Where a bid is made while the hammer is falling in acceptance of a prior bid the auctioneer may in his discretion reopen the bidding or declare the goods sold under the bid on which the hammer was falling.

(3) Such a sale is with reserve unless the goods are in explicit terms put up without reserve. In an auction with reserve the auctioneer may withdraw the goods at any time until he announces completion of the sale. In an auction without reserve, after the auctioneer calls for bids on an article or lot, that article or lot cannot be withdrawn unless no bid is made within a reasonable time. In either case a bidder may retract his bid until the auctioneer's announcement of completion of the sale, but a bidder's retraction does not revive any previous bid.

(4) If the auctioneer knowingly receives a bid on the seller's behalf or the seller makes or procures such a bid, and notice has not been given that liberty for such bidding is reserved, the buyer may at his option avoid the sale or take the goods at the price of the last good faith bid prior to the completion of the sale. This subsection shall not apply to any bid at a forced sale.

PART 4

TITLE, CREDITORS AND GOOD FAITH PURCHASERS

Section 2–401. Passing of Title; Reservation for Security; Limited Applicaton of This Section.

Each provision of this Article with regard to the rights, obligations and remedies of the seller, the buyer, purchasers or other third parties applies irrespective of title to the goods except where the provision refers to such title. Insofar as situations are not covered by the other provisions of this Article and matters concerning title become material the following rules apply:

(1) Title to goods cannot pass under a contract for sale prior to their identification to the contract (Section 2–501), and unless otherwise explicitly agreed the buyer acquires by their identification a special property as limited by this Act. Any retention or reservation by the seller of the title (property) in goods shipped or delivered to the buyer is limited in effect to a reservation of a security interest. Subject to these provisions and to the provisions of the Article on Secured Transactions (Article 9), title to goods passes from the seller to the buyer in any manner and on any conditions explicitly agreed on by the parties.

(2) Unless otherwise explicitly agreed title passes to the buyer at the time and place at which the seller completes his performance with reference to the physical delivery of the goods, despite any reservation of a security interest and even though a document of title is to be delivered at a different time or place; and in particular and despite any reservation of a security interest by the bill of lading

(a) if the contract requires or authorizes the seller to send the goods to the buyer but does not require him to deliver them at destination, title passes to the buyer at the time and place of shipment; but

(b) if the contract requires delivery at destination, title passes on tender there.

(3) Unless otherwise explicitly agreed where delivery is to be made without moving the goods,

(a) if the seller is to deliver a document of title, title passes at the time when and the place where he delivers such documents; or

(b) if the goods are at the time of contracting already identified and no documents are to be delivered, title passes at the time and place of contracting.

(4) A rejection or other refusal by the buyer to receive or retain the goods, whether or not justified, or a justified revocation of acceptance revests title to the goods in the seller. Such revesting occurs by operation of law and is not a "sale".

Section 2–402. Rights of Seller's Creditors Against Sold Goods.

(1) Except as provided in subsections (2) and (3), rights of unsecured creditors of the seller with respect to goods which have been identified to a contract for sale are subject to the buyer's rights to recover the goods under this Article (Sections 2–502 and 2–716).

(2) A creditor of the seller may treat a sale or an identification of goods to a contract for sale as void if as against him a retention of possession by the seller is fraudulent under any rule of law of the state where the goods are situated, except that retention of possession in good faith and current course of trade by a merchant-seller for a commercially reasonable time after a sale or identification is not fraudulent.

(3) Nothing in this Article shall be deemed to impair the rights of creditors of the seller

    (a) under the provisions of the Article on Secured Transactions (Article 9); or

    (b) where identification to the contract or delivery is made not in current course of trade but in satisfaction of or as security for a pre-existing claim for money, security or the like and is made under circumstances which under any rule of law of the state where the goods are situated would apart from this Article constitute the transaction a fraudulent transfer or voidable preference.

Section 2–403. Power to Transfer; Good Faith Purchase of Goods; "Entrusting".

(1) A purchaser of goods acquires all title which his transferor had or had power to transfer except that a purchaser of a limited interest acquires rights only to the extent of the interest purchased. A person with voidable title has power to transfer a good title to a good faith purchaser for value. When goods have been delivered under a transaction of purchase the purchaser has such power even though

    (a) the transferor was deceived as to the identity of the purchaser, or

    (b) the delivery was in exchange for a check which is later dishonored, or

    (c) it was agreed that the transaction was to be a "cash sale", or

    (d) the delivery was procured through fraud punishable as larcenous under the criminal law.

(2) Any entrusting of possession of goods to a merchant who deals in goods of that kind gives him power to transfer all rights of the entruster to a buyer in ordinary course of business.

(3) "Entrusting" includes any delivery and any acquiescence in retention of possession regardless of any condition expressed between the parties to the delivery or acquiescence and regardless of whether the procurement of the entrusting or the possessor's disposition of the goods have been such as to be larcenous under the criminal law.

(4) The rights of other purchasers of goods and of lien creditors are governed by the Articles on Secured Transactions (Article 9), Bulk Transfers (Article 6) and Documents of Title (Article 7).

PART 5

PERFORMANCE

Section 2–501. Insurable Interest in Goods; Manner of Identification of Goods.

(1) The buyer obtains a special property and an insurable interest in goods by identification of existing goods as goods to which the contract refers even though the goods so identified are non-conforming and he has an option to return or reject them. Such identification can be made at any time and in any manner explicitly agreed to by the parties. In the absence of explicit agreement identification occurs

    (a) when the contract is made if it is for the sale of goods already existing and identified;

(b) if the contract is for the sale of future goods other than those described in paragraph (c), when goods are shipped, marked or otherwise designated by the seller as goods to which the contract refers;

(c) when the crops are planted or otherwise become growing crops or the young are conceived if the contract is for the sale of unborn young to be born within twelve months after contracting or for the sale of crops to be harvested within twelve months or the next normal harvest season after contracting whichever is longer.

(2) The seller retains an insurable interest in goods so long as title to or any security interest in the goods remains in him and where the identification is by the seller alone he may until default or insolvency or notification to the buyer that the identification is final substitute other goods for those identified.

(3) Nothing in this section impairs any insurable interest recognized under any other statute or rule of law.

Section 2–502. Buyer's Right to Goods on Seller's Insolvency.

(1) Subject to subsection (2) and even though the goods have not been shipped a buyer who has paid a part or all of the price of goods in which he has a special property under the provisions of the immediately preceding section may on making and keeping good a tender of any unpaid portion of their price recover them from the seller if the seller becomes insolvent within ten days after receipt of the first installment on their price.

(2) If the identification creating his special property has been made by the buyer he acquires the right to recover the goods only if they conform to the contract for sale.

Section 2–503. Manner of Seller's Tender of Delivery.

(1) Tender of delivery requires that the seller put and hold conforming goods at the buyer's disposition and give the buyer any notification reasonably necessary to enable him to take delivery. The manner, time and place for tender are determined by the agreement and this Article, and in particular

(a) tender must be at a reasonable hour, and if it is of goods they must be kept available for the period reasonably necessary to enable the buyer to take possession; but

(b) unless otherwise agreed the buyer must furnish facilities reasonably suited to the receipt of the goods.

(2) Where the case is within the next section respecting shipment tender requires that the seller comply with its provisions.

(3) Where the seller is required to deliver at a particular destination tender requires that he comply with subsection (1) and also in any appropriate case tender documents as described in subsections (4) and (5) of this section.

(4) Where goods are in the possession of a bailee and are to be delivered without being moved

(a) tender requires that the seller either tender a negotiable document of title covering such goods or procure acknowledgment by the bailee of the buyer's right to possession of the goods; but

(b) tender to the buyer of a non-negotiable document of title or of a written direction to the bailee to deliver is sufficient tender unless the buyer seasonably objects, and receipt by the bailee of notification of the buyer's rights fixes those rights as against the bailee and all third persons; but risk of loss of the goods and of any failure by the bailee to honor the non-negotiable document of title or to obey the direction remains on the seller until the buyer has had a reasonable time to present the document or direction, and a refusal by the bailee to honor the document or to obey the direction defeats the tender.

(5) Where the contract requires the seller to deliver documents

    (a) he must tender all such documents in correct form, except as provided in this Article with respect to bills of lading in a set (subsection (2) of Section 2–323); and

    (b) tender through customary banking channels is sufficient and dishonor of a draft accompanying the documents constitutes non-acceptance or rejection.

Section 2–504. Shipment by Seller.

Where the seller is required or authorized to send the goods to the buyer and the contract does not require him to deliver them at a particular destination, then unless otherwise agreed he must

    (a) put the goods in the possession of such a carrier and make such a contract for their transportation as may be reasonable having regard to the nature of the goods and other circumstances of the case; and

    (b) obtain and promptly deliver or tender in due form any document necessary to enable the buyer to obtain possession of the goods or otherwise required by the agreement or by usage of trade; and

    (c) promptly notify the buyer of the shipment.

Failure to notify the buyer under paragraph (c) or to make a proper contract under paragraph (a) is a ground for rejection only if material delay or loss ensues.

Section 2–505. Seller's Shipment Under Reservation.

(1) Where the seller has identified goods to the contract by or before shipment:

    (a) his procurement of a negotiable bill of lading to his own order or otherwise reserves in him a security interest in the goods. His procurement of the bill to the order of a financing agency or of the buyer indicates in addition only the seller's expectation of transferring that interest to the person named.

    (b) a non-negotiable bill of lading to himself or his nominee reserves possession of the goods as security but except in a case of conditional delivery (subsection (2) of Section 2–507) a non-negotiable bill of lading naming the buyer as consignee reserves no security interest even though the seller retains possession of the bill of lading.

(2) When shipment by the seller with reservation of a security interest is in violation of the contract for sale it constitutes an improper contract for transportation within the preceding section but impairs neither the rights given to the buyer by shipment and identification of the goods to the contract nor the seller's powers as a holder of a negotiable document.

Section 2–506. Rights of Financing Agency.

(1) A financing agency by paying or purchasing for value a draft which relates to a shipment of goods acquires to the extent of the payment or purchase and in addition to its own rights under the draft and any document of title securing it any rights of the shipper in the goods including the right to stop delivery and the shipper's right to have the draft honored by the buyer.

(2) The right to reimbursement of a financing agency which has in good faith honored or purchased the draft under commitment to or authority from the buyer is not impaired by subsequent discovery of defects with reference to any relevant document which was apparently regular on its face.

Section 2–507. Effect of Seller's Tender; Delivery on Condition.

(1) Tender of delivery is a condition to the buyer's duty to accept the goods and, unless otherwise agreed, to his duty to pay for them. Tender entitles the seller to acceptance of the goods and to payment according to the contract.

(2) Where payment is due and demanded on the delivery to the buyer of goods or documents of title, his right as against the seller to retain or dispose of them is conditional upon his making the payment due.

Section 2–508. Cure by Seller of Improper Tender or Delivery; Replacement.

(1) Where any tender or delivery by the seller is rejected because nonconforming and the time for performance has not yet expired, the seller may seasonably notify the buyer of his intention to cure and may then within the contract time make a conforming delivery.

(2) Where the buyer rejects a non-conforming tender which the seller had reasonable grounds to believe would be acceptable with or without money allowance the seller may if he seasonably notifies the buyer have a further reasonable time to substitute a conforming tender.

Section 2–509. Risk of Loss in the Absence of Breach.

(1) Where the contract requires or authorizes the seller to ship the goods by carrier
    (a) if it does not require him to deliver them at a particular destination, the risk of loss passes to the buyer when the goods are duly delivered to the carrier even though the shipment is under reservation (Section 2–505); but
    (b) if it does require him to deliver them at a particular destination and the goods are there duly tendered while in the possession of the carrier, the risk of loss passes to the buyer when the goods are there duly so tendered as to enable the buyer to take delivery.

(2) Where the goods are held by a bailee to be delivered without being moved, the risk of loss passes to the buyer
    (a) on his receipt of a negotiable document of title covering the goods; or
    (b) on acknowledgment by the bailee of the buyer's right to possession of the goods; or

(c) after his receipt of a non-negotiable document of title or other written direction to deliver, as provided in subsection (4) (b) of Section 2–503.

(3) In any case not within subsection (1) or (2), the risk of loss passes to the buyer on his receipt of the goods if the seller is a merchant; otherwise the risk passes to the buyer on tender of delivery.

(4) The provisions of this section are subject to contrary agreement of the parties and to the provisions of this Article on sale on approval (Section 2–327) and on effect of breach on risk of loss (Section 2–510).

Section 2–510. Effect of Breach on Risk of Loss.

(1) Where a tender or delivery of goods so fails to conform to the contract as to give a right of rejection the risk of their loss remains on the seller until cure or acceptance.

(2) Where the buyer rightfully revokes acceptance he may to the extent of any deficiency in his effective insurance coverage treat the risk of loss as having rested on the seller from the beginning.

(3) Where the buyer as to conforming goods already identified to the contract for sale repudiates or is otherwise in breach before risk of their loss has passed to him, the seller may to the extent of any deficiency in his effective insurance coverage treat the risk of loss as resting on the buyer for a commercially reasonable time.

Section 2–511. Tender of Payment by Buyer; Payment by Check.

(1) Unless otherwise agreed tender of payment is a condition to the seller's duty to tender and complete any delivery.

(2) Tender of payment is sufficient when made by any means or in any manner current in the ordinary course of business unless the seller demands payment in legal tender and gives any extension of time reasonably necessary to procure it.

(3) Subject to the provisions of this Act on the effect of an instrument on an obligation (Section 3–802), payment by check is conditional and is defeated as between the parties by dishonor of the check on due presentment.

Section 2–512. Payment by Buyer Before Inspection.

(1) Where the contract requires payment before inspection non-conformity of the goods does not excuse the buyer from so making payment unless
    (a) the non-conformity appears without inspection; or
    (b) despite tender of the required documents the circumstances would justify injunction against honor under the provisions of this Act (Section 5–114).

(2) Payment pursuant to subsection (1) does not constitute an acceptance of goods or impair the buyer's right to inspect or any of his remedies.

Section 2–513. Buyer's Right to Inspection of Goods.

(1) Unless otherwise agreed and subject to subsection (3), where goods are tendered or delivered or identified to the contract for sale, the buyer has a right before payment or acceptance to inspect them at any reasonable place and time

and in any reasonable manner. When the seller is required or authorized to send the goods to the buyer, the inspection may be after their arrival.

(2) Expenses of inspection must be borne by the buyer but may be recovered from the seller if the goods do not conform and are rejected.

(3) Unless otherwise agreed and subject to the provisions of this Article on C.I.F. contracts (subsection (3) of Section 2–321), the buyer is not entitled to inspect the goods before payment of the price when the contract provides

    (a) for delivery "C.O.D." or on other like terms; or

    (b) for payment against documents of title, except where such payment is due only after the goods are to become available for inspection.

(4) A place or method of inspection fixed by the parties is presumed to be exclusive but unless otherwise expressly agreed it does not postpone identification or shift the place for delivery or for passing the risk of loss. If compliance becomes impossible, inspection shall be as provided in this section unless the place or method fixed was clearly intended as an indispensable condition failure of which avoids the contract.

Section 2–514. When Documents Deliverable on Acceptance; When on Payment.

Unless otherwise agreed documents against which a draft is drawn are to be delivered to the drawee on acceptance of the draft if it is payable more than three days after presentment; otherwise, only on payment.

Section 2–515. Preserving Evidence of Goods in Dispute.

In furtherance of the adjustment of any claim or dispute

    (a) either party on reasonable notification to the other and for the purpose of ascertaining the facts and preserving evidence has the right to inspect, test and sample the goods including such of them as may be in the possession or control of the other; and

    (b) the parties may agree to a third party inspection or survey to determine the conformity or condition of the goods and may agree that the findings shall be binding upon them in any subsequent litigation or adjustment.

PART 6

BREACH, REPUDIATION AND EXCUSE

Section 2–601. Buyer's Rights on Improper Delivery.

Subject to the provisions of this Article on breach in installment contracts (Section 2–612) and unless otherwise agreed under the sections on contractual limitations of remedy (Sections 2–718 and 2–719), if the goods or the tender of delivery fail in any respect to conform to the contract, the buyer may

    (a) reject the whole; or

    (b) accept the whole; or

    (c) accept any commercial unit or units and reject the rest.

Section 2–602. Manner and Effect of Rightful Rejection.

(1) Rejection of goods must be within a reasonable time after their delivery or tender. It is ineffective unless the buyer seasonably notifies the seller.

(2) Subject to the provisions of the two following sections on rejected goods (Sections 2–603 and 2–604),

   (a) after rejection any exercise of ownership by the buyer with respect to any commercial unit is wrongful as against the seller; and

   (b) if the buyer has before rejection taken physical possession of goods in which he does not have a security interest under the provisions of this Article (subsection (3) of Section 2–711), he is under a duty after rejection to hold them with reasonable care at the seller's disposition for a time sufficient to permit the seller to remove them; but

   (c) the buyer has no further obligations with regard to goods rightfully rejected.

(3) The seller's rights with respect to goods wrongfully rejected are governed by the provisions of this Article on Seller's remedies in general (Section 2–703).

Section 2–603. Merchant Buyer's Duties as to Rightfully Rejected Goods.

(1) Subject to any security interest in the buyer (subsection (3) of Section 2–711), when the seller has no agent or place of business at the market of rejection a merchant buyer is under a duty after rejection of goods in his possession or control to follow any reasonable instructions received from the seller with respect to the goods and in the absence of such instructions to make reasonable efforts to sell them for the seller's account if they are perishable or threaten to decline in value speedily. Instructions are not reasonable if on demand indemnity for expenses is not forthcoming.

(2) When the buyer sells goods under subsection (1), he is entitled to reimbursement from the seller or out of the proceeds for reasonable expenses of caring for and selling them, and if the expenses include no selling commission then to such commission as is usual in the trade or if there is none to a reasonable sum not exceeding ten per cent on the gross proceeds.

(3) In complying with this section the buyer is held only to good faith and good faith conduct hereunder is neither acceptance nor conversion nor the basis of an action for damages.

Section 2–604. Buyer's Options as to Salvage of Rightfully Rejected Goods.

Subject to the provisions of the immediately preceding section on perishables if the seller gives no instructions within a reasonable time after notification of rejection the buyer may store the rejected goods for the seller's account or reship them to him or resell them for the seller's account with reimbursement as provided in the preceding section. Such action is not acceptance or conversion.

Section 2–605. Waiver of Buyer's Objections by Failure to Particularize.

(1) The buyer's failure to state in connection with rejection a particular defect which is ascertainable by reasonable inspection precludes him from relying on the unstated defect to justify rejection or to establish breach

   (a) where the seller could have cured it if stated seasonably; or

    (b) between merchants when the seller has after rejection made a request in writing for a full and final written statement of all defects on which the buyer proposes to rely.

(2) Payment against documents made without reservation of rights precludes recovery of the payment for defects apparent on the face of the documents.

Section 2-606. What Constitutes Acceptance of Goods.

(1) Acceptance of goods occurs when the buyer
    (a) after a reasonable opportunity to inspect the goods signifies to the seller that the goods are conforming or that he will take or retain them in spite of their nonconformity; or
    (b) fails to make an effective rejection (subsection (1) of Section 2-602), but such acceptance does not occur until the buyer has had a reasonable opportunity to inspect them; or
    (c) does any act inconsistent with the seller's ownership; but if such act is wrongful as against the seller it is an acceptance only if ratified by him.

(2) Acceptance of a part of any commercial unit is acceptance of that entire unit.

Section 2-607. Effect of Acceptance; Notice of Breach; Burden of Establishing Breach After Acceptance; Notice of Claim or Litigation to Person Answerable Over.

(1) The buyer must pay at the contract rate for any goods accepted.

(2) Acceptance of goods by the buyer precludes rejection of the goods accepted and if made with knowledge of a non-conformity cannot be revoked because of it unless the acceptance was on the reasonable assumption that the non-conformity would be seasonably cured but acceptance does not of itself impair any other remedy provided by this Article for non-conformity.

(3) Where a tender has been accepted
    (a) the buyer must within a reasonable time after he discovers or should have discovered any breach notify the seller of breach or be barred from any remedy; and
    (b) if the claim is one for infringement or the like (subsection (3) of Section 2-312) and the buyer is sued as a result of such a breach he must so notify the seller within a reasonable time after he receives notice of the litigation or be barred from any remedy over for liability established by the litigation.

(4) The burden is on the buyer to establish any breach with respect to the goods accepted.

(5) Where the buyer is sued for breach of a warranty or other obligation for which his seller is answerable over
    (a) he may give his seller written notice of the litigation. If the notice states that the seller may come in and defend and that if the seller does not do so he will be bound in any action against him by his buyer by any determination of fact common to the two litigations,

then unless the seller after seasonable receipt of the notice does come in and defend he is so bound.

(b) if the claim is one for infringement or the like (subsection (3) of Section 2–312) the original seller may demand in writing that his buyer turn over to him control of the litigation including settlement or else be barred from any remedy over and if he also agrees to bear all expense and to satisfy any adverse judgment, then unless the buyer after seasonable receipt of the demand does turn over control the buyer is so barred.

(6) The provisions of subsections (3), (4) and (5) apply to any obligation of a buyer to hold the seller harmless against infringement or the like (subsection (3) of Section 2–312).

Section 2–608. Revocation of Acceptance in Whole or in Part.

(1) The buyer may revoke his acceptance of a lot or commercial unit whose non-conformity substantially impairs its value to him if he has accepted it

(a) on the reasonable assumption that its non-conformity would be cured and it has not been seasonably cured; or

(b) without discovery of such non-conformity if his acceptance was reasonably induced either by the difficulty of discovery before acceptance or by the seller's assurances.

(2) Revocation of acceptance must occur within a reasonable time after the buyer discovers or should have discovered the ground for it and before any substantial change in condition of the goods which is not caused by their own defects. It is not effective until the buyer notifies the seller of it.

(3) A buyer who so revokes has the same rights and duties with regard to the goods involved as if he had rejected them.

Section 2–609. Right to Adequate Assurance of Performance.

(1) A contract for sale imposes an obligation on each party that the other's expectation of receiving due performance will not be impaired. When reasonable grounds for insecurity arise with respect to the performance of either party the other may in writing demand adequate assurance of due performance and until he receives such assurance may if commercially reasonable suspend any performance for which he has not already received the agreed return.

(2) Between merchants the reasonableness of grounds for insecurity and the adequacy of any assurance offered shall be determined according to commercial standards.

(3) Acceptance of any improper delivery or payment does not prejudice the aggrieved party's right to demand adequate assurance of future performance.

(4) After receipt of a justified demand failure to provide within a reasonable time not exceeding thirty days such assurance of due performance as is adequate under the circumstances of the particular case is a repudiation of the contract.

Section 2–610. Anticipatory Repudiation.

When either party repudiates the contract with respect to a performance not yet due the loss of which will substantially impair the value of the contract to the other, the aggrieved party may

(a) for a commercially reasonable time await performance by the repudiating party; or

(b) resort to any remedy for breach (Section 2–703 or Section 2–711), even though he has notified the repudiating party that he would await the latter's performance and has urged retraction; and

(c) in either case suspend his own performance or proceed in accordance with the provisions of this Article on the seller's right to identify goods to the contract notwithstanding breach or to salvage unfinished goods (Section 2–704).

Section 2–611. Retraction of Anticipatory Repudiation.

(1) Until the repudiating party's next performance is due he can retract his repudiation unless the aggrieved party has since the repudiation cancelled or materially changed his position or otherwise indicated that he considers the repudiation final.

(2) Retraction may be by any method which clearly indicates to the aggrieved party that the repudiating party intends to perform, but must include any assurance justifiably demanded under the provisions of this Article (Section 2–609).

(3) Retraction reinstates the repudiating party's rights under the contract with due excuse and allowance to the aggrieved party for any delay occasioned by the repudiation.

Section 2–612. "Installment Contract"; Breach.

(1) An "installment contract" is one which requires or authorizes the delivery of goods in separate lots to be separately accepted, even though the contract contains a clause "each delivery is a separate contract" or its equivalent.

(2) The buyer may reject any installment which is non-conforming if the non-conformity substantially impairs the value of that installment and cannot be cured or if the non-conformity is a defect in the required documents; but if the non-conformity does not fall within subsection (3) and the seller gives adequate assurance of its cure the buyer must accept that installment.

(3) Whenever non-conformity or default with respect to one or more installments substantially impairs the value of the whole contract there is a breach of the whole. But the aggrieved party reinstates the contract if he accepts a non-conforming installment without seasonably notifying of cancellation or if he brings an action with respect only to past installments or demands performance as to future installments.

Section 2–613. Casualty to Identified Goods.

Where the contract requires for its performance goods identified when the contract is made, and the goods suffer casualty without fault of either party before the risk of loss passes to the buyer, or in a proper case under a "no arrival, no sale" term (Section 2–324) then

(a) if the loss is total the contract is avoided; and

(b) if the loss is partial or the goods have so deteriorated as no longer to conform to the contract the buyer may nevertheless demand inspection and at his option either treat the contract as avoided or accept the goods with due allowance from the contract price for the deterioration or the deficiency in quantity but without further right against the seller.

Section 2–614. Substituted Performance.

(1) Where without fault of either party the agreed berthing, loading, or unloading facilities fail or an agreed type of carrier becomes unavailable or the agreed manner of delivery otherwise becomes commercially impracticable but a commercially reasonable substitute is available, such substitute performance must be tendered and accepted.

(2) If the agreed means or manner of payment fails because of domestic or foreign governmental regulation, the seller may withhold or stop delivery unless the buyer provides a means or manner of payment which is commercially a substantial equivalent. If delivery has already been taken, payment by the means or in the manner provided by the regulation discharges the buyer's obligation unless the regulation is discriminatory, oppressive or predatory.

Section 2–615. Excuse by Failure of Presupposed Conditions.

Except so far as a seller may have assumed a greater obligation and subject to the preceding section on substituted performance:

(a) Delay in delivery or non-delivery in whole or in part by a seller who complies with paragraphs (b) and (c) is not a breach of his duty under a contract for sale if performance as agreed has been made impracticable by the occurrence of a contingency the non-occurence of which was a basic assumption on which the contract was made or by compliance in good faith with any applicable foreign or domestic governmental regulation or order whether or not it later proves to be invalid.

(b) Where the causes mentioned in paragraph (a) affect only a part of the seller's capacity to perform, he must allocate production and deliveries among his customers but may at his option include regular customers not then under contract as well as his own requirements for further manufacture. He may so allocate in any manner which is fair and reasonable.

(c) The seller must notify the buyer seasonably that there will be delay or non-delivery and, when allocation is required under paragraph (b), of the estimated quota thus made available for the buyer.

Section 2–616. Procedure on Notice Claiming Excuse.

(1) Where the buyer receives notification of a material or indefinite delay or an allocation justified under the preceding section he may by written notification to the seller as to any delivery concerned, and where the prospective deficiency substantially impairs the value of the whole contract under the provisions of this Article relating to breach of installment contracts (Section 2–612), then also as to the whole,

(a) terminate and thereby discharge any unexecuted portion of the contract; or

(b) modify the contract by agreeing to take his available quota in substitution.

(2) If after receipt of such notification from the seller the buyer fails so to modify the contract within a reasonable time not exceeding thirty days the contract lapses with respect to any deliveries affected.

(3) The provisions of this section may not be negated by agreement except in so far as the seller has assumed a greater obligation under the preceding section.

PART 7

REMEDIES

Section 2–701. Remedies for Breach of Collateral Contracts Not Impaired.

Remedies for breach of any obligation or promise collateral or ancillary to a contract for sale are not impaired by the provisions of this Article.

Section 2–702. Seller's Remedies on Discovery of Buyer's Insolvency.

(1) Where the seller discovers the buyer to be insolvent he may refuse delivery except for cash including payment for all goods theretofore delivered under the contract, and stop delivery under this Article (Section 2–705).

(2) Where the seller discovers that the buyer has received goods on credit while insolvent he may reclaim the goods upon demand made within ten days after the receipt, but if misrepresentation of solvency has been made to the particular seller in writing within three months before delivery the ten day limitation does not apply. Except as provided in this subsection the seller may not base a right to reclaim goods on the buyer's fraudulent or innocent misrepresentation of solvency or of intent to pay.

(3) The seller's right to reclaim under subsection (2) is subject to the rights of a buyer in ordinary course or other good faith purchaser or lien creditor under this Article (Section 2–403). Successful reclamation of goods excludes all other remedies with respect to them.

Section 2–703. Seller's Remedies in General.

Where the buyer wrongfully rejects or revokes acceptance of goods or fails to make a payment due on or before delivery or repudiates with respect to a part or the whole, then with respect to any goods directly affected and, if the breach is of the whole contract (Section 2–612), then also with respect to the whole undelivered balance, the aggrieved seller may

    (a) withhold delivery of such goods;

    (b) stop delivery by any bailee as hereafter provided (Section 2–705);

    (c) proceed under the next section respecting goods still unidentified to the contract;

    (d) resell and recover damages as hereafter provided (Section 2–706);

    (e) recover damages for non-acceptance (Section 2–708) or in a proper case the price (Section 2–709);

    (f) cancel.

Section 2–704. Seller's Right to Identify Goods to the Contract Notwithstanding Breach or to Salvage Unfinished Goods.

(1) An aggrieved seller under the preceding section may

    (a) identify to the contract conforming goods not already identified if at the time he learned of the breach they are in his possession or control;

    (b) treat as the subject of resale goods which have demonstrably been intended for the particular contract even though those goods are unfinished.

(2) Where the goods are unfinished an aggrieved seller may in the exercise of reasonable commercial judgment for the purposes of avoiding loss and of effective realization either complete the manufacture and wholly identify the goods to the contract or cease manufacture and resell for scrap or salvage value or proceed in any other reasonable manner.

Section 2–705. Seller's Stoppage of Delivery in Transit or Otherwise.

(1) The seller may stop delivery of goods in the possession of a carrier or other bailee when he discovers the buyer to be insolvent (Section 2–702) and may stop delivery of carload, truckload, planeload or larger shipments of express or freight when the buyer repudiates or fails to make a payment due before delivery or if for any other reason the seller has a right to withhold or reclaim the goods.

(2) As against such buyer the seller may stop delivery until

    (a) receipt of the goods by the buyer; or

    (b) acknowledgment to the buyer by any bailee of the goods except a carrier that the bailee holds the goods for the buyer; or

    (c) such acknowledgment to the buyer by a carrier by reshipment or as warehouseman; or

    (d) negotiation to the buyer of any negotiable document of title covering the goods.

(3) (a) To stop delivery the seller must so notify as to enable the bailee by reasonable diligence to prevent delivery of the goods.

    (b) After such notification the bailee must hold and deliver the goods according to the directions of the seller but the seller is liable to the bailee for any ensuing charges or damages.

    (c) If a negotiable document of title has been issued for goods the bailee is not obliged to obey a notification to stop until surrender of the document.

    (d) A carrier who has issued a non-negotiable bill of lading is not obliged to obey a notification to stop received from a person other than the consignor.

Section 2–706. Seller's Resale Including Contract for Resale.

(1) Under the conditions stated in Section 2–703 on seller's remedies, the seller may resell the goods concerned or the undelivered balance thereof. Where the resale is made in good faith and in a commercially reasonable manner the seller may recover the difference between the resale price and the contract price

together with any incidental damages allowed under the provisions of this Article (Section 2-710), but less expenses saved in consequence of the buyer's breach.

(2) Except as otherwise provided in subsection (3) or unless otherwise agreed resale may be at public or private sale including sale by way of one or more contracts to sell or of identification to an existing contract of the seller. Sale may be as a unit or in parcels and at any time and place and on any terms but every aspect of the sale including the method, manner, time, place and terms must be commercially reasonable. The resale must be reasonably identified as referring to the broken contract, but it is not necessary that the goods be in existence or that any or all of them have been identified to the contract before the breach.

(3) Where the resale is at private sale the seller must give the buyer reasonable notification of his intention to resell.

(4) Where the resale is at public sale

(a) only identified goods can be sold except where there is a recognized market for a public sale of futures in goods of the kind; and

(b) it must be made at a usual place or market for public sale if one is reasonably available and except in the case of goods which are perishable or threaten to decline in value speedily the seller must give the buyer reasonable notice of the time and place of the resale; and

(c) if the goods are not to be within the view of those attending the sale the notification of sale must state the place where the goods are located and provide for their reasonable inspection by prospective bidders; and

(d) the seller may buy.

(5) A purchaser who buys in good faith at a resale takes the goods free of any rights of the original buyer even though the seller fails to comply with one or more of the requirements of this section.

(6) The seller is not accountable to the buyer for any profit made on any resale. A person in the position of a seller (Section 2-707) or a buyer who has rightfully rejected or justifiably revoked acceptance must account for any excess over the amount of his security interest, as hereinafter defined (subsection (3) of Section 2-711).

Section 2-707. "Person in the Position of a Seller".

(1) A "person in the position of a seller" includes as against a principal an agent who has paid or become responsible for the price of goods on behalf of his principal or anyone who otherwise holds a security interest or other right in goods similar to that of a seller.

(2) A person in the position of a seller may as provided in this Article withhold or stop delivery (Section 2-705) and resell (Section 2-706) and recover incidental damages (Section 2-710).

Section 2-708. Seller's Damages for Non-acceptance or Repudiation.

(1) Subject to subsection (2) and to the provisions of this Article with respect to proof of market price (Section 2-723), the measure of damages for

non-acceptance or repudiation by the buyer is the difference between the market price at the time and place for tender and the unpaid contract price together with any incidental damages provided in this Article (Section 2–710), but less expenses saved in consequence of the buyer's breach.

(2) If the measure of damages provided in subsection (1) is inadequate to put the seller in as good a position as performance would have done then the measure of damages is the profit (including reasonable overhead) which the seller would have made from full performance by the buyer, together with any incidental damages provided in this Article (Section 2–710), due allowance for costs reasonably incurred and due credit for payments or proceeds of resale.

Section 2–709. Action for the Price.

(1) When the buyer fails to pay the price as it becomes due the seller may recover, together with any incidental damages under the next section, the price

(a) of goods accepted or of conforming goods lost or damaged within a commercially reasonable time after risk of their loss has passed to the buyer; and

(b) of goods identified to the contract if the seller is unable after reasonable effort to resell them at a reasonable price or the circumstances reasonably indicate that such effort will be unavailing.

(2) Where the seller sues for the price he must hold for the buyer any goods which have been identified to the contract and are still in his control except that if resale becomes possible he may resell them at any time prior to the collection of the judgment. The net proceeds of any such resale must be credited to the buyer and payment of the judgment entitles him to any goods not resold.

(3) After the buyer has wrongfully rejected or revoked acceptance of the goods or has failed to make a payment due or has repudiated (Section 2–610), a seller who is held not entitled to the price under this section shall nevertheless be awarded damages for non-acceptance under the preceding section.

Section 2–710. Seller's Incidental Damages.

Incidental damages to an aggrieved seller include any commercially reasonable charges, expenses or commissions incurred in stopping delivery, in the transportation, care and custody of goods after the buyer's breach, in connection with return or resale of the goods or otherwise resulting from the breach.

Section 2–711. Buyer's Remedies in General; Buyer's Security Interest in Rejected Goods.

(1) Where the seller fails to make delivery or repudiates or the buyer rightfully rejects or justifiably revokes acceptance then with respect to any goods involved, and with respect to the whole if the breach goes to the whole contract (Section 2–612), the buyer may cancel and whether or not he has done so may in addition to recovering so much of the price as has been paid

(a) "cover" and have damages under the next section as to all the goods affected whether or not they have been identified to the contract; or

(b) recover damages for non-delivery as provided in this Article (Section 2–713).

(2) Where the seller fails to deliver or repudiates the buyer may also

 (a) if the goods have been identified recover them as provided in this Article (Section 2–502); or

 (b) in a proper case obtain specific performance or replevy the goods as provided in this Article (Section 2–716).

(3) On rightful rejection or justifiable revocation of acceptance a buyer has a security interest in goods in his possession or control for any payments made on their price and any expenses reasonably incurred in their inspection, receipt, transportation, care and custody and may hold such goods and resell them in like manner as an aggrieved seller (Section 2–706).

Section 2–712. "Cover"; Buyer's Procurement of Substitute Goods.

(1) After a breach within the preceding section the buyer may "cover" by making in good faith and without unreasonable delay any reasonable purchase of or contract to purchase goods in substitution for those due from the seller.

(2) The buyer may recover from the seller as damages the difference between the cost of cover and the contract price together with any incidental or consequential damages as hereinafter defined (Section 2–715), but less expenses saved in consequence of the seller's breach.

(3) Failure of the buyer to effect cover within this section does not bar him from any other remedy.

Section 2–713. Buyer's Damages for Non-Delivery or Repudiation.

(1) Subject to the provisions of this Article with respect to proof of market price (Section 2–723), the measure of damages for non-delivery or repudiation by the seller is the difference between the market price at the time when the buyer learned of the breach and the contract price together with any incidental and consequential damages provided in this Article (Section 2–715), but less expenses saved in consequence of the seller's breach.

(2) Market price is to be determined as of the place for tender or, in cases of rejection after arrival or revocation of acceptance, as of the place of arrival.

Section 2–714. Buyer's Damages for Breach in Regard to Accepted Goods.

(1) Where the buyer has accepted goods and given notification (subsection (3) of Section 2–607) he may recover as damages for any non-conformity of tender the loss resulting in the ordinary course of events from the seller's breach as determined in any manner which is reasonable.

(2) The measure of damages for breach of warranty is the difference at the time and place of acceptance between the value of the goods accepted and the value they would have had if they had been as warranted, unless special circumstances show proximate damages of a different amount.

(3) In a proper case any incidental and consequential damages under the next section may also be recovered.

Section 2–715. Buyer's Incidental and Consequential Damages.

(1) Incidental damages resulting from the seller's breach include expenses reasonably incurred in inspection, receipt, transportation and care and custody of goods rightfully rejected, any commercially reasonable charges, expenses or

commissions in connection with effecting cover and any other reasonable expense incident to the delay or other breach.

(2) Consequential damages resulting from the seller's breach include

(a) any loss resulting from general or particular requirements and needs of which the seller at the time of contracting had reason to know and which could not reasonably be prevented by cover or otherwise; and

(b) injury to person or property proximately resulting from any breach of warranty.

Section 2–716. Buyer's Right to Specific Performance or Replevin.

(1) Specific performance may be decreed where the goods are unique or in other proper circumstances.

(2) The decree for specific performance may include such terms and conditions as to payment of the price, damages, or other relief as the court may deem just.

(3) The buyer has a right of replevin for goods identified to the contract if after reasonable effort he is unable to effect cover for such goods or the circumstances reasonably indicate that such effort will be unavailing or if the goods have been shipped under reservation and satisfaction of the security interest in them has been made or tendered.

Section 2–717. Deduction of Damages From the Price.

The buyer on notifying the seller of his intention to do so may deduct all or any part of the damages resulting from any breach of the contract from any part of the price still due under the same contract.

Section 2–718. Liquidation or Limitation of Damages; Deposits.

(1) Damages for breach by either party may be liquidated in the agreement but only at an amount which is reasonable in the light of the anticipated or actual harm caused by the breach, the difficulties of proof of loss, and the inconvenience or nonfeasibility of otherwise obtaining an adequate remedy. A term fixing unreasonably large liquidated damages is void as a penalty.

(2) Where the seller justifiably withholds delivery of goods because of the buyer's breach, the buyer is entitled to restitution of any amount by which the sum of his payments exceeds

(a) the amount to which the seller is entitled by virtue of terms liquidating the seller's damages in accordance with subsection (1), or

(b) in the absence of such terms, twenty per cent of the value of the total performance for which the buyer is obligated under the contract or $500, whichever is smaller.

(3) The buyer's right to restitution under subsection (2) is subject to offset to the extent that the seller establishes

(a) a right to recover damages under the provisions of this Article other than subsection (1), and

(b) the amount or value of any benefits received by the buyer directly or indirectly by reason of the contract.

(4) Where a seller has received payment in goods their reasonable value or the proceeds of their resale shall be treated as payments for the purposes of

subsection (2); but if the seller has notice of the buyer's breach before reselling goods received in part performance, his resale is subject to the conditions laid down in this Article on resale by an aggrieved seller (Section 2–706).

Section 2–719.   Contractual Modification or Limitation of Remedy.

(1) Subject to the provisions of subsections (2) and (3) of this section and of the preceding section on liquidation and limitation of damages,

   (a) the agreement may provide for remedies in addition to or in substitution for those provided in this Article and may limit or alter the measure of damages recoverable under this Article, as by limiting the buyer's remedies to return of the goods and repayment of the price or to repair and replacement of non-conforming goods or parts; and

   (b) resort to a remedy as provided is optional unless the remedy is expressly agreed to be exclusive, in which case it is the sole remedy.

(2) Where circumstances cause an exclusive or limited remedy to fail of its essential purpose, remedy may be had as provided in this Act.

(3) Consequential damages may be limited or excluded unless the limitation or exclusion is unconscionable. Limitation of consequential damages for injury to the person in the case of consumer goods is prima facie unconscionable but limitation of damages where the loss is commercial is not.

Section 2–720.   Effect of "Cancellation" or "Rescission" on Claims for Antecedent Breach.

Unless the contrary intention clearly appears, expressions of "cancellation" or "rescission" of the contract or the like shall not be construed as a renunciation or discharge of any claim in damages for an antecedent breach.

Section 2–721.   Remedies for Fraud.

Remedies for material misrepresentation or fraud include all remedies available under this Article for non-fraudulent breach. Neither rescission or a claim for rescission of the contract for sale nor rejection or return of the goods shall bar or be deemed inconsistent with a claim for damages or other remedy.

Section 2–722.   Who Can Sue Third Parties for Injury to Goods.

Where a third party so deals with goods which have been identified to a contract for sale as to cause actionable injury to a party to that contract

   (a) a right of action against the third party is in either party to the contract for sale who has title to or a security interest or a special property or an insurable interest in the goods; and if the goods have been destroyed or converted a right of action is also in the party who either bore the risk of loss under the contract for sale or has since the injury assumed that risk as against the other;

   (b) if at the time of the injury the party plaintiff did not bear the risk of loss as against the other party to the contract for sale and there is no arrangement between them for disposition of the recovery, his suit or settlement is, subject to his own interest, as a fiduciary for the other party to the contract;

(c) either party may with the consent of the other sue for the benefit of whom it may concern.

Section 2–723. Proof of Market Price: Time and Place.

(1) If an action based on anticipatory repudiation comes to trial before the time for performance with respect to some or all of the goods, any damages based on market price (Section 2–708 or Section 2–713) shall be determined according to the price of such goods prevailing at the time when the aggrieved party learned of the repudiation.

(2) If evidence of a price prevailing at the times or places described in this Article is not readily available the price prevailing within any reasonable time before or after the time described or at any other place which in commercial judgment or under usage of trade would serve as a reasonable substitute for the one described may be used, making any proper allowance for the cost of transporting the goods to or from such other place.

(3) Evidence of a relevant price prevailing at a time or place other than the one described in this Article offered by one party is not admissible unless and until he has given the other party such notice as the court finds sufficient to prevent unfair surprise.

Section 2–724. Admissibility of Market Quotations.

Whenever the prevailing price or value of any goods regularly bought and sold in any established commodity market is in issue, reports in official publications or trade journals or in newspapers or periodicals of general circulation published as the reports of such market shall be admissible in evidence. The circumstances of the preparation of such a report may be shown to affect its weight but not its admissibility.

Section 2–725. Statute of Limitations in Contracts for Sale.

(1) An action for breach of any contract for sale must be commenced within four years after the cause of action has accrued. By the original agreement the parties may reduce the period of limitation to not less than one year but may not extend it.

(2) A cause of action accrues when the breach occurs, regardless of the aggrieved party's lack of knowledge of the breach. A breach of warranty occurs when tender of delivery is made, except that where a warranty explicitly extends to future performance of the goods and discovery of the breach must await the time of such performance the cause of action accrues when the breach is or should have been discovered.

(3) Where an action commenced within the time limited by subsection (1) is so terminated as to leave available a remedy by another action for the same breach such other action may be commenced after the expiration of the time limited and within six months after the termination of the first action unless the termination resulted from voluntary discontinuance or from dismissal for failure or neglect to prosecute.

(4) This section does not alter the law on tolling of the statute of limitations nor does it apply to causes of action which have accrued before this Act becomes effective.

ARTICLE 3

COMMERCIAL PAPER

PART 1

Short Title, Form and Interpretation

Section 3–101.   Short Title.

This Article shall be known and may be cited as Uniform Commercial Code—Commercial Paper.

Section 3–102.   Definitions and Index of Definitions.

(1) In this Article unless the context otherwise requires
  (a) "Issue" means the first delivery of an instrument to a holder or a remitter.
  (b) An "order" is a direction to pay and must be more than an authorization or request. It must identify the person to pay with reasonable certainty. It may be addressed to one or more such persons jointly or in the alternative but not in succession.
  (c) A "promise" is an undertaking to pay and must be more than an acknowledgment of an obligation.
  (d) "Secondary party" means a drawer or indorser.
  (e) "Instrument" means a negotiable instrument.
(2) Other definitions applying to this Article and the sections in which they appear are:
    "Acceptance". Section 3–410.
    "Accommodation party". Section 3–415.
    "Alteration". Section 3–407.
    "Certificate of deposit". Section 3–104.
    "Certification". Section 3–411.
    "Check". Section 3–104.
    "Definite time". Section 3–109.
    "Dishonor". Section 3–507.
    "Draft". Section 3–104.
    "Holder in due course". Section 3–302.
    "Negotiation". Section 3–202.
    "Note". Section 3–104.
    "Notice of dishonor". Section 3–508.
    "On demand". Section 3–108.
    "Presentment". Section 3–504.
    "Protest". Section 3–509.
    "Restrictive Indorsement". Section 3–205.
    "Signature". Section 3–401.

(3) The following definitions in other Articles apply to this Article:
"Account". Section 4–104.
"Banking Day". Section 4–104.
"Clearing house". Section 4–104.
"Collecting bank". Section 4–105.
"Customer". Section 4–104.
"Depositary Bank". Section 4–105.
"Documentary Draft". Section 4–104.
"Intermediary Bank". Section 4–105.
"Item". Section 4–104.
"Midnight deadline". Section 4–104.
"Payor bank". Section 4–105.

(4) In addition Article 1 contains general definitions and principles of construction and interpretation applicable throughout this Article.

Section 3–103. Limitations on Scope of Article.

(1) This Article does not apply to money, documents of title or investment securities.

(2) The provisions of this Article are subject to the provisions of the Article on Bank Deposits and Collections (Article 4) and Secured Transactions (Article 9).

Section 3–104. Form of Negotiable Instruments; "Draft"; "Check"; "Certificate of Deposit"; "Note".

(1) Any writing to be a negotiable instrument within this Article must
  (a) be signed by the maker or drawer; and
  (b) contain an unconditional promise or order to pay a sum certain in money and no other promise, order, obligation or power given by the maker or drawer except as authorized by this Article; and
  (c) be payable on demand or at a definite time; and
  (d) be payable to order or to bearer.
(2) A writing which complies with the requirements of this section is
  (a) a "draft" ("bill of exchange") if it is an order;
  (b) a "check" if it is a draft drawn on a bank and payable on demand;
  (c) a "certificate of deposit" if it is an acknowledgment by a bank of receipt of money with an engagement to repay it;
  (d) a "note" if it is a promise other than a certificate of deposit.
(3) As used in other Articles of this Act, and as the context may require, the terms "draft", "check", "certificate of deposit" and "note" may refer to instruments which are not negotiable within this Article as well as to instruments which are so negotiable.

Section 3–105. When Promise or Order Unconditional.

(1) A promise or order otherwise unconditional is not made conditional by the fact that the instrument

(a) is subject to implied or constructive conditions; or

(b) states its consideration, whether performed or promised, or the transaction which gave rise to the instrument, or that the promise or order is made or the instrument matures in accordance with or "as per" such transaction; or

(c) refers to or states that it arises out of a separate agreement or refers to a separate agreement for rights as to prepayment or acceleration; or

(d) states that it is drawn under a letter of credit; or

(e) states that it is secured, whether by mortgage, reservation of title or otherwise; or

(f) indicates a particular account to be debited or any other fund or source from which reimbursement is expected; or

(g) is limited to payment out of a particular fund or the proceeds of a particular source, if the instrument is issued by a government or governmental agency or unit; or

(h) is limited to payment out of the entire assets of a partnership, unincorporated association, trust or estate by or on behalf of which the instrument is issued.

(2) A promise or order is not unconditional if the instrument

(a) states that it is subject to or governed by any other agreement; or

(b) states that it is to be paid only out of a particular fund or source except as provided in this section.

Section 3–106. Sum Certain.

(1) The sum payable is a sum certain even though it is to be paid

(a) with stated interest or by stated installments; or

(b) with stated different rates of interest before and after default or a specified date; or

(c) with a stated discount or addition if paid before or after the date fixed for payment; or

(d) with exchange or less exchange, whether at a fixed rate or at the current rate; or

(e) with costs of collection or an attorney's fee or both upon default.

(2) Nothing in this section shall validate any term which is otherwise illegal.

Section 3–107. Money.

(1) An instrument is payable in money if the medium of exchange in which it is payable is money at the time the instrument is made. An instrument payable in "currency" or "current funds" is payable in money.

(2) A promise or order to pay a sum stated in a foreign currency is for a sum certain in money and, unless a different medium of payment is specified in the instrument, may be satisfied by payment of that number of dollars which the stated foreign currency will purchase at the buying sight rate for that currency on the day on which the instrument is payable or, if payable

on demand, on the day of demand. If such an instrument specifies a foreign currency as the medium of payment the instrument is payable in that currency.

Section 3–108. Payable on Demand.

Instruments payable on demand include those payable at sight or on presentation and those in which no time for payment is stated.

Section 3–109. Definite Time.

(1) An instrument is payable at a definite time if by its terms it is payable
   (a) on or before a stated date or at a fixed period after a stated date; or
   (b) at a fixed period after sight; or
   (c) at a definite time subject to any acceleration; or
   (d) at a definite time subject to extension at the option of the holder, or to extension to a further definite time at the option of the maker or acceptor or automatically upon or after a specified act or event.

(2) An instrument which by its terms is otherwise payable only upon an act or event uncertain as to time of occurrence is not payable at a definite time even though the act or event has occurred.

Section 3–110. Payable to Order.

(1) An instrument is payable to order when by its terms it is payable to the order or assigns of any person therein specified with reasonable certainty, or to him or his order, or when it is conspicuously designated on its face as "exchange" or the like and names a payee. It may be payable to the order of
   (a) the maker or drawer; or
   (b) the drawee; or
   (c) a payee who is not maker, drawer or drawee; or
   (d) two or more payees together or in the alternative; or
   (e) an estate, trust or fund, in which case it is payable to the order of the representative of such estate, trust or fund or his successors; or
   (f) an office, or an officer by his title as such in which case it is payable to the principal but the incumbent of the office or his successors may act as if he or they were the holder; or
   (g) a partnership or unincorporated association, in which case it is payable to the partnership or association and may be indorsed or transferred by any person thereto authorized.

(2) An instrument not payable to order is not made so payable by such words as "payable upon return of this instrument properly indorsed."

(3) An instrument made payable both to order and to bearer is payable to order unless the bearer words are handwritten or typewritten.

Section 3–111.   Payable to Bearer.

An instrument is payable to bearer when by its terms it is payable to
(a) bearer or the order of bearer; or
(b) a specified person or bearer; or
(c) "cash" or the order of "cash", or any other indication which does not purport to designate a specific payee.

Section 3–112.   Terms and Omissions Not Affecting Negotiability.

(1) The negotiability of an instrument is not affected by
(a) the omission of a statement of any consideration or of the place where the instrument is drawn or payable; or
(b) a statement that collateral has been given to secure obligations either on the instrument or otherwise of an obligor on the instrument or that in case of default on those obligations the holder may realize on or dispose of the collateral; or
(c) a promise or power to maintain or protect collateral or to give additional collateral; or
(d) a term authorizing a confession of judgment on the instrument if it is not paid when due; or
(e) a term purporting to waive the benefit of any law intended for the advantage or protection of any obligor; or
(f) a term in a draft providing that the payee by indorsing or cashing it acknowledges full satisfaction of an obligation of the drawer; or
(g) a statement in a draft drawn in a set of parts (Section 3–801) to the effect that the order is effective only if no other part has been honored.

(2) Nothing in this section shall validate any term which is otherwise illegal.

Section 3–113.   Seal.

An instrument otherwise negotiable is within this Article even though it is under a seal.

Section 3–114.   Date, Antedating, Postdating.

(1) The negotiability of an instrument is not affected by the fact that is undated, antedated or postdated.

(2) Where an instrument is antedated or postdated the time when it is payable is determined by the stated date if the instrument is payable on demand or at a fixed period after date.

(3) Where the instrument or any signature thereon is dated, the date is presumed to be correct.

Section 3–115.   Incomplete Instruments.

(1) When a paper whose contents at the time of signing show that it is intended to become an instrument is signed while still incomplete in any

necessary respect it cannot be enforced until completed, but when it is completed in accordance with authority given it is effective as completed.

(2) If the completion is unauthorized the rules as to material alteration apply (Section 3–407), even though the paper was not delivered by the maker or drawer; but the burden of establishing that any completion is unauthorized is on the party so asserting.

Section 3–116. Instruments Payable to Two or More Persons.

An instrument payable to the order of two or more persons
  (a) if in the alternative is payable to any one of them and may be negotiated, discharged or enforced by any of them who has possession of it;
  (b) if not in the alternative is payable to all of them and may be negotiated, discharged or enforced only by all of them.

Section 3–117. Instruments Payable With Words of Description.

An instrument made payable to a named person with the addition of words describing him
  (a) as agent or officer of a specified person is payable to his principal but the agent or officer may act as if he were the holder;
  (b) as any other fiduciary for a specified person or purpose is payable to the payee and may be negotiated, discharged or enforced by him;
  (c) in any other manner is payable to the payee unconditionally and the additional words are without effect on subsequent parties.

Section 3–118. Ambiguous Terms and Rules of Construction.

The following rules apply to every instrument:
  (a) Where there is doubt whether the instrument is a draft or a note the holder may treat it as either. A draft drawn on the drawer is effective as a note.
  (b) Handwritten terms control typewritten and printed terms, and typewritten control printed.
  (c) Words control figures except that if the words are ambiguous figures control.
  (d) Unless otherwise specified a provision for interest means interest at the judgment rate at the place of payment from the date of the instrument, or if it is undated from the date of issue.
  (e) Unless the instrument otherwise specifies two or more persons who sign as maker, acceptor or drawer or indorser and as a part of the same transaction are jointly and severally liable even though the instrument contains such words as "I promise to pay."
  (f) Unless otherwise specified consent to extension authorizes a single extension for not longer than the original period. A consent to extension, expressed in the instrument, is binding on secondary parties and accommodation makers. A holder may not exercise his option to extend an instrument over the objection of a maker or acceptor or other party

who in accordance with Section 3—604 tenders full payment when the instrument is due.

Section 3-119.   Other Writings Affecting Instrument.

(1) As between the obligor and his immediate obligee or any transferee the terms of an instrument may be modified or affected by any other written agreement executed as a part of the same transaction, except that a holder in due course is not affected by any limitation of his rights arising out of the separate written agreement if he had no notice of the limitation when he took the instrument.

(2) A separate agreement does not affect the negotiability of an instrument.

Section 3-120.   Instruments "Payable Through" Bank.

An instrument which states that it is "payable through" a bank or the like designates that bank as a collecting bank to make presentment but does not of itself authorize the bank to pay the instrument.

Section 3-121.   Instruments Payable at Bank.

Note: *If this Act is introduced in the Congress of the United States this section should be omitted. (States to select either alternative)*

Alternative A—

A note or acceptance which states that it is payable at a bank is the equivalent of a draft drawn on the bank payable when it falls due out of any funds of the maker or acceptor in current account or otherwise available for such payment.

Alternative B—

A note or acceptance which states that it is payable at a bank is not of itself an order or authorization to the bank to pay it.

Section 3-122.   Accrual of Cause of Action.

(1) A cause of action against a maker or an acceptor accrues
   (a) in the case of a time instrument on the day after maturity;
   (b) in the case of a demand instrument upon its date or, if no date is stated, on the date of issue.

(2) A cause of action against the obligor of a demand or time certificate of deposit accrues upon demand, but demand on a time certificate may not be made until on or after the date of maturity.

(3) A cause of action against a drawer of a draft or an indorser of any instrument accrues upon demand following dishonor of the instrument. Notice of dishonor is a demand.

(4) Unless an instrument provides otherwise, interest runs at the rate provided by law for a judgment.

(a) in the case of a maker, acceptor or other primary obligor of a demand instrument, from the date of demand;

(b) in all other cases from the date of accrual of the cause of action.

PART 2
TRANSFER AND NEGOTIATION

Section 3–201. Transfer: Right to Indorsement.

(1) Transfer of an instrument vests in the transferee such rights as the transferor has therein, except that a transferee who has himself been a party to any fraud or illegality affecting the instrument or who as a prior holder had notice of a defense or claim against it cannot improve his position by taking from a later holder in due course.

(2) A transfer of a security interest in an instrument vests the foregoing rights in the transferee to the extent of the interest transferred.

(3) Unless otherwise agreed any transfer for value of an instrument not then payable to bearer gives the transferee the specifically enforceable right to have the unqualified indorsement of the transferor. Negotiation takes effect only when the indorsement is made and until that time there is no presumption that the transferee is the owner.

Section 3–202. Negotiation.

(1) Negotiation is the transfer of an instrument in such form that the transferee becomes a holder. If the instrument is payable to order it is negotiated by delivery with any necessary indorsement; if payable to bearer it is negotiated by delivery.

(2) An indorsement must be written by or on behalf of the holder and on the instrument or on a paper so firmly affixed thereto as to become a part thereof.

(3) An indorsement is effective for negotiation only when it conveys the entire instrument or any unpaid residue. If it purports to be of less it operates only as a partial assignment.

(4) Words of assignment, condition, waiver, guaranty, limitation or disclaimer of liability and the like accompanying an indorsement do not affect its character as an indorsement.

Section 3–203. Wrong or Misspelled Name.

Where an instrument is made payable to a person under a misspelled name or one other than his own he may indorse in that name or his own or both; but signature in both names may be required by a person paying or giving value for the instrument.

Section 3–204. Special Indorsement; Blank Indorsement.

(1) A special indorsement specifies the person to whom or to whose order it makes the instrument payable. Any instrument specially indorsed becomes payable to the order of the special indorsee and may be further negotiated only by his indorsement.

(2) An indorsement in blank specifies no particular indorsee and may consist of a mere signature. An instrument payable to order and indorsed in blank becomes payable to bearer and may be negotiated by delivery alone until specially indorsed.

(3) The holder may convert a blank indorsement into a special indorsement by writing over the signature of the indorser in blank any contract consistent with the character of the indorsement.

Section 3–205. Restrictive Indorsements.

An indorsement is restrictive which either
(a) is conditional; or
(b) purports to prohibit further transfer of the instrument; or
(c) includes the words "for collection", "for deposit", "pay any bank", or like terms signifying a purpose of deposit or collection; or
(d) otherwise states that it is for the benefit or use of the indorser or of another person.

Section 3–206. Effect of Restrictive Indorsement.

(1) No restrictive indorsement prevents further transfer or negotiation of the instrument.

(2) An intermediary bank, or a payor bank which is not the depositary bank, is neither given notice nor otherwise affected by a restrictive indorsement of any person except the bank's immediate transferor or the person presenting for payment.

(3) Except for an intermediary bank, any transferee under an indorsement which is conditional or includes the words "for collection", "for deposit", "pay any bank", or like terms (subparagraphs (a) and (c) of Section 3–205) must pay or apply any value given by him for or on the security of the instrument consistently with the indorsement and to the extent that he does so he becomes a holder for value. In addition such transferee is a holder in due course if he otherwise complies with the requirements of Section 3–302 on what constitutes a holder in due course.

(4) The first taker under an indorsement for the benefit of the indorser or another person (subparagraph (d) of Section 3–205) must pay or apply any value given by him for or on the security of the instrument consistently with the indorsement and to the extent that he does so he becomes a holder for value. In addition such taker is a holder in due course if he otherwise complies with the requirements of Section 3–302 on what constitutes a holder in due course. A later holder for value is neither given notice nor otherwise affected by such restrictive indorsement unless he has knowledge that a fiduciary or other person has negotiated the instrument in any transaction for his own benefit or otherwise in breach of duty (subsection (2) of Section 3–304).

Section 3–207. Negotiation Effective Although It May Be Rescinded.

(1) Negotiation is effective to transfer the instrument although the negotiation is
(a) made by an infant, a corporation exceeding its powers, or any other person without capacity; or

(b) obtained by fraud, duress or mistake of any kind; or

(c) part of an illegal transaction; or

(d) made in breach of duty.

(2) Except as against a subsequent holder in due course such negotiation is in an appropriate case subject to rescission, the declaration of a constructive trust or any other remedy permitted by law.

Section 3–208. Reacquisition.

Where an instrument is returned to or reacquired by a prior party he may cancel any indorsement which is not necessary to his title and reissue or further negotiate the instrument, but any intervening party is discharged as against the reacquiring party and subsequent holders not in due course and if his indorsement has been cancelled is discharged as against subsequent holders in due course as well.

PART 3
RIGHTS OF A HOLDER

Section 3–301. Rights of a Holder.

The holder of an instrument whether or not he is the owner may transfer or negotiate it and, except as otherwise provided in Section 3–603 on payment or satisfaction, discharge it or enforce payment in his own name.

Section 3–302. Holder in Due Course.

(1) A holder in due course is a holder who takes the instrument

(a) for value; and

(b) in good faith; and

(c) without notice that it is overdue or has been dishonored or of any defense against or claim to it on the part of any person.

(2) A payee may be a holder in due course.

(3) A holder does not become a holder in due course of an instrument:

(a) by purchase of it at judicial sale or by taking it under legal process; or

(b) by acquiring it in taking over an estate; or

(c) by purchasing it as part of a bulk transaction not in regular course of business of the transferor.

(4) A purchaser of a limited interest can be a holder in due course only to the extent of the interest purchased.

Section 3–303. Taking for Value.

A holder takes the instrument for value

(a) to the extent that the agreed consideration has been performed or that he acquires a security interest in or a lien on the instrument otherwise than by legal process; or

(b) when he takes the instrument in payment of or as security for an antecedent claim against any person whether or not the claim is due; *or*

(c) when he gives a negotiable instrument for it or makes an irrevocable commitment to a third person.

Section 3–304. Notice to Purchaser.

(1) The purchaser has notice of a claim or defense if

  (a) the instrument is so incomplete, bears such visible evidence of forgery or alteration, or is otherwise so irregular as to call into question its validity, terms or ownership or to create an ambiguity as to the party to pay; or

  (b) the purchaser has notice that the obligation of any party is voidable in whole or in part, or that all parties have been discharged.

(2) The purchaser has notice of a claim against the instrument when he has knowledge that a fiduciary has negotiated the instrument in payment of or as security for his own debt or in any transaction for his own benefit or otherwise in breach of duty.

(3) The purchaser has notice that an instrument is overdue if he has reason to know

  (a) that any part of the principal amount is overdue or that there is an uncured default in payment of another instrument of the same series; or

  (b) that acceleration of the instrument has been made; or

  (c) that he is taking a demand instrument after demand has been made or more than a reasonable length of time after its issue. A reasonable time for a check drawn and payable within the states and territories of the United States and the District of Columbia is presumed to be thirty days.

(4) Knowledge of the following facts does not of itself give the purchaser notice of a defense or claim

  (a) that the instrument is antedated or postdated;

  (b) that it was issued or negotiated in return for an executory promise or accompanied by a separate agreement, unless the purchaser has notice that a defense or claim has arisen from the terms thereof;

  (c) that any party has signed for accommodation;

  (d) that an incomplete instrument has been completed, unless the purchaser has notice of any improper completion;

  (e) that any person negotiating the instrument is or was a fiduciary;

  (f) that there has been default in payment of interest on the instrument or in payment of any other instrument, except one of the same series.

(5) The filing or recording of a document does not of itself constitute notice within the provisions of this Article to a person who would otherwise be a holder in due course.

(6) To be effective notice must be received at such time and in such manner as to give a reasonable opportunity to act on it.

Section 3–305. Rights of a Holder in Due Course.

To the extent that a holder is a holder in due course he takes the instrument free from

(1) all claims to it on the part of any person; and

(2) all defenses of any party to the instrument with whom the holder has not dealt except

    (a) infancy, to the extent that it is a defense to a simple contract; and

    (b) such other incapacity, or duress, or illegality of the transaction, as renders the obligation of the party a nullity; and

    (c) such misrepresentation as has induced the party to sign the instrument with neither knowledge nor reasonable opportunity to obtain knowledge of its character or its essential terms; and

    (d) discharge in insolvency proceedings; and

    (e) any other discharge of which the holder has notice when he takes the instrument.

Section 3–306. Rights of One Not Holder in Due Course.

Unless he has the rights of a holder in due course any person takes the instrument subject to

    (a) all valid claims to it on the part of any person; and

    (b) all defenses of any party which would be available in an action on a simple contract; and

    (c) the defenses of want or failure of consideration, non-performance of any condition precedent, non-delivery, or delivery for a special purpose (Section 3–408); and

    (d) the defense that he or a person through whom he holds the instrument acquired it by theft, or that payment or satisfaction to such holder would be inconsistent with the terms of a restrictive indorsement. The claim of any third person to the instrument is not otherwise available as a defense to any party liable thereon unless the third person himself defends the action for such party.

Section 3–307. Burden of Establishing Signatures, Defenses and Due Course.

(1) Unless specifically denied in the pleadings each signature on an instrument is admitted. When the effectiveness of a signature is put in issue

    (a) the burden of establishing it is on the party claiming under the signature; but

    (b) the signature is presumed to be genuine or authorized except where the action is to enforce the obligation of a purported signer who has died or become incompetent before proof is required.

(2) When signatures are admitted or established, production of the instrument entitles a holder to recover on it unless the defendant establishes a defense.

(3) After it is shown that a defense exists a person claiming the rights of a holder in due course has the burden of establishing that he or some person under whom he claims is in all respects a holder in due course.

PART 4

LIABILITY OF PARTIES

Section 3–401. Signature.

(1) No person is liable on an instrument unless his signature appears thereon.

(2) A signature is made by use of any name, including any trade or assumed name, upon an instrument, or by any word or mark used in lieu of a written signature.

Section 3–402. Signature in Ambiguous Capacity.

Unless the instrument clearly indicates that a signature is made in some other capacity it is an indorsement.

Section 3–403. Signature by Authorized Representative.

(1) A signature may be made by an agent or other representative, and his authority to make it may be established as in other cases of representation. No particular form of appointment is necessary to establish such authority.

(2) An authorized representative who signs his own name to an instrument

    (a) is personally obligated if the instrument neither names the person represented nor shows that the representative signed in a representative capacity;

    (b) except as otherwise established between the immediate parties, is personally obligated if the instrument names the person represented but does not show that the representative signed in a representative capacity, or if the instrument does not name the person represented but does show that the representative signed in a representative capacity.

(3) Except as otherwise established the name of an organization preceded or followed by the name and office of an authorized individual is a signature made in a representative capacity.

Section 3–404. Unauthorized Signatures.

(1) Any unauthorized signature is wholly inoperative as that of the person whose name is signed unless he ratifies it or is precluded from denying it; but it operates as the signature of the unauthorized signer in favor of any person who in good faith pays the instrument or takes it for value.

(2) Any unauthorized signature may be ratified for all purposes of this Article. Such ratification does not of itself affect any rights of the person ratifying against the actual signer.

Section 3–405. Impostors; Signature in Name of Payee.

(1) An indorsement by any person in the name of a named payee is effective if

    (a) an impostor by use of the mails or otherwise has induced the maker or drawer to issue the instrument to him or his confederate in the name of the payee; or

    (b) a person signing as or on behalf of a maker or drawer intends the payee to have no interest in the instrument; or

    (c) an agent or employee of the maker or drawer has supplied him with the name of the payee intending the latter to have no such interest.

(2) Nothing in this section shall affect the criminal or civil liability of the person so indorsing.

Section 3–406. Negligence Contributing to Alteration or Unauthorized Signature.

Any person who by his negligence substantially contributes to a material alteration of the instrument or to the making of an unauthorized signature is precluded from asserting the alteration or lack of authority against a holder in due course or against a drawee or other payor who pays the instrument in good faith and in accordance with the reasonable commercial standards of the drawee's or payor's business.

Section 3–407. Alteration.

(1) Any alteration of an instrument is material which changes the contract of any party thereto in any respect, including any such change in
    (a) the number or relations of the parties; or
    (b) an incomplete instrument, by completing it otherwise than as authorized; or
    (c) the writing as signed, by adding to it or by removing any part of it.
(2) As against any person other than a subsequent holder in due course
    (a) alteration by the holder which is both fraudulent and material discharges any party whose contract is thereby changed unless that party assents or is precluded from asserting the defense;
    (b) no other alteration discharges any party and the instrument may be enforced according to its original tenor, or as to incomplete instruments according to the authority given.
(3) A subsequent holder in due course may in all cases enforce the instrument according to its original tenor, and when an incomplete instrument has been completed, he may enforce it as completed.

Section 3–408. Consideration.

Want or failure of consideration is a defense as against any person not having the rights of a holder in due course (Section 3–305), except that no consideration is necessary for an instrument or obligation thereon given in payment of or as security for an antecedent obligation of any kind. Nothing in this section shall be taken to displace any statute outside this Act under which a promise is enforceable notwithstanding lack or failure of consideration. Partial failure of consideration is a defense pro tanto whether or not the failure is in an ascertained or liquidated amount.

Section 3–409. Draft Not an Assignment.

(1) A check or other draft does not of itself operate as an assignment of any funds in the hands of the drawee available for its payment, and the drawee is not liable on the instrument until he accepts it.
(2) Nothing in this section shall affect any liability in contract, tort or otherwise arising from any letter of credit or other obligation or representation which is not an acceptance.

Section 3–410. Definition and Operation of Acceptance.

(1) Acceptance is the drawee's signed engagement to honor the draft as presented. It must be written on the draft, and may consist of his signature alone. It becomes operative when completed by delivery or notification.

(2) A draft may be accepted although it has not been signed by the drawer or is otherwise incomplete or is overdue or has been dishonored.

(3) Where the draft is payable at a fixed period after sight and the acceptor fails to date his acceptance the holder may complete it by supplying a date in good faith.

Section 3–411. Certification of a Check.

(1) Certification of a check is acceptance. Where a holder procures certification the drawer and all prior indorsers are discharged.

(2) Unless otherwise agreed a bank has no obligation to certify a check.

(3) A bank may certify a check before returning it for lack of proper indorsement. If it does so the drawer is discharged.

Section 3–412. Acceptance Varying Draft.

(1) Where the drawee's proffered acceptance in any manner varies the draft as presented the holder may refuse the acceptance and treat the draft as dishonored in which case the drawee is entitled to have his acceptance cancelled.

(2) The terms of the draft are not varied by an acceptance to pay at any particular bank or place in the United States, unless the acceptance states that the draft is to be paid only at such bank or place.

(3) Where the holder assents to an acceptance varying the terms of the draft each drawer and indorser who does not affirmatively assent is discharged.

Section 3–413. Contract of Maker, Drawer and Acceptor.

(1) The maker or acceptor engages that he will pay the instrument according to its tenor at the time of his engagement or as completed pursuant to Section 3–115 on incomplete instruments.

(2) The drawer engages that upon dishonor of the draft and any necessary notice of dishonor or protest he will pay the amount of the draft to the holder or to any indorser who takes it up. The drawer may disclaim this liability by drawing without recourse.

(3) By making, drawing or accepting the party admits as against all subsequent parties including the drawee the existence of the payee and his then capacity to indorse.

Section 3–414. Contract of Indorser; Order of Liability.

(1) Unless the indorsement otherwise specifies (as by such words as "without recourse") every indorser engages that upon dishonor and any necessary notice of dishonor and protest he will pay the instrument according to its tenor at the time of his indorsement to the holder or to any subsequent indorser who takes it up, even though the indorser who takes it up was not obligated to do so.

(2) Unless they otherwise agree indorsers are liable to one another in the order in which they indorse, which is presumed to be the order in which their signatures appear on the instrument.

Section 3–415. Contract of Accommodation Party.

(1) An accommodation party is one who signs the instrument in any capacity for the purpose of lending his name to another party to it.

(2) When the instrument has been taken for value before it is due the accommodation party is liable in the capacity in which he has signed even though the taker knows of the accommodation.

(3) As against a holder in due course and without notice of the accommodation oral proof of the accommodation is not admissible to give the accommodation party the benefit of discharges dependent on his character as such. In other cases the accommodation character may be shown by oral proof.

(4) An indorsement which shows that it is not in the chain of title is notice of its accommodation character.

(5) An accommodation party is not liable to the party accommodated, and if he pays the instrument has a right of recourse on the instrument against such party.

Section 3–416. Contract of Guarantor.

(1) "Payment guaranteed" or equivalent words added to a signature mean that the signer engages that if the instrument is not paid when due he will pay it according to its tenor without resort by the holder to any other party.

(2) "Collection guaranteed" or equivalent words added to a signature mean that the signer engages that if the instrument is not paid when due he will pay it according to its tenor, but only after the holder has reduced his claim against the maker or acceptor to judgment and execution has been returned unsatisfied, or after the maker or acceptor has become insolvent or it is otherwise apparent that it is useless to proceed against him.

(3) Words of guaranty which do not otherwise specify guarantee payment.

(4) No words of guaranty added to the signature of a sole maker or acceptor affect his liability on the instrument. Such words added to the signature of one of two or more makers or acceptors create a presumption that the signature is for the accommodation of the others.

(5) When words of guaranty are used presentment, notice of dishonor and protest are not necessary to charge the user.

(6) Any guaranty written on the instrument is enforcible notwithstanding any statute of frauds.

Section 3–417. Warranties on Presentment and Transfer.

(1) Any person who obtains payment or acceptance and any prior transferor warrants to a person who in good faith pays or accepts that
- (a) he has a good title to the instrument or is authorized to obtain payment or acceptance on behalf of one who has a good title; and
- (b) he has no knowledge that the signature of the maker or drawer is unauthorized, except that this warranty is not given by a holder in due course acting in good faith
    - (i) to a maker with respect to the maker's own signature; or
    - (ii) to a drawer with respect to the drawer's own signature, whether or not the drawer is also the drawee; or
    - (iii) to an acceptor of a draft if the holder in due course took the draft after the acceptance or obtained the acceptance without knowledge that the drawer's signature was unauthorized; and

(c) the instrument has not been materially altered, except that this warranty is not given by a holder in due course acting in good faith
  (i) to the maker of a note; or
  (ii) to the drawer of a draft whether or not the drawer is also the drawee; or
  (iii) to the acceptor of a draft with respect to an alteration made prior to the acceptance if the holder in due course took the draft after the acceptance, even though the acceptance provided "payable as originally drawn" or equivalent terms; or
  (iv) to the acceptor of a draft with respect to an alteration made after the acceptance.

(2) Any person who transfers an instrument and receives consideration warrants to his transferee and if the transfer is by indorsement to any subsequent holder who takes the instrument in good faith that

(a) he has a good title to the instrument or is authorized to obtain payment or acceptance on behalf of one who has a good title and the transfer is otherwise rightful; and

(b) all signatures are genuine or authorized; and

(c) the instrument has not been materially altered; and

(d) no defense of any party is good against him; and

(e) he has no knowledge of any insolvency proceeding instituted with respect to the maker or acceptor or the drawer of an unaccepted instrument.

(3) By transferring "without recourse" the transferor limits the obligation stated in subsection (2) (d) to a warranty that he has no knowledge of such a defense.

(4) A selling agent or broker who does not disclose the fact that he is acting only as such gives the warranties provided in this section, but if he makes such disclosure warrants only his good faith and authority.

Section 3–418. Finality of Payment or Acceptance.

Except for recovery of bank payments as provided in the Article on Bank Deposits and Collections (Article 4) and except for liability for breach of warranty on presentment under the preceding section, payment or acceptance of any instrument is final in favor of a holder in due course, or a person who has in good faith changed his position in reliance on the payment.

Section 3–419. Conversion of Instrument; Innocent Representative.

(1) An instrument is converted when
  (a) a drawee to whom it is delivered for acceptance refuses to return it on demand; or
  (b) any person to whom it is delivered for payment refuses on demand either to pay or to return it; or
  (c) it is paid on a forged indorsement.

(2) In an action against a drawee under subsection (1) the measure of the drawee's liability is the face amount of the instrument. In any other action under subsection (1) the measure of liability is presumed to be the face amount of the instrument.

(3) Subject to the provisions of this Act concerning restrictive indorsements a representative, including a depositary or collecting bank, who has in good faith and in accordance with the reasonable commercial standards applicable to the business of such representative dealt with an instrument or its proceeds on behalf of one who was not the true owner is not liable in conversion or otherwise to the true owner beyond the amount of any proceeds remaining in his hands.

(4) An intermediary bank or payor bank which is not a depositary bank is not liable in conversion solely by reason of the fact that proceeds of an item indorsed restrictively (Sections 3–205 and 3–206) are not paid or applied consistently with the restrictive indorsement of an indorser other than its immediate transferor.

PART 5

PRESENTMENT, NOTICE OF DISHONOR AND PROTEST

Section 3–501. When Presentment, Notice of Dishonor, and Protest Necessary or Permissible.

(1) Unless excused (Section 3–511) presentment is necessary to charge secondary parties as follows:

    (a) presentment for acceptance is necessary to charge the drawer and indorsers of a draft where the draft so provides, or is payable elsewhere than at the residence or place of business of the drawee, or its date of payment depends upon such presentment. The holder may at his option present for acceptance any other draft payable at a stated date;

    (b) presentment for payment is necessary to charge any indorser;

    (c) in the case of any drawer, the acceptor of a draft payable at a bank or the maker of a note payable at a bank, presentment for payment is necessary, but failure to make presentment discharges such drawer, acceptor or maker only as stated in Section 3–502(1) (b).

(2) Unless excused (Section 3–511)

    (a) notice of any dishonor is necessary to charge any indorser;

    (b) in the case of any drawer, the acceptor of a draft payable at a bank or the maker of a note payable at a bank, notice of any dishonor is necessary, but failure to give such notice discharges such drawer, acceptor or maker only as stated in Section 3–502(1) (b).

(3) Unless excused (Section 3–511) protest of any dishonor is necessary to charge the drawer and indorsers of any draft which on its face appears to be drawn or payable outside of the states and territories of the United States and the District of Columbia. The holder may at his option make protest of any dishonor of any other instrument and in the case of a foreign draft may on insolvency of the acceptor before maturity make protest for better security.

(4) Notwithstanding any provision of this section, neither presentment nor notice of dishonor nor protest is necessary to charge an indorser who has indorsed an instrument after maturity.

Section 3–502. Unexcused Delay; Discharge.

(1) Where without excuse any necessary presentment or notice of dishonor is delayed beyond the time when it is due

(a) any indorser is discharged; and

(b) any drawer or the acceptor of a draft payable at a bank or the maker of a note payable at a bank who because the drawee or payor bank becomes insolvent during the delay is deprived of funds maintained with the drawee or payor bank to cover the instrument may discharge his liability by written assignment to the holder of his rights against the drawee or payor bank in respect of such funds, but such drawer, acceptor or maker is not otherwise discharged.

(2) Where without excuse a necessary protest is delayed beyond the time when it is due any drawer or indorser is discharged.

Section 3–503. Time of Presentment.

(1) Unless a different time is expressed in the instrument the time for any presentment is determined as follows:

(a) where an instrument is payable at or a fixed period after a stated date any presentment for acceptance must be made on or before the date it is payable;

(b) where an instrument is payable after sight it must either be presented for acceptance or negotiated within a reasonable time after date or issue whichever is later;

(c) where an instrument shows the date on which it is payable presentment for payment is due on that date;

(d) where an instrument is accelerated presentment for payment is due within a reasonable time after the acceleration;

(e) with respect to the liability of any secondary party presentment for acceptance or payment of any other instrument is due within a reasonable time after such party becomes liable thereon.

(2) A reasonable time for presentment is determined by the nature of the instrument, any usage of banking or trade and the facts of the particular case. In the case of an uncertified check which is drawn and payable within the United States and which is not a draft drawn by a bank the following are presumed to be reasonable periods within which to present for payment or to initiate bank collection:

(a) with respect to the liability of the drawer, thirty days after date or issue whichever is later; and

(b) with respect to the liability of an indorser, seven days after his indorsement.

(3) Where any presentment is due on a day which is not a full business day for either the person making presentment or the party to pay or accept, presentment is due on the next following day which is a full business day for both parties.

(4) Presentment to be sufficient must be made at a reasonable hour, and if at a bank during its banking day.

Section 3–504. How Presentment Made.

(1) Presentment is a demand for acceptance or payment made upon the maker, acceptor, drawee or other payor by or on behalf of the holder.

(2) Presentment may be made

(a) by mail, in which event the time of presentment is determined by the time of receipt of the mail; or

(b) through a clearing house; or

(c) at the place of acceptance or payment specified in the instrument or if there be none at the place of business or residence of the party to accept or pay. If neither the party to accept or pay nor anyone authorized to act for him is present or accessible at such place presentment is excused.

(3) It may be made

(a) to any one of two or more makers, acceptors, drawees or other payors; or

(b) to any person who has authority to make or refuse the acceptance or payment.

(4) A draft accepted or a note made payable at a bank in the United States must be presented at such bank.

(5) In the cases described in Section 4–210 presentment may be made in the manner and with the result stated in that section.

Section 3–505. Rights of Party to Whom Presentment Is Made.

(1) The party to whom presentment is made may without dishonor require

(a) exhibition of the instrument; and

(b) reasonable identification of the person making presentment and evidence of his authority to make it if made for another; and

(c) that the instrument be produced for acceptance or payment at a place specified in it, or if there be none at any place reasonable in the circumstances; and

(d) a signed receipt on the instrument for any partial or full payment and its surrender upon full payment.

(2) Failure to comply with any such requirement invalidates the presentment but the person presenting has a reasonable time in which to comply and the time for acceptance or payment runs from the time of compliance.

Section 3–506. Time Allowed for Acceptance or Payment.

(1) Acceptance may be deferred without dishonor until the close of the next business day following presentment. The holder may also in a good faith effort to obtain acceptance and without either dishonor of the instrument or discharge of secondary parties allow postponement of acceptance for an additional business day.

(2) Except as a longer time is allowed in the case of documentary drafts drawn under a letter of credit, and unless an earlier time is agreed to by the party to pay, payment of an instrument may be deferred without dishonor

pending reasonable examination to determine whether it is properly payable, but payment must be made in any event before the close of business on the day of presentment.

Section 3–507. Dishonor; Holder's Right of Recourse; Term Allowing Re-Presentment.

(1) An instrument is dishonored when

    (a) a necessary or optional presentment is duly made and due acceptance or payment is refused or cannot be obtained within the prescribed time or in case of bank collections the instrument is seasonably returned by the midnight deadline (Section 4–301); or

    (b) presentment is excused and the instrument is not duly accepted or paid.

(2) Subject to any necessary notice of dishonor and protest, the holder has upon dishonor an immediate right of recourse against the drawers and indorsers.

(3) Return of an instrument for lack of proper indorsement is not dishonor.

(4) A term in a draft or an indorsement thereof allowing a stated time for re-presentment in the event of any dishonor of the draft by nonacceptance if a time draft or by nonpayment if a sight draft gives the holder as against any secondary party bound by the term an option to waive the dishonor without affecting the liability of the secondary party and he may present again up to the end of the stated time.

Section 3–508. Notice of Dishonor.

(1) Notice of dishonor may be given to any person who may be liable on the instrument by or on behalf of the holder or any party who has himself received notice, or any other party who can be compelled to pay the instrument. In addition an agent or bank in whose hands the instrument is dishonored may give notice to his principal or customer or to another agent or bank from which the instrument was received.

(2) Any necessary notice must be given by a bank before its midnight deadline and by any other person before midnight of the third business day after dishonor or receipt of notice of dishonor.

(3) Notice may be given in any reasonable manner. It may be oral or written and in any terms which identify the instrument and state that it has been dishonored. A misdescription which does not mislead the party notified does not vitiate the notice. Sending the instrument bearing a stamp, ticket or writing stating that acceptance or payment has been refused or sending a notice of debit with respect to the instrument is sufficient.

(4) Written notice is given when sent although it is not received.

(5) Notice to one partner is notice to each although the firm has been dissolved.

(6) When any party is in insolvency proceedings instituted after the issue of the instrument notice may be given either to the party or to the representative of his estate.

(7) When any party is dead or incompetent notice may be sent to his last known address or given to his personal representative.

(8) Notice operates for the benefit of all parties who have rights on the instrument against the party notified.

Section 3–509. Protest; Noting for Protest.

(1) A protest is a certificate of dishonor made under the hand and seal of a United States consul or vice consul or a notary public or other person authorized to certify dishonor by the law of the place where dishonor occurs. It may be made upon information satisfactory to such person.

(2) The protest must identify the instrument and certify either that due presentment has been made or the reason why it is excused and that the instrument has been dishonored by nonacceptance or nonpayment.

(3) The protest may also certify that notice of dishonor has been given to all parties or to specified parties.

(4) Subject to subsection (5) any necessary protest is due by the time that notice of dishonor is due.

(5) If, before protest is due, an instrument has been noted for protest by the officer to make protest, the protest may be made at any time thereafter as of the date of the noting.

Section 3–510. Evidence of Dishonor and Notice of Dishonor.

The following are admissible as evidence and create a presumption of dishonor and of any notice of dishonor therein shown:

  (a) a document regular in form as provided in the preceding section which purports to be a protest;

  (b) the purported stamp or writing of the drawee, payor bank or presenting bank on the instrument or accompanying it stating that acceptance or payment has been refused for reasons consistent with dishonor;

  (c) any book or record of the drawee, payor bank, or any collecting bank kept in the usual course of business which shows dishonor, even though there is no evidence of who made the entry.

Section 3–511. Waived or Excused Presentment, Protest or Notice of Dishonor or Delay Therein.

(1) Delay in presentment, protest or notice of dishonor is excused when the party is without notice that it is due or when the delay is caused by circumstances beyond his control and he exercises reasonable diligence after the cause of the delay ceases to operate.

(2) Presentment or notice or protest as the case may be is entirely excused when

  (a) the party to be charged has waived it expressly or by implication either before or after it is due; or

  (b) such party has himself dishonored the instrument or has countermanded payment or otherwise has no reason to expect or right to require that the instrument be accepted or paid; or

  (c) by reasonable diligence the presentment or protest cannot be made or the notice given.

(3) Presentment is also entirely excused when

(a) the maker, acceptor or drawee of any instrument except a documentary draft is dead or in insolvency proceedings instituted after the issue of the instrument; or

(b) acceptance or payment is refused but not for want of proper presentment.

(4) Where a draft has been dishonored by nonacceptance a later presentment for payment and any notice of dishonor and protest for nonpayment are excused unless in the meantime the instrument has been accepted.

(5) A waiver of protest is also a waiver of presentment and of notice of dishonor even though protest is not required.

(6) Where a waiver of presentment or notice or protest is embodied in the instrument itself it is binding upon all parties; but where it is written above the signature of an indorser it binds him only.

PART 6

DISCHARGE

Section 3–601. Discharge of Parties.

(1) The extent of the discharge of any party from liability on an instrument is governed by the sections on

(a) payment or satisfaction (Section 3–603); or

(b) tender of payment (Section 3–604); or

(c) cancellation or renunciation (Section 3–605); or

(d) impairment of right of recourse or of collateral (Section 3–606); or

(e) reacquisition of the instrument by a prior party (Section 3–208); or

(f) fraudulent and material alteration (Section 3–407); or

(g) certification of a check (Section 3–411); or

(h) acceptance varying a draft (Section 3–412); or

(i) unexcused delay in presentment or notice of dishonor or protest (Section 3–502).

(2) Any party is also discharged from his liability on an instrument to another party by any other act or agreement with such party which would discharge his simple contract for the payment of money.

(3) The liability of all parties is discharged when any party who has himself no right of action or recourse on the instrument

(a) reacquires the instrument in his own right; or

(b) is discharged under any provision of this Article, except as otherwise provided with respect to discharge for impairment of recourse or of collateral (Section 3–606).

Section 3–602. Effect of Discharge Against Holder in Due Course.

No discharge of any party provided by this Article is effective against a subsequent holder in due course unless he has notice thereof when he takes the instrument.

Section 3–603. Payment or Satisfaction.

(1) The liability of any party is discharged to the extent of his payment or satisfaction to the holder even though it is made with knowledge of a claim

of another person to the instrument unless prior to such payment or satisfaction the person making the claim either supplies indemnity deemed
adequate by the party seeking the discharge or enjoins payment or satisfaction
by order of a court of competent jurisdiction in an action in which the adverse
claimant and the holder are parties. This subsection does not, however, result
in the discharge of the liability

> (a) of a party who in bad faith pays or satisfies a holder who acquired
> the instrument by theft or who (unless having the rights of a
> holder in due course) holds through one who so acquired it; or
>
> (b) of a party (other than an intermediary bank or a payor bank which
> is not a depositary bank) who pays or satisfies the holder of an
> instrument which has been restrictively indorsed in a manner not
> consistent with the terms of such restrictive indorsement.

(2) Payment or satisfaction may be made with the consent of the holder
by any person including a stranger to the instrument. Surrender of the
instrument to such a person gives him the rights of a transferee (Section
3–201).

Section 3–604. Tender of Payment.

(1) Any party making tender of full payment to a holder when or after
it is due is discharged to the extent of all subsequent liability for interest,
costs and attorney's fees.

(2) The holder's refusal of such tender wholly discharges any party who
has a right of recourse against the party making the tender.

(3) Where the maker or acceptor of an instrument payable otherwise than
on demand is able and ready to pay at every place of payment specified in the
instrument when it is due, it is equivalent to tender.

Section 3–605. Cancellation and Renunciation.

(1) The holder of an instrument may even without consideration discharge
any party

> (a) in any manner apparent on the face of the instrument or the indorse-
> ment, as by intentionally cancelling the instrument or the party's
> signature by destruction or mutilation, or by striking out the party's
> signature; or
>
> (b) by renouncing his rights by a writing signed and delivered or by
> surrender of the instrument to the party to be discharged.

(2) Neither cancellation nor renunciation without surrender of the
instrument affects the title thereto.

Section 3–606. Impairment of Recourse or of Collateral.

(1) The holder discharges any party to the instrument to the extent that
without such party's consent the holder

> (a) without express reservation of rights releases or agrees not to sue
> any person against whom the party has to the knowledge of the
> holder a right of recourse or agrees to suspend the right to enforce
> against such person the instrument or collateral or otherwise dis-
> charges such person, except that failure or delay in effecting any re-

quired presentment, protest or notice of dishonor with respect to any such person does not discharge any party as to whom presentment, protest or notice of dishonor is effective or unnecessary; or

(b) unjustifiably impairs any collateral for the instrument given by or on behalf of the party or any person against whom he has a right of recourse.

(2) By express reservation of rights against a party with a right of recourse the holder preserves

(a) all his rights against such party as of the time when the instrument was originally due; and

(b) the right of the party to pay the instrument as of that time; and

(c) all rights of such party to recourse against others.

PART 7
ADVICE OF INTERNATIONAL SIGHT DRAFT

Section 3–701. Letter of Advice of International Sight Draft.

(1) A "letter of advice" is a drawer's communication to the drawee that a described draft has been drawn.

(2) Unless otherwise agreed when a bank receives from another bank a letter of advice of an international sight draft the drawee bank may immediately debit the drawer's account and stop the running of interest pro tanto. Such a debit and any resulting credit to any account covering outstanding drafts leaves in the drawer full power to stop payment or otherwise dispose of the amount and creates no trust or interest in favor of the holder.

(3) Unless otherwise agreed and except where a draft is drawn under a credit issued by the drawee, the drawee of an international sight draft owes the drawer no duty to pay an unadvised draft but if it does so and the draft is genuine, may appropriately debit the drawer's account.

PART 8
MISCELLANEOUS

Section 3–801. Drafts in a Set.

(1) Where a draft is drawn in a set of parts, each of which is numbered and expressed to be an order only if no other part has been honored, the whole of the parts constitutes one draft but a taker of any part may become a holder in due course of the draft.

(2) Any person who negotiates, indorses or accepts a single part of a draft drawn in a set thereby becomes liable to any holder in due course of that part as if it were the whole set, but as between different holders in due course to whom different parts have been negotiated the holder whose title first accrues has all rights to the draft and its proceeds.

(3) As against the drawee the first presented part of a draft drawn in a set is the part entitled to payment, or if a time draft to acceptance and

payment. Acceptance of any subsequently presented part renders the drawee liable thereon under subsection (2). With respect both to a holder and to the drawer payment of a subsequently presented part of a draft payable at sight has the same effect as payment of a check notwithstanding an effective stop order (Section 4–407).

(4) Except as otherwise provided in this section, where any part of a draft in a set is discharged by payment or otherwise the whole draft is discharged.

Section 3–802. Effect of Instrument on Obligation for Which It Is Given.

(1) Unless otherwise agreed where an instrument is taken for an underlying obligation

- (a) the obligation is pro tanto discharged if a bank is drawer, maker or acceptor of the instrument and there is no recourse on the instrument against the underlying obligor; and
- (b) in any other case the obligation is suspended pro tanto until the instrument is due or if it is payable on demand until its presentment. If the instrument is dishonored action may be maintained on either the instrument or the obligation; discharge of the underlying obligor on the instrument also discharges him on the obligation.

(2) The taking in good faith of a check which is not postdated does not of itself so extend the time on the original obligation as to discharge a surety.

Section 3–803. Notice to Third Party.

Where a defendant is sued for breach of an obligation for which a third person is answerable over under this Article he may give the third person written notice of the litigation, and the person notified may then give similar notice to any other person who is answerable over to him under this Article. If the notice states that the person notified may come in and defend and that if the person notified does not do so he will in any action against him by the person giving the notice be bound by any determination of fact common to the two litigations, then unless after seasonable receipt of the notice the person notified does come in and defend he is so bound.

Section 3–804. Lost, Destroyed or Stolen Instruments.

The owner of an instrument which is lost, whether by destruction, theft or otherwise, may maintain an action in his own name and recover from any party liable thereon upon due proof of his ownership, the facts which prevent his production of the instrument and its terms. The court may require security indemnifying the defendant against loss by reason of further claims on the instrument.

Section 3–805. Instruments Not Payable to Order or to Bearer.

This Article applies to any instrument whose terms do not preclude transfer and which is otherwise negotiable within this Article but which is not payable to order or to bearer, except that there can be no holder in due course of such an instrument.

ARTICLE 4

BANK DEPOSITS AND COLLECTIONS

PART 1

GENERAL PROVISIONS AND DEFINITIONS

Section 4–101.   Short Title.

This Article shall be known and may be cited as Uniform Commercial Code—Bank Deposits and Collections.

Section 4–102.   Applicability.

(1) To the extent that items within this Article are also within the scope of Articles 3 and 8, they are subject to the provisions of those Articles. In the event of conflict the provisions of this Article govern those of Article 3 but the provisions of Article 8 govern those of this Article.

(2) The liability of a bank for action or non-action with respect to any item handled by it for purposes of presentment, payment or collection is governed by the law of the place where the bank is located. In the case of action or non-action by or at a branch or separate office of a bank, its liability is governed by the law of the place where the branch or separate office is located.

Section 4–103.   Variation by Agreement; Measure of Damages; Certain Action Constituting Ordinary Care.

(1) The effect of the provisions of this Article may be varied by agreement except that no agreement can disclaim a bank's responsibility for its own lack of good faith or failure to exercise ordinary care or can limit the measure of damages for such lack or failure; but the parties may by agreement determine the standards by which such responsibility is to be measured if such standards are not manifestly unreasonable.

(2) Federal Reserve regulations and operating letters, clearing house rules, and the like, have the effect of agreements under subsection (1), whether or not specifically assented to by all parties interested in items handled.

(3) Action or non-action approved by this Article or pursuant to Federal Reserve regulations or operating letters constitutes the exercise of ordinary care and, in the absence of special instructions, action or non-action consistent with clearing house rules and the like or with a general banking usage not disapproved by this Article, prima facie constitutes the exercise of ordinary care.

(4) The specification or approval of certain procedures by this Article does not constitute disapproval of other procedures which may be reasonable under the circumstances.

(5) The measure of damages for failure to exercise ordinary care in handling an item is the amount of the item reduced by an amount which could not have been realized by the use of ordinary care, and where there is bad faith it includes other damages, if any, suffered by the party as a proximate consequence.

Section 4–104.   Definitions and Index of Definitions.

(1) In this Article unless the context otherwise requires
    (a) "Account" means any account with a bank and includes a checking, time, interest or savings account;
    (b) "Afternoon" means the period of a day between noon and midnight;
    (c) "Banking day" means that part of any day on which a bank is open to the public for carrying on substantially all of its banking functions;
    (d) "Clearing house" means any association of banks or other payors regularly clearing items;
    (e) "Customer" means any person having an account with a bank or for whom a bank has agreed to collect items and includes a bank carrying an account with another bank;
    (f) "Documentary draft" means any negotiable or non-negotiable draft with accompanying documents, securities or other papers to be delivered against honor of the draft;
    (g) "Item" means any instrument for the payment of money even though it is not negotiable but does not include money;
    (h) "Midnight deadline" with respect to a bank is midnight on its next banking day following the banking day on which it receives the relevant item or notice or from which the time for taking action commences to run, whichever is later;
    (i) "Properly payable" includes the availability of funds for payment at the time of decision to pay or dishonor;
    (j) "Settle" means to pay in cash, by clearing house settlement, in a charge or credit or by remittance, or otherwise as instructed. A settlement may be either provisional or final;
    (k) "Suspends payments" with respect to a bank means that it has been closed by order of the supervisory authorities, that a public officer has been appointed to take it over or that it ceases or refuses to make payments in the ordinary course of business.

(2) Other definitions applying to this Article and the sections in which they appear are:

"Collecting bank"	Section 4–105.
"Depositary bank"	Section 4–105.
"Intermediary bank"	Section 4–105.
"Payor bank"	Section 4–105.
"Presenting bank"	Section 4–105.
"Remitting bank"	Section 4–105.

(3) The following definitions in other Articles apply to this Article:

"Acceptance"	Section 3–410.
"Certificate of deposit"	Section 3–104.
"Certification"	Section 3–411.

"Check"	Section 3–104.
"Draft"	Section 3–104.
"Holder in due course"	Section 3–302.
"Notice of dishonor"	Section 3–508.
"Presentment"	Section 3–504.
"Protest"	Section 3–509.
"Secondary party"	Section 3–102.

(4) In addition Article 1 contains general definitions and principles of construction and interpretation applicable throughout this Article.

Section 4–105. "Depositary Bank"; "Intermediary Bank"; "Collecting Bank"; "Payor Bank"; "Presenting Bank"; "Remitting Bank."

In this Article unless the context otherwise requires:

(a) "Depositary bank" means the first bank to which an item is transferred for collection even though it is also the payor bank;

(b) "Payor bank" means a bank by which an item is payable as drawn or accepted;

(c) "Intermediary bank" means any bank to which an item is transferred in course of collection except the depositary or payor bank;

(d) "Collecting bank" means any bank handling the item for collection except the payor bank;

(e) "Presenting bank" means any bank presenting an item except a payor bank;

(f) "Remitting bank" means any payor or intermediary bank remitting for an item.

Section 4–106. Separate Office of a Bank.

A branch or separate office of a bank [maintaining its own deposit ledgers] is a separate bank for the purpose of computing the time within which and determining the place at or to which action may be taken or notices or orders shall be given under this Article and under Article 3.

Note: *The words in brackets are optional.*

Section 4–107. Time of Receipt of Items.

(1) For the purpose of allowing time to process items, prove balances and make the necessary entries on its books to determine its position for the day, a bank may fix an afternoon hour of two P.M. or later as a cut-off hour for the handling of money and items and the making of entries on its books.

(2) Any item or deposit of money received on any day after a cut-off hour so fixed or after the close of the banking day may be treated as being received at the opening of the next banking day.

Section 4–108. Delays.

(1) Unless otherwise instructed, a collecting bank in a good faith effort to secure payment may, in the case of specific items and with or without the approval of any person involved, waive, modify or extend time limits imposed

or permitted by this Act for a period not in excess of an additional banking day without discharge of secondary parties and without liability to its transferor or any prior party.

(2) Delay by a collecting bank or payor bank beyond time limits prescribed or permitted by this Act or by instructions is excused if caused by interruption of communication facilities, suspension of payments by another bank, war, emergency conditions or other circumstances beyond the control of the bank provided it exercises such diligence as the circumstances require.

Section 4–109. Process of Posting.

The "process of posting" means the usual procedure followed by a payor bank in determining to pay an item and in recording the payment including one or more of the following or other steps as determined by the bank:

  (a) verification of any signature;
  (b) ascertaining that sufficient funds are available;
  (c) affixing a "paid" or other stamp;
  (d) entering a charge or entry to a customer's account;
  (e) correcting or reversing an entry or erroneous action with respect to the item.

PART 2

COLLECTION OF ITEMS: DEPOSITARY AND COLLECTING BANKS

Section 4–201. Presumption and Duration of Agency Status of Collecting Banks and Provisional Status of Credits; Applicability of Article; Item Indorsed "Pay Any Bank".

(1) Unless a contrary intent clearly appears and prior to the time that a settlement given by a collecting bank for an item is or becomes final (subsection (3) of Section 4–211 and Sections 4–212 and 4–213) the bank is an agent or sub-agent of the owner of the item and any settlement given for the item is provisional. This provision applies regardless of the form of indorsement or lack of indorsement and even though credit given for the item is subject to immediate withdrawal as of right or is in fact withdrawn; but the continuance of ownership of an item by its owner and any rights of the owner to proceeds of the item are subject to rights of a collecting bank such as those resulting from outstanding advances on the item and valid rights of setoff. When an item is handled by banks for purposes of presentment, payment and collection, the relevant provisions of this Article apply even though action of parties clearly establishes that a particular bank has purchased the item and is the owner of it.

(2) After an item has been indorsed with the words "pay any bank" or the like, only a bank may acquire the rights of a holder

  (a) until the item has been returned to the customer initiating collection; or
  (b) until the item has been specially indorsed by a bank to a person who is not a bank.

Section 4–202. Responsibility for Collection; When Action Seasonable.

(1) A collecting bank must use ordinary care in

  (a) presenting an item or sending it for presentment; and

  (b) sending notice of dishonor or non-payment or returning an item other than a documentary draft to the bank's transferor [or directly to the depositary bank under subsection (2) of Section 4–212] (*see note to Section 4–212*) after learning that the item has not been paid or accepted, as the case may be; and

  (c) settling for an item when the bank receives final settlement; and

  (d) making or providing for any necessary protest; and

  (e) notifying its transferor of any loss or delay in transit within a reasonable time after discovery thereof.

(2) A collecting bank taking proper action before its midnight deadline following receipt of an item, notice or payment acts seasonably; taking proper action within a reasonably longer time may be seasonable but the bank has the burden of so establishing.

(3) Subject to subsection (1) (a), a bank is not liable for the insolvency, neglect, misconduct, mistake or default of another bank or person or for loss or destruction of an item in transit or in the possession of others.

Section 4–203. Effect of Instructions.

Subject to the provisions of Article 3 concerning conversion of instruments (Section 3–419) and the provisions of both Article 3 and this Article concerning restrictive indorsements only a collecting bank's transferor can give instructions which affect the bank or constitute notice to it and a collecting bank is not liable to prior parties for any action taken pursuant to such instructions or in accordance with any agreement with its transferor.

Section 4–204. Methods of Sending and Presenting; Sending Direct to Payor Bank.

(1) A collecting bank must send items by reasonably prompt method taking into consideration any relevant instructions, the nature of the item, the number of such items on hand, and the cost of collection involved and the method generally used by it or others to present such items.

(2) A collecting bank may send

  (a) any item direct to the payor bank;

  (b) any item to any non-bank payor if authorized by its transferor; and

  (c) any item other than documentary drafts to any non-bank payor, if authorized by Federal Reserve regulation or operating letter, clearing house rule or the like.

(3) Presentment may be made by a presenting bank at a place where the payor bank has requested that presentment be made.

Section 4–205. Supplying Missing Indorsement; No Notice from Prior Indorsement.

(1) A depositary bank which has taken an item for collection may supply any indorsement of the customer which is necessary to title unless the item

contains the words "payee's indorsement required" or the like. In the absence of such a requirement a statement placed on the item by the depositary bank to the effect that the item was deposited by a customer or credited to his account is effective as the customer's indorsement.

(2) An intermediary bank, or payor bank which is not a depositary bank, is neither given notice nor otherwise affected by a restrictive indorsement of any person except the bank's immediate transferor.

Section 4–206. Transfer Between Banks.

Any agreed method which identifies the transferor bank is sufficient for the item's further transfer to another bank.

Section 4–207. Warranties of Customer and Collecting Bank on Transfer or Presentment of Items; Time for Claims.

(1) Each customer or collecting bank who obtains payment or acceptance of an item and each prior customer and collecting bank warrants to the payor bank or other payor who in good faith pays or accepts the item that

    (a) he has a good title to the item or is authorized to obtain payment or acceptance on behalf of one who has a good title; and

    (b) he has no knowledge that the signature of the maker or drawer is unauthorized, except that this warranty is not given by any customer or collecting bank that is a holder in due course and acts in good faith

        (i) to a maker with respect to the maker's own signature; or

        (ii) to a drawer with respect to the drawer's own signature, whether or not the drawer is also the drawee; or

        (iii) to an acceptor of an item if the holder in due course took the item after the acceptance or obtained the acceptance without knowledge that the drawer's signature was unauthorized; and

    (c) the item has not been materially altered, except that this warranty is not given by any customer or collecting bank that is a holder in due course and acts in good faith

        (i) to the maker of a note; or

        (ii) to the drawer of a draft whether or not the drawer is also the drawee; or

        (iii) to the acceptor of an item with respect to an alteration made prior to the acceptance if the holder in due course took the item after the acceptance, even though the acceptance provided "payable as originally drawn" or equivalent terms; or

        (iv) to the acceptor of an item with respect to an alteration made after the acceptance.

(2) Each customer and collecting bank who transfers an item and receives a settlement or other consideration for it warrants to his transferee and to any subsequent collecting bank who takes the item in good faith that

    (a) he has a good title to the item or is authorized to obtain payment or acceptance on behalf of one who has a good title and the transfer is otherwise rightful; and

(b) all signatures are genuine or authorized; and

(c) the item has not been materially altered; and

(d) no defense of any party is good against him; and

(e) he has no knowledge of any insolvency proceeding instituted with respect to the maker or acceptor or the drawer of an unaccepted item.

In addition each customer and collecting bank so transferring an item and receiving a settlement or other consideration engages that upon dishonor and any necessary notice of dishonor and protest he will take up the item.

(3) The warranties and the engagement to honor set forth in the two preceding subsections arise notwithstanding the absence of indorsement or words of guaranty or warranty in the transfer or presentment and a collecting bank remains liable for their breach despite remittance to its transferor. Damages for breach of such warranties or engagement to honor shall not exceed the consideration received by the customer or collecting bank responsible plus finance charges and expenses related to the item, if any.

(4) Unless a claim for breach of warranty under this section is made within a reasonable time after the person claiming learns of the breach, the person liable is discharged to the extent of any loss caused by the delay in making claim.

Section 4–208. Security Interest of Collecting Bank in Items, Accompanying Documents and Proceeds.

(1) A bank has a security interest in an item and any accompanying documents or the proceeds of either

(a) in case of an item deposited in an account to the extent to which credit given for the item has been withdrawn or applied;

(b) in case of an item for which it has given credit available for withdrawal as of right, to the extent of the credit given whether or not the credit is drawn upon and whether or not there is a right of charge-back; or

(c) if it makes an advance on or against the item.

(2) When credit which has been given for several items received at one time or pursuant to a single agreement is withdrawn or applied in part the security interest remains upon all the items, any accompanying documents or the proceeds of either. For the purpose of this section, credits first given are first withdrawn.

(3) Receipt by a collecting bank of a final settlement for an item is a realization on its security interest in the item, accompanying documents and proceeds. To the extent and so long as the bank does not receive final settlement for the item or give up possession of the item or accompanying documents for purposes other than collection, the security interest continues and is subject to the provisions of Article 9 except that

(a) no security agreement is necessary to make the security interest enforceable (subsection (1) (b) of Section 9–203); and

(b) no filing is required to perfect the security interest; and

(c) the security interest has priority over conflicting perfected security interests in the item, accompanying documents or proceeds.

Section 4–209. When Bank Gives Value for Purposes of Holder in Due Course.

For purposes of determining its status as a holder in due course, the bank has given value to the extent that it has a security interest in an item provided that the bank otherwise complies with the requirements of Section 3–302 on what constitutes a holder in due course.

Section 4–210. Presentment by Notice of Item Not Payable by, Through or at a Bank; Liability of Secondary Parties.

(1) Unless otherwise instructed, a collecting bank may present an item not payable by, through or at a bank by sending to the party to accept or pay a written notice that the bank holds the item for acceptance or payment. The notice must be sent in time to be received on or before the day when presentment is due and the bank must meet any requirement of the party to accept or pay under Section 3–505 by the close of the bank's next banking day after it knows of the requirement.

(2) Where presentment is made by notice and neither honor nor request for compliance with a requirement under Section 3–505 is received by the close of business on the day after maturity or in the case of demand items by the close of business on the third banking day after notice was sent, the presenting bank may treat the item as dishonored and charge any secondary party by sending him notice of the facts.

Section 4–211. Media of Remittance; Provisional and Final Settlement in Remittance Cases.

(1) A collecting bank may take in settlement of an item
  (a) a check of the remitting bank or of another bank on any bank except the remitting bank; or
  (b) a cashier's check or similar primary obligation of a remitting bank which is a member of or clears through a member of the same clearing house or group as the collecting bank; or
  (c) appropriate authority to charge an account of the remitting bank or of another bank with the collecting bank; or
  (d) if the item is drawn upon or payable by a person other than a bank, a cashier's check, certified check or other bank check or obligation.

(2) If before its midnight deadline the collecting bank properly dishonors a remittance check or authorization to charge on itself or presents or forwards for collection a remittance instrument of or on another bank which is of a kind approved by subsection (1) or has not been authorized by it, the collecting bank is not liable to prior parties in the event of the dishonor of such check, instrument or authorization.

(3) A settlement for an item by means of a remittance instrument or authorization to charge is or becomes a final settlement as to both the person making and the person receiving the settlement
  (a) if the remittance instrument or authorization to charge is of a kind approved by subsection (1) or has not been authorized by the person receiving the settlement and in either case the person receiving the settlement acts seasonably before its midnight deadline

in presenting, forwarding for collection or paying the instrument or authorization,—at the time the remittance instrument or authorization is finally paid by the payor by which it is payable;

(b) if the person receiving the settlement has authorized remittance by a non-bank check or obligation or by a cashier's check or similar primary obligation of or a check upon the payor or other remitting bank which is not of a kind approved by subsection (1) (b),—at the time of the receipt of such remittance check or obligation; or

(c) if in a case not covered by sub-paragraphs (a) or (b) the person receiving the settlement fails to seasonably present, forward for collection, pay or return a remittance instrument or authorization to it to charge before its midnight deadline,—at such midnight deadline.

Section 4–212. Right of Charge-Back or Refund.

(1) If a collecting bank has made provisional settlement with its customer for an item and itself fails by reason of dishonor, suspension of payments by a bank or otherwise to receive a settlement for the item which is or becomes final, the bank may revoke the settlement given by it, charge back the amount of any credit given for the item to its customer's account or obtain refund from its customer whether or not it is able to return the items if by its midnight deadline or within a longer reasonable time after it learns the facts it returns the item or sends notification of the facts. These rights to revoke, charge-back and obtain refund terminate if and when a settlement for the item received by the bank is or becomes final (subsection (3) of Section 4–211 and subsections (2) and (3) of Section 4–213).

[(2) Within the time and manner prescribed by this section and Section 4–301, an intermediary or payor bank, as the case may be, may return an unpaid item directly to the depositary bank and may send for collection a draft on the depositary bank and obtain reimbursement. In such case, if the depositary bank has received provisional settlement for the item, it must reimburse the bank drawing the draft and any provisional credits for the item between banks shall become and remain final.]

Note: *Direct returns is recognized as an innovation that is not yet established bank practice, and therefore, Paragraph 2 has been bracketed. Some lawyers have doubts whether it should be included in legislation or left to development by agreement.*

(3) A depositary bank which is also the payor may charge-back the amount of an item to its customer's account or obtain refund in accordance with the section governing return of an item received by a payor bank for credit on its books (Section 4–301).

(4) The right to charge-back is not affected by

(a) prior use of the credit given for the item; or

(b) failure by any bank to exercise ordinary care with respect to the item but any bank so failing remains liable.

(5) A failure to charge-back or claim refund does not affect other rights of the bank against the customer or any other party.

(6) If credit is given in dollars as the equivalent of the value of an item payable in a foreign currency the dollar amount of any charge-back or refund

shall be calculated on the basis of the buying sight rate for the foreign currency prevailing on the day when the person entitled to the charge-back or refund learns that it will not receive payment in ordinary course.

Section 4–213. Final Payment of Item by Payor Bank; When Provisional Debits and Credits Become Final; When Certain Credits Become Available for Withdrawal.

(1) An item is finally paid by a payor bank when the bank has done any of the following, whichever happens first:

(a) paid the item in cash; or

(b) settled for the item without reserving a right to revoke the settlement and without having such right under statute, clearing house rule or agreement; or

(c) completed the process of posting the item to the indicated account of the drawer, maker or other person to be charged therewith; or

(d) made a provisional settlement for the item and failed to revoke the settlement in the time and manner permitted by statute, clearing house rule or agreement.

Upon a final payment under subparagraphs (b), (c) or (d) the payor bank shall be accountable for the amount of the item.

(2) If provisional settlement for an item between the presenting and payor banks is made through a clearing house or by debits or credits in an account between them, then to the extent that provisional debits or credits for the item are entered in accounts between the presenting and payor banks or between the presenting and successive prior collecting banks seriatim, they become final upon final payment of the item by the payor bank.

(3) If a collecting bank receives a settlement for an item which is or becomes final (subsection (3) of Section 4–211, subsection (2) of Section 4–213) the bank is accountable to its customer for the amount of the item and any provisional credit given for the item in an account with its customer becomes final.

(4) Subject to any right of the bank to apply the credit to an obligation of the customer, credit given by a bank for an item in an account with its customer becomes available for withdrawal as of right

(a) in any case where the bank has received a provisional settlement for the item,—when such settlement becomes final and the bank has had a reasonable time to learn that the settlement is final;

(b) in any case where the bank is both a depositary bank and a payor bank and the item is finally paid,—at the opening of the bank's second banking day following receipt of the item.

(5) A deposit of money in a bank is final when made but, subject to any right of the bank to apply the deposit to an obligation of the customer, the deposit becomes available for withdrawal as of right at the opening of the bank's next banking day following receipt of the deposit.

Section 4–214. Insolvency and Preference.

(1) Any item in or coming into the possession of a payor or collecting bank which suspends payment and which item is not finally paid shall be

returned by the receiver, trustee or agent in charge of the closed bank to the presenting bank or the closed bank's customer.

(2) If a payor bank finally pays an item and suspends payments without making a settlement for the item with its customer or the presenting bank which settlement is or becomes final, the owner of the item has a preferred claim against the payor bank.

(3) If a payor bank gives or a collecting bank gives or receives a provisional settlement for an item and thereafter suspends payments, the suspension does not prevent or interfere with the settlement becoming final if such finality occurs automatically upon the lapse of certain time or the happening of certain events (subsection (3) of Section 4–211, subsections (1) (d), (2) and (3) of Section 4–213).

(4) If a collecting bank receives from subsequent parties settlement for an item which settlement is or becomes final and suspends payments without making a settlement for the item with its customer which is or becomes final, the owner of the item has a preferred claim against such collecting bank.

PART 3

COLLECTION OF ITEMS: PAYOR BANKS

Section 4–301. Deferred Posting; Recovery of Payment by Return of Items; Time of Dishonor.

(1) Where an authorized settlement for a demand item (other than a documentary draft) received by a payor bank otherwise than for immediate payment over the counter has been made before midnight of the banking day of receipt the payor bank may revoke the settlement and recover any payment if before it has made final payment (subsection (1) of Section 4–213) and before its midnight deadline it

    (a) returns the item; or

    (b) sends written notice of dishonor or nonpayment if the item is held for protest or is otherwise unavailable for return.

(2) If a demand item is received by a payor bank for credit on its books it may return such item or send notice of dishonor and may revoke any credit given or recover the amount thereof withdrawn by its customer, if it acts within the time limit and in the manner specified in the preceding subsection.

(3) Unless previous notice of dishonor has been sent an item is dishonored at the time when for purposes of dishonor it is returned or notice sent in accordance with this section.

(4) An item is returned:

    (a) as to an item received through a clearing house, when it is delivered to the presenting or last collecting bank or to the clearing house or is sent or delivered in accordance with its rules; or

    (b) in all other cases, when it is sent or delivered to the bank's customer or transferor or pursuant to his instructions.

Section 4–302. Payor Bank's Responsibility for Late Return of Item.

In the absence of a valid defense such as breach of a presentment warranty (subsection (1) of Section 4–207), settlement effected or the like, if an item is presented on and received by a payor bank the bank is accountable for the amount of

(a) a demand item other than a documentary draft whether properly payable or not if the bank, in any case where it is not also the depositary bank, retains the item beyond midnight of the banking day of receipt without settling for it or, regardless of whether it is also the depositary bank, does not pay or return the item or send notice of dishonor until after its midnight deadline; or

(b) any other properly payable item unless within the time allowed for acceptance or payment of that item the bank either accepts or pays the item or returns it and accompanying documents.

Section 4–303. When Items Subject to Notice, Stop-Order, Legal Process or Setoff; Order in Which Items May Be Charged or Certified.

(1) Any knowledge, notice or stop-order received by, legal process served upon or setoff exercised by a payor bank, whether or not effective under other rules of law to terminate, suspend or modify the bank's right or duty to pay an item or to charge its customer's account for the item, comes too late to so terminate, suspend or modify such right or duty if the knowledge, notice, stop-order or legal process is received or served and a reasonable time for the bank to act thereon expires or the setoff is exercised after the bank has done any of the following:

(a) accepted or certified the item;

(b) paid the item in cash;

(c) settled for the item without reserving a right to revoke the settlement and without having such right under statute, clearing house rule or agreement;

(d) completed the process of posting the item to the indicated account of the drawer, maker or other person to be charged therewith or otherwise has evidenced by examination of such indicated account and by action its decision to pay the item; or

(e) become accountable for the amount of the item under subsection (1) (d) of Section 4–213 and Section 4–302 dealing with the payor bank's responsibility for late return of items.

(2) Subject to the provisions of subsection (1) items may be accepted, paid, certified or charged to the indicated account of its customer in any order convenient to the bank.

PART 4

RELATIONSHIP BETWEEN PAYOR BANK AND ITS CUSTOMER

Section 4–401. When Bank May Charge Customer's Account.

(1) As against its customer, a bank may charge against his account any item which is otherwise properly payable from that account even though the charge creates an overdraft.

(2) A bank which in good faith makes payment to a holder may charge the indicated account of its customer according to

    (a) the original tenor of his altered item; or

    (b) the tenor of his completed item, even though the bank knows the item has been completed unless the bank has notice that the completion was improper.

Section 4–402. Bank's Liability to Customer for Wrongful Dishonor.

A payor bank is liable to its customer for damages proximately caused by the wrongful dishonor of an item. When the dishonor occurs through mistake liability is limited to actual damages proved. If so proximately caused and proved damages may include damages for an arrest or prosecution of the customer or other consequential damages. Whether any consequential damages are proximately caused by the wrongful dishonor is a question of fact to be determined in each case.

Section 4–403. Customer's Right to Stop Payment; Burden of Proof of Loss.

(1) A customer may by order to his bank stop payment of any item payable for his account but the order must be received at such time and in such manner as to afford the bank a reasonable opportunity to act on it prior to any action by the bank with respect to the item described in Section 4–303.

(2) An oral order is binding upon the bank only for fourteen calendar days unless confirmed in writing within that period. A written order is effective for only six months unless renewed in writing.

(3) The burden of establishing the fact and amount of loss resulting from the payment of an item contrary to a binding stop payment order is on the customer.

Section 4–404. Bank Not Obligated to Pay Check More Than Six Months Old.

A bank is under no obligation to a customer having a checking account to pay a check, other than a certified check, which is presented more than six months after its date, but it may charge its customer's account for a payment made thereafter in good faith.

Section 4–405. Death or Incompetence of Customer.

(1) A payor or collecting bank's authority to accept, pay or collect an item or to account for proceeds of its collection if otherwise effective is not rendered ineffective by incompetence of a customer of either bank existing at the time the item is issued or its collection is undertaken if the bank does not know of an adjudication of incompetence. Neither death nor incompetence of a customer revokes such authority to accept, pay, collect or account until the bank knows of the fact of death or of an adjudication of incompetence and has reasonable opportunity to act on it.

(2) Even with knowledge a bank may for ten days after the date of death

pay or certify checks drawn on or prior to that date unless ordered to stop payment by a person claiming an interest in the account.

Section 4–406. Customer's Duty to Discover and Report Unauthorized Signature or Alteration.

(1) When a bank sends to its customer a statement of account accompanied by items paid in good faith in support of the debit entries or holds the statement and items pursuant to a request or instructions of its customer or otherwise in a reasonable manner makes the statement and items available to the customer, the customer must exercise reasonable care and promptness to examine the statement and items to discover his unauthorized signature or any alteration on an item and must notify the bank promptly after discovery thereof.

(2) If the bank establishes that the customer failed with respect to an item to comply with the duties imposed on the customer by subsection (1) the customer is precluded from asserting against the bank

    (a) his unauthorized signature or any alteration on the item if the bank also establishes that it suffered a loss by reason of such failure; and

    (b) an unauthorized signature or alteration by the same wrongdoer on any other item paid in good faith by the bank after the first item and statement was available to the customer for a reasonable period not exceeding fourteen calendar days and before the bank receives notification from the customer of any such unauthorized signature or alteration.

(3) The preclusion under subsection (2) does not apply if the customer establishes lack of ordinary care on the part of the bank in paying the item(s).

(4) Without regard to care or lack of care of either the customer or the bank a customer who does not within one year from the time the statement and items are made available to the customer (subsection (1)) discover and report his unauthorized signature or any alteration on the face or back of the item or does not within three years from that time discover and report any unauthorized indorsement is precluded from asserting against the bank such unauthorized signature or indorsement or such alteration.

(5) If under this section a payor bank has a valid defense against a claim of a customer upon or resulting from payment of an item and waives or fails upon request to assert the defense the bank may not assert against any collecting bank or other prior party presenting or transferring the item a claim based upon the unauthorized signature or alteration giving rise to the customer's claim.

Section 4–407. Payor Bank's Right to Subrogation on Improper Payment.

If a payor bank has paid an item over the stop payment order of the drawer or maker or otherwise under circumstances giving a basis for objection by the drawer or maker, to prevent unjust enrichment and only to the extent necessary to prevent loss to the bank by reason of its payment of the item, **the** payor bank shall be subrogated to the rights

    (a) of any holder in due course on the item against the drawer or maker; and

    (b) of the payee or any other holder of the item against the drawer or maker either on the item or under the transaction out of which the item arose; and

    (c) of the drawer or maker against the payee or any other holder of the item with respect to the transaction out of which the item arose.

PART 5

COLLECTION OF DOCUMENTARY DRAFTS

Section 4–501. Handling of Documentary Drafts; Duty to Send for Presentment and to Notify Customer of Dishonor.

A bank which takes a documentary draft for collection must present or send the draft and accompanying documents for presentment and upon learning that the draft has not been paid or accepted in due course must seasonably notify its customer of such fact even though it may have discounted or bought the draft or extended credit available for withdrawal as of right.

Section 4–502. Presentment of "On Arrival" Drafts.

When a draft or the relevant instructions require presentment "on arrival," "when goods arrive" or the like, the collecting bank need not present until in its judgment a reasonable time for arrival of the goods has expired. Refusal to pay or accept because the goods have not arrived is not dishonor; the bank must notify its transferor of such refusal but need not present the draft again until it is instructed to do so or learns of the arrival of the goods.

Section 4–503. Responsibility of Presenting Bank for Documents and Goods; Report of Reasons for Dishonor; Referee in Case of Need.

Unless otherwise instructed and except as provided in Article 5 a bank presenting a documentary draft

    (a) must deliver the documents to the drawee on acceptance of the draft if it is payable more than three days after presentment; otherwise, only on payment; and

    (b) upon dishonor, either in the case of presentment for acceptance or presentment for payment, may seek and follow instructions from any referee in case of need designated in the draft or if the presenting bank does not choose to utilize his services it must use diligence and good faith to ascertain the reason for dishonor, must notify its transferor of the dishonor and of the results of its effort to ascertain the reasons therefor and must request instructions.

But the presenting bank is under no obligation with respect to goods represented by the documents except to follow any reasonable instructions seasonably received; it has a right to reimbursement for any expense incurred in following instructions and to prepayment of or indemnity for such expenses.

Section 4–504. Privilege of Presenting Bank to Deal With Goods; Security Interest for Expenses.

(1) A presenting bank which, following the dishonor of a documentary draft, has seasonably requested instructions but does not receive them within a reasonable time may store, sell, or otherwise deal with the goods in any reasonable manner.

(2) For its reasonable expenses incurred by action under subsection (1) the presenting bank has a lien upon the goods or their proceeds, which may be foreclosed in the same manner as an unpaid seller's lien.

ARTICLE 5

LETTERS OF CREDIT

Section 5–101. Short Title.

This Article shall be known and may be cited as Uniform Commercial Code—Letters of Credit.

Section 5–102. Scope.

(1) This Article applies
   (a) to a credit issued by a bank if the credit requires a documentary draft or a documentary demand for payment; and
   (b) to a credit issued by a person other than a bank if the credit requires that the draft or demand for payment be accompanied by a document of title; and
   (c) to a credit issued by a bank or other person if the credit is not within subparagraphs (a) or (b) but conspicuously states that it is a letter of credit or is conspicuously so entitled.

(2) Unless the engagement meets the requirements of subsection (1), this Article does not apply to engagements to make advances or to honor drafts or demands for payment, to authorities to pay or purchase, to guarantees or to general agreements.

(3) This Article deals with some but not all of the rules and concepts of letters of credit as such rules or concepts have developed prior to this act or may hereafter develop. The fact that this Article states a rule does not by itself require, imply or negate application of the same or a converse rule to a situation not provided for or to a person not specified by this Article.

Section 5–103. Definitions.

(1) In this Article unless the context otherwise requires
   (a) "Credit" or "letter of credit" means an engagement by a bank or other person made at the request of a customer and of a kind within the scope of this Article (Section 5–102) that the issuer will honor drafts or other demands for payment upon compliance with the conditions specified in the credit. A credit may be either revocable or irrevocable. The engagement may be either an agreement to honor or a statement that the bank or other person is authorized to honor.
   (b) A "documentary draft" or a "documentary demand for payment" is one honor of which is conditioned upon the presentation of a docu-

ment or documents. "Document" means any paper including document of title, security, invoice, certificate, notice of default and the like.

(c) An "issuer" is a bank or other person issuing a credit.

(d) A "beneficiary" of a credit is a person who is entitled under its terms to draw or demand payment.

(e) An "advising bank" is a bank which gives notification of the issuance of a credit by another bank.

(f) A "confirming bank" is a bank which engages either that it will itself honor a credit already issued by another bank or that such a credit will be honored by the issuer or a third bank.

(g) A "customer" is a buyer or other person who causes an issuer to issue a credit. The term also includes a bank which procures issuance or confirmation on behalf of that bank's customer.

(2) Other definitions applying to this Article and the sections in which they appear are:

"Notation of Credit."	Section 5–108.
"Presenter."	Section 5–112(3).

(3) Definitions in other Articles applying to this Article and the sections in which they appear are:

"Accept" or "Acceptance."	Section 3–410.
"Contract for sale."	Section 2–106.
"Draft."	Section 3–104.
"Holder in due course."	Section 3–302.
"Midnight deadline."	Section 4–104.
"Security."	Section 8–102.

(4) In addition, Article 1 contains general definitions and principles of construction and interpretation applicable throughout this Article.

Section 5–104. Formal Requirements; Signing.

(1) Except as otherwise required in subsection (1) (c) of Section 5–102 on scope, no particular form of phrasing is required for a credit. A credit must be in writing and signed by the issuer and a confirmation must be in writing and signed by the confirming bank. A modification of the terms of a credit or confirmation must be signed by the issuer or confirming bank.

(2) A telegram may be a sufficient signed writing if it identifies its sender by an authorized authentication. The authentication may be in code and the authorized naming of the issuer in an advice of credit is a sufficient signing.

Section 5–105. Consideration.

No consideration is necessary to establish a credit or to enlarge or otherwise modify its terms.

Section 5–106. Time and Effect of Establishment of Credit.

(1) Unless otherwise agreed a credit is established

(a) as regards the customer as soon as a letter of credit is sent to him or the letter of credit or an authorized written advice of its issuance is sent to the beneficiary; and

(b) as regards the beneficiary when he receives a letter of credit or an authorized written advice of its issuance.

(2) Unless otherwise agreed once an irrevocable credit is established as regards the customer it can be modified or revoked only with the consent of the customer and once it is established as regards the beneficiary it can be modified or revoked only with his consent.

(3) Unless otherwise agreed after a revocable credit is established it may be modified or revoked by the issuer without notice to or consent from the customer or beneficiary.

(4) Notwithstanding any modification or revocation of a revocable credit any person authorized to honor or negotiate under the terms of the original credit is entitled to reimbursement for or honor of any draft or demand for payment duly honored or negotiated before receipt of notice of the modification or revocation and the issuer in turn is entitled to reimbursement from its customer.

Section 5–107. Advice of Credit; Confirmation; Error in Statement of Terms.

(1) Unless otherwise specified an advising bank by advising a credit issued by another bank does not assume any obligation to honor drafts drawn or demands for payment made under the credit but it does assume obligation for the accuracy of its own statement.

(2) A confirming bank by confirming a credit becomes directly obligated on the credit to the extent of its confirmation as though it were its issuer and acquires the rights of an issuer.

(3) Even though an advising bank incorrectly advises the terms of a credit it has been authorized to advise the credit is established as against the issuer to the extent of its original terms.

(4) Unless otherwise specified the customer bears as against the issuer all risks of transmission and reasonable translation or interpretation of any message relating to a credit.

Section 5–108. "Notation Credit"; Exhaustion of Credit.

(1) A credit which specifies that any person purchasing or paying drafts drawn or demands for payment made under it must note the amount of the draft or demand on the letter or advice of credit is a "notation credit."

(2) Under a notation credit
  (a) a person paying the beneficiary or purchasing a draft or demand for payment from him acquires a right to honor only if the appropriate notation is made and by transferring or forwarding for honor the documents under the credit such a person warrants to the issuer that the notation has been made; and
  (b) unless the credit or a signed statement that an appropriate notation has been made accompanies the draft or demand for payment the issuer may delay honor until evidence of notation has been procured which is satisfactory to it but its obligation and that of its customer continue for a reasonable time not exceeding thirty days to obtain such evidence.

(3) If the credit is not a notation credit

(a) the issuer may honor complying drafts or demands for payment presented to it in the order in which they are presented and is discharged pro tanto by honor of any such draft or demand;

(b) as between competing good faith purchasers of complying drafts or demands the person first purchasing has priority over a subsequent purchaser even though the later purchased draft or demand has been first honored.

Section 5–109. Issuer's Obligation to Its Customer.

(1) An issuer's obligation to its customer includes good faith and observance of any general banking usage but unless otherwise agreed does not include liability or responsibility

(a) for performance of the underlying contract for sale or other transaction between the customer and the beneficiary; or

(b) for any act or omission of any person other than itself or its own branch or for loss or destruction of a draft, demand or document in transit or in the possession of others; or

(c) based on knowledge or lack of knowledge of any usage of any particular trade.

(2) An issuer must examine documents with care so as to ascertain that on their face they appear to comply with the terms of the credit but unless otherwise agreed assumes no liability or responsibility for the genuineness, falsification or effect of any document which appears on such examination to be regular on its face.

(3) A non-bank issuer is not bound by any banking usage of which it has no knowledge.

Section 5–110. Availability of Credit in Portions; Presenter's Reservation of Lien or Claim.

(1) Unless otherwise specified a credit may be used in portions in the discretion of the beneficiary.

(2) Unless otherwise specified a person by presenting a documentary draft or demand for payment under a credit relinquishes upon its honor all claims to the documents and a person by transferring such draft or demand or causing such presentment authorizes such relinquishment. An explicit reservation of claim makes the draft or demand non-complying.

Section 5–111. Warranties on Transfer and Presentment.

(1) Unless otherwise agreed the beneficiary by transferring or presenting a documentary draft or demand for payment warrants to all interested parties that the necessary conditions of the credit have been complied with. This is in addition to any warranties arising under Articles 3, 4, 7 and 8.

(2) Unless otherwise agreed a negotiating, advising, confirming, collecting or issuing bank presenting or transferring a draft or demand for payment under a credit warrants only the matters warranted by a collecting bank under Article 4 and any such bank transferring a document warrants only the matters warranted by an intermediary under Articles 7 and 8.

Section 5–112. Time Allowed for Honor or Rejection; Withholding Honor or Rejection by Consent; "Presenter."

(1) A bank to which a documentary draft or demand for payment is presented under a credit may without dishonor of the draft, demand or credit

 (a) defer honor until the close of the third banking day following receipt of the documents; and

 (b) further defer honor if the presenter has expressly or impliedly consented thereto.

Failure to honor within the time here specified constitutes dishonor of the draft or demand and of the credit [except as otherwise provided in subsection (4) of Section 5–114 on conditional payment].

 Note: *The bracketed language in the last sentence of subsection (1) should be included only if the optional provisions of Section 5–114(4) and (5) are included.*

(2) Upon dishonor the bank may unless otherwise instructed fulfill its duty to return the draft or demand and the documents by holding them at the disposal of the presenter and sending him an advice to that effect.

(3) "Presenter" means any person presenting a draft or demand for payment for honor under a credit even though that person is a confirming bank or other correspondent which is acting under an issuer's authorization.

Section 5–113. Indemnities.

(1) A bank seeking to obtain (whether for itself or another) honor, negotiation or reimbursement under a credit may give an indemnity to induce such honor, negotiation or reimbursement.

(2) An indemnity agreement inducing honor, negotiation or reimbursement

 (a) unless otherwise explicitly agreed applies to defects in the documents but not in the goods; and

 (b) unless a longer time is explicitly agreed expires at the end of ten business days following receipt of the documents by the ultimate customer unless notice of objection is sent before such expiration date. The ultimate customer may send notice of objection to the person from whom he received the documents and any bank receiving such notice is under a duty to send notice to its transferor before its midnight deadline.

Section 5–114. Issuer's Duty and Privilege to Honor; Right to Reimbursement.

(1) An issuer must honor a draft or demand for payment which complies with the terms of the relevant credit regardless of whether the goods or documents conform to the underlying contract for sale or other contract between the customer and the beneficiary. The issuer is not excused from honor of such a draft or demand by reason of an additional general term that all documents must be satisfactory to the issuer, but an issuer may require that specified documents must be satisfactory to it.

(2) Unless otherwise agreed when documents appear on their face to comply with the terms of a credit but a required document does not in fact

conform to the warranties made on negotiation or transfer of a document of title (Section 7–507) or of a security (Section 8–306) or is forged or fraudulent or there is fraud in the transaction

(a) the issuer must honor the draft or demand for payment if honor is demanded by a negotiating bank or other holder of the draft or demand which has taken the draft or demand under the credit and under circumstances which would make it a holder in due course (Section 3–302) and in an appropriate case would make it a person to whom a document of title has been duly negotiated (Section 7–502) or a bona fide purchaser of a security (Section 8–302); and

(b) in all other cases as against its customer, an issuer acting in good faith may honor the draft or demand for payment despite notification from the customer of fraud, forgery or other defect not apparent on the face of the documents but a court of appropriate jurisdiction may enjoin such honor.

(3) Unless otherwise agreed an issuer which has duly honored a draft or demand for payment is entitled to immediate reimbursement of any payment made under the credit and to be put in effectively available funds not later than the day before maturity of any acceptance made under the credit.

[(4) When a credit provides for payment by the issuer on receipt of notice that the required documents are in the possession of a correspondent or other agent of the issuer

(a) any payment made on receipt of such notice is conditional; and

(b) the issuer may reject documents which do not comply with the credit if it does so within three banking days following its receipt of the documents; and

(c) in the event of such rejection, the issuer is entitled by charge back or otherwise to return of the payment made.]

[(5) In the case covered by subsection (4) failure to reject documents within the time specified in sub-paragraph (b) constitutes acceptance of the documents and makes the payment final in favor of the beneficiary.]

Note: *Subsections (4) and (5) are bracketed as optional. If they are included the bracketed language in the last sentence of Section 5–112(1) should also be included.*

Section 5–115. Remedy for Improper Dishonor or Anticipatory Repudiation.

(1) When an issuer wrongfully dishonors a draft or demand for payment presented under a credit the person entitled to honor has with respect to any documents the rights of a person in the position of a seller (Section 2–707) and may recover from the issuer the face amount of the draft or demand together with incidental damages under Section 2–710 on seller's incidental damages and interest but less any amount realized by resale or other use or disposition of the subject matter of the transaction. In the event no resale or other utilization is made the documents, goods or other subject matter involved in the transaction must be turned over to the issuer on payment of judgment.

(2) When an issuer wrongfully cancels or otherwise repudiates a credit before presentment of a draft or demand for payment drawn under it the bene-

ficiary has the rights of a seller after anticipatory repudiation by the buyer under Section 2–610 if he learns of the repudiation in time reasonably to avoid procurement of the required documents. Otherwise the beneficiary has an immediate right of action for wrongful dishonor.

Section 5–116. Transfer and Assignment.

(1) The right to draw under a credit can be transferred or assigned only when the credit is expressly designated as transferable or assignable.

(2) Even though the credit specifically states that it is nontransferable or nonassignable the beneficiary may before performance of the conditions of the credit assign his right to proceeds. Such an assignment is an assignment of an account under Article 9 on Secured Transactions and is governed by that Article except that

> (a) the assignment is ineffective until the letter of credit or advice of credit is delivered to the assignee which delivery constitutes perfection of the security interest under Article 9; and
>
> (b) the issuer may honor drafts or demands for payment drawn under the credit until it receives a notification of the assignment signed by the beneficiary which reasonably identifies the credit involved in the assignment and contains a request to pay the assignee; and
>
> (c) after what reasonably appears to be such a notification has been received the issuer may without dishonor refuse to accept or pay even to a person otherwise entitled to honor until the letter of credit or advice of credit is exhibited to the issuer.

(3) Except where the beneficiary has effectively assigned his right to draw or his right to proceeds, nothing in this section limits his right to transfer or negotiate drafts or demands drawn under the credit.

Section 5–117. Insolvency of Bank Holding Funds for Documentary Credit.

(1) Where an issuer or an advising or confirming bank or a bank which has for a customer procured issuance of a credit by another bank becomes insolvent before final payment under the credit and the credit is one to which this Article is made applicable by paragraphs (a) or (b) of Section 5–102(1) on scope, the receipt or allocation of funds or collateral to secure or meet obligations under the credit shall have the following results:

> (a) to the extent of any funds or collateral turned over after or before the insolvency as indemnity against or specifically for the purpose of payment of drafts or demands for payment drawn under the designated credit, the drafts or demands are entitled to payment in preference over depositors or other general creditors of the issuer or bank; and
>
> (b) on expiration of the credit or surrender of the beneficiary's rights under it unused any person who has given such funds or collateral is similarly entitled to return thereof; and
>
> (c) a change to a general or current account with a bank if specifically consented to for the purpose of indemnity against or payment of drafts or demands for payment drawn under the designated credit

falls under the same rules as if the funds had been drawn out in cash and then turned over with specific instructions.

(2) After honor or reimbursement under this section the customer or other person for whose account the insolvent bank has acted is entitled to receive the documents involved.

ARTICLE 6

BULK TRANSFERS

Section 6–101. Short Title.

This Article shall be known and may be cited as Uniform Commercial Code —Bulk Transfers.

Section 6–102. "Bulk Transfers"; Transfers of Equiment; Enterprises Subject to This Article; Bulk Transfers Subject to This Article.

(1) A "bulk transfer" is any transfer in bulk and not in the ordinary course of the transferor's business of a major part of the materials, supplies, merchandise or other inventory (Section 9–109) of an enterprise subject to this Article.

(2) A transfer of a substantial part of the equipment (Section 9–109) of such an enterprise is a bulk transfer if it is made in connection with a bulk transfer of inventory, but not otherwise.

(3) The enterprises subject to this Article are all those whose principal business is the sale of merchandise from stock, including those who manufacture what they sell.

(4) Except as limited by the following section all bulk transfers of goods located within this state are subject to this Article.

Section 6–103. Transfers Excepted From This Article.

The following transfers are not subject to this Article:

(1) Those made to give security for the performance of an obligation;

(2) General assignments for the benefit of all the creditors of the transferor, and subsequent transfers by the assignee thereunder;

(3) Transfers in settlement or realization of a lien or other security interest;

(4) Sales by executors, administrators, receivers, trustees in bankruptcy, or any public officer under judicial process;

(5) Sales made in the course of judicial or administrative proceedings for the dissolution or reorganization of a corporation and of which notice is sent to the creditors of the corporation pursuant to order of the court or administrative agency;

(6) Transfers to a person maintaining a known place of business in this State who becomes bound to pay the debts of the transferor in full and gives public notice of that fact, and who is solvent after becoming so bound;

(7) A transfer to a new business enterprise organized to take over and continue the business, if public notice of the transaction is given and the new enterprise assumes the debts of the transferor and he receives nothing from the

transaction except an interest in the new enterprise junior to the claims of creditors;

(8) Transfers of property which is exempt from execution.

Public notice under subsection (6) or subsection (7) may be given by publishing once a week for two consecutive weeks in a newspaper of general circulation where the transferor had its principal place of business in this state an advertisement including the names and addresses of the transferor and transferee and the effective date of the transfer.

Section 6–104. Schedule of Property, List of Creditors.

(1) Except as provided with respect to auction sales (Section 6–108), a bulk transfer subject to this Article is ineffective against any creditor of the transferor unless:

    (a) The transferee requires the transferor to furnish a list of his existing creditors prepared as stated in this section; and

    (b) The parties prepare a schedule of the property transferred sufficient to identify it; and

    (c) The transferee preserves the list and schedule for six months next following the transfer and permits inspection of either or both and copying therefrom at all reasonable hours by any creditor of the transferor, or files the list and schedule in (a public office to be here identified).

(2) The list of creditors must be signed and sworn to or affirmed by the transferor or his agent. It must contain the names and business addresses of all creditors of the transferor, with the amounts when known, and also the names of all persons who are known to the transferor to assert claims against him even though such claims are disputed. If the transferor is the obligor of an outstanding issue of bonds, debentures or the like as to which there is an indenture trustee, the list of creditors need include only tne name and address of the indenture trustee and the aggregate outstanding principal amount of the issue.

(3) Responsibility for the completeness and accuracy of the list of creditors rests on the transferor, and the transfer is not renedered ineffective by errors or omissions therein unless the transferee is shown to have had knowledge.

Section 6–105. Notice to Creditors.

In addition to the requirements of the preceding section, any bulk transfer subject to this Article except one made by auction sale (Section 6–108) is ineffective against any creditor of the transferor unless at least ten days before he takes possession of the goods or pays for them, whichever happens first, the transferee gives notice of the transfer in the manner and to the persons hereafter provided (Section 6–107).

[Section 6–106. Application of the Proceeds.

In addition to the requirements of the two preceding sections:

(1) Upon every bulk transfer subject to this Article for which new consideration becomes payable except those made by sale at auction it is the duty of the transferee to assure that such consideration is applied so far as necessary to pay those debts of the transferor which are either shown on the list furnished by the transferor (Section 6–104) or filed in writing in the place stated in the notice (Section 6–107) within thirty days after the mailing of such notice. This duty

of the transferee runs to all the holders of such debts, and may be enforced by any of them for the benefit of all.

(2) If any of said debts are in dispute the necessary sum may be withheld from distribution until the dispute is settled or adjudicated.

(3) If the consideration payable is not enough to pay all of the said debts in full distribution shall be made pro rata.]

Note: *This section is bracketed to indicate division of opinion as to whether or not it is a wise provision, and to suggest that this is a point on which State enactments may differ without serious damage to the principle of uniformity.*

In any State where this section is omitted, the following parts of sections, also bracketed in the text, should also be omitted, namely:

Section 6–107(2)(e).

6–108(3)(c).

6–109(2).

In any State where this section is enacted, these other provisions should be also.

Optional Subsection (4)

[(4) The transferee may within ten days after he takes possession of the goods pay the consideration into the (specify court) in the county where the transferor had its principal place of business in this state and thereafter may discharge his duty under this section by giving notice by registered or certified mail to all the persons to whom the duty runs that the consideration has been paid into that court and that they should file their claims there. On motion of any interested party, the court may order the distribution of the consideration to the persons entitled to it.]

Note: *Optional subsection (4) is recommended for those states which do not have a general statute providing for payment of money into court.*

Section 6–107. The Notice.

(1) The notice to creditors (Section 6–105) shall state:

(a) that a bulk transfer is about to be made; and

(b) the names and business addresses of the transferor and transferee, and all other business names and addresses used by the transferor within three years last past so far as known to the transferee; and

(c) whether or not all the debts of the transferor are to be paid in full as they fall due as a result of the transaction, and if so, the address to which creditors should send their bills.

(2) If the debts of the transferor are not to be paid in full as they fall due or if the transferee is in doubt on that point then the notice shall state further:

(a) the location and general description of the property to be transferred and the estimated total of the transferor's debts;

(b) the address where the schedule of property and list of creditors (Section 6–104) may be inspected;

(c) whether the transfer is to pay existing debts and if so the amount of such debts and to whom owing;

(d) whether the transfer is for new consideration and if so the amount of such consideration and the time and place of payment; [and]

[(e) if for new consideration the time and place where creditors of the transferor are to file their claims.]

(3) The notice in any case shall be delivered personally or sent by registered or certified mail to all the persons shown on the list of creditors furnished by the transferor (Section 6–104) and to all other persons who are known to the transferee to hold or assert claims against the transferor.

Note: *The words in brackets are optional.*

Section 6–108.   Auction Sales; "Auctioneer".

(1) A bulk transfer is subject to this Article even though it is by sale at auction, but only in the manner and with the results stated in this section.

(2) The transferor shall furnish a list of his creditors and assist in the preparation of a schedule of the property to be sold, both prepared as before stated (Section 6–104)..

(3) The person or persons other than the transferor who direct, control or are responsible for the auction are collectively called the "auctioneer". The auctioneer shall:

  (a) receive and retain the list of creditors and prepare and retain the schedule of property for the period stated in this Article (Section 6–104);

  (b) give notice of the auction personally or by registered or certified mail at least ten days before it occurs to all persons shown on the list of creditors and to all other persons who are known to him to hold or assert claims against the transferor; [and]

  [(c) assure that the net proceeds of the auction are applied as provided in this Article (Section 6–106).]

(4) Failure of the auctioneer to perform any of these duties does not affect the validity of the sale or the title of the purchasers, but if the auctioneer knows that the auction constitutes a bulk transfer such failure renders the auctioneer liable to the creditors of the transferor as a class for the sums owing to them from the transferor up to but not exceeding the net proceeds of the auction. If the auctioneer consists of several persons their liability is joint and several.

Note: *The words in brackets are optional.*

Section 6–109.   What Creditors Protected; [Credit for Payment to Particular Creditors].

(1) The creditors of the transferor mentioned in this Article are those holding claims based on transactions or events occurring before the bulk transfer, but creditors who become such after notice to creditors is given (Sections 6–105 and 6–107) are not entitled to notice.

[(2) Against the aggregate obligation imposed by the provisions of this Article concerning the application of the proceeds (Section 6–106 and subsection (3) (c) of 6–108) the transferee or auctioneer is entitled to credit for sums paid to particular creditors of the transferor, not exceeding the sums believed in good faith at the time of the payment to be properly payable to such creditors.]

Section 6–110.   Subsequent Transfers.

When the title of a transferee to property is subject to a defect by reason of his non-compliance with the requirements of this Article, then:

(1) A purchaser of any of such property from such transferee who pays no value or who takes with notice of such non-compliance takes subject to such defect, but

(2) a purchaser for value in good faith and without such notice takes free of such defect.

Section 6–111. Limitation of Actions and Levies.

No action under this Article shall be brought nor levy made more than six months after the date on which the transferee took possession of the goods unless the transfer has been concealed. If the transfer has been concealed, actions may be brought or levies made within six months after its discovery.

Note to Article 6: *Section 6–106 is bracketed to indicate division of opinion as to whether or not it is a wise provision, and to suggest that this is a point on which State enactments may differ without serious damage to the principle of uniformity.*

In any State where Section 6–106 is not enacted, the following parts of sections, also bracketed in the text, should also be omitted, namely:

> *Sec. 6–107(2) (e).*
> *6–108(3) (c).*
> *6–109(2).*

In any State where Section 6–106 is enacted, these other provisions should be also.

ARTICLE 7

WAREHOUSE RECEIPTS, BILLS OF LADING AND OTHER DOCUMENTS OF TITLE

PART 1

GENERAL

Section 7–101. Short Title.

This Article shall be known and may be cited as Uniform Commerical Code —Documents of Title.

Section 7–102. Definitions and Index of Definitions.

(1) In this Article, unless the context otherwise requires:

(a) "Bailee" means the person who by a warehouse receipt, bill of lading or other document of title acknowledges possession of goods and contracts to deliver them.

(b) "Consignee" means the person named in a bill to whom or to whose order the bill promises delivery.

(c) "Consignor" means the person named in a bill as the person from whom the goods have been received for shipment.

(d) "Delivery order" means a written order to deliver goods directed to a warehouseman, carrier or other person who in the ordinary course of business issues warehouse receipts or bills of lading.

(e) "Document" means document of title as defined in the general definitions in Article 1 (Section 1–201).

(f) "Goods" means all things which are treated as movable for the purposes of a contract of storage or transportation.

(g) "Issuer" means a bailee who issues a document except that in relation to an unaccepted delivery order it means the person who orders the possessor of goods to deliver. Issuer includes any person for whom an agent or employee purports to act in issuing a document if the agent or employee has real or apparent authority to issue documents, notwithstanding that the issuer received no goods or that the goods were misdescribed or that in any other respect the agent or employee violated his instructions.

(h) "Warehouseman" is a person engaged in the business of storing goods for hire.

(2) Other definitions applying to this Article or to specified Parts thereof, and the sections in which they appear are:

"Duly negotiate". Section 7–501.

"Person entitled under the document". Section 7–403(4).

(3) Definitions in other Articles applying to this Article and the sections in which they appear are:

"Contract for sale". Section 2–106.

"Overseas". Section 2–323.

"Receipt" of goods. Section 2–103.

(4) In addition Article 1 contains general definitions and principles of construction and interpretation applicable throughout this Article.

Section 7–103. Relation of Article to Treaty, Statute, Tariff, Classification or Regulation.

To the extent that any treaty or statute of the United States, regulatory statute of this State or tariff, classification or regulation filed or issued pursuant thereto is applicable, the provisions of this Article are subject thereto.

Section 7–104. Negotiable and Non-Negotiable Warehouse Receipt, Bill of Lading or Other Document of Title.

(1) A warehouse receipt, bill of lading or other document of title is negotiable

(a) if by its terms the goods are to be delivered to bearer or to the order of a named person; or

(b) where recognized in overseas trade, if it runs to a named person or assigns.

(2) Any other document is non-negotiable. A bill of lading in which it is stated that the goods are consigned to a named person is not made negotiable by a provision that the goods are to be delivered only against a written order signed by the same or another named person.

Section 7–105. Construction Against Negative Implication.

The omission from either Part 2 or Part 3 of this Article of a provision corresponding to a provision made in the other Part does not imply that a corresponding rule of law is not applicable.

PART 2

WAREHOUSE RECEIPTS: SPECIAL PROVISIONS

Section 7–201. Who May Issue a Warehouse Receipt; Storage Under Government Bond.

(1) A warehouse receipt may be issued by any warehouseman.

(2) Where goods including distilled spirits and agricultural commodities are stored under a statute requiring a bond against withdrawal or a license for the issuance of receipts in the nature of warehouse receipts, a receipt issued for the goods has like effect as a warehouse receipt even though issued by a person who is the owner of the goods and is not a warehouseman.

Section 7–202. Form of Warehouse Receipt; Essential Terms; Optional Terms.

(1) A warehouse receipt need not be in any particular form.

(2) Unless a warehouse receipt embodies within its written or printed terms each of the following, the warehouseman is liable for damages caused by the omission to a person injured thereby:

(a) the location of the warehouse where the goods are stored;

(b) the date of issue of the receipt;

(c) the consecutive number of the receipt;

(d) a statement whether the goods received will be delivered to the bearer, to a specified person, or to a specified person or his order;

(e) the rate of storage and handling charges, except that where goods are stored under a field warehousing arrangement a statement of that fact is sufficient on a non-negotiable receipt;

(f) a description of the goods or of the packages containing them;

(g) the signature of the warehouseman, which may be made by his authorized agent;

(h) if the receipt is issued for goods of which the warehouseman is owner, either solely or jointly or in common with others, the fact of such ownership; and

(i) a statement of the amount of advances made and of liabilities incurred for which the warehouseman claims a lien or security interest (Section 7–209). If the precise amount of such advances made or of such liabilities incurred is, at the time of the issue of the receipt, unknown to the warehouseman or to his agent who issues it, a statement of the fact that advances have been made or liabilities incurred and the purpose thereof is sufficient.

(3) A warehouseman may insert in his receipt any other terms which are not contrary to the provisions of this Act and do not impair his obligation of delivery (Section 7–403) or his duty of care (Section 7–204). Any contrary provisions shall be ineffective.

Section 7–203. Liability for Non-Receipt or Misdescription.

A party to or purchaser for value in good faith of a document of title other than a bill of lading relying in either case upon the description therein of the goods may recover from the issuer damages caused by the non-receipt or misdescription of the goods, except to the extent that the document conspicuously indicates that the issuer does not know whether any part or all of the goods in fact were received or conform to the description, as where the description is in terms of marks or labels or kind, quantity or condition, or the receipt or description is qualified by "contents, condition and quality unknown", "said to contain" or the like, if such indication be true, or the party or purchaser otherwise has notice.

Section 7–204. Duty of Care; Contractual Limitation of Warehouseman's Liability.

(1) A warehouseman is liable for damages for loss of or injury to the goods caused by his failure to exercise such care in regard to them as a reasonably careful man would exercise under like circumstances but unless otherwise agreed he is not liable for damages which could not have been avoided by the exercise of such care.

(2) Damages may be limited by a term in the warehouse receipt or storage agreement limiting the amount of liability in case of loss or damage, and setting forth a specific liability per article or item, or value per unit of weight, beyond which the warehouseman shall not be liable; provided, however, that such liability may on written request of the bailor at the time of signing such storage agreement or within a reasonable time after receipt of the warehouse receipt be increased on part or all of the goods thereunder, in which event increased rates may be charged based on such increased valuation, but that no such increase shall be permitted contrary to a lawful limitation of liability contained in the warehouseman's tariff, if any. No such limitation is effective with respect to the warehouseman's liability for conversion to his own use.

(3) Reasonable provisions as to the time and manner of presenting claims and instituting actions based on the bailment may be included in the warehouse receipt or tariff.

(4) This section does not impair or repeal . . .

Note: *Insert in subsection (4) a reference to any statute which imposes a higher responsibility upon the warehouseman or invalidates contractual limitations which would be permissible under this Article.*

Section 7–205. Title Under Warehouse Receipt Defeated in Certain Cases.

A buyer in the ordinary course of business of fungible goods sold and delivered by a warehouseman who is also in the business of buying and selling such goods takes free of any claim under a warehouse receipt even though it has been duly negotiated.

Section 7–206. Termination of Storage at Warehouseman's Option.

(1) A warehouseman may on notifying the person on whose account the goods are held and any other person known to claim an interest in the goods require payment of any charges and removal of the goods from the warehouse

at the termination of the period of storage fixed by the document, or, if no period is fixed, within a stated period not less than thirty days after the notification. If the goods are not removed before the date specified in the notification, the warehouseman may sell them in accordance with the provisions of the section on enforcement of a warehouseman's lien (Section 7–210).

(2) If a warehouseman in good faith believes that the goods are about to deteriorate or decline in value to less than the amount of his lien within the time prescribed in subsection (1) for notification, advertisement and sale, the warehouseman may specify in the notification any reasonable shorter time for removal of the goods and in case the goods are not removed, may sell them at public sale held not less than one week after a single advertisement or posting.

(3) If as a result of a quality or condition of the goods of which the warehouseman had no notice at the time of deposit the goods are a hazard to other property or to the warehouse or to persons, the warehouseman may sell the goods at public or private sale without advertisement on reasonable notification to all persons known to claim an interest in the goods. If the warehouseman after a reasonable effort is unable to sell the goods he may dispose of them in any lawful manner and shall incur no liability by reason of such disposition.

(4) The warehouseman must deliver the goods to any person entitled to them under this Article upon due demand made at any time prior to sale or other disposition under this section.

(5) The warehouseman may satisfy his lien from the proceeds of any sale or disposition under this section but must hold the balance for delivery on the demand of any person to whom he would have been bound to deliver the goods.

Section 7–207. Goods Must Be Kept Separate; Fungible Goods.

(1) Unless the warehouse receipt otherwise provides, a warehouseman must keep separate the goods covered by each receipt so as to permit at all times identification and delivery of those goods except that different lots of fungible goods may be commingled.

(2) Fungible goods so commingled are owned in common by the persons entitled thereto and the warehouseman is severally liable to each owner for that owner's share. Where because of overissue a mass of fungible goods is insufficient to meet all the receipts which the warehouseman has issued against it, the persons entitled include all holders to whom overissued receipts have been duly negotiated.

Section 7–208. Altered Warehouse Receipts.

Where a blank in a negotiable warehouse receipt has been filled in without authority, a purchaser for value and without notice of the want of authority may treat the insertion as authorized. Any other unauthorized alteration leaves any receipt enforceable against the issuer according to its original tenor.

Section 7–209. Lien of Warehouseman.

(1) A warehouseman has a lien against the bailor on the goods covered by a warehouse receipt or on the proceeds thereof in his possession for charges for storage or transportation (including demurrage and terminal charges),

insurance, labor, or charges present or future in relation to the goods, and for expenses necessary for preservation of the goods or reasonably incurred in their sale pursuant to law. If the person on whose account the goods are held is liable for like charges or expenses in relation to other goods whenever deposited and it is stated in the receipt that a lien is claimed for charges and expenses in relation to other goods, the warehouseman also has a lien against him for such charges and expenses whether or not the other goods have been delivered by the warehouseman. But against a person to whom a negotiable warehouse receipt is duly negotiated a warehouseman's lien is limited to charges in an amount or at a rate specified on the receipt or if no charges are so specified then to a reasonable charge for storage of the goods covered by the receipt subsequent to the date of the receipt.

(2) The warehouseman may also reserve a security interest against the bailor for a maximum amount specified on the receipt for charges other than those specified in subsection (1), such as for money advanced and interest. Such a security interest is governed by the Article on Secured Transactions (Article 9).

(3) A warehouseman's lien for charges and expenses under subsection (1) or a security interest under subsection (2) is also effective against any person who so entrusted the bailor with possession of the goods that a pledge of them by him to a good faith purchaser for value would have been valid but is not effective against a person as to whom the document confers no right in the goods covered by it under Section 7–503.

(4) A warehouseman loses his lien on any goods which he voluntarily delivers or which he unjustifiably refuses to deliver.

Section 7–210. Enforcement of Warehouseman's Lien

(1) Except as provided in subsection (2), a warehouseman's lien may be enforced by public or private sale of the goods in block or in parcels, at any time or place and on any terms which are commercially reasonable, after notifying all persons known to claim an interest in the goods. Such notification must include a statement of the amount due, the nature of the proposed sale and the time and place of any public sale. The fact that a better price could have been obtained by a sale at a different time or in a different method from that selected by the warehouseman is not of itself sufficient to establish that the sale was not made in a commercially reasonable manner. If the warehouseman either sells the goods in the usual manner in any recognized market therefor, or if he sells at the price current in such market at the time of his sale, or if he has otherwise sold in conformity with commercially reasonable practices among dealers in the type of goods sold, he has sold in a commercially reasonable manner. A sale of more goods than apparently necessary to be offered to insure satisfaction of the obligation is not commercially reasonable except in cases covered by the preceding sentence.

(2) A warehouseman's lien on goods other than goods stored by a merchant in the course of his business may be enforced only as follows:

    (a) All persons known to claim an interest in the goods must be notified.

    (b) The notification must be delivered in person or sent by registered or certified letter to the last known address of any person to be notified.

(c) The notification must include an itemized statement of the claim, a description of the goods subject to the lien, a demand for payment within a specified time not less than ten days after receipt of the notification, and a conspicuous statement that unless the claim is paid within that time the goods will be advertised for sale and sold by auction at a specified time and place.

(d) The sale must conform to the terms of the notification.

(e) The sale must be held at the nearest suitable place to that where the goods are held or stored.

(f) After the expiration of the time given in the notification, an advertisement of the sale must be published once a week for two weeks consecutively in a newspaper of general circulation where the sale is to be held. The advertisement must include a description of the goods, the name of the person on whose account they are being held, and the time and place of the sale. The sale must take place at least fifteen days after the first publication. If there is no newspaper of general circulation where the sale is to be held, the advertisement must be posted at least ten days before the sale in not less than six conspicuous places in the neighborhood of the proposed sale.

(3) Before any sale pursuant to this section any person claiming a right in the goods may pay the amount necessary to satisfy the lien and the reasonable expenses incurred under this section. In that event the goods must not be sold, but must be retained by the warehouseman subject to the terms of the receipt and this Article.

(4) The warehouseman may buy at any public sale pursuant to this section.

(5) A purchaser in good faith of goods sold to enforce a warehouseman's lien takes the goods free of any rights of persons against whom the lien was valid, despite noncompliance by the warehouseman with the requirements of this section.

(6) The warehouseman may satisfy his lien from the proceeds of any sale pursuant to this section but must hold the balance, if any, for delivery on demand to any person to whom he would have been bound to deliver the goods.

(7) The rights provided by this section shall be in addition to all other rights allowed by law to a creditor against his debtor.

(8) Where a lien is on goods stored by a merchant in the course of his business the lien may be enforced in accordance with either subsection (1) or (2).

(9) The warehouseman is liable for damages caused by failure to comply with the requirements for sale under this section and in case of willful violation is liable for conversion.

PART 3

BILLS OF LADING: SPECIAL PROVISIONS

Section 7–301. Liability for Non-Receipt or Misdescription; "Said to Contain"; "Shipper's Load and Count"; Improper Handling.

(1) A consignee of a non-negotiable bill who has given value in good faith or a holder to whom a negotiable bill has been duly negotiated relying in

either case upon the description therein of the goods, or upon the date therein shown, may recover from the issuer damages caused by the misdating of the bill or the nonreceipt or misdescription of the goods, except to the extent that the document indicates that the issuer does not know whether any part or all of the goods in fact were received or conform to the description, as where the description is in terms of marks or labels or kind, quantity, or condition or the receipt or description is qualified by "contents or condition of contents of packages unknown", "said to contain", "shipper's weight, load and count" or the like, if such indication be true.

(2) When goods are loaded by an issuer who is a common carrier, the issuer must count the packages of goods if package freight and ascertain the kind and quantity if bulk freight. In such cases "shipper's weight, load and count" or other words indicating that the description was made by the shipper are ineffective except as to freight concealed by packages.

(3) When bulk freight is loaded by a shipper who makes available to the issuer adequate facilities for weighing such freight, an issuer who is a common carrier must ascertain the kind and quantity within a reasonable time after receiving the written request of the shipper to do so. In such cases "shipper's weight" or other words of like purport are ineffective.

(4) The issuer may by inserting in the bill the words "shipper's weight, load and count" or other words of like purport indicate that the goods were loaded by the shipper; and if such statement be true the issuer shall not be liable for damages caused by the improper loading. But their omission does not imply liability for such damages.

(5) The shipper shall be deemed to have guaranteed to the issuer the accuracy at the time of shipment of the description, marks, labels, number, kind, quantity, condition and weight, as furnished by him; and the shipper shall indemnify the issuer against damage caused by inaccuracies in such particulars. The right of the issuer to such indemnity shall in no way limit his responsibility and liability under the contract of carriage to any person other than the shipper.

Section 7–302. Through Bills of Lading and Similar Documents.

(1) The issuer of a through bill of lading or other document embodying an undertaking to be performed in part by persons acting as its agents or by connecting carriers is liable to anyone entitled to recover on the document for any breach by such other persons or by a connecting carrier of its obligation under the document but to the extent that the bill covers an undertaking to be performed overseas or in territory not contiguous to the continental United States or an undertaking including matters other than transportation this liability may be varied by agreement of the parties.

(2) Where goods covered by a through bill of lading or other document embodying an undertaking to be performed in part by persons other than the issuer are received by any such person, he is subject with respect to his own performance while the goods are in his possession to the obligation of the issuer. His obligation is discharged by delivery of the goods to another such person pursuant to the document, and does not include liability for breach by any other such persons or by the issuer.

(3) The issuer of such through bill of lading or other document shall be entitled to recover from the connecting carrier or such other person in possession of the goods when the breach of the obligation under the document occurred, the amount it may be required to pay to anyone entitled to recover on the document therefor, as may be evidenced by any receipt, judgment, or transcript thereof, and the amount of any expense reasonably incurred by it in defending any action brought by anyone entitled to recover on the document therefor.

Section 7–303. Diversion; Reconsignment; Change of Instructions.

(1) Unless the bill of lading otherwise provides, the carrier may deliver the goods to a person or destination other than that stated in the bill or may otherwise dispose of the goods on instructions from
- (a) the holder of a negotiable bill; or
- (b) the consignor on a non-negotiable bill notwithstanding contrary instructions from the consignee; or
- (c) the consignee on a non-negotiable bill in the absence of contrary instructions from the consignor, if the goods have arrived at the billed destination or if the consignee is in possession of the bill; or
- (d) the consignee on a non-negotiable bill if he is entitled as against the consignor to dispose of them.

(2) Unless such instructions are noted on a negotiable bill of lading, a person to whom the bill is duly negotiated can hold the bailee according to the original terms.

Section 7–304. Bills of Lading in a Set.

(1) Except where customary in overseas transportation, a bill of lading must not be issued in a set of parts. The issuer is liable for damages caused by violation of this subsection.

(2) Where a bill of lading is lawfully drawn in a set of parts, each of which is numbered and expressed to be valid only if the goods have not been delivered against any other part, the whole of the parts constitute one bill.

(3) Where a bill of lading is lawfully issued in a set of parts and different parts are negotiated to different persons, the title of the holder to whom the first due negotiation is made prevails as to both the document and the goods even though any later holder may have received the goods from the carrier in good faith and discharged the carrier's obligation by surrender of his part.

(4) Any person who negotiates or transfers a single part of a bill of lading drawn in a set is liable to holders of that part as if it were the whole set.

(5) The bailee is obliged to deliver in accordance with Part 4 of this Article against the first presented part of a bill of lading lawfully drawn in a set. Such delivery discharges the bailee's obligation on the whole bill.

Section 7–305. Destination Bills.

(1) Instead of issuing a bill of lading to the consignor at the place of shipment a carrier may at the request of the consignor procure the bill to be issued at destination or at any other place designated in the request.

(2) Upon request of anyone entitled as against the carrier to control the goods while in transit and on surrender of any outstanding bill of lading or other receipt covering such goods, the issuer may procure a substitute bill to be issued at any place designated in the request.

Section 7–306. Altered Bills of Lading.

An unauthorized alteration or filling in of a blank in a bill of lading leaves the bill enforceable according to its original tenor.

Section 7–307. Lien of Carrier.

(1) A carrier has a lien on the goods covered by a bill of lading for charges subsequent to the date of its receipt of the goods for storage or transportation (including demurrage and terminal charges) and for expenses necessary for preservation of the goods incident to their transportation or reasonably incurred in their sale pursuant to law. But against a purchaser for value of a negotiable bill of lading a carrier's lien is limited to charges stated in the bill or the applicable tariffs, or if no charges are stated then to a reasonable charge.

(2) A lien for charges and expenses under subsection (1) on goods which the carrier was required by law to receive for transportation is effective against the consignor or any person entitled to the goods unless the carrier had notice that the consignor lacked authority to subject the goods to such charges and expenses. Any other lien under subsection (1) is effective against the consignor and any person who permitted the bailor to have control or possession of the goods unless the carrier had notice that the bailor lacked such authority.

(3) A carrier loses his lien on any goods which he voluntarily delivers or which he unjustifiably refuses to deliver.

Section 7–308. Enforcement of Carrier's Lien.

(1) A carrier's lien may be enforced by public or private sale of the goods, in bloc or in parcels, at any time or place and on any terms which are commercially reasonable, after notifying all persons known to claim an interest in the goods. Such notification must include a statement of the amount due, the nature of the proposed sale and the time and place of any public sale. The fact that a better price could have been obtained by a sale at a different time or in a different method from that selected by the carrier is not of itself sufficient to establish that the sale was not made in a commercially reasonable manner. If the carrier either sells the goods in the usual manner in any recognized market therefor or if he sells at the price current in such market at the time of his sale or if he has otherwise sold in conformity with commercially reasonable practices among dealers in the type of goods sold he has sold in a commercially reasonable manner. A sale of more goods than apparently necessary to be offered to ensure satisfaction of the obligation is not commercially reasonable except in cases covered by the preceding sentence.

(2) Before any sale pursuant to this section any person claiming a right in the goods may pay the amount necessary to satisfy the lien and the reasonable expenses incurred under this section. In that event the goods must not be sold, but must be retained by the carrier subject to the terms of the bill and this Article.

(3) The carrier may buy at any public sale pursuant to this section.

(4) A purchaser in good faith of goods sold to enforce a carrier's lien takes the goods free of any rights of persons against whom the lien was valid, despite noncompliance by the carrier with the requirements of this section.

(5) The carrier may satisfy his lien from the proceeds of any sale pursuant to this section but must hold the balance, if any, for delivery on demand to any person to whom he would have been bound to deliver the goods.

(6) The rights provided by this section shall be in addition to all other rights allowed by law to a creditor against his debtor.

(7) A carrier's lien may be enforced in accordance with either subsection (1) or the procedure set forth in subsection (2) of Section 7–210.

(8) The carrier is liable for damages caused by failure to comply with the requirements for sale under this section and in case of willful violation is liable for conversion.

Section 7–309. Duty of Care; Contractual Limitation of Carrier's Liability.

(1) A carrier who issues a bill of lading whether negotiable or non-negotiable must exercise the degree of care in relation to the goods which a reasonably careful man would exercise under like circumstances. This sub-section does not repeal or change any law or rule of law which imposes liability upon a common carrier for damages not caused by its negligence.

(2) Damages may be limited by a provision that the carrier's liability shall not exceed a value stated in the document if the carrier's rates are dependent upon value and the consignor by the carrier's tariff is afforded an opportunity to declare a higher value or a value as lawfully provided in the tariff, or where no tariff is filed he is otherwise advised of such opportunity; but no such limitation is effective with respect to the carrier's liability for conversion to its own use.

(3) Reasonable provisions as to the time and manner of presenting claims and instituting actions based on the shipment may be included in a bill of lading or tariff.

PART 4

Warehouse Receipts and Bills of Lading: General Obligations

Section 7–401. Irregularities in Issue of Receipt or Bill or Conduct of Issuer.

The obligations imposed by this Article on an issuer apply to a document of title regardless of the fact that

  (a) the document may not comply with the requirements of this Article or of any other law or regulation regarding its issue, form or content; or

  (b) the issuer may have violated laws regulating the conduct of his business; or

  (c) the goods covered by the document were owned by the bailee at the time the document was issued; or

(d) the person issuing the document does not come within the definition of warehouseman if it purports to be a warehouse receipt.

Section 7–402. Duplicate Receipt or Bill; Overissue.

Neither a duplicate nor any other document of title purporting to cover goods already represented by an outstanding document of the same issuer confers any right in the goods, except as provided in the case of bills in a set, overissue of documents for fungible goods and substitutes for lost, stolen or destroyed documents. But the issuer is liable for damages caused by his overissue or failure to identify a duplicate document as such by conspicuous notation on its face.

Section 7–403. Obligation of Warehouseman or Carrier to Deliver; Excuse.

(1) The bailee must deliver the goods to a person entitled under the document who complies with subsections (2) and (3), unless and to the extent that the bailee establishes any of the following:

(a) delivery of the goods to a person whose receipt was rightful as against the claimant;

(b) damage to or delay, loss or destruction of the goods for which the bailee is not liable [, but the burden of establishing negligence in such cases is on the person entitled under the document];

Note: *The brackets in (1) (b) indicate that State enactments may differ on this point without serious damage to the principle of uniformity.*

(c) previous sale or other disposition of the goods in lawful enforcement of a lien or on warehouseman's lawful termination of storage;

(d) the exercise by a seller of his right to stop delivery pursuant to the provisions of the Article on Sales (Section 2–705);

(e) a diversion, reconsignment or other disposition pursuant to the provisions of this Article (Section 7–303) or tariff regulating such right;

(f) release, satisfaction or any other fact affording a personal defense against the claimant;

(g) any other lawful excuse.

(2) A person claiming goods covered by a document of title must satisfy the bailee's lien where the bailee so requests or where the bailee is prohibited by law from delivering the goods until the charges are paid.

(3) Unless the person claiming is one against whom the document confers no right under Sec. 7–503 (1), he must surrender for cancellation or notation of partial deliveries any outstanding negotiable document covering the goods, and the bailee must cancel the document or conspicuously note the partial delivery thereon or be liable to any person to whom the document is duly negotiated.

(4) "Person entitled under the document" means holder in the case of a negotiable document, or the person to whom delivery is to be made by the terms of or pursuant to written instructions under a non-negotiable document.

Section 7–404. No Liability for Good Faith Delivery Pursuant to Receipt or Bill.

A bailee who in good faith including observance of reasonable commercial standards has received goods and delivered or otherwise disposed of them according to the terms of the document of title or pursuant to this Article is not liable therefor. This rule applies even though the person from whom he received the goods had no authority to procure the document or to dispose of the goods and even though the person to whom he delivered the goods had no authority to receive them.

PART 5
WAREHOUSE RECEIPTS AND BILLS OF LADING: NEGOTIATION AND TRANSFER

Section 7–501. Form of Negotiation and Requirements of "Due Negotiation".

(1) A negotiable document of title running to the order of a named person is negotiated by his indorsement and delivery. After his indorsement in blank or to bearer any person can negotiate it by delivery alone.

(2) (a) A negotiable document of title is also negotiated by delivery alone when by its original terms it runs to bearer.

(b) When a document running to the order of a named person is delivered to him the effect is the same as if the document had been negotiated.

(3) Negotiation of a negotiable document of title after it has been indorsed to a specified person requires indorsement by the special indorsee as well as delivery.

(4) A negotiable document of title is "duly negotiated" when it is negotiated in the manner stated in this section to a holder who purchases it in good faith without notice of any defense against or claim to it on the part of any person and for value, unless it is established that the negotiation is not in the regular course of business or financing or involves receiving the document in settlement or payment of a money obligation.

(5) Indorsement of a non-negotiable document neither makes it negotiable nor adds to the transferee's rights.

(6) The naming in a negotiable bill of a person to be notified of the arrival of the goods does not limit the negotiability of the bill nor constitute notice to a purchaser thereof of any interest of such person in the goods.

Section 7–502. Rights Acquired by Due Negotiation.

(1) Subject to the following section and to the provisions of Section 7–205 on fungible goods, a holder to whom a negotiable document of title has been duly negotiated acquires thereby:

(a) title to the document;

(b) title to the goods;

(c) all rights accruing under the law of agency or estoppel, including rights to goods delivered to the bailee after the document was issued; and

(d) the direct obligation of the issuer to hold or deliver the goods according to the terms of the document free of any defense or claim by him except those arising under the terms of the document or under this Article. In the case of a delivery order the bailee's obligation accrues only upon acceptance and the obligation acquired by the holder is that the issuer and any indorser will procure the acceptance of the bailee.

(2) Subject to the following section, title and rights so acquired are not defeated by any stoppage of the goods represented by the document or by surrender of such goods by the bailee, and are not impaired even though the negotiation or any prior negotiation constituted a breach of duty or even though any person has been deprived of possession of the document by misrepresentation, fraud, accident, mistake, duress, loss, theft or conversion, or even though a previous sale or other transfer of the goods or document has been made to a third person.

Section 7–503. Document of Title to Goods Defeated in Certain Cases.

(1) A document of title confers no right in goods against a person who before issuance of the document had a legal interest or a perfected security interest in them and who neither

(a) delivered or entrusted them or any document of title covering them to the bailor or his nominee with actual or apparent authority to ship, store or sell or with power to obtain delivery under this Article (Section 7–403) or with power of disposition under this Act (Sections 2–403 and 9–307) or other statute or rule of law; nor

(b) acquiesced in the procurement by the bailor or his nominee of any document of title.

(2) Title to goods based upon an unaccepted delivery order is subject to the rights of anyone to whom a negotiable warehouse receipt or bill of lading covering the goods has been duly negotiated. Such a title may be defeated under the next section to the same extent as the rights of the issuer or a transferee from the issuer.

(3) Title to goods based upon a bill of lading issued to a freight forwarder is subject to the rights of anyone to whom a bill issued by the freight forwarder is duly negotiated; but delivery by the carrier in accordance with Part 4 of this Article pursuant to its own bill of lading discharges the carrier's obligation to deliver.

Section 7–504. Rights Acquired in the Absence of Due Negotiation; Effect of Diversion; Seller's Stoppage of Delivery.

(1) A transferee of a document, whether negotiable or non-negotiable, to whom the document has been delivered but not duly negotiated, acquires the title and rights which his transferor had or had actual authority to convey.

(2) In the case of a non-negotiable document, until but not after the bailee receives notification of the transfer, the rights of the transferee may be defeated

(a) by those creditors of the transferor who could treat the sale as void under Section 2–402; or

(b) by a buyer from the transferor in ordinary course of business if the bailee has delivered the goods to the buyer or received notification of his rights; or

(c) as against the bailee by good faith dealings of the bailee with the transferor.

(3) A diversion or other change of shipping instructions by the consignor in a non-negotiable bill of lading which causes the bailee not to deliver to the consignee defeats the consignee's title to the goods if they have been delivered to a buyer in ordinary course of business and in any event defeats the consignee's rights against the bailee.

(4) Delivery pursuant to a non-negotiable document may be stopped by a seller under Section 2–705, and subject to the requirement of due notification there provided. A bailee honoring the seller's instructions is entitled to be indemnified by the seller against any resulting loss or expense.

Section 7–505. Indorser Not a Guarantor for Other Parties.

The indorsement of a document of title issued by a bailee does not make the indorser liable for any default by the bailee or by previous indorsers.

Section 7–506. Delivery Without Indorsement: Right to Compel Indorsement.

The transferee of a negotiable document of title has a specifically enforceable right to have his transferor supply any necessary indorsement but the transfer becomes a negotiation only as of the time the indorsement is supplied.

Section 7–507. Warranties on Negotiation or Transfer of Receipt or Bill.

Where a person negotiates or transfers a document of title for value otherwise than as a mere intermediary under the next following section, then unless otherwise agreed he warrants to his immediate purchaser only in addition to any warranty made in selling the goods

(a) that the document is genuine; and

(b) that he has no knowledge of any fact which would impair its validity or worth; and

(c) that his negotiation or transfer is rightful and fully effective with respect to the title to the document and the goods it represents.

Section 7–508. Warranties of Collecting Bank as to Documents.

A collecting bank or other intermediary known to be entrusted with documents on behalf of another or with collection of a draft or other claim against delivery of documents warrants by such delivery of the documents only its own good faith and authority. This rule applies even though the intermediary has purchased or made advances against the claim or draft to be collected.

Section 7–509. Receipt or Bill: When Adequate Compliance With Commercial Contract.

The question whether a document is adequate to fulfill the obligations of a contract for sale or the conditions of a credit is governed by the Articles on Sales (Article 2) and on Letters of Credit (Article 5).

PART 6

WAREHOUSE RECEIPTS AND BILLS OF LADING: MISCELLANEOUS PROVISIONS

Section 7–601. Lost and Missing Documents.

(1) If a document has been lost, stolen or destroyed, a court may order delivery of the goods or issuance of a substitute document and the bailee may without liability to any person comply with such order. If the document was negotiable the claimant must post security approved by the court to indemnify any person who may suffer loss as a result of non-surrender of the document. If the document was not negotiable, such security may be required at the discretion of the court. The court may also in its discretion order payment of the bailee's reasonable costs and counsel fees.

(2) A bailee who without court order delivers goods to a person claiming under a missing negotiable document is liable to any person injured thereby, and if the delivery is not in good faith becomes liable for conversion. Delivery in good faith is not conversion if made in accordance with a filed classification or tariff or, where no classification or tariff is filed, if the claimant posts security with the bailee in an amount at least double the value of the goods at the time of posting to indemnify any person injured by the delivery who files a notice of claim within one year after the delivery.

Section 7–602. Attachment of Goods Covered by a Negotiable Document.

Except where the document was originally issued upon delivery of the goods by a person who had no power to dispose of them, no lien attaches by virtue of any judicial process to goods in the possession of a bailee for which a negotiable document of title is outstanding unless the document be first surrendered to the bailee or its negotiation enjoined, and the bailee shall not be compelled to deliver the goods pursuant to process until the document is surrendered to him or impounded by the court. One who purchases the document for value without notice of the process or injunction takes free of the lien imposed by judicial process.

Section 7–603. Conflicting Claims; Interpleader.

If more than one person claims title or possession of the goods, the bailee is excused from delivery until he has had a reasonable time to ascertain the validity of the adverse claims or to bring an action to compel all claimants to interplead and may compel such interpleader, either in defending an action for non-delivery of the goods, or by original action, whichever is appropriate.

ARTICLE 8

INVESTMENT SECURITIES

PART 1

SHORT TITLE AND GENERAL MATTERS

Section 8–101. Short Title.

This Article shall be known and may be cited as Uniform Commercial Code—Investment Securities.

Section 8–102. Definitions and Index of Definitions.

(1) In this Article unless the context otherwise requires
  (a) A "security" is an instrument which
    (i) is issued in bearer or registered form; and
    (ii) is of a type commonly dealt in upon securities exchanges or markets or commonly recognized in any area in which it is issued or dealt in as a medium for investment; and
    (iii) is either one of a class or series or by its terms is divisible into a class or series of instruments; and
    (iv) evidences a share, participation or other interest in property or in an enterprise or evidences an obligation of the issuer.
  (b) A writing which is a security is governed by this Article and not by Uniform Commercial Code-Commercial Paper even though it also meets the requirements of that Article. This Article does not apply to money.
  (c) A security is in "registered form" when it specifies a person entitled to the security or to the rights it evidences and when its transfer may be registered upon books maintained for that purpose by or on behalf of an issuer or the security so states.
  (d) A security is in "bearer form" when it runs to bearer according to its terms and not by reason of any indorsement.

(2) A "subsequent purchaser" is a person who takes other than by original issue.

(3) A "clearing corporation" is a corporation all of the capital stock of which is held by or for a national securities exchange or association registered under a statute of the United States such as the Securities Exchange Act of 1934.

(4) A "custodian bank" is any bank or trust company which is supervised and examined by state or federal authority having supervision over banks and which is acting as custodian for a clearing corporation.

(5) Other definitions applying to this Article or to specified Parts thereof and the sections in which they appear are:

"Adverse claim".	Section 8–301.
"Bona fide purchaser".	Section 8–302.
"Broker".	Section 8–303.
"Guarantee of the signature".	Section 8–402.
"Intermediary bank".	Section 4–105.
"Issuer".	Section 8–201.
"Overissue".	Section 8–104.

(6) In addition Article 1 contains general definitions and principles of construction and interpretation applicable throughout this Article.

Section 8–103. Issuer's Lien.

A lien upon a security in favor of an issuer thereof is valid against a purchaser only if the right of the issuer to such lien is noted conspicuously on the security.

Section 8–104. Effect of Overissue; "Overissue."

(1) The provisions of this Article which validate a security or compel its issue or reissue do not apply to the extent that validation, issue or reissue would result in overissue; but

(a) if an identical security which does not constitute an overissue is reasonably available for purchase, the person entitled to issue or validation may compel the issuer to purchase and deliver such a security to him against surrender of the security, if any, which he holds; or

(b) if a security is not so available for purchase, the person entitled to issue or validation may recover from the issuer the price he or the last purchaser for value paid for it with interest from the date of his demand.

(2) "Overissue" means the issue of securities in excess of the amount which the issuer has corporate power to issue.

Section 8–105. Securities Negotiable; Presumptions.

(1) Securities governed by this Article are negotiable instruments.

(2) In any action on a security

(a) unless specifically denied in the pleadings, each signature on the security or in a necessary indorsement is admitted;

(b) when the effectiveness of a signature is put in issue the burden of establishing it is on the party claiming under the signature but the signature is presumed to be genuine or authorized;

(c) when signatures are admitted or established production of the instrument entitles a holder to recover on it unless the defendant establishes a defense or a defect going to the validity of the security; and

(d) after it is shown that a defense or defect exists the plaintiff has the burden of establishing that he or some person under whom he claims is a person against whom the defense or defect is ineffective (Section 8–202).

Section 8–106. Applicability.

The validity of a security and the rights and duties of the issuer with respect to registration of transfer are governed by the law (including the conflict of laws rules) of the jurisdiction of organization of the issuer.

Section 8–107. Securities Deliverable; Action for Price.

(1) Unless otherwise agreed and subject to any applicable law or regulation respecting short sales, a person obligated to deliver securities may deliver any security of the specified issue in bearer form or registered in the name of the transferee or indorsed to him or in blank.

(2) When the buyer fails to pay the price as it comes due under a contract of sale the seller may recover the price

(a) of securities accepted by the buyer; and

(b) of other securities if efforts at their resale would be unduly burdensome or if there is no readily available market for their resale.

PART 2

ISSUE—ISSUER

Section 8–201. "Issuer."

(1) With respect to obligations on or defenses to a security "issuer" includes a person who

(a) places or authorizes the placing of his name on a security (otherwise than as authenticating trustee, registrar, transfer agent or the like) to evidence that it represents a share, participation or other interest in his property or in an enterprise or to evidence his duty to perform an obligation evidenced by the security; or

(b) directly or indirectly creates fractional interests in his rights or property which fractional interests are evidenced by securities; or

(c) becomes responsible for or in place of any other person described as an issuer in this section.

(2) With respect to obligations on or defenses to a security a guarantor is an issuer to the extent of his guaranty whether or not his obligation is noted on the security.

(3) With respect to registration of transfer (Part 4 of this Article) "issuer" means a person on whose behalf transfer books are maintained.

Section 8–202. Issuer's Responsibility and Defenses; Notice of Defect or Defense.

(1) Even against a purchaser for value and without notice, the terms of a security include those stated on the security and those made part of the security by reference to another instrument, indenture or document or to a constitution, statute, ordinance, rule, regulation, order or the like to the extent that the terms so referred to do not conflict with the stated terms. Such a reference does not of itself charge a purchaser for value with notice of a defect going to the validity of the security even though the security expressly states that a person accepting it admits such notice.

(2) (a) A security other than one issued by a government or governmental agency or unit even though issued with a defect going to its validity is valid in the hands of a purchaser for value and without notice of the particular defect unless the defect involves a violation of constitutional provisions in which case the security is valid in the hands of a subsequent purchaser for value and without notice of the defect.

(b) The rule of subparagraph (a) applies to an issuer which is a government or governmental agency or unit only if either there has been substantial compliance with the legal requirements governing the issue or the issuer has received a substantial consideration for the issue as a whole or for the particular security and a stated purpose of the issue is one for which the issuer has power to borrow money or issue the security.

(3) Except as otherwise provided in the case of certain unauthorized

signatures on issue (Section 8–205), lack of genuineness of a security is a complete defense even against a purchaser for value and without notice.

(4) All other defenses of the issuer including nondelivery and conditional delivery of the security are ineffective against a purchaser for value who has taken without notice of the particular defense.

(5) Nothing in this section shall be construed to affect the right of a party to a "when, as and if issued" or a "when distributed" contract to cancel the contract in the event of a material change in the character of the security which is the subject of the contract or in the plan or arrangement pursuant to which such security is to be issued or distributed.

Section 8–203. Staleness as Notice of Defects or Defenses.

(1) After an act or event which creates a right to immediate performance of the principal obligation evidenced by the security or which sets a date on or after which the security is to be presented or surrendered for redemption or exchange, a purchaser is charged with notice of any defect in its issue or defense of the issuer

   (a) if the act or event is one requiring the payment of money or the delivery of securities or both on presentation or surrender of the security and such funds or securities are available on the date set for payment or exchange and he takes the security more than one year after that date; and

   (b) if the act or event is not covered by paragraph (a) and he takes the security more than two years after the date set for surrender or presentation or the date on which such performance became due.

(2) A call which has been revoked is not within subsection (1).

Section 8–204. Effect of Issuer's Restrictions on Transfer.

Unless noted conspicuously on the security a restriction on transfer imposed by the issuer even though otherwise lawful is ineffective except against a person with actual knowledge of it.

Section 8–205. Effect of Unauthorized Signature on Issue.

An unauthorized signature placed on a security prior to or in the course of issue is ineffective except that the signature is effective in favor of a purchaser for value and without notice of the lack of authority if the signing has been done by

   (a) an authenticating trustee, registrar, transfer agent or other person entrusted by the issuer with the signing of the security or of similar securities or their immediate preparation for signing; or

   (b) an employee of the issuer or of any of the foregoing entrusted with responsible handling of the security.

Section 8–206. Completion or Alteration of Instrument.

(1) Where a security contains the signatures necessary to its issue or transfer but is incomplete in any other respect

   (a) any person may complete it by filling in the blanks as authorized; and

(b) even though the blanks are incorrectly filled in, the security as completed is enforceable by a purchaser who took it for value and without notice of such incorrectness.

(2) A complete security which has been improperly altered even though fraudulently remains enforceable but only according to its original terms.

Section 8–207. Rights of Issuer With Respect to Registered Owners.

(1) Prior to due presentment for registration of transfer of a security in registered form the issuer or indenture trustee may treat the registered owner as the person exclusively entitled to vote, to receive notifications and otherwise to exercise all the rights and powers of an owner.

(2) Nothing in this Article shall be construed to affect the liability of the registered owner of a security for calls, assessments or the like.

Section 8–208. Effect of Signature of Authenticating Trustee, Registrar or Transfer Agent.

(1) A person placing his signature upon a security as authenticating trustee, registrar, transfer agent or the like warrants to a purchaser for value without notice of the particular defect that
(a) the security is genuine; and
(b) his own participation in the issue of the security is within his capacity and within the scope of the authorization received by him from the issuer; and
(c) he has reasonable grounds to believe that the security is in the form and within the amount the issuer is authorized to issue.

(2) Unless otherwise agreed, a person by so placing his signature does not assume responsibility for the validity of the security in other respects.

PART 3

PURCHASE

Section 8–301. Rights Acquired by Purchaser; "Adverse Claim"; Title Acquired by Bona Fide Purchaser.

(1) Upon delivery of a security the purchaser acquires the rights in the security which his transferor had or had actual authority to convey except that a purchaser who has himself been a party to any fraud or illegality affecting the security or who as a prior holder had notice of an adverse claim cannot improve his position by taking from a later bona fide purchaser. "Adverse claim" includes a claim that a transfer was or would be wrongful or that a particular adverse person is the owner of or has an interest in the security.

(2) A bona fide purchaser in addition to acquiring the rights of a purchaser also acquires the security free of any adverse claim.

(3) A purchaser of a limited interest acquires rights only to the extent of the interest purchased.

Section 8–302. "Bona Fide Purchaser."

A "bona fide purchaser" is a purchaser for value in good faith and without notice of any adverse claim who takes delivery of a security in bearer form or of one in registered form issued to him or indorsed to him or in blank.

Section 8–303. "Broker."

"Broker" means a person engaged for all or part of his time in the business of buying and selling securities, who in the transaction concerned acts for, or buys a security from or sells a security to a customer. Nothing in this Article determines the capacity in which a person acts for purposes of any other statute or rule to which such person is subject.

Section 8–304. Notice to Purchaser of Adverse Claims.

(1) A purchaser (including a broker for the seller or buyer but excluding an intermediary bank) of a security is charged with notice of adverse claims if
  (a) the security whether in bearer or registered form has been indorsed "for collection" or "for surrender" or for some other purpose not involving transfer; or
  (b) the security is in bearer form and has on it an unambiguous statement that it is the property of a person other than the transferor. The mere writing of a name on a security is not such a statement.

(2) The fact that the purchaser (including a broker for the seller or buyer) has notice that the security is held for a third person or is registered in the name of or indorsed by a fiduciary does not create a duty of inquiry into the rightfulness of the transfer or constitute notice of adverse claims. If, however, the purchaser (excluding an intermediary bank) has knowledge that the proceeds are being used or that the transaction is for the individual benefit of the fiduciary or otherwise in breach of duty, the purchaser is charged with notice of adverse claims.

Section 8–305. Staleness as Notice of Adverse Claims.

An act or event which creates a right to immediate performance of the principal obligation evidenced by the security or which sets a date on or after which the security is to be presented or surrendered for redemption or exchange does not of itself constitute any notice of adverse claims except in the case of a purchase
  (a) after one year from any date set for such presentment or surrender for redemption or exchange; or
  (b) after six months from any date set for payment of money against presentation or surrender of the security if funds are available for payment on that date.

Section 8–306. Warranties on Presentment and Transfer.

(1) A person who presents a security for registration of transfer or for payment or exchange warrants to the issuer that he is entitled to the registration, payment or exchange. But a purchaser for value without notice of adverse claims who receives a new, reissued or re-registered security on registration of transfer warrants only that he has no knowledge of any unauthorized signature (Section 8–311) in a necessary indorsement.

(2) A person by transferring a security to a purchaser for value warrants only that
  (a) his transfer is effective and rightful; and

(b) the security is genuine and has not been materially altered; and

(c) he knows no fact which might impair the validity of the security.

(3) Where a security is delivered by an intermediary known to be entrusted with delivery of the security on behalf of another or with collection of a draft or other claim against such delivery, the intermediary by such delivery warrants only his own good faith and authority even though he has purchased or made advances against the claim to be collected against the delivery.

(4) A pledgee or other holder for security who redelivers the security received, or after payment and on order of the debtor delivers that security to a third person makes only the warranties of an intermediary under subsection (3).

(5) A broker gives to his customer and to the issuer and a purchaser the warranties provided in this section and has the rights and privileges of a purchaser under this section. The warranties of and in favor of the broker acting as an agent are in addition to applicable warranties given by and in favor of his customer.

Section 8–307. Effect of Delivery Without Indorsement; Right to Compel Indorsement.

Where a security in registered form has been delivered to a purchaser without a necessary indorsement he may become a bona fide purchaser only as of the time the indorsement is supplied, but against the transferor the transfer is complete upon delivery and the purchaser has a specifically enforceable right to have any necessary indorsement supplied.

Section 8–308. Indorsement, How Made; Special Indorsement; Indorser Not a Guarantor; Partial Assignment.

(1) An indorsement of a security in registered form is made when an appropriate person signs on it or on a separate document an assignment or transfer of the security or a power to assign or transfer it or when the signature of such person is written without more upon the back of the security.

(2) An indorsement may be in blank or special. An indorsement in blank includes an indorsement to bearer. A special indorsement specifies the person to whom the security is to be transferred, or who has power to transfer it. A holder may convert a blank indorsement into a special indorsement.

(3) "An appropriate person" in subsection (1) means

(a) the person specified by the security or by special indorsement to be entitled to the security; or

(b) where the person so specified is described as a fiduciary but is no longer serving in the described capacity,—either that person or his successor; or

(c) where the security or indorsement so specifies more than one person as fiduciaries and one or more are no longer serving in the described capacity,—the remaining fiduciary or fiduciaries, whether or not a successor has been appointed or qualified; or

(d) where the person so specified is an individual and is without capacity to act by virtue of death, incompetence, infancy or otherwise,—his executor, administrator, guardian or like fiduciary; or

(e) where the security or indorsement so specifies more than one person as tenants by the entirety or with right of survivorship and by reason of death all cannot sign,—the survivor or survivors; or

(f) a person having power to sign under applicable law or controlling instrument; or

(g) to the extent that any of the foregoing persons may act through an agent,—his authorized agent.

(4) Unless otherwise agreed the indorser by his indorsement assumes no obligation that the security will be honored by the issuer.

(5) An indorsement purporting to be only of part of a security representing units intended by the issuer to be separately transferable is effective to the extent of the indorsement.

(6) Whether the person signing is appropriate is determined as of the date of signing and an indorsement by such a person does not become unauthorized for the purposes of this Article by virtue of any subsequent change of circumstances.

(7) Failure of a fiduciary to comply with a controlling instrument or with the law of the state having jurisdiction of the fiduciary relationship, including any law requiring the fiduciary to obtain court approval of the transfer, does not render his indorsement unauthorized for the purposes of this Article.

Section 8–309. Effect of Indorsement Without Delivery.

An indorsement of a security whether special or in blank does not constitute a transfer until delivery of the security on which it appears or if the indorsement is on a separate document until delivery of both the document and the security.

Section 8–310. Indorsement of Security in Bearer Form.

An indorsement of a security in bearer form may give notice of adverse claims (Section 8–304) but does not otherwise affect any right to registration the holder may possess.

Section 8–311. Effect of Unauthorized Indorsement.

Unless the owner has ratified an unauthorized indorsement or is otherwise precluded from asserting its ineffectiveness

(a) he may assert its ineffectiveness against the issuer or any purchaser other than a purchaser for value and without notice of adverse claims who has in good faith received a new, reissued or re-registered security on registration of transfer; and

(b) an issuer who registers the transfer of a security upon the unauthorized indorsement is subject to liability for improper registration (Section 8–404).

Section 8–312. Effect of Guaranteeing Signature or Indorsement.

(1) Any person guaranteeing a signature of an indorser of a security warrants that at the time of signing

(a) the signature was genuine; and

(b) the signer was an appropriate person to indorse (Section 8–308); and

(c) the signer had legal capacity to sign.

But the guarantor does not otherwise warrant the rightfulness of the particular transfer.

(2) Any person may guarantee an indorsement of a security and by so doing warrants not only the signature (subsection 1) but also the rightfulness of the particular transfer in all respects. But no issuer may require a guarantee of indorsement as a condition to registration of transfer.

(3) The foregoing warranties are made to any person taking or dealing with the security in reliance on the guarantee and the guarantor is liable to such person for any loss resulting from breach of the warranties.

Section 8–313. When Delivery to the Purchaser Occurs; Purchaser's Broker as Holder.

(1) Delivery to a purchaser occurs when
   (a) he or a person designated by him acquires possession of a security; or
   (b) his broker acquires possession of a security specially indorsed to or issued in the name of the purchaser; or
   (c) his broker sends him confirmation of the purchase and also by book entry or otherwise identifies a specific security in the broker's possession as belonging to the purchaser; or
   (d) with respect to an identified security to be delivered while still in the possession of a third person when that person acknowledges that he holds for the purchaser; or
   (e) appropriate entries on the books of a clearing corporation are made under Section 8–320.

(2) The purchaser is the owner of a security held for him by his broker, but is not the holder except as specified in subparagraphs (b), (c) and (e) of subsection (1). Where a security is part of a fungible bulk the purchaser is the owner of a proportionate property interest in the fungible bulk.

(3) Notice of an adverse claim received by the broker or by the purchaser after the broker takes delivery as a holder for value is not effective either as to the broker or as to the purchaser. However, as between the broker and the purchaser the purchaser may demand delivery of an equivalent security as to which no notice of an adverse claim has been received.

Section 8–314. Duty to Deliver, When Completed.

(1) Unless otherwise agreed where a sale of a security is made on an exchange or otherwise through brokers
   (a) the selling customer fulfills his duty to deliver when he places such a security in the possession of the selling broker or of a person designated by the broker or if requested causes an acknowledgment to be made to the selling broker that it is held for him; and

(b) the selling broker including a correspondent broker acting for a selling customer fulfills his duty to deliver by placing the security or a like security in the possession of the buying broker or a person designated by him or by effecting clearance of the sale in accordance with the rules of the exchange on which the transaction took place.

(2) Except as otherwise provided in this section and unless otherwise agreed, a transferor's duty to deliver a security under a contract of purchase is not fulfilled until he places the security in form to be negotiated by the purchaser in the possession of the purchaser or of a person designated by him or at the purchaser's request causes an acknowledgment to be made to the purchaser that it is held for him. Unless made on an exchange a sale to a broker purchasing for his own account is within this subsection and not within subsection (1).

Section 8–315. Action Against Purchaser Based Upon Wrongful Transfer.

(1) Any person against whom the transfer of a security is wrongful for any reason, including his incapacity, may against anyone except a bona fide purchaser reclaim possession of the security or obtain possession of any new security evidencing all or part of the same rights or have damages.

(2) If the transfer is wrongful because of an unauthorized indorsement, the owner may also reclaim or obtain possession of the security or new security even from a bona fide purchaser if the ineffectiveness of the purported indorsement can be asserted against him under the provisions of this Article on unauthorized indorsements (Section 8–311).

(3) The right to obtain or reclaim possession of a security may be specifically enforced and its transfer enjoined and the security impounded pending the litigation.

Section 8–316. Purchaser's Right to Requisites for Registration of Transfer on Books.

Unless otherwise agreed the transferor must on due demand supply his purchaser with any proof of his authority to transfer or with any other requisite which may be necessary to obtain registration of the transfer of the security but if the transfer is not for value a transferor need not do so unless the purchaser furnishes the necessary expenses. Failure to comply with a demand made within a reasonable time gives the purchaser the right to reject or rescind the transfer.

Section 8–317. Attachment or Levy Upon Security.

(1) No attachment or levy upon a security or any share or other interest evidenced thereby which is outstanding shall be valid until the security is actually seized by the officer making the attachment or levy but a security which has been surrendered to the issuer may be attached or levied upon at the source.

(2) A creditor whose debtor is the owner of a security shall be entitled to such aid from courts of appropriate jurisdiction, by injunction or otherwise, in reaching such security or in satisfying the claim by means thereof as is allowed at law or in equity in regard to property which cannot readily be attached or levied upon by ordinary legal process.

Section 8–318. No Conversion by Good Faith Delivery.

An agent or bailee who in good faith (including observance of reasonable commercial standards if he is in the business of buying, selling or otherwise dealing with securities) has received securities and sold, pledged or delivered them according to the instructions of his principal is not liable for conversion or for participation in breach of fiduciary duty although the principal had no right to dispose of them.

Section 8–319. Statute of Frauds.

A contract for the sale of securities is not enforceable by way of action or defense unless

(a) there is some writing signed by the party against whom enforcement is sought or by his authorized agent or broker sufficient to indicate that a contract has been made for sale of a stated quantity of described securities at a defined or stated price; or

(b) delivery of the security has been accepted or payment has been made but the contract is enforceable under this provision only to the extent of such delivery or payment; or

(c) within a reasonable time a writing in confirmation of the sale or purchase and sufficient against the sender under paragraph (a) has been received by the party against whom enforcement is sought and he has failed to send written objection to its contents within ten days after its receipt; or

(d) the party against whom enforcement is sought admits in his pleading, testimony or otherwise in court that a contract was made for sale of a stated quantity of described securities at a defined or stated price.

Section 8–320. Transfer or Pledge within a Central Depository System.

(1) If a security

(a) is in the custody of a clearing corporation or of a custodian bank or a nominee of either subject to the instructions of the clearing corporation; and

(b) is in bearer form or indorsed in blank by an appropriate person or registered in the name of the clearing corporation or custodian bank or a nominee of either; and

(c) is shown on the account of a transferor or pledgor on the books of the clearing corporation;

then, in addition to other methods, a transfer or pledge of the security or any interest therein may be effected by the making of appropriate entries on the books of the clearing corporation reducing the account of the transferor or pledgor and increasing the account of the transferee or pledgee by the amount of the obligation or the number of shares or rights transferred or pledged.

(2) Under this section entries may be with respect to like securities or interests therein as a part of a fungible bulk and may refer merely to a quantity of a particular security without reference to the name of the registered owner, certificate or bond number or the like and, in appropriate cases, may be on a net basis taking into account other transfers or pledges of the same security.

(3) A transfer or pledge under this section has the effect of a delivery of a security in bearer form or duly indorsed in blank (Section 8–301) representing the amount of the obligation or the number of shares or rights transferred or pledged. If a pledge or the creation of a security interest is intended, the making of entries has the effect of a taking of delivery by the pledgee or a secured party (Sections 9–304 and 9–305). A transferee or pledgee under this section is a holder.

(4) A transfer or pledge under this section does not constitute a registration of transfer under Part 4 of this Article.

(5) That entries made on the books of the clearing corporation as provided in subsection (1) are not appropriate does not affect the validity or effect of the entries nor the liabilities or obligations of the clearing corporation to any person adversely affected thereby.

PART 4

REGISTRATION

Section 8–401. Duty of Issuer to Register Transfer.

(1) Where a security in registered form is presented to the issuer with a request to register transfer, the issuer is under a duty to register the transfer as requested if

(a) the security is indorsed by the appropriate person or persons (Section 8–308); and

(b) reasonable assurance is given that those indorsements are genuine and effective (Section 8–402); and

(c) the issuer has no duty to inquire into adverse claims or has discharged any such duty (Section 8–403); and

(d) any applicable law relating to the collection of taxes has been complied with; and

(e) the transfer is in fact rightful or is to a bona fide purchaser.

(2) Where an issuer is under a duty to register a transfer of a security the issuer is also liable to the person presenting it for registration or his principal for loss resulting from any unreasonable delay in registration or from failure or refusal to register the transfer.

Section 8–402. Assurance that Indorsements Are Effective.

(1) The issuer may require the following assurance that each necessary indorsement (Section 8–308) is genuine and effective

(a) in all cases, a guarantee of the signature (subsection (1) of Section 8–312) of the person indorsing; and

(b) where the indorsement is by an agent, appropriate assurance of authority to sign;

(c) where the indorsement is by a fiduciary, appropriate evidence of appointment or incumbency;

(d) where there is more than one fiduciary, reasonable assurance that all who are required to sign have done so; and

(e) where the indorsement is by a person not covered by any of the foregoing, assurance appropriate to the case corresponding as nearly as may be to the foregoing.

(2) A "guarantee of the signature" in subsection (1) means a guarantee signed by or on behalf of a person reasonably believed by the issuer to be responsible. The issuer may adopt standards with respect to responsibility provided such standards are not manifestly unreasonable.

(3) "Appropriate evidence of appointment or incumbency" in subsection (1) means

    (a) in the case of a fiduciary appointed or qualified by a court, a certificate issued by or under the direction or supervision of that court or an officer thereof and dated within sixty days before the date of presentation for transfer; or

    (b) in any other case, a copy of a document showing the appointment or a certificate issued by or on behalf of a person reasonably believed by the issuer to be responsible or, in the absence of such a document or certificate, other evidence reasonably deemed by the issuer to be appropriate. The issuer may adopt standards with respect to such evidence provided such standards are not manifestly unreasonable. The issuer is not charged with notice of the contents of any document obtained pursuant to this paragraph (b) except to the extent that the contents relate directly to the appointment or incumbency.

(4) The issuer may elect to require reasonable assurance beyond that specified in this section but if it does so and for a purpose other than that specified in subsection 3(b) both requires and obtains a copy of a will, trust, indenture, articles of co-partnership, by-laws or other controlling instrument it is charged with notice of all matters contained therein affecting the transfer.

Section 8–403. Limited Duty of Inquiry.

(1) An issuer to whom a security is presented for registration is under a duty to inquire into adverse claims if

    (a) a written notification of an adverse claim is received at a time and in a manner which affords the issuer a reasonable opportunity to act on it prior to the issuance of a new, reissued or re-registered security and the notification identifies the claimant, the registered owner and the issue of which the security is a part and provides an address for communications directed to the claimant; or

    (b) the issuer is charged with notice of an adverse claim from a controlling instrument which it has elected to require under subsection (4) of Section 8–402.

(2) The issuer may discharge any duty of inquiry by any reasonable means, including notifying an adverse claimant by registered or certified mail at the address furnished by him or if there be no such address at his residence or regular place of business that the security has been presented for registration of transfer by a named person, and that the transfer will be registered unless within thirty days from the date of mailing the notification, either

    (a) an appropriate restraining order, injunction or other process issues from a court of competent jurisdiction; or

    (b) an indemnity bond sufficient in the issuer's judgment to protect the issuer and any transfer agent, registrar or other agent of the issuer involved, from any loss which it or they may suffer by complying with the adverse claim is filed with the issuer.

(3) Unless an issuer is charged with notice of an adverse claim from a controlling instrument which it has elected to require under subsection (4) of Section 8–402 or receives notification of an adverse claim under subsection (1) of this section, where a security presented for registration is indorsed by the appropriate person or persons the issuer is under no duty to inquire into adverse claims. In particular

(a) an issuer registering a security in the name of a person who is a fiduciary or who is described as a fiduciary is not bound to inquire into the existence, extent, or correct description of the fiduciary relationship and thereafter the issuer may assume without inquiry that the newly registered owner continues to be the fiduciary until the issuer receives written notice that the fiduciary is no longer acting as such with respect to the particular security;

(b) an issuer registering transfer on an indorsement by a fiduciary is not bound to inquire whether the transfer is made in compliance with a controlling instrument or with the law of the state having jurisdiction of the fiduciary relationship, including any law requiring the fiduciary to obtain court approval of the transfer; and

(c) the issuer is not charged with notice of the contents of any court record or file or other recorded or unrecorded document even though the document is in its possession and even though the transfer is made on the indorsement of a fiduciary to the fiduciary himself or to his nominee.

Section 8–404. Liability and Non-Liability for Registration.

(1) Except as otherwise provided in any law relating to the collection of taxes, the issuer is not liable to the owner or any other person suffering loss as a result of the registration of a transfer of a security if

(a) there were on or with the security the necessary indorsements (Section 8–308); and

(b) the issuer had no duty to inquire into adverse claims or has discharged any such duty (Section 8–403).

(2) Where an issuer has registered a transfer of a security to a person not entitled to it the issuer on demand must deliver a like security to the true owner unless

(a) the registration was pursuant to subsection (1); or

(b) the owner is precluded from asserting any claim for registering the transfer under subsection (1) of the following section; or

(c) such delivery would result in overissue, in which case the issuer's liability is governed by Section 8–104.

Section 8–405. Lost, Destroyed and Stolen Securities.

(1) Where a security has been lost, apparently destroyed or wrongfully taken and the owner fails to notify the issuer of that fact within a reasonable time after he has notice of it and the issuer registers a transfer of the security

before receiving such a notification, the owner is precluded from asserting against the issuer any claim for registering the transfer under the preceding section or any claim to a new security under this section.

(2) Where the owner of a security claims that the security has been lost, destroyed or wrongfully taken, the issuer must issue a new security in place of the original security if the owner (a) so requests before the issuer has notice that the security has been acquired by a bona fide purchaser; and (b) files with the issuer a sufficient indemnity bond; and (c) satisfies any other reasonable requirements imposed by the issuer.

(3) If, after the issue of the new security, a bona fide purchaser of the original security presents it for registration of transfer, the issuer must register the transfer unless registration would result in overissue, in which event the issuer's liability is governed by Section 8–104. In addition to any rights on the indemnity bond, the issuer may recover the new security from the person to whom it was issued or any person taking under him except a bona fide purchaser.

Section 8–406. Duty of Authenticating Trustee, Transfer Agent or Registrar.

(1) Where a person acts as authenticating trustee, transfer agent, registrar, or other agent for an issuer in the registration of transfers of its securities or in the issue of new securities or in the cancellation of surrendered securities

(a) he is under a duty to the issuer to exercise good faith and due diligence in performing his functions; and

(b) he has with regard to the particular functions he performs the same obligation to the holder or owner of the security and has the same rights and privileges as the issuer has in regard to those functions.

(2) Notice to an authenticating trustee, transfer agent, registrar or other such agent is notice to the issuer with respect to the functions performed by the agent.

ARTICLE 9

SECURED TRANSACTIONS; SALES OF ACCOUNTS AND CHATTEL PAPER

PART 1

SHORT TITLE, APPLICABILITY AND DEFINITIONS

Section 9–101. Short Title.

This Article shall be known and may be cited as Uniform Commercial Code —Secured Transactions.

Section 9–102. Policy and Subject Matter of Article.

(1) Except as otherwise provided in Section 9–104 on excluded transactions, this Article applies

(a) to any transaction (regardless of its form) which is intended to create a security interest in personal property or fixtures including goods, documents, instruments, general intangibles, chattel paper or accounts; and also

(b) to any sale of accounts or chattel paper.

(2) This Article applies to security interests created by contract including pledge, assignment, chattel mortgage, chattel trust, trust deed, factor's lien, equipment trust, conditional sale, trust receipt, other lien or title retention contract and lease or consignment intended as security. This Article does not apply to statutory liens except as provided in Section 9–310.

(3) The application of this Article to a security interest in a secured obligation is not affected by the fact that the obligation is itself secured by a transaction or interest to which this Article does not apply.

Note: *The adoption of this Article should be accompanied by the repeal of existing statutes dealing with conditional sales, trust receipts, factor's liens where the factor is given a non-possessory lien, chattel mortgages, crop mortgages, mortgages on railroad equipment, assignment of accounts and generally statutes regulating security interests in personal property.*

Where the state has a retail installment selling act or small loan act, that legislation should be carefully examined to determine what changes in those acts are needed to conform them to this Article. This Article primarily sets out rules defining rights of a secured party against persons dealing with the debtor; it does not prescribe regulations and controls which may be necessary to curb abuses arising in the small loan business or in the financing of consumer purchases on credit. Accordingly there is no intention to repeal existing regulatory acts in those fields by enactment or re-enactment of Article 9. See Section 9–203(4) and the Note thereto.

Section 9–103. Perfection of Security Interests in Multiple State Transactions.

(1) Documents, instruments and ordinary goods.

(a) This subsection applies to documents and instruments and to goods other than those covered by a certificate of title described in subsection (2), mobile goods described in subsection (3), and minerals described in subsection (5).

(b) Except as otherwise provided in this subsection, perfection and the effect of perfection or non-perfection of a security interest in collateral are governed by the law of the jurisdiction where the collateral is when the last event occurs on which is based the assertion that the security interest is perfected or unperfected.

(c) If the parties to a transaction creating a purchase money security interest in goods in one jurisdiction understand at the time that the security interest attaches that the goods will be kept in another jurisdiction, then the law of the other jurisdiction governs the perfection and the effect of perfection or non-perfection of the security interest from the time it attaches until thirty days after the debtor receives possession of the goods and thereafter if the goods are taken to the other jurisdiction before the end of the thirty-day period.

(d) When collateral is brought into and kept in this state while subject to a security interest perfected under the law of the jurisdiction from which the collateral was removed, the security interest remains perfected, but if action is required by Part 3 of this Article to perfect the security interest,

(i) if the action is not taken before the expiration of the period of perfection in the other jurisdiction or the end of four months after the collateral is brought into this state, whichever period first expires, the security interest becomes unperfected at the end of that period and is thereafter deemed to have been unperfected as against a person who became a purchaser after removal;

(ii) if the action is taken before the expiration of the period specified in subparagraph (i), the security interest continues perfected thereafter;

(iii) for the purpose of priority over a buyer of consumer goods (subsection (2) of Section 9–307), the period of the effectiveness of a filing in the jurisdiction from which the collateral is removed is governed by the rules with respect to perfection in subparagraphs (i) and (ii).

(2) Certificate of title.

(a) This subsection applies to goods covered by a certificate of title issued under a statute of this state or of another jurisdiction under the law of which indication of a security interest on the certificate is required as a condition of perfection.

(b) Except as otherwise provided in this subsection, perfection and the effect of perfection or non-perfection of the security interest are governed by the law (including the conflict of laws rules) of the jurisdiction issuing the certificate until four months after the goods are removed from that jurisdiction and thereafter until the goods are registered in another jurisdiction, but in any event not beyond surrender of the certificate. After the expiration of that period, the goods are not covered by the certificate of title within the meaning of this section.

(c) Except with respect to the rights of a buyer described in the next paragraph, a security interest, perfected in another jurisdiction otherwise than by notation on a certificate of title, in goods brought into this state and thereafter covered by a certificate of title issued by this state is subject to the rules stated in paragraph (d) of subsection (1).

(d) If goods are brought into this state while a security interest therein is perfected in any manner under the law of the jurisdiction from which the goods are removed and a certificate of title is issued by this state and the certificate does not show that the goods are subject to the security interest or that they may be subject to security interests not shown on the certificate, the security interest is subordinate to the rights of a buyer of the goods who is not in the business of selling goods of that kind to the extent that he gives value and receives delivery of the goods after issuance of the certificate and without knowledge of the security interest.

(3) Accounts, general intangibles and mobile goods.

(a) This subsection applies to accounts (other than an account described in subsection (5) on minerals) and general intangibles and to goods which are mobile and which are of a type normally used in more than one jurisdiction, such as motor vehicles, trailers, rolling stock, airplanes, shipping containers, road building and construction machinery and commercial harvesting machinery and the like, if the goods are equipment or are inventory leased or held for lease by the debtor to others, and are not covered by a certificate of title described in subsection (2).

(b) The law (including the conflict of laws rules) of the jurisdiction in which the debtor is located governs the perfection and the effect of perfection or non-perfection of the security interest.

(c) If, however, the debtor is located in a jurisdiction which is not a part of the United States, and which does not provide for perfection of the security interest by filing or recording in that jurisdiction, the law of the jurisdiction in the United States in which the debtor has its major executive office in the United States governs the perfection and the effect of perfection or non-perfection of the security interest through filing. In the alternative, if the debtor is located in a jurisdiction which is not a part of the United States or Canada and the collateral is accounts or general intangibles for money due or to become due, the security interest may be perfected by notification to the account debtor. As used in this paragraph, "United States" includes its territories and possessions and the Commonwealth of Puerto Rico.

(d) A debtor shall be deemed located at his place of business if he has one, at his chief executive office if he has more than one place of business, otherwise at his residence. If, however, the debtor is a foreign air carrier under the Federal Aviation Act of 1958, as amended, it shall be deemed located at the designated office of the agent upon whom service of process may be made on behalf of the foreign air carrier.

(e) A security interest perfected under the law of the jurisdiction of the location of the debtor is perfected until the expiration of four months after a change of the debtor's location to another jurisdiction, or until perfection would have ceased by the law of the first jurisdiction, whichever period first expires. Unless perfected in the new jurisdiction before the end of that period, it becomes unperfected thereafter and is deemed to have been unperfected as against a person who became a purchaser after the change.

(4) Chattel paper.

The rules stated for goods in subsection (1) apply to a possessory security interest in chattel paper. The rules stated for accounts in subsection (3) apply to a non-possessory security interest in chattel paper, but the security interest may not be perfected by notification to the account debtor.

(5) Minerals.

Perfection and the effect of perfection or non-perfection of a security interest which is created by a debtor who has an interest in minerals or the like (including oil and gas) before extraction and which attaches thereto as extracted, or which attaches to an account resulting from the sale thereof at the wellhead or minehead are governed by the law (including the conflict of laws rules) of the jurisdiction wherein the wellhead or minehead is located.

Section 9–104. Transactions Excluded from Article.

This Article does not apply

      (a) to a security interest subject to any statute of the United States to the extent that such statute governs the rights of parties to and third parties affected by transactions in particular types of property; or

      (b) to a landlord's lien; or

(c) to a lien given by statute or other rule of law for services or materials except as provided in Section 9–310 on priority of such liens; or

(d) to a transfer of a claim for wages, salary or other compensation of an employee; or

(e) to a transfer by a government or governmental sub-division or agency; or

(f) to a sale of accounts or chattel paper as part of a sale of the business out of which they arose, or an assignment of accounts or chattel paper which is for the purpose of collection only, or a transfer of a right to payment under a contract to an assignee who is also to do the performance under the contract or a transfer of a single account to an assignee in whole or partial satisfaction of a preexisting indebtedness; or

(g) to a transfer of an interest in or claim in or under any policy of insurance, except as provided with respect to proceeds (Section 9–306) and priorities in proceeds (Section 9–312); or

(h) to a right represented by a judgment (other than a judgment taken on a right to payment which was collateral); or

(i) to any right of set-off; or

(j) except to the extent that provision is made for fixtures in Section 9–313, to the creation or transfer of an interest in or lien on real estate, including a lease or rents thereunder; or

(k) to a transfer in whole or in part of any claim arising out of tort; or

(l) to a transfer of an interest in any deposit account (subsection (1) of of Section 9–105), except as provided with respect to proceeds (Section 9–306) and priorities in proceeds (Section 9–312).

Section 9–105. Definitions and Index of Definitions.

(1) In this Article unless the context otherwise requires:

(a) "Account debtor" means the person who is obligated on an account, chattel paper or general intangible;

(b) "Chattel paper" means a writing or writings which evidence both a monetary obligation and a security interest in or a lease of specific goods, but a charter or other contract involving the use or hire of a vessel is not chattel paper. When a transaction is evidenced both by such a security agreement or a lease and by an instrument or a series of instruments, the group of writings taken together constitutes chattel paper;

(c) "Collateral" means the property subject to a security interest, and includes accounts and chattel paper which have been sold;

(d) "Debtor" means the person who owes payment or other performance of the obligation secured, whether or not he owns or has rights in the collateral, and includes the seller of accounts or chattel paper. Where the debtor and the owner of the collateral are not the same person, the term "debtor" means the owner of the collateral in any provision of the Article dealing with the collateral, the obligor in any provision dealing with the obligation, and may include both where the context so requires;

(e) "Deposit account" means a demand, time, savings, passbook or like account maintained with a bank, savings and loan association, credit union or like organization, other than an account evidenced by a certificate of deposit;

(f) "Document" means document of title as defined in the general definitions of Article 1 (Section 1–201), and a receipt of the kind described in subsection (2) of Section 7–201;

(g) "Encumbrance" includes real estate mortgages and other liens on real estate and all other rights in real estate that are not ownership interests;

(h) "Goods" includes all things which are movable at the time the security interest attaches or which are fixtures (Section 9–313), but does not include money, documents, instruments, accounts, chattel paper, general intangibles, or minerals or the like (including oil and gas) before extraction. "Goods" also includes standing timber which is to be cut and removed under a conveyance or contract for sale, the unborn young of animals, and growing crops;

(i) "Instrument" means a negotiable instrument (defined in Section 3–104), or a security (defined in Section 8–102) or any other writing which evidences a right to the payment of money and is not itself a security agreement or lease and is of a type which is in ordinary course of business transferred by delivery with any necessary indorsement or assignment;

(j) "Mortgage" means a consensual interest created by a real estate mortgage, a trust deed on real estate, or the like;

(k) An advance is made "pursuant to commitment" if the secured party has bound himself to make it, whether or not a subsequent event of default or other event not within his control has relieved or may relieve him from his obligation;

(l) "Security agreement" means an agreement which creates or provides for a security interest;

(m) "Secured party" means a lender, seller or other person in whose favor there is a security interest, including a person to whom accounts or chattel paper have been sold. When the holders of obligations issued under an indenture of trust, equipment trust agreement or the like are represented by a trustee or other person, the representative is the secured party;

(n) "Transmitting utility" means any person primarily engaged in the railroad, street railway or trolley bus business, the electric or electronics communications transmission business, the transmission of goods by pipeline, or the transmission or the production and transmission of electricity, steam, gas or water, or the provision of sewer service.

(2) Other definitions applying to this Article and the sections in which they appear are:

"Account".	Section 9–106.
"Attach".	Section 9–203.
"Construction mortgage".	Section 9–313(1).

(3) The following definitions in other Articles apply to this Article:

(4) In addition Article 1 contains general definitions and principles of construction and interpretation applicable throughout this Article.

Section 9–106.   Definitions: "Account"; "General Intangibles".

"Account" means any right to payment for goods sold or leased or for services rendered which is not evidenced by an instrument or chattel paper, whether or not it has been earned by performance. "General intangibles" means any personal property (including things in action) other than goods, accounts, chattel paper, documents, instruments, and money. All rights to payment earned or unearned under a charter or other contract involving the use or hire of a vessel and all rights incident to the charter or contract are accounts.

Section 9–107.   Definitions: "Purchase Money Security Interest".

A security interest is a "purchase money security interest" to the extent that it is
   (a) taken or retained by the seller of the collateral to secure all or part of its price; or
   (b) taken by a person who by making advances or incurring an obligation gives value to enable the debtor to acquire rights in or the use of collateral if such value is in fact so used.

Section 9–108.   When After-Acquired Collateral Not Security for Antecedent Debt.

Where a secured party makes an advance, incurs an obligation, releases a perfected security interest, or otherwise gives new value which is to be secured in whole or in part by after-acquired property his security interest in the after-acquired collateral shall be deemed to be taken for new value and not as security for an antecedent debt if the debtor acquires his rights in such collateral either in the ordinary course of his business or under a contract of purchase made pursuant to the security agreement within a reasonable time after new value is given.

Section 9–109.   Classification of Goods; "Consumer Goods"; "Equipment"; "Farm Products"; "Inventory".

Goods are

(1) "consumer goods" if they are used or bought for use primarily for personal, family or household purposes;

(2) "equipment" if they are used or bought for use primarily in business (including farming or a profession) or by a debtor who is a non-profit organization or a governmental subdivision or agency or if the goods are not included in the definitions of inventory, farm products or consumer goods;

(3) "farm products" if they are crops or livestock or supplies used or produced in farming operations of if they are products of crops or livestock in their unmanufactured states (such as ginned cotton, wool-clip, maple syrup, milk and eggs), and if they are in the possession of a debtor engaged in raising, fattening, grazing or other farming operations. If goods are farm products they are neither equipment nor inventory;

(4) "inventory" if they are held by a person who holds them for sale or lease or to be furnished under contracts of service or if he has so furnished them, or if they are raw materials, work in process or materials used or consumed in a business. Inventory of a person is not to be classified as his equipment.

Section 9–110.   Sufficiency of Description.

For the purposes of this Article any description of personal property or real estate is sufficient whether or not it is specific if it reasonably identifies what is described.

Section 9–111.   Applicability of Bulk Transfer Laws.

The creation of a security interest is not a bulk transfer under Article 6 (see Section 6–103).

Section 9–112.   Where Collateral Is Not Owned by Debtor.

Unless otherwise agreed, when a secured party knows that collateral is owned by a person who is not the debtor, the owner of the collateral is entitled to receive from the secured party any surplus under Section 9–502(2) or under Section 9–504(1), and is not liable for the debt or for any deficiency after resale, and he has the same right as the debtor

   (a) to receive statements under Section 9–208;
   (b) to receive notice of and to object to a secured party's proposal to retain the collateral in satisfaction of the indebtedness under Section 9–505;
   (c) to redeem the collateral under Section 9–506;
   (d) to obtain injunctive or other relief under Section 9–507(1); and
   (e) to recover losses caused to him under Section 9–208(2).

Section 9–113.   Security Interests Arising under Article on Sales.

A security interest arising solely under the Article on Sales (Article 2) is subject to the provisions of this Article except that to the extent that and so long as the debtor does not have or does not lawfully obtain possession of the goods

(a) no security agreement is necessary to make the security interest enforceable; and

(b) no filing is required to perfect the security interest; and

(c) the rights of the secured party on default by the debtor are governed by the Article on Sales (Article 2).

Section 9–114. Consignment.

(1) A person who delivers goods under a consignment which is not a security interest and who would be required to file under this Article by paragraph (3) (c) of Section 2–326 has priority over a secured party who is or becomes a creditor of the consignee and who would have a perfected security interest in the goods if they were the property of the consignee, and also has priority with respect to identifiable cash proceeds received on or before delivery of the goods to a buyer, if

(a) the consignor complies with the filing provision of the Article on Sales with respect to consignments (paragraph (3) (c) of Section 2–326) before the consignee receives possession of the goods; and

(b) the consignor gives notification in writing to the holder of the security interest if the holder has filed a financing statement covering the same types of goods before the date of the filing made by the consignor; and

(c) the holder of the security interest receives the notification within five years before the consignee receives possession of the goods; and

(d) the notification states that the consignor expects to deliver goods on consignment to the consignee, describing the goods by item or type.

(2) In the case of a consignment which is not a security interest and in which the requirements of the preceding subsection have not been met, a person who delivers goods to another is subordinate to a person who would have a perfected security interest in the goods if they were the property of the debtor.

PART 2

VALIDITY OF SECURITY AGREEMENT AND RIGHTS OF PARTIES THERETO

Section 9–201. General Validity of Security Agreement.

Except as otherwise provided by this Act a security agreement is effective according to its terms between the parties, against purchasers of the collateral and against creditors. Nothing in this Article validates any charge or practice illegal under any statute or regulation thereunder governing usury, small loans, retail installment sales, or the like, or extends the application of any such statute or regulation to any transaction not otherwise subject thereto.

Section 9–202. Title to Collateral Immaterial.

Each provision of this Article with regard to rights, obligations and remedies applies whether title to collateral is in the secured party or in the debtor.

Section 9–203. Attachment and Enforceability of Security Interest; Proceeds; Formal Requisites.

(1) Subject to the provisions of Section 4–208 on the security interest of a collecting bank and Section 9–113 on a security interest arising under the Article on Sales, a security interest is not enforceable against the debtor or third parties with respect to the collateral and does not attach unless

(a) the collateral is in the possession of the secured party pursuant to agreement, or the debtor has signed a security agreement which contains a description of the collateral and in addition, when the security interest covers crops growing or to be grown or timber to be cut, a description of the land concerned; and

(b) value has been given; and

(c) the debtor has rights in the collateral.

(2) A security interest attaches when it becomes enforceable against the debtor with respect to the collateral. Attachment occurs as soon as all of the events specified in subsection (1) have taken place unless explicit agreement postpones the time of attaching.

(3) Unless otherwise agreed a security agreement gives the secured party the rights to proceeds provided by Section 9–306.

(4) A transaction, although subject to this Article, is also subject to . . . . . *, and in the case of conflict between the provisions of this Article and any such statute, the provisions of such statute control. Failure to comply with any applicable statute has only the effect which is specified therein.

Note: *At * in subsection (4) insert reference to any local statute regulating small loans, retail installment sales and the like.*

The foregoing subsection (4) is designed to make it clear that certain transactions, although subject to this Article, must also comply with other applicable legislation.

This Article is designed to regulate all the "security" aspects of transactions within its scope. There is, however, much regulatory legislation, particularly in the consumer field, which supplements this Article and should not be repealed by its enactment. Examples are small loan acts, retail installment selling acts and the like. Such acts may provide for licensing and rate regulation and may prescribe particular forms of contract. Such provisions should remain in force despite the enactment of this Article. On the other hand if a retail installment selling act contains provisions on filing, rights on default, etc., such provisions should be repealed as inconsistent with this Article except that inconsistent provisions as to deficiencies, penalties, etc., in the Uniform Consumer Credit Code and other recent related legislation should remain because those statutes were drafted after the substantial enactment of the Article and with the intention of modifying certain provisions of this Article as to consumer credit.

Section 9–204. After-Acquired Property; Future Advances.

(1) Except as provided in subsection (2), a security agreement may provide that any or all obligations covered by the security agreement are to be secured by after-acquired collateral.

(2) No security interest attaches under an after-acquired property clause

to consumer goods other than accessions (Section 9–314) when given as additional security unless the debtor acquires rights in them within ten days after the secured party gives value.

(3) Obligations covered by a security agreement may include future advances or other value whether or not the advances or value are given pursuant to commitment (subsection (1) of Section 9–105).

Section 9–205. Use or Disposition of Collateral without Accounting Permissible.

A security interest is not invalid or fraudulent against creditors by reason of liberty in the debtor to use, commingle or dispose of all or part of the collateral (including returned or repossessed goods) or to collect or compromise accounts or chattel paper, or to accept the return of goods or make repossessions, or to use, commingle or dispose of proceeds, or by reason of the failure of the secured party to require the debtor to account for proceeds or replace collateral. This section does not relax the requirements of possession where perfection of a security interest depends upon possession of the collateral by the secured party or by a bailee.

Section 9–206. Agreement Not to Assert Defenses against Assignee; Modification of Sales Warranties Where Security Agreement Exists.

(1) Subject to any statute or decision which establishes a different rule for buyers or lessees of consumer goods, an agreement by a buyer or lessee that he will not assert against an assignee any claim or defense which he may have against the seller or lessor is enforceable by an assignee who takes his assignment for value, in good faith and without notice of a claim or defense, except as to defenses of a type which may be asserted against a holder in due course of a negotiable instrument under the Article on Commercial Paper (Article 3). A buyer who as part of one transaction signs both a negotiable instrument and a security agreement makes such an agreement.

(2) When a seller retains a purchase money security interest in goods the Article on Sales (Article 2) governs the sale and any disclaimer, limitation or modification of the seller's warranties.

Section 9–207. Rights and Duties When Collateral Is in Secured Party's Possession.

(1) A secured party must use reasonable care in the custody and preservation of collateral in his possession. In the case of an instrument or chattel paper reasonable care includes taking necessary steps to preserve rights against prior parties unless otherwise agreed.

(2) Unless otherwise agreed, when collateral is in the secured party's possession

    (a) reasonable expenses (including the cost of any insurance and payment of taxes or other charges) incurred in the custody, preservation, use or operation of the collateral are chargeable to the debtor and are secured by the collateral;

    (b) the risk of accidental loss or damage is on the debtor to the extent of any deficiency in any effective insurance coverage;

 (c) the secured party may hold as additional security any increase or profits (except money) received from the collateral, but money so received, unless remitted to the debtor, shall be applied in reduction of the secured obligation;

 (d) the secured party must keep the collateral identifiable but fungible collateral may be commingled;

 (e) the secured party may repledge the collateral upon terms which do not impair the debtor's right to redeem it.

(3) A secured party is liable for any loss caused by his failure to meet any obligation imposed by the preceding subsections but does not lose his security interest.

(4) A secured party may use or operate the collateral for the purpose of preserving the collateral or its value or pursuant to the order of a court of appropriate jurisdiction or, except in the case of consumer goods, in the manner and to the extent provided in the security agreement.

Section 9–208. Request for Statement of Account or List of Collateral.

(1) A debtor may sign a statement indicating what he believes to be the aggregate amount of unpaid indebtedness as of a specified date and may send it to the secured party with a request that the statement be approved or corrected and returned to the debtor. When the security agreement or any other record kept by the secured party identifies the collateral a debtor may similarly request the secured party to approve or correct a list of the collateral.

(2) The secured party must comply with such a request within two weeks after receipt by sending a written correction or approval. If the secured party claims a security interest in all of a particular type of collateral owned by the debtor he may indicate that fact in his reply and need not approve or correct an itemized list of such collateral. If the secured party without reasonable excuse fails to comply he is liable for any loss caused to the debtor thereby; and if the debtor has properly included in his request a good faith statement of the obligation or a list of the collateral or both the secured party may claim a security interest only as shown in the statement against persons misled by his failure to comply. If he no longer has an interest in the obligation or collateral at the time the request is received he must disclose the name and address of any successor in interest known to him and he is liable for any loss caused to the debtor as a result of failure to disclose. A successor in interest is not subject to this section until a request is received by him.

(3) A debtor is entitled to such a statement once every six months without charge. The secured party may require payment of a charge not exceeding $10 for each additional statement furnished.

PART 3

RIGHTS OF THIRD PARTIES; PERFECTED AND UNPERFECTED SECURITY INTERESTS; RULES OF PRIORITY

Section 9–301. Persons Who Take Priority over Unperfected Security Interest; Rights of "Lien Creditor".

(1) Except as otherwise provided in subsection (2), an unperfected security interest is subordinate to the rights of

(a) persons entitled to priority under Section 9–312;

(b) a person who becomes a lien creditor before the security interest is perfected;

(c) in the case of goods, instruments, documents, and chattel paper, a person who is not a secured party and who is a transferee in bulk or other buyer not in ordinary course of business or is a buyer of farm products in ordinary course of business, to the extent that he gives value and receives delivery of the collateral without knowledge of the security interest and before it is perfected;

(d) in the case of accounts and general intangibles, a person who is not a secured party and who is a transferee to the extent that he gives value without knowledge of the security interest and before it is perfected.

(2) If the secured party files with respect to a purchase money security interest before or within ten days after the debtor receives possession of the collateral, he takes priority over the rights of a transferee in bulk or of a lien creditor which arise between the time the security interest attaches and the time of filing.

(3) A "lien creditor" means a creditor who has acquired a lien on the property involved by attachment, levy or the like and includes an assignee for benefit of creditors from the time of assignment, and a trustee in bankruptcy from the date of the filing of the petition or a receiver in equity from the time of appointment.

(4) A person who becomes a lien creditor while a security interest is perfected takes subject to the security interest only to the extent that it secures advances made before he becomes a lien creditor or within 45 days thereafter or made without knowledge of the lien or pursuant to a commitment entered into without knowledge of the lien.

Section 9–302. When Filing Is Required to Perfect Security Interest; Security Interests to Which Filing Provisions of This Article Do Not Apply.

(1) A financing statement must be filed to perfect all security interests except the following:

(a) a security interest in collateral in possession of the secured party under Section 9–305;

(b) a security interest temporarily perfected in instruments or documents without delivery under Section 9–304 or in proceeds for a 10 day period under Section 9–306;

(c) a security interest created by an assignment of a beneficial interest in a trust or a decedent's estate;

(d) a purchase money security interest in consumer goods; but filing is required for a motor vehicle required to be registered; and fixture filing is required for priority over conflicting interests in fixtures to the extent provided in Section 9–313;

(e) an assignment of accounts which does not alone or in conjunction with other assignments to the same assignee transfer a significant part of the outstanding accounts of the assignor;

(f) a security interest of a collecting bank (Section 4–208) or arising under the Article on Sales (see Section 9–113) or covered in subsection (3) of this section;

(g) an assignment for the benefit of all the creditors of the transferor, and subsequent transfers by the assignee thereunder.

(2) If a secured party assigns a perfected security interest, no filing under this Article is required in order to continue the perfected status of the security interest against creditors of and transferees from the original debtor.

(3) The filing of a financing statement otherwise required by this Article is not necessary or effective to perfect a security interest in property subject to

(a) a statute or treaty of the United States which provides for a national or international registration or a national or international certificate of title or which specifies a place of filing different from that specified in this Article for filing of the security interest; or

(b) the following statutes of this state; [list any certificate of title statute covering automobiles, trailers, mobile homes, boats, farm tractors, or the like, and any central filing statute*.]; but during any period in which collateral is inventory held for sale by a person who is in the business of selling goods of that kind, the filing provisions of this Article (Part 4) apply to a security interest in that collateral created by him as debtor; or

*Note: *It is recommended that the provisions of certificate of title acts for perfection of security interests by notation on the certificates should be amended to exclude coverage of inventory held for sale.*

(c) a certificate of title statute of another jurisdiction under the law of which indication of a security interest on the certificate is required as a condition of perfection (subsection (2) of Section 9–103).

(4) Compliance with a statute or treaty described in subsection (3) is equivalent to the filing of a financing statement under this Article, and a security interest in property subject to the statute or treaty can be perfected only by compliance therewith except as provided in Section 9–103 on multiple state transactions. Duration and renewal of perfection of a security interest perfected by compliance with the statute or treaty are governed by the provisions of the statute or treaty; in other respects the security interest is subject to this Article.

Section 9–303. When Security Interest Is Perfected; Continuity of Perfection.

(1) A security interest is perfected when it has attached and when all of the applicable steps required for perfection have been taken. Such steps are specified in Sections 9–302, 9–304, 9–305 and 9–306. If such steps are taken before the security interest attaches, it is perfected at the time when it attaches.

(2) If a security interest is originally perfected in any way permitted under this Article and is subsequently perfected in some other way under this Article, without an intermediate period when it was unperfected, the security interest shall be deemed to be perfected continuously for the purposes of this Article.

Section 9–304. Perfection of Security Interest in Instruments, Documents, and Goods Covered by Documents; Perfection by Permissive Filing; Temporary Perfection without Filing or Transfer of Possession.

(1) A security interest in chattel paper or negotiable documents may be perfected by filing. A security interest in money or instruments (other than instruments which constitute part of chattel paper) can be perfected only by the secured party's taking possession, except as provided in subsections (4) and (5) of this section and subsections (2) and (3) of Section 9–306 on proceeds.

(2) During the period that goods are in the possession of the issuer of a negotiable document therefor, a security interest in the goods is perfected by perfecting a security interest in the document, and any security interest in the goods otherwise perfected during such period is subject thereto.

(3) A security interest in goods in the possession of a bailee other than one who has issued a negotiable document therefor is perfected by issuance of a document in the name of the secured party or by the bailee's receipt of notification of the secured party's interest or by filing as to the goods.

(4) A security interest in instruments or negotiable documents is perfected without filing or the taking of possession for a period of 21 days from the time it attaches to the extent that it arises for new value given under a written security agreement.

(5) A security interest remains perfected for a period of 21 days without filing where a secured party having a perfected security interest in an instrument, a negotiable document or goods in possession of a bailee other than one who has issued a negotiable document therefor

    (a) makes available to the debtor the goods or documents representing the goods for the purpose of ultimate sale or exchange or for the purpose of loading, unloading, storing, shipping, transshipping, manufacturing, processing or otherwise dealing with them in a manner preliminary to their sale or exchange, but priority between conflicting security interests in the goods is subject to subsection (3) of Section 9–312; or

    (b) delivers the instrument to the debtor for the purpose of ultimate sale or exchange or of presentation, collection, renewal or registration of transfer.

(6) After the 21 day period in subsections (4) and (5) perfection depends upon compliance with applicable provisions of this Article.

Section 9–305. When Possession by Secured Party Perfects Security Interest without Filing.

A security interest in letters of credit and advices of credit (subsection (2)(a) of Section 5–116), goods, instruments, money, negotiable documents or chattel paper may be perfected by the secured party's taking possession of the collateral. If such collateral other than goods covered by a negotiable document is held by a bailee, the secured party is deemed to have possession from the time the bailee receives notification of the secured party's interest. A security interest is perfected by possession from the time possession is taken without relation back and continues only so long as possession is retained, unless otherwise specified in this Article. The security interest may be otherwise perfected as provided in this Article before or after the period of possession by the secured party.

Section 9-306. **"Proceeds"; Secured Party's Rights on Disposition of Collateral.**

(1) "Proceeds" includes whatever is received upon the sale, exchange, collection or other disposition of collateral or proceeds. Insurance payable by reason of loss or damage to the collateral is proceeds, except to the extent that it is payable to a person other than a party to the security agreement. Money, checks, deposit accounts, and the like are "cash proceeds." All other proceeds are "non-cash proceeds."

(2) Except where this Article otherwise provides, a security interest continues in collateral notwithstanding sale, exchange or other disposition thereof unless the disposition was authorized by the secured party in the security agreement or otherwise, and also continues in any identifiable proceeds including collections received by the debtor.

(3) The security interest in proceeds is a continuously perfected security interest if the interest in the original collateral was perfected but it ceases to be a perfected security interest and becomes unperfected ten days after receipt of the proceeds by the debtor unless

    (a) a filed financing statement covers the original collateral and the proceeds are collateral in which a security interest may be perfected by filing in the office or offices where the financing statement has been filed and, if the proceeds are acquired with cash proceeds, the description of collateral in the financing statement indicates the types of property constituting the proceeds; or

    (b) a filed financing statement covers the original collateral and the proceeds are identifiable cash proceeds; or

    (c) the security interest in the proceeds is perfected before the expiration of the ten day period.

Except as provided in this section, a security interest in proceeds can be perfected only by the methods or under the circumstances permitted in this Article for original collateral of the same type.

(4) In the event of insolvency proceedings instituted by or against a debtor, a secured party with a perfected security interest in proceeds has a perfected security interest only in the following proceeds:

    (a) in identifiable non-cash proceeds and in separate deposit accounts containing only proceeds;

    (b) in identifiable cash proceeds in the form of money which is neither commingled with other money nor deposited in a deposit account prior to the insolvency proceedings;

    (c) in identifiable cash proceeds in the form of checks and the like which are not deposited in a deposit account prior to the insolvency proceedings; and

    (d) in all cash and deposit accounts of the debtor in which proceeds have been commingled with other funds, but the perfected security interest under this paragraph (d) is

(i) subject to any right of set-off; and

(ii) limited to an amount not greater than the amount of any cash proceeds received by the debtor within ten days before the institution of the insolvency proceedings less the sum of (I) the payments to the secured party on account of cash proceeds received by the debtor during such period and (II) the cash proceeds received by the debtor during such period to which the secured party is entitled under paragraphs (a) through (c) of this subsection (4).

(5) If a sale of goods results in an account or chattel paper which is transferred by the seller to a secured party, and if the goods are returned to or are repossessed by the seller or the secured party, the following rules determine priorities:

(a) If the goods were collateral at the time of sale, for an indebtedness of the seller which is still unpaid, the original security interest attaches again to the goods and continues as a perfected security interest if it was perfected at the time when the goods were sold. If the security interest was originally perfected by a filing which is still effective, nothing further is required to continue the perfected status; in any other case, the secured party must take possession of the returned or repossessed goods or must file.

(b) An unpaid transferee of the chattel paper has a security interest in the goods against the transferor. Such security interest is prior to a security interest asserted under paragraph (a) to the extent that the transferee of the chattel paper was entitled to priority under Section 9–308.

(c) An unpaid transferee of the account has a security interest in the goods against the transferor. Such security interest is subordinate to a security interest asserted under paragraph (a).

(d) A security interest of an unpaid transferee asserted under paragraph (b) or (c) must be perfected for protection against creditors of the transferor and purchasers of the returned or repossessed goods.

Section 9–307. Protection of Buyers of Goods.

(1) A buyer in ordinary course of business (subsection (9) of Section 1–201) other than a person buying farm products from a person engaged in farming operations takes free of a security interest created by his seller even though the security interest is perfected and even though the buyer knows of its existence.

(2) In the case of consumer goods, a buyer takes free of a security interest even though perfected if he buys without knowledge of the security interest, for value and for his own personal, family or household purposes unless prior to the purchase the secured party has filed a financing statement covering such goods.

(3) A buyer other than a buyer in ordinary course of business (subsection (1) of this section) takes free of a security interest to the extent that it secures future advances made after the secured party acquires knowledge of the purchase, or more than 45 days after the purchase, whichever first occurs, unless made

pursuant to a commitment entered into without knowledge of the purchase and before the expiration of the 45 day period.

Section 9–308. Purchase of Chattel Paper and Instruments.

A purchaser of chattel paper or an instrument who gives new value and takes possession of it in the ordinary course of his business has priority over a security interest in the chattel paper or instrument

    (a) which is perfected under Section 9–304 (permissive filing and temporary perfection) or under Section 9–306 (perfection as to proceeds) if he acts without knowledge that the specific paper or instrument is subject to a security interest; or

    (b) which is claimed merely as proceeds of inventory subject to a security interest (Section 9–306) even though he knows that the specific paper or instrument is subject to the security interest.

Section 9–309. Protection of Purchasers of Instruments and Documents.

Nothing in this Article limits the rights of a holder in due course of a negotiable instrument (Section 3–302) or a holder to whom a negotiable document of title has been duly negotiated (Section 7–501) or a bona fide purchaser of a security (Section 8–301) and such holders or purchasers take priority over an earlier security interest even though perfected. Filing under this Article does not constitute notice of the security interest to such holders or purchasers.

Section 9–310. Priority of Certain Liens Arising by Operation of Law.

When a person in the ordinary course of his business furnishes services or materials with respect to goods subject to a security interest, a lien upon goods in the possession of such person given by statute or rule of law for such materials or services takes priority over a perfected security interest unless the lien is statutory and the statute expressly provides otherwise.

Section 9–311. Alienability of Debtor's Rights; Judicial Process.

The debtor's rights in collateral may be voluntarily or involuntarily transferred (by way of sale, creation of a security interest, attachment, levy, garnishment or other judicial process) notwithstanding a provision in the security agreement prohibiting any transfer or making the transfer constitute a default.

Section 9–312. Priorities among Conflicting Security Interests in the Same Collateral.

(1) The rules of priority stated in other sections of this Part and in the following sections shall govern when applicable: Section 4–208 with respect to the security interests of collecting banks in items being collected, accompanying documents and proceeds; Section 9–103 on security interests related to other jurisdictions; Section 9–114 on consignments.

(2) A perfected security interest in crops for new value given to enable the debtor to produce the crops during the production season and given not more than three months before the crops become growing crops by planting or otherwise takes priority over an earlier perfected security interest to the extent that

such earlier interest secures obligations due more than six months before the crops become growing crops by planting or otherwise, even though the person giving new value had knowledge of the earlier security interest.

(3) A perfected purchase money security interest in inventory has priority over a conflicting security interest in the same inventory and also has priority in identifiable cash proceeds received on or before the delivery of the inventory to a buyer if

    (a) the purchase money security interest is perfected at the time the debtor receives possession of the inventory; and

    (b) the purchase money secured party gives notification in writing to the holder of the conflicting security interest if the holder had filed a financing statement covering the same types of inventory (i) before the date of the filing made by the purchase money secured party, or (ii) before the beginning of the 21 day period where the purchase money security interest is temporarily perfected without filing or possession (subsection (5) of Section 9–304); and

    (c) the holder of the conflicting security interest receives the notification within five years before the debtor receives possession of the inventory; and

    (d) the notification states that the person giving the notice has or expects to acquire a purchase money security interest in inventory of the debtor, describing such inventory by item or type.

(4) A purchase money security interest in collateral other than inventory has priority over a conflicting security interest in the same collateral or its proceeds if the purchase money security interest is perfected at the time the debtor receives possession of the collateral or within ten days thereafter.

(5) In all cases not governed by other rules stated in this section (including cases of purchase money security interests which do not qualify for the special priorities set forth in subsections (3) and (4) of this section), priority between conflicting security interests in the same collateral shall be determined according to the following rules:

    (a) Conflicting security interests rank according to priority in time of filing or perfection. Priority dates from the time a filing is first made covering the collateral or the time the security interest is first perfected, whichever is earlier, provided that there is no period thereafter when there is neither filing nor perfection.

    (b) So long as conflicting security interests are unperfected, the first to attach has priority.

(6) For the purposes of subsection (5) a date of filing or perfection as to collateral is also a date of filing or perfection as to proceeds.

(7) If future advances are made while a security interest is perfected by filing or the taking of possession, the security interest has the same priority for the purposes of subsection (5) with respect to the future advances as it does with respect to the first advance. If a commitment is made before or while the security interest is so perfected, the security interest has the same priority with respect to advances made pursuant thereto. In other cases a perfected security interest has priority from the date the advance is made.

Section 9–313.   Priority of Security Interests in Fixtures.

(1) In this section and in the provisions of Part 4 of this Article referring to fixture filing, unless the context otherwise requires

    (a) Goods are "fixtures" when they become so related to particular real estate that an interest in them arises under real estate law.

    (b) A "fixture filing" is the filing in the office where a mortgage on the real estate would be filed or recorded of a financing statement covering goods which are or are to become fixtures and conforming to the requirements of subsection (5) of Section 9–402.

    (c) A mortgage is a "construction mortgage" to the extent that it secures an obligation incurred for the construction of an improvement on land including the acquisition cost of the land, if the recorded writing so indicates.

(2) A security interest under this Article may be created in goods which are fixtures or may continue in goods which become fixtures, but no security interest exists under this Article in ordinary building materials incorporated into an improvement on land.

(3) This Article does not prevent creation of an encumbrance upon fixtures pursuant to real estate law.

(4) A perfected security interest in fixtures has priority over the conflicting interest of an encumbrancer or owner of the real estate where

    (a) the security interest is a purchase money security interest, the interest of the encumbrancer or owner arises before the goods become fixtures, the security interest is perfected by a fixture filing before the goods become fixtures or within ten days thereafter, and the debtor has an interest of record in the real estate or is in possession of the real estate; or

    (b) the security interest is perfected by a fixture filing before the interest of the encumbrancer or owner is of record, the security interest has priority over any conflicting interest of a predecessor in title of the encumbrancer or owner, and the debtor has an interest of record in the real estate or is in possession of the real estate; or

    (c) the fixtures are readily removable factory or office machines or readily removable replacements of domestic appliances which are consumer goods, and before the goods become fixtures the security interest is perfected by any method permitted by this Article; or

    (d) the conflicting interest is a lien on the real estate obtained by legal or equitable proceedings after the security interest was perfected by any method permitted by this Article.

(5) A security interest in fixtures, whether or not perfected, has priority over the conflicting interest of an encumbrancer or owner of the real estate where

    (a) the encumbrancer or owner has consented in writing to the security interest or has disclaimed an interest in the goods as fixtures; or

    (b) the debtor has a right to remove the goods as against the encumbrancer or owner. If the debtor's right terminates, the priority of the security interest continues for a reasonable time.

(6) Notwithstanding paragraph (a) of subsection (4) but otherwise subject to subsections (4) and (5), a security interest in fixtures is subordinate to a construction mortgage recorded before the goods become fixtures if the goods become fixtures before the completion of the construction. To the extent that it is given to refinance a construction mortgage, a mortgage has this priority to the same extent as the construction mortgage.

(7) In cases not within the preceding subsections, a security interest in fixtures is subordinate to the conflicting interest of an encumbrancer or owner of the related real estate who is not the debtor.

(8) When the secured party has priority over all owners and encumbrancers of the real estate, he may, on default, subject to the provisions of Part 5, remove his collateral from the real estate but he must reimburse any encumbrancer or owner of the real estate who is not the debtor and who has not otherwise agreed for the cost of repair of any physical injury, but not for any diminution in value of the real estate caused by the absence of the goods removed or by any necessity of replacing them. A person entitled to reimbursement may refuse permission to remove until the secured party gives adequate security for the performance of this obligation.

Section 9–314.   Accessions.

(1) A security interest in goods which attaches before they are installed in or affixed to other goods takes priority as to the goods installed or affixed (called in this section "accessions") over the claims of all persons to the whole except as stated in subsection (3) and subject to Section 9–315(1).

(2) A security interest which attaches to goods after they become part of a whole is valid against all persons subsequently acquiring interests in the whole except as stated in subsection (3) but is invalid against any person with an interest in the whole at the time the security interest attaches to the goods who has not in writing consented to the security interest or disclaimed an interest in the goods as part of the whole.

(3) The security interests described in subsections (1) and (2) do not take priority over

  (a) a subsequent purchaser for value of any interest in the whole; or
  (b) a creditor with a lien on the whole subsequently obtained by judicial proceedings; or
  (c) a creditor with a prior perfected security interest in the whole to the extent that he makes subsequent advances

if the subsequent purchase is made, the lien by judicial proceedings obtained or the subsequent advance under the prior perfected security interest is made or contracted for without knowledge of the security interest and before it is perfected. A purchaser of the whole at a foreclosure sale other than the holder of a perfected security interest purchasing at his own foreclosure sale is a subsequent purchaser within this section.

(4) When under subsections (1) or (2) and (3) a secured party has an interest in accessions which has priority over the claims of all persons who have interests in the whole, he may on default subject to the provisions of Part 5 remove his collateral from the whole but he must reimburse any encumbrancer or owner of the whole who is not the debtor and who has not otherwise agreed

for the cost of repair of any physical injury but not for any diminution in value of the whole caused by the absence of the goods removed or by any necessity for replacing them. A person entitled to reimbursement may refuse permission to remove until the secured party gives adequate security for the performance of this obligation.

Section 9–315.   Priority When Goods Are Commingled or Processed.

(1) If a security interest in goods was perfected and subsequently the goods or a part thereof have become part of a product or mass, the security interest continues in the product or mass if

  (a) the goods are so manufactured, processed, assembled or commingled that their identity is lost in the product or mass; or
  (b) a financing statement covering the original goods also covers the product into which the goods have been manufactured, processed or assembled.

In a case to which paragraph (b) applies, no separate security interest in that part of the original goods which has been manufactured, processed or assembled into the product may be claimed under Section 9–314.

(2) When under subsection (1) more than one security interest attaches to the product or mass, they rank equally according to the ratio that the cost of the goods to which each interest originally attached bears to the cost of the total product or mass.

Section 9–316.   Priority Subject to Subordination.

Nothing in this Article prevents subordination by agreement by any person entitled to priority.

Section 9–317.   Secured Party Not Obligated on Contract of Debtor.

The mere existence of a security interest or authority given to the debtor to dispose of or use collateral does not impose contract or tort liability upon the secured party for the debtor's acts or omissions.

Section 9–318.   Defenses against Assignee; Modification of Contract after Notification of Assignment; Term Prohibiting Assignment Ineffective; Identification and Proof of Assignment.

(1) Unless an account debtor has made an enforceable agreement not to assert defenses or claims arising out of a sale as provided in Section 9–206 the rights of an assignee are subject to

  (a) all the terms of the contract between the account debtor and assignor and any defense or claim arising therefrom; and
  (b) any other defense or claim of the account debtor against the assignor which accrues before the account debtor receives notification of the assignment.

(2) So far as the right to payment or a part thereof under an assigned contract has not been fully earned by performance, and notwithstanding notification of the assignment, any modification of or substitution for the contract made in good faith and in accordance with reasonable commercial standards is effective against an assignee unless the account debtor has otherwise agreed but the assignee acquires corresponding rights under the modified or substituted contract. The assignment may provide that such modification or substitution is a breach by the assignor.

(3) The account debtor is authorized to pay the assignor until the account debtor receives notification that the amount due or to become due has been assigned and that payment is to be made to the assignee. A notification which does not reasonably identify the rights assigned is ineffective. If requested by the account debtor, the assignee must seasonably furnish reasonable proof that the assignment has been made and unless he does so the account debtor may pay the assignor.

(4) A term in any contract between an account debtor and an assignor is ineffective if it prohibits assignment of an account or prohibits creation of a security interest in a general intangible for money due or to become due or requires the account debtor's consent to such assignment or security interest.

PART 4

FILING

Section 9–401. Place of Filing; Erroneous Filing; Removal of Collateral.

First Alternative Subsection (1)

(1) The proper place to file in order to perfect a security interest is as follows:

    (a) when the collateral is timber to be cut or is minerals or the like (including oil and gas) or accounts subject to subsection (5) of Section 9–103, or when the financing statement is filed as a fixture filing (Section 9–313) and the collateral is goods which are or are to become fixtures, then in the office where a mortgage on the real estate would be filed or recorded;

    (b) in all other cases, in the office of the [Secretary of State].

Second Alternative Subsection (1)

(1) The proper place to file in order to perfect a security interest is as follows:

    (a) when the collateral is equipment used in farming operations, or farm products, or accounts or general intangibles arising from or relating to the sale of farm products by a farmer, or consumer goods, then in the office of the ...... in the county of the debtor's residence or if the debtor is not a resident of this state then in the office of the .... in the county where the goods are kept, and in addition when the collateral is crops growing or to be grown in the office of the ...... in the county where the land is located;

    (b) when the collateral is timber to be cut or is minerals or the like (including oil and gas) or accounts subject to subsection (5) of Section 9–103, or when the financing statement is filed as a fixture filing

(Section 9–313) and the collateral is goods which are or are to become fixtures, then in the office where a mortgage on the real estate
would be filed or recorded;

(c) in all other cases, in the office of the [Secretary of State].

Third Alternative Subsection (1)

(1) The proper place to file in order to perfect a security interest is as
follows:

(a) when the collateral is equipment used in farming operations, or
farm products, or accounts or general intangibles arising from or relating to the sale of farm products by a farmer, or consumer goods,
then in the office of the ...... in the county of the debtor's
residence or if the debtor is not a resident of this state then in the
office of the .... in the county where the goods are kept,
and in addition when the collateral is crops growing or to be grown
in the office of the .... in the county where the land is located;

(b) when the collateral is timber to be cut or is minerals or the like
(including oil and gas) or accounts subject to subsection (5) of
Section 9–103, or when the financing statement is filed as a fixture
filing (Section 9–313) and the collateral is goods which are or are
to become fixtures, then in the office where a mortgage on the real
estate would be filed or recorded;

(c) in all other cases, in the office of the [Secretary of State] and in addition, if the debtor has a place of business in only one county of this
state, also in the office of .... of such county, or, if the debtor
has no place of business in this state, but resides in the state, also in
the office of .... of the county in which he resides.

Note: *One of the three alternatives should be selected as subsection (1).*

(2) A filing which is made in good faith in an improper place or not in all
of the places required by this section is nevertheless effective with regard to any
collateral as to which the filing complied with the requirements of this Article
and is also effective with regard to collateral covered by the financing statement
against any person who has knowledge of the contents of such financing statement.

(3) A filing which is made in the proper place in this state continues effective even though the debtor's residence or place of business or the location of
the collateral or its use, whichever controlled the original filing, is thereafter
changed.

Alternative Subsection (3)

[(3) A filing which is made in the proper county continues effective for
four months after a change to another county of the debtor's residence or place
of business or the location of the collateral, whichever controlled the original
filing. It becomes ineffective thereafter unless a copy of the financing statement
signed by the secured party is filed in the new county within said period. The
security interest may also be perfected in the new county after the expiration of

the four month period; in such case perfection dates from the time of perfection in the new county. A change in the use of the collateral does not impair the effectiveness of the original filing.]

(4) The rules stated in Section 9–103 determine whether filing is necessary in this state.

(5) Notwithstanding the preceding subsections, and subject to subsection (3) of Section 9–302, the proper place to file in order to perfect a security interest in collateral, including fixtures, of a transmitting utility is the office of the [Secretary of State]. This filing constitutes a fixture filing (Section 9–313) as to the collateral described therein which is or is to become fixtures.

(6) For the purposes of this section, the residence of an organization is its place of business if it has one or its chief executive office if it has more than one place of business.

Note: *Subsection (6) should be used only if the state chooses the Second or Third Alternative Subsection (1)*

Section 9–402. Formal Requisites of Financing Statement; Amendments; Mortgage as Financing Statement.

(1) A financing statement is sufficient if it gives the names of the debtor and the secured party, is signed by the debtor, gives an address of the secured party from which information concerning the security interest may be obtained, gives a mailing address of the debtor and contains a statement indicating the types, or describing the items, of collateral. A financing statement may be filed before a security agreement is made or a security interest otherwise attaches. When the financing statement covers crops growing or to be grown, the statement must also contain a description of the real estate concerned. When the financing statement covers timber to be cut or covers minerals or the like (including oil and gas) or accounts subject to subsection (5) of Section 9–103, or when the financing statement is filed as a fixture filing (Section 9–313) and the collateral is goods which are or are to become fixtures, the statement must also comply with subsection (5). A copy of the security agreement is sufficient as a financing statement if it contains the above information and is signed by the debtor. A carbon, photographic or other reproduction of a security agreement or a financing statement is sufficient as a financing statement if the security agreement so provides or if the original has been filed in this state.

(2) A financing statement which otherwise complies with subsection (1) is sufficient when it is signed by the secured party instead of the debtor if it is filed to perfect a security interest in

(a) collateral already subject to a security interest in another jurisdiction when it is brought into this state, or when the debtor's location is changed to this state. Such a financing statement must state that the collateral was brought into this state or that the debtor's location was changed to this state under such circumstances; or

(b) proceeds under Section 9–306 if the security interest in the original collateral was perfected. Such a financing statement must describe the original collateral; or

(c) collateral as to which the filing has lapsed; or

      (d) collateral acquired after a change of name, identity or corporate structure of the debtor (subsection (7)).

    (3) A form substantially as follows is sufficient to comply with subsection (1):

Name of debtor (or assignor) ....

Address ....

Name of secured party (or assignee) ....

Address ....

1. This financing statement covers the following types (or items) of property:
       (Describe) ....
2. (If collateral is crops) The above described crops are growing or are to be grown on:
       (Describe Real Estate) ....
3. (If applicable) The above goods are to become fixtures on*
       (Describe Real Estate) ....
   and this financing statement is to be filed [for record] in the real estate records. (If the debtor does not have an interest of record) The name of a record owner is ....
4. (If products of collateral are claimed) Products of the collateral are also covered.

(use   ....

whichever   Signature of Debtor (or Assignor)

is   ....

applicable)   Signature of Secured Party (or Assignee)

   * Where appropriate substitute either "The above timber is standing on . . . . ." or "The above minerals or the like (including oil and gas) or accounts will be financed at the wellhead or minehead of the well or mine located on . . . . ."

    (4) A financing statement may be amended by filing a writing signed by both the debtor and the secured party. An amendment does not extend the period of effectiveness of a financing statement. If any amendment adds collateral, it is effective as to the added collateral only from the filing date of the amendment. In this Article, unless the context otherwise requires, the term "financing statement" means the original financing statement and any amendments.

    (5) A financing statement covering timber to be cut or covering minerals or the like (including oil and gas) or accounts subject to subsection (5) of Section 9–103, or a financing statement filed as a fixture filing (Section 9–313) where the debtor is not a transmitting utility, must show that it covers this type of collateral, must recite that it is to be filed [for record] in the real estate records, and the financing statement must contain a description of the real estate [sufficient if it were contained in a mortgage of the real estate to give constructive notice of the mortgage under the law of this state]. If the debtor does not have an interest of record in the real estate, the financing statement must show the name of a record owner.

    (6) A mortgage is effective as a financing statement filed as a fixture filing from the date of its recording if

(a) the goods are described in the mortgage by item or type; and

(b) the goods are or are to become fixtures related to the real estate described in the mortgage; and

(c) the mortgage complies with the requirements for a financing statement in this section other than a recital that it is to be filed in the real estate records; and

(d) the mortgage is duly recorded.

No fee with reference to the financing statement is required other than the regular recording and satisfaction fees with respect to the mortgage.

(7) A financing statement sufficiently shows the name of the debtor if it gives the individual, partnership or corporate name of the debtor, whether or not it adds other trade names or names of partners. Where the debtor so changes his name or in the case of an organization its name, identity or corporate structure that a filed financing statement becomes seriously misleading, the filing is not effective to perfect a security interest in collateral acquired by the debtor more than four months after the change, unless a new appropriate financing statement is filed before the expiration of that time. A filed financing statement remains effective with respect to collateral transferred by the debtor even though the secured party knows of or consents to the transfer.

(8) A financing statement substantially complying with the requirements of this section is effective even though it contains minor errors which are not seriously misleading.

Note: *Language in brackets is optional.*

Note: *Where the state has any special recording system for real estate other than the usual grantor-grantee index (as, for instance, a tract system or a title registration or Torrens system) local adaptations of subsection (5) and Section 9–403(7) may be necessary. See Mass. Gen. Laws Chapter 106, Section 9–409.*

Section 9–403. What Constitutes Filing; Duration of Filing; Effect of Lapsed Filing; Duties of Filing Officer.

(1) Presentation for filing of a financing statement and tender of the filing fee or acceptance of the statement by the filing officer constitutes filing under this Article.

(2) Except as provided in subsection (6) a filed financing statement is effective for a period of five years from the date of filing. The effectiveness of a filed financing statement lapses on the expiration of the five year period unless a continuation statement is filed prior to the lapse. If a security interest perfected by filing exists at the time insolvency proceedings are commenced by or against the debtor, the security interest remains perfected until termination of the insolvency proceedings and thereafter for a period of sixty days or until expiration of the five year period, whichever occurs later. Upon lapse the security interest becomes unperfected, unless it is perfected without filing. If the security interest becomes unperfected upon lapse, it is deemed to have been unperfected as against a person who became a purchaser or lien creditor before lapse.

(3) A continuation statement may be filed by the secured party within six

months prior to the expiration of the five year period specified in subsection (2). Any such continuation statement must be signed by the secured party, identify the original statement by file number and state that the original statement is still effective. A continuation statement signed by a person other than the secured party of record must be accompanied by a separate written statement of assignment signed by the secured party of record and complying with subsection (2) of Section 9–405, including payment of the required fee. Upon timely filing of the continuation statement, the effectiveness of the original statement is continued for five years after the last date to which the filing was effective whereupon it lapses in the same manner as provided in subsection (2) unless another continuation statement is filed prior to such lapse. Succeeding continuation statements may be filed in the same manner to continue the effectiveness of the original statement. Unless a statute on disposition of public records provides otherwise, the filing officer may remove a lapsed statement from the files and destroy it immediately if he has retained a microfilm or other photographic record, or in other cases after one year after the lapse. The filing officer shall so arrange matters by physical annexation of financing statements to continuation statements or other related filings, or by other means, that if he physically destroys the financing statements of a period more than five years past, those which have been continued by a continuation statement or which are still effective under subsection (6) shall be retained.

(4) Except as provided in subsection (7) a filing officer shall mark each statement with a file number and with the date and hour of filing and shall hold the statement or a microfilm or other photographic copy thereof for public inspection. In addition the filing officer shall index the statement according to the name of the debtor and shall note in the index the file number and the address of the debtor given in the statement.

(5) The uniform fee for filing and indexing and for stamping a copy furnished by the secured party to show the date and place of filing for an original financing statement or for a continuation statement shall be $....... if the statement is in the standard form prescribed by the [Secretary of State] and otherwise shall be $....., plus in each case, if the financing statement is subject to subsection (5) of Section 9–402, $..... The uniform fee for each name more than one required to be indexed shall be $..... The secured party may at his option show a trade name for any person and an extra uniform indexing fee of $..... shall be paid with respect thereto.

(6) If the debtor is a transmitting utility (subsection (5) of Section 9–401) and a filed financing statement so states, it is effective until a termination statement is filed. A real estate mortgage which is effective as a fixture filing under subsection (6) of Section 9–402 remains effective as a fixture filing until the mortgage is released or satisfied of record or its effectiveness otherwise terminates as to the real estate.

(7) When a financing statement covers timber to be cut or covers minerals or the like (including oil and gas) or accounts subject to subsection (5) of Section 9–103, or is filed as a fixture filing, [it shall be filed for record and] the filing officer shall index it under the names of the debtor and any owner of record shown in the financing statement in the same fashion as if he were the mortgagor in a mortgage of the real estate described, and, to the extent that the

law of this state provides for indexing of mortgages under the name of the mortgagee, under the name of the secured party as if he were the mortgagee thereunder, or where indexing is by description in the same fashion as if the financing statement were a mortgage of the real estate described.

Note: *In states in which writings will not appear in the real estate records and indices unless actually recorded the bracketed language in subsection (7) should be used.*

Section 9–404. Termination Statement.

(1) If a financing statement covering consumer goods is filed on or after ...., then within one month or within ten days following written demand by the debtor after there is no outstanding secured obligation and no commitment to make advances, incur obligations or otherwise give value, the secured party must file with each filing officer with whom the financing statement was filed, a termination statement to the effect that he no longer claims a security interest under the financing statement, which shall be identified by file number. In other cases whenever there is no outstanding secured obligation and no commitment to make advances, incur obligations or otherwise give value, the secured party must on written demand by the debtor send the debtor, for each filing officer with whom the financing statement was filed, a termination statement to the effect that he no longer claims a security interest under the financing statement, which shall be identified by file number. A termination statement signed by a person other than the secured party of record must be accompanied by a separate written statement of assignment signed by the secured party of record and complying with subsection (2) of Section 9–405, including payment of the required fee. If the affected secured party fails to file such a termination statement as required by this subsection, or to send such a termination statement within ten days after proper demand therefor he shall be liable to the debtor for one hundred dollars, and in addition for any loss caused to the debtor by such failure.

(2) On presentation to the filing officer of such a termination statement he must note it in the index. If he has received the termination statement in duplicate, he shall return one copy of the termination statement to the secured party stamped to show the time of receipt thereof. If the filing officer has a microfilm or other photographic record of the financing statement, and of any related continuation statement, statement of assignment and statement of release, he may remove the originals from the files at any time after receipt of the termination statement, or if he has no such record, he may remove them from the files at any time after one year after receipt of the termination statement.

(3) If the termination statement is in the standard form prescribed by the [Secretary of State], the uniform fee for filing and indexing the termination statement shall be $..... and otherwise shall be $....., plus in each case an additional fee of $..... for each name more than one against which the termination statement is required to be indexed.

Note: *The date to be inserted should be the effective date of the revised Article 9.*

Section 9–405. Assignment of Security Interest; Duties of Filing Officer; Fees.

(1) A financing statement may disclose an assignment of a security interest in the collateral described in the financing statement by indication in the financing statement of the name and address of the assignee or by an assignment itself or a copy thereof on the face or back of the statement. On presentation to the filing officer of such a financing statement the filing officer shall mark the same as provided in Section 9–403(4). The uniform fee for filing, indexing and furnishing filing data for a financing statement so indicating an assignment shall be $ . . . . . if the statement is in the standard form prescribed by the [Secretary of State] and otherwise shall be $ . . . . ., plus in each case an additional fee of $ . . . . . for each name more than one against which the financing statement is required to be indexed.

(2) A secured party may assign of record all or part of his rights under a financing statement by the filing in the place where the original financing statement was filed of a separate written statement of assignment signed by the secured party of record and setting forth the name of the secured party of record and the debtor, the file number and the date of filing of the financing statement and the name and address of the assignee and containing a description of the collateral assigned. A copy of the assignment is sufficient as a separate statement if it complies with the preceding sentence. On presentation to the filing officer of such a separate statement, the filing officer shall mark such separate statement with the date and hour of the filing. He shall note the assignment on the index of the financing statement, or in the case of a fixture filing, or a filing covering timber to be cut, or covering minerals or the like (including oil and gas) or accounts subject to subsection (5) of Section 9–103, he shall index the assignment under the name of the assignor as grantor and, to the extent that the law of this state provides for indexing the assignment of a mortgage under the name of the assignee, he shall index the assignment of the financing statement under the name of the assignee. The uniform fee for filing, indexing and furnishing filing data about such a separate statement of assignment shall be $ . . . . . if the statement is in the standard form prescribed by the [Secretary of State] and otherwise shall be $ . . . . ., plus in each case an additional fee of $ . . . . . for each name more than one against which the statement of assignment is required to be indexed. Notwithstanding the provisions of this subsection, an assignment of record of a security interest in a fixture contained in a mortgage effective as a fixture filing (subsection (6) of Section 9–402) may be made only by an assignment of the mortgage in the manner provided by the law of this state other than this Act.

(3) After the disclosure or filing of an assignment under this section, the assignee is the secured party of record.

Section 9–406. Release of Collateral; Duties of Filing Officer; Fees.

A secured party of record may by his signed statement release all or a part of any collateral described in a filed financing statement. The statement of release is sufficient if it contains a description of the collateral being released, the name and address of the debtor, the name and address of the secured party, and the file number of the financing statement. A statement of release signed by a person other than the secured party of record must be accompanied by a separate written statement of assignment signed by the secured party of record and complying with subsection (2) of Section 9–405, including payment of the required fee. Upon presentation of such a statement of release to the filing officer he shall mark the statement with the hour and date of filing and shall note the same upon the margin of the index of the filing of the financing statement. The uniform fee for filing and noting such a statement of release shall be $..... if the statement is in the standard form prescribed by the [Secretary of State] and otherwise shall be $....., plus in each case an additional fee of $..... for each name more than one against which the statement of release is required to be indexed.

[Section 9–407.   Information from Filing Officer.]

[(1)   If the person filing any financing statement, termination statement, statement of assignment, or statement of release, furnishes the filing officer a copy thereof, the filing officer shall upon request note upon the copy the file number and date and hour of the filing of the original and deliver or send the copy to such person.]

[(2)   Upon request of any person, the filing officer shall issue his certificate showing whether there is on file on the date and hour stated therein, any presently effective financing statement naming a particular debtor and any statement of assignment thereof and if there is, giving the date and hour of filing of each such statement and the names and addresses of each secured party therein. The uniform fee for such a certificate shall be $..... if the request for the certificate is in the standard form prescribed by the [Secretary of State] and otherwise shall be $.....]

Note: *This section is proposed as an optional provision to require filing officers to furnish certificates. Local law and practices should be consulted with regard to the advisability of adoption.*

Section 9–408.   Financing Statements Covering Consigned or Leased Goods.

A consignor or lessor of goods may file a financing statement using the terms "consignor," "consignee," "lessor," "lessee" or the like instead of the terms specified in Section 9–402. The provisions of this Part shall apply as appropriate to such a financing statement but its filing shall not of itself be a factor in determining whether or not the consignment or lease is intended as security (Section 1–201(37)). However, if it is determined for other reasons that the consignment or lease is so intended, a security interest of the consignor or lessor which attaches to the consigned or leased goods is perfected by such filing.

PART 5

DEFAULT

Section 9–501.   Default; Procedure When Security Agreement Covers Both Real and Personal Property.

(1)   When a debtor is in default under a security agreement, a secured party has the rights and remedies provided in this Part and except as limited by subsection (3) those provided in the security agreement. He may reduce his

claim to judgment, foreclose or otherwise enforce the security interest by any available judicial procedure. If the collateral is documents the secured party may proceed either as to the documents or as to the goods covered thereby. A secured party in possession has the rights, remedies and duties provided in Section 9–207. The rights and remedies referred to in this subsection are cumulative.

(2) After default, the debtor has the rights and remedies provided in this Part, those provided in the security agreement and those provided in Section 9–207.

(3) To the extent that they give rights to the debtor and impose duties on the secured party, the rules stated in the subsections referred to below may not be waived or varied except as provided with respect to compulsory disposition of collateral (subsection (3) of Section 9–504 and Section 9–505) and with respect to redemption of collateral (Section 9–506) but the parties may by agreement determine the standards by which the fulfillment of these rights and duties is to be measured if such standards are not manifestly unreasonable:

(a) subsection (2) of Section 9–502 and subsection (2) of Section 9–504 insofar as they require accounting for surplus proceeds of collateral;

(b) subsection (3) of Section 9–504 and subsection (1) of Section 9–505 which deal with disposition of collateral;

(c) subsection (2) of Section 9–505 which deals with acceptance of collateral as discharge of obligation;

(d) Section 9–506 which deals with redemption of collateral; and

(e) subsection (1) of Section 9–507 which deals with the secured party's liability for failure to comply with this Part.

(4) If the security agreement covers both real and personal property, the secured party may proceed under this Part as to the personal property or he may proceed as to both the real and the personal property in accordance with his rights and remedies in respect of the real property in which case the provisions of this Part do not apply.

(5) When a secured party has reduced his claim to judgment the lien of any levy which may be made upon his collateral by virtue of any execution based upon the judgment shall relate back to the date of the perfection of the security interest in such collateral. A judicial sale, pursuant to such execution, is a foreclosure of the security interest by judicial procedure within the meaning of this section, and the secured party may purchase at the sale and thereafter hold the collateral free of any other requirements of this Article.

Section 9–502. Collection Rights of Secured Party.

(1) When so agreed and in any event on default the secured party is entitled to notify an account debtor or the obligor on an instrument to make payment to him whether or not the assignor was theretofore making collections on the collateral, and also to take control of any proceeds to which he is entitled under Section 9–306.

(2) A secured party who by agreement is entitled to charge back uncollected collateral or otherwise to full or limited recourse against the debtor and who undertakes to collect from the account debtors or obligors must proceed in

a commercially reasonable manner and may deduct his reasonable expenses of realization from the collections. If the security agreement secures an indebtedness, the secured party must account to the debtor for any surplus, and unless otherwise agreed, the debtor is liable for any deficiency. But, if the underlying transaction was a sale of accounts or chattel paper, the debtor is entitled to any surplus or is liable for any deficiency only if the security agreement so provides.

Section 9–503.   Secured Party's Right to Take Possession after Default.

Unless otherwise agreed a secured party has on default the right to take possession of the collateral. In taking possession a secured party may proceed without judicial process if this can be done without breach of the peace or may proceed by action. If the security agreement so provides the secured party may require the debtor to assemble the collateral and make it available to the secured party at a place to be designated by the secured party which is reasonably convenient to both parties. Without removal a secured party may render equipment unusable, and may dispose of collateral on the debtor's premises under Section 9–504.

Section 9–504.   Secured Party's Right to Dispose of Collateral after Default; Effect of Disposition.

(1) A secured party after default may sell, lease or otherwise dispose of any or all of the collateral in its then condition or following any commercially reasonable preparation or processing. Any sale of goods is subject to the Article on Sales (Article 2). The proceeds of disposition shall be applied in the order following to

- (a) the reasonable expenses of retaking, holding, preparing for sale or lease, selling, leasing and the like and, to the extent provided for in the agreement and not prohibited by law, the reasonable attorneys' fees and legal expenses incurred by the secured party;
- (b) the satisfaction of indebtedness secured by the security interest under which the disposition is made;
- (c) the satisfaction of indebtedness secured by any subordinate security interest in the collateral if written notification of demand therefor is received before distribution of the proceeds is completed. If requested by the secured party, the holder of a subordinate security interest must seasonably furnish reasonable proof of his interest, and unless he does so, the secured party need not comply with his demand.

(2) If the security interest secures an indebtedness, the secured party must account to the debtor for any surplus, and, unless otherwise agreed, the debtor is liable for any deficiency. But if the underlying transaction was a sale of accounts or chattel paper, the debtor is entitled to any surplus or is liable for any deficiency only if the security agreement so provides.

(3) Disposition of the collateral may be by public or private proceedings and may be made by way of one or more contracts. Sale or other disposition may be as a unit or in parcels and at any time and place and on any terms but every aspect of the disposition including the method, manner, time, place and terms must be commercially reasonable. Unless collateral is perishable or threatens to decline speedily in value or is of a type customarily sold on a recognized marke reasonable notification of the time and place of any public sale or reasonable notification of the time after which any private sale or other intended disposition is to be made shall be sent by the secured party to the debtor, if he has not signed after default a statement renouncing or modifying his right to notification of sale. In the case of consumer goods no other notification need be sent. In other cases notification shall be sent to any other secured party from whom the secured party has received (before sending his notification to the debtor or before the debtor's renunciation of his rights) written notice of a claim of an interest in the collateral. The secured party may buy at any public sale and if the collateral is of a type customarily sold in a recognized market or is of a type which is the subject of widely distributed standard price quotations he may buy at private sale.

(4) When collateral is disposed of by a secured party after default, the disposition transfers to a purchaser for value all of the debtor's rights therein, discharges the security interest under which it is made and any security interest or lien subordinate thereto. The purchaser takes free of all such rights and interests even though the secured party fails to comply with the requirements of this Part or of any judicial proceedings

 (a) in the case of a public sale, if the purchaser has no knowledge of any defects in the sale and if he does not buy in collusion with the secured party, other bidders or the person conducting the sale; or

 (b) in any other case, if the purchaser acts in good faith.

(5) A person who is liable to a secured party under a guaranty, indorsement, repurchase agreement or the like and who receives a transfer of collateral from the secured party or is subrogated to his rights has thereafter the rights and duties of the secured party. Such a transfer of collateral is not a sale or disposition of the collateral under this Article.

Section 9–505. Compulsory Disposition of Collateral; Acceptance of the Collateral as Discharge of Obligation.

(1) If the debtor has paid sixty per cent of the cash price in the case of a purchase money security interest in consumer goods or sixty per cent of the loan in the case of another security interest in consumer goods, and has not signed after default a statement renouncing or modifying his rights under this Part a secured party who has taken possession of collateral must dispose of it under Section 9–504 and if he fails to do so within ninety days after he takes possession the debtor at his option may recover in conversion or under Section 9–507(1) on secured party's liability.

(2) In any other case involving consumer goods or any other collateral a secured party in possession may, after default, propose to retain the collateral in satisfaction of the obligation. Written notice of such proposal shall be sent to the debtor if he has not signed after default a statement renouncing or modifying his rights under this subsection. In the case of consumer goods no other notice need be given. In other cases notice shall be sent to any other secured party from whom the secured party has received (before sending his notice to the debtor or before the debtor's renunciation of his rights) written notice of a claim of an interest in the collateral. If the secured party receives objection in writing from a person entitled to receive notification within twenty-one days after the notice

was sent, the secured party must dispose of the collateral under Section 9–504. In the absence of such written objection the secured party may retain the collateral in satisfaction of the debtor's obligation.

Section 9–506. Debtor's Right to Redeem Collateral.

At any time before the secured party has disposed of collateral or entered into a contract for its disposition under Section 9–504 or before the obligation has been discharged under Section 9–505(2) the debtor or any other secured party may unless otherwise agreed in writing after default redeem the collateral by tendering fulfillment of all obligations secured by the collateral as well as the expenses reasonably incurred by the secured party in retaking, holding and preparing the collateral for disposition, in arranging for the sale, and to the extent provided in the agreement and not prohibited by law, his reasonable attorneys' fees and legal expenses.

Section 9–507. Secured Party's Liability for Failure to Comply with This Part.

(1) If it is established that the secured party is not proceeding in accordance with the provisions of this Part disposition may be ordered or restrained on appropriate terms and conditions. If the disposition has occurred the debtor or any person entitled to notification or whose security interest has been made known to the secured party prior to the disposition has a right to recover from the secured party any loss caused by a failure to comply with the provisions of this Part. If the collateral is consumer goods, the debtor has a right to recover in any event an amount not less than the credit service charge plus ten per cent of the principal amount of the debt or the time price differential plus ten per cent of the cash price.

(2) The fact that a better price could have been obtained by a sale at a different time or in a different method from that selected by the secured party is not of itself sufficient to establish that the sale was not made in a commercially reasonable manner. If the secured party either sells the collateral in the usual manner in any recognized market therefor or if he sells at the price current in such market at the time of his sale or if he has otherwise sold in conformity with reasonable commercial practices among dealers in the type of property sold he has sold in a commercially reasonable manner. The principles stated in the two preceding sentences with respect to sales also apply as may be appropriate to other types of disposition. A disposition which has been approved in any judicial proceeding or by any bona fide creditors' committee or representative of creditors shall conclusively be deemed to be commercially reasonable, but this sentence does not indicate that any such approval must be obtained in any case nor does it indicate that any disposition not so approved is not commercially reasonable.

ARTICLE 10

EFFECTIVE DATE AND REPEALER

Section 10–101. Effective Date.

This Act shall become effective at midnight on December 31st following its enactment. It applies to transactions entered into and events occurring after that date.

Section 10–102. Specific Repealer; Provision for Transition.

(1) The following acts and all other acts and parts of acts inconsistent herewith are hereby repealed:

(Here should follow the acts to be specifically repealed including the following:

    Uniform Negotiable Instruments Act

    Uniform Warehouse Receipts Act

    Uniform Sales Act

    Uniform Bills of Lading Act

    Uniform Stock Transfer Act

    Uniform Conditional Sales Act

    Uniform Trust Receipts Act

Also any acts regulating:

    Bank collections

    Bulk sales

    Chattel mortgages

    Conditional sales

    Factor's lien acts

    Farm storage of grain and similar acts

    Assignment of accounts receivable)

(2) Transactions validly entered into before the effective date specified in Section 10–101 and the rights, duties and interests flowing from them remain valid thereafter and may be terminated, completed, consummated or enforced as required or permitted by any statute or other law amended or repealed by this Act as though such repeal or amendment had not occurred.

Note: *Subsection (1) should be separately prepared for each state. The foregoing is a list of statutes to be checked.*

Section 10–103. General Repealer.

Except as provided in the following section, all acts and parts of acts inconsistent with this Act are hereby repealed.

Section 10–104. Laws Not Repealed.

[(1)] The Article on Documents of Title (Article 7) does not repeal or modify any laws prescribing the form or contents of documents of title or the services or facilities to be afforded by bailees, or otherwise regulating bailees' businesses in respects not specifically dealt with herein; but the fact that such laws are violated does not affect the status of a document of title which otherwise complies with the definition of a document of title (Section 1–201).

[(2) This Act does not repeal...............................

....*,

cited as the Uniform Act for the Simplification of Fiduciary Security Transfers, and if in any respect there is any inconsistency between that Act and the Article of this Act on investment securities (Article 8) the provisions of the former Act shall control.]

Note: *At * in subsection (2) insert the statutory reference to the Uniform Act for the Simplification of Fiduciary Security Transfers if such Act has previously been enacted. If it has not been enacted, omit subsection (2).*

ARTICLE 11

Notes

This material has been numbered Article 11 to distinguish it from Article 10, the transition provision of the 1962 Code, which may still remain in effect in some states to cover transition problems from pre-Code law to the original Uniform Commercial Code. Adaptation may be necessary in particular states. The terms "[old Code]" and "[new Code]" and "[old U.C.C.]" and "[new U.C.C.]" are used herein, and should be suitably changed in each state.

This draft was prepared by the Reporters and has not been passed upon by the Review Committee, the Permanent Editorial Board, the American Law Institute, or the National Conference of Commissioners on Uniform State Laws. It is submitted as a working draft which may be adapted as appropriate in each state.

EFFECTIVE DATE AND TRANSITION PROVISIONS

Section 11-101.   Effective Date.

This Act shall become effective at 12:01 A.M. on   , 19 .

Section 11-102.   Preservation of Old Transition Provision.

The provisions of [here insert reference to the original transition provision in the particular state] shall continue to apply to [the new U.C.C.] and for this purpose the [old U.C.C. and new U.C.C.] shall be considered one continuous statute.

Section 11-103.   Transition to [New Code]—General Rule.

Transactions validly entered into after [effective date of old U.C.C.] and before [effective date of new U.C.C.], and which were subject to the provisions of [old U.C.C.] and which would be subject to this Act as amended if they had been entered into after the effective date of [new U.C.C.] and the rights, duties and interests flowing from such transactions remain valid after the latter date and may be terminated, completed, consummated or enforced as required or permitted by the [new U.C.C.]. Security interests arising out of such transactions which are perfected when [new U.C.C.] becomes effective shall remain perfected until they lapse as provided in [new U.C.C.], and may be continued as permitted by [new U.C.C.], except as stated in Section 11–105.

Section 11–104. Transition Provision on Change of Requirement of Filing.

A security interest for the perfection of which filing or the taking of possession was required under [old U.C.C.] and which attached prior to the effective date of [new U.C.C.] but was not perfected shall be deemed perfected on the effective date of [new U.C.C.] if [new U.C.C.] permits perfection without filing or authorizes filing in the office or offices where a prior ineffective filing was made.

Section 11–105. Transition Provision on Change of Place of Filing.

(1) A financing statement or continuation statement filed prior to [effective date of new U.C.C.] which shall not have lapsed prior to [the effective date of new U.C.C.] shall remain effective for the period provided in the [old Code], but not less than five years after the filing.

(2) With respect to any collateral acquired by the debtor subsequent to the effective date of [new U.C.C.], any effective financing statement or continuation statement described in this section shall apply only if the filing or filings are in the office or offices that would be appropriate to perfect the security interests in the new collateral under [new U.C.C.].

(3) The effectiveness of any financing statement or continuation statement filed prior to [effective date of new U.C.C.] may be continued by a continuation statement as permitted by [new U.C.C.], except that if [new U.C.C.] requires a filing in an office where there was no previous financing statement, a new financing statement conforming to Section 11–106 shall be filed in that office.

(4) If the record of a mortgage of real estate would have been effective as a fixture filing of goods described therein if [new U.C.C.] had been in effect on the date of recording the mortgage, the mortgage shall be deemed effective as a fixture filing as to such goods under subsection (6) of Section 9–402 of the [new U.C.C.] on the effective date of [new U.C.C.].

Section 11–106. Required Refilings.

(1) If a security interest is perfected or has priority when this Act takes effect as to all persons or as to certain persons without any filing or recording, and if the filing of a financing statement would be required for the perfection or priority of the security interest against those persons under [new U.C.C.], the perfection and priority rights of the security interest continue until 3 years after the effective date of [new U.C.C.]. The perfection will then lapse unless a financing statement is filed as provided in subsection (4) or unless the security interest is perfected otherwise than by filing.

(2) If a security interest is perfected when [new U.C.C.] takes effect under a law other than [U.C.C.] which requires no further filing, refiling or recording to continue its perfection, perfection continues until and will lapse 3 years after [new U.C.C.] takes effect, unless a financing statement is filed as provided in subsection (4) or unless the security interest is perfected otherwise than by filing, or unless under subsection (3) of Section 9–302 the other law continues to govern filing.

(3) If a security interest is perfected by a filing, refiling or recording under a law repealed by this Act which required further filing, refiling or recording to continue its perfection, perfection continues and will lapse on the date provided by the law so repealed for such further filing, refiling or recording unless a financing statement is filed as provided in subsection (4) or unless the security interest is perfected otherwise than by filing.

(4) A financing statement may be filed within six months before the perfection of a security interest would otherwise lapse. Any such financing statement may be signed by either the debtor or the secured party. It must identify the security agreement, statement or notice (however denominated in any statute or other law repealed or modified by this Act), state the office where and the date when the last filing, refiling or recording, if any, was made with respect thereto, and the filing number, if any, or book and page, if any, of recording and further state that the security agreement, statement or notice, however denominated, in another filing office under the [U.C.C.] or under any statute or other law repealed or modified by this Act is still effective. Section 9–401 and Section 9–103 determine the proper place to file such a financing statement. Except as specified in this subsection, the provisions of Section 9–403(3) for continuation statements apply to such a financing statement.

Section 11–107. Transition Provisions as to Priorities.

Except as otherwise provided in [Article 11], [old U.C.C.] shall apply to any questions of priority if the positions of the parties were fixed prior to the effective date of [new U.C.C.]. In other cases questions of priority shall be determined by [new U.C.C.].

Section 11–108. Presumption that Rule of Law Continues Unchanged.

Unless a change in law has clearly been made, the provisions of [new U.C.C.] shall be deemed declaratory of the meaning of the [old U.C.C.].

UNIFORM PARTNERSHIP ACT (1914)*

PART I

Preliminary Provisions

SECTION 1. *Name of act.*—This act may be cited as Uniform Partnership Act.

SECTION 2. *Definition of terms.*—In this act, "Court" includes every court and judge having jurisdiction in the case.

"Business" includes every trade, occupation, or profession.

"Person" includes individuals, partnerships, corporations, and other associations.

"Bankrupt" includes bankrupt under the Federal Bankruptcy Act or insolvent under any state insolvent act.

"Conveyance" includes every assignment, lease, mortgage, or encumbrance.

"Real property" includes land and any interest or estate in land.

SECTION 3. *Interpretation of knowledge and notice.*—(1) A person has "knowledge" of a fact within the meaning of this act not only when he has actual knowledge thereof, but also when he has knowledge of such other facts as in the circumstances shows bad faith.

(2) A person has "notice" of a fact within the meaning of this act when the person who claims the benefit of the notice:

(a) States the fact to such person, or

(b) Delivers through the mail, or by other means of communication, a written statement of the fact to such person or to a proper person at his place of business or residence.

SECTION 4. *Rules of construction.*—(1) The rule that statutes in derogation of the common law are to be strictly construed shall have no application to this act.

(2) The law of estoppel shall apply under this act.

(3) The law of agency shall apply under this act.

(4) This act shall be so interpreted and construed as to effect its general purpose to make uniform the law of those states which enact it.

(5) This act shall not be construed so as to impair the obligations of any

---

* Reproduced with permission of the National Conference of Commissioners on Uniform State Laws.

contract existing when the act goes into effect, nor to affect any action or proceedings begun or right accrued before this act takes effect.

SECTION 5. *Rules for cases not provided for in this act.*—In any case not provided for in this act the rules of law and equity, including the law merchant, shall govern.

PART II

Nature of Partnership

SECTION 6. *Partnership defined.*—(1) A partnership is an association of two or more persons to carry on as co-owners a business for profit.

(2) But any association formed under any other statute of this state, or any statute adopted by authority, other than the authority of this state, is not a partnership under this act, unless such association would have been a partnership in this state prior to the adoption of this act; but this act shall apply to limited partnerships except in so far as the statutes relating to such partnerships are inconsistent herewith.

SECTION 7. *Rules for determining the existence of a partnership.*—In determining whether a partnership exists, these rules shall apply:

(1) Except as provided by section 16 persons who are not partners as to each other are not partners as to third persons.

(2) Joint tenancy, tenancy in common, tenancy by the entireties, joint property, common property, or part ownership does not of itself establish a partnership, whether such co-owners do or do not share any profits made by the use of the property.

(3) The sharing of gross returns does not of itself establish a partnership, whether or not the persons sharing them have a joint or common right or interest in any property from which the returns are derived.

(4) The receipt by a person of a share of the profits of a business is prima facie evidence that he is a partner in the business, but no such inference shall be drawn if such profits were received in payment:

(a) As a debt by installments or otherwise,

(b) As wages of an employee or rent to a landlord,

(c) As an annuity to a widow or representative of a deceased partner,

(d) As interest on a loan, though the amount of payment vary with the profits of the business,

(e) As the consideration for the sale of a good-will of a business or other property by installments or otherwise.

SECTION 8. *Partnership property.*—(1) All property originally brought into the partnership stock or subsequently acquired by purchase or otherwise, on account of the partnership, is partnership property.

(2) Unless the contrary intention appears, property acquired with partnership funds is partnership property.

(3) Any estate in real property may be acquired in the partnership name. Title so acquired can be conveyed only in the partnership name.

(4) A conveyance to a partnership in the partnership name, though without

words of inheritance, passes the entire estate of the grantor unless a contrary intent appears.

PART III

Relations of Partners to Persons Dealing with the Partnership

SECTION 9. *Partner agent of partnership as to partnership business.*—(1) Every partner is an agent of the partnership for the purpose of its business, and the act of every partner, including the execution in the partnership name of any instrument, for apparently carrying on in the usual way the business of the partnership of which he is a member binds the partnership, unless the partner so acting has in fact no authority to act for the partnership in the particular matter, and the person with whom he is dealing has knowledge of the fact that he has no such authority.

(2) An act of a partner which is not apparently for the carrying on of the business of the partnership in the usual way does not bind the partnership unless authorized by the other partners.

(3) Unless authorized by the other partners or unless they have abandoned the business, one or more but less than all the partners have no authority to:

(a) Assign the partnership property in trust for creditors or on the assignee's promise to pay the debts of the partnership,

(b) Dispose of the good-will of the business,

(c) Do any other act which would make it impossible to carry on the ordinary business of a partnership,

(d) Confess a judgment,

(e) Submit a partnership claim or liability to arbitration or reference.

(4) No act of a partner in contravention of a restriction on authority shall bind the partnership to persons having knowledge of the restriction.

SECTION 10. *Conveyance of real property of the partnership.*—(1) Where title to real property is in the partnership name, any partner may convey title to such property by a conveyance executed in the partnership name; but the partnership may recover such property unless the partner's act binds the partnership under the provisions of paragraph (1) of section 9, or unless such property has been conveyed by the grantee or a person claiming through such grantee to a holder for value without knowledge that the partner, in making the conveyance, has exceeded his authority.

(2) Where title to real property is in the name of the partnership, a conveyance executed by a partner, in his own name, passes the equitable interest of the partnership, provided the act is one within the authority of the partner under the provisions of paragraph (1) of section 9.

(3) Where title to real property is in the name of one or more but not all the partners, and the record does not disclose the right of the partnership, the partners in whose name the title stands may convey title to such property, but the partnership may recover such property if the partners' act does not bind the partnership under the provisions of paragraph (1) of section 9, unless the purchaser or his assignee, is a holder for value, without knowledge.

(4) Where the title to real property is in the name of one or more or all the partners, or in a third person in trust for the partnership, a conveyance executed by a partner in the partnership name, or in his own name, passes the equitable

interest of the partnership, provided the act is one within the authority of the partner under the provisions of paragraph (1) of section 9.

(5) Where the title to real property is in the names of all the partners a conveyance executed by all the partners passes all their rights in such property.

SECTION 11. *Partnership bound by admission of partner.*—An admission or representation made by any partner concerning partnership affairs within the scope of his authority as conferred by this act is evidence against the partnership.

SECTION 12. *Partnership charged with knowledge of or notice to partner.*—Notice to any partner of any matter relating to partnership affairs, and the knowledge of the partner acting in the particular matter, acquired while a partner or then present to his mind, and the knowledge of any other partner who reasonably could and should have communicated it to the acting partner, operate as notice to or knowledge of the partnership, except in the case of a fraud on the partnership committed by or with the consent of that partner.

SECTION 13. *Partnership bound by partner's wrongful act.*—Where, by any wrongful act or omission of any partner acting in the ordinary course of the business of the partnership or with the authority of his co-partners, loss or injury is caused to any person, not being a partner in the partnership, or any penalty is incurred, the partnership is liable therefor to the same extent as the partner so acting or omitting to act.

SECTION 14. *Partnership bound by partner's breach of trust.*—The partnership is bound to make good the loss:

(a) Where one partner acting within the scope of his apparent authority receives money or property of a third person and misapplies it; and

(b) Where the partnership in the course of its business receives money or property of a third person and the money or property so received is misapplied by any partner while it is in the custody of the partnership.

SECTION 15. *Nature of partner's liability.*—All partners are liable

(a) Jointly and severally for everything chargeable to the partnership under sections 13 and 14.

(b) Jointly for all other debts and obligations of the partnership; but any partner may enter into a separate obligation to perform a partnership contract.

SECTION 16. *Partner by estoppel.*—(1) When a person, by words spoken or written or by conduct, represents himself, or consents to another representing him to any one, as a partner in an existing partnership or with one or more persons not actual partners, he is liable to any such person to whom such representation has been made, who has, on the faith of such representation, given credit to the actual or apparent partnership, and if he has made such representation or consented to its being made in a public manner he is liable to such person, whether the representation has or has not been made or communicated to such person so giving credit by or with the knowledge of the apparent partner making the representation or consenting to its being made.

(a) When a partnership liability results, he is liable as though he were an actual member of the partnership.

(b) When no partnership liability results, he is liable jointly with the other persons, if any, so consenting to the contract or representation as to incur liability, otherwise separately.

(2) When a person has been thus represented to be a partner in an existing partnership, or with one or more persons not actual partners, he is an agent of

the persons consenting to such representation to bind them to the same extent and in the same manner as though he were a partner in fact, with respect to persons who rely upon the representation. Where all the members of the existing partnership consent to the representation, a partnership act or obligation results; but in all other cases it is the joint act or obligation of the person acting and the persons consenting to the representation.

SECTION 17. *Liability of incoming partner.*—A person admitted as a partner into an existing partnership is liable for all the obligations of the partnership arising before his admission as though he had been a partner when such obligations were incurred, except that this liability shall be satisfied only out of partnership property.

PART IV

Relations of Partners to One Another

SECTION 18. *Rules determining rights and duties of partners.*—The rights and duties of the partners in relation to the partnership shall be determined, subject to any agreement between them, by the following rules:

(a) Each partner shall be repaid his contributions, whether by way of capital or advances to the partnership property and share equally in the profits and surplus remaining after all liabilities, including those to partners, are satisfied; and must contribute towards the losses, whether of capital or otherwise, sustained by the partnership according to his share in the profits.

(b) The partnership must indemnify every partner in respect of payments made and personal liabilities reasonably incurred by him in the ordinary and proper conduct of its business, or for the preservation of its business or property.

(c) A partner, who in aid of the partnership makes any payment or advance beyond the amount of capital which he agreed to contribute, shall be paid interest from the date of the payment or advance.

(d) A partner shall receive interest on the capital contributed by him only from the date when repayment should be made.

(e) All partners have equal rights in the management and conduct of the partnership business.

(f) No partner is entitled to remuneration for acting in the partnership business, except that a surviving partner is entitled to reasonable compensation for his services in winding up the partnership affairs.

(g) No person can become a member of a partnership without the consent of all the partners.

(h) Any difference arising as to ordinary matters connected with the partnership business may be decided by a majority of the partners; but no act in contravention of any agreement between the partners may be done rightfully without the consent of all the partners.

SECTION 19. *Partnership books.*—The partnership books shall be kept, subject to any agreement between the partners, at the principal place of business of the partnership, and every partner shall at all times have access to and may inspect and copy any of them.

SECTION 20. *Duty of partners to render information.*—Partners shall render on demand true and full information of all things affecting the partnership to any partner or the legal representative of any deceased partner or partner under legal disability.

SECTION 21. *Partner accountable as a fiduciary.*—(1) Every partner must account to the partnership for any benefit, and hold as trustee for it any profits derived by him without the consent of the other partners from any transaction connected with the formation, conduct, or liquidation of the partnership or from any use by him of its property.

(2) This section applies also to the representatives of a deceased partner engaged in the liquidation of the affairs of the partnership as the personal representatives of the last surviving partner.

SECTION 22. *Right to an account.*—Any partner shall have the right to a formal account as to partnership affairs:

(a) If he is wrongfully excluded from the partnership business or possession of its property by his co-partners,

(b) If the right exists under the terms of any agreement,

(c) As provided by section 21,

(d) Whenever other circumstances render it just and reasonable.

SECTION 23. *Continuation of partnership beyond fixed term.*—(1) When a partnership for a fixed term or particular undertaking is continued after the termination of such term or particular undertaking without any express agreement, the rights and duties of the partners remain the same as they were at such termination, so far as is consistent with a partnership at will.

(2) A continuation of the business by the partners or such of them as habitually acted therein during the term, without any settlement or liquidation of the partnership affairs, is prima facie evidence of a continuation of the partnership.

PART V

Property Rights of a Partner

SECTION 24. *Extent of property rights of a partner.*—The property rights of a partner are (1) his rights in specific partnership property, (2) his interest in the partnership, and (3) his right to participate in the management.

SECTION 25. *Nature of a partner's right in specific partnership property.*—(1) A partner is co-owner with his partners of specific partnership property holding as a tenant in partnership.

(2) The incidents of this tenancy are such that:

(a) A partner, subject to the provisions of this act and to any agreement between the partners, has an equal right with his partners to possess specific partnership property for partnership purposes; but he has no right to possess such property for any other purpose without the consent of his partners.

(b) A partner's right in specific partnership property is not assignable except in connection with the assignment of rights of all the partners in the same property.

(c) A partner's right in specific partnership property is not subject to attachment or execution, except on a claim against the partnership. When partnership property is attached for a partnership debt the partners, or any of them, or the representatives of a deceased partner, cannot claim any right under the homestead or exemption laws.

(d) On the death of a partner his right in specific partnership property vests in the surviving partner or partners, except where the deceased was the last surviving partner, when his right in such property vests in his legal representative. Such surviving partner or partners, or the legal representative of the last surviving partner, has no right to possess the partnership property for any but a partnership purpose.

(e) A partner's right in specific partnership property is not subject to dower, curtesy, or allowances to widows, heirs, or next of kin.

SECTION 26. *Nature of partner's interest in the partnership.*—A partner's interest in the partnership is his share of the profits and surplus, and the same is personal property.

SECTION 27. *Assignment of partner's interest.*—(1) A conveyance by a partner of his interest in the partnership does not of itself dissolve the partnership, nor, as against the other partners in the absence of agreement, entitle the assignee, during the continuance of the partnership, to interfere in the management or administration of the partnership business or affairs, or to require any information or account of partnership transactions, or to inspect the partnership books; but it merely entitles the assignee to receive in accordance with his contract the profits to which the assigning partner would otherwise be entitled.

(2) In case of a dissolution of the partnership, the assignee is entitled to receive his assignor's interest and may require an account from the date only of the last account agreed to by all the partners.

SECTION 28. *Partner's interest subject to charging order.*—(1) On due application to a competent court by any judgment creditor of a partner, the court which entered the judgment, order, or decree, or any other court, may charge the interest of the debtor partner with payment of the unsatisfied amount of such judgment debt with interest thereon; and may then or later appoint a receiver of his share of the profits, and of any other money due or to fall due to him in respect of the partnership, and make all other orders, directions, accounts and inquiries which the debtor partner might have made, or which the circumstances of the case may require.

(2) The interest charged may be redeemed at any time before foreclosure, or in case of a sale being directed by the court may be purchased without thereby causing a dissolution:

(a) With separate property, by any one or more of the partners, or

(b) With partnership property, by any one or more of the partners with the consent of all the partners whose interests are not so charged or sold.

(3) Nothing in this act shall be held to deprive a partner of his right, if any, under the exemption laws, as regards his interest in the partnership.

PART VI

Dissolution and Winding Up

SECTION 29. *Dissolution defined.*—The dissolution of a partnership is the change in the relation of the partners caused by any partner ceasing to be associated in the carrying on as distinguished from the winding up of the business.

SECTION 30. *Partnership not terminated by dissolution.*—On dissolution the partnership is not terminated, but continues until the winding up of partnership affairs is completed.

SECTION 31. *Causes of dissolution.*—Dissolution is caused: (1) Without violation of the agreement between the partners,

(a) By the termination of the definite term or particular undertaking specified in the agreement,

(b) By the express will of any partner when no definite term or particular undertaking is specified,

(c) By the express will of all the partners who have not assigned their interests or suffered them to be charged for their separate debts, either before or after the termination of any specified term or particular undertaking,

(d) By the expulsion of any partner from the business bona fide in accordance with such a power conferred by the agreement between the partners;

(2) In contravention of the agreement between the partners, where the circumstances do not permit a dissolution under any other provision of this section, by the express will of any partner at any time;

(3) By any event which makes it unlawful for the business of the partnership to be carried on or for the members to carry it on in partnership;

(4) By the death of any partner;

(5) By the bankruptcy of any partner or the partnership;

(6) By decree of court under section 32.

SECTION 32. *Dissolution by decree of court.*—(1) On application by or for a partner the court shall decree a dissolution whenever:

(a) A partner has been declared a lunatic in any judicial proceeding or is shown to be of unsound mind,

(b) A partner becomes in any other way incapable of performing his part of the partnership contract,

(c) A partner has been guilty of such conduct as tends to affect prejudicially the carrying on of the business,

(d) A partner wilfully or persistently commits a breach of the partnership agreement, or otherwise so conducts himself in matters relating to the partnership business that it is not reasonably practicable to carry on the business in partnership with him,

(e) The business of the partnership can only be carried on at a loss,

(f) Other circumstances render a dissolution equitable.

(2) On the application of the purchaser of a partner's interest under sections 27 or 28:

(a) After the termination of the specified term or particular undertaking,

(b) At any time if the partnership was a partnership at will when the interest was assigned or when the charging order was issued.

SECTION 33. *General effect of dissolution on authority of partner.*—Except so far as may be necessary to wind up partnership affairs or to complete transactions begun but not then finished, dissolution terminates all authority of any partner to act for the partnership,

(1) With respect to the partners,

(a) When the dissolution is not by the act, bankruptcy or death of a partner; or

(b) When the dissolution is by such act, bankruptcy or death of a partner, in cases where section 34 so requires.

(2) With respect to persons not partners, as declared in section 35.

SECTION 34. *Right of partner to contribution from co-partners after disso-lution.*—Where the dissolution is caused by the act, death or bankruptcy of a partner, each partner is liable to his co-partners for his share of any liability created by any partner acting for the partnership as if the partnership had not been dissolved unless

(a) The dissolution being by act of any partner, the partner acting for the partnership had knowledge of the dissolution, or

(b) The dissolution being by the death or bankruptcy of a partner, the part-ner acting for the partnership had knowledge or notice of the death or bank-ruptcy.

SECTION 35. *Power of partner to bind partnership to third persons after dissolution.*—(1) After dissolution a partner can bind the partnership except as provided in Paragraph (3).

(a) By any act appropriate for winding up partnership affairs or completing transactions unfinished at dissolution;

(b) By any transaction which would bind the partnership if dissolution had not taken place, provided the other party to the transaction

(I) Had extended credit to the partnership prior to dissolution and had no knowledge or notice of the dissolution; or

(II) Though he had not so extended credit, had nevertheless known of the partnership prior to dissolution, and, having no knowledge or notice of dissolu-tion, the fact of dissolution had not been advertised in a newspaper of general circulation in the place (or in each place if more than one) at which the partner-ship business was regularly carried on.

(2) The liability of a partner under Paragraph (1b) shall be satisfied out of partnership assets alone when such partner had been prior to dissolution

(a) Unknown as a partner to the person with whom the contract is made; and

(b) So far unknown and inactive in partnership affairs that the business reputation of the partnership could not be said to have been in any degree due to his connection with it.

(3) The partnership is in no case bound by any act of a partner after disso-lution

(a) Where the partnership is dissolved because it is unlawful to carry on the business, unless the act is appropriate for winding up partnership affairs, or

(b) Where the partner has become bankrupt; or

(c) Where the partner has no authority to wind up partnership affairs; ex-cept by a transaction with one who

(I) Had extended credit to the partnership prior to dissolution and had no knowledge or notice of his want of authority; or

(II) Had not extended credit to the partnership prior to dissolution, and, having no knowledge or notice of his want of authority, the fact of his want of authority has not been advertised in the manner provided for advertising the fact of dissolution in Paragraph (1bII).

(4) Nothing in this section shall affect the liability under section 16 of any

person who after dissolution represents himself or consents to another representing him as a partner in a partnership engaged in carrying on business.

SECTION 36. *Effect of dissolution on partner's existing liability.*—(1) The dissolution of the partnership does not of itself discharge the existing liability of any partner.

(2) A partner is discharged from any existing liability upon dissolution of the partnership by an agreement to that effect between himself, the partnership creditor and the person or partnership continuing the business; and such agreement may be inferred from the course of dealing between the creditor having knowledge of the dissolution and the person or partnership continuing the business.

(3) Where a person agrees to assume the existing obligations of a dissolved partnership, the partners whose obligations have been assumed shall be discharged from any liability to any creditor of the partnership who, knowing of the agreement, consents to a material alteration in the nature or time of payment of such obligations.

(4) The individual property of a deceased partner shall be liable for all obligations of the partnership incurred while he was a partner but subject to the prior payment of his separate debts.

SECTION 37. *Right to wind up.*—Unless otherwise agreed the partners who have not wrongfully dissolved the partnership or the legal representative of the last surviving partner, not bankrupt, has the right to wind up the partnership affairs; provided, however, that any partner, his legal representative or his assignee, upon cause shown, may obtain winding up by the court.

SECTION 38. *Rights of partners to application of partnership property.*—(1) When dissolution is caused in any way, except in contravention of the partnership agreement, each partner, as against his co-partners and all persons claiming through them in respect of their interests in the partnership, unless otherwise agreed, may have the partnership property applied to discharge its liabilities, and the surplus applied to pay in cash the net amount owing to the respective partners. But if dissolution is caused by expulsion of a partner, bona fide under the partnership agreement and if the expelled partner is discharged from all partnership liabilities, either by payment or agreement under section 36 (2), he shall receive in cash only the net amount due him from the partnership.

(2) When dissolution is caused in contravention of the partnership agreement the rights of the partners shall be as follows:

(a) Each partner who has not caused dissolution wrongfully shall have,

(I) All the rights specified in Paragraph (1) of this section, and

(II) The right, as against each partner who has caused the dissolution wrongfully, to damages for breach of the agreement.

(b) The partners who have not caused the dissolution wrongfully, if they all desire to continue the business in the same name, either by themselves or jointly with others, may do so, during the agreed term for the partnership and for that purpose may possess the partnership property, provided they secure the payment by bond approved by the court, or pay to any partner who has caused the dissolution wrongfully, the value of his interest in the partnership at the dissolution, less any damages recoverable under clause (2aII) of this section, and in like manner indemnify him against all present or future partnership liabilities.

(c) A partner who has caused the dissolution wrongfully shall have:

(I) If the business is not continued under the provisions of Paragraph (2b) all the rights of a partner under Paragraph (1), subject to clause (2aII), of this section,

(II) If the business is continued under Paragraph (2b) of this section the right as against his co-partners and all claiming through them in respect of their interests in the partnership, to have the value of his interest in the partnership, less any damages caused to his co-partners by the dissolution, ascertained and paid to him in cash, or the payment secured by bond approved by the court, and to be released from all existing liabilities of the partnership; but in ascertaining the value of the partner's interest the value of the good-will of the business shall not be considered.

SECTION 39. *Rights where partnership is dissolved for fraud or misrepresentation.*—Where a partnership contract is rescinded on the ground of the fraud or misrepresentation of one of the parties thereto, the party entitled to rescind is, without prejudice to any other right, entitled,

(a) To a lien on, or right of retention of, the surplus of the partnership property after satisfying the partnership liabilities to third persons for any sum of money paid by him for the purchase of an interest in the partnership and for any capital or advances contributed by him; and

(b) To stand, after all liabilities to third persons have been satisfied, in the place of the creditors of the partnership for any payments made by him in respect of the partnership liabilities; and

(c) To be indemnified by the person guilty of the fraud or making the representation against all debts and liabilities of the partnership.

SECTION 40. *Rules for distribution.*—In settling accounts between the partners after dissolution, the following rules shall be observed, subject to any agreement to the contrary:

(a) The assets of the partnership are:

(I) The partnership property,

(II) The contributions of the partners necessary for the payment of all the liabilities specified in clause (b) of this paragraph.

(b) The liabilities of the partnership shall rank in order of payment, as follows:

(I) Those owing to creditors other than partners,

(II) Those owing to partners other than for capital and profits,

(III) Those owing to partners in respect of capital,

(IV) Those owing to partners in respect of profits.

(c) The assets shall be applied in order of their declaration in clause (a) of this paragraph to the satisfaction of the liabilities.

(d) The partners shall contribute, as provided by section 18 (a) the amount necessary to satisfy the liabilities; but if any, but not all, of the partners are insolvent, or, not being subject to process, refuse to contribute, the other partners shall contribute their share of the liabilities, and, in the relative proportions in which they share the profits, the additional amount necessary to pay the liabilities.

(e) An assignee for the benefit of creditors or any person appointed by the court shall have the right to enforce the contributions specified in clause (d) of this paragraph.

(f) Any partner or his legal representative shall have the right to enforce the contributions specified in clause (d) of this paragraph, to the extent of the amount which he has paid in excess of his share of the liability.

(g) The individual property of a deceased partner shall be liable for the contributions specified in clause (d) of this paragraph.

(h) When partnership property and the individual properties of the partners are in possession of a court for distribution, partnership creditors shall have priority on partnership property and separate creditors on individual property, saving the rights of lien or secured creditors as heretofore.

(i) Where a partner has become bankrupt or his estate is insolvent the claims against his separate property shall rank in the following order:

(I) Those owing to separate creditors,

(II) Those owing to partnership creditors,

(III) Those owing to partners by way of contribution.

SECTION 41. *Liability of persons continuing the business in certain cases.* —(1) When any new partner is admitted into an existing partnership, or when any partner retires and assigns (or the representative of the deceased partner assigns) his rights in partnership property to two or more of the partners, or to one or more of the partners and one or more third persons, if the business is continued without liquidation of the partnership affairs, creditors of the first or dissolved partnership are also creditors of the partnership so continuing the business.

(2) When all but one partner retire and assign (or the representative of a deceased partner assigns) their rights in partnership property to the remaining partner, who continues the business without liquidation of partnership affairs, either alone or with others, creditors of the dissolved partnership are also creditors of the person or partnership so continuing the business.

(3) When any partner retires or dies and the business of the dissolved partnership is continued as set forth in Paragraphs (1) and (2) of this section, with the consent of the retired partners or the representative of the deceased partner, but without any assignment of his right in partnership property, rights of creditors of the dissolved partnership and of the creditors of the person or partnership continuing the business shall be as if such assignment had been made.

(4) When all the partners or their representatives assign their rights in partnership property to one or more third persons who promise to pay the debts and who continue the business of the dissolved partnership, creditors of the dissolved partnership are also creditors of the person or partnership continuing the business.

(5) When any partner wrongfully causes a dissolution and the remaining partners continue the business under the provisions of section 38 (2b), either alone or with others, and without liquidation of the partnership affairs, creditors of the dissolved partnership are also creditors of the person or partnership continuing the business.

(6) When a partner is expelled and the remaining partners continue the business either alone or with others, without liquidation of the partnership affairs, creditors of the dissolved partnership are also creditors of the person or partnership continuing the business.

(7) The liability of a third person becoming a partner in the partnership continuing the business, under this section, to the creditors of the dissolved partnership shall be satisfied out of partnership property only.

(8) When the business of a partnership after dissolution is continued under any conditions set forth in this section the creditors of the dissolved partnership, as against the separate creditors of the retiring or deceased partner or the representative of the deceased partner, have a prior right to any claim of the retired partner or the representative of the deceased partner against the person or partnership continuing the business, on account of the retired or deceased partner's interest in the dissolved partnership or on account of any consideration promised for such interest or for his right in partnership property.

(9) Nothing in this section shall be held to modify any right of creditors to set aside any assignment on the ground of fraud.

(10) The use by the person or partnership continuing the business of the partnership name, or the name of a deceased partner as part thereof, shall not of itself make the individual property of the deceased partner liable for any debts contracted by such person or partnership.

SECTION 42. *Rights of retiring or estate of deceased partner when the business is continued.*—When any partner retires or dies, and the business is continued under any of the conditions set forth in section 41 (1, 2, 3, 5, 6), or section 38(2b) without any settlement of accounts as between him or his estate and the person or partnership continuing the business, unless otherwise agreed, he or his legal representative as against such persons or partnership may have the value of his interest at the date of dissolution ascertained, and shall receive as an ordinary creditor an amount equal to the value of his interest in the dissolved partnership with interest, or, at his option or at the option of his legal representative, in lieu of interest, the profits attributable to the use of his right in the property of the dissolved partnership; provided that the creditors of the dissolved partnership as against the separate creditors, or the representative of the retired or deceased partner, shall have priority on any claim arising under this section, as provided by section 41(8) of this act.

SECTION 43. *Accrual of actions.*—The right to an account of his interest shall accrue to any partner, or his legal representative, as against the winding up partners or the surviving partners or the person or partnership continuing the business, at the date of dissolution, in the absence of any agreement to the contrary.

PART VII

Miscellaneous Provisions

SECTION 44. *When act takes effect.*—This act shall take effect on the . . . day of . . . , one thousand nine hundred and. . . .

SECTION 45. *Legislation repealed.*—All acts or parts of acts inconsistent with this act are hereby repealed.

EXCERPTS FROM UNIFORM FRAUDULENT CONVEYANCE ACT (1918)*

SECTION 2. *Insolvency.*—(1) A person is insolvent when the present fair salable value of his assets is less than the amount that will be required to pay his probable liability on his existing debts as they become absolute and matured.

(2) In determining whether a partnership is insolvent there shall be added to the partnership property the present fair salable value of the separate assets of each general partner in excess of the amount probably sufficient to meet the claims of his separate creditors, and also the amount of any unpaid subscription to the partnership of each limited partner, provided the present fair salable value of the assets of such limited partner is probably sufficient to pay his debts, including such unpaid subscription.

SECTION 3. *Fair consideration.*—Fair consideration is given for property, or obligation,

(a) When in exchange for such property, or obligation, as a fair equivalent therefor, and in good faith, property is conveyed or an antecedent debt is satisfied, or

(b) When such property, or obligation is received in good faith to secure a present advance or antecedent debt in amount not disproportionately small as compared with the value of the property, or obligation obtained.

SECTION 4. *Conveyances by insolvent.*—Every conveyance made and every obligation incurred by a person who is or will be thereby rendered insolvent is fraudulent as to creditors without regard to his actual intent if the conveyance is made or the obligation is incurred without a fair consideration.

SECTION 5. *Conveyances by persons in business.*—Every conveyance made without fair consideration when the person making it is engaged or is about to engage in a business or transaction for which the property remaining in his hands after the conveyance is an unreasonably small capital, is fraudulent as to creditors and as to other persons who become creditors during the continuance of such business or transaction without regard to his actual intent.

SECTION 6. *Conveyances by a person about to incur debts.*—Every conveyance made and every obligation incurred without fair consideration when the person making the conveyance or entering into the obligation intends or believes that he will incur debts beyond his ability to pay as they mature, is fraudulent as to both present and future creditors.

---

* Reproduced with permission of the National Conference of Commissioners on Uniform State Laws.

SECTION 7. *Conveyance made with intent to defraud.*—Every conveyance made and every obligation incurred with actual intent, as distinguished from intent presumed in law, to hinder, delay, or defraud either present or future creditors, is fraudulent as to both present and future creditors.

SECTION 8. *Conveyance of partnership property.*—Every conveyance of partnership property and every partnership obligation incurred when the partnership is or will be thereby rendered insolvent, is fraudulent as to partnership creditors, if the conveyance is made or obligation is incurred,

(a) To a partner, whether with or without a promise by him to pay partnership debts, or

(b) To a person not a partner without fair consideration to the partnership as distinguished from consideration to the individual partners.

SECTION 9. *Rights of creditors whose claims have matured.*—(1) Where a conveyance or obligation is fraudulent as to a creditor, such creditor, when his claim has matured, may, as against any person except a purchaser for fair consideration without knowledge of the fraud at the time of the purchase, or one who has derived title immediately or mediately from such a purchaser,

(a) Have the conveyance set aside or obligation annulled to the extent necessary to satisfy his claim, or

(b) Disregard the conveyance and attach or levy execution upon the property conveyed.

(2) A purchaser who without actual fraudulent intent has given less than a fair consideration for the conveyance or obligation, may retain the property or obligation as security for repayment.

SECTION 10. *Rights of creditors whose claims have not matured.*—Where a conveyance made or obligation incurred is fraudulent as to a creditor whose claim has not matured he may proceed in a court of competent jurisdiction against any person against whom he could have proceeded had his claim matured, and the court may,

(a) Restrain the defendant from disposing of his property,

(b) Appoint a receiver to take charge of the property,

(c) Set aside the conveyance or annul the obligation, or

(d) Make any order which the circumstances of the case may require.

EXCERPTS FROM THE BANKRUPTCY ACT
(*1898, AMENDED*)

SECTION 5. *Partners.*—a. A partnership, including a limited partnership containing one or more general partners, during the continuation of the partnership business or after its dissolution and before the final settlement thereof, may be adjudged a bankrupt either separately or jointly with one or more or all of its general partners.

b. A petition may be filed by one or more or all of the general partners in the separate behalf of a partnership or jointly in behalf of a partnership and of the general partner or partners filing the same: *Provided, however,* That where a petition is filed in behalf of a partnership by less than all of the general partners, the petition shall allege that the partnership is insolvent. A petition may be filed separately against a partnership or jointly against a partnership and one or more or all of its general partners.

c. The creditors of the bankrupt partnership shall appoint the trustee, who shall be the trustee of the individual estate of a general partner being administered in the proceeding: *Provided, however,* That the creditors of a general partner adjudged a bankrupt may, upon cause shown, be permitted to appoint their separate trustee for his estate. In other respects, so far as possible, the partnership estate shall be administered as herein provided for other estates.

d. The court of bankruptcy which has jurisdiction of one of the general partners may have jurisdiction of all the general partners and of the administration of the partnership and individual property.

e. The trustee or trustees shall keep separate accounts of the partnership property and of the property belonging to the individual general partners.

f. The expenses shall be paid from the partnership property and the individual property in such proportions as the court shall determine.

g. The net proceeds of the partnership property shall be appropriated to the payment of the partnership debts and the net proceeds of the individual estate of each general partner to the payment of his individual debts. Should any surplus remain of the property of any general partner after paying his individual debts, such surplus shall be added to the partnership assets and be applied to the payment of the partnership debts. Should any surplus of the partnership property remain after paying the partnership debts, such surplus shall be distributed among the individual partners, general or limited, or added to the estates of the general partners, as the case may be, in the proportion of their respective interests in the partnership and in the order of distribution provided by the laws of the State applicable thereto.

h. The court may permit the proof of the claim of the partnership estate against the individual estates, and vice versa, and may marshal the assets of the partnership estate and individual estates so as to prevent preferences and secure the equitable distribution of the property of the several estates.

i. Where all the general partners are adjudged bankrupt, the partnership shall also be adjudged bankrupt. In the event of one or more but not all of the general partners of a partnership being adjudged bankrupt, the partnership property shall not be administered in bankruptcy, unless by consent of the general partner or partners not adjudged bankrupt; but such general partner or partners not adjudged bankrupt shall settle the partnership business as expeditiously as its nature will permit and account for the interest of the general partner or partners adjudged bankrupt.

j. The discharge of a partnership shall not discharge the individual general partners thereof from the partnership debts. A general partner adjudged a bankrupt either in a joint or separate proceeding may, pursuant to the provisions of this Act, obtain a discharge from both his partnership and individual debts.

k. If a limited partnership is adjudged bankrupt, any limited partner who is individually liable under the laws of the United States or of any State for any of the partnership debts shall be deemed a general partner as to such debts and, if he is insolvent, shall be subject to the provisions and entitled to the benefits of this Act, as in the case of a general partner.

INDEX

INDEX

A

Abandonment, personal property, 171–72
Abstract of title, 915
Accession, property, 173, 760
Accord and satisfaction; *see* Contracts
Account stated; *see* Contracts
Accountant, 965–66
Accountant's legal responsibility
  duties and liabilities of public accountant
    application of federal statutes, 970–76
    to his client, 966–69
    to third persons, 969–70
    privileged communications, 968–69
    professional ethics, 976–77
  public accountant
    duties and liabilities, 966–976
    lien, 967–68
    professional ethics for C.P.A.s, 976–77
    status, 965–66
    working papers, etc., 968
Accounts; *see* Security
Act, 505 (n. 2)
Act of God, 191–92
Administrator
  defined, 937
  when promise within statute of frauds, 107
Administratrix, 937
Adverse possession, of land, 917–18
Agency
  accountant, *see* Accountant's legal responsibility
  actual authority
    defined, 514
    express, 515
    implied, 515–25
    interpretation, 525–26
    general agent, 508
    non-servant agent, 507–8
    servant, 507
    special agent, 508–10
    termination, 580–725
  agent's disobedience justified, 546–47
  agent's possessory lien on principal's property, 543

Agency—*Cont.*
  apparent authority
    creation, 515–16, 525–27
    estoppel compared, 529–30
    origins, 529–30
    principles applicable, 526–27
    termination, 584–88
  by appointment, 510
  attorney in fact, 509
  attorney at law, 509
  auctioneer, 509
  authority
    to act for joint principals, 516
    actual, 514–25
    apparent, 525–27
    estoppel, application of, 527–30
    express, 515
    implied, 515–25
    interpretation, 514–15
    ostensible, 526
    ratification, application of, 530–39
  bailment distinguished, 503
  broker, 509
  contracts, disclosed principal
    actual authority to make, 550–51
    apparent authority to make, 550–51
    defenses, 564–65
    duty of third persons to ascertain agency and authority, 551–53
    inherent agency power, liability for, 554–64
    notice to agent, 552
    parties, 549–50
    unauthorized conduct of agent, liability for, 553–64
  contracts, undisclosed principal
    defenses, 571–74
    election by third person, 567
    liability, 567–74
    parties, 566–67
    unauthorized conduct of agent, liability for, 568–71
  to convey interest in land; *see* statute of frauds
  creation
    of agency, 505–13

This book has been set in 12 and 10 point Garamond No. 3, leaded 1 point. Chapter numbers and titles are in 14 point Garamont italics. Part numbers, titles, and outlines, and the cut-in sideheads, are in Spartan Medium. The size of the type page is 27 by 46½ picas.